CW00336247

TROPICAL RESORTS

TAN HOCK BENG

TROPICAL RESORTS

PAGE ONE PUBLISHING

For Maria, Brent and Gale

Fly title:
Stone carving at Baan Taling Ngam, Koh Samui
Overleaf:
Laguna Beach Club, Phuket, Thailand

Deckblatt:
Steinskulpturen am Baan Taling Ngam, Koh Samui
Umseitig:
Laguna Beach Club, Phuket, Thailand

Feuille volante:
Sculptures en pierre à Baan Taling Ngam, Koh Samui
Verso:
Laguna Beach Club, Phuket, Thaïlande

Block 4 Pasir Panjang Road
#06-35 Alexandra Distripark
Singapore 118491
Tel: (65) 274-3188
Fax: (65) 274-1833

Distributed in Asia by:

Page One The Bookshop Pte Ltd
Block 4 Pasir Panjang Road
#08-33 Alexandra Distripark
Singapore 118491

Cover design: Peter Feierabend, Berlin
Layout: K. C. Sin, Singapore
Contributing editor: Regine Ermert, Cologne
German translation: Jutta Hein, Hamburg
French translation: France Varry, Cologne
Colour separation by Columbia Offset, Singapore
Printed by Amilcare Pizzi, Italy
Printed in Italy

ISBN 981-00-6326-1

Contents

Inhalt

Sommaire

"The human task of architecture is not to beautify or to humanise the world of everyday facts, but to open up a view into the second dimension of our consciousness, the reality of images, memories and dreams."

Juhani Pallasmaa

»In der Architektur besteht die Aufgabe für den Menschen nicht darin, die Alltagswelt schöner oder humaner zu gestalten, sondern den Blick in die zweite Dimension unseres Bewußtseins zu öffnen, für die Wirklichkeit von Bildern, Erinnerungen und Träumen.«

Juhani Pallasmaa

Preface
Vorwort
Préface

This book is a natural evolution from *Tropical Architecture and Interiors*. While compiling materials for the first book, it became obvious that some of the most beautiful works in the region are intimate resorts. With the bloom in the global tourist industry, these buildings are challenging the dreary monotony of conventional hotel architecture. Hence they deserve a more detailed record within these pages.

While writing the epilogue for the same book, it was also apparent that these hotels raise an important issue – the notion of authenticity. The chapter in this book – "Re-Presentation And Authenticity" – is a further expansion on this issue. The collection of resorts is grouped to graphically support the argument set out in the same chapter.

Mass tourism has become one of the most highly developed and fastest growing industries. Travel and tourism alone stimulate some US$693 billion investment in new facilities and equipment. Hotels and resorts are built at an alarming rate to cater to holiday-makers in search of natural beauty spots. A recent spate of resort building in Southeast Asia looks set to follow in the tradition of the ultimate luxury resorts such as Eden Roc on the Cote d'Azur.

Resorts do not belong to the category in which much of contemporary debate on architecture is centred. The nature of the resort is different from most building types. Buildings in this particular genre are usually luxurious places designed for the privileged few; they have generous design budgets; they are located in idyll, exotic sites of unsurpassed beauty; they are theatrical and stage set-like, exuding a blissful serenity and meditative quality.

The production of tourist architecture usually distorts both time and place. There is a powerful tendency to homogenity behind the false fronts. Termed 'troppo chic' by some observers, these exotic hideaways for the world-weary are truly sumptuous. The architectural resolution, based on traditional skills, invariably necessitates the involvement of traditional craftsmen at an early stage. The architects are all consciously espousing a respect for the indigenous culture and the local vernacular. In *Hotel Planning and Design*, Rutes and Penner argue that "when all the research, financial feasibility studies, facilities programmes, technical standards and management systems are completed, it is the specific *design* that makes the big difference."

Dieses Buch ist eine Fortsetzung von *Tropische Architektur und Interieurs*. Bei der Materialsammlung für das erste Buch stellte sich heraus, daß einige der schönsten Bauwerke der Region Ferienanlagen mit privatem Charakter sind. Die Tourismusindustrie boomt weltweit, und diese Häuser bilden einen Kontrast zu der tristen Monotonie herkömmlicher Hotelarchitektur. Daher verdienen sie eine genauere Betrachtung.

Beim Schreiben des Nachworts für das erwähnte Buch wurde auch klar, daß diese Hotels sich ein hohes Ziel gesteckt haben – die Vermittlung von Authentizität. Das Kapitel »(Re)Präsentation und Authentizität« befaßt sich ausführlicher damit. Die Ferienanlagen wurden so ausgewählt und zusammengestellt, daß sie die Argumente dieses Kapitels anschaulich stützen.

Der Massentourismus ist eine hoch entwickelte und schnell wachsende Industrie geworden. Allein Reise und Tourismus verzeichnen Investitionen in Höhe von etwa 693 Milliarden US-Dollar für neue Anlagen und Einrichtungen. In alarmierendem Umfang werden Hotels und Ferienanlagen gebaut, um solche Urlauber zu versorgen, die Orte von natürlicher Schönheit suchen. In jüngster Zeit schossen Ferienanlagen in Südostasien wie Pilze aus dem Boden, die offenbar die Tradition edelster Luxusherbergen wie des Eden Roc an der Côte d'Azur fortsetzen wollen.

Die gegenwärtige Diskussion über Architektur befaßt sich kaum mit Ferienanlagen. Sie haben einen anderen Charakter als die meisten Bauten. Sie sind häufig Luxusunterkünfte für wenige Privilegierte, verfügen über einen großzügigen Entwicklungsetat und liegen an idyllischen, exotischen Orten von unvergleichlicher Schönheit. Sie wirken dramatisch wie Theaterkulissen und strahlen doch eine meditative Gelassenheit aus.

Die Touristenarchitektur verfälscht im allgemeinen Zeit und Ort. Es besteht ein starker Hang zur Einheitlichkeit hinter den falschen Fassaden. Von einigen Beobachtern als »troppo chic« bezeichnet, sind diese exotischen Zufluchtsorte für die Weltverdrossenen wahrlich luxuriös. Wenn die architektonische Entscheidung auf traditionellem Handwerk basiert, ist es unumgänglich, schon in einem sehr frühen Stadium auch traditionelle Handwerker einzubeziehen. Die Architekten respektieren ganz bewußt die gewachsene Kultur und die Landschaft vor Ort. In *Hotel Planning and Design* stellen Rutes und Penner fest, »wenn Vorplanung, Kostenaufstellung, Ausführungsprogramm, technische Standards und

"La tâche humaine de l'architecture n'est pas d'embellir ou d'humaniser le monde quotidien, mais d'ouvrir une perspective dans la seconde dimension de notre conscience, la réalité des images, des souvenirs et des rêves."

Juhani Pallasmaa

Ce livre est la conséquence naturelle de *Architecture et intérieurs tropicaux*. Les recherches pour le premier livre ont révélé que quelques-uns des plus beaux ouvrages de la région sont des complexes hôteliers. Depuis l'essor de l'industrie du tourisme, ces édifices défient la monotonie terne de l'architecture d'hôtel conventionnelle. C'est pourquoi ils méritent un regard plus appuyé dans ces pages.

Lors de la rédaction de l'épilogue du premier livre, il est également apparu que ces hôtels soulèvent un point important – la notion d'authenticité – sur lequel le chapitre de ce livre, "Re-Présentation et Authenticité", s'étend davantage. La sélection des villégiatures matérialise l'argumentation développée dans ce chapitre.

Le tourisme est une des industries qui connaît une croissance extrêmement rapide. Quelque 630 billions de dollars US ont été investis dans de nouveaux équipements et services, uniquement pour les voyages et séjours d'agrément. On construit des hôtels et stations balnéaires à une rapidité alarmante aux fins d'accueillir la masse des vacanciers à la recherche des beautés de la nature. Une catégorie de nouvelles villégiatures du Sud-Est asiatique semblerait faire bientôt partie des stations balnéaires de grand luxe telles qu'Eden Roc sur la Côte d'Azur.

La création de villégiatures n'entre pas dans le débat actuel sur l'architecture. Par sa nature, le complexe hôtelier de luxe diffère de la plupart des types de construction. C'est un ouvrage d'un genre particulier réservé à un petit nombre de privilégiés. Il est réalisé avec de gros moyens financiers, est situé dans des sites idylliques et exotiques et offre des décors scéniques, enrobés de sérénité et de paix exquises.

L'architecture hôtelière altère souvent le temps et le lieu. Les façades trompeuses dissimulent une forte tendance à l'homogénéité. Qualifiées de "chic tropical" par d'aucuns, ces retraites exotiques sont des endroits vraiment somptueux. Leur réalisation basée sur des techniques traditionnelles, nécessite toujours la participation d'une main-d'œuvre spécialisée dans des métiers traditionnels dès le départ. Les architectes respectent sciemment la culture indigène de la région concernée. Dans leur livre *Hotel, Planning and Design*, Rutes et Penner affirment que "lorsque les recherches – études de possibilités financières, plans d'installations, critères techniques et systèmes de management – sont achevés, c'est le style spécifique qui fait la grande différence."

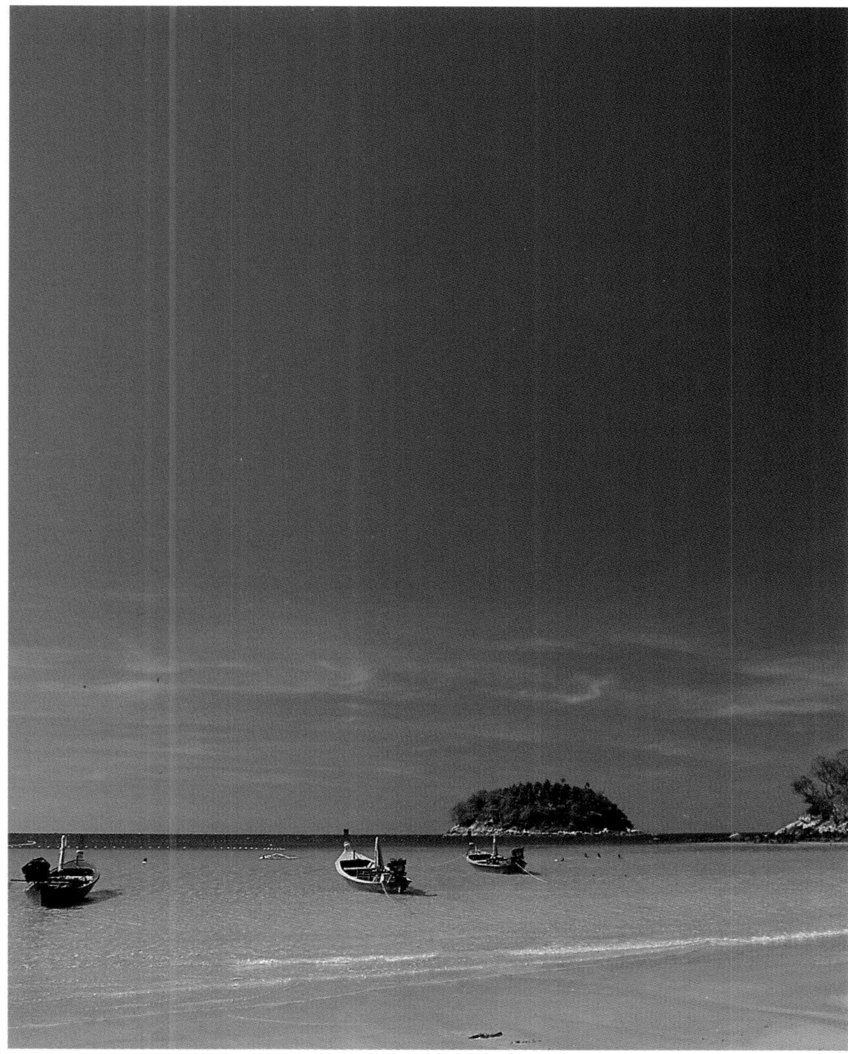

Southeast Asia has many attributes conducive to tourism - beautiful beaches and clear waters are two of them.

Südostasien hat viele Attraktionen, die den Tourismus fördern - wunderschöne Strände und klares Wasser gehören dazu.

Le Sud-Est asiatique a de nombreux atout touristiques - des plages magnifiques et des eaux cristallines.

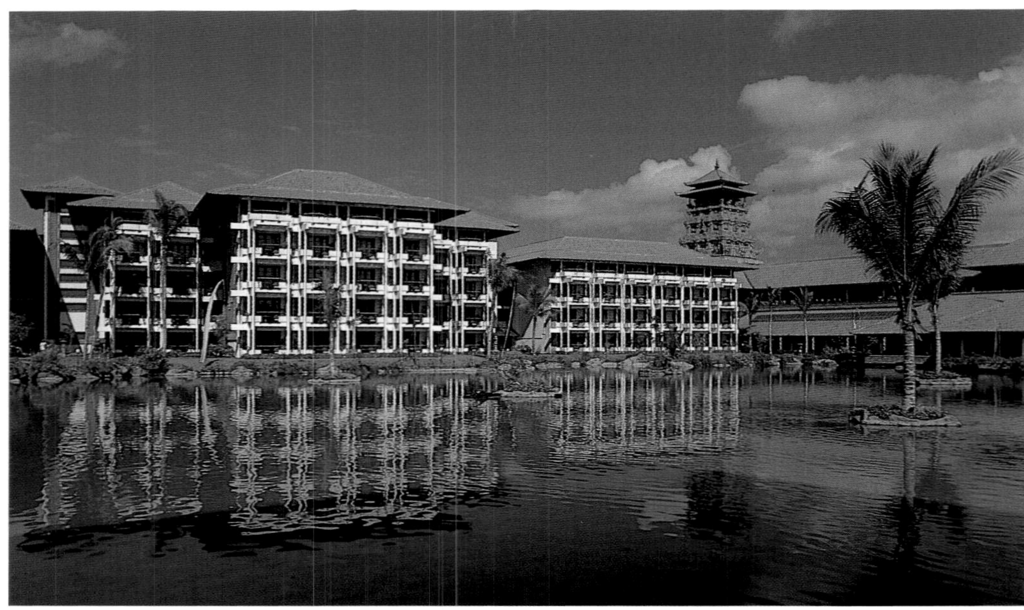

Resort markets are burgeoning in the region, resulting in huge hotels being built in all countries.

Der Markt für Ferienanlagen blüht in der Region. Als Folge davon entstehen in allen Ländern riesige Hotels.

Le marché du tourisme est en plein essor; de vastes complexes hôteliers sont érigés dans tous les pays.

Because the programme and site are relatively uncomplicated, the result is usually an exquisitely well-crafted resort that is a tribute to timeless craftsmanship and fine artisanry. This burgeoning variety of 'good' works are usually small but highly exclusive retreat resorts in remote locations. Termed boutique hotels, they were treated as an exotic refuge for affluent vacationers. Most of them are variations on the theme of the 'village'. The pavilion is treated as a unit of accommodation, each self-contained, with privacy assured by the careful placement of openings and walls. Many of them are influenced by important precedents.

The influence of Sri Lankan architect Geoffrey Bawa, whose deep concern for an architecture that is an integral part of the landscape, has been profound although largely under-rated. Many architects of these new resorts have been influenced by Bawa's corpus of works in Sri Lanka as well as his design at Batujimbar Estate in Bali for the late artist Donald Friend. This residence is noted for its blend of modern sensibilities and traditional elements as well as its sequence of carefully composed vistas. His design concept of different pavilions set in a lush landscape has been an important signpost.

Brian Brace Taylor, in his book *Geoffrey Bawa*, argues that a "unique and modernist quality of Bawa'a architecture is his *redeploying* of components, salvaged ancient artefacts, columns, a window or a jar in newly circumscribed contexts." The same strategy of incorporating vestiges of an ancient culture can be discerned in most of these resorts, where a sense of authenticity is derived from such historical artefacts.

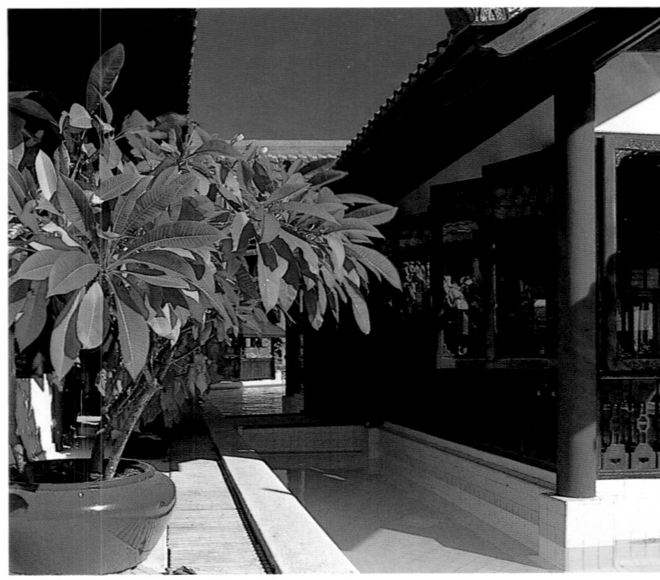

Many of the new resorts, such as Club Med Phuket, possess a sensual refinement and a sure sense of place.

Viele der neuen Anlagen, wie der Club Med Phuket, strahlen eine sinnliche Qualität und Gespür für die Umgebung aus.

Nombre de nouveaux complexes hôteliers tels que le Club Med à Phuket se distinguent par un raffinement sensuel et une recherche architectonique précise.

Australian architect Peter Muller, designer of the enigmatic and sybaritic haven of the luxurious Amandari, was the pioneer in promoting the "Bali" style to an international audience after his work at The Oberoi in Seminyak. The Amandari, officially opened in 1989, with its architecture of pavilions located at the picturesque Sayan ridge, and its famous 'knife-edge' pool, has spawned a number of progency and its variations. Frequented by high-powered jetsetters, the resort's outdoor baths flanked by water gardens have also proved to be an enduring model.

Other important precedents built during the early 1970s include the Hyatt Bali and Tanjung Sari at Sanur. Kerry Hill, designer of many resorts such as Amanusa and Chedi Ubud, as well as Ed Tuttle, designer of Amankila, are also involved in noted works in Bali. Together with landscape designers like

Managementsystem abgeschlossen sind, macht allein das besondere *Design* den entscheidenden Unterschied aus«.

Weil Programm und Lage keine besonderen Herausforderungen stellen, entstehen im allgemeinen hervorragend gebaute Ferienanlagen, mit denen zeitloses handwerkliches Können und großartiges Kunsthandwerk gewürdigt werden. Diese Form des »guten« Bauens nimmt zumeist in kleinen, aber hochst exklusiven Ferienanlagen an weit entfernten Orten zu. Man bezeichnet sie als Boutique-Hotels, die als exotische Zufluchtsorte für finanzkräftige Urlauber gelten. Die meisten variieren das Thema »Dorf«. Jeder Pavillon stellt eine unabhängige Wohneinheit dar, deren Privatatmosphäre mittels durchdachter Anbringung von Öffnungen und Wänden erzielt wird. Viele der neuen Bauten orientieren sich an wichtigen Vorgängern.

Der weitreichende Einfluß des srilankischen Architekten Geoffrey Bawa, der immer eine Architektur als integralen Bestandteil der Landschaft angestrebt hat, wurde stets unterschätzt. Viele Architekten der neuen Ferienanlagen ließen sich sowohl von Bawas Bauten auf Sri Lanka beeinflussen als auch von seinem Design im Batujimbar Estate auf Bali, entworfen für den inzwischen verstorbenen Künstler Donald Friend. Diese Residenz ist bemerkenswert, weil sie einerseits moderne Strömungen und traditionelle Elemente mischt, und weil sie andererseits eine Reihe sorgfältig geplanter und gestalteter Ausblicke bietet. Bawas Konzept von verschiedenen Pavillons in einer üpigen Landschaft war ein wichtiger Meilenstein. Seine Strategie, Antiquitäten und archäologische Fundobjekte in die Architektur miteinzubeziehen, läßt sich in den meisten Ferienanlagen erkennen, in denen historische Kunstwerke für ein Gefühl von Authentizität sorgen.

Der australische Architekt Peter Muller, Gestalter des rätselhaften, schwelgerischen und luxuriösen Zufluchtsorts Amandari, war der Erste, der weltweit für den »Bali-Stil« warb. Das 1989 eröffnete Amandari mit seinen Pavillons in den malerischen Bergen und mit seinem berühmten »Messerschneiden«-Pool hat eine Reihe von Nachkommen samt Varianten hervorgebracht.

Zu den weiteren wichtigen Vorgängern aus den frühen 70er Jahren gehören das Hyatt Bali und Tanjung Sari in Sanur. Kerry Hill, Erbauer vieler Ferienanlagen, darunter Amanusa und Chedi Ubud, und Ed Tuttle, Architekt von Amankila, waren auch an

Les programmes de réalisation et les sites créant rarement de difficultés, il en résulte des complexes hôteliers de construction raffinée qui rendent hommage à un savoir-faire manuel indestructible et à l'art artisanal. Cette nouvelle catégorie de "bons" ouvrages inclut des complexes hôteliers souvent de taille modeste, mais très luxueux et situés dans des lieux isolés. Appelés "boutique hotels " en anglais, ils sont conçus comme refuges exotiques pour vacanciers fortunés. La plupart d'entre eux sont construits comme des villages. Le pavillon est une unité d'hébergement indépendante, dont l'intimité est assurée par un choix réfléchi de l'emplacement des ouvertures et des murs. Dans un grand nombre de ces réalisations, on remarque l'influence d'importants projets précédents.

L'architecte Geoffrey Bawa de Sri Lanka, qui cherche notamment à intégrer l'architecture dans le paysage, a exercé une influence profonde bien que largement sous-estimée. Un grand nombre d'architectes des nouvelles stations balnéaires se sont inspirés de ses travaux au Sri Lanka et au Batujimbar Estate à Bali pour l'artiste défunt Donald Friend. Cette résidence révèle un mariage remarquable de perception moderne et d'éléments traditionnels ainsi qu'une composition élaborée de successions de vues. Le concept de Bawa – placer différents pavillons dans un cadre verdoyant – représente une innovation majeure.

Dans son livre *Geoffrey Bawa*, Brian Brace Taylor explique "que l'architecture de Bawa présente une qualité unique et moderne de par la redistribution d'éléments – objets anciens récupérés, colonne, fenêtre ou jarre – dans des contextes nouveaux". Une stratégie identique a été utilisée dans ces complexes hôteliers auxquels des objets historiques apportent un air d'authenticité.

L'Australien Peter Muller, architecte du havre énigmatique et sensuel qu'est le complexe hôtelier luxueux Amandari, a été le promoteur du style "Bali" auprès d'un public international, après avoir achevé l'Oberoi à Seminyak. Avec sa disposition architecturale de pavillons sur le pittoresque Sayan Ridge et sa célèbre piscine qui déborde en cascade, l'Amandari, inauguré en 1989, a été imité maintes fois, sous différentes variations. Fréquentés par la jet-society, les piscines et jardins aquatiques de l'hôtel sont également devenus un modèle classique.

Construits au début des années 70, le Hyatt Bali et le Tanjung Sari à Sanur font aussi partie des précurseurs. Kerry Hill, architecte de plusieurs complexes tels qu'Amanusa et Chedi Ubud ainsi

Bill Bensley and Michael White, they employed native craftsmen to build houses and hotels that have exerted strong influences in resort architecture in various parts of Southeast Asia.

The wave of upmarket resorts in Southeast Asia, probably started by the Hong Kong-based Amanresorts chain, continue unabated in this age of unconstrained mobility. The pioneering concept of Amanpuri, Amanresorts' first venture into the boutique hotel market in the region, has caught on rapidly. Its exclusive villa concept, the brainchild of hotel developer Adrian Zecha, depends very much on well-crafted architecture in spectacular settings. Even though the rates are extremely pricey, the concept proves to be highly popular. Today, major hotel groups such as the Four Seasons/Regent, the Mandarin Oriental and Singapore-based Banyan Tree Resorts are getting into the same market niche.

Many hotels are drearily homogenised and dog-eared, and merely become excuses for indulgence in Neo-Vernacular kitsch. However, at the top end of the market, the individual villa concept has also become trite and formulaic. It tends to lose its resonance when used indiscriminately. Having visited some 100 hotels and resorts, there are certainly more discernible, and sometimes disturbing similarities than marked differences. Besotted with nostalgia and often couched in the plaintive terms of "tradition" and "identity", many offer superficial reassurance of well-crafted buildings in our impoverished times. But most fail to address the pressing concerns of contemporary architecture.

Looking at the collection of resorts in this book, there is much to learn as well as to lament. While many offer a sensual physicality and sheer *joie de vivre* that are thoroughly absorbing, there is regrettably too little creative reinterpretation of regional history, local forms and materials. This is perhaps best summed up by David Klob, who argues that "traditional vocabularies might be used and metaphorically changed in ways that affirm a solidarity that is not that of shared immediate belief, a solidarity that remains comfortable with future reinterpretation. There is room for buildings that are neither naive celebrations nor elitst games."

Tan Hock Beng

Singapore 1995

bemerkenswerten Bauten in Bali beteiligt. Zusammen mit Landschaftsarchitekten wie Bill Bensley und Michael White haben sie einheimische Handwerker beschäftigt und Häuser und Hotels gebaut, die die Architektur der Ferienanlagen in verschiedenen Regionen Südostasiens stark beeinflußt haben.

Die Welle der anspruchsvollen Ferienanlagen in Südostasien, vermutlich von Amanresorts, Hongkong, ausgelöst, rollt in dieser Zeit der uneingeschränkten Mobilität ungebrochen weiter. Das wegbereitende Konzept von Amanpuri, der erste Vorstoß von Amanresorts in den Markt der Boutique-Hotels in der Region, wurde sehr schnell aufgenommen. Das exklusive Villen-Konzept, Erfindung des Hotelplaners Adrian Zecha, hängt von gekonnt ausgeführter Architektur in außergewöhnlich schöner Umgebung ab. Obwohl die Kosten extrem hoch sind, erweist es sich als sehr beliebt. Heute dringen größere Hotelgruppen wie Four Seasons/Regent, Mandarin Oriental und Banyan Tree Resorts aus Singapur in eben diese Marktlücke vor.

Viele Hotels sind in trauriger Eintönigkeit gebaut und nur noch ein Vorwand für ein Schwelgen in neo-folkloristischem Kitsch. Doch auch das individuelle Villen-Konzept der Marktführer ist schon abgedroschen und zur Formel verkommen. Es verliert immer mehr an Resonanz, wenn es wahllos eingesetzt wird. Beim Besuch von einigen hundert Hotels und Ferienanlagen waren mehr offensichtliche, manchmal ärgerliche Übereinstimmungen als deutliche Unterschiede zu erkennen. Berauscht von Nostalgie und dem Publikum mit den Begriffen »Tradition« und »Individualität« angepriesen, vermitteln viele nur oberflächlich den Eindruck von gekonnt konstruierten Häusern.

Wirft man einen Blick auf die Auswahl von Ferienanlagen in diesem Buch, so stellt man fest, daß zwar viele eine körperliche Sinnlichkeit und reine *joie de vivre* vermitteln, aber gleichzeitig leider zu wenig neue Interpretationen regionaler Geschichte, einheimischer Formen und Materialien bieten. David Klob faßt das vermutlich am besten zusammen, wenn er sagt, daß »das traditionelle Vokabular benutzt und bildlich auf eine Art verändert werden konnte, so daß ein Zusammengehörigkeitsgefühl entsteht, das nicht nur auf heutigen gemeinsamen Überzeugungen beruht, sodern auch mit zukunftigen neuen Interpretationen gut leben kann. Fur Bauwerke, die weder ein naives Zelebrieren noch Elitespiele sind, ist Platz.«

Tan Hock Beng

Singapur 1995

qu'Ed Tuttle, bâtisseur d'Amankila, ont également travaillé à des ouvrages réputés de Bali. En collaboration avec les paysagistes Bill Bensley et Michael White, ils ont employé des artisans du pays pour construire des maisons et hôtels qui ont fortement influencé l'architecture hôtelière dans le Sud-Est asiatique.

La vague de complexes hôteliers de première classe dans le Sud-Est asiatique, sans doute commencée par la chaîne Amanresorts de Hong Kong, ne cesse de se propager dans notre époque de mobilité constante. On a rapidement repris le concept innovateur de l'Amanpuri qui a été la première entreprise sur le marché régional de "l'hôtel boutique" de la chaîne Amanresorts. Son concept de villas élégantes, idée du promoteur hôtelier Adrian Zecha, repose essentiellement sur une architecture soignée dans des décors spectaculaires. Le concept remporte un immense succès en dépit de la cherté des séjours. Aujourd'hui, de grands groupes tels que le Four Seasons/Regent, le Mandarin Oriental et le Banyan Tree Resorts dont le siège est à Singapour, sont en train de pénétrer cette branche du marché.

Un grand nombre d'hôtels ne présentent aucune harmonie d'éléments et utilisent un kitsch néo-indigène tout juste acceptable. De toute façon, le concept de la villa individuelle s'est également banalisé en haut de l'échelle du marché. Il tend à perdre de sa valeur lorsqu'on l'utilise sans discernement. L'étude de quelque 100 hôtels et stations balnéaires a révélé plus de similarités parfois fâcheuses que de différences marquantes. Misant sur la nostalgie, la tradition et l'identité, beaucoup n'offrent que la garantie d'être des édifices bien construits, ce qui est devenu rare aujourd'hui. Mais les problèmes urgents de l'architecture contemporaine ne sont pas abordés dans la plupart.

Les complexes hôteliers présentés dans ce livre enseignent autant qu'ils soulèvent la critique. Nombre d'entre eux comblent les sens de la vue et du toucher et dégagent une véritable joie de vivre; néanmoins, on déplore la rareté d'interprétation créative de l'histoire régionale, des formes locales et des matériaux. Une citation de David Klob résume peut-être au mieux la situation: "Les langages traditionnels peuvent être utilisés et changés métaphoriquement de façon à exprimer une dépendance compatible avec de futures interprétations nouvelles. On peut construire des projets qui ne sont ni des glorifications naïves, ni des entreprises élitistes."

Tan Hock Beng

Singapour 1995

There is an increasing body of sensitively designed works in resort architecture, like the Amanpuri in Phuket, Thailand.

Es gibt immer mehr behutsam gebaute Ferienanlagen wie das Amanpuri in Phuket, Thailand.

Le nombre des complexes hôteliers conçus avec discernement augmente. Un exemple est l'Amanpuri à Phuket, Thaïlande.

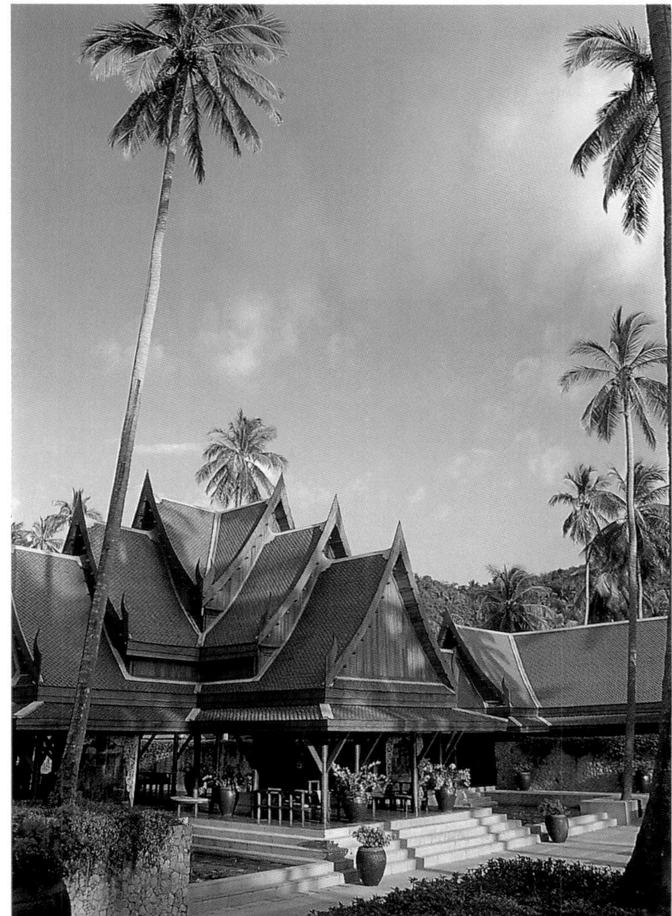

Amanpuri, Amanresorts's first foray into the boutique hotel, is an influential precursor to many subsequent development.

Amanpuri, das erste Boutique-Hotel von Amanresorts, hat viele weitere Entwicklungen stark beeinflußt.

Amanpuri, premier projet d'Amanresorts dans la branche de "l'hôtel boutique", a inspiré maintes réalisations ultérieures.

Tourism and Resort Architecture in Southeast Asia

Tourismus und die Architektur von Ferienanlagen in Südostasien

Introduction
Einleitung
Introduction

Today 21 million people around the world are employed in the travel and tourism industry, one that generates a staggering US$3.4 trillion annually. (1) The most rapidly developing tourism region globally is East Asia and the Pacific area, which has experienced an average annual growth rate of between 6% to 9% in recent years. Its rapid economic development has stimulated business travel and increased domestic and intraregional holiday travel of an unprecedented scale.

The "Seven Dragons" of East Asia have economies that enjoy the world's highest growth rates. As a result, East Asians are enjoying the new-found affluence they have created. Resort markets are burgeoning in the region, imposing unprecedented strains on the environment and infrastructure. The Brussels-based World Travel & Tourism Council predicts that the Asia-Pacific region's current 23% share of the world's travel market would increase to 27% in 2005, putting the Asia-Pacific ahead of America and not far behind Western Europe.

Some of the reasons for this especially strong market are the region's proximity to Japan, where it is reckoned that some 13.6 million Japanese travel abroad each year. Southeast Asia also has many attributes conducive to tourism — it has plenty of natural beauty in its mountains, tropical rainforests, sandy beaches and underwater coral gardens, as well as a rich historical and varied cultural heritage. All the countries of Southeast Asia are thus encouraging the active growth of their tourism industries.

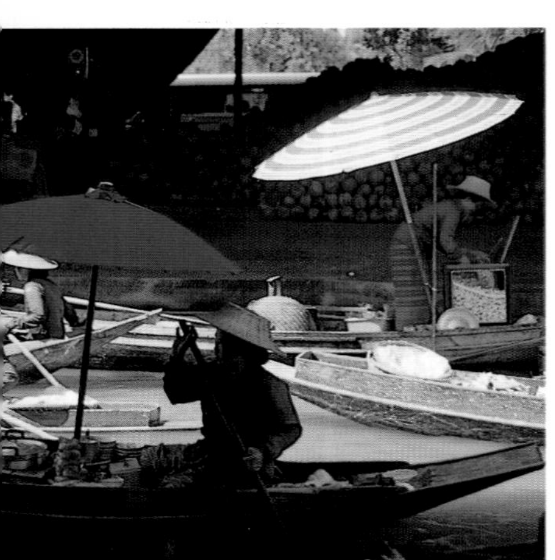

The rich historical and varied cultural heritage of Southeast Asia continues to attract tourists.

Das reiche historische und vielfältige Erbe Südostasiens zieht immer noch Touristen an.

Un nombre croissant de touristes désire découvrir le riche héritage historique et culturel du Sud-Est asiatique.

Indonesia, the world's largest archipelago of 13, 667 islands, has embarked on ambitious plans to attract tourists to more remote destinations and the lesser known parts of the country other than Bali and the places around its capital of Jakarta. Bali, "Island of the Gods", helps boost Indonesia's tourism industry that brings in more than US$3 billion (S$4.7 billion) a year from foreign exchange. (2) In the early 1980s, the sleepy fishing village of Nusa Dua on the dry Bukit Peninsula was selected as the site for major tourist development.

This project has been remarkably successful. The Bali Tourism Development Corporation (BTDC) has done an excellent job in managing Nusa Dua Beach Resort, having fully repaid its loan to the World Bank within 6 years instead of the 30-year grace period. (3) The Nusa Dua resort is an example of a large scale beach resort planned as an integrated development to be implemented over a long period of time. After years of concentrating their interest and investment on Bali, the

Heutzutage arbeiten 21 Millionen Menschen auf der ganzen Welt in der Reise- und Tourismusindustrie, die jährlich die schwindelerregende Summe von 3,4 Billionen US-Dollar umsetzt (1). Südostasien und der pazifische Raum ist die Tourismus-Region, die sich weltweit am schnellsten entwickelt; sie verzeichnet in letzter Zeit jährlich eine durchschnittliche Wachstumsrate zwischen 6 und 9 Prozent.

Die »Sieben Drachen« Ostasiens (Südkorea, Taiwan, Singapur, Hongkong, Malaysia, Thailand und Vietnam) verzeichnen weltweit die höchsten Wachstumsraten. Als Folge davon genießen die Menschen Ostasiens den selbst geschaffeneu neuen Wohlstand. Der Markt für Ferienanlagen blüht und belastet Umwelt und Infrastruktur auf ungeahnte Weise. Der World Travel & Tourism Council, Brüssel, sagt voraus, daß der Anteil des asiatisch-pazifischen Raums am weltweiten Reisemarkt von gegenwärtig 23 auf 27 Prozent im Jahr 2005 steigen wird, womit diese Region dann vor Amerika und nur wenig hinter Westeuropa liegt.

Einer der Gründe für diesen starken Markt ist die Nähe zu Japan: Jedes Jahr reisen rund 13,6 Millionen Japaner ins Ausland. Außerdem verfügt Südostasien über Reize, die dem Tourismus förderlich sind: eine wunderschone, abwechslungsreiche Natur und ein reiches historisches und kulturelles Erbe. Alle Länder Südostasiens fördern dabei ganz bewußt das Wachstum der Tourismusindustrie.

Indonesien, mit 13 667 Inseln der größte Archipel der Welt, hat den ehrgeizigen Plan entwickelt, Touristen nicht mehr nur nach Bali und in die Orte rund um die Hauptstadt Jakarta zu locken, sondern an entferntere Ziele und in weniger bekannte Teile des Landes. Bali, »Insel der Götter«, ist ein wichtiger Werbeträger für Indonesiens Tourismusindustrie, die jährlich 3 Milliarden US-Dollar Devisen einbringt (2). Zu Beginn der 80er Jahre wurde das verschlafene Fischerdorf Nusa Dua auf der Halbinsel Bukit dazu auserwählt, Schauplatz bedeutender touristischer Entwicklung zu werden - mit bemerkenswertem Erfolg. Die Bali tourism development Corporation (BTDC) leislete ganze Arbeit bei der Ferienanlage Nusa Dua Beach: Statt erst innerhalb der vereinbarten 30 Jahre konnte man die gesamte Anleihe bei der Weltbank schon nach sechs Jahren zurückzahlen (3). Nusa Dua ist ein Beispiel für eine Strand-Anlage im großen Stil; die Planung sah eine integrierte Entwicklung über einen langen Zeitraum vor. Nachdem die indonesische Regierung ihr Interesse und ihre Investitionen viele Jahre auf Bali konzentriert

Tourisme et architecture hôtelière dans le Sud-Est asiatique

Aujourd'hui, l'industrie du tourisme et des voyages emploie 21 millions de personnes dans le monde entier et rapporte la somme faramineuse de 3,4 trillions de dollars US par an (1). Les régions touristiques au développement le plus rapide sont l'Asie orientale et la région du Pacifique, avec un taux de croissance annuel de 6 à 9% au cours des dernières années. L'essor économique de ces régions a entraîné une augmentation sans précédent des voyages d'affaires et d'agrément nationaux et interrégionaux.

Les "sept dragons" du Sud-Est asiatique jouissent des taux de croissance les plus élevés du monde en matière d'économie. Par conséquent, les habitants d'Asie orientale profitent de la nouvelle prospérité qu'ils ont créée. Des complexes hôteliers surgissent partout dans ces pays, mettant l'environnement et les infrastructures à rude épreuve. Selon le Conseil international pour les voyages et le tourisme dont le siège est à Bruxelles, la part actuelle de 23% du marché mondial du tourisme de la région Asie-Pacifique aura augmenté de 27% en 2005. Cette région se retrouvera ainsi devant l'Amérique et sur les talons de l'Europe occidentale.

L'essor énorme du marché touristique dans cette région s'explique notamment par la présence proche du Japon dont 13,6 millions des habitants voyagent à l'étranger chaque année. Le Sud-Est asiatique a de nombreux atouts: des paysages merveilleux de montagne, de forêts tropicales, de rivages de sable et de parcs de coraux sous-marins ainsi qu'un riche héritage culturel et historique. Tous les pays du Sud-Est asiatique encouragent le développement actif de leur industrie du tourisme.

L'Indonésie qui est le plus grand archipel du monde avec 13667 îles, a élaboré des plans ambitieux pour attirer les touristes dans des lieux plus éloignés et moins connus que Bali et les environs de sa capitale Jakarta. Bali, "l'île des Dieux", joue un rôle majeur dans l'industrie touristique indonésienne qui rapporte plus de 3 billions de dollars US (4,7 billions de dollars de Singapour) en devises. (2) Au début des années 80, Nusa Dua, un paisible village de pêcheurs situé sur la péninsule non-marécageuse de Bukit, a été choisi comme site principal du développement touristique.

Ce projet a obtenu un succès remarquable. La Corporation balinaise du Développement du Tourisme (BTDC) a si bien administré Nusa Dua Beach qu'elle a entièrement remboursé l'emprunt pris auprès de la Banque mondiale en six ans au lieu

Southeast Asia is full of colossal but elegantly proportioned shrines, like this one at Prambanan, which are among the most impressive structures created by man.

In Südostasien gibt es zahllose Schreine, die trotz ihrer Monumentalität elegant proportioniert sind, wie dieser in Prambanan, der zu den eindrucksvollsten von Menschenhand geschaffenen Bauten gehört.

Le Sud-Est asiatique abrite une profusion de temples colossaux, mais aux proportions élégantes comme cette pagode à Prambanan, un des édifices les plus impressionnants que l'Homme ait jamais créé.

Located on a breathtaking site, the Tanah Lot temple is one of the six holiest temples in Bali.

In atemberaubender Lage: der Tanah Lot Tempel, einer der sechs heiligsten Tempel Balis.

Situé dans un site d'une beauté incomparable, le temple de Tanah Lot est l'un des six lieux saints de Bali.

The Barong Dance in Bali is staged primarily for tourists.

Der Barong-Tanz wird vor allem für Touristen aufgeführt.

La danse Barong à Bali est une véritable attraction touristique.

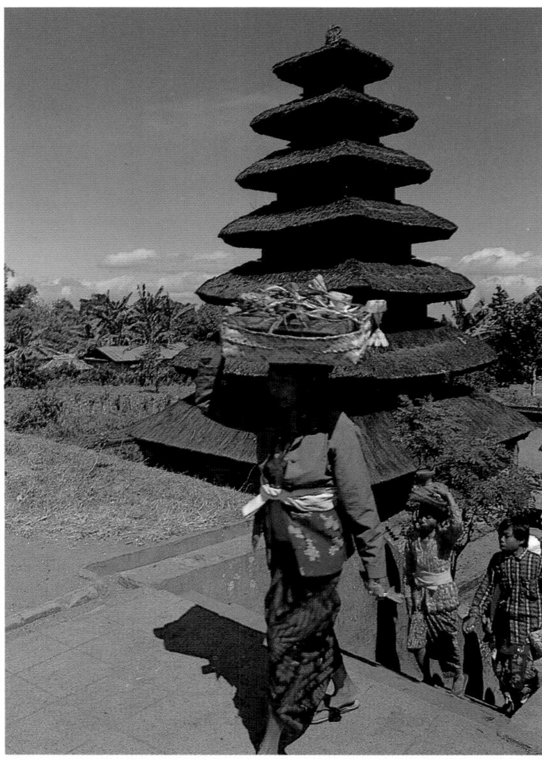

Villagers on their way to make offerings at the holiest Balinese temple at Bersakih.

Dorfbewohner mit Opfergaben auf dem Weg zu Balis heiligstem Tempel in Bersakih.

Des villageois vont porter leurs offrandes au temple de Bersakih, le premier lieu saint de Bali.

Indonesian government is developing new resort areas like Senggigi, Manado, Parangtritis, Biak and Bintan.

The 23,000 hectares Bintan Beach International Resort (BBIR) on the Indonesian island of Bintan, 45 km south-east of Singapore, is the first and largest project to be launched under the 1990 framework agreement between Singapore and Indonesia to jointly develop tourism on the island. The integrated lifestyle destination resort will be completed over a 20-year time-frame, and will boast more than 20 hotels, 10 condominium complexes, 30 village clusters and 10 golf courses. It intends to turn "an entire stretch of marshy wasteland into the Hawaii of the Orient." (4)

In June 1994, Singapore and Indonesia announced wide-ranging proposals to help boost the level of tourism in the two countries. These include joint identification of new tourist destinations and the development of hotels and resorts in Indonesia. Indonesia had singled out existing tourist destinations and those with potential which could benefit from the co-operation. These were in West Sumatra province, Yogjakarta and Solo in Central Java, Lombok Island off Bali, and Ujung Pandang in South Sulawesi province.(5) Parangtritis, which is less than half an hour's drive from Yogjakarta, already has the new Queen of the South hotel perched on cliffs above a beautiful black sand beach. Solo will be developed as an international entry point and serve as a gateway to attractions in the neighbouring cities of Yogjakarta and Semarang.

The mega-resort concept is also expanded to include high-altitude districts like Baturaden in the highlands of Central Java and Anai in the mountains of western Sumatra. New Tourism Development Corporations are being established in many parts of Indonesia, like Manado in North Sulawesi, Tanjung Bunga in South Sulawesi, Belitung Island in the straits between Sumatra and Borneo, Padang Beach on the western shore of Sumatra and Biak in West Irian. Manado has already benefited from the commencement of direct international air service from Singapore in 1994. It is targeted that by the end of the 90s, there will be another ten carefully planned, self-contained "Nusa Duas" all over the world's largest archipelago. They will be joint ventures between government and private industry, where the former will provide infrastructure like airports, highways, water and sewage treatment, power and telecommunications while the latter will build hotels, holiday homes and golf courses. Indonesia's long-term objectives are 6.5 million foreign tourists

hat, erschließt sie nun neue Gebiete für Ferienanlagen.

Das 23 000 Hektar große Bintan Beach International Resort (BBIR) auf der indonesischen Insel Bintan, 45 km südöstlich von Singapur, ist das erste und größte Projekt, das nach dem Rahmenabkommen von 1990 zwischen Indonesien und Singapur in Angriff genommen wird; dieses Abkommen sieht vor, den Tourismus auf der Insel gemeinsam zu entwickeln. Für die integrierte Lifestyle-Anlage ist ein Zeitraum von 20 Jahren vorgesehen; dann wird sie über mehr als 20 Hotels, zehn Komplexe mit Eigentumswohnungen, 30 Dorfgruppen und zehn Golfplätze verfügen. Man will »einen ganzen Bereich von sumpfigem Ödland in das Hawaii des Ostens« verwandeln (4).

Im Juni 1994 kündigten Singapur und Indonesien weitreichende Hilfen an, um das Niveau des Tourismus in beiden Ländern anzuheben. Dazu gehören gemeinsame Festlegung neuer Tourismusziele und die Entwicklung von Hotels und Ferienanlagen in Indonesien. Indonesien hatte bereits bestehende Ziele und solche, die von der Zusammenarbeit profitieren könnten, ausgewählt: West-Sumatra, Yogyakarta und Solo auf Zentraljava, die Insel Lombok vor Bali und Ujung Pandang in Süd-Sulawesi (5). Parangtritis, weniger als eine halbe Stunde Autofahrt von Yogyakarta entfernt, verfügt bereits über das neue Hotel Queen of the South oben auf den Klippen über einem wunderschönen schwarzen Sandstrand. Solo wird als internationaler Ausgangspunkt entwickelt und soll als Pforte zu den Attraktionen der benachbarten Städte dienen.

Das Konzept der Mega-Ferienanlage wird auch auf hochgelegene Regionen wie Baturaden im Hochland Zentraljavas und Anai in den Bergen West-Sumatras ausgedehnt. Neue Gesellschaften zur Tourismus-Entwicklung entstehen in vielen Teilen Indonesiens, beispielsweise in Manado in Nord-Sulawesi, Tanjung Bunga in Süd-Sulawesi, auf der Insel Belitung in der Meerenge zwischen Sumatra und Borneo, in Padang Beach an der Westküste Sumatras und in Birian in West-Irian. Manado profitiert bereits von der Einrichtung einer direkten internationalen Flugverbindung aus Singapur im Jahr 1994. Ziel bis zum Ende der 90er Jahre sind zehn sorgfältig geplante, unabhängige »Nusa Duas« im größten Archipel der Welt. Es wird zu Joint-ventures zwischen Regierung und Privatindustrie kommen, wobei die Regierung mit Flughäfen, Autobahnen, Wasser und Kläranlagen, Strom und Telekommunikation für die Infrastruktur sorgt, während die Industrie Hotels, Ferienhäuser und Golfplätze baut. Indonesien strebt auf lange Sicht 6,5

du délai accordé de 30 ans. (3) La station balnéaire Nusa Dua est l'exemple d'un vaste projet aux structures intégrées, planifié pour être réalisé à long terme. Après avoir concentré ses efforts et investissements sur Bali durant des années, le gouvernement indonésien a commencé la mise en valeur touristique de sites comme Senggigi, Manado, Parangtritis et Bintan.

Le site dit Bintan Beach International Resort (BBIR), d'une superficie de 23 000 hectares, s'étend sur l'île indonésienne de Bintan, à 45 km au Sud-Est de Singapour. Il est le premier et le plus important des projets réalisés dans l'accord-cadre passé entre Singapour et l'Indonésie en 1990 pour le développement commun du tourisme sur l'île. L'aménagement de la station balnéaire intégrée est prévu sur une période de vingt années et comprendra plus de 20 hôtels, 10 complexes hôteliers, 30 villages de vacances et 10 terrains de golf. Ce projet a pour objectif de transformer "une région entière de marécages" en l'Hawaï de l'Orient. (4)

En juin 1994, Singapour et l'Indonésie ont annoncé des plans de grande envergure pour promouvoir davantage le tourisme dans les deux pays. Ils incluent le choix commun de nouvelles destinations touristiques et le développement d'hôtels et de villégiatures en Indonésie. L'indonésie a sélectionné des lieux touristiques existants et d'autres sites potentiels qui pourraient profiter de la coopération. Ils sont situés dans l'Est de la province de Sumatra, à Yogjakarta et à Solo au centre de Sumatra et comprennent l'île Lombok au large de Bali et Ujung Pandang dans le Sud de la province de Sulawesi. (5)

Parangtritis, située à moins d'une demi-heure en voiture de Yogjakarta, abrite déjà le nouvel hôtel Queen of the South qui est perché sur des falaises dominant une magnifique plage de sable noir. Solo va devenir une porte d'entrée internationale et sera le point de départ vers les villes voisines de Yogjakarta et Semarang.

Le développement de vastes complexes hôteliers englobera également des régions à haute altitude comme Baturaden sur les hauts-plateaux du centre de Java et Anai dans les montagnes à l'Ouest de Sumatra. De nouvelles sociétés de promotion du tourisme s'établissent dans de nombreux endroits d'Indonésie tels que Manado au Nord et Tanjung Bunga au Sud de Sulawesi, Belitung Island dans le détroit entre Sumatra et Bornéo, Padang Beach sur la côte occidentale de Sumatra et Biak dans l'Ouest d'Irian. Manado a d'ores et déjà tiré profit de la ligne aérienne

With the influx of tourists, traditional artefacts in many parts of Southeast Asia rapidly become consumable items made specifically for tourism.

Der Massentourismus hat dazu geführt, daß traditionelle Kunstwerke Südostasiens eigens als Konsumware hergestellt werden.

Dans de nombreuses parties du Sud-Est asiatique, l'essor du tourisme a entraîné la fabrication en masse d'objets traditionnels.

and US$8.9 billion in tourism revenue by 1998. (6)

In Thailand, the main resort destinations are Chiangmai, Pattaya, Phuket and recently, Koh Samui and Krabi Province. Other new target areas are Rayong, Cha Am, Songkhla and the Phi Phi Islands. There are more than 30 major hotel and resort properties on the island of Phuket, not including the many bungalows and three-star hotels. It is playing host to more than 1.63 million visitors a year.[7] Some of the new five star projects include the Wah Chang property group's Bang Tao Beach Resort, on the site of a once abandoned tin mine at Laguna Bay. The Dusit Hotel and Resort Group has also recently opened a new resort on the province of Krabi.

Malaysia has several renowned resorts like the Tanjong Jara Beach Hotel in Trengganu and the Berjaya on Pulau Tioman. Penang, "the Pearl of the Orient", has long been considered Malaysia's premier tourist destination. However, its 96 hotels have to compete with the development of new hotels in Langkawi Island. With strong federal government backing, several new development on Langkawi have been completed since early 1994, including Westin Langkawi and The Datai.

The Philippines' medium-term tourism masterplan hopes to achieve its target of some 3.1 million foreign visitors by 1998. Massive investments have to be made by both the public and private sectors. Some 60,000 hotel rooms will be required to fulfill the numbers set. A 20-year tourism masterplan has been adopted as the blueprint for the sustainable development of tourism. It identifies six priority destinations that will be developed with massive foreign investments. These are Samal Island in Davao in southern Philippines; Panglao Island in Bohol in central Philippines; Palawan in western Philippines; Batangas-Taal-Tagaytay in the eastern coast of Luzon; Baguio, Ilocos and Pangasinan in northern Luzon; and the Bicol Peninsula.

Countries like Myanmar and Vietnam are also likely to be opened up rapidly for visitors. Cities like Hanoi, Ho Chi Minh City and Da Nang are already part of tour itineraries. Other potential tourist spots include Dalat, a hill resort that once served the French officials, and Hoa Binh in the interior of the country.

The main criticisms against enormous luxury hotels are aesthetic and environmental. While many hotels are gross fatuities, others are deemed inappropriate and ecologically wasteful amidst the poverty-stricken villages of many

Millionen Touristen aus dem Ausland und damit 8,9 Milliarden US-Dollar an Devisen an (6).

Die Hauptanlagen in Thailand sind Chiang Mai, Pattaya, Phuket und seit kurzem Koh Samui und Krabi. Vorgesehen sind weiterhin als neue Ziele Rayong, Cha Am, Songkhla und die Phi Phi Islands. Es gibt mehr als 30 größere Hotels und Ferienanlagen auf Phuket, wobei die Bungalows und Drei-Sterne-Hotels noch gar nicht mitgezählt sind. Die Insel ist Gastgeber für mehr als 1,63 Millionen Besucher jährlich (7). Zu den neuen Fünf-Sterne-Projekten gehört das Bang Tao Beach Resort der Wah-Chang-Gruppe in einer verlassenen Zinnmine in Laguna Bay.

Malaysia verfügt über mehrere bekannte Ferienanlagen wie das Tanjong Jara Beach Hotel in Trengganu und Berjaya auf Pulau Tioman. Penang, »die Perle des Ostens«, galt lange als Malaysias Touristenziel Nummer eins. Doch die 96 Hotels müssen mit neuen Hotels auf der Insel Langkawi in Konkurrenz treten. Dort wurden seit Anfang 1991 mehrere neue Projekte fertiggestellt, darunter Westin Langkawi und The Datai.

Der mittelfristige Tourismusplan der Philippinen hat sich zum Ziel gesetzt, 1998 etwa 3,1 Millionen ausländische Besucher begrüßen zu können. Kräftige Investitionen durch die öffentliche Hand und private Geldgeber sind nötig, um den angestrebten Plan zu erfüllen. Als Grundlage für langfristige Tourismusentwicklung wurde ein Zwanzigjahresplan aufgestellt. Er legt sechs vorrangige Ziele fest, die mit Hilfe massiver ausländischer Investitionen entwickelt werden: Samal Island in Davao auf den südlichen Philippinen, Panglao Island in Bohol auf den zentralen Philippinen, Palawan im Westen, Batangas-Taal-Tagaytay an der Ostküste von Luzon, Baguio, Ilocos und Pangasinan im Norden Luzons und die Halbinsel Bicol.

Auch Länder wie Birma und Vietnam werden sich Besuchern wahrscheinlich schnell öffnen. Städte wie Hanoi und Ho-Chi-Minh-Stadt (das ehemalige Saigon) und Da Nang sind bereits Stationen touristischer Rundreisen. Weitere mögliche Touristenziele sind Dalat, ein Ort in den Bergen, in dem früher Franzosen lebten, und Hoa Binh im Inneren des Landes.

Die Hauptkritik gegen riesige Luxushotels wird aus ästhetischen und umweltpolitischen Gründen erhoben. Ihnen wird vorgeworfen, sie paßten nicht mitten in unter Armut leidende Dörfer vieler Entwicklungsländer und betrieben ökologische Verschwendung. Sie benötigen große Mengen Wasser, Energie,

directe de Singapour, mise en service en 1994. L'objectif est de parsemer le plus grand archipel du monde d'ici à la fin des années 90, d'une autre dizaine de "Nusa Dua", chacune indépendante et planifiée avec soin. Elles seront des joint-ventures entre le gouvernement et l'industrie privée. Le gouvernement se chargera de l'infrastructure telle que les aéroports, les autoroutes, la distribution des eaux, la voirie, l'énergie et les télécommunications tandis que l'industrie bâtira les hôtels, les villages de vacances et les terrains de golf. L'objectif à long terme de l'Indonésie est d'accueillir 6,5 millions de touristes étrangers et de réaliser un revenu de 8,9 billions de dollars US pour le secteur du tourisme d'ici à 1998. [(6)]

Les principaux sites touristiques de la Thaïlande sont Chiangmai, Pattaya, Phuket et plus récemment Koh Samui et la province de Krabi. Les nouvelles régions-cibles s'appellent Rayong, Cha Am, Songkhla et les îles Phi Phi. L'île de Phuket abrite 30 hôtels et complexes hôteliers importants ainsi que de nombreux bungalows et établissements trois étoiles. Elle accueille 1,63 million de visiteurs chaque année. [(7)] Quelques-uns des nouveaux projets cinq étoiles incluent la station balnéaire Bang Tao du groupe immobilier Wah Chang qui sera aménagée sur le site d'une mine d'étain désaffectée à Laguna Bay. Le Dusit Hotel et Resort Group vient également d'ouvrir un complexe touristique dans la province de Krabi.

La Malaisie possède plusieurs endroits de villégiature renommés tels que le Tanjong Jara Beach Hotel à Trenganu et le Berjaya sur Pulau Tioman. Penang, la "Perle de l'Orient", est depuis longtemps la première destination touristique de la Malaisie. Cependant, ses 96 hôtels sont soumis à une forte concurrence depuis la création de nouveaux complexes hôteliers sur l'île de Langkawi. Ces nouvelles villégiatures qui incluent le Westin Langkawi et le Datai, ont été créées au début de 1994 avec un important soutien du gouvernement fédéral.

Aux Philippines, un plan à moyen terme vise à accueillir 3,1 millions de visiteurs étrangers d'ici à 1998. Les secteurs public et privé auront à faire d'importants investissements. Il s'agit de créer quelque 60 000 lits d'hôtels pour atteindre les objectifs fixés. Un plan sur 20 années a été adopté pour un développement continu du tourisme. Il donne la priorité à six sites qui seront mis en exploitation avec d'importants investissements étrangers: Samal Island à Davao dans le Sud des Philippines, Panglao Island sur Bohol au Centre des Philippines, Palawan dans l'Ouest des Philippines, Batangas-Taal-Tagaytay sur la côte orientale de l'île

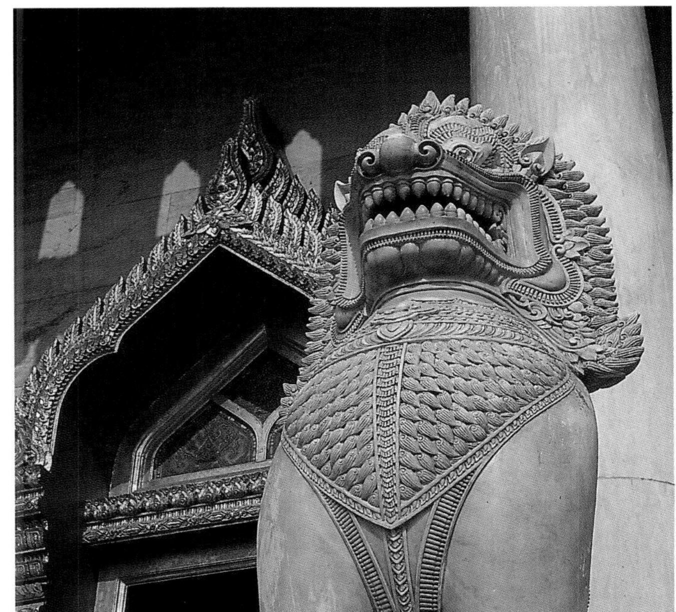

Religious buildings like this temple in Bangkok have become important stops in most tour itineraries.

Sakrale Bauten wie dieser Tempel in Bangkok gehören zu fast jedem Besuchsprogramm.

Les visites d'édifices religieux comme ce temple de Bangkok font partie du programme de la plupart des circuits touristiques.

A Balinese entrance gate leads into the temple compound.

Eine balinesische Eingangspforte führt ins Innere des Tempels.

Portes d'un temple de style balinais.

A Thai temple is a sanctuary of calm.

Ein Thai-Tempel ist ein Ort der Stille.

Un temple siamois est un sanctuaire de paix.

developing countries. They generally require large amounts of water, energy, food, monetary support, land and construction materials. If not carefully controlled, many of these buildings are going to be a blight to the environment. In March 1994, students from the Indonesian Arts Institute protested against plans to build a luxury resort in Bali and the alleged erosion of Balinese culture. (8) They demanded that the planned luxury Bali Nirwana resort be stopped. The resort will be sited close to the Tanah Lot temple which Balinese consider as one of the six holiest temples on the island.

Richard England have argued that "much of the onus and responsibility in avoiding these tragic situations and of consequently producing solutions for housing these travelling masses, without committing environmental suicide, rests squarely on members of the architectural profession. As planners, designers and policy-makers, there is much we can contribute to ensure that while the necessary economic aspect of foreign-exchange earnings and employment is not stunted, accommodation can be achieved without spoilation and pollution, and that the preservation of natural and man-made beauty spots together with the retention of the essential qualities of the genius loci are carefully preserved."

Environmental and ecological impacts aside, the socio-cultural and economic impacts of tourism also need to be continually monitored. The influx of mass tourism to Third World countries has created many problems ranging from the commercialisation of traditions to the degradation of social values. Tourism should be perceived as an instrument to enhance the quality of life, especially of the local populace, and the quality of the environment.

To quote from the editorial of the UNESCO International Social Science Journal No. 1, *The Anatomy of Tourism*: "Tourism has become an industry, a vast, globe-encircling "system", the direct and indirect effects of which are still poorly understood and even less well controlled. It regenerates as it pollutes, pays off as it undermines its very base, represents a source both of constructive experience and cultural enrichment as of alienation and degradation. In short, tourism is a mirror of the contradictions inherent in the present state of world development..."

Borobudur, the world's largest Buddhist monument, bears witness to the powerful foreign influences that shaped the cultures of Southeast Asia.

Borobudur, das größte Buddhistische Bauwerk der Welt, ist Zeuge für die mächtigen ausländischen Einflüsse, die Südostasiens Kulturen geformt haben.

Borobudur, le plus grand monument bouddhiste du monde, révèle la profondeur des influences étrangères dans les cultures du Sud-Est asiatique.

Nahrung, finanzielle Unterstützung, Land und Baumaterial. Wenn keine sorgfältige Kontrolle stattfindet, werden viele dieser Anlagen zum Fluch für ihre Umgebung. Im März 1994 protestierten Studenten des indonesischen Kunst-Instituts gegen die Planung einer Luxusanlage auf Bali und gegen die angebliche schleichende Zerstörung der einheimischen Kultur (8). Sie verlangten, den Bau der Luxusanlage Bali Nirwana einzustellen. Die Anlage liegt in der Nähe des Tempels Tanah Lot, einem der sechs heiligsten Tempel der Insel.

Richard England führte an, daß »ein großer Teil der Verpflichtung und der Verantwortung, solche tragischen Situationen zu vermeiden und dennoch Lösungen für die Unterbringung der reisenden Massen zu schaffen, ohne ökologischen Selbstmord zu begehen, eindeutig auf den Schultern der Architekten ruht. Mit Plänen, Entwürfen und politischem Handeln können wir viel dazu beitragen, daß Unterkünfte ohne Zerstörung und Umweltvergiftung entstehen, ohne daß der notwendige ökonomische Aspekt von Verdienst und Arbeit vernachlässigt wird; und wir können dazu beitragen, daß die natürliche und die vom Menschen geschaffene Schönheit erhalten bleibt und daß die ureigenste Atmosphäre eines Ortes sorgfältig bewahrt wird.«

Abgesehen von Auswirkungen auf Umwelt und Ökologie müssen auch die soziokulturellen und wirtschaftlichen Folgen des Tourismus ständig überwacht werden. Der Strom der Massentouristen in Länder der sogenannten Dritten Welt schafft viele Probleme, von der Kommerzialisierung der Traditionen bis zum Niedergang gesellschaftlicher Werte. Tourismus sollte als ein Instrument verstanden werden, mit dessen Hilfe die Lebensqualität, besonders der Bevölkerung vor Ort, und die Qualität der Umwelt gesteigert werden.

Zitat aus dem Leitartikel des UNESCO International Social Science Journal No 1, *The Anatomy of Tourism*: »Tourismus ist eine Industrie geworden, ein breites, weltumspannendes ›System‹, dessen direkte und indirekte Auswirkungen immer noch wenig verstanden und noch weniger kontrolliert werden. Tourismus schafft Neues, und er vergiftet gleichzeitig, er zahlt sich aus und gräbt sich auch selbst das Wasser ab, er ist eine Quelle konstruktiver Erfahrung und kultureller Bereicherung und Ursache von Entfremdung und Erniedrigung. Kurz, Tourismus ist ein Spiegel der Widersprüche, wie sie im gegenwärtigen Zustand der Weltentwicklung zu erkennen sind.«

Luçon, Baguio, Ilocos et Pangasinan dans le Nord de Luçon et la péninsule de Bicol.

Des pays tels que Myanmar et le Viêt-nam commencent à ouvrir leurs portes aux visiteurs étrangers. Hanoï, Hô Chi Minh Ville et Da Nang font déjà partie des circuits touristiques. D'autres lieux potentiels incluent Dalat, une villégiature dans les montagnes, et Hoa Binh à l'intérieur du pays.

Les critiques majeures contre les grands complexes hôteliers de luxe sont d'ordre esthétique et écologique. Si beaucoup d'hôtels n'étaient qu'un luxe ostentatoire, certains nuisent à l'environnement et paraissent très incongrus parmi les villages souvent démunis des pays en développement. En mars 1994, des étudiants de l'Institut des Arts indonésiens ont protesté contre le projet de construction du complexe hôtelier de luxe Bali Nirwana sur Bali et contre la détérioration de la culture balinaise. (8) Le complexe avoisinera le temple de Tanah Lot, l'un des six temples les plus sacrés de l'île.

Richard England a écrit: "Il revient en grande partie aux membres de la profession d'architecte d'éviter ces situations tragiques et de trouver des solutions d'hébergement des masses de voyageurs sans détruire l'environnement. En tant que planificateurs, bâtisseurs et 'décideurs', nous pouvons faire beaucoup pour garantir la création de lieux de villégiature sans spoliation et pollution, la conservation de sites naturels ou dessinés par l'homme et la préservation des qualités fondamentales du "genus loci", tout en tenant compte de la nécessité de l'aspect économique, à savoir les profits en devises et l'emploi."

Outre l'impact écologique et environnemental, il s'agit d'observer continuellement les effets socio-culturels et économiques du tourisme. Le flux du tourisme dans le Tiers Monde a entraîné de nombreux problèmes, depuis la commercialisation des traditions jusqu'à la détérioration des valeurs sociales. Le tourisme devrait être un instrument destiné à rehausser la qualité de l'environnement et la qualité de vie, notamment des populations locales.

On peut lire dans l'éditorial du Journal International de Sciences Sociales n° 1 de l'UNESCO, *Anatomie du tourisme*: "Le tourisme est devenu une industrie, un vaste 'système' englobant le monde entier, dont les effets directs et indirects sont encore peu compris et encore moins contrôlés.

Primitive and ethnic art has become ubiquitous touristic objects.

Primitive Kunstwerke und Volkskunst werden Touristen überall angeboten.

L'art indigène occupe désormais une place omniprésente dans l'industrie du tourisme.

"The poetic image is not subject to an inner thrust. (That is, its relation to an archetype lying dormant in the depths of the unconscious is not a casual one.) It is not an echo of the past. On the contrary; through the brilliance of an image, the distant past resounds with echoes..."

Gaston Bachelard

»Das poetische Bild ist nicht von einem inneren Anstoß abhängig. (Das bedeutet, seine Beziehung zu einem Urbild, das in den Tiefen des Unbewußten ruht, ist keine zufällige.) Es ist nicht ein Echo der Vergangenheit. Im Gegenteil, durch die Brillanz eines Bildes erklingen die Echos aus der fernen Vergangenheit...«

Gaston Bachelard

Re-Presentation and Authenticity

(Re)Präsentation und Authentizität

Re-Présentation et Authenticité

"Time-space convergence", as defined by Giddens, is the way in which time-space distantiation occurs in capitalist modernity; a phenomenon of the "shrinking of distance" between locales under the influence particularly of advanced transportation and communication technology. (9) Time-space convergence and commodification have arguably led to tourism becoming a general phenomenon.

As Wolfgang Schivelbusch comments, "From now on, the places visited by the traveller become ever more similar to the commodities that are part of the same circulatory system. For twentieth century tourism, the world has become one big department store of landscapes and cities." (10)

As we move into a new epoch of global culture, tourist amenities, in particular, are readily subjected to the rigors of the global marketplace. The "international standard" hotel, whether owned by the state but run by an international hotel chain, or privately owned, is one of the most conspicuous symbol of modernity in many parts of the Third World. Such buildings bring into sharp focus the definitions of terms such as "tradition/al" and "modern/ity", as well as redefining notions of "authenticity" within the culture involved.

CONCEPT OF AUTHENTICITY

In Southeast Asia, established locations like Bali in Indonesia, as well as prospective locations like Langkawi in Malaysia, are earmarked for even more elaborate development in order to attract the growing share of regional and international travellers. Over the last couple of years, there is without doubt an increasing body of well-crafted works in the resort industry of the region.

However, the issue is really how have these buildings contributed to the generation of vital forms of regional culture, and at the same time, merit claims of authenticity. To attract the ever-increasing number of tourists, entrepreneurs and tour operators often use traditions and heritage, both authentic and manufactured, for mass consumption. Resorts are building types that are precisely tailored to fulfil this need. Being intrinsically contrived, many of them are now paradoxically marketed for their architectural merits, which are being hailed for their "authenticity".

The increasingly anthropological interest of the world's

»Zeit-Raum-Konvergenz« ist nach der Definition von Giddens die Art und Weise, in der sich die Entfernung Zeit Raum in der kapitalistischen Moderne zeigt; ein Phänomen des »Schrumpfens der Entfernung« zwischen Schauplätzen besonders unter dem Einfluß verbesserter Transportverhältnise und Kommunikationstechnologie (9). Zeit-Raum-Konvergenz und die Umwandlung von Werten in stets verfügbare Ware haben dazu geführt, daß der Tourismus ein Phänomen wurde.

Wolfgang Schivelbusch kommentiert: »Ab jetzt werden die von den Reisenden besuchten Orte den Waren immer ähnlicher, die Teil desselben Kreislaufs sind. Für den Tourismus des 20. Jahrhunderts ist die Welt ein einziges riesiges Warenhaus mit Landschaften und Städten geworden.« (10)

Touristische Annehmlichkeiten werden bereitwillig den Zwängen des globalen Marktes unterworfen. Das Hotel mit »internationalem Standard«, ob in Staatsbesitz, von einer internationalen Kette betrieben oder in Privathand, ist in vielen Teilen der sogenannten Dritten Welt eines der verdächtigsten Symbole von Modernität. Solche Bauwerke rücken Begriffe wie »Tradition/traditionell« und »Modernität/modern« in den Mittelpunkt, und sie definieren Vorstellungen von »Authentizität« in der entsprechenden Kultur neu.

KONZEPT DER AUTHENTIZITÄT

In Südostasien soll in bereits bekannten Orten wie Bali in Indonesien und zukünftigen Urlaubszielen wie Langkawi in Malaysia die Entwicklung noch besser geplant werden, damit der Anteil regionaler und internationaler Reisender wächst. Die Zahl der guten Ferienanlagen nahm in den letzten Jahren in dieser Region zweifellos zu.

Eigentlich geht es jedoch darum, wie man diese Bauten mit den lebendigen Formen der regionalen Kultur verbindet und dabei den Anspruch auf Authentizität durchsetzt. Um für die Touristen attraktiv zu sein, setzen Unternehmer und Reiseveranstalter oft Tradition und kulturelles Erbe, ob authentisch oder künstlich produziert, für den Massenkonsum ein. Ferienanlagen sind genau auf das Bedürfnis nach Tradition und Erbe zugeschnitten. Zwar sind sie eigentlich gekünstelt, aber so paradox es klingt, ihre Architektur wird auf dem Markt angepriesen, und löst ob ihrer »Authentizität« sogar Jubel aus.

Die reisende Mittelklasse sucht zunehmend den Tourismus

"L'image poétique ne dépend pas d'une impulsion intérieure. (Sa relation avec un archétype dormant dans les profondeurs de l'inconscient n'est pas fortuite.) Elle n'est pas un écho du passé. Au contraire: le passé lointain résonne d'échos créés par la brillance d'une image."

D'après Gaston Bachelard

Selon Giddens, la "convergence temps-espace" traduit la distanciation temps-espace dans le monde moderne capitaliste. C'est un phénomène de "distance qui se réduit" entre les lieux grâce aux transports modernes et à la technologie de communications. (9) Sa banalisation et la convergence temps-espace ont fait du tourisme un phénomène général.

Wolfgang Schivelbusch commente que: "Désormais, les endroits visités par les voyageurs sont de plus en plus assimilés aux produits appartenant au même circuit économique. Le monde est devenu un grand magasin de paysages et de villes pour le tourisme du 20e siècle." (10)

Alors que nous entrons dans une ère nouvelle de culture universelle, les aménagements touristiques sont d'ores et déjà assujettis aux lois du marché mondial. Qu'il soit propriété de l'Etat, mais géré par une chaîne hôtelière internationale, ou qu'il appartienne à des particuliers, l'hôtel "conforme aux normes internationales" constitue un des symboles les plus marquants du monde moderne dans de nombreuses régions du Tiers Monde. Ces édifices obligent à définir des termes tels que "tradition/nel" et "modern/ité" ainsi que la notion "d'authenticité" dans les cultures concernées.

Tour operators continue to market intimate new resorts as beingmore authentic than ill-conceived large developments.

Reiseveranstalter werben damit, daß kleine neue Ferienanlagen authentischer sind als schlecht geplante große Bauten.

Dans leur mercatique, les tours-opérateurs vantent l'aspect authentique des nouveaux hôtels de taille modeste, absent des grands complexes de conception médiocre.

CONCEPT D'AUTHENTICITE

Dans le Sud-Est asiatique, des lieux touristiques connus tels que Bali en Indonésie et certains endroits potentiels comme Langkawi en Malaisie, vont être encore plus exploités et mis en valeur afin d'attirer la masse croissante des voyageurs nationaux et internationaux. Le nombre des complexes hôteliers de première catégorie a déjà énormément augmenté dans cette région au cours des dernières années.

Cependant, la question est de savoir comment ces édifices ont contribué à l'évolution de la culture régionale tout en pouvant prétendre en même temps à l'authenticité. En vue d'attirer les touristes de plus en plus nombreux, les entrepreneurs et tours-opérateurs se servent fréquemment des traditions et de l'héritage culturel, authentiques ou fabriqués pour la société de consommation. Les complexes hôteliers sont spécialement construits pour répondre à ces besoins. Leur conception repose sur des données artificielles alors que la mercatique en souligne les qualités architecturales saluées pour leur "authenticité".

La classe moyenne en voyage montre un intérêt accru pour

Historic sites, such as this bathing pool in Bali, have been reproduced countless times in the grounds of resorts.

Historische Anlagen wie dieses Schwimmbecken auf Bali wurden in Ferienanlagen ungezählte Male nachgebaut.

Des sites historiques tels que ces bassins à Bali, ont été reproduits maintes fois sur les sites des complexes hôteliers.

In their rush to embrace an aesthetic for a new touristic consciousness through the use of pre-existing elements, architects have isolated form from meaning.

In ihrem Bemühen, mit Hilfe bereits bestehender Elemente eine Ästhetik für ein neues touristisches Bewußtsein zu schaffen, haben die Architekten Form und Bedeutung voneinander getrennt.

Les architectes ont isolé la forme du contenu en voulant utiliser des éléments préexistants pour créer une esthétique qui réponde aux exigences accrues des touristes.

The concept of authenticity offer tourists a more culturally sensitive form of travel accommodation.

Das Konzept der Authentizität bietet den Touristen eine kulturell sensiblere Form der Ferienunterkunft.

Le concept d'authenticité offre aux touristes une forme d'hébergement plus influencée par la culture locale.

travelling middle class, in search of ethnic tourism, go to the host countries "experiencing" and pursuing proofs of their "authentic" contact with exotic cultures. Many host countries are providing such material symbols, both for touristic consumption as well as for their own cultural self-fulfillment in the development of "secondary ethnicity". MacCannell describes the phenomena as having a "front stage" for outsiders to experience, and the "back stage" where "things really happen".[11] He argues that touristic consciousness is motivated by the desire for the latter. Increasingly, more tourists are actively seeking "authenticity" in these back-stage regions. However, many of such back-stage regions are often just as inauthentic, staged purely for another form of touristic consumption.

Tour operators continue to market new resorts, especially those of a more intimate scale, that claim to be more authentic than many ill-conceived large developments. This claim to "authenticity" is usually substantiated and validated by comparisons with two other categories of buildings — the "placeless" Modernist high-rise structures and the bogus regionalist works which are often flaccidly designed in an eclectic agglomeration of kitsch.

The tourism industry has thus successfully constructed a new niche by marketing the concept of authenticity which offers tourists a more "culturally sensitive" and "politically correct" form of travel accommodation. Authenticity has become one of the primary concerns of architects practising in many parts of Southeast Asia today. However, the attempt to be "authentic" is often well-intentioned but usually misguided.

The concept of "authenticity" is itself a minefield of conflicting notions. It is a nebulous, emotive and elusive term. Yet the mapping out of the term's limits is essential if we are to enter into any discourse on the difference between the genuine and the fake, as well as to fuel the search for a culturally vital contemporary architectural expression for Southeast Asian societies.

The root of this concern for authenticity can be traced to a major shift that occurred within the American arts and material cultural scene from the late 19th century to the 20th century. The then popular arts of imitation and illusion were replaced by a quest for values of authenticity, one that was obsessed with "the real thing". "Authenticity" is hence an essentially modern

mit völkerkundlichem Anspruch, weshalb sie in bestimmte Gastländer reist, um »authentischen« Kontakt mit fremden Kulturen zu »erfahren« und Beweise dafür zu sammeln. Viele Gastländer stellen diese materiellen Symbole zur Verfügung, nicht nur für den Konsum durch die Touristen, sondern auch für die eigene kulturelle Befriedigung. MacCannell vergleicht diese Art der Begegnung mit einem Theater, das über eine Vorderbühne verfügt, auf der die Außenstehenden (Touristen) etwas erleben, und eine Hinterbühne, auf der sich das »richtige Leben« (der Einheimischen) abspielt, wobei die Touristen Sehnsucht nach der hinteren Bühne empfinden. (11) Durch diese Sehnsucht motiviert, suchen immer mehr Touristen aktiv die »Authentizität« in den Bereichen der »hinteren Bühne«, doch sind viele dieser Bereiche genauso wenig authentisch wie die »Vorderbühne«, denn sie werden oft nur als Bühne für eine andere Form des touristischen Konsums aufgebaut.

Reiseveranstalter preisen vor allem kleine, intime Ferienanlagen an, die den Anspruch erheben, »authentischer« als viele der schlecht gestalteten großen Anlagen zu sein. Um diesen Anspruch auf »Authentizität« auch zu beweisen und positiv darzustellen, werden sie mit zwei anderen Kategorien von Bauwerken verglichen – mit den überall errichteten modernistischen Hochbauten und den »unechten« regionalen Anlagen, die oft eine unerschöpfliche, zusammengewürfelte Anhäufung von Kitsch vorzuweisen haben.

Die Tourismusindustrie hat mit der Vermarktung der Authentizität erfolgreich eine neue Nische geschaffen, in der den Touristen eine »kulturell sensiblere« und »politisch korrektere« Form der Reiseunterkunft angeboten wird. Heute ist Authentizität einer der wichtigsten Punkte für die Architekten in vielen Teilen Südostasiens geworden. Doch der Versuch, »authentisch« zu sein, ist oft beste Absicht, geht aber meistens in die falsche Richtung.

Das Konzept der »Authentizität« ist in sich selbst ein Minenfeld widersprüchlicher Vorstellungen. Es ist ein nebulöser, gefühlsbetonter, schwer faßbarer Begriff. Doch es ist wichtig, die Grenzen dieses Begriffs abzustecken, wenn wir in eine Diskussion über den Unterschied zwischen dem Echten und dem Falschen eintreten und damit die Suche nach einer kulturell lebendigen, zeitgemäßen architektonischen Ausdrucksform für südostasiatische Gesellschaften beschleunigen wollen.

Das Bemühen um Authentizität ist eine Reaktion auf die

l'anthropologie. Elle veut du tourisme ethnographique, vivre des "expériences" et rechercher un contact "authentique" avec les cultures exotiques. Un grand nombre des pays hôtes offrent ces symboles matériels destinés à la consommation touristique, mais aussi à créer une "culture secondaire". MacCannell décrit ce phénomène d'un "devant de scène" à montrer aux étrangers et de "coulisses" où "les choses réelles se passent". (11) Il déclare que les touristes recherchent cette dernière situation. Ils sont toujours plus nombreux à partir explorer les coulisses, en quête "d'authenticité". Cependant, beaucoup de ces régions "coulisses" sont également inauthentiques et mises en scène pour une autre forme de consommation touristique.

Les tours-opérateurs poursuivent la promotion de nouvelles villégiatures, notamment du genre intime, qui se prétendent plus authentiques qu'un grand nombre de vastes complexes hôteliers de conception médiocre. Cette revendication "d'authenticité" se justifie dans la comparaison avec deux autres catégories de constructions: les énormes structures en hauteur de style moderne et les ouvrages bidon régionalistes qui ne sont souvent qu'un assemblage syncrétique d'éléments kitsch.

L'industrie du tourisme a donc créé un nouveau créneau avec la mercatique du concept d'authenticité qui offre au touriste une forme d'hébergement "plus sensibilisée à la culture" et "plus juste". L'authenticité est devenue une priorité des architectes qui œuvrent aujourd'hui dans de nombreuses régions de l'Asie du Sud-Est. Toutefois, si les tentatives "d'authenticité" partent de bonnes intentions, elles se révèlent souvent malencontreuses.

Le concept "d'authenticité" est formé d'un embrouillement de notions antagoniques. C'est un terme évasif, empreint de nébulosité et de sentiment. Pourtant il faut en délimiter son sens afin de pouvoir débattre sur la différence entre le vrai et le faux et découvrir une expression architecturale contemporaine qui soit vitale aux cultures des sociétés du Sud-Est asiatique.

Ce souci d'authenticité remonte à un changement profond qui s'est opéré dans les arts et l'architecture américains au tournant du siècle. Les courants artistiques alors en vogue – imitation et création d'illusion – furent remplacés par une quête de l'authenticité, une recherche de la "chose réelle". L'authenticité est donc une valeur essentiellement moderne, associée aux répercussions de la modernité, et dans le contexte actuel – la post-modernité – à la société contemporaine.

Traditional architecture is used as inspiration for many large resorts, but usually reproduced at a scale that is without any historical precedence.

Die traditionelle Architektur dient vielen großen Anlagen als Anregung, wird im allgemeinen jedoch ohne jeglichen historischen Bezug einfach nachgebaut.

Un grand nombre de vastes complexes hôteliers s'inspirent de l'architecture traditionnelle, mais elle est reproduite sans tenir compte de l'Histoire.

At Amanusa, Bali, traditional elements are used to provide visual and tactile links with the past.

In Amanusa, Bali, werden traditionelle Elemente verwendet, um sichtbare und greifbare Verbindungen mit der Vergangenheit herzustellen.

A Amanusa, Bali, les éléments traditionnels constituent des liens visuels et tangibles avec le passé.

value, associated with the impacts of modernity, and in today's context —postmodernity— upon contemporary society.

Many writers have echoed that modern life is filled with an overwhelming sense of fragmentation and transitoriness. If change and ephemerality formed the material basis of modernity, then the successful artist was one who understood such chaos and fragmentation and at the same time managed to extract the universal and the eternal.

Harvey argues that "Modernism from its very beginning, therefore, became preoccupied with language, with finding some special mode of representation of eternal truths." (12) In order to be authentic to its age, the aesthetic response exhibited a fascination with modern techniques, new conditions for production, new transport and communication systems and other new commodities of daily life.

The impact of modernity upon social existence has resulted in this consuming effort to get beyond imitation. Berger has said, " If nothing on 'the outside' can be relied upon to give weight to the individual's sense of reality, he is left no option but to burrow into himself in search of the real. Whatever this *ens realissimum* may then turn out to be, it must necessarily be in opposition to any external (modern) social formation. The opposition between self and society has now reached its maximum. The concept of authenticity is one way of articulating this experience." (13)

In the current literature on the postmodern condition, many critics have reiterated that postmodernist thought, just like the modernist value, also accepts ephemerality, fragmentation and discontinuity. The world is seen as comprising of perpetually shifting fragments. The loss of temporality and the search for instantaneous impact have also given rise to a loss of depth. Jameson describes contemporary cultural production's fixation with appearances and Postmodern architecture's preoccupation with surfaces as 'contrived depthlessness'. Kenneth Frampton concurs in noting that "stripped by science of its magical coalescence, the modern world began to fragment. Since appearance now belied truth, it became necessary to regard form as being separate from content..." (14) History and cultural forms are hence commercialised. Through the media, past architectural styles are viewed as an archive to be raided in order to achieve historical legitimacy, and thus authenticity.

großen Veränderungen in der materiellen Kultur Europas und Amerikas an der Wende vom 19. zum 20. Jahrhundert und wurde zuerst in der Kunstszene gefordert. Dort war man seinerzeit besessen von »the real thing«, dem Echten, und so trat an die Stelle von Imitation und Illusion in der Kunst das Streben nach Authentizitat. »Authentizität« ist somit ein noch junger Wert, entstanden durch die Auswirkungen der Moderne auf die zeitgenössische Gesellschaft. Viele Autoren haben immer wieder darauf hingewiesen, daß das moderne Leben von einem überwältigenden Gefühl von Zersplitterung und Vergänglichkeit erfüllt sei. Wenn Wandel und Kurzlebigkeit die materielle Basis für Modernität sind, dann ist der erfolgreiche Künstler jemand, der Chaos und Zersplitterung begreift und gleichzeitig das Wesentliche des Universellen und des Ewigen darstellt.

Harvey führt aus, daß »Modernismus von Anfang an vor allem mit Sprache beschäftigt war, damit, eine besondere Form zu finden, um ewige Wahrheiten auszudrücken.« (12) Um zeitgenössisch authentisch zu sein, entwickelte die Ästhetik eine Faszination für moderne Techniken, neue Produktionsformen, neue Transport- und Kommunikationssysteme und andere neue Angebote des täglichen Lebens.

Der Einfluß der Modernität auf die soziale Existenz führte zum Konsumstreben. Berger schrieb, »wenn der Einzelne sich auf nichts ›Äußerliches‹ verlassen kann, durch das sein Gefühl von Realität Gewicht bekommt, dann hat er keine Wahl, sondern er muß sich in die Suche nach dem Wirklichen vertiefen. Als was immer sich dieses absolut Wirkliche dann herausstellt, es muß notwendigerweise im Gegensatz zu jeder äußeren (modernen) gesellschaftlichen Form stehen. Der Gegensatz zwischen dem Selbst und der Gesellschaft ist jetzt am größten. Das Konzept der Authentizität ist eine Möglichkeit, diese Erfahrung zum Ausdruck zu bringen.« (13) Jameson beschreibt die Fixierung der zeitgenössischen Kulturproduktion auf äußere Erscheinungsformen und die Beschäftigung der postmodernen Architektur mit Oberflächen als »künstliche Tiefenlosigkeit«. Kenneth Frampton merkt an, daß »die moderne Welt anfing zu zersplittern, als ihr die Naturwissenschaft ihre magische Verschmelzung raubte. Da das äußere Erscheinungsbild die Wahrheit nun falsch darstellte, wurde es notwendig, Form unabhängig vom Inhalt zu betrachten«. (14) Folglich wurden Geschichte und kulturelle Formen kommerzialisiert. Durch die Medien werden architektonische Stilrichtungen der Vergangenheit zu einem Archiv, das man plündern kann, um historische Legitimität und damit »Authentizität« zu erreichen.

Un grand nombre d'écrivains ont écrit que la vie moderne est faite de fragmentations et de transitions. Si le changement et l'éphémère ont formé la base matérielle de la modernité, l'artiste qui réussissait était celui capable de comprendre le chaos et la fragmentation tout en exprimant l'universel et l'éternel.

Harvey déclare que "dès son commencement, le mouvement moderne s'est préoccupé du langage, de trouver un mode spécial de représentation des vérités éternelles" (12). Afin d'être authentique dans son époque, la démarche esthétique a consacré une large place aux techniques modernes, aux nouvelles méthodes de production, aux nouveaux moyens de transport et communications et autres nouvelles commodités de la vie quotidienne.

L'impact de la modernité sur l'existence sociale a entraîné ce désir de vouloir à tout pris dépasser l'imitation. Berger a dit: "A défaut de pouvoir se reposer sur quelque chose venant de 'l'extérieur' pour avoir un sens de la réalité, on est obligé de chercher le réel à l'intérieur de soi. Mais quelle que soit la forme de cette réalité, elle s'oppose nécessairement à toute structure sociale (moderne) externe. Le soi et la société n'ont jamais été autant en opposition. Le concept d'authenticité est une manière d'exprimer cette expérience." (13)

Dans la littérature sur la période postmoderne, de nombreux critiques ont répété que la pensée postmoderne, tout comme la valeur moderne, accepte également l'éphémère, la fragmentation et la discontinuité. Le monde est vu comme un ensemble de fragments continuellement en mouvement. La perte de la temporalité et la recherche d'effets immédiats ont entraîné une perte de la profondeur. Jameson décrit l'obsession avec les apparences de la production culturelle contemporaine et la préoccupation de l'architecture postmoderne avec les surfaces comme étant " un manque de profondeur intentionnel ". Kenneth Frampton ajoute que "le monde moderne s'est fragmenté lorsque la Science l'a dépouillé de sa fusion magique. Puisque l'apparence démentait désormais la vérité, il a fallu considérer que la forme était séparée du contenu..." (14) Par conséquent, les formes historiques et culturelles se sont commercialisées. Avec les médias, les styles architecturaux anciens ont pris la valeur d'archives dans lesquelles on puise pour obtenir une légitimation historique, à savoir l'authenticité.

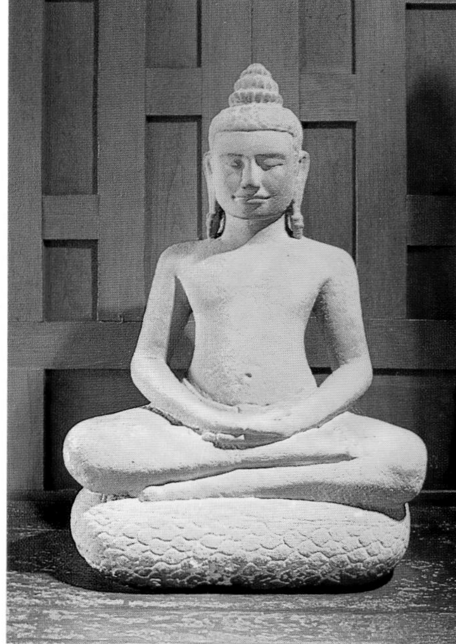

Authenticity in ethnic art is being conceived in ever more rigorous terms. Absence of commoditisation has become an important factor.

Authentizität in der Volkskunst wird immer strengeren Kriterien unterworfen. Wichtig ist, daß sie nicht zur Handelsware gemacht wird.

Des normes sévères définissent l'authenticité dans l'art indigène. La valeur intrinsèque des choses est devenue un facteur crucial.

AUTHENTICITY AS A "NEGOTIABLE" CONCEPT

Modern man, since the 19th century, is thus seen as a being in quest of authenticity while living in 'inauthentic' societies. MacCannell has forcefully argued that this quest for authenticity has become an important characteristic of modern tourism.(15) In tourism studies, the concept of authenticity is used to characterise a criterion of evaluation used by the modern tourist as observer. Erik Cohen has however objected to MacCannell's conceptual framework which did not raise the possibility that the tourist may conceive of authenticity in different terms.

Cohen suggesed that " 'authenticity' is a socially constructed concept and its social (as against philosophical) connotation is, therefore, not given, but 'negotiable'...It follows that intellectuals and other more alienated individuals will engage in a more serious quest for authenticity than most rank-and-file members of society. It is hypothesized further that, the greater their concern for authenticity, the stricter will be the criteria by which they conceive of it. Less alienated and hence less concerned individuals, including most rank-and-file tourists, will be content with much wider, less strict criteria of authenticity." (16)

Hence, tourists seek authenticity in varying degrees of intensity. It is also argued that they will also conceive it in varying degrees of rigour and adopt different criteria for the judgement of authenticity. Cohen argues that "since authenticity is not a given, but negotiable, one has to allow for the possibility of its gradual emergence in the eyes of visitors to the host culture. In other words, a cultural product, or a trait thereof, which is at one point generally judged as contrived or inauthentic may, in the course of time, become generally recognised as authentic." (17)

Cohen looks into the approach to "authenticity" among curators and ethnographers as a means to clarify the socially constructed nature of the concept. An increasing number of objects were declared to be "fakes" by curators and art historians not because new information on the objects was discovered, but because the concept of fakery has slowly changed. Authenticity in primitive and ethnic art is being conceived in ever more rigorous criteria. One such criterion is that the product should not be manufactured specifically for commercial purposes. Hence, absence of commoditisation has become an important factor in evaluating authenticity. Authenticity, for curators, is thus seen as a quality of pre-

AUTHENTIZITÄT ALS »VERHANDELBARES« KONZEPT

Der moderne Mensch wird also seit dem 19. Jahrhundert als jemand gesehen, der auf der Suche nach Authentizität ist, während er in »nicht authentischen« Gesellschaften lebt. MacCannell hat nachdrücklich darauf hingewiesen, daß diese Suche zu einem wichtigen Charakteristikum des modernen Tourismus geworden ist. (15) In Studien zum Tourismus wird das Konzept der Authentizität dazu benutzt, dieses Beurteilungskriterium, das der moderne Tourist als Beobachter gebraucht, zu erklären.

Eric Cohen hat MacCannell, der in seiner konzeptionellen Arbeit nicht die Möglichkeit in Betracht gezogen hat, daß der Tourist Authentizität auf unterschiedliche Weise erfahren kann, widersprochen. Cohen meint: »›Authentizität‹ ist ein gesellschaftlich konstruiertes Konzept und seine soziale (im Gegensatz zur philosophischen) Bedeutung ist nicht vorgegeben, sondern ›verhandelbar‹ ... Daraus folgt, daß Intellektuelle oder andere mehr aus der Masse herausgehobene Menschen der Gesellschaft sich ernsthafter auf die Suche nach Authentizität begeben als die meisten einfachen Mitglieder der Gesellschaft. Je größer ihr Streben nach Authentizität ist, so die Hypothese, desto strenger sind die Kriterien, die sie anlegen. Weniger herausgehobene und somit weniger nachdenkliche Menschen, und dazu gehören die meisten einfachen Touristen, werden sich mit viel weiter gefaßten strengen Kriterien für Authentizität zufriedengeben.« (16)

Touristen suchen also Authentizität unterschiedlich intensiv. Ebenso wird argumentiert, daß ihre Maßstäbe unterschiedlich strikt sind und daher nicht alle dieselben Kriterien bei der Beurteilung von Authentizität anlegen. Cohen meint, »da Authentizität nicht vorgegeben, sondern verhandelbar ist, muß man auch die Möglichkeit erwägen, daß sie für die Besucher der Gastkultur erst schrittweise erkennbar wird. Mit anderen Worten, ein Kulturprodukt oder ein Teil davon, das zu einem bestimmten Zeitpunkt allgemein als gekünstelt oder nicht authentisch beurteilt wird, kann im Laufe der Zeit als authentisch anerkannt werden.« (17)

Cohen meint, die Art, wie Museumsdirektoren und Völkerkundler mit Authentizität umgehen, sei ein Mittel, die soziale Konstruktion dieses Konzepts zu erklären: Sie deklarierten eine steigende Anzahl von Objekten als »Fälschung«, nicht, weil neue Informationen zu den Objekten aufgetaucht wären, sondern

L'AUTHENTICITE EN TANT QUE CONCEPT NEGOCIABLE

Depuis le 19e siècle, l'Homme moderne est en quête d'authenticité alors qu'il vit dans des sociétés 'inauthentiques'. MacCannell affirme que la recherche d'authenticité est devenue un élément déterminant du tourisme moderne. (15) Des études sur le tourisme révèlent que le concept d'authenticité est un critère d'évaluation pour le touriste moderne en tant qu'observateur. Toutefois, Erik Cohen a critiqué la structure conceptuelle de MacCannell qui omet la possibilité que le touriste puisse concevoir l'authenticité sous des formes différentes.

Cohen a suggéré que " l'authenticité est un concept à caractère social; sa connotation sociale (à l'opposé de philosophique) n'est donc pas déterminée, mais 'négociable'... Par conséquent, certains groupes tels que les intellectuels s'engageront dans une recherche plus profonde de l'authenticité que les classes populaires. En outre, les critères sont sans doute d'autant plus sévères que le souci d'authenticité est grand. Les individus moins concernés comme la plupart des touristes moyens se satisfont de critères d'authenticité bien moins rigoureux." (16)

Ainsi, les touristes recherchent l'authenticité avec plus ou moins d'intensité. Ils donnent également une signification plus ou moins stricte au concept et l'évaluent selon des critères différents. Cohen écrit: "Puisque l'authenticité n'est pas établie, mais négociable, les visiteurs peuvent très bien croire graduellement à l'authenticité des choses dans un pays. En d'autres termes, un produit culturel, estimé artificiel ou inauthentique à un certain moment, sera généralement considéré authentique avec le temps." (17)

Selon Cohen, la façon dont les conservateurs de musée et les ethnographes définissent "l'authenticité", explique le caractère social du concept d'authenticité. De plus en plus d'objets estimés "faux" par les conservateurs de musées et historiens d'art, ne le sont pas en raison de nouvelles informations découvertes sur ces objets, mais parce que le concept d'inauthenticité a lentement évolué. Des critères encore plus rigoureux déterminent l'authenticité dans les arts populaires. Par exemple, le produit ne doit pas être fabriqué pour des raisons commerciales. Par conséquent, la non-commercialisation est un facteur important dans l'évaluation de l'authenticité. Pour les conservateurs de musée, l'authenticité est donc une qualité n'appartenant pas au monde moderne ou à des objets culturels dénotant une influence occidentale. La différence faite entre les objets de

The new and the old are almost indistinguishable.
(top): The one on the right is a recent reproduction of the traditional Balinese bell-tower.
(bottom): The Balinese bale or pavilion on the right is a facsimile of the original shown on the left.

Altes und Neues ist kaum zu unterscheiden.
(oben): Der balinesische Glockenturm ist eine moderne Nachbildung des traditionellen Turms.
(unten): Der balinesische bale oder Pavillon rechts gleicht dem Original links aufs Haar.

On peut à peine distinguer l'ancien du nouveau.
(en haut): sur la droite, une reproduction récente d'un campanile balinais.
(en bas): le "bale" ou pavillon balinais sur la droite est une reproduction de l'original montré à gauche.

The roof forms of Amanpuri in Phuket are based on traditional Thai temple roofs, seen in the photograph above.

Die Dachformen des Amanpuri in Phuket gehen zurück auf die traditionellen Dächer der Thai-Tempel.

Le toit de l'Amanpuri à Phuket s'inspire des toits traditionnels des temples balinais montrés sur la photographie ci-dessus.

modern life, and of cultural artefacts untainted in any way by Western influences. Emphasis is also placed on the difference between hand-made objects and those produced by machines.

It can be seen that there are various interpretations of the term "authenticity", where their form and content vary greatly, depending on the mode and object, as well as operational structure of the relationship. Posing the question "What is the notion of authenticity ?" is hence unsatisfactory. The question should instead be directed at uncovering the qualitative and quantitative aspects of different notions of authenticity and to comprehend the intricate intercausal relationships between them.

FORM AND CONTENT IN AUTHENTICITY

Resorts are essentially luxurious architectural stage-sets. Because of their manifestations of a unique life-style, they have always serve as models in a 'filtering down' effect. They are an important source of inspiration for many subsequent local works. The moment such exquisite works are perceived as constituting a particular style, they possess an ability to create an illusory transcendence of class. When touted as being "authentic", these consumable styles enter the popular imagination as "the real thing", assuming a forceful validity of their own.

In an incisive essay, Hassan-Uddin Khan wrote: "Constructing buildings using the same materials, the same colours, the same vocabularies ... but with everything obviously more sophiscated, polished, shinier, and so on, means that historical information so absorbed it assumes the aspect of reincarnation." (18) He goes on to question the relationship between this architectural expression and the "real thing — the vernacular born of the tradition of a hundred years. Or is this the real thing?"

Many of these buildings are definitely improved versions of the vernacular, at least at the perceptual level. Umberto Eco echoes this point when writing about the Palace of Living Arts in Los Angeles. He describes its philosophy as not "We are giving you the reproduction so you will want the original", but rather, "We are giving you the reproduction so that you will no longer feel any need for the original." (19) The reproduction always conditions perceptions of the original, to the extent that the former can even replace the latter to become 'the real thing', "where the referents are swept away by the signs, where the artificial is more 'real' than the real." (20)

weil sich die Vorstellung von Fälschung langsam gewandelt hat. Authentizität in der Ethnokunst wird nach immer strengeren Kriterien beurteilt. Dazu gehört, daß das Produkt nicht für kommerzielle Zwecke hergestellt sein sollte. Daher ist die mangelnde Verwertbarkeit als reine Ware ein wichtiger Faktor bei der Beurteilung von Authentizität geworden. Für Museumsdirektoren gehört Authentizität zum vor-modernen Leben und zu kulturellen Objekten, die von jeglichen westlichen Einflüssen unberührt sind. Besonders betont wird auch der Unterschied zwischen von Hand und maschinell hergestellten Objekten.

Es sind auch verschiedene Interpretationen des Begriffs »Authentizität« zu erkennen, bei denen Form und Inhalt sehr unterschiedlich sind, je nach Mode und Objekt und nach der Wechselwirkung zwischen beiden. Die Frage »Wie sieht die Vorstellung von Authentizität aus?« ist daher unbefriedigend. Besser wäre es, die qualitativen und quantitativen Aspekte unterschiedlicher Vorstellungen aufzudecken und die verschlungenen, kausalen Beziehungen zwischen ihnen zu begreifen.

FORM UND INHALT VON AUTHENTIZITÄT

Ferienanlagen sind im wesentlichen luxuriöse architektonische Bühnenbilder. Weil sie einen einzigartigen Life-Style demonstrieren, haben sie immer als Modelle in einem Filterungsprozeß gedient. Sie sind eine wichtige Quelle der Inspiration für zahlreiche nachfolgende örtliche Bauwerke. In dem Augenblick, in dem diese herausragenden Bauten als besonders stilbildend wahrgenommen werden, bekommen sie die Kraft, eine illusorische Durchlässigkeit der Klassen herzustellen. Wenn sie dann auch noch aufdringlich als »authentisch« beworben werden, können diese konsumierbaren Stilarten als »the real thing«, das Echte, in die allgemeine Vorstellung eindringen und bekommen dann einen starken eigenen Wert.

Hassan-Uddin Khan schrieb in einem prägnanten Essay: »Wenn bei der Errichtung von Neubauten dieselben Materialien, dieselben Farben, dasselbe Vokabular verwendet wird .., aber alles offensichtlich ein bißchen raffinierter, glatter, glänzender usw. ist, dann bedeutet das, daß die so aufgenommene historische Information von dem Aspekt der Reinkarnation ausgeht.« (18) Weiterhin stellt er die Frage nach der Beziehung zwischen dieser architektonischen Ausdrucksform und dem »real thing, dem Charakteristischen für das Land, das einer Tradition von

fabrications artisanale et industrielle représente également un critère important.

Il y a donc de nombreuses interprétations du terme "authenticité" qui diffèrent par leur forme et contenu, selon le mode et l'objet, ainsi que par la structure de la relation entre ces notions. Par conséquent, il est impossible de donner de réponse satisfaisante à la question: "Quelle est la définition de l'authenticité?". Il faut plutôt essayer de découvrir les aspects qualitatifs et quantitatifs des concepts différents d'authenticité et de comprendre la complexité de leurs relations causales.

FORME ET CONTENU DANS L'AUTHENTICITE

Les complexes hôteliers présentent souvent des décors d'architecture luxueuse. Evoquant un style de vie incomparable, ils servent de modèles à des niveaux moins élevés et deviennent une source d'inspiration majeure pour de nombreux autres ouvrages locaux. Et puisque ces ouvrages exquis possèdent un style unique, il s'ensuit l'illusion d'une transcendance des classes. Déclarés "authentiques", ces styles à consommer se fixent en tant que "chose réelle" dans l'imaginaire populaire et s'approprient une vérité puissante.

Hassan-Udin Khan écrit dans un essai incisif: "La construction d'édifices, utilisant les mêmes matériaux, les mêmes couleurs, les mêmes langages trouvés dans les informations historiques...mais d'une manière plus sophistiquée, plus léchée, plus éclatante, etc., équivaut à une réincarnation." (18) Il s'interroge ensuite sur la relation entre l'expression architecturale et la "chose réelle – la culture indigène née de siècles de traditions. Mais est-ce bien la chose réelle?"

Un grand nombre de ces constructions sont sans aucun doute des versions améliorées du style indigène, du moins sont-elles perçues ainsi. Umberto Eco souligne ce point dans son évocation du Palace of Living Arts à Los Angeles. Son concept philosophique ne se traduit pas par: "Nous vous donnons la reproduction pour que vous ayez envie de l'original", mais plutôt: "Nous vous donnons la reproduction pour que vous n'ayez plus envie de l'original." (19) L'original étant toujours perçu à travers la reproduction, cette dernière peut même remplacer l'original pour devenir la 'chose réelle', "quand les signes chassent les référents et que l'artificiel devient plus réel que le réel." (20)

Authenticity for art curators is increasingly seen as a qualtiy of pre-modern life, and of cultural artefacts untainted by Western influence.

Kunsthistoriker sehen die Authentizität immer mehr als typische Eigenschaft des vor-modernen Lebens und der kulturellen Objekte, die von westlichem Einfluß frei sind.

Pour les conservateurs de musée, l'authenticité devient un attribut appartenant à l'ère antérieure à la vie moderne et aux objets culturels qui n'ont pas subi d'influence occidentale.

However, in their rush to embrace an aesthetic for a new touristic consciousness through the use of pre-existing elements, architects have irrevocably isolated form from production and meaning. These sumptuous tourist developments are unable to reconcile form with content, or technique with technology. Such superficial mimicry is a sign of regressive sentimentalism, and this merely results in hackneyed works. Authenticity certainly cannot be sought in the self-conscious application of such signs.

Authenticity comes from the Greek root, *authentes*, which refers to "one who does anything with his own hand." (21) It thus suggests a strong association with craft. Human identity in the production of architecture has always been an instrumental aspect of its authenticity. Trilling argues that "the machine... could make only inauthentic things, dead things..." (22) However, contemporary methods of building production are more opaque than traditional ones. Hence, the links between fabrication and signification, construction and metaphor, are increasingly separated.

In a similar argument, Hannah Arendt, in The Human *Condition*, observes that the societal concerns of modern collective systems have devalued "labour" (a natural, almost biological concomitant of life) to "work" (an artificial, static separation of life from the natural world around us). Contemporary architecture represents "the world of work" (which is artificial) more than "the world of labour" (which is biological). Vernooy has also argued that "the metaphysical implications of material and detail are reduced to gestures which imply, but do not denote; they express ideas which represent architecture's customary functions — the registration of built form with its physical and cultural context — but they are phenomenally weak." (23)

An authentic architecture would thus appears to be the product of labour, in which the building acts as a mediation between the natural world and the artificial world. The role of representation in architecture must include societal intentions produced by labour and technical intentions produced by work. However, in the process of distinguishing each notion of authenticity relative to the other – the social/cultural necessities versus the technical/ethical necessities – they become irrevocably dislocated. Vernooy points out that architectural authenticity expects cultural recognition and presumes technical originality. Recent stylistic ideologies attempt to define an authentic architecture by reconfiguring the

Hunderten von Jahren entstammt. Oder ist das ›the real thing‹.«

Viele dieser Anlagen sind mit Sicherheit verbesserte Varianten des Einheimischen, zumindest auf der von außen wahrnehmbaren Ebene. Umberto Eco wiederholt diesen Punkt in seiner Schrift über den Palace of Living Arts in Los Angeles. Er beschreibt dessen Philosophie nicht als »Wir geben euch die Reproduktion, also werdet ihr das Original wollen«, sondern eher als »Wir geben euch die Reproduktion, also werdet ihr das Original nicht mehr brauchen«. (19) Die Reproduktion beeinflußt immer die Wahrnehmung des Originals, und das in einem Maß, daß sie sogar das Original ersetzen und selbst »the real thing« werden kann, »wobei das Echte von den Symbolen weggefegt wird, das Künstliche ›wahrer‹ ist als das Wahre«. (20)

Doch in ihrem Eifer, für ein neues touristisches Bewußtsein durch die Verwendung bereits bestehender Elemente eine Ästhetik zu entwickeln, haben die Architekten unwiderruflich die Form von der Herstellung und der Bedeutung losgelöst. Diese luxuriösen Touristenanlagen können Form und Inhalt oder Technik und Technologie nicht miteinander versöhnen. Oberflächliche Nachahmung bis ins Detail ist ein Zeichen für rückwärtsgewandte Sentimentalität, und das führt nur zu abgedroschenen, immer wiederkehrenden Ergebnissen – aber auf keinen Fall Authentizität.

Authentizität kommt aus dem Griechischen, und *authentes* bedeutet soviel wie »wer mit eigener Hand etwas vollbringt«. (21) Es besteht also eine enge Verbindung mit Handwerk. Der Mensch war bei der Produktion von Architektur immer förderlich für ihre Authentizität. Trilling führt an, daß »die Maschine nur nicht authentische Dinge herstellen kann, tote Dinge... «. (22) Doch zeitgenössische Baumethoden sind durchsichtiger als traditionelle. Daher entfernen sich die Verbindungen zwischen Herstellung und Bedeutung, Bau und Metapher immer mehr voneinander.

Ähnlich argumentiert Hannah Arendt in *The Human Condition*, wenn sie beobachtet, daß die modernen kollektiven Gesellschaftssysteme die schwere Arbeit, die Mühe und Plage »labour« (ein natürlicher, fast biologischer Begleitumstand des Lebens) abgewertet haben zur einfachen Arbeit »work« (eine künstliche, statische Abtrennung des Lebens von der natürlichen Welt um uns herum). Zeitgenössische Architektur repräsentiert eher die »Welt der Arbeit« (work), die künstlich ist als die »Welt der Mühe« (labour), die biologisch ist. Vernooy hat auch

Néanmoins, dans leur empressement à concevoir une esthétique pour un nouveau genre de tourisme en se servant d'éléments préexistants, les architectes ont entièrement séparé la forme de la réalisation et de la signification. Ces complexes touristiques somptueux n'associent ni la forme au contenu, ni la technique à la technologie. Cette imitation superficielle découle d'un sentimentalisme régressif qui se traduit par des ouvrages gâchés. L'authenticité n'a certainement rien à voir avec cette démarche forcée.

Authenticité a pour racine le mot grec *authentes* signifiant "quelqu'un qui fait tout avec ses mains". (21) Il révèle une forte association avec le travail manuel. L'aspect humain a toujours été un instrument d'authenticité en architecture. Trilling dit que "la machine... ne peut fabriquer que des choses inauthentiques, des choses mortes..." (22) Cependant, les méthodes modernes de construction sont plus obscures que les méthodes traditionnelles. Ainsi, les liens entre la fabrication et la signification, entre la construction et la métaphore, ne cessent de se relâcher.

Dans la même pensée, Hannah Arendt écrit dans *La condition humaine* que les intérêts communautaires de systèmes collectifs modernes ont dévalorisé "l'ouvrage" (un concomitant naturel, virtuellement biologique de la vie) par rapport au "travail" (une séparation artificielle, statique de la vie du monde naturel autour de nous). Les architectes contemporains représentent davantage "le monde du travail" (qui est artificiel) que le "monde de l'ouvrage" (qui est biologique). Veernooy argumente également que "les implications métaphysiques du matériel et du détail se réduisent à des gestes qui suggèrent sans déterminer. Ils expriment des idées qui représentent les fonctions habituelles de l'architecture – la construction de formes avec son contexte physique et culturel – mais sans aucune vigueur." (23)

Il semblerait qu'une architecture authentique soit le produit de l'ouvrage, la construction servant de médiation entre le monde naturel et le monde artificiel. La fonction de l'architecture doit inclure des intentions sociales produites par l'ouvrage et des intentions techniques produites par le travail. Toutefois, les notions d'authenticité se disloquent irrémédiablement lorsqu'on essaie de distinguer leur corrélation – les nécessités sociales/culturelles opposées aux nécessités techniques/éthiques. Veernooy signale que la reconnaissance culturelle et l'originalité technique appartiennent à l'authenticité architecturale. Dans une

Critics have questioned the relationship between contemporary architectural expression that replicate the old and the "real thing". Superficial mimicry is a sign of regressive sentimentalism.

Die Beziehung zwischen zeitgenössischem architektonischem Ausdruck, der das Alte nur wiederholt, und dem Echten, dem »real thing«, wurde von Kritikern oft diskutiert. Oberflächliche Nachahmung ist ein Zeichen von nach rückwärts gewandter Sentimentalität.

Les critiques s'interrogent sur la relation entre l'architecture contemporaine, reproductrice de l'ancien, et la "chose réelle". Une imitation superficielle traduit un sentimentalisme régressif.

At Amanusa, Bali, the designers attempt to incorporate lessons of the past as mere input in their search for a contemporary expression.

Bei ihrer Suche nach einer zeitgenössischen Ausdrucksform versuchen die Architekten in Amanusa, Bali, die Lektionen der Vergangenheit als Produktionsmittel einzubeziehen.

L'Amenusa, Bali, montre une vague tentative des architectes de se servir des leçons du passé dans leur recherche d'une expression contemporaine.

An authentic architecture must address unique contexts, not homogenise them.

Eine authentische Architektur muß einzigartige Zusammenhänge schaffen, nicht alles gleich gestalten.

Une architecture basée sur l'authenticité devrait considérer des contextes uniques, sans les homogénéiser.

built world such that they express particular aspects of contemporary culture. Each contributes an aspect to the discourse, but each fails as well.

Authenticity is also commonly viewed as the result of specificities to place and time. Juhani Pallasmaa argues that "Authenticity is frequently identified with the ideas of artistic autonomy and originality. But I understand authenticity more as the quality of deep rootedness in the stratifications of culture." (24) Ismail Serageldin, in *Space For Freedom*, suggests that "the issue is not whether the structure conforms exactly to the criteria of the past; it clearly cannot do so and remain relevant to today's concerns. Instead, the issue is whether the designer has learnt the lessons of the past, internalised them, and used them as an input, although partial, in defining the solution to a contemporary problem for contemporary clients." (25)

Vernooy feels that the problem of authenticity cannot be addressed by formal idealisations; they can only be addressed by opening the references of figuration to the multiple imperatives of our contemporary culture. These imperatives include that of technology, economics and culture. Architecture is the physical manifestation of multitudinous factors pertaining to the temporal, cultural, climatic, geographic, social, political and economic milieu of a society. Hence, any attempt at defining authenticity in an architectural project must address such contexts. An authentic architecture explores how spaces can heighten, not blur the relationships of man to these contexts.

ausgeführt, daß »die metaphysischen Bedeutungen von Material und Detail auf Gesten reduziert wurden, die etwas andeuten, aber nichts bedeuten; sie drücken Ideen zu den üblichen Funktionen der Architektur aus, aber sie sind in ihrer Wirkung schwach«. (23)

Eine authentische Architektur würde daher so aussehen, als sei sie ein Ergebnis von Mühe (labour). Die Repräsentation in der Architektur muß gesellschaftliche Absichten einschließen, die durch Mühe (labour) entstanden sind, und technische Absichten, entstanden durch Arbeit (work). Doch in dem Prozeß, jede Vorstellung von Authentizität in ihrer Beziehung zu einer anderen-gesellschaftliche/kulturelle Notwendigkeiten gegen technische/ethische Notwendigkeiten – abzugrenzen, werden diese Absichten erschüttert. Vernooy weist darauf hin, daß architektonische Authentizität kulturelle Anerkennung erwartet und technische Originalität voraussetzt. Neuere Stilideologien versuchen, eine authentische Architektur zu definieren, indem sie die gebaute Welt so neu gestalten, daß sie spezielle Aspekte der zeitgenössischen Kultur ausdrückt.

Authentizität wird auch oft gesehen als das Ergebnis von Zugeständnissen an Ort und Zeit. Juhani Pallasmaa führt aus, daß »Authentizität oft gleichgesetzt wird mit den Vorstellungen von künstlerischer Autonomie und Originalität. Aber ich verstehe Authentizität eher als die tiefe Verwurzeltheit in den Schichten der Kultur«. (24) Ismail Serageldin schreibt, daß »es nicht darum geht, ob die Struktur genau mit den Kriterien der Vergangenheit übereinstimmt; das kann sie einfach nicht und gleichzeitig reevant für heutige Belange sein. Statt dessen geht es eher darum, ob der Architekt die Lektionen aus der Vergangenheit gelernt, sie verinnerlicht und als Eingangsleistung, wenn auch nur teilweise, benutzt hat, um eine Lösung für zeitgenössische Probleme zeitgenössischer Kunden zu finden«. (25)

Vernooy meint, die Probleme der Authentizität könnte man nicht durch formale Idealisierung lösen, sondern nur, indem man die alten Vorstellungen von Form für die vielschichtigen Anforderungen unserer gegenwärtigen Kultur öffnet. Zu diesen Anforderungen gehören Technologie, Wirtschaft und Kultur. Architektur ist der materielle Ausdruck vielfältiger Faktoren, die zum zeitlichen, kulturellen, klimatischen, geographischen, sozialen, politischen und wirtschaftlichen Milieu einer Gesellschaft gehören. Daher muß sich jeder Versuch, die Authentizität einer Architektur zu definieren, um solche Zusammenhänge kümmern.

tentative de définir l'authenticité dans l'architecture, des idéologies récentes utilisent certains aspects de la culture contemporaine pour retracer l'univers architectural. Chacune contribue à un aspect du débat, mais aucune n'apporte de véritable réponse.

L'authenticité est donc considérée comme la conséquence de facteurs spécifiques à l'endroit et à l'époque. Juhani Pallasmaa écrit: "On identifie fréquemment l'authenticité aux idées d'autonomie et d'originalité artistiques. Mais pour moi, l'authenticité constitue davantage une racine profonde dans les stratifications de la culture." (24) Dans *Space for freedom* (Espaces de liberté), Ismail Serageldin suggère que: "la question n'est pas de savoir si la construction est exactement conforme aux critères du passé; elle ne peut évidemment pas l'être puisqu'elle est contemporaine. La question est plutôt de savoir si l'architecte a appris les leçons du passé, les a assimilées et utilisées, ne seraitce qu'en partie, pour trouver une solution à un problème actuel visant des clients d'aujourd'hui." (25)

Selon Vernooy, on ne peut pas considérer le problème d'authenticité selon des idéaux anciens; il faut prendre en compte les impératifs multiples de notre culture contemporaine. Ces impératifs sont dictés par la technologie, l'économie et la culture. L'architecture est la manifestation physique d'une foule de facteurs qui relèvent des données temporelle, culturelle, climatique, géographique, sociale, politique et économique d'une société. Toute tentative pour définir l'authenticité dans un projet architectural doit considérer ces contextes. Une architecture authentique cherche à intensifier et non pas à altérer la relation de l'Homme avec ces contextes.

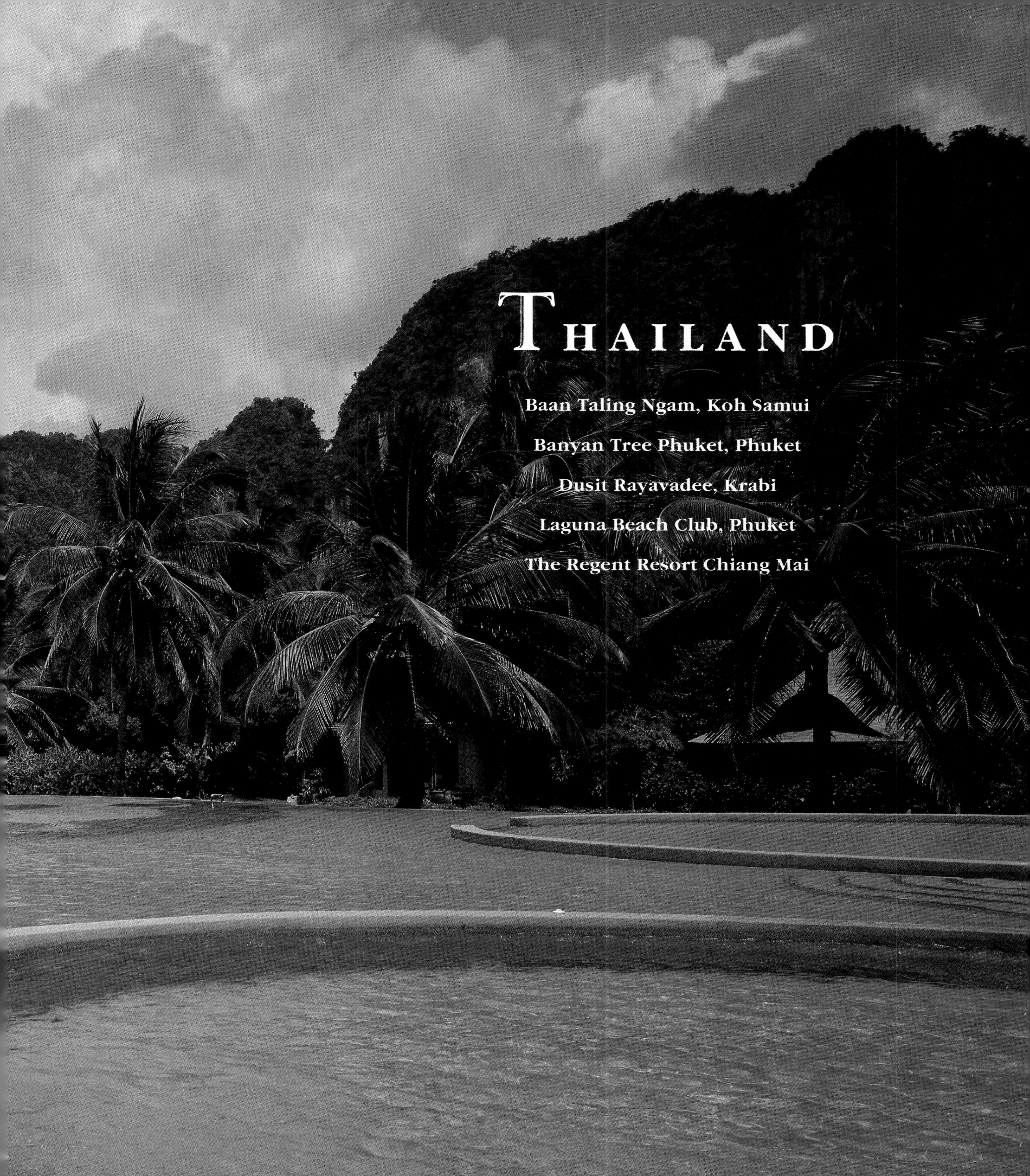

THAILAND

Baan Taling Ngam, Koh Samui

Banyan Tree Phuket, Phuket

Dusit Rayavadee, Krabi

Laguna Beach Club, Phuket

The Regent Resort Chiang Mai

Baan Taling Ngam, Koh Samui

Baan Taling Ngam is located on a hillslope overlooking crystal-clear waters.

Baan Taling Ngam liegt an einem Abhang oberhalb des kristallklaren Meers.

Baan Taling Ngam s'accroche sur un versant de colline surplombant des eaux cristallines.

Together with Krabi and Phuket, Koh Samui forms Thailand's trio of top beach destinations. A beautiful island off the eastern coast of the southern peninsula, Koh Samui is blessed with exquisite white sand, crystal-clear waters and palm groves.

Known as the "Land of a Million Coconuts", it is Thailand's third largest island, measuring 21 kilometres at its widest point and 25 kilometres at its longest. Its reputation as an idyllic retreat was for years confined to the back-pack set. However, the opening of its airport in 1988 has resulted in the accelerated development of deluxe resorts like Santiburi Dusit Resort and Baan Taling Ngam. It is earmarked to be one of the new destinations heavily promoted by the Thai Tourism Authority.

In 1992, RMJM was appointed as architects to masterplan Baan Taling Ngam Resort, the Mandarin Oriental's first foray into the boutique hotel market. Opened in November 1993, this resort is made up of 40 guestrooms and two suites. It is set on the forested hillslopes at the southwest corner of Thailand's most environmentally protected island. Most of the hotels are located on the east coast of the island on the famous beaches of Chaweng and Lamai. For the moment, Baan Taling Ngam is the only major development on the west coast, thus achieving a high level of exclusivity.

Of the 42 rooms that are housed on three cliffside levels, six have ten-metre high Thai-style roofs. All the rooms have generous terraces overlooking the sea. The resort also has 42 residential villas of varying sizes built on stilts over the precipitous terrain. They are grouped in clusters and centred around several swimming pools. There is also a beach accommodation with seven single-storey suites, a beach club and a swimming pool.

Baan Taling Ngam, translates as "house on a beautiful cliff", is located on a truly breathtaking site of more than six hectares. Certainly, the most impressive aspect of the resort is its location. As the management explains, the resort is all about space, place and pace. It is sited on a verdant ridge with spectacular views of the island-dotted waters of the Samui archipelago. No matter where one is, the aquamarine blue of the sea remains visible.

Located about 60 metres above the beach, the resort is accessed from a steep winding road that makes one anticipate the final approach with great expectations. However, the design

Baan Taling Ngam, Koh Samui

Zusammen mit Krabi und Phuket gehört Koh Samui zu Thailands Spitzentrio der Sandstrände. Als wunderschöne Insel vor der Ostküste der Halbinsel ist Koh Samui gesegnet mit feinem, weißem Sand, kristallklarem Wasser und Palmenhainen.

Als »Land der Kokosnüsse« ist Koh Samui die drittgrößte Insel Thailands und mißt an der breitesten Stelle 21 Kilometer und 25 Kilometer an der längsten. Jahrelang diente sie als idyllischer Zufluchtsort nur den Rucksacktouristen. Doch nach der Eröffnung des Flughafens 1988 kam es zu einer schnellen Entwicklung von Luxus-Anlagen wie dem Santiburi Dusit Resort und Baan Taling Ngam. Die Insel gehört zu den neuen Zielen, die von der thailändischen Tourismusbehörde kräftig gefördert und beworben werden.

1992 bekamen die Architekten von RMJM den Auftrag, das Baan Taling Ngam Resort zu planen; es war der erste Vorstoß von Mandarin Oriental in den Markt der Boutique-Hotels. Das Haus, im November 1993 eröffnet, verfügt über 40 Gästezimmer und zwei Suiten. Es liegt am bewaldeten Abhang in der südwestlichen Ecke der Insel, auf der die Umwelt am meisten geschützt wird. Die meisten Hotels befinden sich an der Ostküste an den berühmten Stränden von Chaweng und Lamai. Gegenwärtig ist Baan Taling Ngam die einzige größere Einrichtung an der Westküste und verfügt daher über ein hohes Maß an Exklusivität.

Sechs der 42 Räume auf drei Ebenen der Kliffseite haben zehn Meter hohe Dächer im Thai-Stil. Zu allen Zimmern gehören große Terrassen mit Meerblick. Die Anlage verfügt außerdem über 42 Wohnhäuser unterschiedlicher Größe, auf dem abschüssigen Gelände auf Pfählen errichtet. Sie sind in Gruppen um mehrere Swimming-pools angeordnet. Außerdem gibt es eine Unterkunft am Strand mit sieben einstöckigen Suiten, einem Beach Club und einem Swimming-pool.

Baan Taling Ngam, was »Haus auf einem schönen Kliff« bedeutet, liegt auf einem wahrlich atemberaubenden Gelände von sechs Hektar. Am eindrucksvollsten ist hier zweifellos die Lage. Wie das Management erklärt, dreht sich in dieser Anlage alles um Raum, Ort und viele, viele Schritte. Sie liegt auf einem grünen Bergkamm mit großartigen Ausblicken auf den Samui-Archipel mit seinen Inseln, die wie Punkte im Meer wirken. Ganz gleich, wo man sich aufhält, die aquamarinblaue See ist immer zu sehen.

(previous page):
Dusit Rayavadee, Krabi.

(vorherige Seite):
Dusit Rayavadee, Krabi.

(page précédente):
Dusit Rayavadee à Krabi.

Baan Taling Ngam, Kob Samui

Avec Krabi et Phuket, Koh Samui fait partie des trois lieux touristiques principaux de la Thaïlande. C'est une île magnifique au large de la côte est de la péninsule méridionale, dotée de plages splendides de sable blanc, d'eaux cristallines et de vastes palmeraies.

Surnommée "le pays des millions de cocotiers", elle est la troisième île de Thaïlande, mesurant 21 kilomètres en sa partie la plus large et 25 kilomètres en sa partie la plus longue. Sa réputation de retraite idyllique est restée longtemps le secret des "routards". Cependant, l'ouverture de l'aéroport en 1988 a accéléré le développement de stations estivales luxueuses telles que Santiburi Dusit Resort et Baan Taling Ngam. Kob Samui est une nouvelle destination touristique que l'office du tourisme thaïlandais a décidé de promouvoir à grande échelle.

En 1992, les architectes de RMJM ont été choisis pour planifier le Baan Taling Ngam Resort. C'était la première incursion de Mandarin Oriental sur le marché de ce qu'on appelle "l'Hôtel boutique". L'établissement, ouvert en novembre 1993, comprend 40 chambres et deux suites. Il se dresse sur des collines boisées, dans la partie sud-ouest de l'île qui a l'environnement le plus protégé de Thaïlande. La plupart des hôtels se trouvent sur la côte orientale, le long des célèbres plages de Chaweng et Lamai. Pour l'heure, Baan Taling Ngam est l'unique complexe hôtelier majeur sur la côte occidentale, ce qui en fait un lieu très exceptionnel.

Des 42 chambres qui s'accrochent sur trois paliers à flanc de colline, six sont surmontées de toits de style thaïlandais de 10 mètres de haut. Toutes les chambres ont de vastes terrasses donnant sur la mer. Le complexe comprend également 42 villas privées, de dimensions différentes, construites sur pilotis sur le terrain escarpé. Elles se regroupent autour de plusieurs piscines. Sur la plage, on trouve aussi sept suites en rez-de-chaussée, un "beach club" et une piscine.

Baan Taling Ngam, qui signifie "la maison de la belle colline" s'étend sur un site merveilleux de plus de six hectares de superficie. Cette situation est sans aucun doute son aspect le plus impressionnant. La direction explique que l'hôtel conjugue l'espace, la place et le calme. Il se dresse sur une crête verdoyante offrant des panoramas spectaculaires de la mer parsemée d'îles de l'archipel Samui. Où que l'on se trouve, on découvre le bleu aigue-marine de la mer.

The aquamarine blue of the sea is visible from nearly every part of the resort.

Von fast jeder Stelle in der Anlage sieht man das aquamarinblaue Meer.

On découvre la mer aigue-marine de presque tous les endroits du complexe.

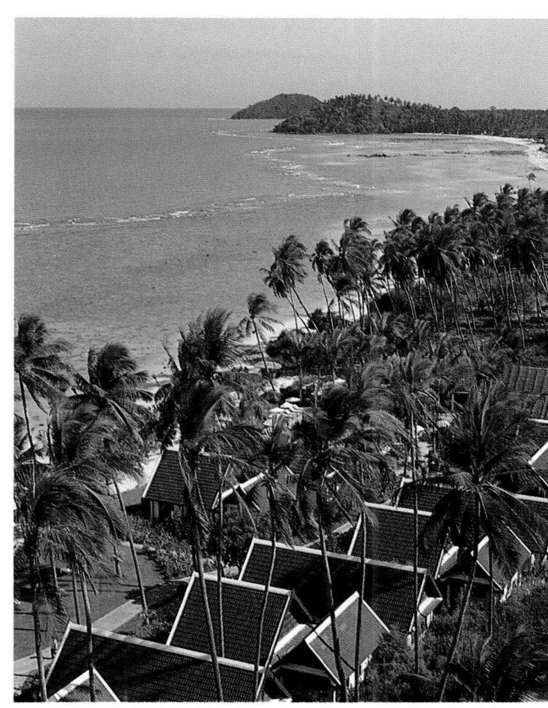

View of the Beach Club from the lobby.

Blick aus der Halle auf den Beach Club.

Vue sur le Beach Club depuis la réception.

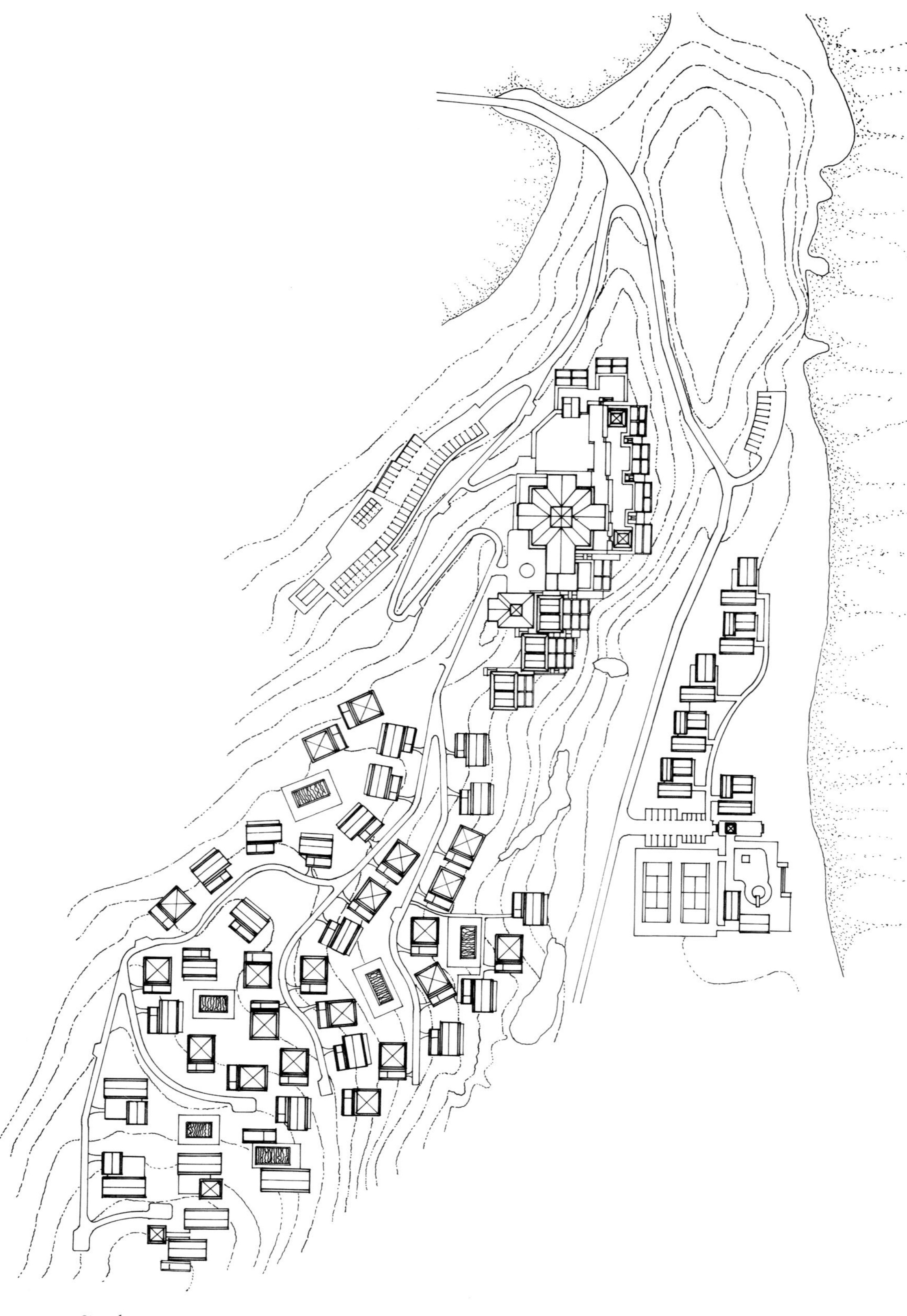

Site plan.

Plan der Anlage.

Plan du site.

of the entrance lobby lacks the drama implicit in the approach sequence. One has to enter deep into the lobby before being confronted by the much anticipated view of the sea. But the panoramic view is certainly a spectacular sight. There are views of the Gulf of Thailand as well as the Ang Thong Marine National Park, a protected archipelago of 38 uninhabited islands.

The lobby, housed under a voluminous traditional Thai roof, is grouped together with a restaurant and a cocktail bar. The restaurant overlooks a swimming pool set at the edge of a cliff. This 'knife-edge' pool, a precedent provided by the much publicized pool at the Amandari Resort in Bali, has now become a widely used design device in many resorts. It forms the main focus of the architectural set-piece. Each evening, the setting sun casts a delightful glow over the water surface.

The single-loaded guestroom blocks look distinctly different from the residential villas. The use of concrete and white plastered walls impart a certain Mediterranean character to these blocks while the timber villas retain more of the charm evident in traditional Thai architecture.

Each of the two-storey residential villa attempts to replicate traditional Thai architecture, with teak floors and wide sliding doors opening onto spacious timber-decked terraces overlooking the sea. Every villa is more than 250 square metres in size and is tastefully furnished with exquisite furniture and objects. However, the maze of interconnecting walkways and lanes is dauntingly steep and guests have to depend very much on electric carts to move around the complex.

The siting of these villas is a deftly orchestrated exercise, considering the steep and difficult nature of the terrain. Some of the concrete stilts supporting the villas are nearly three-storey high. On the whole, the architecture exudes a general feeling of repose in a unique setting.

Die Anlage befindet sich etwa 60 Meter oberhalb des Strands, und der Zugang führt über eine steile, gewundene Straße, auf der man sich schon mit großen Erwartungen auf die Ankunft freut. Doch der Anlage der Eingangshalle fehlt es an der Dramatik, die man bei der Annäherung erwartet hatte. Man muß tief in die Lobby hineingehen, bis man den Meeresblick hat, auf den man sich so gefreut hatte. Doch der Panoramablick ist wahrhaftig spektakulär. Man schaut auf den Golf von Thailand und auf den Ang Thong Marine National Park, einen geschützten Archipel mit 38 unbewohnten Inseln.

Zu der Lobby unter einem riesigen, traditionellen thailändischen Dach gehören ein Restaurant und eine Cocktail-Bar. Vom Restaurant aus hat man einen Blick auf einen Swimming-pool am Rand einer Klippe. Dieser "Messerschneiden"-Pool, dem vielfach erwähnten Pool im Amandari Resort in Bali nachgebaut, findet sich inzwischen in vielen Ferienanlagen. Er liegt im Zentrum des architektonischen Meisterstücks. Die untergehende Sonne läßt allabendlich die Wasseroberfläche wunderschön erstrahlen.

Die Häuser mit den Gästezimmern sehen vollkommen anders aus als die Villen. Die Verwendung von Beton und weißen Gipswänden verleiht diesen Blocks einen gewissen mediterranen Charakter, während die Holzvillen mehr den Charme der traditionellen Thai-Architektur ausstrahlen.

Mit Teakböden und weißen Schiebetüren, die auf geräumige, mit Holz gedeckte Terrassen mit Blick auf das Meer führen, versucht jedes der einstöckigen Wohnhäuser die traditionelle Thai-Architektur nachzuahmen. Jede Villa ist 250 Quadratmeter groß und mit erlesenen Möbeln und Kunstgegenständen geschmackvoll eingerichtet. Doch das Labyrinth der miteinander verbundenen Wege und Pfade ist beängstigend steil, und die Gäste sind weitgehend auf Elektrokarren angewiesen, wenn sie sich auf dem Gelände bewegen wollen.

Diese Villen sind sehr geschickt angelegt, wenn man bedenkt, wie steil und schwierig das Gelände ist. Einige der tragenden Betonpfähle sind fast so hoch wie zweistöckige Häuser. Insgesamt strahlt die Architektur ein allgemeines Gefühl von Ruhe in einer einzigartigen Umgebung aus.

Une route escarpée et sinueuse mène à l'hôtel qui est situé à environ 60 mètres au-dessus du rivage. La beauté du trajet rehausse le désir d'arriver à destination. Cependant, l'architecture du hall de réception n'est pas aussi impressionnante qu'on aurait pu le croire. Il faut pénétrer assez loin dans la réception avant d'avoir la vue tant attendue de la mer. Mais le panorama est alors spectaculaire. On découvre le golfe de Thaïlande ainsi que le "Ang Thong Marine National Park", un archipel protégé de 38 îles désertes.

Le hall de réception est surmonté d'un toit volumineux de style traditionnel thaïlandais sous lequel sont regroupés un restaurant et un cocktail bar. Le restaurant surplombe une piscine construite sur l'arête d'une colline. Cette piscine dont un côté déborde en cascade est construite sur le plan de la célèbre piscine de l'Amandari Resort à Bali qui est devenue un modèle très utilisé dans de nombreux hôtels. Elle constitue le point principal de la composition architecturale. Tous les soirs, le soleil couchant enrobe la surface de l'eau d'une lumière resplendissante.

Les édifices abritant les chambres individuelles ne ressemblent aucunement aux villas. L'utilisation du béton et des murs peints en blanc leur donnent un certain caractère méditerranéen tandis que les villas en bois présentent davantage le charme de l'architecture thaïlandaise traditionnelle.

Les villas à un étage tentent de reproduire l'architecture traditionnelle thaïlandaise, avec des planchers en teck et de larges portes coulissantes ouvrant sur des terrasses spacieuses en bois qui surplombent la mer. Chaque villa a plus de 250 mètres carrés de superficie et est meublée avec un goût exquis. Cependant, les passages et les chemins sont très raides, ce qui oblige fréquemment les hôtes à emprunter les voitures électriques pour se déplacer dans le complexe.

L'arrangement de ces villas a été fait avec beaucoup d'habileté, vu la configuration accidentée du terrain. Quelques-uns des pilotis en béton qui supportent les maisons, s'élèvent sur près de trois étages. Dans l'ensemble, l'architecture dégage une impression de paix dans un décor unique.

Traditional roof forms are used as important architectural devices in the private villas.

Traditionelle Dachformen sind wichtige architektonische Elemente der Privatvillen.

Les toits traditionnels sont une partie inhérente de l'architecture des villas.

(opposite page):
The entrance to the beach club is flanked by two huge earthern jars.

(gegenüberliegende Seite):
Zwei riesige Tonkrüge stehen am Eingang des Beach Club.

(page ci-contre):
Deux énormes jarres en terre cuite ornent l'entrée du beach club.

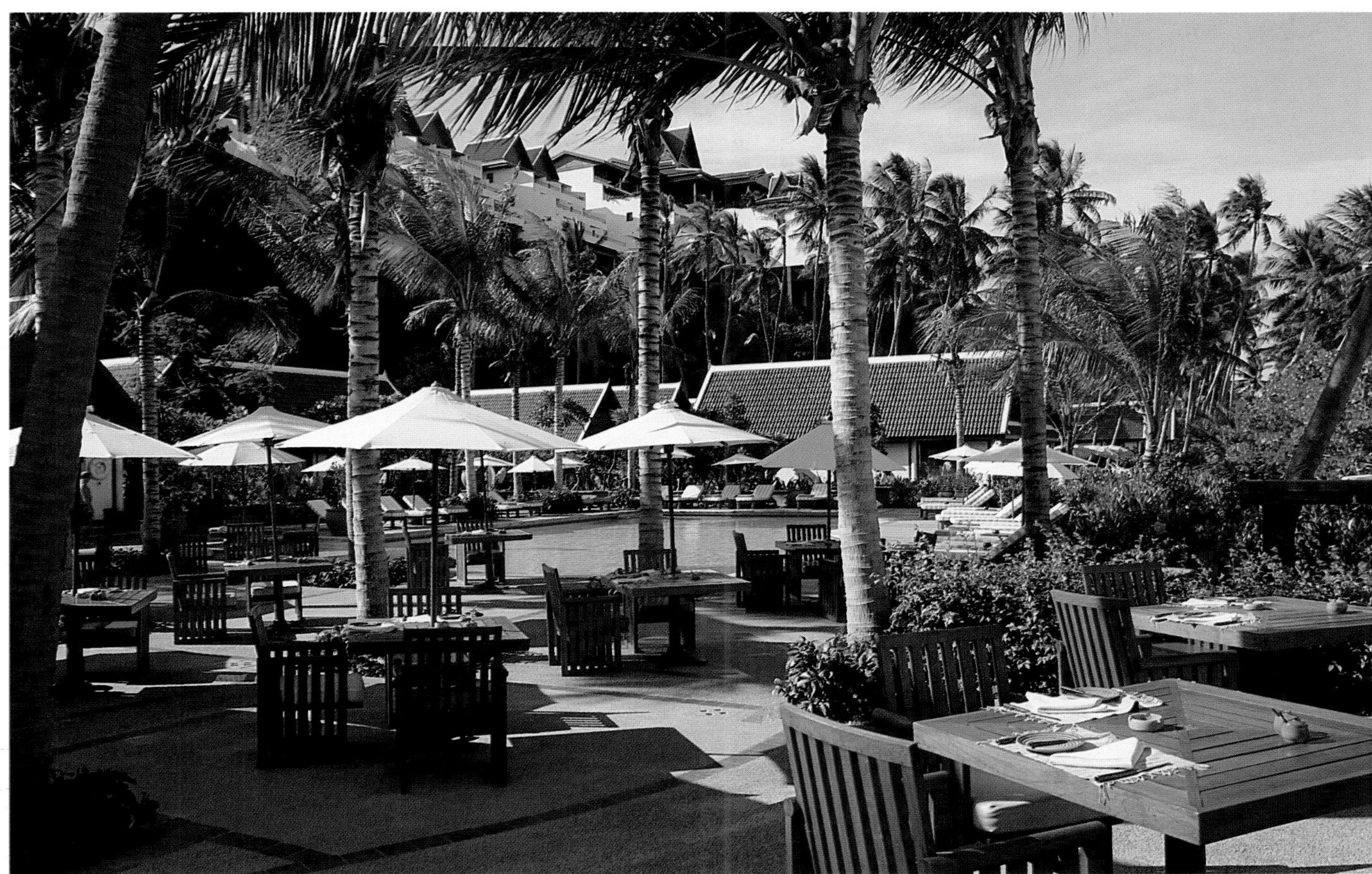

The Beach Club is centred around a rectangular pool fringed by coconut palms.

Der Beach Club liegt rund um einen rechteckigen Pool, umgeben von Kokospalmen.

Le Beach Club entoure une piscine rectangulaire ombragée de cocotiers.

(back page):
The private villas are lifted off the sloping terrain by concrete stilts.

(folgende Seite):
Die Privatvillen am Hang werden von Betonpfeilern getragen.

(page précédente):
Des pilotis en béton supportent les villas privées accrochées au versant.

Views across the pool to the verdant valleys.

Blick über den Pool auf die grünen Hänge.

Vue depuis la piscine sur les vallées verdoyantes.

Most of the private villas have spectacular views of the sea.

Aus den meisten Privatvillen hat man einen grandiosen Blick auf das Meer.

La plupart des résidences privées jouissent de merveilleux panoramas sur la mer.

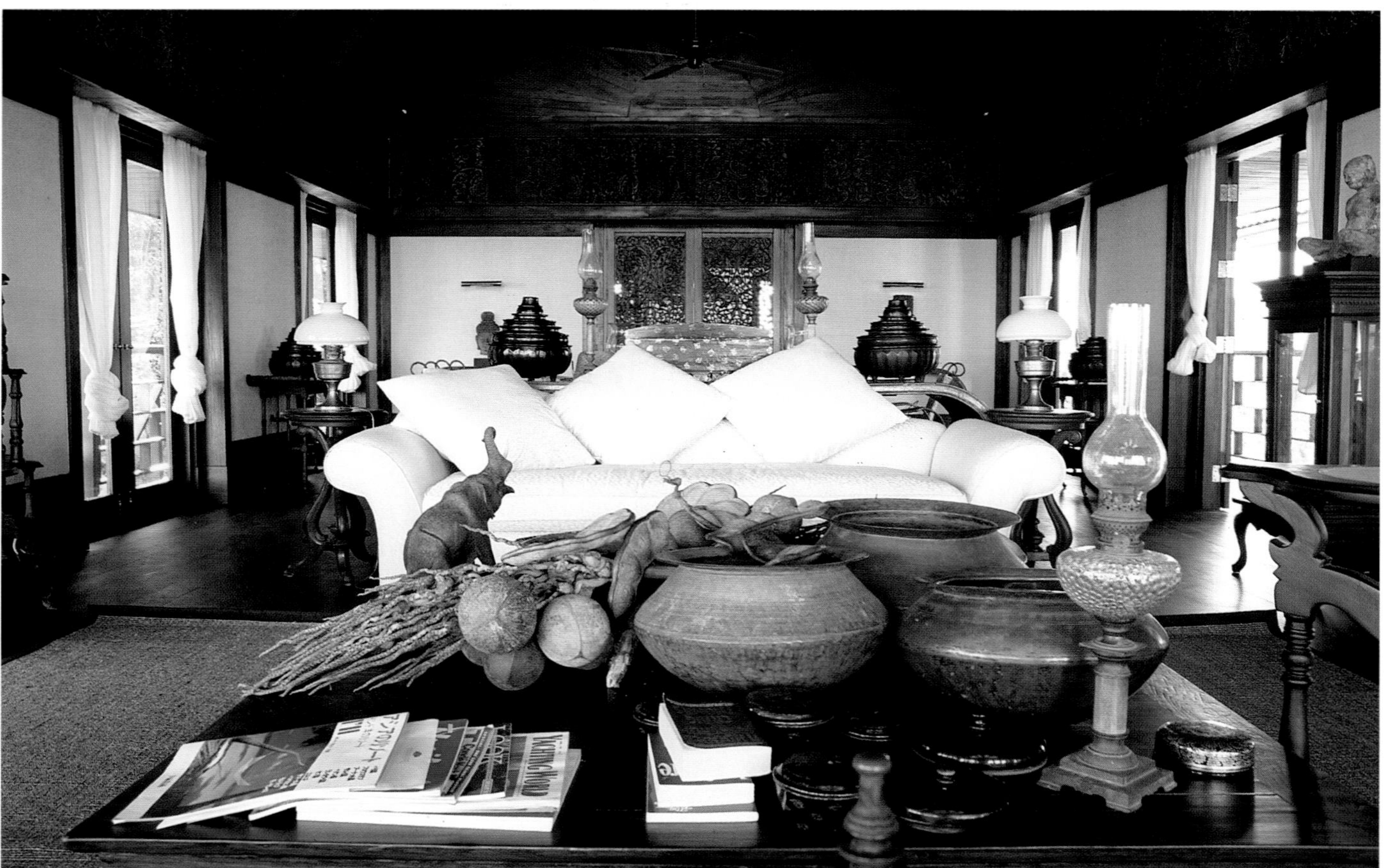

The interiors of the villas are luxuriantly furnished with traditional objects and elements, evoking a spirit of delightful eclecticism.

Die Villen sind luxuriös mit traditionellen Kunstgegenständen und Elementen eingerichtet, in einer zwar bunten, aber charmanten Mischung.

L'intérieur des villas abonde en objets traditionnels et en éléments qui créent un éclectisme charmant.

Baan Taling Ngam is located on a hillslope overlooking crystal-clear waters.

Baan Taling Ngam liegt an einem Hang oberhalb des kristallklaren Meers.

On découvre la mer aigue-marine de presque tous les endroits du complexe.

An evening view of the pool, which is delightfully set at the edge of a steep cliff.

Abendlicher Blick auf den Teich, der an einem steilen Hügel angelegt ist.

Vue nocturne de la piscine agréablement placée sur la crête d'une colline escarpée.

Seen from the pool, the lobby pavilion is the focus of the entire composition.

Vom Pool aus gesehen, ist der Pavillon mit der Halle das Zentrum der Gesamtanlage.

Vue depuis la piscine du pavillon de réception qui forme le cœur de la composition architecturale.

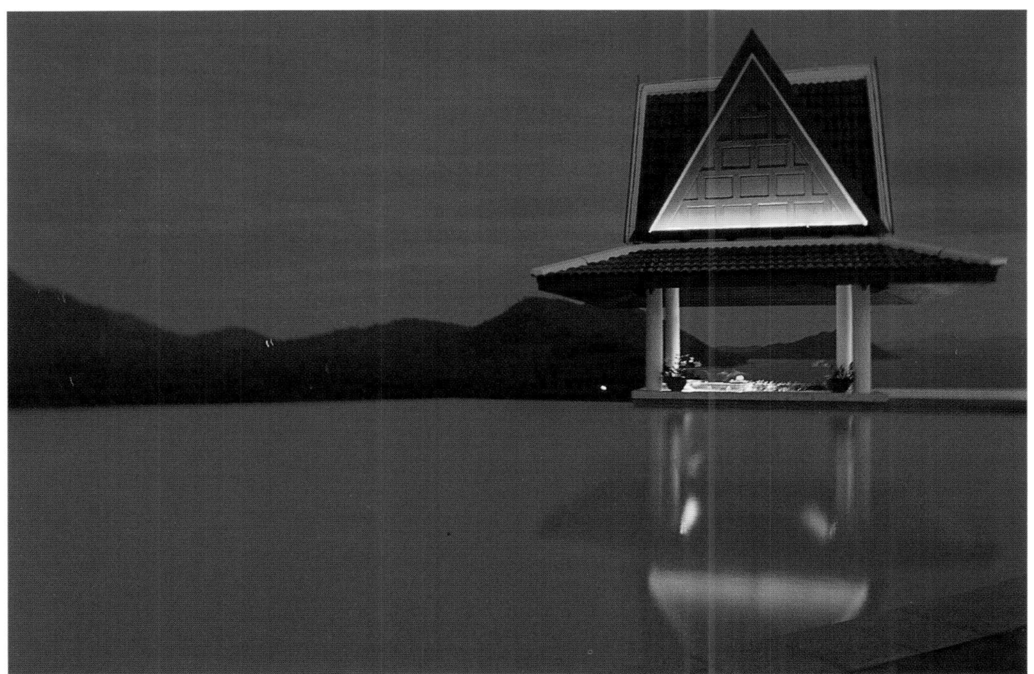

The pool bar provides an important architectural counterpoint to the tranquility of the pool.

Die Bar ist ein wichtiger architektonischer Kontrast zu der Ruhe des Pools.

Le bar de la piscine crée un fort contraste architectural avec les lignes sereines de la pièce d'eau.

Banyan Tree Phuket, Phuket

View of the lobby blocks from across a man-made lagoon.

Blick über die künstliche Lagune auf die Pavillons mit der Lobby.

Vue depuis la lagune artificielle sur les pavillons abritant la réception.

Phuket, billed as Thailand's "tropical paradise", remains the country's most popular beach resort. Located off the southwest coast, the stunningly beautiful island has magnificent bays, unspoiled sandy beaches and limpid blue waters. It attracts two million foreign tourists a year.

The Banyan Tree is one of the four luxury hotels in Laguna Phuket, Asia's first integrated resort. Located within the same three-kilometre stretch of beachland, it comprises of Banyan Tree Phuket, Dusit Laguna, Laguna Beach Club and Sheraton Grande Laguna Beach. There are also The Allamanda Apartment Suites, Banyan Tree Club, an 18-hole championship golf course and a canal village shopping complex. The developer Wah Chang bought a very large piece of ravaged tin-mining wasteland in 1984 and transformed it into a large resort complex. A 1977 United Nations Survey had written off the site as being too environmentally damaged to have any development potential. The integrated resort now occupies a 400-hectare site, including six lagoons. Guest activities are integrated and certain core activities like laundry operations and waste treatment disposal are centralised.

In 1992, the US$300 million development won the International Hotel Association Environment Award for Environmental Conservation. It has transformed the abandoned and devastated site into a resort property and restored the flora and fauna, including the return of wild birds to the area. The Banyan Tree Phuket, designed by Architrave Design and Planning, is probably the most impressive project in the complex.

Located on Bang Tao Bay on the northwestern coast of Phuket, the Banyan Tree Phuket is the first of the new luxury Banyan Tree chain, and in many ways it is a showcase for the group's concept. Its individual guest villas are spread over the vast landscape designed around a man-made lagoon. Altogether they exude a monastic solemnity. Spread over both sides of the lagoon, the wall-enclosed villas are grouped in tight clusters, evoking images of Balinese villages, except that they are roofed over by ostensibly Thai structures.

The hotel lobby, comprising of four simple pyramidal roofs clad in strongly hued orange tiles, is designed around a central reflecting pool. But behind this formal reticence, its open-sided spaces are intricately layered to provide a captivating depth of vision from various vantage points. The lighting at night is

Banyan Tree Phuket, Phuket

Phuket, das sogenannte »tropische Paradies« Thailands, ist immer noch die beliebteste Badeinsel des Landes. Die überwältigend schöne Insel liegt vor der Südwestküste und hat traumhafte Buchten, unzerstörte Sandstrände und klares blaues Wasser. Jährlich zieht sie zwei Millionen ausländische Touristen an.

Das Banyan Tree ist eines der vier Luxushotels in Laguna Phuket, Asiens erster integrierter Ferienanlage an einem drei Kilometer langen Sandstrand. Dazu gehören neben dem Banyan Tree auch das Dusit Laguna, der Laguna Beach Club und das Sheraton Grande Laguna Beach. Außerdem sind da The Allamanda Apartment Suites, der Banyan Tree Club, ein 18-Loch-Meisterschaftsgolfplatz und ein Einkaufszentrum in einem Dorf am Kanal. Der Bauherr Wah Chang kaufte 1984 eine große Fläche Ödland, auf der vorher Zinnminen waren, und machte daraus eine riesige Ferienanlage. 1977 hatte eine Studie der Vereinten Nationen die Gegend abgeschrieben, weil die Umwelt so verschmutzt war, daß hier keine Entwicklungen mehr möglich schienen. Die integrierte Anlage umfaßt heute 400 Hektar, darunter sechs Lagunen. Alle Aktivitäten der Gäste finden hier statt, und Dienstleistungen wie Wäscherei und Abfallbeseitigung sind zentral organisiert.

Die Anlage für 300 Millionen US-Dollar gewann 1992 den International Hotel Association Environment Award for Environmental Conservation, einen internationalen Preis für Umweltschutz. Aus dem verlassenen und verwüsteten Landstrich wurde eine vorbildliche Anlage, in der auch Fauna und Flora zu neuem Leben erwachten, und selbst die wilden Vögel der Gegend kehrten zurück. Das Banyan Tree Phuket, entwickelt von Architrave Design and Planning, ist vermutlich das eindrucksvollste Projekt in dem gesamten Komplex.

Das Banyan Tree Phuket liegt an der Bang Tao Bay an der nordwestlichen Küste von Phuket und ist die erste Anlage der neuen Luxus-Kette Banyan Tree. In vieler Hinsicht ist Banyan Tree Phuket das Vorzeigeobjekt für das Konzept der Gruppe. Die individuellen Gästevillen sind in einer weiten Landschaft verteilt, die um eine künstlich geschaffene Lagune angelegt wurde. Alles in allem strahlen sie eine geradezu klösterliche Feierlichkeit aus. Auf beiden Seiten der Lagune stehen die von Mauern umgebenen Villen in engen Gruppen zusammen und erinnern an balinesische Dörfer, nur die Dächer sind eindeutig thailändische Konstruktionen.

Banyan Tree Phuket, Phuket

Phuket, considéré comme le "paradis tropical de la Thaïlande", est encore la station balnéaire la plus fréquentée du pays. Située au large de la côte sud-ouest, l'île à la beauté merveilleuse possède des baies magnifiques, des plages de sable fin et des eaux bleues limpides. Elle attire deux millions de touristes étrangers par an.

Le Banyan Tree est un des quatre hôtels de luxe de Laguna Phuket, la première station balnéaire d'Asie avec une structure intégrée. Elle s'étend sur une plage continue de trois kilomètres et comprend les hôtels Banyan Tree Phuket, Dusit Laguna, Laguna Beach Club et Sheraton Grande Laguna Beach. On trouve également les Allamandaa Apartment Suites, Banyan Tree Club, un terrain de golf de 18 trous et un complexe commercial bâti entre des canaux. En 1984, le promoteur Wah Chang acquit une large surface d'un territoire ravagé par des mines d'étain pour le transformer en un vaste complexe hôtelier. En 1977, une expertise des Nations unies avait considéré l'environnement du site trop endommagé pour offrir un potentiel de développement. La station balnéaire aux structures intégrées occupe aujourd'hui un site de 400 hectares, y compris six lagunes. Les aménagements pour la détente et les loisirs sont intégrés tandis que certaines installations de base comme le traitement des ordures et la blanchisserie sont centralisées.

Le projet qui a coûté 300 millions de dollars US, a recu le "International Hotel Association Environnement Award" (Prix international de l'association hôtelière pour l'environnement). Il a transformé un site abandonné et ravagé en une station balnéaire de valeur et a restauré la flore et la faune, permettant également le retour d'oiseaux sauvages dans la région. Le Banyan Tree Phuket, conçu par le bureau Architrave Design and Planning, est sans doute l'hôtel le plus captivant du complexe.

Le Banyan Tree Phuket s'étend dans la baie Bang Tao, sur la côte nord-ouest de Phuket. Le premier projet de la nouvelle chaîne d'hôtels de luxe Banyan Tree est représentatif du concept du groupe sur bien des points. Ses villas individuelles sont parsemées dans un vaste paysage qui entoure une lagune artificielle. L'ensemble a beaucoup de sobriété. S'étendant de chaque côté de la lagune, les villas entourées de murs et bâties en groupes serrés, évoquent des villages balinais, à l'exception des toits qui sont de pur style thaïlandais.

La réception de l'hôtel, un ensemble surmonté de quatre toits pyramidaux recouverts de tuiles d'un orange brillant, est

especially enchanting, imbuing the place with a special ambience.

The 86-villa resort has 52 garden villas and 34 pool villas. The 170-square metre garden villa contains a private garden within its walled compound, whereas the 270-square metre pool villa (34 in number) has a private 9 x 3 metre swimming pool. Each villa has its own garden and an open-air sunken bath. The Pool Villa also features a raised Thai-style 'sala' and dining area, as well as a paved patio with built-in barbeque pit.

The interior of the villa is a sanctuary of uninvaded calm, sensitively detailed and subtly lit at night. Careful detailing and clean, controlled execution of the finishes ensure a thoroughly pleasant and luxurious interior layout. Especially delightful is the sleeping area, which is a raised timber platform overlooking the private pool and the 'sala'.

A unique facility of the resort is the Banyan Tree Spa, one of Asia's largest garden spas. Four spa pavilions, equipped with saunas, steam rooms, jacuzzi, and loofah areas, offer a wide range of massage and beauty treatments like hydrotherapy and aromatherapy. Guests also have access to the 18-hole championship Banyan Tree Club golf course.

The Banyan Tree Phuket is a provocative piece of work in more ways than one. An assured piece of work, the end result is both elegant and inviting. Yet in fusing Balinese-inspired layouts with literal variants of traditional Thai architecture, the resort poses several ideological issues even while it seeks to provide reassurance of identity.

Die Hotellobby, bestehend aus vier einfachen Pyramidendächern mit Ziegeln in kräftigem Orange, ist um einen zentralen glitzernden Pool herum angelegt. Hinter dieser formalen Schlichtheit sind die an den Seiten offenen Räume versetzt angelegt, so daß man von verschiedenen Aussichtspunkten aus einen wunderbaren Blick in die Weite hat. Die nächtliche Beleuchtung ist besonders bezaubernd und verleiht dem Ganzen eine spezielle Atmosphäre.

Von den insgesamt 86 Villen verfügen 52 über einen Garten und 34 über einen Pool. Die Gartenvillen sind 170 Quadratmeter groß, und die Privatgärten sind von Mauern umgeben. Die Pool-Villen dagegen sind 270 Quadratmeter groß und haben ein eigenes 9 x 3 Meter großes Schwimmbecken. Zu den Pool-Villen gehört auch eine etwas höher angelegte Plattform mit Eßbereich im Thai-Stil und eine Veranda mit Steinfußboden und eingebautem Grillplatz.

Innen wirkt die Villa wie ein Zufluchtsort ungestörter Ruhe, ist schön eingerichtet und bei Nacht sanft beleuchtet. Die Einrichtung ist bis ins Detail sauber und sorgfältig ausgeführt und vermittelt den Eindruck von Luxus. Besonders angenehm ist der Schlafbereich auf einer erhöhten Holzplattform, von der aus man einen Blick auf den privaten Pool hat.

Einzigartig in dieser Anlage ist das Banyan Tree Spa, eine Badeanlage im Garten, die zu den größten Asiens gehört. In vier Badepavillons mit Sauna, Dampfbädern, Whirlpools und Ruheräumen werden Massagen und Schönheitsbehandlungen wie Hydro- und Aromatherapie angeboten. Gäste haben auch Zutritt zu dem 18-Loch-Meisterschaftsgolfplatz des Banyan Tree Club.

In mehr als einer Weise war das Banyan Tree Phuket eine Herausforderung. Das Endergebnis ist elegant und einladend zugleich. Doch da die Anlage Anregungen aus Bali mit echten Varianten der thailändischen Architektur verbindet, vermischt sie unterschiedliche ideologische Ziele, während sie gleichzeitig eigene Identität zu vermitteln versucht.

construite autour d'un bassin d'agrément où se reflètent les édifices. A côté de cette rigueur des formes, les espaces qui s'ouvrent sur les côtés présentent un agencement compliqué de plusieurs niveaux, destiné à offrir différents très beaux points de vue. L'éclairage, la nuit, est particulièrement enchanteur; il enrobe l'endroit d'une atmosphère unique.

L'hôtel comprend 86 unités: 52 villas de 170 m^2 avec un jardin privé entouré de mur et 34 villas de 270 m^2 avec une piscine privée de 9 mètres sur 3. Chaque villa a son propre jardin avec un bain encastré dans le sol. Les villas avec piscine ont également un *sala* et un coin-repas surélevés de style thaïlandais ainsi qu'un patio pavé avec barbecue intégré.

L'intérieur des villas est un véritable sanctuaire de paix, d'un goût parfait et à l'éclairage raffiné. L'agencement très soigné jusque dans les détails assure une ambiance agréable et luxueuse. Tout particulièrement plaisant est l'espace repos qui est une plate-forme en bois surplombant la piscine privée et le *sala*.

Le Banyan Tree Spa, un des plus grands parcs thermaux d'Asie, dote la station balnéaire d'un ensemble unique. Dans quatre pavillons équipés de saunas, bains de vapeur, jacuzzis et zones de luffa, les hôtes ont le choix entre différentes méthodes de massage et de soins de beauté comme l'hydrothérapie et l'aromathérapie. Le terrain de golf à 18 trous du Banyan Tree Club est également ouvert à la clientèle des hôtels.

Le Banyan Tree Phuket est un ouvrage captivant à plusieurs égards. De conception sûre, l'ensemble est à la fois élégant et accueillant. Cependant, en associant un agencement d'inspiration balinaise à des éléments d'architecture traditionnelle thaïlandaise, le complexe soulève plusieurs questions idéologiques alors qu'il cherche à assurer son identité.

The spaces of the resort are intricately layered to provide a captivating depth of vision from various vantage points

Die Räume sind geschickt gegeneinander versetzt, um Tiefe zu erreichen und von verschiedenen Punkten einen guten Ausblick zu ermöglichen.

Les espaces présentent un agencement compliqué de plusieurs niveaux, destinés à offrir de très beaux points de vue.

Each of the 34 pool villas has a private 9 x 3 metre swimming pool.

Jede der 34 Pool-Villen hat ein 9 x 3 Meter großes Schwimmbecken.

Les 34 villas ont toutes une piscine de 9 mètres sur 3.

Spread over both sides of the lagoon, the wall-enclosed villas are grouped in tight clusters.

Auf beiden Seiten der Lagune stehen die von Mauern umgebenen Villen in Gruppen dicht beieinander.

Les villas forment des groupes serrés autour de la lagune.

(opposite page):
Located at one end of the pool, the raised platform is also placed on axis with the bedroom.

(gegenüberliegende Seite):
An einem Ende des Pools gelegen, bildet die Plattform eine Achse mit dem Schlafraum.

(page ci-contre):
Située à un bout de la piscine, la plate-forme prolonge la chambre.

View of the pool villa from a raised platform, or sala.

Blick auf die Pool-Villa von einer erhöhten Plattform aus.

Vue sur la piscine depuis la plate-forme surélevée appelée sala.

The distinctive Thai roof is used as a recurrent design motif.

Das charakteristische Thai-Dach ist immer wieder zu sehen.

Le toit thaïlandais est un motif récurrent.

(opposite page):
The open-sided lobby restaurant is surrounded by reflecting pools that imbue an overall sense of lightness to the structure.

(gegenüberliegende Seite):
Das an den Seiten offene Restaurant ist umgeben von glitzernden Wasserbecken, die dem Bau insgesamt eine gewisse Leichtigkeit verleihen.

(page ci-contre):
Ouvert sur un côté, le restaurant attenant à la réception est entouré de bassins d'agrément qui allègent la structure.

Landscaping is used to complement the harshness of the wall-enclosed villas.

Die Gartengestaltung bildet ein Gegengewicht zu der Schroffheit der von Mauern umgebenen Villen.

La végétation luxuriante adoucit les lignes sévères des villas entourées de murs.

Privacy is carefully maintained through sensitive use of architectural elements like walls and thick vegetation.

Durch einfühlsamen Einsatz von architektonischen Elementen wie Mauern und dichter Begrünung bleibt die Privatsphäre erhalten.

Des éléments architecturaux tels que des murs et une végétation épaisse assurent l'intimité.

The lobby is designed with minimal fuss, as well as a strong axial quality.

Die Lobby ist mit einem Minimum an Aufwand gestaltet.

Décorée dans un style dépouillé, la réception forme également un axe du complexe.

Subtle lighting modulate the tranquil mood of the library.

Sanfte Beleuchtung unterstreicht die Ruhe der Bibliothek.

Un éclairage subtil crée une atmosphère sereine dans la bibliothèque.

Evening is probably one of the most enchanting period in the resort, as evident the delightful play of light in the lobby.

Am Abend ist es vermutlich am stimmungsvollsten, wie das Spiel des Lichts in der Halle zeigt.

La nuit, le complexe s'enveloppe d'une ambiance enchanteresse, créée par des jeux de lumière comme ici, dans la réception.

The sleeping area inside the villa consists of a raised platform overlooking the pool.

Der Schlafbereich in der Villa liegt auf einer erhöhten Plattform mit Blick auf den Pool.

L'espace repos dans la villa est une plate-forme qui surplombe la piscine.

An outdoor bath, in the tradition of wall-enclosed Balinese baths, is fringed by lush vegetation.

Ein Bad im Freien steht in der Tradition der von Wänden umschlossenen balinesischen Bäder und ist von üppiger Vegetation umgeben.

Une végétation luxuriante entoure le bain en plein air qui rappelle les bains traditionnels balinais enfermés dans des murs.

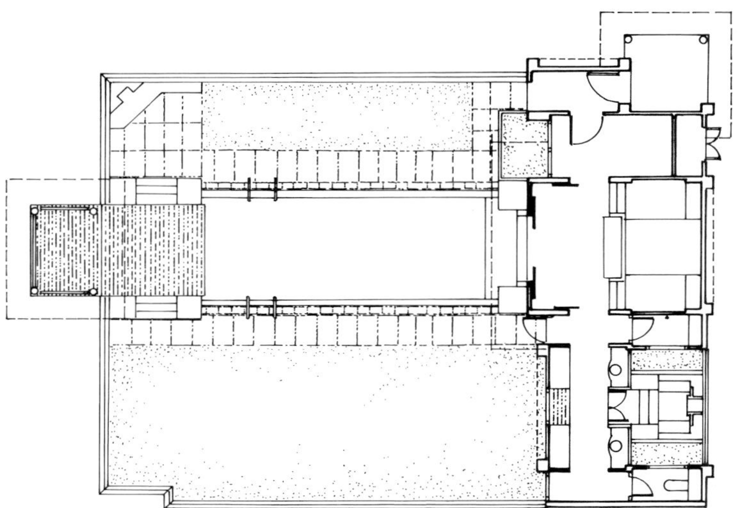

Plan of a typical guestroom.

Plan eines typischen Gästezimmers.

Plan d'une chambre type.

The interior is a sanctuary of calm. It is sensitively detailed and elegantly furnished.

Innen herrscht angenehme Ruhe. Der Raum ist gut aufgeteilt und elegant eingerichtet.

L'intérieur est un sanctuaire de paix, au mobilier élégant et décoré avec une recherche étudiée des détails.

Dusit Rayavadee, Krabi

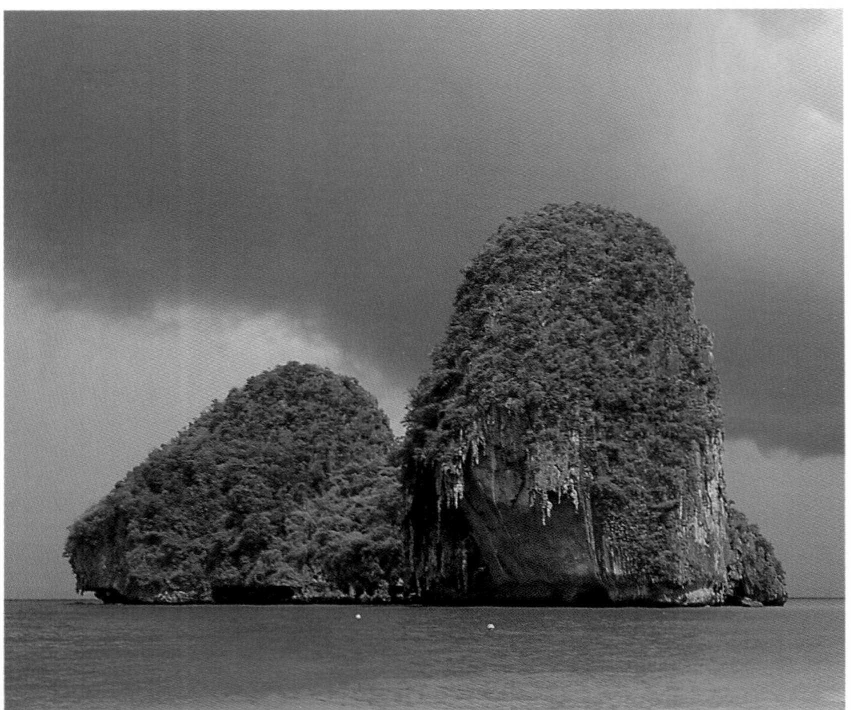

Krabi is a region of towering limestone outcrops, many of them jutting out spectacularly from the sea.

Krabi ist eine Region mit hoch aufragendem Kalkgestein, das sich manchmal spektakulär aus dem Meer erhebt.

Krabi est notamment connue pour ses hautes falaises et ses concrétions de calcaire qui se hérissent dans la mer.

Lying over 800 kilometres south of Bangkok, the coastal province of Krabi offers some of the region's most outstanding natural scenery. A distinctive region of densely forested hills, palms and rubber plantations and towering limestone outcrops, it reputedly has the most beautiful beach in the world as well. This extraordinary location is the latest southern resort to attract international attention ever since the recent opening of its first luxury hotel, the Dusit Rayavadee.

The hotel is located 163 kilometres east of Phuket by road and 55 kilometres by sea. However, the peninsula is completely cut off from all land transport by soaring cliffs, necessitating entry by boat. The scenic sea trip takes just over an hour from Phuket's Laem Preaw jetty.

The 100-pavilion Dusit Rayavadee Resort, designed by Four Aces Consultants Co Ltd, is located on an alluring nine-hectare site that is part of the Had Nopparat Thara National Park. Raya in Thai means "princess" while vadee is a village. This "Village of the Princess" is surrounded on two sides by spectacular limestone outcrops towering between 150-200 metres. The untamed splendour of the surrounding environment has a particular potency. Nature dominates, and dominates completely. Wildlife is all around, as the resort shares its site with troops of macaques and a family of endangered gibbons.

The resort is built on a headland nestling between three sandy beaches, namely Nam Mao, Phra Nang and Ray Lei. The most striking of the three, Phra Nang is regularly quoted as being the most beautiful beach in the world. Its powdery soft white sands and crystal-clear waters are convincing evidence that this is no empty boast. The hotel reception lounge and central guest area are located in Nam Mao beach, which is not used for recreation as it turns into mangrove flats at low tides. Guest and staff transfers by boat are handled through this beach.

The wilderness of the surroundings provide the pavilions with an even more dramatic ambience.

Die Wildnis um die Pavillons herum macht die Atmosphäre noch aufregender.

La nature sauvage entoure les pavillons d'un décor merveilleux.

On arrival by boat, guests board a timber cart waiting at shallow waters. The ensemble is then dragged onto the beach by a tractor. As this is a national park, no jetty is allowed to be constructed. The pavilions, hidden by dense foliage, are hardly discernible. Set amidst an existing coconut plantation, they offer wondrous views of the rugged multi-colored limestone cliffs and weirdly-shaped rock formations jutting above the sea.

Conceptualised by Bangkok-based Thai architect, M. L. Chainimit Navarat, the design aims to make the resort

Dusit Rayavadee, Krabi

Mehr als 800 Kilometer südlich von Bangkok gelegen, bietet die Küstenprovinz Krabi einige der ungewöhnlichsten Landschaften der Region. Die Gegend mit dichtbewaldeten Hügeln, Palmen, Gummiplantagen und hoch aufragendem Kalkgestein ist unverwechselbar, und sie hat angeblich auch noch den schönsten Strand der Welt. An diesem außergewöhnlichen Ort liegt die jüngste südliche Ferienanlage, die international Aufmerksamkeit erregt, seit das erste Luxushotel, das Dusit Rayavadee, eröffnet wurde.

Das Hotel liegt östlich von Phuket, in einer Entfernung von 163 Kilometern auf dem Landweg und 55 Kilometern auf dem Seeweg. Doch wegen hoher Klippen ist die Halbinsel von Land aus vollkommen unzugänglich und nur mit dem Schiff zu erreichen. Die malerische Überfahrt von der Anlegestelle Laem Preaw in Phuket dauert etwas über eine Stunde.

Das Dusit Rayavadee Resort mit seinen 100 Pavillons wurde von Four Aces Consultants Co. Ltd. geplant und liegt auf einem reizvollen, neun Hektar großen Gelände, das zum Had Nopparat Thara National Park gehört. Das thailändische Wort raya bedeutet "Prinzessin", vadee heißt "Dorf". An zwei Seiten des "Dorfes der Prinzessin" sieht man spektakuläres Kalkgestein, 150 - 200 Meter hoch. Die wilde Schönheit der Umgebung hat einen ganz besonderen Reiz. Hier herrscht die Natur, und zwar auf ganzer Linie. Wildlebende Tiere sind allgegenwärtig, da auf dem Gelände Scharen von Makaken und eine Familie gefährdeter Gibbons leben.

Die Anlage wurde errichtet auf einer Landzunge oberhalb von drei Sandstränden, Nam Mao, Phra Nang und Ray Lei. Der aufregendste, Phra Nang, wird immer wieder als der schönste Strand der Welt bezeichnet. Der puderfeine, weiße Sand und das kristallklare Wasser sind überzeugender Beweis, daß es sich dabei nicht um reine Prahlerei handelt. Die Empfangshalle des Hotels und der zentrale Gästebereich liegen am Strand Nam Mao; er wird nicht zur Freizeitgestaltung genutzt, denn bei Ebbe breiten sich hier die Mangroven aus. Diesen Strand laufen auch die Schiffe mit Gästen und Angestellten an.

Nach der Ankunft per Schiff besteigen die Gäste einen Holzwagen, der im flachen Wasser wartet und dann von einem Trecker an Land gezogen wird. Da es sich hier um einen Nationalpark handelt, darf kein Anlegesteg gebaut werden. Versteckt unter dichtem Laub, sind die Pavillons kaum zu erkennen. Mitten auf einer Kokosnuß-Plantage gelegen, bieten

Dusit Rayavadee, Krabi

La province côtière de Krabi qui s'étend à 800 kilomètres au Sud de Bangkok, offre quelques-uns des plus beaux paysages de la région. Une région qui se distingue par des collines recouvertes de forêts épaisses, des palmeraies, des plantations de caoutchouc et de hautes concrétions de calcaire. Elle est également réputée pour avoir les plus belles plages du monde. Grâce à cette situation splendide, la dernière station balnéaire au Sud attire un public international depuis l'ouverture récente de son premier hôtel de luxe, le Dusit Rayavadee.

L'hôtel est situé à 163 kilomètres de Phuket par la route et à 55 kilomètres par la mer. Cependant, le seul accès possible est par la mer car des rochers escarpés empêchent d'atteindre la péninsule par transport terrestre. Le très beau trajet en bateau prend un peu plus d'une heure depuis la jetée Laem Preaw à Phuket.

Le Dusit Rayavadee Resort a été construit par la firme Four Aces Consultants CO Ltd. Ses cent pavillons s'étendent sur un site de neuf hectares qui fait partie du Parc national Had Nopparat Thara. "Raya" signifie princesse et "Vadee" village en thaïlandais. Des rochers de calcaire spectaculaires de 150 à 200 mètres de haut entourent le "Village de la Princesse" sur deux côtés. La nature environnante a une splendeur sauvage. La faune est aussi présente car l'hôtel partage le site avec des hordes de macaques et une famille de gibbons, en voie de disparition.

L'hôtel se dresse sur un promontoire entouré de trois plages de sable: Nam Mao, Phra Nang et Ray Lei. Phra Nang a la réputation d'être la plus belle plage du monde. On lui accorde volontiers ce titre quand on voit l'admirable rivage de sable blanc très fin et ses eaux claires comme du cristal. Le hall de réception et les zones communes pour les hôtes sont situés sur la plage Nam Mao qui n'est pas utilisée pour les loisirs car elle se transforme en étendues de mangroves à marée basse. C'est ici que les bateaux qui transportent clients et personnel de l'hôtel accostent.

A l'arrivée, les hôtes montent dans une charrette qui attend dans les eaux basses. Un tracteur tire le véhicule jusqu'à la plage. La construction d'une jetée est interdite car l'endroit est un parc national. Les pavillons sont à peine visibles derrière le rideau de végétation dense. Ils sont bâtis dans une plantation de cocotiers entourée d'un paysage merveilleux de falaises escarpées aux multiples couleurs et de rochers aux formes étranges surgissant de la mer.

Viewed from the adjacent limestone cliff, the sensitively sited pavilions are hardly discernible.

Vom nahegelegenen Kalksteinkliff aus sind die Pavillons kaum zu erkennen.

Les pavillons sont si bien cachés qu'on peut à peine les voir depuis la falaise.

appropriately non-intrusive and visually not apparent when viewed from the sea, especially along the Ray Lei and Phra Nang beaches. Awarded the Royal Gold Medal for environmentally sympathetic construction by the Association of Siamese Architects, the resort demonstrates an earnest concern and a keen sensitivity to the pristine environment.

Existing vegetation was kept intact along the beach front, providing both visual barrier as well as acting as a buffer against the impact of the wind during the monsoon months. A great effort was also made to keep as many of the existing trees as possible. The pavilions are hence scattered amongst brilliant displays of indigenous foliage. The environmental consciousness is also reflected in various concerns. For example, treated waste water is circulated around the resort grounds in a meandering series of lily pools filled with fishes. All forms of engine watersports and beach umbrellas are also not allowed on the property.

An obvious architectural treatment is the circular plan used in the design of the pavilion. A "semi-prefabricated" technique was used in the construction because all the building materials have to be transported by boat and assembled on site. A fully-furnished prototype pavilion was even set up in Bangkok to get the specifications as precise as possible as it would be difficult to make any adjustments on site.

The structures draw inspiration from local design precepts in an organic relationship with the surroundings. The two-storey design was inspired by traditional Thai architecture as well as the mosques of Southern Thailand. The first storey of the typical pavilion, consisting of a living space and a pantry, is linked by a wooden spiral staircase to a sumptuous bedroom with attached bathroom. The interior design, executed by Leo Design Co. Ltd., and Nature Touch Co. Ltd., is luxurious without being opulent.

There are eight deluxe pavilions with their own outdoor whirlpool and four larger two-bedroom pavilions. There are also two special pavilion suites, the Phra Nang Villa and the Rayavadee Villa. The external wall finishes are wood substitution panels made of composite fibreglass and cement materials in a warm yellow colour. Industrialised wood products have been extensively used so as to conserve endangered hardwood. The roof-form evokes associations with Oriental structures in subtle ways. At night, the lighting around the meandering footpaths

sie wunderbare Ausblicke auf die zerklüfteten, bunten Kalksteinklippen und wilde Felsformationen, die aus dem Meer ragen.

Die Planung stammt von dem in Bangkok lebenden thailändischen Architekten M. L. Chainimit Navarat, und die Anlage ist so konzipiert, daß sie so wenig wie möglich in die Landschaft eingreift und vom Meer aus nicht zu sehen ist, vor allem von den Stränden Ray Lei und Phra Nang aus. Die Association of Siamese Architects hat die Anlage mit der Royal Gold Medal für umweltverträgliches Bauen ausgezeichnet, und hier demonstriert man wirklich ernsthaftes Interesse und wachsame Sensibilität für die ursprüngliche Umwelt.

Entlang der Strände blieb bereits vorhandene Vegetation erhalten, und sie dient so gleichzeitig als Sichtschutz und Abwehr gegen den Sturm während der Monsunmonate. Die Pavillons sind zwischen heimischen Laubbäumen verstreut, und das Umweltbewußtsein läßt sich auch an anderen Dingen ablesen. Geklärtes Abwasser beispielsweise zirkuliert auf dem Gelände durch eine Reihe von miteinander verbundenen Seerosenteichen, in denen Fische schwimmen. In der Anlage sind jeder motorbetriebene Wassersport und Sonnenschirme verboten.

Eine besondere architektonische Leistung war der Aufbau der Pavillons. Man setzte eine »halb vorgefertigte« Bautechnik ein, weil das gesamte Material per Schiff transportiert und auf der Anlage montiert werden mußte. In Bangkok baute man sogar einen voll eingerichteten Prototyp eines Pavillons auf, um alle Einzelheiten so genau wie möglich durchzuplanen, denn Nachbesserungen vor Ort wären schwierig gewesen.

Die Bauten sind inspiriert von bestehenden örtlichen Vorbildern und stehen in einer organischen Beziehung zu der Umgebung. Die einstöckigen Gebäude sind sowohl von der traditionellen Thai-Architektur als auch von den Moscheen im südlichen Thailand beeinflußt. Das Erdgeschoß des typischen Pavillons hat einen Wohnbereich und eine kleine Küche; eine Wendeltreppe aus Holz verbindet es mit einem prachtvollen Schlafzimmer mit Bad. Die Inneneinrichtung, durchgeführt von Leo Design Co. Ltd. und Nature Touch Co. Ltd., ist luxuriös, ohne jedoch übertrieben zu wirken.

Es gibt acht Pavillons der Luxusklasse mit eigenem Whirlpool im Freien und vier größere Pavillons mit zwei Schlafzimmern, außerdem spezielle Pavillon-Suiten, die Phra Nang Villa

M.L. Chainimit Navarat, architecte thaïlandais résidant à Bangkok, a conçu l'ensemble de façon à ce qu'il se fonde dans le paysage et ne soit pas visible de la mer, notamment des plages Ray Lei et Phra Nang. L'Association des architectes siamois a décerné la Médaille d'Or Royale pour la construction écologique de la station qui témoigne d'un grand souci de protection de l'environnement.

La végétation existante est restée intacte le long du rivage; elle constitue un rideau naturel qui masque la vue et forme obstacle au vent pendant les mois de la mousson. De grands efforts ayant été faits pour conserver un maximum d'arbres, les pavillons sont parsemés dans un magnifique paysage de végétation exotique. On retrouve également cette conscience de l'environnement dans d'autres aspects. Par exemple, les eaux usées traitées coulent dans une succession de bassins remplis de nénuphars et de poissons, qui méandre à travers le site de l'hôtel. Les sports nautiques à moteur et les parasols de plage sont également interdits.

L'architecture des pavillons construits selon un plan circulaire, saute immédiatement aux yeux. On a utilisé une technique de "semi-préfabriqué" car tous les matériaux de construction ont dû être transportés par bateau et assemblés sur place. Un pavillon prototype entièrement meublé a même été créé à Bangkok afin d'obtenir des spécifications aussi précises que possible, puisqu'il aurait été difficile d'opérer des modifications sur place.

Les structures suivent les principes architecturaux locaux et s'harmonisent avec l'environnement. Les constructions à un étage s'inspirent de l'architecture traditionnelle thaïlandaise et des mosquées de la Thaïlande du Sud. Le rez-de-chaussée d'un pavillon typique comprend un salon et un office. Un escalier tournant en bois mène à une somptueuse chambre à coucher avec salle de bains attenante. Leo Design Co. Ltd., et Nature Touch Co. Ltd., ont conçu le design intérieur d'un luxe discret.

Huit pavillons de luxe ont leur propre bassin à remous et quatre pavillons plus vastes ont deux chambres à coucher. On trouve également deux pavillons de grand standing abritant une suite: les villas Phra Nang et Rayavadee. Peints dans un jaune éclatant, les murs extérieurs sont recouverts de ciment et de panneaux de fibre de verre imitant le bois. La large utilisation de produits industriels substitutifs du bois s'explique par un désir de ne pas contribuer au déboisement excessif. La forme des toits évoque subtilement des structures orientales. La nuit, les

and the silhouette of the buildings' forms are reminiscent of a Japanese garden. A charming Thai restaurant, located next to the beach, is especially engimatic at night.

Leisure facilities include two tennis courts situated next to a limestone cliff and a large pool overlooking the sea at Rai Lay Beach, with a whirlpool extension and a separate children's pool. Rock-climbing, snorkelling and scuba-diving are the main activities. The waters of the surrounding islands are crystal-clear during the calm season, with colourful fishes frolicking next to the swimmers. Another enchanting activity is exploring the numerous *hongs*, or "rooms" of collapsed cave systems open to the sky, and accessible only in purpose-designed inflatable canoes through sea-caves at low tides.

In the final analysis, the project is informed by a sense of respect for the fragile environment. While the tectonic gestures are finely judged, the attention the architect lavishes on details compels greater admiration. With great discipline and few extraneous elements, the architect has interwoven sensitivity and simplicity to create a thoughtful piece of work that achieves a resonance with the environment.

Since its inception eight years ago, Navarat has taken pains to ensure that the project is ecologically sensitive. The commitment towards conservation is certainly palpable. The end result engenders deep satisfaction. It is a powerful and convincing step in the right direction towards a realistic and sensible form of ecotourism.

und die Rayavadee Villa. Die Außenwände haben eine warme, gelbe Verkleidung aus Holzersatz, hergestellt aus Fiberglas und Zementstoffen. In großem Umfang wurden industriell hergestellte Holzprodukte verwendet, um die gefährdeten Harthölzer zu schützen. Die Dachformen zitieren auf subtile Weise orientalische Strukturen. Nachts erinnern die Beleuchtung an den verschlungenen Wegen und die Silhouetten der Gebäude an japanische Gärten. Ein zauberhaftes Thai-Restaurant in der Nähe des Strandes wirkt zur Nachtzeit besonders geheimnisvoll.

Für die Freizeitbeschäftigung stehen zwei Tennisplätze in der Nähe von Kalksteinklippen zur Verfügung, ebenso ein großer Pool mit angeschlossenem Whirlpool und separatem Kinderbecken in Rai Lay Beach mit Blick auf das Meer. Felsenkletterei, Schnorcheln und Sporttauchen sind die Hauptaktivitäten. Das Wasser rund um die Inseln in der Umgebung ist während der ruhigen Jahreszeit kristallklar, und bunte Fische kommen ganz nahe an die Schwimmer heran. Faszinierend ist auch die Erforschung der zahllosen *hongs*. Das sind »Zimmer« eingestürzter Höhlensysteme, zum Himmel offen und nur bei Ebbe mit speziell entwickelten, aufblasbaren Kanus vom Meer aus durch Höhlen zu erreichen.

Alles in allem zeichnet sich das Hotel durch Respekt vor der empfindlichen Umwelt aus. Die Gliederung des Baus ist ausgewogen, doch die große Aufmerksamkeit, die der Architekt den Details schenkt, kann man nur aufs höchste bewundern. Mit großer Disziplin und nur wenigen fremden Elementen hat er Sensibilität und Einfachheit miteinander verbunden und so eine durchdachte Anlage geschaffen, die in Einklang mit der Umwelt steht.

Seit den Anfängen vor acht Jahren hat Navarat sich darum bemüht, daß das Projekt umweltverträglich ist. Die Verpflichtung gegenüber der Bewahrung ist offensichtlich. Das Endergebnis löst tiefe Zufriedenheit aus. Hier wurde ein großer und überzeugender Schritt in die richtige Richtung getan, hin zu einer realistischen und vernünftigen Form des Öko-Tourismus.

chemins sinueux éclairés et la silhouette des édifices rappellent un jardin japonais. Dans l'obscurité, une atmosphère énigmatique entoure tout particulièrement le restaurant thaïlandais près de la plage.

Les aménagements pour les loisirs comprennent deux courts de tennis situés près de la falaise, une vaste piscine qui surplombe la mer à Rai Lay Beach, avec un bassin à remous attenant et un bassin pour enfants séparé. Les activités principales sont l'escalade et la plongée sous-marine. En dehors de la saison des moussons, les eaux sont claires comme du cristal et l'on peut voir des poissons multicolores virevolter autour des baigneurs. Une très belle excursion à faire est de partir explorer les nombreuses *hongs*, des grottes ouvertes sur le ciel, accessibles seulement par des caves sous-marines que l'on traverse à marée basse dans des canoës pneumatiques de formes spéciales.

Analyse finale: le projet révèle un grand respect pour l'environnement fragile. L'architecte a équilibré les structures d'une façon admirable tout en accordant une attention particulière aux détails. Avec rigueur et sans éléments superflus, il a uni sensibilité et simplicité pour créer une œuvre en parfaite harmonie avec l'environnement.

Dès le début du projet, il y a huit ans, Navarat a énormément tenu compte de l'aspect écologique. Les efforts entrepris pour la conservation sont tangibles. Le résultat final engendre une satisfaction profonde. C'est un pas important et convaincant vers une forme d'écotourisme réaliste et judicieuse.

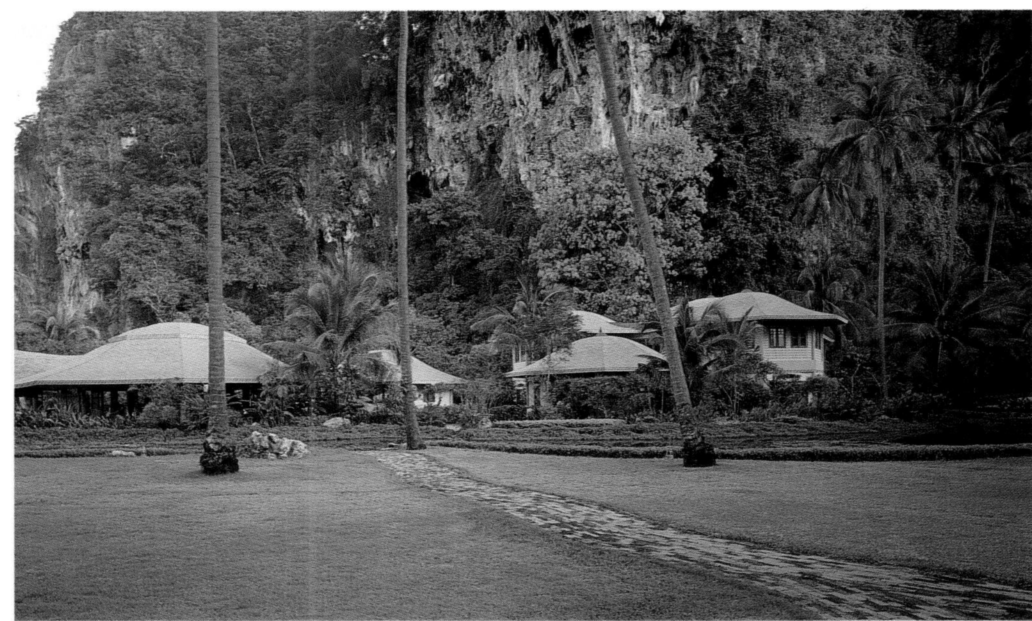

A distant view of the administrative and reception areas.

Ein Blick aus der Ferne auf den Verwaltungs- und Empfangsbereich.

Une vue à distance de la réception et du pavillon de l'administration.

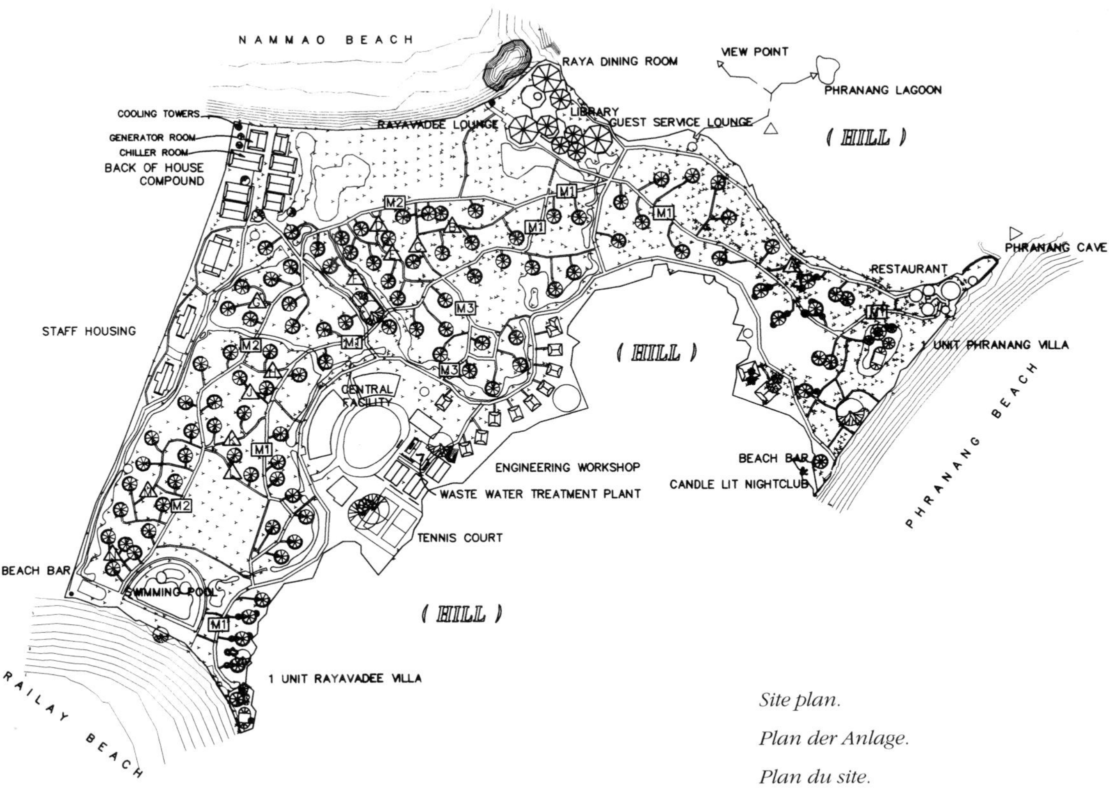

Site plan.

Plan der Anlage.

Plan du site.

(opposite page):
The structures draw inspiration from local design precepts in an organic relationship with the surroundings.

(gegenüberliegende Seite):
Die Bauten stehen in einer organischen Beziehung zur Umgebung und sind von einheimischen Vorbildern inspiriert.

(page ci-contre):
S'inspirant des principes architecturaux locaux, les constructions se fondent dans le paysage.

The Rayavadee Suite is a luxurious retreat designed around a private pool.

Die Rayavadee Suite ist ein luxuriöser Zufluchtsort an einem privaten Pool.

La suite Rayavadee, une retraite luxueuse construite autour d'une piscine.

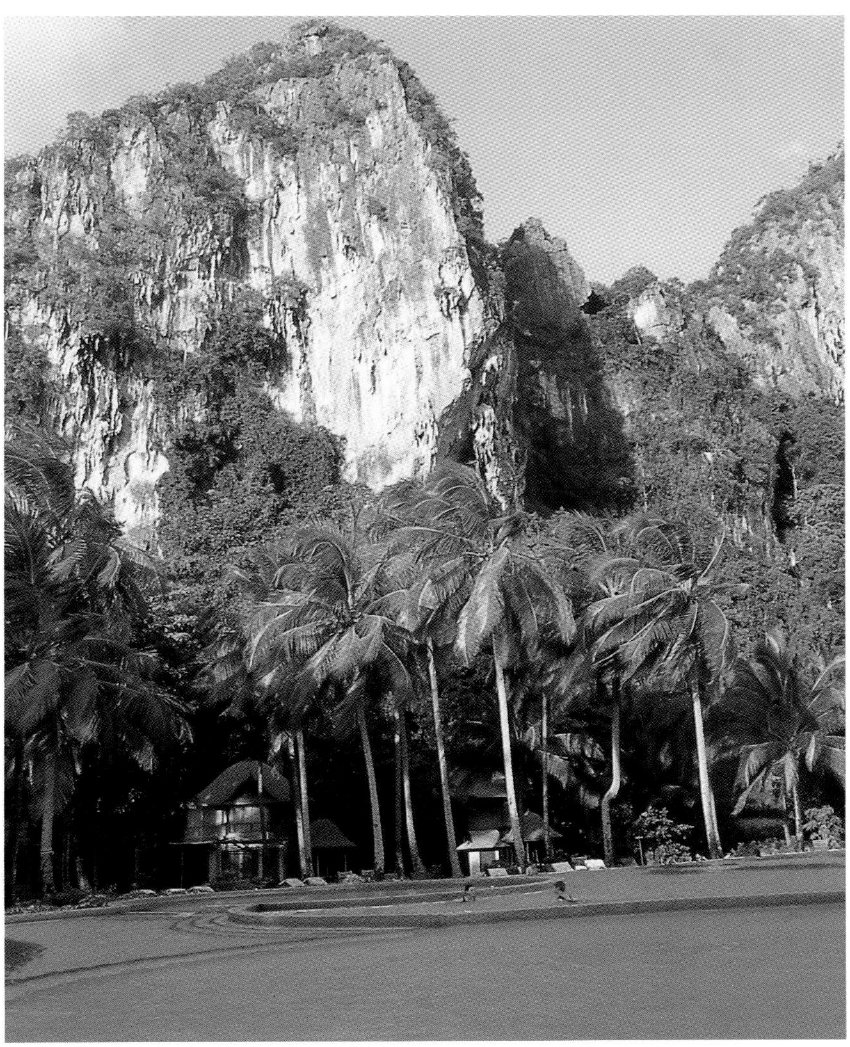

The untamed splendour of the surrounding environment has a particular potency.

Die ungezähmte Pracht der Umgebung hat eine besondere Ausstrahlung.

L'environnement n'est que nature sauvage.

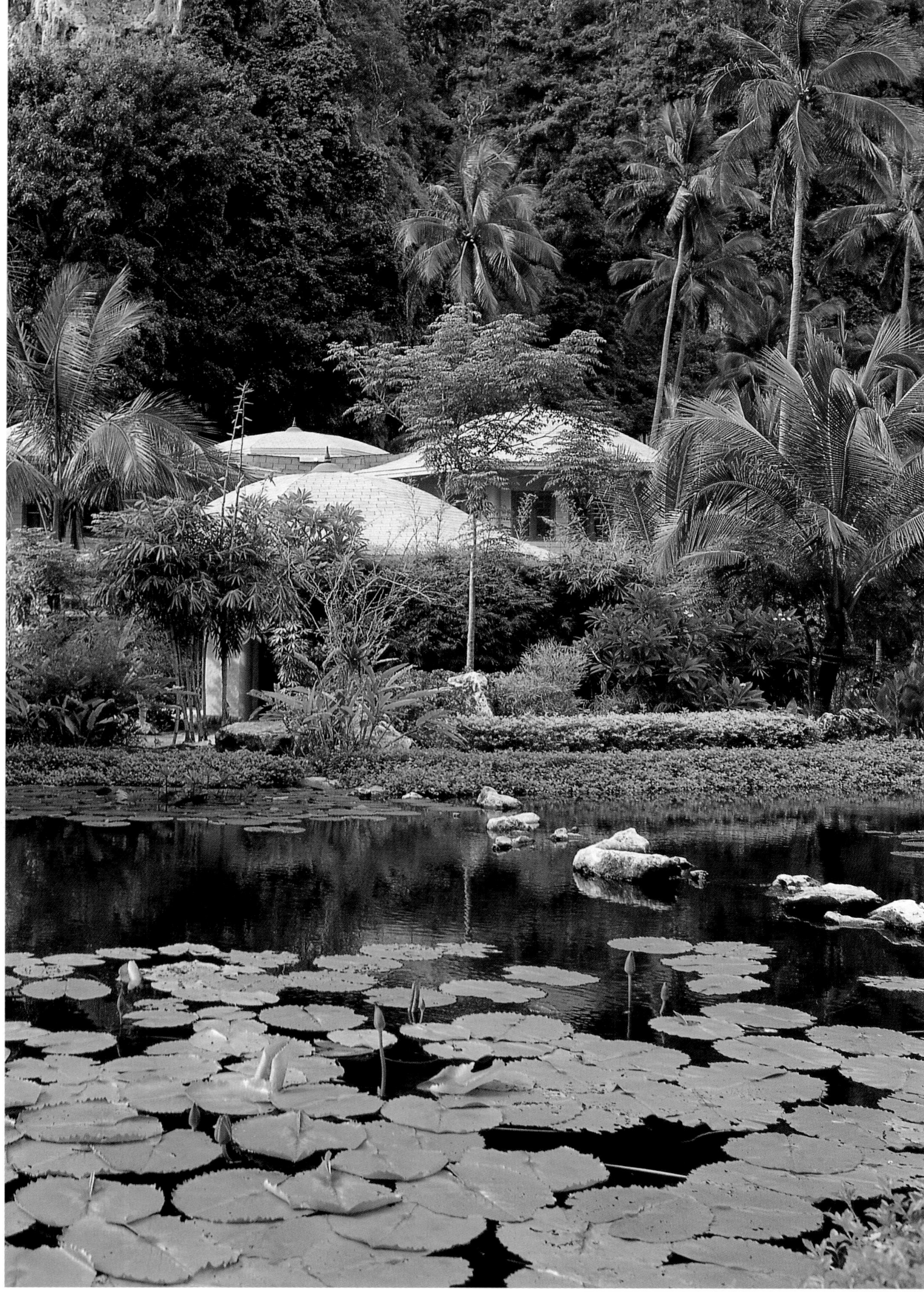

The administrative area is cleverly tucked away to one corner of the site.

Der Verwaltungsbereich liegt gut versteckt in einer Ecke der Anlage.

Le pavillon de l'administration de l'hôtel se cache dans la verdure du parc.

(previous page):
The two-storey design was inspired by traditional Thai architecture as well as the mosques of Southern Thailand .

(vorherige Seite):
Der einstöckige Bau bezieht Anregungen aus der traditionellen Thai-Architektur und von den Moscheen im Süden Thailands.

(page précédente):
Les édifices à un étage s'inspirent de l'architecture traditionnelle thaïlandaise et des mosquées de la Thaïlande du Sud.

(top & bottom):
Upon arrival, the visitors is greeted by the low silhouette of the lounge pavilion.

(oben und unten):
Bei der Ankunft werden die Gäste von der niedrigen Silhouette des Lounge-Pavillons begrüßt.

(en haut et ci-dessous):
La silhouette trapue du pavillon abritant le salon accueille les visiteurs à leur arrivée.

At night, the lounge is lit in dramatic ways that highlight the intricately carved timber columns.

Nachts ist die Halle spektakulär beleuchtet, so daß die geschnitzten Holzsäulen besonders gut zur Geltung kommen.

La nuit, l'éclairage du salon révèle toute la beauté des colonnes en bois sculpté.

An interior view of the restaurant, which is also circular on plan.

Ein Blick in das runde Restaurant.

Une vue intérieure du restaurant, construit selon un plan circulaire.

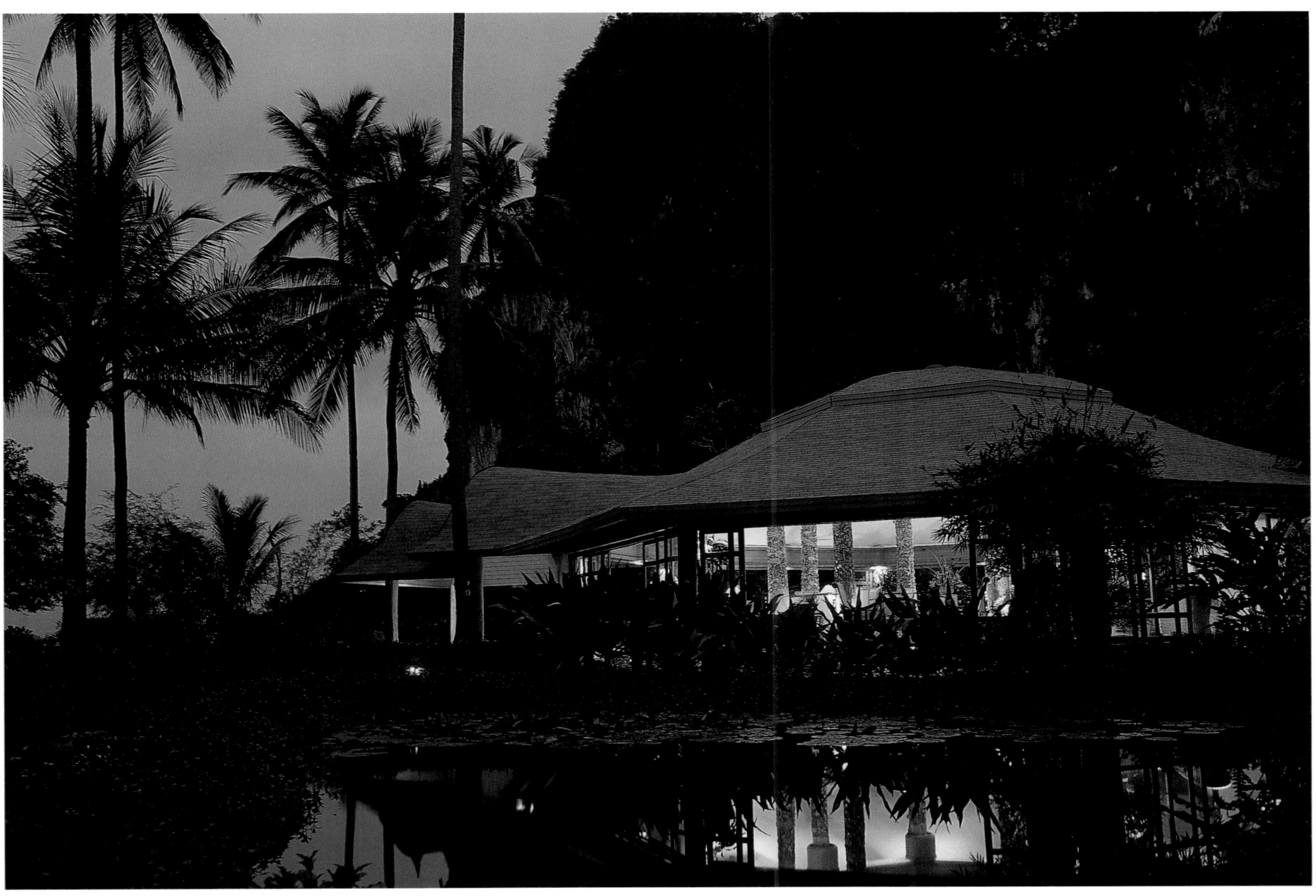

The resort is thoroughly enigmatic at night, taking on a surreal atmosphere.

Nachts wirkt die Anlage geheimnisvoll, hat eine fast surreale Atmosphäre.

La nuit, le complexe est empreint d'une atmosphère mystérieuse.

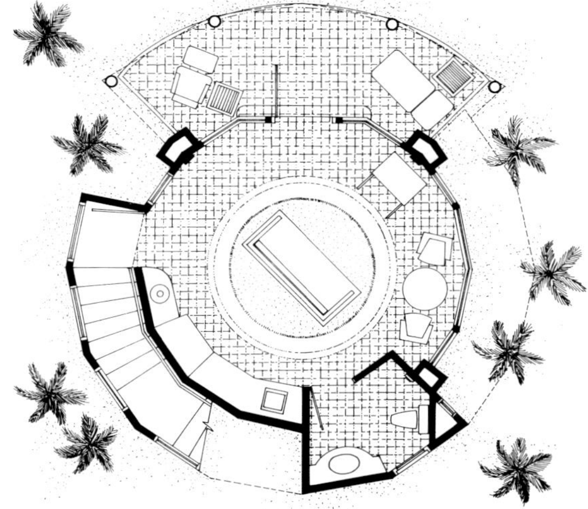

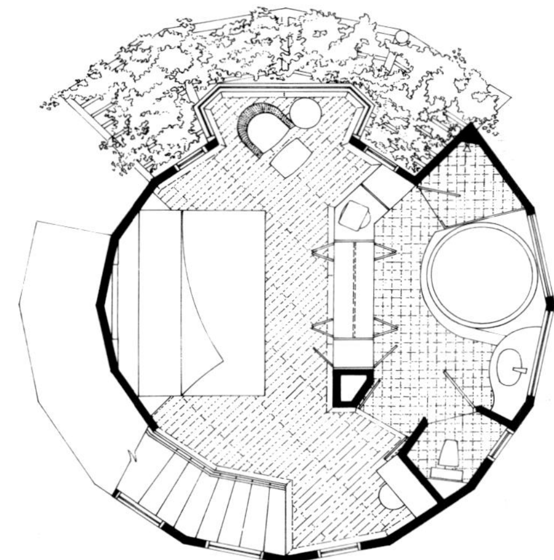

Plan of a typical guestroom.

Grundriß eines typischen Gästezimmers.

Plan d'une chambre type.

The lounge area on the first storey is sparingly, but luxuriously furnished.

Der Wohnbereich ist sparsam mit luxuriösen Möbeln eingerichtet.

Le salon au rez-de-chaussée est meublé avec un luxe sobre.

(opposite page):
Several of the pavilions are specially designed with an outdoor jacuzzi set in a lush garden. Bamboo fence and the natural terrain provide the necessary privacy.

(gegenüberliegende Seite):
Einige Pavillons haben im Freien in einem üppigen Garten einen kleinen Whirlpool. Bambuszäune und die umgebende Natur sorgen für die notwendige Privatatmosphäre.

(page ci-contre):
Plusieurs pavillons possèdent un jacuzzi en plein air entouré d'une végétation luxuriante. Des parois en bambou et le relief du terrain assurent l'intimité.

The interiors of the suite are furnished with exquisite objects that evoke a casual but dignified atmosphere.

Exquisite Einrichtungsgegenstände geben der Suite eine zwanglose, dennoch würdevolle Atmosphäre.

Des objets exquis meublent les intérieurs des suites à l'ambiance élégante, mais dépourvue de contrainte.

Laguna Beach Club, Phuket

Part of Laguna Phuket integrated resort, Laguna Beach Club at Bangtao Bay is located within the same three-kilometre stretch of beachland as three other hotels. It is linked to all these hotels in the complex by a ferry ride across man-made lagoons.

This resort's key emphasis is on its extensive recreational facilities. The architecture was hence designed to exude an air of vibrancy and festivity. The imagery was ostensibly inspired by a mixture of Central and Northern Thai architectural styles. Enclosing a two-hectare plot of beachfront property, the main focus of the guest activities is a huge Water Park. It is designed as a ruined Khmer fortress, complete with toppling stone walls, reproductions of old statues and elephant carvings. A rock art studio carefully fashioned concrete blocks into various types of simulated rocks.

Waterfalls, water slides and swimming pools contribute to the overall aquatic theme. Luxuriant landscaping, designed by Belt Collins & Associates, complements the rock pools, creating a convivial environment. The pivotal piece in the landscape design is the multi-tiered roof of the poolside Andaman Bar, which overlooks both the main swimming pool and the sea.

The landscape features are perhaps the most important design elements in the resort. They are truly scenographic settings, sumptuous and luxuriant. The interplay of landscape and architecture successfully creates a place that is full of unfolding vistas. Lawns interspersed with balmy coconut groves provide the architectural backdrop to the standard guestroom blocks.

The guestrooms are housed in conventional concrete four-storey blocks roofed by traditional Thai structures. Inspired by the combined building styles of Central and Northern Thailand, the different stylistic languages can be visually distracting. Serenely located at the edge of the expansive man-made lagoon, these guestroom blocks are dispersed away from the public areas.

The reception lobby is the first space to confront the guests. It is a voluminous space supported by complex roof trusses. The overall ambience is slightly dim, and at the same time, the spatial enclosure is narrow and long, thus drawing guests quickly into the deeper recesses of the complex. As such, it is not a space that encourages lounging activities.

Laguna Beach Club, Phuket

Ein Teil der Anlage Laguna Phuket, der Laguna Beach Club an der Bangtao Bay, liegt zusammen mit drei weiteren Hotels an einem drei Kilometer langen Strand. Er ist durch eine Fähre über die künstlich angelegten Lagunen mit allen Hotels verbunden.

Den Schwerpunkt dieser Anlage bilden die umfangreichen Freizeitangebote. Mit Hilfe der Architektur soll ein Gefühl von Lebensfreude und Festlichkeit entstehen. Das äußere Erscheinungsbild bezieht eindeutig Anregungen aus einer Mischung der Stilformen von Mittel- und Nord-Thailand. Der zentrale Punkt für die Aktivitäten der Gäste ist ein riesiger Wasserpark, zu dem auch ein zwei Hektar großes Strandgelände gehört. Der Park ist angelegt wie die Ruine einer Khmer-Festung, mit eingestürzten Steinmauern, Nachbildungen alter Statuen und Elefantenreliefs. Ein Studio für Felsenkunst modellierte Betonblöcke sorgfältig zu verschiedenen Felsenformen.

Wasserfälle, Wasserrutschen und Swimmingpools unterstreichen das allgegenwärtige Thema Wasser. Üppige Landschaftsgestaltung durch Belt Collins & Associates ergänzt die Felsen-Pools und schafft eine heitere Umgebung. Dreh – und Angelpunkt in der Landschaftsgestaltung ist das vielschichtige Dach der Andaman Bar am Pool, von wo aus man einen Blick auf die großen Swimming-pools und das Meer hat.

Die landschaftliche Schönheit ist vermutlich das wichtigste Element der Anlage. Sie ist wahrlich atemberaubend, üppig und voller Reichtum. Durch das Wechselspiel von Landschaft und Architektur entstehen überraschende Ausblicke. Eingestreute Rasenflächen mit sanften Kokospalmenhainen liefern den Hintergrund für die Standardhäuser mit den Gästezimmern.

Die Gästezimmer liegen in herkömmlichen dreistöckigen Betonbauten mit traditionellen Thai-Dächern. Angeregt von den kombinierten Baustilen Mittel- und Nord-Thailands, sind die unterschiedlichen stilistischen Sprachen für das Auge sehr abwechslungsreich. Von den öffentlichen Bereichen sind diese Häuser am Rande der ausgedehnten, künstlichen Lagune entfernt gelegen.

Der Gast betritt als erstes die Empfangshalle. Es ist ein riesiger Raum, getragen von dicken Dachbalken. Die allgemeine Atmosphäre ist etwas gedämpft, gleichzeitig ist der Raum eng und lang, so daß die Gäste schnell tiefer in die Anlage hineingezogen werden.

Laguna Beach Club, Phuket

Le Laguna Beach Club à Bangtao Bay, qui fait partie de la station balnéaire intégrée de Laguna Phuket, est situé sur la même plage de trois kilomètres que les trois autres hôtels. Un bac assure la liaison entre les hôtels par des lagunes artificielles.

Le complexe hôtelier met l'accent sur ses importants aménagements pour les loisirs. L'architecture a donc été conçue pour dégager une atmosphère de fête et d'animation. Le décor s'inspire d'un mélange de styles architecturaux du Centre et du Nord de la Thaïlande. S'étendant sur deux hectares de rivage un vastes parc nautique est le centre des activités. Il est bâti sur le modèle d'une forteresse khmère en ruine, avec des murs croulants, des reproductions de statues anciennes et des sculptures d'éléphants. En fait, tout ce décor de pierres et de rochers a été façonné dans des blocs de béton par un atelier de roches d'art.

L'eau est le thème dominant, accentué par les nombreuses cascades, les toboggans nautiques et les piscines. Un paysage luxuriant dessiné par Belt Collins and Associates complète les bassins entourés de rochers pour créer un environnement très engageant. Le pivot de ce paysage est le toit en gradins du Bar Andaman qui surplombe la piscine principale et la mer.

Le paysage constitue sans doute l'élément le plus important du complexe. On découvre de véritables décors scéniques exubérants et somptueux. Le jeu de la nature et de l'architecture crée un site rempli d'images magnifiques. Des pelouses parsemées de bosquets de cocotiers odorants forment l'arrière-plan des édifices abritant les chambres standard.

Ces édifices en béton de trois étages sont coiffés de toits de style traditionnel thaïlandais. Leur style s'inspire des architectures du Centre et du Nord de la Thaïlande, ce qui produit un mélange de styles très intéressant. Les habitations se dressent à l'écart des espaces collectifs, au bord d'une vaste lagune artificielle.

A l'arrivée, on ne voit d'abord que le hall de réception. C'est un espace volumineux reposant sur une charpente ouvragée. L'ambiance y étant assez obscure et la salle longue et étroite, les hôtes ne s'y attardent pas, mais s'enfoncent rapidement dans le reste du complexe. Ce n'est pas un endroit qui incite à la détente.

Alors que le toit de la réception est construit dans le style des toits pointus du Centre de la thaïlande, les ailes abritant les

The lobby terminates in a huge reflecting pool.

Die Lobby liegt am Ende eines riesigen, glitzernden Teichs.

Un immense bassin d'agrément prolonge la réception.

Guestrooms have wonderful views of the lagoon.

Die Gästezimmer haben einen wundervollen Ausblick auf das Meer.

Les chambres s'ouvrent sur de merveilleuses vues de la lagune.

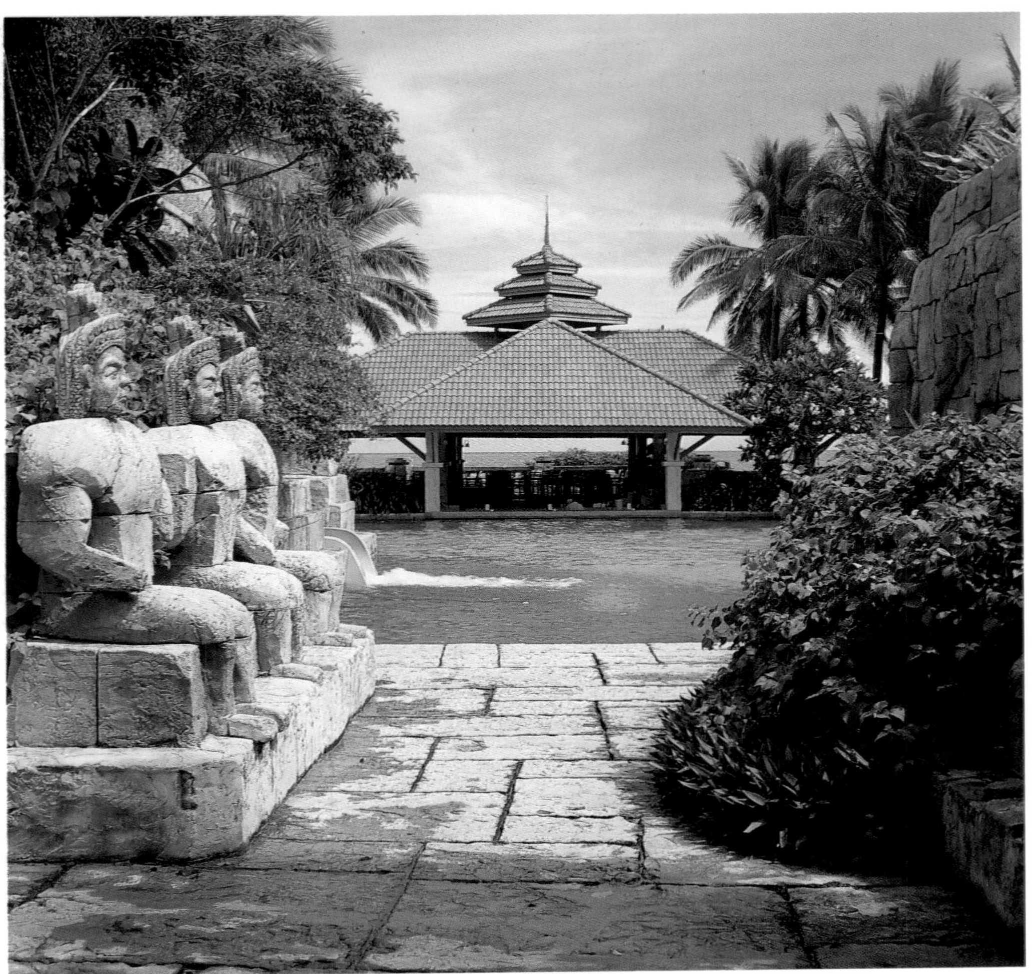

Designed as a ruined Khmer fortress, the resort's landscape reveals tantalising vistas at every corner.

Die Ferienanlage ist gebaut als Ruine einer Khmer-Festung, und die Landschaft gibt an jeder Ecke hinreißende Ausblicke auf das Meer frei.

Conçu sur le modèle d'une forteresse kmère en ruine, le paysage du complexe offre une multitude de vues splendides.

While the reception lobby's roof is based on the steep roof of the Central Thai style, the guestroom wings are based on the Northern style of distinctive crossbows at the roof's apex. The south wing offers views of the lagoon while the north wing faces the Andaman Sea.

Every room of the 265 guestrooms features a *dang* — a Thai-style sitting platform — that projects out of the room. Each room also features a sunken bathtub. The furnishings, selected by Mary Philpotts & Associates from Hawaii in collaboration with Abacus, Bangkok, are based on traditional Thai decor mixed with a contemporary touch. Brightly-coloured cushions contrast strongly with the rustic theme of natural finishes.

The overall architectural treatment of the resort exhibits an urbane quality, which is perhaps heightened by the eclecticism apparent in the articulation of elements. As a medium-size resort, the overall planning certainly works well. Pragmatically it responds to the exigencies of brief, site and locality, although architecturally the project offers few surprises. At the same time, it has not tested new grounds. Ultimately though, what impresses most is the rich allusiveness of the landscape.

Während das Dach der Empfangshalle den steilen Dächern des Stils Zentral-Thailands nachgebildet ist, orientieren sich die Gästeflügel am nördlichen Stil mit deutlich erkennbaren Kreuzbögen am Scheitelpunkt. Vom Südflügel aus blickt man auf die Lagune, der Nordflügel geht zum Meer.

In jedem der 265 Gästezimmer befindet sich ein *dang*, eine Sitzplattform im Thai-Stil, die aus dem Raum herausragt, und eine in den Boden eingelassene Badewanne. Die Einrichtung, ausgewählt von Mary Philpotts & Associates, Hawaii, in Zusammenarbeit mit Abacus, Bangkok, basiert auf traditioneller Thai-Ausstattung mit einem Hauch von Moderne. Kissen in kräftigen Farben stehen in starkem Kontrast zu der rustikalen, natürlichen Einrichtung.

Die allgemeine Architektur der Anlage strahlt urbane Atmosphäre aus, die durch den Rückgriff auf die Stilmittel verschiedener Epochen bei einzelnen Elementen noch verstärkt wird. Für eine mittelgroße Anlage funktioniert die Gesamtplanung gut. Pragmatisch betrachtet erfüllt sie die Anforderungen an die Lage und die örtlichen Gegebenheiten, auch wenn sie architektonisch wenig Überraschungen bietet. Man ist auch keine neuen Wege gegangen. Was letzten Endes am meisten imponiert, ist die Vielfalt und Schönheit der Landschaft.

chambres sont dotées de toits à arcs transversaux, typiques dans le Nord du pays. L'aile sud donne sur la lagune tandis que l'aile nord fait face à la mer Andaman.

Chacune des 265 chambres possède une baignoire encastrée dans le sol et un *dang*, une plate-forme en bois de style thaïlandais qui prolonge la pièce au dehors et sert d'espace détente. La firme hawaïenne Mary Philpotts and Associate et la firme Abacus de Bangkok ont réalisé l'agencement intérieur qui allie le style traditionnel thaïlandais à quelques éléments modernes. Des coussins de couleurs éclatantes forment un vif contraste avec les finitions rustiques en bois naturel.

L'architecture du complexe hôtelier présente une certaine élégance que rehausse l'éclectisme manifeste dans l'articulation des éléments. La conception d'ensemble est très adéquate pour un complexe de taille moyenne. Bien qu'il n'offre guère de surprises du point de vue architectural, il répond pragmatiquement aux exigences imposées par l'espace restreint, le site et la situation. Mais il n'est pas novateur. En fin de compte, l'aspect le plus impressionnant est la beauté grandiose du paysage.

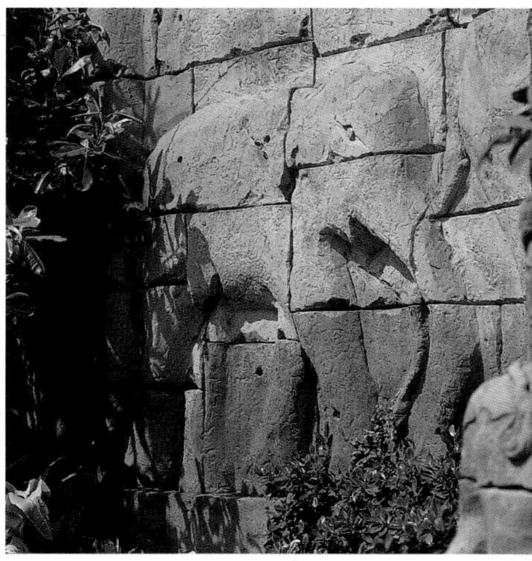

Stone carving depicting elephants are common sights.

In Stein gehauene Elefanten sieht man oft.

Des éléphants sculptés dans la pierre sont un motif récurrent du complexe.

The water theme is carried through at many levels, exuding an air of vibracy. The two-hectare plot is turned into a sprawling landscape of tiered pools, jacuzzis, water features and luxuriant vegetation.

Das Thema Wasser wird auf verschiedenen Ebenen durchgespielt und sorgt für Lebendigkeit. Das zwei Hektar große Gelände wurde zu einer ausgedehnten Landschaft mit Teichen, Whirlpools, Wasserspeiern inmitten einer üppigen Vegetation gestaltet.

Le thème de l'eau est décliné de multiples façons dans le parc de deux hectares. Les piscines à cascades, les jacuzzis, les bassins d'agrément et la végétation luxuriante ravissent le regard.

The guestrooms are housed in conventional concrete blocks roofed by traditional Thai structures.

Die Gästezimmer liegen in herkömmlichen Häusern mit traditionellen Thai-Dächern.

Des bâtiments en béton classiques, coiffés de toits traditionnels siamois, abritent les chambres.

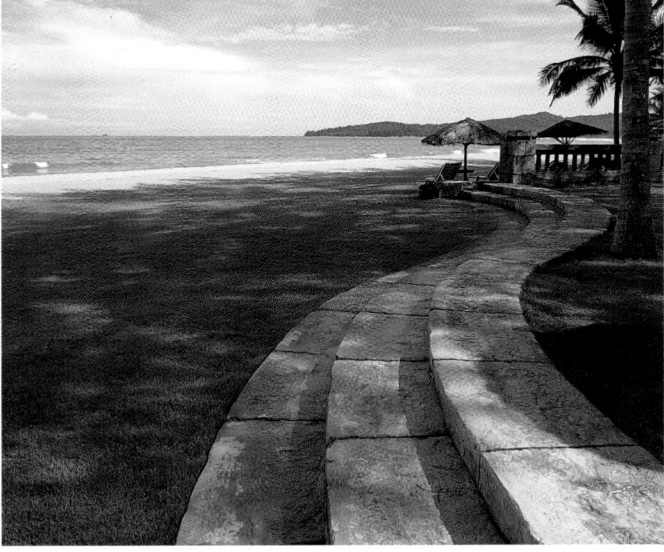

Serpentine steps mark the transition between the landscaped grounds and the beach.

Serpentinenstufen bilden die Grenze zwischen der gestalteten Landschaft und dem Strand.

Une allée sinueuse de larges marches en pierre relie les jardins à la plage.

Stone figurines serve as delightful water features in this narrow stretch of pool.

An dieser schmalen Stelle am Pool dienen Steinfiguren als fröhliche Wasserspeier.

De jolies statues en pierre décorent ce bassin étroit.

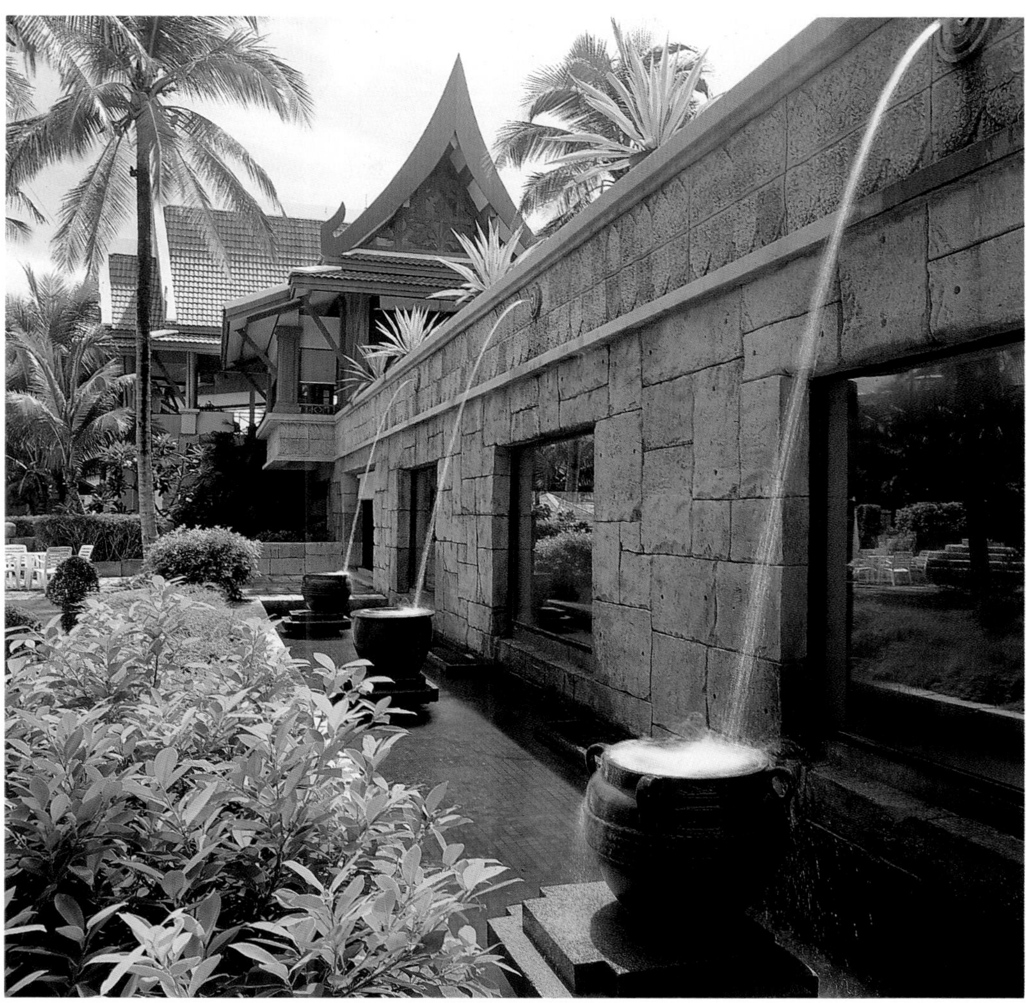

Water sprouts enliven stone-clad walls.

Wasser belebt die Steinwände.

Des fontaines animent la simplicité du mur en pierre.

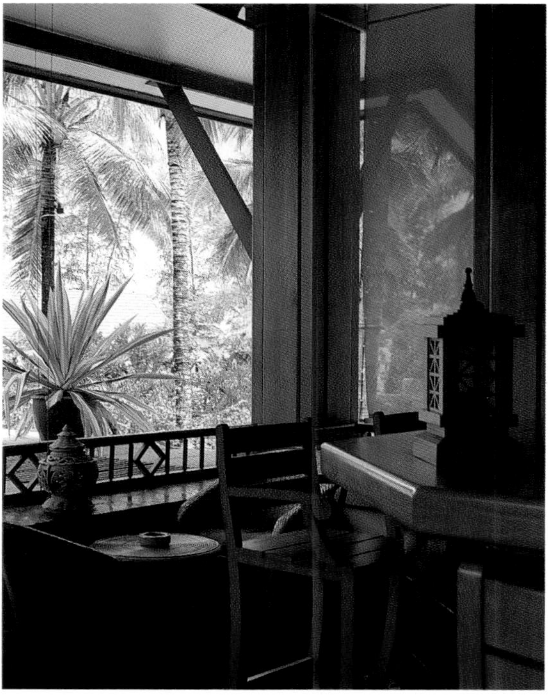

Views of the gardens from the cosy niche in the guestroom.

Blick auf die Gärten von der gemütlichen Ecke im Gästezimmer aus.

Vue sur le jardin depuis l'alcôve douillette d'une chambre.

(opposite page):
Whimsical stone carvings provide a sense of festivity to the pools of the water park.

(gegenüberliegende Seite):
Witzge Steinskulpturen lassen die Pools im Wasserpark fröhlich wirken.

(page ci-contre):
De curieuses sculptures rehaussent le décor ludique des piscines.

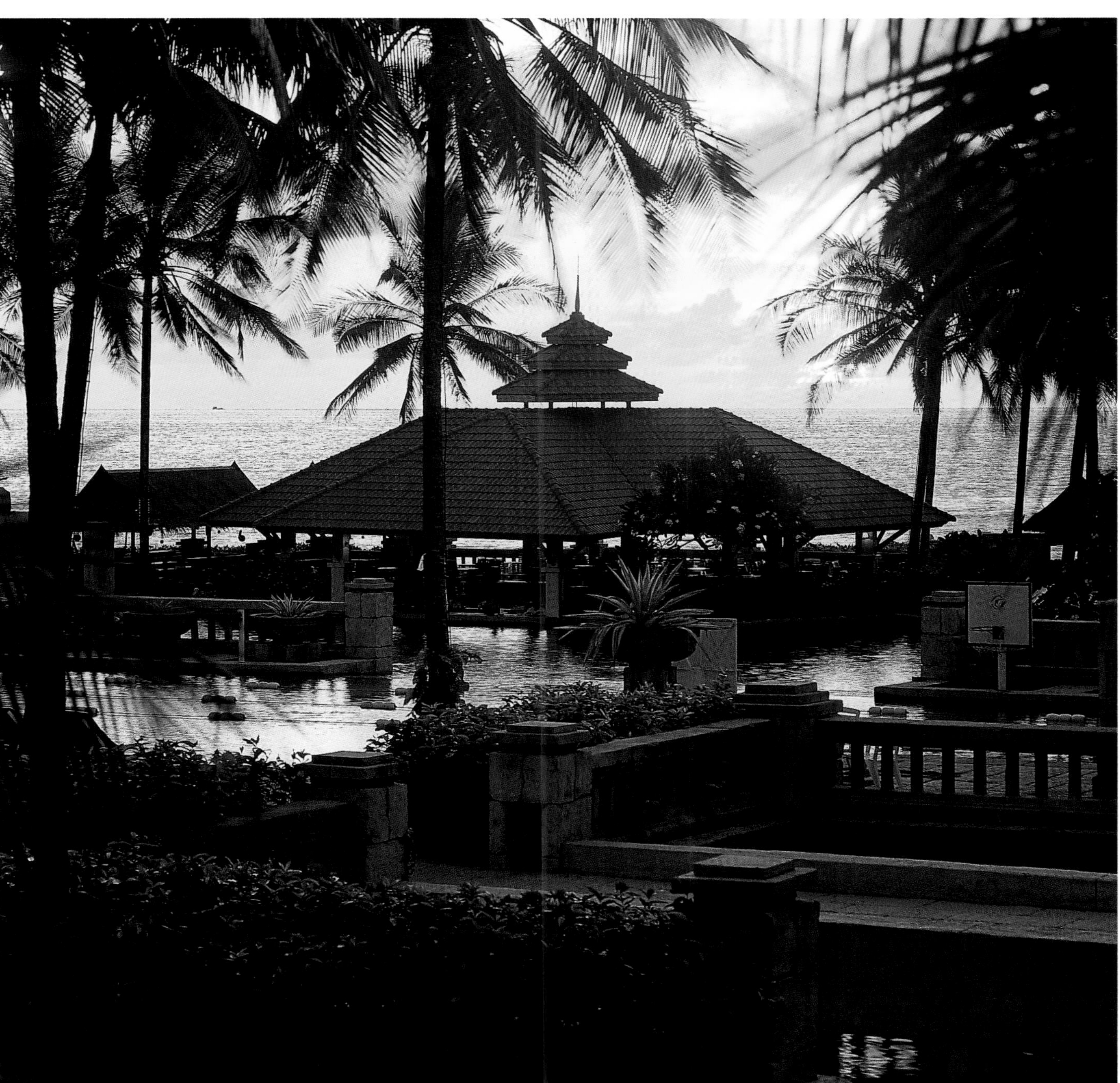

The muti-tiered roof of the pool bar is the main architectural focus of the landscape grounds.

Das mehrschichtige Dach der Bar setzt einen architektonischen Schwerpunkt in der Landschaft.

Le toit en gradins du bar de la piscine constitue l'élément architectural principal du complexe.

The narrow and high-volume lobby channels guests straight into the heart of the resort.

Die enge, hohe Lobby führt die Gäste wie durch einen Tunnel direkt in das Herz der Anlage.

La haute salle étroite de la réception conduit directement les hôtes au cœur du complexe.

(previous page):
At dusk, the reflecting lights of the various hotels in the Laguna Phuket development provide spectacular sights across the man-made lagoon.

(vorherige Seite):
In der Dämmerung sorgen die reflektierenden Lichter der Hotels für einen aufregenden Blick über die künstliche Lagune.

(page précédente):
Au crépuscule, les lumières des hôtels miroitant dans les eaux de la lagune, produisent un spectacle magnifique.

(opposite page):
Simply furnished, the suite looks out into different parts of the resort. The furnishings, selected by Mary Philpotts & Associates from Hawaii in collaboration with Abacus, Bangkok, are based on traditional Thai decor

(gegenüberliegende Seite):
Die schlicht eingerichtete Suite erlaubt Ausblicke auf verschiedene Bereiche der Anlage. Die Möbel, ausgewählt von Mary Philpotts & Associates, Hawaii, in Zusammenarbeit mit Abacus, Bangkok, basieren auf traditionellem Thai-Dekor.

(page ci-contre):
La suite s'ouvre sur différentes vues du complexe. Les firmes Mary Philpotts & Associates de Hawaï et Abacus de Bangkok ont réalisé l'agencement intérieur de style traditionnel siamois.

Wonderful views in the restaurant.

Wundervolle Ausblicke aus dem Restaurant.

Des vues magnifiques dans le restaurant.

The Regent Resort Chiang Mai, Chiang Mai

The 67 pavilion suites of the resort are laid out amidst the undulating valleys of the Mae Rim Valley.

Die 67 Pavillon-Suiten liegen mitten in den sanften Senken des Mae Rim Valley.

Les 67 pavillons du complexe se cachent dans les vallons ondulés de la Mae Rim Valley.

Chiang Mai, located in northern Thailand in a region of densely forested hills and beautiful landscapes, was founded in the late 13th century as the capital of the Lanna Kingdom. This Kingdom, which is a historically significant period of Thai history, began in 1296 when it was established by King Mengrai. Today, Chiang Mai is a modern metropolis and Thailand's second largest city with a population of 1.3 million. It is also the country's cottage-industry capital, producing a staggering variety of quality handicrafts.

Located on a five-hectare plot of land in the beautiful Mae Rim Valley, which is about 20 minutes' drive north of Chiang Mai International Airport, the Regent pays tribute to the city's ethnic and cultural heritage. There are altogether 67 pavilion suites in clusters of two-storey structures with either king or twin-bed accommodation, each offering a luxurious 70 square metres of living space. The pavilions are based on the style of the Lanna Kingdom. They were designed by Arjarn Chulatat Kitibutre of Chiang Mai Collaborative, who is a keen conservationist in the preservation of Lanna-style northern Thai architecture.

In the interior of each pavilion, a spacious bedroom and sitting room lead into a separate dressing room and generous bathroom. A private Thai *sala*, or covered verandah, provides additional external space. The word *sala* literally means a traveller's shelter in the rice fields. It has been used in different variations all over Thailand.

The resort, located on a striking terrain, is surrounded by lushly landscaped gardens designed by Bill Bensley of Bensley Design Group. Delighful landscape elements offer surprises at every junction. The main bulk of the property is devoted to the main landscape feature of Bali-inspired terraced rice and flower fields. There is also a small lake and a meandering series of lily ponds.

Other features of the resort include a Thai restaurant, cocktail lounge, an all-day poolside dining facility, two flood-lit tennis courts, a contoured swimming pool, fitness club and massage rooms.

The project, in reinvigorating almost lost craft skills, is informed by a constructive logic based on traditional craftsmanship. The robust timber structure of the pavilions are elegantly proportioned, while the concern for details impresses. The overall

Das Regent Resort Chiang Mai, Chiang Mai

Chiang Mai, im Norden Thailands in einer Region mit dichtbewaldeten Hügeln und wunderschönen Landschaften gelegen, wurde im 13. Jahrhundert als Hauptstadt des Königreichs Lan Na gegründet. Dieses Königreich, eine historisch wichtige Ära in der Geschichte Thailands, entstand 1296 unter König Mengrai. Heute ist Chiang Mai eine moderne Metropole und mit 1,3 Millionen Einwohnern die zweitgrößte Stadt Thailands. Gleichzeitig ist sie die Hauptstadt der Heimarbeit, in der kunsthandwerkliche Gegenstände von großer Vielfalt hergestellt werden.

Etwa zwanzig Autominuten nördlich von Chiang Mais internationalem Flughafen auf einem Gelände von fünf Hektar im schönen Mae Rim Valley gelegen, zollt das Regent dem ethnischen und kulturellen Erbe der Stadt Tribut. Es gibt insgesamt 67 Pavillons, angeordnet in Gruppen von einstöckigen Gebäuden. Angeboten werden entweder ein großes Doppelbett oder zwei Einzelbetten auf großzügigen 70 Quadratmetern Wohnraum. Die Pavillons orientieren sich am Stil des Königreichs Lan Na. Arjarn Chulatat Kitibutre von der Chiang Mai Collaborative hat sie entworfen, und er ist ein harter Verfechter der Erhaltung von nordthailändischer Architektur im Lan-Na-Stil.

Im Inneren jedes Pavillons führt ein Ankeidezimmer in ein geräumiges Schlafzimmer mit einem großen angrenzenden Bad und in einen Wohnraum. Eine thailändische *sala*, eine überdachte Veranda, bietet draußen zusätzlichen Raum. Das Wort *sala* bedeutet wörtlich »Schutzhütte für den Reisenden im Reisfeld«, und sie wurde in verschiedenen Varianten in ganz Thailand gebaut.

Die Ferienanlage auf einem eindrucksvollen Gelände ist umgeben von üppig gestalteten Gärten, entwickelt von Bill Bensley von der Bensley Design Group. Wunderschöne Elemente sorgen an jeder Kreuzung für Überraschungen. Von Bali inspiriert, ist die Landschaft in Terrassen mit Reis und Blumen angelegt, und dem passen sich die meisten Bauten an. Es gibt auch einen kleinen See und miteinander verbundene Seerosenteiche. Weiterhin gehören zu der Anlage ein Thai-Restaurant, eine Cocktail-Bar, ein Swimmingpool mit ganztägig geöffnetem Restaurant, zwei Tennisplätze, ein Fitneß-Club und ein Massageraum.

Das Projekt hat fast vergessene Fertigkeiten zu neuem Leben erweckt, und beim Bau hat man auf traditionelle Handwerkskunst zurückgegriffen. Die robusten Holzstrukturen der Pavillons sind

Le Regent Resort Chiang Mai, Chiang Mai

Chiang Mai est située au Nord de la Thaïlande, dans une très belle région de collines recouvertes de forêts épaisses. Cette ancienne capitale du royaume de Lân-Na fut fondée à la fin du 13e siècle. Le royaume qui est une page d'histoire importante de la Thaïlande, fut créé en 1296 par le roi Mengray. Aujourd'hui, Chiang Mai est une métropole moderne et la deuxième ville du pays avec une population de 1,3 million d'habitants. Elle est également la capitale de la fabrication artisanale, produisant une énorme variété de marchandises de haute qualité.

Le Regent occupe un site de cinq hectares dans la belle vallée de Mae Rim qui est à environ vingt minutes de voiture de l'aéroport international de Chiang Mai. Le complexe hôtelier honore l'héritage ethnique et culturel de la ville. Il comprend 67 pavillons à un étage, chacun d'une superficie généreuse de 70 m^2. Les pavillons sont construits selon le style du royaume de Lân-Na. Ils sont l'œuvre d'Arjarn Ghulatat Kitibutre de la Chiang Mai Collaborative, un architecte qui s'attache à conserver le style de Lân-Na dans l'architecture du Nord de la Thaïlande.

Un salon, une vaste chambre à grand lit ou à lits jumeaux, avec salle de bains attenante et un dressing-room constituent l'intérieur du pavillon. Un *sala* ou véranda couverte, offre un espace extérieur privé supplémentaire. Le mot *sala* se traduit littéralement par abri pour voyageurs dans les rizières. Mais il a plusieurs significations différentes selon les régions de la Thaïlande.

Le complexe, situé dans un site impressionnant, est entouré de jardins à la végétation luxuriante, dessinés par Bill Bensley du Bensley Design Group. Des arrangements splendides surprennent continuellement le regard. Le décor principal s'inspire des rizières et champs de fleurs en terrasses de Bali. On trouve également un petit lac et une suite en méandres de bassins à nénuphars.

Les autres agencements de l'hôtel sont un restaurant thaïlandais, un bar, un snack servant des repas toute la journée près de la piscine, deux courts de tennis, une piscine, un club de mise en forme et une salle de massage.

Le complexe qui a été réalisé selon des méthodes de construction traditionnelles, a fait renaître des métiers manuels virtuellement disparus. Dans les pavillons, on remarque les proportions élégantes de la structure en bois et le soin minutieux

design of the resort is an appropriate response to the tropical climate. There is a thoughtful consideration of use, place and climate. The architect has successfully translated and carried through the tropical theme at all levels, pursuing a return to the essentials of vernacular architecture based on an immediate sensual engagement with natural materials as well as the setting.

Although the architecture has not really steered away from the trap of revivalism and nostalgia, it exhibits a basic constructional rationalism and stylistic consistency that are exemplary. The outcome is a handsomely detailed resort of great confidence and competence, where site, form and materials have been integrated into an indissoluble whole.

elegant proportioniert, während gleichzeitig das Bemühen um Details beeindruckt. Insgesamt entspricht die Ferienanlage dem tropischen Klima. Nutzung, Ort und Klima werden sinnvoll berücksichtigt. Auf allen Ebenen hat der Architekt das tropische Thema umgesetzt und durchgeführt, und er verfolgt dabei die Rückkehr zum Wesentlichen der einheimischen Architektur unter Einbeziehung der sinnlichen Wirkung von Naturmaterialien und der Umgebung.

Auch wenn die Architektur die Klippe Wiederbelebung und Nostalgie nicht ganz umschifft hat, zeigt sie doch eine grundlegende Vernunft beim Bauen und eine stilistische Konsequenz, die beispielhaft sind. Das Ergebnis ist eine in Details schöne Ferienanlage von großer Ausstrahlung und Echtheit, wobei Lage, Form und Material ein untrennbares Ganzes bilden.

accordé aux détails. La conception du complexe répond avec bonheur aux demandes du climat tropical. L'architecte a également attaché une importance particulière aux facteurs utilisation, espace et climat. A tous les niveaux, il a su traduire et réaliser l'idée primaire d'exalter l'environnement tropical en retournant aux sources de l'architecture indigène qui est basée sur la liaison sensuelle des matériaux naturels et du paysage.

Bien que l'architecture n'ait pas entièrement évité le piège de la reproduction et de la nostalgie, la construction rationnelle et la continuité dans le style sont exemplaires. Le résultat est un complexe hôtelier splendide, admirablement agencé, dans lequel site, formes et matériaux s'intègrent à la perfection.

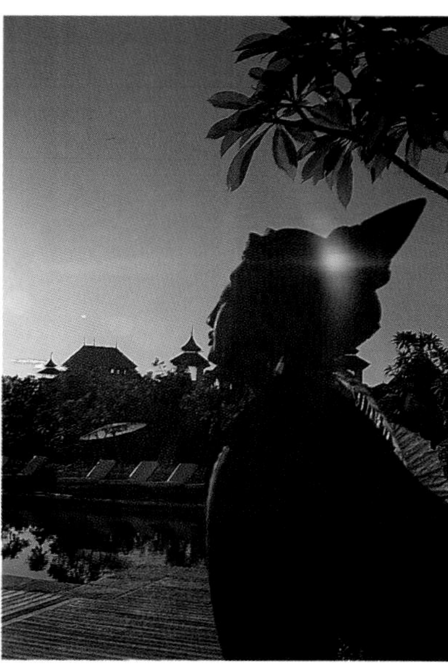

Scattered throughout the grounds of the resort are delightful sculptural objects conceptualised by landscape architect Bill Bensley.

Entsprechend der Planung des Landschaftsarchitekten Bill Bensley stehen hübsche Skulpturen verstreut in der Anlage.

De belles sculptures parsèment le parc du complexe dessiné par le paysagiste Bill Bensley.

The main bulk of the strikingly stunning property is devoted to the main landscape feature of Bali-inspired terraced rice and flower fields.

Schwerpunkt in der Landschaftsgestaltung der unglaublich schönen Anlage sind die von Bali inspirierten Reis- und Blumenterrassen.

Le paysage qui s'inspire des rizières et champs de fleurs en terrasses de Bali est l'atout principal de ce splendide complexe.

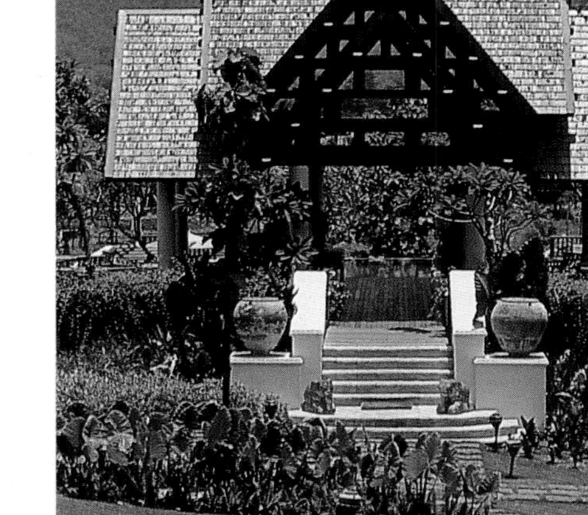

The robust timber structure of the various public pavilions are elegantly proportioned, while the concern for details impresses.

Die robuste Holzkonstruktion der Gemeinschaftspavillons fällt durch elegante Proportionen auf, und auch die Sorgfalt im Detail ist beeindruckend.

On remarque les proportions élégantes des robustes structures en bois et le soin minutieux accordé aux détails dans les pavillons abritant les espaces collectifs.

The sensitively executed landscape design plays a role of paramount importance in providing a verdant and tranquil setting for the pavilions.

Als grüne, ruhige Kulisse für die Pavillons spielt die einfühlsame Landschaftsgestaltung eine extrem wichtige Rolle.

Admirablement dessiné, le paysage a une importance cruciale. Il compose un décor serein et verdoyant pour les pavillons.

The project, in reinvigorating almost lost craft skills, is informed by a constructive logic based on traditional craftmanship. This is evident in the way elements are carefully put together to evoke a sensual visual appeal.

Fast vergessenes handwerkliches Können wurde wiederbelebt, und man griff auf das traditionelle Handwerk zurück. Das ist erkennbar an der Weise, in der Elemente sorgfältig zusammengefügt wurden, um eine sinnliche Optik zu erreichen.

Basée sur des méthodes de construction traditionnelle, la réalisation du complexe a fait renaître des métiers manuels virtuellement disparus. Le résultat est un ensemble d'éléments qui se lient en une harmonie parfaite.

(opposite page):
67 pavilion suites in clusters of two-storey structures each offers a luxurious 70 square metres of living space. The pavilions are based on the style of the Lanna Kingdom.

(gegenüberliegende Seite):
67 Pavillon-Suiten stehen in Gruppen von einstöckigen Bauten. Jede Suite verfügt über 70 Quadratmeter Wohnraum. Die Bauweise des Königreichs Lan Na lieferte die Anregungen.

(page ci-contre):
Les 67 pavillons à un étage ont une superficie généreuse de 70m^2. Ils sont construits d'après le style du royaume de Lân-Na.

Landscape and architecture blends into a seamless whole throughout.

Landschaft und Architektur verbinden sich nahtlos zu einem Ganzen.

Architecture et paysage se fondent en une entité.

This traditional Thai art object is one of the many pleasant surprises that greet visitors at every junction of the resort.

Dieses traditionelle Thai-Kunstobjekt gehört zu den zahlreichen angenehmen Überraschungen, denen der Gast an jeder Ecke der Anlage begegnet.

Parsemées dans le complexe, des sculptures d'art traditionnel siamois surprennent plaisamment le regard.

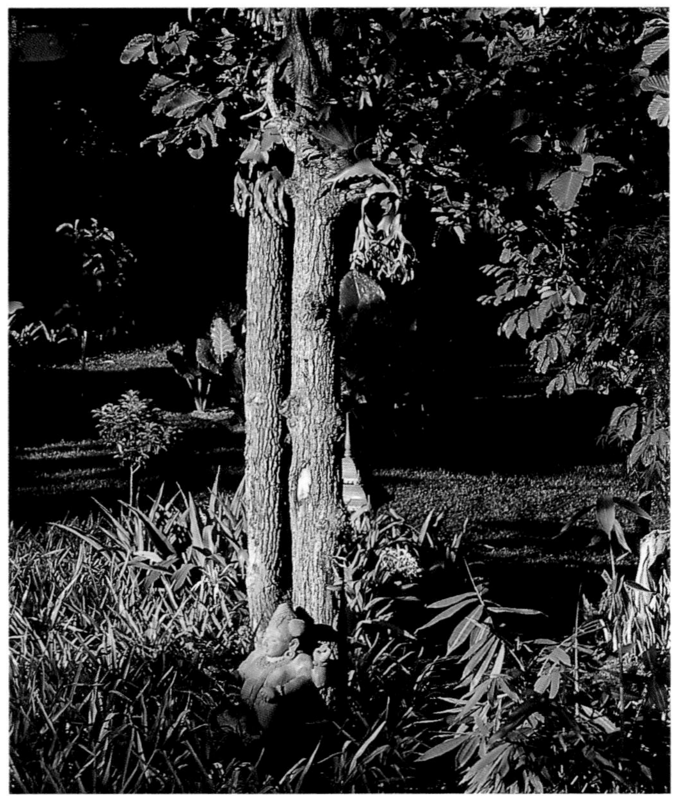

The lush vegetation evokes a naturalistic setting that is a far cry from the contrived landscape features of many resorts.

Die üppige Vegetation bildet eine natürliche Kulisse, die weit entfernt ist von den gekünstelten Landschaften in vielen anderen Anlagen.

Le paysage luxuriant crée un décor naturel très différent des jardins aménagés de maints complexes hôteliers.

The bedroom also has a bright, generous attached bathroom that has glimpses of the surroundings.

Aus dem großen, hellen Bad hat man Ausblicke auf die Umgebung.

Le paysage entre par les baies de la salle de bains emplie de clarté.

In the interior of each pavilion, a separate dressing room leads into the spacious bedroom and sitting room. The bedroom also has a generous attached bathroom.

In den Pavillons führt ein Ankleidezimmer in den geräumigen Schlafraum, dem sich ein großes Bad anschließt, und in das Wohnzimmer.

A l'intérieur de chaque pavillon, un vestibule s'ouvre sur un salon et une chambre à coucher spacieuse avec une salle de bains attenante.

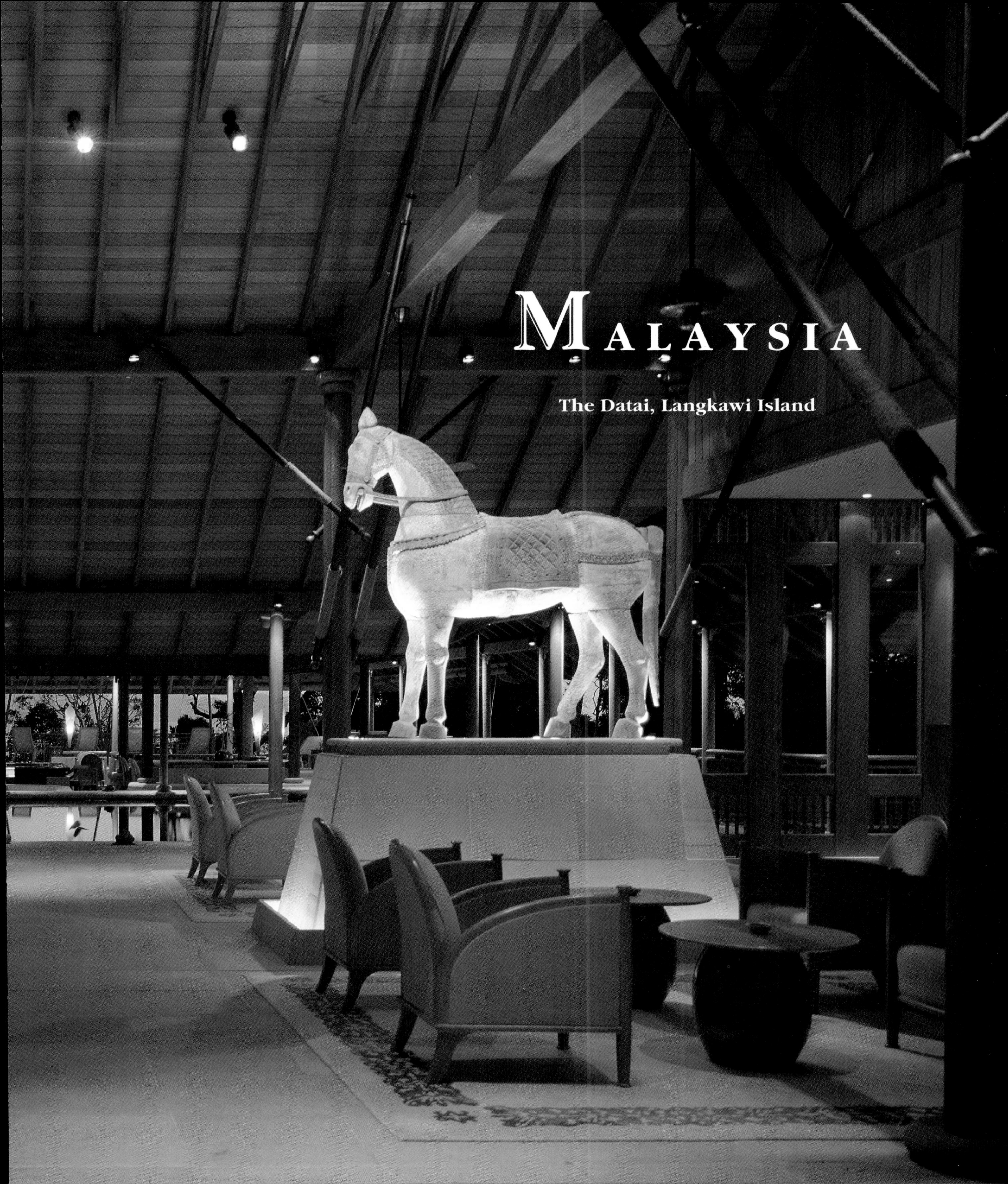

MALAYSIA

The Datai, Langkawi Island

The Datai, Langkawi Island

Langkawi Island is part of an archipelago of 104 islands in peninsular Malaysia, of which only three are inhabited. Luxuriantly forested, this largest west coast island faces the Andaman Sea and boasts of wonderful beaches and relatively untouched natural landscapes. It manages to remain blissfully unspoilt by commercial razzmatazz despite being promoted as a tourist destination for the past ten years. To further encourage tourism, the Malaysian government declared the island a duty-free haven in 1987, and since then it has been actively promoting tourist development on the island.

One of the latest and certainly architecturally most distinguished tourist additions on Langkawi is The Datai. This dramatic resort was designed by the Singapore-based firm Kerry Hill Architects with Akitek Jururancang (M'sia) Sdn Bhd.

Situated on the northwestern tip of the island, The Datai enjoys exclusivity because most of the other hotels and villages are located on the southern side of the island. The resort complex is perched on a ridge, 40 meteres above sea level and 300 metres away from the beach. It consists of 84 rooms contained within slab blocks and 40 pavilion suites scattered at the foot of an artificial mound on which the main building sits.

Conceptualised as a jungle retreat, much of the surroundings of the resort are retained in their original conditions. Set in 700 hectares of primary rainforest, conservation of this fragile environment was a critical design consideration.

The health club and services are tucked within the artificial mound which has rubble walls all around it. The swimming pool and sundecks are located above this mound. A series of monumental steps descends down to the ground, where a pathway meandering through the trees leads guests to the beach where the beach club is located. Essentially composed of simple pavilions containing a restaurant, bar and changing rooms supported by timber columns salvaged from site clearances during construction, the beach club further reinforces the rustic theme.

On arrival, a low but massive shingled roof made of Belian wood greets the visitors. An open courtyard with a landscaped pool separates the reception from the lobby lounge. Pale limewashed timber and pink sandstone are used for the finishes. A Thai restaurant, called The Pavilion, is spectacularly

Das Datai, Langkawi Island

Langkawi Island gehört zu einem Archipel mit 104 Inseln der Halbinsel Malaysia. Nur drei von ihnen sind bewohnt. Dichtbewaldet, liegt diese größte Insel der Westküste gegenüber der Andaman Sea und verfügt über wunderbare Strände und relativ unberührte natürliche Landschaften. Obwohl während der letzten zehn Jahre Werbung für die Insel als Touristenziel gemacht wurde, ist sie von kommerziellem Rummel glücklicherweise verschont geblieben. Zur weiteren Förderung des Tourismus erklärte die malaysische Regierung die Insel 1987 zu einem zollfreien Gebiet und hat seitdem touristische Entwicklungen aktiv unterstützt.

Eines der neuen und architektonisch zweifellos auffälligsten Angebote für Touristen auf Langkawi ist das Datai. Diese eindrucksvolle Ferienanlage wurde von der Firma Kerry Hill Architects, Singapur, zusammen mit Akitek Jururancang (M'sia) Sdn Bhd entworfen.

Schon durch seine Lage auf der Nordwestspitze der Insel verfügt das Datai über Exklusivität, weil sich die meisten anderen Hotels und Dörfer im Süden der Insel befinden. Standort der Anlage ist eine Hügelkette, 40 Meter über dem Meeresspiegel und 300 Meter vom Strand entfernt. Es verfügt über 84 Zimmer in flachen Gebäuden und 40 Pavillons, die am Fuß eines künstlichen Hügels verstreut sind. Auf diesem Hügel befindet sich das Hauptgebäude.

Das Konzept sieht eine Anlage im Dschungel vor, daher blieb ein großer Teil der Umgebung im Originalzustand erhalten. Bei 700 Hektar Regenwald war die Erhaltung dieser empfindlichen Umwelt ein kritischer Punkt bei der Planung.

Der Gesundheitsclub und die Dienstleistungseinrichtungen sind innerhalb des künstlichen Hügels untergebracht, der vollständig von Steinmauern umgeben ist. Swimmingpool und Sonnenterrassen liegen oberhalb des Hügels. Eine Reihe von monumentalen Stufen führt nach unten, wo ein gewundener Pfad zwischen den Bäumen die Gäste zum Strand und zum Beach Club leitet. Dieser Club besteht im wesentlichen aus einfachen Pavillons mit Restaurant, Bar und Umkleideräumen. Sie werden von Säulen aus Holz getragen, das bei der Rodung anfiel und für den Bau eingesetzt wurde. So unterstreicht der Club die rustikale Note.

Bei der Ankunft wird der Gast von einem niedrigen, aber massiven Schindeldach aus Holz begrüßt. Ein offener Hof mit

Distant view of the Thai restaurant's dining pavilion.

Blick aus der Ferne auf den Pavillon des Thai-Restaurants.

Vue du restaurant thaïlandais

(previous page): *The Datai.*

(vorherige Seite): *Das Datai.*

(page précédente): *Le Datai.*

Le Datai, île Langkawi

L'île Langkawi fait partie d'un archipel de 104 îles de la péninsule malaise, dont trois seulement sont habitées. Recouverte de forêts épaisses, cette large île de la côte occidentale en face de la mer Andaman, a des plages merveilleuses et une nature presque intacte. Elle est parvenue à conserver son caractère sauvage en dépit de l'essor touristique des dix dernières années. Pour encourager davantage le tourisme, le gouvernement malais en a fait un port sans droits de douane en 1987 et travaille activement depuis au développement du tourisme.

Le Datai est une des dernières additions architecturales de grande classe de Langkawi. Ce complexe hôtelier a été conçu par le bureau Kerry Hill Architects de Singapour et Akitek Jururancang (M'sia) Sdn Bhd.

S'étendant à la pointe nord-ouest de l'île, le Datai jouit d'une situation exceptionnelle car la plupart des autres hôtels et villages de vacances se trouvent sur le côté sud de l'île. Le complexe est perché sur une crête à 40 mètres au-dessus du niveau de la mer et à 300 mètres du rivage. Il comprend 80 chambres standard et 40 pavillons parsemés au pied d'une butte artificielle sur laquelle se dresse le bâtiment principal.

Le complexe ayant été conçu comme une retraite dans la jungle, son décor naturel n'a pratiquement subi aucune modification. Il est situé dans 700 hectares de forêts tropicales. La conservation de cet environnement fragile a été un critère majeur lors de la conceptualisation.

Le club de mise en forme et les services matériels se trouvent à l'intérieur de la butte artificielle qui est entourée de murs en pierre. La piscine et les solariums surplombent cette hauteur. Un escalier monumental rejoint le chemin qui serpente entre des arbres jusqu'à la plage où se trouve le "beach club" avec un bar, un restaurant et des vestiaires. Composé de pavillons simples construits avec des poteaux en bois récupérés lors du déblaiement du site, le beach club souligne également l'idée d'architecture rustique.

Les visiteurs sont accueillis sous un toit bas et massif construit en bardeaux de bois de belian. Un patio avec un bassin d'agrément sépare la réception du salon. Le bois blond et le grès rose ont été utilisés pour les finitions. Le restaurant thaïlandais appelé le "Pavillon" est construit en encorbellement sur le mont artificiel. Il repose sur une construction audacieuse de troncs d'arbres de 14 mètres de hauteur, abattus durant le déboisement

Conceptualised as a jungle retreat, much of the surroundings of the resort are retained in their original rainforest conditions.

Die Ferienanlage ist als Dschungelsiedlung konzipiert, daher wurde in der Umgebung der Regenwald erhalten.

Le paysage autour du complexe n'a presque pas été modifié. Conçu comme une retraite dans la jungle, l'hôtel est entouré de forêts tropicales.

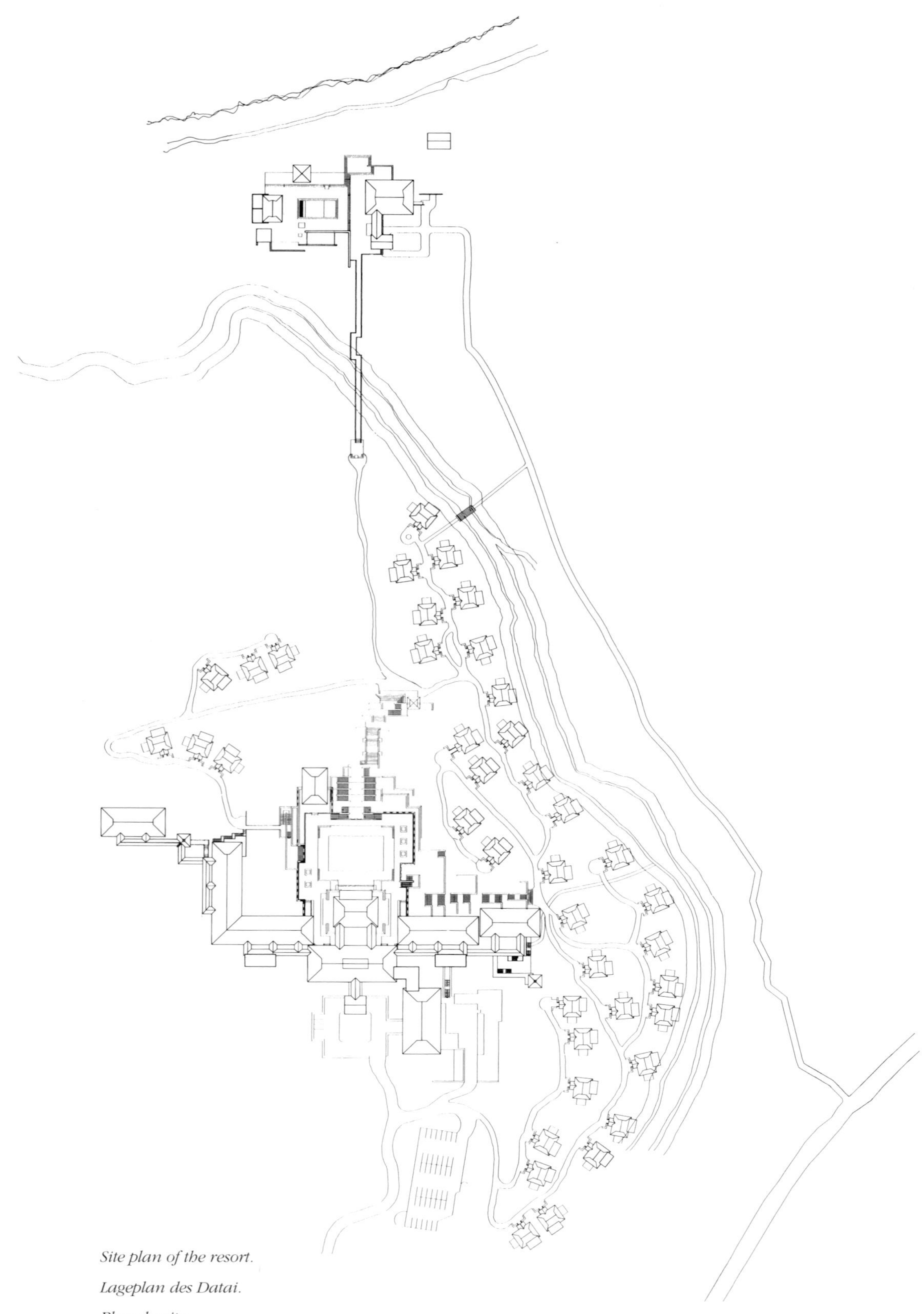

Site plan of the resort.
Lageplan des Datai.
Plan du site.

cantilevered from the mound and is daringly supported by the 14 m tall trunks of hardwood trees felled during clearing of the site. This pavilion is perhaps the most memorable structure in the whole complex.

The traditional Malay house serves as the inspiration for the design of the individual villas, which are picturesquely scattered along the slopes. Planned in an apparently casual manner, they are elevated on concrete piles and connected to the public facilities by timber bridges and meandering walkways. Each villa is air-conditioned and has an attached bath and a private sun-deck.

Other guestrooms are placed in wings to the east and west of the main lobby. They are accessed by long timber walkways, separated from the building walls to create a series of court-yards as well as to provide each room with a semi-public domain at the doorway. The interiors were designed by Frenchmen Didier Lefort and Luc Vaichere of Lefort-Vaichere Architects Associes, who have worked on various projects in Pakistan and for the Aga Khan. Timbers like the red balau wood and nyatoh, two common types of local hardwood, are used extensively for interior panelling and built-in furniture.

The resort responds very well to the difficult terrain and the tropical climate. Architecturally, it is a superbly commanding piece of building, surprising guests at every junction with tantalising vistas and wonderful qualities of tactility and a real sense of place. Walls, columns, beams and roofs vaunt their materiality, eliciting a great sense of delight. It possesses a pervasive sensuality and understated elegance that thrills the senses.

While ostensibly avoiding superficial mimcry of the traditional Malay house form, the architecture is still trapped within the language and imagery of traditional architecture of the region. There is no doubt that a creative process of cultural cross-fertilisation exists. Nevertheless, it has an uneasy air of eclecticism. This quibble aside, the resort is executed with sheer confidence and elan, and represents the necessary struggle in the search for a new mode of representation.

einem landschaftlich gestalteten Pool trennt den Empfang von der Lounge. Für die Außengestaltung wurden helles, gekalktes Holz und rosa Sandstein verwendet. Ein spektakulär freischwebendes Thai-Restaurant, ragt über den Hügel hinaus und wird von 14 Meter hohen Baumstämmen aus Hartholz getragen, die bei der Rodung gefällt wurden. Dieser Pavillon wird vermutlich von allen Bauten der Anlage am meisten in Erinnerung bleiben.

Das traditionelle malaysische Haus liefert die Anregungen für die Einzelvillen, die malerisch an den Hängen verstreut sind. In der Anlage leicht und unbeschwert, stehen sie auf Betonpfeilern und sind durch Holzbrücken und gewundene Wege mit den allgemeinen Einrichtungen verbunden. Jede Villa verfügt über eine Klimaanlage, ein Bad und eine eigene Sonnenterrasse.

In den Flügeln östlich und westlich der Haupthalle liegen weitere Gästezimmer. Sie sind über lange Holzgänge an den tragenden Mauern zu erreichen. Dadurch entstehen weitere Innenhöfe, und vor jedem Eingang befindet sich ein halböffentlicher Bereich. Die Inneneinrichtung stammt von den Franzosen Didier Lefort und Luc Vaichere von Lefort-Vaichere Architects Associés, die an verschiedenen Projekten in Pakistan und für den Aga Khan gearbeitet haben. Für die Innenverkleidung und die Einbaumöbel wurden vor allem einheimische Harthölzer verwendet.

Die Ferienanlage berücksichtigt das schwierige Gelände und das tropische Klima sehr gut. Architektonisch ist sie wahrlich beeindruckend und überrascht den Gast an jeder Ecke mit grandiosen Aussichten; es macht Spaß, Dinge anzufassen, und man spürt die wunderbare Atmosphäre. Das Material von Wänden, Säulen, Balken und Dächern kommt voll zur Wirkung und macht Freude. Die allgegenwärtige Sinnlichkeit und die zurückhaltende Eleganz bieten Anregung für alle Sinne.

Die Architektur vermeidet ganz offensichtlich jede oberflächliche Nachahmung der traditionellen malaysischen Hausform, dennoch verwendet sie die Sprache und die Bilder der alten Bauweise. Hier ist zweifellos ein kreativer Prozeß von wechselseitiger kultureller Befruchtung zustande gekommen. Dennoch bleibt ein unangenehmes Gefühl, daß Elemente früherer Epochen aufgegriffen und bunt zusammengewürfelt wurden. Davon abgesehen,wirkt die Anlage selbstbewußt und schwungvoll und ist ein Beispiel für die notwendige Auseinandersetzung bei der Suche nach neuen Ausdrucksformen.

du site. Cet édifice est l'ouvrage le plus impressionnant de tout le complexe.

La maison malaise traditionnelle a inspiré le style des villas individuelles disséminées sur les versants selon un schéma qui ne présente aucun ordre apparent. Elles sont surélevées par des piliers de béton et reliées aux espaces communs par des ponts en bois et des chemins sinueux. Toutes les villas sont climatisées et possèdent un bain et un solarium privés.

Les chambres standard se trouvent dans des ailes situées de part et d'autre de la réception principale. On y accède par de longues galeries en bois qui forment une succession de petites cours et offrent un espace semi-privé devant chaque chambre. Les architectes français Didier Lefort et Luc Vaichere, auteurs de divers projets au Pakistan et pour l'Aga Khan, ont réalisé la décoration intérieure. Ils ont employé des variétés courantes de bois locaux tels le balau rouge et le nyatoh, pour les boiseries et le mobilier intégré.

Le complexe est parfaitement adapté à la topographie difficile du terrain et au climat tropical. C'est une œuvre architecturale superbe, qui offre de multiples panoramas surprenants, un environnement intérieur merveilleux et une impression de vaste espace. Les matériaux révèlent leurs beautés dans les murs, les colonnes, les poutres et les toits. L'endroit dévoile une sensualité délicate et une élégance discrète, véritable plaisir des sens.

Bien que l'architecture évite une imitation superficielle de la demeure traditionnelle malaise, elle reste prisonnière de l'expression abstraite et concrète de l'architecture traditionnelle de la région. On remarque incontestablement une créativité qui découle de la rencontre fertile de cultures différentes. Néanmoins, un certain syncrétisme y est associé. Mais hormis cette critique, le complexe hôtelier a été réalisé avec sûreté et brio et dévoile le désir de recherche nécessaire à la création d'un nouveau mode de représentation.

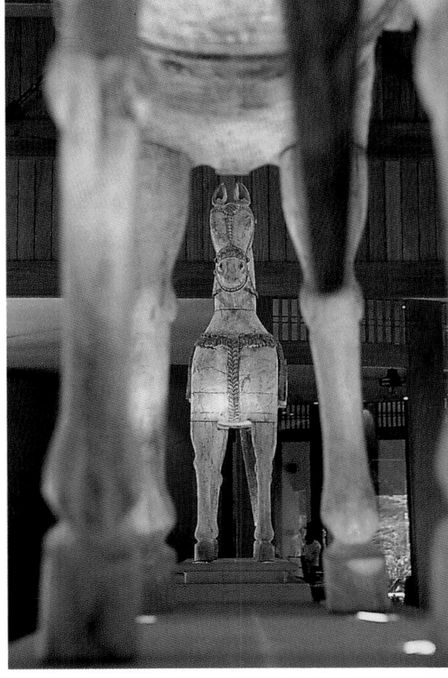

Sculptural objects provide visual focal points in the lobby.

Skulpturen setzen optische Schwerpunkte in der Lobby.

Des sculptures attirent le regard dans la réception.

(previous page):
The dining pavilion is probably the most spectacular building in the entire complex.

(vorherige Seite):
Der Speisepavillon ist vermutlich der spektakulärste Bau des gesamten Komplexes.

(page précédente):
Le pavillon abritant le restaurant est le bâtiment le plus spectaculaire du complexe.

(opposite page):
Balconies are cantilevered from a base clad in rubble, reminiscent of Himalayan architecture.

(gegenüberliegende Seite):
Die freischwebenden Balkons über einer Steinbasis erinnern an Himalaja-Architektur.

(page ci-contre):
Des balcons surmontent une base en pierre qui évoque le style d'architecture de l'Himalaya.

The end walls of the guestroom blocks are sensitively designed, providing a dramatic architectural statement.

Die abschließenden Wände der Blocks mit den Gästezimmern sind einfühlsam gestaltet und treffen eine klare architektonische Aussage.

Les murs cernant les pavillons qui abritent les chambres créent un tableau architectural superbe.

A walkway linking the main facilities of the complex.

Ein Weg verbindet die Hauptfreizeitangebote mit dem Wohnkomplex.

Ce chemin relie les différentes zones du complexe.

The beach club is a simple structure overlooking the pool.

Der Beach Club ist ein einfacher Bau mit Blick auf den Pool.

Le bâtiment sans fioriture du beach club domine la piscine.

(opposite page):
At The Datai,the simplicity of the architectural details elicit a great sense of delight.

(gegenüberliegende Seite):
Die Schlichtheit der architektonischen Details verleiht dem Datai eine große Leichtigkeit.

(page ci-contre):
Le Datai, La sobriété des éléments architecturaux engendre une beauté sereine.

Architectural elements are designed to frame views.

Architektonische Elemente bilden den Rahmen für Ausblicke.

Les éléments architecturaux servent de cadres aux vues.

(opposite page):
Evening view of the lobby and its reflections on the calm surface of the reflecting pool.

(gegenuberliegende seite):
Abendlicher Blick auf die Lobby und ihre Spiegelung im ruhigen Wasser des Pools.

(page ci-contre):
Une vue nocturne de la réception et le reflet de la lumière sur la surface paisible du bassin.

The evening lights show off to maximum effects the controlled drama of the resort.

Die abendlichen Lichter unterstreichen die kontrollierte Dramatik der Anlage optimal.

La beauté sobre du complexe se révèle dans toute sa splendeur sous les éclairages.

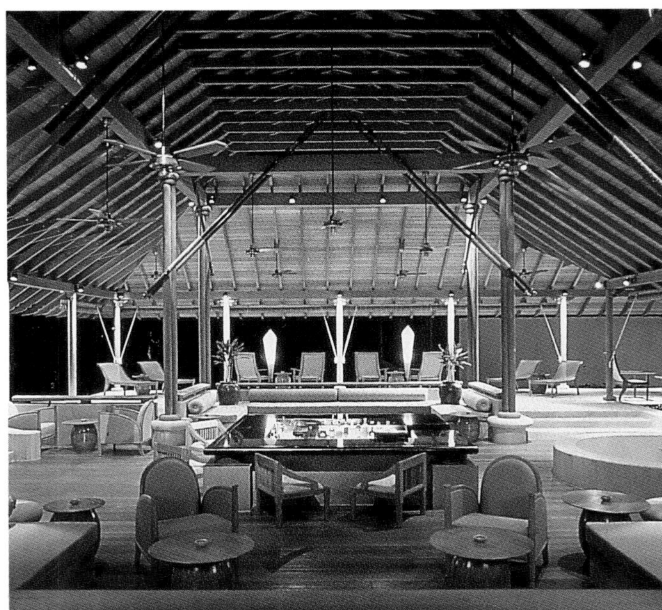

The voluminous roof of the lobby is supported by elegantly proportioned timber structures.

Das große Dach der Lobby wird von elegant proportionierten Holzkonstruktionen getragen.

Une armature en bois aux proportions élégantes supporte le toit volumineux.

The skilful manipulations of the details and finishes is evident in every aspect of the project, including the retail shop.

Die gekonnte Behandlung der Einzelheiten und der Gesamtausführung ist überall in der Anlage erkennbar, selbst in dem Geschäft.

Les moindres détails et finitions sont admirablement façonnés, comme on peut le voir dans la boutique.

Section across the site.

Ausblick auf einen Teil der Anlage.

Coupe du site.

The roof structure, drawing inspiration from the local vernacular, achieves an understated elegance through controlled use of elements.

Die Dachkonstruktion nach Vorbild einheimischer Bauten bekommt durch die kontrollierte Verwendung der Elemente eine zurückhaltende Eleganz.

Les éléments utilisés avec maîtrise confèrent une élégance discrète à la structure du toit qui s'inspire du style indigène local.

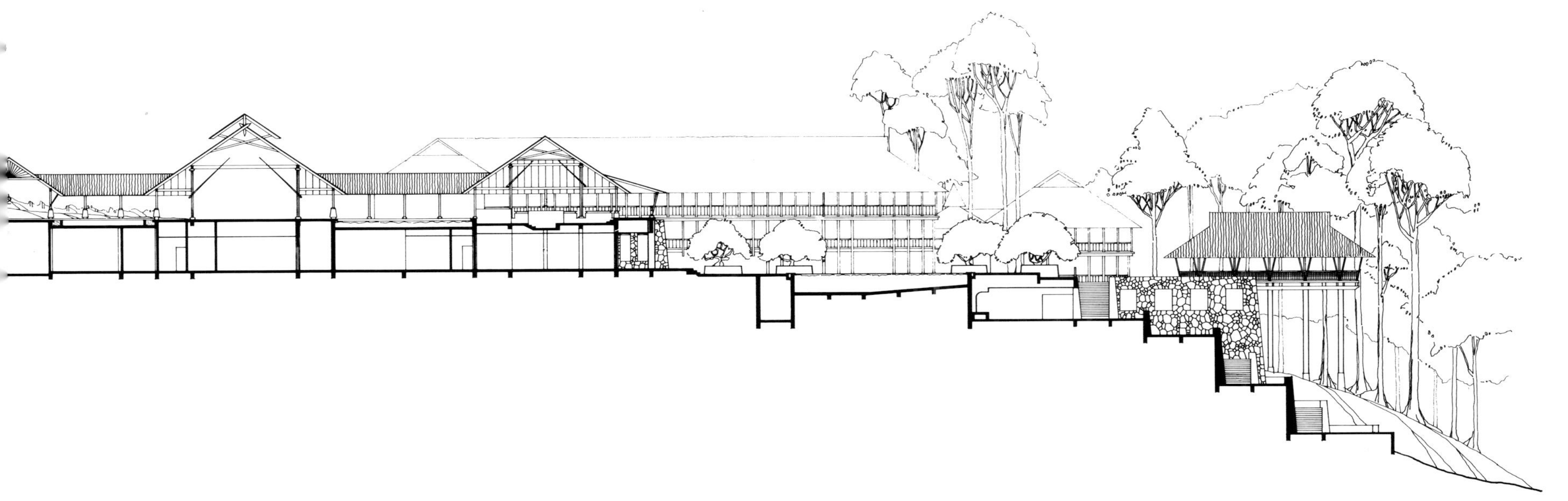

The structural system of a typical walkway demonstrates the care with which elements are used in a deliberate manner to achieve a wonderful sense of proportion, scale and rhythm.

Die Gliederung einer Wegüberdachung zeigt, mit welcher Sorgfalt Elemente bewußt eingesetzt werden, um ein Gefühl von Proportion, Maßstab und Rhythmus zu erzeugen.

La composition architecturale de l'allée témoigne d'un sens admirable des proportions, de l'équilibre et du rythme grâce à une utilisation judicieuse des éléments.

The overall planning of the individual villas contributes immensely to the general feeling of repose, possessing a directness that engages the senses in a sensual manner. The affinity of the architecture to the site is inescapable. The typical floor plan of the villa shows how it is designed to open up to the surroundings.

Die Gesamtplanung der Einzelvillen vermittelt intensiv ein allgemeines Gefühl der Ruhe, die sich direkt auf die Sinne überträgt. Unübersehbar ist, wie gut Architektur und Landschaft zusammenpassen. Der Grundriß der Villa läßt erkennen, daß das Haus sich zur Umgebung hin öffnet.

La disposition des villas contribue beaucoup à créer l'atmosphère de charme et de quiétude. Architecture et site se lient étroitement. Le plan montre comment une villa est bâtie pour s'ouvrir sur l'extérieur.

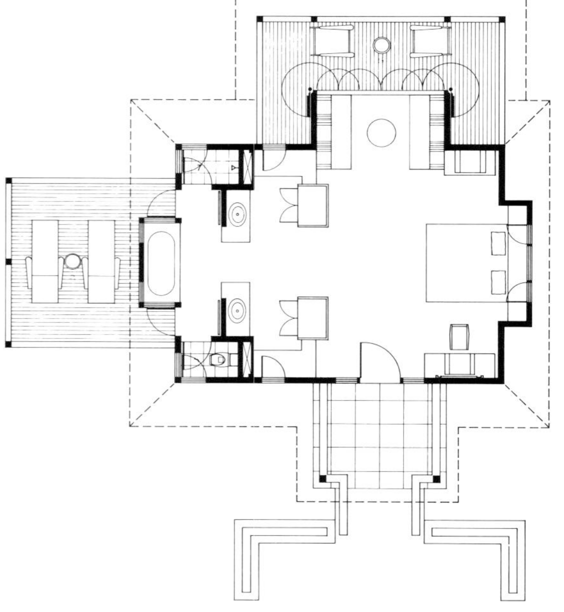

The interiors were designed by Frenchmen Didier Lefort and Luc Vaichere of Lefort-Vaichere Architects Associes. Common types of local hardwood are used extensively for interior panelling and built-in furniture.

Die Franzosen Didier Lefort und Luc Vaichere von Lefort-Vaichere Architects Associés entwarfen die Inneneinrichtung. Für Verkleidung und Einbaumöbel wurden einheimische Hartholzsorten verwendet.

Les architectes français Didier Lefort et Luc Vaichere ont réalisé la décoration intérieure. Des variétés courantes de bois locaux ont servi pour les lambris intérieurs et le mobilier intégré.

Repetitive use of similar elements achieve a pleasing visual complexity.

Immer wieder werden ähnliche Elemente verwendet, um eine optische Einheit zu erzielen.

La répétition d'éléments analogues forme des tableaux très étudiés.

SINGAPORE

The Beaufort, Sentosa

The Beaufort, Sentosa

The open-sided lounge is fitted with bamboo blinds, which are rolled down in the evenings to reduce the glare of the setting sun.

Die Bambus-Jalousetten der an den Seiten offenen Lounge werden abends heruntergelassen, um das blendende Licht der untergehenden Sonne zu mildern.

Le salon ouvert sur un côté a des jalousies en bambou que l'on descend le soir pour réduire l'éclat éblouissant du soleil couchant.

The Beaufort is Singapore's first resort style hotel and is located on Sentosa, a leisure isle off the main land. Designed in the manner of idyll beach resorts found in popular travel destinations like Bali and Phuket, The Beaufort differs significantly in its treatment of architectural imagery in a non-pastiche manner.

Set on a sprawling 11-hectare site, the low-rise development is located along the southern escarpment of the island with panoramic views of the sea and the Singapore mainland. It is broken up into separate masses that respect the topography and draw subtle lessons from the old British military buildings and barracks that exist on the isle. Some pre-War buildings on the adjacent site has been restored to accommodate the health club, squash and tennis courts, lap pool and hotel staff facilities.

A symmetrical and cross-axial composition is imposed rather rigidly and forcefully onto the site. Based on the notion of framing views, rhythmic sequence of columns capture frames that include picturesque tropical forests, harbour scenes and unruffled expanse of reflecting pools.

Designed as a complex of understated buildings with a maximum height of five storeys, the Beaufort has six guestroom blocks housing 214 rooms, five separate blocks housing the public spaces and four super-luxurious private villas that have individual swimming pools. These 160 square metres villas face a quiet meandering road that brings guests right to the lobby. Delightful use of verdigris finish and mirror tiles at the lobby heighten the sense of grandeur in a non-ostentatious manner. Long axial walkways lead guests to the Pavilion lobby lounge, a huge building open on all sides. Located at the heart of the hotel, the Pavilion overlooks the pool and coast. Its vaulted ceiling is hung with fans and the main area is teak floored, with teak and cane chairs upholstered in Thai fabric. Roll chick blinds modulate the amount of light streaming in from all sides.

The open spaces between the buildings are filled with vast expanse of reflecting pools. The unruffled calm of the main swimming pool, lined with iridiscent blue-black tiles commisioned from Thai craftsmen, has a deep sense of quietude. Set on a cliff which overlooks a newly developed beach below, this most appropriately captured the pervading mood of the understated resort, whose serenity has not really been appreciated by many Singaporeans.

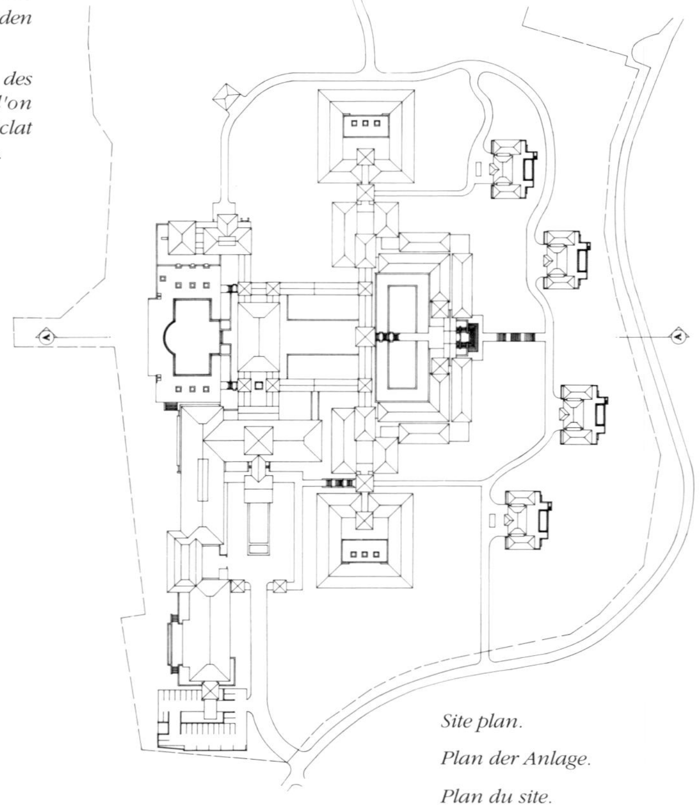

Site plan.

Plan der Anlage.

Plan du site.

(previous page):
The Beaufort.

(vorherige Seite):
Das Beaufort.

(page précédente):
Le Beaufort.

Das Beaufort, Sentosa

Das Beaufort ist Singapurs erstes Hotel im Stil einer Ferienanlage und liegt auf Sentosa, einer Freizeitinsel vor der Küste. Es ist im Stil der idyllischen Strandanlagen gebaut, wie man sie in beliebten Urlaubsorten wie Bali und Phuket findet. Aber das Beaufort unterscheidet sich in seiner architektonischen Erscheinungsweise deutlich, weil es ohne stilistischen Mischmasch auskommt.

Auf einem weitläufigen Gelände von elf Hektar liegt der flache Bau am südlichen Steilabbruch der Insel und bietet einen weiten Blick auf das Meer und auf Singapur. Es ist in einzelne Baukörper aufgeteilt, berücksichtigt damit die Topographie und zieht so vorsichtige Lehren aus den alten britischen Militärbauten und Kasernen, die es auf der Insel noch gibt. Einige Vorkriegsbauten auf dem benachbarten Gelände wurden restauriert. Dort sind der Gesundheitsclub, Squash- und Tennisplätze, ein Pool und Unterkünfte für die Angestellten untergebracht.

Dem Gelände wurde ziemlich hart und kraftvoll eine symmetrische Komposition mit Kreuzachse aufgezwungen. Ausgehend von der Vorstellung gerahmter Bilder, liefern sich wiederholende Säulenreihen die Rahmung für malerische Tropenwälder, Hafenszenen und große, glitzernde Pools.

Das Beaufort ist ein Komplex von zurückhaltenden Gebäuden mit höchstens vier Etagen. Es gibt sechs Häuser mit 214 Gästezimmern, fünf einzelne Blocks für Gemeinschaftsaktivitäten und vier höchst luxuriöse Villen mit eigenen Swimmingpools. Diese 160 Quadratmeter großen Villen liegen an einer ruhigen, gewundenen Straße, die die Gäste direkt in die Lobby führt. Die hübsche Verwendung von vorgetäuschtem Grünspan und Spiegelkacheln in der Halle verstärkt auf unaufdringliche Weise den Eindruck von Größe. Lange überdachte Wege verbinden den Pavillon mit der Lounge, einem großen Bau, der nach allen Seiten offen ist. Der Pavillon liegt im Herzen der Hotelanlage und bietet Ausblick auf Pool und Küste. An der gewölbten Decke hängen Ventilatoren, der Boden ist im Hauptbereich aus Teak, und die Teak – und Bambusstühle sind mit thailändischen Stoffen bezogen. Rollos dämpfen das Licht, das von allen Seiten hereinströmt.

Überall zwischen den Gebäuden liegen große, glitzernde Teiche. Die ungestörte Stille des größten Swimmingpools mit den schimmernden blauschwarzen Kacheln, die thailändische Handwerker hergestellt haben, vermittelt ein tiefes Gefühl der Ruhe. Unterhalb der Klippen wurde ein Strand neu angelegt.

Le Beaufort, Sentosa

Premier hôtel de style et lieu de détente de Singapour, le Beaufort se trouve à Sentosa, une île de villégiature au large du continent. Conçu à la façon des stations balnéaires paradisiaques que l'on trouve dans des endroits touristiques à la mode comme Bali et Phuket, le Beaufort s'en démarque toutefois nettement dans la mesure où le langage architectural utilisé n'a rien du pastiche.

Bâti sur un vaste site de 11 hectares, le complexe, de faible hauteur, longe l'escarpement sud de l'île, s'ouvrant sur une vue panoramique de la mer et de Singapour. Il est constitué de plusieurs parties qui épousent le relief, et tire habilement parti des anciens bâtiments et casernes de l'armée britannique construits sur l'île. Plusieurs constructions datant d'avant-guerre ont été restaurées pour abriter le club de mise en forme, les terrains de squash et de tennis, une longue piscine étroite et les installations du personnel hôtelier.

Sa composition symétrique et en forme de croix est quelque peu plaquée sur le site, donnant une certaine impression de rigidité. Conçues dans l'idée de former des tableaux, des colonnes s'échelonnent à un rythme régulier, découpant des vues sur la forêt tropicale, le port ou le miroir lisse de pièces d'eau étincelantes.

Formé de bâtiments peu élevés ne dépassant pas 5 étages, le Beaufort comprend 6 constructions accueillant 214 chambres, 5 autres aménagées pour les espaces collectifs et 4 villas privées de grand luxe dotées chacune d'une piscine. Ces villas de 160 m2 font face à une route tranquille qui serpente doucement jusqu'à la réception. Utilisés avec art, la tonalité gris vert et les carreaux miroitants accroissent sans ostentation l'impression de magnificence. De longues allées conduisent les hôtes au pavillon abritant le salon, un vaste bâtiment ouvert de tous côtés. Situé au cœur de l'hôtel, le pavillon domine la piscine et la côte. Son plafond voûté est ponctué de ventilateurs; l'espace central est garni de teck au sol, et meublé de sièges en rotin et en teck tendus d'étoffes thaï. Des jalousies modulent la quantité de lumière qui afflue de tous côtés.

Dans les espaces libres entre les constructions se déploient de vastes bassins aux surfaces miroitantes. Un profond sentiment de quiétude émane des eaux paisibles de la grande piscine soulignée de carreaux bleu noir aux reflets irisés, œuvre d'artisans thaïs. Située sur une falaise qui surplombe une plage récemment aménagée, elle traduit parfaitement la douceur qui

Landscaped pools are filled with water lilies.

In gestalteten Teichen wachsen Seerosen.

Des nénuphars décorent la surface des bassins.

The equally understated, albeit more tactile interiors are designed by Ed Tuttle of Design Realisation, who is also responsible for the design of the Amanpuri resort in Phuket and the interiors of the Sukhothai Hotel in Bangkok. The latter is also designed by Kerry Hill Architects.

At The Beaufort, the rich interplay of materials and muted tones in the interiors provide a good complement to the simple guestroom blocks that are proportioned and detailed with minimalist rigour. The restrained use of materials includes black granite, celandon tiles, teak and burlwood camphor floors. Distinctive furniture and interiors such as hand-made tortoiseshell desks, teak drum-like stools, French banquette sofas and upholstered wooden screens give each room an individual character.

However, the most obvious architectural triumph is the building's lack of stylistic cliches, paper-thin embellishments and other contrivances so pervasive in resorts in all parts of South-east Asia. Its simplicity proves that Mies's adage of "Less is More" is certainly still valid in today's re-working of Modernism. Yet, every deliberate move has been thought through at so many different levels. There is careful consideration of use, place and climate. Moreover, its architectural idiom is contemporary and carefully judged, without any overt attempts at incorporating cultural symbols.

Insgesamt atmet diese Anlage ohne jegliche Übertreibung eine Heiterkeit, die von vielen Leuten aus Singapur noch gar nicht richtig gewürdigt wurde.

Genauso dezent, allerdings viel greifbarer ist die Inneneinrichtung von Ed Tuttle von Design Realisation, der auch für die Planung von Amanpuri in Phuket und die Ausstattung des Sukhotai Hotels in Bangkok verantwortlich zeichnet. Das zuletzt genannte Hotel wurde ebenfalls von Kerry Hill Architects entworfen.

Im Beaufort runden die gut aufeinander abgestimmten Materialien und die gedämpften Farben die schlichten, gut proportionierten Häuser mit den Gästezimmern ab. Bei der Auswahl der Materialien hat man sich beschränkt und sich für schwarzen Granit, blaßgrüne Kacheln sowie Teak und Kampferholz für die Böden entschieden. Unverwechselbare Einrichtungsgegenstände wie handgearbeitete Schreibtische mit Schildpatt, trommelförmige Hocker aus Teak, französische Sofas und grün bespannte Zwischenwände aus Holz verleihen jedem Zimmer einen individuellen Charakter.

Doch die sichtbarste architektonische Glanzleistung ist der Verzicht auf alle stilistischen Klischees, hauchdünne Verzierungen und anderen Zierat die man so oft in den Ferienanlagen überall in Südostasien findet. Die Schlichtheit des Beaufort beweist, daß der alte Spruch »Weniger ist mehr« auch heute noch gilt. Und doch wurde alles auf verschiedenen Ebenen immer wieder durchdacht. Nutzung, Ort und Klima wurden sorgfältig berücksichtigt. Außerdem ist die architektonische Sprache zeitgemäß und überlegt, ohne offensichtliche Versuche, kulturelle Symbole einzubauen.

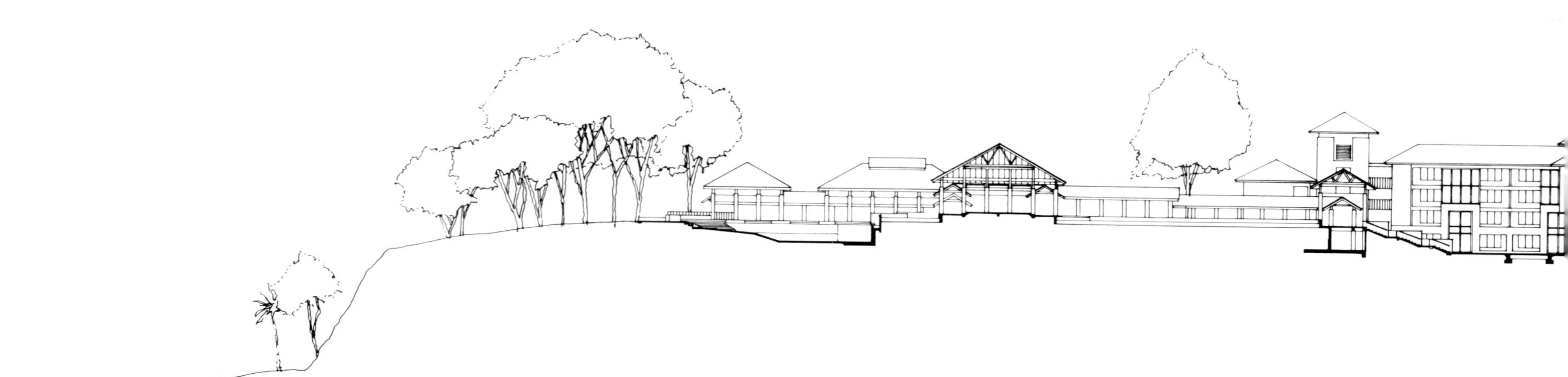

imprègne ce lieu de villégiature dont, jusqu'alors, la sérénité n'a pas vraiment été appréciée des Singapouriens.

Les intérieurs tout aussi feutrés, mais plus sensuels sont dus à Ed Tuttle of Design Realisation, qui a également conçu la station d'Amanpuri à Phuket et les intérieurs du Sukhothai Hotel à Bangkok. Ce dernier porte également la signature du bureau Kerry Hill Architects.

Au Beaufort, les subtils mariages de matériaux et les tons doux dans les intérieurs complètent avec bonheur la simplicité des bâtiments abritant les chambres, dont les proportions et les détails relèvent d'un minimalisme rigoureux. Granit noir, carreaux vert céladon, teck et bois de camphrier pour les parquets, la sélection de matériaux se caractérise avant tout par une grande sobriété. Le choix de meubles différents et une décoration propre à chaque chambre – secrétaires en carapace de tortue façonnés à la main, tabourets en teck en forme de tambour, canapés – confèrent à chaque pièce un caractère unique.

Cependant, le véritable tour de force est d'avoir su préserver l'ensemble architectural des clichés stylistiques, des ornements bon marché et autres inventions si envahissantes dans les stations touristiques de toute l'Asie du Sud-Est. Sa simplicité montre bien que l'adage de Mies "Less is more" est encore valable dans la recherche actuelle sur le modernisme. Cependant, chaque élément a été pensé et repensé à plusieurs niveaux. La finalité, l'emplacement et le climat ont été pris en considération avec soin. En outre, le langage architectural utilisé est contemporain sans être excessif et a le mérite de ne pas chercher à intégrer des symboles culturels coûte que coûte.

The Beaufort, as seen in the pool's reflections.

Das Beaufort, wie es sich im Pool spiegelt.

Le Beaufort se reflète dans les eaux de la piscine.

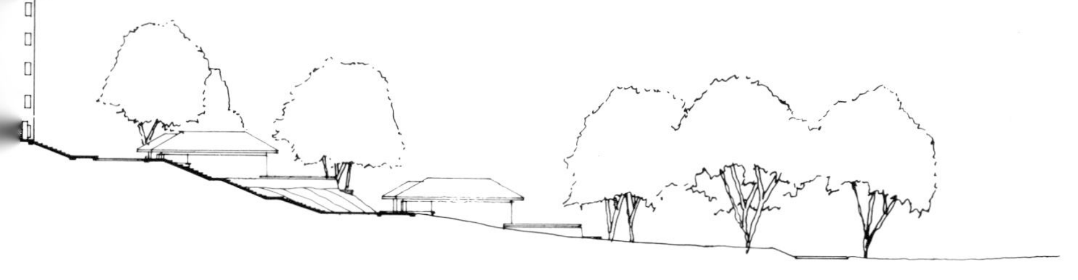

(opposite page):
The landscape of the hotel is carefully orchestrated to complement the built structure.

(gegenüberliegende Seite):
Die Landschaft ist sorgfältig als Ergänzung zu den Bauten gestaltet.

(page ci-contre):
Le dessin du paysage se marie à merveille avec l'architecture.

(above and below): The open spaces between the buildings are filled with vast expanse of reflecting pools, which create an overall ambience of serenity.

(oben und unten): Zwischen den Gebäuden liegen glitzernde Wasserbecken, die für eine heitere Atmosphäre sorgen.

(au-dessus et au-dessous): Tous les bâtiments collectifs et galeries sont ouverts sur un côté; une architecture qui lie étroitement les espaces intérieurs et extérieurs.

The large landscaped pool provides an important foreground for the pavilion lounge.

Der große künstlich angelegte Teich ist der ideale optische Vordergrund für den Pavillon mit der Lounge.

Le vaste bassin constitue une avant-scène idéale pour le pavillon abritant le salon.

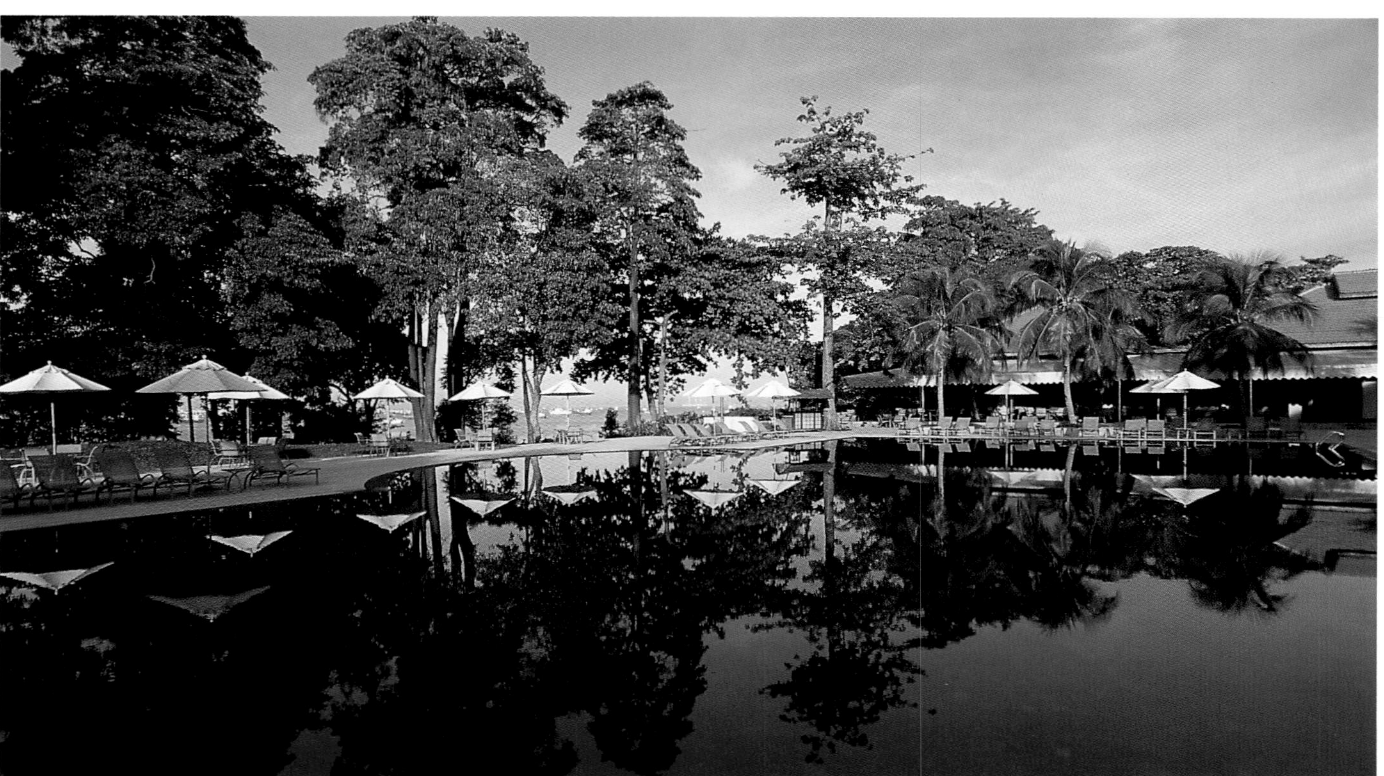

The unruffled calm of the main swimming pool, lined with iridescent blue-black tiles, has a deep sense of quietude.

Die ungestörte Stille des Swimming-pools mit den schillernden blauschwarzen Kacheln wirkt ungeheuer beruhigend.

Un profond sentiment de quiétude émane des eaux paisibles de la grande piscine décorée de carreaux bleu noir aux reflets irisés.

(opposite page):
The guestroom blocks are sensitively articulated to reduce the visual blandness associated with such buildings.

(gegenüberliegende Seite):
Die Blocks mit den Gästezimmern sind einfühlsam gestaltet, um die bei solchen Bauten drohende Langeweile zu mildern.

(page ci-contre):
La disposition judicieuse des bâtiments abritant les chambres d'hôtes réduit l'aspect neutre que présente souvent ce type de construction.

Landscaped areas and reflecting pools act as intermediary elements in the spaces between activity pockets.

Gestaltete Landschaften und glitzernde Wasserbecken liegen zwischen den Freizeitbereichen.

Des jardins et bassins d'agrément servent d'éléments intermédiaires entre les différents centres d'activités.

The open spaces between the buildings are filled with vast expanse of reflecting pools, which create an overall ambience of serenity.

Zwischen den Gebäuden liegen glitzerde Wasserbecken, die für eine heitere Atmosphäre sorgen.

Les nombreux bassins d'agrément qui séparent les bâtiments, créent une ambiance sereine.

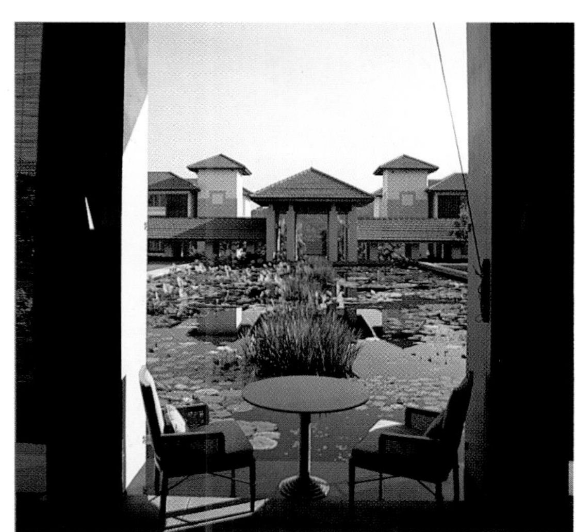

Columns become visual frames for guests lounging in the Pavilion.

Für Gäste, die sich im Pavillon aufhalten, werden Säulen zu optischen Bilderrahmen.

Les colonnes découpent des vues que les hôtes découvrent depuis le Pavillon.

In all of Kerry Hill's projects, the understated elegance and minimalist rigour are a result of careful considerations ofmaterials and details. The seemingly sparse interiors reveal a certain complexity in their details upon closer examination. The interior of the restaurant reveals sensitive consideration in its choice of finishes.

Bei allen Anlagen von Kerry Hill sind die zurückhaltende Eleganz und der sparsame Einsatz von Mitteln das Ergebnis der sorgfältigen Einschätzung von Materialien und Details. Die scheinbar spärliche Inneneinrichtung erweist sich bei genauerem Hinsehen als recht vielseitig. Die Einrichtung des Restaurants läßt einen einfühlsamen Einsatz von Material erkennen.

Toutes les œuvres de Kerry Hill témoignent d'une élégance discrète et d'une rigueur minimaliste qui résultent d'un choix minutieux des matériaux et des détails. Les intérieurs, dépouillés à première vue, dévoilent une certaine complexité dans les détails au second regard. Le choix des finitions du restaurant a fait l'objet d'une grande attention.

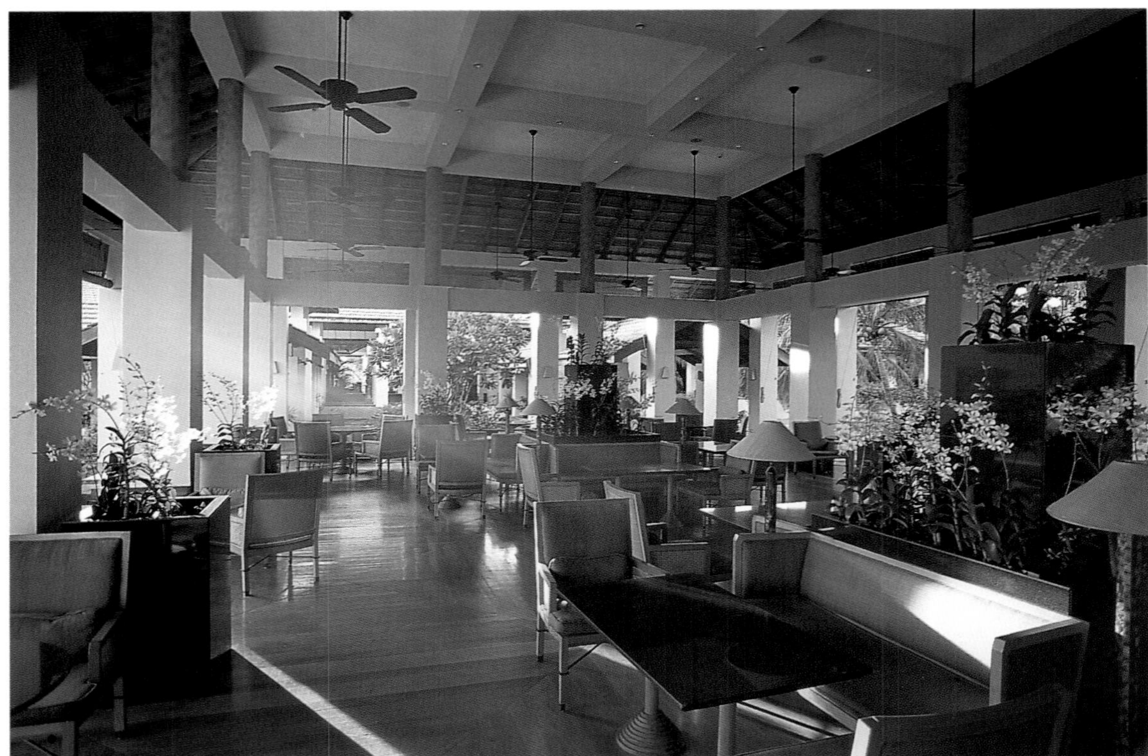

Delightful use of verdigris finish and mirror tiles at the lobby heightens the sense of grandeur in a non-ostentatious manner.

Die Verwendung von Grünspan-anstrich und Spiegelkacheln verstärkt unaufdringlich den Eindruck von Größe.

La tonalité gris vert et les carreaux miroitants rehaussent sans ostentation l'impression de magnificence dans la réception.

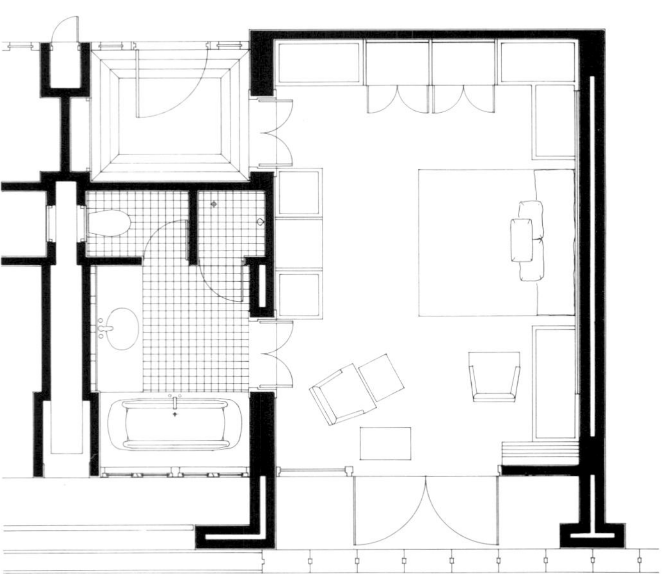

Plan of a typical guestroom.

Grundriß eines typischen Gästezimmers.

Plan d'une chambre type.

Located at the heart of the hotel, the Pavilion overlooks the swimming pool on one side and a huge landscaped pool on the other.

Der Pavillon im Herzen der Anlage liegt zwischen dem Swimmingpool und einem riesigen künstlichen Teich.

Situé au cœur de l'hôtel, le Pavillon se dresse entre la piscine et un immense bassin d'agrément.

INDONESIA

Bali Hyatt, Sanur, Bali

Bali Imperial Hotel, Legian, Bali

Bali Intercontinental Resort, Jimbaran, Bali

Balina Serai, Candi Desa, Bali

Chedi Bandung, Bandung, Java

Four Seasons Resort Bali, Jimbaran, Bali

Grand Hyatt Bali, Nusa Dua, Bali

Bali Hyatt, Sanur, Bali

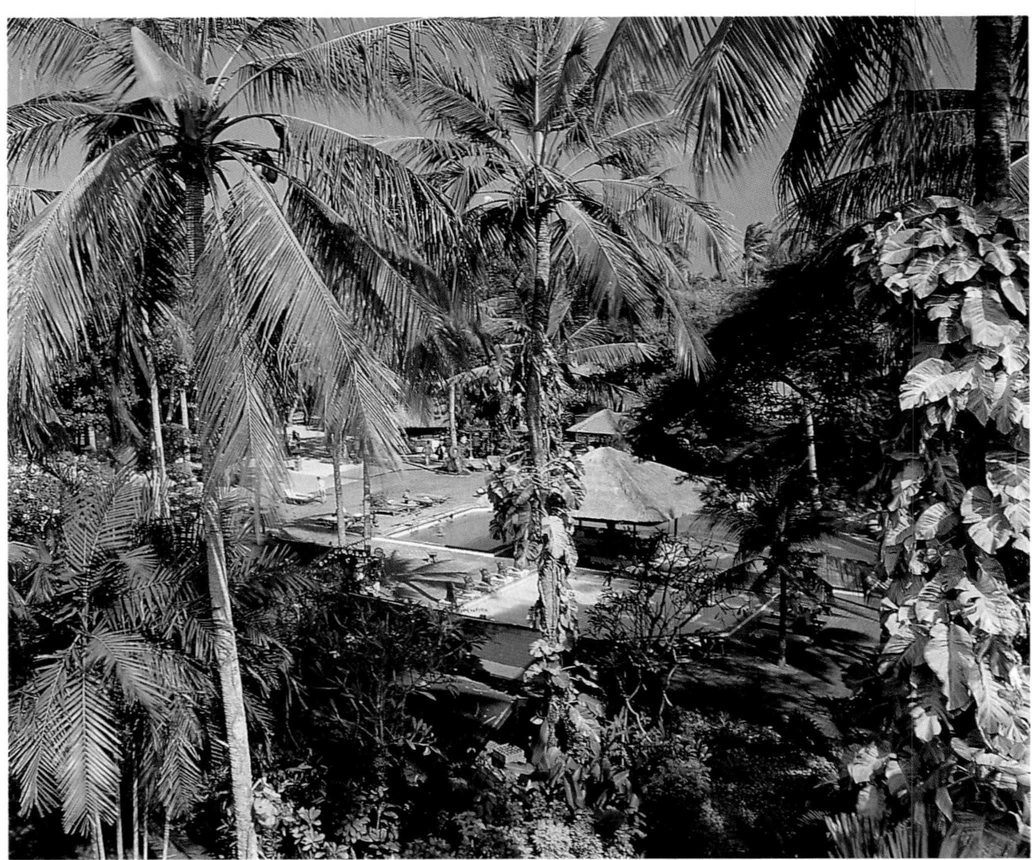

Built on a former coconut plantation of over 2000 trees, the resort boasts of one of the best tropical gardens in Southeast Asia.

Die Anlage wurde auf einer ehemaligen Kokosnußplantage mit mehr als 2000 Bäumen errichtet und kann auf einen der besten tropischen Gärten in Südostasien verweisen.

Construit su une ancienne plantation de plus de 2000 cocotiers, le complexe possède un des plus beaux parcs tropicaux du Sud-Est asiatique.

Opened in 1973, the 390-room Bali Hyatt is located in Sanur, a former fishing village and home to Brahman priests. Built on a former coconut plantation of over 2000 trees, with a 500-metre long white beach, the hotel is probably one of the most important architectural precedents for all subsequent hotels in Bali.

Touted by the management for "its authenticity and its unique Balinese ambience", Bali Hyatt demonstrates convincingly how the architecture of a large hotel can assume an unobtrusive but complementary role in the landscape.

Designed by the Hong Kong-based Palmer and Turner, the simple architecture is successfully integrated into 15 hectares of spectacular landscaped gardens overflowing with orchids, hibiscus, frangipani and bougainvillaea. These gardens, sensitively designed oases full of surprises, add immeasurably to the ambience of the hotel.

In 1981, a new phase of planting and design was carried out by landscape architect Michael White, his associate Ketut Marsa and a large team of gardeners. Stone carvings and other objects by Bali's renowned sculptors were added to complement the brilliant displays of tropical abundance. Plants were grouped in masses of similar species to create interesting patterns.

This concept of lush landscaping was further reinforced by the establishment of the Tropical Horticultural Garden of decorative plants in 1983 which houses the hotel's amazing collection of tropical plants. Many of these plants were initially brought from Singapore and Hawaii and cultivated here before being introduced throughout the gardens of Bali.

The architecture of the hotel is fundamentally straightforward and manages to preserve in the interiors the languorous feeling of its beautiful landscaped gardens. Its low-key guestroom blocks are housed in three internal courts. Architecturally undistinguished, the single-loaded corridors overlook these lushly landscaped courtyards.

The lobby pavilion is a voluminous structure inspired by the traditional Balinese meeting hall. Supported by timber columns, the huge thatched roof is a unique feature amongst large hotels. Open-sided, the space is surprisingly cool and comfortable. It forms the focal point of most activities.

(previous page):
Balina Serai, Candi Desa.
(vorberige Seite):
Balina Serai, Candi Desa.
(page précédente):
Balina Serai, Candi Desa.

Bali Hyatt, Sanur, Bali

Das Bali Hyatt wurde 1973 eröffnet, es hat 390 Zimmer und liegt in Sanur, einst ein Fischerdorf und die Heimat brahmanischer Priester. Es wurde auf einer alten Kokosnußplantage mit über 2000 Bäumen und einem 500 Meter langen Sandstrand gebaut. Vermutlich ist dieses Hotel das wichtigste architektonische Vorbild aller späteren Bauten auf Bali.

Das Management des Bali Hyatt wirbt mit der »Authentizität und der einzigartigen balinesischen Atmosphäre«, und hier wird überzeugend demonstriert, wie die Architektur eines großen Hotels eine unaufdringliche, ergänzende Rolle in einer Landschaft spielen kann.

Entworfen von Palmer and Turner, Hongkong, ist die schlichte Architektur erfolgreich in ein Gelände von 15 Hektar mit großartig gestalteten Gärten einbezogen worden. Hier blühen Orchideen, Hibiskus, Jasmin und Bougainvilleas in Hülle und Fülle, und diese Gärten, einfühlsam als Oasen voller Überraschungen angelegt, tragen viel zu der Atmosphäre des Hotels bei.

1981 führten Landschaftsarchitekt Michael White, sein Partner Ketut Marge und ein großes Gärtnerteam eine Neugestaltung durch. Steinskulpturen und andere Objekte von Balis bekannten Bildhauern wurden als Ergänzung zu der tropischen Fülle aufgestellt. Pflanzen derselben Art wurden in großen Gruppen gepflanzt, so daß interessante Muster entstanden.

Dieses Konzept der üppigen Landschaftsgestaltung wurde 1983 erweitert. Damals entstand der Tropical Horticultural Garden, ein Garten für dekorative Pflanzen, in dem die beachtliche Sammlung tropischer Pflanzen des Bali Hyatt untergebracht ist. Viele dieser Pflanzen wurden ursprünglich aus Singapur und Hawaii geholt und hier weitergezüchtet. Inzwischen findet man sie in vielen Gärten Balis.

Die Architektur des Hotels ist sehr klar, und es gelingt, auch im Inneren die Stimmung der wunderschönen Gärten zu erhalten. Die architektonisch wenig interessanten, in gedämpften Farben gehaltenen Häuser mit den Gästezimmern liegen an drei Innenhöfen. Von den Korridoren aus schaut man in die Gärten.

Der Pavillon mit der Lobby ist ein riesiger Bau nach dem Vorbild der traditionellen balinesischen Gemeinschaftshalle. Das große, von Holzsäulen getragene Strohdach ist einzigartig unter den großen Hotels. Die Lobby ist nach allen Seiten offen,

Bali Hyatt, Sanur, Bali

Ouvert en 1973, le Bali Hyatt compte 390 chambres. Il se trouve à Sanur, ancien village de pêcheurs et lieu de résidence de prêtres brahmanes. Construit sur le site d'une ancienne plantation de cocotiers de plus de 2000 arbres bordée de 500 mètres de plage de sable blanc, l'hôtel constitue sans doute l'un des précédents architecturaux les plus importants pour tous les hôtels édifiés par la suite.

Vanté par la direction pour "son authenticité et son ambiance typiquement balinaise", le Bali Hyatt est la preuve convaincante que l'architecture d'un grand hôtel peut non seulement s'intégrer de façon discrète dans le paysage, mais aussi y jouer un rôle complémentaire.

Conçue par le bureau d'architectes Palmer and Turner de Hong Kong, l'architecture simple de l'hôtel s'insère avec art dans les 15 hectares de splendides jardins paysagers où abondent orchidées, hibiscus, frangipaniers et bougainvilliers. Oasis conçues avec raffinement et regorgeant de surprises, ces jardins constituent un atout remarquable pour l'atmosphère de l'hôtel.

En 1981, une nouvelle phase de plantation et de composition a été exécutée par toute une équipe de jardiniers placée sous la direction du paysagiste Michael White et de son associé Ketut Marsa. Des sculptures et autres objets réalisés par des artistes de renom balinais sont venus compléter ce splendide déploiement de végétation tropicale. Les plantes ont été regroupées en buissons de variétés analogues, créant ainsi des compositions florales originales.

Cette idée de jardin paysager luxuriant a été renforcée ensuite par la création en 1983 du Jardin Tropical Horticole de plantes décoratives qui rassemble l'extraordinaire collection de plantes tropicales de l'hôtel. Pour nombre d'entre elles, ces plantes proviennent de Singapour et de Hawaii, et ont d'abord été cultivées ici avant d'être introduites dans tous les jardins de Bali.

L'architecture de l'hôtel est simple par essence, mais sait préserver à l'intérieur l'impression de langueur suscitée par la merveilleuse composition des jardins. L'ensemble discret des chambres est réparti en trois cours intérieures. Construit sur le même modèle architectural, les galeries à claire-voie donnent sur le foisonnement végétal des jardins.

Le pavillon qui abrite la réception est un édifice imposant, construit sur le modèle des salles publiques traditionnelles

A stone carving provides the backdrop to the spa pool.

Eine Steinskulptur bildet den Hintergrund für ein Schwimmbecken.

Des reliefs sculptés constituent la toile de fond de la piscine.

The hotel was closed for renovation and a general facelift programme during the latter half of 1994. Hirsch Bedner and Associates was commissioned as interior designers for the rejuvenation of all existing guestrooms. The hotel's US$12 million restoration project retains much of the original character and atmosphere, yet augmenting and upgrading facilities to keep abreast of new developments in the hotel industry.

The highlight of the renovation programme was the transformation of 50 superior rooms into the deluxe Regency Club class. Intricate batik and ikat fabrics are used in a rich palette of colours for upholstery and wall-hangings. A new Regency Club Lounge was also constructed over an artificial lake, amidst the existing gardens.

The most impressive landscaped feature of the hotel is probably the pool deck, where a replica of Goa Gajah, a famous tourist's attraction, has been carved out of stone and used as a waterfall entrance to an artificial cave. Located a stone's throw away from the main lobby, the Telaga Naga is a delightful restaurant set in beautifully landscaped grounds.

Despite being one of the early forerunners of hotels in Bali, the Bali Hyatt is still arguably one of the most well-designed hotels. Its gardens demonstrate the possibilities and potential of architecture playing a secondary, but critical supporting role, to landscape design in the tropics. They are convincingly integrated with the built forms, capturing both the spirit and the romance of Balinese landscape design.

überraschend kühl und bequem und dient als Treffpunkt für viele Aktivitäten.

Im zweiten Halbjahr 1994 war das Hotel wegen Renovierung und einer allgemeinen Verschönerung geschlossen. Hirsch Bedner and Associates hatten als Innenarchitekten den Auftrag, die vorhandenen Gästezimmer zu modernisieren. Auch nach der Renovierung für 12 Millionen US-Dollar ist viel von dem ursprünglichen Charakter und der Atmosphäre erhalten geblieben. Gleichzeitig hat man neue Entwicklungen der Hotel-Industrie berücksichtigt.

Höhepunkt des Renovierungsprogramms war die Umwandlung von 50 Zimmern der gehobenen Klasse in Unterkünfte de Luxe. Für Polster und Wandbehänge wurden Batikstoffe in vielen Farben verwendet. Mitten in bereits vorhandenen Gärten wurde über einem künstlichen See die neue Regency Club Lounge gebaut.

Am eindrucksvollsten wurde wohl der Pool-Bereich gestaltet. Eine Nachbildung der Touristenattraktion Goa Gaja wurde in Stein geschlagen. Von hier aus stürzt ein Wasserfall in eine künstliche Höhle. Einen Steinwurf entfernt liegt das Restaurant Telaga Naga in wunderschön gestalteter Umgebung.

Das Bali Hyatt ist ein früher Vorgänger der heutigen Hotels auf Bali, aber es gehört mit Sicherheit zu den schönsten. Die Gärten zeigen, welche Möglichkeiten die Architektur bei der Landschaftsgestaltung in den Tropen hat, wenn sie eine untergeordnete, kritisch begleitende Rolle spielt. Gärten und Bauten sind eine überzeugende Verbindung eingegangen und fangen Geist und Romantik der balinesischen Landschaftsarchitektur ein.

A replica of Goa Gajah, a famous tourist attraction, has been carved out of stone and used as a waterfall entrance.

Eine steinerne Nachbildung der Touristenattraktion Goa Gaja dient als Öffnung für einen Wasserfall.

Une réplique de Goa Gajah, une célèbre curiosité touristique, a été sculptée dans la pierre et forme la bouche d'une cascade.

balinaises. Posé sur des colonnes de bois, l'énorme toit de chaume n'a pas d'égal dans les autres grands hôtels. Ouvert sur tous les côtés, le pavillon, étonnamment frais et confortable, constitue le cœur de la plupart des activités.

L'hôtel a été fermé pour des travaux de réfection et une remise à neuf générale pendant la seconde moitié de 1994. Le décorateur Hirsch Bedner et son équipe ont été ainsi chargés de réaménager toutes les chambres. Le projet de rénovation de l'hôtel, qui aura coûté quelque 12 millions de dollars, a su conserver le caractère et l'atmosphère d'origine tout en développant et modernisant les services, afin de tenir compte des dernières innovations de l'hôtellerie.

La transformation de 50 chambres haut de gamme en la somptueuse classe Regency Club constitue l'apogée du programme de rénovation. Les *batiks* et *ikats* raffinés dont les murs sont tendus ou décorés, offrent une riche palette de couleurs. Un nouveau salon Regency Club a également été construit au-dessus d'un lac artificiel, au milieu des jardins.

Un des aménagements de l'hôtel les plus spectaculaires est sans doute le promontoire où une réplique de Goa Gajah, une célèbre curiosité touristique, a été sculptée dans la pierre et dont la cascade rafraîchit l'entrée d'une grotte artificielle. Situé à quelques minutes à peine du principal pavillon de réception, le Telaga Naga est un charmant restaurant caché au fond d'un superbe parc.

Bien que le Bali Hyatt figure parmi les premiers hôtels construits à Bali, il est sans doute l'un des mieux conçus. Ses jardins révèlent comment l'architecture peut jouer un rôle à la fois secondaire, mais non moins crucial dans la conception de paysages sous les tropiques. Ils forment un ensemble harmonieux avec les bâtiments, reflétant à la fois l'esprit et le charme de l'art paysager à Bali.

The other side of the entrance to an artificial cave is framed by another elaborate stone carving.

Auf der anderen Seite des Eingangs zu einer künstlichen Höhle steht eine weitere kunstvolle Skulptur.

Un magnifique relief sculpté décore l'autre côté de l'entrée de la grotte artificielle.

The pool bar is located at the centre of the gardens.

Die Pool-Bar liegt mitten im Garten.

Le bar de la piscine se dresse au milieu des jardins.

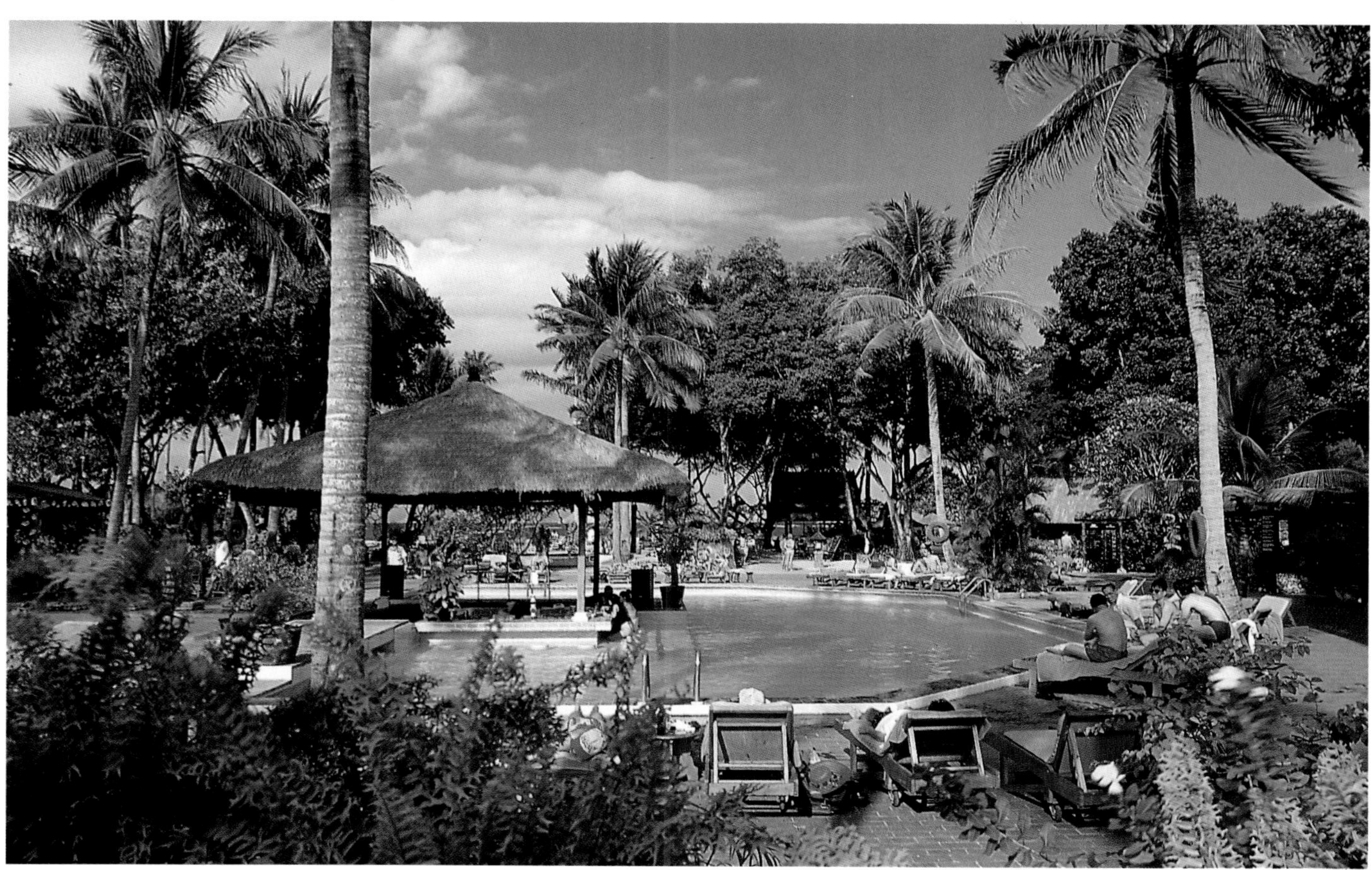

View of the pool area from the wide lawn.

Der Pool-Bereich vom großen Rasen aus gesehen.

Vue de la piscine depuis la vaste pelouse.

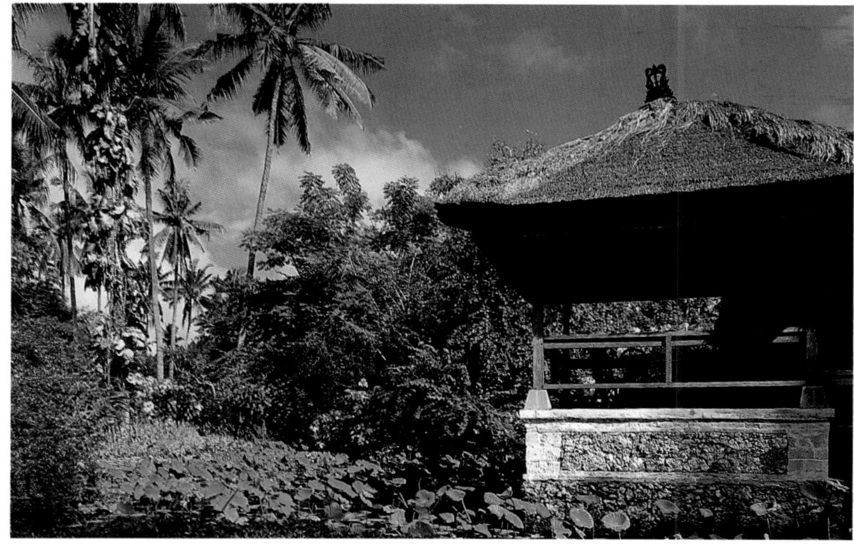

The Telaga Naga is a charming restaurant surrounded by lotus ponds.

Das bezaubernde Restaurant Telaga Naga ist von Seerosenteichen umgeben.

Le Telaga Naga est un charmant restaurant entouré de bassins de lotus.

Located a stone's throw away from the main lobby, the Telaga Naga is a separate pavilion set in beautifully landscaped grounds.

Der Pavillon mit dem Telaga Naga liegt nur einen Steinwurf entfernt von der Haupthalle und ist von wunderschöner Landschaft umgeben.

Situé à proximité de la réception principale, le pavillon du Telaga Naga se cache dans un parc superbe.

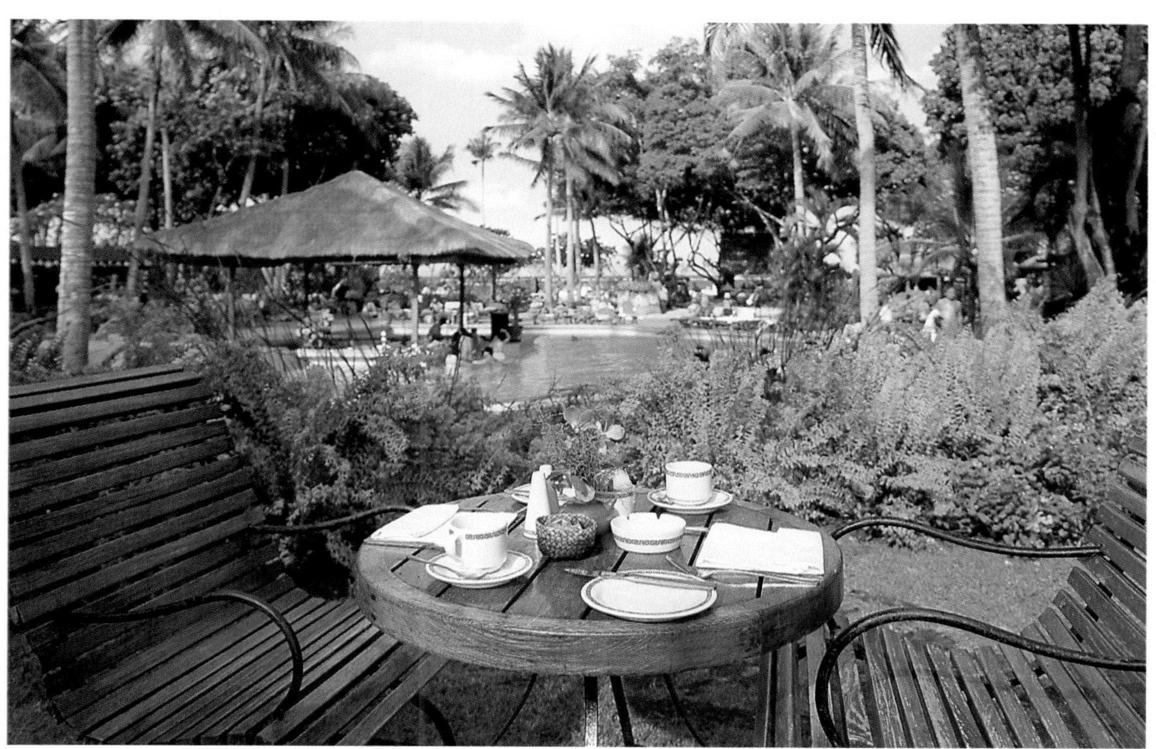

Outdoor breakfast areas overlook the swimming pool.

Frühstück im Freien mit Blick auf den Swimmingpool.

Les hôtes peuvent prendre le petit déjeuner sur des terrasses surplombant la piscine.

The restaurant is housed under a huge pyramidal roof supported by traditional structural systems.

Das große Pyramidendach des Restaurants wird von traditionellen Konstruktionen getragen.

Le restaurant est coiffé d'un immense toit pyramidal avec une armature de style traditionnel.

Bali Imperial Hotel, Legian, Bali

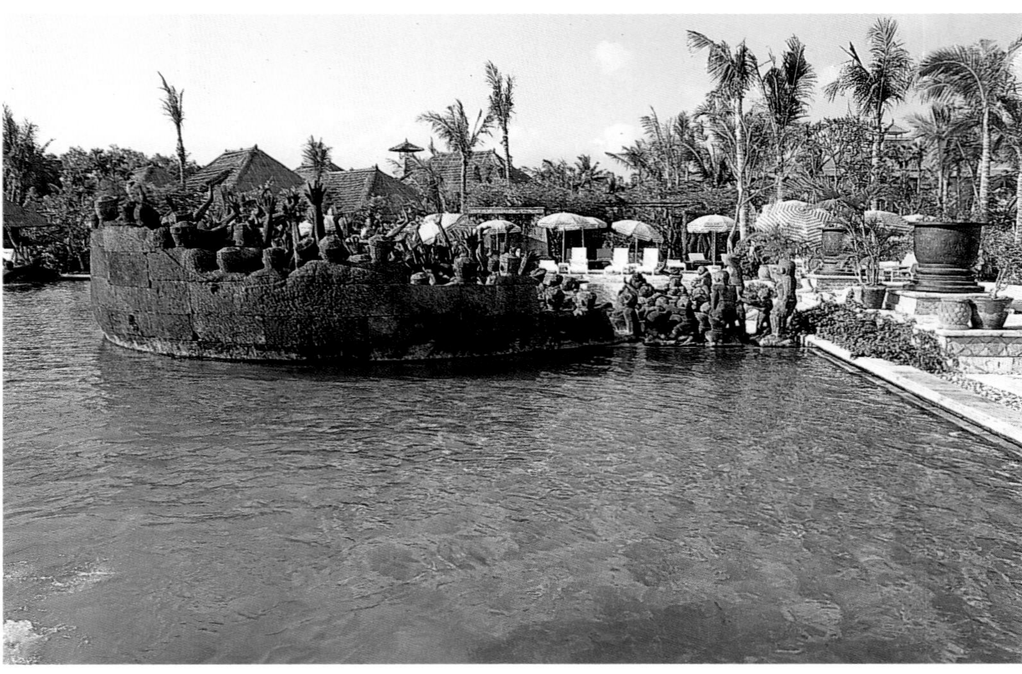

The open amphitheatre is fringed by 60 andesite figures depicting the 'kecak' dance.

Das offene Amphitheater wird von 60 Andesin-Figuren gerahmt, die den ›kecak‹–Tanz darstellen.

L'amphithéâtre est entouré de 60 statues en andésite représentant la danse 'kecak'.

Located at Legian Beach, Seminyak, the resort lies between the town of Kuta and the famous Tanah Lot Temple. Managed by the Imperial Hotel Tokyo, it covers over 4.5 hectares of beachfront property amidst verdant landscaping.

There are altogether 138 rooms, among which are seven maisonette suites, one garden suite, 16 villas and a huge double-storey Imperial Villa. The main block of the hotel was designed by Atelier 6, while the villas were designed by Alan Gilbert. Bensley Design Studios was responsible for the master planning and the landscape design.

Most of the villas have their own private pools and jacuzzis. Other leisure facilities include two swimming pools and a children's pool, as well as two tennis courts and a mini-putting green.

The lobby is filled with highly ornamental details. Elaborate patterns on the granite floors also contribute to the profusion of details. Fully air-conditioned, it evokes the ambience of an urban hotel rather than a tropical resort. A glass-enclosed lift further adds to this sense of business-like politeness.

Most of the guestrooms have breeze-swept views across the gardens to the surf and beyond. These rooms, with single-loaded corridors, are located in standard three-storey high blocks that are dispersed across the grounds in a staggered layout. Capped by orange-tiled roofs, these concrete blocks are not particularly outstanding or different in terms of architectural quality.

However, the grounds are beautifully landscaped. Different varieties of foliage are grouped in various manners to frame views, obstruct views and soften the architecture. Designed by Bill Bensley, the landscape is a pleasure to experience.

There is an open amphitheatre fringed by a dense mass of 60 andesite figures depicting the 'kecak' dance. This centrepiece of the landscape feature protrudes out into the main swimming pool, providing an animated qualtiy to the surroundings. During performances, dancers adorn costumes in a special room under the pool and appear on stage amidst the kecak dance setting. Water features play a prominent role here, both in the form of decorative pools and swimming pools, as evidenced by eight swimming pools and 12 jacuzzi spas. Delightful wall reliefs and reclining figurines further add a touch of whimsy to these water features.

Bali Imperial Hotel, Legian, Bali

Das Hotel liegt am Legian Beach, Seminyak, zwischen der Stadt Kuta und dem berühmten Tempel Tanah Lot und wird vom Imperial Hotel Tokyo betrieben. Strände und eine grüne Landschaft bedecken eine Fläche von mehr als 4,5 Hektar.

Die Anlage verfügt über 138 Zimmer, darunter sieben Maisonette-Suiten, eine Garten-Suite, 16 Villen und die riesige einstöckige Imperial Villa. Atelier 6 entwarf die Haupthäuser, Alan Gilbert die Villen, Bensley Design Studios waren verantwortlich für die Gesamtplanung und die Landschaftsarchitektur.

Die meisten Villen verfügen über eigene Pools und Whirlpools. Zu den weiteren Freizeitangeboten gehören zwei Swimmingpools, ein Kinderbecken, zwei Tennisplätze und ein kleines Putting green.

Viele dekorative Einzelheiten schmücken die Lobby. Kunstvoll gemusterte Steinböden unterstreichen den Eindruck von Luxus. Das voll klimatisierte Haus hat eher die Atmosphäre eines Stadthotels als die einer tropischen Ferienanlage. Ein gläserner Aufzug trägt zu diesem Eindruck bei.

Die meisten Gästezimmer bieten einen Blick auf die Brandung und das offene Meer. Diese Gästezimmer befinden sich in zweistöckigen Standardhäusern, die gestaffelt auf dem Gelände verteilt sind. Diese Betonhäuser mit den orangefarbenen Ziegeldächern zeichnen sich nicht gerade durch eine hervorragende oder eigenwillige Architektur aus.

Jedoch ist das Gelände wunderschön gestaltet. Unterschiedliche Laubbäume stehen in Gruppen zusammen und rahmen Ausblicke ein oder versperren den Blick, so daß die Architektur weicher wirkt. Von Bill Bensley entworfen, ist diese Landschaft eine reine Freude.

Das offene Amphitheater ist umgeben von 60 dichtgedrängten Andesin-Figuren, die den *kecak*-Tanz darstellen. Dieser Mittelpunkt der Landschaft ragt in den Hauptswimmingpool hinein und belebt die Umgebung. Wenn Aufführungen stattfinden, legen die Tänzer ihre Kostüme in einem Spezialraum unter dem Pool an und erscheinen dann mitten in der *kecak*-Tanzgruppe auf der Bühne. Wasser spielt hier eine große Rolle, in Zierteichen, acht Swimming-pools und zwölf Whirlpools. Hübsche Wandreliefs und Figurinen verleihen all diesen Wasseranlagen etwas Phantastisches.

Bali Imperial Hotel, Legian, Bali

Situé sur la plage Legian à Seminyak, le complexe hôtelier s'étend entre la ville de Kuta et le célèbre temple de Tanah Lot. Il est administré par l'Imperial Hotel Tokyo et occupe plus de 4,5 hectares de bord de mer entouré d'un paysage verdoyant.

Le complexe comprend 138 unités d'hébergement dont sept suites en duplex, une suite-jardin, 16 villas et la Villa Impériale qui est une immense demeure à un étage. Le bureau Atelier 6 a conçu l'édifice principal de l'hôtel tandis que les villas sont l'œuvre d'Alain Gilbert. La firme Bensley Design Studios a été chargée du schéma directeur et du dessin du paysage.

La plupart des villas sont dotées d'une piscine et d'un jacuzzi privés. Les aménagements pour les loisirs comprennent deux piscines, un bassin pour les enfants, deux courts de tennis et un mini-putting green.

La réception a une multitude de détails ornementaux. Des dessins recherchés sur le sol de granit ajoutent à la profusion des détails. Entièrement climatisé, le hall présente davantage l'atmosphère d'un grand hôtel dans une métropole que celle d'un lieu de villégiature tropicale. Un ascenseur en verre contribue également à l'impression d'élégance citadine.

La plupart des chambres jouissent de vues sur les jardins et le rivage d'où souffle une brise marine. Elles se rangent le long de galeries à claire-voie et sont situées dans des édifices standard de deux étages dispersés dans le parc. Ces constructions en béton aux toits de tuiles oranges ne sont pas exceptionnelles et n'offrent rien de particulier au niveau de leur architecture.

Cela n'est pas le cas pour le parc à l'aménagement remarquable. Diverses variétés de plantes sont disposées de façon à encadrer ou obstruer des vues et à adoucir l'architecture. Le paysage dessiné par Bill Bensley, est un véritable plaisir des yeux.

Un amphithéâtre est entouré de 60 statues imposantes en andésite représentant la danse *kecak*. Ce point principal du paysage surplombe la piscine principale et anime les alentours. Pendant les représentations, les danseurs se changent dans une loge située sous la piscine et apparaissent sur scène au milieu du décor de danse *kecak*. L'eau joue un rôle prédominant qui se manifeste dans des bassins décoratifs, huit piscines et 12 jacuzzis.

An adaption of a traditional bell-tower is used as a landscape feature.

Eine Nachbildung eines traditionellen Glockenturms ist ein Element in der Landschaftsgestaltung.

La reproduction d'un campanile traditionnel est un élément essentiel du paysage.

Lavishly detailed, the interiors of the rooms are decorated with all kinds of Balinese artefacts. The wide palette of colours and finishes, intended to evoke opulence, certainly has a strong eclectic touch. Some elements seem gratuitously styled. Architecturally, the most interesting part of the resort is the private villas that offer both secluded privacy and Balinese opulence.

Enclosed by luxuriant foliage and high stone walls, the villas and their private gardens are designed to be introspective. While all the gardens use a similar palette of materials, they have their own distinct character. There is an 'L'-shaped pool , 20 metres in each direction, with a villa located at each end of the 'L'. The Imperial Villa features a long black lap pool with an andesite, Sri Lankan-inspired spa at one end.

The use of natural materials like *paras rabo, paras kerobokan* and *batu palimanan*, are well handled and the sense of tactility is certainly enhanced by sensitive detailing. Traditional thatched roofs and volcanic stones are used extensively. The level of craft is applaudable. The landscaping is lush and succeeds in many instances in screening out the views of the guestroom blocks from within the villas.

The Bali Imperial Hotel is a good example of an increasingly popular trend of mixing standard guestroom block design with a mix of private villas. On the whole, it is a resort that is perhaps fastidiously detailed and done with celebratory exuberance.

Die Inneneinrichtungen sind großzügig mit balinesischen Kunstwerken ausgestattet. Die Vielfalt von Farben und Materialien soll den Eindruck von Überfluß erwecken, bedient sich aber zweifellos bereits vorhandener künstlerischer Formen. Manche Elemente wirken wenig überzeugend. Architektonisch am interessantesten sind zweifellos die Privatvillen, die sowohl Abgeschiedenheit als auch balinesischen Luxus bieten.

Unter dichtem Laub und hinter hohen Steinmauern verborgen, sorgen diese Villen für Privatatmosphäre. Während in allen Gärten dieselben Materialien verwendet wurden, haben diese Villen einen ganz eigenen Charakter. Es gibt einen Pool in L-Form, 20 Meter lang in jeder Richtung, und jeweils an den Enden des L liegt eine Villa. Zur Imperial Villa gehört ein langer, schwarzer Pool mit einem von Sri Lanka beeinflußten Bad aus Andesin.

Natürliche Materialien werden gut und einfühlsam eingesetzt, und sie schaffen Atmosphäre. Überall sind die traditionell gedeckten Dächer und Vulkangestein zu sehen. Und das Niveau der Handwerkskunst ist sehr zu loben. Die Landschaftsgestaltung ist üppig, und sie kann an vielen Stellen verhindern, daß man von den Privatvillen aus die Häuser mit den Gästezimmern sieht.

Das Bali Imperial Hotel ist ein gutes Beispiel für die steigende Beliebtheit der Verbindung von Standardhäusern mit Gästezimmern und Privatvillen. Insgesamt handelt es sich hier um eine Ferienanlage, die anspruchsvoll geplant und luxuriös ausgeführt ist.

Reclining figurines add an animated quality to the poolside.

Skulpturen ruhender Mädchen beleben die Pool-Landschaft.

Des statues allongées apportent une note fantaisiste aux plans d'eau.

De jolis reliefs et des statues dans des positions différentes apportent une touche de fantaisie aux plans d'eau.

Les chambres sont décorées d'une profusion d'objets balinais. Le vaste éventail de couleurs et de finitions, destiné à créer une atmosphère opulente, paraît très syncrétique. Certains éléments semblent superflus. Quant à l'architecture, les villas privées qui offrent à la fois intimité et opulence balinaise, constituent la partie la plus intéressante du complexe.

Les villas sont cachées derrière une végétation luxuriante et de hauts murs et regardent vers l'intérieur. Les jardins ont chacun leur propre caractère, bien que conçus avec les mêmes matériaux. Une villa se dresse à chaque bout d'une piscine en forme de "L", mesurant vingt mètres dans chaque longueur. La Villa Imperial possède une longue piscine noire avec une andésite; le style de Sri Lanka a inspiré le décor à un bout du plan d'eau.

Les matériaux naturels tels que le *paras rabo*, le *paras kerobokan* et le *batu palimanan* sont très bien employés, tandis que la recherche du détail rehausse le sens de la tangabilité. Un grand usage est fait des toits en chaume traditionnels et des roches volcaniques. On peut en applaudir le niveau d'exécution. Les aménagements paysagers sont luxuriants et remplissent leur fonction de rideau entre les édifices abritant les chambres d'hôtel et les villas.

Le Bali Imperial Hotel illustre positivement la tendance de plus en plus populaire à réunir des chambres d'hôtel standard et des villas privées. Dans l'ensemble, c'est un complexe construit avec une grande exubérance de formes et une recherche un peu fastidieuse du détail.

Banyan Tree Bintan est à environ 45 kilomètres de Singapour. Il est situé sur un site côtier en hauteur de 240 hectares, dans une baie à Tanjong Said sur Bintan Islands. 27 villas de style balinais traditionnel ont d'abord été construites. 13 autres villas et un hôtel 5 étoiles de hauteur limitée, qui comprendra 200 chambres, sont prévus d'ici à 1996.

A close-up view of the andesite figures at the amphitheatre.

Nahansicht der Andesin-Figuren des Amphitheaters.

Vue rapprochée des statues en andésite de l'amphithéâtre.

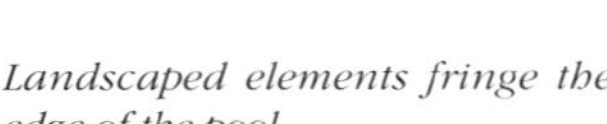

Landscaped elements fringe the edge of the pool.

Die Landschaftselemente fügen sich zu einer Bühnenbild-ähnlichen Szenerie.

Les caractéristiques du paysage s'harmonisent en un superbe décor.

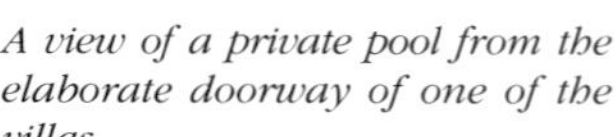

A view of a private pool from the elaborate doorway of one of the villas.

Ein Blick auf den privaten Pool vom Eingang einer Villa aus.

Vue d'une piscine privée depuis l'entrée sculptée d'une des villas.

An L-shaped swimming pool links two units of private villas.

Ein Blick auf den privaten Pool vom Eingang einer Villa aus.

Une piscine en "L" relie deux villas.

(opposite page):
A rest pavilion located in the gardens of one of the private villas.

(gegenüberliegende Seite):
Ein Ruhe-Pavillon im Garten einer Privatvilla.

(page ci-contre):
Un pavillon de repos dans les jardins d'une villa privée.

Enclosed by stone walls, the lush garden setting of the private villa offers both secluded privacy and Balinese opulence.

Umgeben von Steinmauern, bietet die üppige Gartenlandschaft der Privatvillen sowohl abgeschiedene Privatspäre als auch balinesische Opulenz.

Entourés de murs, les jardins luxurianis des villas privées allient l'opulence balinaise à l'intimité.

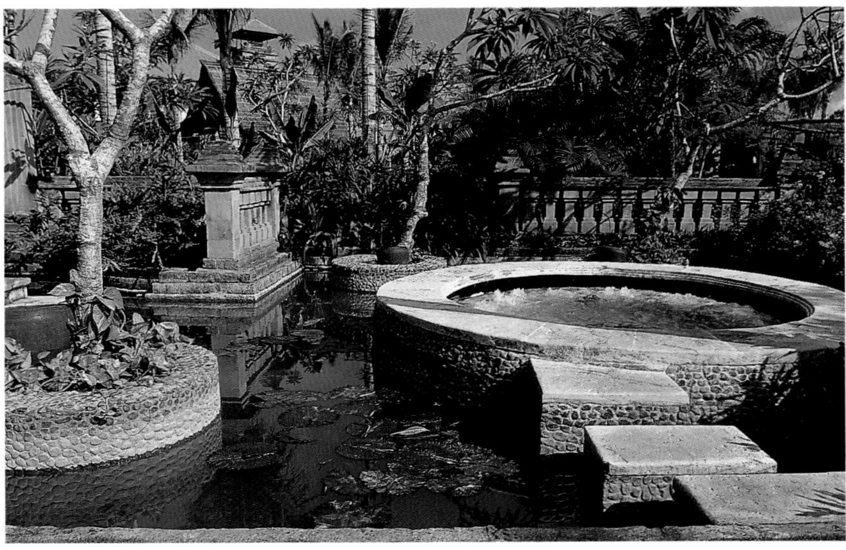

Each of the villa is provided with an outdoor jacuzzi located in the middle of landscaped pools.

Jede der Villen verfügt über einen Whirlpool inmitten der in die Landschaft integrierten Swimming-pools.

Chaque villa possède un jacuzzi situé au milieu de la piscine intégrée dans le paysage.

Bali Intercontinental Resort, Jimbaran, Bali

Based on the theme of water palaces, the hotel features several huge pools and water elements.

Das Hotel ist nach dem Vorbild von Wasserpalästen gebaut und verfügt über mehrere große Teiche und Wasserelemente.

Conçu d'après les "palais d'eau", l'hôtel comprend plusieurs piscines immenses et une multitude d'autres éléments aquatiques.

Located at Jimbaran Bay, the Bali Intercontinental Resort has a capacity of 451 rooms, with 14 hectares of beachfront. The luxury resort is owned by Mr. Bambang Trihatmodjo, whose company, PT Bimantara Citra, hopes to attract international sporting events to the resort.

The huge project was designed by Hendra Hadiprana of PT Grahacipta Hadiprana. Hadiprana , a widely respected authority on Balinese and Javanese culture, directed local craftsmen to interpret their cultural heritage in the context of a mega-resort.

The suitably dignified resort is a low rise four-storey structure that is sensibly arranged, with most of the 368 standard rooms having a view of the bay. The design has four conventional "fingers" directed towards the beach so that most of the rooms and public areas have views of the sea.

Occupying key locations throughtout the resort are 58 split-level Loft Rooms, each a generous 90 square metres in size. There are double and king-size bedrooms, ten junior suites, nine executive suites, four Japanese suites and two presidential suites.

Food and beverage facilities include an informal restaurant, a continental restaurant, a Japanese restaurant with sushi bar and teppanyaki tables, an Oriental seafood restaurant, an informal outdoor restaurant, a casual pub and a beachfront snack bar.

There are also extensive recreational facilities like three swimming pools, three outdoor jacuzzis, an amphitheatre, six tennis courts, three squash courts and a golf driving range. These are all set within an Arcadian setting that is overwhelming in scale. Located next to the beach is the main pool and a children's pool. This pool is huge and forms the main pivotal point in the design of the landscape. Water courts and water features are also extensively used as part of the landscape concept. The resort also has its own helicopter pad.

According to the architect, the design is a mix of the simplicity inherent in Balinese architecture and the formality of Javanese court architecture. Hence the reception lobby evokes a certain pomposity that is obviously intentional. It is a space of great luminosity and grand gesture. An interesting attempt at fusing two distinctive architectural heritage in a celebratory way, the outcome is both lavish and well-mannered, achieving a cheerful monumentalism.

Bali Intercontinental Resort, Jimbaran, Bali

Das Bali Intercontinental Resort an der Jimbaran Bay verfügt über 451 Zimmer und hat 14 Hektar Strandfläche. Die Luxusanlage gehört Mr. Bambang Trihatmodjo, dessen Firma, PT Bimantara Citra, hofft, Ausrichter von internationalen Sportveranstaltungen zu werden.

Entwickelt wurde das umfangreiche Projekt von Hendra Hadiprana von der PT Grahacipta Hadiprana. Er ist eine anerkannte Autorität auf dem Gebiet der Kultur Balis und Javas und leitete einheimische Handwerker dazu an, ihr kulturelles Erbe bei der Errichtung einer Mega-Anlage einzusetzen.

Die ausgesprochen würdevolle Anlage ist ein dreistöckiger Bau, der den meisten der 368 Standardzimmern einen Blick auf die Bucht bietet. Das wird durch vier »Finger«, d.h. lange, schmale Häuser mit Ausrichtung auf das Meer, erreicht.

An den schönsten Stellen der Anlage befinden sich 58 Lofts mit zwei Ebenen, jede 90 Quadratmeter groß. Es gibt Doppelzimmer, zehn Junior-Suiten, neun Manager-Suiten, vier japanische Suiten und zwei Präsidenten-Suiten. Für das leibliche Wohl sorgen ein zwangloses, ein kontinentales und ein japanisches Restaurant mit Sushi-Bar und Teppanyaki-Tischen, außerdem ein orientalisches Meeresfrüchte-Restaurant, ein zwangloses Restaurant im Freien, ein Pub und eine Snack-Bar.

Die Freizeitangebote sind sehr umfangreich. Es gibt drei Swimmingpools, drei Whirlpools im Freien, ein Amphitheater, sechs Tennisplätze, drei Squash-Plätze und eine Driving Range für Golfer. All das liegt in einer idyllischen Umgebung von wahrhaft überwältigenden Ausmaßen. Der Haupt-Pool und ein Kinderbecken sind dem Strand am nächsten. Dieser riesige Pool ist der Dreh- und Angelpunkt der landschaftlichen Gestaltung. Auch Wasserläufe und Wasserspiele gehören zum landschaftlichen Konzept. Die Anlage hat sogar einen eigenen Landeplatz für Hubschrauber.

Nach Aussage des Architekten ist die Anlage eine Mischung aus der schlichten balinesischen Architektur und der Strenge javanischer Hofarchitektur. Daher wirkt die Empfangshalle auch ein wenig pompös, was wohl beabsichtigt ist. Jedenfalls ist sie ein Raum von strahlender Leuchtkraft und Generosität. Sie stellt einen interessanten Versuch dar, zwei unterschiedliche architektonische Überlieferungen miteinander zu verschmelzen.

Bali Intercontinental Resort, Jimbaran, Bali

Situé dans la baie de Jimbaran, le Bali Intercontinental Resort est un hôtel de 451 chambres, construit sur 14 hectares de terrain en bordure de mer. L'établissement de luxe est la propriété de monsieur Bambang Trihatmodjo dont la société PT Bimantara Citra espère attirer des manifestations sportives internationales à la station balnéaire.

Hendra Hadiprana de PT Grahacipta Hadiprana, qui fait autorité en matière de cultures javanaise et balinaise, a réalisé les plans et dirigé les travaux effectués par des artisans locaux qui ont interprété leur héritage culturel dans le contexte d'un projet de grande envergure.

L'hôtel de grande classe est un édifice de trois étages judicieusement conçu qui abrite 368 chambres standard dont la plupart donnent sur la baie. Les quatre ailes, longues et étroites, étant orientées vers la plage, la plupart des salles et espaces collectifs ont des vues sur la mer.

58 duplex de 90 m^2 occupent des positions-clés au dernier étage de l'établissement. On trouve des chambres à lits jumeaux ou à grand lit, dix suites "juniors", neuf suites de luxe, quatre suites japonaises et deux suites de grand luxe.

L'hôtel comprend un restaurant "simple", un restaurant de cuisine européenne, un restaurant japonais avec un bar à sushi et des tables de teppanyaki, un restaurant oriental offrant des produits de la mer, un restaurant en plein air, un bistro et un snack bar sur la plage.

Les aménagements pour la détente et les loisirs incluent trois piscines, trois jacuzzis en plein air, un amphithéâtre, six courts de tennis, trois courts de squash et un terrain de golf, disséminés dans un vaste décor champêtre. La piscine principale et un bassin pour enfants avoisinent la plage. Cet immense ensemble nautique constitue la charnière dans le dessin du paysage où abondent également les pièces d'eau et les cascades. L'hôtel possède aussi un terrain d'atterrissage pour hélicoptères.

Selon l'architecte, le concept allie la simplicité de l'architecture balinaise à l'architecture imposante des palais javanais. La réception est empreinte d'une certaine solennité sans doute intentionnelle. C'est un espace très généreux et lumineux. Le complexe illustre la démarche visant à marier noblement deux héritages architecturaux distincts; le résultat est un ouvrage aussi imposant que gai, à la fois somptueux et élégant.

The lobby is filled with highly ornamental details and furnished with intricate and elaborate objects from the region.

In der Lobby sind überall Ornamente und so einzigartige wie kunstvolle Objekte der Region zu bewundern.

Des éléments ornementaux et de très beaux meubles de style balinais décorent la réception.

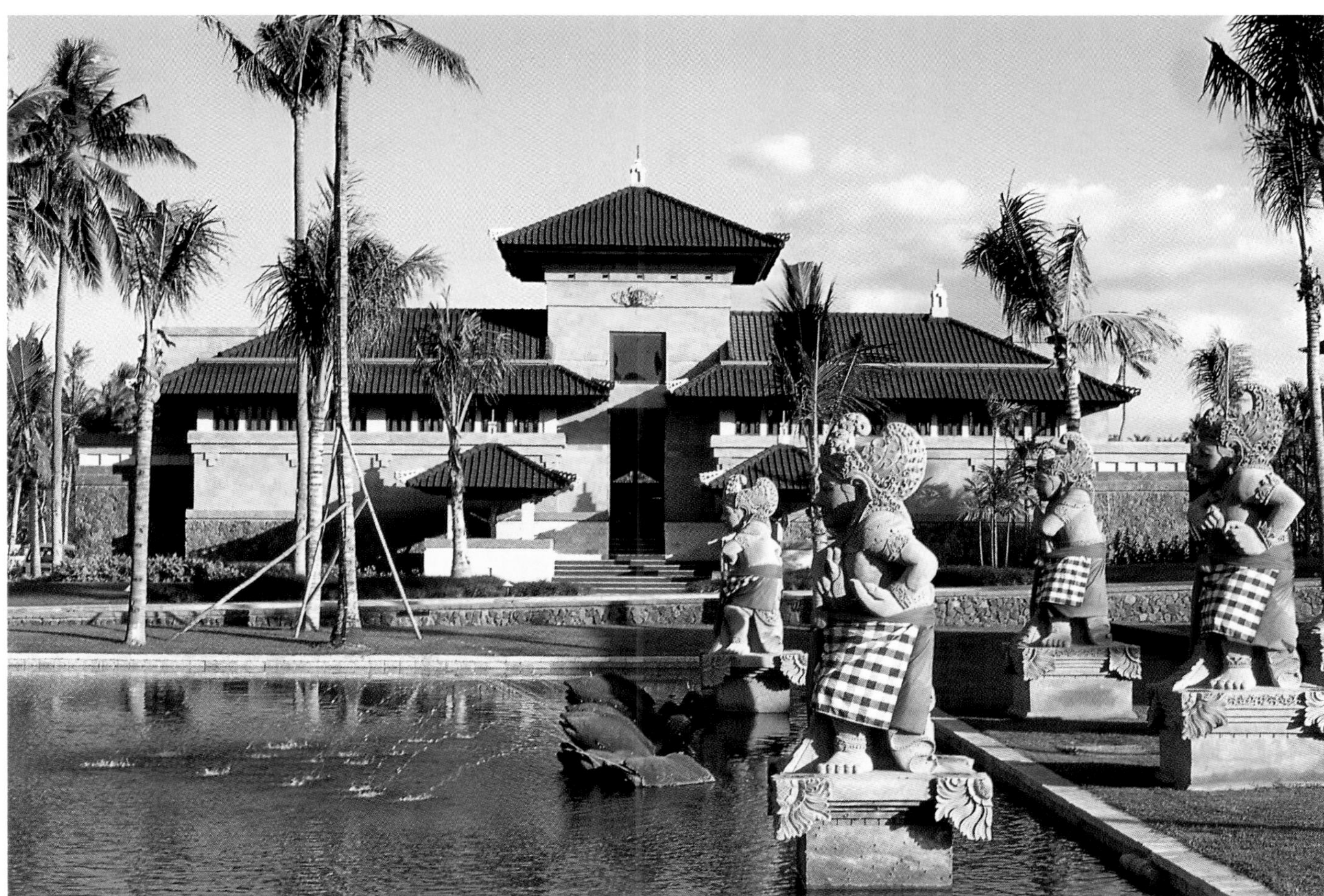

Dispersed throughout the complex are a wide range of sculptural objects and traditional carvings.

Überall auf dem Gelände stehen Skulpturen und traditionelle Schnitzereien.

Une profusion de sculptures et de reliefs en pierre ornement le complexe.

(left):
Plants help to soften the impact of the heavy masonry structure.

(links):
Pflanzen mildern die Schwere der Häuser.

(a gauche):
La végétation adoucit la lourdeur de la maçonnerie.

(right):
Planter boxes are articulated with details taken from traditional Balinese architecture.

(rechts):
Die Balkonkästen sind mit Elementen der traditionellen balinesischen Architektur gestaltet.

(a droite):
Des bacs à plantes présentent des détails d'architecture traditionnelle balinaise.

Pavilions are scattered around different parts of the swimming pools.

Pavillons liegen verstreut an verschiedenen Stellen rund um den Swimmingpool.

Les pavillons sont disséminés autour des piscines.

Cascading water features provide a pervasive background sound throughout the resort's grounds.

Herabstürzendes Wasser liefert das allgegenwärtige Hintergrundgeräusch.

Partout sur le site, on entend le murmure des fontaines.

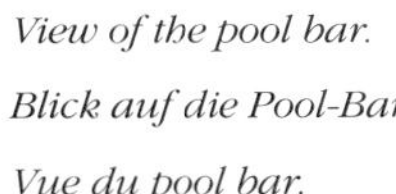

View of the pool bar.

Blick auf die Pool-Bar.

Vue du pool bar.

Vew of the generously proportioned bedroom.

Noch ein Blick auf einen großen Schlafraum.

Une autre vue de la chambre aux dimensions généreuses.

The opulence of the decor is also evident in the bedroom.

Auch der Schlafraum zeichnet sich durch reichhaltiges Dekor aus.

La chambre à coucher a le même décor somptueux.

The interiors of the luxurious suite are highly elaborate and evoke the ambience of an urban hotel.

Die Luxussuite ist kunstvoll eingerichtet und hat die Atmosphäre eines Stadthotels.

La chambre àcoucher a le même décor somptueux.

Balina Serai, Candi Desa, Bali

Located on the east coast of Bali, the Balina Serai is a short distance from Candi Desa, an outpost of rural charm and beautiful beaches.

Known for their distaste for explicit iconography, Kerry Hill Architects do not consciously attempt to achieve a creative interpretation of specific models in all their resort projects. Instead the tendency is inclined towards designing from general principles using a reductionist palette. This approach was similarly used in the design of the Balina Serai, completed in November 1994.

The resort was meant to be a three-star hotel. Sited on a small two-hectare plot of land, it is an interesting experiment in creating a new niche market, where architecture is an important selling point. The reductionist palette of the architect is thus taken to an even more acute level of minimalism, although the result is far from being reductionist.

It must be admitted that, on first impact, the legibility of the planning is less than apparent. One gets the feeling that the formal moves are deliberately very safe. On first impression, the most striking aspect of the building is that it appears uneffacingly too simple and rather reticent, almost too minimal in its details. But it soon became apparent that this is a welcome virtue.

The gross floor area of the resort is approximately 4,500 square metres. There are altogether 56 standard guestrooms of 27 square metres each, and two suites of 54 square metres each. The public areas include an open-sided reception lobby, lounge and a restaurant.

Appreciation of the careful choice of materials and articulation of joints is made much more easier because of the economy of means in which the entire resort is executed. The detailing is everywhere very understated, and demonstrates an impressive use of making the few and relatively cheap materials to achieve maximum effects. Lavish attention is spent on subtle details that dignify simple construction.

The architectural language is developed through exploitation of traditional constructional logic and close considerations of use and site conditions. The carefully proportioned and elegantly articulated blocks are set facing a 20-metre square swimming pool. Each block is immutably related to the surrounding environment and to each other in the

Balina Serai, Candi Desa, Bali

Das Balina Serai an der Ostküste Balis liegt in der Nähe von Candi Desa, einem Ort von ländlichem Charme und mit wunderschönen Stränden.

Kerry Hill Architects sind bekannt für ihre Abneigung gegen übermäßige bildliche Darstellung, und in all ihren Ferienanlagen versuchen sie bewußt nicht, bestimmte Vorbilder kreativ umzudeuten. Statt dessen geht die Planung eher von allgemeinen Prinzipien mit Tendenz zum sparsamen Einsatz der Mittel aus. Das gilt auch für das im November 1994 fertiggestellte Balina Hotel.

Es wurde als Drei-Sterne-Hotel konzipiert, liegt auf einem Gelände von nur zwei Hektar und ist ein interessanter Versuch, eine neue Lücke im Markt zu erschließen, in der Architektur ein wichtiges Verkaufsargument ist.

Zugegeben, das Ziel der Planung ist nicht auf Anhieb erkennbar. Man hat das Gefühl, daß in formalen Dingen auf Nummer Sicher gesetzt wurde. Beim ersten Eindruck ist das Auffälligste an dem Bau, daß er zu schlicht und unauffällig wirkt und sich in den Einzelheiten zu sehr auf ein Minimum beschränkt. Doch schon bald erkennt man, daß dieses eine willkommene Tugend ist.

Das Haus hat eine Fläche von 4500 Quadratmetern. Es gibt 56 Standardzimmer von 27 Quadratmetern und zwei Suiten mit je 54 Quadratmetern. Zu den Gemeinschaftsbereichen gehören eine zur Seite offene Empfangshalle, eine Lounge und ein Restaurant.

Die Sparsamkeit der Mittel in der gesamten Anlage erleichtert es, die sorgfältige Auswahl der Materialien und die Ausführung zu würdigen. Alles ist sehr maßvoll, und es ist eindrucksvoll zu sehen, wie mit den wenigen und relativ billigen Materialien eine optimale Wirkung erzielt wird. Die Sorgfalt, die auf kleine Einzelheiten verwendet wurde, geben der gesamten Anlage eine gewisse Würde.

Die architektonische Sprache ergibt sich aus der Auswertung der Prinzipien traditionellen Bauens und der Berücksichtigung von Nutzung und Lage. Die gut proportionierten und elegant ausgeführten Blocks liegen gegenüber einem 20 Meter langen Swimmingpool. Alle Häuser beziehen sich sowohl auf ihre Umgebung als auch aufeinander, so daß die Gesamtanlage Ruhe ausstrahlt.

Balina Serai, Candi Desa, Bali

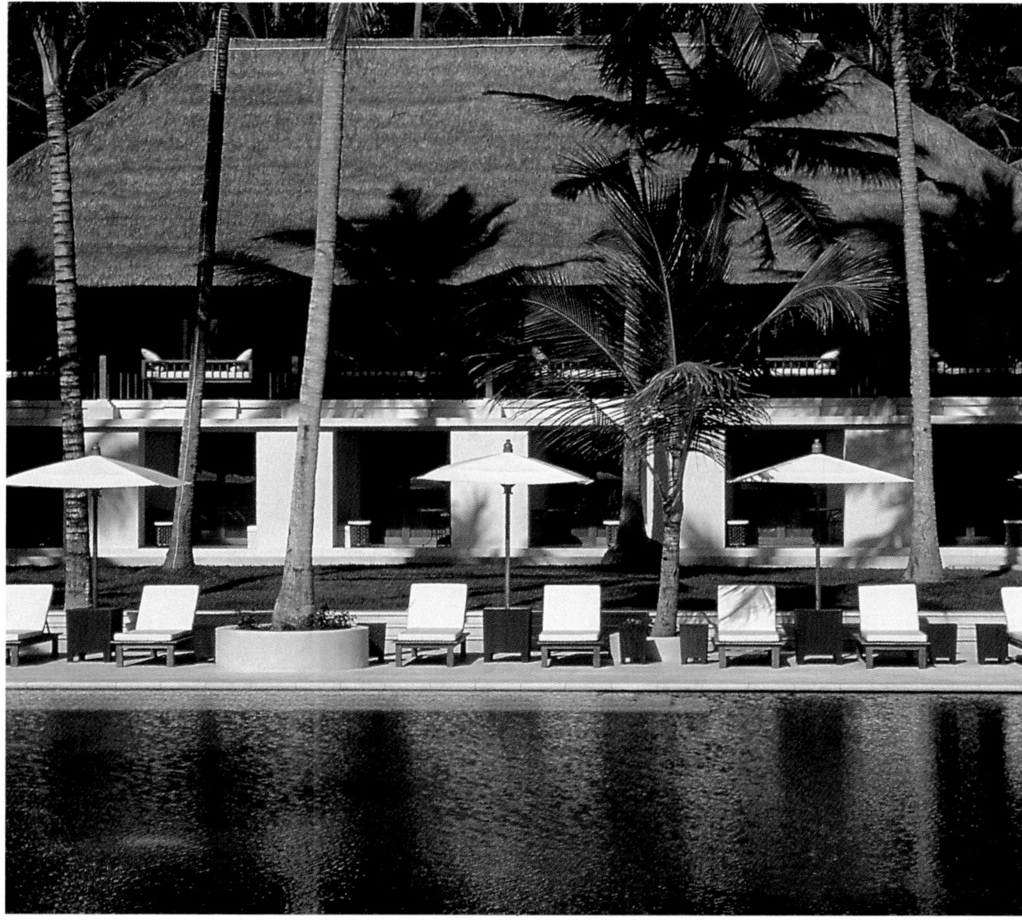

The reductionist palette has produced a simplicity of form, which stands out as tectonic blocks with a strong sense of horizontality counter-balanced by the verticality of the coconut palms.

Die schlichten Formen fügen sich zu Bauteilen mit starker Betonung der Waagerechten zusammen, denen die Kokospalmen ein Gegengewicht zu geben scheinen.

Une recherche du minimalisme a créé une simplicité des formes, évidentes dans l'architecture des édifices dont la ligne horizontale contrebalance la verticalité des cocotiers.

Situé sur la côte orientale de Bali, le Serai Hotel se trouve à proximité de Candi Desa, un endroit au charme champêtre et aux plages magnifiques.

Le bureau Kerry Hill Architects, connu pour refuser l'iconographie explicite, n'essaie pas de réaliser des adaptations créatives de modèles spécifiques dans ses projets de complexes hôteliers. Sa tendance est plutôt de se servir d'un minimum de principes généraux architecturaux. On retrouve ces orientations dans l'architecture du Serai Hotel achevé en novembre 1994.

Il s'agissait de construire un hôtel trois étoiles. Situé sur une petite superficie de deux hectares, le projet est une expérience intéressante qui s'inscrit dans la création d'un nouveau créneau du marché où l'architecture est un facteur important de vente. L'architecte a donc misé sur le minimalisme bien que le résultat final soit loin d'être infime.

Il faut admettre qu'à première vue, on ne réalise pas le bien-fondé du concept. Le choix des formes semble très prévisible et la construction bien trop simple et austère, presque trop dépouillée dans ses détails. Mais on se rend compte bientôt que cela est un véritable mérite.

L'hôtel en lui-même a une superficie d'environ 4500 m^2. Il comprend 56 chambres standard de 27 m^2 et deux suites de 54 m2. Un hall de réception ouvert sur un côté, un salon et un restaurant constituent les espaces collectifs.

Vu l'économie de moyens avec laquelle l'hôtel a été réalisé, il est facile d'apprécier le choix pertinent des matériaux et l'articulation architecturale. Les détails sont très sobres partout et démontrent comment l'emploi ingénieux d'un nombre restreint de matériaux, relativement bon marché, peut créer de très beaux effets. Une grande attention est donnée à des détails subtils qui rehaussent la sobriété des lignes.

Le langage architectural se traduit par l'utilisation de principes de construction traditionnelle et par une considération attentive du site. Les pavillons aux proportions harmonieuses forment un ensemble élégant devant la piscine longue de 20 mètres. Chaque construction semble être une partie inhérente de son environnement et constitue un groupe architectural homogène empreint de quiétude.

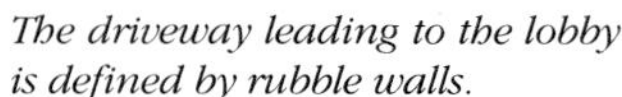

L'assemblage des différents éléments ressemble à un collage de

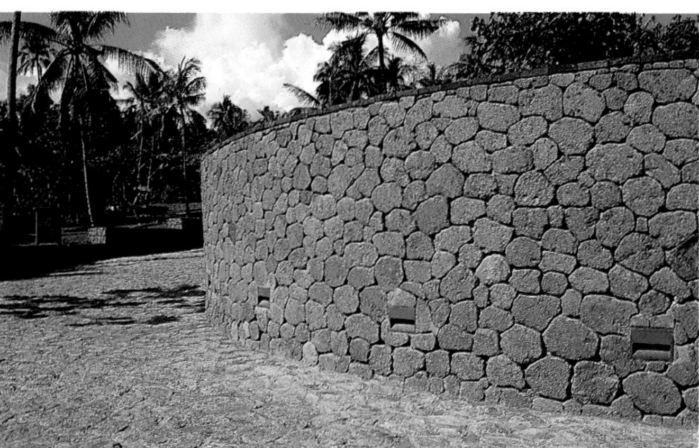

The driveway leading to the lobby is defined by rubble walls.

Die Straße zur Lobby wird von Steinwänden begrenzt.

L'allée menant à la réception suit des murs en pierre.

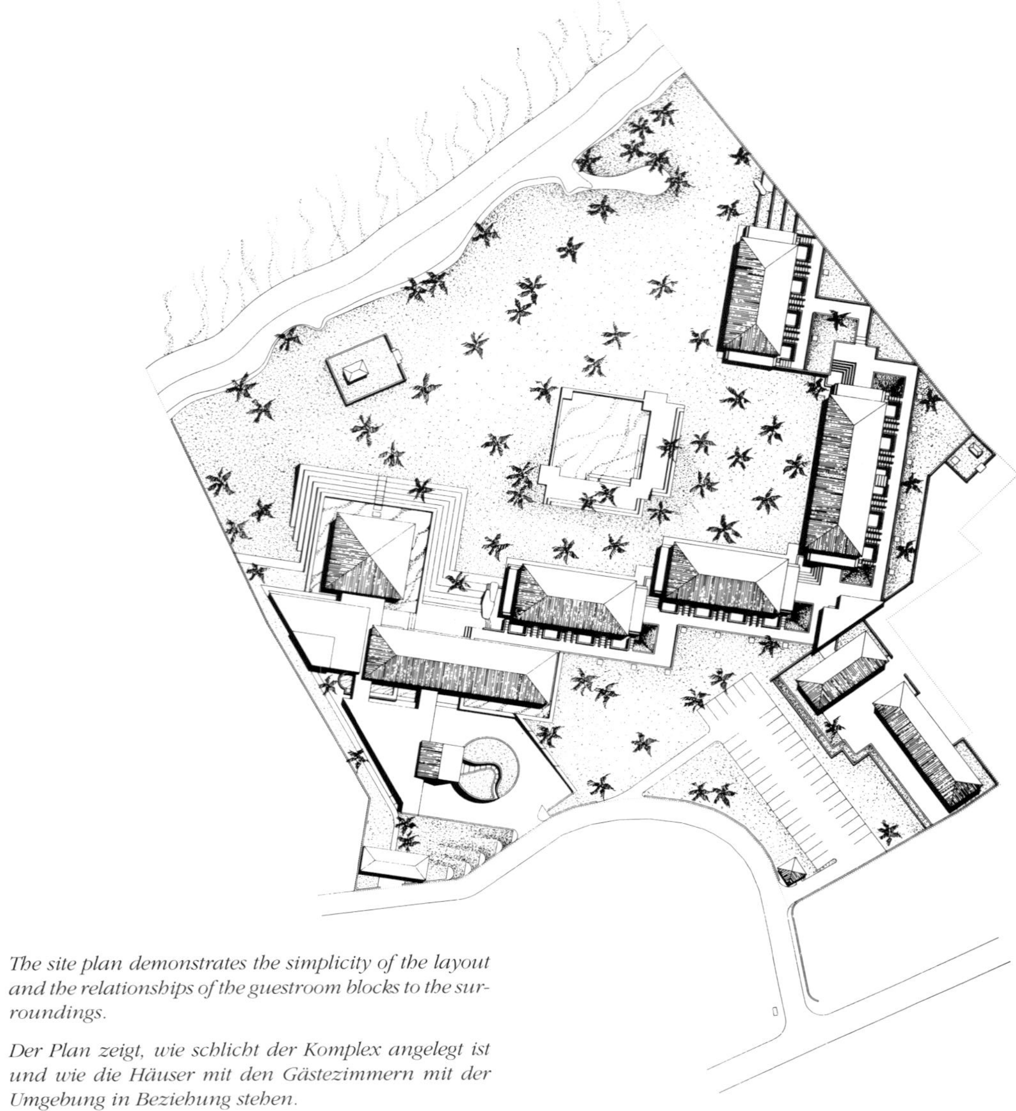

The site plan demonstrates the simplicity of the layout and the relationships of the guestroom blocks to the surroundings.

Der Plan zeigt, wie schlicht der Komplex angelegt ist und wie die Häuser mit den Gästezimmern mit der Umgebung in Beziehung stehen.

Le plan du site dévoile la simplicité de son agencement et la liaison étroite entre les bâtiments qui abritent les chambres et le paysage environnant.

compositional sense. There is an overall languorous quality about the entire composition.

The arrangement of the component parts is also akin to a Modernist collage of urban fragments reduced to simplicity. At the same time, it evokes reminiscences of Geoffrey Bawa's works in Sri Lanka. This is interesting because the architecture manages to transcend the "Balinese" style that has become so formulaic. Even though traditional *alang-alang* roof has been used as a design feature, the abstract monumentalism of the guestroom blocks negates the overall reading as a Balinese pavilion.

There is a clear expressiveness in the use of architecural elements. Wide overhanging eaves contribute to the pronounced horitzontality that creates a close relationship to the ground. Carefully constructed views also offer surprises at various points along the promenade.

The work is noteworthy for its sense of asceticism. It is a contemplative sort of architecture that seems so unselfconscious in its effects. Without mimicking the traditional Balinese forms or descending into kitsch, the architect uses an abstract and austere vocabulary to evoke the local nuance. The outcome seems so uncontrived that it has a sense of inevitability.

Die Anordnung der Einzelkomponenten ähnelt einer modernen Collage von urbanen Elementen, die auf ein Minimum reduziert wurden. Gleichzeitig werden Erinnerungen wach an Geoffrey Bawas Arbeiten in Sri Lanka. Das ist interessant, denn die Architektur geht erfolgreich über den »balinesischen« Stil hinaus, der inzwischen zum Schema F geworden ist. Obwohl das traditionelle *alang-alang*–Dach verwendet wurde, läßt die Konstruktion der Häuser mit den Gästezimmern nicht den Eindruck balinesischer Pavillons aufkommen.

Die architektonischen Elemente werden ganz bewußt eingesetzt. Breite, überhängende Dachgesimse betonen die waagerechten Linien, so daß eine enge Beziehung zum Boden entsteht. Sorgfältig angelegte Aussichtspunkte bieten an mehreren Stellen des Weges Überraschungen.

Die Anlage ist wegen der äußersten Sparsamkeit der Mittel bemerkenswert. Diese Art von Architektur wirkt gar nicht schüchtern und zurückhaltend. Ohne die traditionellen balinesischen Formen nachzuahmen oder sich in die Niederungen des Kitsch zu begeben, verwendet der Architekt eine abstrakte, strenge Sprache, um eine einheimische Atmosphäre zu schaffen. Das Ergebnis wirkt so ungekünstelt, daß man denkt, es müsse einfach so sein.

fragments modernes utilisés avec parcimonie. Il évoque en même temps les travaux de Goeffrey Bawa à Sri Kanka. Cela est intéressant car l'architecture réussit à transcender le style "balinais" qui est devenu une formule banale. Malgré les toits *alang-alang* traditionnels, l'architecture abstraite des bâtiments abritant les chambres s'éloigne du pavillon balinais classique.

L'emploi des éléments architecturaux dénote une forte expressivité. Les larges auvents contribuent à l'impression d'horizontalité qui crée une relation étroite avec le sol. A différents endroits de la promenade, on peut admirer des vues élaborées comme des tableaux.

L'ouvrage est remarquable par la rigueur de ses formes. Son architecture dégage une impression de sérénité et de naturel. Sans plagier les formes traditionnelles balinaises, ni tomber dans le kitsch, l'architecte utilise un expression abstraite et austère pour évoquer le style régional. Le résultat paraît si naturel qu'il devient partie inhérente de l'environnement.

Close-up view of a wall junction.

Ein Wandstück aus der Nähe gesehen.

Un raccordement de murs vu de près.

A pair of whimsical carvings provide a visual focus to the rectangular pool.

Zwei phantasievolle Skulpturen schaffen einen optischen Schwerpunkt an dem rechteckigen Pool.

Rompant le contour rectangulaire de la piscine, de curieuses sculptures attirent le regard.

(opposite page):
The pool is an important part of the design, as the reflections extend the spatial perception considerably.

(gegenüberliegende Seite):
Wasser ist ein wichtiger Teil der Anlage, da die Spiegelungen die räumliche Wahrnehmung beträchtlich erweitern.

(page ci-contre):
La piscine est un élément important de la conception; sa surface miroitante accroît la perception spatiale.

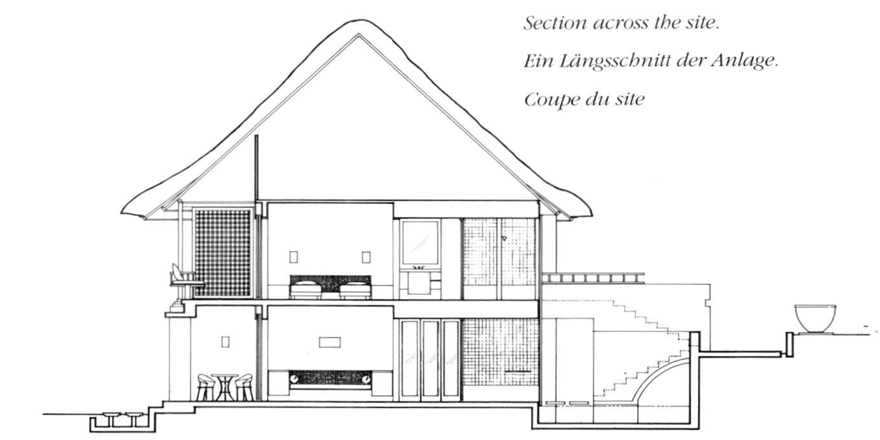

Section across the site.

Ein Längsschnitt der Anlage.

Coupe du site

(previous page):
View of the grounds and the pool from one of the guestrooms' balcony.

(vorherige Seite):
Blick vom Balkon eines Gästezimmers auf die Anlage und den Pool.

(page précédente):
Vue sur le parc et la piscine depuis le balcon d'une chambre.

Gaps between buildings are treated as vista-framing devices.

Freiräume zwischen den Gebäuden dienen als Rahmen für die Ausblicke.

Les espaces entre les édifices sont conçus de façon à s'ouvrir sur des panoramas.

(left):
Considerable attention has been lavished on minor details.

(links):
Auch Details wurden mit großer Sorgfalt behandelt.

(a gauche):
Une attention minutieuse a été accordée aux moindres détails.

(right):
Junctions between columns and floors are treated in a direct manner.

(rechts):
Verbindungen zwischen Säulen und Boden sind klar und schlicht gestaltet.

(a droite):
La liaison pure des colonnes et des sols.

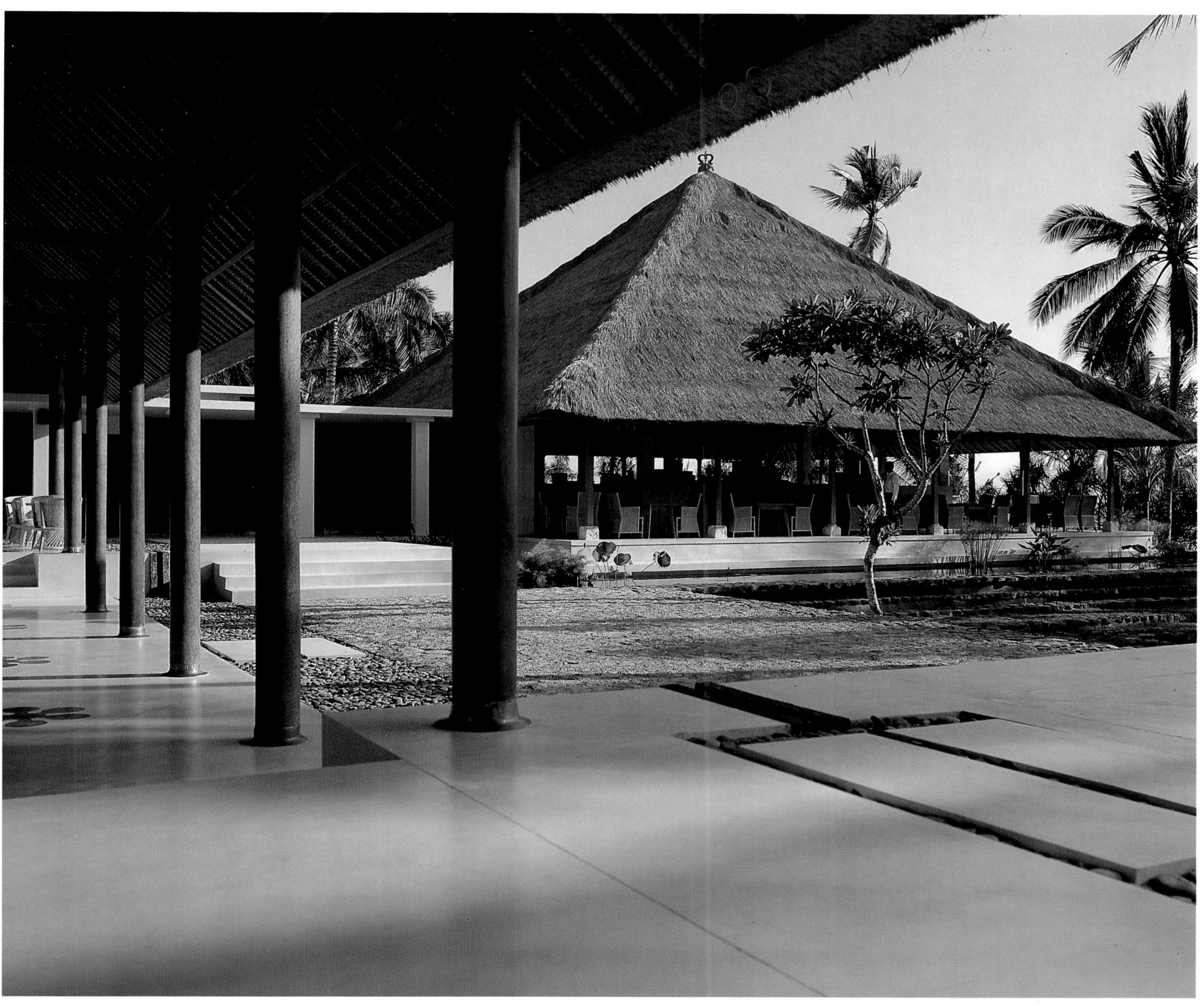

The powerful roof form of the restaurant is the visual focus in the overall composition.

Das mächtige Dach des Restaurants bildet den optischen Schwerpunkt.

Le forme puissante du toit du restaurant domine l'ensemble de la composition.

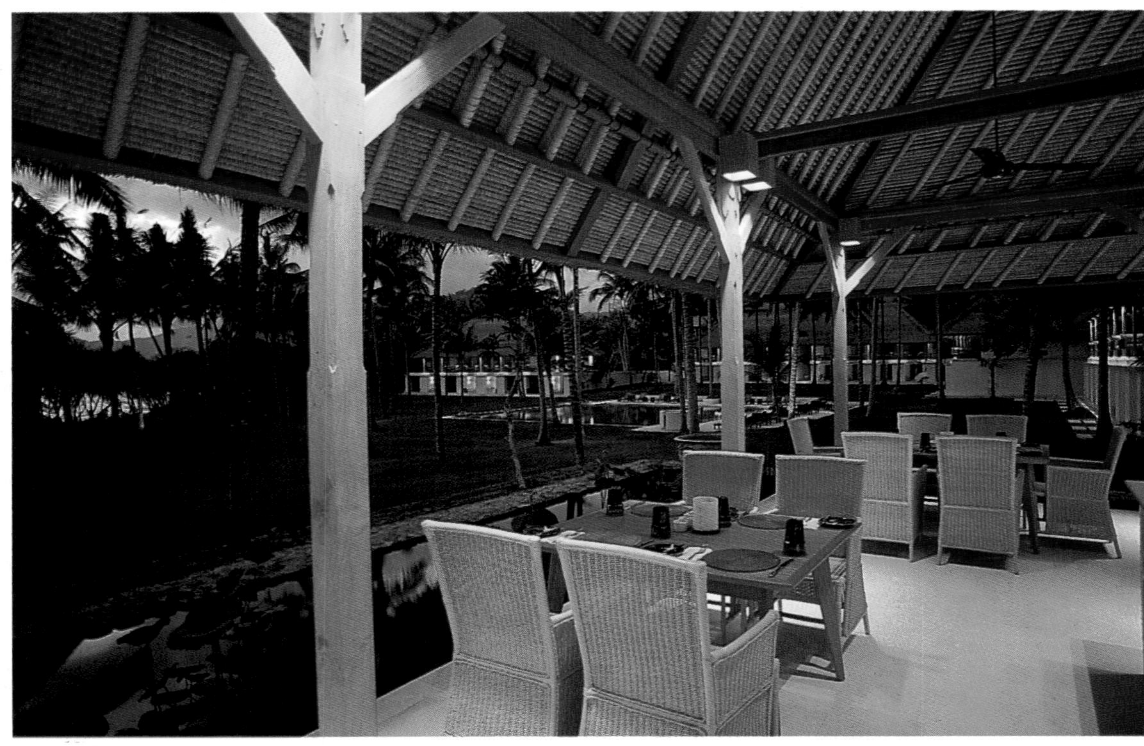

The restaurant has the best views in the entire complex.

Vom Restaurant aus hat man den besten Blick auf die Anlage.

On découvre les plus beaux panoramas depuis le restaurant.

(opposite page):
An austere simplicity pervades throughout the lobby.

(gegenüberliegende Seite):
Die Lobby zeichnet sich durch strenge Einfachheit aus.

(page ci-contre):
Une simplicité austère émane de la réception.

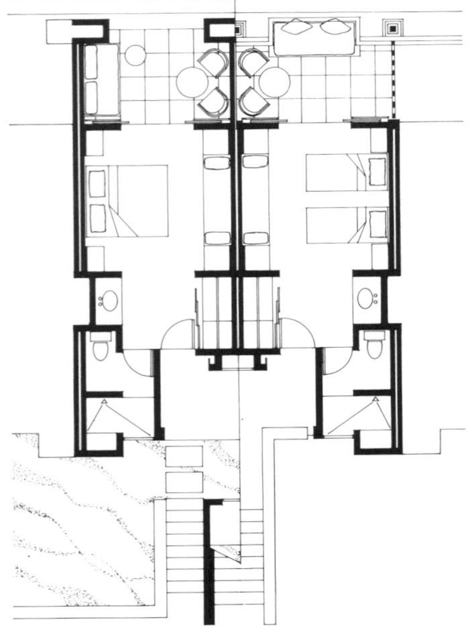

Plan of a typical room.

Grundriß eines typischen Zimmers.

Plan d'une chambre type.

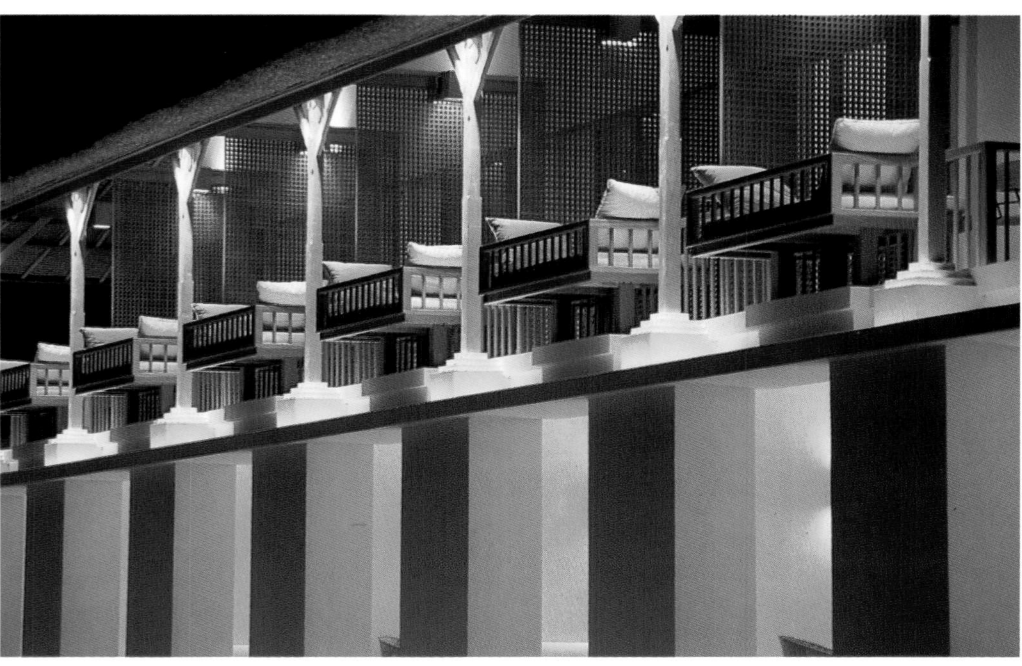

The architectural elements in the facade of the guestroom block provide an interesting geometrical pattern that is heightened by repetition.

Die Fassade des Blocks mit den Gästezimmern zeigt ein interessantes geometrisches Muster, dessen Eindruck durch Wiederholung verstärkt wird.

L'édifice des chambres d'hôtes. La répétition des éléments architecturaux de sa façade forme un dessin géométrique intéressant.

The elevational treatment of the guestroom blocks has decidedly steer away from replicating the Balinese prototype.

Die Blocks mit den Gästezimmern wurden erhöht angelegt, man hat also das balinesische Vorbild nicht nur einfach nachgebaut.

La conception des façades de l'édifice des chambres d'hôtes évite de reproduire le modèle balinais.

View of the complex from the restaurant.

Blick aus dem Restaurant auf die Anlage.

Vue du complexe depuis le restaurant.

The architectural language of the restaurant block is developed through exploitation of traditional constructional logic.

Die architektonische Sprache des Restaurants zitiert die traditionelle Bauweise.

Les méthodes de construction traditionnelles dictent le langage architectural du restaurant.

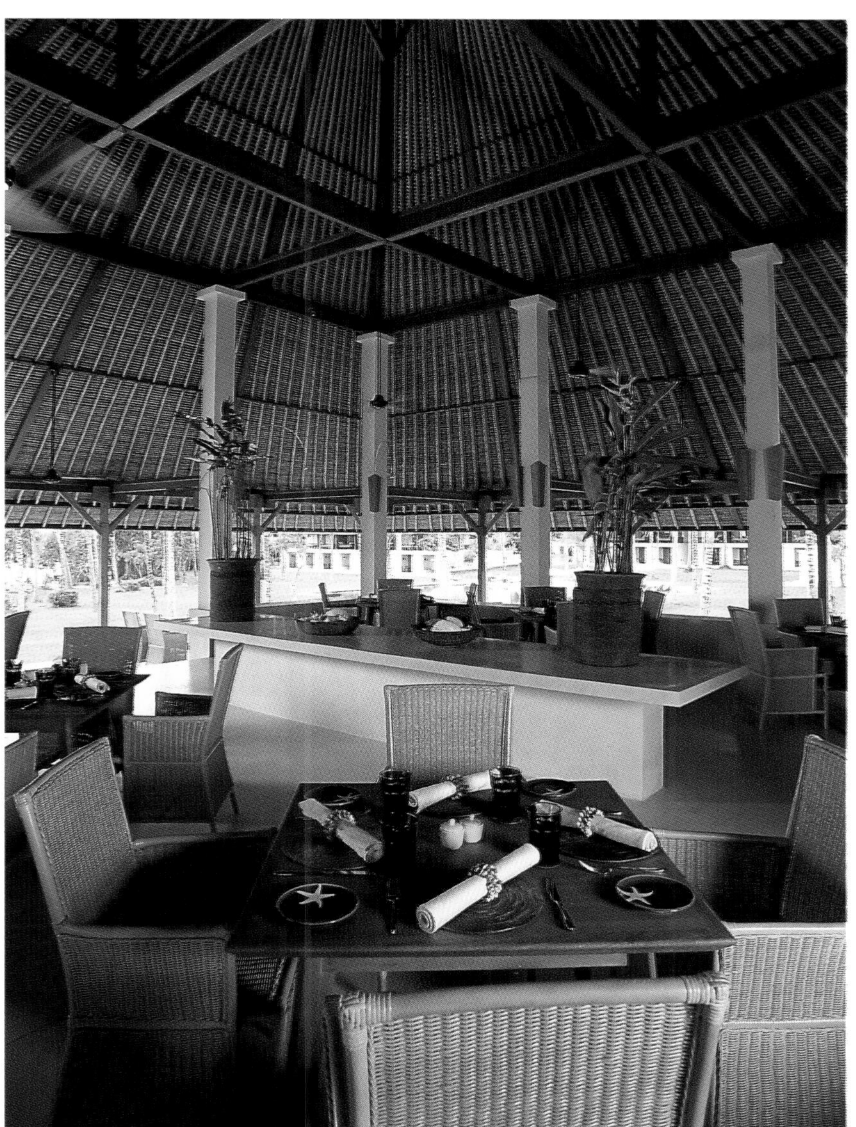

Chedi Bandung, Bandung, Java

The hotel building boom in Indonesia, mainly concentrated in the three "gateway" destinations of Bali, Jakarta and the Riau Archipelago, has also spread to other second-tier destinations like Surabaya, Yogjakarta, Manado, Lombok and Bandung.

Prior to 1990, there was only one international standard hotel in the city of Bandung, Indonesia's leading university town. There are now several new hotels and many more are under construction in this city in Central Java. The Chedi Bandung, completed in August 1993, is a distinct and particularly memorable newcomer.

The crisply tectonic assemblage consists of urban blocks inserted into a 8400-square metre plot of land. Articulated in an abstracted Art-Deco style, there are a total of 44 standard guestrooms and seven large suites. Public areas include an intimate lobby, a lobby lounge, business centre, two meeting rooms, a poolside lounge, a restaurant and a 25-metre long swimming pool.

Richly nuanced, the medium-rise structure utilises an early Modernist sensibility in a confident interweaving of formal themes. Openings are simply punched into flat planes in a controlled elevational treatment. The architects and interior designers, Kerry Hill Architects, deploy these basic architectural elements into a sumptuous scenographic setting, evoking the sense of exuberance of the Art-Deco period. The detailing, minimal yet immaculate, is well complemented by the sparse landscape design of Karl Princic Design Ltd.

While its allegiance clearly belongs to Modernism, the 5230-square metre project is informed by, and engages with the concerns of history, place, climate and site. The measured use of concrete structure is unmistakably associated with the early throes of Modernism. But the lithingly curved concrete roofs impart a sense of lightness to the heaviness of the base. At the same time, they imbue a delightful sense of *joie de vivre*. Yet, the juxtaposition of traditional materials like crafted timber details and local materials evoke a decidedly Javanese touch to the whole ensemble.

Without resorting to nostalgia, the final result is an immensely satisfying whole. It is at the same time a poetic interpretation of the functionalist approach that shows much reverence for the history and culture. Muted colours also play an important role

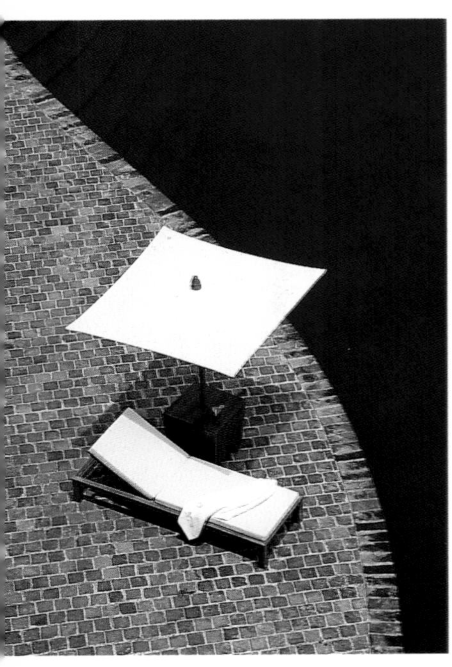

Serpentine edge of the pool.
Der geschwungene Rand des Pools.
Le bord sinueux de la piscine.

Chedi Bandung, Bandung, Java

Der Boom im Hotelbau in Indonesien, vorwiegend in den drei "Eingangsbereichen" von Bali, Jakarta und im Archipel Riau, hat sich auch auf Ziele in der zweiten Reihe der Region ausgedehnt, beispielsweise auf Surabaya, Yogjakarta, Manado, Lombok und Bandung.

Vor 1990 gab es in Bandung, Indonesiens führender Universitätsstadt, nur ein Hotel von internationalem Standard. Inzwischen sind mehrere neue entstanden, weitere sind in dieser Stadt in Zentraljava im Bau. Das Chedi Bandung, im August 1993 fertiggestellt, ist ein eigenwilliger und besonders erwähnenswerter Neubau.

Die unregelmäßig strukturierte Anlage besteht aus urbanen Häuserblocks auf einem Gelände von 8400 Quadratmetern. Es gibt 44 Standard-Zimmer und sieben große Suiten, alle in einem abstrahierten Art-déco-Stil. Zum Gemeinschaftsbereich gehören eine intime Lobby, eine Lounge, ein Geschäftszentrum, zwei Gesellschaftsräume, eine Lounge am Pool, ein Restaurant und ein 25 Meter langer Swimmingpool.

In dieser mittelhohen Anlage mit ihren zahlreichen Nuancen wurden formale Strukturen in der Art der frühen modernistischen Sensibilität miteinander kombiniert. Die Architekten und Inneneinrichter, Kerry Hill Architects, erinnern damit an den Reichtum der Art-déco-Zeit. Die Landschaftsgestaltung durch Karl Princic Design Ltd. liefert eine wunderbare Ergänzung dazu.

Während sich die 5230 Quadratmeter große Anlage eindeutig der Moderne verpflichtet fühlt, berücksichtigt sie auch Geschichte, Ort und Klima. Die maßvolle Verwendung von Beton hängt zweifellos mit den Geburtswehen des Modernismus zusammen. Aber die Betondächer mit ihrem geschmeidigen Schwung verleihen dem schweren unteren Teil einen Hauch von Leichtigkeit. Gleichzeitig lösen sie ein angenehmes Gefühl von *joie de vivre* aus. Der Kontrast zwischen traditionellem Material wie bearbeitetem Holz und einheimischen Baustoffen erzeugt eine eindeutig javanische Atmosphäre.

Ohne auf Nostalgisches zurückzugreifen, ist das Endergebnis außerordentlich zufriedenstellend. Es ist eine poetische Umsetzung des Funktionalismus und zeigt gleichzeitig viel Respekt vor Geschichte und Kultur. Dabei spielen gedämpfte Farben sowohl bei der Gliederung der äußeren Formen als auch bei der Innenraumgestaltung eine wichtige Rolle.

Chedi Bandung, Bandung, Java

La vague de construction d'hôtels en Indonésie, jusqu'alors concentrée sur les trois "portes" Bali, Jakarta et l'archipel Riau, s'est propagée vers des lieux moins connus tels que Surabaya, Yogjakarta, Manado, Lombok et Bandung.

Bandung est située au centre de Java. Jusqu'en 1990, la première ville universitaire d'Indonésie ne possédait qu'un hôtel de classe internationale. Elle en abrite à présent plusieurs, beaucoup sont en construction. Le Chedi Bandung, achevé en 1993, se distingue par son style remarquable.

Son ensemble bien équilibré de bâtiments s'élève sur 8400 m^2. Il comprend 44 chambres standard et sept vastes suites de style Art déco. Une réception intime, un salon, un centre d'affaires, deux salles de conférences, une piscine de 25 mètres de long avec salon et restaurant, constituent les espaces publics.

Richement nuancée, la structure de taille moyenne montre un ensemble sûr de thèmes formels construits dans le style du début du modernisme. Les ouvertures superposées sont simplement construites dans des plans plats. Avec ces éléments, la firme d'architectes et décorateurs Kerry Hill Architects a créé un décor somptueux évoquant la magnificence de la période Art déco. Les jardins sobres dessinés par Karl Princic Design Ltd complètent à merveille la structure aux lignes pures et dépouillées.

Bien que le projet de 5230 m^2 soit indéniablement inspiré du modernisme, on remarque un souci de l'histoire, du site et du climat dans sa réalisation. La structure en béton rappelle les débuts du modernisme, mais les toits aux courbes légères donnent un sens de légèreté à la lourdeur de la base, apportant à l'ensemble une délicieuse atmosphère de joie de vivre. En même temps, la juxtaposition de matériaux traditionnels tels que le bois façonné dans certains détails et d'autres matériaux locaux, évoque un style purement javanais.

Le résultat final est très satisfaisant sans avoir recours à la nostalgie. Il révèle une interprétation poétique d'une approche fonctionnelle qui respecte l'histoire et la culture. Des couleurs douces jouent également un rôle important dans l'articulation des proportions externes et dans les configurations spatiales intérieures.

Un sens très fort de l'harmonie est attaché à tout l'ensemble qui est rempli d'un charme discret grâce à l'emploi judicieux de

The elevational treatment of the block is interesting in the way various openings are designed within an overall coherent language.

Die Fassade ist dahingehend interessant, daß die Öffnungen trotz ihrer Verschiedenartigkeit ein harmonisches Ganzes bilden.

Un aspect très intéressant est la conception des façades dont les diverses ouvertures forment un tout parfaitement cohérent.

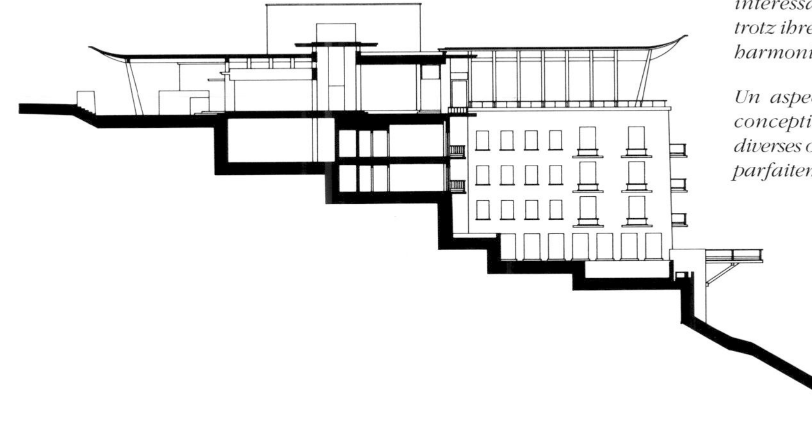

Section across the site.

Ein Längsschnitt der Anlage.

Coupe du site

in articulating the external proportions as well as defining internal spatial configurations.

There is an inherently strong sense of sonority. Deft manipulation of simple materials has resulted in a place full of understated charm. At the same time, it evokes a decidedly theatrical atmosphere reminiscent of the charming old hotels of the mythical Orient.

The disciplined restraint with which the whole hotel has been articulated and detailed has resulted in an elegant and truly inviting piece of work. Composed with vigour and skill, it is a sanctuary of absolute calm in an essentially urban setting.

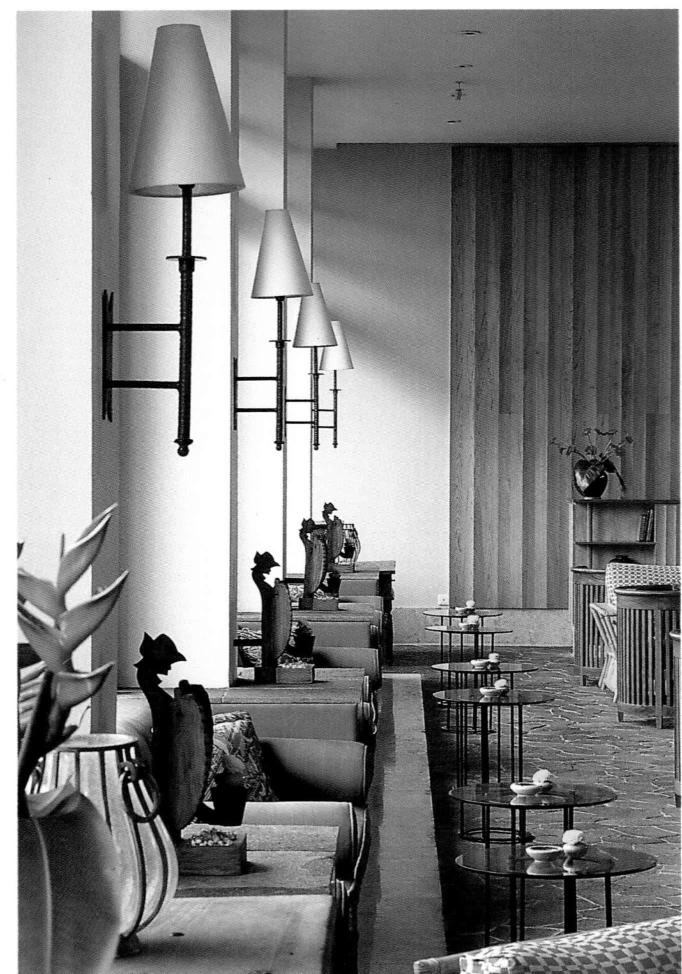

Richly nuanced, the interiors are designed as a sumptuous scenograhic setting.

Die Inneneinrichtung ist luxuriös und reich nuanciert.

Richement nuancés, les intérieurs présentent des décors scéniques somptueux.

Every piece of furniture is carefully designed to evoke the intended mood.

Jedes Möbelstück ist so entworfen, daß es gezielt eine gewisse Stimmung hervorruft.

Chaque pièce du mobilier contribue à créer l'ambiance particulière.

Geschickte Verarbeitung der einfachen Materialien verleiht der Gesamtanlage einen zurückhaltenden Charme. Gleichzeitig ist eine fast dramatische Atmosphäre entstanden, die an die bezaubernden alten Hotels des geheimnisvollen Orient erinnert.

Dank der disziplinierten Zurückhaltung bei Planung und Ausführung ist eine elegante, wirklich einladende Anlage entstanden. Kraftvoll und gekonnt gestaltet, ist diese Anlage ein Zufluchtsort voller Ruhe in einer urbanen Kulisse.

matériaux simples. Néanmoins, il dégage une certaine atmosphère théâtrale qui évoque les charmants vieux hôtels de l'Orient mythique.

La retenue qui a guidé l'articulation des éléments architecturaux et la décoration, fait de cet hôtel un lieu élégant et très accueillant. Elaboré avec vigueur et habileté, c'est un sanctuaire de calme au cœur d'un environnement urbain.

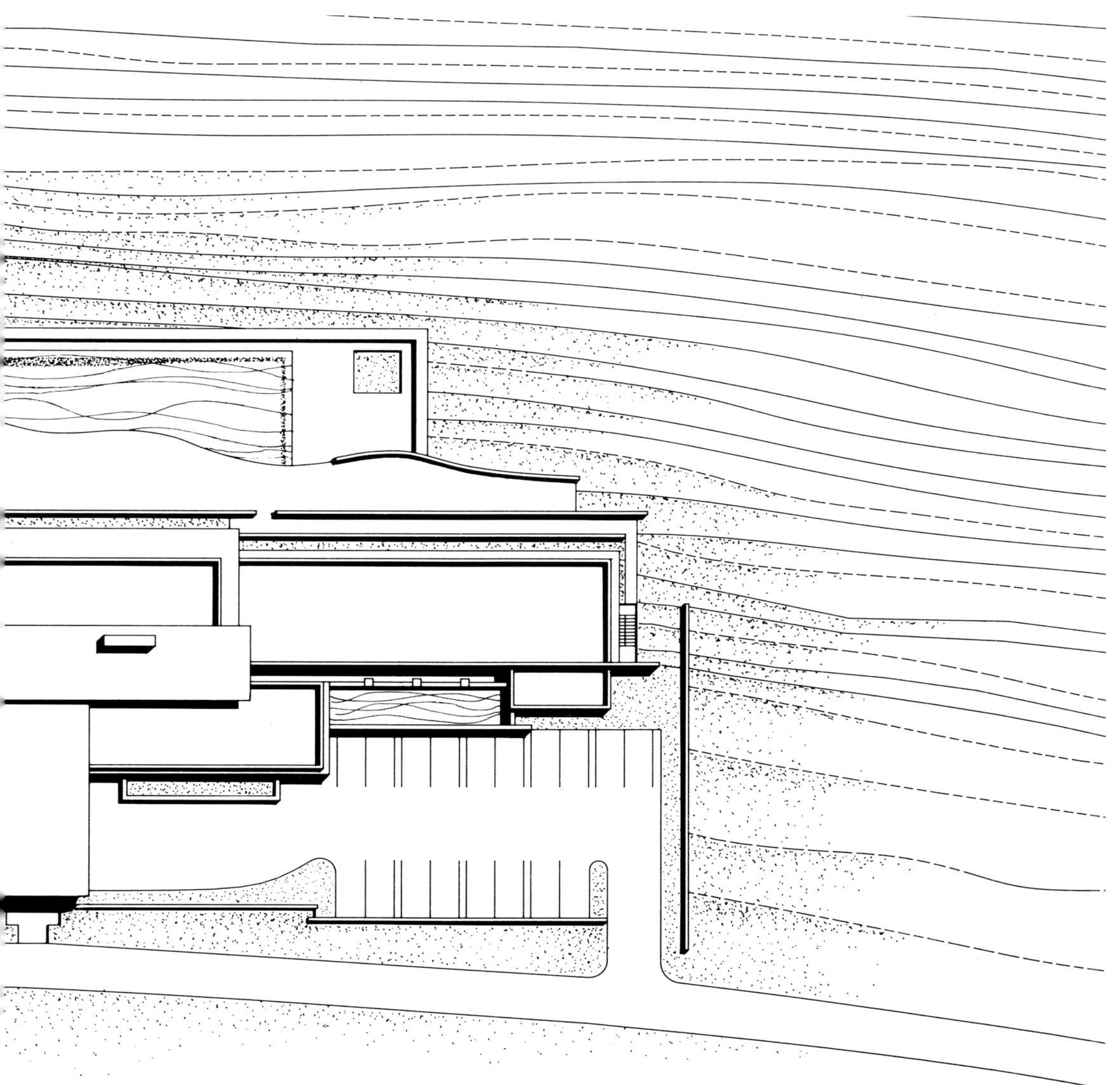

The site plan of the hotel reveals a strong Modernist tendency in its planning.

Der Plan des Hotels zeigt eine starke modernistische Tendenz.

Le plan de l'hôtel révèle une influence profonde du mouvement moderne en architecture.

(previous page):
The crisply tectonic assemblage consists of urban blocks articulated in an abstract Art-Deco style.

(vorherige Seite):
Die Gesamtanlage besteht aus urbanen Häusern, die in einem abstrahierten Art-déco-Stil ausgeführt sind.

(page précédente):
L'abstraction du style Art déco se révèle dans l'assemblage précis des édifices.

The lithingly curved concrete roof of the entrance porch immediately announces the building's character.

Das leicht geschwungene Dach der Eingangsveranda läßt den Charakter des Baus sofort erkennen.

La courbe légère du toit de l'entrée annonce le caractère du complexe.

Light streaming in from the exteriors, emphasising the important role of the columns in articulating the in-between realm.

Von außen strömt Licht herein und unterstreicht die wichtige Rolle der Säulen und des Raums, den sie umgeben.

Les jeux de la lumière rehaussent le rôle important des colonnes qui relient les espaces.

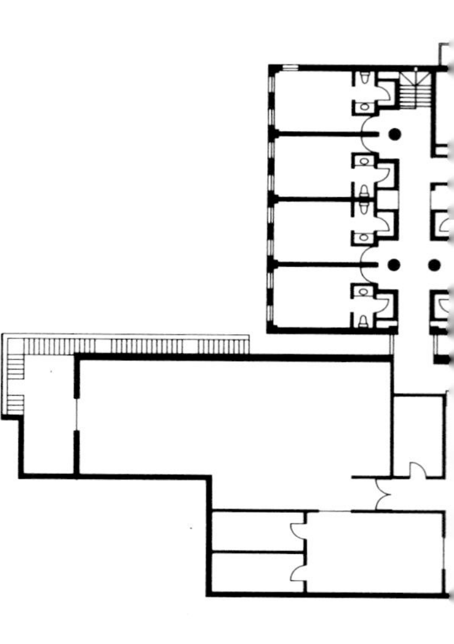

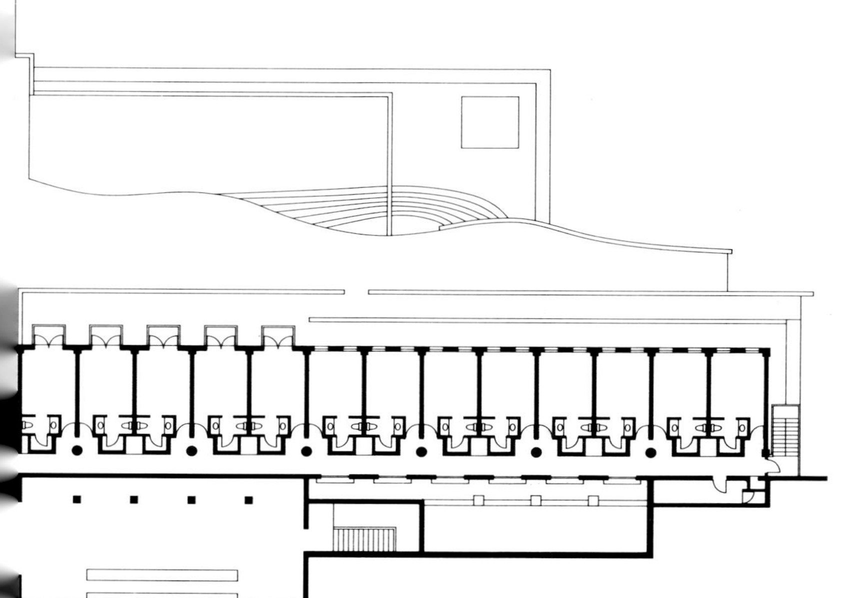

The simple plan of the typical guestroom floor cannot capture the elegance of the three-dimensional expression.

Der schlichte Grundß einer typischen Etage mit Gästezimmern läßt die Eleganz der dreidimensionalen Wirkung nicht erkennen.

La représentation graphique ne dévoile pas les proportions élégantes des chambres.

(opposite page):
The rectilinearity of the architectural elements is offset by an organically inflected roof.

(gegenüberliegende Seite):
Die Gradlinigkeit der architektonischen Elemente wird durch das organisch geschwungene Dach ausgeglichen.

(page ci-contre):
Le toit incliné souligne les lignes droites des éléments architecturaux.

Night view of the hotel from the pool.

Nächtlicher Blick auf das Hotel vom Pool aus.

Vue nocturne de l'hôtel depuis la piscine.

The disciplined restraint with which the elevation is composed has resulted in a hotel that evokes a great sense of calm.

Die disziplinierte Zurückhaltung in der Gestaltung macht das Hotel zu einem Ort, der Ruhe ausstrahlt.

Par la retenue de ses éléments architecturaux, la façade de l'hôtel dégage une impression de calme.

The interiors of the hotel, detailed with a disciplined restraint, is full of understated charm.

Das Innere des Hotels, mit disziplinierter Einfachheit ausgestattet, strahlt einen zurückhaltenden Charme aus.

Un charme discret émane de la décoration intérieure de l'hôtel qui est d'une grande sobriété.

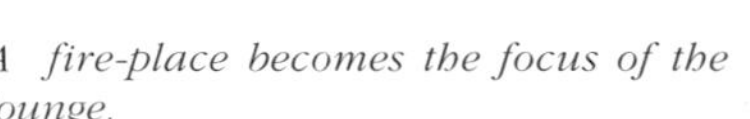

A fire-place becomes the focus of the lounge.

Der Kamin wird zum Mittelpunkt des Salons.

La cheminée est le cœur du salon.

Sparse furnishings in the room follow the same minimalist palette.

Auch die Zimmer sind zurückhaltend eingerichtet.

Le concept minimaliste se retrouve dans l'ameublement très sobre du salon.

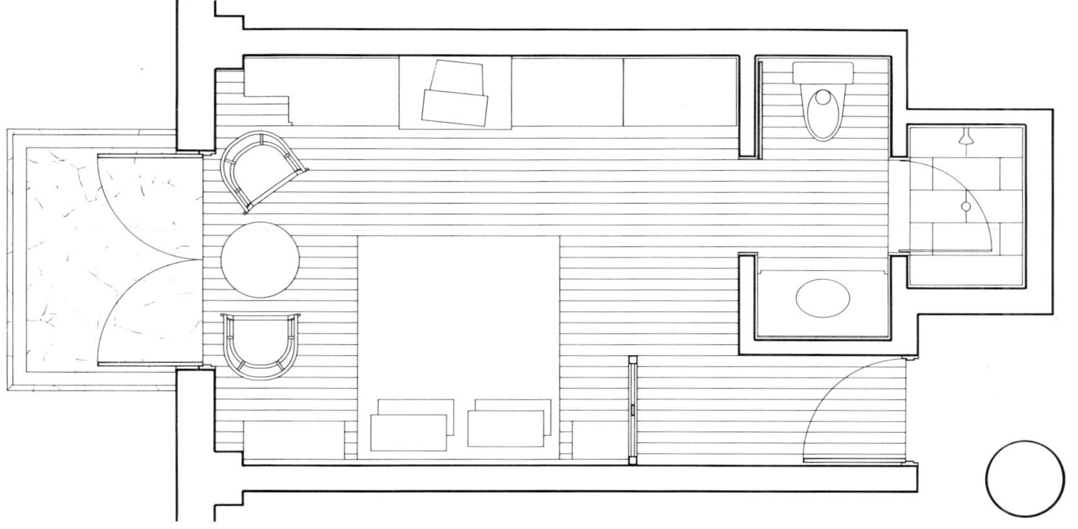

Typical plan of the guestroom.

Grundriß eines typischen Gästezimmers.

Plan d'une chambre type.

Four Seasons Resort Bali, Jimbaran, Bali

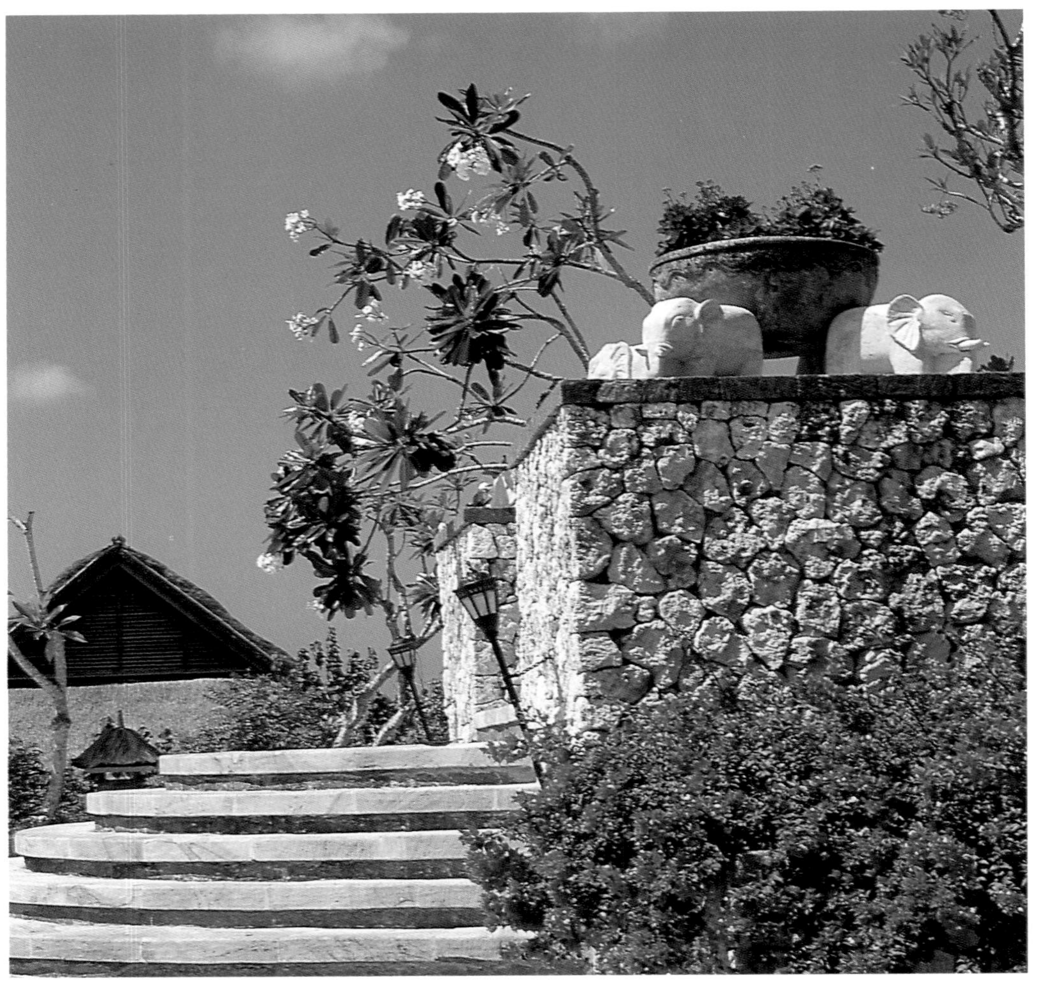

Steps leading down from the lobby lounge.

Stufen führen zur großen Halle.

Cet escalier mène à la réception.

Even though Bali has been overwhelmed by tourists, especially in the last couple of years, the island's legendary charms can still be savoured. Many of the mega-resorts are monotonous and lacking in character. But several of the exclusive luxury hotels are outstanding in their celebration of the island's architectural heritage and natural beauty. They combine ultimate luxury with sensitive use of local materials. The idea is to evoke the perceived romanticism and pace of the local lifestyle without any of its inconveniences, of course.

Located in Bali, Jimbaran Bay, the Four Seasons Resort is one of them. With the acquisition of Regent International Hotels in August 1992, Canada's Four Seasons is now one of the world's leading luxury hotel chains. Originally a Regent project, the Four Seasons Resort Bali is only about ten minutes' drive from crowded Kuta Beach and about 15 kilometres from Ngurah Rai International Airport. It is designed by Australian architects Martin Grounds and Jack Kent of Perth-based Grounds Kent Architects.

The 14-hectare site is a coraline headland, set on a gradual slope rising to 45 metres above the waters of Jimbaran Bay. The bay is a deep, semi-circular cove with six kilometres of white sandy beach. On a clear day, Mount Agung, the spiritual and sacred heart of Bali, can be seen. The Four Seasons Resort is inspired by traditional Balinese village layout and construction methods, yet with all the amenities of a five-star resort.

The traditional Balinese village planning provides an important precedent in the design of the US$70 million resort. Notions of the "courtyard house", the "village square" and the "village lane" are used as part of the major design framework. The resort is laid out as a series of seven villages surrounding the central facilities building.

Within each village, there is a village square surrounded by 20-25 courtyard units. There are a total of 147 private villas, among which 139 are one-bedroom villas of about 200 square metres each. The interior design, undertaken by Hong Kong-based Dale Keller & Associates, evokes a traditional Balinese theme in a restrained palette of materials and objects.

There are also six two-bedroom villas with 370 square metres, and two sumptous Royal Villas, each containing 600 square metres of self-contained spaces tastefully furnished with local artefacts and sculptural pieces. They each have two bed-

Four Seasons Resort Bali, Jimbaran, Bali

Obwohl Bali vor allem in den letzten paar Jahren von Touristen überrannt wurde, ist der legendäre Charme der Insel noch zu spüren. Doch sind viele der Mega-Anlagen eintönig und ohne eigenen Charakter.

Aber einige der exklusiven Luxus-Hotels berücksichtigen das architektonische Erbe und die Naturschönheiten auf hervorragende Weise. Sie verbinden höchsten Luxus mit der einfühlsamen Verwendung einheimischer Materialien. Ziel ist es, die sichtbare Romantik und den Frieden des einheimischen Lebensstils heraufzubeschwören, aber ohne seine Unbequemlichkeiten in Kauf zu nehmen.

Zu diesen Anlagen gehört auch das Four Seasons an der Jimbaran Bay, Bali. Mit dem Erwerb der Regent International Hotels im August 1992 ist die kanadische Four Seasons inzwischen eine der weltweit führenden Luxushotel-Ketten. Das ursprüngliche Regent-Projekt Four Seasons ist nur zehn Autominuten von der belebten Kuta Beach und etwa 15 Kilometer vom Ngurah Rai International Airport entfernt. Es wurde von den australischen Architekten Martin Grounds und Jack Kent von Grounds Kent Architects, Perth, entworfen.

Das 14 Hektar große Gelände liegt auf der Landspitze eines Korrallenriffs an einem sanften Hang, der sich bis zu 45 Meter über das Wasser der Jimbaran Bay erhebt. Die tiefe, halbkreisförmige Bucht verfügt über sechs Kilometer weißen Sandstrand. An klaren Tagen ist der Mount Agung, das geistliche und heilige Herz Balis, zu sehen. Traditionelle balinesische Dorfanlagen und Baumethoden haben das Four Seasons beeinflußt, aber es verfügt über alle Annehmlichkeiten eines Fünf-Sterne-Hauses, in das 70 Millionen US-Dollar investiert wurden.

Anklänge an das »Hofhaus«, den »Dorfplatz« und die »Dorfstraße« sind ein Teil der Gesamtplanung. Die Anlage besteht aus sieben Dörfern, die um ein Zentralgebäude gruppiert sind. In jedem Dorf gibt es einen Dorfplatz, umgeben von 20 bis 25 Wohneinheiten. Von den insgesamt 147 Privatvillen haben 139 nur ein Schlafzimmer und sind 200 Quadratmeter groß. Die Inneneinrichtung, ausgeführt von Dale Keller & Associates, Hongkong, nimmt mit einer eingeschränkten Palette von Materialien und Gegenständen balinesische Traditionen wieder auf.

Die Villen mit zwei Schlafräumen sind 370 Quadratmeter

Four Seasons Resort Bali, Jimbaran, Bali

On peut encore savourer les charmes légendaires de Bali bien que l'île ait été envahie par les touristes, notamment au cours des dernières années. Si un grand nombre de grands hôtels sont ennuyeux et manquent de cachet, plusieurs établissements de grande classe célèbrent à souhait l'héritage architectural et la beauté merveilleuse de l'île. Ils allient le luxe à une utilisation appropriée des matériaux locaux. L'idée est de reproduire le romantisme et la douceur du style de vie du pays, sans aucun de ses inconvénients.

Un de ces palaces est le Four Seasons Resort situé à Bali, sur la Jimbaran Bay. Après avoir acquis la chaîne Regent International Hotels en 1992, le groupe canadien de Four Seasons est un des leaders de l'hôtellerie de luxe dans le monde. Le Four Season Resort Bali, un ancien établissement de la chaîne Regent, se trouve à dix minutes en voiture de la plage animée de Kuta Beach et à 15 kilomètres de l'aéroport international de Ngurah Rai. Il est l'œuvre des architectes australiens Martin Grounds et Jack Kent du bureau Grounds Kent Architects à Perth.

Le site de 14 hectares s'étend sur le versant d'un promontoire de corail à 45 mètres au-dessus du rivage de la Jimbaran Bay. La baie semi-circulaire a une plage de sable blanc de six kilomètres de longueur. Par temps clair, on peut voir le Mount Agung, la montagne sacrée de Bali. Conçu sur les plans d'un village balinais classique et avec des méthodes de construction traditionnelles, le Four Seasons Resort offre toutefois le confort d'un hôtel cinq étoiles.

Le plan en forme de village de l'hôtel qui a coûté 70 millions de dollars US, a été une innovation majeure. Les éléments principaux de la disposition incluent la "maison avec cour-jardin", la "place du village" et la "grand-rue du village". Le complexe comprend sept villages entourant un édifice principal qui abrite les zones communes.

20 à 25 cours-jardins cernent une place de village. Le complexe possède au total 147 villas dont 139 sont des unités d'environ 200 m^2, avec une chambre. La décoration intérieure effectuée par la firme Dale Keller et Associés de Hong Kong, est de style balinais avec un minimum de matériaux et d'objets.

Il y a également six villas de 370 m^2 comprenant deux chambres, et deux Villas Royales somptueuses de 600 m^2 renfermant des meubles et des sculptures splendides du pays. Elles ont chacune deux chambres avec salle de bain, deux

Stone figurine in the courtyard of the villa.

Steinfigur im Hof der Villa.

Statue en pierre dans la cour d'une villa.

rooms with attached bathrooms, two sundecks, a private swimming pool, hot and cold spa pools, sauna and a fully equipped pantry as well.

The courtyard unit, designed in the manner of a Balinese dwelling, contains a series of three pavilions laid out within a private courtyard enclosed by high walls, and entered through a traditional courtyard gate. These are the open-sided living/dining pavilion; an enclosed air-conditioned bedroom leading into a private sundeck, and a bathroom pavilion with glass walls looking into a private garden with an outdoor shower. The bathroom is fitted with an oversized soaking bath tub and double vanities.

The landscaped courtyard within each compound provides a lush and contemplative setting. The courtyard wall is omitted on the side facing the bay. A small yet delightful plunge pool is located here. Every unit enjoys the panoramic sea view because all the pavilions are set on terraced tiers on the gradual slope. However, the rather tightly packed individual pavilions are perhaps sited too close to one another.

Its lush landscaping,with over 200 species of plants, shrubs and trees, is designed by Michael White. The grounds are designed for long strolls, punctuated by thatch-roofed gazebos. One of the main features of the landscape is the 34-m wide main swimming pool, which spills over a ledge and cascades in a seven metres waterfall into a free-form pool below. Other facilities include three restaurants and cafes, meeting rooms and banquet seating for 90 people, art gallery, late check-out lounge, tennis courts and a beauty spa.

Four Seasons Resort Bali is certainly one of the largest hotels, in terms of its number of rooms, for a hotel in the 'boutique resort' category. A totally consistent work of architecture, the resort embodies forms and materials in ways that characterise and honour the essence of tradition while meeting the needs of a contemporary luxury hotel.

groß, und die beiden luxuriösen Royal Villas verfügen über 600 Quadratmeter Wohnfläche und sind geschmackvoll mit einheimischen Kunstwerken und Skulpturen dekoriert. Zu den beiden Schlafräumen gehört jeweils ein Bad, es gibt zwei Sonnenterrassen, einen eigenen Pool, heiße und kalte Whirlpools und eine voll eingerichtete Küche.

Die Wohneinheiten nach balinesischem Vorbild bestehen aus drei Pavillons innerhalb eines Hofes, der von hohen Mauern umgeben ist. Der Zugang erfolgt durch eine traditionelle Pforte. Da sind der an den Seiten offene Wohn-Pavillon, ein geschlossener, klimatisierter Schlafraum, der zu einer privaten Sonnenterrasse führt, und ein Badepavillon mit Glaswänden, von dem aus man auf den privaten Garten mit Dusche im Freien blickt. Das Bad ist mit einer Maxi-Wanne und doppeltem Waschbecken ausgestattet.

Der Hof innerhalb jeder Einheit ist üppig gestaltet. Zur Bucht hin ist die Mauer unterbrochen. An der Stelle liegt ein kleines Planschbecken. Jede Unterkunft hat Meeresblick, denn alle Pavillons liegen terrassenförmig am Hang. Die Einzelpavillons allerdings liegen vielleicht zu dicht beieinander.

Die üppige Landschaft mit über 200 Pflanzenarten, Büschen und Bäumen wurde von Michael White gestaltet. Das Gelände, auf dem es überall strohgedeckte Ausblickhütten gibt, bietet sich für lange Spaziergänge an. Einer der Hauptpunkte ist der 34 Meter breite Swimming-pool, dessen Wasser über den Rand läuft und sich als Wasserfall sieben Meter tief in einen Teich ergießt. Zu den Angeboten auf dem Gelände gehören drei Restaurants und Cafés, Gesellschafts- und Bankettträume für 90 Personen, eine Kunstgalerie, eine Lounge für spät Abreisende, Tennisplätze und ein Schönheitssalon.

Für ein Hotel der »Boutique«-Kategorie ist das Four Seasons Resort Bali sicherlich eines der größten, was die Anzahl der Zimmer angeht. In der in sich vollkommen stimmigen Anlage wurden Formen und Materialien auf eine Weise verwendet, die das Wesentliche der Tradition darstellt und in Ehren hält und gleichzeitig den Anforderungen eines modernen Luxushotels entspricht.

solariums, une piscine privée, des bains thermaux chaud et froid et une cuisine entièrement équipée.

Une unité cour-jardin, conçue comme une demeure balinaise, contient trois pavillons dans un jardin privé entouré de hauts murs, où l'on pénètre par un portail de style traditionnel. Un pavillon abrite la salle de séjour avec un côté ouvert sur l'extérieur, un autre la chambre climatisée s'ouvrant sur un solarium privé et le dernier une salle de bains avec des murs en verre qui donnent sur un jardin privé avec une douche extérieure. La salle de bains a une immense baignoire et deux lavabos.

Dans chaque cour, la végétation crée un décor luxuriant et reposant. Une agréable petite piscine remplace le mur sur le côté de la cour faisant face à la baie. Toutes les unités jouissent d'un panorama sur la mer car elles sont construites en terrasses sur le versant. Cependant, les pavillons sont peut-être bâtis trop proches les uns des autres.

Michael White a dessiné les jardins luxuriants qui abritent plus de 200 espèces de plantes et arbres. On y trouve un réseau de longues allées parsemées de belvédères aux toits de chaume. Un des points principaux du paysage est la piscine de 34 mètres de large qui cascade sur un côté jusqu'à un bassin situé sept mètres plus bas. Le complexe comprend également trois restaurants et cafés, des salles de conférence et de banquet pour 90 personnes, une galerie d'art, un salon de départ, des courts de tennis et un institut de beauté.

Le Four Season Resort Bali est certainement un des plus grands hôtels, vu son nombre de chambres, de la catégorie "hôtel boutique". Néanmoins, cette très belle œuvre architecturale concrétise des formes et matériaux qui caractérisent et honorent l'essence de la tradition tout en offrant ce qu'on attend d'un hôtel de luxe contemporain.

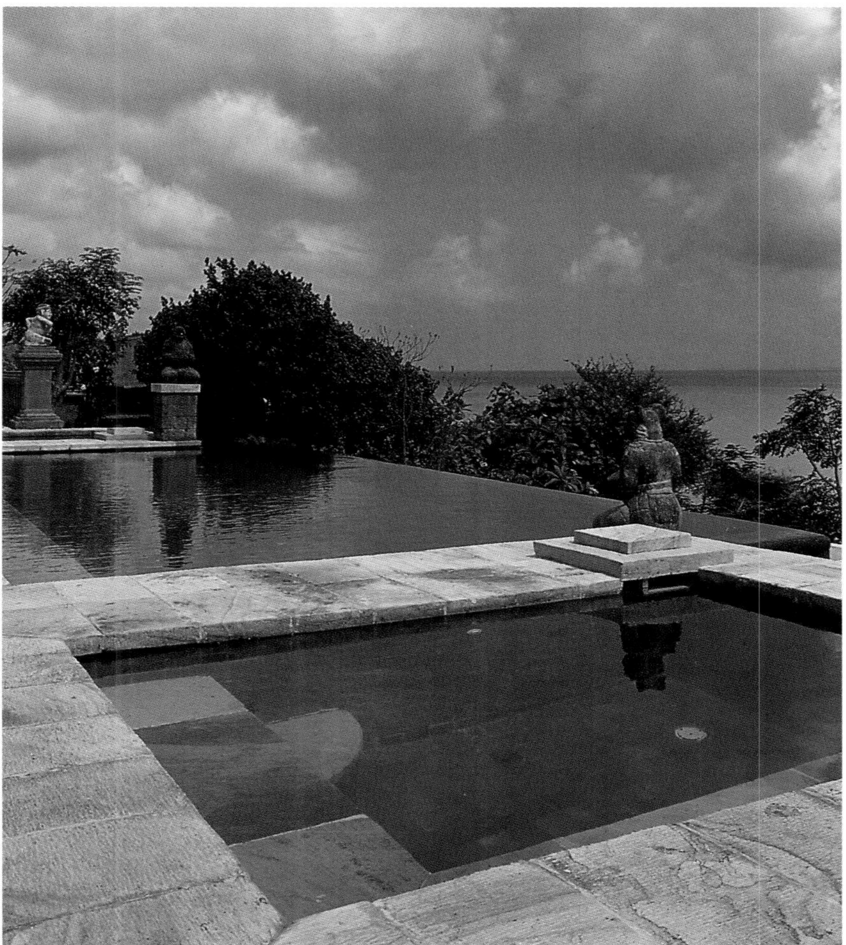

The private plunge pool of the Royal Villa is located next to the swimming pool.

Das private Planschbecken der Royal Villa liegt neben dem Swimmingpool.

Le bassin privé avec plongeoir de la Villa Royale est situé près de la piscine.

View of the open court next to the restaurant.

Blick auf den offenen Hof neben dem Restaurant.

Vue de la terrasse avoisinant le restaurant.

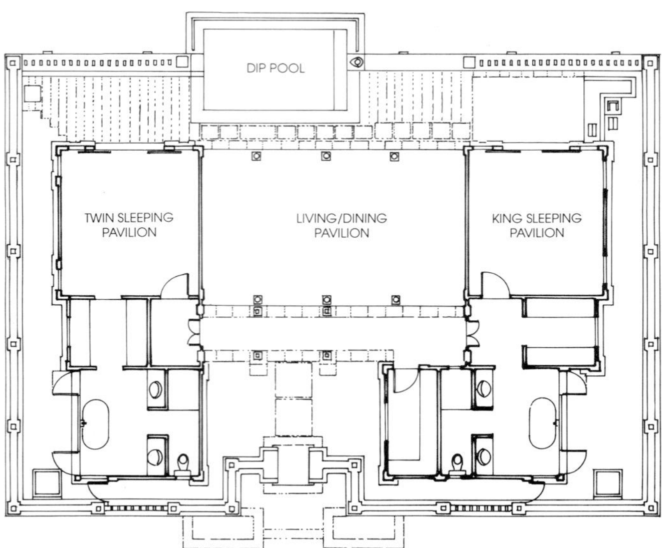

Plan of a typical guestroom.

Grundriß eines typischen Gästezimmers.

Plan d'une chambre type.

Water features provide a forecourt to the restaurant.

Teichanlage vor dem Restaurant.

Un décor aquatique devant le restaurant.

(opposite page): The tiered roof of the lobby pavilion is a conspicuous structure.

(gegenüberliegende Seite): Das Ziegeldach des Lobby-Pavillons ist eine eindrucksvole Konstruktion.

(page ci-contre): Le toit en gradins du pavillon de la réception domine le paysage.

The lower swimming pool is designed as a landscaped feature as well.

Der untere Swimming-pool ist als Teil der Landschaft angelegt.

La piscine inférieure ressemble à un bassin d'agrément.

Meandering paths are designed for long strolls. Designed by Michael White, they also provide views of the sea. Thatch-roof gazebos provide shelters.

Geschwungene Pfade, angelegt von Michael White, laden zu langen Spaziergängen ein und geben auch den Blick auf das Meer frei. Strohgedeckte Hütten bieten Schutz.

Dessinées par Michael White, des allées sinueuses invitent à la promenade et offrent de belles vues sur la mer.

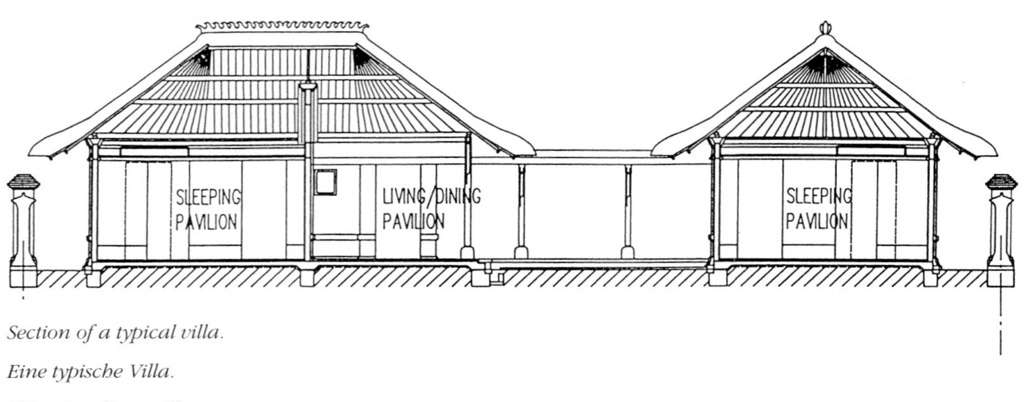

Section of a typical villa.

Eine typische Villa.

Elévation d'une villa type.

Close-up view of a water spout.

Ein Wasserspeier aus der Nähe gesehen.

Une jolie fontaine sculptée.

Grand Hyatt Bali, Nusa Dua, Bali

Situated on the Nusa Dua Beach, with a 650-metres beachfront, Grand Hyatt Bali is one of the largest hotels in Southeast Asia. With its opening, it brings the number of hotels operated by the chain in Indonesia to five. The brand name "Grand Hyatt" is used exclusively for large-scale properties located only in the major capitals and recreation centres of the world.

Grand Hyatt Bali's 750 rooms are set in four huge villages, spread over 16 hectares of gardens and water features. Each village is designed to be self-contained, with its own swimming pool and restaurant. In addition, there are two private villas set next to the beach. Construction started at the end of 1989, and the resort soft-opened 20 months later, in 1991. The combined facilities of both the Bali Hyatt and the Grand Hyatt properties are fully available to all guests residing in either resorts. The former is marketed as "A Garden of Eden" while the latter is billed as "A Water Palace".

Designed by Wimberly Allison Tong and Goo of Hawaii, the resort's water theme is based on Balinese water-palaces reminiscent of the ancient palace of Tirta Gangga in Karangasem. This is emphasised through an interlinked system of lagoons, waterfalls and cascades. There are also five swimming pools and a large Balinese-style bathing pool.

The entire composition is held together by the reception lobby, an open-sided pavilion capped by a pyramidal roof. Here, it feels expansively spacious. It is raised some five metres above the original ground level to create the vantage point. The guest is confronted immediately by views of a reflecting pool, cascades, a river pool, free-form swimming pools and the sea. Concrete is used in an ubiquitous manner, thus imbuing the place with a certain sense of solidity so different from that of Bali Hyatt's lobby. Howver, the lack of ornamentation is probably a visual strength, as the minimalist treatment of surfaces provide the languorous feeling so vital in resort architecture.

The external design of the four-storey high guestroom blocks, roofed with orange-hued tiles, are no different from most large hotels. But the planning has been skillfully articulated to dispose the blocks in such a manner that they do not intrude too much upon the landscape. The landscape architecture was designed by Tongg Clarke & Mechler of Honolulu, and executed by Indo Sekar, Bali.

Grand Hyatt Bali, Nusa Dua, Bali

Das Grand Hyatt Bali liegt an der Nusa Dua Beach mit 650 Metern Strand, und es ist eins der größten in Südostasien. Es ist das fünfte, das von der Hotelkette in Indonesien betrieben wird. Der Markenname »Grand Hyatt« wird ausschließlich an Luxushäuser in Großstädten und wichtigen Erholungszentren der Welt vergeben.

Die 750 Zimmer des Grand Hyatt Bali befinden sich in vier großen Dörfern, die auf einem 16 Hektar großen Gelände mit Gärten und Wasseranlagen verteilt sind. Jedes Dorf ist in sich abgeschlossen, verfügt über eigenen Swimmingpool und Restaurant. Am Strand gibt es außerdem zwei Privatvillen. Ende 1989 wurde mit dem Bau begonnen, und zwanzig Monate später, im Jahr 1991, fand die Eröffnung statt. Alle Gäste, die im Bali Hyatt oder Grand Hyatt Bali wohnen, können die Angebote beider Anlagen nutzen. Das Bali Hyatt wird als »Garten Eden« vermarktet, das Grand Hyatt als »Wasserpalast«.

Von Wimberly Allison, Tong and Goo Hawaii, entworfen, orientiert sich das gestalterische Thema Wasser an einem balinesischen Wasserpalast, der an den alten Palast Tirta Gangga in Karangasem erinnert. Das wird deutlich an dem System von miteinander verbundenen Lagunen, Wasserfällen und Kaskaden. Außerdem gibt es fünf Swimmingpools und ein großes Badebecken in balinesischem Stil.

Das Ganze wird zusammengehalten durch die Empfangshalle, einen an den Seiten offenen Pavillon mit einem Pyramidendach. Hier bekommt man den Eindruck von großer Weite. Er wurde etwa fünf Meter über dem Boden errichtet, um einen Aussichtspunkt zu schaffen. Der Gast blickt sofort auf einen glitzernden Teich, einen Fluß, verschiedene Swimmingpools und auf das Meer. Überall wurde Beton verwendet, was diesem Ort einen Eindruck von Festigkeit gibt, der so ganz anders ist als in der Lobby des Bali Hyatt. Doch der Verzicht auf Dekoration ist vermutlich eine optische Stärke, denn die sparsamste Behandlung von Oberflächen erzeugt ein Gefühl der Muße, das für Ferienanlagen so wichtig ist.

In der äußeren Gestaltung unterscheiden sich die dreistöckigen Gästehäuser mit den orangefarbenen Dachziegeln wenig von denen anderer großer Hotelanlagen. Aber in der Planung wurde Wert darauf gelegt, die Häuser so zu plazieren, daß sie in der Landschaft nicht stören. Die Landschaftsarchitektur wurde von Tongg Clarke & Mechler, Honolulu, konzipiert und von Indo Sekar, Bali, ausgeführt.

Grand Hyatt Bali, Nusa Dua, Bali

Le Grand Hyatt Bali est un des plus grands hôtels du Sud-Est asiatique. Il est situé sur la Nusa Dua Beach dont il occupe 650 mètres de rivage. Il est le cinquième des hôtels que la chaîne Hyatt dirige en Indonésie. Le nom de marque "Grand Hyatt" est exclusivement réservé aux grands complexes hôteliers situés dans les principaux sites touristiques et métropoles du monde.

Le Grand Hyatt Bali est un ensemble de quatre villages abritant 750 chambres, parsemés sur 16 hectares de jardins et d'aménagements nautiques. Chaque village est indépendant avec ses propres piscine et restaurant. On trouve en outre deux villas privées près de la plage. La construction de l'hôtel a démarré fin 1989 et s'est achevée 20 mois plus tard, en 1991. Le Bali Hyatt et le Grand Hyatt ont des installations communes ouvertes à la clientèle des deux hôtels. Dans la publicité, le Bali Hyatt est qualifié de "Jardin d'Eden" et le Grand Hyatt de "palais aquatique".

Conçus par Wimberleyn Allison Tong et Goo de Hawaï, les aménagements nautiques s'inspirent du paysage aquatique traditionnel de l'ancien palais balinais de Tirta Gangga à Karangasem. On découvre une succession de lagunes et de cascades, cinq piscines et un vaste bain de style balinais.

Le cœur du complexe est le hall de réception qui domine l'environnement en étant construit sur une butte de cinq mètres de hauteur. L'édifice ouvert sur un côté et coiffé d'un toit pyramidal, offre une impression d'espace à l'arrivant qui découvre immédiatement des vues sur un bassin d'agrément, sur des cascades, sur une rivière, sur des piscines et sur la mer. Le béton a été largement utilisé et donne à l'endroit un certain air de solidité que l'on ne retrouve pas dans la réception du Bali Hyatt. Néanmoins, l'absence de décoration est un atout car la sobriété des lignes procure ce sentiment de sérénité si important dans l'architecture hôtelière.

Des édifices de trois étages, surmontés de toits en tuiles oranges, abritent les chambres d'hôtes. Leur architecture ne diffère guère de celle des autres grands hôtels, mais ils ont été répartis d'une façon si ingénieuse qu'ils ne s'imposent pas dans le paysage. Tongg Clarke et Mechler de Honolulu ont dessiné les jardins qui ont été réalisés ensuite par Indo Sekar de Bali.

Dans les intérieurs conçus par Hirsch Bedner Associates de Hong Kong, les chambres spacieuses ont toutes un balcon qui donne sur la mer ou sur les jardins. Les aménagements particuliers

Grand Hyatt's 750 rooms are spread out over four 'villages' consisting of four-storey structures. This is a view of the Regency Club rooms.

Die 750 Zimmer sind auf vier »Dörfer« mit dreistöckigen Häusern verteilt. Hier ein Blick auf die Zimmer des Regency Club.

Les 750 chambres du Grand Hyatt sont réparties sur quatre "villages" dans des édifices à trois étages. Ici: le Regency Club.

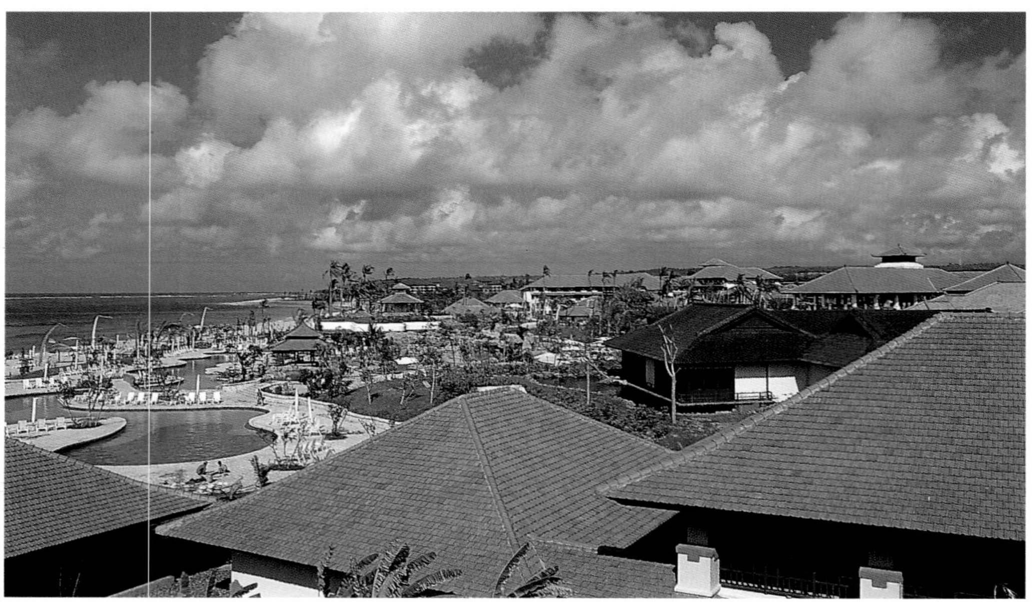

An overall view of the main swimming pool next to the beach.

Ein Blick auf den Swimmingpool in der Nähe des Strandes.

Vue d'ensemble de la piscine principale près de la plage.

In the interiors designed by Hirsch Bedner Associates of Hong Kong, each spacious guestroom has its own private balcony looking out to the sea or landscaped gardens. Unique features include a cozy lounge area next to the balcony, and a huge bathroom that opens up to the bedroom.

Among the restaurant outlets, the Nelayan Seafood Restaurant is probably the most interesting structure. Built of timber posts and beams, and roofed over with the traditional 'alang-alang' thatch, the open-sided pavilions are surrounded by lotus ponds. Other facilities include a grand ballroom with a seating capacity of 750, a fitness and health club and a night bazaar. This bazaar is made up of individual Balinese structures housing all kinds of shops.

Designing a mega-resort of this scale is no easy task. The design of Grand Hyatt Bali has ably demonstrates the importance of breaking down the scale of the complex and spreading the bulk of the accommodation through individual clusters. However, the need for easy orientation is another important consideration that is perhaps not entirely well resolved in this instance. Of course, the use of traditional forms in such a massive complex raises several philosophical and technical problems as well.

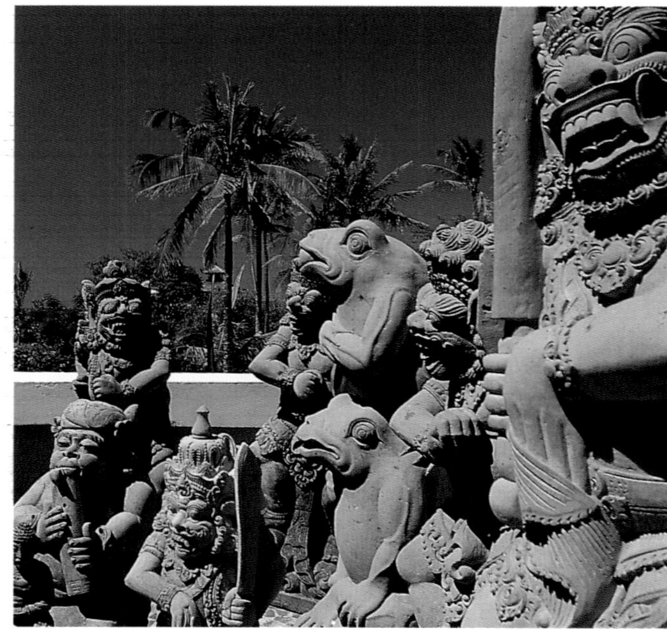

Stone carvings and statues in the bazaar.

Skulpturen und Statuen im Basar.

Sculptures et reliefs en pierre dans le bazar.

Die Inneneinrichtung stammt von Hirsch Bedner Associates, Hongkong. Jedes der geräumigen Gästezimmer hat einen eigenen Balkon mit Blick auf das Meer oder die Gärten. Einzigartig sind eine gemütliche Sitzecke neben dem Balkon und ein sehr großes Badezimmer mit Zugang zum Schlafraum.

Unter den Restaurants ist das Nelayan Seafood Restaurant vermutlich der interessanteste Bau. Aus Holzpfählen und -balken gebaut und mit dem traditionellen *alang-alang*–Strohdach versehen, ist der Pavillon an den Seiten offen und wird von Lotos-Teichen umgeben. Zu den weiteren Angeboten gehören ein Ballsaal mit 750 Sitzplätzen, ein Fitneß- und Gesundheitsclub und ein Nachtbasar. Dieser Basar besteht aus einzeln stehenden balinesischen Häusern, in denen viele unterschiedliche Läden untergebracht sind.

Eine Mega-Anlage von diesen Ausmaßen zu entwerfen, ist keine leichte Aufgabe. Das Grand Hyatt Bali zeigt, wie wichtig es ist, einen Komplex dieser Größe aufzubrechen und die Unterkünfte an mehreren Stellen zu verteilen. Ein weiterer wichtiger Aspekt ist die Notwendigkeit schneller Orientierung, und dieses Problem ist für den Augenblick noch nicht befriedigend gelöst. Und natürlich stellen sich bei der Verwendung traditioneller Formen in so einem massiven Komplex auch verschiedene philosophische und technische Fragen.

comprennent un espace salon intime près du balcon et une immense salle de bains contiguë à la chambre.

Des restaurants, le Nelayan Seafood Restaurant est sans aucun doute la construction la plus intéressante. Entourés de bassins couverts de lotus, les pavillons ouverts sur un côté sont construits en poteaux et madriers de bois et coiffés du toit en chaume traditionnel *alang-alang*. Il y a également une grande salle de bal où 750 personnes peuvent s'asseoir, un club de mise en forme et un bazar nocturne composé de maisons individuelles de style balinais qui abritent toutes sortes de boutiques.

Ce n'est pas une tâche facile que de réaliser un complexe hôtelier d'aussi grande envergure. La conception du Grand Hyatt Balia démontre l'importance de morceler un projet de cette taille et réussit avec bonheur à remplacer un ensemble volumineux par des groupes d'éléments individuels. Néanmoins, il n'est pas très facile de s'y orienter. Cet autre point principal a été assez mal résolu dans ce cas. L'utilisation de formes traditionnelles dans un complexe aussi énorme soulève aussi, naturellement, plusieurs problèmes philosophiques et techniques.

Spread over 16 hectares of gardens, the dense development is hardly perceptible.

Auf dem Gartengelände von 16 Hektar ist die dichte Bebauung kaum erkennbar.

On remarque à peine la taille importante du complexe dont les bâtiments sont disséminés dans un parc de 16 hectares.

Water features at the entrance lobby convey the aquatic theme of the resort.

Wasser an der Eingangshalle unterstreicht das Hauptthema der Anlage.

Le complexe est construit autour du thème de l'eau. Ici, le bassin d'agrément devant l'entrée de la réception.

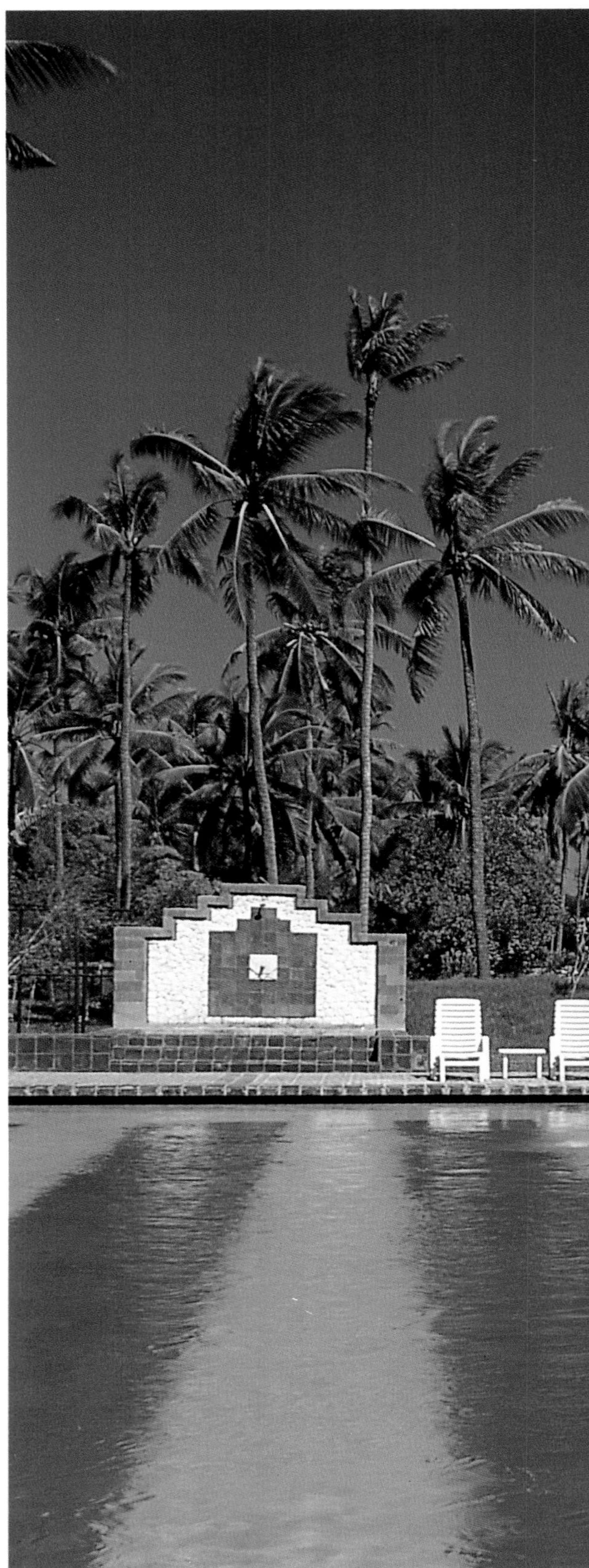

One of the five swimming pools in the resort.

Einer der fünf Swimmingpools.

Une des cinq piscines du complexe.

The Balinese bathing pool is modelled after traditional pools.

Das balinesische Bad wurde nach traditionellem Vorbild gebaut.

Les bains balinais sont conçus dans le style traditionnel.

One of the private villas in the grounds of the resort.

Eine der Privatvillen.

Une des villas privées dans les jardins du complexe.

Large conference facilities are also available at the resort.

Auch große Konferenzräume stehen zur Verfügung.

Le complexe comprend de vastes salles de conférence.

View of the pool from a restaurant.

Blick auf den Pool vom Restaurant aus.

Vue d'une piscine depuis son restaurant.

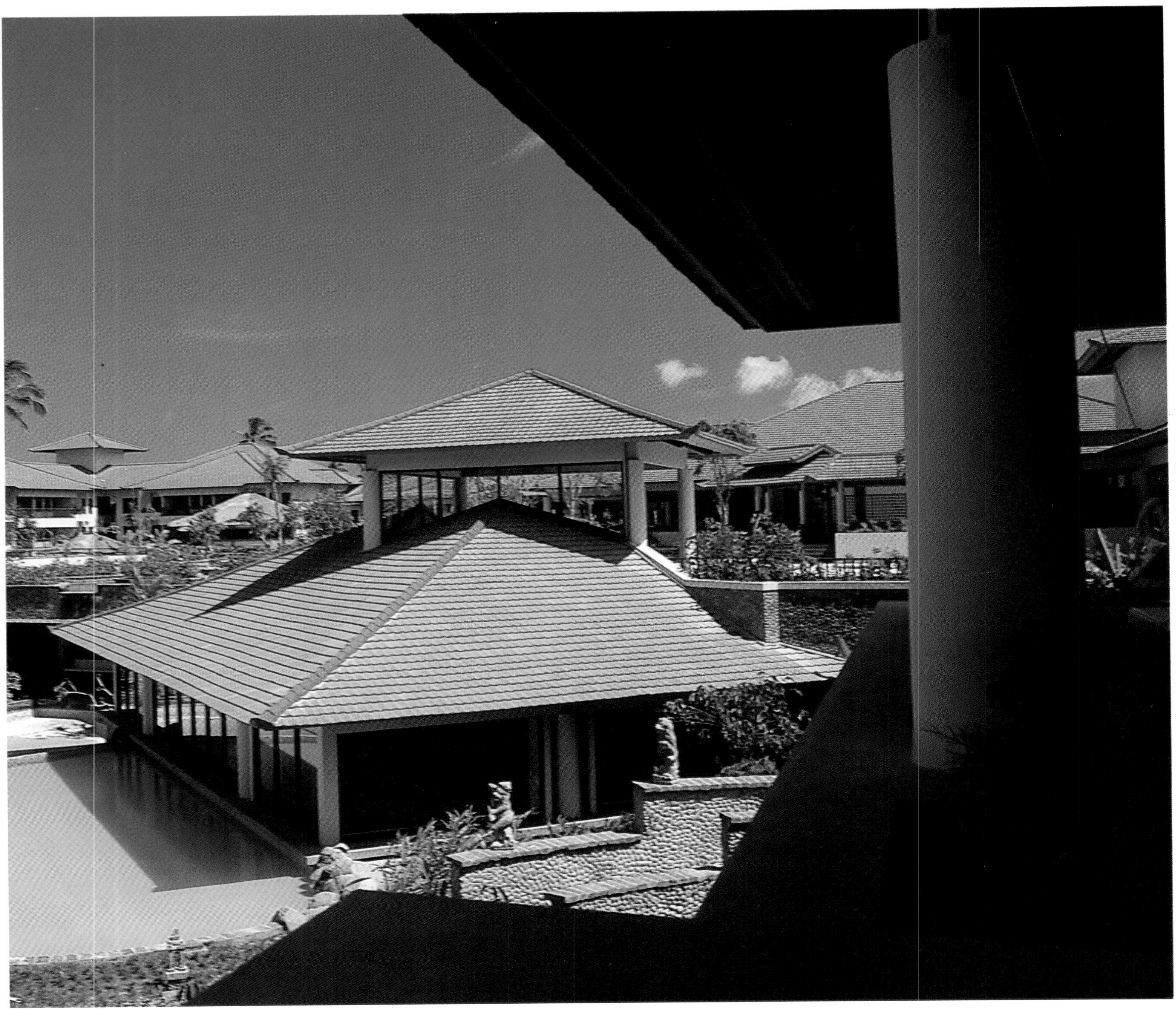

A variety of roof forms are used in the formal treatment.

Die Dächer wurden in verschiedenen Formen gebaut.

Les formes variées des toits font partie du concept architectural.

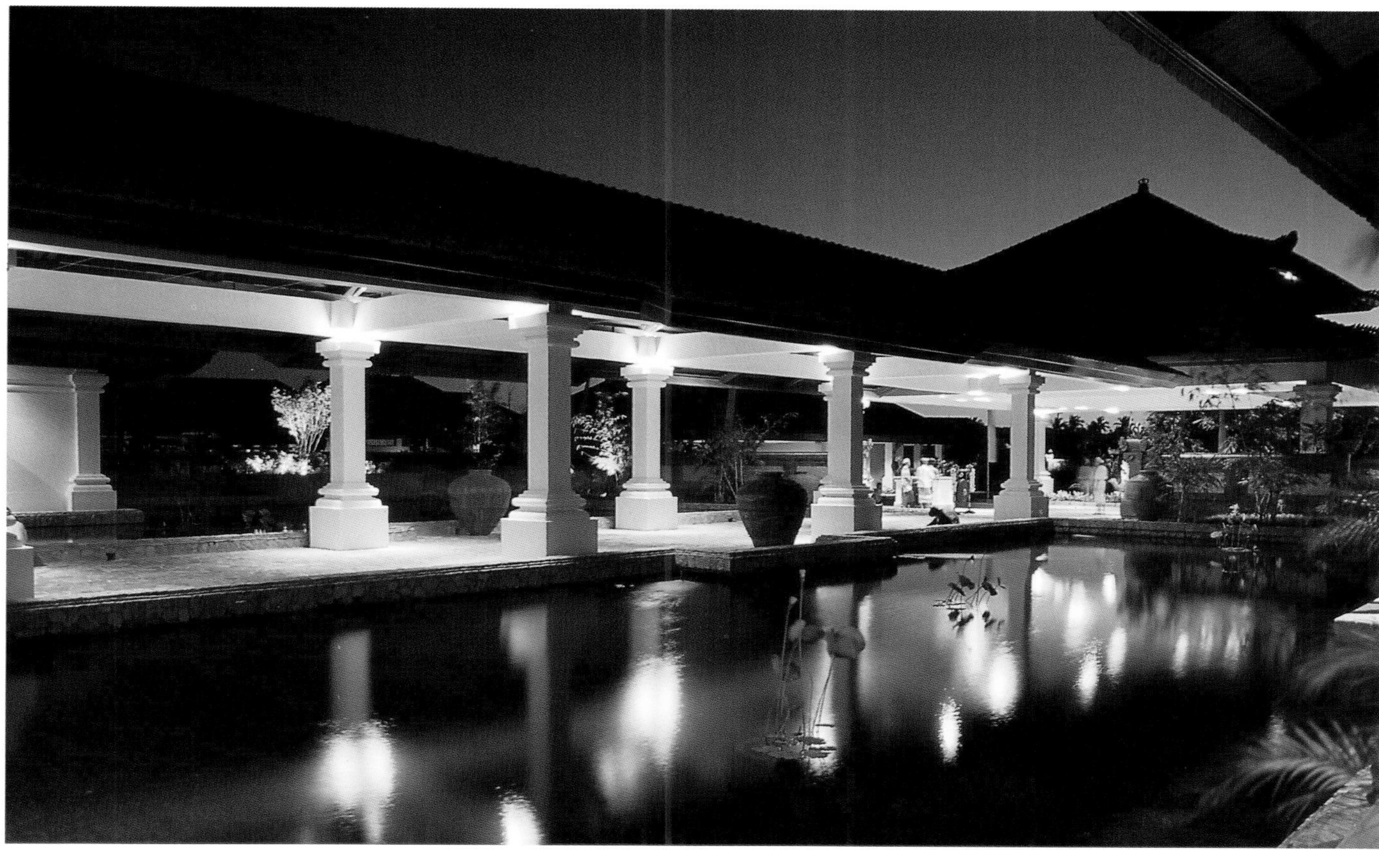

A long walkway surrounded by reflecting pools lead guests from the entrance porch into the lobby.

Ein langer Gang, umgeben von glitzernden Wasserbecken, führt die Gäste von der Eingangsveranda in die Lobby.

Une longue allée entourée de bassins d'agrément relie le portail d'entrée à la réception.

Part of the lobby lounge is visible from the bazaar.

Vom Basar aus ist ein Teil der Lounge zu sehen.

Une partie de la réception est visible depuis le bazar.

PHILIPPINES

Pearl Farm Beach Resort,
Samal Island, Davao City,
Mindanao

Pearl Farm Beach Resort, Samal Island, Davao City, Mindanao

The jagged profile of the roof provides an especially interesting silhouette when viewed against the backdrop of verdant hills.

Vor dem Hintergrund der grünen Hügel bildet das gezackte Dach eine besonders interessante Silhouette.

La silhouette dentelée des toits se découpant devant les collines verdoyantes compose un tableau captivant.

The Philippines is an archipelago of more than 7,000 islands, many of which are endowed with spectacular scenery and clear waters. The Pearl Farm Beach Resort lies in a scenic cove on one of such islands - Samal Island. It is only a 40-minute boat ride from Davao City in Mindanao. The regional office of the Department of Tourism has earmarked the island and other surrounding isles to be the centrepiece of a major tourism programme to lure tourists to Davao City. About 20 resorts in the same genre as the Pearl Farm are expected to be built over the next ten years.

Once a breeding farm for cultured pearls, the 11-hectare property of Pearl Farm is located on a secluded cove on the beautiful island. It used to produce cultured pearls from white-lipped oysters of the Sulu Seas. But it was subsequently bought over by the Florendo family, known more as the banana magnates of the country, and upgraded into a luxury resort. The waters of the Sulu Sea offer varied diving spots, while the dazzling coral gardens are a delight to underwater photography enthusiasts.

Conceptualised by Bobby Manosa, who is probably the most outspoken champion of indigenous Filipino architecture, the resort's Samal Houses are inspired by the stilt houses of the seafaring Samal tribes of the Sulu archipelago. The idea is evoke a semblance of an indigenous community built over the water. The sense of isolation and the pervasive presence of the sea imbues the resort with a special ambience. The design also reflects Manosa's long interest in evolving a specifically Filipino architecture by experimenting and creating new possibilites of handling native materials like rattan, bamboo and hardwoods of various sorts.

Each individual pavilion thus uses architectonic devices that both explicitly and subtly recall the traditional forms of regional habitations. Ethnic motifs reflecting the cultural heritage of indigenous tribes are used throughout the resort. There are 19 Samal Houses and six Samal Suites. The suites are two-storey duplexes, with the upper chambers consisting of spacious bathrooms. The lower rooms each consists of a sitting room and a bedroom with an attached bathroom. In addition, there are 15 standard hotel-type rooms at two main blocks located at the hilltop. Here, the natural terrain has been preserved in its original conditions. Every room has sliding glass doors that provide panoramic views of the turquoise sea. Schools of fishes swimming among the stilts of the Samal Houses are delightful

(previous page):
Pearl Farm Beach Resort, Samal Island.

(vorherige Seite):
Pearl Farm Beach Resort, Samal Island.

(page précédente):
Pearl Farm Beach Resort, Samal Island.

Pearl Farm Beach Resort, Samal Island, Davao City, Mindanao

Die Philippinen sind ein Archipel mit mehr als 7000 Inseln, viele davon mit einer spektakulären Landschaft und klarem Wasser. Das Pearl Farm Beach Resort befindet sich auf einer solchen Insel, Samal Island. Die Fahrt mit dem Schiff von Davao City in Mindanao dauert nur 40 Minuten. Das Regionalbüro des Department of Tourism hat diese und andere Inseln in der Umgebung als Zentrum für ein größeres Tourismusprogramm ausgewählt, um Gäste nach Davao City zu locken. Etwa zwanzig Anlagen im Stil der Pearl Farm sollen in den nächsten zehn Jahren gebaut werden.

Einst eine Zuchtperlenfarm, liegt die Pearl Farm auf einem elf Hektar großen Gelände in einer abgeschiedenen Bucht. Hier züchtete man früher in den Austern der Sulu Sea Perlen. Doch später wurde das Gelände von der Familie Florendo, bekannt als Bananen-Könige des Landes, aufgekauft und zu einer Hotel-Anlage der Luxusklasse umgebaut. Die Sulu Sea bietet Gelegenheit zum Tauchen, und an den prachtvollen Korallengärten wird jeder Unterwasserfotograf seine Freude haben.

Bobby Manosa, der wohl größte Meister echter philippinischer Baukunst, hat die Anlage geplant. Die Pfahlbauten der seefahrenden Samal-Stämme im Sulu-Archipel lieferten die Vorlage für die Samal Houses in der Ferienanlage. Das Gefühl der Einsamkeit und das allgegenwärtige Meer verleihen der Anlage eine ganz besondere Atmosphäre. Deutlich wird auch Manosas großes Interesse daran, eine typische philippische Architektur zu entwickeln. Dazu experimentiert er und schafft neue Möglichkeiten im Umgang mit einheimischem Material wie Rattan, Bambus und verschiedenen Harthölzern.

Jeder einzelne Pavillon hat daher architektonische Elemente, die absichtlich und subtil an traditionelle regionale Wohnformenen erinnern. Überall finden sich Motive aus dem kulturellen Erbe der einheimischen Stämme. Es gibt 19 Samal-Häuser und sechs Samal-Suiten. Zwei Haupthäuser oben auf dem Hügel, wo die Natur in ihrem ursprünglichen Zustand erhalten ist, verfügen über 15 Hotelzimmer des Standardtypes. Jedes Zimmer hat eine gläserne Schiebetür, die den Blick auf das türkisfarbene Meer freigibt. Fischschwärme schwimmen zwischen den Pfählen und sind eine unterhaltsame Ablenkung für die Gäste. Wenn die Wellen abends schlagen, klingt das wie ein beruhigendes Schlaflied. Am Eingang jedes Zimmers stehen ein Krug mit Wasser und eine Kokosschale als Schöpflöffel bereit, damit die Gäste sich die Füße reinigen können.

Pearl Farm Beach Resort, Ile Samal, Davao City, Mindanao

Les Philippines sont un archipel de plus de 7000 îles dont un grand nombre offrent une nature merveilleuse et une mer de cristal. Le Pearl Beach Resort s'étend dans un golfe pittoresque de l'île Samal qui est à 40 minutes en bateau de Davao City située sur Mindaneo. L'office régional du Ministère du Tourisme a choisi cette île et quelques autres environnantes pour développer un programme majeur de tourisme autour de Davao City. La construction d'une vingtaine de complexes hôteliers, du genre de Pearl Farm, est prévue au cours des dix prochaines années.

Pearl Farm est une ancienne ferme de culture perlière de 11 hectares, située dans une baie solitaire de l'île splendide. La ferme produisait des perles de culture des huîtres de la mer Sulu avant d'être achetée par la famille Florendo (les magnats de la banane de la région) qui l'ont transformée en une villégiature de luxe. La mer de Sulu est un paradis de plongée sous-marine tandis que les merveilleux jardins de coraux font la joie des amateurs de photographie sous-marine.

Bobby Manosa, sans doute le champion le plus ardent de l'architecture indigène philippine, a réalisé l'ensemble qui s'inspire des maisons à pilotis du peuple marin de Samal et évoque une communauté indigène construite sur l'eau. L'endroit est enrobé d'une ambiance particulière créée par la mer infinie et l'impression de solitude. Le complexe dévoile également la démarche de Manosa qui s'est toujours attaché à faire évoluer l'architecture philippine en expérimentant et en créant de nouveaux procédés d'utilisation des matériaux locaux tels que le rotin, le bambou et différentes espèces d'arbres exotiques.

Chaque pavillon est construit selon des méthodes architecturales, utilisées avec subtilité, qui rappellent les formes traditionnelles des habitations locales. Partout, des motifs évoquent l'héritage culturel des tribus autochtones. On trouve 19 maisons Samal et 6 suites Samal. Les suites sont des duplex, avec de spacieuses salles de bains au niveau supérieur et un salon, une chambre avec salle de bain attenante au niveau inférieur. Il y a également 15 chambres standard occupant deux édifices principaux situés en haut de la colline. Ici, la topographie du terrain n'a pas été modifiée. Chaque chambre a des portes en verre coulissantes qui s'ouvrent sur des vues panoramiques de la mer turquoise. Les résidents jouissent du spectacle charmant de bancs de poissons évoluant entre les maisons à pilotis et s'endorment la nuit au bruit des vaguelettes qui viennent lécher les maisons. Pour se laver les pieds, on trouve devant chaque

distractions for the guests. At night, the sound of lapping waves provides a soothing lullaby. A jar of water and a coconut shell dipper are placed at the entrance of each unit for guests to clean their feet.

The pervasive use of bamboo, left in their natural colour, as the main building material is highly ingenious. It imbues the resort with a natural charm and poignancy that are truly unique in Southeast Asia. The jagged profile of the roof provides an especially interesting silhouette when viewed against the backdrop of verdant hills. The multi-tiered roof of the elegantly proportioned Parola Bar, which is an individual pavilion jutting out above the water, acts the main visual focus of the resort. Named after the local term for lighthouse, it was once a lookout post when the place was still a pearl farm.

The large swimming pool, located next to the sea, is designed with the now popular "knife-edge" effect of water cascading over the edge of the pool. To heighten the aquatic theme, a fish pond is also stocked with rare aquatic species like the *pawikan* (marine turtle) and the giant *taklobo* clams. The lush landscaping in the property is complemented by numerous wooden footbridges and walkways. Island structures are built of natural materials like bamboo, wood, stone and coral.

From the overall conception to the level of its detailing, Pearl Farm Beach Resort reflects a determined but controlled effort to showcase the rich architectural heritage of the region in an uncontrived manner that is both simple and refined. An economy of means is employed to subtle effects. The outcome is a handsomely detailed resort of great confidence and competence.

The overall layout of the exemplary resort contributes immensely to the general feeling of repose. The engagement of architecture with the sea possesses a directness and rawness that thrill the senses in a thoroughly absorbing manner. Site, form and materials have been crafted and integrated into a seamless whole.

Die reichliche Verwendung von naturfarbenem Bambus als Hauptbaumaterial entspricht ganz dem einheimischen Stil. Dadurch bekommt die Ferienanlage einen natürlichen Charme, wie er in Südostasien wirklich einmalig ist. Vor dem Hintergrund grüner Hügel zeichnet sich das gezackte Dach als interessante Silhouette ab. Das vielschichtige Dach der eleganten Parola Bar, die allein direkt über dem Wasser steht, ist der Hauptblickfang der gesamten Anlage. Der Name ist das einheimische Wort für Leuchtturm, und als hier noch eine Perlenfarm betrieben wurde, war die Bar ein Beobachtungsposten.

Der große Swimmingpool am Meer ist mit dem inzwischen beliebten »Messerschneiden«-Effekt angelegt, wobei Wasser über den Beckenrand strömt. In einem Fischteich leben seltene Tiere wie der *pawikan* (Seeschildkröte) und die riesigen *taklobo*-Muscheln. In die üppige Landschaft fügen sich zahlreiche hölzerne Fußgängerbrücken und Spazierwege ein. Für Bauten auf der Insel werden natürliche Materialien wie Bambus, Holz, Stein und Korallen verwendet.

Von der Gesamtkonzeption bis ins Detail ist die Pearl Farm ein entschlossener, aber kontrollierter Versuch, das reiche architektonische Erbe der Region schlicht und zugleich raffiniert vorzuführen. Die Sparsamkeit der Mittel schafft subtile Wirkungen. Das Ergebnis ist eine schöne Ferienanlage mit Selbstbewußtsein und Charakter.

Die Gesamtausstattung der beispielhaften Anlage vermittelt ein allgemeines Gefühl der Ruhe. Die Verbindung von Architektur mit dem Meer ist von einer Unmittelbarkeit und Rauhheit, die die Sinne ansprechen. Lage, Form und Materialien bilden eine nahtlose Einheit.

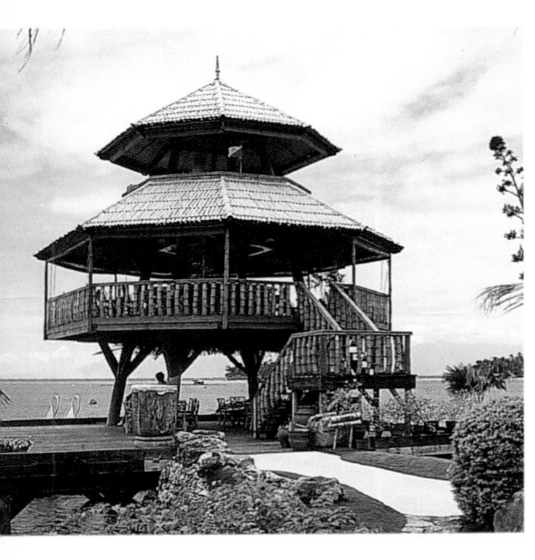

The Parola Bar announces the presence of the resort in a dramatic manner.

Die Parola Bar ist besonders bemerkenswert und eindrucksvoll.

Le bar Parola est le premier tableau spectaculaire que l'on voit en arrivant au complexe.

porte, un pot d'eau et une coque de noix de coco pour puiser l'eau.

Utilisé avec ingéniosité, le bambou constitue le principal matériau de construction. Il apporte au complexe ce charme naturel typique du Sud-Est asiatique. La silhouette dentelée des toits se découpant devant les collines verdoyantes, compose un tableau captivant. Le toit en gradins du bar Parola domine l'ensemble. Le pavillon aux proportions élégantes qui surplombe la mer servait de "phare" comme son nom l'indique, lorsque l'endroit était une ferme de culture de perles.

Située près de la mer, la vaste piscine a un côté qui déborde en cascades, une forme à présent très populaire. Pour le plaisir du regard, un bassin à poissons abrite des espèces aquatiques rares telles que la *pawikan* (une tortue marine) et la *taklobo* (une palourde géante). De nombreux passerelles et passages en bois sillonnent le paysage à la végétation luxuriante. Les autres structures sont construites en matériaux naturels comme le bambou, le bois, la pierre et le corail.

Le Pearl Farm Beach Resort révèle, jusque dans ses moindres détails, une maîtrise de l'utilisation à la fois simple et raffinée du riche héritage culturel de la région. Le résultat est un complexe hôtelier harmonieux sur toute la ligne, réalisé avec brio et sûreté.

Le concept d'ensemble de cet hôtel exemplaire contribue beaucoup à l'atmosphère paisible qui s'en dégage. L'interaction étroite de l'architecture et de la mer compose un décor d'une nature sauvage émouvante. Le site, les structures et les matériaux sont travaillés et intégrés en un ensemble parfait.

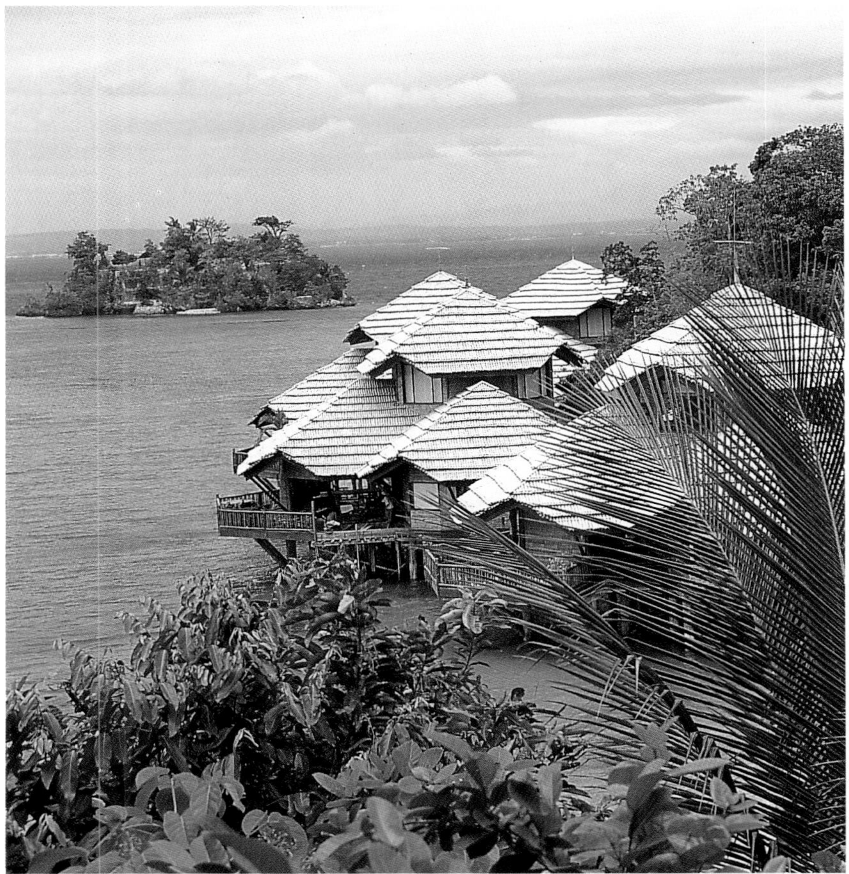

Architecturally, the design uses various materials and features that both explicitly and subtly recall the traditional forms of regional habitations.

Verschiedene Materialien und Elemente werden eingesetzt, die ganz bewußt und subtil an die traditionellen Formen einheimischer Unterkünfte erinnern.

L'architecture utilise avec précision et subtilité divers matériaux et structures que l'on retrouve dans les formes traditionnelles des habitations locales.

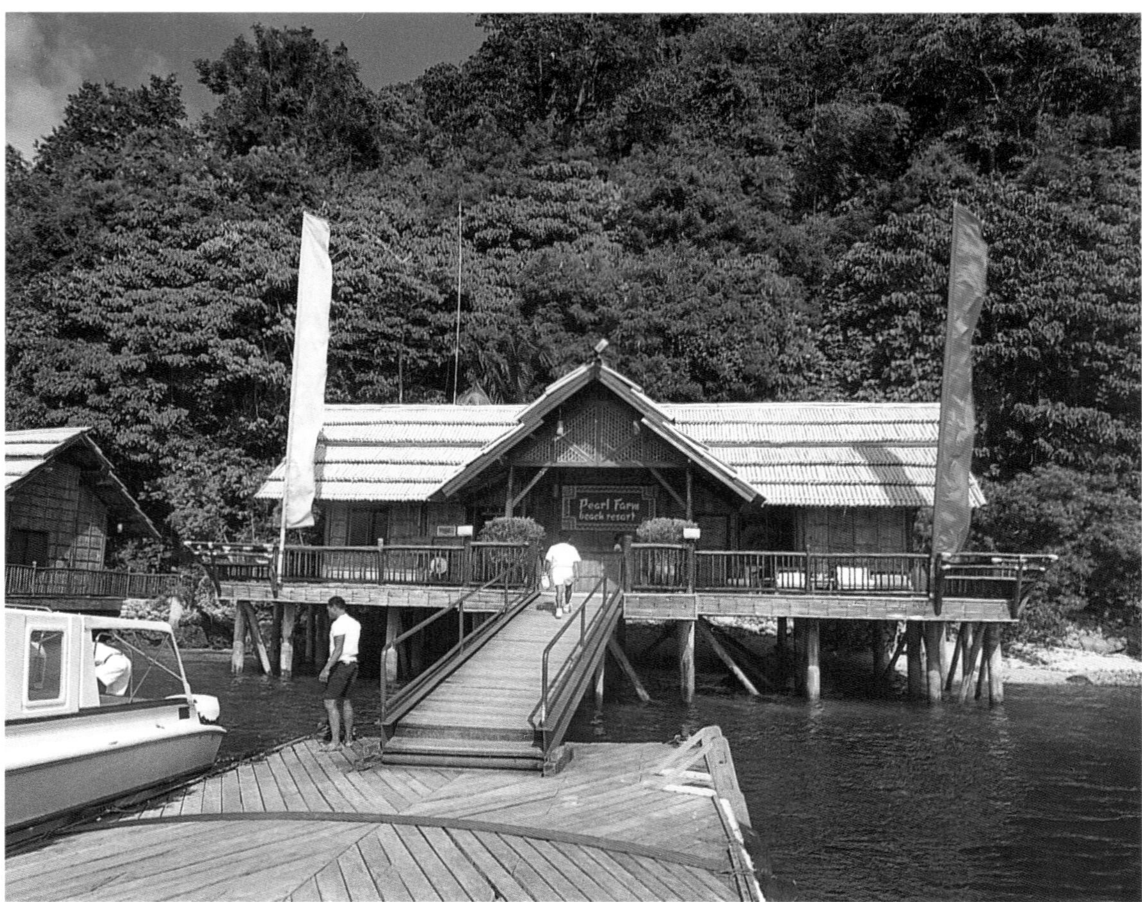

Guests are greeted by a simple jetty that leads to the reception lobby set against the lush hills.

Die Gäste werden von einem schlichten Steg begrüßt, der sie zu der Empfangshalle vor den üppig grünen Hügeln führt.

Une jetée toute simple conduit les hôtes à la réception construite devant un paysage de collines verdoyantes.

The design reflects the architect's interest in evolving a specifically Filipino architecture by creating new possibilites of handling native materials like rattan and bamboo.

Hier ist das Bemühen des Architekten erkennbar, eine spezielle philippinische Bauweise zu entwickeln. Er schafft neue Möglichkeiten im Umgang mit einheimischem Material wie Rattan und Bambus.

La conception dévoile la démarche de l'architecte visant à faire évoluer l'architecture philippine en créant de nouveaux procédés d'utilisation de matériaux locaux tels que le rotin et le bambou.

The multi-tiered roof of the elegantly proportioned Parola Bar, which is an individual pavilion jutting out above the water, acts as the main visual focus of the resort.

Das Ziegeldach der eleganten Parola Bar, die als Einzelpavillon aus dem Wasser ragt, ist der optische Blickfang der Anlage.

Le pavillon aux proportions élégantes du bar Parola surplombe la mer. Son toit en gradins domine le complexe.

The Suites are two-storey duplexes, with the upper chambers consisting of spacious bathrooms. The lower rooms each consists of a sitting room and a bedroom with an attached bathroom.

Die Suiten liegen in einstöckigen Doppelhäusern. In den oberen Räumen befinden sich geräumige Badezimmer, unten jeweils ein Wohnzimmer und ein Schlafraum mit Bad.

Les suites sont des duplex, avec de vastes salles de bains au niveau supérieur. Le niveau inférieur abrite un salon et une chambre avec salle de bains attenante.

Spacious timber-decked terraces overlook the sea.

Von den großen Holzterrassen hat man Meeresblick.

De spacieuses terrasses en bois surplombent la mer.

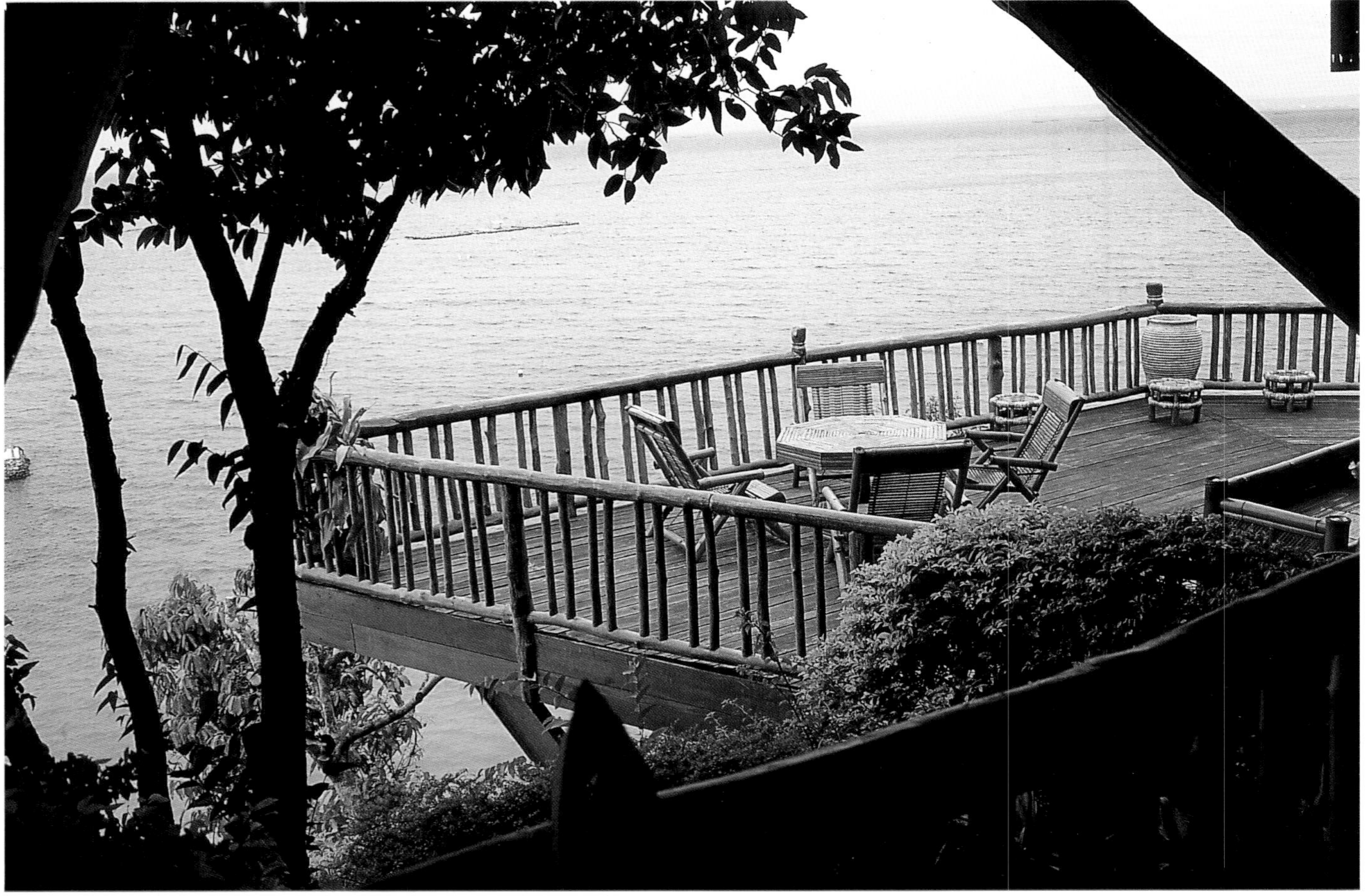

Ethnic motifs reflecting the cultural heritage of indigenous tribes are used throughout the resort. Existing trees are also kept intact where possible.

Überall findet man Motive aus dem kulturellen Erbe der einheimischen Stämme. Auch Baumbestand wird erhalten, wo es möglich ist.

Le complexe abonde en motifs évoquant l'héritage culturel des tribus autochtones. Les arbres ont été conservés dans la mesure du possible.

(opposite page):
Stairways connecting various parts of the resort are designed with traditional materials like bamboo and various hardwoods.

(gegenüberliegende Seite):
Die Treppen, die die verschiedenen Bereiche der Anlage miteinander verbinden, wurden mit traditionellem Material wie Bambus und verschiedenen Hartholzsorten gebaut.

(page ci-contre):
Les escaliers qui relient les différent parties du complexe sont construits avec les matériaux traditionnels de la région tels que le bambou et les différentes variétés de bois dur.

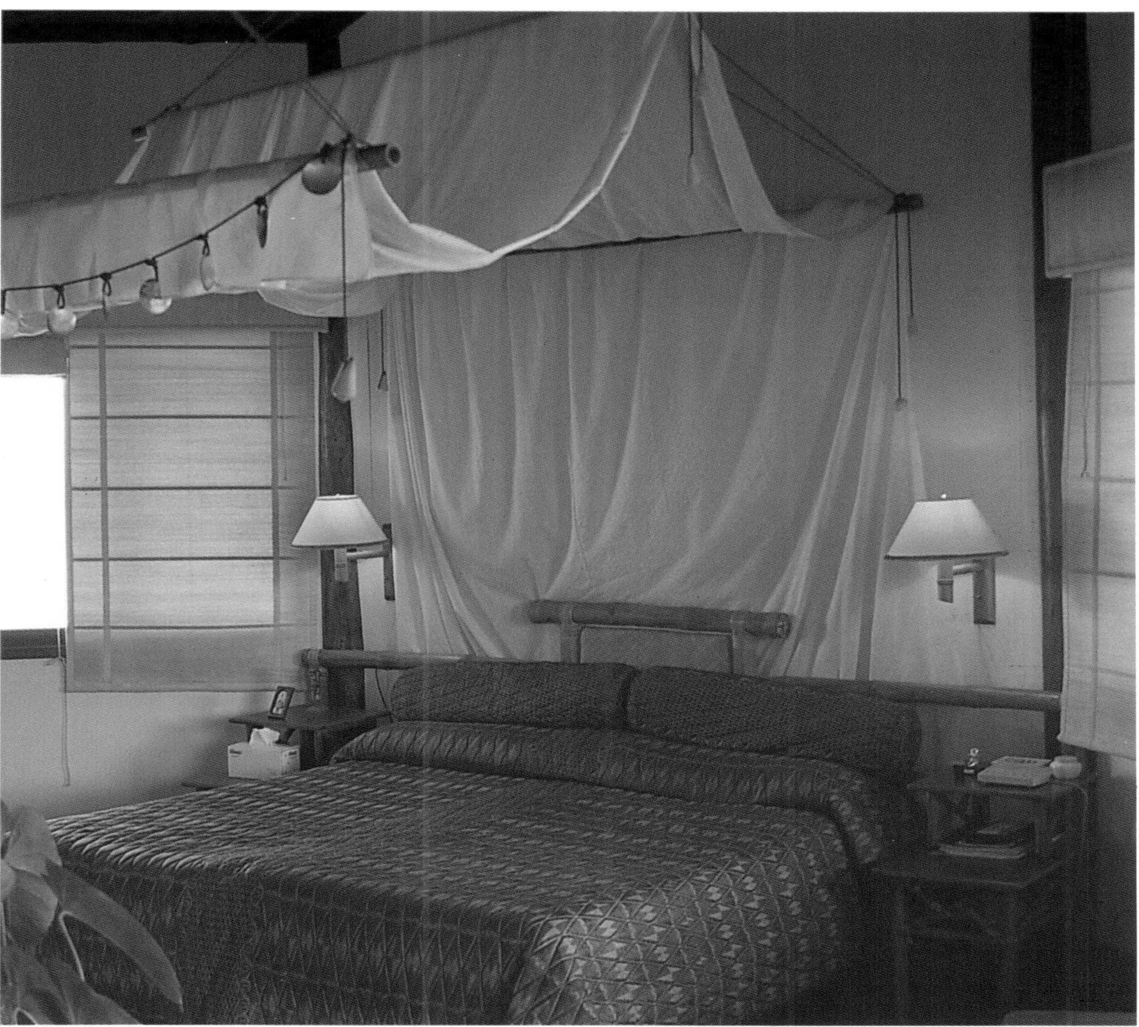

The interiors are simply furnished with ethnic materials, evoking a rustic charm that is understated but elegant.

Die Innenräume sind mit einheimischem Material schlicht möbliert und strahlen einen zurückhaltenden rustikalen Charme aus, der dennoch elegant ist.

Des matériaux locaux ont servi à l'ameublement des intérieurs d'une élégance sobre.

A close-up view of the roof structure at the ceiling of the bedroom.

Eine Nahaufnahme der Dachstruktur im Schlafraum.

Un gros plan de la structure du toit dans une chambre.

"No matter where we look, it is becoming increasingly difficult to recognise an original from a copy, or from a copy of a copy. Mimicry has replaced innovation as a creative value. We recycle everything."

Thomas Lawson,
'Nostalgia as Resistance in Modern Dreams'

Conclusions
Zusammenfassung
Conclusions

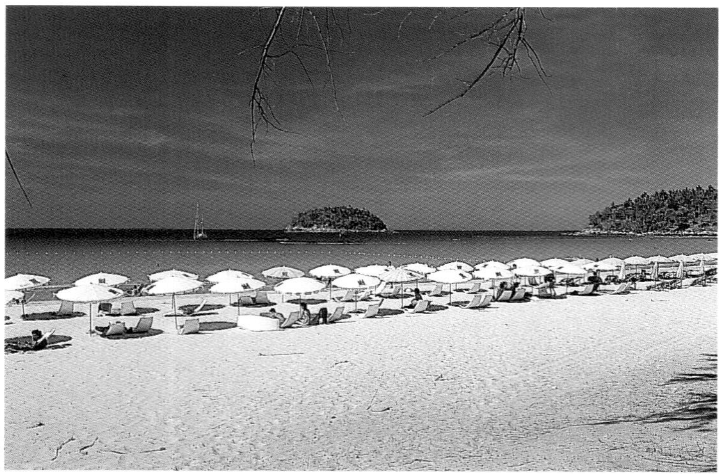

Increasingly sophisticated tourists will demand new destinations and different forms of resorts.

Zunehmend anspruchsvolle Touristen werden nach neuen Reisezielen und anderen Hotelanlagen verlangen.

Des touristes toujours plus exigeants demanderont de nouvelles destinations et d'autres formes de villégiature.

The sensitivity of architects designing resorts in pristine environments will be tested.

Architekten werden mit ihrem ganzen Können herausgefordert sein, wenn sie Hotelanlagen in unberührter Natur planen.

Les architectes devront prouver leur sensibilité quand ils dessineront les plans d'un complexe situé dans un environnement intact.

In this era of rapid expansion of the international hotel trade, resorts are constantly in a process of evolution. The success of a resort is dependent on several factors: location, market segmentation, facilities and standards of service. Recent trends indicate that resorts are beginning to specialise and reinforcing niche marketing. Two broad trends in the resort industry are likely in the near future. One is the establishment of increasingly elaborate large-scale developments involving theme-parks.

Large integrated resorts offering a wide range of recreation and leisure facilities and activities are also likely to be popular. 'Activity' resorts, like the US-based Pacific Islands Club resorts in Guam and Saipan, will definitely increase in number. These integrated resort development in emerging destinations of Southeast Asia, in the mould of Phuket's Laguna Beach Resort, will test the sensitivity and creativity of architects in problems of scale, representation and authenticity.

Another trend is the emergence of environmentally sensitive, small specialised resorts. These will be centred around unique recreational activities or cultural attractions. These special interest market segments for more sophisticated and demanding travellers are likely to flourish, especially in remote or hitherto off-limits regions like Myanmar and Vietnam.

Several tourism trends are already discernible in the first half of the nineties. Tourists are becoming more sophisticated and are increasingly seeking new opportunities and demanding high quality and well-planned destinations. These consumers will demand specialised hotels that are designed for their specific needs. Fragmentation of tourist markets and the proliferation of special interest tours are the obvious trends. There is also an increasing interest in forms of alternative eco-tourism and convention tourism.

The search for new market niches will see an accelerated trend toward market segmentation through new types of hotels. Already major chains have established new subchains with slightly different emphasis. Amanresorts has started a 'no-frills' chain of resorts, exemplified by Balina Serai Hotel and Chedi Ubud in Bali.

Craftsmanship is highly evident in most of the projects shown in this book, due to the availability of a large pool of skilled craftsmen and artisans capable of executing high quality worksmanship, especially in Indonesia and Thailand. It will continue to be an important architectural criteria in the design of new resorts, especially in small scale boutique hotels.

Currently, buildings around the world are rarely produced by craftsmen. Traditional forms no longer represent how buildings are now being constructed. The logic of construction of traditional architecture was visually apparent to everyone — the architecture represented directly the materials used and the method of construction employed. These "transparent" technologies are being displaced

»Ganz gleich, wohin wir sehen, es wird immer schwieriger, ein Original von einer Kopie oder von der Kopie einer Kopie zu unterscheiden. Nachahmung scheint als kreativer Wert an die Stelle der Erneuerung getreten zu sein. Wir recyceln alles.«

Thomas Lawson,
›Nostalgia as Resistance in Modern Dreams‹

In dieser Zeit der schnellen Expansion des internationalen Hotelmarkts werden die Ferienanlagen ständig weiterentwickelt. Der Erfolg einer Anlage hängt von mehreren Faktoren ab: Lage, Größe des Marktanteils, Annehmlichkeiten und Standard des Service. Neuere Trends zeigen, daß Ferienanlagen anfangen, sich zu spezialisieren und Marktlücken zu suchen. Für die Zukunft scheinen sich zwei Hauptrichtungen abzuzeichnen. Eine ist die Errichtung immer raffinierterer Anlagen in großem Stil, zu denen auch Themen-Parks gehören.

Wahrscheinlich werden große Anlagen mit zahlreichen Freizeitangeboten und Aktivitäten sehr beliebt sein. Die Zahl dieser Anlagen, wie die amerikanischen Pacific Island Clubs in Guam und Saipan, wird mit Sicherheit steigen. Diese Entwicklung von Ferienanlagen an neuen Zielen in Südostasien nach dem Vorbild von Laguna Beach in Phuket wird ein Test sein, wie sensibel und kreativ Architekten Probleme wie Größe, Repräsentation und Authentizität angehen.

Der zweite Trend geht in die Richtung umweltfreundlicher, spezialisierter kleiner Anlagen. In ihnen dreht sich alles um einzigartige Freizeitbeschäftigungen oder kulturelle Ereignisse. Diese speziellen Marktanteile für anspruchsvolle Reisende werden wahrscheinlich kräftig wachsen, vor allem in entfernten oder bislang nicht zugänglichen Ländern wie Birma und Vietnam.

Einige Touristentrends sind schon in der ersten Hälfte der 90er Jahre erkennbar. Die Reisenden werden anspruchsvoller, sie suchen immer neue Möglichkeiten, verlangen hohe Qualität und gut geplante Ziele. Diese Konsumenten werden Hotels wählen, die auf ihre spezifischen Bedürfnisse zugeschnitten sind. Die Aufteilung des Tourismusmarktes und die weitere Verbreitung von Spezialreisen sind die offensichtlichen Trends. Ebenso steigt das Interesse an alternativen Öko-Reisen und Kongreßtourismus.

Die Suche nach neuen Marktlücken wird den Trend beschleunigen, daß Hotels eines neuen Typs die Marktanteile unter sich ausmachen. Große Ketten haben bereits neue Tochterketten mit etwas anderen Schwerpunkten. Amranresorts hat eine Kette mit Hotels »ohne Kinkerlitzchen« gegründet, dazu gehören das Balina Serai Hotel und das Chedi Ubud, Bali.

Bei den meisten der hier vorgestellten Anlagen ist die gekonnte Ausführung offensichtlich. Das liegt daran, daß eine große Zahl geschickter Handwerker und Künstler zur Verfügung steht, um die Arbeiten von hoher Qualität auszuführen, besonders in Indonesien und Thailand. Die gekonnte Ausführung wird auch weiterhin ein architektonisches Kriterium bei der Planung neuer Anlagen sein, besonders bei Boutique-Hotels in kleinerem Maßstab.

Gegenwärtig werden Bauten auf der ganzen Welt nicht mehr von Handwerkern errichtet. Traditionelle Formen geben keine Auskunft mehr darüber, wie heute gebaut wird. In der traditionellen Architektur war die Logik des Bauens für jeden zu sehen – die Architektur ließ das verwendete Material und die Baumethode

"Où que l'on regarde, il devient de plus en plus ardu de distinguer un original d'une copie ou une copie d'une copie. L'imitation a remplacé l'innovation en tant que valeur créative. Nous recyclons tout."

Thomas Lawson
'Nostalgie, résistance des rêves modernes'

Les stations balnéaires ne cessent d'évoluer à notre époque d'expansion rapide de l'industrie hôtelière internationale. Le succès d'une station dépend de plusieurs facteurs: le lieu, l'importance des parts, de marche, les facilités et la qualité des services. Des tendances récentes montrent que les complexes hôteliers commencent à se spécialiser et entrer dans des créneaux différents de marché. Deux tendances principales se dessinent pour l'avenir. L'une est la réalisation de vastes complexes de plus en plus raffinés avec des parcs de loisirs à thème.

De grands complexes intégrés offrant un large éventail d'activités et de facilités pour la détente et les loisirs, vont devenir de plus en plus populaires. On verra une augmentation du nombre de villégiatures à "activités" telles que les Pacific Islands Clubs de Guam et Saipan dont le siège est aux USA. Comme le Laguna Beach Resort de Phuket, ces complexes intégrés dans des lieux touristiques du Sud-Est asiatique, imposeront aux architectes de tester leurs sensibilité et créativité en matière de dimension, représentation et authenticité.

L'autre tendance souligne l'apparition de petits complexes spécialisés, construits avec un souci de l'environnement. Ceux-ci se concentreront autour d'activités récréatives et d'attractions culturelles spécifiques. Ces branches du marché qui s'adressent à des touristes plus exigeants, vont se développer, notamment dans des régions lointaines ou jusqu'à présent isolées comme Myanmar (Birmanie) et le Viêt-nam.

Plusieurs tendances touristiques s'affirment d'ores et déjà dans cette première moitié des années 90. Les touristes sont de plus en plus évolués; ils recherchent de nouvelles expériences et exigent des séjours d'agrément de haute qualité et bien planifiés. Ces consommateurs désirent des hôtels qui répondent à leurs besoins spécifiques. Deux tendance évidentes sont la fragmentation des marchés touristiques et la prolifération de circuits axés sur des intérêts particuliers. On remarque également une croissance de "l'éco-tourisme" et du tourisme conventionnel.

La recherche de nouveaux créneaux va accélérer la segmentation du marché, à savoir la création de nouveaux types d'hôtels. Les grands groupes ont d'ores et déjà établi des chaînes secondaires qui mettent l'accent sur des points légèrement différents. Amanresorts a créé une chaîne d'hôtels "sans fioritures" dont deux exemples sont le Balina Şerai Hotel et le Chedi Ubud à Bali.

La plupart des projets présentés dans ce livre révèlent un haut niveau de réalisation artisanale. Cela est dû à la nombreuse main-d'œvre spécialisée, notamment en Indonésie et en Thaïlande, qui est en mesure d'effectuer des travaux de qualité. Ce travail "bien fait" continuera d'être un critère architectural crucial dans la conceptualisation des nouveaux complexes, surtout dans ceux de taille plus modeste.

A l'heure actuelle, les édifices construits de par le monde sont rarement l'œuvre

by the evolution of material science. Quality is not judged by the skill of fabrication, but more the skill of installation. Workmanship is valued above craftsmanship. Figuration in architecture hence becomes less to do with response to materials and more to do with the associative attributes of particular shapes and forms. This is very apparent in the mega-resorts featured in the book.

Hence, it is easy to categorise the resorts into two types. The smaller resorts utilise craftsmen in a greater, or perhaps, more visible and "transparent" manner than the mega-resorts. The former are able to achieve material authenticity through the logic of traditional construction. In the discourse on authenticity, there appears an implicit acknowledgement that the craftsman's role is of paramount importance.

There is an incredibly rich range of possibilities to which architects are beginning to respond, albeit too slowly and too slavishly. But the search for an authentic architecture must combine aspects of contemporary culture and traditions into works of significance not just in the local cultural milieu, but also in the wider spatial and temporal contexts.

In these resorts, even though they are undeniably exquisitely crafted works of architecture, the problem of authenticity has been addressed only by formal idealisations. It has not been tackled by opening the references of figuration to the multiple imperatives of our contemporary culture. Such historicism can be avoided if the design has been based on the generating principles of the past rather than on acknowledged forms and symbols. The continued regeneration of traditional forms or literal, kitsch variants of past models, no matter how sensually or carefully crafted, can only at its best, result in the stagnation of the operational idea of tradition. At its worst, it debases both itself and the past model.

As Peter Davey argues, "Replicated forms have very limited use in any society; they only have any kind of authenticity when they are restricted to replacing decayed elements of past compositions which must be preserved because of their historical and cultural importance. . . kitsch revivalism is one of the ways that, in the West, design is being reduced to consumerism, and culture to a supermarket commodity." In the East, it is now in danger of being reduced to the same status, paradoxically, of a very high formal order.

A search for authenticity can be seen as a self-conscious commitment to uncover a particular tradition's unique response to place and climate, and thereafter exteriorise these formal and symbolic underpinnings into creative new forms through a designer's eye that is very much in touch with contemporary realitites and modern sensibilities. Authenticity can perhaps be viewed as the attainment of an integrated, unstrained totality derived from a meaningful dialectical relationships between these different contexts.

unmittelbar erkennen. Diese »transparenten« Technologien wurden verdrängt durch die Weiterentwicklung der Materialkenntnis. Qualität wird nicht nach der Qualität des Bauens beurteilt, sondern nach der Geschicklichkeit beim Zusammenfügen. Arbeitskraft wird höher bewertet als handwerkliches Können. Gestaltung in der Architektur hat daher weniger mit der Reaktion auf das Material zu tun, sondern mehr mit den typischen Eigenschaften spezieller Formen. Das ist in den hier vorgestellten Mega-Ferienanlagen deutlich erkennbar.

Daher lassen sich die Ferienanlagen leicht in zwei Kategorien einteilen: Die kleineren Anlagen beschäftigen Handwerker in einem größeren oder vielleicht sichtbareren und »transparenten« Maß als die Mega-Anlagen. Sie erreichen Authentizität durch die Logik des traditionellen Bauens. In der Diskussion um die Authentizität scheint Übereinstimmung darüber zu herrschen, daß die Rolle des Handwerkers von größter Wichtigkeit ist.

Es gibt unglaublich viele Möglichkeiten, auf die Architekten langsam wieder zurückgreifen, wenn auch zu langsam und zu sklavisch. Aber bei der Suche nach authentischer Architektur müssen die Aspekte zeitgenössischer Kultur und die Traditionen in Werken von Bedeutung miteinander verbunden werden.

Obwohl viele dieser Anlagen handwerklich hervorragend gearbeitet sind, wurde das Problem der Authentizität nur mit formalen Idealisierungen gelöst. Keineswegs hat man die zahlreichen Notwendigkeiten unserer zeitgenössischen Kultur in die Gestaltung miteinbezogen. Ein solcher Historismus läßt sich vermeiden, wenn die Planung Prinzipien der Vergangenheit weiterführt und nicht nur die anerkannten Formen und Symbole wiederholt. Die ständige Wiederbelebung von traditionellen Formen oder von Kitschvarianten vergangener Modelle, wie kunstvoll sie auch immer gestaltet sein mögen, kann im besten Falle dazu führen, daß sich diese Methode totläuft. Im schlimmsten Falle diskreditiert diese Methode ihre historischen Grundlagen und auch sich selbst.

Peter Davey schreibt: »Kopierte Formen haben in jeder Gesellschaft nur einen begrenzten Wert; sie besitzen nur dann Authentizität, wenn sie einzig als Ersatz für zerstörte Elemente alter Kompositionen dienen, die wegen ihrer historischen und kulturellen Bedeutung erhalten werden müssen ... Wiederbelebung von Kitsch ist eine der Methoden, mit der im Westen Design zum Konsumgut wurde und Kultur ein Supermarktangebot.« Im Osten besteht jetzt dieselbe Gefahr, wenn auch auf einem sehr hohen formalen Niveau.

Die Suche nach »Authentizität kann man als selbstkritische Verpflichtung sehen, die Reaktion auf Ort und Klima in einer bestimmten Region aufzudecken und danach diese formalen und symbolischen Grundprinzipien in kreative neue Formen zu verwandeln; dazu muß ein Planer Beziehung zu zeitgenössischen Realitäten und modernen Empfindungen haben. Authentizität kann man vielleicht sehen als das Erreichen eines integrierten, natürlichen Ganzen, das aus einer sinnvollen Beziehung zwischen diesen beiden Zusammenhängen entwickelt wurde.

d'artisans. Les formes traditionnelles ne sont plus utilisées. Auparavant, la logique de la construction dans l'architecture classique était évidente - l'architecture montrait les matériaux et les méthodes de construction utilisés. Ces technologies "transparentes" reculent devant l'évolution de la science des matériaux. La compétence quant à l'installation prévaut sur la fabrication artisanale lorsqu'il s'agit de juger la qualité. Désormais, la représentation architecturale mise bien moins sur la valeur du matériau en soi que sur la forme qu'il va constituer. Ceci est très visible dans les immenses complexes hôteliers présentés dans le livre.

Il est donc très facile de catégoriser les complexes en deux types. Les plus petits sont davantage l'œuvre d'artisans aux techniques "transparentes". Ils obtiennent une authenticité matérielle grâce à la logique de construction traditionnelle. Le débat sur l'authenticité révèle implicitement que le rôle de l'artisan est d'importance capitale.

.es architectes commencent, bien trop lentement, à se servir de l'incroyable richesse des possibilités. Mais la recherche d'une architecture authentique doit marier des aspects de la culture contemporaine aux traditions pour constituer des ouvrages qui ne seront pas seulement significatifs dans le milieu culturel local, mais aussi dans des contextes temporaux et spatiaux plus vastes.

Dans ces complexes hôteliers qui comprennent indéniablement des ouvrages d'architecture exquis, le problème d'authenticité n'est considéré qu'au travers de l'idéalisation des formes. Il n'est pas abordé en se référant aux représentations des impératifs multiples de notre culture contemporaine. On peut éviter un tel historisme si le concept est basé sur les principes du passé plutôt que sur des formes et symboles désignés. La reconstitution de formes traditionnelles ou de variantes kitsch d'anciens modèles, même réalisée avec perception et habileté, ne peut au mieux que causer la stagnation de l'idée de tradition. Au pire, elle se dévalorise ainsi que le modèle ancien.

Peter Davey affirme que: "les sociétés n'ont guère besoin de formes reproduites. Elles ne deviennent authentiques que lorsqu'elles sont utilisées pour remplacer des éléments détériorés de structures anciennes qu'il faut sauvegarder en raison de leur importance culturelle et historique... En Occident, le kitsch est une des manières de réduire l'architecture à un article de consommation et la culture à une marchandise de supermarché." L'architecture risque le même sort en Orient, mais paradoxalement avec des formes de haut niveau.

Dans la recherche de l'authenticité, on peut voir l'engagement de découvrir comment chaque tradition relève du milieu géographique et climatique. Un architecte sensible aux réalités contemporaines saura ensuite exprimer les substrats formels et symboliques dans la création de nouvelles formes. L'authenticité peut être considérée comme la réalisation d'une intégralité dérivée d'une relation dialectiquement positive entre les différents contextes.

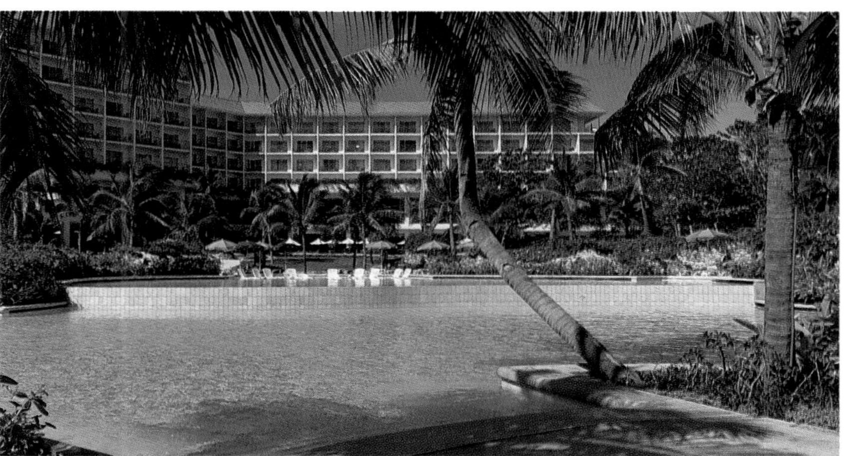

Large, integrated resorts like this one in Mactan Island, Philippines, will be a common trend.

Große Anlagen wie diese auf Mactan Island, Philippinen, sind typisch für die allgemeine Entwicklung.

La tendance ira vers les grands complexes hôteliers, comme celui-ci à Mactan Island, Philippines.

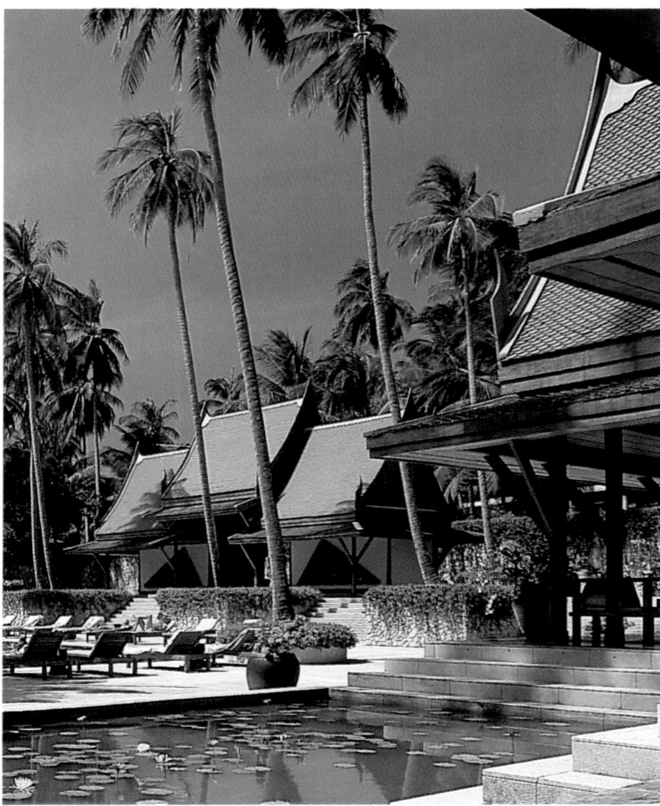

Skilled craftsmen are still available in various parts of Southeast Asia. Their contribution to contemporary architecture should be harnessed into extending traditions, rather than re-duplicating them.

Erfahrene Handwerker gibt es überall in Südostasien. Ihr Beitrag zur zeitgenössischen Architektur sollte dazu führen, die Tradition weiterzuentwickeln statt sie nur zu vervielfältigen.

Les artisans de haut niveau existent encore dans le Sud-Est asiatique. Leur contribution à l'architecture contemporaine doit être utilisée comme un élargissement des traditions et non comme leur simple reproduction.

Vernooy observes that "authenticity is an issue of perception and social consciousness that invokes technical, economic and cultural considerations. These are the imperatives of the modern world. They are the obligations that motivate the configuration of architecture, and they are the conceptual poles that direct the development of its technology." (26)

The predicament cannot simply be assuaged by the re-presentation of the vernacular. The resultant work is image-based and merely serves to embalm traditions and aestheticises the landscape. The famous quotation from French historian Paul Ricoeur, in his essay "Universal Civilization and National Cultures," remains a challenge : "There is the paradox: how to become modern and to return to sources; how to revive an old, dormant civilisation and take part in universal civilisation..." (27)

The unbuilt congress hotel in Agadir, Morocco, designed by Rem Koolhaas is perhaps the most visionary and boldest scheme for this building type. The structure consists of three zones stacked on top of one another. The lowest of these comprises auditoria and congress halls dug into the ground. Its curving forms resemble the surrounding dunes. Irregulary shaped columns support a roof slab, which houses the hotel. The intermediate zone is lit by skylights that produce an atmosphere reminiscent of Islamic cities and mosques. The hotel itself is an abstracted version of an Arab settlement, consisting of guestrooms arranged around courtyards. This contemporary interpretation of Islamic spatial precepts is highly exhilarating and illustrates explicitly the notion of authenticity that is proposed.

Meaningful directions in contemporary architecture in Southeast Asia can only evolve if there is a deeper understanding and protracted re-evaluation of indigenous building traditions in an ever-expanding field of possibilities than is practised at the moment. The challenge lies in dismantling many of the existing false fronts designed to project a superficial reassurance of identity, and seeking instead new modes of representation. Architects must understand the fundamental lessons found in the rich local traditions of Southeast Asia, and learn to synthesise them into convincing forms determinedly contemporary and appropriate to changing conditions.

The task of architectural reinterpretation is inevitably a difficult and tenuous one. But with more resorts being designed in various parts of Southeast Asia, the growing consciousness and tentative discourse in this part of the world look set to intensify, and hopefully will bring about greater transformations. As Christopher Alexander once noted, "There is no perfect static language, which once defined will stay defined forever. No language is ever finished."

Vernooy merkt an, daß »Authentizität eine Frage von Wahrnehmung und sozialem Bewußtsein ist, wobei technische, wirtschaftliche und kulturelle Überlegungen einbezogen werden. Das sind die Anforderungen der modernen Welt. Das sind die Verpflichtungen, die zur Gestaltung von Architektur anregen, und das sind die konzeptionellen Pole, die die Entwicklung ihrer Technologie lenken«. (26)

Die mißliche Lage kann nicht einfach durch die Re-Präsentation des Einheimischen entschärft werden. Die so entstandene Arbeit basiert auf Bildern und dient nur dazu, Traditionen zu konservieren und die Landschaft zu verschönern. Das bekannte Zitat des französischen Historikers Paul Ricœur bleibt eine Herausforderung: »Da liegt das Paradox: wie modern werden und zu den Quellen zurückkehren, wie eine alte, ruhende Zivilisation wiederbeleben und an der universellen Zivilisation teilhaben ...« (27)

Das noch nicht fertiggestellte Kongreßhotel in Agadir, Marokko, geplant von Rem Koolhaas, ist vielleicht der visionärste und mutigste Entwurf für diesen Bautyp. Das Gebäude besteht aus drei übereinander liegenden Zonen. Die unterste mit Hörsälen und Kongreßräumen wird in den Boden gegraben. Die geschwungenen Formen ähneln den Dünen in der Umgebung. Unregelmäßig geformte Säulen tragen eine Dachkonstruktion, unter der das Hotel untergebracht ist. Die mittlere Zone wird von Oberlicht erhellt, wodurch eine Atmosphäre entsteht, die an islamische Städte und Moscheen erinnert. Das Hotel selbst ist eine Anlehnung an eine arabische Siedlung und besteht aus Gästezimmern, die um einen Hof herum angeordnet sind. Diese zeitgenössische Interpretation von islamischen Raum aufteilungen ist höchst erfrischend und illustriert deutlich die Vorstellung von Authentizität, die angestrebt wird.

Die zeitgenössische Architektur Südostasiens kann nur dann eine sinnvolle Richtung einschlagen, wenn es auf einem immer weiter expandierenden Feld von Möglichkeiten ein tieferes Verständnis und eine ausführlichere Neubewertung einheimischer Bautraditionen gibt. Die Herausforderung liegt im Abbau vieler bestehender falscher Fronten, die oberflächlich Echtheit vermitteln sollen, und in der Suche neuer Formen der Repräsentation. Architekten müssen die grundlegenden Lektionen verstehen, die in den reichen örtlichen Traditionen Südostasiens stecken, und sie müssen lernen, sie umzuwandeln in überzeugende Formen, die eindeutig zeitgenössisch und den wechselnden Bedingungen angepaßt sind.

Die Aufgabe architektonischer Neuinterpretation ist zweifellos schwierig und mühsam. Aber da weitere Ferienanlagen in verschiedenen Teilen Südostasiens geplant sind, sieht es so aus, als würde das Problembewußtsein wachsen und die vorsichtige Diskussion in diesem Teil der Welt intensiver. Und daraus entstehen dann hoffentlich größere Veränderungen. Wie Christopher Alexander einmal anmerkte: »Es gibt keine perfekte statische Sprache, die, einmal festgelegt, für immer festgelegt bleibt. Keine Sprache ist je vollendet.«

Vernooy observe que "l'authenticité est une question de perception et conscience sociale qui implique des considérations techniques, économiques et culturelles. Ces impératifs du monde moderne déterminent la configuration architecturale et sont les pôles conceptuels qui dirigent le développement de sa technologie." (26)

On ne peut résoudre cette situation par le simple fait de re-présenter l'aspect autochtone. Le résultat, créé sur des clichés, ne fait qu'embaumer les traditions et esthétiser le paysage. La citation célèbre tirée de l'essai *Civilisation universelle et cultures nationales* de l'historien français Paul Ricoeur, constitue encore une gageure: " C'est un paradoxe: comment devenir moderne et retourner aux sources, comment faire revivre une vieille civilisation dormante et participer à la civilisation universelle..." (27)

Le projet novateur et audacieux de Rem Koolhaas pour l'hôtel de congrès d'Agadir au Maroc, apporte une réponse. La structure consiste en trois zones superposées. La première, creusée dans le sol, comprend un auditorium et des salles de congrès. Ses lignes courbes ressemblent aux dunes environnantes. Des colonnes de formes différentes supportent un toit qui surmonte la partie hôtel. Eclairée par des lucarnes, la zone intermédiaire évoque l'atmosphère des mosquées et des cités islamiques. L'hôtel lui-même est une version plus abstraite d'une demeure arabe avec des chambres s'ouvrant sur des patios. Cette adaptation contemporaine des principes architecturaux arabes est très réussie et illustre explicitement la notion d'authenticité proposée.

L'architecture contemporaine en Asie du Sud-Est ne se développera de manière positive qu'avec une compréhension et une nouvelle évaluation plus profondes des traditions architecturales indigènes dans ce champ des possibilités qui ne cesse de s'étendre. Il s'agit de démanteler les fausses façades existantes qui projettent une assurance d'identité superficielle et de les remplacer par de nouveaux modes d'expression. Il faut que les architectes assimilent les leçons fondamentales dictées par les riches traditions locales du Sud-Est asiatique et apprennent à les synthétiser en formes convaincantes, contemporaines et adaptées aux conditions changeantes.

Réaliser une interprétation neuve de styles architecturaux est une tâche difficile et précaire. Néanmoins, le nombre de complexes hôteliers ne cessant d'augmenter dans les différentes parties d'Asie du Sud-Est, il semblerait que la réflexion et le débat s'intensifient dans cette partie du monde, ce qui permet d'espérer des changements accrus. Comme Christopher Alexander l'énonçait: "Il n'existe pas de langage statique parfait, où les définitions restent immuables à jamais. Un langage n'est jamais achevé."

Bibliography
Bibliographie
Bibliographie

A. Abraben, *Resort Hotel Planning and Management*, Van Nostrand Reinhold, New York, 1965.

Jiro Akiyama, *Small and Luxury Hotels as a Home*, Process Architecture Co. Ltd, Tokyo, 1993.

Manuel Baud-Bovey & Fred Lawson, *Tourism and Recreation Development*, The Architectural Press & CBI Publishing Co Inc, London, 1977.

Clare A. Gunn, *Vacationscape: Designing Tourist Regions*, Van Nostrand Reinhold, New York, 1988.

Edward Inskeep, *Tourism Planning*, Van Nostrand Reinhold, New York, 1991.

Edward D. Mills, *Design for Holidays and Tourism*, Butterworth & Co. (Publishers) Ltd, London,1983.

Walter A. Rutes and Richard H. Penner, *Hotel Planning and Design*, Watson-Guptill Publications, New York, 1985.

Tan Hock Beng, *Tropical Architecture and Interiors*, Page One Publishing Pte Ltd, Singapore, 1994.

Anthony Wylson, *Design for Leisure Entertainment*, Butterworth & Co. (Publishers) ltd., London, 1980.

Footnotes
Fußnoten
Notes

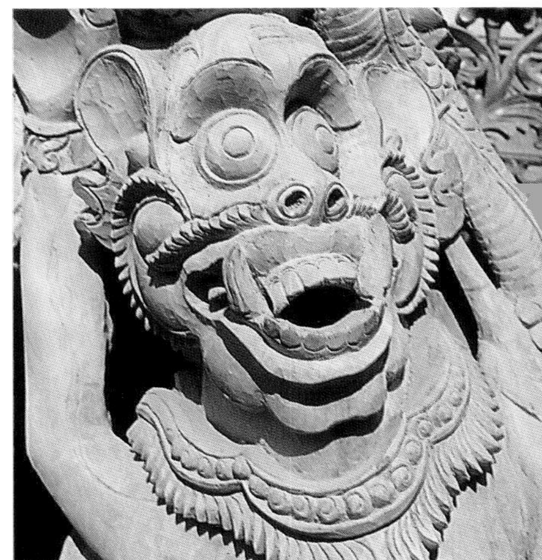

1 George M. Taber, "A Whole New World" in *TIME*, Time Inc., New York, June 12, 1995, pp 50.
2 A Reuter report published in *The Straits Times*, Singapore, Mar 8 1994.
3 Winarta Adisubrata, "Nusa Dua Resort: The Secret of Success" in *Asia Travel Trade*, June 1994, Eastern Publishing Associates Pte Ltd, pp 36.
4 Tan Sung, "Bintan resort emerging as one of S'pore's biggest overseas ventures", *The Straits Times*, Singapore, March 14 1994, pp 39.
5 Paul Jacob, "Singapore, Jakarta to co-operate on tourism", *The Sunday Times*, pp 1.
6 Joseph R. Yogerst, "Indonesia Marks A Vintage Year" in *International Herald Tribune*, November 1994, pp 11.
7 Ron Corben, "Phuket and Pattaya: Prized Possessions" in *Asia Travel Trade*, June 1994, Eastern Publishing Associates Pte Ltd, pp 40.
8 A Reuter report published in *The Straits Times*, Singapore, Mar 8 1994.
9 Giddens, *Sociology : A Brief, But Critical Introduction* , 1982, pp 142.
10 Wolfgang Schivelbusch, "Railroad Space And Railroad Time" in *New German Critique 14*, 1978, pp. 40.
11 Dean MacCannell, *The Tourist : A New Theory of the Leisure Class*, Schocken. Smith, V. L., ed., 1976.
12 *Ibid*, pp 20.
13 P. L. Berger, B. Berger, and H. Kellner, *The Homeless Mind*, Harmondsworth: Penguin, 1973, pp 88.
14 Kenneth Frampton, "The Status of Man and the Status of His Objects" in *Modern Architecture and the Critical Present*, Architectural Design Profiles, Garden House Press, London, 1982, pp 6-19.
15 Dean MacCannell, *The Tourist : A New Theory of the Leisure Class*, Schocken. Smith, V. L., ed., 1976.
16 Erik Cohen, "Authenticity and Commoditization in Tourism" in *Annals of Tourism Research*, 1988, 15: 371-386.
17 *Ibid*.
18 Hassan-Uddin Khan, "Houses: A Synthesis of Tradition and Modernity" in *MIMAR: Architecture in Development*, No. 39, June 1991, Concept Media Pte Ltd., pp 28.
19 Umberto Eco, *Travels in Hyper-Reality*, Picador, 1987, pp 3-58.
20 Chambers, I.,"Maps for the Metropolis: A Possible guide to the Postmodern', *Cultural Studies*.
21 Webster's New International Dictionary, Second edition, G. & C. Merriam Company, 1934, pp 185.
22 L. Trilling, *Sincerity and Authenticity*, London, Oxford University Press, 1972; as quoted in Erik Cohen, "Authenticity and Commoditisation in Tourism".
23 D. Andrew Vernooy, "Crisis of Figuration in Contemporary Architecture", pp 95.
24 Juhani Pallasmaa, "Six Themes for the next Millennium" in *The Architectural Review*, London, July 1994, pp 78.
25 Ismail Serageldin, "The Collective Message of the Award" in *Space For Freedom: The Search For Architectural Excellence in Muslim Societies*, Butterworth Architecture, 1989, pp 58.
26 D. Andrew Vernooy, "Crisis of Figuration in Contemporary Architecture", pp 99.
27 Paul Ricoeur, "Universal Civilization and National Cultures", in *History and Truth*, trans. Charles A. Kelbley, Evanston, Ill.: Northwestern University Press, 1965, pp 277.

Photo Credits
Fotonachweis
Crédits Photographiques

P. 2 Shusse Publishing Pte Ltd

Tourism and Resort Architecture in Southeast Asia

P. 13 K. C. Sin
P. 18 K. C. Sin (*Borobudur*)
P. 34 Four Aces Consultants Ltd

Dusit Rayavadee

P. 64 Four Aces Consultants Ltd
P. 68 Four Aces Consultants Ltd
P. 70 Four Aces Consultants Ltd
P. 73 Four Aces Consultants Ltd

Laguna Beach Club

P. 81-91 Shusse Publishing Pte Ltd

The Regent Resort Chiang Mai

P. 92-100 Bensley Design Group
P. 101 The Regent Resort Chiang Mai, Regent International, Hong Kong.

The Datai

P. 102-119 Albert Lim (*Courtesy of Kerry Hill Architects*)

The Beaufort

P. 120-133 Albert Lim (*Courtesy of Kerry Hill Architects*)

Indonesia

P. 134	Rio Helmi (*Courtesy of Kerry Hill Architects*)

Bali Imperial Hotel

P. 144-145	Bensley Design Group
P. 147	Bensley Design Group

Bali Intercontinental Resort

P. 152-159	Grahacipta Hadiprana

Balina Serai

P. 161-164	Rio Helmi (*Courtesy of Kerry Hill Architects*)
P. 166-173	Rio Helmi (*Courtesy of Kerry Hill Architects*)

Chedi Bandung

P. 174-185	Albert Lim (*Courtesy of Kerry Hill Architects*)

Four Seasons Resort Bali

P. 193	Four Seasons Resort Bali

Pearl Farm Beach Resort

P. 204-209	Robert Powell
P. 210-211	Blain Crellin
P. 212-215	Robert Powell

Conclusions

P. 219	Shangri-La Mactan Island, Cebu and Couldrey Jones Ltd., Hong Kong.

Acknowledgements
Danksagungen
Remerciements

Completing this book within the relatively short time-frame has been an arduous task. Many people have shared their time and profound knowledge with me. Their myriad conversations, experiences, insights and friendships have been great inspiration. The book would not have been possible without them. I owe tremendous debts to the following :

Foremost among them is Mark Tan, who was responsible for conceptualising the book; Violet Tan, who oversees the entire project; K. C. Sin, whose design and layout of the book is highly commendable. Thanks are also due to my wife, Maria Hartati, for her support and encouragement and also for preparing some wonderful ink drawings.

I acknowledge with sincere thanks the contributions and encouragement of many friends. They are William Lim, Robert Powell, Karan Grover, Jimmy Lim, Kerry Hill, Justin Hill, Karen Lim, Wong Chiu Man, Maria Warner, Michael Oh, Sunshine Wong, Russell Smith, Foo May Leng, Trina Dingler Ebert, Ricky Yeo, Hendra Hadiprana, Sindhu Hadiprana, Bobby Manosa, Cecilia Leong-Faulkner, Ho Kwon Cjan, Alicia Poon, Cathi Anderson, Sara Mastriforte, Armando Kraenzlin, Teeraphol Rattanyoo, Nadim X. Salhani, Nicola Parker, Trina Dingler Ebert, Joseph Lo, Tang Guan Bee, Bill Bensley and Lek Mathar Bunnag.

Special thanks are due to M.L. Chainimit Navarat for his kind hospitality and for sharing his deep insight into conservation, ecotourism and the design of Dusit Rayavadee. I am also especially grateful to Kerry Hill for his time and for patiently helping me select suitable material. His delightful works in this region are probably more influential than he realised.

Over the last three years, I have been inspired and provoked by many of my students, both during field trips in Malaysia and Bali, and in the intense environment of our design studios. Their inquiring minds have been thoroughly engaging. Several names immediately come to mind : Cheng Hsing Yao, Louise Wong, Mok Wei Terk, Yeo Pei Shan, Chang Jiat Hwee, Abel Law, David Chin, Billie Khoo, Lim Yin Shi, Jane Wong, Phillip Yong, Lim Hong Kian and Carol Chng.

Perhaps most importantly, thanks are also gratefully expressed to the various architects and hotel personnel who have kindly supplied material for publication.

Die Fertigstellung dieses Buchs innerhalb relativ kurzer Zeit war eine schwierige Aufgabe. Viele Leute haben ihre Zeit und ihr profundes Wissen mit mir geteilt. Ihre zahllosen Gespräche, Erfahrungen, Einsichten und Freundschaften waren eine großartige Anregung. Ohne sie wäre dieses Buch nicht möglich gewesen. Ich stehe tief in der Schuld folgender Personen:

Zuerst wären zu nennen: Mark Tan, der für das Konzept des Buchs verantwortlich war; Violet Tan, die das gesamte Projekt überwachte; K. C. Sin für das höchst lobenswerte Design und Layout des Buchs. Dank auch an meine Frau Maria Hartati für ihre Hilfe und Ermutigung und auch für einige wundervolle Tuschezeichnungen.

Mit ehrlichem Dank erwähne ich die Beiträge und die Unterstützung vieler Freunde. Es sind: William Lim, Robert Powell, Karan Grover, Jimmy Lim, Kerry Hill, Justin Hill, Karen Lim, Wong Chiu Man, Maria Warner, Michael Oh, Sunshine Wong, Russell Smith, Foo May Leng, Trina Dingler Ebert, Ricky Yeo, Hendra Hadiprana, Sindhu Hadiprana, Bobby Manosa, Cecilia Leong-Faulkner, Ho Kwon Cjan, Alicia Poon, Cathi Anderson, Sara Mastriforte, Armando Kraenzlin, Teeraphol Rattanyoo, Nadim X. Salhani, Nicola Parker, Joseph Lo, Tang Guan Bee, Bill Bensley und Lek Mathar Bunnag.

Besonderen Dank schulde ich M. I. Chainimit Navarat für seine Gastfreundschaft und dafür, daß er mir seine klugen Erkenntnisse über Erhaltung, Ökotourismus und die Anlage von Dusit Rayavadee mitteilte. Besonders dankbar bin ich auch Kerry Hill für die Zeit und die Geduld, die er aufbrachte, um mir bei der Auswahl von geeignetem Material zu helfen. Seine erfreulichen Arbeiten in dieser Region sind vermutlich einflußreicher als er vermutet.

In den letzten drei Jahren haben mich vieler meiner Studenten inspiriert und herausgefordert, sowohl bei Studienreisen in Malaysia und Bali als auch in der intensiven Atmosphäre unserer Design-Ateliers. Ihr forschender Geist war ein großer Gewinn. Mehrere Namen fielen mir auf Anhieb ein: Cheng Hsing Yao, Louise Wong, Mok Wei Terk, Yeo Pei Shan, Chang Jiat Hwee, Abel Law, David Chin, Billie Khoo, Lim Yin Shi, Jane Wong, Phillip Yong, Lim Hong Kian und Carol Chng.

Und was vielleicht am wichtigsten ist: Den vielen Architekten und Hotelangestellten, die mir freundlicherweise Material für die Veröffentlichung zur Verfügung gestellt haben, drücke ich meinen ehrlichen Dank aus.

Ce livre, réalisé dans un espace de temps relativement court, a représenté une tâche ardue. Un grand nombre de personnes m'ont offert leur temps et leur savoir. Leurs multiples conversations, leurs expériences, leurs idées et leur amitié m'ont été d'une grande inspiration. Je n'aurais pu réaliser ce livre sans elles et dois une profonde reconnaissance aux personnes suivantes:

d'abord à Mark Tan qui s'est chargé de la conceptualisation du livre et à Violet Tan qui l'a contrôlé et puis à K.C. Sin pour son admirable conception et mise en page du livre. Je remercie également ma femme, Maria Hartati, pour son soutien, ses encouragements et ses merveilleux dessins à l'encre.

J'adresse mes plus sincères remerciements aux nombreux amis qui m'ont encouragé et apporté leur contribution: William Lim, Robert Powell, Karan Grover, Jimmy Lim, Kerry Hill,Justin Hill, Karen Lim, Wong Chiu Man, Maria Werner, Michael Oh, Sunshine Wong, Russel Smith, Foo May Leng, Trina Dingler Ebert, Ricky Yeo, Hendra Hadiprana, Sindhu Hadiprana, Bobby Manosa, Cecilia Leong-Faulkner, Ho Kwon Cjan, Alicia Poon, Cathi Anderson, Sara Mastriforte, Armando Kraenzlin, Teeraphol Rattanyoo, Nadim X. Salhani, Nicola Parker, Joseph Lo, Tang Guan Bee, Bill Bensley et Lek Mathar Bunnag.

Je remercie tout spécialement M.L. Chainimit Navarat pour son aimable hospitalité et pour m'avoir fait partager ses connaissances profondes de la conservation, de l'éco-tourisme et de la conception du Dusit Rayavadee. Ma profonde gratitude à Kerry Hill qui m'a accordé son temps et aidé, avec beaucoup de patience, dans le choix du matériel. Au travers des ouvrages admirables qu'il a créés dans la région, il a exercé une bien plus grande influence qu'il ne le réalise.

Au cours des dernières trois années, nombre de mes étudiants m'ont également apporté leurs idées et critiques lors de nos voyages d'études en Malaisie et à Bali et durant les séances de travail dans nos studios d'architecture. Leur soif de connaissances m'a fait énormément plaisir. Plusieurs noms me viennent immédiatement à l'esprit: Cheng Hsing Yao, Louise Wong, Mok Wei Terk, Yeo Pei Shan, Chang Jiat Hwee, Abel Law, David Chin, Billie Khoo, Lim Yin Shi, Jane Wong, Phillip Yong, Lim Hong Kian et Carol Chng.

Je n'oublierai pas ce qui est peut-être le plus important: adresser tous mes remerciements aux architectes et au personnel hôtelier qui ont eu l'amabilité de fournir le matériel nécessaire pour à réalisation de ce livre.

GW00357146

READER'S DIGEST
DIY
MANUAL

READER'S DIGEST
DIY
MANUAL

Published by The Reader's Digest Association, Inc.
London • New York • Sydney • Montreal

Contents

How planning and building regulations will affect your major improvements. Plus what you need to consider when planning a loft conversion, home extension, adding a conservatory and more.

Everything you need to know about calling in the professionals, including how to cost a project, finding and hiring contractors, what to do before work starts, sorting out contracts and keeping track of progress. Plus, what you can do if things go wrong.

LOOK OUT FOR THE GREEN LEAF SYMBOL FOR GREENER DIY AND ENERGY SAVING TIPS.

Know your home 1

Foundations

Foundations are as old as houses – literally. They carry the weight of the building, transferring the load safely to the soil beneath so the structure stands securely.

A three-bedroom detached house typically weighs around 120 tonnes, so adequate foundations are clearly essential. Yet until the late 19th century, all that was required of them was that they should 'rest on solid ground'. Only in 1879 were statutory requirements introduced for houses to have a concrete strip foundation that we would recognise today. It had to be just 230mm thick.

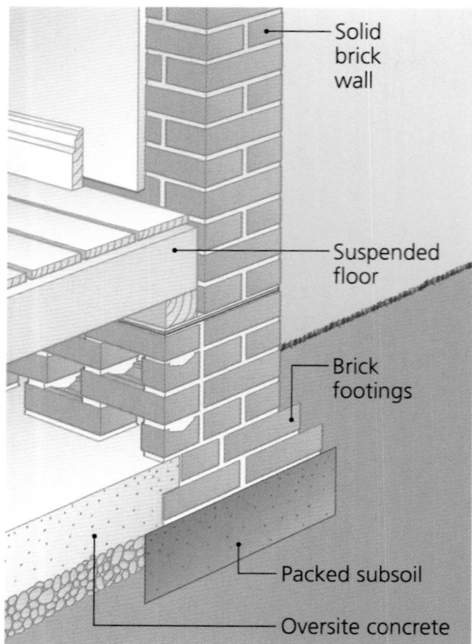

Many older properties may have little more than rammed earth or stone foundations, with stepped brickwork built up to ground level to help to spread the load of the walls. By contrast, modern homes often have deep concrete trench foundations, especially on clay or gravel subsoils that do not carry loads well. The area within modern concrete foundations is usually covered with a reinforced concrete ground slab; older properties usually had suspended timber ground floors (see pages 10–11).

What to do when cracks appear

If your house starts to develop cracks in external or internal walls, or around the edges of solid floor slabs, seek professional help without delay. The best place to start is the building control department of your local authority. Not only will the inspectors have a thorough knowledge of local soil conditions; they will also be able to put you in contact with approved contractors if remedial work is necessary.

THE TROUBLE WITH FOUNDATIONS

Because foundations are out of sight, the only time they cause any concern is when they appear to be failing to do their job. They can suffer from several problems, in which cause and effect may be unclear. All produce similar symptoms: small cracks in the house walls to begin with, then larger ones – often linking door and window openings, and following a zig-zag path up the walls as mortar joints fail. Finally, if the problem is very severe, parts of the structure seem about to separate as cracks extend to the full height of the building. Here are some of the commonest problems affecting house foundations.

Settlement All new houses settle to some degree. Slight movement in the ground occurs as it is compacted to a uniform degree by the new load imposed on it. The result is usually a few small cracks in the structure which stop developing when settlement is complete, and which can be repaired with no risk of recurrence.

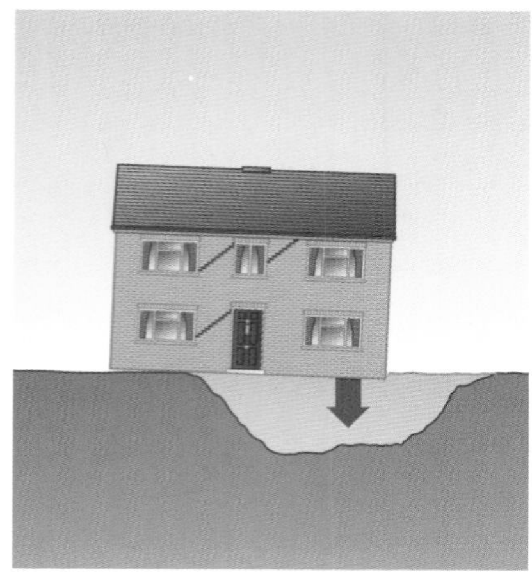

Differential settlement An extension or addition to a property may be built with different foundations to the original, and the new part may settle and start to separate from the existing building over time. The problem was common with bay windows and back additions in Victorian houses, and is seen today with home extensions built on inadequate foundations and not tied properly to the existing structure, or where changes occur in the ground.

Ground movement The moisture content of the ground beneath the house changes with the seasons. This is especially pronounced with clay soils, which contract and expand more than other soil types, especially during and after a severe drought. A similar problem is called frost heave, caused by water within the soil freezing and expanding upwards, displacing the foundations; it occurs mainly in porous sandy and chalk subsoils. Ground movement can also be caused by trees too close to the house, either sucking moisture from the ground as they grow, or no longer doing so if they are felled. Lastly, cracked and leaking underground drains can saturate the subsoil or cause soil erosion, depending on the soil type.

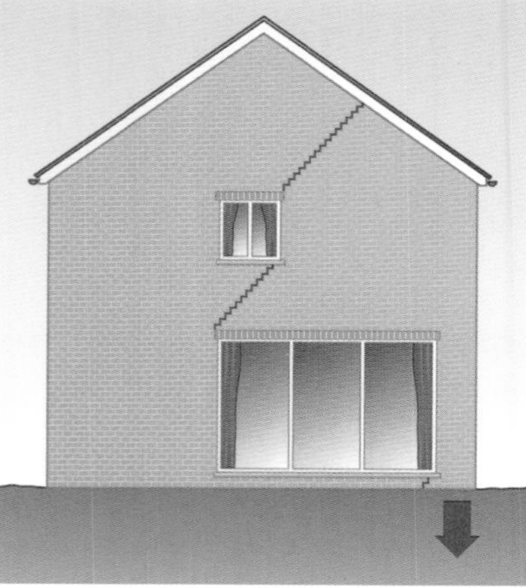

Overloading Foundations may become overloaded when structural alterations are carried out to the building. For example, removing a load-bearing internal wall and installing a rolled steel joist (RSJ) to carry the weight of upper floors transfers that load to the walls at each end of the RSJ and thence to their foundations, which may not have been designed to take that sort of load.

Subsidence True subsidence is the result of the collapse of underground chambers – either natural ones such as caves, or man-made ones such as disused mine shafts. The effects on a building can be catastrophic.

Exterior walls

Walls vary in construction and finish, which may be purely decorative or have weather-proofing properties. The way the outside walls are built reveal your house's age with some accuracy.

Solid walls Houses built before about 1920 have solid walls of brick or stone – brick walls are usually about 230mm thick; the thickness of stone walls depends on the type of stone used. Buildings taller than two storeys, such as Georgian terraced houses, often have thicker walls in the lower storeys to carry the extra load.

Cavity walls Houses built since about 1920 have cavity walls – developed as a way to prevent damp penetrating solid wall structures. Early examples have two brick walls (called leaves) about 100mm thick separated by an open cavity 50–75mm wide. The two leaves were held together by metal wall ties for extra stability.
Blockwork Newer houses have the inner leaf of the cavity wall (and the outer one too if the exterior is rendered or has tiling or weather-boarding) built of insulating blockwork rather than brick. This reduces heat losses through the walls, and their thermal efficiency can be increased still further by using insulation in the wall cavities. This may fill the cavity completely, or may be held against the inner leaf so that water penetrating the outer leaf can run down to ground level rather than across to the inner leaf. The two leaves of the wall are tied together with galvanised wire, stainless steel or plastic wall ties.

THE TROUBLE WITH WALLS

Water and frost are the biggest enemies of exterior walls. Defective pointing (page 408), damaged rendering (page 409) and failed weatherproofing (page 204) can allow moisture to penetrate the structure, causing damp patches to appear indoors. Damp masonry can be damaged by frost, which freezes water within the wall structure and makes it expand, splitting the faces off bricks and detaching rendering from the masonry.

Settlement of the foundations (see opposite) can cause severe cracking in external walls. Failure of the wall ties can cause a cavity wall to bow outwards.

What to do

Most minor faults can be repaired by a competent do-it-yourselfer; the cross-references above will take you to the relevant pages of the book.

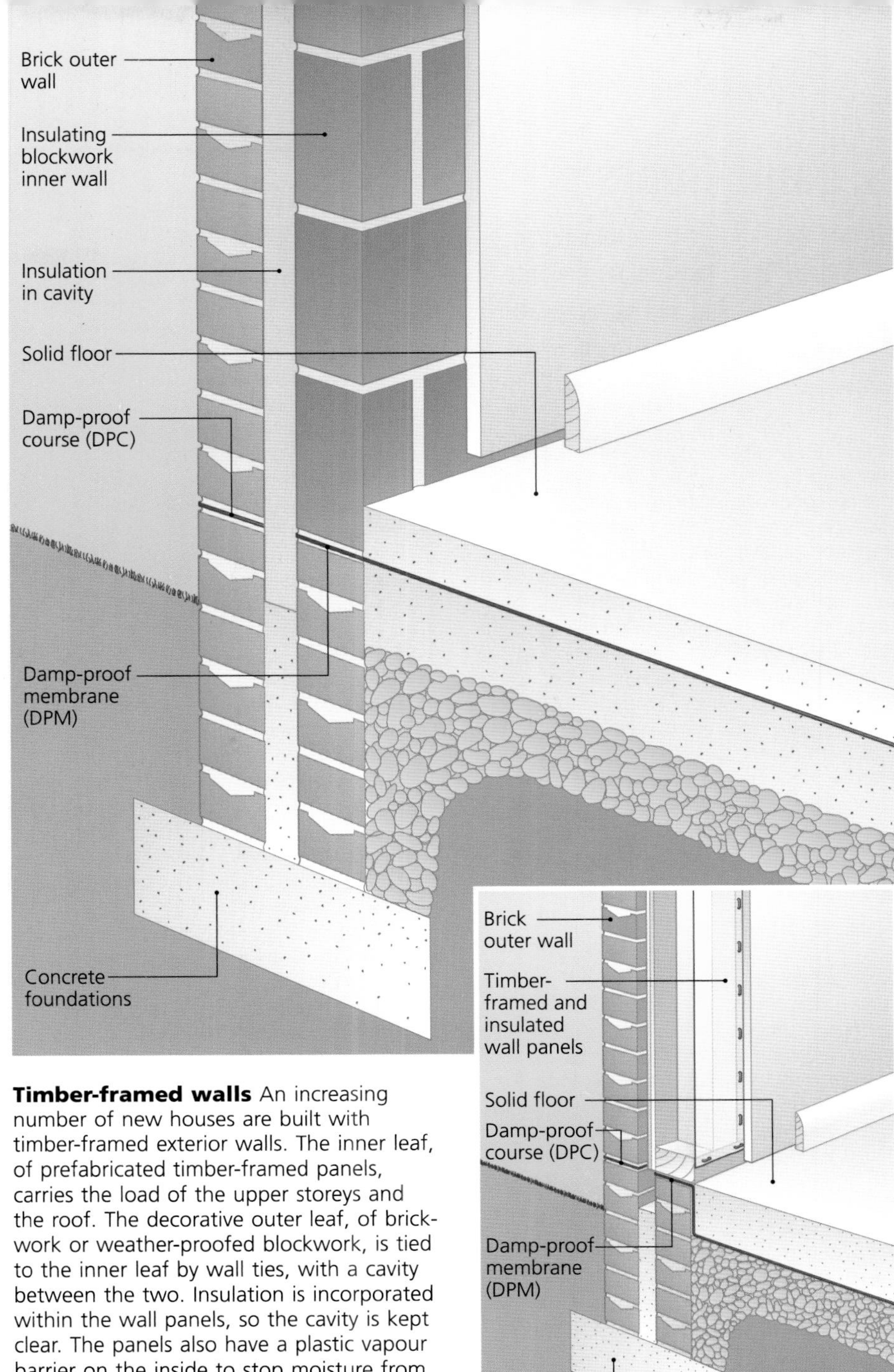

Timber-framed walls An increasing number of new houses are built with timber-framed exterior walls. The inner leaf, of prefabricated timber-framed panels, carries the load of the upper storeys and the roof. The decorative outer leaf, of brick-work or weather-proofed blockwork, is tied to the inner leaf by wall ties, with a cavity between the two. Insulation is incorporated within the wall panels, so the cavity is kept clear. The panels also have a plastic vapour barrier on the inside to stop moisture from the house condensing within the insulation and causing the timber frame to rot.

Wall finishes

External finishes The walls may be exposed brick or stone with mortar pointing. Solid brick walls will show headers (the ends of the bricks) alternating with stretchers (their long sides) laid in one of several regular patterns called bonds. Cavity brick walls will show only stretchers, laid with a half-brick overlap in what is known as stretcher bond.
Rendering Cement or lime mortar applied as a weatherproof coating may be smooth or textured, and there are many regional variations. A universal rendered finish is pebble-dashing, created by bedding small stones in the mortar coat. Rendering and pebble-dashing are often painted to improve their looks and weather resistance.

Other external wall finishes include clay tiles hung on timber battens, timber weather-boarding, timber shingles and plastic cladding. Timber finishes may be left to weather, or may be stained or painted for decorative effect.

Internal finishes Masonry walls are usually given an internal finish of plaster – one or two undercoats and a thin finish coat. Lime plasters are found in older houses, whereas modern houses have gypsum-based plaster which is thinner and harder. Some older houses have plaster applied over wooden laths fixed to wall battens; these walls sound hollow when tapped. A similar effect is achieved in some modern houses by dry-lining exterior walls with plasterboard on wall battens, as an alternative to wet plastering. Timber-framed houses have plasterboard cladding on the inner face of the wall panels. Both these wall finishes sound hollow when tapped, and require special care when making wall fixings.

Ground floors

Ground floors in very old buildings are simply that: the ground beneath the house, levelled and covered with flagstones or a layer of rough concrete.

Solid floors like these were notoriously damp and extremely cold. Only slate kept the dampness out. During the early 19th century, asphalt was introduced to form a damp-proof layer in the floor construction, and the use of quarry and ceramic tiles became widespread as a surface for ground floors. But the Victorians acknowledged the difficulty of damp-proofing solid floors effectively, and turned to timber ground floors as an alternative. Properly constructed, these floors were not only free from damp; they were also much warmer underfoot. However, they were prone to rot, and solid concrete ground floors are once again the norm in most modern houses.

Timber ground floors

A traditional timber ground floor is supported on joists. The ground beneath the floor is covered with hardcore and concrete (the oversite concrete, usually laid level with the ground). The ends of the joists are either fitted directly into holes left in the brickwork or are supported on (and nailed to) a horizontal timber wall plate resting on a ledge of masonry. The resulting underfloor void (called the crawl space for obvious reasons) is a minimum of 300mm deep, and often more. A damp-proof course (also known as a DPC) between the wall plate and the masonry protects the timber from damp. Intermediate supports called sleeper walls are built up off the oversite concrete at roughly 3m intervals to prevent the relatively shallow joists from sagging across large spans. These are of honeycomb construction to allow air movement through the underfloor void – essential to keep the floor timbers dry and free from rot. They also carry a wall plate (resting on a DPC) to which the joists are nailed.

The floor surface is formed of softwood boards which are nailed to the joists. These were made from square-edged boards until the 1930s, and generally tongued-and-grooved thereafter. Square-edged boards became unpopular because they usually shrank and created gaps, which caused draughts.

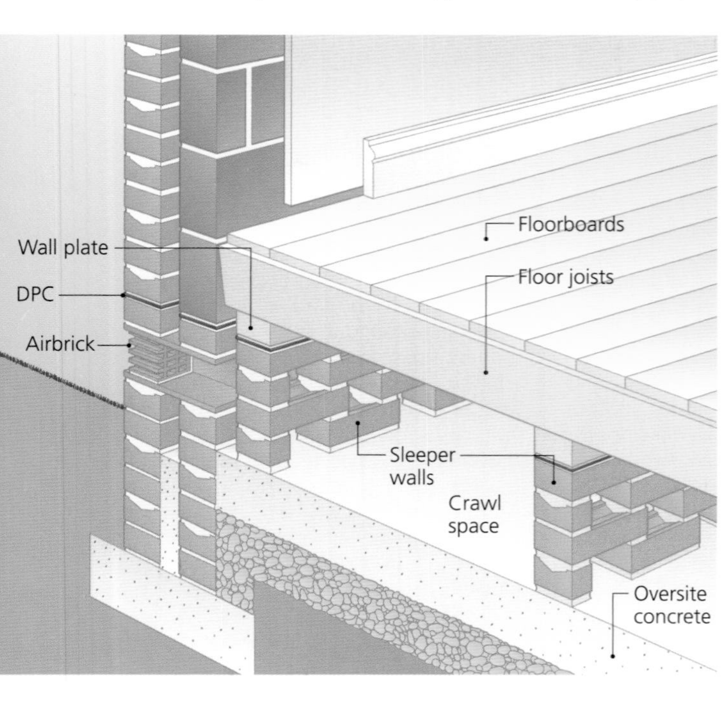

THE TROUBLE WITH TIMBER FLOORS

If the ventilation of the underfloor void is inadequate, the structure will often become plagued by dry rot, a ravenous form of wood-destroying fungus which can eventually cause its total collapse.

Joist ends are prone to attacks of wet rot, which are often linked to localised failures in the damp-proof course in the house walls. Another problem is that the void can be invaded by rodents and other pests, which use it as an easy access route into the house itself.

What to do

Make sure that the void is well ventilated by keeping airbricks clear of obstructions. Replace damaged airbricks to deny pests entry. If the floor appears springy at the edges, wet rot may be affecting the joist ends. It may be possible to reinforce them with new wood, but large-scale replacement of the floor structure may be necessary.

If there is a tell-tale musty smell in ground-floor rooms and you find dry rot, the entire floor structure will have to be replaced and the area sterilised before a new floor is constructed. Both these jobs are best left to specialist contractors.

Minor faults involving damage to floorboards can be repaired by a competent do-it-yourselfer (see pages 126–7).

Modern solid ground floors

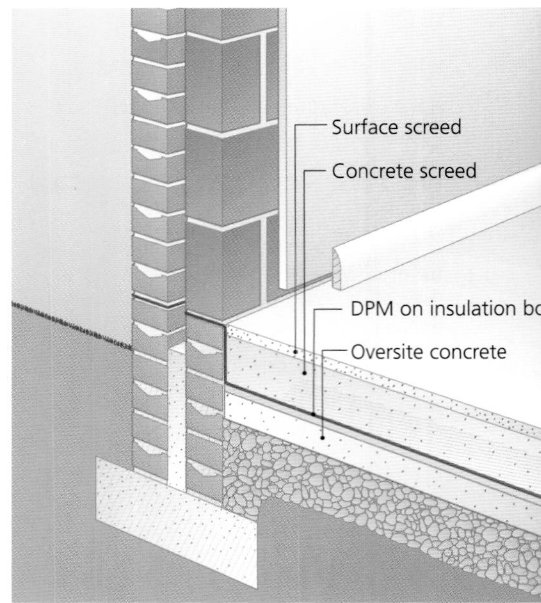

By the end of the 19th century, it had become obvious that timber ground floors caused more problems than they solved, and a solid floor – waterproofed initially with asphalt and later with heavy-duty plastic membranes – once again became the norm in house construction.

These floors consist of a bed of rammed hardcore, filled with sand (a process known as blinding) and topped by a layer of concrete 100–150mm thick. A damp-proof membrane (DPM) is laid over the concrete, and a further screeding layer of mortar or fine concrete up to 63mm thick is added to form the final floor surface.

The latest Building Regulations require solid floors to be insulated, and the structure now includes a thick layer of rigid polystyrene or other foam insulation. This is placed between the concrete and the screed.

THE TROUBLE WITH SOLID FLOORS

The commonest problem with solid ground floors is a failed DPM. This can usually be remedied by sealing the floor slab with a liquid damp-proofer, covered with a new thin surface screed (see page 247).

Damp may also be caused by leaks in buried plumbing or heating pipes, which will have to be excavated and repaired. It is possible to hire a concrete breaker (with vibration damping) to do this job yourself. Wear protective clothing and goggles, and make sure you know where water and gas pipes have been laid.

An uneven concrete floor can be treated with a self-levelling compound which will raise the floor level by about 10mm.

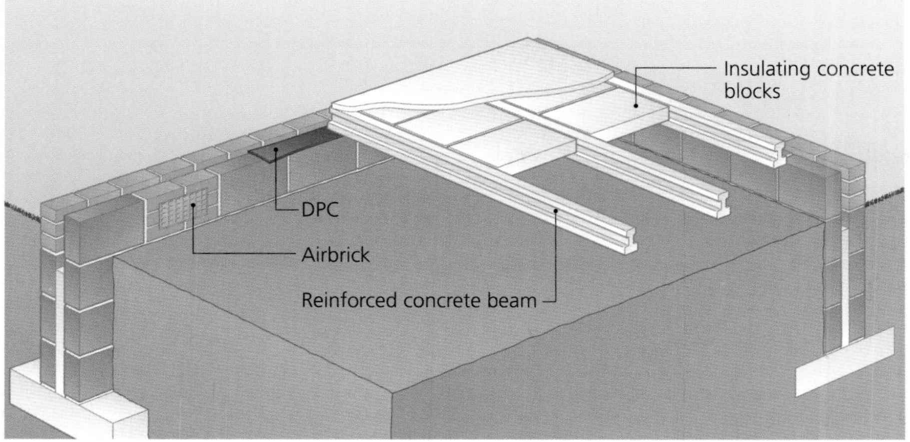

Another recent development is the use of suspended concrete ground floors, mainly on sloping sites where a solid infill would be prohibitively expensive. The floor is formed by inverted T-shaped beams of reinforced concrete that span the underfloor void, like traditional timber floor joists. Insulating concrete blocks rest on the flanges of the beams to form the floor slab, which is then topped with a fine screed as for solid floors.

THE TROUBLE WITH UPPER FLOORS

The only major problem likely to affect upper floors is sagging of the floor structure, caused either by overloading of inadequately sized joists or by alteration work involving the removal of supporting partitions. Excessive notching of joists during plumbing or wiring installation work can also lead to joists being weakened and sagging under a load. Minor damage to floorboards is usually the result of boards having been lifted for the installation of wiring and pipework.

What to do

It may be possible to strengthen a sagging floor structure by bolting new joists alongside the existing ones, or by installing a transverse support beam in the room below to support the centres of the affected joists. Both these jobs are best left to a builder. Minor repairs to floorboards are straightforward DIY jobs (see pages 126–7).

Upper floors

Two and three-storey houses invariably have upper floors supported on timber joists. These span individual rooms and are supported by load-bearing walls between rooms on the ground floor.

Floorboards
Strutting
Joist hanger
Joists
Ceiling

In older houses, the joist ends rest either in sockets in the outer walls, or on ledges in the masonry if the wall thickness decreases as the storeys rise.

In more modern buildings, they are supported by metal joist hangers built into the masonry. The joists are usually deeper (up to 230mm) than those in a suspended timber ground floor because they often have no intermediate supports.

The whole structure may be stiffened by the insertion of solid or herringbone strutting between the joists; this has another advantage – it also helps to prevent the joists from warping and distorting the floor surface. It will be covered with square-edged or tongued-and-grooved floorboards in older homes, or with sheets of flooring-grade chipboard in more modern ones.

Openings in the floor structure – round a stairwell, for example, or a chimney stack – are formed with doubled joists called trimming joists running parallel with the floor joists at either side of the opening. Trimmer joists are fixed at right angles to the trimming joists to form the other sides of the opening. The trimmer joists also support the cut (trimmed) ends of the floor joists adjoining the opening. The trimmer and trimmed joists are supported on joist hangers in modern homes and are fixed with cut timber joints in older buildings. The ends of upper floor joists in the modern home are tied into the masonry with special restraint joist hangers at 2m intervals to give the external walls extra support. Joists running parallel with the walls are tied to them with transverse steel strapping, which usually extends over two or three joists.

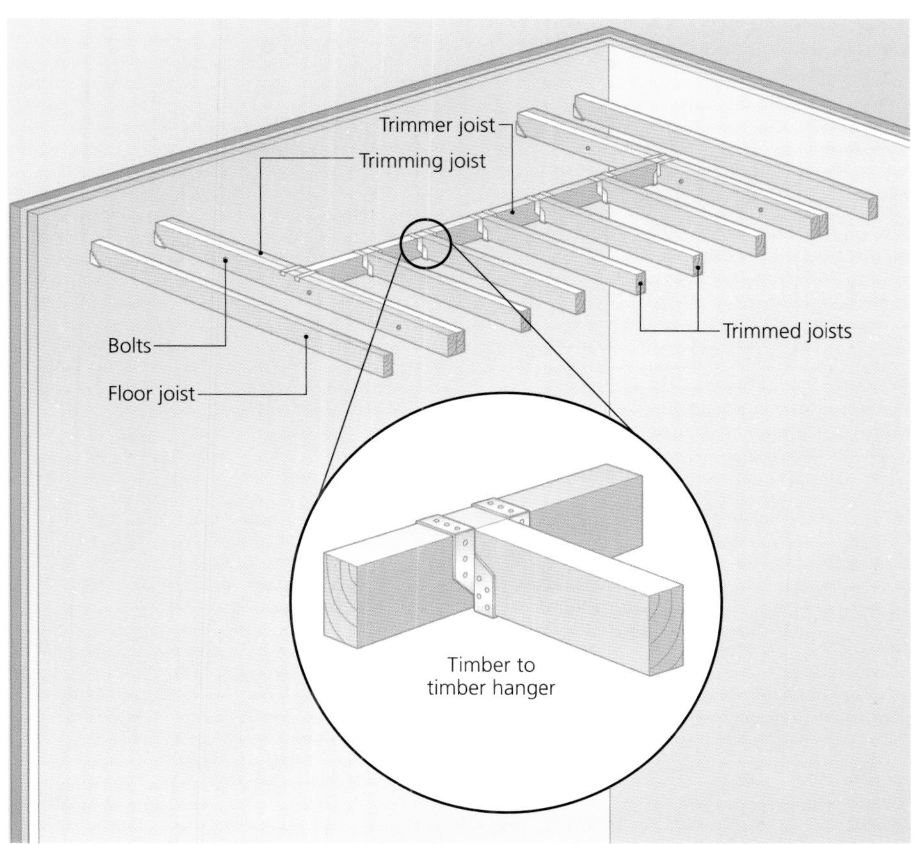

Internal walls and ceilings

Internal walls divide the space within the house into rooms of different sizes. They also contribute significantly to the stability of the building, and may support the structure of the storey above.

The way internal walls are built depends largely on the age of the house, and knowing about their structure can affect how you carry out DIY work on them.

Internal partitions

You can discover what type of partition walls you have by tapping the wall surface to see if it is solid or hollow, and then following this with test-drilling to reveal the materials used to construct it.

Brick walls In most properties built before the 1930s, internal partitions in ground-floor rooms are generally of brickwork, one brick thick, built in stretcher bond. With plaster on both faces, they are about 140mm thick overall. They support the floor joists of first floor rooms, and most of them are load-bearing. At least one of these walls will continue into the first storey (and higher storeys in multi-storey buildings), and will help to carry the load of the roof structure, so they, too, are load-bearing. Bear this in mind if you are considering removing walls to alter room layouts.

Block walls In properties built later than about 1930, 100mm thick concrete blockwork is used instead of brick for ground-floor load-bearing partitions and, again, these may be extended into upper storeys to support the roof structure. The plaster is generally thinner (and harder) than on old brick partitions, so the walls will measure about 125mm thick. You may also find non-loadbearing blockwork partitions, which are built in thinner blockwork.

You can confirm whether you have brick or block partition walls by making some test drillings into them. Drill three holes in an equilateral triangle, each hole about 50mm from the others; this guarantees that at least one hole will miss a mortar joint. Brick dust will be reddish or yellowish, whereas block dust will be grey or black.

Timber stud partitions Timber-framed walls, built with 100 x 50mm or 75 x 50mm sawn timber, are used as internal partitions in houses of all ages. The vertical studs are fixed at regular intervals (commonly 400mm, although spacings vary in older properties) between a timber head plate nailed to the ceiling joists and a corresponding sole plate fixed to the floor. Horizontal noggings are fitted between the studs to stiffen the structure and prevent warping of the studs.

Timber stud partitions may be load-bearing, although partitions in upper floor rooms are usually not, especially if their position does not coincide with a partition in the floor below. As a general rule, partitions of 75 x 50mm timber are never

THE TROUBLE WITH PARTITIONS

Apart from the usual (and expected) problems of superficial damage to the plaster or plasterboard surfaces of the wall, partitions can suffer from structural problems. The most serious is settlement of solid walls, caused by inadequate support being provided for the wall when it was built, or by subsequent ground movement. This causes cracks in the wall and at junctions with the ceiling and other walls, and doors may become difficult to shut as the frames are distorted. Settlement can also be caused by load-bearing walls being overloaded if the original roof covering has been replaced with a heavier material.

Lateral movement in solid walls can result from inadequate tying of the partitions to the external walls of the house during construction. In timber-framed walls, such movement is usually due to shrinkage of the timber frame, which may result from the use of poorly-stored timber on a wet building site.

What to do

Superficial damage to wall surfaces can be repaired easily on a DIY basis (see page 222). Settlement of solid walls usually requires some form of underpinning, and is a job for a surveyor to assess and an underpinning specialist to carry out. The work is likely to be expensive and disruptive. Lateral movement can often be cured by introducing lateral ties between the affected parts of the structure – again work for an expert. Shrinkage in timber-framed walls will cease once the wood has dried out, and the resulting cracks can then be filled and concealed.

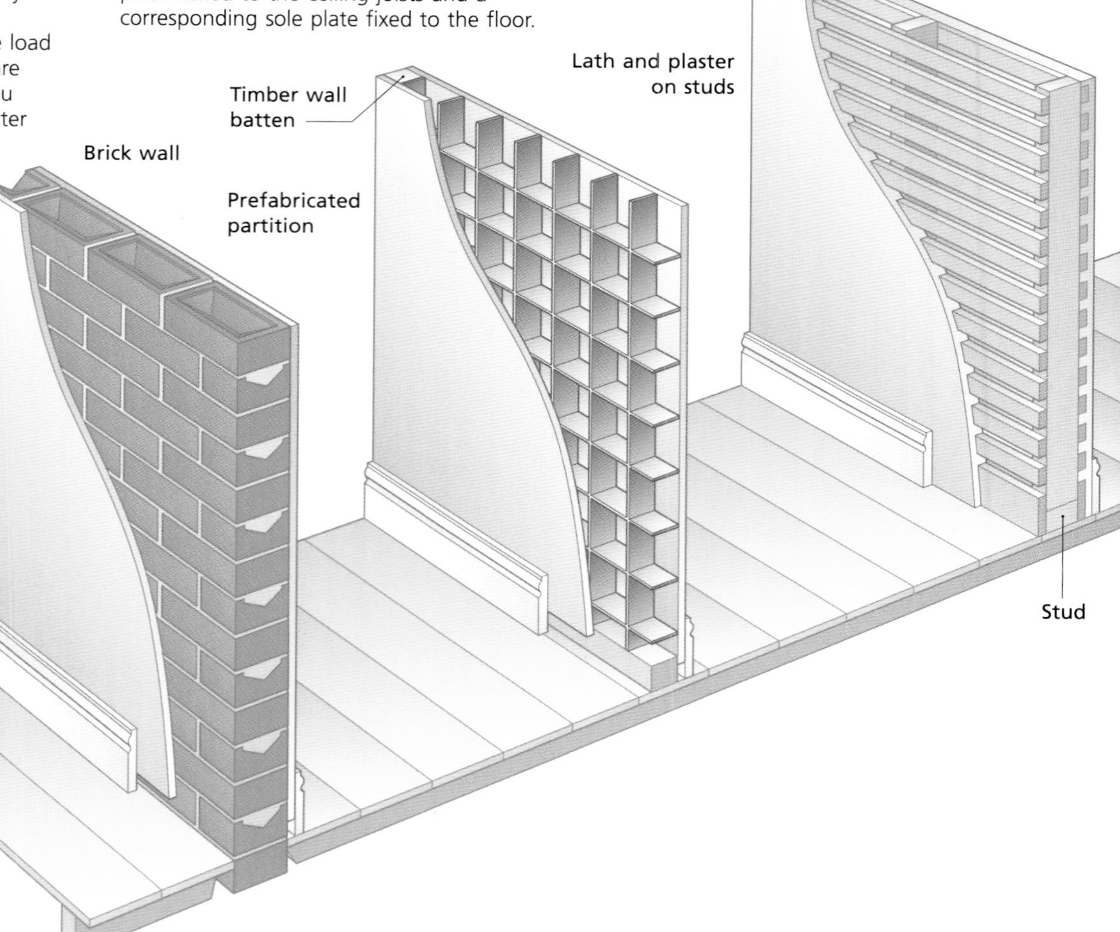

load-bearing. The framework will be clad in lath and plaster up to 20mm thick in older houses, and in 9.5 or 12.7mm thick plasterboard in those built since the late 1940s. A single test drilling will instantly reveal which type of cladding you have.

In houses built since the late 1960s, the roof structure is generally built using trussed rafters, which span the external walls of the house and do away with the need for load-bearing partition walls in upper floors. In houses with this type of roof structure, all upstairs partitions are timber-framed.

Prefabricated partitions In houses built in the last 20 years or so, you may encounter internal partitions built using prefabricated wall panels instead of the usual plasterboard on a timber frame. They consist of outer layers of plasterboard bonded to a cardboard core of egg-box construction, and are 1200mm wide and only 50mm thick. The panels rest on a timber sole plate and are fixed to timber battens at each end and at panel junctions.

Plasterboard on studs

Lightweight blockwork

Openings in partitions

In old internal brick partitions, door openings are commonly spanned by stout timber beams. Blockwork partitions have openings spanned by short lintels, of reinforced concrete or galvanised steel. Openings in timber-framed partition walls are suitably spaced between a pair of vertical studs, with the sole plate cut away and a cross-piece fixed between the studs to create the door head.

The opening is lined with a timber frame fixed to the masonry or the wall studs. The joint between wall surface and door frame is covered by an architrave moulding.

Ceilings

There is much less variation in the construction of ceilings, compared with partition walls. The age of the house is the key to the method used.

Ceilings are probably the most neglected surface in the house. They get little more than the most perfunctory decoration compared with walls, floors and woodwork, and tend to get noticed only when they start to cause trouble. However, they are a very good indicator of when things are going wrong. Check your ceilings regularly for sagging, damp marks and stains. Cracks in a plastered ceiling should be checked and monitored, to see if they worsen.

Lath and plaster ceiling

Lath and plaster Until the use of plasterboard became commonplace after the 1940s, ceilings were formed of lath and plaster in the same way as timber stud partition walls. Split or sawn timber laths 25–40mm wide and up to 13mm thick were nailed to the undersides of the ceiling joists, spaced about 10mm apart. The first coat of plaster was then applied and forced up between the laths to provide a fixing key. You can see these plaster ridges clearly if you view the ceiling surface from above – in a loft, for example. Two further coats of plaster were then applied to give a ceiling thickness of up to about 25mm.

Timber You may come across boarded ceilings in unrestored Victorian houses, especially in cellars and basement rooms. These consist of tongued-and-grooved boards nailed directly to the ceiling joists, and were generally gloss-painted.

Plasterboard Ceilings in modern houses consist of sheets of 9.5mm plasterboard nailed to the ceiling joists, and to noggings fixed between the joists to support the board ends. The joints between the boards are taped to prevent movement cracks from developing, and the plasterboard is either skim-coated with plaster or decorated directly – often with a textured coating such as Artex.

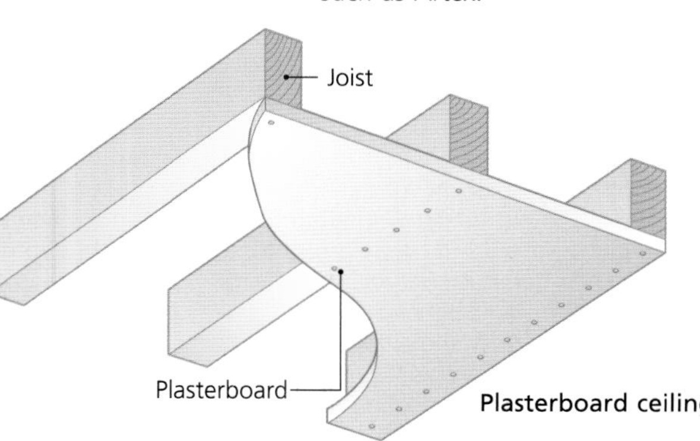

Plasterboard ceiling

THE TROUBLE WITH CEILINGS

Lath and plaster ceilings often fail with age because of the loss of the key between the plaster and the laths. Plasterboard ceilings may crack along the board joints, especially if these were not properly taped during installation. Both types can be holed by physical damage, and are badly affected by plumbing leaks. Minor leaks can cause staining which is difficult to conceal, and major ones can cause the ceiling to collapse.

What to do

Minor damage to any ceiling can be patched with plaster or plasterboard. Old lath and plaster ceilings in poor condition are best replaced with a new plasterboard ceiling. See pages 230–1 for details of the work involved.

Doors

An external door has to be thoroughly weatherproof and secure. An internal door is a decorative feature of the room where it is installed. Both come in a wide range of types and styles, in a number of standard sizes.

External door frames

The timber frame for an external door is prefabricated, and consists of a sill, two side members called jambs and a door head. The components are jointed with mortise and tenon joints or held together with steel dowels. The sill is usually made from hardwood for durability, and projects from the frame like a window sill to throw rainwater clear of the wall below.

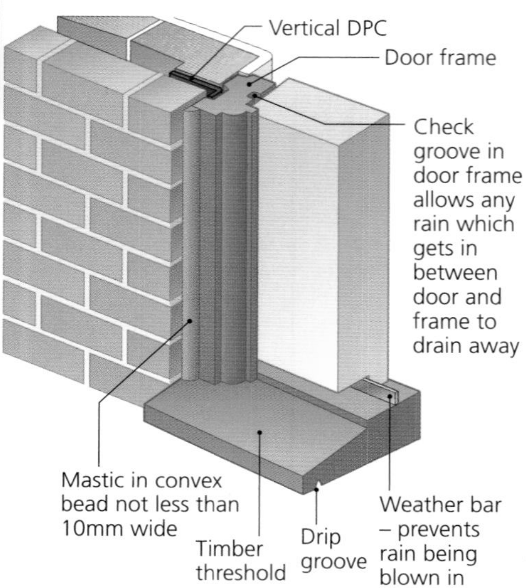

The door sill has grooves machined in its underside. The outermost is the drip groove which stops water from running back under the sill, while the inner one helps to fix the frame on its mortar bed when it is set in place in the wall just above the level of the house damp-proof course. A plastic or metal strip called a weather bar is set in a groove in the upper surface of the sill. This stops water from blowing under the door when it is closed.

The sides and head of the frame are rebated, allowing the door to close securely against the frame. This rebate also contains a drip groove or, on modern frames, integral weatherstripping.

Aluminium and steel-framed plastic (PVCu) door frames are made up in a similar way from specially-formed cross sections, and usually incorporate weatherstripping as part of the design.

The frame of an external door is set in place before the walls are built up around it, and is tied into the masonry with galvanised steel ties screwed to the frame and bedded into the mortar courses.

Internal door frames

Internal doors usually have simple three-sided timber frames, made from two jambs and a door head. The frame is commonly referred to as a door lining. In older houses it may be rebated like an external frame, but in modern houses it is usually formed from plain timber. Slim timber battens called stop beads are pinned to the door lining after installation to form a rebate against which the door closes.

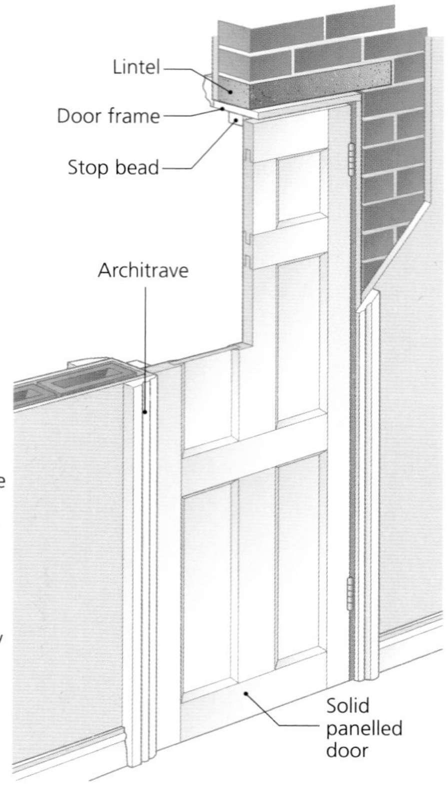

In a masonry wall The lining is fixed direct to the masonry – probably with large cut nails in older properties, and with screws and wallplugs or nailable frame fixings in a modern house. The timber used is usually about 25mm wider than the wall thickness, creating an edge against which the wall plaster can be finished. This joint is covered with architrave mouldings pinned to the edges of the door lining once plastering is complete.

In thin (75mm) blockwork partitions, the sides of the frame may extend from floor to ceiling, with the door head fixed between them and the space above it filled with blockwork. This type of storey-height frame is stronger than one built into an opening with a lintel over it.

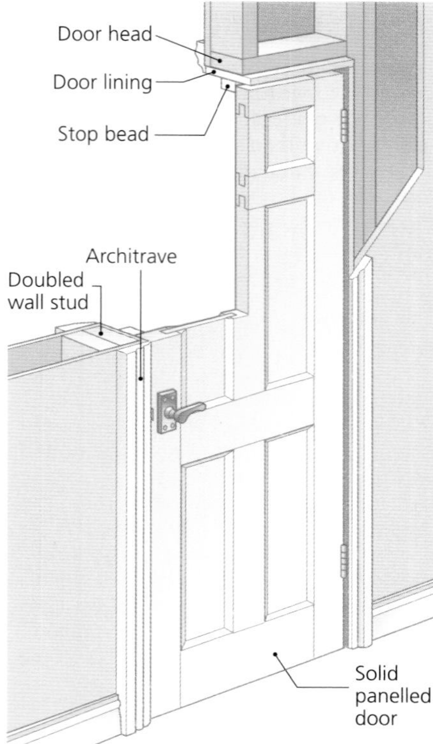

In timber-framed partition walls Vertical studs form the sides of the opening and the door head is nailed between them. Sometimes thicker studs are used here, or double studs are fitted for extra strength and rigidity. A thin door lining is nailed within the opening, providing an edge to which the plasterboard cladding on the partition can be abutted.

Again, architrave mouldings cover the join and stop beads form a rebate against which the door closes.

Safe glazing

Part N of the Building Regulations lays down strict rules about the use of glass in and next to doors. It applies to all new and replacement work.

Briefly, glass panels in all doors and in fixed panes beside door openings should be of toughened glass marked 'Made to British Standard BS6206 Class A'. This requirement also applies to any double-glazed panels.

Ordinary 6mm glass may be used in small panes (up to 0.5m^2 in size and with one side no more than 250mm long).

THE TROUBLE WITH DOORS

Rot is the main enemy of external doors and their frames if they are not kept in good decorative order, or if the sealant between frame and masonry fails. Internal and external doors can suffer from warping or binding in their frames, and may be affected by worn or damaged hinges. Most minor faults can be repaired by a competent do-it-yourselfer (see pages 188–91).

Replacing a damaged or unfashionable door requires moderate carpentry skills (pages 192–5), and you may prefer to leave the job to a carpenter.

Choosing doors

If a door is to be fitted at an entrance, style is not the only criterion – choose it with resistance to weather (and burglars) in mind as well. For inside the house, you need an interior grade door which is cheaper and lighter. Flush interior doors are generally less expensive than panelled doors. For an older house, you may be able to find suitable secondhand doors.

External doors

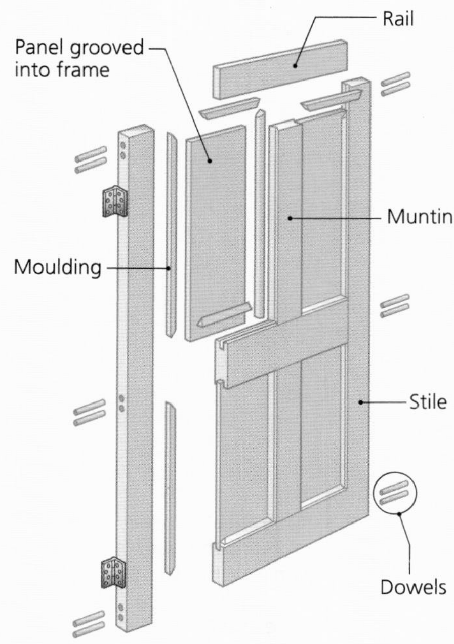

There are several types of external door. The traditional timber front door is a solid or glazed door, usually of panelled construction. It is available in many different styles, in hardwood and softwood.

It consists of two vertical outer components called stiles, linked by top and bottom rails and sometimes also a centre rail. Central vertical components called muntins link the rails in a traditional panelled door, but may be omitted if the door is fully glazed. All these components were traditionally assembled with mortise-and-tenon joints, but nowadays dowel joints are often substituted.

The inner edges of the components are machined – either with grooves to hold solid panels of timber or plywood, or with rebates to accept panes of glass which are held in place with beading on the inner face of the door. Multi-paned doors have no centre rail or muntins. An interlocking framework of glazing bars is fixed between the stiles and the top and bottom rails, as in a multi-paned window.

Flush doors are sometimes fitted as external doors, especially where they lead to the side or rear of the house. The door may be solid or part-glazed, and usually has a softwood frame with plywood facings.

Aluminium external doors are usually simple frames containing solid and glazed panels. Steel-framed PVCu and GRP (glass-reinforced plastic) doors may be of similar design, and are also available in a variety of panelled styles in imitation of traditional timber door styles.

External timber and aluminium doors Made in a range of standard sizes. The most widely available are 1981 x 762mm and 1981 x 838mm – the metric equivalents of traditional imperial sizes. Door thickness is a standard 44mm, to allow for the fitting of mortise locks without weakening the door structure.

Steel-framed PVCu doors are available in similar sizes for installation in timber frames, or can be supplied complete with matching frames (2085 x 920 is a typical overall size).

Patio doors The modern equivalent of French doors, consisting of two or more large glazed panels fitted into an outer frame. The doors may be of timber or PVCu, and are invariably double-glazed. In two-door units, one panel is fixed and the other slides. In multi-door units one or two panels may slide. Units are available in widths from 1530mm upwards.

French doors Double doors, usually fitted at the back of the house. The doors are side-hung within an outer frame, and have rebated meeting edges. They are usually part or fully glazed. The outer frame may incorporate fixed glazed panels at each side of the doors. Timber and PVCu types are available, in widths from 1220 to 1830mm.

Internal doors

Internal doors are usually only 35mm thick compared with the standard 44mm of an external door. This makes them lighter and easier to hang.

Internal doors may be panelled like a traditional front door, or flush-faced. Panelled doors are made in softwood and hardwood, with a choice of two, four or six panels which may be solid or glazed. Construction is similar to that of an external door.

Flush doors Have a lightweight softwood outer frame clad on each side with a layer (called a skin) of man-made board. Hardboard skins are used on the cheapest flush doors, and plywood – often with a decorative surface veneer – on more expensive ones. The doors are lipped in solid timber to protect the edges of the skins. The core of the door is usually a cardboard egg-box filling, with a solid block of wood glued to the inside of one of the frame stiles to take a lock or latch. The edge with the lock block is marked clearly, so it can be hung the correct way round.

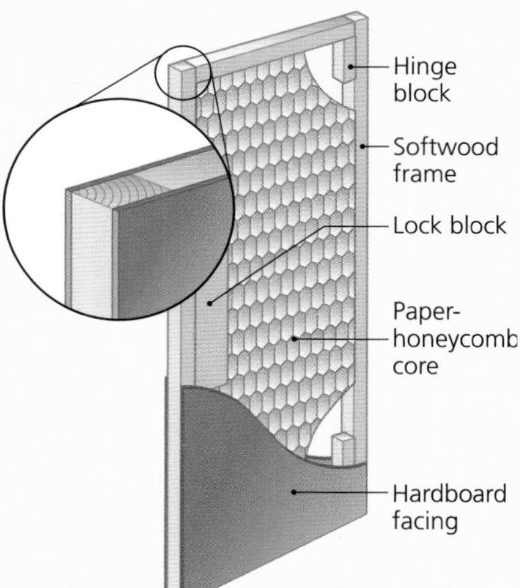

You can also buy 'flush' doors with moulded or embossed facing panels made from medium-density fibreboard (MDF). They are a very good imitation of panelled doors, and do not suffer from shrinkage round the panels as solid wood doors do. They are sold ready-primed.

Internal doors are also made in standard sizes. The most common heights are 1981 and 2032mm, and standard widths are 686, 762, 813 and 838mm. Narrower internal doors are also available, intended to be hung in pairs from bi-fold door gear. They are often fitted as doors to alcove cupboards, or where there is no room for a standard door to open.

Windows

Windows come in more shapes, sizes and styles than almost any other component of a typical house.

They are also often more troublesome than other parts of the house because they are made from a complex mix of components. This is multiplied by the fact that even a small terraced house will have half a dozen windows, and a detached house may have twice as many.

TYPES OF LINTEL

Standard pressed steel

Steel and block

Steel and wood

Steel and concrete

Through-the-wall concrete lintel

Concrete boot lintel

Window and door openings are spanned by lintels – load-bearing beams that support the masonry above them. They are made from galvanised steel or reinforced concrete, and sometimes both. Steel lintels are virtually invisible from outside, since the metal lip supports facing brickwork over the opening. Hollow types incorporate insulation material to prevent condensation inside. Plain concrete lintels have a visible outer face that can look unsightly. In a cavity wall, a damp-proof barrier, called a cavity tray, stops any rainwater that penetrates the outer leaf from crossing the cavity at the lintel.

Openings in internal masonry walls are spanned by a timber lintel in old houses, and by a slim concrete or box steel lintel in newer ones.

Window frames

Window frames are built into the house walls in much the same way as an external door (see page 14). Modern windows are positioned so that the frame is set back from the face of the masonry by only about 25mm – a fact that contributes significantly to the often short life of wooden casement windows when compared with Victorian sash windows. These were set back so that the inside of the frame was flush with the internal wall surface, and as a result the frame was much less exposed to the weather. In areas of the country rated as having severe weather exposure (mainly Scotland and Northern Ireland), Building Regulations require windows to be recessed for this very reason.

Wood is still the most popular material for making window frames. Modern high-performance hardwood windows treated with microporous paints or stains offer excellent durability, and their integral draught-stripping ensures efficient weatherproofing. Cheaper softwood windows need more regular maintenance, but they are the lowest cost choice for new or replacement work.

Steel windows were briefly popular during the 1930s and 1940s, but suffered severely from rust even when they were galvanised. Their slim, fashionable appearance was more than outweighed by the fact that the frames ran with condensation, and they could not readily be double-glazed. They are still to be found in many unmodernised properties of the period, often with the opening casements rusted (or painted) permanently shut.

Aluminium windows took their place by the 1960s, creating a trend for uncluttered picture windows. They tended to weather badly, and needed a timber sub-frame because the metal frames were not very strong. They endured for some years in patio door format, but even here other materials have now taken their place.

Plastic (PVCu) windows have a stranglehold on the replacement window market, where they offer a unique combination of comfort and warmth with a promise of being virtually maintenance-free. They are less widely used in new work, because they are more expensive to specify and their looks are not as aesthetically pleasing as a well-proportioned wooden window. Their longevity is not yet proven.

Casement windows

The casement window is the most widely used type in modern housing. In its simplest form it consists of a square or rectangular outer frame containing a single framed pane of glass called a casement. This is side-hung in the same way as a door. The frame may be divided into two or more sections by vertical mullions, and each section may contain an opening casement or a fixed pane. Further variety is introduced by fitting horizontal transoms near the top of each section, allowing the fitting of a small opening top light above

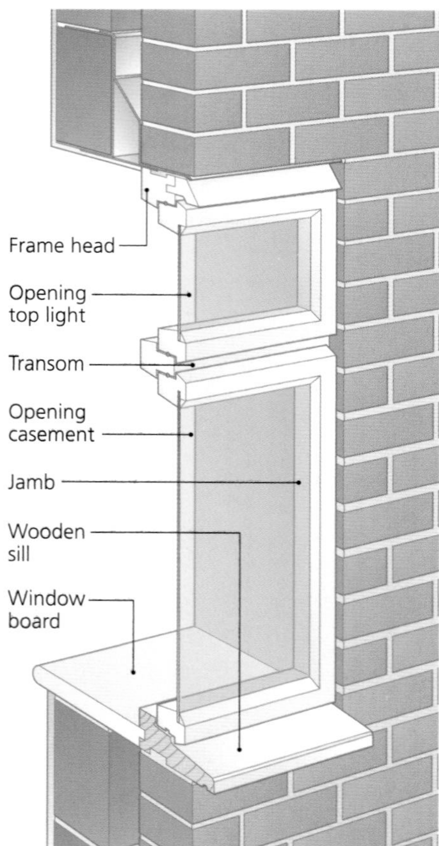

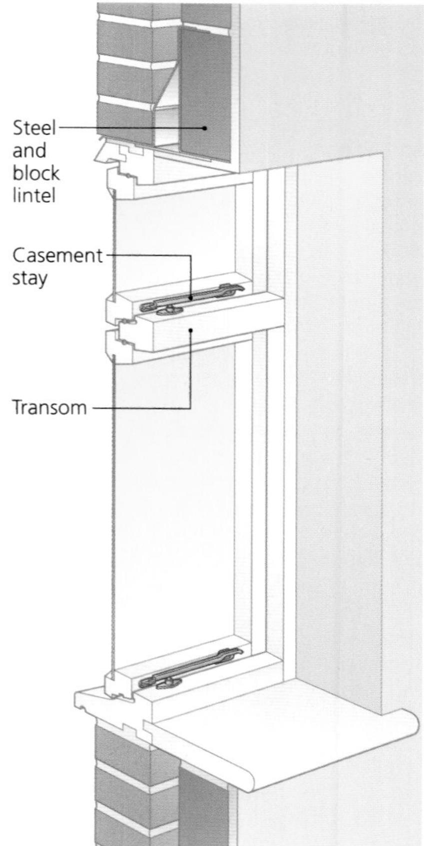

Components of a casement window

the side-hung casement – an arrangement that covers every ventilation requirement.

Individual casements may contain glazing bars and a number of smaller panes of glass, rather than a single large pane – styles known generally as cottage (four panes) or Georgian (six or eight panes). Casements are held closed by a simple handle and wedge, and held in an open position with a casement stay and peg. Top ventilators usually have just a casement stay.

A casement frame consists of a head, two side jambs and a sill. These components, and any mullions and transoms, are joined with mortise and tenon joints. To help to prevent rain penetration round the opening casements and top ventilators, drip grooves are machined round the inner faces of the frames, mullions and transoms. There are additional grooves round the edges of casements and top ventilators. On high-performance windows, integral weatherstripping is also fitted to make the opening parts of the window weatherproof.

In new buildings, casement frames are usually built into the walls as they rise, and are secured with galvanised ties screwed to the frame and anchored in the mortar courses. Replacement windows are generally secured at the sides by screws and wallplugs or nailable frame fixings.

A variation on the casement style is created by arranging the frame sections at a slight angle to each other to form a projecting bow window, or at bigger angles (up to 90°) to create a bay window.

Sash windows

The sash window was the favoured window style in homes until early in the 20th century. It is a highly complex construction, built into the inner face of the house wall in a rebate in the masonry. This contains the concealed channels for the counterweights that balance the two sliding sashes. Because the frame is set back in this way, there is usually a sub-sill of stone or quarry tiles on which the frame sill rests.

The window frame consists of a head, a sill and two jambs. Each jamb is a vertical box, consisting of an outer lining, a pulley stile, an inner lining and a back lining. A moulding called the parting bead is pinned down the centre of the visible face of the pulley stile. This forms a track between it and the projecting lip of the outer lining to form a vertical track in which the outer (top) sash slides. A second moulding called the staff bead is fixed down the inner edge of the pulley stile to create a parallel track for the inner (bottom) sash.

Near the top of each track, a pulley is fitted into a slot in each pulley stile. This allows the sash cords that connect each sash to its weights to run in and out of the weight compartments as the sashes are raised and lowered. At the bottom of each track is a removable cut-out pocket that gives access to the weight compartments if the sash cords need replacing.

The sashes are square or rectangular frames, sometimes sub-divided by glazing bars into two, four or six smaller panes. The stiles at the top of the inner sash and the bottom of the outer sash are often extended into decorative horns. A catch mounted on the meeting rails allows the windows to be secured in the closed position.

The modern version of the sliding sash window replaces the cords and weights with clever spring-loaded spiral balances, which are mounted on the faces of the frame sides. Each sash is attached to its two spiral balances by fixing plates at its bottom corners.

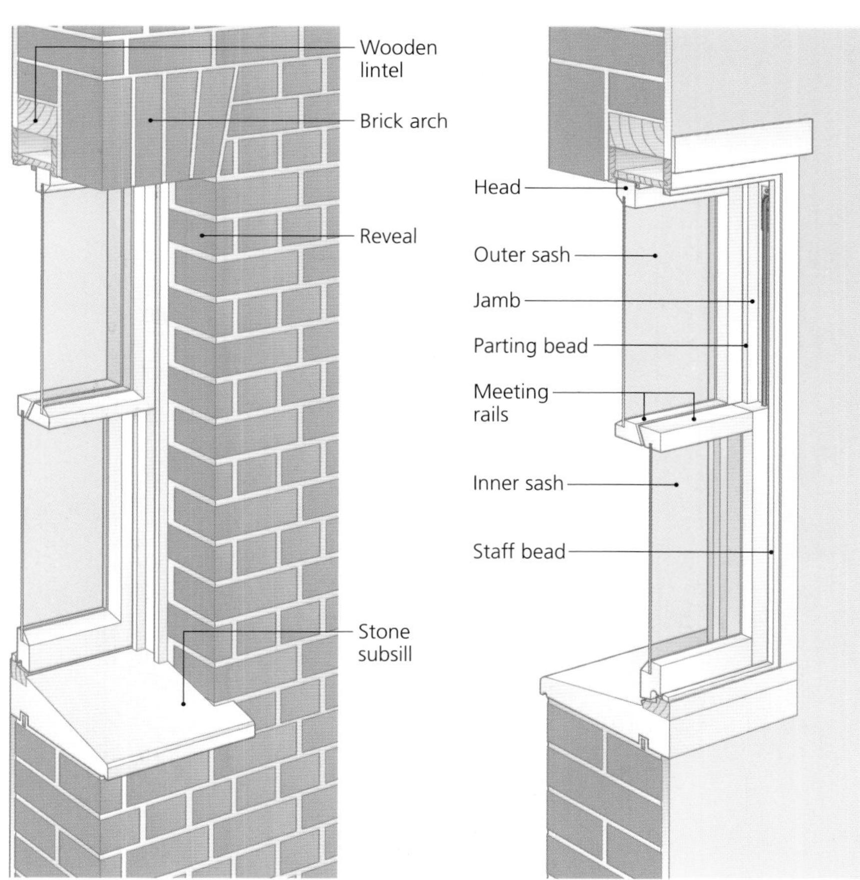

Components of a sash window

THE TROUBLE WITH WINDOWS

The commonest problem with all wooden windows is rot. It can attack the frame, its casements or sashes at the joints if water is able to penetrate, and at any point where the glazing putty fails.

Casements can bind or stick in their frames, much as a door does, making them difficult to open and close. Hinges can be damaged if the casement is allowed to swing open violently or any weight is put on it.

Sashes can bind against the pulley stiles, rattle in high winds and let in draughts. However, their biggest problem is failed sash cords, which can be tricky and time-consuming to replace.

Lastly, glass in any window may be cracked or broken by an impact, or by the window slamming shut.

What to do

The most important thing you can do to give your windows the longest life is to maintain them regularly, especially as far as their decoration is concerned (see pages 414–15). It is failed paintwork that allows rot to gain an initial foothold in window woodwork.

You can carry out most of the everyday repairs a window might need yourself (see pages 203–11 and 412–13). Replacing a window is a fairly major undertaking subject to Building Regulations (see pages 211 and 214–15), and is one you may prefer to leave to a carpenter, builder or professional installer.

Draughtproofing of sashes can also prevent rattling and will cut down on the amount of noise that comes in. This is a task best undertaken by professionals as it involves removing sashes from their frames and lining them with strips of insulation.

Pitched roofs

Most houses have pitched roofs, sloping on one or more sides and clad with tiles or slates.

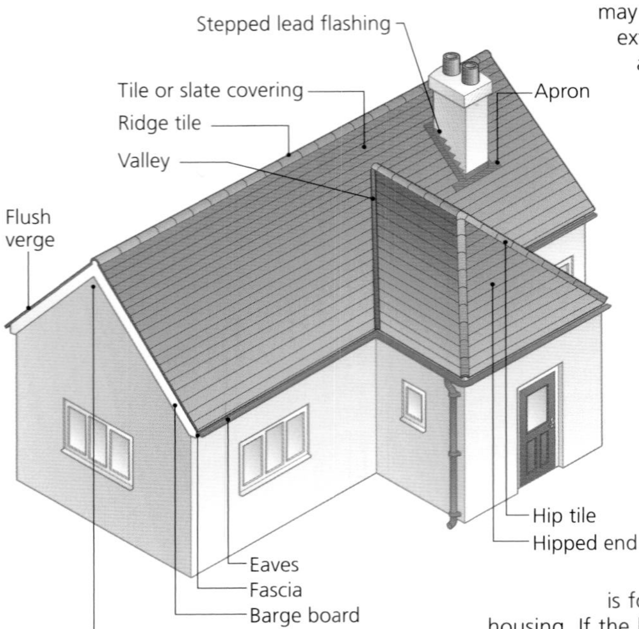

Until around the 1960s, pitched-roof construction was a job for skilled carpenters, who would cut and fix the individual timbers one by one to form the roof structure the house required. Modern houses are built almost exclusively using prefabricated roof trusses, which allow the roof structure to be erected much more quickly and also eliminate the need for internal load-bearing walls in all but the largest properties.

Traditional roof construction

The simplest pitched roof is called a lean-to or mono-pitch roof. It is a slope that usually abuts a wall at its higher end. The roof consists of sloping rafters, resting at each end on a horizontal timber wallplate. It may be installed on single-storey extensions, porches and attached garages and, in the past, was often used to roof the additions at the rear of Victorian terraces.

The span of a pitched roof can be increased considerably by butting two mono-pitch roofs together to form a so-called double-pitch roof. The two roof slopes meet at a ridge board, and the bottom ends of the rafters forming each slope are tied together by joists to create a rigid triangular structure. Gable walls fill in the open ends of the roof. This type of roof structure is limited in span to about 4m, and is found mainly in terraced housing. If the house has an internal load-bearing wall, struts can be added between the purlins and a wallplate resting on top of the internal wall. The addition of a collar tie between the rafters at the level of the purlins creates a roof structure that can comfortably span the width of most houses.

THE EAVES OF THE HOUSE

At the eaves, the rafters either project beyond the walls or are cut off flush with them. A vertical fascia board protects the cut ends of the rafters and carries the roof gutters.

If the eaves project, a horizontal soffit board fills the gap between the fascia board and the house wall. In modern construction, the soffit incorporates ventilation strips to allow an air flow through the loft.

No soffit board is fitted to open eaves, where the underside of the rafters is visible. Bricks (or ventilators) fill the gaps between the rafters.

1 Flush eaves

2 Closed eaves

3 Open eaves

A duo-pitch roof may have sloping ends (called hips) instead of gables. Each hip is formed by two diagonal hip rafters that support the end of the ridge board, and short jack rafters are fitted between the hip rafters and the wallplates to complete the roof structure.

Where two duo-pitched roofs meet in an L-shape, they form an external hip and an internal valley, which is supported by a valley rafter and jack rafters in the same way as a hip is formed. The valley is either lined with a lead gutter or with specially shaped valley tiles (see Roof coverings, right).

Ridge board
Wall plate
Binder
Hanger
Purlin
Common rafter
Joist
Strut
Loadbearing internal wall

Purlin roof The commonest type of duo-pitch roof is the purlin roof. This has a horizontal beam called a purlin running between the gable ends along each slope of the roof, midway between the ridge board and the eaves, to provide extra support for the rafters. This increases the unsupported span of the roof to about 7m.

Prefabricated roofs

Almost all modern (post 1960s) house roofs are built using roof trusses, which are prefabricated in a variety of shapes to cater for most roof designs. Each roof truss combines rafters, joists and struts in a W-pattern to create a frame that is extremely strong and can span the external walls of the building with no need for internal load-bearing walls. The triangular structure does not deform under load, so the timbers used can be slimmer in cross-section than those in a traditional roof. This has the advantages of lower cost, lighter weight and ease of handling on site. The trusses can also be fixed by relatively unskilled workers, as little carpentry is involved in installing them.

The components of each roof truss are butt-jointed and fixed together with galvanised steel connector plates. The trusses are positioned 600mm apart on wallplates at each side of the span, and are nailed into place. There is no ridge board, but the row of trusses has to be braced to prevent it from collapsing sideways. Horizontal braces are fitted where the W-shaped internal supports meet the rafters and the ceiling joists, and diagonal braces are added across the underside of each section of the roof slope, running from the ridge to the eaves. The roof structure is tied to the house walls with galvanised steel straps to prevent the roof from lifting or gable walls collapsing in high winds.

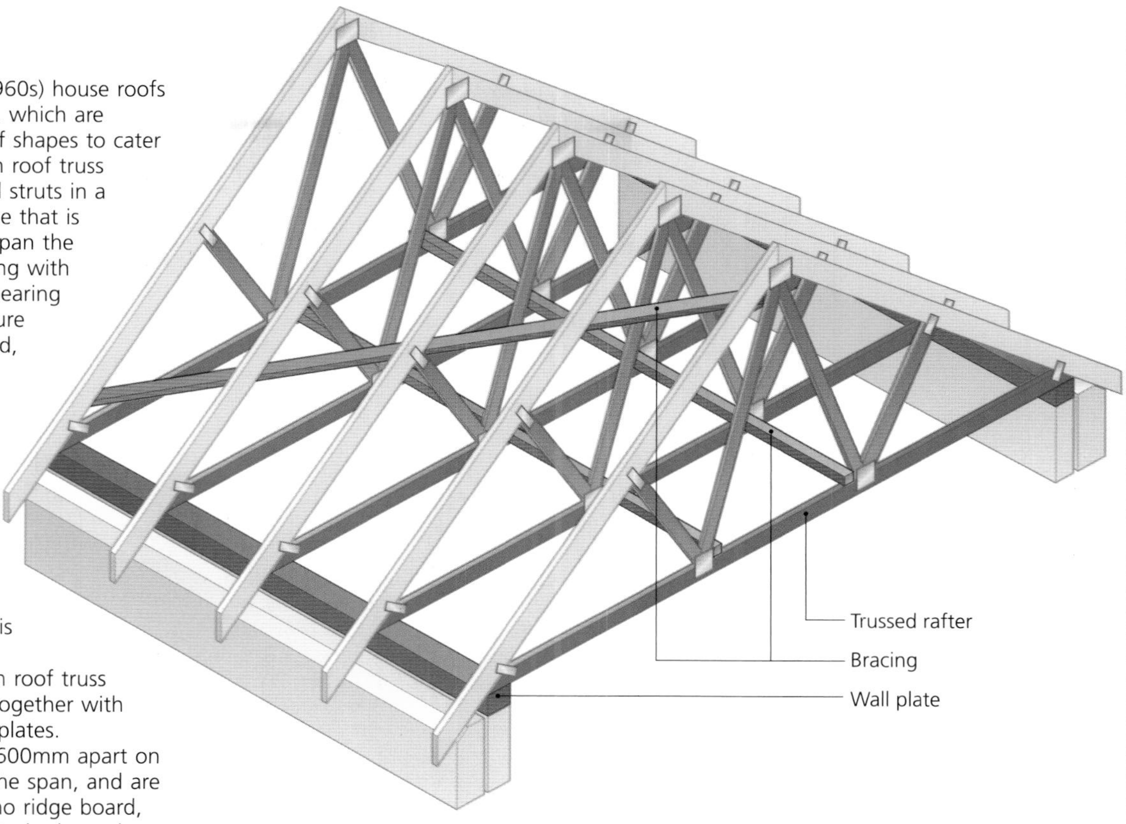

Roof coverings

Pitched roofs are traditionally covered with tiles or slates (see page 388). Other materials such as split stone and thatch are found in localised areas of the country, but their installation, maintenance and repair are beyond the scope of this book and are best left to specialist contractors.

In older houses, the roof covering is laid on closely spaced horizontal battens nailed across the upper edges of the rafters. In old roofs, this method allowed fine rain and snow to blow through the gaps between the tiles or slates and into the roof space. This was prevented by trowelling a mixture of mortar and animal hair into the gaps from inside the roof (a process called torching) or by boarding the roof slope – an expensive solution found only on better-quality houses. Since the 1930s it has been usual to lay underfelt (called sarking) over the rafters before the battens are fixed.

Slates and plain tiles

There are always two layers of tile or slate at any point on the roof, and three layers directly over each batten. This double-lapping prevents the water running off one tile or slate from entering the roof space through the gap between the tile or slate in the course below. Slates are nailed to the battens at every course. Plain tiles have nibs on the back which hook over the roof battens, and are usually nailed only at every third or fourth course.

Other types of tile, such as traditional pantiles and large modern concrete tiles, overlap or interlock with their neighbours in each course. This prevents rain penetrating between their edges, so they can be laid with a single lap. This saves on both labour and materials when covering the roof. Tiles are fixed to the battens with nails or, more commonly on modern roofs, with side-fixing clips. Usually every third course is fixed, plus all perimeter tiles.

Flashings

Where a roof slope meets a wall or a chimney stack, the join must be waterproof. This is what flashings do. Lead, zinc, copper and mortar have all been used, but lead is the most common material in use today. It is cut into strips that are let into the mortar joints of the wall and shaped to overlap the roof covering.

Ridges and hips

Special half-round or L-shaped tiles are bedded on mortar or dry-fixed to the ridge board and hip rafters. Hips on plain-tiled roofs may be finished with specially-shaped bonnet hip tiles, which continue the tile coursing neatly round the hip. Valleys may also be tiled or lined with lead sheeting. At verges – where the roof slope meets a gable wall – the gaps between the tiles and the masonry may be filled with mortar, or the roof edge may be finished with special verge tiles. See pages 391–3 for more details.

THE TROUBLE WITH ROOFS

A well-built pitched roof will last for decades (or longer), but several problems are commonplace. Individual slates and tiles can slip out of position if their fixings fail, allowing water to penetrate the roof structure, and ridge and hip tiles can be dislodged by high winds if their mortar bedding fails. Slates can become brittle with age, and both tiles and slates can be damaged by careless roofing contractors or reckless householders climbing on the roof surface. Metal flashings can be torn or lifted by high winds, and mortar flashings may simply crack and fall out.

What to do

Unless you have the proper access equipment (see page 387) and are experienced in working at heights, it is safest to leave all roofing work to professional roofing contractors. You may be able to carry out minor repairs close to the eaves via a ladder. If you feel you are capable of carrying out work on the roof slope, you can replace tiles and slates (see pages 389–92) and repair flashings (page 394).

Flat roofs

Flat roofs are relatively uncommon on new homes today. In the 1960s and 1970s, every home extension had one because it was cheap and quick to erect.

Poor quality felting on these roofs led to a host of problems, and many owners of flat roofs eventually gave up the constant round of repairs and put on a pitched roof instead. Planners, too, grew disillusioned with flat roofs on domestic buildings and it is now very difficult to get consent to build anything new with a flat roof. Despite this, there are many flat roofs still in existence and giving reasonable service.

Flat roof construction

A flat roof is not truly horizontal; it needs a slight slope to drain rainwater off its surface. The basic structure consists of a series of parallel joists, usually running across the shorter dimension of the roof and spaced at 400, 450 or 600mm centres. On spans of more than about 2.5m, solid or herringbone strutting is fixed between the joists to prevent them from warping.

Where an extension roof abuts a house wall, the ends of the joists nearest the house are supported on joist hangers or on a wall plate bolted to the wall. The other ends rest on a wall plate on top of the outer wall of the extension. This wall plate is secured to the wall with galvanised strapping to prevent strong winds from lifting the roof structure.

To create the required slope, which should be 1 in 60 for a felted roof, tapered battens called furring strips are fixed to the top edges of the joists. If the roof slope is to run at right angles to the joist direction, the strips also run at right angles to the joists.

The roof decking is then nailed in place. It may be tongued-and-grooved softwood boards, roofing-grade chipboard (which is coated with bitumen) or exterior-grade plywood. Softwood should be 19mm thick, while boards are usually 18mm thick. Boards are normally laid with their long edges across the joists, and solid struts or noggings can be positioned at 1220mm centres to provide extra support for the board edges.

Roof coverings

There are two materials commonly used on new domestic flat roofs; built-up felt and mastic asphalt. You may find lead, copper or zinc sheet roofs on older properties, especially on flat-topped window bays and porches.

Felt is usually built up in three layers, bonded together with hot or cold bitumen. Felt is available in several types, and the choice (and cost) will affect the life of the roof. The cheapest felts are based on mineral or glass fibre, and are generally used nowadays only for outbuildings. More expensive high-performance felts based on polyester fibres and fabrics are much more durable. As an alternative to bonding each felt layer to the one below with bitumen, torch-on felts have been developed. These have extra bitumen on one face that is melted with a blowtorch as the felt is unrolled into position.

The top layer of felt needs protecting against the effects of sunlight. Solar protection is usually provided by dressing the roof surface with a layer of small stone chippings, or by applying a solar reflective paint. Chippings are best bonded to the felt surface to prevent them from drifting

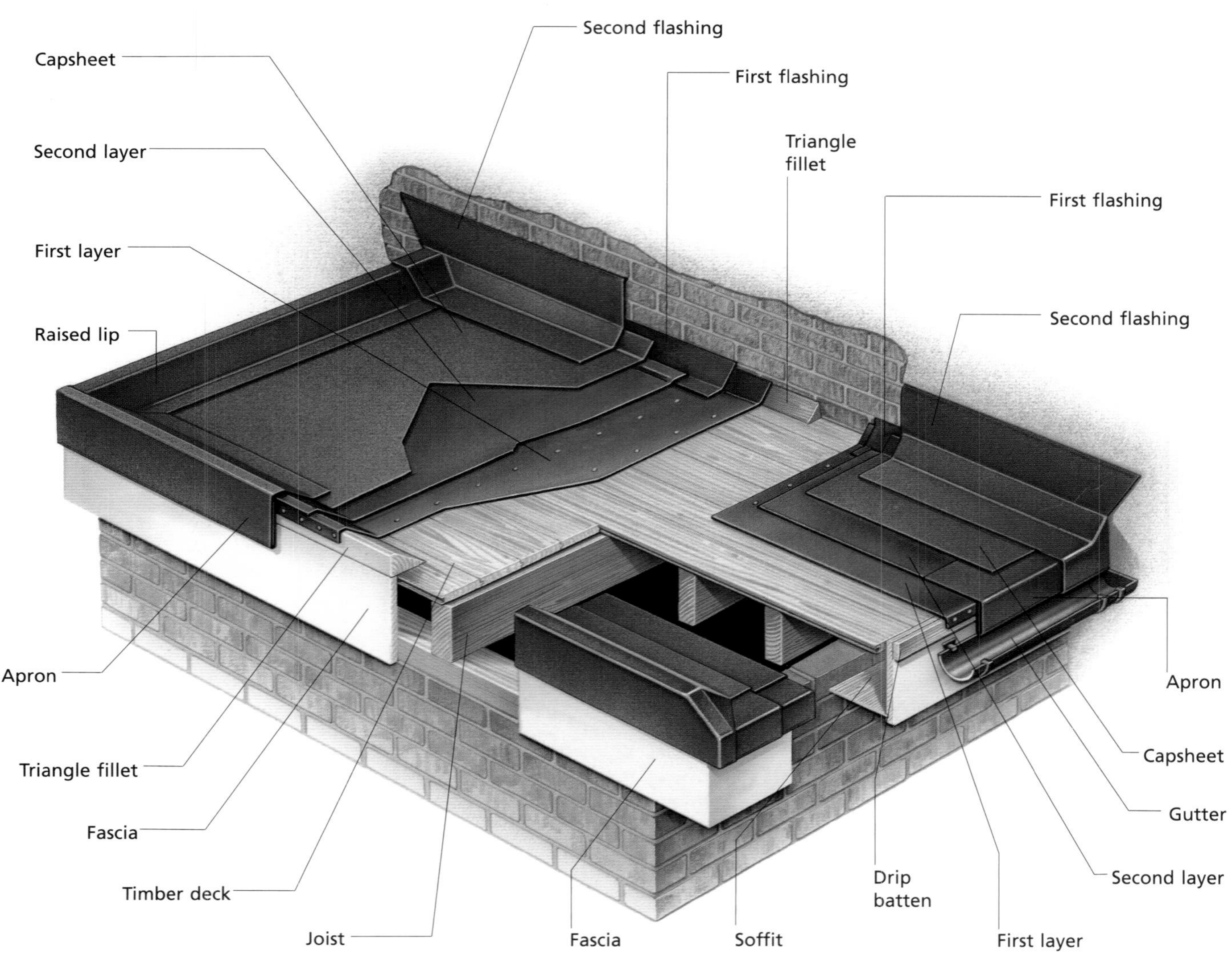

into gutters, but bonded chippings are more difficult to remove if the roof needs repairing.

Asphalt is a seamless roof covering made from natural or synthetic bitumen. It is melted in a cauldron and applied hot, over a layer of sheathing felt, in two layers to a total thickness of 18-20mm. It is used as an alternative to built-up felt on roofs that are used as balconies or roof gardens.

THE TROUBLE WITH FLAT ROOFS

Failure of the roofing felt is the commonest problem with existing flat roofs. A standard bitumen-bonded three-layer roof has a life expectancy of 10 to 15 years if well maintained, and less if it is subjected to regular foot traffic and the careless use of ladders or other access equipment, both of which can damage the felt. Weathering of the felt opens up cracks and pinholes that allow moisture to penetrate, causing blisters in the felt when the moisture is turned to vapour in hot sun. Seams and edges can be lifted in high winds, causing the felt to tear and allowing water penetration. Once water has penetrated, dampness in the roof structure can allow rot to develop. This initially causes the decking to subside between the joists, and may eventually lead to collapse of the roof structure if not remedied.

What to do

It is important to inspect flat roofs regularly – at least once a year – so that small defects can be identified and treated before they cause major trouble. You can repair blisters and splits yourself (see page 396) and carry out other minor repairs such as fixing faulty flashings (page 393). More widespread problems may need an overall waterproofing treatment (page 397). Full-scale replacement of an existing felted roof is a major project which you may prefer to leave to a professional roofing contractor.

Insulation and ventilation

A basic flat roof is a poor insulator, with just decking above the joists and a plasterboard ceiling below to keep the heat in. Old flat roofs may contain no insulation at all, or just a thin layer of glass fibre blanket laid above the ceiling. As a result, the rooms below it will be cold and expensive to heat. New or recently-built flat roofs always incorporate insulation, and this is provided in a number of different ways.

Cold roof

Insulated flat roofs are divided into two categories – cold roofs and warm roofs – according to where the insulation layer is placed.

In a cold roof, the insulation is placed above the ceiling and between the joists, so that the decking and the cavity between it and the insulation will be cold in winter. Unless the ceiling incorporates a vapour barrier, moisture rising through it will form condensation within the roof structure, rendering fibre insulation useless, saturating the ceiling and encouraging rot in the roof timbers. Since the fascia boards effectively seal the cavity, ventilation must be provided by openings equivalent to a 25mm wide strip all round the eaves of the roof. Condensation is still a potential problem, however, and because of this warm roofs are now preferred on new buildings.

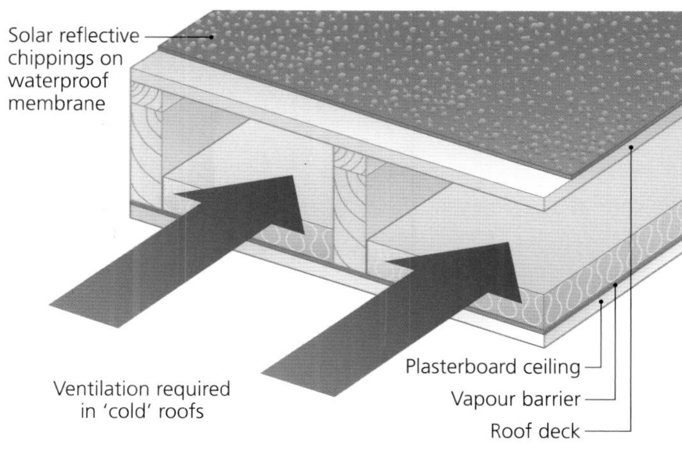

Warm roof There are two main types of warm roof construction. In both, the insulation is placed above the roof deck, keeping it and the roof structure warm. This means a greatly reduced incidence of condensation, so ventilation of the roof space is no longer required, although a vapour barrier is still incorporated in the structure.

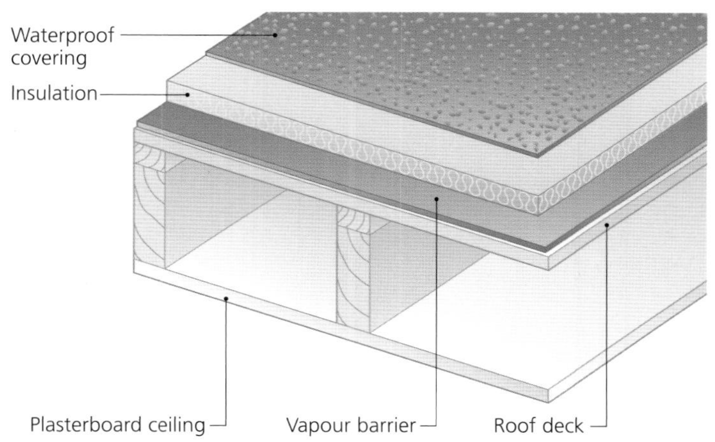

Sandwich roof
Insulation in the form of rigid boards is placed over a vapour barrier on top of the deck, and is protected by the final roof covering

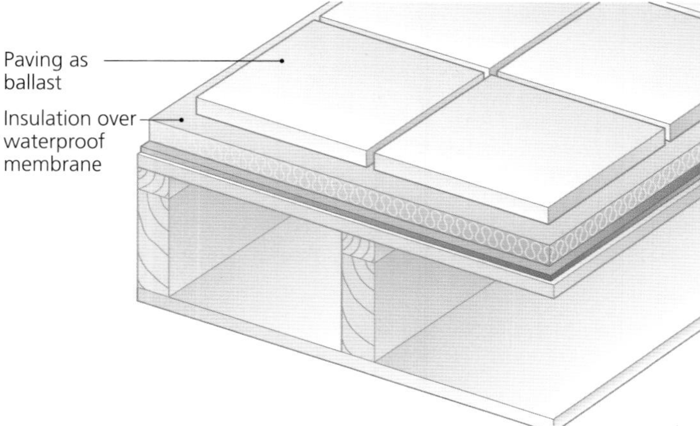

Inverted roof
The insulation is placed above the roof covering, and is held down by ballast in the form of paving stones or a layer of pebbles. This protects the roof covering from extremes of temperature and accidental damage, and can be used to upgrade the insulation of an existing roof without any structural work. It has two drawbacks. Firstly, repairs to the roof, if needed, are more difficult to carry out because the ballast and insulation must first be removed. Secondly, the ballast may impose too great a load on an insubstantial roof structure; a surveyor should always check this aspect before an inverted roof is used on an existing roof structure.

Rainwater and drainage systems

In heavy rain, a lot of water falls on the roof of your house. 25mm of rain – a good cloudburst by British standards – means the whole of your roof area is covered to a depth of 25mm.

On a typical roof with an area of, say, 160m², that 25mm of water adds up to a total of 4m³ of water, or a volume of 4000 litres. Collecting it safely and getting rid of it is the job of the house's rainwater system.

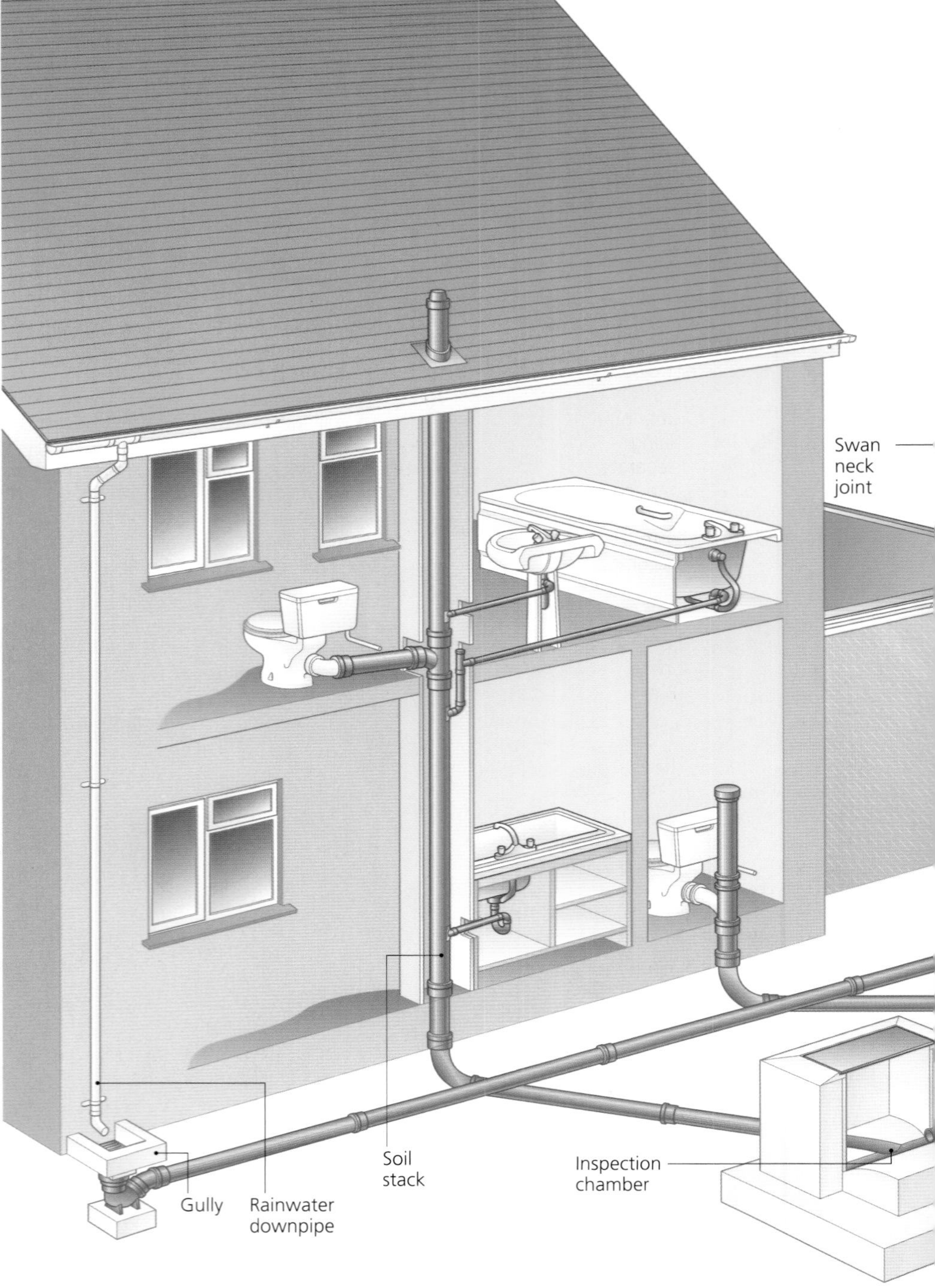

Gutters and downpipes

Water running off a roof is collected in gutters fixed to the fascia boards. The gutters must be big enough to collect the occasional downpour without overflowing, and for most houses a gutter 100 or 112mm in width will do the job.

They discharge the water they collect into downpipes, which run down the house walls to ground level. A downpipe 68-75mm in diameter is usually big enough to carry the discharge from 100 or 112mm gutters.

Gutter outlets These are fitted at downpipe positions, discharging directly into the downpipe if the house eaves are flush with the wall. If the eaves overhang, an offset double-bend pipe called a swan neck links the gutter to the downpipe.

Where two roof slopes meet in a valley, the rainwater is usually discharged from the valley gutter into a fitting called a hopper head. A downpipe runs from the hopper head down to ground level. A rainwater hopper head may also collect waste water from upstairs baths and washbasins.

Cast-iron downpipes Iron pipes have integral fixing lugs that are secured to the house walls with large pipe nails driven into wooden wedges in the mortar joints of the wall. Each pipe end fits loosely into the top of the length below. Bends divert the pipe where necessary, and single branch fittings allow two downpipes to be joined. At the base of the pipe, an angled fitting called a shoe discharges the water over the grate of an underground gully (see right).

PVCu rainwater systems In modern houses, gutter systems are plastic. They are very similar to their cast-iron counterparts in terms of the components used, but are much lighter. They are available in black, grey, white and brown.

Joints are made using fittings with integral rubber seals and plastic clips. The gutters may be half-round, or may have a deep oval or square trough cross-section. All are supported on brackets screwed to the fascia boards. The gutters discharge into downpipes that are fixed to the wall with separate brackets.

Aluminium gutters These are seamless, and are formed on site by passing lengths of aluminium strip through a shaping machine. The lengths are joined to special outlet, angle and stop-end fittings to make up the gutter run. Matching downpipes are available to complete the system.

Check gutters and downpipes regularly – preferably during heavy rain – to see that they are working properly.

Gullies

At ground level, downpipes discharge into an underground fitting called a gully. If rainwater and waste water flow into the same drains, the gully contains a U-bend which prevents drain smells from rising up the downpipes. The bend also acts as a trap for debris washed down from the roof slope, preventing it from being washed into the drains.

• In old houses, the gullies will be made of earthenware (called vitrified clay), also used for the underground drains (below).

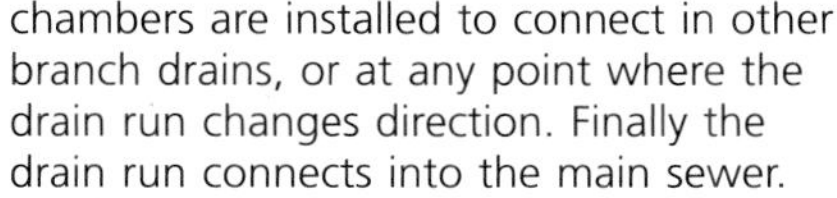

Modern houses have plastic (PVCu) gullies and drains.

• If the house has separate rainwater and waste water drains, a trap is not needed and the downpipes can be connected directly to the underground rainwater drain by an underground elbow fitting. The gully may be a single round or square pot, with the downpipe shoe discharging over it through a grating that can be removed for cleaning if the trap becomes blocked.

• If the gully also drains water from a garden, it may have two inlets – one for the downpipe and another to take surface water. This type is a back-inlet gully.

• In modern plastic installations, the downpipe does not discharge over a grating, but passes through it, straight into the gully. A removable grating allows access to the trap for cleaning.

• If the house has separate rainwater drains, the downpipe is connected to the drains via an underground elbow, with a ground-level access point nearby to allow blockages to be cleared if they occur.

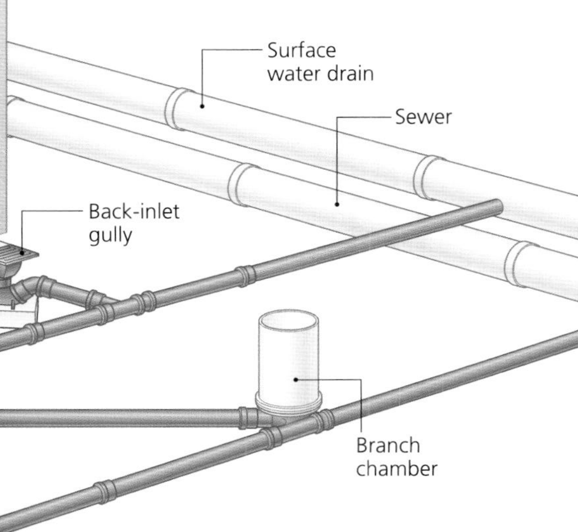

Underground drains

Drains are a mysterious underworld to most homeowners, and are noticed only if they get blocked. Knowing where they run and how they work makes dealing with this occasional occurrence much less traumatic.

Soil stacks Homes built since about the 1950s have one or more PVCu soil stacks to gather all the household waste water and carry it into the drains. All appliances – including WCs – are connected directly into the stack, which is often sited inside the house to do away with all the unsightly external plumbing of the old two-pipe system.

Inspection chamber Each stack discharges into a traditional rectangular brick chamber or a plastic moulded chamber fitted with a round metal cover. With either type, extra chambers are installed to connect in other branch drains, or at any point where the drain run changes direction. Finally the drain run connects into the main sewer.

Soakaways In many modern homes, rainwater is collected separately from waste water, and is taken by buried pipes to a main surface water drain or into a sunken chamber called a soakaway. They are usually buried in both front and rear gardens, and allow the collected rainwater to soak away into the subsoil.

If you build an extension, you may be required to have a soakaway to take the rainwater, even if your existing gutters go to the main drains.

Cesspools and septic tanks

In areas where there is no mains drainage system, household waste water can be led into an underground cesspool – a large holding tank that has to be emptied regularly for disposal elsewhere.

A septic tank is a tiny sewage treatment plant, breaking down the material piped into it by a combination of filtration and bacterial action. The effluent is safe enough to be discharged into the subsoil, and residual solid material has to be cleaned out of the tank from time to time.

THE TROUBLE WITH GUTTERS AND DRAINS

By far the most common problem with both rainwater and drainage systems is a blockage, leading to an overflow from the affected part of the system. This may be caused by leaves and wind-blown debris in gutters and hopper heads, or by unsuitable materials being flushed into the drainage system.

Leaks are another problem, easily solved in rainwater systems but more difficult to tackle in underground drains.

Old cast-iron gutters often suffer from serious (and sometimes terminal) rust.

What to do

Clearing blockages, fixing leaks and dealing with other rainwater system problems is generally a simple matter of routine maintenance (see pages 400–5) You can tackle most drain blockages yourself with the aid of a set of drain rods, which you can buy or hire when required (see pages 406–7).

OLDER HOMES

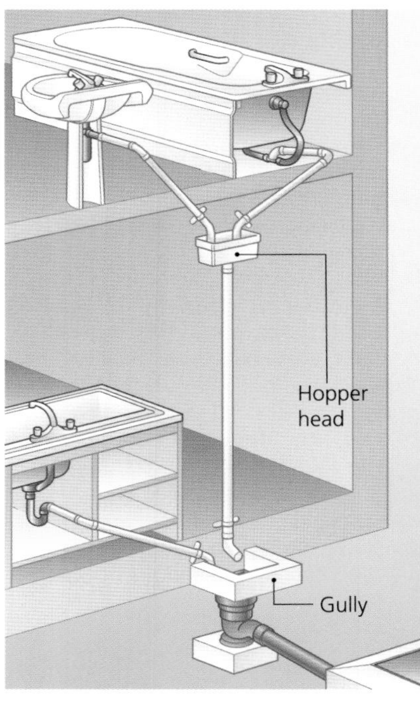

In houses built before about 1950, a two-pipe system carried waste water from the house (and often rainwater from the roof as well) to the underground drains. One large-diameter pipe called the soil pipe took waste from WCs directly into the drains by an underground elbow; a trap to keep drain smells out was not needed because the WC pan contained one, but the pipe was extended to eaves level to ventilate the drain section.

Waste water discharged directly into a trapped gully from appliances such as a sink at ground-floor level, or into a wall-mounted hopper head from basins and other appliances in upstairs rooms.

A downpipe linked the hopper head to the gully below, which was connected to a separate section of the drains. All these pipes were mounted on the walls of the house, and looked extremely unsightly.

The underground section of the soil pipe and the drain run from each gully met at an underground brick chamber called an inspection chamber, fitted with a cast-iron cover. Inside the chamber, the branch pipes run into an open channel, allowing each section of the drains to be cleared via the chamber using drain rods if it became blocked. The outlet from the chamber ran on as a single underground drain, via further chambers installed to connect in other branch drains or where the drain run changed direction. The last chamber before the main sewer was built as an interceptor chamber, and contained a trap to prevent sewer gases from entering the drainage system of individual houses. This type of chamber was prone to frequent blockages, and has not been used for many years.

Fireplaces, flues and chimneys

Central heating has made the fireplace almost redundant in modern homes, although consumer demand means that one is still often provided in the main living room.

In older homes there was a fireplace in every room, and the construction of the flues that were needed to discharge the smoke was the most complex part of the whole house structure.

In terraced houses, the flues were built into the party walls between the properties. In larger houses, there would often be two or more chimney stacks, each containing two or four flues and serving downstairs and upstairs fireplaces, plus a separate chimney for the coal-fired boiler that heated the house's hot water supply.

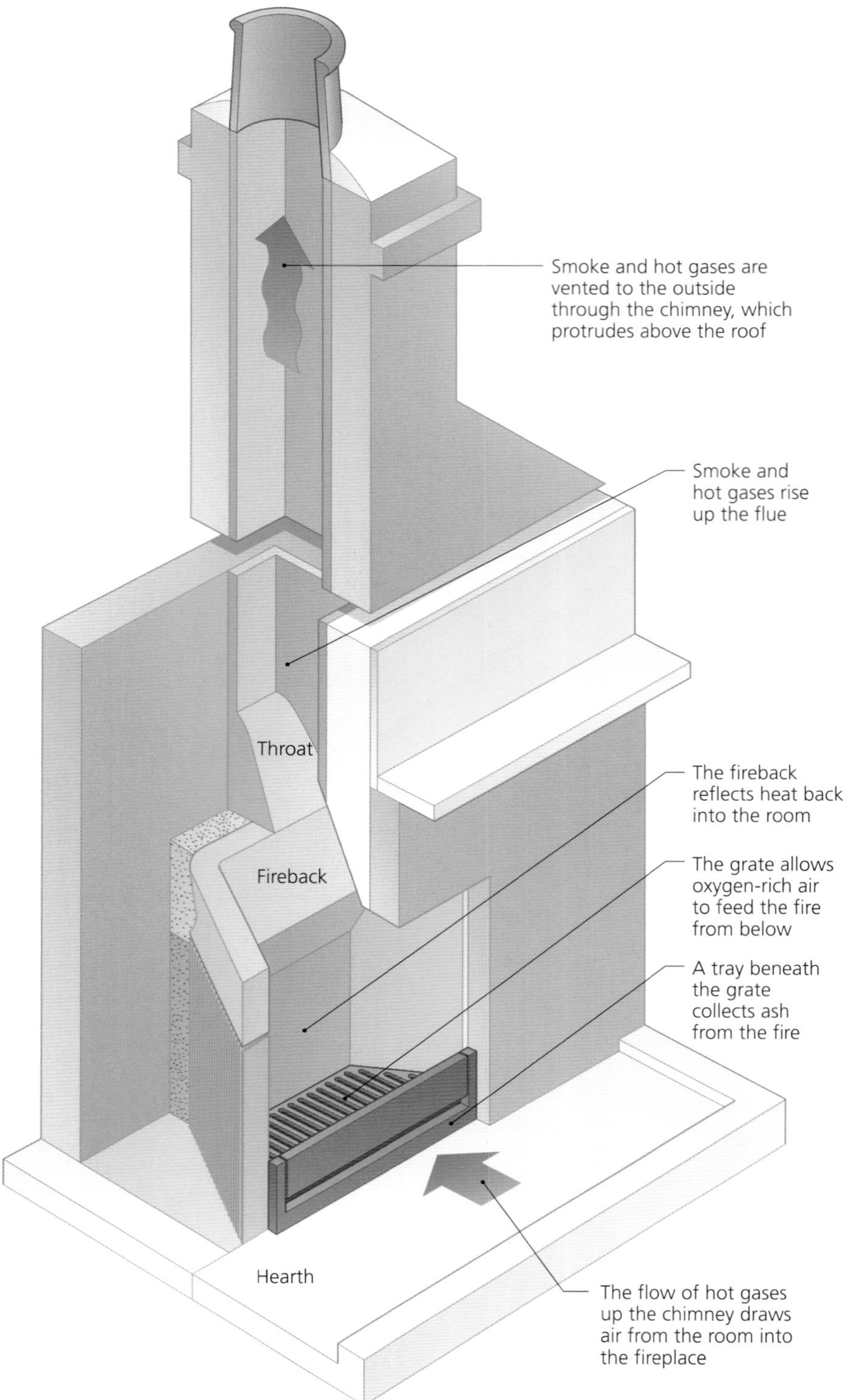

Fireplaces

The simplest type of fireplace, found in old and unmodernised homes, is just a brick opening at the base of the flue. A free-standing grate is set on a concrete hearth, and the fire is built within the grate. As it burns, the hot gases it creates rise into the flue and draw fresh air in from the room through the base of the grate to keep the fire burning.

This arrangement is very wasteful of heat, and often suffers from smoke blowing back into the room. Birds also have a habit of falling down the open flue.

Firebacks

Most fireplaces have a shaped fireback built into the basic brick recess. This is a shaped fireclay unit, available in several pieces that are bonded together with fire cement at assembly. The fireback helps to retain the heat of the fire, reflecting it back into the room. The void between the fireback and the brick recess is usually filled with a mixture of sand, lime and broken brick (or simply builder's rubble) in older homes, or with lightweight insulating concrete in newer ones.

Flues

The fireplace is linked to the open flue above it with a sloping connector called a throat. This was formed from mortar in older homes, but in modern chimneys a pre-cast concrete throat unit is built in as the chimney is constructed. The joints between the fireback and the throat are sealed with fireproof rope. This also seals the joint between the fireback and a decorative fire surround fitted round the fireplace opening.

The concrete hearth is often topped with a decorative 'superimposed' hearth of ceramic or quarry tiles or stone slabs.

Chimney construction

Modern chimneys are lined with special interlocking clay flue blocks, which allow for a smooth upward flow of smoke and prevent soot and tar from collecting. Such deposits are in any case less of a problem today, thanks to the widespread use of processed fuels rather than raw coal.

The chimney stack projects above the roof line so that down-draughts do not affect the upwards draw of the flue. Each flue within the chimney is topped by a chimney pot, which is set on a mortar bed and secured by a shaped cap of mortar called flaunching round its base. If the flue has become disused, the pots may have been removed and replaced by a cowl or a cover slab. The latter is likely to be found where the fireplaces have themselves been decommissioned and blocked up.

The traditional chimney is a hollow brick column with an open hearth or fireplace at the bottom and a chimney pot at the top. Generally speaking, the higher the chimney is, the more efficient it is at drawing smoke and fumes up and away. The chimney may be free-standing (especially in a timber-framed house), but is usually built into an external or internal wall for support. On an external wall, the flue may be built on the inside of the wall or on the outside.

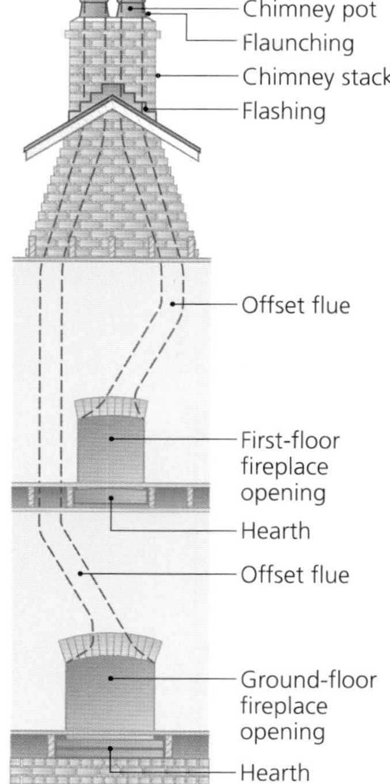

An inside flue creates a projecting chimney breast flanked by two alcoves within the room, whereas an outside flue leaves the fireplace opening flush with the wall surface. The chimney is straight if it has a single flue. If it contains multiple flues, each is offset so that the downstairs flue by-passes the upstairs fireplace.

Old flues were unlined, or were rendered internally with mortar, which cracked and failed as time went by. Condensation within the flue could eventually carry tar and soot stains through the unprotected masonry to ruin room decorations. Soot would accumulate within the flue, often leading to messy soot falls and eventually to chimney fires.

THE TROUBLE WITH CHIMNEYS

Indoors, the main problem with chimneys, especially disused ones, is tar and soot staining being carried through to the inner face of the flue by condensation occurring within it. Externally, the exposed part of the chimney stack can suffer from failed pointing and flaunching, loose chimney pots, damage to the brickwork and to the flashings that weatherproof the junction between the stack and the roof slope.

What to do

Make sure that disused flues are properly capped off and have adequate ventilation at top and bottom. Inspect the chimney stack regularly so that faults can be spotted and rectified before they become serious. Unless you are experienced in working at heights, it is best to leave chimney stack repairs to a professional builder.

Insulation and ventilation

Your house would be cold in winter without insulation, and unhealthy without ventilation. These unseen but vital aspects of your home need to be understood and maintained.

Roof insulation

Roofs in new homes will be insulated to current Building Regulations standards. A house with a pitched roof and a loft used for storage will have insulation between (and possibly over) the ceiling joists, to a thickness of about 270mm. If the loft has been converted for use as habitable rooms, the underside of the roof slope and the walls forming the loft room(s) will be insulated to a similar standard. Flat roofs will incorporate insulation, probably as a warm roof structure.

If you have a pitched roof with less insulation than the current standards require, you can lay extra insulation over what is there already, or insulate the roof slope if the roof space is to be used as a loft conversion (see pages 243–5). Use sleeved blanket insulation for convenience and ease of handling. If you have a flat roof with inadequate insulation, consider converting it to a warm roof structure by adding insulation above the existing roof covering (see page 21).

Wall insulation

Modern homes incorporate insulation within their cavity walls to meet Building Regulations requirements. Timber-framed houses have insulation within their load-bearing wall panels. Older houses with unfilled cavity walls can be insulated by pumping insulation material into the cavity through holes drilled in the outer leaf of the wall. This is a job that must be carried out by an approved installer, and requires Building Regulations approval to ensure that the walls are in suitable condition, and that the installation fills the cavity entirely.

Houses with solid walls have poor insulation performance, and improving this is a major undertaking. It can be done by insulating and dry-lining the external wall surfaces indoors – a highly disruptive job, but one which can be carried out on a DIY basis (see page 232).

External insulation is a less disruptive but more expensive option which will materially alter the appearance of the house, and which may need planning consent.

It involves fixing insulation material to the wall surfaces and waterproofing it with timber or tile cladding, or with a layer of rendering applied over expanded metal mesh. It is a job for a specialist contractor.

Floor insulation

Houses with solid ground floors built since the early 1990s have to include a layer of insulation to meet Building Regulations requirements. Older houses have no such insulation, so ground floor slabs can feel very cold. Adding insulation involves laying rigid polystyrene boards over the existing floor surface and adding a new floating floor of chipboard – a process that raises the existing floor level by at least 70mm.

Suspended timber ground floors are easier to insulate, because insulation can be placed between the floor joists. However, the job will involve lifting and re-laying floorboards unless there is an accessible crawl space or cellar below the floor. Adding 100mm thick rigid insulation will improve the floor's insulation significantly.

Window and door insulation

Recently-built and modernised houses will be fitted with double-glazed windows, and efficiently draughtproofed door and window frames. In older houses, replacing existing single-glazed windows with double-glazed ones will significantly improve their insulation performance (see page 211). Replacing the glass in existing windows with double-glazed sealed units may be possible depending on the design of the frames, but may be as expensive as replacing the windows. Installing secondary glazing inside the existing windows (see pages 212–13) will be cheaper but is not as effective and tends to look intrusive.

If existing doors and windows are not draughtproofed, installing the relevant products is a simple job to tackle on a DIY basis (see pages 216–17).

Ventilation

Appropriate ventilation is essential in four main areas of the home.

- Lofts must be ventilated to prevent condensation within the roof space – achieved by eaves ventilation in new houses. In older houses, ensure that the eaves are not blocked by loft insulation.
- Voids beneath suspended timber ground floors need ventilation to prevent rot from attacking the floor timbers. This is provided by airbricks in the house walls; ensure that these are not obstructed or blocked.
- Kitchens and bathrooms need ventilation to disperse cooking odours and steam. This ventilation can be provided by openable windows, but it is useful to supplement this with extractor fans. These are essential in internal rooms with no windows.
- Efficient ventilation is a matter of life and death in rooms containing fuel-burning appliances such as boilers and gas fires. Installers of new equipment (who must be Gas Safe registered) will ensure that appropriate levels of ventilation are provided, and you can call in a gas safety inspector to check an existing installation.

How energy-efficient is your home?

A house that uses energy inefficiently, by allowing heat to escape through a poorly insulated loft, for example, will be expensive to run. All homes for sale in the UK must have an Energy Performance Certificate (EPC) which includes an energy efficiency rating. There are several steps you can take to ensure your house has the best possible rating.

A thermal image shows where this house is efficiently insulated (the roof) and where it is not (the windows).

The first step is to assess your home's energy efficiency and identify its weak points. Start by considering the age and construction of your home. A new home with cavity walls, floor insulation and other energy-saving measures that has been constructed to the latest Building Regulations requirements will be more energy-efficient than a Victorian property with draughty wooden floorboards and solid brick walls.

You cannot change the fabric of your home, but once you understand what you have you can work within those limits to make improvements where you can and reduce the amount of energy you use.

Windows and doors

Look closely at all the windows and doors in the house and consider replacing any with decaying frames.

If windows are double-glazed, check the size of the gap between the panes – the larger the gap, the better the insulation the window will provide. All new windows must comply with Part L (conservation of fuel and power) of the Building Regulations, so if you are planning to replace any windows (page 214) ask your supplier for advice.

Finally, make sure that all windows and doors are fitted with draught excluders to keep in as much heat as possible.

Walls

Consider how the walls of your home are constructed. Cavity walls (page 9) provide the best insulation, particularly if the cavity has been filled with insulating material. The walls may be a double skin of brick or brick on the outside and concrete blocks inside, but both methods are effective insulators.

Solid walls heat up on the inside and allow the heat to radiate from the outside, making them much less effective at keeping heat in. There are options for insulating solid walls (page 241), so check whether your walls have been adequately clad.

Roof and loft

All lofts should be well insulated (page 244), although it is also important to allow a little ventilation into the roof space to prevent condensation. Check the thickness of any loft insulation. If your loft is not currently insulated, installing a 270mm thickness of insulation (the standard required by Building Regulations in new builds) across the whole area could cut your bills by up to a third. Topping up existing insulation to at least 250-270mm deep will also help and some grants are available to contribute to the cost of the work. Your own energy provider may also have a scheme providing discounts to encourage customers to fit adequate loft insulation.

REGULATIONS

Replacing a boiler, installing new windows and inserting cavity wall insulation are all categories of work that are subject to Building Regulations control (pages 482-497). If you are uncertain whether you need approval for work you are planning, call your local council's Building Control Officer for advice.

Lights

Now that incandescent light bulbs are being phased out (see page 296), the potential for making savings by switching to energy-saving bulbs is reduced, but there are still choices to be made, especially as the market for highly-efficient and very long-lasting light-emitting diodes (LEDs) develops. Consider, too, whether you have too many multiple light fittings, which could be replaced by single fittings – and always switch off lights when not needed.

Hot water

If you have a hot-water tank, lag it, along with as many exposed hot-water pipes as you can locate. Pipes should be lagged either with a fibre bandage wrapped around them or, better still, lengths of foam that fit around the pipes. Most modern hot water cylinders have a hard coat of sprayed-on lagging – tap the cylinder to see whether it feels solid. If you have a bare metal cylinder, wrap it in a lagging jacket immediately (pages 365 and 368).

Central heating

The central heating system is one of the main energy users in the home and your boiler is the powerhouse. The most efficient type is a condensing boiler. These are expensive to fit, but over their lifetime they will pay for themselves in savings.

Look at the central heating controls, too. At the least, you should have a time controller and a room thermostat. If the thermostat is positioned opposite a fire or in another warm place it will turn off the heating before the rest of the house is warm enough and you will find yourself turning up the temperature across the whole house to compensate. Consider how you use your house, whether you are at work during the day, and whether there are elderly people or young children in the family, who may need the temperature to be a little warmer. The most efficient programmers allow you to specify different temperatures at different times of day and to adjust the on/off timing for weekends (page 371). For maximum efficiency, combine a single main room thermostat with individual thermostatic radiator valves (TRVs), to control each room separately.

ECO LIGHTING AND HEATING

Sun pipes are an ingenious and environmentally sound way to provide light and air to dark or windowless areas of the home. The system consists of a translucent dome fitted above the roof, connected by a mirror-finish aluminium tube to a diffuser on the ceiling below. All the parts you need are supplied in a kit for you to fit yourself. Versions are also available including a solar-powered extractor fan and two low-energy downlighters. Go to www.sunpipe.co.uk for details.

Alternative methods of heating include solar panels, which are a particularly efficient system for heating water. Panels using crystalline technology require only daylight to generate electricity, not direct sunlight, making them a good choice for the northern European climate. They may be installed on the roof of the house or on a convenient outbuilding. Initial setup costs are high, but you will recoup your outlay in the long term. Most solar panels need professional installation, but DIY kits are available.

Woodburning stoves can also be used to heat water, as well as providing good room heat. Again, while purchase and installation costs may be high, burning seasoned wood from a sustainable source is economic and good for the environment.

THE ENERGY PERFORMANCE CERTIFICATE

European Law now stipulates that every home sold in the EU must have an EPC, or Energy Performance Certificate. The EPC uses the government-approved Standard Assessment Procedure (SAP) to assess the energy-efficiency of a property and to gauge its environmental impact in terms of CO_2 emissions. The report considers the building itself, the presence (or absence) of insulation (including double glazing), the heating system (and the controls with which it is fitted), the hot water heating system and the types of lighting used. Energy-saving additions and home improvements, such as solar panels for heating water or generating energy, will also be taken into account. The more energy-efficient the home the higher the SAP rating, which promises potential purchasers lower fuel bills and reduced carbon emissions.

The EPC will rate a property on a 100 point scale, divided into seven categories. These range from A (most efficient) to G (least efficient) – this is the same A-G scale that is used to rate electrical appliances, such as washing machines, dishwashers and fridges. Two figures are given for energy efficiency and environmental impact – the current rating and the potential rating your home could achieve if energy-saving measures were put in place. The cost of an EPC varies from under £50 to more than £100, so it is worth shopping around – the certificate must be issued by an accredited Domestic Energy Assessor.

Where appropriate, the Energy Performance Certificate will recommend measures that can be taken to increase the property's efficiency. These are graded by cost of installation and potential annual cost savings in reduced energy use. Only major works, such as replacing an old boiler with a new, more efficient one or installing cavity wall insulation, are likely to raise your rating from one band to another, but even simple things like improving your loft insulation will make a difference to your score.

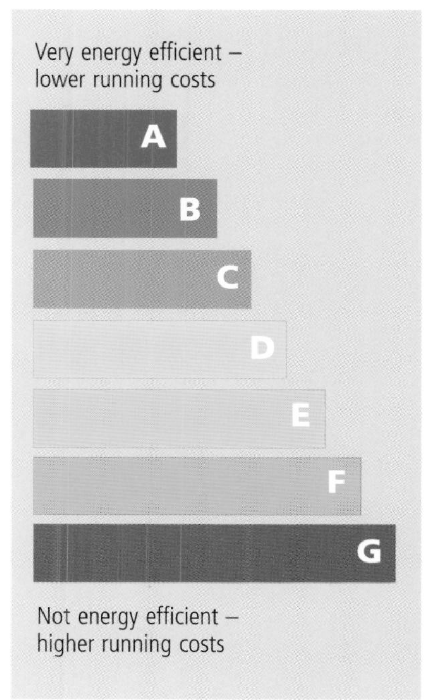

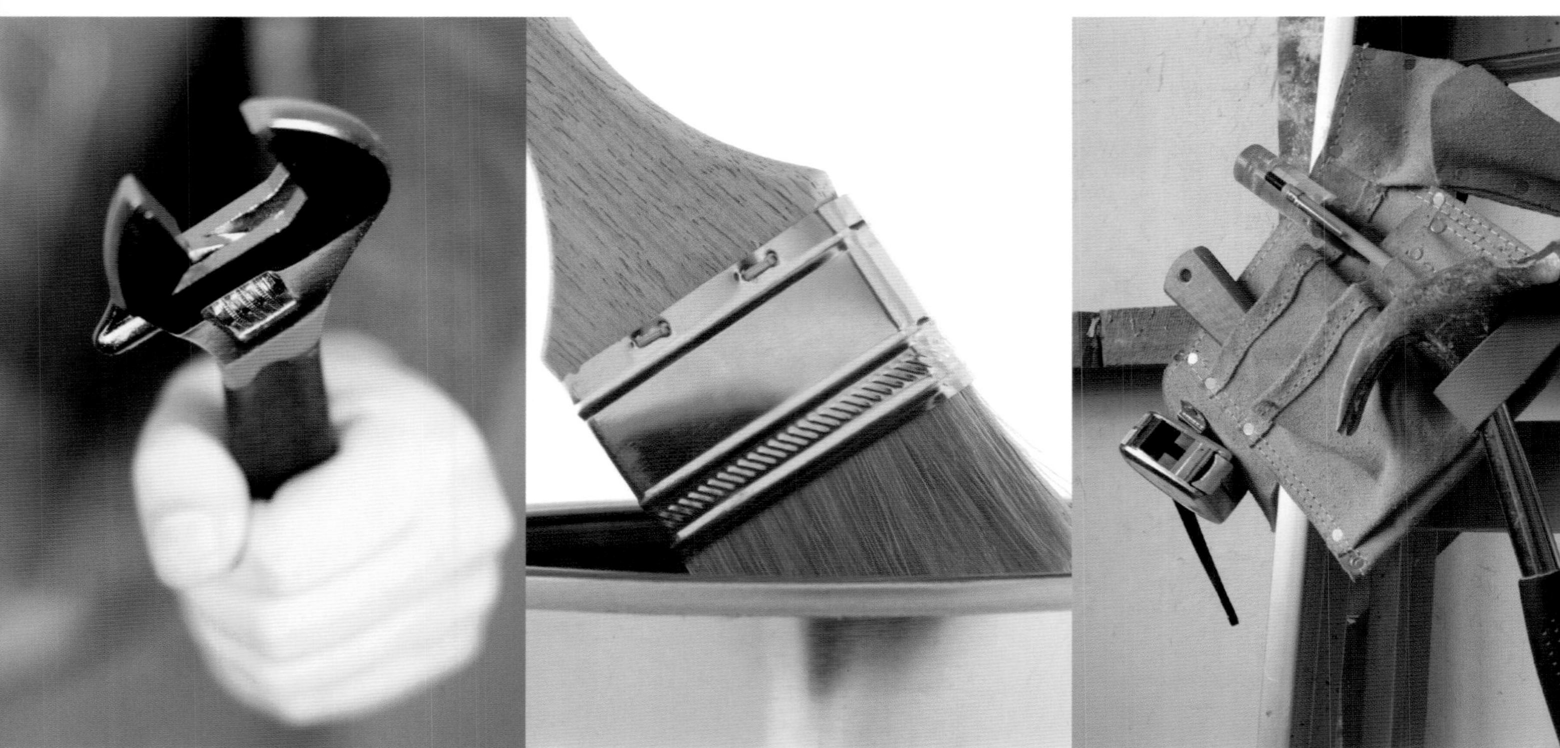

Basic skills and tools 2

The basic tool kit

This section introduces the tools you will need to tackle all the run-of-the-mill DIY jobs you are likely to face as a householder. Some are essentials that no home should be without, while others can be bought as and when you need them. You will find tools for woodwork dealt with on pages 50 to 65.

General purpose tools

The tool box

You will need a sturdy tool box in which to store your DIY hand tools. Many sizes and styles are available; to start with, pick a light but sturdy plastic case with a lift-out tray for small tools. You can always buy a second or a bigger one as your tool kit grows. Avoid metal tool boxes; they are heavy to carry around and they rust.

Pincers

Looking more like an instrument of torture than a DIY tool, pincers are extremely useful jacks of all trades. They are designed primarily for pulling out unwanted pins, tacks and nails – from floorboards, for example – but can also be put to other tasks, such as pulling out picture hooks without damaging the plaster. Pincers are usually about 200mm long, and are inexpensive to buy.

Pliers

A pair of combination pliers is another multi-purpose tool that is well worth having in your tool kit. Their serrated jaws are useful for gripping all sorts of things, such as the wire loop that holds the bath plug on its chain, the corroded piston on a faulty ball valve or the shattered remains of a light bulb stuck in its lampholder. You can use them as a makeshift spanner if none is to hand. You can twist and cut wire, and straighten bent metal. Most combination (or general-purpose pliers) sold these days have soft grip or 'comfort' handles.

Trimming knife

A trimming knife with replaceable blades is a DIY essential. A standard blade will cut paper, card and thin sheet materials such as plasterboard, and will mark clear cutting lines on all sorts of surfaces. Fitted with special blades, the knife can cut sheet flooring, plastic laminates, even wood and metal. Knives are available with fixed blades (initially covered by a slip-on blade guard, which is often

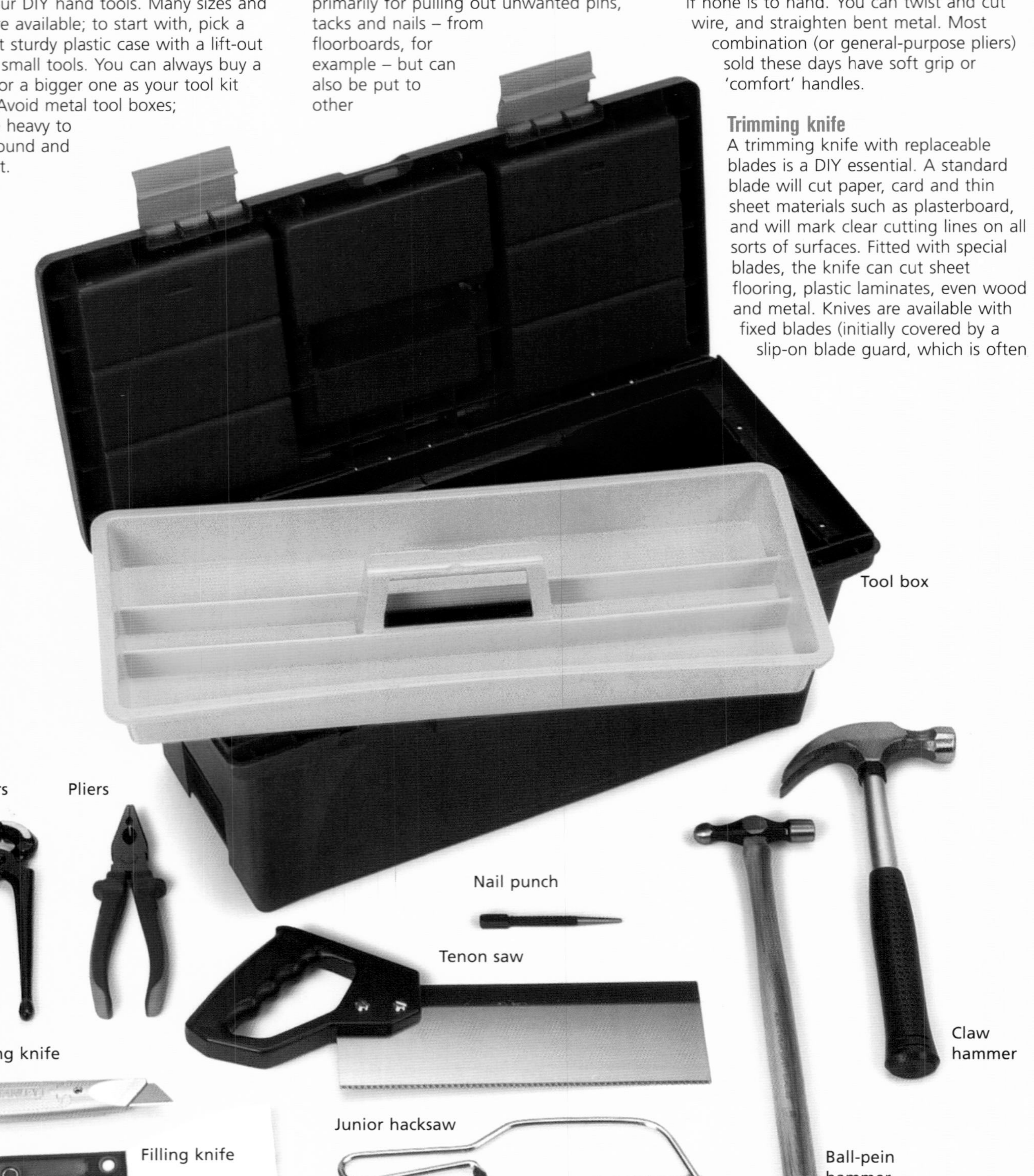

lost), or with retractable blades which are safer to use and to carry around. Most knives allow you to store spare blades (except long wood and metal-cutting ones) inside the knife handle. Make sure you have plenty of spares.

Hacksaw

Hacksaws take replaceable blades, and are designed to cut metal. You might need one to cut through a rusty nail or bolt, or an unwanted pipe. A hacksaw will also cut through plastic – a curtain rail, for example – and can even be used for cutting small pieces of wood such as timber mouldings. For all these jobs, an inexpensive junior hacksaw is ideal. It takes slim 150mm long blades, which are held in tension by the spring of the one-piece steel frame. Buy a pack of spare blades too.

Saws

If you plan to cut any wood larger than a slim moulding (which your junior hacksaw will deal with), you need a proper saw. Invest in a tenon saw, which has a rectangular blade about 250mm long stiffened along the top with a strip of brass or steel. The handle is either wood or moulded plastic. As its name implies, the tenon saw is designed primarily for cutting woodworking joints, but it will cope with all sorts of other minor woodwork jobs such as trimming wall battens or cutting a shelf to length. The thickness it will cut is limited by the depth of the blade.

Hammers

The most versatile hammer to have is a claw hammer, which will drive all but the smallest pins and can also be used to lever out old nails by fitting the grooved claw under the nail head. Choose one with a metal or glass-fibre shaft and a rubber grip, with a head weighing 16 or 20oz (hammers still come in imperial sizes).

To accompany your claw hammer, buy a nail punch (also known as a nail set). This is a small steel tool about 100mm long, with a knurled shaft and a tapered point. It is used with a hammer to drive nail heads below the wood surface, preventing the hammer head from striking and denting it.

Add a small pin hammer or ball-pein hammer to your tool kit if you drive a lot of small nails and panel pins. They will have wooden handles and lightweight heads.

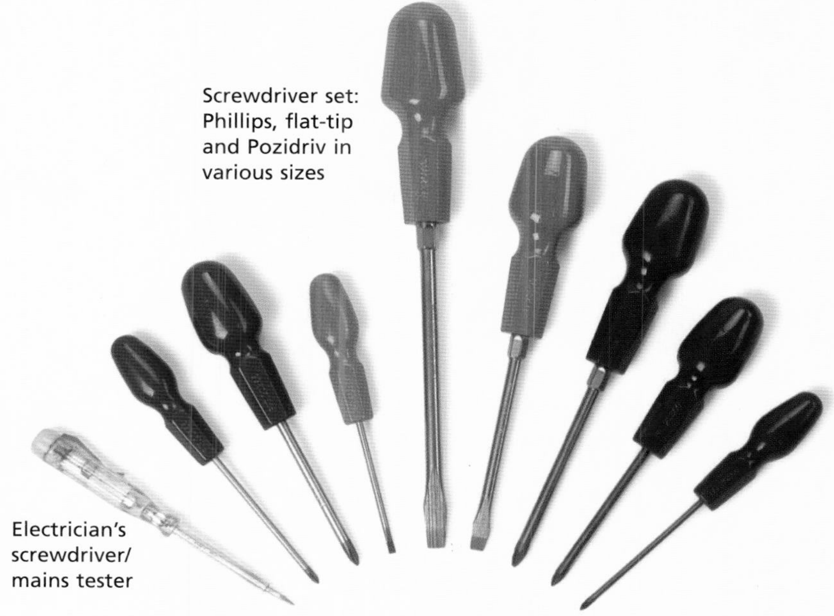

Screwdriver set: Phillips, flat-tip and Pozidriv in various sizes

Electrician's screwdriver/ mains tester

Screwdrivers

Within reason, you can never have too many screwdrivers. Screws come with head recesses of different types, ranging from straight slots to cross and hexagon shapes, and in different sizes.

To start with, you need a flat-tip screwdriver with a blade about 125mm long for slotted-head screws, such as Pozidriv and Prodrive.

You will also need a small slotted screwdriver for fiddly jobs. An electrician's screwdriver can double as a mains tester – see page 269.

If you need more screwdrivers, it is worth looking out for screwdriver sets sold in a storage case. These typically include two or three drivers for slotted-head screws, plus Phillips and Pozidriv drivers in two sizes for large and small cross-head screws of different types. The set may have a master handle, into which you slot the blade you need for the task. This type of set saves space but can be fiddly to use if you have a large or complicated project in hand.

Filling knife

This tool has a wood or plastic handle and a flexible steel blade, and is used for applying filler to holes and defects in wood or plaster. Buy a 25mm and a 50mm knife for everyday use. Do not confuse a filling knife with a stripping knife, which has a stiffer blade.

Measuring and marking

Straightedge

A long steel or aluminium straightedge is essential for many DIY jobs, from checking the flatness of surfaces (a tiled wall, for example) to guiding a trimming knife when cutting things like vinyl flooring. Buy one 1m long for maximum usefulness, with both metric and imperial markings along it.

Tape measure

You need a steel tape measure for measuring and estimating jobs. An ideal size is a 5m tape, which will cope with measuring up a room as well as taking smaller measurements. Most have metric and imperial markings, so you can use the tape as a handy conversion device. Pick one with a lock that keeps the blade extended while you use it.

Spirit level

This tool is essential if you are to get things like shelves and curtain tracks level, and for checking anything that needs to be truly vertical. It is a plastic or alloy bar with vials containing an air bubble set into the long edge and at one or both ends. The level is horizontal or vertical when the bubble is exactly centred between the marks on the appropriate vial. The most useful sizes of spirit level for DIY are 250mm and 600mm long: to check levels over longer distances, balance the tool on a timber batten.

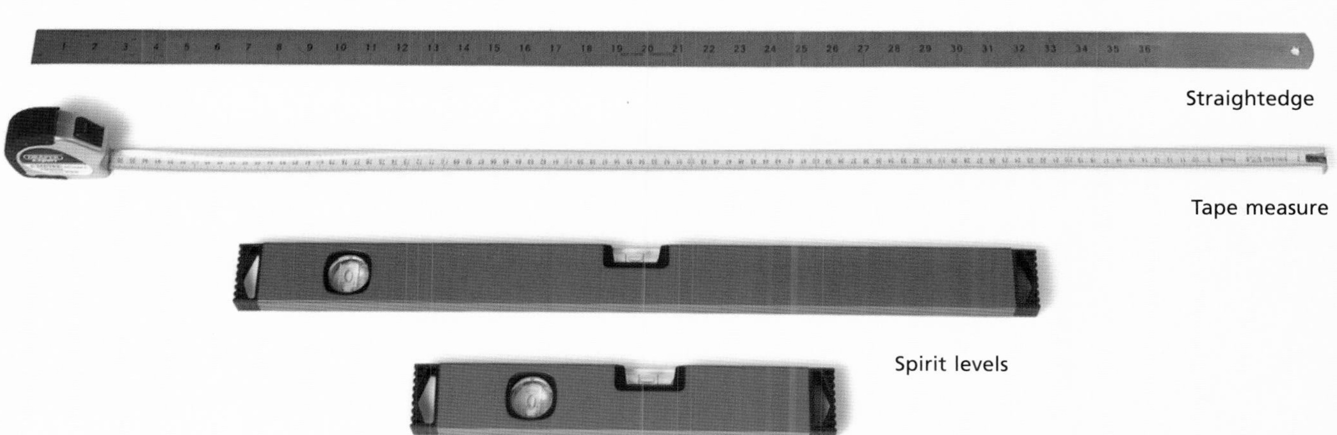

Straightedge

Tape measure

Spirit levels

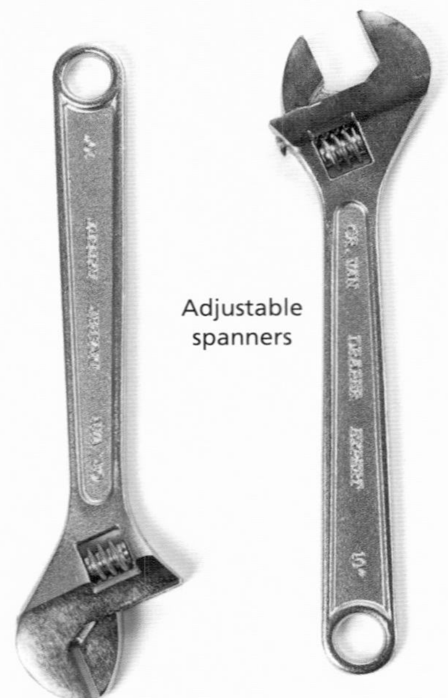

Adjustable spanners

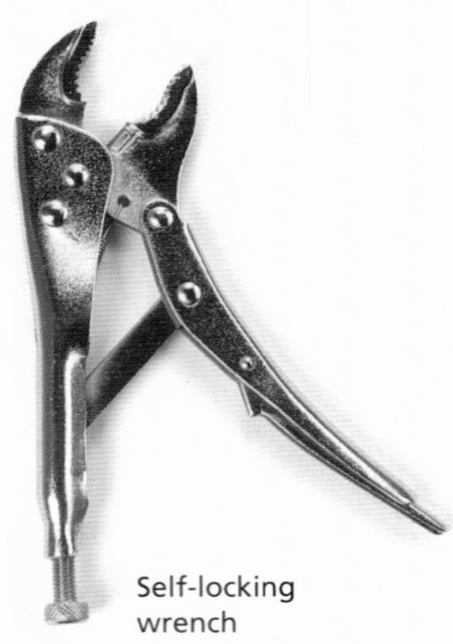

Self-locking wrench

Holding and gripping

Spanners

Spanners are better for turning nuts and bolts without damage, and you will probably have to undo something that's bolted together or tighten a leaky plumbing fitting sooner or later. What you need is an adjustable spanner with a jaw opening up to about 30mm – big enough to grip the nuts on plumbing fittings, yet capable of tackling smaller nuts too. The so-called crescent pattern with its offset head is best at getting into awkward positions.

Self-locking wrench

This versatile tool, commonly known as a Mole wrench from the name of the original maker, can be used like a pair of pliers or as a makeshift extra spanner. Its serrated jaws will grip round things and large knurled nuts, and its lockable jaws mean you can use it as a clamp when you need an extra pair of hands.

Power tools

Jigsaw

A jigsaw is one of the most useful of all power tools. Even if you do not do much woodwork, you can justify its purchase for its all-round versatility. It has a relatively short blade that protrudes from the baseplate of the saw, and this cuts on the upstroke. Because of the thinness of the blade, you can make curved cuts with it as well as straight ones, simply by driving the saw blade along a marked cutting line. You can also make cuts away from the edge of the workpiece – to fit a letterbox in a front door, for example, or make a cut-out in a worktop for an inset sink or hob.

Although the jigsaw is primarily designed for cutting wood and man-made boards, it will also cut materials such as metal, rigid plastic and ceramic tiles as long as the correct type of blade is fitted.

Features to look out for when choosing a jigsaw are adequate power (at least 500 watts), variable speed, a dust bag or vacuum cleaner attachment to help to collect dust, and a blade fitting arrangement that does not need tools. Keep a stock of standard wood-cutting blades for general work, and buy specialist blades only when you need them.

Cordless jigsaws are a little more expensive than mains-powered saws, but they work well and can be used anywhere without extension leads and trailing flexes.

Sander

Finishing new wood, keying the surface of paintwork before redecorating it, and removing surplus material such as plaster filler are all jobs that require sanding – using an abrasive paper to create a smooth surface. You can do the job by hand, but for all but the smallest areas this is one of the most tedious and time-consuming DIY jobs. A power sander does all the work in a fraction of the time, and even gathers up the dust if you buy the right type.

Power sanders come in more varieties than any other tool, ranging from tiny hand-sized finishing sanders to high-powered belt sanders. There are even sanders with interchangeable heads for sanding awkward areas. As a first choice for general smoothing work, an eccentric or random-orbit sander is probably the best. This combines the fine finish of an orbital sander with the fast stock removal of a disc sander, and can be fitted with a wide range of abrasive sheets.

Most random-orbit sanders take circular sanding discs 115 or 125mm in diameter. You attach the discs to the baseplate with touch-and-close (Velcro) fastenings. Holes in the discs line up with holes in the baseplate through which the sander's motor extracts dust, either depositing it in a small dust bag or delivering it via a hose connection to a vacuum cleaner.

Drill

You will need a power drill for all sorts of DIY jobs. The most versatile choice is a cordless drill, which has a rechargeable battery and can be used anywhere without the need for a power supply. Cordless drills are not as powerful as mains-powered models (see page 58), and can be more expensive. However, they double up as a power screwdriver thanks to their low chuck speed, and their reverse gear allows you to undo screws as well. A model with hammer action will drill holes in all but the hardest walls. Battery sizes range from 9.6V (volts) up to a massive 24V; a drill rated at 14.4 or 16.5V will be powerful enough to cope with almost every job. Choose one that is comfortable and well-balanced to hold, and is not too heavy to handle easily. Keep a spare battery, so that one can be kept fully charged while the other is in use.

Jigsaw

Random orbit sander

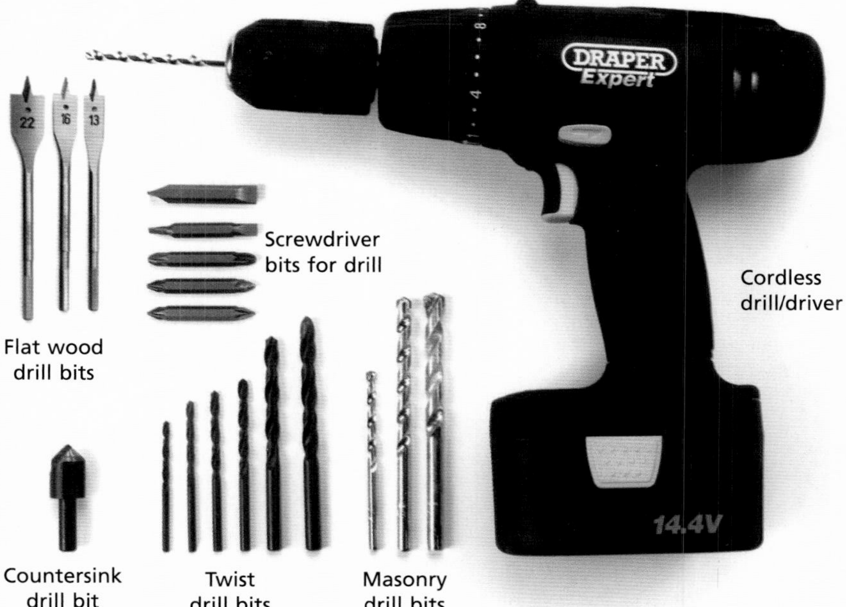

Drill bits

Your cordless drill will need a range of drill bits for the various jobs it can do.

Twist drill bits Make small holes in wood, man-made boards and metal. Buy a set of HSS (high-speed steel) drill bits containing sizes up to 10mm, stored in a metal case which will last longer than a plastic one. Carbon steel bits are cheaper than HSS ones, but become blunt more quickly.

Flat wood bits Drill larger holes in wood and boards, and come in sizes from 6mm up to 38mm. Buy them as and when you need them and store them in their packaging – usually a plastic sleeve.

Masonry drill bits Make holes in solid walls, usually to take wallplugs when making wall fixings. Do not buy a boxed set, which will contain sizes you will never use. Instead, match the sizes you buy to the wallplugs and other fixings you usually use – probably 6, 7 and 8mm. You may need longer and larger drills to make holes in walls for pipes and cables; buy them when you need them. Store them all in a tray in your tool box.

Screwdriver bits enable you to drive and remove screws using your cordless drill as a power screwdriver. One two-ended bit will probably be supplied with your drill; add a set containing bits for slotted-head, Phillips, Pozidriv and Torx screws.

Lastly, you will also need a countersink drill bit. This makes cone-shaped recesses in wood or metal to accept the heads of countersunk screws.

Work and access

Stepladders

A light but sturdy stepladder is essential for high-level work. Choose one that is versatile – some can be used in various conformations, for use in stairwells, for example – and has a grab rail and platform for resting tools or paint pots at the top. Make sure the feet have non-skid covers. Accessories such as clip-on trays, stand-offs (which keep the ladder away from the wall) and paint hooks are useful.

Workbench

The last essential for everyday DIY is a portable workbench. You can use it to support things while you cut, drill and assemble them, and its jaws will act as a large vice for gripping anything from a length of pipe to a room door. You can even stand on it at a pinch. Small basic types are surprisingly cheap; larger models cost more, but may have extra features, such as dual height settings and movable jaws.

Other useful tools

Staple gun

The DIY version of the office stapler has all sorts of uses. It will fix webbing or fabric to furniture frames, trellis to fences and low-voltage wires to skirting boards, all the time leaving one hand free to hold whatever you are fixing. You will also find it ideal for securing carpet underlay to floorboards, attaching fabric to roller blinds and even making small picture frames. The most versatile will fire staples of different sizes.

Electronic detector

One of these devices can help you avoid drilling into pipes or cables and enable you to screw directly into floor joists or wall studs. They work in three ways: metal detection (pipes and cables), density detection (studs and joists) and voltage detection (live electric cables). You will find detectors with one, two or all three of the functions. Note that metal detectors may not work with foil-backed plasterboard.

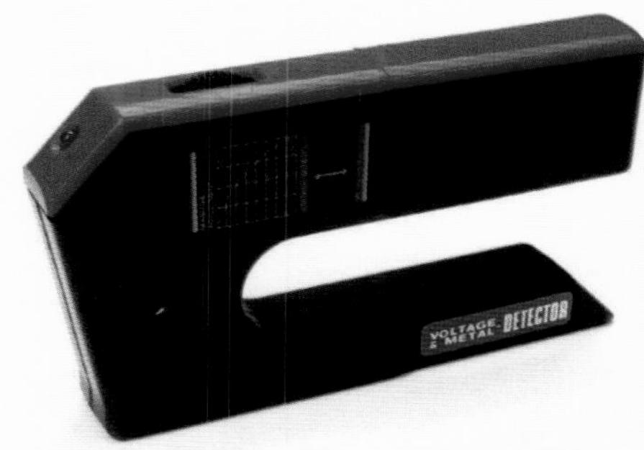

Cartridge gun

Many ready-to-use fillers, sealants and adhesives are now sold in standard-sized cartridges. To be able to use them, you need a cartridge gun. This inexpensive tool has an open metal or plastic frame which holds the cartridge, and is fitted with a simple trigger and piston mechanism which extrudes the contents of the cartridge as the trigger is squeezed. Cartridges come in two standard sizes, and you may need two gun sizes to take them.

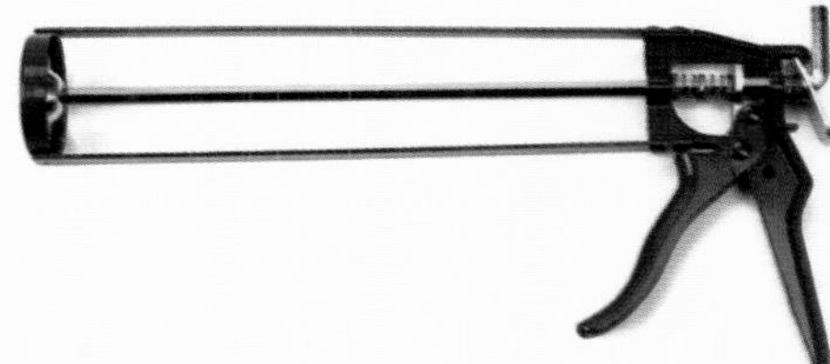

Sizing up

Many DIY jobs involve three essential but unrelated jobs: measuring the size of things, positioning them to a true horizontal or vertical, and checking that making fixings will not cause damage to cables or pipework concealed within the house structure. Here are the tools you need for these jobs, and how to use them.

Measuring up

A retractable tape measure consists of a coil of printed steel stored on a spring-loaded drum within a plastic or metal case. The spring retracts the extended tape back into the case, which usually has a simple lock to hold the tape in the extended position if required. The strip has a slight curve in cross-section to keep it stiff when in use, and measurements are printed on the concave face, usually in metric and imperial. A 5m tape is long enough to take room measurements without being unnecessarily bulky to carry in the pocket.

1 To take an internal measurement (of an alcove, for example), hold the free end against one surface and extend the tape until the side of the case is against the opposite surface. Add the width of the case to the last measurement visible on the tape where it emerges from the case. The case width is usually printed on the case, but is typically 50 or 65mm. Always read off and mark measurements with the eye vertically above the tape if it is horizontal, or level with the tape if it is vertical. If you do not do this, a visual error called parallax occurs and the mark you make will be inaccurate. Always measure and mark twice to eliminate the risk of introducing this error.

2 The end of the tape is fitted with a small metal lug. To take an external measurement (of a piece of wood, for example), hook the lug over one end of the wood and draw the tape out until you can read off and mark the measurement.

Checking horizontals and verticals

A spirit level tells you whether surfaces are truly horizontal or vertical. It consists of a metal or plastic bar with parallel edges into which one or more clear plastic vials are set. The vial in the long edge of the level indicates a true horizontal, while vials at the ends indicate a true vertical. Each vial contains an air bubble and is marked with two parallel lines. When the bubble is centred between the marks, the tool is level or vertical according to which vial is being used. Long spirit levels are more accurate than short ones; buy one spirit level at least 600mm long and ideally 1m long.

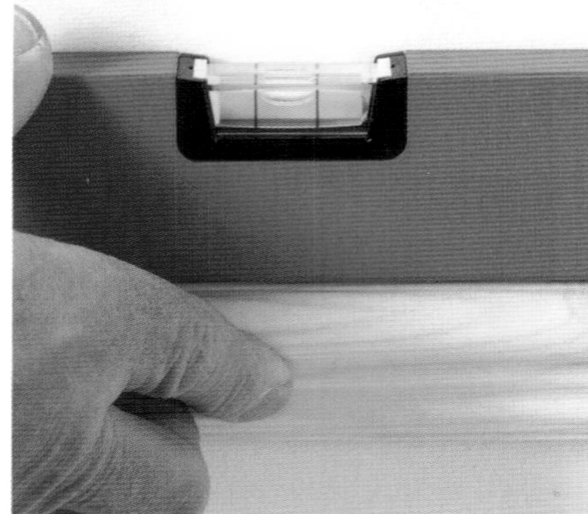

1 To check a horizontal, rest the level on the surface being checked and view the vial in the long edge from directly above or beside the level. Adjust the surface until the bubble is precisely centred between the marks on the vial.

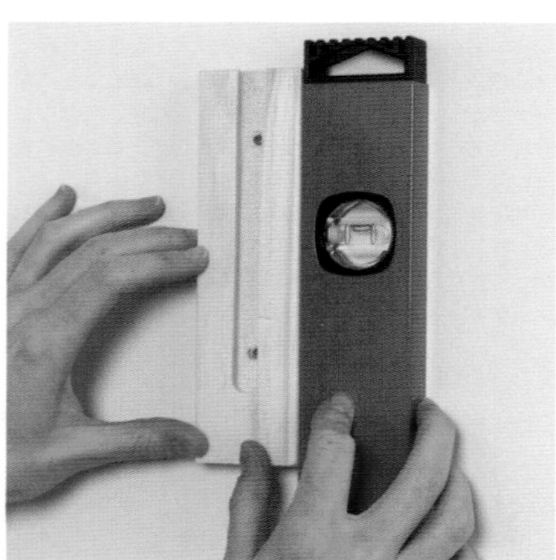

2 To check a vertical, hold the level against the surface and view the vial at the end with the eye at the same level. Adjust the position of the surface until the bubble is centred in the vial.

3 Some spirit levels have one end vial set in a movable mounting marked with an angle scale. Rotate the mounting to the required angle and use the level to set a surface to that specific angle. However, this is less accurate than other tools for this job (see page 54).

Locating concealed hazards

A pipe/cable detector is a hand-held battery-powered electronic device that will reveal the presence of electricity cables or plumbing pipework concealed in the house structure. It is important to be aware of their presence whenever you are making fixings (with nails or with screws and wallplugs) into a wall, floor or ceiling, since piercing one could cause personal injury, physical damage or both.

In some cases it is obvious where buried services are located. For example, you can expect there to be a vertical cable run immediately above a light switch, or pipework above or below a flush-mounted thermostatic shower mixer valve. In other cases, using the detector can avoid a potential accident.

If you want to find where wall studs (or floor/ceiling joists) are, use a stud detector: this finds the solid wood, which you may want to put screws into if hollow wall plugs will not support whatever you are fixing.

Switch the detector on and set its sensitivity according to the manufacturer's instructions. Pass it slowly back and forth over the area you are testing. The detector will bleep and may flash a light when it senses a hazard, enabling you to mark and avoid its route when making any fixings.

Cutting

Once you have measured how big something needs to be, your next job is to cut it to size. The tools you need for this depend on what you are cutting, and on how thick it is. Whichever tool you are using, make sure that it is sharp. A blunt tool requires more effort to use, and is more likely to slip or cut off course as a result – either injuring you or damaging the workpiece.

Using a trimming knife

A sharp trimming knife will cut all sorts of thin sheet materials, from wallpaper and soft floorcoverings to plasterboard. You can use it freehand, but you will get better results if you place a steel straightedge over the cutting line and draw the knife blade along its edge. Make sure your free hand is anchoring the straightedge securely, and that your fingertips are out of the way of the knife blade.

1 When using a trimming knife on the workbench or on the floor, always place a cutting board or a piece of scrap hardboard beneath whatever you are cutting. This will allow the knife to cut cleanly through the workpiece without scoring or damaging the surface below.

2 Hold the knife securely and draw it along the straightedge in one continuous movement. If necessary, make two or three passes rather than trying to cut the material in one go; the harder you have to press, the more risk there is that the blade will slip off line. Always cut against the side of the straightedge next to the waste material.

Using a tenon saw

A tenon saw will cut wood and man-made boards. Its cutting depth is limited to about 75mm by the presence of the stiffening along the top edge of the blade. This also limits the width of the workpiece that can be cut; in practice, it is difficult to make a cut longer than about 300mm with this tool.

Whatever you are cutting must be held securely. You can clamp it in the jaws of your workbench. However, it is easier to hold small workpieces using a simple aid called a bench hook (page 51). You can buy one, or make one from scrap wood and board. To make one, glue and screw two pieces of softwood batten to opposite faces of a rectangle of plywood measuring about 250 x 150mm.

1 To cut a piece of wood to length, mark the cutting line on it (see page 54). Hold it securely on your workbench with the thumb of your free hand next to the cutting line to guide the saw blade. Position the saw blade so it will cut just on the waste side of the cutting line, and draw it towards you at about 45° to start the cut.

2 Once the saw teeth begin to bite, start to cut the wood with light but firm strokes. Remember that it cuts on the forward stroke only. Start to flatten out the angle of the saw. Complete the cut with gentle strokes, holding the saw almost level with the wood surface, to avoid splitting the underside of the wood. Support the off-cut with your free hand if the workpiece is held in the jaws of the workbench.

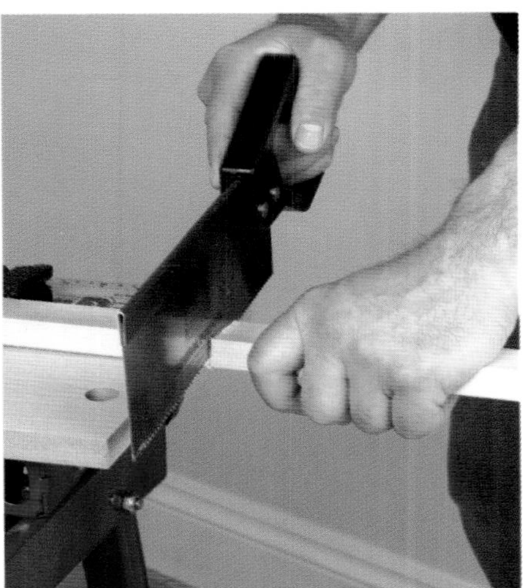

Using a hacksaw

A junior hacksaw will cut metal and rigid plastic – and wood with a small cross-section, such as timber mouldings. Make sure that the blade is fitted with the points of the teeth facing away from the handle, so it will cut on the forward stroke.

1 The hacksaw blade tends to snatch when cutting thin metal, so it is best to secure the workpiece in the jaws of your workbench. Most have grooves machined in the mating edges of the jaws for holding round objects such as copper pipe or a metal wardrobe rail.

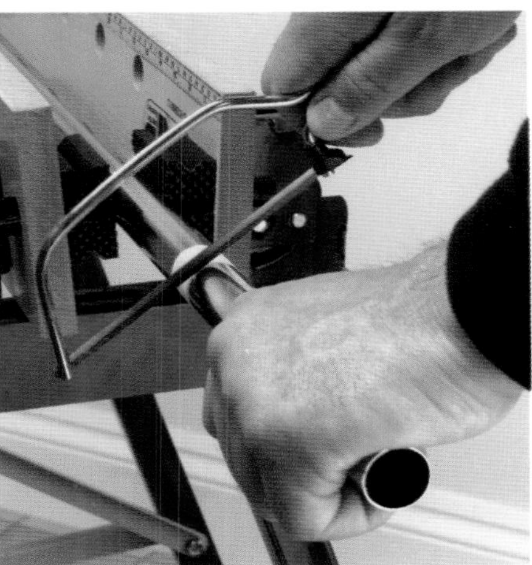

2 Start the cut on the waste side of the marked line, as for cutting wood with a tenon saw. A strip of masking tape makes a good cutting guide. Draw the blade towards you two or three times to start the cut, taking care to keep the blade on line.

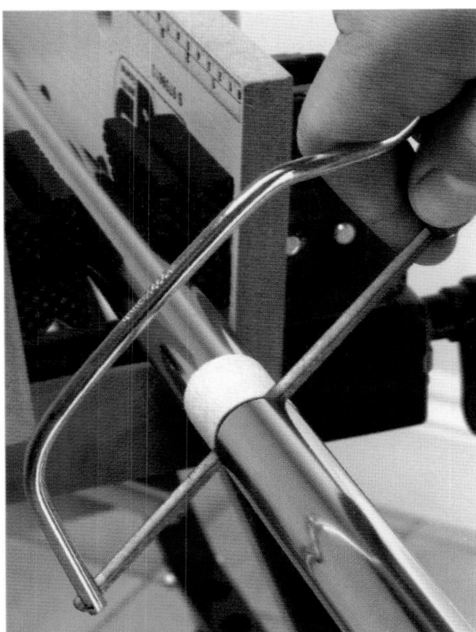

3 Saw with firm forward strokes. On metal tubing, the teeth will tend to snatch as you start the cut. Do not let the blade jump out of the cut as you proceed. Complete the cut with a few gentle strokes.

Nailing

A nail is one of the simplest fixing devices. Its point is driven through whatever you are fixing and on into the material beneath until its head is flush with the surface. Different nail types and sizes are used for different jobs, but in practice you will need only a small range to cope with everyday DIY jobs – see Choosing nails, opposite. You need a hammer to drive nails in, and a small tool called a nail punch to enable you to finish driving the nail without marking the surface with the hammer head.

Using a claw hammer

A claw hammer will drive all but the smallest nails with ease, and its claw will extract nails that are misaligned or bent while being driven in. Hold it near the end of the handle and watch the hammer head to make sure that it strikes the nail head squarely.

1 Hold the nail between your thumb and forefinger and start it with a few gentle taps of the hammer head. Check that it is at right angles to the surface.

2 Release the nail and drive it in with harder blows. For large nails, keep your wrist stiff and swing hammer and forearm from the elbow. On rough work, hammer the nail head in flush with the surface.

Using a ball-pein or pin hammer

A pin hammer or lightweight ball-pein hammer (shown here) is easier to handle when driving small panel pins, tacks, upholstery nails and glazing sprigs (used to hold glass panes in wooden window frames).

1 Hold the pin between your thumb and forefinger and tap it in with the flat end of the hammer head.

2 When it stands by itself, drive it in with the hammer head, flexing your wrist to control the hammer. Drive the pin fully home, or use a nail punch to recess its head in the wood, if necessary.

Removing a bent nail

If you bend a nail as you drive it, stop and remove it. Do not try to straighten a bent nail or drive it fully home at an angle. Pull it out and replace it with a new nail.

Place a piece of card or thin wood on the surface beside the nail. Hook the hammer claw under the nail head and pull the handle towards you to draw out the nail. Keep the handle vertical so you do not widen the opening of the nail hole.

Using a staple gun

A hand-operated staple gun fires metal staples, and can be used for many light fixing jobs. The staples work like two-pronged nails, relying on the crossbar between the pins to fix the material in place. The staple is ejected at high speed, so take care not to fire the gun unless its baseplate is securely pressed against the workpiece.

1 If the model accepts staples of different lengths, select the correct size for the job in hand. Load the magazine and test the gun by firing a staple into some scrap material.

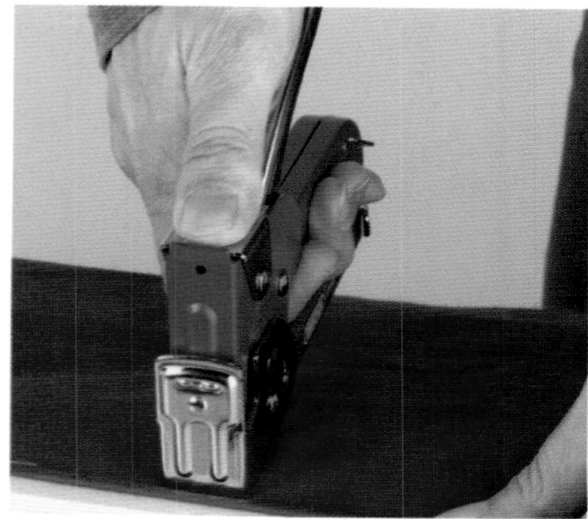

2 Position the material to be fixed. Place the staple gun over the fixing position and squeeze the trigger to fire the staple. Repeat the process to make further fixings, reloading the magazine if it runs out.

Choosing nails

The two nail types you are likely to use most frequently are oval wire nails and panel pins. For everyday fixings, keep a supply of these in a compartmentalised storage box. Buy other types of nail as and when you need them.

Oval wire nails Have an oval cross-section and a stubby head. These are the most commonly used nails. Position them with the oval parallel with the wood grain to avoid splitting the wood. Punch in the nail head and fill over it for an invisible fixing. Use these nails for securing the joints in light timber frames, and for other general woodwork jobs.
Sizes From 25 to 150mm; useful sizes to keep are 50 and 75mm.

Masonry nails Specially hardened round steel nails, used to fix wood to masonry and preferred nowadays to cut clasp nails for similar jobs. They are very hard to remove without damaging the masonry, and can shatter while being driven if not struck straight.
Sizes From 25 to 100mm.

Annular (ring-shank) nails Have a ridged shank which grips wood better than a smooth wire nail. They are used in situations where the fixing has to resist being pulled apart, and are almost impossible to remove once driven. They are particularly good for making fixings into man-made boards.
Sizes From 20 to 100mm.

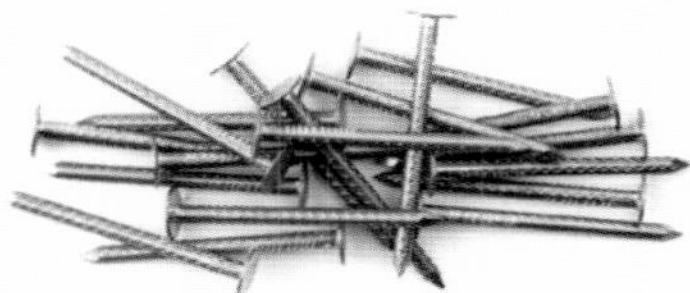

Clout nails Short galvanised nails with a wide flat head, used for fixing roof tiles and slates.
Felt nails are shorter versions, which are designed for fixing roofing felt.
Sizes 50 and 75mm for clout nails and 12 and 25mm for felt nails.

Cut nails Traditional nails cut from flat metal sheet. Cut clasp nails are still used to fix wood to masonry (skirting boards, for example), while cut floor nails – also known as floor brads – are used to fix floorboards to their joists.
Sizes Various sizes are available.

Panel pins Have a round cross-section and a small flat head. As the name implies, they are used chiefly for fixing thin sheet materials to an underlying timber framework. They are also ideal for fixing timber mouldings in place, although pilot holes for the pins may be needed in small mouldings to avoid splitting the wood. Hardboard panel pins have a diamond-shaped head that is driven in flush with the board surface, and often have a coppered finish.
Sizes From 15 to 50mm; useful sizes to keep are 20, 25 and 40mm.

Plasterboard nails Have a cone-shaped head (like a countersunk screw) and a jagged shank to grip the framing to which the board is being fixed. They have a galvanised finish.
Sizes 30 and 40mm, for fixing 9.5 and 12.7mm thick plasterboard respectively.

Round wire nails Have a round cross-section and a large flat head. They are used on rough woodwork, such as the framework for a partition wall or a garden pergola.
Sizes From 25 to 150mm.

Using masonry nails

Choose a nail long enough to penetrate solid masonry to a depth of at least 25mm. Fixing a 25mm batten to a plastered wall therefore requires a nail at least 65mm long to allow for the thickness of the plaster. On bare brickwork, drive nails into the bricks, not into the mortar courses.

1 Drill pilot holes in the wood at each fixing position to accept the nail shank. Insert the nails, hold the wood in position against the wall and check that it is horizontal or vertical as required.

2 Drive in one end nail, striking its head squarely and hammering it flush with the surface of the wood.

3 Drive in the other end nail next. This ensures that the wood is not forced out of position as intermediate nails are driven in.

Using picture hooks

Picture hooks are pinned to walls with hardened steel pins, usually about 25mm long. Traditional single-pin and twin-pin metal picture hooks are designed to hold the pin at an angle to the wall surface; plastic varieties hold a group of small headless masonry pins at right angles to the wall, and may be secured by a longer pin once they are fixed in position.

1 Hold the picture on the wall where you want to hang it. Place a small spirit level on top of the frame to check that it is level, then lightly mark the positions of its top corners on the wall.

2 Place the picture face down. Mark the centre of its top edge and fit the hook to the cord. Pull the hook towards the mark until the cord is taut. Measure the distance between the top of the hook and the top of the frame.

3 On the wall, mark the centre point between the two marks made in step 1. Measure down from it the distance taken in step 2, and mark the wall there. Pin the hook in place with its top level with this mark. Hang and level the picture.

Fixing with screws

A screw is a stronger fixing device than a nail. Its thread grips the material into which it is driven, and its head secures the item being fixed. Unlike a nail, a screw can be withdrawn easily to undo the fixing.

As with nails, different types and sizes of screws are used for different jobs, but for everyday DIY you will need only a small selection. You need a screwdriver to drive screws, and to work successfully the screwdriver tip must match the size and shape of the recess in the screw head. You can drive (and remove) screws by hand, or with a cordless screwdriver or drill.

Screwing wood to wood

Start by choosing a screw with a countersunk head that is long enough to pass through the piece you are fixing, and halfway through the piece you are fixing it to. The screw head will be flush with the surface once the screw has been driven in. Screws are now mainly sold in metric sizes and the most useful sizes are 4mm (old No 8 gauge) up to 50mm long and 5mm (old No 10 gauge) up to 75mm long. Keep a stock of these two sizes in different length and buy other sizes only when needed.

1 Mark where you want the screw hole in the piece of wood you are fixing. Fit a twist drill bit the same size as the screw shank in your drill, and drill a clearance hole right through the wood. Place scrap wood beneath the workpiece so you do not drill into your workbench. See page 42 for more information about using a drill.

2 Exchange the twist drill bit for a countersink bit and drill the cone-shaped recess for the screw head in the mouth of the clearance hole. It should be only as wide as the screw head.

3 Hold the piece of wood you are fixing in position over the piece you are fixing it to. Push a nail (or a bradawl if you have one) through the clearance hole you drilled in step 1 to mark the screw position on the piece below. Drill a pilot hole 2mm in diameter at the mark, to half the depth of the wood.

4 Reposition the two pieces of wood and insert the screw through the clearance hole in the top piece so it enters the pilot hole in the piece beneath. Tighten it fully with your screwdriver until the screw head is fully recessed in the countersunk hole.

Screwing metal to wood

Most metal fixtures – such as door handles, window catches, coat hooks and shelf supports – have countersunk holes for their fixing screws.

You can use a countersunk screw to attach them, but screws with raised countersunk heads look more attractive. They are available in brass, chrome and stainless steel, and matching screws are often supplied with the fixture.

If you have to supply your own, make sure the screw shank will pass through the clearance holes in the fixture. The screws should be long enough to pass halfway through the wood you are fixing into.

Door hinges are an exception; they are always fixed with countersunk screws.

Some metal fixtures – particularly those used out of doors, such as gate hinges – do not have countersinks, and are fixed with round-head screws. The hemispherical screw heads sit proud of the surface.

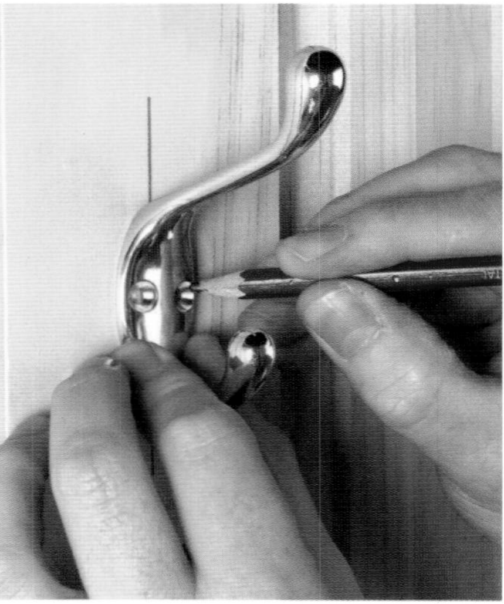

1 Decide where you are going to position the fixture. Hold the fixture in position and mark each screw position on the wood in pencil through the clearance holes.

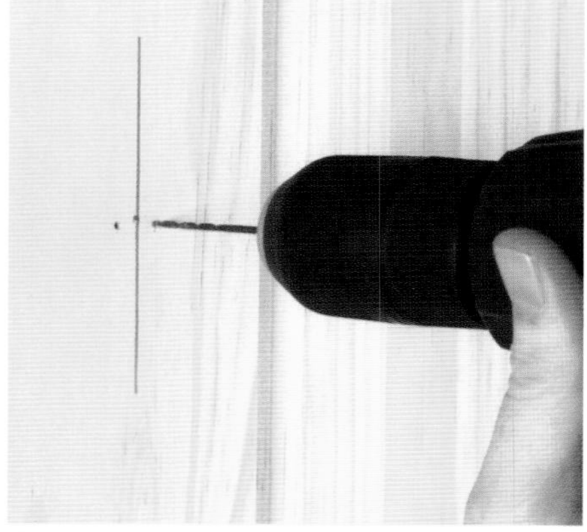

2 Drill a pilot hole at each mark, to half the thickness of the wood. If you find it difficult to gauge the depth, use a guide on the drill bit – a strip of masking tape, for example. Stop when the guide touches the wood. the wood. Use a 2mm drill bit for the pilot hole with 4mm screws and a 2.5mm bit for 5mm screws.

3 Replace the fixture over the holes and drive in the screws. If there is more than one, only tighten them fully when you are sure the fixture is straight and level.

Screwing into metal or plastic

You may want to make a fixing into a metal or plastic surface – for example, to mount a roller blind to a uPVC window. You need a special self-tapping screw for this sort of job. The screw needs a pilot hole, and cuts its own thread as it is driven in. Self-tapping screws are made from hardened steel, and come with countersunk, raised countersunk and pan heads (the last resembles a roundhead screw, but with the head flattened).

Screwing into walls and ceilings

You cannot simply drive a screw into most walls or ceilings to make a fixing. There are two exceptions: if you have a timber-framed partition wall and the fixing position coincides with one of the vertical frame members, or if you are making a ceiling fixing directly into a joist. Otherwise you have to drill a hole and insert a special fixing device to hold the screw in place. See pages 44–45 for more details.

Using a power screwdriver

Driving screws with a power screwdriver is much quicker and easier than driving them by hand, especially when using cross-head screws. You can use a cordless drill on a slow speed setting, or buy a cordless screwdriver instead. Both tools use interchangeable screwdriver bits, which are available to fit all common screw heads. It is actually cheaper to buy a set of these bits and a cordless tool than it is to buy individual screwdrivers. You can use a power driver with slotted-head screws, but there is a greater risk of the bit slipping out of the slot and damaging the workpiece than with hand screwdriving.

1 Select the screwdriver bit to match the screw size and recess type. Fit it in the drill chuck, or use the magnetic bit holder supplied with the bits.

2 If you are using a cordless drill, set it to the drill symbol and choose an intermediate torque setting (for example, 3 on a scale of 1 to 5).

3 Fit the screw onto the tip of the screwdriver bit and offer it up to its pre-drilled hole.

4 Start the drill or screwdriver and drive in the screw. With a cordless drill, the torque setting selected should allow the clutch to slip when the screw is tight. If this does not happen, select a different torque setting until it does.

5 Set the screwdriver or drill to reverse to undo a screw.

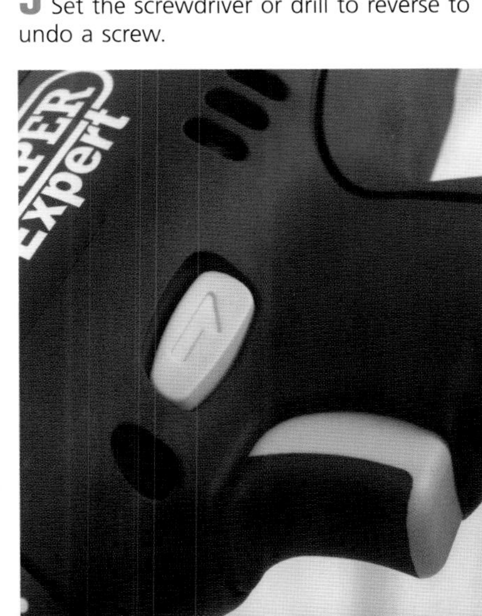

Choosing screws

Most of the fixings you make will require countersunk screws. Traditionally, all screws had slotted heads and were driven with a flat-tip screwdriver. Today, screws are designed for driving with a power screwdriver, and their heads have a specially shaped recess to engage the screwdriver tip more positively than a flat-tip driver does in a slot. The most common recesses are cross-shaped.

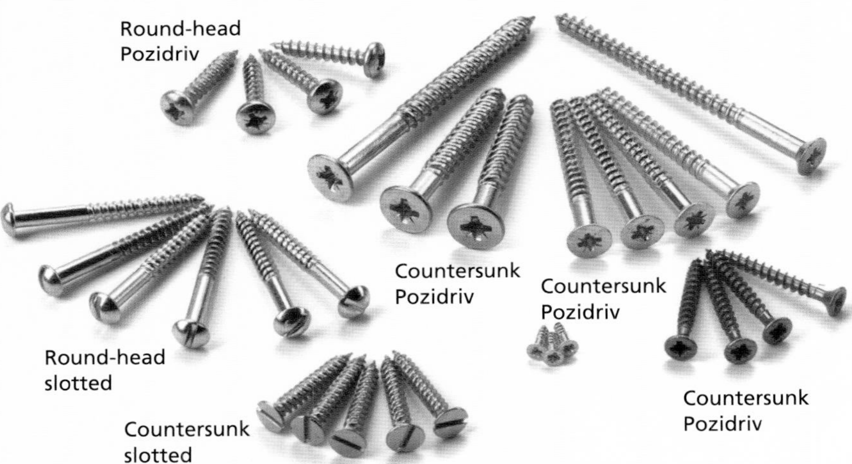

Phillips These screws have a simple cross, and are found mainly in flat-pack furniture kits and on domestic appliances.

Pozidriv and Prodrive A star-shaped recess grips the screwdriver tip more securely than a slotted head. Drivers for Pozidriv and Prodrive screws are interchangeable. In each case the No 2. size will drive screws up to 5mm diameter.

Woodscrews Traditional woodscrews are threaded only for part of their length. Many modern countersunk screws have continuously-threaded shanks and other features such as twin threads that are designed to make them quicker and easier to drive.

For everyday use, store a small selection of Pozidriv or Prodrive countersunk woodscrews in individual containers. The most useful sizes are: 19, 25, 38 and 50mm for 4mm diameter; 50 and 75mm for 5mm diameter.

Other screw head types Raised countersunk and round-head woodscrews usually have slotted heads. Other head types you may encounter – especially in flat-pack furniture kits and on domestic appliances – include: internal-hex screws with a plain hexagonal recess, driven with an Allen key; Torx screws and Uni-screws with specially shaped hexagonal recesses; Robertson screws with a square recess. Each type requires a special screwdriver bit.

Undoing fixings

Many DIY jobs involve undoing an existing fixing. How you go about this depends on analysing how the fixing was originally made. It also depends on whether you need to do the job with care, or whether you can take a 'wrecking' approach. Here are some of the options.

Removing old screws

In most cases, there are three things that make old screws hard to remove.

- Their heads are often over-painted, making it difficult to engage a screwdriver tip positively.
- Plain steel screws tend to corrode with time, so their screw threads grip the wood tightly and are very difficult to free.
- The screw head may have been damaged as the screw was driven in, with the result that the screwdriver tip slips out of the slot or recess as you try to undo the screw.

1 Use a pointed tool such as a bradawl or a small screwdriver to scrape paint out of the slot or recess in the screw head, so that the screwdriver tip fits it properly. Then try to undo the screw.

2 Before attempting to undo a rusty screw, place the screwdriver in the slot or recess and strike the end of the handle firmly two or three times with a hammer. This often breaks the grip of the threads in the wood and makes it easier to undo the screw. With slotted-head screws, try angling the screwdriver blade in the slot before you strike its handle. This will turn the screw slightly and should have the same effect.

3 If the screw head is damaged and the screwdriver tip will not allow any torque to be applied to it, you will have to drill it out. Fit a twist drill bit about half the diameter of the screw head in your drill. Hold it against the centre of the screw head and drill slowly into it. When you reach the screw shank, the drilled-off head will spin off on the drill shank. Continue drilling until you have completely drilled out the screw shank, and separate the components it was securing.

Alternatively You can use a screw extractor – a left-hand cutter or a threaded bolt that fits the chuck of a cordless drill. It is screwed into a pilot hole drilled in the screw head, and is then reverse-driven to draw out the damaged screw.

Removing old nails

Because nails are driven flush with the surface, removing them without damaging what they are fixing is almost impossible.

1 The best approach is to try to prise away whatever the nail is securing – for example, by levering up a floorboard or pulling a skirting board away from the wall. One of two things will happen.

2 The nail head may be lifted slightly, allowing you to grip it with a claw hammer or pincers and pull it out.

3 Often the nail will not move but will tear through the material it is fixing, allowing you to remove this and then tackle the exposed nail as before. Use this approach to remove old carpet that has been tacked down, to tear hardboard off an old panelled door or to pull plasterboard away from partition walls and ceiling joists.

4 You can try another approach if it is not essential to remove the nail. Use a nail punch and hammer to drive the nail head through the material it is fixing so you can free it. This is the best way of lifting old floorboards that are to be saved and re-laid, as it minimises damage to the boards.

5 If large nails have been used to assemble a framework – in a partition wall that is being demolished, for example – it may be possible to free the fixings by knocking the individual joints apart. The nails are often driven in at an angle in structures of this sort, and a few carefully aimed blows with a club hammer will open up joints and make them easy to separate.

Gripping and tightening

Around the house you will have to tackle a variety of small jobs where you need to get a grip on something.

You might need to tighten up a plumbing fitting that has started to weep a little water, or to dismantle a tap to change a tap washer. If you have taken down something fixed to a wall, you may want to remove the old wallplugs and fill the holes before fixing it somewhere else. Your tool kit should contain an assortment of gripping tools to help you to improvise solutions to problems like these.

Adjustable spanners

Spanners tighten and loosen nuts and bolts, which generally have hexagonal or square heads. There are more types of spanner than almost any other tool, but you can cover yourself for most domestic jobs with a couple of adjustable spanners. These have one fixed and one movable jaw, which you adjust with a worm-drive screw.

The largest nuts you are likely to have to tackle around the house are those on plumbing fittings and connectors, which are generally between 25 and 30mm 'across the flats' – measured from opposite sides of the nut. An adjustable spanner big enough to cope with these can also be used on smaller nuts.

1 To work on a nut, open the jaws of the spanner and slip it into place.

2 Tighten the movable jaw so the spanner grips opposite flats on the nut securely.

3 Work out which way to turn the nut. A nut is screwed on in a clockwise direction, so your spanner must move in the same direction to tighten the nut, and counter-clockwise to loosen it. Use reasonable force to turn the spanner as required.

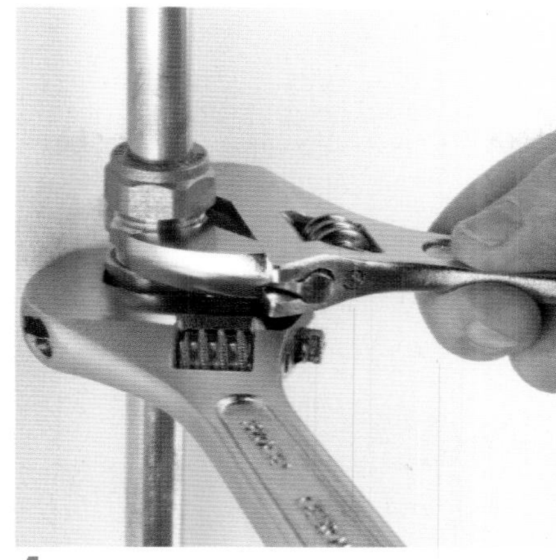

4 Some jobs need two spanners. For example, to tighten a leaking brass compression fitting joining two lengths of copper pipe, you need one spanner to grip the hexagonal section in the middle of the fitting, and the other to tighten the leaking nut where the pipe enters it. See Chapter 10 for more information on using spanners for a variety of plumbing jobs.

Pliers

Pliers were originally designed for cutting, bending and twisting wire, and electricians use them for all those jobs when doing wiring work. However, you can use pliers for all sorts of everyday gripping jobs. Here are a few practical examples.

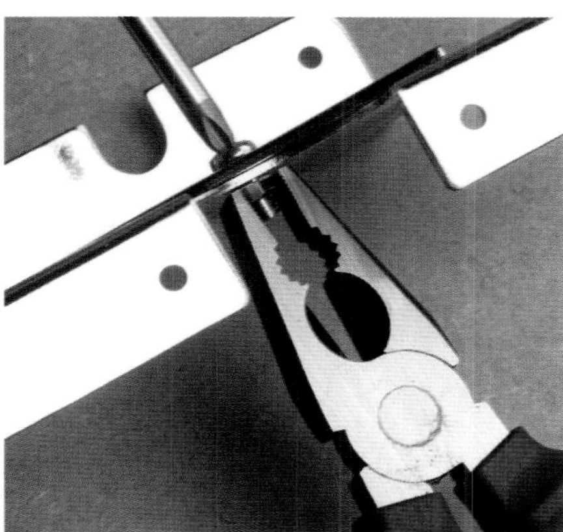

1 Use pliers to grip small nuts if you do not have a suitable spanner. For example, attaching a metal curtain track to its wall brackets may involve tightening a nut onto a small screw with a slotted head. Here pliers are ideal for holding the nut while you do up the screw with a screwdriver. Pliers are also useful for home plumbing – for example, when dismantling a piston-type ball valve (page 339) or when opening or closing the lockshield valve of a central heating radiator (page 374).

2 Use pliers to remove the metal base of a broken light bulb from its lampholder. Turn off the power at the mains before you do this. Then push the tip of the pliers into the base of the bulb and turn it counter-clockwise to remove the bulb base from either a bayonet or screw lampholder.

3 Use pliers to pull unwanted wallplugs out of the wall. When you have unscrewed whatever was fixed to the wall, drive the screw back into the plug for a few turns. Then grip the screw head with the pliers and pull screw and plug straight out. Fill the hole for an invisible repair.

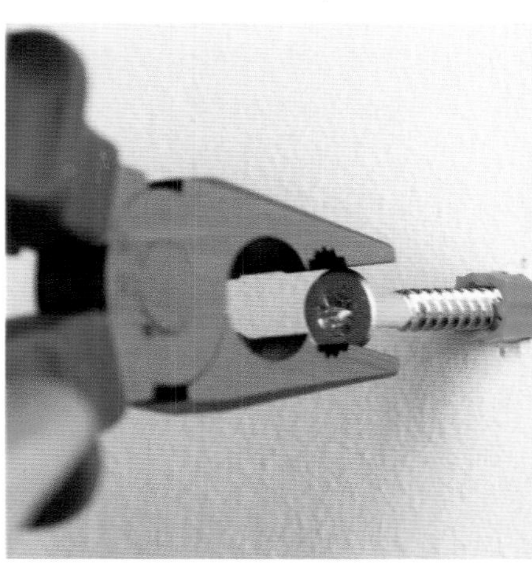

Self-locking wrench

This tool can be used as a spanner, as a wrench (for gripping round objects such as metal tubing, for example), as pliers and even as a simple clamp. The jaws can be adjusted to a range of settings, and then locked into place.

1 Close the jaws onto whatever you want to grip by squeezing the handles, and turn the adjuster screw counter-clockwise until the handles close.

2 If the workpiece is too small for the tool to lock on with the handles closed, keep squeezing the handles and turn the adjuster screw clockwise until the jaws touch the work. Operate the release lever, turn the adjuster a little more and squeeze the handles to lock the jaws onto the workpiece.

3 To release the locking action, hold the handles together and operate the release lever.

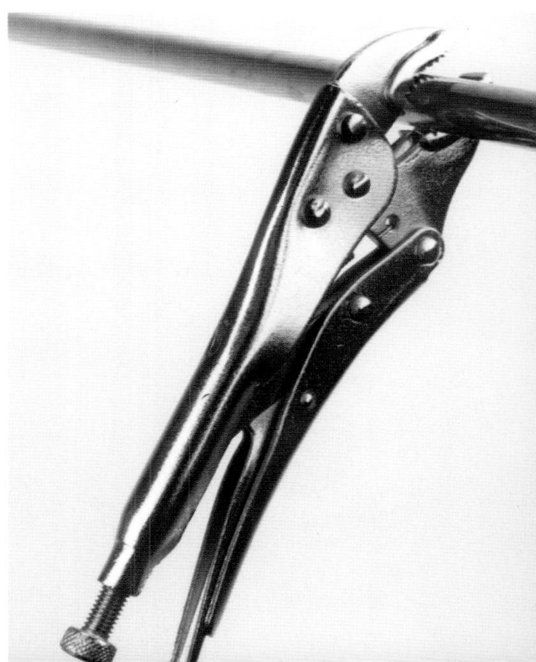

Drilling holes

There are few DIY jobs that do not involve drilling a hole at some stage. Your cordless drill is the power source for all these operations, used in conjunction with a range of drill bits and other accessories.

Get to know your drill

Cordless drills run on rechargeable batteries, and all but the cheapest come with two batteries. Make sure you know how to remove and insert the batteries, and how to operate the battery charger. Check whether the battery can be left to trickle-charge for hours, or whether it has a fixed recharge time.

Next, read the instructions. These will tell you how to select the following:
- Forward and reverse gears.
- The correct speed setting for drilling, screwdriving and, if the drill has the option, hammer action for making holes in masonry.
- The correct torque setting, which enables you to apply the optimum turning force when driving screws into different materials.

Most cordless drills come with a carry case. Keep the drill in it when you are not using it. If you do not have a case, buy one. DIY stores stock a selection; take your drill in to test its fit before you buy.

Fitting drill bits

Select the right type of drill bit for the job you are doing (page 33).

1 Open the chuck by twisting the knurled ring and fit the end of the drill bit inside it.

2 Tighten the knurled ring until you feel it start to slip. The drill bit is now secure. Select forward gear and the drilling or hammer-drilling option, and you are ready to start work.

Drilling freehand

Most people drill holes by simply pointing the drill at the surface and squeezing the trigger. With very few exceptions, drilled holes have to be at 90° to the surface.

1 If you have a good eye, check from two angles that you are holding the drill at more or less the right angle. This is good enough for many drilling jobs.

2 If you want to check the angle more accurately, hold the drill in position and set a try square against the surface you are drilling into. The drill bit should be parallel with the metal blade of the try square.

Drilling small holes in wood or metal

Fit a twist drill bit of the required diameter and select the drilling setting on the drill.

1 Secure the workpiece on your workbench, with some scrap wood underneath if you are drilling a hole right through it. This prevents you from damaging your bench jaws, and also guarantees a clean exit hole through the workpiece.

2 Hold the drill tip at the mark and check that you are holding it upright. Drill the hole through the workpiece and on into the scrap wood. In metal, withdraw the drill bit while it is still running so that it does not jam in the hole.

Drilling large holes in wood

Fit a flat wood bit of the required size and select the drilling setting on the drill.

1 Secure the workpiece on the bench with scrap wood beneath it.

2 Position the lead point of the drill bit at the mark and start drilling. As the cutting blades begin to bite and cut the hole, they will cut evenly if you are holding the drill upright. Drill on into the scrap wood, which will guarantee a clean exit hole through the workpiece.

Alternatively Clamp the wood so the drill can emerge from the underside into free air. Drill the hole until the lead point just penetrates the wood. Turn it over, locate the lead point in the hole and drill out the rest of the hole. This will reduce the risk of leaving a rough exit hole. Use this technique for jobs such as fitting a cylinder lock to a front door (see page 198).

Drill bit varieties

Apart from the basic selection of drill bits outlined on page 33, you may need to buy others for specific DIY jobs.

Long twist drills are available in lengths of up to 165mm (and 8mm in diameter). They are used for making holes in thick components such as timber-framed partition walls.

Reduced-shank drills are available in diameters up to 20mm (most standard twist drills go up to 10 or 13mm only). They have 13mm diameter shanks to fit the maximum chuck size on most cordless drills.

Drill accessories

Apart from drilling holes, your cordless drill can do a number of other jobs if fitted with the right accessory. Here are some of the most useful.

Wire brushes

Remove rust or old paint from metal surfaces with one of these. There are two types, cups and wheels, both available in a range of sizes. Between them they will allow you to get into awkward corners as well as tackling flat surfaces. Most have a built-in spindle; some have a separate spindle called an arbor so you can fit different brushes on one spindle.

Sanding attachments

These good all-rounders allow you to carry out small-scale sanding jobs on flat surfaces if you do not have a power sander. Sanding discs fit on a stiff rubber backing disc and are held on by a washer and screw. Their only disadvantage is that they can leave swirl marks across the grain of the wood if you use too coarse a paper. Make sure you finish a job with medium or fine grades for a very smooth, unmarked surface. Paper discs are fine for sanding wood if the job is reasonably small. For bigger jobs with wood, or with metal or masonry surfaces, choose more durable abrasive-coated metal discs instead. Coarse discs can remove material very quickly. Flap-wheel sanders have tongues of double-sided abrasive paper fixed to a centre spindle, and are good for sanding curved surfaces. Also good for curves are drum sanders. They consist of a thick disc of foam plastic, coated with abrasive paper.

Polishing pads

Take the hard work out of polishing your car's paintwork or the furniture with a lambswool pad or bonnet, which fits over a rubber backing pad held in the chuck. Foam drum polishers work in a similar way.

Paint mixers

To mix and stir paint and other mixes such as wallpaper paste and tile grout, fit one of these to your drill. They are made of plastic or metal and will give paint or other liquids a thorough mixing. Use them only with a slow speed setting on your drill to avoid splashing.

Light-duty pump

This accessory can cope with jobs such as emptying a garden pond or mopping up after a plumbing disaster. The drill drives an impeller inside the pump casing, which has inlet and outlet spigots to take lengths of standard garden hose. Make sure you use the manufacturer's recommended setting on your drill.

Hole saws

If you have to cut a large perfectly round hole in a piece of wood, the best way to do it is with a hole saw. It is a cylinder of steel with teeth at one end and a central twist drill that makes the starting hole. Hole saws can be bought singly or in sets, and can cut holes of up to 76mm in diameter. For more information, see page 50.

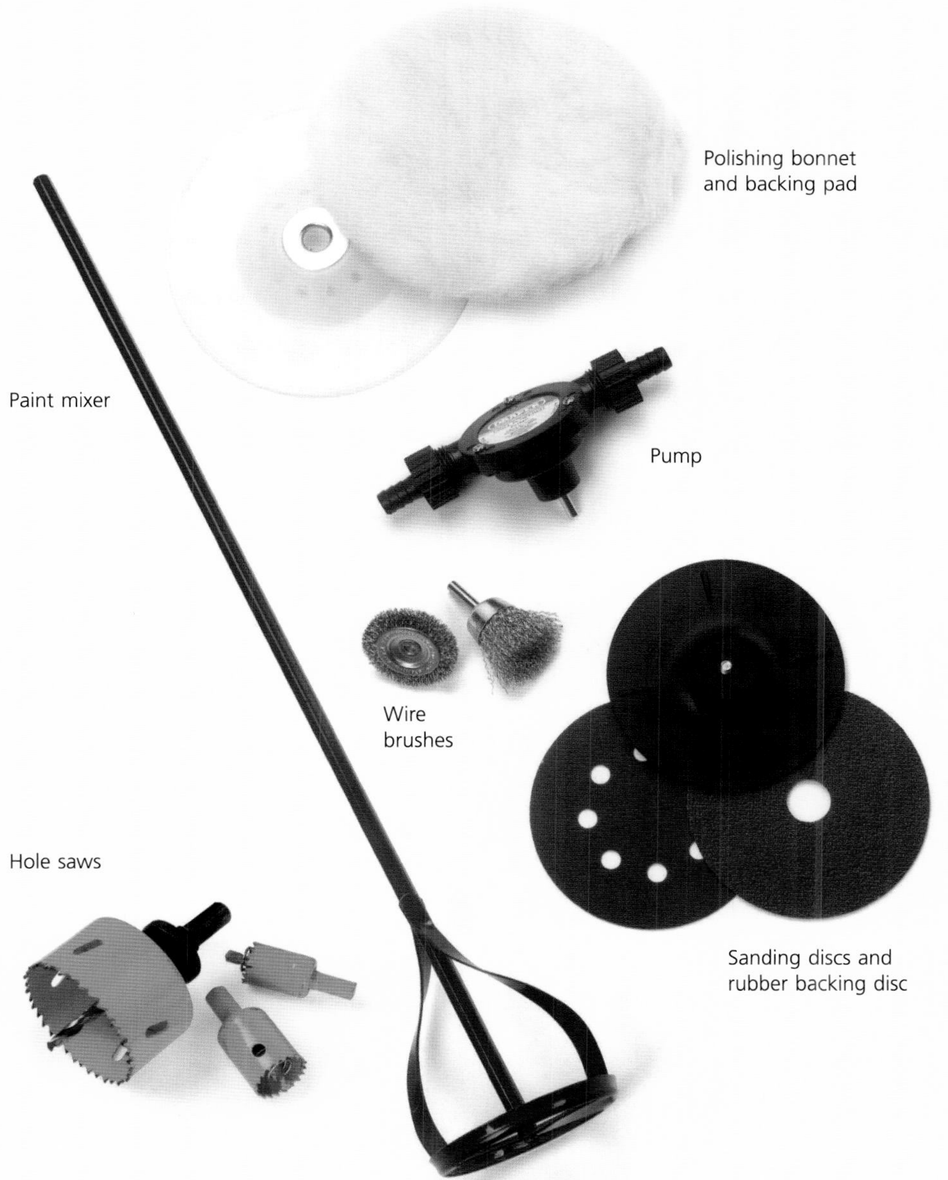

Polishing bonnet and backing pad

Paint mixer

Pump

Wire brushes

Hole saws

Sanding discs and rubber backing disc

AIDS TO ACCURATE DRILLING

If you do a lot of woodwork, it will be worth investing in a bench-mounted drill stand (see page 58). For everyday drilling jobs, a drill guide is a cheaper and more versatile option. It has a flat baseplate and a spring-loaded clamp to hold the drill body at 90° to the baseplate. Fit the drill in the guide and tighten the securing clamp. Press the baseplate against the surface you are drilling – wood on the workbench, or a tiled wall in the bathroom – and start drilling a perfect 90° hole. Use the centring guide to drill holes in the centre of the workpiece edge.
The guide rods can be extended beyond the base (to centre on an edge) and the baseplate has V-grooves for holding round items.

Making wall fixings

Fixing things to walls is the key part of many everyday DIY jobs, from fitting shelves and curtain tracks to putting up a mirror or hanging a display cabinet. It is an easy job as long as you use the right fixings and the correct technique. Done wrongly, the fixing will fail, with potentially serious consequences.

Assessing the job

The first step is to discover what sort of wall is involved, because this dictates how you make a fixing into it.

- Masonry walls sound solid when tapped; most exterior walls and internal ground-floor walls are of this type.
- Timber-framed internal partition walls and ceilings sound hollow, whether they are clad with plasterboard or the lath and plaster found in pre-1945 houses.
- Dry-lined masonry walls can also sound hollow. This is because they have a layer of lath and plaster (in pre-1945 houses) or plasterboard on a framework of timber battens attached to the masonry, instead of solid plaster.
- Timber-framed houses have dry-lined plasterboard walls throughout.

Masonry walls

For fixings in solid masonry, you have to drill a hole in the wall and insert a hollow wallplug that will grip a screw when one is driven into it. To make a secure fixing, the plug and screw must penetrate solid masonry to a minimum depth of 25mm. On a plastered wall you must therefore make an allowance for the thickness of the plaster (about 13mm in a modern house, and up to 20mm in older houses). For heavy-duty fixings the screw must penetrate up to 40mm, so use a 50 or 60mm screw.

Choosing wallplugs

Moulded plastic wallplugs are available in a range of sizes in two main types: smooth and flanged. Smooth plugs fit entirely within the drilled hole, with the end of the plug just below the wall surface. Flanged plugs have a surface flange that fits flush with the wall surface. Choose a plug to match the length and gauge of the screw you intend to use. The drill diameter to use will be marked on the plastic 'tree' to which the plugs are fixed, or on the packaging.

Frame fixers are moulded plastic wallplugs with an extended sleeve, and are designed for fixing timber door and window frames to walls – see right.

Making the fixing

Fit a masonry drill bit of the required size in the drill chuck. Select the drilling setting (or hammer action if you have it) on the drill. If it has two speed settings, select the lower speed.

1 Measure the length of the wallplug you intend to use, and wrap a piece of visible tape round the drill bit to act as a depth mark. Position it at a distance of 5mm plus the plug length from the tip of the bit.

2 Press the tip of the bit against the wall where you plan to drill and check by eye that the drill is at right angles to the surface.

3 Start the drill and apply firm pressure to drill out the hole. On deep holes, withdraw the bit once or twice so the flutes on the drill bit can clear dust from the hole.

4 Drill until the tape reaches the wall surface. Then withdraw the bit while the drill is still running to clear drill dust from the hole.

5 Insert the wallplug to check that it will fit. Pass the screw through whatever you are fixing and drive it into the wallplug. If the plug turns in the hole as you tighten the screw you have made the hole too large and the fixing will fail. Pull the plug out and fit a larger one.

Using frame fixers

These fixers come in a range of sizes to suit different frame thicknesses. They are sold complete with long wood screws or special hammer-in screws.

1 Set the frame in position and mark the locations of the fixings. If possible, ensure that they will be made into solid masonry, not into the mortar joints between courses.

2 Choose a twist drill bit to match the diameter of the frame fixer. Select drilling and high speed on your drill. Drill a clearance hole through the frame at each fixing location. Stop drilling and withdraw the still-rotating drill bit to clear the debris.

3 Switch to a long masonry drill bit of the same diameter. Select hammer action (if you have it) and low speed on your drill. Measure the length of the frame fixer, and wrap a piece of tape round the drill bit to act as a depth mark. Position it at a distance of 5mm plus the plug length from the tip of the bit.

4 Insert the drill bit through the clearance hole until it touches the masonry, and start drilling the hole there. Withdraw the drill bit at intervals to clear the debris. Drill until the tape depth stop reaches the surface of the frame.

5 Insert the frame fixer and tap it fully home with a hammer so its flange is flush with the frame. Drive in the wood screw or the hammer-in screw to complete the fixing.

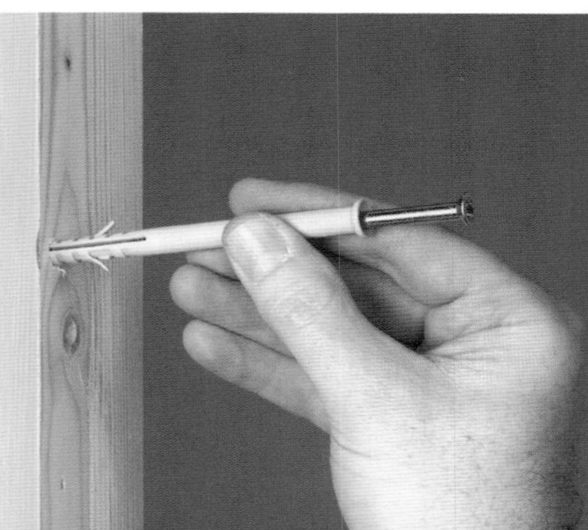

Partition walls and ceilings

You can make fixings into internal partition walls and ceilings in one of two ways.
• Locate the wall frame members (the studs) or the ceiling joists, and screw through the cladding into solid timber. To do this, you need to use an electronic stud detector, or to make some test drillings through the cladding. In modern houses, wall studs and ceiling joists are at 400mm centres. In older houses the spacings may be as wide as 450mm or even 600mm.
• If the stud or joist positions do not coincide with where you want to make your fixings, drill a hole in the cladding and insert a cavity fixing device that will expand and grip the inner face of the cladding. The device must be strong enough to support the load on the fixing.

Choosing cavity fixings

A wide range of cavity fixings is available, made from moulded plastic or metal. The fixing is inserted through a hole in the wall cladding, and a wood screw (or the machine screw supplied with the fixing) is tightened into it. This draws up and compresses part of the fixing against the inner face of the wall cladding, providing a firm grip for the screw. The fixing remains in place in the wall if the screw is removed.

Spring toggles (right) have two spring-loaded wings that flip outwards once the fixing is inserted, to grip the inner face of the wall cladding. The toggle is lost in the cavity if the screw is removed.

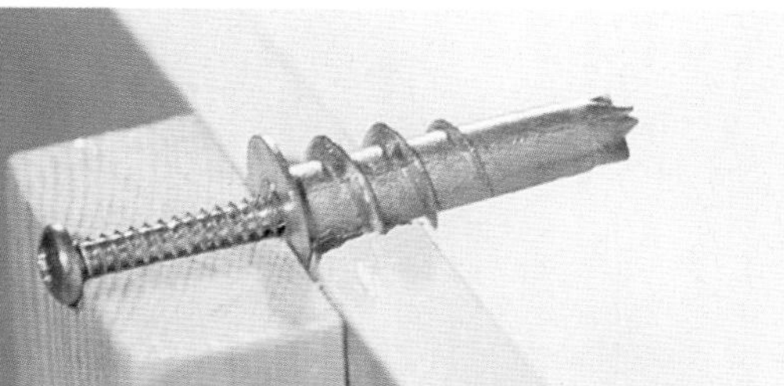

Cavity fixings are sold as suitable for light, medium or heavy loads. As a general rule, use plastic or metal screw-in fixings (above) for light loads. Use plastic anchor fixings or spring toggles for medium loads, and metal anchor fixings for heavy loads such as a wall cabinet or radiator. The metal anchor fixing has four wings that grip against the inner face of the wall cladding as the machine screw is tightened.

Making the fixing

You can drill through plasterboard or lath-and-plaster with a twist drill bit. Match the drill size to the fixing you are using. Select the drilling setting on your drill, and high speed on a two-speed drill.

1 Press the tip of the drill bit into the surface and check by eye that the drill is at right angles to the surface. Drill until the drill bit breaks through the cladding, and withdraw it while it is still rotating to clear debris from the hole.

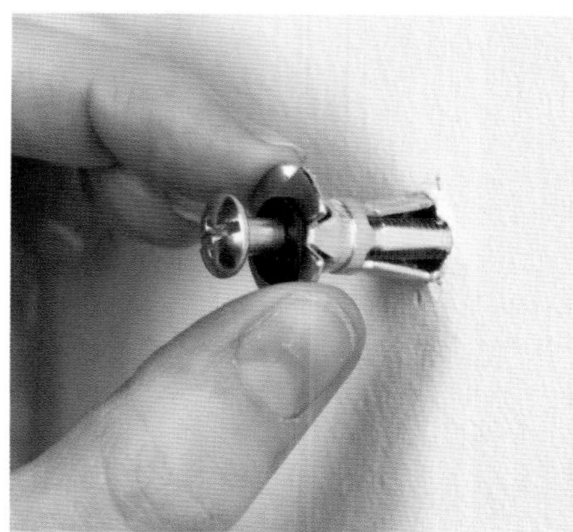

2 Push the fixing into the hole until its flange is flush with the surface. Remove the machine screw if one is supplied (except for spring toggles).

3 Pass the machine screw (or wood screw) through whatever you are fitting. Drive the screw into the fixing and tighten it fully.

Spring toggles

1 Do not put a spring toggle straight into its hole. Instead, remove the machine screw and pass this through whatever you are fitting.

2 Reattach the toggle to the screw, fold up its wings and push them through the hole. Check that the wings have opened by pulling on the fixing, then tighten the screw fully.

Dry-lined walls

Dry-lined walls have a cavity 25–40mm wide between the lining and the solid masonry behind. How you make a fixing depends on the load to be supported. For lightweight items you can use plastic or metal screw-in fixings, as for partition walls. Medium-weight items need a cavity anchor, but the cavity depth restricts the types of fixing you can use. Heavyweight items must be supported on fixings made into the masonry using a long screw and wallplug. The best type is a frame fixer long enough to pass through wall cladding and cavity, and penetrate masonry by about 40mm.

Making the fixing

Use a twist drill to match the diameter of the frame plug to make a hole in the wall cladding at the fixing location. Then switch to a long masonry drill bit of the same size and wrap tape round it to indicate the total drilling depth (cladding plus cavity plus 40mm). Select drilling (or hammer action if your drill has it) and slow speed.

1 Insert the long masonry drill bit through the hole in the wall cladding and check that it is at right angles to the surface.

2 Drill the hole to the depth indicated by your tape depth stop. Withdraw the drill bit from time to time to clear the hole of debris, which will fall into the cavity.

3 Insert the frame plug and check that its flange fits flush with the surface of the wall cladding. Pass the screw through whatever you are fixing and drive it into the plug.

Timber-framed houses

In a timber-framed house, internal walls are timber-framed partitions and you should make fixings into them as described, left. External walls are lined with plasterboard, but behind this is a vapour barrier and a layer of glass fibre insulation. Fixings should be made into the vertical timber frame members wherever possible. Otherwise use cavity fixings, as for other partition walls.

Fixings in external walls

Use a twist drill bit to match the size of the fitting. Select drilling and high speed on the drill. Press the tip of the drill bit into the wall surface and check by eye that the drill is at right angles to the surface.

Drill until the drill bit just breaks through the wall cladding. If you drill any deeper, you will penetrate the vapour barrier and the drill bit will pull tufts of insulation out of the hole. Insert the cavity fixing and screw whatever you are fitting into place.

Making good

Making good means restoring something to its original state, and it is a task that is involved in many everyday DIY jobs. Woodwork can be dented or split. Plaster can crack or come away from the surface beneath. Gaps can open up where skirting boards and architraves meet the wall. All these defects need making good, using the appropriate filler or sealant and the right tools. The basic techniques for making good minor defects are described here; for more details, see pages 78–79.

Choosing fillers

There is a daunting array of fillers available in DIY stores, ranging from traditional dry powder that you mix with water, to ready-mixed products in tubes, tubs, tins and cartridges. Powder fillers can be kept for a long time if they are stored in dry conditions, but ready-mixed fillers have a finite shelf life. Buy them only if you have a lot of filling to do in a short space of time, and are likely to use up most of the filler.

You need three basic types of filler for everyday DIY – a filler for wood, a filler for plaster and a filler for gaps. So-called 'all-purpose' fillers are available, but as with all products of this type their performance is a compromise. They will fill anything adequately, but you will get better results with a one-job filler designed specifically for its purpose.

FILLERS FOR WOODWORK

Most of the woodwork round the house will be painted or varnished, and unless it is brand new will need to have dents and scratches filled before being finished.

- If the wood is to be painted over, standard wood filler in a tub will be adequate. Some are white and others come in a neutral woody colour.
- If you are filling wood that is stained or varnished, you need a matching filler – called wood stopping. It comes in a range of colours, and you can mix in a little woodstain to get a perfect match.
- A specialist filler is linseed oil putty – used for fixing glass into wooden window frames. Soft enough to allow the glass to be bedded into it, it sets rock hard and can be painted after a fortnight.

Repairing woodwork

Existing woodwork, whether painted or varnished, can become dented or chipped from everyday wear and tear. These defects need filling before the surface is given a new finish. Use interior wood filler on woodwork that will be painted, and wood stopper in a matching wood shade for woodwork that will be varnished.

There are also two-part products for really tough filling jobs. They consist of a basic filler and a chemical hardening agent. You add a small amount of the hardening agent to activate the ingredients of the filler, to start the setting process. This type of filler is particularly good for repairing damage caused by wet rot.

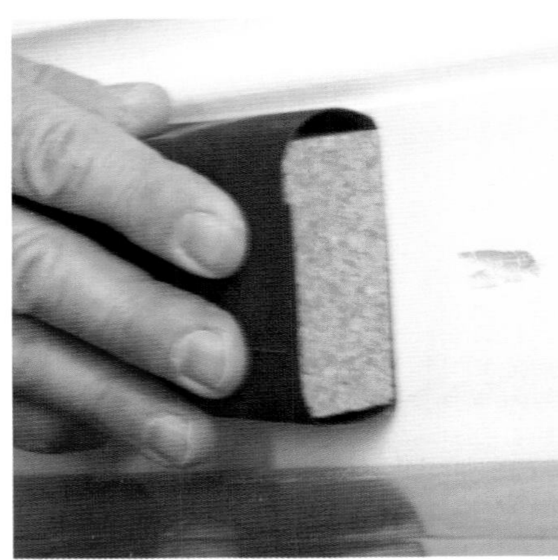

1 Sand the damaged area with fine wet-and-dry abrasive paper. This will smooth any rough edges to the damage, and will key the surface so that the filler will bond better to it. Wipe away any dust with kitchen roll moistened with white spirit.

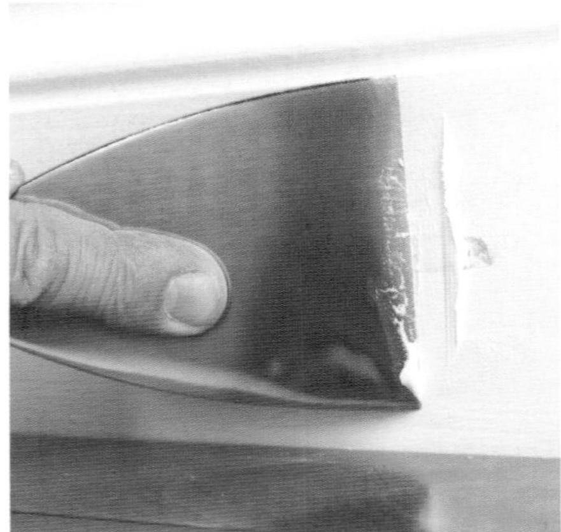

2 Use your filling knife to press wood filler or stopper into the damage, leaving it a little proud of the surrounding surface. Leave it to set hard.

3 Sand the filled area smooth with fine abrasive paper, then wipe away dust with kitchen roll as in step 1. The repair is now ready for redecorating.

Repairing plaster

The plaster on your walls and ceilings is a hard but fairly brittle material, so it may develop cracks or dents if it is knocked. It will also crack if the structure to which it is stuck moves, as often happens with the plaster on timber-framed walls and ceilings.

Use a ready-mixed wall filler for repairing small cracks and dents, and ready-mixed plaster for patching larger areas. To fill gaps where a hard-setting filler keeps falling out, use a non-setting flexible sealant instead (see Filling gaps, opposite).

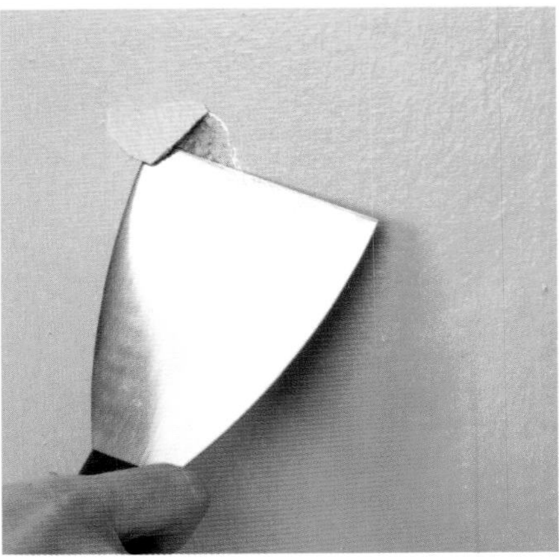

1 To fill a surface crack in plaster, rake out loose material with the blade of your filling knife, leaving only the sound plaster.

2 Use an old paintbrush to brush out any dust remaining in the crack. It is important to make the area as clean as possible.

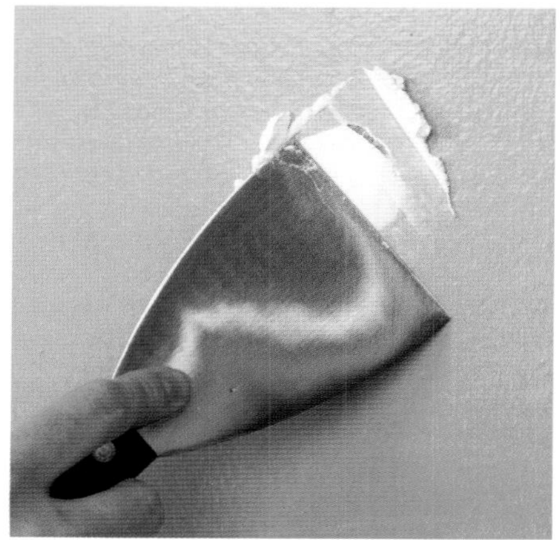

3 Load some filler onto your knife and draw the blade firmly across the crack to press the filler into it. Repeat as necessary to fill the entire length of the crack, then draw the blade along it to smooth off any excess filler.

4 Allow the filler to set hard, then sand the surface by hand or with a power sander, using fine abrasive paper. Dust off any fine particles. The surface is now ready for redecoration.

Filling gaps

Houses are full of problem gaps – where walls and ceilings meet, along the join between skirting boards or architraves and walls, around window frames and along the edges of baths and kitchen worktops.

They are difficult to fill with conventional hard-setting fillers because the gap expands or contracts as temperature and humidity changes, and this cracks the filler.

A non-setting flexible sealant bonds to both surfaces and stretches to accommodate the movement. Different types are available for different jobs, but a decorator's acrylic sealant is ideal for most interior filling jobs in areas that will remain dry. Apply it with a cartridge gun. It comes in white only but can be painted over.

For areas that get damp, such as a bathroom or kitchen, there is a waterproof silicone sealant that is claimed by its manufacturer to last for up to 30 years. It is white, and can be painted over if desired.

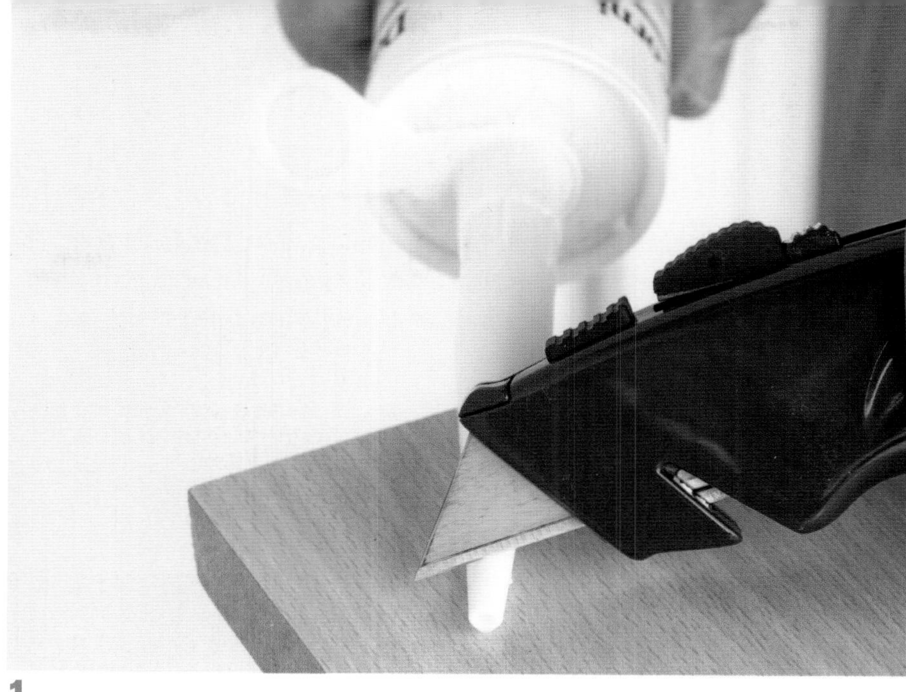

1 Once you have chosen which sealant is suitable for the job, cut the nozzle of the cartridge at an angle so it will extrude a bead of sealant a little wider than the gap you need to fill.

2 Most cartridges are made to fit a standard gun, so once you have the gun, all you need each time is the appropriate cartridge. Insert the cartridge in the gun and pump the trigger until the plunger touches the base of the cartridge.

3 Gently squeeze the trigger. This will push the plunger down through the cartridge and begin to force sealant out of the nozzle.

4 Hold the nozzle at 45° to the crack and draw the nozzle along it, squeezing the trigger to maintain a steady flow of sealant. The flow rate should match the speed of the nozzle as you move it along the gap. Do not leave any gaps. If you do, go back and fill them.

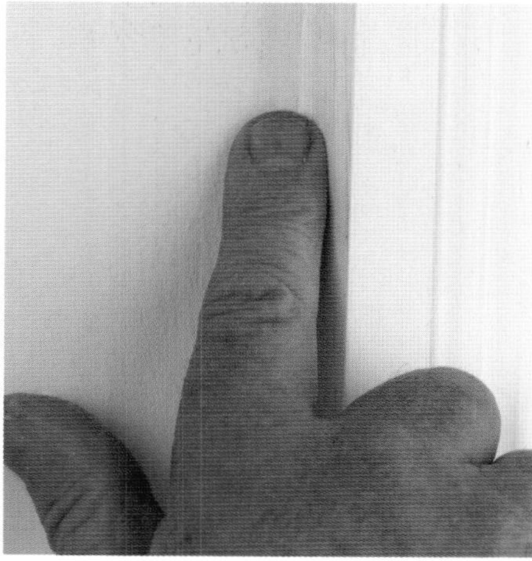

5 When you have filled the gap, press the piston release lever on the gun to stop the flow of sealant. Smooth the surface of the sealant with a clean, wetted fingertip. When the sealant has hardened sufficiently, you can paint over it. Reverse the cut-off tip and push it into the end of the nozzle to keep the remaining sealant fresh.

Power tool basics

Many DIY tools need sharp blades or powerful motors to be able to do their jobs properly. This means that they can cause injury if they are not used correctly and with care. Never bypass or deactivate any safety guard fitted to the tool.

Using a jigsaw

A jigsaw with a 400-500 watt motor is adequate for most DIY tasks, though you may want extra power when you discover how useful this tool is.

A jigsaw will cut wood, man-made boards and several other materials if it is fitted with the correct type of blade. You can buy a basic model very cheaply. Key features to look out for are variable speed, an adjustable sole plate so you can make cuts at angles other than 90°, and some means of collecting or extracting sawdust – either a dust bag or an adaptor so you can connect it to a vacuum cleaner. Some jigsaws now feature blade clamps that do not need tools. Some have variable speed (useful for different materials) and some have pendulum action, which gives a faster, cleaner cut.

Making a short cut

Select the right blade for the job and fit it in the blade clamp. Secure whatever you are sawing to the workbench with a clamp, or by holding it in the bench jaws. The saw will tend to snatch at the workpiece if you simply hold it with your free hand.

1 You can make short cuts freehand – for example, to cut a wall batten or a piece of skirting board to length. Mark the cutting line and rest the front of the saw's sole plate on the edge of the workpiece.

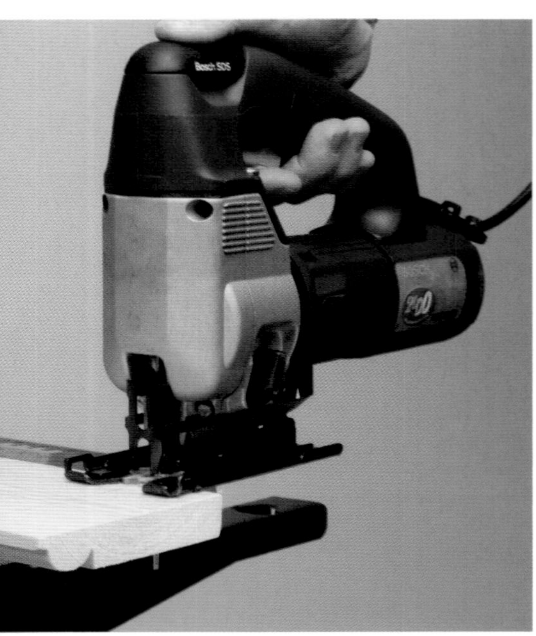

2 Start the saw at a slow speed and move it forwards so that the blade starts to cut just on the waste side of the cutting line. Make sure the sole plate is flat on the surface of the workpiece.

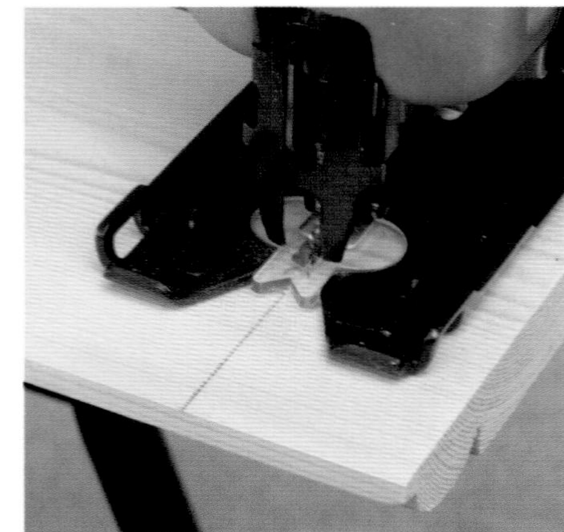

3 As the cut proceeds, increase the saw speed and check that you are keeping the blade on line. As you complete the cut, support the offcut with your free hand. Stop the saw as soon as the blade is free.

CHOOSING JIGSAW BLADES

Blades for cutting wood and man-made boards come in fine, medium and coarse versions; the closer the teeth, the finer the cut. The maximum cutting depth is usually between 50 and 75mm, depending on the blade. Wood-cutting blades will also cut plastic sheet materials. You need extra-fine blades for cutting metal, and there are also special blades available for cutting ceramic tiles and glass-reinforced plastics (GRP). Check that any blades you buy are compatible with your make of saw; not all are interchangeable between brands.

Making a long straight cut

Because the saw blade is narrow, it can wander off-line on long, straight cuts made freehand. On thick materials, there is also a tendency for the blade to deform under load, giving a cut that is not at 90° to the surface of the workpiece. To prevent the first problem, use a saw guide. To counteract the second, let the saw cut at its own speed rather than forcing it.

1 If the jigsaw is supplied with a side fence – a tee-shaped bar projecting from the side of the sole plate – you can use it to make cuts up to about 150mm from the edge of the workpiece. Clamp the fence in the required position and make a test cut on some scrap wood to check the setting.

2 Position the saw so the blade is aligned with the cutting line and the fence lies against the edge of the wood.

3 Move the saw forwards as the cut proceeds, keeping the fence against the edge of the workpiece. Allow the blade to run out of the cut at the far end.

Using a guide batten

To make a cut further from the edge of the workpiece than the fence will allow, use a guide batten. This is a strip of wood clamped across the workpiece to guide the edge of the saw's sole plate along the cut.

1 Mark the cutting line, align the saw blade with it and place the batten next to the side of the sole plate.

2 When you are happy with its position, clamp it to the workpiece and check that the clamps will not interfere with the travel of the saw. Make the cut by running the edge of the sole plate against the batten.

Making a curved cut

Mark the cutting line on the workpiece. Avoid starting a curved cut at the edge; the blade will skate off it as you try to start the cut. Instead, drill a hole in the waste area large enough to admit the saw blade and begin the cut there.

1 Start the cut as for a straight cut, positioning the blade on the waste side of the cutting line. Move the saw forward at its own speed – don't attempt to push it – following the cutting line by eye.

2 Cut more slowly on sharp curves, turning the saw body gradually so the blade can follow it closely. In this instance, the curve was a continuation of a straight cut, so no starter hole was required.

Making an internal cut-out

Mark the cut-out on the workpiece; if you are cutting a square or a rectangle, draw a line in from each corner at 45°. You will be placing the point of the drill bit on this line.

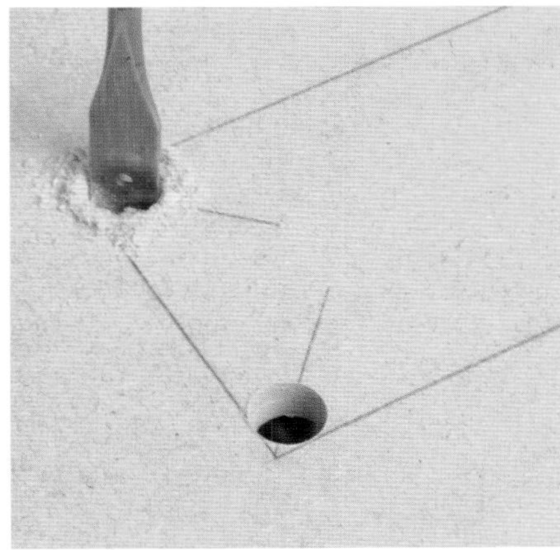

1 If you use a 16mm spade bit, place the point of the bit at least 8mm into the waste area from the corner, on the 45° line. Drill all four holes.

2 Insert the saw blade and rest the sole plate on the workpiece. Follow the cutting line to the next drill hole for straight cuts, or carry on cutting round a curve.

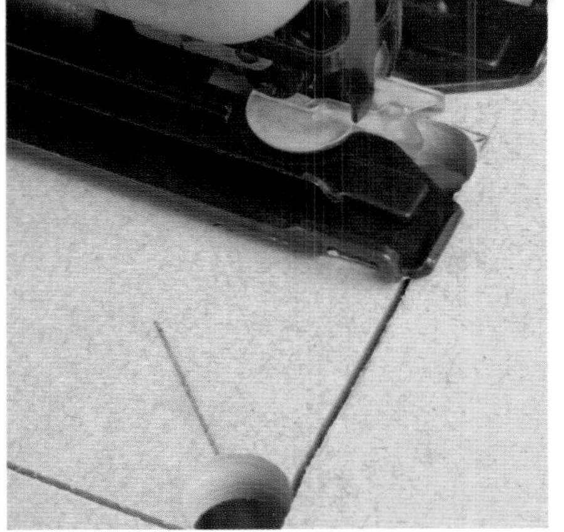

3 At the next corner, let the saw blade run right into the angle. Then turn the saw in the drill hole and start the next straight cut. Repeat at the third corner to run the saw back to your starting point.

4 Use abrasive paper to smooth the edges of the cut and to square up the internal corners.

Using a power sander

A random orbit sander will cope with most everyday sanding jobs. You can buy a basic tool quite cheaply.

Key features to look for are a 125mm diameter backing pad, a locking switch for continuous operation, and some form of dust extraction via a dust bag or vacuum cleaner attachment. Random orbit sanders now use touch-and-close (Velcro) fastenings to attach the abrasive discs to the backing pad, with holes in the abrasive disc lining up with holes in the pad.

CHOOSING ABRASIVES

The sanding discs for this type of sander use aluminium oxide grit as the abrasive, bonded to a strong backing fabric. If the sander has a through-the-pad dust extraction system, the sheets have holes in them that coincide with holes in the backing pad, allowing the machine to draw dust up through the pad as you work. Make sure that the discs you buy are compatible with your make of sander; not all brands are interchangeable.

There is a range of disc grades, from coarse, for fast removal of material, to extra fine for finishing work. Abrasive discs use a numbering system to indicate the coarseness of the abrasive grit; the lower the number, the coarser the grit. Typical figures are 60 (coarse), 120 (medium) and 180 (fine).

Sanding without scratches

A random-orbit sander is the simplest of all power tools to use. Its action is designed to leave no scratch marks on the surface of wood when used with a fine grade abrasive disc.

1 Select the correct grade of abrasive disc for the finish you want to achieve, and attach it to the backing pad so the holes in disc and pad are aligned. Press the disc firmly into place on the pad.

2 Connect the sander to the hose of your vacuum cleaner using the adaptor provided, and switch the vacuum cleaner on. Alternatively, fit the dust bag if the tool has one.

3 Hold the disc against the surface you want to sand and switch on the power. Keep the sander moving backwards and forwards over the surface.

4 Be prepared to switch discs as you work to achieve the finish you want. For example, you may need to start with a coarse disc to remove an old surface finish, followed by medium and then fine discs to create a perfectly smooth surface.

Woodworking tools

These are the extra tools you will need if you plan to be more than an occasional weekend woodworker, cutting a wall batten to size or trimming the odd shelf to length. They complement the basic tool kit described on pages 30–33, and can be built up tool by tool as your woodworking horizons expand.

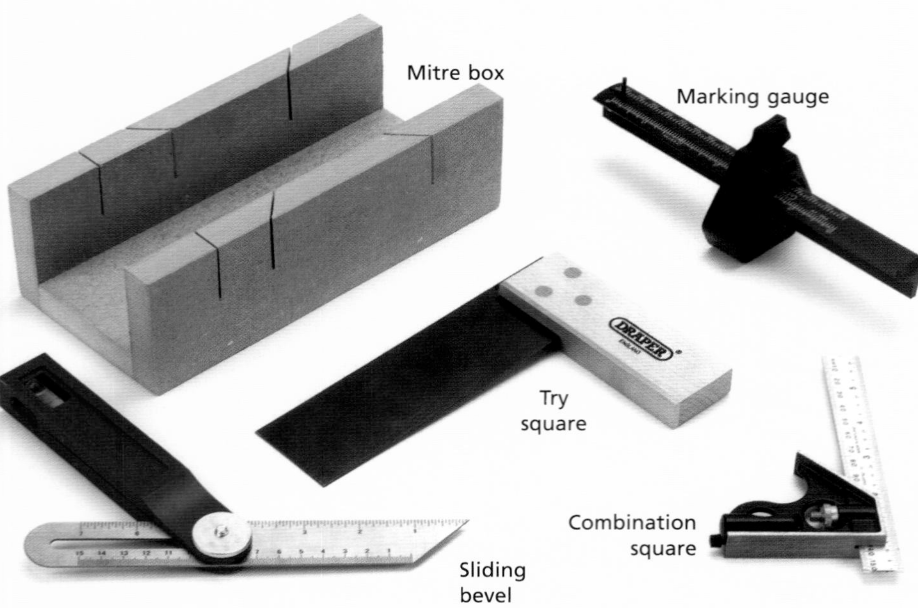

Tools for marking

Marking gauge
This tool has a hardwood or plastic beam with a hardened steel pin set into it near one end, and a block that slides along the beam and can be secured to it with a thumbscrew. The pin scribes a line at a fixed distance from the edge of the workpiece. It is used when marking out woodworking joints, and is also useful for jobs such as centring locks on door edges and marking the depth of hinge recesses.

Mitre box
A three-sided open-ended box with guide slots pre-cut in its opposite sides, used to guide a tenon saw blade when making 45° mitre cuts. The size of the box restricts the size of pieces that can be cut with it.

Try square and combination square
A try square has a rectangular metal blade fixed at 90° to a wooden, metal or plastic stock. It is an essential tool for marking a cutting line at right angles to the edge of a workpiece, and is also used for checking internal and external corners. A combination square is a variation on the theme, with a moveable stock that can also mark 45° angles and be used for measuring depths.

Sliding bevel
This tool is a sort of adjustable try square with a metal blade that can be set at any angle and locked in place with a wing nut. It is particularly useful for fitting shelves in out-of-square alcoves, and for fitting staircase balusters.

Tools for sawing

Circular saw
A circular saw is essential if you plan to cut up sheets of man-made boards, fit your own kitchen worktops or lay floorboards. A circular saw makes accurate, straight cuts, and its tilting soleplate can be set to allow cuts at any angle between 45° and 90°.

A basic circular saw takes blades 150mm diameter and has a maximum cutting depth of about 45mm. Larger and more powerful semi-professional models take blades 185mm or 190mm diameter, giving a cutting depth of around 65mm at 90° (45mm at 45°). Most have dust extraction.

Cordless circular saws have smaller blades – typically 136mm to 140mm – and a 90° cutting depth of around 40mm, but can be used anywhere.

Blades are available for fine cutting, cross cutting and rip cutting wood and man-made boards, and for cutting laminated chipboard kitchen worktops. Check that any blades you buy are compatible with your make of saw.

Coping saw
Designed for making curved cuts in wood and boards, it has a slim replaceable blade mounted in a U-shaped steel frame with a handle at one side. The frame holds the blade in tension, and allows the blade to be rotated to prevent the frame from fouling the edge of the workpiece.

Hole saw
This attachment for a power drill is used to cut holes in wood and boards that are larger than the maximum size of a flat wood bit (around 38mm). The blade is a short length of saw formed into a cylinder and fitted into a blade holder. This carries a twist drill at its centre which starts the hole and guides the saw blade into the wood. Hole saws are sold in sets of several blades, up to about 75mm in diameter.

Mitre saw
This useful tool (see page 65) consists of a framed saw with a fine-toothed blade mounted on guide bars over a steel base. The guide bars can be rotated to position the saw at any angle between 45° and 90° to the workpiece, which is clamped in place between the blade and the base while the cut is made. It is more accurate than a mitre box, and can cut wider components.

Padsaw
The padsaw has a short tapered blade fitted into a handle, and is used mainly for cutting holes in the centre of the workpiece, such as a keyhole in a door. You need a starter hole to insert the blade and start the cut.

Panel saw
The panel saw has a plain steel blade about 560mm long, typically with around 10 teeth per inch (tpi), fitted to a wooden or plastic handle. As its name implies, it is used mainly for cutting up panels of man-made boards by hand, as a low-cost alternative to using a circular saw. The blade may be PTFE-coated to minimise friction, and the best saws have hard-point teeth that will stay sharp for longer than standard teeth. On most saws, the handle doubles as a simple 45°/90° try square.

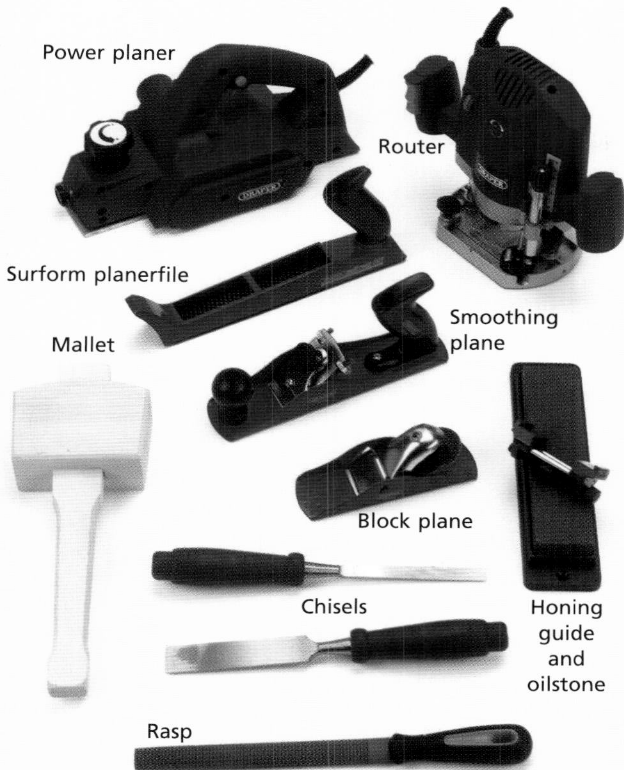

Tools for shaping

Chisels
Chisels are essential for cutting many woodworking joints. They also chop out slots (mortises) for door locks, form recesses for hinges and do all sorts of general paring and shaping jobs. To start with, buy a set of bevel-edge chisels in 6, 12, 19 and 25mm sizes, ideally contained in a storage case so they do not get muddled up with other tools in your tool box. Keep the plastic blade guards on their tips when they are not in use.

Mallet
This wooden hammer with a square beechwood head is used mainly for striking chisel handles when cutting woodworking joints, and for assembling joint components.

Planes and power planers
The bench plane is the traditional tool for reducing wood to the cross-sectional size you want, and for finishing it with flat, smooth edges. It consists of a steel blade held at an angle to the tool's soleplate in an adjustable mount. The 250mm long smoothing plane is the most useful (a larger version – the jack plane – is 355mm long); shorter block planes, with the blade at a lower angle, are designed for smoothing end grain.

The power planer does the work of a bench plane much more quickly. It has a rotating cylinder into which two replaceable cutting blades are fitted, and can be used to remove up to 2–3mm of wood in each pass of the tool. It can also cut rebates when fitted with a detachable guide, and the groove in its soleplate allows it to chamfer edges too.

Router
The router is a power tool with a motor that drives a cutter at very high speed. Straight cutters produce slots and grooves; shaped cutters create a wide range of edge mouldings. The tool is mounted on a baseplate on springs, allowing it to be 'plunged' into the work to a pre-set depth. Edge and circle guides allow the tool to follow the shape of the workpiece or to cut circular recesses. Many routers now feature dust extraction, and come with a few router bits. Extra bits can be bought singly or in sets as required.

Rasp
This tool is a coarse file used for shaping wood, especially curved surfaces. Buy a half-round rasp with one flat and one curved surface, which will shape convex and concave curves.

Surforms
The Surform range of shaping tools all have perforated blades that work like a miniature cheese grater, removing wood in a series of fine shavings. The range includes planes and files in several styles; the planerfile with its reversible handle is the most versatile. The blades are all replaceable when blunt.

Honing guide and oilstone
This wheeled guide holds a chisel or plane blade at the correct angle while it is being sharpened on an oilstone. It also holds it square to the surface of the stone. The oilstone is made of natural or synthetic abrasive material and usually has a fine and a coarse face; it is lubricated with light machine oil.

Workbench tools

Bench hook
This simple wooden bench aid is used to hold small workpieces on the workbench, for example when cutting them to length with a tenon saw (see page 33). The hook is positioned on the workbench with the lower batten against its front edge. The workpiece is held against the upper batten.

Clamps
Clamps come in many different styles and sizes, and are used for two main jobs. The first is holding workpieces securely on the workbench while they are cut, drilled or shaped. The second is clamping components such as woodworking joints together while the adhesive sets. G-clamps and screw clamps are traditional designs, but fast-action trigger clamps and spring clamps are quicker and easier to use.

Drill stand
This bench aid clamps your power drill in an upright position on your workbench, making it easy to drill holes in workpieces at precisely 90° to the work surface – something that is difficult to judge accurately by eye. The running drill is moved up and down in the stand with a lever, and the depth of drilling can be pre-set to create stopped holes if required. Take your drill with you when buying a stand, so you can check that it will fit. You can also get a dowelling jig which allows you to drill correctly aligned holes for the three most common dowel sizes (6, 8 and 10mm).

Glue gun
This mains-powered tool dispenses blobs of hot-melt adhesive at the squeeze of a trigger, and is invaluable when assembling woodworking joints. The adhesive comes in sticks which you insert into the back of the gun. They are melted and extruded from the nozzle when you squeeze the trigger.

Vice
You can grip large workpieces in the jaws of your portable workbench. However, for smaller items it is useful to have a bench-mounted vice, which you can attach to the workbench as needed. Traditional metalworkers (engineers) vices are bolted in place; you can get smaller versions that clamp to a table or a workbench jaw.

Drill stand

Bench hook

Clamps (fast action)

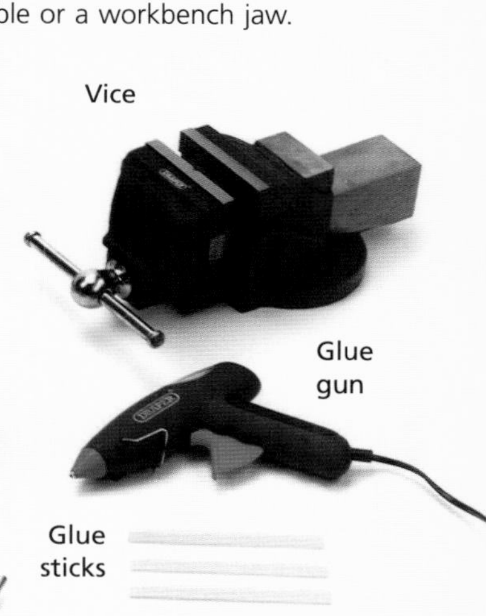

Choosing and buying wood

The basic raw materials for most DIY woodworking projects are softwood – cut from coniferous trees such as pine and spruce – and man-made boards. Hardwood from deciduous trees such as oak, beech, teak and mahogany is expensive and harder to work than softwood, and is used mainly for making furniture. However, hardwood mouldings are widely available, and are popular because they hold detail better than the softwood equivalent.

Softwood

Softwood is not only easy to work, but it almost invariably comes from renewable sources, so is not depleting valuable stocks of rare woods or destroying forests.

Buying softwood

You can buy softwood from DIY stores or from local timber merchants. Wood from timber merchants is generally cheaper, and they are much more welcoming to the do-it-yourselfer than they used to be. They also stock a wider range of wood types and sizes.

However, for small amounts of wood, the convenience of the DIY store probably outweighs the extra cost involved.

Softwood sizes

Softwood is available in sawn and planed finishes, in a range of cross-sections that are described in millimetres but are still commonly referred to by their imperial equivalents – 2 x 1in equals 50 x 25mm, for example.

It is important to realise that the quoted sizes are the actual dimensions of the wood when it leaves the sawmill. A piece of sawn wood described as 100 x 50mm will be that size, give or take a millimetre or so to allow for shrinkage. Planing the rough-sawn wood removes from 3mm to 6mm from each dimension, so a piece of planed wood described as 100 x 50mm (its nominal size) will actually measure about 95 x 47mm in cross-section.

Many DIY stores now sell timber marked with its actual rather than its nominal size, but it's still worth taking a tape measure with you when buying so you can carry out a double check. Think in millimetres.

Commonly available widths for softwood are 25, 38, 50, 75, 100, 150 and 225mm (the last usually available only in Parana pine). Common thicknesses are 12, 19, 25, 38 and 50mm.

Softwood is sold in lengths that are multiples of 300mm (known as a metric foot, and about 5mm shorter than the old imperial one). Commonly available lengths are 1.8, 2.4 and 3m.

Structural timbers such as floor joists are available in longer lengths.

Softwood faults

When buying softwood, check it for faults. The most serious is warping, where the wood is bent or twisted along its length.

This can be disguised when wood is sold in bundles, as in many DIY stores. Do not be afraid to open bundles and examine individual lengths before you buy, because warped wood is useless for most projects. Try to hold the timber at eye level, and look along its length to check for warping. It helps to have someone with you, to hold the other end.

Other faults that can spoil softwood are excessive knots – especially dead ones where the heart of the knot has fallen out – and end splits (called shakes).

Reject any wood with these faults because you will find you cannot use it when you get it home.

Hardwood

Hardwood is used in the home mainly in the form of decorative mouldings and as veneers on man-made boards. If you want a particular hardwood as an alternative to softwood – for shelves or a windowsill, for example – look for a specialist timber merchant in your local *Yellow Pages*.

Man-made boards

Man-made boards allow you to use wood wider than that available from any tree. There are two main types: boards made from real wood, glued together in thin veneers or solid strips, and boards made from ground-up wood chips or fibres bonded together into a uniform sheet. Each has its uses, its advantages and disadvantages.

Buying man-made boards

Boards of all types are available from DIY stores and timber merchants. As with softwood, timber merchants are generally cheaper and stock a wider range of types and board sizes.

The standard board size for all types is 2440 x 1220mm, a straightforward conversion from the old imperial 8 x 4ft sheet. Most board types are also available in smaller sizes, equal to one half or one quarter of a full-sized sheet (nominally 2440 x 610mm and 1220 x 610mm), and also in 1830 x 610mm panels.

So-called furniture panels – mainly plastic-faced or veneered chipboard (see opposite) intended for shelving and making kitchen cabinets – are now made in metric sizes which are fractionally smaller than their imperial-based equivalents.

Real wood boards

The oldest of the man-made boards is plywood. Blockboard is little used today, its place in the woodworker's stockroom has been taken by timberboard (also known as pineboard.

Plywood Sheets that consist of a number of thin wood veneers called plies, bonded together with adhesive. The grain direction in each layer is at right angles to that of its

neighbours, resulting in a board that is stable and equally strong in either direction. The grain direction of the outer plies (there is always an odd number) runs the length of the board.

The board surface is smooth, but the edges tend to splinter when cut and can be difficult to finish neatly.

Exterior-grade (WBP) plywood is made with water-resistant adhesives, and is used in damp situations indoors (such as under ceramic floor tiles) as well as for outdoor structures. Marine ply is made with waterproof adhesive, but still needs protecting with paint or varnish when used outside. Both are expensive.

Blockboard A board with a core of softwood strips bonded together edge to edge, and finished with one or two veneer plies on each face. Blockboard is stronger along the length of the board than across it. It is expensive to buy and has now largely been replaced by timberboard for shelving and MDF for other uses.

Timberboard A composite board made by gluing together parallel softwood strips to form wide boards suitable for shelving, table tops and worktops as an alternative to blockboard.

The boards are usually 18mm thick, and are intended for staining and varnishing.

Fibreboard and particle board

Hardboard and chipboard were once the most widely used board types, but medium-density fibreboard (known to everyone as MDF) has now taken its place for many DIY projects.

Hardboard Made from heavily compressed wood fibres, with one smooth surface and one with a mesh texture. It is widely available but it only comes in one thickness: 3mm (sometimes 3.2mm).

Hardboard has little strength, and is mainly used to form the back panels of cabinets and bookcases and the bases of drawers (especially in its white plastic-faced form). It is also used for jobs such as boxing in pipes or lining timber floors where the strength of the board is unimportant. It is possible to get perforated hardboard, which is useful in workshops where tools are to be kept on the wall. Hooks fitted into the holes at the appropriate spots can make a place for every tool.

Also available is oil-tempered hardboard, which is stronger and denser than standard hardboard, and white-faced hardboard used for cupboard backs.

Chipboard Consists of wood chips bonded together with resins. It has relatively smooth surfaces but rough, crumbly edges which can make it difficult to produce a neat finish.

Chipboard is commonly available in 12 and 18mm thicknesses. It is a heavy and dense board that blunts tools quickly, because of its high resin content. It is not as strong as plywood and has poor load-bearing strength – chipboard shelves always tend to sag unless they are well supported – and is mainly used in its plastic-faced form for kitchen units and flat-pack furniture, and in plain 22mm thick sheets for flooring. Extra-thick 28 and 38mm chipboard forms the core of laminated kitchen worktops and 18mm and 22mm tongue-and-groove sheets of flooring-grade chipboard are used in place of floorboards.

SHOPPING FOR SUSTAINABLE WOOD

Wood is considered a natural, ecologically friendly building material, yet up to a fifth of all the timber sold in the UK is illegally produced. To ensure the wood you buy comes from an ethically managed and sustainable forest, look for the Forest Stewardship Council (FSC) logo. The FSC tracks the wood from forest to store to ensure best production practice at every stage. Labelled timber is widely available in DIY stores.

Medium-density fibreboard (MDF) Made from fine wood fibres bonded together with resin under high pressure to create a board with a fine, even texture and smooth faces and edges. MDF is easier to cut and shape than other board types, and is now widely used for all indoor panel work as well as a wide range of flat-pack furniture.

It is available in 6, 9, 12 and 18mm thicknesses. Cutting, drilling and sanding the board produces a fine dust that can be unpleasant to inhale, so it is advisable to wear a face mask when working with it.

Wood mouldings

Most of the wood used in woodworking is square or rectangular in cross section. Mouldings are made by machining wood to create a variety of other cross sections.

Many of these are used for structural jobs as diverse as making windows and doors and forming skirting boards and wall cladding. Other mouldings are purely decorative, being used to edge boards, to cover gaps or to trim and finish things like built-in furniture.

Structural mouldings are generally relatively large in section and machined from softwood, although hardwood versions are available at a price. They include skirting boards, architraves, dado and picture rails, staircase handrails and balusters, windowsills and wall cladding. You can also buy structural mouldings machined from MDF and factory-primed ready for painting. They have well-finished edges and are free from knots, warping and other defects.

Decorative mouldings are machined from hardwoods such as ramin, and include small trim mouldings in quadrant, scotia, half-round and corner profiles.

Embossed trim mouldings are created by impressing decorative designs onto the face of pre-machined mouldings.

Measuring and marking wood

The first step in making anything using wood or a man-made board is to measure and mark your workpiece so that you can cut it to size. Take as much care with this as with every other stage in the woodworking process; making a mistake at the start can spoil the entire job.

Starting square

You can generally assume that man-made boards have edges that are square to each other. The same applies to the ends of full lengths of sawn and planed softwood. However, wood or board offcuts in your workshop may not have square ends or edges, and it is very important to square them up before using them.

1 To check whether an end or edge is square, hold the stock of your try square against the adjacent edge and align the blade with the edge you are checking.

2 If it is not square, move the try square away from the corner by about 5mm and mark a line across the workpiece against the try-square blade with a trimming knife or a sharp pencil.

3 On softwood, use the try square and marker to continue the squared line onto the other faces of the workpiece. The line on the fourth face should meet up with the one on the first face.

4 Cut off the waste to leave a perfectly square end or edge (see facing page).

Measuring

Use a steel ruler for measurements of less than about 300mm, and a tape measure for longer measurements. Always work in millimetres, even if you prefer to think in feet and inches; it is only too easy to get confused with fractions of an inch, but an exact measurement in millimetres is easier to work with.

1 Align the end of the ruler with the squared-up end of the workpiece, or hook the end of the tape over the end and extend it as required. Make sure that your eye is vertically above the figure on the ruler or tape that you want to use, and mark the workpiece at that point with a knife or pencil.

2 Hold the try square with its blade aligned with the mark, and square the cutting line across the face of the workpiece. On softwood, continue the line round the workpiece as in step 3, left.

Multiple components

Every saw cut you make removes a small amount of wood, equal to the width of the saw teeth. If you want four pieces of wood each 300mm long and you mark up four successive cutting lines 300mm apart on a length of softwood, three of the pieces will be marginally shorter than 300mm when you cut them off. To avoid this, always mark and cut each component before marking and cutting the next.

You must also allow for the width of the saw cut when marking out man-made boards, ready for cutting into a number of smaller panels. Mark parallel guide lines 3mm apart at the edge of each panel, instead of a single line, so you can saw between the lines when you cut the panels.

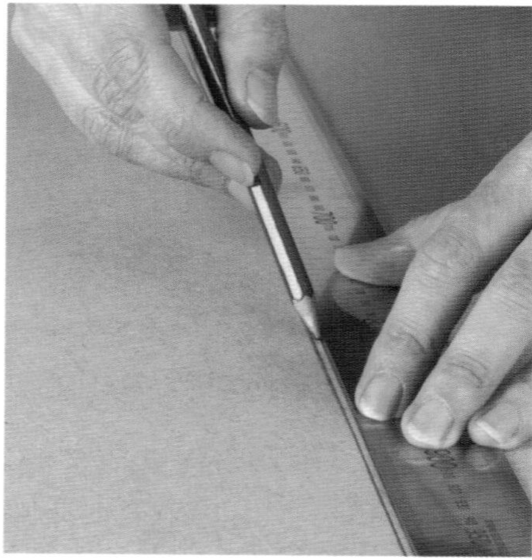

Using a combination square

You can use a combination square in the same way as a try square to mark lines at 90° to the edge of the workpiece. The design of the square also allows you to mark cutting lines at 45° for mitres.

1 Make a mark on the edge of the workpiece where you want the cutting line to begin.

2 Slide the stock to the end of the blade and hold the 45° face against the edge of the workpiece in line with the mark and with the blade extending across its width.

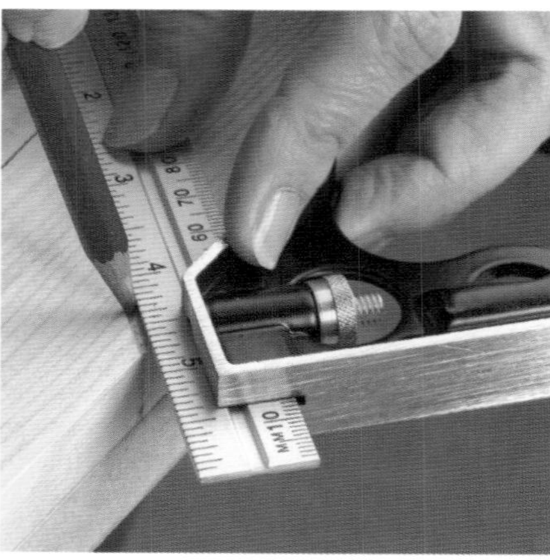

3 Mark the cutting line across the workpiece with a knife or sharp pencil. Alternatively, use the removable scribing pin fitted into the tool's stock.

Using a sliding bevel

A sliding bevel allows you to copy an existing cutting angle – on a replacement staircase baluster, for example – or to set a new angle using a protractor.

1 To copy an existing angle, loosen the wing nut or knurled nut on the tool. Hold the stock against one surface forming the angle and move the blade to touch the other surface. Tighten the wing nut to lock the blade in place.

2 To set a new angle, use a protractor to position the blade at the required angle and lock it in place.

3 Transfer the tool to the workpiece and use it like a try square to transfer the angle of the cutting line to the new wood.

Cutting wood and boards

You can use a hand or power saw to cut wood to length and board panels to size. Power saws save time and effort, but for smaller jobs you may not want the trouble of setting up a power saw. Whichever you use, it is important that the workpiece is held securely so that the saw blade cannot snatch it loose and damage it.

Using a bench hook

The best way of holding mouldings and other small workpieces – up to about 50 x 25mm in size – is to use a bench hook. You can buy one or make one from a piece of timber and two offcuts.

1 Place the lower batten against the near edge of your workbench and place the workpiece against the upper batten. If the batten is inset from the edge of the base, position the cutting line just beyond the end of the batten. If it is not, let the workpiece project beyond the edge of the base by about 25mm.

2 Position the saw blade just on the waste side of the cutting line, guiding it against the side of the thumb of your spare hand. Start the cut with a few light backward strokes of the saw.

3 Saw with the blade at 45° to begin with, then lower it closer to the horizontal once the cut is established. If the bench hook batten is inset, complete the cut by sawing into the base of the bench hook. This ensures a clean cut with no splinters on the underside of the workpiece.

If the batten is not inset, complete the cut with gentle strokes to minimise splitting on the underside.

Using a mitre box

You can hold and cut small workpieces in a mitre box, which is itself clamped in the jaws of your workbench. The guide slots in the box allow you to make accurate cuts at 90° as well as at 45°.

1 Mark the cutting line on the workpiece (see opposite). Place it in the box with the cutting line aligned with the slots you want to use. As these do not extend to the base of the box, place a piece of scrap wood beneath the workpiece so that you can saw into it, to avoid leaving a ragged finish.

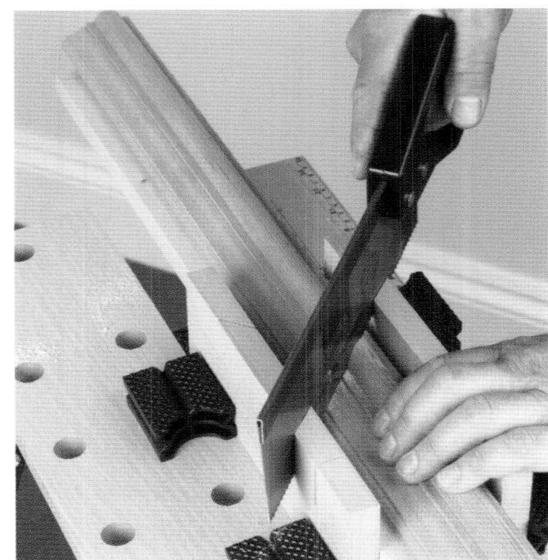

2 Fit the tenon saw into the slots in the mitre box and use your free hand to hold the workpiece in place. Make the cut with the saw held horizontally. Take care not to widen the mitre box slots by letting the saw wander off line.

Using a vice

The jaws of a portable workbench (page 33) can be used to hold most things, but sometimes it is easier to hold small mouldings or pieces of wood in a metalworkers (engineers) vice. Buy some plain jaw covers if you are going to do this – the normal serrated jaws will leave permanent marks on softwood mouldings.

Using a panel saw

A panel saw is used to cut wood that is too big for the tenon saw, and to cut man-made boards into smaller panels. It can be used for both cross-cutting (cutting across the grain) and ripping (cutting with the grain). Wood should not be allowed to vibrate while it is being cut, so securing it firmly is essential to a good, clean cut and a satisfactory result.

Even when you take the greatest amount of care, it is possible that the exit cut may be a little rough. To avoid this, always start with the good side of the wood facing upwards in the bench – this way, any minor defects in the cut won't affect the finished job quite as much.

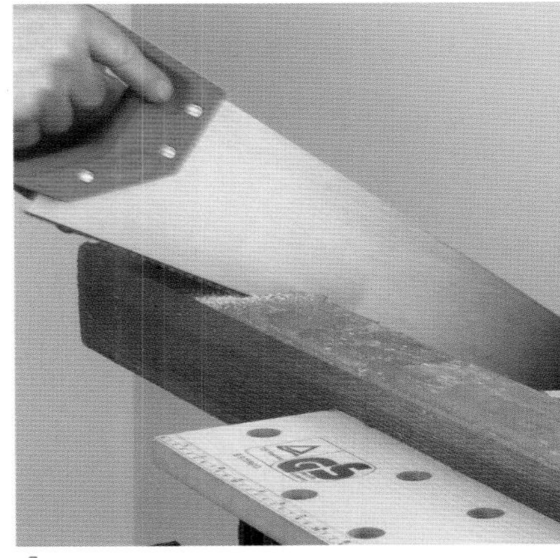

1 To cut wood across the grain, clamp it in the jaws of your workbench with the cutting line clear of the bench frame. Start the cut with a few gentle backwards strokes of the saw blade, then continue cutting with the blade at an angle of about 45°. Hold the offcut with your free hand as you complete the cut to prevent the wood from splintering on the underside.

2 To cut smaller panels from a larger sheet of board, you need to support it on both sides of the cut unless you are sawing close to the board edge. You can rest the panel over the open jaws of your portable workbench and saw between them, but you need to take care not to hit the bench framework. Alternatively, rest the board on two planks supported at each end, or use an open stepladder laid on its side as a makeshift support (below).

3 Kneel on the workpiece so that your eye is above the cutting line and your arm in line with it. Start the cut on the waste side of the marked line and saw as far as is comfortable. Reposition yourself and the board to continue the cut, and complete it using short saw strokes to avoid splintering the board.

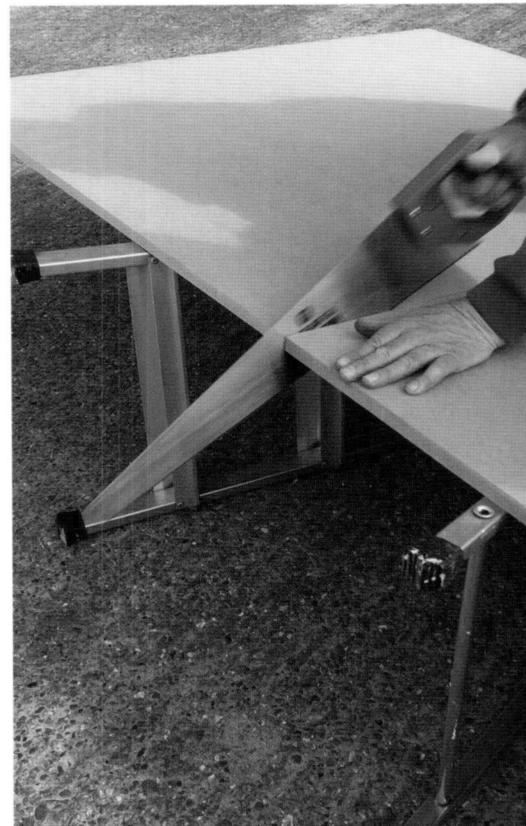

Using a coping saw

If the saw is already fitted with a blade, check the blade tension by tightening the screw-up handle on the tool. To fit a new blade, unscrew the handle fully and unhook the ends of the old blade from their holders. Hook the ends of the new blade into the holders, with the teeth facing away from the handle, and tighten it fully.

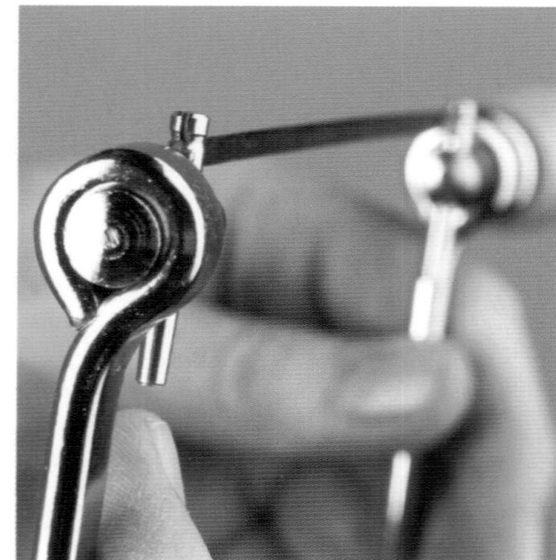

1 To make a cut starting at the edge of the workpiece, check that the pins on the blade holders are aligned with the frame. Start the cut with the blade at right angles to the edge. Follow the marked cutting line carefully.

2 As you saw along the cutting line, you may need to rotate the blade to stop the frame from fouling the edge of the workpiece. Unscrew the handle slightly, rotate both blade holder pins to the required angle and re-tighten the handle. Repeat as necessary to allow the blade to follow the curve.

3 To make an internal cut-out, mark its outline and drill a hole through the workpiece within the waste area large enough to admit the saw blade. Unhook the blade from the frame, thread it through the hole and re-attach it to the frame.

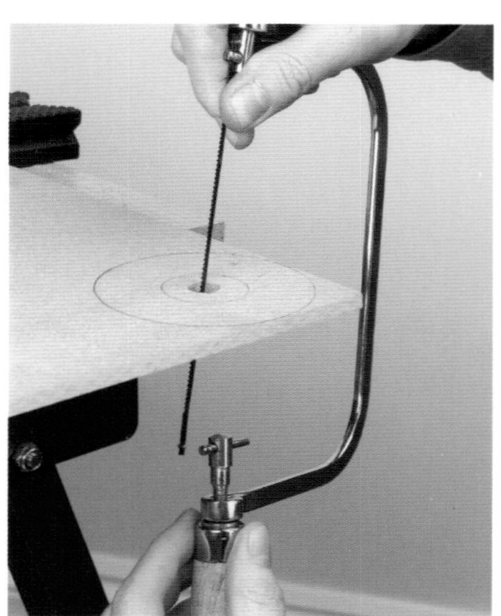

4 Cut from the hole towards the marked outline, then follow it round until you return to your starting point. To allow the blade to turn corners in straight-sided cut-outs, drill a hole within the outline at each corner. Square up the corners with a chisel when you have removed the cut-out.

Using a padsaw

The padsaw is ideal for making cut-outs and cutting curves where it is not possible or practicable to use a coping saw. Two typical jobs for it are making cut-outs in plasterboard walls to fit electrical wiring accessories, and cutting keyholes in doors.

Cutting a hole in a wall

1 To make an enclosed cut, mark its outline and drill a starter hole within the waste area big enough to admit the saw blade. If the cut-out is to be square or rectangular, drill a hole at each corner so that you can turn the blade to cut along the next side.

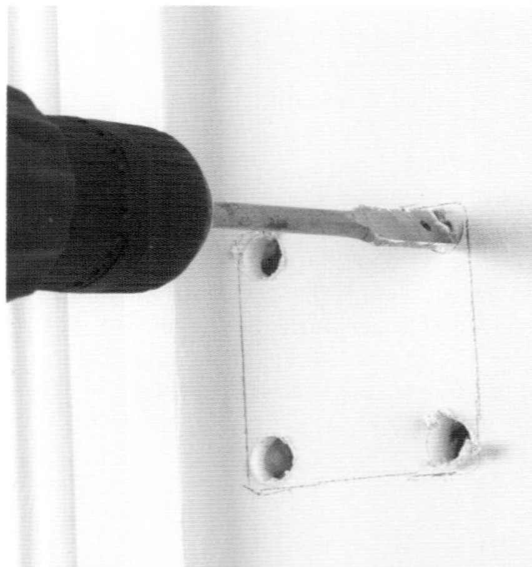

2 Insert the saw blade and start cutting along the marked line. Use short saw strokes in a plasterboard wall to avoid damaging the cladding on the opposite side of the frame.

Cutting a keyhole

To cut a keyhole, drill the starter hole at the top and mark the sides of the slot needed to admit the tongue of the key. Insert the saw blade right through the hole and cut down both sides of the slot. Use a narrow chisel (page 60) to chop out the waste wood, working from both sides of the door.

Using a hole saw

The hole saw will cut perfectly round holes in wood, man-made boards, plasterboard and sheet metal or plastic. Select the blade diameter that matches the hole you want to make and clip it into the circular arbor, or blade holder. Fit the arbor into the chuck of your power drill.

1 Locate the pilot drill bit at the centre of the cut-out and start the drill slowly.
As the drill penetrates the surface, the saw teeth will start to cut into it. The cut will be even all round if you are holding the drill at a 90° angle to the surface.

2 If you are cutting a workpiece on your bench, clamp some scrap wood beneath it and saw through the workpiece into the scrap to ensure a clean exit hole.

Using a circular saw

Before you use a circular saw for the first time, read the instructions supplied with it and familiarise yourself with all the controls and safety features. Check that you have the correct type of blade (see panel below).

CIRCULAR SAW BLADES

Use tungsten carbide tipped (TCT) blades of the correct diameter for your saw. The number of teeth is a general guide to its cutting performance: many small teeth ensure a fine cut; fewer large teeth give a fast but coarse cut. Special blades are available for cutting man-made boards and laminates.

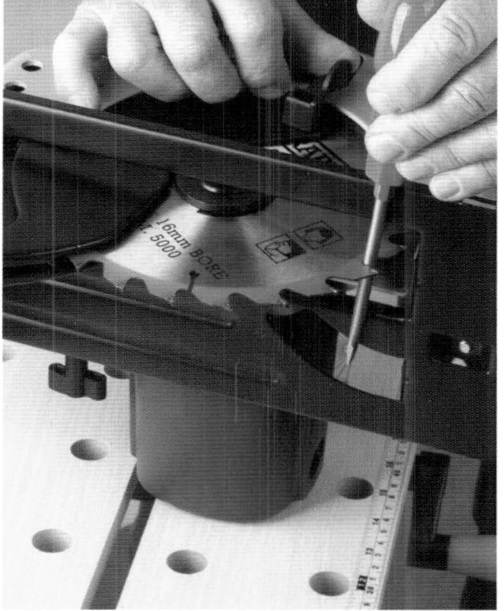

1 To remove or change a blade, make sure that the saw is unplugged. Use the Allen key provided with the saw to loosen the retaining nut. For blades with large teeth, jam a screwdriver blade between the saw teeth and the soleplate to stop it turning. For fine blades, hold the saw blade down firmly on some scrap wood. Release the old blade from its spindle, fit the replacement with the teeth pointing forwards and tighten the nut fully.

2 To set the cutting depth you require, place the saw on its side and loosen the lever that locks the saw body to the soleplate. Move the saw body until the saw teeth just project beyond the thickness of the material you are cutting. Tighten the lever again.

3 To make a cut up to about 150mm from the edge of the workpiece, fit the adjustable side fence in its clamp. Set it the required distance from the saw blade and tighten the wing nut. Clamp the workpiece to your workbench.

4 Rest the front edge of the soleplate on the edge of the workpiece and align the narrow guide notch with the marked cutting line. Hold the fence against the side edge of the workpiece.

5 Start the saw and let it run up to full speed, then move it forward until the blade begins to cut. Move the saw forward slowly, with its soleplate flat on the workpiece and the fence running against its side edge. Let the saw do the work.

6 Let the saw run out at the end of the cut before releasing the trigger. Make sure that the blade has stopped before setting the saw down.

7 To make a cut beyond the reach of the fence, clamp a guide batten across the workpiece, parallel with the marked cutting line, and run the edge of the soleplate against it. Align the guide notch with the cutting line and check the position of the batten before starting the cut. Check that the clamps will not foul the saw body as you make the cut.

8 To make an angled cut, loosen the wing nuts at the front and back of the soleplate and rotate the saw body to the setting you want. Lock the nuts and test the cutting angle on some scrap wood.

9 Align the left-hand edge of the wider guide notch on the front of the soleplate with the marked cutting line. Start the saw and feed the blade into the workpiece, then move the saw forward to make the cut. Keep the notch aligned with the cutting line. Remember that cutting depths are reduced when making angled cuts.

Drilling wood

Almost every woodworking project involves drilling holes, and much of this will be done on your workbench.

You can of course use your cordless drill (see pages 32 and 42), but for workshop use, a corded drill is a worthwhile addition to your tool kit. Its higher drilling speeds allow you to work faster and more accurately, and the extra power means that you can drill bigger holes than a cordless drill can manage. It will also drill large or deep holes in dense masonry (page 44) that are beyond the capacity of a cordless drill.

Get to know your drill

Mains drills have power ratings in watts (W), ranging from about 500W for small single-speed drills up to 1,000W or more for big semi-professional models. Most have variable speed control from 0 to about 3000rpm; some have two speed ranges. The more powerful drills have the advantage of a 13mm chuck (most cordless drills have only a 10mm chuck) that will take larger-diameter twist and masonry drill bits.

Before you use the drill for the first time, read the instructions. These will tell you how to select and use the following:

- The correct speed setting for the material you are drilling.
- Drilling or hammer-drilling.
- Variable speed (a good 'soft start' is essential if a mains-powered drill is to be used for screwdriving).
- The correct torque setting (if available) for driving screws.
- Forward or reverse gear (for removing screws and freeing jammed drill bits).

Most corded drills come with a carry case; keep the drill in it when you are not using it. If you do not have a case, buy one and keep a set of drill bits in it. DIY stores stock a selection, so take your drill in to test its fit before you buy.

Using your drill

Follow the instructions given on pages 42–43 for cordless drills. These explain how to fit drill bits into the drill chuck, and how to carry out a range of basic drilling operations in wood and metal. Some mains drills (as the one shown on this page) have chucks that require the use of a chuck key to fit the drill bit.

The main differences between the drill types are that mains drills tend to be larger and heavier to handle than cordless drills, and they operate at much higher speeds. This last point makes it essential to clamp your workpiece to the bench before carrying out any drilling operation. The power of the drill can snatch a hand-held workpiece from your grasp.

Using a drill stand

A drill stand holds the drill in a movable clamp mounted on a vertical pillar. It can be clamped in place on your workbench, or can be bolted to it if you have a permanent bench rather than a portable one. The stand allows you to drill holes at precisely 90° to the surface of the workpiece, which is placed on the stand's base. This accuracy is particularly important for jobs such as making dowel joints or drilling the recesses in cabinet doors for spring-loaded hinges.

The stand can also be set up to allow you to drill stopped holes to a precise depth.

Take your drill with you when you shop for a drill stand, to ensure that it will fit in the clamp. Some drill stands may not accept drills with keyless chucks.

1 Mount the drill in the stand and fit the drill bit you want to use (see page 33 and panel right). Check the travel of the drill in the stand to ensure that the drill bit will penetrate the workpiece without drilling into the bench beneath the stand's base.

2 Place the workpiece beneath the drill and lower the drill bit so it just touches the surface. Adjust its position until the bit is at the drilling mark; then clamp the workpiece to the bench.

3 Set the depth of travel on the stand if you want to drill a stopped hole. Test the result on some scrap wood first.

4 Raise the drill, squeeze the trigger and lock it on. Lower it and drill the hole, then raise the drill while it is still running to clear sawdust from the hole. Release the trigger lock.

EXTRA DRILL BITS YOU MAY NEED

Dowel drill bits These resemble twist drill bits, but have a centre point and cutting spurs (like a miniature flat wood bit) that enable them to drill holes more accurately than a twist drill bit when making dowel joints (page 64). They are available in 6, 8 and 10mm diameters to match ready-cut hardwood dowel sizes.

Auger drill bits Used to drill deep holes in wood up to 25mm in diameter, for which a flat wood bit would be too inaccurate. They have a screw-threaded lead point and a cutting spur, with deep spiral flutes to clear the debris from the hole. They are available in diameters up to 25mm, in lengths of 120 and 200mm.

End mill bits Used to drill shallow stopped holes such as those required when fitting recessed cabinet hinges and certain assembly fittings (page 67). They come in a range of sizes, but the most widely used sizes are 25, 26 and 35mm.

Smoothing wood

Whether you are working with wood or man-made boards, you will need to sand the surface smooth before you can apply a decorative finish to it. Do this by hand, or use one of the many different power sanders now available.

Sanding by hand

The traditional way of smoothing wood is to wrap a piece of abrasive paper round a cork sanding block and to rub it along the direction of the grain. Sanding across the grain can leave scratches which are difficult to remove and can mar a clear finish. Glasspaper (often incorrectly still called sandpaper) is the cheapest sheet abrasive available, but aluminium oxide abrasives cut better and last longer. Both types are sold in standard 280 x 230mm sheets.

Glasspaper Made in a series of grades: 3, 2½ and S2 are coarse; M2, F2 and 1½ are medium; 1, 0 and 00 are fine.

Aluminium oxide paper Graded by numbers, running from 40, 50 and 60 (coarse) through 80, 100 and 120 (medium) to 150, 180 and beyond (fine).

You will usually need only fine grades for finishing planed timber and board surfaces, but you may need other grades for smoothing cut ends and board edges.

Note that silicon carbide abrasive paper, also known as wet-and-dry paper, is not intended for use in sanding bare wood. Its main DIY use is for smoothing metal and keying existing painted or varnished surfaces prior to redecoration.

Power sanding

For rapid removal of material without scratches, use a random orbit sander (see page 49) or a belt sander (see below). For getting a really smooth surface quickly, a finishing sander is the tool to use.

Using a finishing sander

This sander scrubs the surface of the wood, moving its baseplate in small orbits to give a very fine, scratch-free surface finish. Most sanders take pre-cut sheets of aluminium oxide abrasive paper equal to one third of a standard sheet in size, larger sanders take half sheets and smaller sanders (called palm sanders) take quarter sheets or special own-brand shaped sheets. Those with a dust extraction facility use perforated sanding sheets, often attached with touch-and-close (Velcro) fastenings. Make sure the sheets you buy will fit your sander.

1 Select the correct grade of abrasive sheet for the finish you want to achieve, and attach it to the sanding pad so that the holes in sheet and pad are aligned. Press it firmly into place on the pad.

2 Connect the sander to the hose of your vacuum cleaner using the adaptor provided, and switch the vacuum cleaner on. Or fit the dust bag if the tool has one.

3 Hold the tool against the surface you want to sand and switch on the power. Keep the sander moving backwards and forwards over the surface until it is smooth.

Using a belt sander

A belt sander is ideal for fast removal of material – for example, smoothing rough-sawn timber in the garden – and it will also strip paint and sand other materials such as plastic or metal if fitted with the appropriate abrasive belt. Note that there are more than a dozen different belt sizes available to fit different belt sander makes and models, so make sure you buy the correct size for your machine.

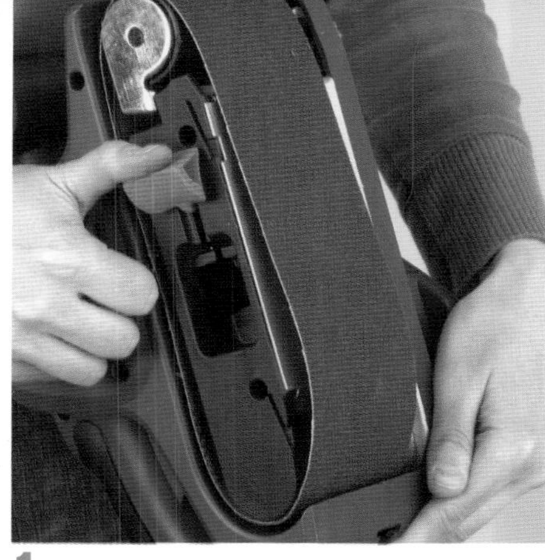

1 Release the roller tension lever and fit the belt over the rollers. Check that it is aligned with the edges of the rollers and tension the belt. Also check the tracking adjustment to ensure that the belt is positioned correctly. If it is not, it will run off the rollers in use.

2 Fit the dust bag or connect the sander to your vacuum cleaner hose via the adaptor supplied.

3 Switch the sander on and drive it over the surface you are sanding, working only along the grain direction. Keep the tool moving, or you will gouge out more material than necessary and leave an uneven finish. Change to finer grades of belt to achieve the finish you want.

Using a detail sander

This small orbital sander uses triangular sanding sheets attached to a matching pad, and is used for sanding into corners where an orbital sander will not reach. It does not usually have a dust bag. Some models have a rotating head that allows you to use all three corners of the sheet before replacing it; on fixed-head machines you reposition the abrasive sheet.

Shaping wood by hand

Most of the wood you use will be in standard sizes or will be a ready-machined moulding, and the range of sizes and cross-sections available will meet most of your requirements.

Sometimes, however, you need to shape a piece of wood for a particular purpose. Chisels, rasps and Surforms will help you to do this. If you need a component that is not available as a standard size or profile, you will have to alter its cross-section or shape. For this you need a plane and a router respectively. You can cut curves with a suitable saw (see pages 48 and 56). Rounded ends or surfaces curved in more than one direction need another approach.

Paring with a chisel

The simplest way to form a rounded end or corner is to trim (pare) it with a chisel.

1 Mark the shape you want to cut on your workpiece. Clamp it securely on your workbench, with some scrap wood or board underneath it to protect the bench surface. Cut off the bulk of the area with a saw before you use the chisel.

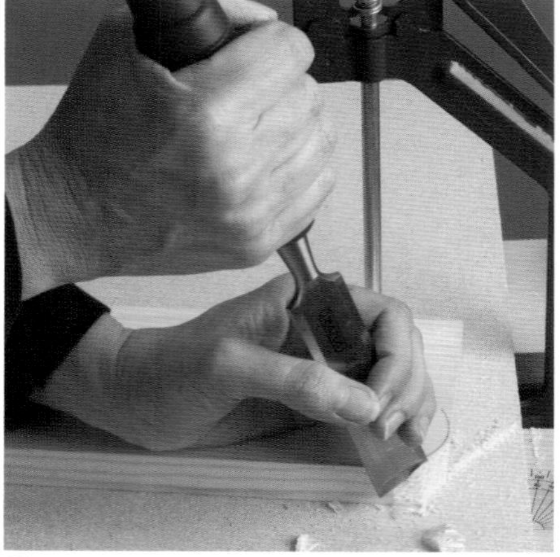

2 Use a sharpened chisel (see opposite) to pare the remaining wood. Continue trimming off finer and finer shavings until you have cut back to the marked line.

3 Smooth the resulting curve with a fine rasp (see below) and then abrasive paper.

Shaping with a wood rasp

A rasp is often confused with a file, which is a metalworking tool and has parallel cutting edges machined across its blade. Rasp blades have individual raised teeth, which remove wood in the same manner as a very coarse abrasive paper. The tool cuts on the forward stroke. If the teeth become clogged with wood fibres as you work, clean them with a wire brush.

1 Mark the curve you want to shape on the workpiece, and clamp it securely in a vice or the jaws of your workbench.

2 Hold the handle in one hand and place the tool on the work. Steady the tip of the blade with your other hand to keep the blade flat on the surface.

3 Push the tool forwards to start shaping the wood, repeating the stroke and moving the contact point round the curve as you work to create the required shape.

4 To shape a concave curve, use a round rasp or the rounded face of a half-round rasp and work from both sides of the workpiece to prevent splintering.

Shaping with a Surform

A Surform is a rasp with a difference, having individual cutting teeth stamped out of a thin steel sheet. Different tools in the range have a blade that is flat, gently rounded, curved along its length or rolled into a cylinder, and each is used in a different way. The blades are replaceable.

1 Hold the tool parallel with the wood grain and push it along the wood in a series of steady strokes.

2 Clear shavings from the inside of the blade from time to time. As you near the shape you want, turn the tool slightly to alter the cutting angle and produce finer shavings.

HELPFUL TIP

There are different Surforms for specific jobs. Use a half-round blade to shape concave curves, as for a rasp (see step 4 above). Use a round file to shape tight curves and holes – again work from both sides of the wood to avoid splintering. The Surform shaver tool has a smaller blade, and is designed to cut on the pull stroke. Use it in tight corners where the larger tools cannot reach.

Using a plane

A bench (jack) plane about 350mm long is used to reduce the cross-section of wood from an off-the-peg size to the dimensions required. Its blade must be sharp to cut the wood cleanly (see right) and must be correctly adjusted.

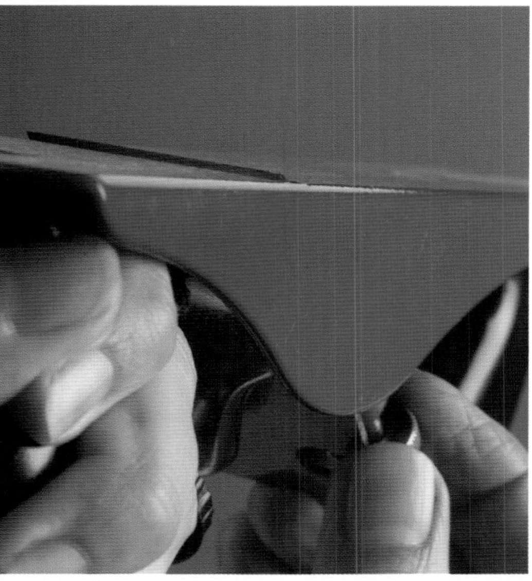

1 Sight along the sole plate of the plane to check that the blade is set square to it, and that it projects by the correct distance. Use the lateral adjustment lever behind the blade to set the cutting edge squarely, and the knurled nut between blade and handle to alter the blade projection.

2 Mark the cutting line on both faces of the workpiece and clamp it securely in your workbench. Hold the plane on the near end of the workpiece and use your free hand to grasp the front handle. Press the fingers of this hand against the side of the workpiece to guide the plane along its edge.

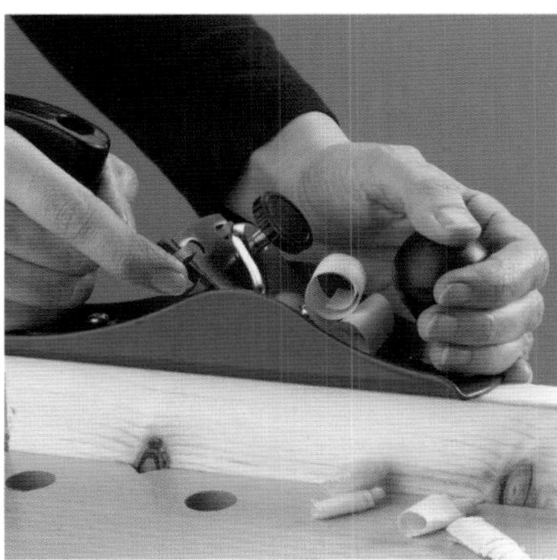

3 Plane from one end of the workpiece to the other in smooth, steady strokes. Let the plane run off the wood at each end of the stroke. Regularly check your progress towards the marked lines. Remove shavings from the jaws as you work.

Sharpening blades

Chisel and plane blades must be kept sharp if they are to cut well – and safely. You are more likely to force a blunt tool, with the increased risk of it slipping and injuring you or damaging the workpiece. To sharpen them you need an oilstone, a honing guide and some light machine oil.

Prepare a new oilstone for use by pouring a teaspoon of oil onto it and smearing it over the stone. Leave it to soak in, then apply a second teaspoon and repeat the process. Wipe off any excess oil with absorbent paper.

1 Clamp the blade in the honing guide, following the instructions. Check that the blade projects by the correct distance and tighten the clamping nuts fully.

2 Pour a little oil on the stone (use the fine side if it has two different faces). Move the guide up and down the stone in a figure of 8 pattern so you use as much of the surface as possible. You will wear a groove in the stone if you simply run the blade up and down the middle. Press down on the honing guide to keep the chisel tip flat against the stone.

3 Release the blade from the guide and rub its flat side back and forth across the stone to remove the curl of metal (the burr) formed on the cutting edge by the sharpening process.

Using a power planer

A power planer is useful for re-sizing work as well as jobs such as fitting doors. Read the instructions and ensure you know how to fit and change the cutting blades. For general bench work, use the planer in the same way as a bench plane. If you are working on a door, stand it on its edge and clamp it securely at one end in a portable workbench. Fit the dust collection bag or flexible extraction tube from a vacuum cleaner.

1 Mark the cutting line on the workpiece and set the cutting depth on the planer.

2 Place the front of the sole plate on the door's edge (the stiles), switch on the tool and with both hands guide it forwards along the length of the door taking care to keep the plane square. Let the planer run off the end of the workpiece before switching off. Repeat until you reach the marked lines.

3 Plane the top and bottom edges of the door from each side towards the centre. This will avoid splitting wood at the edge of the stiles where you will be planning across the grain.

4 You can use a power planer to chamfer edges at 45°, too, by letting the groove in the sole plate run along the edge of the workpiece. Mark guide lines on each face and plane down to them.

Using a router

Depending on which accessories and bits you fit, you can use a router to create edge profiles, grooves and recesses in solid wood and in man-made boards – MDF takes routed effects especially well. The bit rotates at extremely high speed, so the tool needs careful handling. Read the instructions and practise on some scrap before tackling your first job.

Setting up the router

1 To fit your selected cutting bit, use the spanner and locking pin provided. Place the router on its side and lock the chuck (called the collet) with the pin. Loosen the collet with the spanner and insert the bit as far as it will go. Tighten the collet fully and remove the locking pin.

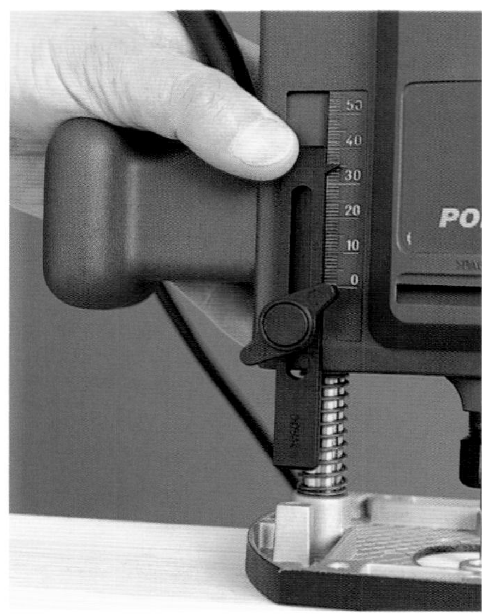

2 To set the routing depth, stand the router on the workbench and undo the winged nut securing the depth rod so it is free to move. Loosen the side handle, press the body of the router down until the bit touches the bench surface and tighten the handle again.

3 Read off the value indicated on the depth scale and add the required routing depth to it. Set the pointer on the depth rod to this combined figure and tighten the winged nut below the scale. Loosen the side handle and allow the router body to rise up on its springs. Check that the routing depth is correct by making test cuts on some scrap wood.

4 If the machine has a dust extractor facility, fit the adaptor and connect it to the hose of your vacuum cleaner.

Routing an edge profile

The router cutter rotates counter-clockwise when viewed from above the tool. Always feed the cutter into the wood from the right, so it is turning into the wood it is about to cut away. If you work in the opposite direction, the speed of the machine may wrench it from your grasp with some force, and you are likely to damage your work. When using a router for any job, make several shallow passes, lowering the cutter for each one.

1 Select the cutter you want to use and fit it in the collet. Set the cutting depth required (see step 2, below left). Clamp the work securely to your workbench, and check that the clamps will not impede the router as you move it along the edge.

2 Rest the edge of the soleplate on top of the workpiece. Switch the router on, press the body down on its springs and guide it sideways into the edge you are shaping. Cut in until the guide pin touches the edge of the workpiece.

3 Move the router slowly forwards, with the baseplate flat on the surface of the workpiece. Let the cutter run off at the far end of the cut and switch off the power.

Using a guide fence

To machine a groove parallel with the edge of the workpiece, fit the guide fence to the router soleplate using the guide plates and winged screws. Mark the position of the groove on the workpiece and set the cutting depth required.

1 Place the router on the workpiece with the cutter aligned with the marked line. Move the fence in against the edge of the workpiece and tighten the securing screws.

2 Position the router soleplate on the end of the workpiece with the fence pressed against its edge. Start the motor, loosen the side handle and press the router body down to the pre-set cutting depth. Tighten the handle again.

3 Start the motor and move the router forwards slowly to cut the groove. Keep the fence pressed against the edge of the workpiece. Let the cutter run out at the end of the groove and switch off the motor.

Using a guide batten

If you want to cut grooves further in from the edge of the workpiece than the fence will allow, use a guide batten instead (see page 48). Clamp it across the workpiece and guide the flat side of the router soleplate against it as you machine the groove. Check that the clamps will not impede the movement of the router.

Choosing router bits

Bits for DIY routers usually have 6mm diameter shafts and tungsten carbide cutting tips. Grooving cutters are plain, while shaping (edge) cutters have a guide wheel that runs against the edge of the workpiece and stops the bit from cutting too deeply. You can buy bits singly, but it is better to buy a set complete with a storage case.

Making joints

Joining wood to wood is an essential skill to master, but you do not need the skills of a cabinet-maker to make a good job. The type of joint you choose will depend on how strong you want it to be, and on how important its appearance is. This section will help you to make those choices, and demonstrate some basic skills that will be useful for a wide range of woodworking projects.

Basic joints

Butt joints These are the easiest joints to make. They are formed by aligning the two components (such as the sides of a box) so that the edge of one meets the end of the other. Butt joints can also be used to join wood edge to edge – to make a table top, for example. There are several options for joining the components:

- Fix the corner joint together with nails or screws and strengthen with wood glue.
- Reinforce a corner or edge joint with hardwood dowels or oval-shaped slips of compressed wood called biscuits.
- Use one of the ingenious knock-down fittings that were originally designed for use in flat-pack furniture (page 67).
- Use a metal angle bracket or a corrugated fastener (below), although these remain visible unless you take steps to hide them.

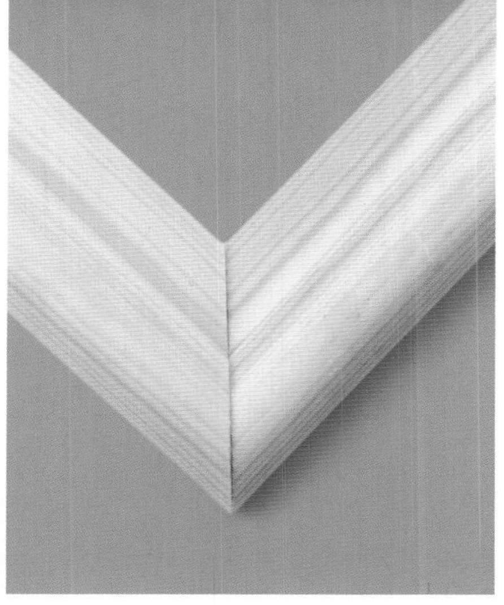

Mitre joints Butt joints that meet at a 45° angle are called mitre joints. They are used mainly in frames where the appearance of the corner joint is important – in a picture frame, for example, or where the architrave mouldings round a door opening meet. Like butt joints they can be nailed, screwed, dowel-jointed or biscuit-jointed, and are usually glued as well.

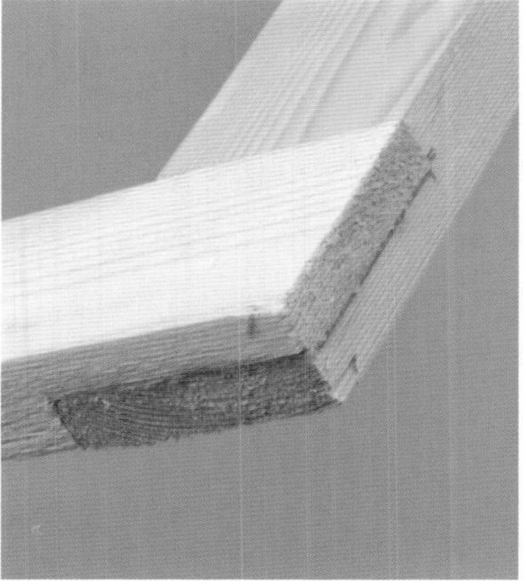

Halving joints As their name implies, halving joints are made by cutting away half of each component so they fit together neatly. The joint is stronger than a butt joint because the parts interlock. If the joint is also glued, it is even stronger because the glued contact area between the parts is bigger. The joint can also be nailed or screwed. Halving joints are used mainly in frames, and components can be joined in L, T or X shapes. The last two – called tee halving joints and cross halving joints respectively – need a slot cut in one or both components (see page 66).

Mortise-and-tenon joints These are serious woodworking joints, formed by fitting a shaped peg (the tenon) into a matching slot (the mortise). They are used mainly in fine furniture making, and are also found in framed doors, sash windows and the like. You are unlikely ever to need the complete joint, but cutting a mortise is essential for fitting a front door lock (page 198).

Using a try square to mark up joints

The most important feature of any woodworking joint is that it should be square, and the try square (page 50) is the tool to use for checking this. You also need a try square for marking cutting lines at 90°, both when cutting wood to length and when marking out halving joints.

1 Mark where you want to cut your workpiece to length. Hold the stock of the try square against its edge at the mark, with the blade across the width, and mark the line with a trimming knife or sharp pencil.

2 Turn the workpiece through 90°, align the try square with the marked line on its face and mark the line on its edge. Repeat the process to continue the marked line all the way round the workpiece. This continuous line will help you to cut the wood squarely to length.

3 To mark out a corner halving joint, clamp the two pieces together and check with the try square that they are at 90° to each other. Mark the edge of each piece on the face of the other.

4 Separate the two pieces and use the try square to continue the marked lines onto the edge of each piece.

Using a marking gauge

To mark out a halving joint, you need a marking gauge (page 50). This enables you to mark the thickness of the wood you want to cut away from each component to make the joint.

1 Loosen the thumbscrew on the block and slide it along the beam so the pin is approximately half the thickness of the workpiece away from the block. Tighten the screw.

2 Hold the block against one face of the workpiece and mark the edge with the pin. Then hold it against the opposite face and repeat the mark. If they coincide, the gauge is correctly set. If they do not, move the block slightly and repeat the process until they do. Tighten the screw fully.

3 Hold the block against the face of each component in turn, and slide it along so the pin marks the halving line on each edge of each component, extending to the end from the cutting line you marked with the try square.

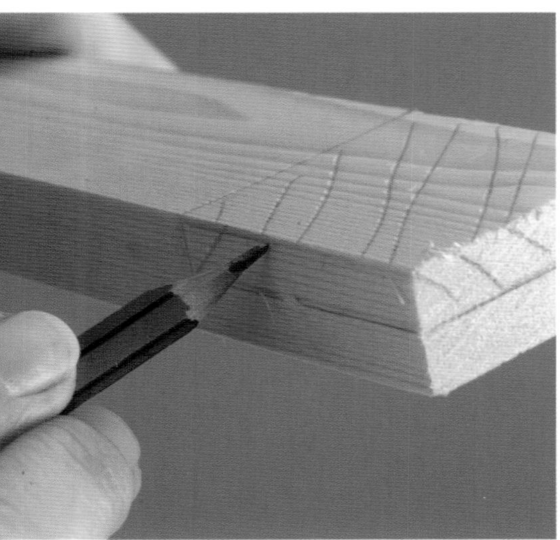

4 Join the edge marks across the end grain of each component. Then cross-hatch the area to be cut away in pencil on each component, ready for the joint to be cut.

Using a mortise gauge

The mortise gauge has two pins, one of which is movable, and is designed for marking the width of a mortise on the edge of the workpiece (or a door, if you are fitting a mortise lock). You set the pin separation first to match the width of the tenon (or the lock body). You then position the block so the two pins mark the mortise in the centre of the edge, in the same way as using a marking gauge to mark a centre line when marking out a halving joint. However, most woodworkers today drill out mortises with a flat wood bit that matches the mortise width, rather than cutting them with a chisel, so there is no need to mark it in the traditional way.

Making dowel joints

The positions of the dowel holes must be carefully matched in the two components being joined. Use a drill bit that matches readily available sizes of hardwood dowel – commonly 6 or 8mm in diameter. It's a good idea to use a drill stand or a dowelling jig to ensure that the holes are drilled at precise right angles to the face of the workpiece, and to the correct depth.

1 Use a combination square to mark a centre line on the end or edge of the first component to be drilled. Mark the dowel positions on this line and corresponding marks on the second component.

2 Drill a hole at each cross in the first component, making the holes a little deeper than half the length of the dowel. Use a drill stand or clamp the dowelling jig to the workpiece and use it to guide the drill bit.

3 Squeeze some wood glue into the holes and insert the dowels. Drill the dowel holes in the second component, ready for the joint to be assembled.

4 Check the alignment of the two components before squeezing some glue into the holes and assembling the joint.

5 Use a wooden mallet to drive the dowels home. Wipe away any surplus adhesive with a damp cloth.

HELPFUL TIP

One way to ensure accurate holes is to drill dowel holes in one of the pieces to join, then put specially designed metal marker pins in the holes. Offer up the pieces in exactly the position you want and knock them together firmly. The markers will leave indentations in the other piece of wood, ready for perfectly-matched holes to be drilled in it.

Making biscuit joints

You need a power tool called a biscuit jointer to cut the slots for the biscuits in the two components. Follow the instructions supplied with the tool to cut the slots. Then squirt woodworking adhesive into the slots, insert the biscuits and assemble the joint. Clamp the joint until the adhesive has set.

Making mitre joints

You can cut mitre joints freehand after marking the cutting angles with a combination square (see advice on using a try square on page 50), or by using a protractor and ruler. Alternatively, you can use a mitre box (page 50) to guide the saw. For the best results a mitre saw (page 50) is the ideal tool to use.

1 Mark the joint positions on each component. Set the cutting angle to 45° by rotating the saw's baseplate, then lock it.

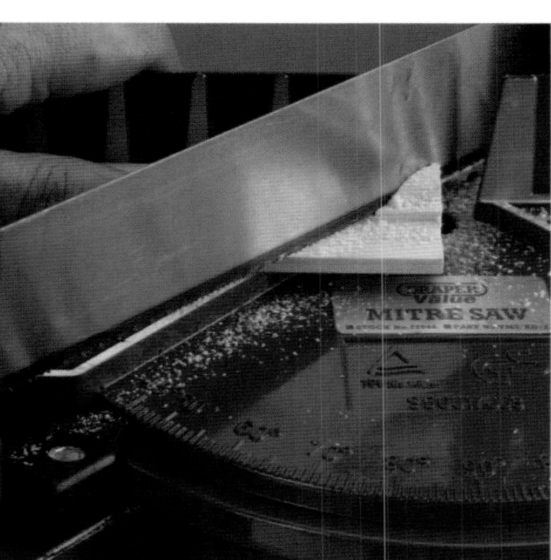

2 Clamp the workpiece in place on the base of the mitre saw and lower the saw blade to check that the cut will be aligned with the mark. Then make the cut. Repeat for the other component of the joint.

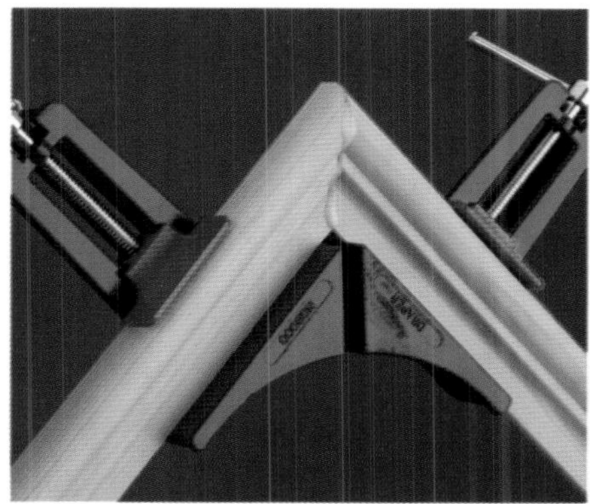

3 Apply adhesive to one mitred end and assemble the joint. Check that it is square, set it aside and leave it until the adhesive has set. You can reinforce the joint by driving a panel pin or a screw in from each side of the joint, or you can drill holes in each mitred face to take dowels. You can also reinforce mitre joints with biscuits (see above left). Special cramps are available (above) that will hold the joint accurately while the adhesive sets.

Making corner halving joints

Once you have marked out the two components (page 63), you can cut and assemble the joint. You need a tenon saw and some wood adhesive (or a glue gun).

1 Clamp each component on its edge and, starting the cut at an angle, begin to saw along the grain.

2 Then complete the cut down to the shoulder marks, holding the saw blade at right-angles to the workpiece.

3 Using a bench hook (page 51) to steady the workpiece, cut carefully across the width to form the shoulder.

4 Squirt some adhesive onto the cut faces of one component and assemble the joint. Clamp it for maximum bond strength, with cardboard or scrap wood between the clamp jaws and the workpieces to prevent dents. Use your try square to check that the joint is a perfect right angle. Wipe away excess adhesive with a damp cloth.

Making tee halving joints

As with a corner halving joint, use the two components you wish to join to mark the outline of the joint.

1 Clamp the two components together, check that they are at right angles and mark the edges of each component on the face of the other one.

2 Use a marking gauge to mark the joint thickness on the edge of each component. Cut the piece forming the leg of the tee in the same way as for a corner halving joint (page 65).

3 Using a tenon saw, make two parallel cuts on the waste side of the marks on the piece forming the cross-bar of the tee. Saw down to the halfway line. Then make several more cuts to the same depth within the waste area (below).

4 Clamp the workpiece securely and, using a sharp chisel, begin to chisel out the waste wood between the outer saw cuts.

5 Work from opposite sides in turn so as to avoid splintering, until the base of the notch is flat and is level with the halfway lines on the edges.

6 Test the fit of the two components, and shave away any excess wood with your chisel if necessary.

7 Glue and assemble the joint as for a corner halving joint (page 65).

Making cross halving joints

Mark out the joint from the two components as before, then use your tenon saw and chisel to create two matching notches as for cutting the cross-piece of a tee halving joint. Test the fit and assemble the joint as before.

USING A CHISEL

When using a chisel for making joints (or a recess for something like a hinge, page 193), it's important you hold it the right way round.

For perpendicular cuts, the bevel should be on the opposite side to the waste material: if it's on the same side, the recess could end up too large.

For removing the waste between perpendicular cuts or between saw cuts (as in Steps 4 and 5, left), use the chisel bevel down – or it will dig in.

Using knock-down fittings

As the use of man-made boards – especially veneered and plastic-coated chipboard – for making furniture became widespread in the 1970s, it was clear that traditional woodworking joints were not appropriate for joining this type of material. Manufacturers began to devise various mechanical means of connecting the panels, and the knock-down (KD) fitting was born.

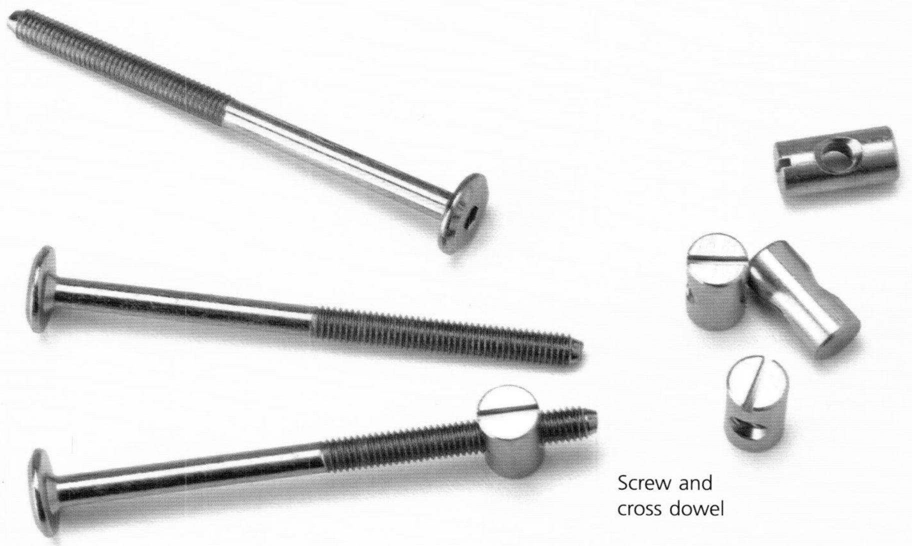

Screw and cross dowel

Types of knock-down fitting

These fittings are now widely used throughout the furniture industry, particularly in flat-pack furniture which the user assembles at home.

Early fittings were surface-mounted and obtrusive, but many of the newest fittings are completely concealed once assembly is complete. They are strong and easy to use, although the wordless instructions that often accompany flat-pack furniture do not always make this clear.

Here are some of the most common types, with details of how they are fitted and assembled. Familiarise yourself with them to make assembling flat-pack furniture easier. For more information on using knock-down fittings and assembling flat-pack furniture, see page 168-9.

Screwed fittings

One of the problems of using faced chipboard in furniture is that it does not hold screws very well. You can buy special countersunk chipboard screws (with raised threads) or thicker 'Confirmat' screws (secured with an Allen key). Or you can use an insert nut screwed into a hole in one piece, with a matching machine screw passing through the other piece.

An alternative (for fixing unit sides) is the cross dowel. An internally threaded steel dowel is set in a hole drilled in the face of one component, close to the edge. This receives the threaded end of a machine screw passing through a hole in the second component and into the edge of the first one. A slot in the dowel allows its threaded hole to be aligned with the machine screw. See page 169 for details of how to use this.

Cam fittings

A cam fitting is one of the neatest types of knock-down fitting. Various designs are available, but all work on a similar principle. A screwed peg is inserted into one component of the joint, and its peg located in a bush (the cam) inserted in a hole drilled in the other component. The cam is rotated through 90° to lock the two components together. See page 169 for some of the variants available.

One of the most popular cam fittings is the cam lock shown below and on page 169. The peg is screwed into a hole in one component and passes through a clearance hole into the cam lock fitted in the other component; rotating the cam secures the joint. A dowel-and-bush fitting is similar, except that the dowel passes right through the bush and is clamped by the screw.

Using any of these fittings from scratch requires very accurate drilling of holes.

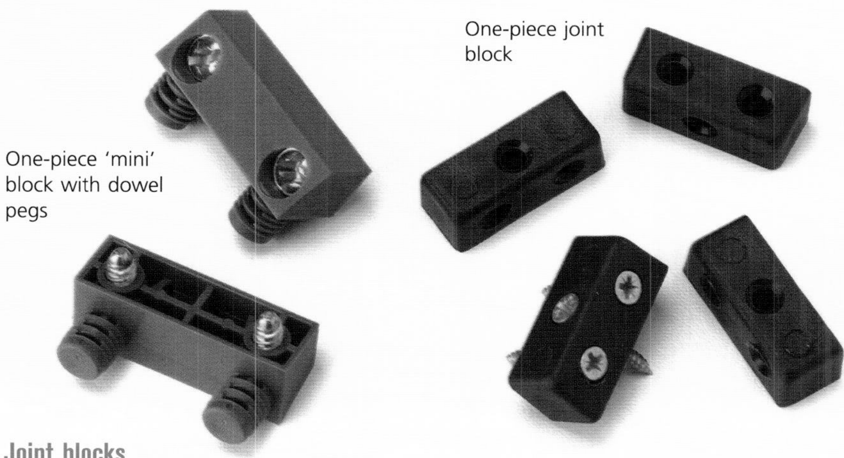

One-piece joint block

One-piece 'mini' block with dowel pegs

Joint blocks

The joint block was the earliest type of knock-down fitting. Its simplest form is a single rectangular block which fits into the internal angle between two butt-jointed components, and is fixed to each one with wood screws. The two-part block (see page 168) is stronger and easier to assemble once fitted in place. One block is screwed to each panel; then a short screw connects the two blocks together.

Another surface-mounted joint is the 'mini' block. This has one (or two) moulded plastic dowel pegs on one face which fit into 10mm holes drilled in one component with one (or two) thick screws (Euro screws) going at an angle into 5mm holes in the other. A single-peg variant of this can be used for securing worktops (using woodscrews).

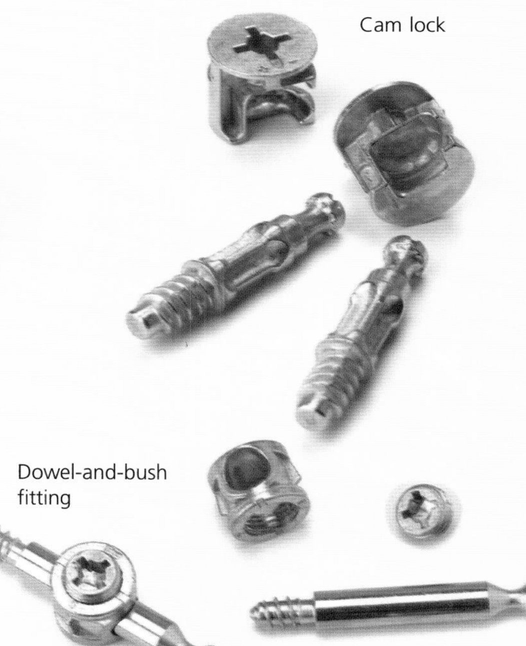

Cam lock

Dowel-and-bush fitting

Home decorating 3

Tools and preparation

There is a huge variety of tools available in DIY stores, and new ones are being introduced all the time. Choosing the right tools can make a job both faster and easier.

Steam stripper This is the most effective tool for stripping wallpaper or papered surfaces that have been painted.

It consists of a water reservoir and a hose, which is connected to a steam plate held against the wall. When the water heats up, steam is forced up the hose and out through the plate. This penetrates the wall covering and softens the adhesive underneath (painted paper must first be scored). It's worth buying a steam stripper if you plan to strip more than one room. They can also be hired.

Sanding tools Have a variety of abrasive papers to hand for smoothing filler or any roughness on stripped walls or woodwork. Wet-and-dry paper can be used dry or damped with water. A flexible sanding block has an abrasive coating on four sides. Rinse and squeeze out before using to rub down a painted surface before repainting. This destroys the glaze while removing dirt. Powered sanding tools clean stripped surfaces quickly. But don't try to strip paint with a sander as the abrasive will become clogged.

Wire brush Used to remove loose or flaking material, it is available as a hand tool or as a fitting for an electric drill.

Flexible sanding block

Filling knife A filling knife is like a scraper with a more flexible blade. Use it to press filler into holes and cracks and to level it flush with the surface.

Glass scraper

Combination shave hook

Triangular shave hook

Broad blade paint scraper

Narrow blade paint scraper

Broad blade filling knife

Narrow blade filling knife

Scrapers/strippers Scrapers or stripping knives have a flat, slightly sprung blade, which may be broad or narrow, for stripping paint from flat surfaces. Broad blade scrapers can also be used for stripping wallpaper. Glass scrapers are fitted with trimming knife blades and used for removing dried paint from glass surfaces.

Shave hooks, with triangular or curved blades set at right angles to the handle, are used to strip paint from moulded woodwork such as window or door frames and banisters. You can now buy a super-efficient scraper with a long handle and strong, sharp replaceable blades.

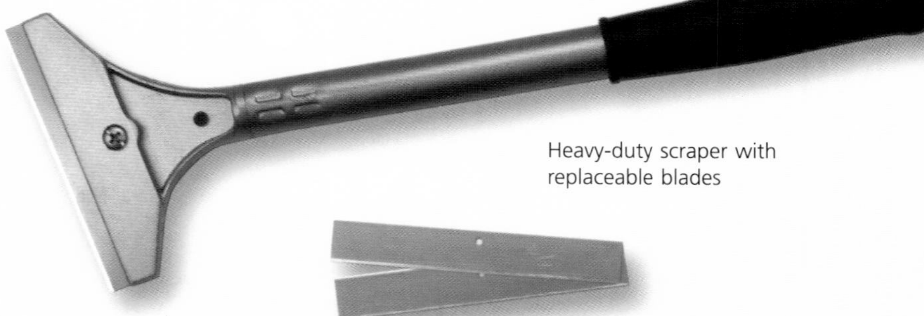

Heavy-duty scraper with replaceable blades

Hot-air guns Hot-air guns have completely superseded blowtorches to soften paint before stripping. They work like a superheated hair dryer and are much safer than blowtorches as there is no naked flame.

Hot-air gun

Protect yourself Each year thousands of injuries are caused by falls from chairs or insecure ladders, rust particles or tile chips flying into eyes or burns from paint stripping chemicals. Wear safety goggles to protect your eyes; wear a face mask if there is a lot of dust; protect your hands with suitable gloves; keep dirt out of your hair with a cap or scarf; and don ear defenders for noisy jobs.

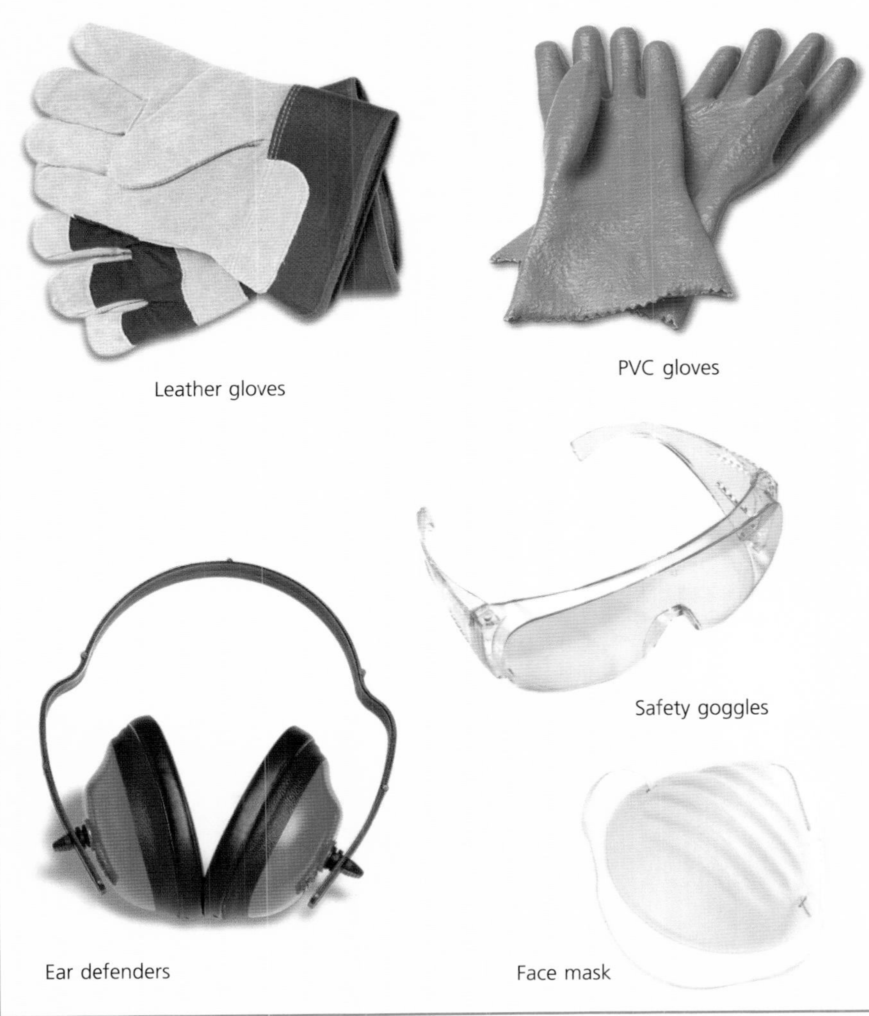
Leather gloves

PVC gloves

Safety goggles

Ear defenders

Face mask

Before you start to decorate

Most preparatory work creates mess and dust. Clear out everything you can and put remaining furniture in the middle of the room and cover with dustsheets. Tape plastic bags over wall and ceiling lights, sockets and switches to keep water out.

If you can, it is a good idea to lift carpets. Otherwise, protect them with dustsheets and possibly plastic sheeting as well. Take down curtains and lampshades and take off door furniture. All surfaces must be clean, dry and stable before you begin decorating. Treat damaged or problem areas and strip old paint and paper if necessary. If the surface of a stripped wall is rough in places, rub it with coarse abrasive paper on a sanding block.

Be height conscious

Use a stepladder that is high enough for you to reach the ceiling without stretching or standing on the top rung. In a stairwell, a combination ladder is useful. A stepladder can also act as a trestle for a scaffold board. Borrow another stepladder or hire a trestle for the other end of the board, which must be at least 38mm thick.

You can hire scaffold towers to use in some stairwells. The tower must be vertical, so take time to adjust the feet. Never reach forwards from a scaffold tower, or lean sideways from a ladder or stepladder.

Preparing walls and ceilings

Any professional decorator will tell you that preparation is crucial to a good finish. It's time-consuming and hard work stripping off old finishes – and even new, bare plaster needs priming – but your job will be far easier if you know what to do.

Painted or wallpapered surfaces

Gloss/eggshell painted
• If repainting and existing paint is sound, wash with sugar soap and water.
• If the emulsion is sound, wash the surface with sugar soap and water. Turn off the electricity before washing down walls.

Emulsion painted
• If emulsion is peeling, strip back to a sound base. There may be distemper underneath.
• If the emulsion is sound, wash the surface with sugar soap and water. Turn off the electricity before washing down walls.
• If papering, use heavy-duty paste with minimum water.

Distemper
Distemper forms a chalky barrier which prevents paint or paper adhering to the wall.
• Scrub off with a rough cloth or a nylon pan scourer and water.
• If there is a thick coating, damp the whole area, then scrape with a wide stripping knife. Never scrape bad cases of distemper without wetting it; it makes too much mess.
• Coat any remaining distemper with stabilising solution and leave to dry.

LEAD IN PAINT
Paint with a high lead content can cause lead poisoning. All household paint available in this country is now completely lead-free. However, paint in older houses – as a rough benchmark, pre-1960s – may have lead painted surfaces. Use a Lead Paint Test Kit to check. If the surface is sound, paint over it. If you need to strip the paint, take precautions: always wear a face mask conforming to BS EN149 and open the windows. Use a liquid chemical stripper, put all waste into a sealed bag and consult your local Environmental Health Department for details of safe disposal.

Standard wallpaper
• Soften ordinary wallpaper with water and a little washing-up liquid.
• Add a handful of cellulose paste to each bucket of water – it helps to hold the water on the wall.
• Use a scraper to lift off the paper.

Painted wallpaper
• Roughen the surface with coarse abrasive paper before you wet it or use a steamer.
• If the paint is thick, you may have to score the surface with a wallpaper scorer.
• Never use a wire brush – if slivers of metal become embedded in the plaster, they will rust and stain wall coverings.

Vinyls, washables and wipe-clean papers
• Vinyls are easy to strip – the vinyl skin can be pulled from its backing, then the backing can be soaked and stripped.
• With some modern papers and vinyls (called easy-strip), the backing can be left on the wall as lining paper for the next wallcovering. This only works if the paper is well stuck. If there are any loose areas, strip the whole lot off.
• For washable and wipe-clean wallpaper, use a steam wallpaper stripper. Score the surface so the steam can penetrate.

Tiles, textures and bricks

Imitation tiling
This can be hard to remove as it is often put up with strong adhesive.
• Pull the top layer from its backing.
• Soak off the backing and old adhesive with hot water, scraping it away as it softens.
• Try using a steam wallpaper stripper.
• If the adhesive is very stubborn, use a hot-air gun to soften it.

Textured coatings
Thick coatings applied by brush or roller on ceilings and walls are difficult to remove.
• Modern products are based on emulsion paint and may be removed with a proprietary textured-paint remover, which works like a chemical paint stripper.
• You could try using a steam wallpaper stripper (see right).
• Textures applied before the 1970s may contain asbestos. It is safe to remove them using a steam stripper (right) but never remove a textured coating by sanding as this may release asbestos fibres into the air.
• If you simply want to repaint the textured surface, lightly scrub it with a mild solution of sugar soap and water and allow to dry.

Polystyrene tiles
Expanded polystyrene ceiling tiles can only be painted with emulsion paint. To remove tiles, lever each one from the surface and scrape off the glue (see page 76).

Ceramic tiles
If tiles are to be painted, make sure they are clean and dry, then use a specialist tile paint. You cannot hang wallpaper over tiles so you may wish to remove them (page 76). This is hard work, and may necessitate replastering the wall.

Cork tiles
Cork tiles cannot be painted over, though you may be able to cover them with lining paper and wallpaper.
• Prise each tile away from the wall with a wide stripping knife or a bolster chisel.
• To remove hard lumps of adhesive, follow the instructions for taking down expanded polystyrene tiles (page 76).

Exposed brick
• Brush the bricks to remove dust.
• Paint interior bricks with emulsion or leave unpainted.

Steam-stripping a ceiling

Use a steam wallpaper stripper to remove old painted or washable wallpaper from a ceiling. Because you will be using the steaming plate above head level, take precautions to stop yourself being splashed by hot water. Wear a baseball cap or similar headgear, safety goggles, a long-sleeved shirt and work gloves. Set up a work platform across the room so you can hold the steaming plate in front of you as you work across the ceiling strip by strip. Put down plenty of dustsheets.

A steam stripper will also help to remove old textured ceiling finishes such as Artex, allowing you to scrape the softened coating off area by area. Be warned, however; this is a messy and time-consuming job, and you may prefer to use one of the specialist textured coating smoothing compounds now available – see page 74 for details.

Problems with surfaces

Efflorescence
Damp can cause chemicals in mortar or plaster to come to the surface and form a whitish fluff called efflorescence. Brush this off the wall, then apply an alkali-resisting primer or a stabilising solution.

Stains
Cover stains made by tar deposits in a flue or rust marks on a wall, for instance, with an aluminium primer-sealer. This stops the stain from bleeding through the new paint.

Damp
Do not isolate damp by applying an impervious coating – this will cause it to move elsewhere, creating fresh problems. Find and cure the cause (page 246).

Holes and cracks
Brush away any loose or crumbling plaster from small holes and cracks, and repair the area with an appropriate filler (page 78).

Larger holes, gaps and cracks require more extensive treatment (pages 222–7).

Uneven plaster
Level out slight irregularities with a skimming coat of ready-mixed plaster.

Preparing and stripping wood and metal

Whether your woodwork or pipework is brand new or old and coated with layers of paint, it will need some preparation before you decorate. Adding another layer of paint to a door, window frame or radiator will seldom hide imperfections in the layer beneath.

Woodwork

New bare wood

• Apply knotting solution to all visible knots to stop resin bleeding from them.
• Look for cracks and blemishes which need filling. Use fine surface filler for interior wood.
• Smooth the wood by hand, using fine abrasive paper, working with the grain. Alternatively, use an orbital or multi-purpose power sander, again working with the grain. Be gentle, because with power tools even the finer grades of abrasive paper remove wood very fast.

Old bare wood

• If there are signs of wet rot – soft patches easily penetrated by a penknife blade – then these will need dealing with: see page 412.
• Fill all cracks and gaps with a flexible wood filler. When set, smooth with fine abrasive paper.
• As soon as preparatory work is complete, apply a coat of wood primer.

Painted wood

If paint is sound and in good condition, do not strip it unless the thickness causes an obstruction – making windows hard to open, for instance. Instead, clean with sugar soap and water. This removes dirt and keys the existing paint so that new paint will adhere to it.

Keying (roughening a gloss surface very finely) is essential: without it, new paint is easily damaged and scratched off.

Where paintwork is slightly damaged but mainly sound, only work on the damaged areas. Rub with a damp flexible sanding pad to remove all loose material, wipe clean and allow to dry. Prime bare wood where it is exposed. Then lightly rub the whole area with very fine abrasive paper and wash with sugar soap, as for sound paintwork. Fill small chips with fine surface filler.

Varnished wood

Use a chemical paint stripper or varnish remover to get back to bare wood.

Stained wood

If the wood is to be painted and the stain is old, rub down with a flexible sanding pad. If the wood is to be sealed to give a natural finish, remove the stain with a wood bleach. Follow the instructions on the can.

Wood treated with preservative

Coat the wood with an aluminium primer-sealer. Otherwise the preservative may bleed through.

Metal

New iron and steel

Wipe off grease with white spirit on a lint-free rag, then use abrasive paper to remove rust and wipe clean. Apply metal primer.

Old rusted iron and steel

• Wear safety goggles and leather gloves for protection.
• Use wire brushes and abrasive paper to remove all rust.
• Fill any serious pitting with epoxy-based filler. If it is left untreated, rust can eat through thin metal, leaving holes. This quite often happens to old steel window frames.
• Epoxy-based filler is a rust inhibitor, so it can be applied to sound surfaces still showing signs of rust discoloration.
• Before painting the metal, apply a metal primer. This contains zinc to prevent further rusting. Different primers are available for different types of metal.

Alternatively Use a rust-killing paint (such as Hammerite) directly on the rusted metal. No primer or undercoat needed; paint can be brushed on or sprayed from an aerosol.

Aluminium alloy and anodised aluminium (such as windows and patio doors)

These materials have a very shiny surface and, in good condition, do not need painting. But if you want to match a decorating scheme, clean them first with white spirit, dry off and then apply enamel paint direct. No primer or undercoat is necessary.

Copper (such as central heating pipes)

Remove any protective grease with white spirit and rub away any discoloration with fine abrasive paper or wire wool. Wipe clean, then apply gloss paint or enamel paint direct. No primer or undercoat is necessary. Ordinary gloss can withstand the heat of water passing through the pipes.

Stainless and chromium-plated steel

This should not require painting but, if desired, apply gloss paint or enamel paint direct after removing any grease with white spirit.

Painted metal window frames

Do not interfere with sound paint on metal, unless a build-up of paint is making frames too tight. If the paint does not need stripping, clean down the frames with sugar soap and water. Key the surface with fine abrasive paper or wire wool, then apply a primer and gloss paint.

Where rust is lifting paint

This may be found in older houses where window frames were not galvanised. Wear safety goggles and brush away flaking paint with a wire brush. Scrape back the remaining paint to reveal bright metal. Do not ignore any hidden rust; it can lead to a new attack. Treat with rust inhibitor, apply a metal primer and finish with gloss paint.

A hot-air gun will make paint bubble up from the surface. It can then be scraped away with a stripping knife – or a shave hook for tricky shaped mouldings.

GREEN STRIPPING

Water-based paint strippers are a safe, non-irritant alternative to traditional chemical strippers. Suitable for wood, metal and stone, they will remove all kinds of paints, varnishes and waxes. Take care, though, with the disposal of old lead and solvent-based paint after stripping (page 72).

Stripping wallpaper

Stripping wallpaper cannot be rushed. If the paper is not wet enough, it will be difficult to remove. You can use a scraper and water or a steam stripper. In either case, it's a good idea to perforate the paper first using an orbital wallpaper scorer. This allows water or steam to penetrate the surface and soften the paste.

Tools *Bucket; sponge or old paintbrush; dust sheets; wide stripping knife; wallpaper scorer (serrated scraper or orbital scorer).*

Materials *Water; wallpaper paste; washing-up liquid.*

Stripping standard wallpaper

1 Cover the floor with dustsheets.

2 Go over the surface of the paper with a scoring tool.

3 Fill a bucket with warm water. Add a handful of wallpaper paste and a squirt of washing-up liquid. The paste helps to hold the water on the wall and the detergent acts as a wetting agent which speeds up the penetration of the water.

HELPFUL TIP

Wetting the wall with a hand-held garden spray gun is quicker than using a brush or sponge.

4 Wet a whole wall, applying water generously with a large sponge or an old paintbrush.

TEXTURED WALL COATINGS

Removing a thick textured coating is a messy job. You can use a textured-paint remover on modern paint-based coatings or a steam wallpaper stripper (see page 72). Clear the furniture and protect the floor with newspaper, which can be thrown away as it becomes covered. Wear a cap, gloves and goggles.

Removing the coating

• If using paint remover, apply thickly with a large paintbrush and leave it to penetrate as indicated on the container. When the surface has softened, strip it off with a wide-bladed wallpaper scraper. Wash the surface with water and washing-up liquid before redecorating.

• If using a steam wallpaper stripper, allow the steam to break through the paint barrier and soften the material underneath. Then scrape it off with a stripping knife.

Alternatively You can cover a textured coating with a thin skim of plaster, or by putting up sheets of plasterboard using battens, but for a cheaper solution, there is a smoothing compound which can be applied to a wall or ceiling with a wide flexible knife.

SAFETY NOTE Never sand a textured coating to smooth it. Many old (pre-1970s) coatings contain asbestos which is dangerous if inhaled. Removing it wet, using a steam stripper, is safe. If you suspect the coating you are removing may contain asbestos, bag up the material you strip away and contact your council for advice on disposal.

5 Leave the water to soak into the surface for at least five minutes.

6 Test to see whether the paper is ready to be stripped. Slide the edge of a wide stripping knife under the wet paper either at the bottom of the length or at a seam.

7 Hold the knife at an angle of about 30° and push it away from you, up the wall. Do not let the blade gouge the plaster. If the paper does not wrinkle and is hard to lift, it needs to soak for longer.

8 Sponge on more water if necessary and try the test again – if the paper wrinkles, pull it away from the wall upwards. It should come away in a fairly big strip.

9 Ease the stripper under the wet covering again and continue to peel away paper. If the paper won't come off the wall despite a good soaking, use a steam wallpaper stripper.

SAFETY TIP

If you have to get paper out from behind a light switch or socket, switch off electricity at the consumer unit (fuse box) before loosening the faceplate screws.

Stripping washable, heavy relief and painted paper

Wallpaper that has been covered with paint can be removed in the same way as standard wallpaper, but the coating must be scored vigorously to allow the water to penetrate.

Tools *Bucket; sponge or old paintbrush; wide stripping knife; water; wallpaper paste; washing-up liquid; scoring tool, serrated scraper or wallpaper scorer.*

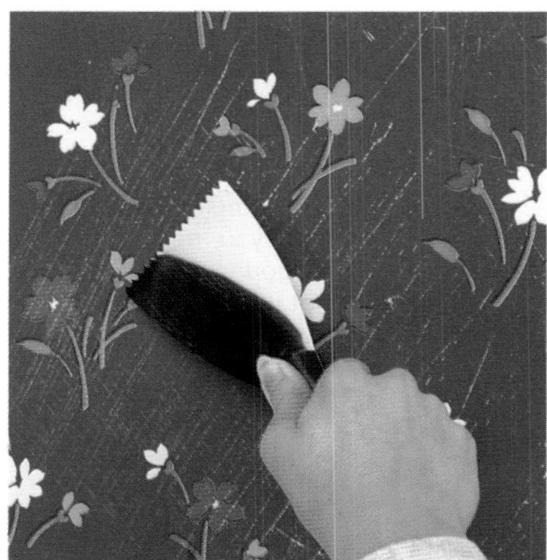

1 Score the surface with a serrated scraper or orbital scorer so that water can soak through into the paper. Do not use a wire brush or wire wool – small pieces of metal may become embedded in the plaster underneath and cause stains on the new paper surface.

2 Apply water and strip the covering as for standard wallpaper. If the covering comes off easily, it may be that it was not put up properly. Alternatively, the walls may be damp, in which case find the cause and remedy the problems before redecorating.

USING A STEAM STRIPPER

If you want to strip a room in a day, your best bet is to use a steam stripper.

Tools *Steam stripper; wallpaper scorer; rubber gloves; safety goggles; wide stripping knife; dustsheets.*

Before you start Cover the area with dustsheets and put on some old work clothes and a pair of rubber gloves. Read the instruction leaflet carefully.

1 Fill the tank, switch the stripper on and wait for the light to come on, indicating that the stripper is ready. This usually takes about ten minutes, when steam begins to come out of the perforated plate. While you are waiting, score the surface of the paper with a scoring tool.

2 Strip a length at a time, working from the bottom up, loosening stubborn areas with a stripping knife. Hold the plate at the bottom of the length. Keep it in position until the paper around it shows signs of damp – usually after about a minute.

3 Holding the plate in one hand over the next area you are going to strip, use the other to start scraping the paper from the first area.

4 Top up the tank as necessary, first switching off and leaving the stripper to cool for half a minute.

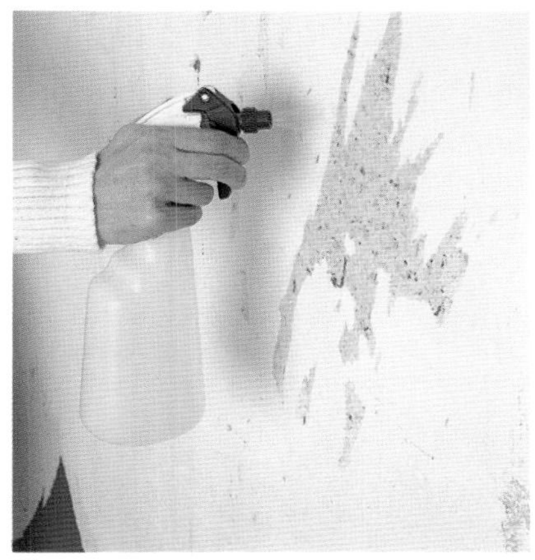

5 If you find you've missed any bits, spray them with a garden spray gun. This will soak in and allow you to scrape them off easily.

TIP Take care when using a stripper on plasterboard. The steam will soften the surface, so use a stripping knife as little as possible and do not dig it in.

Vinyls and easy-strip papers

1 With a fingernail or knife blade, lift a corner of the covering away from its backing paper.

2 Peel the covering away from the backing, keeping it as close as possible to the wall. If you stand back and pull the strip of top paper towards you, it may pull the backing paper with it.

3 If the backing paper is stuck securely to the wall and in good condition, use it as lining paper for the next covering. But if it is damaged or not stuck firmly, strip it off as for standard wallpaper.

SAFETY TIP

If you are stripping wallpaper around power points, wall lights or light switches, protect them with plastic bags taped on with masking tape, and switch off electricity at the consumer unit (fuse box) before using water or steam around them.

Removing tiles from walls and ceilings

Leaving tiles in place and painting or tiling over them is often the easiest option, but if you want a flat finish for painting or wallpapering the tiles will need to be removed.

Ceramic tiles

Tiles in older houses may be stuck to the wall with cement mortar – sometimes 15mm thick. If you remove them you will probably need to have the wall plastered before you can decorate. Tiles stuck with adhesive are easier to get off, but they may pull plaster with them. In this case, the surface will need to be made good.

Tools *Heavy duty gloves; safety goggles; dust mask; wide steel masonry chisel (bolster); club hammer; paint scraper. Possibly also: power sander.*

Before you start Put on protective clothing – splinters of glass from the glaze will fly in all directions as you chip away at the tiles. Close doors to prevent dust escaping from the room.

1 Prise the tiles away from the wall one at a time with a bolster chisel and a club hammer. Some will come away in one piece, others may crack and break. There is no easy technique – continue to chisel until you have removed all of the tiles.

2 Use a paint scraper to remove any adhesive left on the wall. If the tiles were stuck with cement mortar you will need to continue chipping with the bolster chisel.

Polystyrene tiles and cork tiles

Tools *Wide stripping knife or bolster chisel; safety goggles; possibly a hot-air gun.*

1 Lever tiles away from the surface using a wide stripping knife or bolster chisel. They are more likely to break into pieces than come off as one complete tile. Although the tiles will come away relatively easily, some adhesive – which is difficult to remove – is likely to remain on the walls after that.

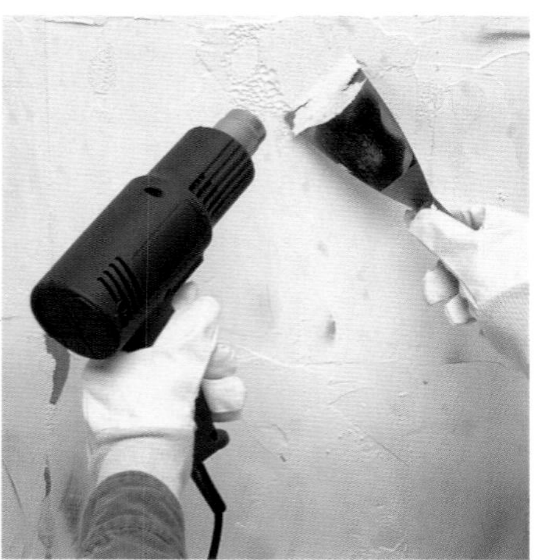

2 Use a hot-air gun to apply heat direct to the remaining adhesive and then scrape it off with a stripping knife.

Stripping poor paintwork

Paint can be stripped with the help of chemicals or heat – often it is best to use a combination of methods. If wood is to be repainted, you won't have to strip off every bit of paint, as you must if you want to varnish the wood.

Using a hot-air gun

A hot-air gun will soften paint so that scrapers can remove it more easily. Some have an attachment to shield glass from heat when stripping window frames. Because of the risk of fire, do not put any newspaper on the floor. Instead, keep a steel tray (an old baking sheet is fine) below to catch paint peelings. Wear cotton gloves (rubber gloves will make your hands too hot in the heat caused by the gun).

1 Soften the paint by moving the hot-air gun backwards and forwards. The heat is very strong so do not concentrate in one area or you may burn the surface. The paint should soften in seconds.

2 Strip the paint from flat areas with a broad-bladed scraper. Push the tool away from you or upwards. When scraping a vertical surface, make sure your hand is not immediately below the hot paint, which may drop onto it.

3 When using a shave hook on mouldings, hold it at an angle when pulling so that hot paint cannot fall onto your hand.

4 If you accidentally scorch the surface, rub fine abrasive paper along the grain to remove charred wood.

5 Apply a wood primer and paint.

> **SAFETY TIP**
>
> Any pre-1960s paintwork is likely to contain lead. Wear gloves and a face mask when stripping old paint. Seal the waste in a bag and contact your local council for details of how to dispose of it – don't burn it.

Paint strippers

Chemical strippers are good at removing paint completely from wood, especially if you want to varnish it. They are applied in liquid form or as a gel or paste and are useful for stripping window frames, where heat could crack the glass. However, this method can be slow and costly. Always neutralise strippers – as directed on the container – before redecorating.

Use gels or pastes on heavily-painted surfaces: some are left on for some time with a blanket covering and claim to be able to remove up to 18 coats of paint in one go.

Using paint strippers Wear safety goggles and protect your hands with PVC or rubber gloves. If you spill any on your skin, wash off immediately. Open all the windows because these products give off strong fumes.

1 Use an old paintbrush to apply liquid stripper. The paint wrinkles and breaks up about 15 minutes after application. Give the stripper enough time to work – if you try to strip the paint too soon it will not come away and another application of stripper will be needed. If you leave it too long, it will dry and begin to harden again.

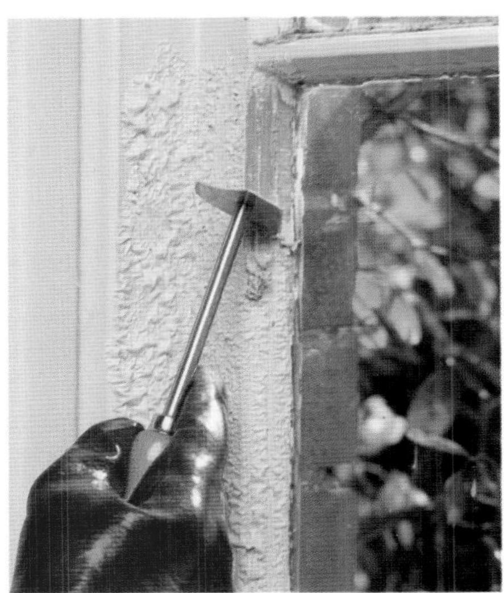

2 Remove the paint using a shave hook on moulded surfaces – pulling the tool towards you.

3 On flat surfaces, push a paint scraper away from you. A heavy build-up of paint will need more than one application.

Using paste or gel strippers Use this type of stripper on vertical surfaces. It will not run to the floor, is easier to control and more effective.

1 Protect the surrounding area with newspaper. Apply the stripper in a thick coat, which will slowly set on the surface while the chemicals work beneath.

2 Follow the manufacturer's instructions; it is usually best to cover the paste with cling film and occasionally spray it with water.

3 After the recommended time (hours rather than minutes), scrape or peel away the paste – it will bring the old paint with it.

Choosing fillers

A huge range of fillers is available, with new ones being brought out all the time. Here are the main ones.

Hairline crack/fine surface filler For fine cracks in walls or woodwork.
• Either applied as liquid from a tin (no sanding required) or with filling knife.
• Dries in less than an hour.
• Not suitable for use outside.

Paste filler For cracks up to 2mm, small blemishes indoors and gaps in wood.
• Comes in tubes and tubs.
• Surface dry in 30–60 minutes; rapid repair versions dry in 5–20 minutes.

Internal plaster repair Gives a smooth finish to damaged plaster surfaces.
• Sold in ready mixed and powder form.
• Fill deep holes (over 50mm) in layers.
• Dry in 24 hours.

Exterior filler General filling for external masonry, concrete and paving.
• Available ready mixed or as powder.
• Sets in 1 hour and is drillable.
• Dries to a grey, weatherproof finish.

All-purpose filler For cracks and holes in most materials, inside and out.
• Powder or paste; some types are mixed with a diluted adhesive for outside use.
• Dries to a tough, weather-resistant surface that should be painted.
• Do not expose to permanent damp.

Polyester-based metal filler Cracks in metal gutters and downpipes.
• Chemically bonded filler and catalyst.
• Quick setting – use within 5 minutes.
• Can be sanded after about 20 minutes.

Wood fillers Repairs cracks and small holes in wood, inside and out.
• Flexible wood fillers are for cracks and holes in wood and can be used both inside and out. Ready for sanding in two hours.
• Wood stopping can be used on natural wood surfaces. Comes in a range of colours to match wood and sets quickly.
• High-performance wood filler is used for serious wood repairs and sets quickly. Can be sanded or planed and will take screws.

Frame sealant Fills gaps between masonry and window or door frames.
• Flexible, rubbery paste applied from container fitted into cartridge gun.
• Forms a skin after about 4 hours and can then be painted.
• Available in white and other colours.

Foam filler Largely used for holes or gaps round pipes through a wall, inside or out.
• Sticky foam applied to dampened surface from pressure spray.
• Expensive but good for awkward areas.
• Workable for about 5–7 minutes.
• Expands to 60 times its original volume

Filling small holes and cracks

Small cracks, dents, holes or gouges in plaster walls or ceilings can be repaired with interior filler.

Tools *Old paintbrush; filling knife; abrasive paper and block, or power sander. Possibly also: trimming knife; large paintbrush; cold chisel; garden spray gun; length of wood.*

Materials *Suitable filler.*

1 Rake out the crack with a filling knife. If the crack is in plasterboard and the paper surface has been torn, cut off jagged edges with a sharp trimming knife.

2 Brush the crack with a dry brush to remove dust.

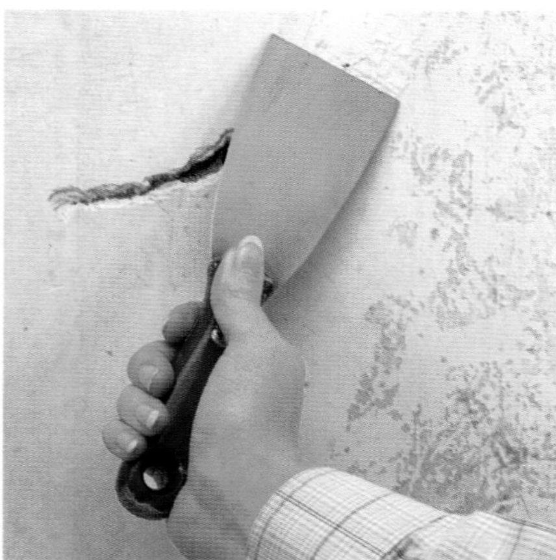

3 Load filler onto the end of the filling knife blade and draw the blade across the crack. Scrape the excess off the blade, then draw it down the crack to remove excess filler from the wall and smooth the surface.

4 For deeper holes, build up the surface in layers, working from the edges. Wait about two hours for each layer to dry before applying the next.

5 When the filler is completely dry, smooth it to the level of the surrounding surface with medium or fine abrasive paper wrapped round a wooden block, or use a power sander with fine-grade sandpaper.

> **HELPFUL TIP**
>
> If the filler pulls away from the wall as you smooth it with your filling knife, try wetting the blade.

Filling awkward gaps and holes

Some holes cannot be filled properly with standard interior fillers. You can buy special fillers to deal with them.

Awkward gaps include the long cracks running from the top to the bottom of a wall – especially in stairwells. These can be filled, but if they open up again, this could indicate a structural problem and you need advice from a builder or surveyor.

Settlement cracks often occur at wall joints or wall-and-ceiling joints and between walls and woodwork. All these can be filled with a flexible sealant.

Foam filler

Deep cavities – around a pipe through a wall, for example – can be difficult to fill but the job is easier if you use foam filler. Wear the gloves supplied – the foam is very sticky until it sets.

Before you start Experiment to see how fast the foam comes out of the nozzle and how much it expands.

1 Brush any dust out of the hole and dampen the surface with water.

2 Allowing for expansion, release foam into the hole. You may only need a thin bead.

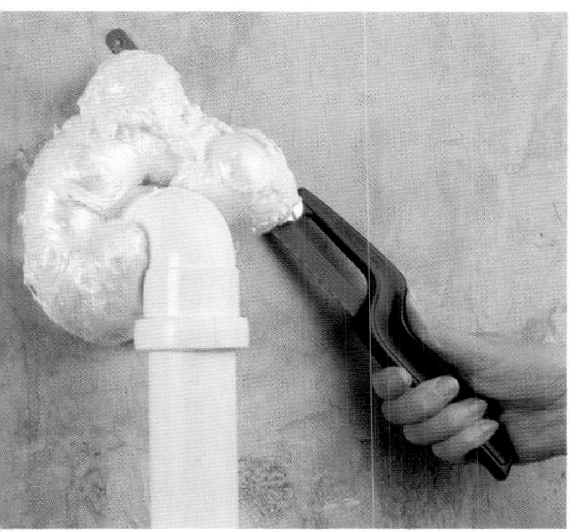

3 Leave the foam for 1 to 2 hours. When it has set, cut any excess away with a hacksaw blade or a sharp knife. Wear a mask to avoid inhaling the dust.

Flexible sealant

Gaps between walls and window frames, skirting boards, door frames and staircases, move. Therefore they should be filled with a flexible sealant that sticks well and resists cracking. The sealant is applied with a cartridge gun.

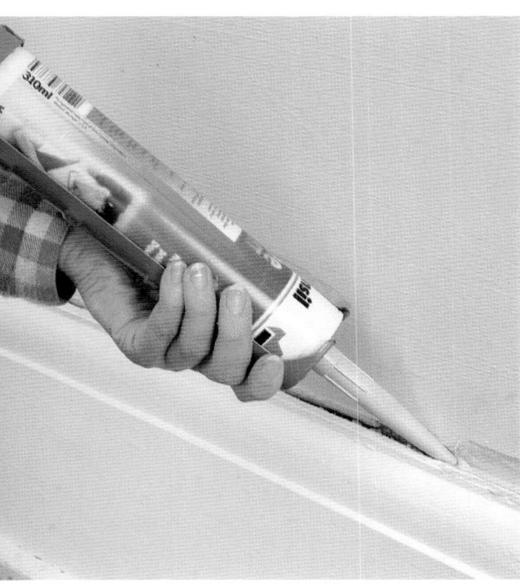

- If the cracks are deep, half-fill them with thin strips of expanded polystyrene before applying the sealant.
- Make sure the sealant reaches to both sides of the gap. Press it in and smooth the surface with a wetted fingertip.

> **HELPFUL TIP**
>
> Instead of licking your fingertip to run along a bead of sealant, dip it in a solution of 50:50 water and washing-up liquid. If you have sensitive skin, use the back of a wetted teaspoon instead.

Using wood filler

The type of wood filler you choose depends on whether the wood is going to be painted or simply waxed or varnished.

Wood must have a well-prepared surface before the final finish is applied. This means filling any holes before the wood is finally sanded smooth. If the wood is to be left its natural colour, buy a wood filler that matches. If it is going to be painted, fill with an interior filler.

Tools *Filling knife; abrasive paper; electric sander.*

Materials *Interior filler or wood filler.*

1 If you plan to paint the wood, use a power sander with fine abrasive paper to key existing paintwork. Then wash it with a solution of hot water and sugar soap.

2 If you are repainting the area, use flexible wood filler to fill any defects such as cracks or dents. Be sure to press the filler in firmly and scrape away any excess.

3 Once the filler has set hard, sand it smooth ready for painting.

4 If you intend to apply a finish through which the wood can be seen – stain, wax or varnish – then sand it smooth and fill it with a wood filler (known as stopping) that matches the colour of the bare wood as closely as possible.

5 Press the stopping into the holes and cracks, taking care not to spread it into the surrounding grain.

6 Wait until the stopping has dried to the same colour all over – usually about 30 minutes – then sand it flat.

Filling an open woodgrain

If a wooden door has a very open grain, and you want to achieve a smooth painted finish, you will need to work in a paste of fine-surface filler. Apply the filler with a flexible filling knife, pushing it right into the grain. Then wipe away the excess with a damp rag.

Tools for painting

As with all tools, quality counts. Buy the best painting tools you can afford and take care of them.

Brushes Good quality bristle brushes improve with use, as the tips become rounded and any loose bristles come out. Cheap brushes usually contain far less bristle for a given width, and they are often badly anchored so that the bristles tend to fall out. Use cheap brushes for applying wood preservatives to rough timber or removing dust after sanding down. Bristle brushes are best for solvent-based paints.

Angled cutting-in brush This brush has an angled tip which gives more control on an edge – useful on window frames or along an edge.

Radiator brush Bristles are at an angle to the handle for painting awkward places, such as behind radiators and pipes.

Synthetic fibre brushes
- Easy to clean.
- Bristles are locked-in.
- Especially good with water-based paints.
- Standard 50mm, 25mm and 12mm brushes are ideal for painting woodwork.
- Wide 100mm or 150mm brushes are used for walls and ceilings.

Radiator brush

Paint kettle Pour paint into a paint kettle as required. The kettle has a handle, unlike most small paint tins. Line the kettle with foil before pouring in the paint. This can be removed and thrown away after use.

Paint shield Use a plastic or metal shield to keep paint off glass when painting window frames. You can also use one to prevent your brush from picking up dirt from a floor when painting a skirting board.

Paint pads A pad is a fine layer of mohair bonded to a foam strip, which is mounted on a handle. Pads vary in size from about 25mm square up to a width of 180mm and also come in useful shapes, such as a crevice pad for painting into corners. You need a tray for the paint.
- Pads are best for water-based paints; most solvents used for cleaning oil-based paints will attack the adhesive.
- Like rollers, some pads have hollow handles for extension poles.

150mm paint pad

Corner pad

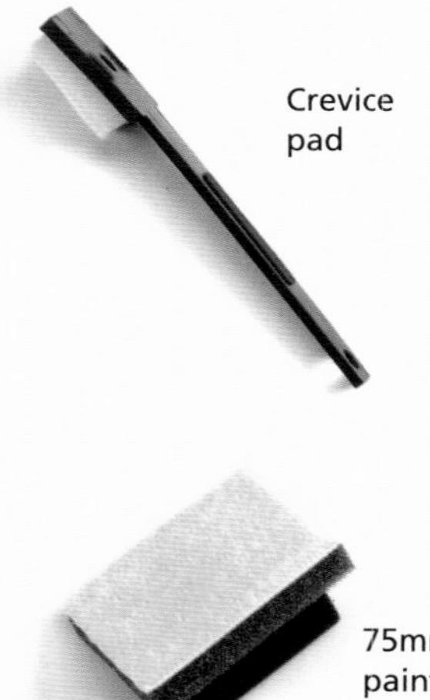

Crevice pad

75mm paint pad

Rollers An easy way to spread emulsion paint quickly over large areas is with a paint roller. A metal or plastic roller tray is needed for painting with a roller.

Foam rollers These are good general-purpose rollers if a high finish is not important. They can only be used on smooth and lightly textured surfaces. Patterned foam rollers will apply textured paint in relief over a smooth surface.

Pile rollers Synthetic or natural pile rollers last longer than foam and are excellent for covering large areas with emulsion paint. Also work well on woodchip paper.

Mohair rollers The very fine pile of mohair rollers (which are mostly synthetic) gives a high-quality finish. Suitable for paints with a sheen, such as silk emulsion and gloss.

Radiator rollers Small rollers on a longer handle are useful for painting areas difficult to reach, such as behind radiators.

Extension handles Many rollers have a hollow handle that will take a telescopic extension pole so you can reach the tops of walls or ceilings.

Pile roller sleeve

Fine foam roller sleeve

Mohair roller sleeve

Roller frame

Patterned foam roller for textured coating

Radiator roller and replacement head

Telescopic extension handle for roller

Paint Pod A paint pod roller system makes light work of covering large areas of wall with emulsion. Paint is fed along the hollow delivery tube by a pump, so you never need to stop to reload the roller. You control the paint flow with a trigger and the machine can be set to clean itself with warm water.

Roller tray and pile roller

What goes on before the paint?

Most surfaces require a preparatory coating to make sure they are stable and sealed before you can apply any paint. Be sure to choose a coating suitable for the surface and consider whether it is indoors or out.

Take special care with any painted surface that will be exposed to the weather. The end grain of wood must be thoroughly soaked with primer to prevent the rain from penetrating. Primer by itself is not particularly weather-resistant, so do not leave a primed surface exposed to rain and wind for long. Cover it with an undercoat and a topcoat as soon as possible.

New windows, doors and other wooden fittings are usually supplied ready primed. Check for scratches and other damage and prime any areas that have become exposed. Give a second coat of primer to any areas that will become hidden by brickwork after the fitting is installed.

When using a microporous paint on bare wood, no primer or undercoat is needed. Do not apply more than two coats.

All bare or new wood needs a sealing coat of primer before it can be painted. First, coat any knots with knotting. Then apply a wood primer or an all-purpose acrylic primer. This is water-based and dries fast.

Choosing primers and other sealers

Knotting

- Paint onto resinous areas, especially knots, in wood.
- Prevents resin in wood from seeping out and discolouring paint.
- When dry, coat knotting with primer.

Primer

- Apply to new or bare wood, plaster (see below) or metal.
- Seals pores in absorbent surfaces and forms a key to which other coats grip.
- Buy primer for a specific surface or use all-purpose primer.
- Prime bare plaster with proprietary sealer or a coat of emulsion diluted to one part water and four parts paint.

Primer-sealer

- For stained walls and plaster, old bituminous coatings and areas treated with preservative.
- Contains fine scales of aluminium and forms a barrier to seal the surface.
- Apply a second coat if stain is still visible after the first has dried.

Stabilising solution

- Sometimes used to seal distemper.
- Binds together surfaces to provide a firm support for paint.
- Apply fungicide before stabilising solution on a mould-affected surface.

Fungicide

- Kills mould on any affected surface.
- When spores are dead, brush them away and apply another coat.

How much paint do you need?

Work out how much paint you need before you buy any at all. It's better to overestimate than underestimate, so as to be sure that you can complete an entire room, or the outside of your house, with paint from the same batch.

Most paint tins indicate the average area of wall or other surface they will cover, but the table below offers a rough general guide for different types of paint. Porosity, texture and the base colour of the surface will affect the amount you actually need. Highly porous surfaces, such as bare plaster, will absorb a considerable amount – especially when priming. Rough surfaces, such as woodchip or pebbledash, are also very thirsty. Two or three undercoats may be necessary to cover a very strong base colour, and always allow for at least two topcoats for good protection against the weather on external surfaces.

COVERAGE PER LITRE

Coating	Coverage
Primer	8–12m²
Undercoat	16m²
Gloss	14m²
Non-drip gloss	12m²
Emulsion	10–13m²
Masonry paint	5–10m²

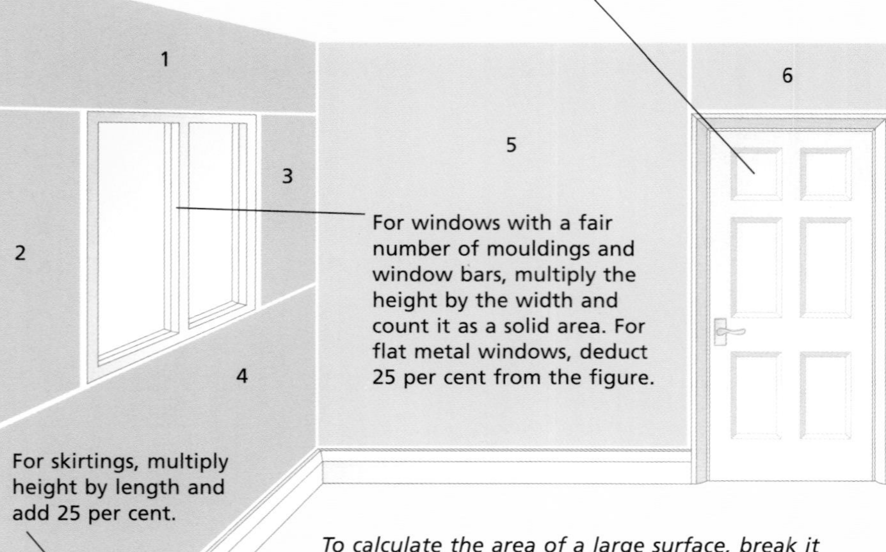

To calculate the area of a large surface, break it down into smaller parts, numbered 1–6 on this plan. Multiply the height by the width of each part and add all the totals together to get the final area.

Choosing paints for every purpose

Before you buy paint, study colour charts, or buy some tester pots to try out on the wall. Paint tends to look darker once it is applied, so if you are doubtful about which shade to buy, choose the paler one.

Solvent-based paint, or gloss, is used for wood or metalwork and water-based emulsions for walls and ceilings. Solvent-based paint must be used with an undercoat, but this is not necessary for emulsion. Water-based gloss paints are also now available. They are faster to dry and easier to clean, but tend to give a less glossy finish.

Non drip (or 'thixotropic') paints are jelly-like in consistency and ideal for less experienced decorators. They may be more expensive per litre, but seldom need an undercoat or second topcoat, so may not cost more in the long run.

Solid non-drip emulsion is sold in wide shallow trays designed to take a standard decorating roller – they are ideal for painting ceilings.

The final coat of paint – the topcoat – can have a gloss, semi-gloss or matt finish. Other names for semi-gloss include eggshell, silk, satin and sheen. The glossier the paint, the tougher and more durable the surface will be. Also, look out for moisture-resistant paints developed for kitchens and bathrooms.

Common types of paint

Undercoat

- A full-bodied paint with more pigment than topcoat and good covering power.
- Used on primed surfaces, before applying topcoat, or on dark surfaces which are to be painted a paler colour.
- Apply a second coat if undercolour shows through the first coat.
- Clean brushes with brush cleaner.

Solvent-based (or synthetic) gloss

- Used for woodwork and metalwork. Gloss is suitable indoors and out, though some are specially designed for exterior use.
- Can also be applied to walls and ceilings.
- On wood, always use with an undercoat.
- Apply two thin coats, rather than one thick one.
- Clean brushes with brush cleaner.

HELPFUL TIP

Don't stir non-drip paint, even if it looks lumpy in the tin. If the paint becomes liquid because it has been accidentally stirred or shaken, leave it to re-set before using.

Water-based gloss

- Used for woodwork and furniture.
- Dries much faster than solvent-based gloss.
- Gives a hardwearing finish; glossy, but not as much as the solvent-based equivalent.
- Clean brushes with water and detergent.

Emulsion

- Water-based paint used for walls and ceilings.
- Dries quickly and does not leave brush marks.
- Can be diluted with 20 per cent water to form its own primer for bare plaster.
- Use a roller for fast coverage.
- Two or three coats may be needed.
- Clean tools with water and soap or detergent.

One-coat paints

- Have better covering power than normal paints, so need only one coat.
- Available both as gloss solvent-based paints (normally non-drip) and as water-based emulsion paints.
- No undercoat needed for gloss paint.

Anti-condensation paint

- Used in kitchens and bathrooms where hot moist air can cause condensation.
- Reduces condensation by insulating the wall surface (making it warmer). Some types absorb water allowing it to evaporate when the air is drier.
- Only available in white, but can be overpainted with a colour of your choice.
- Often contains fungicide to deter mould.
- Apply in the same way as emulsion.
- Clean tools with water and detergent.

Textured (plastic) coating

- Can be applied to walls and ceilings with uneven or unattractive surfaces. Exterior weatherproof versions available.
- Much thicker than paint: it forms a permanent coating which is extremely difficult to remove.
- Apply with a shaggy roller, unless the manufacturer specifies otherwise.
- Coat with emulsion once dry.
- Clean tools with brush cleaner.

Masonry paint

- Used for render and pebbledash.
- Two main types – textured and smooth.
- Textured paint is good for concealing minor blemishes like hairline cracks.
- Smooth paint goes a lot further.

Enamel paint

- Used for metal and wood, especially children's toys and furniture.
- Has very glossy hard finish.
- Non-toxic.
- No primer or undercoat needed.
- Clean brushes with brush cleaner.

Other special paints

There are also special paints for floors, garage floors, tiles and melamine (for revitalising kitchen units). Matt black is used for beams and blackboards, radiator enamel stays white when hot; anti-damp paint seals in minor surface dampness.

SAFER PAINTS

Petrochemical-based paints contain volatile organic compounds, or VOCs, that are emitted as gases and contribute to indoor air pollution. EU rules have led to a reduction in VOC levels in many decorating products in recent years, and many manufacturers now offer natural paint alternatives that are free of environmental pollutants.

Milk paint
A mixture of casein, a protein found in milk, and earth pigments, milk paint has a smooth matt finish suitable for interior walls and furnishings. Unsuitable for humid rooms or those susceptible to damp.

Lime wash
Made from lime and natural pigments, lime wash gives walls – exterior and interior – a soft, weathered look.

Natural/organic paints
Usually made from vegetable and mineral extracts bound with natural oils or resins. Some natural paints still contain conventional pigments such as titanium oxide and natural solvents that can be low-level irritants, though VOC emissions are much lower than conventional paints.

VOC-free paints
These have the same make-up as conventional paints, but exclude the harmful VOCs.

Use natural paints soon after purchase, as they contain few preservatives and don't last as long as conventional paints. Allow for extended drying times as these paints contain no chemical drying agents.

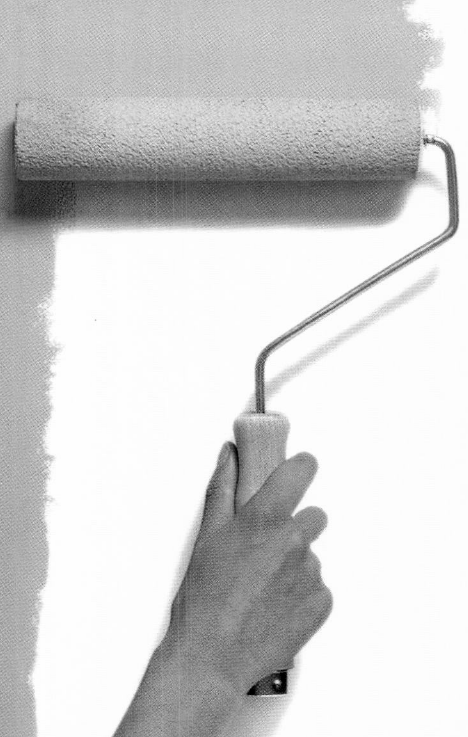

Painting techniques

A paintbrush is a versatile tool for applying primers, undercoats and varnishes, as well as topcoats to a variety of surfaces. Use one for applying gloss to wood and metalwork and for painting where colours or surfaces meet – around windows and doors, for instance.

Using a brush

1 Stir the paint – unless it is non-drip. Make sure any liquid on the surface is thoroughly mixed into the paint by lifting the stick as you stir.

2 Choose a brush which is the right size. As a rough guide, paint window frames with a 25mm brush, door panels with a 75mm brush, and walls and other large surfaces with a 100mm brush. Grip large brushes around the handle and hold smaller brushes more like a pencil.

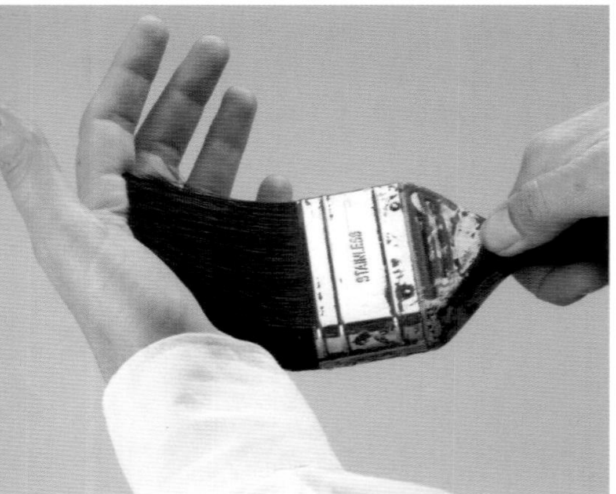

3 Flick the bristles against your hand to remove dust and any loose bristles or dried paint particles.

4 Dip the brush into a paint kettle, to about one-third of the bristle depth, to load it with paint.

5 Press the brush against the kettle wall to remove surplus paint. Do not scrape the brush over the rim of the kettle because too much paint will come off.

Painting with non-drip paint

Do not stir non-drip paint and do not remove any excess paint from the brush; it is meant to be heavily loaded. Apply the paint in horizontal bands. Don't overbrush or the paint will run.

Painting with gloss

1 Start at the top of the surface. Paint three vertical strips parallel with each other, leaving a gap just narrower than the brush width between the strips.

2 Do not reload the brush. Working from the top, brush across the painted area horizontally to fill the gaps and smooth the paint.

3 With the brush now almost dry, lightly go over the section you have just painted with vertical strokes to ensure an even coating, stopping on an upward stroke. This is called 'laying off'.

4 Using the same technique, paint a similar sized section underneath the one you have completed. Work the wet paint into the dry.

HELPFUL TIP

Line a paint kettle with aluminium foil – to make cleaning easier – and pour in paint to fill about one-third of the kettle. Do not work from the tin; you may contaminate the paint with dried paint, dirt and possibly rust from around the rim.

Painting with emulsion

1 Start at the top of the wall. Apply the paint in all directions, working horizontally across the surface and moving down when one band is complete. Do not put the paint on too thickly.

2 Lay off the paint with light brush strokes and a fairly dry brush, working in a criss-cross pattern. Lift the paint finally on upward strokes.

Painting a textured surface

When painting a surface with a heavy texture or relief, load the brush with more paint than for a smooth ceiling or wall. This cuts down the time it takes to coat the surface and fill all the little indentations. But dip to only a third of the bristle depth.

If you are painting a relief wallpaper, Anaglypta for example, use a brush as wide as you can comfortably manage without putting too much strain on your wrist. A 100mm paintbrush is ideal. With a textured coating on a wall or a ceiling, you can use a shaggy pile roller.

USING OLD PAINT

Wipe the rim before you open an old tin of paint. If a skin has formed, cut around the edge and lift it out. Stir the paint well and then strain it through an old stocking to remove any bits of hardened paint.

'Beading' where colours meet

Where walls meet the ceiling and where adjacent walls are of different colours, keep the meeting edge as straight and as neat as possible. Do not rush the job.

1 Turn the paintbrush edge on, holding it like a pen.

2 Load the brush with enough paint to cover about one-third of the bristle depth.

3 Press the brush flat against the surface so that a small amount of paint (the bead) is squeezed from the bristles. Work towards the edge gradually, rather than trying to get close immediately.

4 Draw the brush sideways or downwards along the surface, keeping your hand steady.

Cutting in

Achieve a neat finish along wall and ceiling edges by first painting the edges with a brush, before switching to a roller or pad.

1 Paint four or five overlapping strokes at right angles to the edge.

2 Cross-brush over the painted area in a long, sweeping motion, keeping parallel with the edge.

Painting with other tools

Using a roller

You can cover an area more quickly with a roller than with a brush, but you may need to apply more coats because the paint goes on quite thinly. Use a foam or mohair pile on a smooth surface and a lamb's-wool or nylon pile on a textured one.

1 Thoroughly stir the paint (unless it is a non-drip or solid roller paint).

2 Fill about one-third of the roller tray with paint. Do not overfill, or it will spill.

3 Dip the roller into the paint, then run it lightly on the ridged part of the tray. This spreads the paint evenly on the roller sleeve.

4 Push the roller backwards and forwards, alternating diagonal strokes at random.

5 Do not apply too much in one coat. And do not work too fast, or paint will be thrown off the sleeve and spatter. Try not to press the roller too hard or paint will be forced off the ends in ridges.

6 Use a small paintbrush to cut in the edges around doors, windows, corners and where walls meet the ceiling.

Using a paint pad

Paint pads are suitable for applying water-based paints. They quickly cover large areas like walls and ceilings and will cope with lightly textured surfaces.

1 Stir the paint and pour some into a flat tray or the speed tray sometimes supplied.

2 Run the pad backwards and forwards on the roller in the speed tray or hold the pad flat against the paint in the tray. Do not let it sink below the pile level. If the pad absorbs too much paint it will drip. A pad needs to be reloaded more often than a brush or roller.

3 Start painting near a corner. Move the pad in all directions with a gentle scrubbing action. Work in strips about four times the width of the pad.

4 Do not press too hard or paint may be forced off the pad in drips. With practice you should get no drips at all.

CUTTING IN WITH A PAINT PAD

As as alternative to using a brush to obtain a neat finish along wall and ceiling edges, try using an edging pad with guide wheels, which is specially designed for the job. The wheels guide the pad along the ceiling line as you push it along the wall.

Looking after brushes, rollers and pads

Always thoroughly clean paintbrushes, rollers and pads after each painting session. Use cold water to wash off water-based paint immediately and never leave any of your painting tools to soak in water.

Before you start Check the instructions on the paint container to see what solvent is needed for cleaning painting tools. Some paints (Hammerite, for example) need special cleaners – so make sure you buy this with the paint. Emulsion and acrylic paints need only water; solvent-based gloss paints need only white spirit, but it is much easier to use a proprietary brush cleaner which can then be rinsed out with water.

Leaving a brush loaded with paint

Pads, rollers and trays must not be left loaded with paint, but you can keep a wet brush or roller sleeve for an hour or two so long as you wrap it in tin foil or a plastic bag to prevent the paint from drying.

Cleaning a brush

1 Gently scrape excess paint from a brush onto paper. Use the back of a knife and work from the heel (the base of the bristles) to the tip.

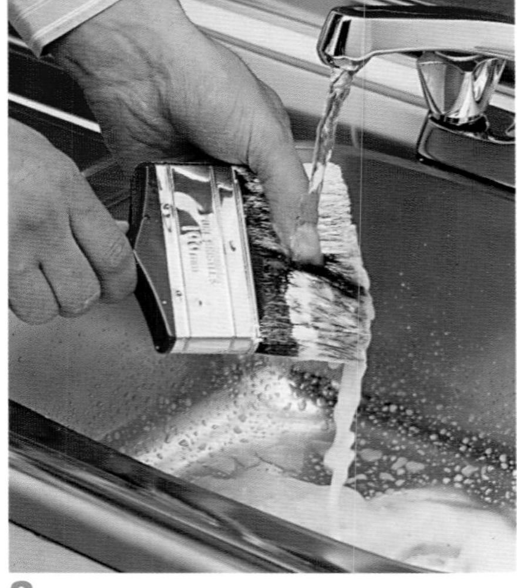

2 Wash emulsion paint out of a brush under a running tap. Rub a little soap or washing-up liquid into the bristles and rinse in clean water.

3 Clean off a solvent-based paint with white spirit or proprietary brush cleaner.

4 All brushes will benefit from a final wash in soap and a rinse in clean water. Use your fingers to work out any remaining paint. Once a brush is clean, shake it vigorously outdoors to get rid of excess water.

5 When the paintbrush is dry, slip a loose rubber band over the tip of the bristles to hold them together and keep the brush in shape.

Cleaning a roller

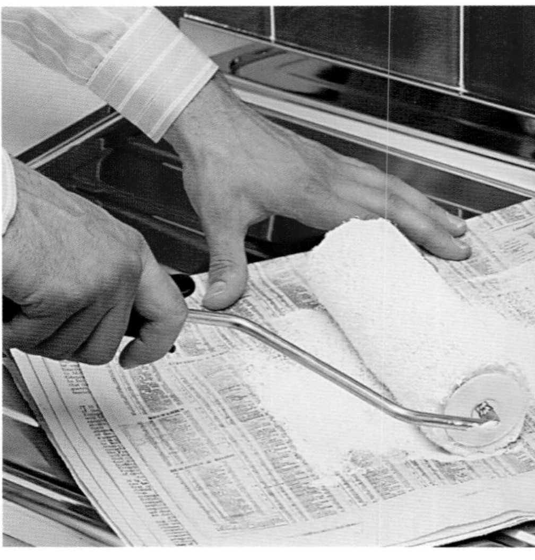

Run the roller over the ribbed part of the paint tray and then over sheets of newspaper to remove excess paint. Remove the roller sleeve if possible. Wash under running water, working the paint out of the sleeve with your hands.

Cleaning a paint pad

1 Run the pad over paper to get rid of most of the paint (or see below).

2 Wash the pad in clean water, taking care not to separate the mohair from the base. The process will be faster if you use a little soap, but make sure you rinse it all out in clean water.

THE GREEN WAY TO CLEAN

Brushes, rollers and pads take a lot of rinsing in order to preserve their condition, and this generally means using a lot of water and losing a lot of excess paint down the drain. Always try to remove as much paint as possible before you start cleaning to keep rinsing to a minimum. To clean rollers, a paint roller cleaner – either a 6-in-1 painters tool (with a semi-circular cut-out in the blade) or a plastic nozzle. Both of these allow you to scrape paint off the sleeve back into its container.

If you're doing a lot of painting, use a paintbrush and roller cleaner kit. This is essentially a drill attachment with a mechanism that clamps your brush or roller in its jaws then spins the excess paint away. You will need to hold the drill inside a cardboard box so as not to spin the paint everywhere, then give the roller or brush a final – minimal – rinse under the tap.

Storing brushes, rollers and pads

Leave clean brushes and rollers to dry and then wrap them in brown paper or lint-free cloth, such as old sheeting. Store the tools flat in a warm dry place.

Paint pads are an awkward shape to wrap, so store them in sealed plastic bags to keep off dust.

How to revive a neglected brush

A brush which has not been cleaned well after use will become hard. The best way to soften a brush is to use a proprietary restorer, following the instructions on the pack. Tease out any paint particles in the base of the brush with a fine brass suede brush. Only use a restored paintbrush for rough work, like applying primer.

Painting walls and ceilings

To avoid spoiling newly painted surfaces with drips and spatters, paint the ceiling first, then the walls and finally the woodwork. It is a good idea to paint the ceiling (which can be a messy job) before stripping any wall coverings. But this is the only exception to the rule that all preparatory work must be done before you start painting.

Painting a ceiling

Make sure that you can safely and comfortably reach the area you are decorating. Use a scaffold board supported by trestles or stepladders. Your head should be about 75mm from the ceiling.

If you do not like working at a height, you can use an extension handle (or broomstick) fitted to the hollow handle of a roller or pad, for most of the painting. But you will need to stand on steps or a board to cut-in where the walls and ceiling meet and around the tops of doors and windows.

Paint the ceiling in strips starting near the window. If there is more than one window in the room, begin nearest the one where most light comes in. Cut in the edges as you work.

WHEN TO PAINT COVING

If you paint coving and ceiling roses after you have painted the ceiling, you will avoid getting splashes on the new paintwork. If coving is to be the same colour as the ceiling, paint it before you paint the walls, otherwise it is easier to paint coving at the end of the job.

Painting a wall

When using a roller, paint horizontal bands about 500mm wide across the wall. Work from the top to the bottom. With a brush, paint blocks about 500mm square. Start in the top right corner (or the top left one if you are left-handed). Paint the blocks from the top of the wall down and then across.

Painting different surfaces

Bare plaster Dilute emulsion to one part water and four parts paint and use it as a priming and sealing coat. Follow this with at least two coats of full strength emulsion. Use a foam or mohair roller or a paintbrush or pad as large as you can comfortably work with. Do any touching up with a small paintbrush while paint is still wet.

Paper Lining paper is the ideal surface for painting, as it hides small cracks and blemishes. Apply at least two coats of paint, using whichever tool you prefer. Do not worry if small bubbles appear on the paper. They disappear as the paint dries.

- Paint high relief papers such as Anaglypta with a shaggy pile roller.
- Old wallpaper can be painted but does not give great results. Test an area first to see that the paper does not bubble or come away from the wall. If it does, you must strip the wall, but if not, apply full-strength emulsion as the first coat. The less water getting onto the wall the better. Use a roller, pad or brush.
- Do not paint over wallpapers that contain a metallic pattern – the pattern tends to show through the paint.

Painted surface New emulsion paint can be applied straight onto old provided the surface has been washed down. If there is a drastic colour change, two or three coats will be needed. Never paint over distemper – it must be removed (page 72). As a general rule, do not paint walls or ceilings with gloss; it enhances blemishes in the surface and is prone to condensation. If you want to paint an old gloss surface, first rub it down with a flexible sanding pad or fine wet-and-dry abrasive paper, damped with clean water. This destroys the glaze on the paint and helps the new paint film to grip the old. Wipe away dust before painting.

Textured coatings Use a brush or shaggy pile roller to put on the paint; you will find that emulsion gives the best result. Textured coatings are sometimes abrasive so they may rip foam rollers and can be difficult to coat thoroughly.

Ceiling tiles Paint polystyrene tiles with emulsion, as long as they are clean. Use a roller, and a small brush for the joins between the tiles. Never use a gloss paint – it creates a fire hazard when it is put on expanded polystyrene. If you plan to stick polystyrene tiles on the ceiling, it is much easier to paint them before you put them up, especially if they have chamfered edges.

Painting walls with glazes

A glaze is a thin, almost transparent film of oil-based colour. The oil slows the glaze's drying time but you still have to work fast. Glazes can be put over surfaces coated with a matt or eggshell solvent-based paint, but will not adhere to a gloss finish. The surface must be thoroughly prepared, as glazing will highlight any imperfections.

Whether or not you need to buy special tools for applying a glaze depends on which techniques you are going to use. You can sponge, rag, drag or stipple a glaze, using normal household materials – such as old cloths – or specialist products. Good stippling and dragging brushes are expensive, but cheaper versions may give poor results.

You can buy transparent oil-based glaze, called scumble glaze, which varies in shade from pale to mid-brown. As a rough guide, a 2.5 litre tin of glaze will be enough to cover all the walls in a room 3.5m x 3.5m.

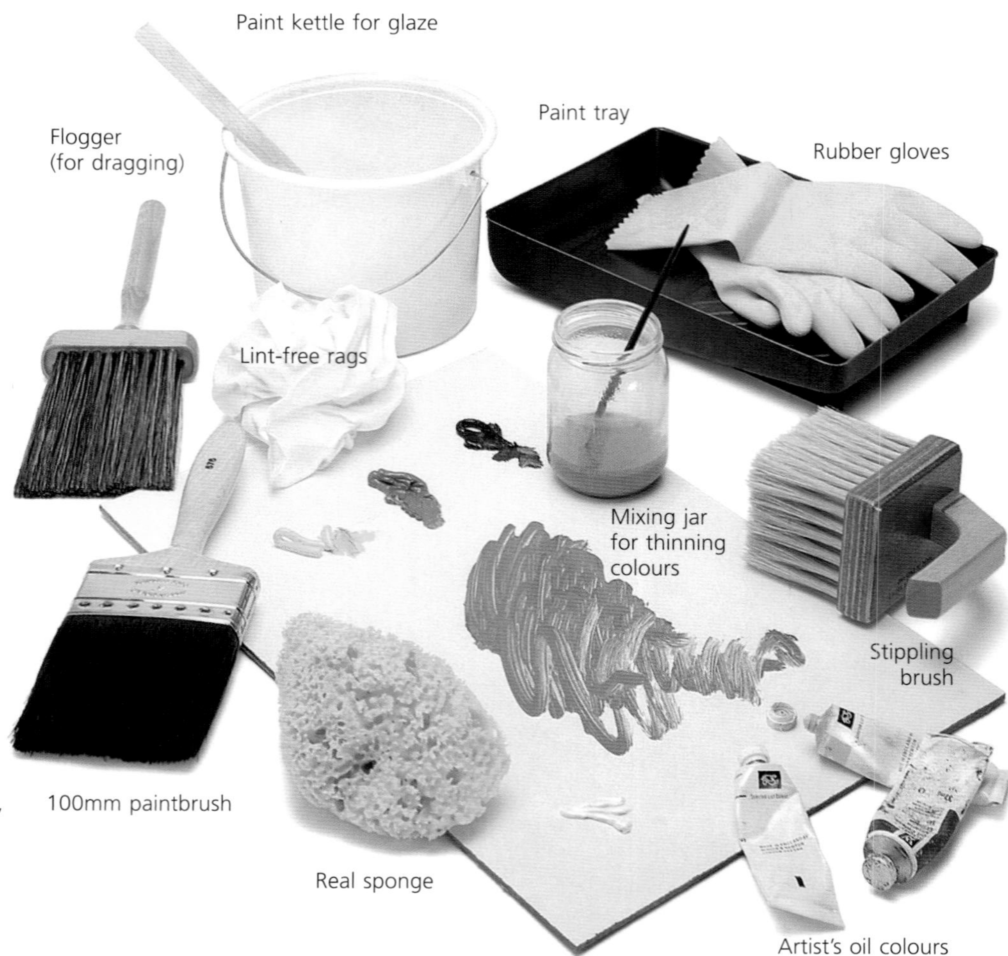

All the painting techniques with glazes require basic tools and materials – a paint kettle, white spirit and rags for mopping up spills, for example – as well as the particular painting tool needed to achieve the desired decorative effect.

Tinting the glaze

Use artist's oil colours or universal stainers to tint the glaze to the colour you want. Mixing a glaze to achieve a particular colour is a matter of trial and error which becomes easier with practice. Always mix up more glaze than you think you need – it is impossible to match a colour if you run out halfway through the job.

1 Blend a small blob of colour – a little goes a long way – with white spirit.

2 Add this to the rest of the glaze in the paint kettle, stirring all the time to mix them well.

3 Test the result on the surface to be painted and repeat the process, if necessary, adding more of the same or a different colour until you are satisfied.

4 Glaze is usually diluted with some white spirit before you apply it to a surface. The consistency should be easy to work with – about the same as single cream.

5 If the glaze thickens as you work (because the white spirit has evaporated) stir in some more white spirit – but be careful with the amount because too much will weaken the colour.

Alternatively You can achieve similar painting effects with eggshell solvent-based paint, although the mixture is not strictly a glaze.

- Mix one part paint to two parts white spirit. It is best to choose white paint and then to tint it to the required colour.
- As with an ordinary glaze, blend a blob of colour with white spirit, add it to the paint mixture and try out the result. Keep blending more colour with the diluted paint until you achieve the colour you want.
- This 'glaze' dries quickly so it is more suited to sponging and ragging than to dragging or stippling.

You can produce decorative effects with emulsion paint as well – one part diluted with three or four parts water – but this dries even faster. Tint the emulsion paint with water-soluble paints – use gouache, acrylic or poster paints – and dilute the emulsion with water, not with white spirit. Always apply an emulsion 'glaze' over an emulsion base coat – not a solvent-based one.

SAFETY TIP

Glaze is highly flammable. Never leave rags soaked with glaze lying around – they may suddenly burst into flame without warning. When you have finished with a rag, do not keep it to use again – always use a clean rag. Put used rags in a tin with a tightly fitting lid and throw it away. Never put used rags straight into a dustbin.

Protecting the surface It is advisable – but not essential – to protect a decorative finish with varnish. Make sure the glazed surface is completely dry (this may take 24 hours or longer) before you do so.

Choose gloss, semi-gloss or matt varnish, depending on how shiny you want the result to be, and buy varnish with as little colour in it as possible.

Brush on a thin coat, working from the top of the wall down. If you use two coats of varnish, allow the first to dry thoroughly before applying the second. Matt varnish, which gives a good flat finish but not a tough one, will not need a second coat.

Sponging a wall

Glaze applied to the wall with a sponge produces a soft, dappled effect.

Tools *Real (not synthetic) sponge; paint kettle, flat paint tray or baking tin; rags; rubber gloves.*

Materials *Glaze tinted the desired colour; white spirit.*

Before you start Find an inconspicuous area and practise the technique until you feel confident that you are achieving an effect that you're happy with.

1 Thin the glaze with white spirit in the paint kettle, stir well and pour some into the flat tray.

2 Wear rubber gloves to protect your hands. Dip the sponge into the glaze and squeeze out the excess.

3 Dab the sponge onto the wall – do not press too hard. Work in a circular pattern to prevent the prints from becoming too regular.

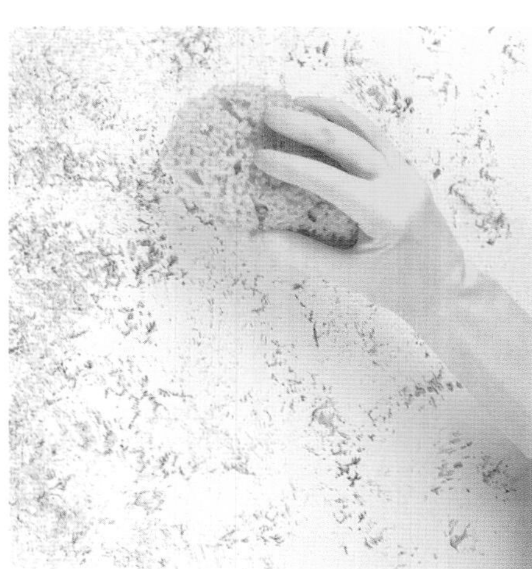

4 Reload the sponge as the glaze runs out. Vary the position of the sponge on the wall so that the impressions it makes are not all the same.

5 Wash the sponge in white spirit when it becomes saturated with glaze. Squeeze it out well or you will over-dilute the glaze.

6 For a marbled effect, leave the surface to dry and then sponge on a second colour, using the same technique as before.

Ragging a wall

With ragging, the pattern is irregular, rather than even, which makes it one of the easiest and fastest decorative techniques.

Tools *A large supply of lint-free rags (all the same texture); 100mm paintbrush; paint kettle; rubber gloves.*

Materials *Glaze tinted the desired colour; white spirit.*

1 Pour the glaze into the paint kettle and thin it with white spirit.

2 Brush glaze onto the surface, beginning at the top of the wall and covering a strip about 500mm wide down to the floor.

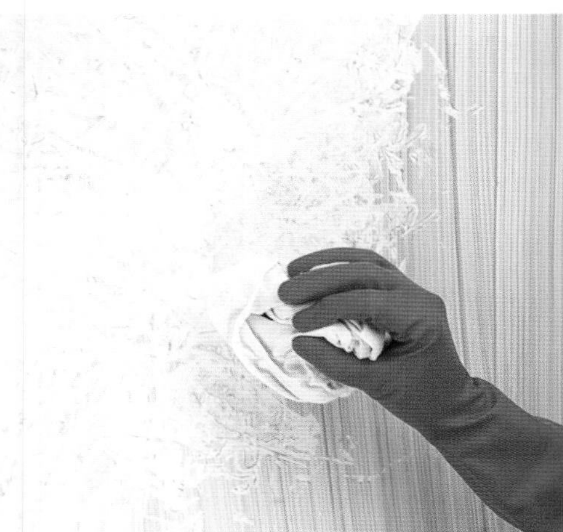

3 Bunch up a rag into a ball and dab it over the surface to pick up glaze while it is still wet. Use one or both hands to move the rag in all directions. This is a messy job so wear rubber gloves. You may find it easier if you crumple one rag into a ball and then wrap another rag around it.

4 Change the rag whenever it becomes full and too wet to pick up more glaze. It is also a good idea to unwrap the rag and crumple it again in a different way so that the patterns you make are not all the same.

5 Continue to apply and rag off glaze until the whole wall is covered.

Dragging a wall

This technique will show up the slightest imperfection in a surface, so it is best kept for only the smoothest walls. If possible, try to get someone else to brush the glaze onto the wall, while you drag it off immediately afterwards.

Tools *Paint kettle; 100mm paintbrush; brush with extra-long bristles (called a flogger) or another wide, coarse-haired paintbrush; clean lint-free rags.*

Materials *Glaze tinted the desired colour; white spirit.*

1 Thin the glaze with white spirit in the paint kettle. It should be a thin, cream-like consistency – if it is too thick or if one of the bristles in the brush is bent, some of the dragged lines of glaze may break into droplets and spoil the effect.

2 Start in a top corner and apply a strip of glaze about 500mm wide, from the top of the wall to the bottom.

3 Again, moving from the top down, drag the dry flogger through the glaze. You may need to stand on steps to reach the top and climb down carefully as you drag the wall.

4 Keep the movement flowing and as straight as possible. However, the results will be more successful if you relax and do not concentrate too much on keeping the lines steady.

5 Do not worry if the lines are slightly crooked in places – they will not spoil the effect from a distance. Hold the flogger against the wall with light, consistent pressure.

6 If you cannot drag the whole wall in one movement, break off and then brush from the bottom up to where you stopped, overlapping slightly at the join. If you have to do this with the next strip as well, break off at a different height, so that you do not get a line running across the wall where the joins meet.

7 Wipe the flogger frequently on a lint-free rag so that the bristles remain as dry as possible and do not lose their shape.

HELPFUL TIP

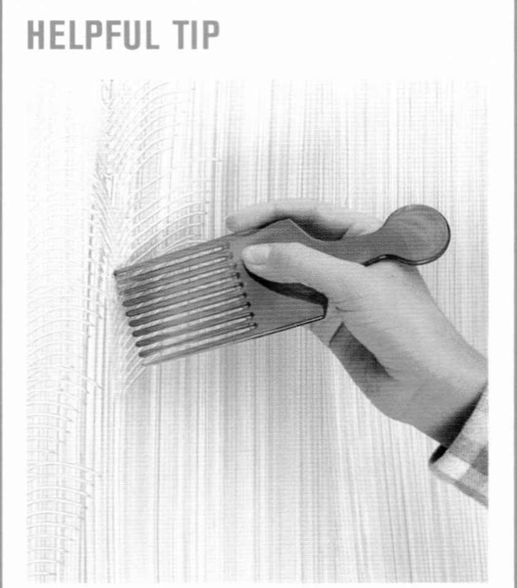

You can create a similar effect to dragging by using a comb with firm teeth. Rubber or steel combs are sold by some artists' suppliers but you can also use plastic ones. You need not confine yourself to vertical lines – experiment with scallop shapes, wavy lines, ticks or criss-cross patterns.

Stippling a wall

This technique creates a uniform, soft effect. The special brush required can be bought from specialist paint shops and larger builders' merchants. Use a white or pale base coat for best results. As with dragging, speed is essential so it is easier if you have a helper.

Tools *Paint kettle; stippling brush; 100mm paintbrush; clean lint-free rags.*

Materials *Glaze tinted the desired colour; white spirit.*

1 Pour the glaze into the paint kettle and thin it with white spirit.

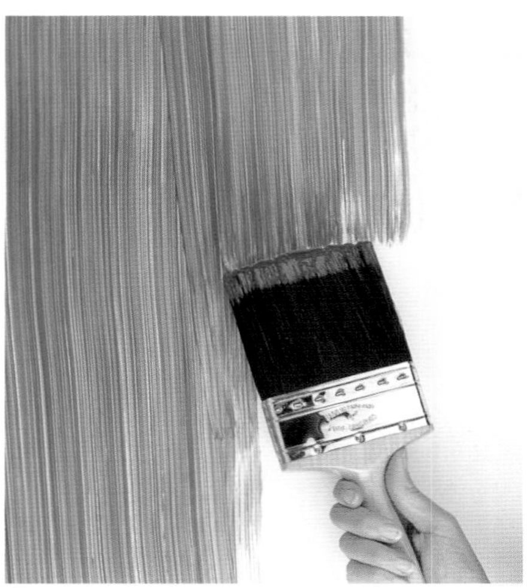

2 Brush the glaze onto the wall in a vertical strip about 500mm wide.

3 Go over the wet area with the stippling brush, stabbing at the surface. Keep the bristles at right angles to the wall, otherwise the brush will skid.

4 Wipe the brush clean on a dry lint-free rag as the picked-up glaze accumulates on the bristles, otherwise they will begin to stick.

5 Continue the process in strips across the wall.

6 Clean the brush immediately after use with white spirit, followed by a little washing-up liquid and warm water.

Stencilling

Using stencils is a quick and easy way of decorating furniture, walls and floors. Buy stencils pre-cut, or make your own.

Tools *Stencil brushes.*

Materials *Plastic stencils; paint; low-tack (easily detachable) tape or spray adhesive; masking tape; paper towel.*

1 Position the first stencil and secure it with tape or low-tack spray adhesive.

2 Use masking tape to cover any cut-outs within the stencil that you intend to paint with another colour.

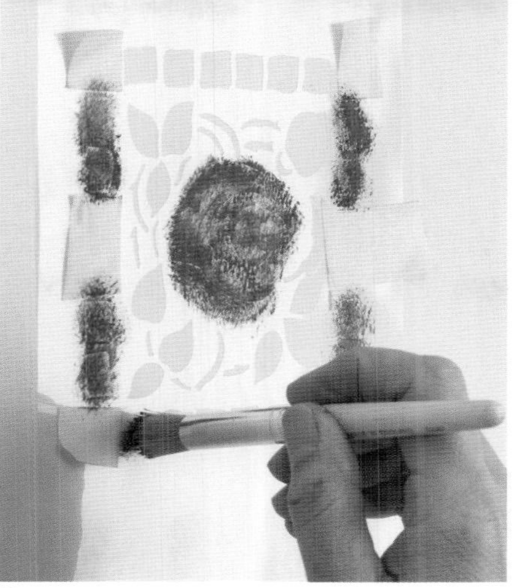

3 Hold the stubby head of the brush at right angles to the stencil and dab paint onto the cut-out areas, working outwards from the centre of each cut-out.

4 Wait until paint is dry to the touch, then repeat the process for the next colour.

PAINT FOR STENCILLING

You can use any paint, so long as it is not so thin that it will run down behind the stencil. There are also stenciling paints available that are specially designed for the job. Spray paint can be used for large areas, but take care not to apply too much, or it will run. Most shop-bought stencils are made from plastic sheets, so it is easy to clean off the paint when you have finished. If you are stencilling onto woodwork, apply a finishing coat of varnish to protect the design.

Painting cornices and mouldings

Plaster or imitation plasterwork cornices and ceiling roses can be painted with emulsion to match or contrast with the ceiling and walls. Or pick out details in a second colour. Never use gloss paint on polystyrene coving – it creates a fire hazard.

Tools *25mm brush with no straggly bristles; artist's sable brush; mahl stick (see right).*

Materials *Emulsion paint(s).*

Before you start Make sure the surface is clean and smooth. Fill small cracks in plaster with interior filler, wait for it to dry and then rub down with fine abrasive paper. If a part of the cornice is broken away, repair it before you do the painting.

1 Apply the paint in thin coats, so that it does not form drips or runs. Let the paint dry between coats.

2 If you are using two colours, either paint the raised parts first or paint the whole area and fill in the recesses, when dry, with an artist's sable brush.

3 To keep your hand steady, lean on a mahl stick (a signwriter's rest). To make a mahl stick, pad the end of a piece of dowel with sponge or cotton wool wrapped in a lint-free rag.

Painting woodwork

Once the ceiling and walls are painted, move on to the woodwork, which should have been well prepared before you started work on the walls and ceiling. Whatever the surface, the order of painting remains the same.

Tools *Paintbrushes; abrasive paper; wood sanding block; thin piece of wood; dusting brush; lint-free cloth or tack rag.*

Materials *Filler for wood painted indoors; knotting; primer; undercoat; topcoat.*

FOR A PERFECT FINISH

To avoid a disappointing final appearance, sand wood smooth and fill any holes before painting.

1 Wrap a piece of abrasive paper around a wood sanding block and rub it along the grain of the wood.

2 After sanding, use a fine brush to remove all the dust, brushing in the direction of the grain to clear all crevices.

3 Press the filler into the holes, taking care not to spread it into the surrounding grain.

4 Wait until the filler has dried to the same colour all over – perhaps 15–30 minutes – then sand it flat and dust once more.

1 Brush a coat of knotting over any resinous areas or knots in the wood so they are sealed and resin cannot seep through.

2 Apply an even coat of primer to bare wood and leave it to dry.

3 Use fine grade abrasive paper wrapped around a block of wood to rub lightly over primed areas to remove any rough bits.

4 Remember to sand moulded areas as well. Use abrasive paper round a thin piece of wood, or a flexible sander.

5 Put one undercoat on light surfaces and two on dark ones. Use an undercoat appropriate to the colour of the paint.

6 When the undercoat is dry, gently rub with abrasive paper. Remove dust with a dusting brush. To pick up remaining dust, wipe with a damp lint-free cloth (a clean old handkerchief is ideal) or a tack rag impregnated with resins that remove dust.

7 Apply the topcoat with a brush that is an appropriate size for the surface.

IF THE WALLS ARE TO BE PAPERED

When a room is to be papered, take about 15mm of paint onto the wall around door and window frames, above skirting boards and below any picture rail. Then, if you leave any small gaps in the papering, the paint will show through, making the imperfection less obvious.

Varnishing woodwork

If you leave woodwork bare, it will become marked and stained over time. Varnish will protect the surface as well as bringing out the wood's natural colour and showing its grain.

Tools *Paint kettle; measuring jug; rubber gloves; paintbrushes; fine wet-and-dry sanding sponge; tack cloth; 0000-grade wire wool; duster.*

Materials *Varnish; white spirit; wax polish.*

Before you start Consider which type of varnish you want to use. The two main choices are acrylic and polyurethene. Acrylic is quick drying and odour-free; polyurethene is harder wearing but smells strongly when you apply it.

1 For best results, thin the varnish before you apply the first coat (there is no need to thin varnish for the second coat). Measure a small quantity of varnish into a measuring jug, note the volume, and pour it into the paint kettle. Next, measure about a tenth of this volume in water (if you are using acrylic varnish) or white spirit (for polyurethane) and add the water or white spirit to the varnish. Stir thoroughly. Wash out the measuring jug immediately.

2 Fold the lint-free cloth into a ball, dip it into the diluted varnish and wipe it along the grain of the wood in smooth, parallel bands. Wear rubber gloves, as this is a messy job. Discard the cloth afterwards.

CHECK THE TINT FIRST

Using a tinted varnish rather than a clear one will add colour without permanently staining the wood. There are wood shades and paintbox colours available. Before you start, test the tint of the varnish by painting patches of one, two and three coats of varnish on a piece of spare wood. If the tinted varnish is slightly too dark, add a little water to acrylic varnish or white spirit to polyurethane, and then paint more patches to see if the colour has lightened sufficiently.

3 When the first coat is dry, sand the surface lightly with a fine sanding sponge, to 'key' the surface for the next coat.

4 Wipe away all the dust with a tack cloth. If you can't find one in your DIY shop, you can make one by dipping a lint-free cloth in white spirit.

5 Brush on the second coat of varnish as soon as possible, before dust has a chance to settle back onto the surface. Apply the varnish along the grain, then brush across the grain to make sure the bands have blended. Finish off with light brush strokes along the grain.

6 It is almost impossible to achieve a perfect finish. Once the varnish has set hard, feel for any blemishes with your fingertips and rub them gently with a pad of fine wire wool dipped in wax polish.

HELPFUL TIPS

- If you need to fill wood that is to be varnished, buy a wood filler that will match the colour of the finish. Fillers are made in a limited colour range, so look at the filler colour chart in the shop and choose the nearest. If you can, take a piece of the wood with you. Do not match the wood against wet filler; it will become paler as it dries.
- To avoid creating bubbles in the varnish, don't scrape the loaded brush against the rim of the tin or across a string tied across a paint kettle; instead, just load your brush and then tap the sides of the container with the brush. The excess varnish will drip off the brush.
- If the wood looks too shiny after varnishing, you can reduce the sheen with fine wire wool. Rub gently, with the grain, to cut back the gloss so that there is hardly any reflection at all. This is particularly suitable for pale woods.
- Commercial dip-stripping in hot caustic soda is a quick and easy way to remove layers of paint from moulded doors and leave a bare wood finish suitable for varnishing. Not all doors are worth stripping, so test one before paying for a whole set; also, joints may become loose and doors may warp, so check with the company that your doors are suitable. Mark each door with a chiselled Roman numeral in the top edge to keep a note of which door belongs with which frame.

Using waxes and oil finishes

Wax and oil finishes are most often used on furniture and wood with a natural finish, where the grain of the wood is visible. Oil finishes are best suited to wood that will be subjected to moisture and frequent handling. Wax is easier to apply but the surface must be completely smooth and clean before application. Most finishes are safe to apply but always read the manufacturer's instructions first.

Applying an oil finish

Tools *Plastic cups; foam brushes; clean lint-free rags; abrasive paper; latex gloves.*
Materials *Oil finish.*

Before you start Spread out plenty of newspaper in the work area. Most oil finishes are non-toxic but wear latex gloves and dispose of used rags and brushes in an airtight container as they can spontaneously combust if left crumpled in a ball.

1 Strip off any old finish and sand the wood until smooth. Start with 80 grit paper, then 120, and finally finish with 180 grit paper, sanding in the direction of the grain to remove any scratch marks.

2 Dust off then wipe down the surface with a tack rag or a cloth, which has been sprinkled with a little linseed oil. Turn the cloth often to expose a clean surface.

3 Use a foam brush to apply a coat of oil in the direction of the grain. Avoid over brushing and do not stop halfway through the job or a line will appear in the finish.

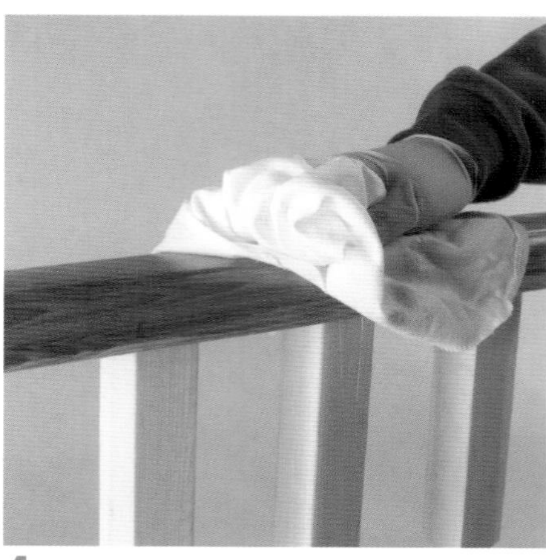

4 After 15 minutes use a clean rag to wipe any excess oil from the surface. When one rag becomes saturated replace it with a clean one.

5 Leave the oil to soak in for 3 hours then apply a second coat and wipe down as before.

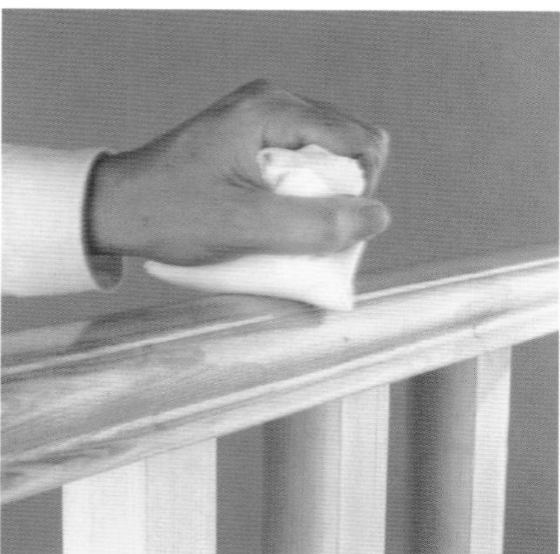

6 Leave for 24 hours and then use a soft clean cloth to buff to a smooth shine.

> **HELPFUL TIP**
>
> Waxes and oils will alter the colour of the wood, so test them on a scrap piece of wood or on an area which will not be visible before you start the job.

Applying a wax finish

Tools *Abrasive paper; soft cloths; latex gloves.*
Materials *Wax; methylated spirit.*

1 Strip off any previous finishes and sand the surface smooth. Make sure that you remove any surface imperfections and scratches that will show through the finish.

2 Wipe down the surface with methylated spirit to remove any residual surface impurities.

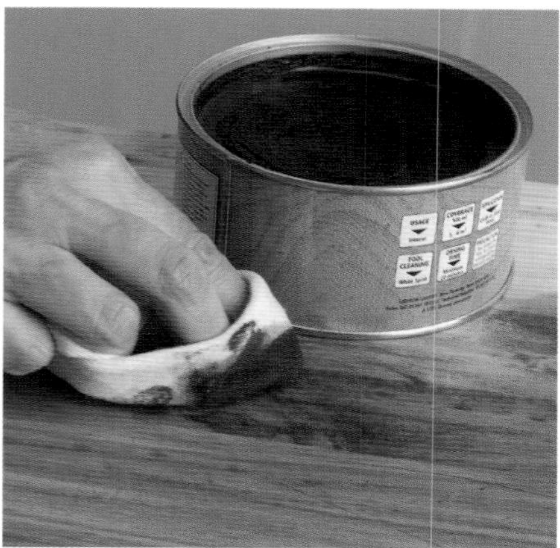

3 Immediately rub on the wax, as detailed in the manufacturer's instructions. Be careful not to apply too much; two thin coats are better than one thick one.

4 Use a soft lint-free cloth and buff to a smooth shine until all the wax has penetrated into the surface of the wood.

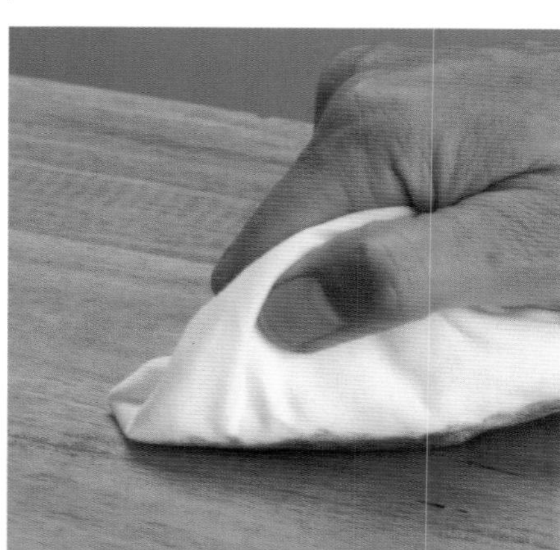

Painting doors and door frames

Doors have several faces and grain patterns going in different directions, each of which needs to be painted separately in a particular sequence for a good finish. Always open a door before you paint it. Leave the door frame until last.

Tools *Suitable brushes; perhaps cutting-in brush; paint shield.*

Materials *Masking tape; wire wool; white spirit; knotting; primer; undercoat; topcoat.*

Before you start Take off any door furniture, put down a dust sheet and hold the door open with a wedge on either side. It's a good idea to keep the door handle nearby in case the door closes.

Panelled doors

Paint the sections of the door in the sequence illustrated, for best results.

Use a brush of a suitable size to paint each part of the door – use a smaller one for the mouldings than for the panels, for instance.

Do not overload the mouldings with paint; this is a common cause of drips and runs. Keep the brush lightly loaded.

Glass panelled doors

Use a paint shield, an angled cutting-in brush or masking tape to keep paint off the glass. Whichever you use, allow paint to go onto about 2mm of the glass to seal where the glass and frames meet.

Paint the rest of the door with a broader brush – about 75mm wide. To avoid drips, do not overload the brush with paint.

If gloss paint gets on the glass, remove it with a rag damped with white spirit before it dries. If paint dries on the glass, scrape it off with a glass scraping tool.

Panelled doors Paint the panels and the mouldings, then the rest of the surfaces.

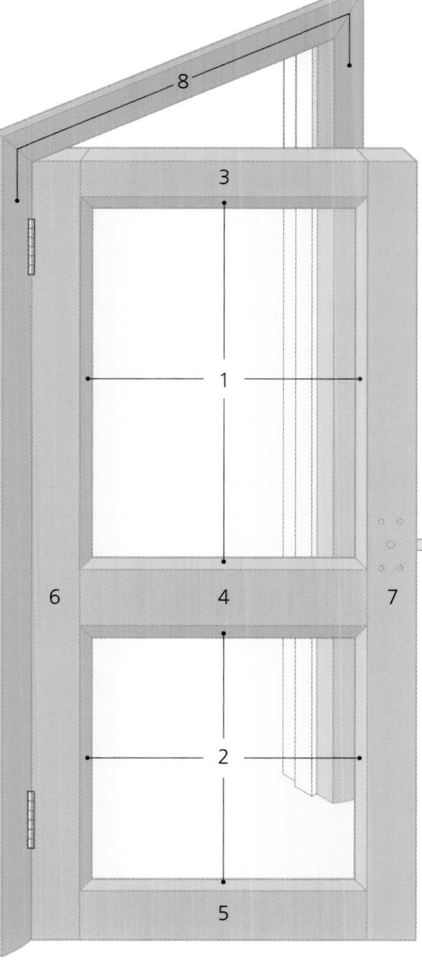

Glass doors Paint the moulding around the glass before the remainder of the door.

USING TWO COLOURS

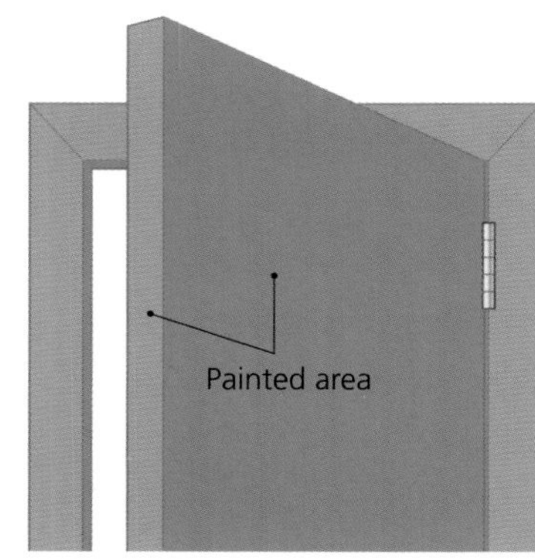

1 If the door is painted a different colour on each side, paint the lock edge the same colour as the side of the door which opens into the room.

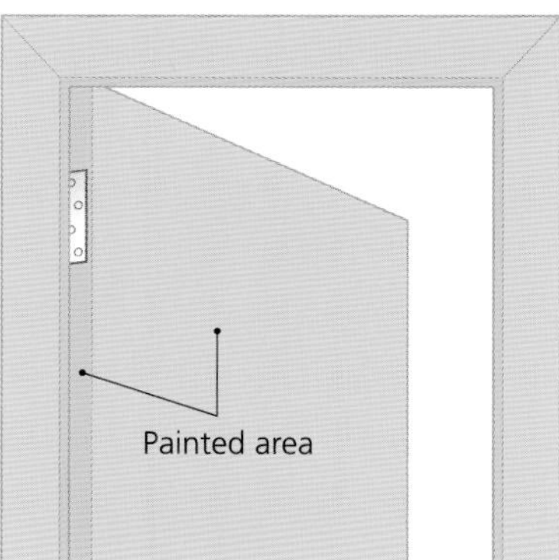

2 Paint the hinge edge of the door so that it is the same colour as the adjacent, visible face of the door.

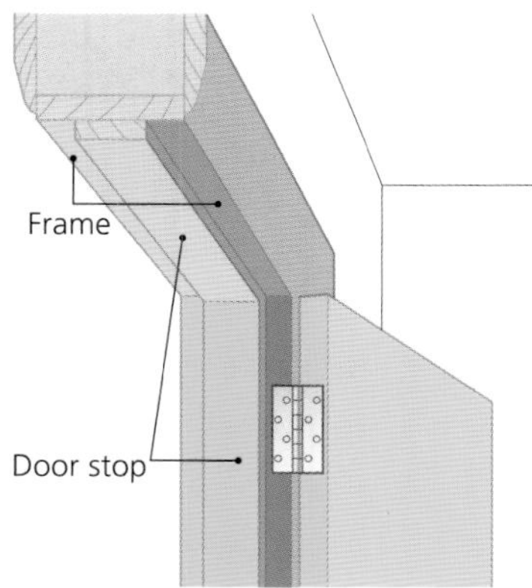

3 If the door frame is also painted a different colour on each side, all the parts which can be seen from one side when the door is closed should be painted the same colour.

In general, you don't have to paint the top and bottom edges of a door. However, if the top edge is overlooked (from a staircase, for example) paint it, so it does not stand out as bare wood.

Painting wooden mouldings

Skirting boards and picture rails are usually painted with gloss to match any other painted woodwork in the room. Balustrades are painted to match doors and other woodwork in the hall. If the walls are to be papered, paint woodwork first.

Tools *Suitable brushes; pieces of old card.*
Materials *Paint; white spirit.*

Before you start Fill damaged woodwork with fine surface filler then rub down to give a smooth finish ready for painting – gloss paint is unforgiving of imperfections and will show up every chip and dent.

Skirting boards

If you can, lift fitted carpets before painting a skirting board. When the carpet cannot be lifted, protect it with dust sheets.

1 The gap between the skirting board and the floor is likely to be full of dust. To remove the worst of it, vacuum along the skirting board before beginning. Then use a piece of card to stop the paintbrush from touching the floor.

2 Apply paint with a 50mm or 75mm paintbrush, depending on the height of the skirting board. Brush lengthways along the run of the board.

Picture and dado rails

1 With a 25mm brush, paint two or three thin coats, not one thick one, allowing each coat ample time to dry.

2 Finish off with fine brush strokes along the run of the picture or dado rail.

Balustrades

The wooden uprights and handrail of a staircase balustrade suffer a lot of wear and tear. It may seem like a fiddly job, but giving them a fresh coat of paint will help to keep them in good condition.

Tools *Bucket; cloths; paintbrushes; filling knife.*
Materials *Sugar soap; fine abrasive paper; white spirit; fine surface filler; wood primer.*

Before you start Remove the stair carpet and thoroughly clean (and vacuum) the bare stairs. Make sure that all the uprights (balusters) are secure and in sound condition, and prime any areas of bare wood.

1 Wash down the woodwork with a sugar soap solution before you paint. Grease and dirt will have collected, particularly on the handrail, and will prevent the new paint from taking hold. Use fine abrasive paper to key the surface all over, then wipe it with a little white spirit.

2 Start by painting the balusters, working from the top of the staircase down, and from the top of each one in turn. Don't overload your brush with paint, or you will end up with drips and runs. If the balusters are turned in an ornate shape, let your brush follow the curves to apply paint to all the recesses.

3 You will need to move round the balustrade to paint from the staircase side as well to make sure that each baluster is completely covered.

4 Once you have painted all the balusters, move on to the handrail. Paint the underside first then give the top and sides of the handrail two coats of paint to give it a hard-wearing finish. Allow the first coat to dry thoroughly and rub it down lightly with fine abrasive paper before applying the second coat.

5 Paint the newel posts after the handrail, working from the top down and making sure that any recesses on a decorative finial at the top are well covered.

6 Finish by painting the strings – the edges of the staircase. Paint the outside of the outer string first, plus any panelling that reaches down to the floor, and then the inside of this string and the wall string.

Painting interior windows

It nearly always takes more time to paint a window than you think, because of the number of surfaces and because you have to keep paint off the glass. For security, you will probably want to close windows at night, so start work as early in the day as possible.

Tools *25mm or 50mm brush or an angled cutting in brush; paint shield.*

Materials *Masking tape; wire wool; white spirit; primer; undercoat; topcoat; cling film or talcum powder.*

Before you start Put down dust sheets, and protect the glass with masking tape. Fix the tape about 2mm from the frame so that a thin line of paint goes onto the glass. This will seal any gap between the glass and the frame. If you can, remove handles, stays and locks.

Casement windows

1 Open the window. Paint the window in the order illustrated below. Do not apply too much paint in one coat or it will run and take longer to dry.

2 The painting sequence is largely determined by the fact that the brush strokes should follow the construction of the joinery; so the vertical brush strokes will 'cut off' the horizontal ones.

Order of work
Paint casement windows in this order: **1** glazing bars and rebates; **2** top and bottom rails; **3** hanging stile and hinge edge; **4** meeting stile; **5** frame. The colours on the drawing indicate the extent of the numbered areas.

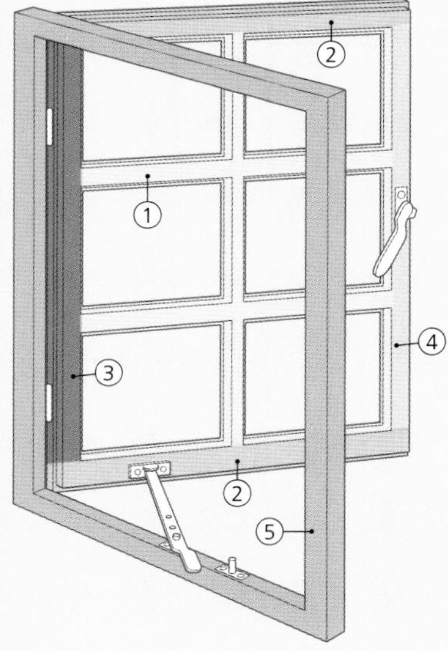

3 If you were not able to remove handles and stays, remove any unwanted paint from them using wire wool dipped in white spirit.

4 If you have to close casements and the paint is touch-dry but not absolutely hard, rub a little talc on the meeting surfaces. Alternatively, place a sheet of cling film between the surfaces most likely to stick.

Sash windows

1 Paint the frame following the order shown below. Almost close the window to paint the inside runners; give them a very thin coat to prevent surfaces from sticking.

2 Do not paint the sash cords or they will harden and fail earlier than they should.

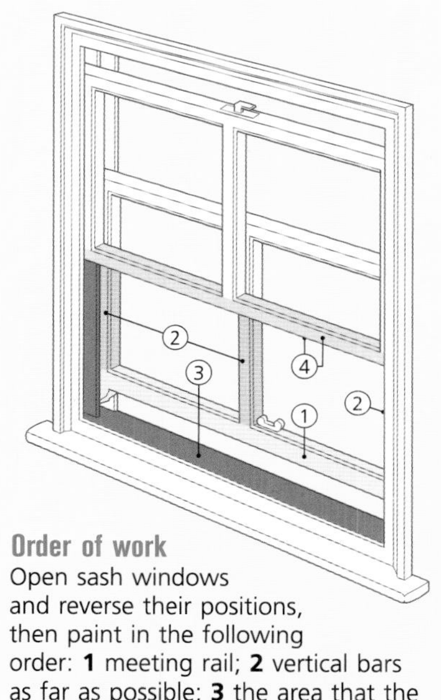

Order of work
Open sash windows and reverse their positions, then paint in the following order: **1** meeting rail; **2** vertical bars as far as possible; **3** the area that the inner sash sits on, and lower runners; **4** bottom rail and underside.

Reverse the windows, then paint: **5** meeting rail; **6** vertical bars; **7** head rail; **8** rest of vertical bars; **9** soffit, top runners and behind cords; **10** frame. The colours on the windows indicate the extent of the numbered areas.

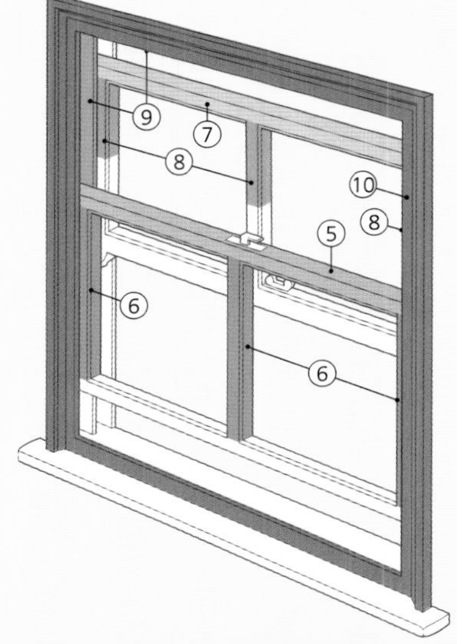

Painting metalwork

Make sure that all metalwork is clean and free from grease before painting.

Windows

Metal windows tend to be tighter fitting than wooden ones, so do not let paint layers build up on them. If the paint layers are very thick, remove the paint with a chemical stripper (page 77). In all other respects, the painting procedure remains the same as for wooden frames (see left).

Radiators

Never paint a hot radiator – always let it cool first. Wait for about an hour after you finish painting, then turn on the heating to speed up the drying process. Special radiator paint is available that will keep its whiteness despite the heat.

Before you start Check for patches of rust or bare metal that may be showing through. Rub them down with a fine wet-and-dry abrasive paper, and then touch them up with metal primer.

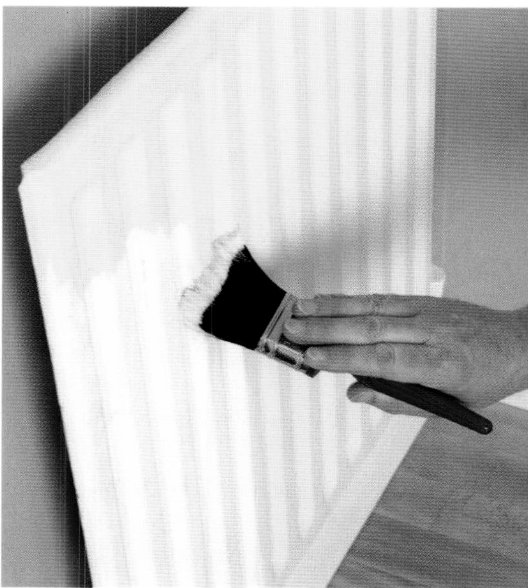

1 Apply gloss direct to new and already painted radiators unless there is to be a colour change, in which case apply an undercoat first.

2 Use a 50mm brush and keep the coat as thin as possible to avoid runs. You can paint a flat panel radiator with a small roller; this will not give quite as good a finish, but takes less time than painting with a brush.

3 Do not paint over control valves; they must be left free to turn.

Painting metal pipes

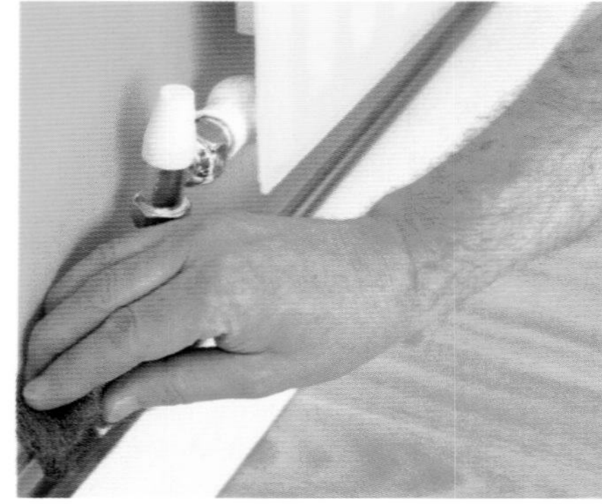

1 Make sure that steel and copper pipes are clean and free from corrosion. Use fine wire wool to clean them.

2 Apply gloss paint direct with a 25mm or 50mm brush. There is no need for a primer unless the pipe is lead. Start by brushing up and down, then smooth the paint along the length of the pipe.

3 Never paint over stop taps or controls or they will not work.

Cast-iron fire surrounds and wrought ironwork

1 Rub down and remove any rust (page 73) and prime the metal if necessary.

2 Use a suitably sized brush to coat the surface with gloss or enamel paint direct, without an undercoat.

3 If possible, remove intricate wrought ironwork and take it outside. Then spray it with an aerosol, shielding the area behind. Always use thin coats to prevent runs. Hold the can at right angles to the work and at a distance of about 300mm.

4 Keep the can parallel with the surface – moving up and down or from side to side. Never swing the can in an arc or hold it in one position for any length of time.

5 If you cannot move intricate wrought ironwork, put on two thin coats of gloss with a small paintbrush.

Dealing with paint problems

The main causes of paint breaking down are incompatible paints being applied on top of one another, poor preparation of the surface, damp or trapped moisture, grease, rot or rust.

Flaking The paint has not been keyed to the surface, which may be too smooth (as with old gloss paint) or may be chalky (as with untreated distemper). Alternatively, rotting timber may be pushing the paint off or rust may have formed underneath.
- Strip small areas by rubbing with fine abrasive paper, fill with a fine surface filler, apply a primer and repaint.
- Larger areas must be completely stripped and prepared again from scratch.

Blistering Prick a blister – if water emerges, damp is trapped under the paint or is finding its way in from behind.
- Strip the blistered paint with a hot-air gun and leave the wood until it has dried.
- Prime the surface and then repaint the whole of the repaired area.

Crazing (sometimes called orange peel) When a paint surface breaks up like mini crazy paving, incompatible paints have been used. The top layer of paint breaks up because it expands at a different rate from the one underneath.
- Usually, you must strip all the paint with chemicals or a hot-air gun and start again.
- Rub down very small areas – no more than a few centimetres square – with a flexible sanding pad or with wet-and-dry paper damped with water.
- When the surface is smooth, fill the stripped area with a fine surface filler, prime and repaint.

Visible under-colour To cover a strong colour, use a one-coat paint or an undercoat before liquid gloss.
- Put on another layer of topcoat, but switch to a one-coat paint, which has more body and covering power.

Runs Too much paint applied in a thick coat results in runs that are hard to disguise.
- If the paint is still wet, brush out runs; but not if the paint has started to dry. Instead, wait until it is completely dry and then rub down with very fine abrasive paper until the surface is smooth.
- Clean with a damp rag.
- Apply a new thin topcoat.

Stains Stains occur when water in emulsion activates impurities in a wall; areas rubbed with a wire brush or wire wool develop rust stains; or deposits in an unlined flue come through the paint surface.
- Prevent stains by applying an aluminium primer-sealer before you start painting.
- If the problem occurs afterwards, brush a primer-sealer over the stain and then repaint.

Mould and discoloration Spores settling on paintwork that is damp – possibly due to condensation – often lead to mould patches.
- Treat the affected area with a fungicide as directed by the manufacturer, wash the surface clean, let it dry and then repaint.

Loss of gloss sheen Gloss paint will sink into the surface and lose its shine if the surface was not primed – or if either primer or undercoat was not left to dry completely.
- Rub down with damp wet-and-dry abrasive paper.
- Brush off the dust and wipe with a clean, damp rag, then apply a new topcoat.

Wrinkled paint Usually caused by applying a second coat of paint before the first has dried. Solvents in the wet paint underneath attack the second coat when they try to pass through it and make it wrinkle.
- Strip the paint with a chemical stripper or heat and redecorate, this time allowing each coat to dry before applying the next.

Gritty paint surface If a newly painted surface feels rough and gritty, paint has been applied with a dirty brush or has become contaminated by the surrounding areas. Or there may have been bits of skin in the paint. Always paint with clean brushes and use a paint kettle. Strain old paint through a paint strainer or a pair of tights. Use a paint shield or piece of card to guard against picking up dirt from a floor.
- When a gritty surface is dry, rub down with a damp wet-and-dry abrasive paper until it is smooth, wipe clean, then apply a new coat of paint.

Dark patches on painted wood Knots in wood which have not been sealed before you decorate may ooze resin when the sun warms them, and the resin will force its way through the paint film.
- Strip paint away with the edge of a scraper blade, then with fine abrasive paper to expose the knot.
- Brush knotting over the area to seal it, leave it to dry and repaint.

Paint will not dry The room is badly ventilated or very cold.
- Open all the windows and doors or put a heater in the room.
- If this does not solve the problem, the paint has been applied to a dirty – and probably greasy – surface.
- Strip it off with chemical stripper or heat and start again, taking great care to clean the surface thoroughly.

Insects on painted surface If you can, remove insects that get stuck to fresh paint while the paint is still wet and touch up the surface with a brush and new paint. If the paint has started to dry, wait until it has set hard and then brush away the insects – they make less of a mess that way.

Wallpapering tools

For any wallpapering job, you will need a steel measuring tape, a pencil – not a pen – to make marks and a metal straightedge to act as a guide when you trim paper. Depending on the type of wallcovering, you will need only some of the tools listed below. Have a supply of old towels and sponges to hand for removing paste from skirting boards and for other general cleaning.

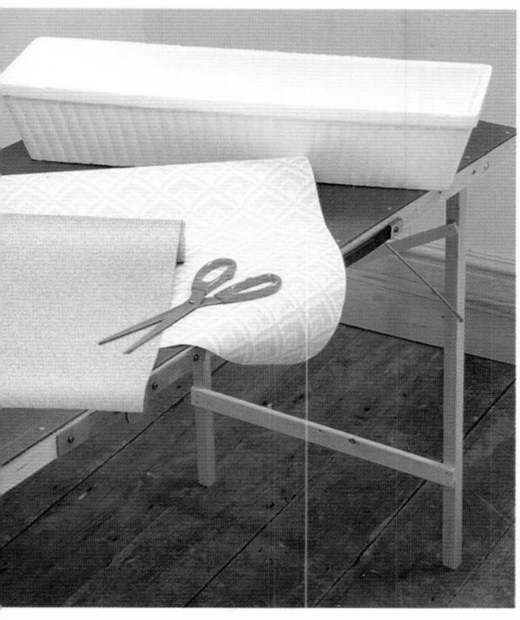

Pasting table A folding table – about 2m long and 500mm wide – is the best type because it is easily moved around. As well as being light to carry, the table must be solid enough to stand firmly on the floor.

Water trough If you are using a pre-pasted wall covering, you will need a trough for wetting each length before hanging.

Plumb line and bob Use a plumb line to mark the true vertical on a wall before hanging the first length of wallpaper – few walls are straight. Buy one or make one by tying a small weight – a metal nut or a small screwdriver – to a length of string.

Paste brush Use a 125mm or 150mm brush to apply paste. If you use an old paintbrush, make sure that it is clean. Wash the brush well in warm water after use.

Plastic bucket Any clean household bucket is fine for mixing the paste. Tie a piece of string across the rim, between the handle anchor points, and rest the brush on the string when you are not using it. Wiping the brush across the string will remove surplus paste.

Cutting guide A Y-shaped graduated length of aluminium just under 600mm long designed specifically for trimming wall coverings at their bottom edge. Place the guide against the skirting board before brushing the wallcovering down the wall and then over the guide. Hold the wallcovering and guide in place and use a very sharp trimming knife along its edge. Remove the guide carefully and the wall covering should now fit perfectly.

Scissors Paperhanger's scissors with 250mm long blades are best for the main cutting work. The longer the blades, the easier it is to cut a straight line. If possible, use stainless steel scissors because they will not rust. Wipe scissors clean after each use when cutting pasted paper, or the paste will harden on the blades and they will tear the next length. Have a pair of small scissors handy for fine trimming.

Trimming knife A knife with a razor-sharp blade is useful for trimming and cutting vinyl wall coverings. It is also sometimes easier to trim pasted paper neatly with a knife and straight-edge than with a pair of scissors – provided the paper is not too thin. Keeping the knife sharp is essential so make sure that you have plenty of spare blades; or use a knife which has a continuous blade that snaps off at intervals to give a sharp new cutting edge.

Paperhanger's scissors

Paperhanging brush

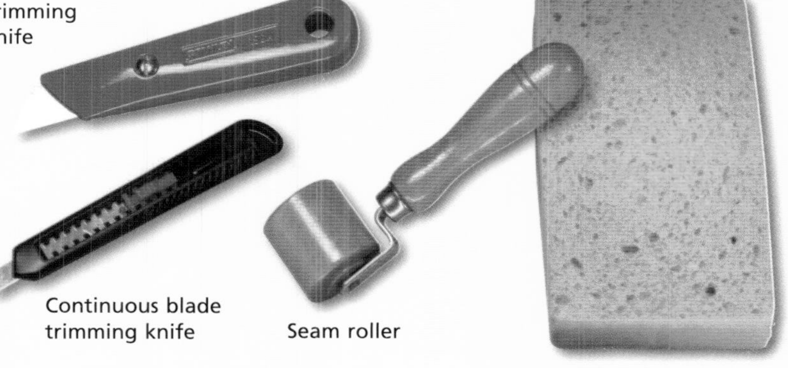

Trimming knife

Continuous blade trimming knife

Seam roller

Sponge

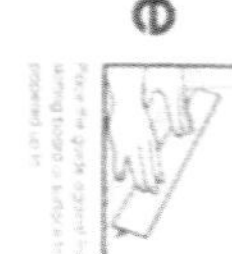

Cutting guide

Paperhanging brush For smoothing out bubbles and creases in newly hung wall coverings. A large brush – between 180mm and 250mm wide – gives best results. Never use the brush for anything else and take care not to get paste on the bristles.

Seam roller For pressing down the seams of wall coverings, once they have been smoothed into place. Never use a roller on embossed and relief wall coverings: it will flatten the pattern.

Sponge Use a clean damp sponge to wipe excess paste from the surface of vinyls and washable wall coverings.

Choosing paper and paste

Lining paper Plain lining paper is designed to cover poor wall surfaces before they are papered. Sold in five thicknesses, heavier and thicker paper is less likely to tear.
Paste Use cold-water or all-purpose.

Woodchip Useful for covering uneven walls, this paper has two layers bonded together with a sprinkling of wood chippings between them. Paint with emulsion. Rough to the touch, so not suitable in children's rooms or in narrow passages.
Paste Use all-purpose, cold-water, heavy-duty or ready mixed.

Standard wallpaper Quality varies with price: cheap paper is thin and tears easily, especially when damp. It is also more difficult to hang. None of these papers is washable, so avoid using them in kitchens.
Paste Use all-purpose, cold-water or ready-mixed.

Duplex paper The top surface – often with a relief pattern – is bonded to a backing paper. It is strong, easy to hang and holds its shape. Easier to hang than other relief wallpapers.
Paste Use all-purpose, cold-water, heavy-duty or ready-mixed.

GREEN WALLPAPERING

Several manufacturers make environmentally friendly wallpapers using a range of materials and methods. Some are made from sustainably sourced wood and use water-based inks, others from recycled paper and even flax. Paste them with natural non-toxic methyl cellulose wallpaper paste, an adhesive mainly obtained from wood pulp and cotton.

Paste-the-wall papers Available in a wide range of colours and designs. They are easy to hang (and strip off) and can be wiped clean. Paste the wall, not the paper.
Paste Use all-purpose, cold-water or ready-mixed.

Relief wall coverings Heavy papers, such as Anaglypta, embossed with a pattern during manufacture. Suitable for uneven walls and ceilings. Can be painted.
Paste Use all-purpose, cold-water or ready-mixed.

High relief wall coverings Made from material that feels like hard putty. Many designs available. Lincrusta is more durable than other relief wall coverings.
Paste Use cold-water, heavy-duty, ready-mixed or Lincrusta adhesive.

Vinyl PVC layer, with pattern or texture, bonded to paper. Durable and washable.
Paste Use all-purpose or ready-mixed (both with fungicide) or vinyl adhesive.

Hessian Available as just a roll of material, or bonded to a backing paper that keeps it from sagging. With unbacked hessian, paste the wall, not the material.
Paste Use all-purpose, cold-water, heavy-duty or ready-mixed.

Silk wall covering Silk, bonded to a fine backing paper. Expensive and delicate; joins are always visible. Best in small areas.
Paste Use all-purpose, cold-water or ready-mixed.

Japanese grasscloth Made of real grasses, bonded and stitched to a fine paper. Joins are always visible.
Paste Use all-purpose, cold-water, heavy-duty or ready-mixed.

Cork wall coverings A fine veneer of cork, stuck to a plain or painted backing paper. Colour shows through the holes. Apply paste to the wall, not the paper.
Paste Use all-purpose, cold-water, heavy-duty or ready-mixed.

Metallic wall coverings Foil bonded to a paper backing. Use only on perfect walls, as any unevenness will spoil the effect. Paste the wall, not the covering.
Paste Use all-purpose or ready-mixed (both with fungicide) or heavy-duty.

Flock wall coverings Fabric pile, bonded to backing paper. Hang as standard wallpaper but try to keep splashes of paste off the surface. Expensive, but effective.
Paste Use all-purpose, cold-water, heavy-duty or ready-mixed.

Special effects wall coverings Papers and vinyls in a wide range that give the effect of wood, stone or tiling. Used to create optical illusions. Can be overpowering, and more expensive than standard coverings.
Paste Use all-purpose, cold-water, heavy-duty or ready-mixed.

Choosing the right paste

What you need to know

- Use a paste recommended by the manufacturer of the wall covering you have chosen. In general, the heavier the wall covering, the stronger the paste will need to be.
- Many pastes can be mixed to different strengths to suit standard wallpaper or heavy vinyls by adding more or less water. Follow the instructions on the packet.
- Many wall coverings must be left to one side after they have been pasted to allow the paste to soak into the paper. The paper expands slightly when it is damp and if it is not left to soak it will continue to expand on the wall, making matching difficult and perhaps forming bubbles. In general, heavy thick coverings need to soak for longer than thin ones. Vinyls need no soaking time because vinyl does not expand when damp.

Glue size Apply to bare wall surfaces before papering. Size adds to the adhesive quality of the paste and makes surfaces slippery so the covering can be slid into place. Mix with cold water. A pack that makes 5 litres will cover enough wall for 8 rolls.

All-purpose paste For all wall coverings. Powder or flakes are mixed with varying quantities of cold water to suit the particular wall covering. Follow the instructions on the packet. Contains a fungicide. Water content varies between 4–7 litres a sachet, covering 2–10 rolls.

Cold-water paste The traditional starch-based wallpaper paste, still favoured by many professionals. For all weights of wallpaper, depending on water content. Mix with cold water, stirring well to avoid lumps. Use with glue size, to provide extra slip and adhesion. A 4.5 litre pack will do for 5–6 rolls of medium-weight paper.

Heavy-duty paste For high relief wall coverings; duplex paper; woodchip; corks; flocks; special effects wall coverings such as imitation wood panelling; imitation tiling; and imitation brick. Will hold heavy materials. Mix with cold water. A 4.5 litre pack is enough for 4–6 rolls.

Ready-mixed paste For paper and fabric-backed vinyls; paper-backed hessian; grasscloth; special wall coverings; expanded polystyrene tiles; veneers; coving. Contains a fungicide. Usually supplied in a tub. More expensive than powdered paste. A 2.5kg pack is enough for 3–4 rolls.

Vinyl adhesive For vinyl wall coverings. A powder or ready-mixed paste containing fungicide to discourage mould – essential when hanging impervious materials. 4.5 litres is enough for 4 rolls.

Lincrusta adhesive For Lincrusta relief decoration and very heavy relief wall coverings. Thick ready-mixed paste. 1 litre is enough for one roll; 2 litres for 2–3 rolls.

How many rolls do you need?

How much paper you need to buy will be affected by whether the wallpaper design has a pattern that repeats down the length of the roll and must be matched up between lengths. The larger the pattern repeat, the more paper you need and the more wastage there will be.

Most British wall coverings are sold in rolls 10.05m x 530mm, though the size may vary slightly. If your chosen paper has these dimensions, use the chart (right) to calculate how many rolls you need to buy. It is better to have too much paper than to run out and find you can't get any more. You can use any leftover paper for future repair work, or as drawer liners.

Use a steel tape to measure the height of the walls from the skirting board to the picture rail, coving or ceiling.

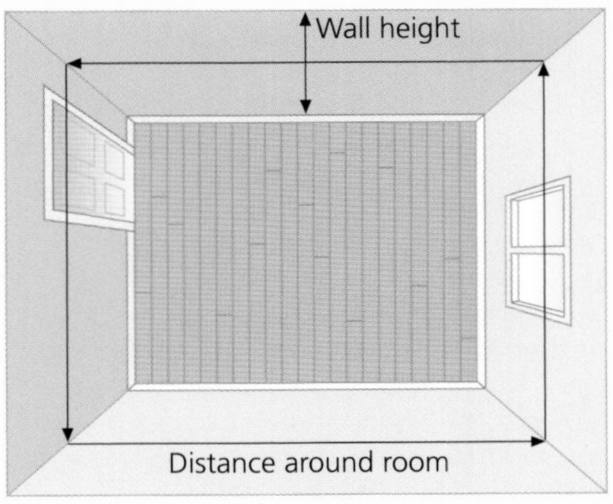

When measuring the perimeter of the room, include the width of the doors and all standard size windows – the extra paper will be needed for the trimming at the top and bottom of each length.

Only deduct the width of a window from your calculations if it is a French window, occupying a large part of a wall.

If you are papering a ceiling, measure the perimeter of the room and use the chart (above).

If you are papering a passage ceiling, measure the width of the ceiling at various places, to make sure it does not vary. Divide this measurement by the width of a roll. A narrow passage, less than a metre wide, will need only two widths. A wider passage may need three widths.

Measure the length of the passage, multiply it by the number of widths, and you will be able to work out how many rolls you will need.

HOW MANY ROLLS DO YOU NEED?

Estimate the number of rolls you will need, including the areas covered by doors and windows. Always buy a little extra to allow for experimentation and mistakes.

Walls

Wall height in metres	Measurement round room in metres										
	10	11	12	13	14	15	16	17	18	19	20
2.0 to 2.2	5	5	5	6	6	7	7	7	8	8	9
2.2 to 2.4	5	6	6	6	7	7	8	8	9	9	9
2.4 to 2.6	5	6	6	7	7	8	8	9	9	10	10
2.6 to 2.8	5	6	7	7	8	8	9	9	10	11	11
2.8 to 3.0	5	5	7	8	8	9	9	10	11	11	12

Ceilings

	Measurement round room in metres						
	9-12	13-15	17-18	20-21	22-24	26-27	29-30
Rolls needed	2	3	4	5	7	9	10

Tips on buying wallpaper

Remember the repeat

If your chosen paper has a random pattern – a sponging effect for example – or if it is plain stripes, you will need fewer rolls of paper than if there is a pattern with a drop between the repeats. Pattern repeats vary from around 75mm to 500mm or more. The pattern repeat length is generally noted on the wallpaper wrapper.

If the paper you have chosen has a large repeat, you will probably get one fewer full length out of each roll than you think, so always buy an extra roll or two. Some stores will allow you to return unused rolls if they are left unopened and you have retained your receipt.

The majority of patterned wallpapers have a straight pattern match: the same part of the design occurs along both edges, which means that each length you hang starts at the same point of the design as the length beside it.

Wallpapers with a drop pattern match have the design offset by half the pattern repeat on the two long edges of the paper. Therefore matching lengths of paper as you paste them on the wall uses up more paper. A way to reduce the amount of wallpaper wasted in this way is to cut alternate lengths from two rolls.

Special coverings

If you choose from a Continental or American pattern book – or have decided upon a special wall covering, such as hessian – check the size and use the chart provided in the pattern book to work out how many rolls you need. Rolls may be wider than standard wallpaper.

Keep to one batch

Check that all the paper comes from the same batch, to avoid colour variation between rolls. If you have to buy rolls with a different batch number, because the store does not have enough from the same batch, aim to use them in areas where any slight shading variations will not show, such as behind furniture, tucked away in a corner or in a passageway.

Lining paper

Lining paper can improve the end result of your wallpapering immensely. It comes in five thicknesses, and is often twice the length of a roll of ordinary wallpaper. So check the length on the roll and work out how many rolls you will need – you will buy too much if you assume that you need the same number of rolls as the wallpaper you choose.

Hanging standard wallpaper

Papering the walls is normally the last stage in decorating. Once you have mastered the simple techniques, the job is quick and easy.

Tools *Pasting table; bucket; brush; paper-hanger's brush; steel tape measure; plumb line; pencil; wallpaper scissors and small scissors; sponge; seam roller.*

Materials *Size; wallpaper paste; wallpaper.*

Before you start Size bare walls to prevent them from absorbing paste from the wallcovering. Size also makes the surface slippery so that the covering can be slid into place. You can either buy size or use a dilute form of the paste you plan to use to hang the wall covering.

Apply size with the paste brush or a short-pile paint roller to cover the whole surface and spread the size evenly. If the size gets onto painted woodwork, wipe it off immediately with a damp cloth.

Cutting paper to length

1 Take a roll of paper and check which way the pattern goes. Decide where definite motifs should be in relation to the top of the wall.

2 With a steel tape, measure the wall height down to the top of the skirting board. Add an extra 100mm to allow for final trimming.

3 Unroll the paper on the pasting table, pattern-side down, measure the length and draw a line with a pencil and straight-edge across the back.

4 Cut along the line with a pair of long-bladed scissors.

5 Turn the paper over, unroll the next length and match the pattern by placing it edge to edge with the first length. Using the cut length as a measuring guide, cut off the second length.

Continue in this way until several lengths are ready for pasting. Number them on the back so that you know the hanging order, and note which end is the top.

HELPFUL TIP

If the ceiling in a room is very uneven or sloping, do not cut lengths of paper in advance. It is much easier to hang one piece, and then match the next against it on the wall.

Pasting the paper

1 Lay the first cut length on the pasting table, pattern side down.

2 Align it so that the end very slightly overlaps the left-hand edge of the table (reverse if you are left-handed).

3 Slide the paper so that one long edge very slightly overlaps the far edge of the pasting table.

4 Load the paste brush and wipe off excess paste by dragging the brush across the string on the bucket.

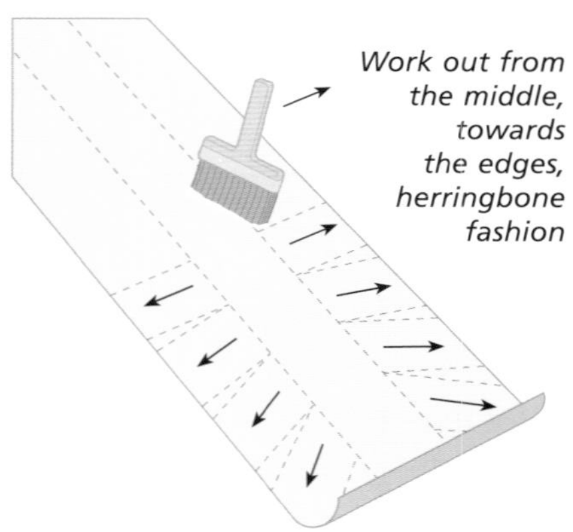

5 Start applying paste in the centre and then brush out to the far edge. Realign the paper to overlap the near edge of the pasting table and brush out to that too.

6 Check that all the paper on the table is evenly covered with paste, then pick up the left-hand end and fold the paper back on itself – paste-to-paste – such that around two-thirds of it is folded like this.

7 Slide the paper to the left of the table so that the pasted part hangs off the edge.

8 Paste the right-hand end of the paper as you did the left, brushing in a herringbone pattern until the paper is all pasted.

9 Fold the paper over – without creasing it – so the top and bottom edges meet. Wipe any paste off the table before pasting the next length.

10 Leave the pasted paper to soak for as long as the manufacturer recommends. Thin paper and vinyl will be ready to hang almost immediately but heavier materials need to be left for 10 to 15 minutes.

LINING PAPER

If you are going to paper a room after lining it, make sure that the seams in the two papers won't fall in the same place.

• Start with a half-width of lining paper to stagger the joints.

• Do not overlap the edges: raised areas will show through.

• Do not take lining paper around corners. Trim away any excess paper so that the edges fit neatly.

Hanging the first length

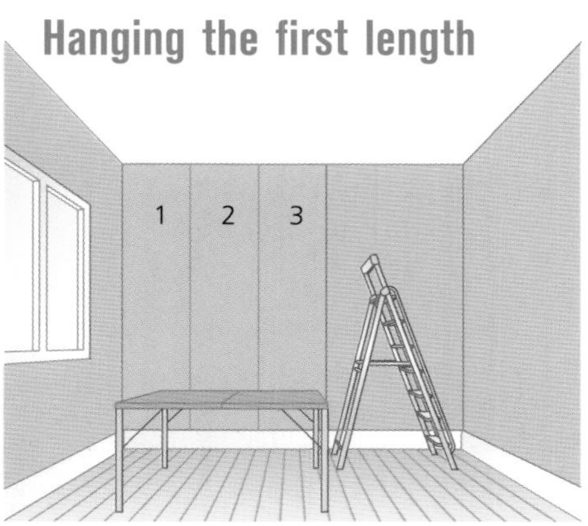

Start hanging the paper on a wall next to the main window wall and work away from the light source, so that any slight overlaps will not cast shadows, which make the joins obvious. Remember that a strong pattern will also need to be centred on features like chimney breasts – see page 106.

1 Pencil a mark near the top of the wall, 515mm out from the corner, so that around 15mm of paper will turn onto the window wall.

2 Pin the plumb line to the mark and let the bob hang free about 1.2m down the wall. When the bob settles, make another pencil mark directly behind the string. Check the distance to the corner all the way down the wall. If it is greater than 515mm at any point because the corner is not true, not enough paper will turn. So make the top measurement shorter, use the plumb line again and draw new pencil marks.

3 Carry the pasted length to the wall and release the (longer) top fold gently, holding it at both sides. Do not let the lower part drop suddenly – it may tear, or stretch and cause matching problems.

4 Hold the top right corner against the wall so that the right-hand edge of the paper aligns with the pencil mark. Make sure about 50mm of excess paper is left at the top of the wall for trimming.

5 Keep the left edge of the paper off the wall while you align the right-hand edge on the lower pencil mark.

6 Once the right edge is in place, smooth the paper with your hand or paperhanging brush diagonally up until the top left corner of the paper is on the wall.

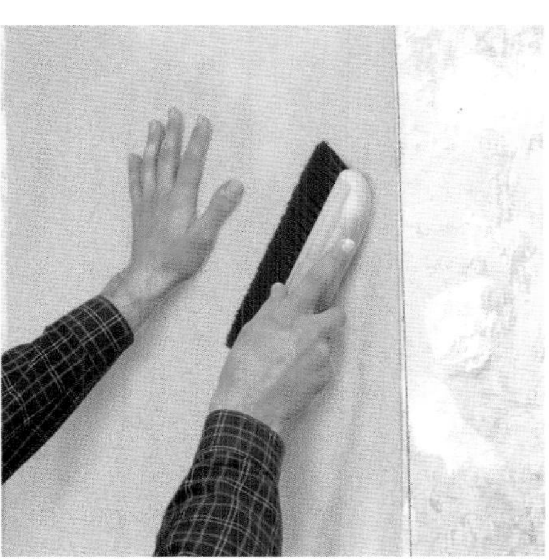

7 Let go of the paper and smooth out the top half of the length with the paper-hanging brush, working from the centre outwards. Make sure the paper stays on the pencil mark.

8 Release the lower fold. Brush down the centre of the length, then out to the edges as you did when pasting, ensuring that any bubbles are brushed out. Dab down the edges with the tip of the brush or a dry, clean cloth made into a pad.

9 With the length in place, run the back of a pair of scissors along the paper where it meets the skirting board, to crease it.

10 Pull the paper gently away from the wall and cut along the crease, with the underside of the paper facing you. Brush the trimmed edge back in place. Repeat this process at the top of the length.

Alternatively A trimming guide gives a neater edge once you have learnt how to handle it properly. Slide the guide under the paper and cut off the excess with a trimming knife. The blade must be razor-sharp or it will tear the damp wallpaper. If you feel the knife pulling at the paper, change the blade immediately.

Hanging the next lengths

1 Hang the second length of paper to the right of the piece on the wall, following the same procedure but without using the plumb line. Match the top section of the left edge of the new length with the length on the wall, then run your hand diagonally up and to the right to press the top of the paper to the wall.

2 Smooth out the paper from the centre with the paperhanging brush.

3 Release the lower fold, check that the edges match and continue to brush over the paper. Trim top and bottom as before.

4 With two or three pieces hung, run the seam roller lightly down the joins of smooth papers. Do not press down the edges of textured materials, like Anaglypta, or lines will show where the pattern has been flattened.

HELPFUL TIP

Use matchsticks to mark where fittings have been taken down from a wall. Push a matchstick into each hole or wallplug, leaving it just proud of the surface. Ease the matchsticks through the paper when you smooth it over the wall. Snap the tip off each matchstick to prevent it from staining the paper.

Wallpapering around corners

All rooms have internal corners and often external ones as well – on a chimney breast for example.

Internal corners

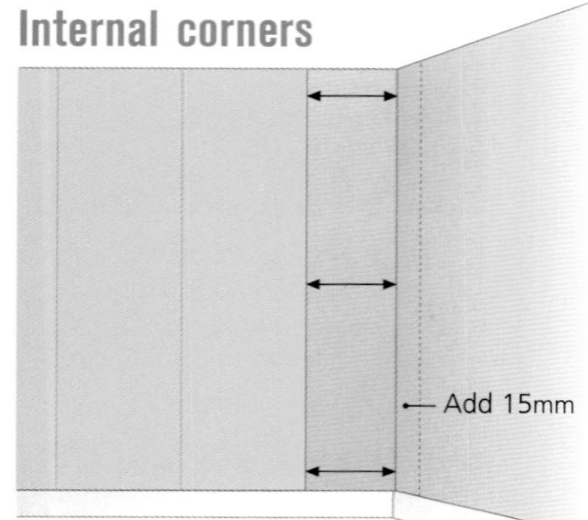

1 Measure the distance between the last length you have hung and the corner at the top, middle and bottom of the wall. Note the widest distance and add 15mm to allow for the turn onto the next wall.

2 Cut a length to this width. Keep the offcut for papering the first section of the adjoining wall.

3 Paste and hang the length. Take the overlap onto the next wall. Use the brush to smooth the paper well into the corner. If creases form, tear the paper – but cut vinyl – and overlap the torn pieces so that they lie flat.

4 Measure the offcut and hang the plumb line this distance away from the corner to find a vertical. Make pencil marks behind the line at intervals down the wall.

5 Hang the offcut with the right-hand edge aligning with the pencil marks. The length will overlap the paper turned from the previous wall. If the paper is patterned, match the two pieces as closely as possible. Use special overlap adhesive with vinyls to make the overlap stick down firmly.

External corners

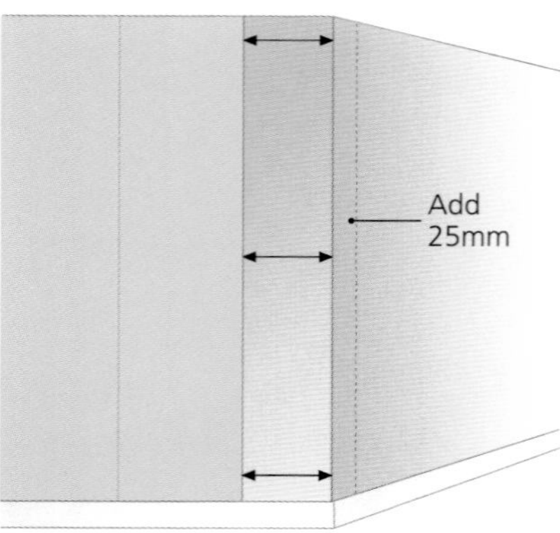

Never try to turn more than 25mm around an external corner – the turned paper is likely to slant and look crooked.

1 Paper the wall until there is less than one width to the corner.

2 Measure the distance between the edge of the last hung length and the corner, at the top, middle and bottom of the wall. Add 25mm to the smallest distance and mark the cutting line in pencil on the back of the paper. Paste the paper first before cutting it – cut just before you fold it over.

3 Hang the length as far as the corner and take the overlap around onto the next wall. Smooth away any bubbles with the paperhanging brush.

4 Mark a vertical plumb line on the new wall and check the width between the line and the edge of the turned-round paper. If it is the same at the top, middle and bottom, you can butt join the offcut piece up to the edge. If not, you will have to overlap it. Choose the less obvious wall to do this – either taking the paper just round the corner or starting it just to the side of the corner. Mark a new vertical plumbline as appropriate, so that the lengths on the rest of this new wall will be true – vital if you have a vertical pattern. Once you have hung this offcut, continue hanging full-width lengths on this wall until you come to a door, a window or the next corner.

APPLYING BORDERS

You can buy friezes and borders to match a fabric or the colours or motif of a wallpaper. You can also buy sticky-back borders, which are a great way to brighten up a child's room.

A deep frieze at the top of a wall will make the ceiling seem lower. A 'frame' of frieze on the wall, set in about 250mm from the edge, will help to 'shrink' the long wall of a narrow hall or landing.

The frieze must go on a sound, flat surface; a heavily embossed paper is not a suitable surface.

Applying a frieze

1 For a frieze at the top of a wall, draw a straight pencil guideline; make it slightly lower than the depth of the frieze to allow for an uneven ceiling edge and apply a band of paint to match the ceiling at the top of the wall. If the frieze is to go along the skirting and round a door, no guideline is needed.

2 Cut the frieze to length, using one piece from corner to corner.

3 Paste the frieze, fold it like a concertina and leave it for ten minutes to soak.

4 Apply it along the guideline, brushing it out well and letting out folds as you work along.

Making a frame

1 Draw guidelines that run parallel to the nearest wall edge.

2 Apply the frieze. At the corners, cut both layers at 45° with a trimming knife and remove the excess.

Peel and stick borders

Borders that are all-plastic have stronger adhesive than paper-backed vinyl. Peel off only a little of the release paper at a time, as they cannot be repositioned without damaging the paper beneath.

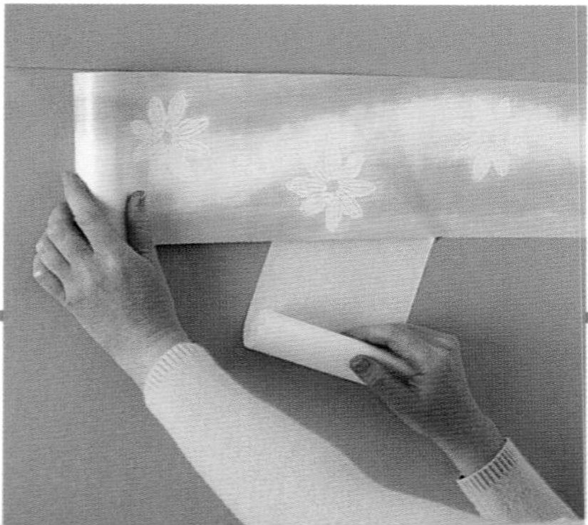

Wallpapering in awkward places

Square light switches or sockets

1 Turn off the electricity at the mains. Hang the paper from the top of the wall down as far as the switch or socket.

2 Cut the paper to the corners of the switch and pull back the flaps.

3 Partially unscrew the switch cover and pull it about 5mm away from the wall.

SAFETY TIP

Never put metallic or foil wall coverings behind light switches. They may conduct electricity. Always turn off the electricity at the consumer unit (fuse box) before undoing light switches or sockets.

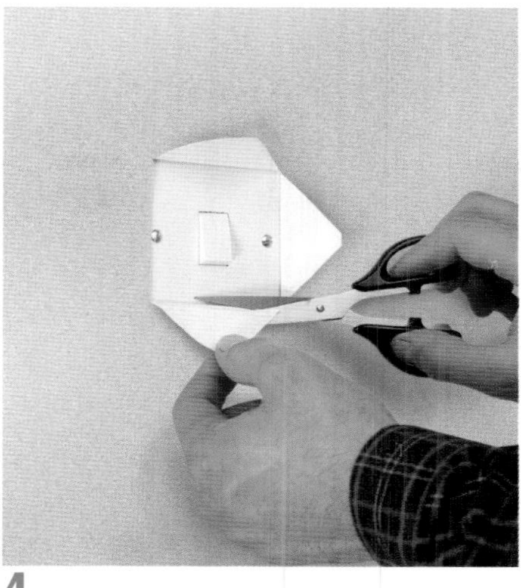

4 Trim away excess paper so that about 3mm of paper will sit behind the cover.

5 Gently ease the switch cover through the hole in the paper.

6 Push the paper behind the switch cover with a piece of flat wood, like a lolly stick, and then brush the paper flat against the wall, smoothing away any air bubbles.

7 Hang the remainder of the length. Tighten the switch cover screws and turn the electricity supply back on.

Circular fittings

1 Turn off the electricity at the mains. Hang the length of wallpaper in the ordinary way until you reach the fixture. Pierce a hole in the paper over it with a pair of small scissors. Then make star-like cuts out to the edge of the fitting.

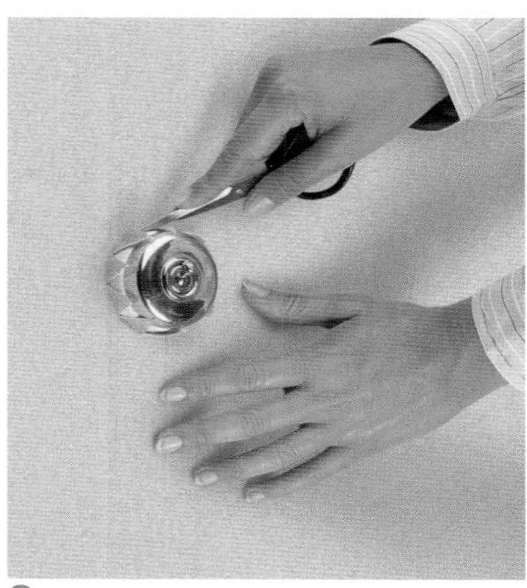

2 Crease the outline of the fitting on the paper with the back of a pair of scissors.

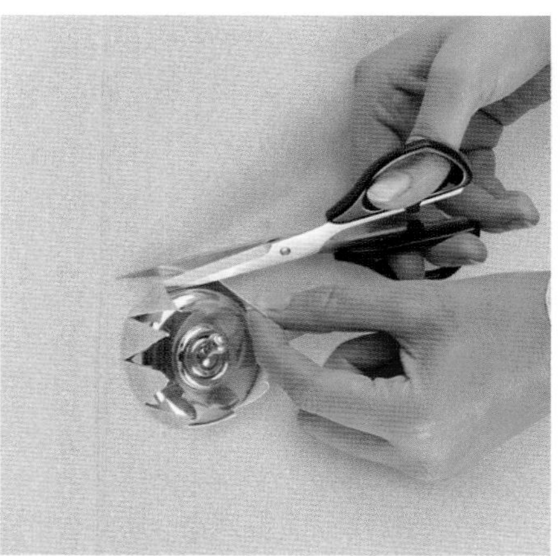

3 Cut off the surplus paper with small pointed scissors – they must be sharp or you may tear the wet paper. Follow the marked outline but allow for just a fraction of paper to turn onto the fitting so that the wall cannot show through a gap.

4 Smooth the paper flat around the fitting with a paperhanging brush. Then hang the rest of the length.

Radiators

1 Tuck the paper in behind the radiator until you reach the supporting bracket. Hang the next piece over the radiator, brushing it flat as far down as possible.

2 Use a pencil to mark the position of the wall bracket on the back of the paper and make a vertical cut in the paper from the bottom edge to the top of the bracket.

3 Feed the paper down behind the radiator and smooth down with a radiator roller. Trim it at the skirting board. Alternatively, if the radiator overhangs the skirting board, save paper by trimming it off 150mm below the top of the radiator.

4 Sponge any paste off the radiator before it dries.

HELPFUL TIP

When wallpapering a room with a radiator, turn off the radiator and allow it to cool completely before you start. Not only will it be more comfortable than working round a hot radiator, but your results will be better, because there will be no risk that the paper may dry too fast and start to curl.

Fireplaces

1 Cut the lengths of paper which are to go round the fireplace roughly to size before applying paste – so that you do not have to cope with a lot of pasted paper when trimming. Leave a margin of at least 25mm for trimming in situ.

2 Paste and hang the paper in the ordinary way as far as you can, then mark the outline of the fireplace on the paper using the back of a scissor blade.

3 Peel a little of the paper away from the wall so you can work comfortably. Cut along the marked outline. Use small, sharp scissors if there are lots of small cuts; otherwise, use paperhanging scissors. If the trimming takes some time and the paste is beginning to dry, apply a little more paste to the wall, rather than to the paper.

4 Smooth the paper in place all around the fireplace, using the points of bristles of a paperhanging brush to push the paper into awkward corners. Continue down to the skirting board.

CHIMNEY BREASTS

If you have chosen a strongly patterned wallpaper, centre it on the chimney breast and hang subsequent lengths from here towards the room corners. If there is no dominant pattern, hang the wallpaper round the chimney breast in the same way as for other corners (page 104).

Door frames

1 When you get to the door, hang a pasted full-length strip next to the last length, allowing the strip to flap over the door. Press the paper against the top corner of the architrave. Make a diagonal cut from the loose edge to the architrave top corner.

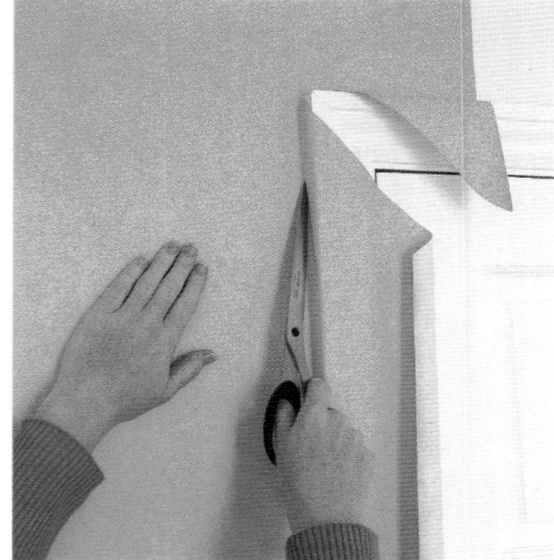

2 Brush paper into the angles between the wall and the architrave above and beside the door. Use scissors to crease the paper.

3 Trim off the excess paper along the side of the door, working from the bottom upwards. Then cut off the waste paper above the door opening.

4 Using a paperhanging brush, press the trimmed edges back into place against the edges of the architrave. Then cut the top edge of the length to fit at ceiling level, and the bottom edge at the skirting board.

5 You will probably need to hang a short length of wallpaper above the door. Use scissors to crease the paper into the angle between wall and ceiling, then into the angle between wall and architrave. Trim the paper to fit. When cutting above the architrave, leave the paper slightly over-long, so that it covers the top edge of the architrave.

6 Repeat steps 1 to 4 to hang another full-length strip at the opposite side of the door opening, again letting it overlap the door architrave so you can mark the corner and cut the waste paper away. Brush the cut edges back into place, then carry on papering the rest of the wall.

Recessed windows

1 When you reach a window recess, hang a full length drop of paper so that it overlaps the opening. If the overlap is large, you may need a helper to support the weight of the pasted paper.

2 Make a neat, horizontal scissor cut level with the top edge of the recess.

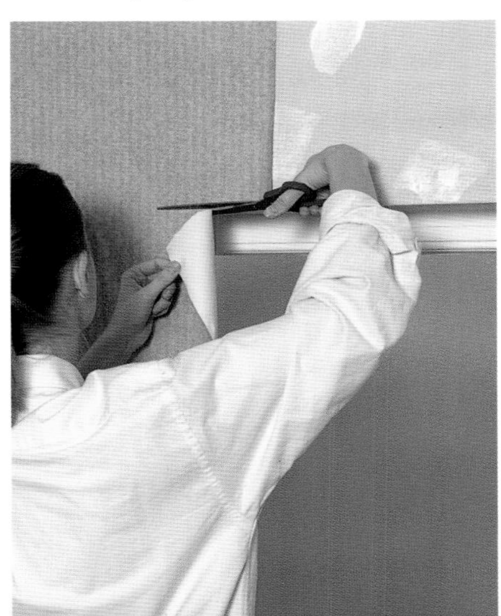

3 Make a second cut level with the top surface of the window sill.

4 If the flap of paper that you have created is enough to cover the depth of the recess, crease it into the angle with a paperhanging brush. If it is not deep enough to reach the window frame, cut and paste a strip a little wider than the gap and hang it on the side of the reveal, matching it to the pattern, if there is one.

5 Run scissors along the crease to make a defined cutting line. Peel back the paper and make a neat scissor cut to trim off the excess. Brush the paper back into place.

6 Cut a piece of wallpaper long enough to reach from the ceiling to the top of the window, into the recess and up to the frame, with extra for trimming. Hang this next to the previous full-length strip, and brush into the recess. Trim at ceiling level and where paper meets the frame. Repeat until you need another full-length piece.

7 Paper under the windowsill. Measure from the underside of the sill to the top of the skirting board, then add 50mm or so for trimming. Cut strips of paper to this length and hang them under the window, matching the pattern if necessary. Repeat to cover the rest of the wall below the window opening, stopping when the next piece needed is a full-length one.

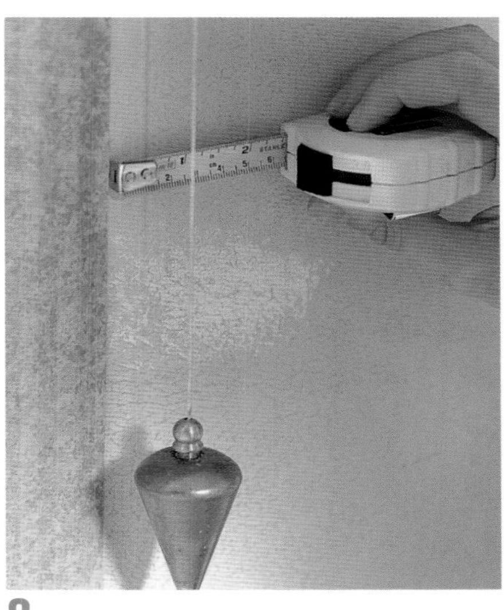

8 Check that the last piece hung above the window is in line with the last piece below it by hanging a plumb line. If it is not, measure the discrepancy at its widest point and subtract this from the width of a piece of paper. Mark a plumb line on the wall to the right of the window at this distance from the edge of the overhanging piece of paper.

9 Hang the next whole length. Butt it up to the previous pieces if they were in line, or position its right hand edge level with the plumb line you have drawn if the paper above and below the window was misaligned.

10 There will be a gap in each top corner of the reveal. Cut a strip of paper the width of the gap at top left, but 50mm deeper than the recess. Position the paper over the gap, allowing about 25mm to turn up at the front edge onto the wall above, matching the pattern, if there is one.

11 Use a trimming knife and straight-edge to cut through both the patch and the paper above it, 15mm above the edge of the recess. Peel away the offcuts from each piece and then press the edges flat for an invisible butt join. Cover the gap in the other corner of the reveal in the same way.

Hanging special coverings

Some wallcoverings require special techniques, such as pasting the wall instead of the paper. Other papers come ready-pasted and you don't even need a pasting table to hang them successfully.

Hanging paste-the-wall paper

This type differs from standard wallpaper because you do not cut lengths from the roll before you hang it. You also paste the wall and not the wall covering.

1 Hang a plumb line and mark a true vertical on the wall as for hanging standard wallpaper (page 103).

2 Paste the area of the wall which the first length is to cover, taking the paste just beyond the width of the covering. Use an adhesive containing a fungicide and apply it with a paint roller or brush.

3 Hold the roll of paper up to the pasted area. Align the edge with the pencil marks on the wall. Smooth the covering into place with a brush or damp sponge.

4 Gradually unroll the paper as you move down the wall, wiping away any bubbles under the surface as you work. You may find it easier if a helper holds the roll.

5 Crease the covering at the top and bottom of the length as for standard wallpaper and trim.

6 Paste an adjacent width of the wall and hang the next length as before. Make sure the pattern matches, and butt join the edges of the two pieces.

Hanging ready-pasted papers

Ready-pasted papers and vinyls are water-resistant so they do not expand in water. This reduces the chance of bubbles forming and they do not have to be left to soak.

Tools *Water trough (cheap polystyrene troughs are widely available in DIY stores); scissors; pasting brush; sponge.*

Before you start Hang a plumb line to find a true vertical and make pencil marks to act as a guide for the first length as for hanging standard wallpaper (page 103). Put down plenty of dust sheets and fill the water trough with cold water. Position it near the wall where you are going to start.

1 Measure the wall height, add 100mm for trimming and cut a length of the paper or vinyl. Check which way up it is to be hung on the wall.

2 Roll the cut length up loosely, paste side out, from bottom to top, and immerse it in the trough for the recommended time.

3 Use both hands to lift the covering out of the trough. Hold the length above the trough for a few seconds so that surplus water drains into it.

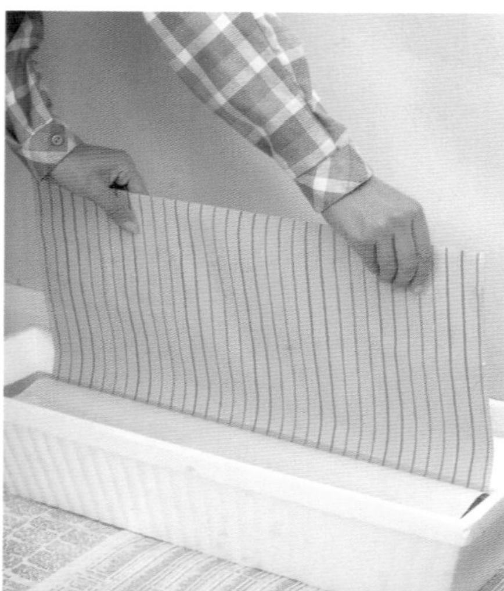

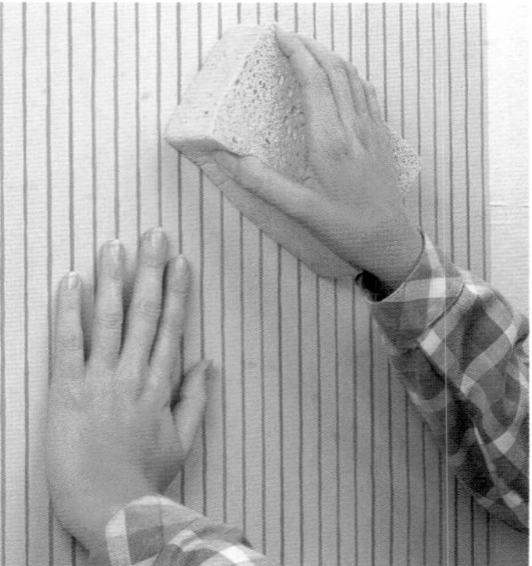

4 Hang the length, smoothing away air bubbles with a clean sponge. Work from the middle of the length out to the edges as for standard wallpaper.

5 Wipe away any excess paste at the seams with a damp rag. The paste will not stain the surface of the covering.

6 Trim the edges as you would standard wallpaper. Then cut the next length. Roll, soak and hang it following the same procedure as for the first length.

7 Keep the water trough topped up with water as you hang the lengths. Move the trough along as you work your way from one end of the wall to the other.

8 Use special overlap adhesive to get a good bond where vinyl overlaps vinyl (around corners for example) or where a seam is not lying flat.

9 Cut vinyl with scissors around awkward angles. You cannot tear it. If you have to overlap vinyl, you can make the join less noticeable by tearing off the backing paper of the top layer of vinyl, to reduce its thickness.

10 When you have hung three or four lengths, go over the seams with a seam roller to ensure that the edges are firmly stuck down.

HELPFUL TIP

Mix a small amount of paste even when you are hanging ready-pasted papers. Use it to revive areas that may have dried out while you have been trimming. Brush the paste onto the dried areas and then smooth the length into place.

Wallpapering a ceiling

Ceilings are hard to decorate – you have to work at a height and against gravity. Also, because the ceiling is usually well lit, any imperfections in your work will show up. If the ceiling is smooth, consider painting it rather than papering it. You may want to paper a ceiling for a decorative effect or line a ceiling that has hairline cracks before painting it.

Tools *Dustsheets; tacks and chalk-line; scissors; pasting brush; wallpaper hanging brush; stepladders and trestle boards; pasting table; sponge.*

Materials *Paper; wallpaper paste.*

Before you start Cover the floor with plenty of cotton dust sheets. Set up a safe working platform. Use two trestles or two stepladders and arrange a scaffold board between them so that the ceiling clears your head by about 75mm. If possible, the board should allow you to paper the length of the ceiling without rearranging the platform. Use two boards – one on top of the other – to give a firmer support if the trestles are more than 1.5m apart. Fill any holes and cracks and seal any stains first.

Tips for a professional finish

1 Hang paper beginning at the main window and working away from it. If there are windows in two walls, hang the paper across the narrower width.

2 If you are hanging a decorative wallpaper, make a line parallel with the wall as a guide for the first length (this is not necessary for lining paper or woodchip – just align the paper with the wall). The wall is unlikely to be perfectly straight, so pin one end of the chalk line to the ceiling 25mm closer to the corner than the width of your paper. Take the line to the other side of the room, position it at the same measurement from the opposite corner and snap the chalk line to make a straight line to work from.

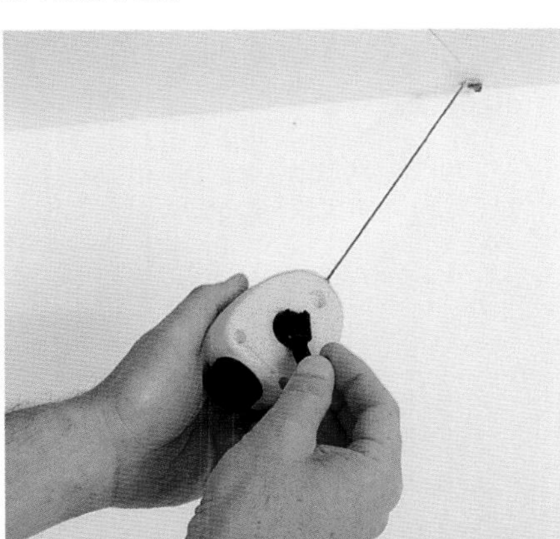

Hanging the paper

1 Brush the whole ceiling with glue size (see page 100) – this gives good slip and helps the adhesion.

2 Measure the ceiling, add 50mm for trimming at each end, and cut the first length.

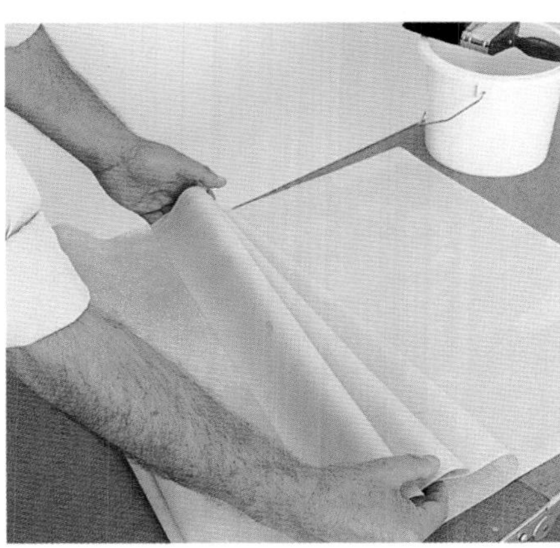

3 Paste as for paper going on a wall but, because of the length of the paper, fold it concertina fashion as you apply the paste. Keep the width of the folds to about 450mm and do not crease the folds.

4 If you are right-handed, hold the pile of folded paper in your left hand. Stand on the right hand end of the board, facing the window. If you are left-handed, hold the paper in your right hand and begin at the other end.

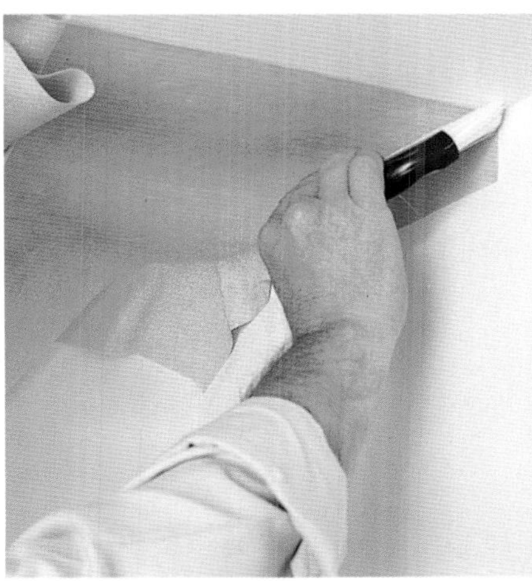

5 Release the top fold of paper. Hold it up to the ceiling and position it so that the right-hand edge aligns with the marks. Smooth the paper into the corner with your fingers. When you are satisfied that the paper is positioned correctly, gently go over it with the paperhanging brush.

6 Carefully move your left hand away to release the next fold of paper. Smooth out the paper with the brush as you move slowly to the left, checking that the paper is following the guideline. The paper will not pull away from the ceiling as long as you keep holding the rest of the paper fairly close. If the paper pulls away easily, the paste is not strong enough, so mix up some more, adding less water. Apply the paste to the ceiling, then smooth the paper back into its position.

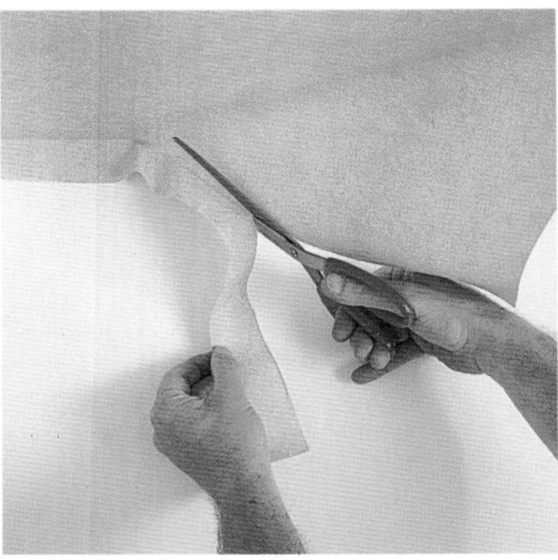

7 When the whole length is stuck to the ceiling, trim the edges against the wall and the ends. Make a crease with the back of a pair of scissors, pull the paper slightly away from the ceiling and cut away the excess.

8 Continue to hang paper in the same way, butt joining the edges.

Papering around a ceiling rose

> **SAFETY TIP**
>
> If you plan to fit paper behind a ceiling rose rather than around it, turn off the electricity at the consumer unit (fuse box) before unscrewing the rose cover.

1 Hang the first part of the length as far as the ceiling rose.

2 Make a cut in from the nearest edge of the length to the point where the fitting has to go through the paper.

3 Make a series of star-shaped cuts to go round the fitting.

4 Hang the remainder of the length. Go back to the rose and trim away the surplus paper with small sharp scissors to make a neat fit.

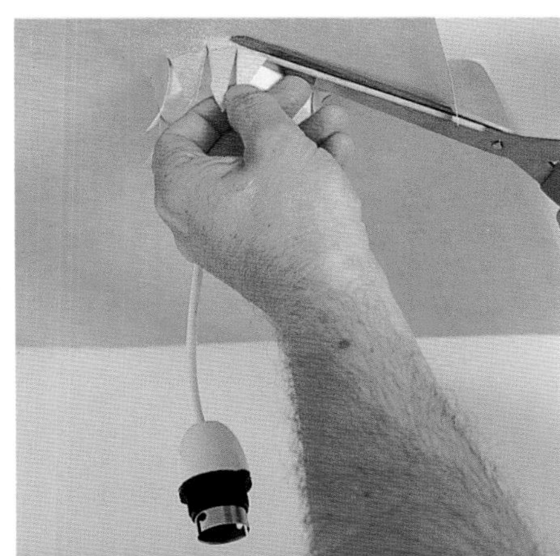

Wallpapering a stairwell

Two problems must be overcome when you paper a stairwell – how to cope with long lengths of pasted paper and how to reach the walls.

Hanging the paper

Until you are experienced, choose a good quality wall covering with a non-matching pattern. Matching long lengths is difficult because they tear easily if the paper is thin and tend to stretch. Hang the paper as on an ordinary wall, but take care when cutting lengths to size. Because stairs rise at an angle, each length of paper will need to be longer at its lower edge. Papering a stairwell is easier with two people. Long lengths of pasted paper are heavy to handle, so if possible get someone to stand on the stairs below where you are hanging the paper to hold the bulk of it while you hang the top and then to fix the lower half in place.

Reaching the walls

You need to be able to reach both the head wall and the well wall from a safe working platform.

You may prefer to reach the walls from a staircase platform, especially if the ceiling is high, although it can be difficult to walk up and down the stairs while it is in place. You can hire a staircase platform designed for use on stairs, with a base only 610mm wide and adjustable feet.

SAFETY TIP

Make sure that the ladder or platform is firm and safe before you step onto it. If you hire a staircase platform, get advice on how to erect it safely. Always move the platform to get to an area out of reach – you risk overbalancing and falling if you lean over or stretch out.

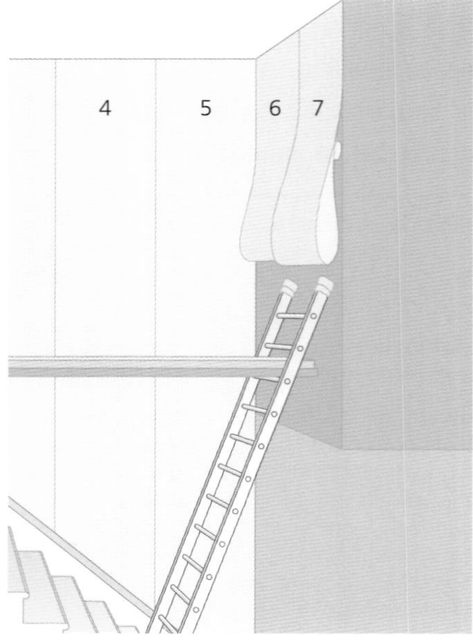

Upper head wall
Paper the top of the head wall first.
- You will probably need two or three lengths of paper. Paste and fold them before climbing onto the platform.
- Get a helper to pass them up one at a time and hang the top of each strip.
- Let them hang there.

Well wall
Head wall
Wrap the ends of the ladder in rags to protect the wall
1
2
3
4
5
Use two scaffold boards if the span is more than 1.5m
Get a second person to fix the lower half in place

Well wall
With a straight staircase, stand a stepladder on the landing – safely back from the top step – and put a straight ladder on the staircase with the top resting against the head wall and the feet against a riser halfway down the stairs. Place scaffold boards between them. Use one board on top of another for stronger support if the gap is wider than 1.5m.
- Hang the top of the paper from the board then move the platform back and smooth the bottom of the strip.

Staircase with landing
On a staircase with a landing, you may have to support the platform over the balustrade. In this situation, the straight ladder must be supported at the bottom by a wooden batten screwed securely to one of the stairs.

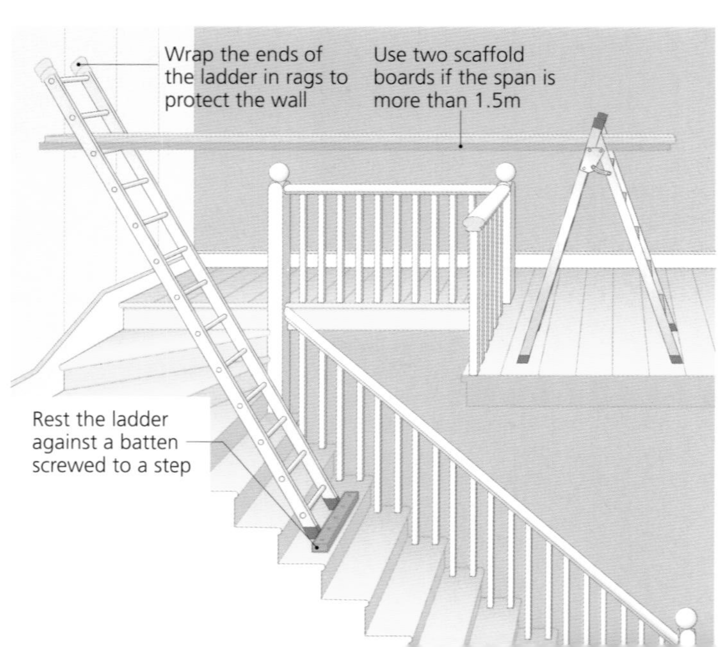

Lower head wall
- Remove the ladder and place one end of the scaffold board on a stair tread and the other on steps at the bottom of the stairs. Adjust the height of the board so that you can comfortably reach the lower half of the head wall to hang the bottom lengths.
- Hang the bottom of the paper from the new position.

Curing papering problems

Persistent bubbles
Small bubbles in wallpaper should disappear as the paper dries out. If they persist, the paper has expanded, either because it was not left to soak long enough or because new paper was applied over old.

- Cut small bubbles with a trimming knife or scalpel blade.
- Insert new paste behind the flaps with a fine artist's brush.
- Press the paper into place and wipe away excess paste with a damp rag.
- If a whole length of paper is badly affected, pull it off and hang another length, increasing the soaking time.

Paper will not slide
Water in the paste is being absorbed by the wall, or the paste is drying out too quickly. Either the wall has not been sized or the paste is too watery. Make sure you mix the paste as recommended by the maker; do not add more water to make it go farther.

- Put the problem paper back on the table.
- Mix a thicker paste and apply it to the wall, then re-hang the paper.
- If you suspect that the room's warmth is causing the paste to dry too quickly, open windows or turn off the heating.

Flattened relief pattern
Caused by too much pressure being applied when pressing the paper into position, particularly at the seams. Use very gentle pressure when applying relief papers, especially those that are heavily embossed. Do not use a seam roller on the edges; dab with a dry rag.

Expanded vinyls will regain their shape as the foam recovers, but nothing can be done to restore the relief pattern on others.

Shiny patches on matt wallpaper
The surface has been rubbed too vigorously when being hung. Shine marks cannot usually be removed completely, but rubbing the area with a ball of white bread may lessen the shine. This method can also be used to clean non-washable wallpaper.

Next time, smooth matt papers carefully with a clean, dry sponge or a dry pile paint roller. Or dab with a rag.

Staining at the seams
Old size has been reactivated by the water in the new paste. Stains cannot be totally removed, but wiping them gently with a clean, damp rag may make them less visible. To avoid this problem, wash down walls with hot water to remove any old size, and then re-size them.

Gaps at the seams
The wallpaper might have shrunk slightly as it dried out, because the paste was not strong enough to hold it in place. Depending on the colour of the wallpaper, try painting the gap with watercolour, using a fine artist's brush, so that it is less obvious. Always use a paste suitable for the type of wallpaper being used (page 100).

Seams that lift
This often happens with vinyls and relief papers, and is caused by too little paste being applied to the edges of the paper. To re-stick the seams, lift the edge gently with the blade of a kitchen knife and apply new paste with a small paint brush. For overlapping edges of vinyls use a special overlap adhesive.

Creases in the paper
Possibly caused by applying paper to a wall which is not perfectly flat, but more often caused by careless hanging. To avoid the problem, fill all indentations with filler or a skimming coat of plaster before papering.

Creases can be treated in the same way as bubbles. Tear the paper, or cut the vinyl, along the crease, re-paste if necessary, and smooth down.

Damp patches on wallpaper
If wet patches remain after most of the paper has dried, damp may be coming through the wall, or the patches may be condensation forming on a cold surface.

Do not ignore the problem: find the cause of the damp immediately and cure it. If treated immediately the damp patch will dry out without trace, but if left too long it will leave a stain.

Paper comes away from the wall
There are four possible causes: the paste is too weak to hold the weight of the paper; the surface has not been sized; the paper has been applied over old distemper or gloss paint; condensation has formed on the wall after it has been prepared.

If only small areas of the paper are coming away from the wall, mix a new batch of paste, apply it to the wall and press the paper back into place. If whole sheets are peeling off, strip the walls and prepare the surface thoroughly.

Brown spots showing through paper
Impurities in the plaster may be the cause, left from using a wire brush or wire wool during preparation.

Alternatively, the marks may be made by mould, formed because the surface is cold and damp.

If the spots are excessive and obvious, strip the walls and prepare them thoroughly before redecorating. Treat them with a fungicide before repapering if damp is a problem. And if the wall is cold, line it with thin expanded polystyrene in roll form. Use a fungicide paste on condensation-prone walls, such as a bathroom or kitchen.

Repairing damaged wallpaper

Torn wallpaper can be patched using a piece of matching paper.

1 Tear off the paper from the damaged area, leaving only the paper which is firmly attached to the wall.

2 Hold a fresh piece of paper over the hole and adjust it so that the pattern matches the surrounding paper on the wall.

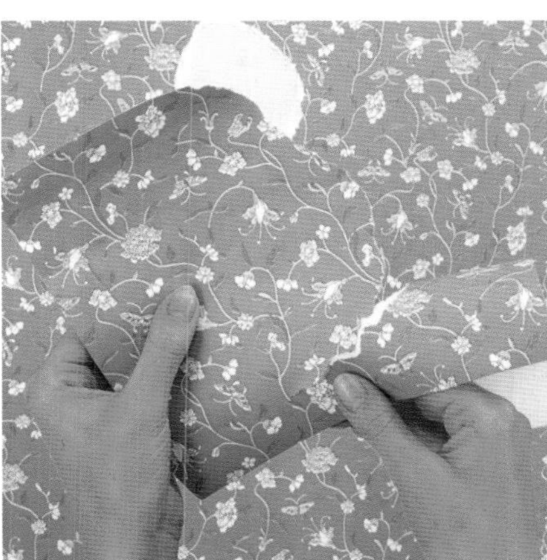

3 Tear (do not cut) a patch from the new paper so that it does not have any straight line edges.

4 Paste the patch and place it over the hole so that the pattern matches all round. Smooth down, working from the centre of the patch to the edges.

Patching vinyl wall covering

1 Cut a square piece of vinyl larger than the damaged area. (You cannot tear vinyl wall covering as you can paper.)

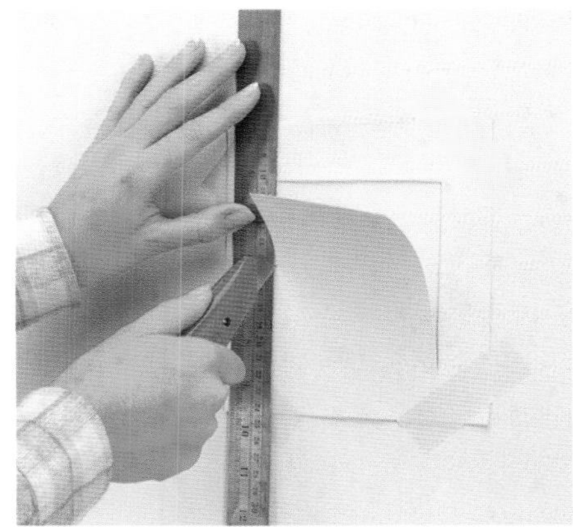

2 Tape the square over the hole and cut a square shape through both layers with a trimming knife.

3 Remove the damaged piece of old vinyl within the square.

4 Coat the patch with vinyl paste and fit it to the wall.

Tools for tiling

Many of the simple tools required for tiling – such as pincers or pliers – may already be in your toolkit. You will also need straight battens and a plumb line to help you with positioning. The specialist tools listed here will help to make the job easier.

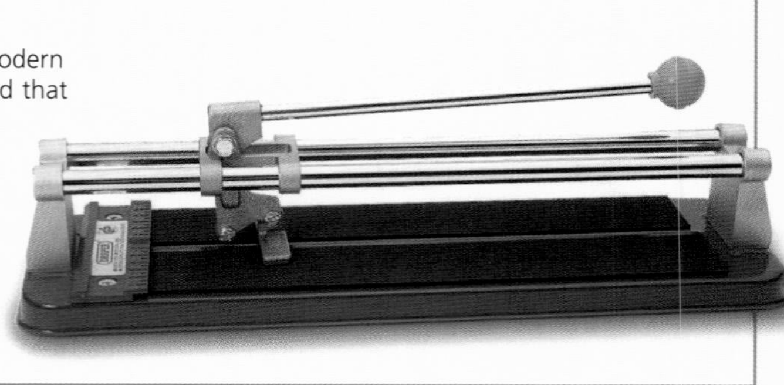

Platform tile cutter Modern ceramic tiles are so hard that they are more or less impossible to cut using a traditional, hand-held cutter. A platform tile cutter will cut both wall and floor tiles.

Profile gauge Useful for cutting tiles to fit around awkward shapes such as pipes or curved basins. The thin strips of plastic are slid into place to match the awkward shape which can then be drawn on the tile.

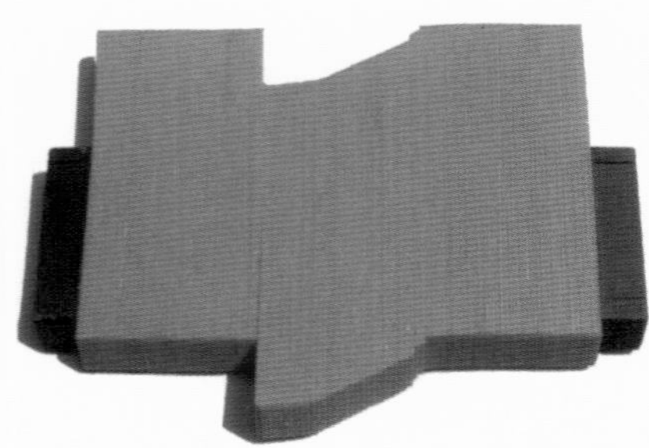

Spacers Small plastic crosses inserted at the corners of straight-edged tiles as they are applied to the wall to ensure that there is an even gap between tiles.

Tile file Removes rough edges from a cut tile. If a cut tile is just a little bit too big, you can also file it down to the correct size.

Tile drills and hole saws Special drill bits and diamond-edged hole saws create holes in ceramic tiles to accommodate pipes or fittings. Hole saws come as a set containing different diameter cutters.

Chinagraph pencil and steel rule For marking where tiles should be cut. Never use a felt-tipped pen to mark a tile – if the ink gets onto the back of the tile it may penetrate and show beneath the glazed surface.

Adhesive spreader and grouter A plastic tool with one notched edge for spreading tile adhesive, and the other edge fitted with a rubber blade for grouting. Small spreaders are usually supplied with tubs of adhesive. The notches on the spreader ensure that the adhesive is spread evenly.

Tiling gauge The gauge is simply a length of wooden batten. Mark the width of the tiles on the wood, plus gaps for spacers if necessary, and use the gauge to set out tiling and to position tiles around windows or any similar breaks in the tiling.

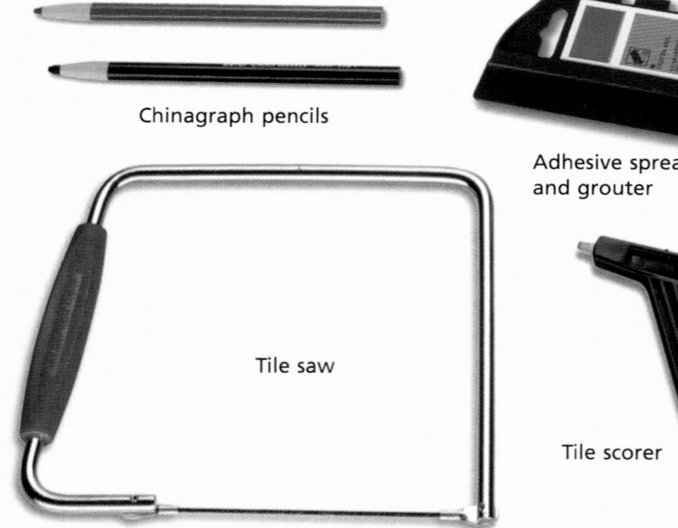

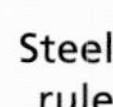

Tile saw A tungsten-carbide coated rod, mounted in a large metal frame, which acts as a cutting blade. It is the ideal tool for shaping curved tiles to fit awkward shapes. You can also get tile-cutting blades for jigsaws.

Tile cutters Cutters vary in size and shape. They are used to score a clearly defined scratch across the glaze of a tile. A cutter may resemble a slim pencil with a cutting tip or have a hardened wheel set into a handle. Tile snappers have two jaws to hold the tile when you break it after it has been scored. Place the scored tile between the jaws and squeeze the handles together. For the toughest tiles, use a platform tile cutter (above). If you have a lot of tiles to cut, consider hiring (or buying) a diamond tile cutter.

Tile nibbler Tungsten carbide edged pincers are used for making very narrow cuts, removing waste from a curved cut or for cutting individual mosaic tiles.

Choosing ceramic wall tiles and trim

Ceramic tiles are a versatile form of wall covering, particularly useful in bathrooms and kitchens. An enormous range is available in prices that vary according to size, colour and quality.

Tile sizes Wall tiles are available in sizes from 100mm square to 330 x 445mm. Choosing a size that neatly fits the space you have to cover can save a lot of cutting and wastage. Remember to allow for your desired grout width when calculating how many tiles will fit your space.

Decorative tiles Although ceramic wall tiles provide a easy-to-clean surface, they can be extremely attractive as well. Some tiles give an overall pattern; with others you can get individual tiles, which may have a raised or printed motif that is painted by hand or machined. They can make attractive insets in a plain tiled wall.

Imported tiles Foreign ceramics are often harder, thicker and heavier than standard ceramic tiles, so experiment on a couple of tiles to see whether you can cut and shape them before you buy in bulk. Occasionally imported tiles are glazed on one or more edges. If the tiles have plain square edges you will need to use spacers.

Insert tiles In some ranges, manufacturers supply special tiles to which bathroom accessories like towel rails, soap dishes and lavatory-paper holders are attached. Even though they are heavier than ordinary tiles, they can be fixed to the wall with standard adhesive. Check that the particular insert tile you want is available in the colour you have chosen before you buy the tiles.

Mosaic tiles Small ceramic or glass tiles, known as chips, usually 20 to 25mm square. They are supplied bonded to nylon or paper mesh or faced with paper, in sheets about 300mm square or rectangles 300 x 610mm. The mesh or paper controls the spacing between the tiles.

HOW MANY TILES DO YOU NEED?

- Tiles are sold singly, or in boxes containing a specified number, or by the square metre.
- Before you buy or order tiles, measure the height and width of each part to be tiled and multiply the two figures to give the area in square metres. Add all the figures together to give the total area. Coverage is also stated on boxes. Allow 5 to 10 per cent extra for cutting and breakages.
- If you are going to use contrasting coloured or patterned tiles among plain ones, decide where they are to go and how many you need. This is easier if you make a plan of the wall on graph paper. Alternatively, cut pieces of paper into tile shapes and stick them to the wall to help you to get the height and spacing of the patterned tiles right. It will probably take a couple of hours, but it gives a better impression of how the tiles will look when the job is complete.
- There is always a slight colour variation between tiles. If you can, buy tiles in boxes with the same batch number. Then shuffle the tiles to disperse and hide any differences before you start to tile.

Borders and trims

Ceramic trims You can finish off the top edge of a half-tiled wall with a row of border tiles, or use a slim pencil bead trim in a matching or contrasting colour if you prefer. Border tiles can also be used between areas of standard tiles on a fully tiled wall, for example to create the effect of a decorative dado. Border and trim tiles are made in sizes to match standard tile widths so vertical joints will align.

Plastic and metal profile trim Strips of edging trim are available in a variety of colours and finishes, from white plastic to shiny chrome and in 2.4m lengths. A curved bead is attached at right angles to a thin perforated backing plate, which is fixed to the wall behind the last tile in each row, using tile adhesive. The tiles butt up against the edging strip, protecting their unglazed edges and creating a neat finish.

Worktop trim The neatest way of edging a tiled worktop is with a timber moulding. Paint, varnish or stain the moulding first, then screw it to the edge of the worktop to help you to position the tiles and bed them to the correct level. Use epoxy grout to fill all the joints to give the worktop a hard-wearing and hygienic finish.

EDGING A BATH OR SHOWER TRAY

The gap between a bath or shower tray and the wall can be filled with flexible silicone sealant (white or coloured), but this can become stained and unsightly in time. If the wall is tiled, you can get small matching quadrant tiles to fit along the gap after the main wall tiles are fitted, or a selection of metal or plastic trims (called bath seals) which are fitted before the bottom row of tiles is installed in the same way as profile trims (see left). Self-adhesive plastic trims can also be used – applied after all the tiles have been fitted and sealed with silicone.

All these trims will need to be mitred where they meet at corners.

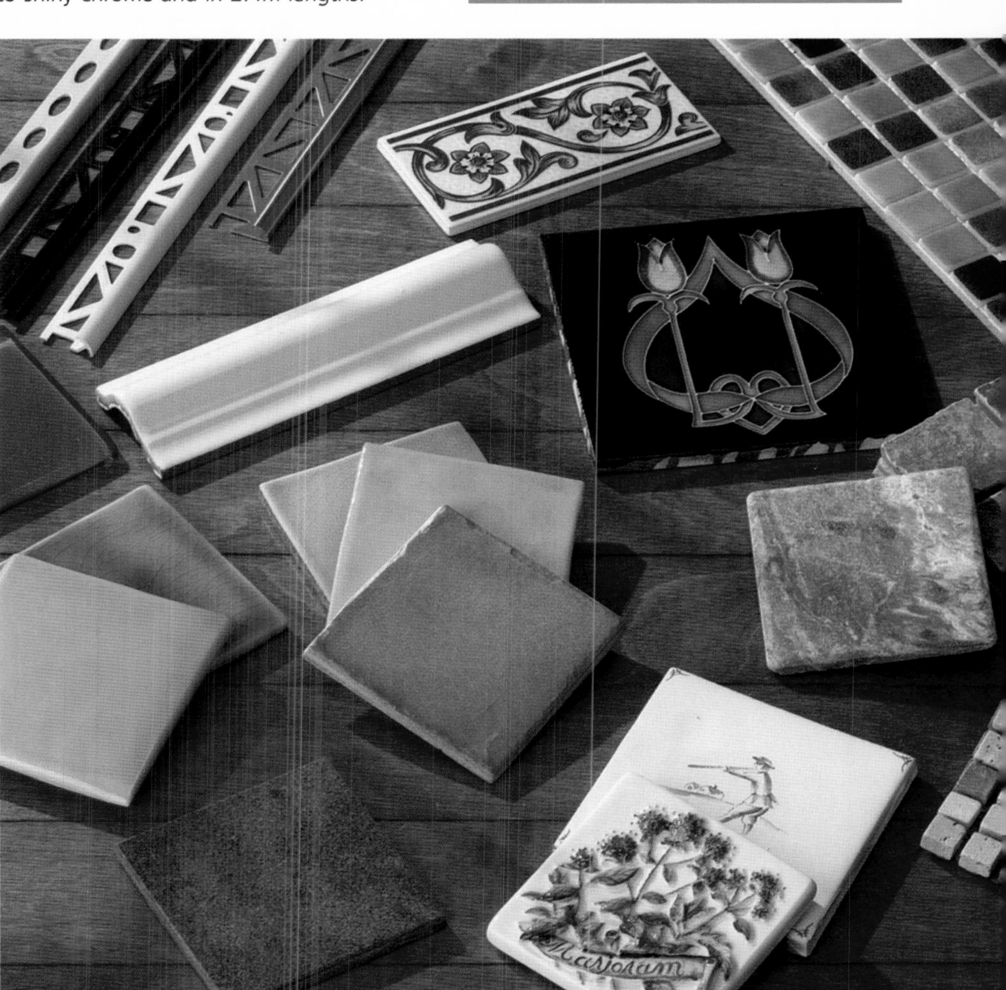

Preparing the surface

The glaze on tiles will highlight even tiny undulations in a wall so the surface must be as flat as possible.

Plaster
Sound, bare plaster is an ideal surface for tiling. The tile adhesive will fill minor cracks and holes; patch larger defects with a skim of ready-mixed repair plaster. Hack off any hollow areas and replaster them. Seal the surface with plaster primer. Scrape any loose paint from painted plaster. Key gloss-painted walls with coarse wet-and-dry abrasive paper.

Plasterboard
You can tile over painted plasterboard; seal bare plasterboard with two coats of emulsion paint. Use water-resistant boards such as Aquapanel instead of ordinary plasterboard for shower cubicle walls.

Papered walls
Strip all wallcoverings before tiling, and seal bare surfaces as described above.

Worktops
Before tiling a laminated worktop, score it with a metal abrasive disc fitted to a power drill. Coarse abrasive paper or a file will also do the job but will take longer.

Old ceramic tiles
You can tile over old tiles so long as they are securely bonded to the surface behind. Re-stick any loose tiles and fill the recesses left by missing tiles with repair plaster. Wash the surface with sugar soap to remove grease and soap deposits.

Man-made boards
Seal board surfaces with wood primer or diluted PVA building adhesive. Use moisture-resistant boards for bath panels and similar uses in damp areas.

CHOOSING TILE ADHESIVE, GROUT AND SEALANT

Tile adhesive and grout come in several forms. The most widely used is an all-in-one ready-mixed product that sticks the tiles and fills the joints, and is water and mould-resistant. It is an ideal choice for most tiling jobs. One 10 litre tub will cover an area of $10–12m^2$.

Separate grouts and adhesives You can also buy adhesive and grout as separate products, in ready-mixed or powder form, which you mix with water. Do this only if you want to use coloured grout, or if you are tiling a kitchen worktop where a special epoxy grout is recommended for hygiene reasons. Powder products are cheaper than ready-mixed options, so may be worth considering for large tiling projects.

Sealing joints Use flexible silicone sealant, not grout, to seal the joints between tiles and bathroom fittings or kitchen worktops (see also page 113 for specialist bath seals). Use flexible sealant also to fill internal corners and the joins between tiles and skirting boards or door architraves.

Tile spacers X-shaped plastic spacers are essential for spacing tiles evenly. They come in sizes from 2 to 5mm thick. Use 2mm spacers with 100mm square tiles, and larger sizes with bigger tiles.

Planning the tile layout

Whether you are tiling a simple splashback or an entire wall, deciding where to start is always the first step. Because an area of tiling is made up of regular units, it always looks best if the tile pattern is centred on the wall – or in the case of a splashback, on the washbasin, sink or bath that it is complementing.

Tiling around a bath

A bath is usually sited either in a corner or in an alcove. If the bath fits exactly in an alcove, the tiling should finish in line with the front edge of the bath at the head and foot; if it is in a corner, the tiling should finish flush with the front edge and the end of the bath.

1 Start each row with a whole tile at the outer edge of the bath or alcove. Centre the tiling on the back wall.

2 Once all the whole tiles are in place, finish the rows with cut tiles in each internal corner.

Tiling a splashback

A simple splashback for a washbasin or sink usually consists of two or three rows of tiles on the wall above it. Because the tiled area is self-contained, you can complete the job using only whole tiles. There are two choices for centring the tile layout (see below). If the basin is in an alcove, centre the tiles in the alcove, positioning cut tiles of equal width at either edge.

1 Mark the centre of the basin or sink on the wall above and draw a vertical line there. Place a whole tile at either side of the line, then add more whole tiles in a row until the tiling reaches (or extends just beyond) the edge of the basin or sink (below). Add a second or third row of tiles to complete the splashback.

2 If this layout means that tiles finish just short of the edges of the basin or sink or extend too far on either side, place the first tile astride the centre line instead (bottom). This has the effect of moving the tile row along by half the width of a tile, and may create a better-looking layout. Add extra rows of tiles to reach the required height.

Positioning tiles for a splashback

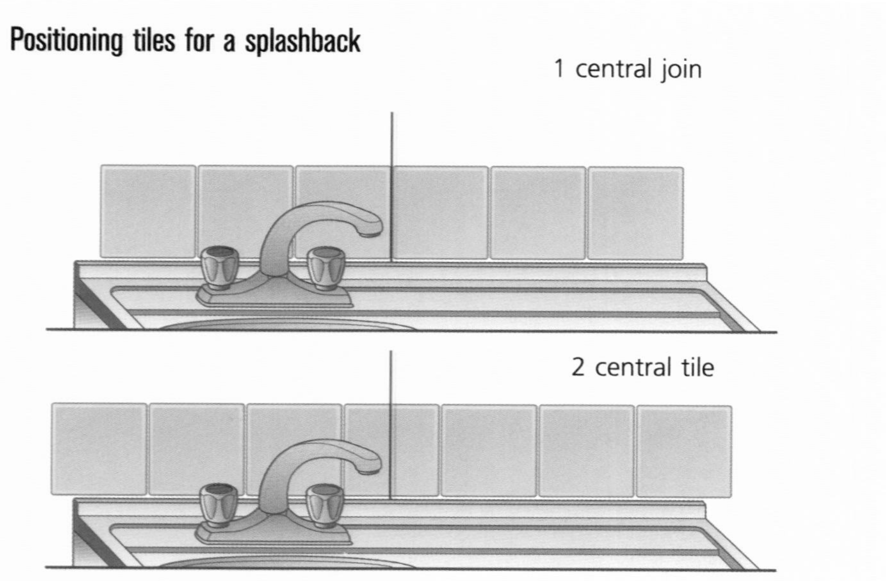

Tiling a wall

You can set out and centre tiles for a splashback by eye, standing tiles in a row along the back edge of the fixture to work out the best layout. On a wall, a simple home-made tiling gauge makes the setting out much easier.

Tiling a wall to full or part height of about 1.2m is a popular project in a bathroom or separate WC. If the wall is unobstructed, the centring rule is simple to apply. Each row should have cut tiles of equal width at each end (except in the unlikely event that a row of whole tiles exactly fills the available space). For part-tiled walls, each column should have a whole tile at the top (and a cut tile at the bottom); for full-height tiling, you'll need to cut tiles both top and bottom.

You may be tempted to save work and start each column with a whole tile at floor or skirting board level, but there is a good reason why you should not do this. The floor or skirting board may not be truly level, and the effect of using it as a baseline will gradually force the tile rows and columns off square. You might get away with this on a single tiled wall, but if you are tiling all round the room the cumulative effect can be disastrous.

Using guide battens

The secret of success is to use a horizontal timber guide batten fixed to the wall beneath the bottom edge of the lowest row of whole tiles. Position it so that the gap to be filled between this row and the floor or skirting board is about three-quarters of a tile width.

You have to place all the whole tiles on the wall before you can fit any cut tiles at the ends of the rows. It is therefore a good idea to add a vertical guide batten at one side of the area, to ensure that the columns of tiles are all precisely vertical. Once all the whole tiles have been placed, both the vertical and horizontal battens are removed so the cut tiles can be measured, cut and fixed in place.

Using a tiling gauge

1 Measure the width of the wall to be tiled and mark the centre point. Hold the tile gauge horizontally, with one end less than a tile width from a corner, and align a joint mark with the centre line. If the gap at the end of the gauge is between one-third and two-thirds of a tile wide, you have a satisfactory tile layout. Mark the wall in line with the end of the gauge. This indicates where the vertical guide batten will be fixed.

2 If the gap is very narrow, or is almost a whole tile wide, it will be difficult to cut tiles to fit. You will get a better layout by moving the gauge along by half a tile width. Do this, then mark the wall in line with the end of the gauge to indicate where to fix the vertical guide batten.

3 Part-height tiling is usually up to around 1.2m from the floor. Hold the gauge vertically to mark the position of the top full tile, allowing a gap of around three-quarters of a tile above the skirting board (or floor) at the bottom. Mark the top of this gap on the wall. For full-height tiling, work out the spacing (see left) and use the gauge to mark the bottom of the lowest full tile. The mark is the position of the horizontal batten.

Fixing the battens

You now have pencil marks on the wall indicating the level of the lowest row of whole tiles, and also the edge of the column of whole tiles nearest the corner.

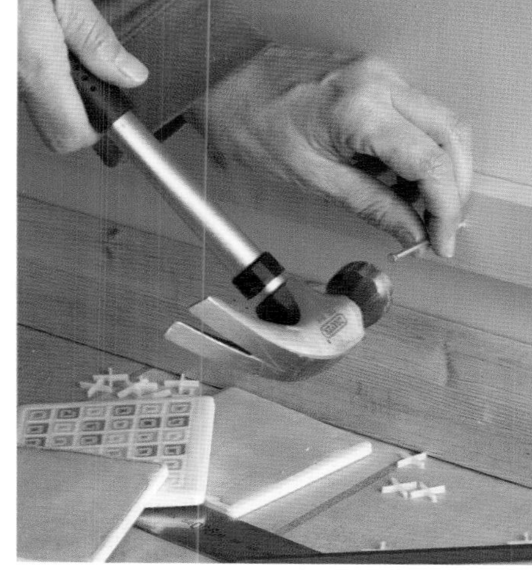

1 Fix the horizontal guide batten first, using a spirit level to get it truly horizontal. If you are tiling more than one wall, fix guide battens to each wall, and check that they are precisely aligned with each other.

2 Use a spirit level or plumb line to mark a true vertical line down to the horizontal guide batten from the end mark you made on the wall with your tiling gauge.

3 Fix a vertical guide batten at this point, long enough to reach up to the top of the area to be tiled. Secure the battens with masonry nails on solid walls, and with wire nails on timber-framed partitions. Leave the nail heads projecting so that they can be pulled out easily when it is time to remove the battens.

MAKING A TILING GAUGE

To make it, you need a piece of 50 x 25mm planed softwood about 2m long. Choose a piece that is straight and not warped in either direction. Place it on the floor and lay a row of tiles alongside it, with tile spacers between the tiles to create uniform gaps of the correct width. Mark a pencil line on the batten to coincide with each joint. Cut the gauge to length at the last pencil mark. You can then hold the gauge against the wall to see how whole tiles will fit in the space available. It is also invaluable for centring tiles on walls with obstacles such as windows, doors and bathroom or kitchen equipment (see page 116).

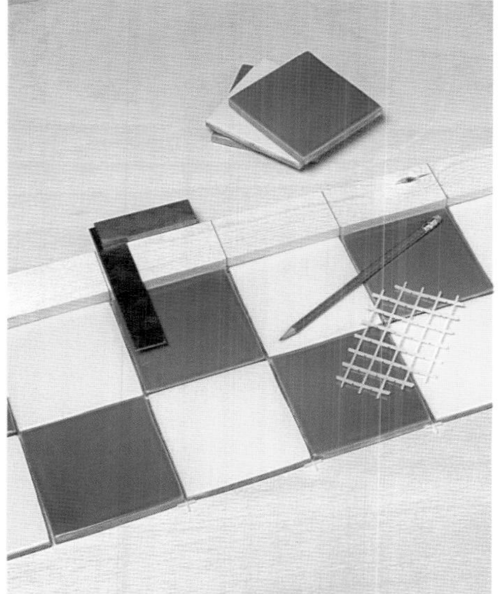

Fixing the tiles

With the setting-out complete and the vertical and horizontal guide battens fixed in place, you can start to put all the whole tiles on the wall.

Before you start Put down a dust sheet to catch stray blobs of adhesive, unpack your tiles and spacers and place them nearby.

Tools *Notched spreader; stripping knife; damp cloth.*

Materials *Tiles; tile adhesive; spacers.*

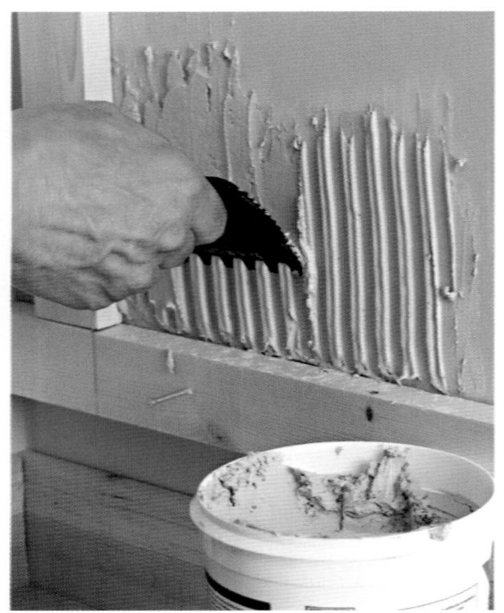

1 Scoop some adhesive from the tub with your spreader and spread it on the wall in a band a little more than one tile wide. The notches form ridges in the adhesive which will be compressed to an even thickness as you place the tiles.

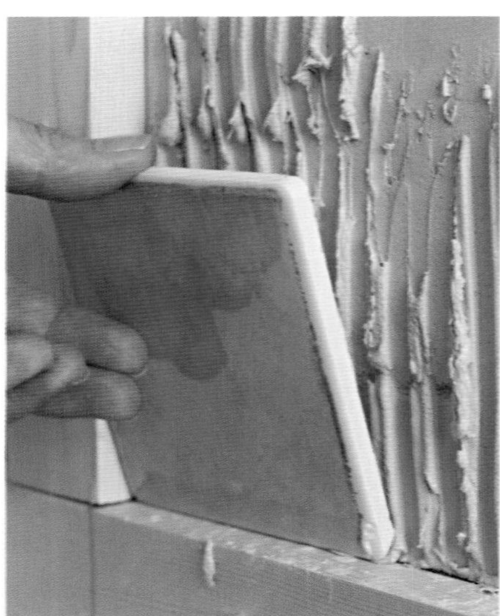

2 Place the first tile in the angle between the guide battens. Rest its lower edge on the horizontal batten, then press it into the adhesive. Check that its edge is against the vertical batten.

3 Place more tiles one by one along the row, fitting a spacer between them, until you reach the room corner. Press the spacers at the top corners into the adhesive so they will be covered when you fill the joints with grout (page 119). At the bottom corners, push one leg of each spacer into the gap between the tiles; these will be pulled out when the batten is removed.

4 Hold the edge of your tiling gauge across the faces of the tiles to check that they are flush with each other. Press in any that are proud of their neighbours.

5 Apply another band of adhesive and place the second row of tiles. Align the bottom edge of each one between the spacers in the row below before pressing it into place. Then fit spacers between the top corners as before.

6 Continue tiling to the highest row of full tiles (using a trim – see page 113 – if part tiling a wall), scrape off any excess adhesive from the wall with a stripping knife and wipe off the remaining traces with a damp cloth.

7 Allow the adhesive to set for 24 hours. Then prise out the nails that are holding the guide battens in place, taking care not to dislodge the tiles. Measure and cut individual tiles one at a time (page 117), to fit the width of the gaps remaining at the ends of each row. Fit tile spacers between each row of whole tiles at the edges.

8 As each tile is cut, spread some adhesive on the back of it and fit the cut tile into its place between adjacent spacers, pressing it down so it is level with its neighbours. Repeat the procedure for the bottom row of cut tiles (adding spacers between columns) and, for whole tiled walls, for the top row of cut tiles.

POSITIONING TILES AROUND A WINDOW

Tiles look best if they are centred around a window opening. Use a tiling gauge (page 115) to span the window and adjust its position until there is an equal width of tile on either side of the opening. Mark the wall to indicate the outer edge of the tiles that will need to be cut. Drop a plumb line through the first of the lines to transfer the mark to the horizontal batten at the bottom of the wall. Work from this mark towards the corner of the room, measuring full tile widths and grout joints to determine the position of the last whole tile in each row. Fix the vertical batten to the wall at this point.

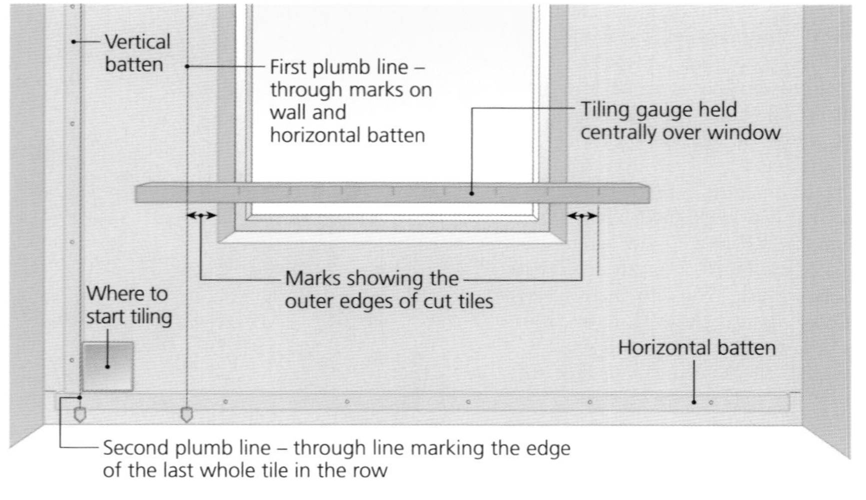

Cutting tiles to fit

Tiling a splashback is easy – you probably won't even have to cut a tile. But if you are tiling a wall, you will encounter various obstacles.

Tools *Chinagraph pencil; steel rule; platform tile cutter; tile saw; tile nibbler; pencil; G-cramp.*

Materials *Tiles; adhesive.*

Finishing a row

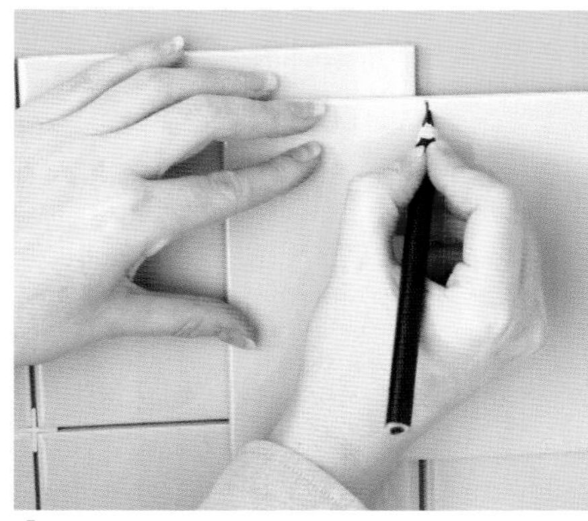

1 When you reach the end of a row, place the final tile over the previous tile and butt it up to the corner. Allow for the width of a grout joint and mark the cutting line.

2 Use a platform tile cutter to make a neat straight cut. Score the tile with the cutting wheel then use the lever to snap the tile along the line. Position the tile on the wall with the cut edge into the corner.

3 Measure the final tile in each row separately. Few walls are perfectly square, so your measurements are unlikely to be the same all the way up.

HELPFUL TIP

If you are filling gaps with cut tiles, butter the back of each tile with adhesive, then press it into place. It is much easier than trying to apply adhesive to a narrow strip of wall.

Taking a sliver off a tile

1 Platform tile cutters will not make fine cuts, less than 15mm wide. Use a hand-held tile scorer and steel straightedge. Score the tile much more deeply than you would for an ordinary cut – you need to cut right through the glaze in order to get a clean break.

2 Nibble away at the sliver of tile that is being removed, using a tile nibbler. Smooth any sharp edges with a tile file.

Cutting a curved line

1 Use a profile gauge or cut a piece of paper to the size of a tile to make a template to fit around the curved object.

2 Make a series of cuts in the edge that will butt up to the obstacle. Press the tongues against the obstacle so that the creases define its outline.

3 Use the paper as a guide to transfer the curved line with a chinagraph pencil onto the glazed tile surface.

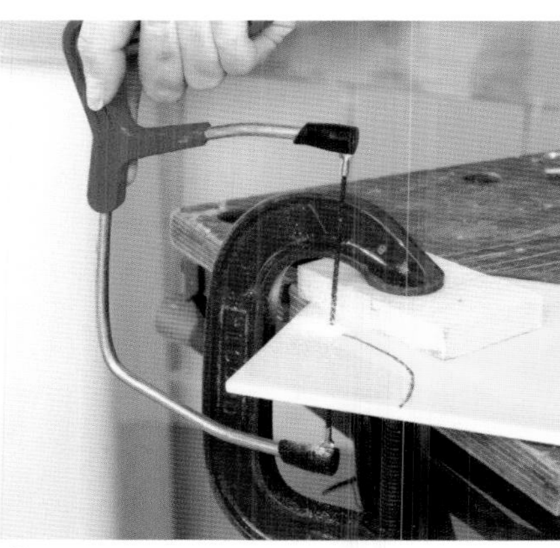

4 Clamp the tile face-up to a workbench, protecting the glaze with a board offcut sandwiched between tile and cramp. Cut along the marked line with a tile saw. Work slowly and with as little pressure as possible to avoid chipping the glaze. File away any excess if necessary to get a perfect fit.

Making holes

1 When you tile around plumbing – in a shower, for example – you may need to make holes in the tiles to allow pipes to run through. Offer up the tile from the side and from below, and mark each edge in line with the centre of the pipe. Draw straight lines to extend the marks: where they intersect is the pipe centre. Trace round an offcut of pipe – or a coin or other round object of about the same diameter – to mark a cutting line at this point.

2 Cut the tile in two along one of the lines drawn through the centre of the marked pipe hole. Score the outline of each resulting semi-circle with a pencil-type tile cutter. Use a tile nibbler to cut the hole.

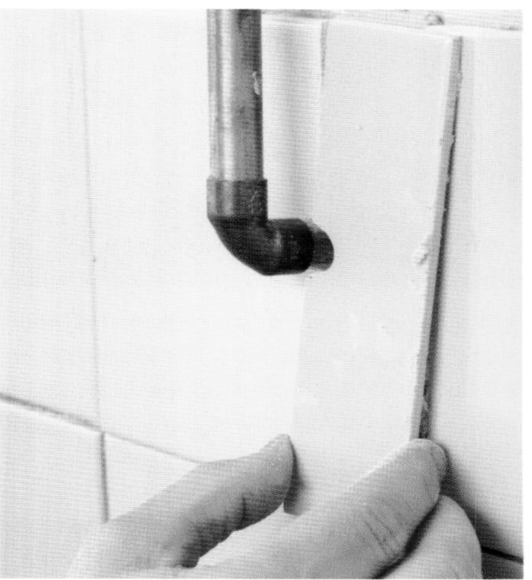

3 Fit the two cut pieces together around the pipe. Grout around the pipe or use a silicone sealant for a water-tight finish.

POWER CUTS FOR TILES

For cutting straight lines, an electric diamond wheel cutter can be bought for little more than a quality platform tile cutter. It gives a clean straight cut and can also chamfer the edge of tiles at 45° (to give really neat internal and external corners) and be used for cutting out L-shapes (useful when fitting tiles around sockets and switches).

For curves, a tungsten-carbide edged jigsaw blade is faster than a tile saw, and for large holes, you can use a diamond-edged hole saw as shown on page 112. For making small holes, a special tile drill (shown on page 119) will give a better result than a masonry bit.

If you have a multi-tool (such as a Dremel), you can buy a tile cutting attachment for cutting shapes in tiles up to a depth of 20mm.

Tiling around corners

Internal corners

Place all the whole tiles on both walls, then remove the guide battens so that you can cut and fit the tiles in the corner.

1 Measure and cut a tile to fit the width of the gap to be filled (page 117). Butter the back of the cut tile with adhesive and press it into place with the cut edge facing into the corner.

2 When the adhesive has dried, seal the angle between the two walls with a flexible waterproof sealant. This will allow for a little wall movement over time. Use masking tape to define the joint, apply the sealant, smooth it and peel off the tape once a skin has formed.

External corners

External corners should, ideally, start with whole tiles on each wall, though this may not be possible at a window rebate. Joins can be made by butting the tiles, using plastic corner trim or sticking on a strip of timber beading.

Butt joint A simple overlapping butt joint works well if the corner is true and the tiles have glazed edges. Tile the less visible wall first, placing whole tiles flush with the corner. Then tile the other wall, overlapping these tiles to conceal the edges of those on the first wall.

Plastic corner trim Coloured plastic or chrome corner trims will protect tiles on external corners from damage and give the edge a neat finish. You can use the trim along the edges of tiled door and window recesses as well.

1 Push the perforated base of the trim into the tile adhesive on one corner so that the outer edge of the rounded trim lines up perfectly with the faces of the tiles on the adjacent wall.

2 Start tiling the second wall, easing each tile into the corner trim as you place it. Don't push it too hard – you don't want to dislodge the trim. When you have laid all the corner tiles, make sure the trim lines up with the tile faces on both walls.

A window recess

1 Tile the wall as far as the window, cutting tiles to fit. If you have to cut a tile to an L shape, cut a line from the edge to the centre of the tile using a tile saw then score a line at right angles to the cut and snap off the unwanted piece. Use lengths of plastic edging strip designed for external corners to give the edges a neat finish.

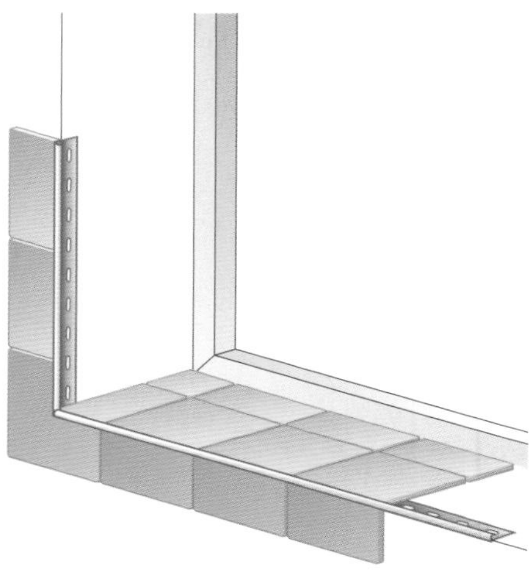

2 Lay the tiles at the bottom of the recess first. Put any cut tiles nearest the window, with cut edges against the frame.

3 Line up the first course of tiles on the side walls with the tiles on the main wall. Fill gap between tiles and window frame with flexible sealant.

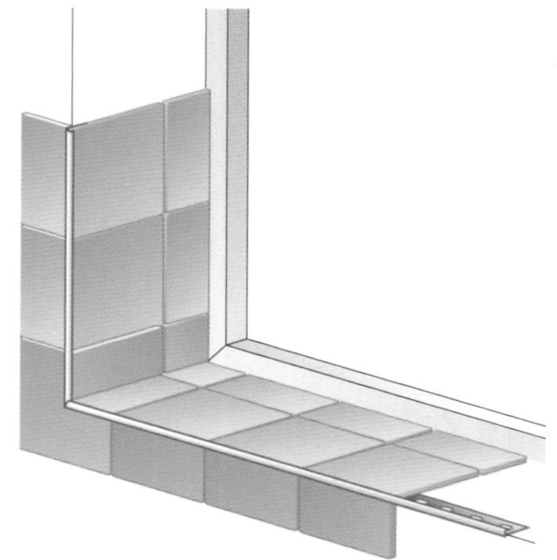

Grouting between tiles

When the tiles have been in place for at least 12 hours, fill the gaps between them with grout. This gives an attractive finished appearance and prevents dirt from collecting in the cracks.

Tools *Pieces of sponge or a squeegee; larger sponge; thin dowel or something similar for finishing; soft dry cloth.*

Materials *Grout (waterproof for kitchens or bathrooms).*

1 If the grout is not ready-mixed, prepare as recommended. With waterproof epoxy-based grout, mix only a little at a time – it sets hard quickly.

2 Press the grout firmly into the gaps between the tiles. Professionals use a rubber-edged squeegee, but if you have never grouted before you may find it easier to get the grout well into the cracks with a small piece of sponge.

3 Wipe away any grout that gets onto the surface of the tiles with a clean, damp sponge while the grout is still wet. Wipe away combined adhesive and grout or waterproof grout quickly – these are hard to clean off the tile surface once set.

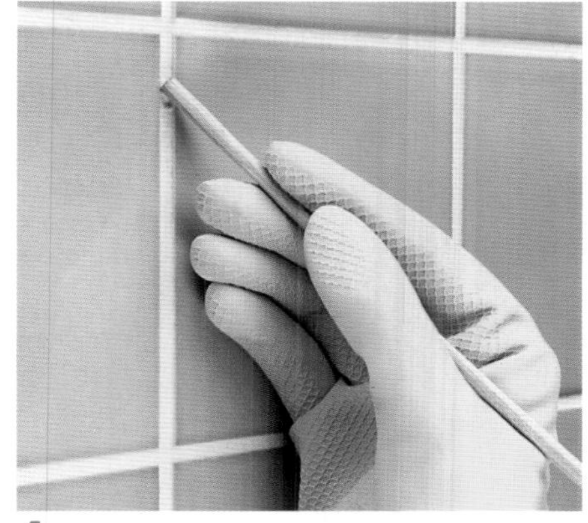

4 To give the tiling a neat professional finish, run a thin piece of dowelling over each grout line. Wipe surplus off the tiles as you go. A plastic proprietary grout finisher has a rounded end for shaping the line and a flat end for removing excess grout.

5 Leave ordinary grout to dry, then polish it off using a clean, dry cloth. Another way to polish tiles effectively is to use a screwed-up ball of newspaper.

> **HELPFUL TIP**
>
> You can restore discoloured grout with a grout whitener (or grout reviver). This is simple to apply and is left to dry before excess is removed with a sponge.

Drilling holes through tiles

Many bathroom and kitchen accessories, like soap dishes, must be screwed to the wall – in which case you may have to drill holes through ceramic tiles.

It's a good idea to make fixings in tiled walls by drilling into grout lines wherever possible, but sometimes drilling through the glaze is unavoidable. Drilling through tiles creates a lot of fine dust, which may stain nearby grouting. To catch the dust, make a simple cardboard tray and stick it to the wall with masking tape or get someone to hold a vacuum-cleaner nozzle near the drill tip as you drill the hole.

Tools *Drill; small masonry bit to make pilot hole and larger one to suit the screw, or sharp spear point bit; chinagraph pencil; screwdriver; possibly steel ruler.*

Materials *Masking tape; wall plugs; screws.*

1 Decide where you want to make the screw fixing and mark its position on the surface of the tile with a chinagraph pencil.

2 Stop the point of the masonry bit from skating over the smooth tile surface by sticking a piece of masking tape over the mark, which should show through it. Remake the mark on the surface of the tape. If you need to make more than one screw hole, use a strip of tape to cover both hole positions and mark them on the tape.

3 Make a pilot hole with the small masonry bit. Press the tip firmly against the mark on the tape. Check the drill isn't on hammer action, and start at a low speed. Drill slowly and carefully through the glazed surface of the tile. Stop drilling when the bit starts to penetrate the plaster. Using a small bit to do this minimises the risk of cracking the glaze. Repeat the process if necessary to drill a second hole through the other mark on the tape.

4 Switch to the bit that matches the screw or wallplug size you intend to use. Position its tip in the hole and drill slowly and carefully through the tile and the plaster and well into the masonry.

Alternatively You can buy a special ceramic tile bit with a sharp spear point. Its shape is designed to break through the glaze immediately. This minimises the risk of skidding across or cracking the tile. The bits are available in a range of sizes.

> **HELPFUL TIP**
>
> If you are putting a wall plug into a tiled wall, make the hole at least 6mm deeper than the length of the plug so that it can be pushed into the wall and beyond the tile. Or use a nylon wallplug where the first part of the plug does not expand. Otherwise, when you drive in the screw, the sideways pressure may crack the tile.

Laying mosaic tiles

Mosaic tiles come in sheets with a fabric mesh backing. They are a good DIY option, being much easier to fit around obstacles than full-size ceramic tiles.

Tools *Straightedge; spirit level; tape measure; pencil; notched adhesive spreader; wood batten; trimming knife; cutting board; tile-cutting pliers; grouting tools.*

Materials *Mosaic tiles; tile adhesive; grout.*

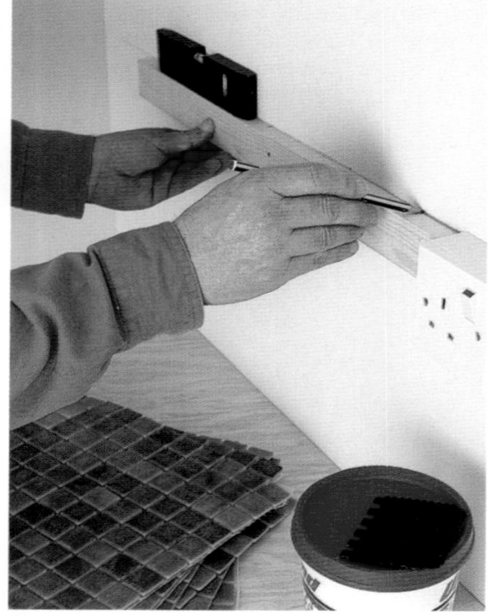

1 Use a batten and spirit level to mark out in pencil the area you want to tile. This simple kitchen splashback is the height of a sheet of tiles above the worktop.

2 Apply tile adhesive, holding the notched spreader at an angle of 45 degrees to create ridges of an even depth.

3 Put up the first sheet of tiles, lining it up with the guideline. Press it into place with your hand, then use a wood offcut to tamp the tiles level – especially those at the edges of the sheet.

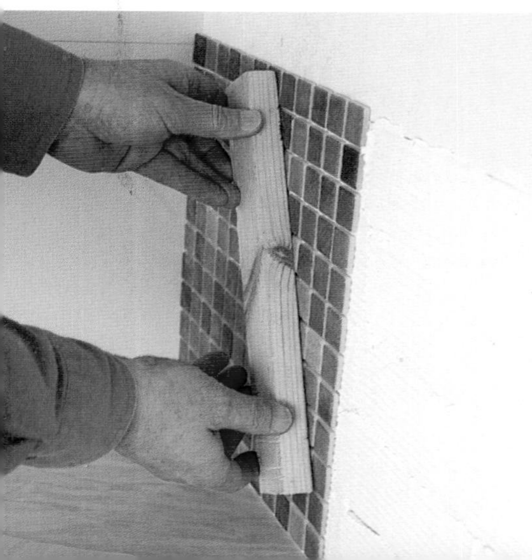

4 When you reach an obstacle, such as a socket outlet, use a sharp trimming knife to cut out sections of whole mosaic tiles. Lay the sheet of tiles on a hardboard sheet and run the blade along the gaps.

5 Once you have cut out the section of tiles, check the fit. There will be gaps, but you can fill these later. Spread adhesive on the wall and put the cut sheet in place.

6 Lay all the whole sheets until the area is covered. Then measure the gaps left round any obstacles. You will need to cut individual mosaic tiles to fit (see box, right).

7 When all the tiles are in place, leave the adhesive to dry for 24 hours. Then grout the gaps between the tiles. Load a rubber-edged grout spreader with grout (use waterproof grout for bathrooms or kitchens), and draw it across the tiles. Clean surplus grout off the tile surfaces as you work. Before the grout sets, use a piece of slim dowel or a proprietary grout finisher to neaten the grout lines (see page 119).

SCORE AND SNAP

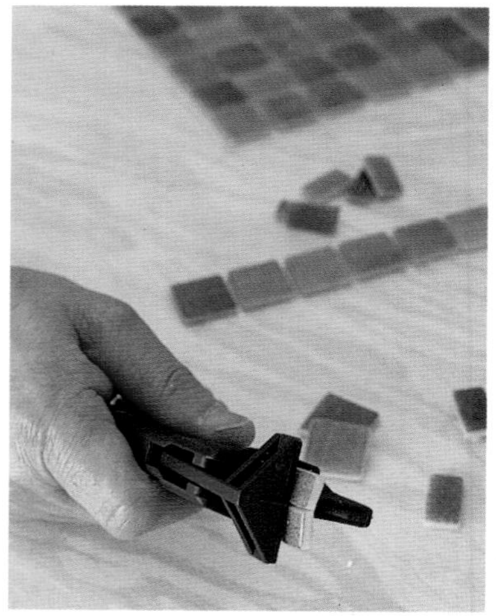

If you need to cut individual mosaic tiles to fill narrow gaps around obstacles, the best tool is a pair of tile cutting pliers. Trim off a strip of tiles and score a cutting line along the whole strip. Then detach individual tiles and use the v-shaped jaws of the pliers to snap the tiles one at a time.

Common tiling problems and cures

Because tiles are so hard-wearing, they are often used in areas that are damp, dirty and prone to damage. There are some common problems to look out for – treat them promptly to minimise the damage.

Mould on grout

Dark stains on grout lines may be caused by mould, which thrives in the damp and warmth of kitchens and bathrooms. Kill the mould with a proprietary fungicide, following the manufacturer's instructions. Do not use bleach. It will not destroy the roots of the mould.

Any stains left on the grout can be hidden by using grout whitener or reviver. When the whitener is dry, apply some more fungicide to prevent further mould.

Dirty grout

Clean grease and dirt from grout with an old toothbrush and liquid detergent in warm water, or a non-abrasive cream cleaner. When dry, treat the grout with a grout whitener or reviver.

Missing grout

If there are gaps in the grout, rake out all old grout with a proprietary grout rake (below), a small-toothed tool designed specifically for the job. Draw the rake along the grout lines, first vertically and then horizontally, to remove the old grout to a depth of about 3mm.

Grout rake

Use a small, stiff-bristled brush or a vacuum cleaner with a narrow nozzle attachment to remove all the debris from the joints before regrouting.

Crazed tiles

Tiles may become crazed because they are old, but new tiles may also be affected if water gets behind them. Nothing can be done to repair tiles damaged by crazing. You can paint tiles with special tile paint, though this is not as tough a finish as the original glaze. If you have spare matching tiles, you can remove the damaged ones and replace them.

Replacing a damaged tile

If you work carefully, it is a fairly straightforward task to replace a single cracked tile or remove and replace one with holes drilled in it that are no longer needed. You can also replace interspersed patterned tiles with matching plain ones to create a uniform effect.

Tools *Power drill; large masonry bit; cold chisel; hammer; safety goggles; work gloves; notched adhesive spreader; tools for applying grout.*

Materials *New tile; adhesive; grout.*

Before you start Always wear safety goggles as protection against slivers of glaze that are likely to splinter away from the tile surface as you chip away at the tile you are removing. Protect your hands with sturdy work gloves.

1 Drill holes in the centre of the tile you want to remove, using a power drill and masonry bit.

2 Insert the cold chisel, and hammer from the holes outwards towards the edges to get behind the tile. If you need to get more leverage, pack pieces of scrap wood behind the chisel as you work. Remove loose pieces of tile as they break away.

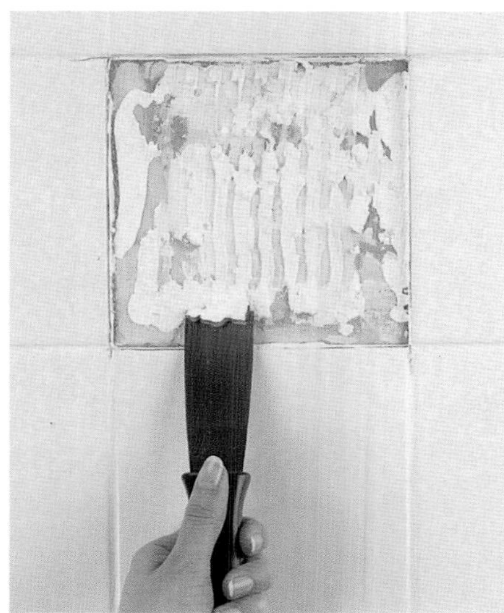

3 When you have removed the tile, use a paint scraper to carefully chisel out the old adhesive until you reveal bare wall.

CHECK THE DEPTH

If you can see an edge of a tile anywhere on the existing tiled area, check how deep the tiles are and make sure you buy a replacement to match. If you have to guess, don't buy a tile thicker than 4mm or you risk it sticking out proud of the surrounding area.

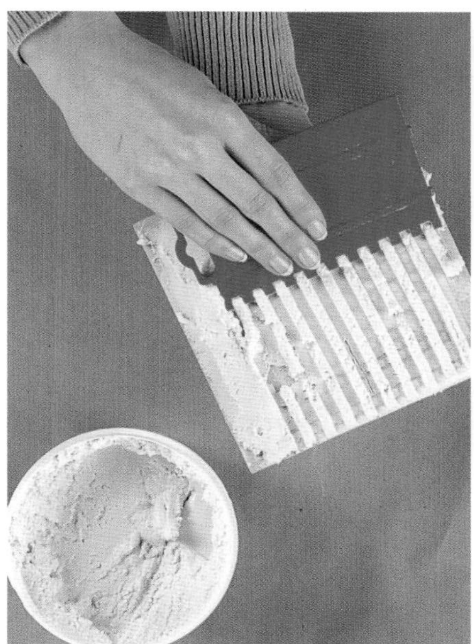

4 Butter the back of a new tile with adhesive, using the notched spreader, and fit it in place. Put spacers around the tile to ensure even spacing.

5 Lay an offcut of timber across the repair to check that the wall is flat, adding or removing adhesive as necessary. Gently tap it flat if necessary.

6 Use a damp cloth to wipe excess adhesive from the surface of the tiles. Leave the adhesive to set for about 12 hours before grouting the joins.

Floor coverings 4

Choosing floor coverings

There are many types of floor covering, with new materials being introduced all the time. Replacing an old carpet with a new wood laminate floor, or stripping old floorboards, can give a room a terrific lift. Here is a summary of what is available.

Sanded and varnished floorboards

• Suitable way of using boards in good condition and without gaps.
• The floor is sanded with a heavy-duty sanding machine that can be hired for a day or weekend. Cheap, and fairly simple to do yourself. Sanding a floor is noisy and dusty work, however.
• The finished surface is noisy underfoot. Can be draughty on a ground floor if boards are not tongued-and-grooved.
• Sweep or vacuum-clean frequently to remove grit, which can scratch the surface. Wipe up spillages with a damp cloth. Polish regularly. Lightly sand worn areas and re-varnish.

Vinyl tiles

• Huge range of colours, patterns and price. Available in imitation ceramic, wood or stone as well as cheaper smooth vinyl.
• Hygienic, easily cleaned. Resistant to spillages. Good for kitchens and bathrooms.
• Smooth vinyl is slippery when wet. Cushion-backed types are warmer, safer and quieter underfoot.
• Clean as for sheet vinyl (right), but beware of using too much water when you wash it; water could get under the joins.

Ceramic tiles

• Range from traditional square or rectangular tiles to specialist, handmade tiles of various shapes. Ceramic tiles can be very slippery, but anti-slip tiles are available.
• Long lasting, easily cleaned and highly resistant to stains and spillages. Wide choice of patterns and colours.
• Unglazed ceramic tiles tend to be porous, and are not suitable for kitchens and bathrooms.
• Expensive. Timber sub-floor needs a 9mm plywood underlay before laying. Noisy underfoot. Cold if walked on in bare feet. Crockery breaks if dropped on it.
• Remove surface grit by sweeping or vacuum cleaning, then wash with non-abrasive detergent in water. Keep water to a minimum to prevent seepage under tiles. Scrub stubborn marks and ingrained dirt round edges of tiles.

Terracotta and quarry tiles

• Terracotta tiles and their budget-priced alternative, quarry tiles, are a more rustic alternative to ceramic tiles. Quarry tiles are less porous than terracotta tiles, but do not have the subtle shading of terracotta.
• Terracotta is warmer underfoot than other hard floor tiles. Both types are hard-wearing and can be cleaned easily. Good choice of brown and red shades.

• Noisy when walked on and not kind to dropped crockery. Their thickness makes them difficult to cut. If laid on a timber floor, these tiles require a 9mm plywood underlay.
• Terracotta tiles need a primer or treatment applied before installation (page 139), plus wax or sealant every few months to maintain their surface finish.

Sheet vinyl

• Smooth vinyl is cheaper; cushioned vinyl is softer underfoot. Wide range of patterns and colours. Linoleum is a traditional floor covering that is recently regaining popularity. It can be more difficult to lay but is very durable and more resistant to burns than vinyl. It comes in a range of colours and patterns.
• Hygienic, easily cleaned, resistant to spillages. Inexpensive flooring for kitchens and bathrooms.
• Smooth vinyl is slippery when wet. Cushion-backed varieties are warmer, safer and quieter underfoot.
• Vacuum-clean or sweep to remove grit, which can scratch. Wash with detergent. Remove scuff marks by gently rubbing with fine steel wool lubricated with white spirit, taking care not to rub through top surface.

Carpet

• Wide range of colour and price. Available as fitted carpet, carpet squares or carpet tiles. Gives feeling of warmth and comfort. Graded according to use – from heavily used stairs to low-use spare bedrooms.
• Good-quality carpet is expensive. Spillages may cause permanent staining.
• Vacuum-clean frequently to remove grit which can harm fibres. Remove stains with proprietary cleaner. Rearrange carpet tiles to even out wear.
• Carpets are the least environmentally friendly floorcovering option. Their manufacture generates pollution and they emit varying levels of volatile organic compounds (VOCs). Production methods are improving, but check the manufacturer's specifications if you have any concerns.

Wood

• Wood floors come as strips or mosaic panels. Some are nailed down, some are stuck down, and some simply interlock and 'float' on the floor below. Because solid wood is so expensive, most wood floors are laminate floors, consisting of a thin top veneer layer fixed to a strong bottom layer of softwood or high-density fibreboard (HDF), known as 'engineered' flooring. For more about choosing laminate and wood flooring see page 130.
• Luxurious and long-lasting in living rooms, dining rooms and halls.
• Natural wood is expensive. Laminated wood effect flooring is cheaper, but the cheapest printed types do not wear well. Noisy underfoot.
• Remove surface dirt with vacuum cleaner to minimise scratching. Varnished floors can be wiped with a damp cloth.

ENVIRONMENTALLY FRIENDLY OPTIONS

A wide range of natural, renewable flooring materials is available. If you're concerned about VOCs (volatile organic compounds) make sure the materials have not been treated with chemicals and avoid synthetic adhesives.

Bamboo

Flooring made from this prolific type of grass is strong, durable and moisture-resistant. It doesn't warp and is free of knots and other flaws found in wood. See page 130 for a picture and more details.

Coir

A coarse material derived from the outer husk of the coconut, coir is very hard-wearing. It's ideal for heavy traffic areas such as halls and living spaces.

Cork

Renewable and recyclable, the bark of the cork tree is harvested once every nine years, then regenerates. Cultivation requires no irrigation, fertilisers or pesticides. Cork flooring is soft, warm and resilient, a good heat and sound insulator and does not collect dust. Non-PVC-coated tiles are the greenest option.

Jute

The woven yarn made from fibres of the stalks of the Cochorus or jute plant provides a soft, absorbent material that is ideal for bedrooms but less appropriate for kitchens, bathrooms, stairs or living areas.

Seagrass

Woven from the fibres of various species of seagrass, this material is tough, hard-wearing and naturally antistatic and stain-resistant. Not suited to damp rooms, nor to high-traffic areas, as its waxy fibres can be slippery.

Sisal

The tightly woven yarn made from the fibres of the agave plant produces durable flooring that is naturally antibacterial and antistatic – but it marks and stains easily.

Preparing a solid floor before laying a covering

A direct-to-earth floor can suffer from three faults that make it unsuitable for a floor covering to be laid. It can be damp; a concrete floor can suffer from a condition called 'dusting'; or the floor could be uneven.

Is the floor damp?

If a floor is damp there is no point in laying a covering. The moisture will eventually destroy the covering itself and any adhesive that was used to hold it down.

Damp in a floor is not always obvious, but if a direct-to-earth floor was laid before 1940 it is unlikely to have a damp-proof membrane, and will have to be treated. Ways of dealing with damp in floors are given on page 247.

A cure for 'dusting'

A concrete floor may suffer from a condition known as dusting, in which dust continually forms on the surface, no matter how often you sweep it.

This can be cured by applying a concrete floor sealer sold by builders' merchants. Apply it following the manufacturer's instructions. Alternatively, you can use a PVA bonding agent diluted with water.

Levelling a solid floor

For most DIY jobs, the best solution for an uneven solid floor is to choose a self-levelling compound, supplied as a powder to mix with water.

Self-levelling compound is very straightforward to use. Follow the manufacturer's instructions that come with the materials.

Be absolutely sure that you really want to use it because once the new surface is laid and has set, it's there to stay.

Tools *Bucket; scrubbing brush; steel float and/or trowel.*

Materials *Self-levelling compound; sugar soap; water.*

HELPFUL TIP

If you do not obtain a good, smooth finish after trowelling the levelling compound, sprinkle water on the surface and try again.

Before you start Fill any deep indentations in the floor with a sand-and-cement mix; bags of mortar to which you merely add water are ideal. To ensure a good bond, first brush a priming coat of PVA adhesive on the patch to be filled, and add a little of it to the mortar. Trowel the surface of the mortar patch as smooth as possible.

1 Clean the floor by scrubbing with a solution of sugar soap and water. Rinse and allow the floor to dry thoroughly.

2 Pour some of the runny compound in the corner farthest from the door. Use a trowel to spread it to a depth of about 10mm – most brands include a spatula for this – and leave it to find its own level.

3 Make sure you use enough to fill in all the dips.

4 Continue working across the floor, smoothing the edges as you work.

5 The compound will be hard enough to walk on after an hour or so, but leave for the time specified on the packet before laying a floor covering.

Preparing a wood floor before laying a covering

Material laid on a properly prepared floor will look better and will last longer. Vinyl or cork flooring will show any ridges in the sub-floor, and will wear unevenly. Even carpet wears more quickly on the ridges.

The instructions below relate to wooden floorboards. Modern homes have chipboard floors which are likely to be in better condition (but must be covered).

1 Make sure that the floor is structurally sound. If it moves as you walk across it, there may be a defective joist, and you should call in a builder. If there is a feeling of sponginess, there could be an outbreak of woodworm or rot below the surface. Take up a board to check.

2 Any damp in the floor must be cured.

3 Loose boards must be fixed.

4 Remove old tacks left behind from a previous covering. Prise them up with a claw hammer, pincers or tack lifter.

5 Any damaged boards will have to be replaced (page 254). If you are sanding the floor, any new boards are unlikely to match exactly the colour of the old. So replace a faulty board in a prominent place with an existing board from a less obvious spot (one that will be hidden by furniture or a rug, for example). This less conspicuous board can be replaced with the new one.

Fill knots Use car body filler to block knot holes in wooden boards before laying vinyl sheet flooring. If you don't, pressure from chair legs and similar objects could pierce and damage the floor covering.

TAKING UP OLD FLOORINGS

Old tiles and woodblock that are firmly stuck can form a sound base for a new floor. But carpets and sheet vinyls – and any other flooring that is not well stuck down – must be removed before you lay a new one.

A garden spade is an excellent tool for lifting a floor covering such as vinyl tiles or lino, when the glue is not holding well. Its blade has a sharp edge that you can push under the material (file it sharper if necessary) and the long handle allows plenty or leverage for lifting. For a large area, hire a powered floor tile stripper.

Old quarry tiles are difficult to remove, and may only reveal an unsatisfactory sub-floor underneath. It is probably best to leave them in place. If a few tiles are damaged or missing, remove damaged pieces with a bolster and club hammer – wearing safety goggles. Then replace them with new tiles (page 137), or fill the gaps with sand and cement mix. If a quarry-tiled floor is in a very bad state, clear out badly broken and crumbling patches, clean thoroughly, fill deeper holes with sand and cement, and then apply a self-levelling compound (page 125).

HARDBOARD AND PLYWOOD

Hardboard (page 52) and plywood (page 53) both come in large (2440 x 1220mm) sheets, but both are also available in smaller sheets, which are easier to transport and handle. Common sizes are 1830 x 610mm and 1220 x 610mm.

Hardboard provides a smooth flat surface for sheet materials and soft tiles; exterior-grade plywood gives extra stiffness for hard heavy tiles.

Hardboard is secured by nailing (left); plywood needs to be screwed down. Be aware that access to underfloor electrical and plumbing connections will now be extremely difficult: you may need to incorporate 'inspection hatches' in the sub-floor, the floor lining and the floorcovering itself.

Lining a wood floor with hardboard

Lining the floor with hardboard levels off boards that are curling at the edges, covers small gaps between boards and even masks minor damage.

Hardboard also covers old stains and polishes. Lay hardboard with its mesh side up. This forms a better key for adhesives than the smooth side, and when you nail down the sheets the nail heads will sink below the mesh and not create pimple marks in the final floor covering. After laying the boards, leave them at least overnight before laying the floor covering.

Tools *Hammer; panel saw; large paintbrush; measuring jug; bowl or paint kettle.*

Materials *Sheets of hardboard 3mm thick; water; 20mm annular nails – these have ringed shafts for extra grip – about 250g for an average sized room.*

1 The boards must be given a moisture content suitable for the room – a process known as conditioning. Otherwise they may become distorted. Brush half a litre of water into the mesh side of the sheets, and stack them mesh side to mesh side, perfectly flat on the floor of the room they will occupy. Leave them for 48 hours before laying. The boards will adjust to the humidity of the room, and dry out further when nailed down, tightening up like a drum skin to form a perfect surface for the final floor covering.

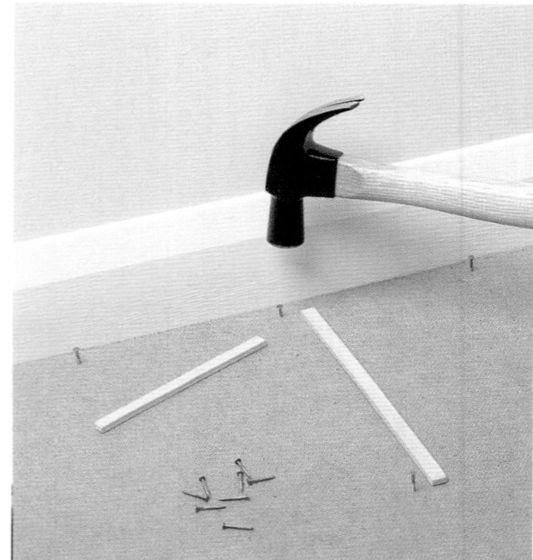

2 Begin laying the boards in a corner of the room, and start nailing along one edge of a sheet, 15mm in from the edge. Work sideways and forwards, in pyramid fashion. The nails should be about 150mm apart along the edges of the board and 250mm apart in the middle of the board.

3 Use the offcut from the previous board to start the next row. This avoids waste, and prevents the joins from lining up across the room. Butt the second board firmly against the first, and begin nailing along

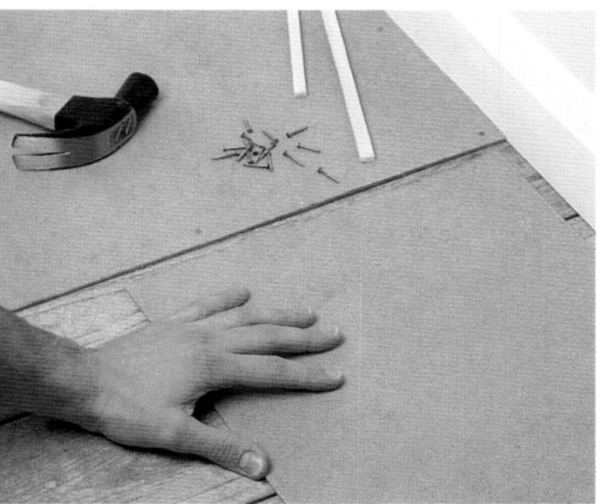

the meeting edge.

4 Continue in this way until, at the end of the row, you will have to cut a board to fit. You do not need to cut the boards to a perfect fit to the skirting board. Gaps up to 5mm do not matter.

5 You will have to cut each sheet in the final row to fit the remaining space.

Restoring a wood floor

An attractive floor can be created by restoring existing floorboards. Floorboards may be stripped and varnished, or you could stain or paint them before sealing with a hardwearing clear coating.

Filling holes in floorboards

Use a flexible wood filler to cover all nail and screw heads – nail heads should be punched below the surface, and screws may need countersinking so that their heads are below the surface. If you are painting the floor, the filler colour does not matter; if you are varnishing it, choose a filler slightly lighter in colour than the surrounding floor. Once dry, sand filler flush with the floor.

Plugging gaps between boards

There are two ways to deal with gaps between floorboards: you can fill the gaps, or you can lift and relay the entire floor.

Fill narrow gaps with flexible sealant; wider gaps are best filled with thin lengths of square-edge moulding.

Filling gaps with moulding

1 Plane moulding strips into a slight wedge shape.

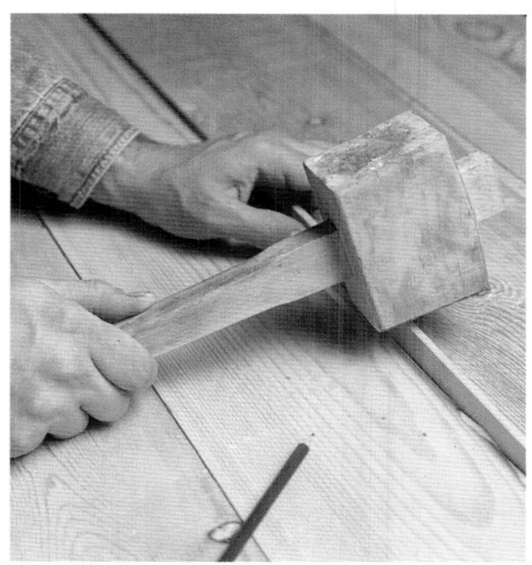

2 Apply a little woodworking adhesive before tapping a wedge into a gap, thin edge first and leave to dry.

3 Use a power sander (see page 257) or a plane to level the wedges to the floor and then stain them to match the boards.

Filling snall gaps with sealant

Use a clear flexible sealant or a wood-coloured flooring filler (page 257) applied with a sealant gun. If you intend to varnish the boards, use a filler that you can stain to match the colour of the boards.

> **RE-LAYING FLOORBOARDS**
>
> If you decide to re-lay the floorboards, you need to fit the first board tight to the wall, and using a tool called a floor cramp – which can be hired – butt each board up against the previous one.
>
> Traditional cut brads are the best nails for fixing floorboards. The length of the brads should be two-and-a-half times the thickness of the boards.
>
> If you are laying a floor above an old ceiling, use screws, countersinking the heads, instead of nails so as not to risk cracking the ceiling beneath as you hammer.

Restoring a woodblock floor

A herringbone-pattern woodblock floor that is not too badly damaged can be rejuvenated by sanding and sealing. The job is worth while, as such flooring is expensive and rarely fitted today. The floor may only need sanding and finishing, or you may need to replace one or more blocks.

Tools *Dust mask; nail punch and claw hammer; floor sanding machine and edging sander (a weekend's hire should be sufficient for one room); earmuffs; sanding belts (coarse, medium and fine); edging sander; old chisel; old paintbrush (for adhesive).*

Materials *Flooring varnish or other sealer; woodblock flooring adhesive.*

Before you start If blocks are missing, a local wood yard may be able to make replacements, or you may find them in a reclamation yard or via the Internet (try typing 'old parquet flooring' into the search engine on your computer).

1 Remove any loose blocks and scrape off the adhesive – probably black pitch – with an old chisel.

2 Spread a layer of adhesive into the space in the floor, about 5mm thick, using a filler knife or spatula.

3 Spread a thin layer of adhesive on the back of the block with a paintbrush and immediately put the block in place. Weigh it down by covering with a piece of plastic, a sheet of ply and several bricks, until the adhesive sets.

4 Fill any small gaps with wood filler.

5 Then use the floor sander, following directions given for sanding and varnishing a wooden floor (page 128). Because the grain lies in two directions, the floor must be sanded twice, running the second pass of the machine at right angles to the first.

6 The final sanding, with a very fine belt, will also need to be done in two directions to remove scratch marks.

7 Once the floor is clean and free of dust, apply your chosen finish.

Sanding and varnishing floorboards

Sound floorboards can be sanded to reveal a beautiful natural floor.

Sanding a floor is hard, dusty, noisy work. On fairly new boards that have not been stained or become too dirty, sanding may not be necessary. Get rid of surface dirt by scrubbing with detergent and hot water. Pay particular attention to removing dirt from nail holes. If sanding is the only way to restore the boards, warn the neighbours before you start.

Tools *Floor-sanding machine and edging sander (a weekend's hire should be enough for one room); sanding belts and discs (coarse, medium and fine); paint roller and wide paintbrush; fine steel wool; dust mask; goggles; earmuffs; gloves; knee pads; nail punch and claw hammer.*

Materials *Flooring-grade varnish or other finish.*

Before you start Punch in all the nails in the floor, otherwise they will tear the sanding belts. Any tacks should also be removed. If there are any traces of old polish, remove them with steel wool dipped in white spirit; otherwise the polish will clog up the sanding belt. Wear protective gloves.

1 Start at the edge of the room with your back against the wall. Keep the sander slightly away from the skirting board at the side otherwise you may damage it.

2 It is normal to work along the length of the boards, as sanding across them causes scratches. But if the boards curl up at the edges, make the first runs diagonally across them with a coarse belt. Finish with medium and fine belts along the length of the boards.

3 On a floor where not very much stripping is needed, let the machine go forwards at a slow steady pace to the far end of the room, lifting up the drum as soon as you reach the skirting board.

4 If the boards are badly marked, wheel the sander backwards to your start point, lower the drum and make a second pass over the first one. Never pull the sander backwards when the drum is rotating, or the machine may pull sideways out of control and score the floor surface badly.

5 When the strip looks clean, move on to the next one, and continue to the end of the room. Raise the belt as you change direction, or it may damage the boards. You will have started each run about a metre out from the wall behind you. When you have covered the room, turn the machine round, and deal with that area.

Sanding the edges

Eventually, you will be left with a narrow border all round the room that the sander cannot reach. This must be stripped with an edging sander. Do not try to use a disc on an electric drill; it is not powerful enough.

1 Use the edging sander all round the edges of the room, taking care not to damage the paint on the skirting boards.

2 When the sanding is finished, vacuum the floor to get rid of all the wood dust. Do not damp the floor as the water may leave marks.

3 Finally, mop the floor with a clean, dry, lint-free cloth. Be sure to shake it frequently outdoors to get rid of the last particles.

Applying floor varnish

The quickest way of sealing a newly stripped floor is to use a paint roller to apply the varnish. Thin the first coat as recommended on the container to aid penetration, and apply full-strength for the second and third coats. Use a power sander fitted with fine abrasive paper to sand the surface lightly between coats, and wipe it with a damp cloth to remove dust before re-coating it.

1 Apply the varnish with criss-cross passes of the roller, then finish off by running it parallel with the boards.

2 Use a paintbrush to finish the floor edges and to cut in around obstacles such as central heating pipes.

WARNING

Empty the dust bag as soon as it is about a third full. Bulked wood dust can ignite spontaneously, especially if it is impregnated with old stain or varnish. Also empty the bag whenever you stop work for more than a few minutes.

HELPFUL TIP

When a floor sander is switched on, the sanding belt starts to move, but does not come into contact with the floor until you lower the drum. Never let a moving belt touch the floor while the machine is stationary, or it will gouge a hollow in the wood. The moment the belt starts to bite into the wood – and there will be enough noise to indicate this – make sure that the machine moves forwards. It will begin to do so anyway, but an inexperienced user will tend to hold it back.

Laying a wood mosaic floor

A wood mosaic floor (sometimes, wrongly, called parquet) is an inexpensive way of achieving a real-wood floor. The panels are easy to handle and easy to lay.

Tools *Tape measure; chalk line; workbench; fine-toothed tenon saw; trimming knife; pencil; rag. Possibly also orbital sander or sanding block; abrasive paper (medium and fine grades); hammer; paintbrush.*

Materials *Wood mosaic panels; adhesive (with spreader); wood moulding or cork strip for the edges. Possibly also panel pins for wood moulding; floor varnish.*

Before you start Wood mosaic comes in square panels about 10mm thick. They are usually backed by felt, paper or netting, but some makes are wired and glued together. The pieces are flexible, and can compensate for slight unevenness in the sub-floor. If the sub-floor is very uneven, cover it with hardboard first (page 127). As wood absorbs moisture from the atmosphere, buy the mosaic panels at least two days before laying, and leave them unwrapped in the room where they are to be laid. This should prevent sudden expansion or contraction.

1 Mosaic panels are laid in the same way as vinyl and other tiles (page 133). First set them out, unglued, to ensure the widest border of cut tiles all around the room. As with most wood floors, a border of 15mm must be left between the edge of the mosaic and the skirting board to allow for expansion.

BUYING WOOD MOSAIC

If you can, check mosaics carefully before buying. Reject any with black marks on the face. This occurs if they are stacked with the felt backing of one against the face of the other, instead of face to face, and marks can be difficult to remove. Check, too, that the panels have been cut to the same size. Take one panel and hold all the others to it in turn, back to back. Rotate each panel through 90° for a further check of squareness. Inspect the surface for chips or scratches.

Prepacked panels usually have transparent wrapping, so you can see if the panels are face to face, and you should be able to see if they are all the same size.

2 Where possible, arrange the laying so that the panels can be cut between 'fingers' of wood, which only involves cutting the backing with a trimming knife.

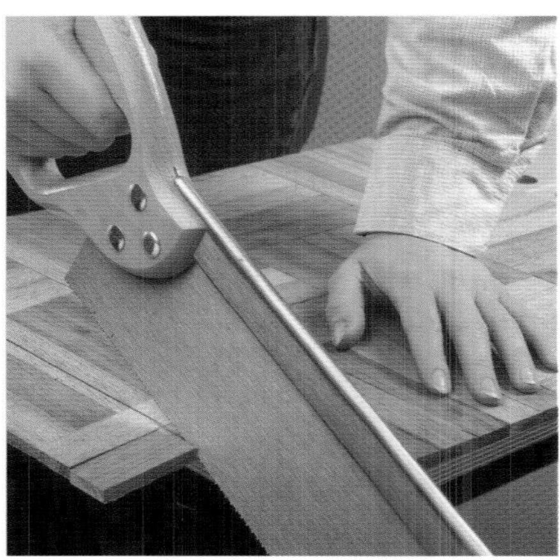

3 When you have to cut through wood, hold the panel firmly on a workbench and use a tenon saw.

4 Use the manufacturer's recommended adhesive and spread a little at a time on the prepared floor. Lay the tiles in position, pressing them into place.

5 When you have laid the floor, cover the gap around the edges with wood moulding or fill it with strips of cork.

6 Seal the surface of the finished floor with three coats of polyurethane floor varnish, thinning the first coat with 10 per cent white spirit. Sand the floor lightly between each coat and wipe off any dust with a rag dampened with white spirit.

HOW TO REPAIR A DAMAGED MOSAIC FLOOR

If a wood mosaic floor is damaged, repair it by replacing a complete square of strips. Keep any panels left over from the original laying for repairs.

1 If possible, cut around the damaged square with a trimming knife. Cut right through the felt or paper backing.

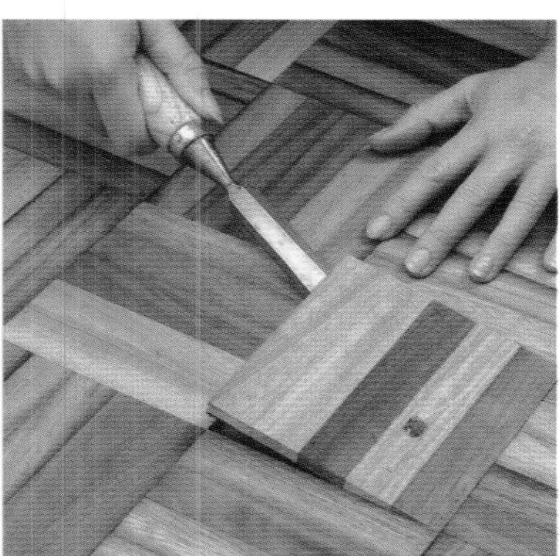

2 Lever out the damaged square as best you can, using an old chisel. Be careful not to damage the adjoining piece. Scrape off the old backing and adhesive from the sub-floor.

3 Cut a new square from a spare panel, together with its backing, and glue it in place.

Choosing laminate and wood flooring

Laminate flooring consists of layers joined together. The base layers are softwood and/or fibreboard to give the flooring strength and resilience, the top layer is the decorative layer and is covered with a tough clear protective finish. The least expensive laminate floorings have a paper decorative layer, on which is printed a wood-effect or other pattern; more expensive laminates, known as 'engineered' flooring have a real wood or bamboo decorative layer. Some laminates have a water-resistant core, allowing them to be used in kitchens and bathrooms. It is laid 'floating' (i.e. not glued or nailed down) over the existing sub-floor (floorboards, flooring-grade chipboard or concrete). A gap must be left at the edges for natural expansion.

Laminate flooring is made from lengths of high density fibreboard (HDF). There are locking or tongue-and-groove versions. Locking planks have tongues on their sides and ends that lock together, so you don't need to glue them. It is easy to unlock them if, for example, you want to replace a damaged board or need access to the floor beneath. Tongue-and-groove boards are glued together at each join, and so cannot be lifted easily.

The flooring is generally sold in packs. The pack will state the area it covers and whether or not the product is suitable for bathrooms and kitchens. Estimate the amount you need by multiplying the width of the room by its length, and buy about 10 per cent extra to allow for wastage. Solid wood flooring can be softwood or hardwood and can either be laid floating or be nailed down to replace existing floorboards or chipboard.

Solid wood

Softwood floorboards (normally 150mm wide and 18mm thick) available in various lengths with square or T&G (tongue-and-groove) edges to replace floorboards. Check size required if replacing single board.
- T & G hardwood floorboards (18 to 22mm thick) can also be used to replace existing floorboards (secret nailed to joists) or can be laid 'floating' over existing floor, glued together and with expansion gap at the edges (NB doors may need to be shortened). Expensive to very expensive.
- Can be sanded several times.
- Suitable for all rooms, but may need extra protection in wet areas.

Real-wood laminate (Often known as 'engineered' flooring)

- Available in wide range of woods including various oaks, beech, maple, cherry, walnut and parawood (rubberwood).
- Plank sizes vary from single widths (around 100mm) up to 250mm (3-strip).
- Normal thicknesses is from 7mm to 14mm (typical wood layer 2.5 to 3.5mm).
- Plank lengths typically from 1.2m.
- Either glued or with simple locking system and designed to be laid as 'floating' floor.
- Not normally suitable for kitchens and bathrooms.
- Thicker types may allow future sanding.

Laminate flooring

- Uses printed paper layer instead of real wood veneer to create a wide range of wood effects (left).
- Also available in various tile effects (above), including anthracite, limestone, travertine, stone and slate
- Range of widths available; common length is around 1.2m.
- Most have highly water-resistant core, making them suitable for use in kitchens, bathrooms and conservatories, but not suitable for saunas or areas of very high humidity.
- Normally supplied with easy-to-lay glue-free locking system (various designs).
- Cannot be sanded.

BAMBOO

A new environmentally-friendly material, but becoming more common.
- Available in T & G boards to be nailed down to replace normal floorboards – typically 18mm thick and 120mm wide – or to lay 'floating' over existing floor with boards glued together.
- Also available in 'engineered' versions with thin top veneer on a high-density fibreboard base. Usually has easy-to-lay glue-free locking system.
- Warm underfoot and can be used in most rooms, including kitchens and bathrooms.

Laying a laminate floor

A quick way to give a room a fresh, modern makeover is to lay laminate flooring. There are two main laying systems for laminate floors: locking and tongue-and-groove.

Tools *Tape measure; pencil; scissors; trimming knife; tenon saw; hand saw or jigsaw with laminate blade; hammer; tapping block or board offcut; pulling bar; power drill with flat wood bit.*

Materials *Enough underlay and laminate flooring to cover the room; adhesive tape; PVA woodworking adhesive; edging; threshold strip; panel pins; expansion strip (optional); fitting kit (which includes wedges or spacers and pulling bar).*

Putting down an underlay

An underlay must be put down before laying any type of laminate floor. This cushions the new floor and absorbs slight irregularities in the sub-floor. If you are covering a solid floor, lay a damp-proof membrane before putting down underlay. Most underlays are foam; wood fibre underlay gives enhanced soundproofing. You can buy a combined underlay and damp-proof membrane, which means fitting one layer instead of two.

1 Prepare timber floors by punching in any floorboard nails with a nail punch.

2 If you have a solid concrete floor, cover it with a layer of heavy-duty polythene sheeting to protect the laminate from any dampness within the floor. Cut 75mm extra on each edge and tape it up the walls.

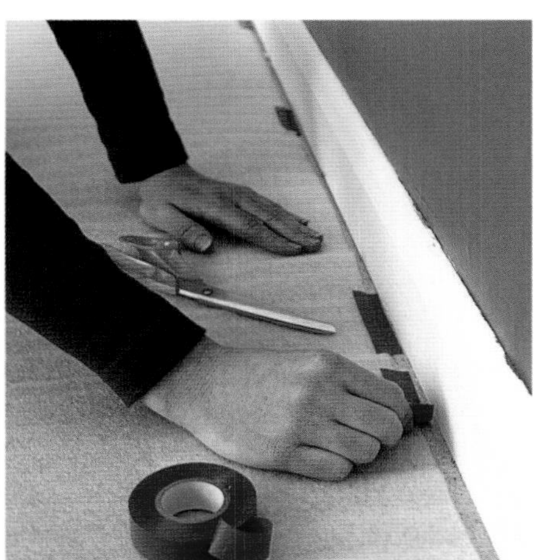

3 Lay the underlay recommended by the flooring manufacturer over the whole floor, trimming to fit with scissors or a trimming knife and leaving a 10mm gap round pipes.

4 Butt underlay joins together – do not overlap them. Secure joins with tape. If using a wood fibre underlay, allow the boards to acclimatise for 24 hours in the room before laying them, and leave an expansion gap of 5mm between the boards and 10mm round the room.

Laying locking laminate

1 Start laying the first board parallel to the longest wall in the room, in a left-hand corner, putting the end with the short tongue against the wall. Insert spacers at intervals between the skirting board and the long edge and end of the board to create an expansion gap.

2 Add more boards until you reach the end of the row, where you will probably need to cut a board.

3 If the offcut is longer than 300mm, use it to start the second row. Otherwise, cut a board in half and use that. This ensures that the joints will be staggered between the rows. Fit spacers at the end.

4 Carry on placing the boards row by row. As you finish each row, enlist help to lift the row so that the long edge is at an angle of about 30° to the previous row, and lower and push down the boards to lock the rows together.

5 At the last row you will probably have to cut the final boards down in width. Lay each board in turn *exactly* over the last whole board laid, and mark the width required on it by using a pencil and a board offcut held against the skirting board to scribe the wall profile on it. This vital technique is used for floor tiles as well as strips – see photograph for Method 2 on page 134.

6 Redraw the line 5mm nearer the exposed edge of the board to recreate the expansion gap. Cut each board to width with a jigsaw or panel saw and fit in place.

7 Remove the spacers from the edge of the flooring and conceal the expansion gap with strips of plain, scotia or quadrant trim to match or to contrast with the floor – see also page 357. At room corners, cut the moulding at 45°, using a mitre block. Use glue or nails to fix the trim to the skirting, not to the floor.

Laying tongue-and-groove laminate

The process is largely the same as for locking laminate (left). However, because gluing does not allow for mistakes, prepare and lay two or three rows without gluing to check the fit first. Always lay boards with the tongue protruding into the room.

1 Lay the first board parallel to the longest wall in the room, with its groove facing the wall. Insert spacers to create a 10mm expansion gap.

2 Lay the next plank end-on to the first one, fitting the tongue into the groove.

3 When you have laid three whole rows, take them up and re-lay them using wood adhesive. Tap them together with the hammer and tapping block.

4 Wipe off any oozing adhesive straight away with a damp rag. Do this again once you have closed up the joints (overleaf).

5 At the end of the row, use the pulling bar to close up the joint by hooking it over the end of the board and tapping the upstand with a hammer or mallet.

6 Start the next row with the offcut from the previous row to create offset joints. Glue the grooved edge and push it into place.

7 As you work across the room, tap the boards closely together by using a proprietary tapping block and hammer to close up the joints.

8 Follow steps 5, 6 and 7 of Laying locking laminate (page 131) to fit the last row and hide the expansion gap.

Fitting boards round pipes

1 To cut round a radiator pipe, align the board with its neighbour and slide it up against the pipe.

2 Mark the pipe centre on the board edge. Then remove the board, butt it up against the skirting board and mark the pipe centre on the board's short end. Join up the marks to indicate the pipe centre.

3 Use a 22mm flat wood bit to drill a hole through the board at the mark. Cut across the board and fit the two sections round the pipe. When you buy your flooring, you should also be able to buy two-part pipe covers in matching wood colours. These simply slide into place to cover the hole after you have fitted the flooring round the pipe.

At door openings

Rather than trying to shape the board to match a door frame, it is easier to cut off the bottom of the door frame so the board can be slid underneath. Place an offcut of board on the underlay and use a panel saw flat against this to do the cutting.

If the flooring finishes at the doorway, use a threshold strip appropriate to the flooring thickness in the next room (there is a whole range available in matching wood colours) and nail, screw or glue this to the sub-floor to protect the edge of the flooring. Two-part threshold strips are easiest to fit.

SOLID WOOD FLOORING

Solid wood flooring (see page 130) can be laid on a timber sub-floor in the same way as laminate flooring with an expansion gap around the perimeter of the room. Or it can be secured to the sub-floor (or directly to the joists to replace existing floorboards) by a technique known as secret nailing.

1 Drive panel pins down through the tongue of each board at an angle to the floor so it passes through the body of the strip and into the sub-floor. Use 30mm pins for boards up to 20mm thick, and 50mm pins for thicker boards.

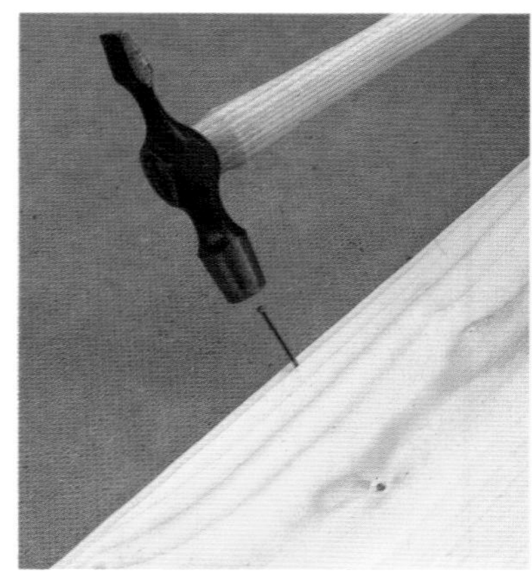

2 Start the pins with the hammer. Use a nail punch to finish driving each pin so its head finishes flush with the top edge of the tongue. You can then slot the grooved edge of the next board over the tongue and repeat the fixing to secure it to the sub-floor.

Setting out floor tiles

Lay floor tiles 'dry' from the centre of the room before you start to stick them in place, so you can achieve the best layout.

Where to start laying

Finding the centre point

Whatever type of tile you are laying, you always begin in the middle of the room, so you need to find the centre point.

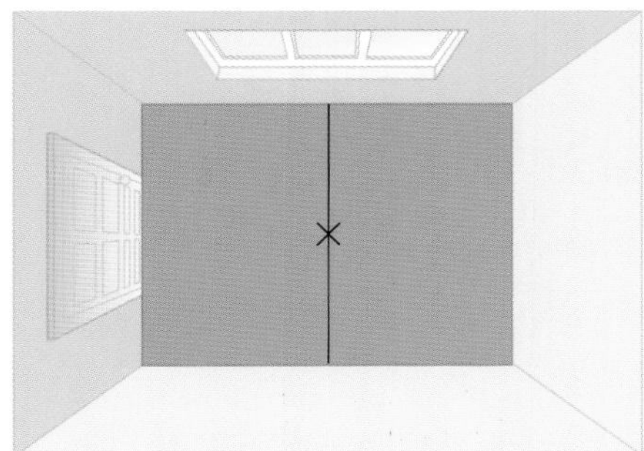

1 Measure two opposite walls and mark their centres. Snap a chalk line (see box, right) between these points.

2 Measure the line and mark its centre. That is the middle of the room.

Alternatively

- If the room has a chimney breast, snap the chalk line parallel to that wall.

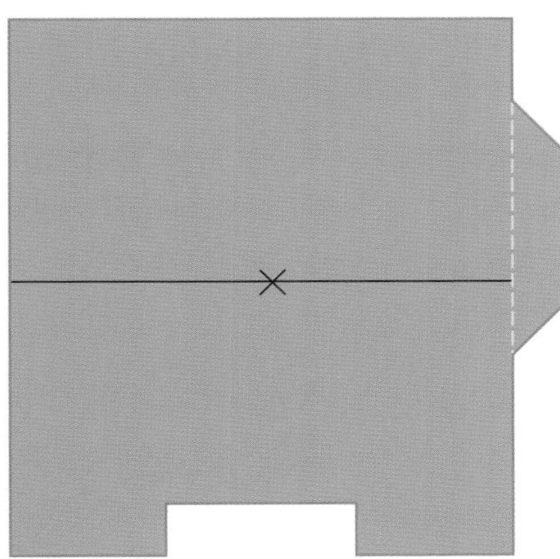

- If the room also has a bay, square it off with a line between the ends of the bay and measure along this false wall line.
- If the room is even more irregular in shape, choose one wall as the base wall. Snap a chalk line parallel to it, about 75mm away, and mark its centre point. Draw a short chalk line at right angles to this base line. To obtain the right angle, use a few tiles as a guide. Extend this line the full length of the room by snapping a chalk line. Measure this line and mark the centre.

Marking the cross-line

Once the main chalk line has been laid, a second line needs to be drawn across it at right angles. To do this, place two tiles on the floor, each with one side along the centre line and one corner on the centre point. Then snap a chalk line across the room, passing through the centre point and following the edge of the tiles.

Placing the key tile

You must now decide the position of the first (or key) tile, which will determine the position of all other tiles in the room. Ideally, all the tiles around the edge of the room should be equal in size, and at least a half tile width. Experiment by laying tiles from the centre to all edges of the room.

The key tile can be placed in any of several positions:

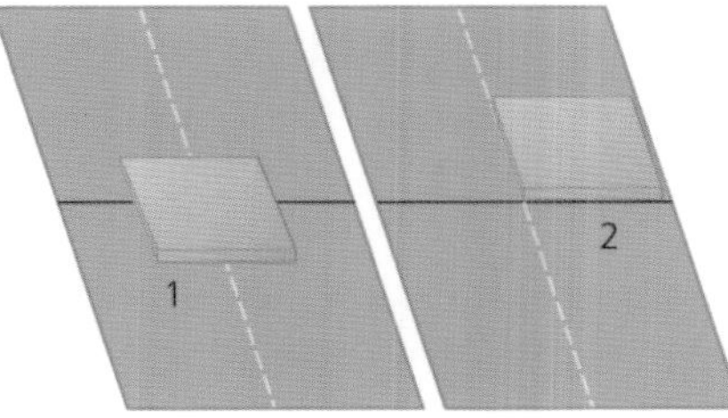

1 Centrally on the middle point of the room.

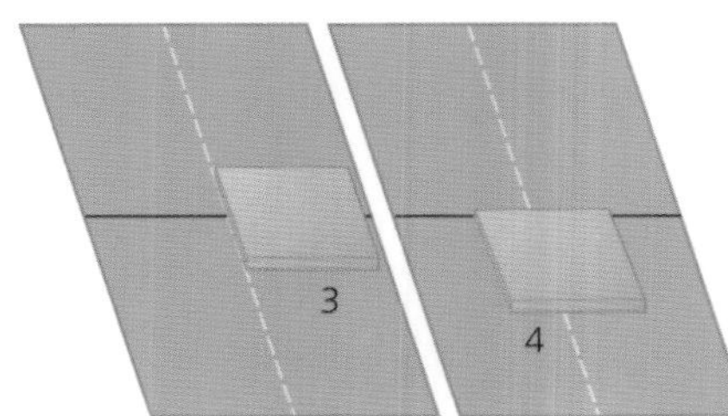

2 In an angle formed by the two chalk lines.

3 Centrally on the main chalk line, and on one side of the line that crosses it.

4 Centrally on the crossing line, and on one side of the main one.

SNAPPING A CHALK LINE

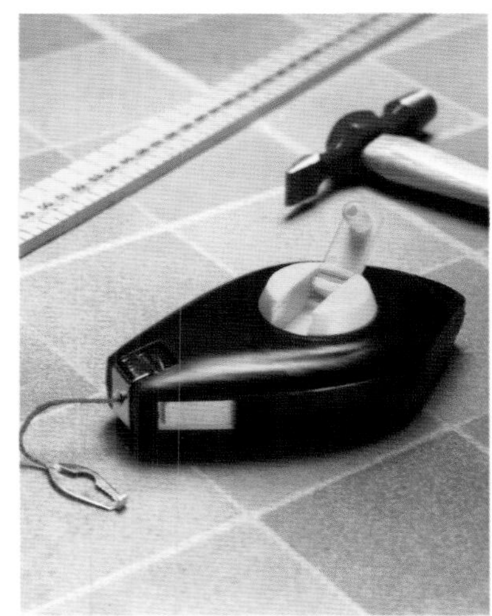

For many jobs, you need a line across the room. Rub chalk along a length of string or buy a chalk-line reel which chalks the string for you. Tie one end to a nail in the floor and hold the other end at the far side of the room, pulling it taut. Pull the string straight up and let go. It will mark a straight line on the floor as it snaps back into place.

Centring the tiles on a feature

- Some rooms have a dominant feature such as a fireplace, or bay window. To obtain an attractive result, adjust the appropriate base line – keeping it parallel to the original line – to ensure that the tiles are centred on the feature. Once again, ensure that you get the biggest possible cut tiles at the edges.

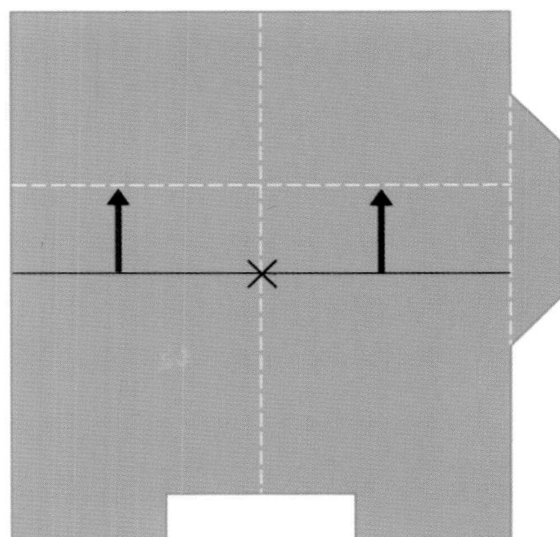

- A room may have two features. If this is the case, adjust both base lines so that the tiles can be centred on both features.
- It is not possible to centre tiles on more than two features, except by accident.

Patterns in tiles

Design your own floor patterns by combining tiles of different colours. The simplest is the 'chessboard', alternating tiles in two colours, but many other arrangements are possible.

Laying tiles diagonally

Laying tiles on the diagonal is not difficult once you have marked the floor using a homemade 'compass' or scriber.

Before you start To prevent mistakes when laying the floor, draw a scale plan of your pattern on squared paper. Then you can work out exactly how many of each colour or design you will need.

1 First improvise a compass using a thin piece of batten about 1m long with a nail in each end. Drill pilot holes, smaller than the diameter of the nails, to avoid splitting the wood.

2 Mark the cross-lines in the middle of the room in the normal way. (See Where to start laying, page 133).

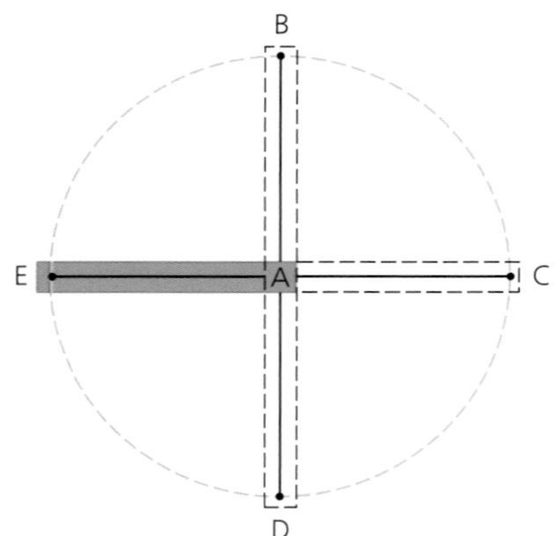

3 Put one nail of the scriber on the point where the lines cross (A), and mark four points on the cross-lines – at B,C,D and E.

4 Put one nail of your scriber on B and make arcs at F and G. Move the scriber to C and make arcs at G and H. From D make arcs at H and I, and from E at I and F.

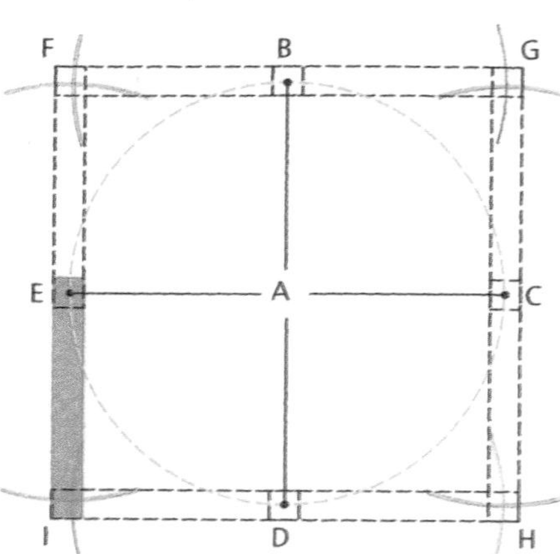

5 Snap diagonal chalk lines on the floor through the points where the arcs meet at G and I and at F and H.

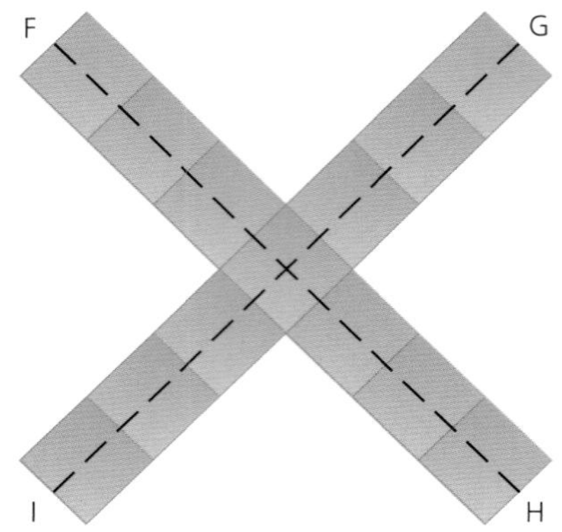

6 Lay out rows of unglued tiles along the diagonal lines, adjusting their position to get the largest cut tiles round the border, then glue down all the whole tiles.

Border tile patterns: method 1

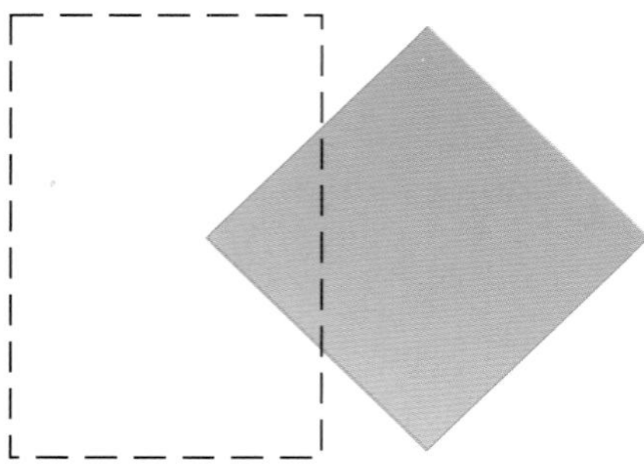

1 To cut border tiles, first make a template. Cut a piece of card with two opposite edges parallel. The distance between the edges must be the same as the distance across the tiles from corner to corner.

2 Place the tile to be cut exactly on to top of the whole tile nearest to the gap to be filled.

3 Place one edge of the template against the skirting board and score along the opposite edge across the face of the tile. When cut, the piece of tile farthest from the skirting board will fit the empty space.

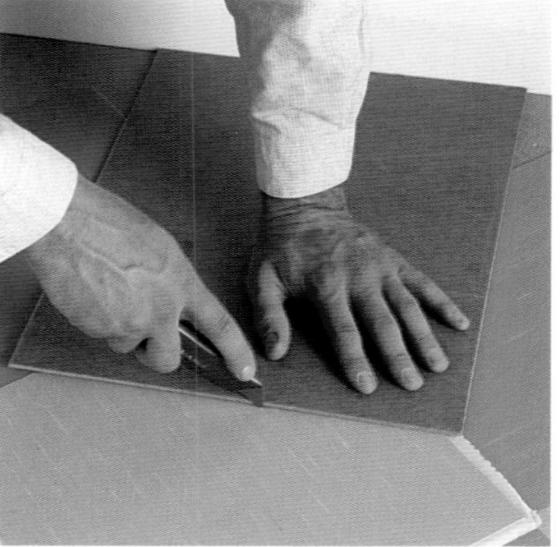

Border tile patterns: method 2

Diagonal tiles can be finished off with a border of part tiles laid square to the wall.

1 When you are setting out the tiles initially, place the first tile in the centre of the room to ensure that the tiles around the wall will be wider than half a tile.

2 Lay all the whole tiles.

3 Cut some tiles in half from corner to corner and lay them to square off the diagonal pattern.

4 Finally, cut the border tiles square to the wall, measuring each one individually, but sticking all of them down one at a time.

> **HOW MANY TILES WILL YOU NEED?**
>
> To calculate the number of tiles required, measure the room and multiply the width by the length to give the area. If the room has a bay or chimney breast, calculate it separately and add or subtract it from the main area. Each pack of tiles gives the area they will cover. (Most tile packs cover a square metre.) Divide the area of the room by the area a pack will cover to get the total number of packs you will need. Remember to buy a few extra tiles to allow for wastage and repairs.

Laying vinyl and cork tiles

Tiles take longer to lay than sheet material, but they are easier to handle and cut to fit, there is less wastage, and, if you make a mistake, ruining one tile is not nearly as serious as damaging a large sheet.

Vinyl and cork tiles are both laid in the same way. Some are self-adhesive.

Tools *Tape measure; chalk line; adhesive spreader; rag; pencil; trimming knife; scrap hardboard; metal straightedge.*

Materials *Tiles; adhesive recommended by tile manufacturer (if tiles are not self-adhesive); perhaps white spirit.*

1 Decide on the best arrangement (see Where to start laying, page 133).

2 Dust the floor then spread the tile adhesive across a metre-square area.

3 Place the first tile at the start point and lay it down flat.

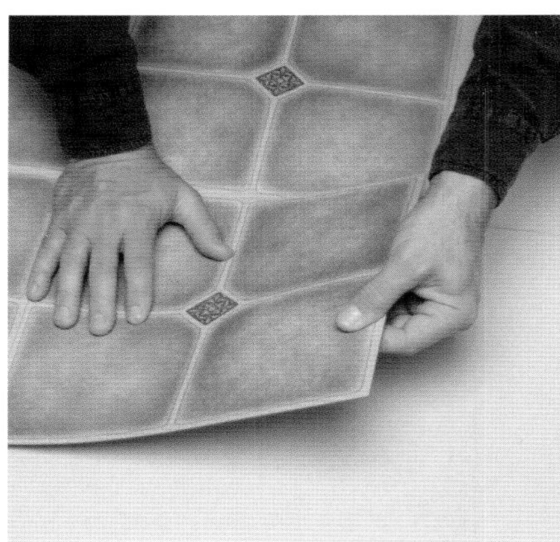

4 With the first tile stuck down, add adjacent tiles to form a square of four. Then work outwards from it to the walls. Where adhesive has to be spread on the floor, spread a square metre at a time.

5 If any adhesive oozes up through the joins, wipe it up immediately, using a cloth damped with water or white spirit depending on the adhesive.

Cutting border tiles to fit

The cut tiles around the edge can be dealt with in two ways. Use method 1 if adhesive is being used, and method 2 in small areas such as WCs and narrow corridors.

Method 1

Lay all the tiles except for a border of one whole tile and one part tile all the way round the room.

1 Place the tile to be cut against the last one in the row, and place another tile on top of it, pressed against the wall.

2 Draw a pencil line across the face of the tile to be cut. With some tiles you do not need to draw a line; score with a knife then snap. If the tile will not break, cut it on a piece of scrap board.

3 The two tiles now change places so the part tile lies against the wall. Put them to one side and prepare the whole row (numbering them on the back as you go), then stick them down one at a time.

Method 2

With this method, you lay all the whole tiles, then deal with the border of part tiles.

1 Place the tile to be cut squarely on the last tile in the row. Put a third on top, pressed against the wall.

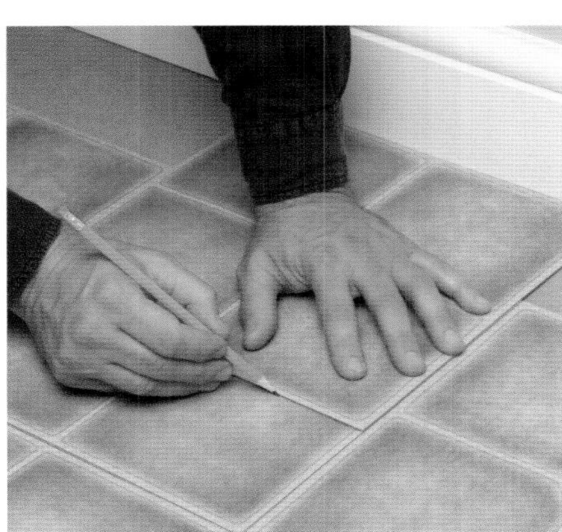

2 Draw a pencil line across the face of the tile to be cut (or score it lightly with a trimming knife). Then either snap a scored tile in two or cut through it (on a piece of hardboard) with a straightedge as a guide.

3 The part of the cut tile closer to the centre of the room will fit the empty space perfectly. Prepare the whole row, then slot them into place.

At doorways Either cut the door frame (as for laminate flooring, page 132) or use a profile gauge (shown on page 112) to transfer the shape of the door frame and architrave to the tile before cutting it.

Corner tiles Tiles in corners will have to be cut to length as well as width, using the same method as above.

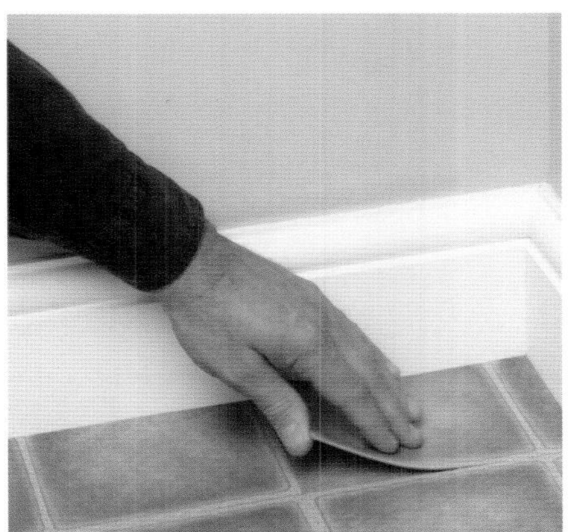

Cutting round a curve

You may have to cut round an irregular shaped object such as a WC or washbasin.

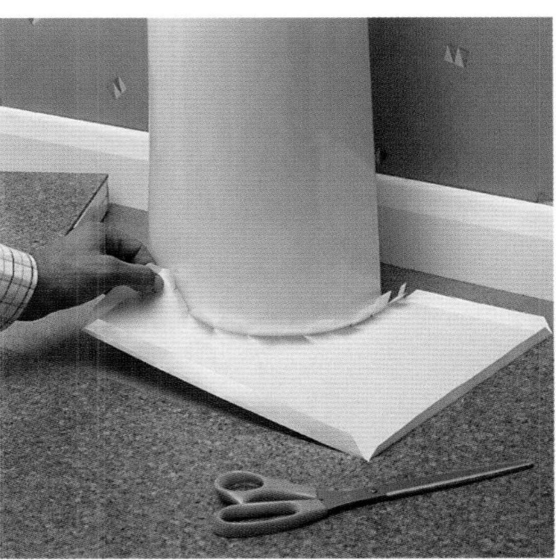

1 Take a sheet of paper a bit larger than a tile. Place it over the area the cut tile will occupy, and fold it along the edges of the adjacent tiles. Tear out the corner to fit the obstacle approximately, and crease the paper firmly against its outline.

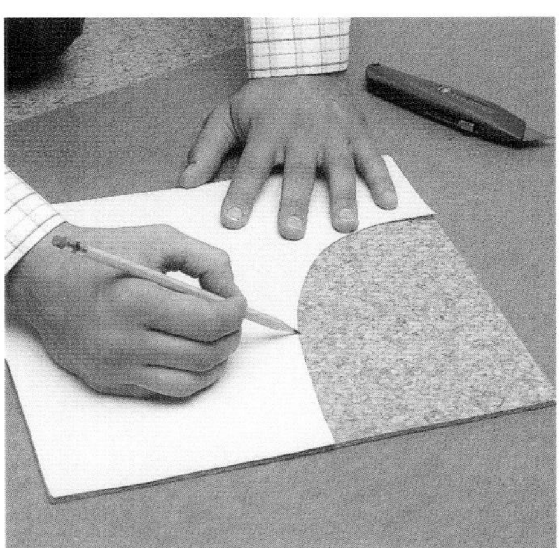

2 Cut the paper along the folds to create the template. Use it to mark the tile for cutting.

FIRE HAZARD WITH ADHESIVES

Solvent-based adhesives are highly flammable. When laying a floor with this type of adhesive, open all the windows and doors in the room and switch off any pilot lights in the room, including those in a gas cooker, gas fire or central-heating boiler. Don't smoke while you work. When you have finished, hang your working clothes outdoors to air.

Water-based adhesives are not flammable, but they take longer to dry, which slows a job down in cold weather.

Cutting round a pipe

A pipe rising from the floor will normally be at the edge of a room, so first cut a tile to fit the border.

1 Place the cut tile square on the last whole tile and push it against the pipe. Make a pencil mark where it touches.

2 Put the cut tile against the wall and push its end against the pipe. Make another mark where it touches.

3 With a try square, draw a line across the tile from the mark on the side. Then put the try square on the uncut long edge and draw a line through the other mark. (Do not put the try square on the cut edge as it may not be square.)

4 Where the lines cross is the centre of the pipe. Drill a hole the right diameter (with the tile held down on a piece of scrap wood), or draw round a coin of the appropriate size, and cut with a knife. Cut a slit from the hole to the edge of the vinyl or cork so you can fit it round the pipe.

Alternatively You can make a very accurate hole by punching through the vinyl or cork with a pipe offcut the same diameter. Use a round file on the inside of the pipe to sharpen the cutting edge, then strike the other end with a hammer.

HOW TO LIFT A DAMAGED VINYL TILE

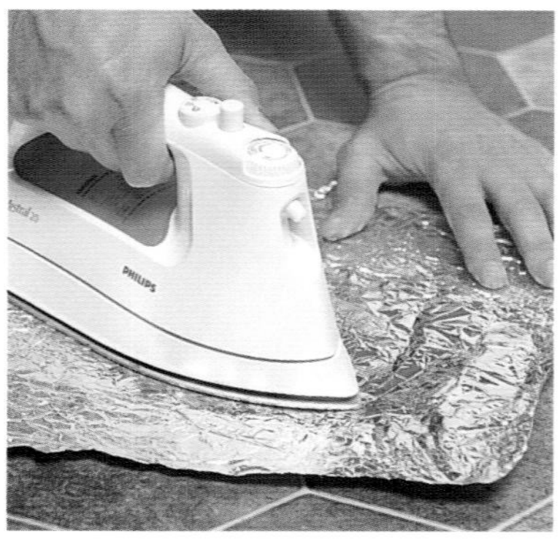

To remove a damaged vinyl tile without disturbing the rest of the floor, put a piece of aluminium kitchen foil over it and press with a hot iron. Wait until the heat penetrates the tile (this will take longer on concrete than wood), then lever up a corner with a filling knife or wallpaper stripper, and pull the tile away. Lift the remaining adhesive with a filling knife heated with a hot-air gun. A larger area can be softened with a hot-air gun. The technique will not work on cork tiles, which insulate too effectively against the heat.

Lay a new tile with fresh adhesive. Do not slide it into place, or adhesive may be forced up at the edges.

CARPET TILES

Carpet tiles are laid in much the same way as vinyl and cork (page 134). Because they are loose laid, worn or damaged tiles can be replaced. It's a good idea to buy several spare tiles and swap them regularly. That way, any colour change or wear is evened out and if a tile needs replacing, the replacement will match the existing floor.

The job will be much easier if you make yourself a carpet tile pusher.

Cut a 300mm length of 150 x 25mm timber. Drill a hole in the centre 15mm deep and glue in a piece of broom handle. Drive a nail through the wood into the handle. Drive four nails through the front, projecting by 3mm, to act as teeth.

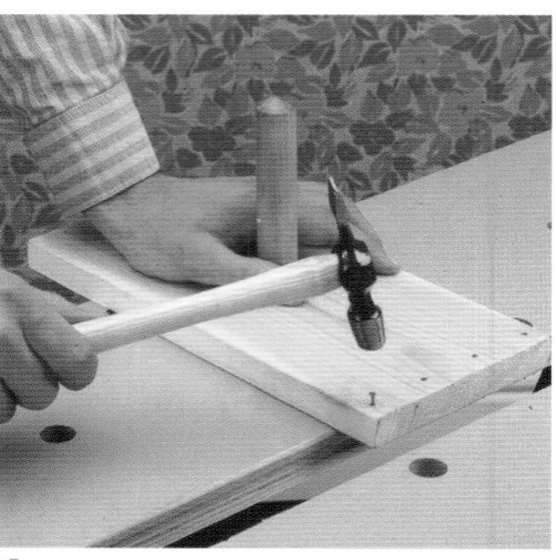

1 Set out the tiles (page 133). You can lay all the tiles with the pile running in the same direction to give the effect of a fitted carpet. Or place them chequer-board style with the pile running at right angles on alternate tiles.

2 Stick down the first tile in the centre of the room with double sided carpet tape to stop it from shifting during laying.

3 Start laying the tiles. Put the tile pusher on top of each tile you lay so that its teeth grip, then push the tile forwards into position.

4 When all the whole tiles have been laid, measure the border tiles using one of the methods on page 135. Mark the cutting line on the face of the tile by making a nick with a trimming knife on each edge. Turn the tile upside down, lay a steel rule across the two nicks, and cut with the knife. Fit a metal carpet threshold bar in the doorway.

Laying ceramic floor tiles

As with vinyl tiles, it's important to get the setting out right before you begin laying ceramic floor tiles.

Before laying ceramic tiles on a timber floor, you need to lay a base of 9mm exterior grade plywood. This provides a level, stable surface and prevents movement of the boards from cracking the tiles. Fix the plywood sheet with screws every 300mm.

You can lay ceramic tiles directly on clean concrete floors or old quarry or vinyl tiles – as long as these are stuck down firmly, and are thoroughly scrubbed with sugar soap.

Tools *String; pencil; straightedge; guide battens (50 x 25mm); claw hammer; spirit level; stripping knife; trimming knife; felt-tip pen; tile-cutting jig (can be hired); notched adhesive spreader; rubber-bladed grout spreader.*

Materials *Tiles (to work out how many you need, see page 134); tile spacers; flooring-grade tile adhesive; waterproof grout; non-setting silicone mastic.*

Where to start

1 Find the centre of the floor by pinning string lines across the room from the midpoint of each wall (page 133). Draw guidelines along the strings, then remove them. Put one tile in the angle between the lines and dry-lay a row of tiles – with spacers in between – towards one wall, to see how wide the edge gap will be.

2 Lay a second row from the centre of the room at right angles to the first row, and check the edge gap. Cutting narrow strips off ceramic tiles is difficult, so you want to avoid very narrow edge pieces, or ones that are almost a tile wide.

3 If the edge gaps will prove difficult, the answer is to shift the whole tile layout by the width of half a tile. Cross out the original guidelines and draw new ones, parallel to them but half a tile's width away. Lay out the tile rows again in order to check the fit.

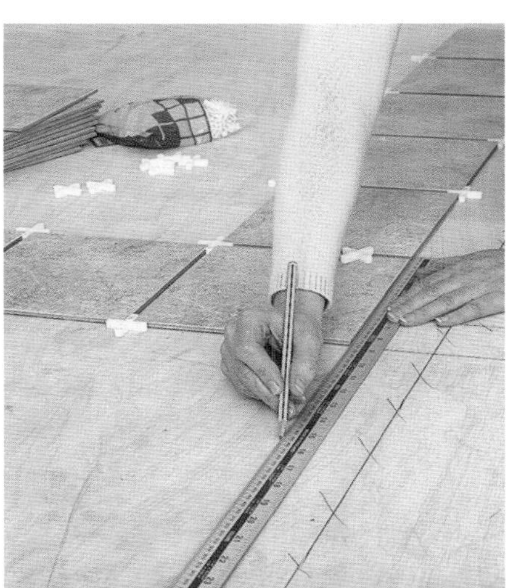

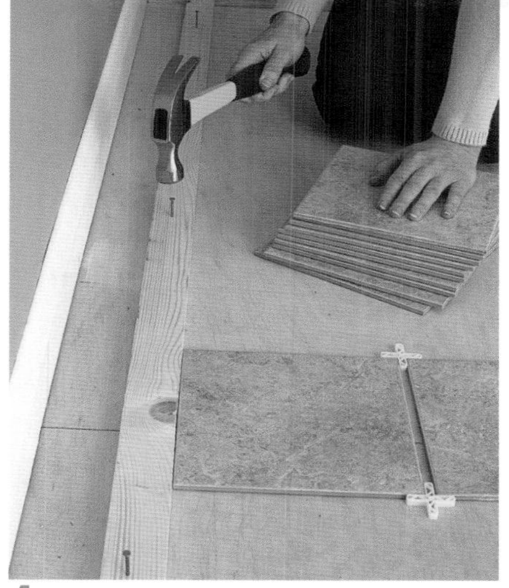

4 Start work in the corner of the room farthest from the door. Nail down one timber batten at the end of one row of tiles, and the second at the end of the other. If you leave the nails proud, you can pull them out easily later on.

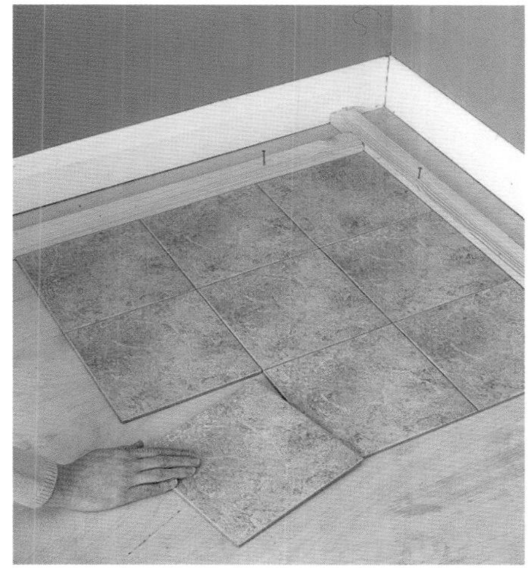

5 Dry-lay a square of nine tiles in the angle between the battens. If the battens don't line up perfectly against the tiles, reposition them so the tiles sit squarely.

Laying whole tiles

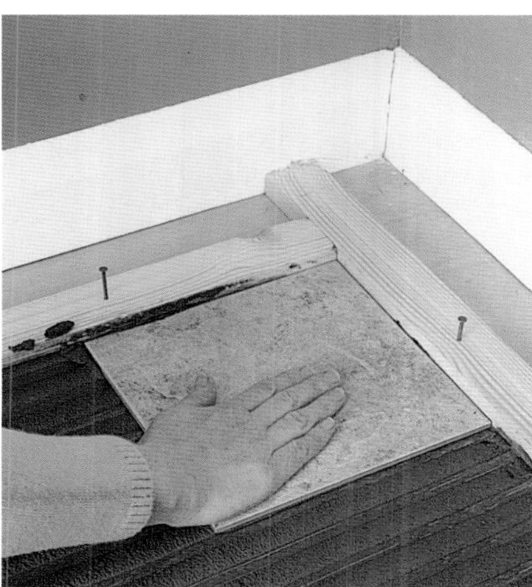

1 Spread enough adhesive for a square of nine (3 x 3) or sixteen (4 x 4) tiles. Hold the notched spreader at an angle of about 45° to the floor. Press the first tile into the right-angle created by the battens.

2 Using tile spacers to ensure even joint sizes, lay two or three more tiles in lines next to each batten.

3 Complete the nine or sixteen tile square, being sure to use spacers at each corner. If you push the spacers deep into the adhesive, the grout will conceal them.

4 Now that the square is complete, use a spirit level to check each row in turn, and across the diagonals. Tamp down any tiles that are standing proud.

5 Continue, a square block at a time, until you cannot fit another whole tile. Run a narrow blade paint scraper between the tiles and the wood battens to stop the adhesive bonding the two together. It's also a good idea to check the edges of each square block with a straightedge to make sure that the tiles are perfectly aligned.

Cutting and fitting edge tiles

Do not attempt to deal with the edges until the whole tiles have had at least 24 hours to set hard enough to walk on.

1 Use a claw hammer to remove the timber guide battens from the edges of the whole tiles.

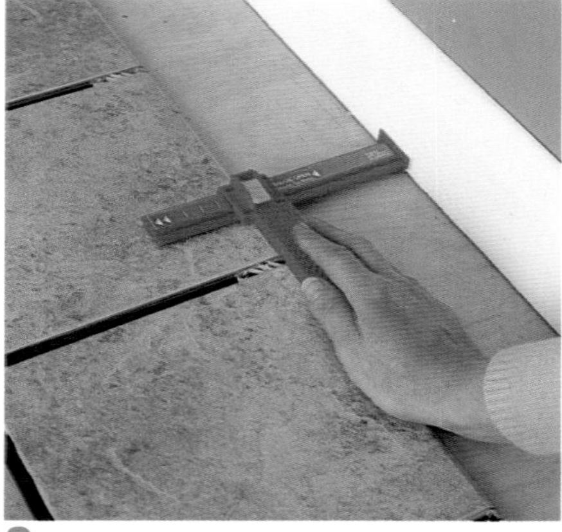

2 Measure the width of the cut pieces. Some cutting jigs come with a sliding tile gauge which makes the job easier. Otherwise use a steel rule, allowing for the spacer width and a small expansion gap.

3 Slot the tile gauge into the cutting jig and position the tile with one edge against the sliding arm of the gauge. Score the cutting line across the surface using the cutting wheel. Fit the tile into the cutter's jaws and press down the lever to snap it along the scored line.

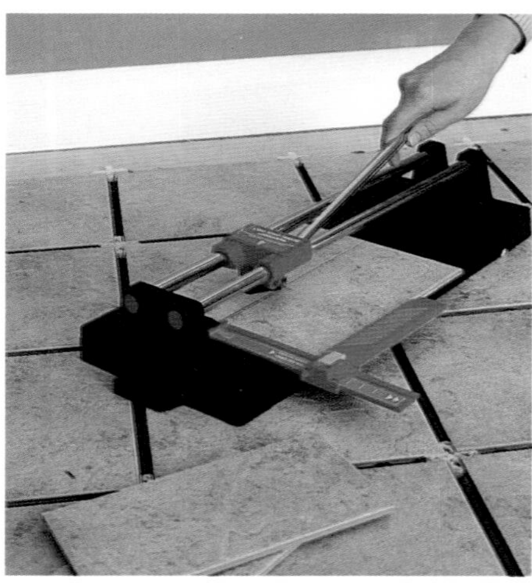

HELPFUL TIP

Measure each tile to be cut individually: the room is unlikely to be perfectly square. Allow for the width of a tile spacer in each joint, and for a small expansion gap next to the skirting board. Mark the width on the tile with a felt-tip pen.

4 Apply adhesive to the back of the cut tile, not to the floor. Use the notched spreader to make uniform ridges.

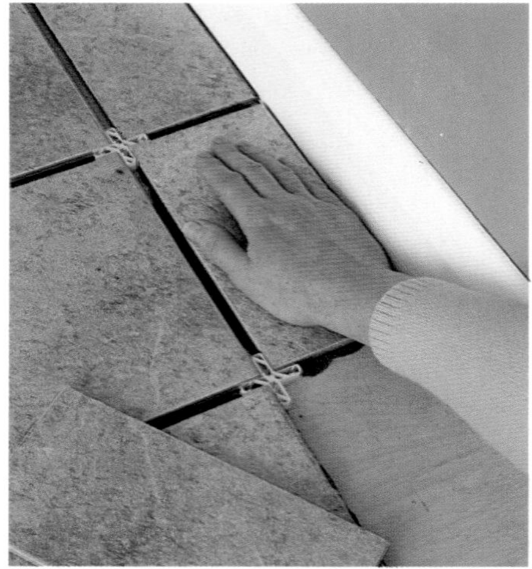

5 Put spacers in each joint between the whole tiles. Leaving the corners for now, work around the perimeter of the room, laying each cut tile in place, in turn. Ensure there is a small gap between each tile and the skirting board.

6 Cut tiles for the corners of the room, and lay them in place.

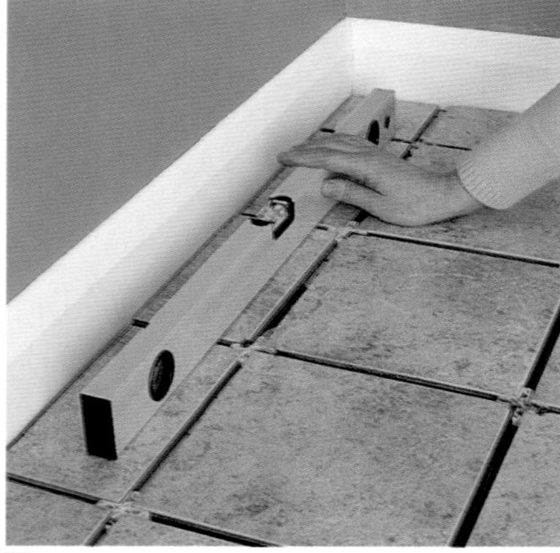

7 Use a spirit level to check that none of the edge tiles stands proud of its neighbours or the rest of the floor. Tap down tiles that are too high. Lift up a tile that is too low and add a little more adhesive.

8 Allow 24 hours for the adhesive to set hard before adding grout to the joints.

9 Fill the joints between tiles with waterproof grout, which will resist staining. Use a rubber bladed spreader to force the grout into the gaps. Clean up as you go, scraping off the excess grout with the spreader. When the grout is dry, polish off smears with an old towel. Seal the gap between the tiles and the skirting board with flexible silicone sealant.

Laying quarry and terracotta tiles

The principles of laying quarry and terracotta tiles are no different from those of laying ceramic floor tiles. Traditionally, they are often laid on the diagonal.

If you wish to lay quarry or terracotta tiles over a timber floor, then check the depth of the joists before you buy the tiles. Joists less than 125mm will not be strong enough to support the weight of these thick, heavy tiles, and your floor will sag and crack.

A timber floor must be covered with plywood, as with ceramic tiles (page 137).

Tools *String; pencil; straightedge; guide battens (50 x 25mm); claw hammer; spirit level; felt-tip pen; notched adhesive spreader; grout spreader; tile-cutting jig or power tile-cutting saw (if tiles more than 6mm thick).*

Materials *Tiles (to work out how many you need, see page 134); tile spacers; masonry nails (for a concrete floor); flooring-grade tile adhesive and grout.*

HELPFUL TIP

Mix up tiles from different boxes before laying them. Quarry tiles have natural colour variations, and a floor looks best if the shades are randomly scattered rather than in concentrated blocks.

GUARD AGAINST STAINING

Seal porous terracotta tiles before laying them. This will prevent them becoming stained later on by the grout. Buy a branded sealer, or make up your own by mixing two parts of boiled linseed oil to one part of white spirit.

Once the tiles are laid and grouted, give them as many additional coats as they can absorb, allowing each to dry before applying the next one. Consult a specialist tile supplier about waxes and other preparations that will protect the seal and enhance the colour.

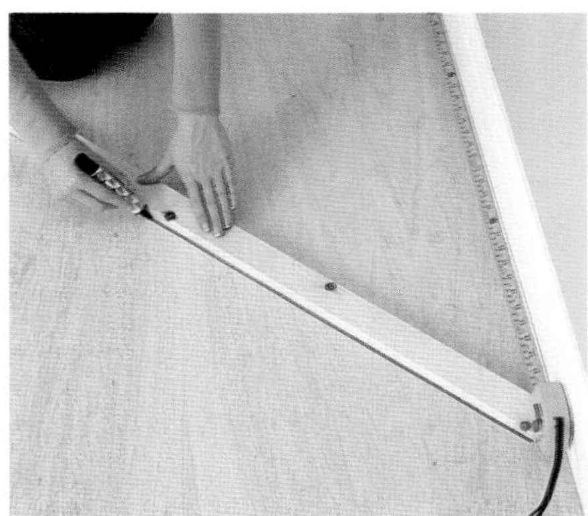

1 Measure one wall and mark its mid point. Mark the half-wall distance along the adjacent wall. If you join these marks with a straightedge, you will have a guideline at exactly 45° to the walls of the room.

2 Dry lay tiles in both directions across the centre of the room to check how the pattern falls between the walls and when you are happy with this, nail the guide batten to the floor along the line, using masonry nails if the floor is concrete. Leave the nail heads proud – they will be easier to pull out later.

3 Apply a band of tile adhesive a little over one tile wide next to the batten. Press the first row of tiles into it, using spacers to ensure even gaps.

4 Once you have laid the first row, remove the batten. Spread adhesive between the row you have laid and the room corner. (If the room is very large, you may have to lay these tiles after you have completed the rest of the whole tiles in the room, and they have had 24 hours to dry.)

5 Lay all the whole tiles, working one row at a time and inserting tile spacers at each joint. In this room, whole tiles stretch from wall to wall leaving half-tile triangles next to the skirting boards. In other rooms, the gaps may be smaller or larger than half a tile – see page 134 for the method of cutting tiles laid diagonally.

6 As you complete each row, use a timber batten and a hammer to tamp it down. After every four or five rows, check the levels with a spirit level. If a tile is too low, prise it up, apply a blob of adhesive to its back and replace it.

Cutting and grouting

With all the whole tiles laid, you can cut and fit the border tiles, and finish the floor by filling the joints with grout.

1 Measure the space for the infill triangle, allowing room for grout. Measure its short sides and transfer the marks onto the tile; then join the marks.

2 It is worth hiring a power tile-cutting saw for cutting quarry or terracotta tiles: its diamond cutting disc creates perfect cuts much more easily than a normal platform tile cutter.

3 Spread adhesive into the back of each cut tile and press it into place, leaving a small gap between the tile and the skirting board.

4 After the adhesive has had 24 hours to set, you can fill the joints with grout. Use a rubber-bladed squeegee to force grout between the tiles. Clean up as you work, and after each square metre or so, finish the join by recessing it slightly with a piece of dowel or a grout shaping tool.

Quarry tiled skirting

You can buy coved skirting to edge a quarry tiled floor. These are great in a kitchen or anywhere that gets wet.

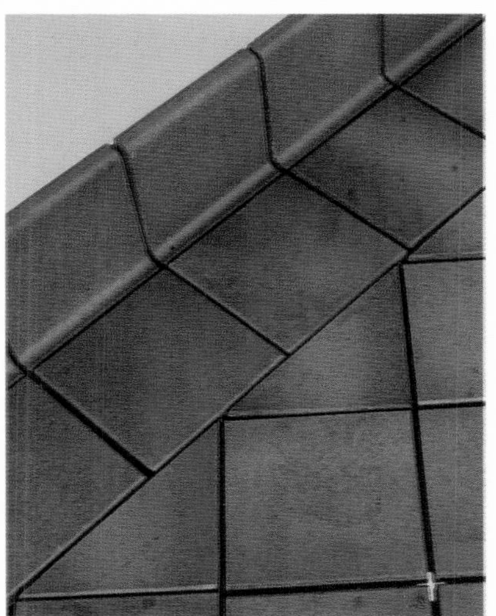

STONE FLOORING

A stone floor is one of the most expensive types of floor, but one of the most durable. Stone floors are heavy and hard to lay – especially when the slabs are of random sizes and thicknesses. They must be laid properly or the joints will crack. The job is generally best left to a professional.

A stone floor can be laid over a wooden floor, but joists will have to be strengthened to support the considerable load. Usually, stone floors are laid in kitchens and high traffic areas on the ground floor, where a concrete slab foundation makes the perfect sub-base.

A stone floor is thick – usually around 40mm. You will need to cut the bottoms off any doors that open over it. Another disadvantage is that stone feels cold underfoot. This can be solved by installing underfloor heating (right) beneath the slabs.

Granite Very hardwearing. It comes highly polished and tends to be used in minimalist kitchens and hallways.

Limestone Comes in hard and soft versions, in a range of colours. It can give a room a contemporary, minimalist feel or a traditional look.

Marble Highly polished. It comes in a range of colours and can be laid in chequerboard or other designs.

Slate Tiles are either split (riven) or cut. Riven slate has a distinctive grain and traditional look; cut slate is smooth, sleek and contemporary.

Travertine Geologically, a cross between limestone and marble. It is a low porosity stone, pale and neutral in colour. Slabs come flat and sleek, or 'pillowed' (where the profile edges of a slab are smoothed into a slight curve) for a softer look.

Tumbled stone mosaic Supplied on a mesh backing in various sizes and colours. Can be used for floors or walls, making it a popular choice for wet rooms.

SAFETY TIP

Before working on electrical systems, isolate electrical circuits and check with a tester before touching any wires or cables. If you are in any doubt about what you are doing, seek specialist advice.

The basics of underfloor heating

Underfloor heating warms the entire surface of the floor. Even in a small room, this is a large radiant surface, which means that its temperature needs to be only slightly higher than the room. By contrast, a radiator transfers heat from a very small surface, and has to be much hotter than the room it is heating.

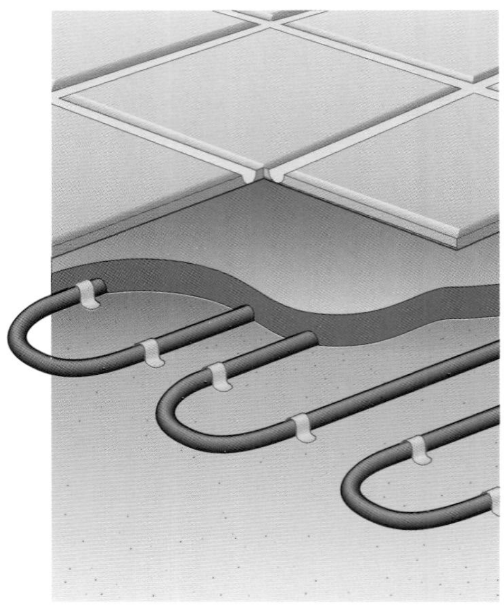

Typically, the temperature of the water in an underfloor heating system pipe is 55-55°C compared to the 80°C surface temperature of a radiator. Most underfloor systems warm the floor to 25–28°C, which is comfortable to walk on.

There are two main underfloor heating systems – water and electric.

Underfloor heating: advantages

- Underfloor heating is unobtrusive, freeing up walls which might otherwise have radiators against them. In addition, it is quiet in use. There is even distribution of heat across each room, and individual room temperature control.
- It is safer than other systems of central heating: there is no risk of contact with surfaces that are too hot.
- The electric system is easy to install and requires no special skills.

Underfloor heating: disadvantages

- Heating systems cannot respond rapidly to quick temperature changes, and have longer heat-up and cooling-down periods than other forms of central heating.
- There is greater disruption when installing an underfloor heating system in an existing building than with other systems.
- The choice of floor finishing requires careful consideration, and changes of floor finish may affect performance.

Water heated systems

Water systems use warm water pumped through small diameter (usually 10mm) plastic pipes which run up and down the sub-floor. The pipes are linked into the building's central heating system. They warm the floor, which in turn warms the room above. Pipes can be installed when the building is constructed or, in some cases, fitted later.

In a new construction (such as a conservatory extension) with a solid ground floor, pipes are laid within the sand-and-cement screed. Insulation beneath the pipework ensures that heat is directed into the room and energy is not wasted in heating the concrete foundations.

On upper floors and suspended wood floors (with joists and floorboards), heating pipes can be laid between the joists. An insulation layer underneath the pipework prevents the ceiling of the room below from getting warm and directs heat to where it is needed: the room above.

A water system is best installed by a qualified contractor.

Electric systems

An alternative to a wet system is an electric system. This is easier to fit, and is a more realistic DIY option. An electric mat, similar in appearance to an electric blanket, is laid on the floor, and your chosen floor covering laid on top.

Many companies supply their products to both the trade and DIY consumer, and most have technical departments that supply installation instructions and even check the completed system.

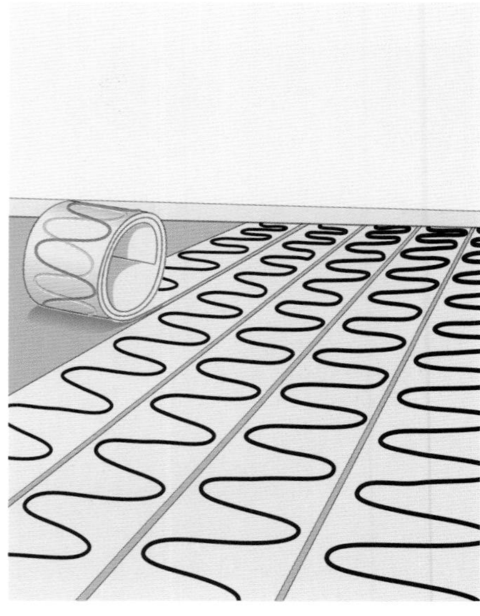

Sheet vinyl

Sheet vinyl comes in myriad designs and colours – and prices. It is faster to lay than tiles, and makes an ideal wall-to-wall floor covering for kitchens and bathrooms. Cushioned varieties are also warm and quiet underfoot.

Buying sheet vinyl

Sheet vinyl is sold in three widths – 2m, 3m or 4m – which means that in most rooms you can lay a seamless floor. If the width of the room is greater than 4m, you can lay vinyl in strips. A large sheet is heavy and unwieldy, so you may feel more confident about laying strips, even if the room is less than 4m wide. Only lengths bought from the same roll should be used on one floor: rolls may be manufactured on different machines, and therefore there may be slight differences in the colours.

You can buy backed or unbacked vinyl. Backed vinyl is cushioned by a built-in underlay which makes it softer underfoot, and is usually more expensive than the unbacked types. Some vinyls have an extra durable coating – ask the retailer which sort is best for your purposes.

Some vinyls are not stuck down – their weight holds them in place. This is useful if it is necessary to gain access to the floor underneath. Other vinyls must be glued down using adhesive recommended by the manufacturer.

HOW MUCH TO BUY

Measure the width of the room to decide how many strips you will need. Measure right into any alcoves and to the halfway point under a door. To take 2m-wide strip vinyl as an example: for every 2m or portion of 2m you will need one strip of 2m-wide vinyl. So if the room width is 3.5m, you need two strips (0.5m will be waste). Allow an extra 75mm trimming allowance on each width.

Then measure in the other direction and multiply by the number of strips. If the length is 3.3m you will need 6.6m (2 x 3.3m), plus 75mm trimming allowance on each strip – a total of 6.75m. Vinyl is usually sold by the nearest metre, so you will have to buy 7m.

If there is a pattern you will need extra for matching up – ask the retailer for advice.

Order the flooring in advance. It can then be stood upright (still tied in a roll) for at least two days in the room where it will be laid so it can reach room temperature. It will then be flexible and easier to lay; cold vinyl tends to be stiff to handle.

Laying sheet vinyl in strips

Tools *Steel tape measure; soft pencil; string longer than the room; chalk; small block of wood; a second piece of wood about 100mm long; sharp trimming knife; ruler; screwdriver; hammer.*

Materials *Vinyl to cover the floor; perhaps adhesive and notched spreader; metal cover strip and screws.*

Before you start It is best to line the floor with hardboard (page 126), but if you decide that your floor is in sufficiently good condition, lay the vinyl at right angles to the floorboards. Be aware that any gaps or ridges will make the vinyl wear unevenly. Decide how the strips of vinyl will be set out. Ideally, strips should run away from the window (or the main window if there is more than one). Joins will be less obvious than if the light strikes them at the side. Avoid having a join running into a doorway as this is an area of heavy traffic.

Marking the base line

1 Snap a chalk line (page 133) between the middle of the two walls that will be at the ends of the strips. This provides a base line to work from, as the walls will almost certainly be out of true.

2 If the first length of vinyl will cover the line, snap a second line parallel to the first where it can be seen.

3 Cut the first strip to length – the distance across the room plus 75mm for trimming.

4 Put it on the floor about 25mm away from the wall on the long side exactly parallel to the chalk line. Let each end ride up the wall by an equal amount.

Fitting to the wall on the long side

1 At two or three points, draw a pencil line across the floor and the edge of the vinyl. These are crosschecks that will allow you to bring the vinyl back to its original position later.

2 Find out where the gap between the wall on the long side and the vinyl is greatest. Cut a small block of wood slightly longer than that measurement. This will be used for scribing the sheet to make the vinyl fit exactly.

Alternatively Use a pair of compasses and set them to the same measurement.

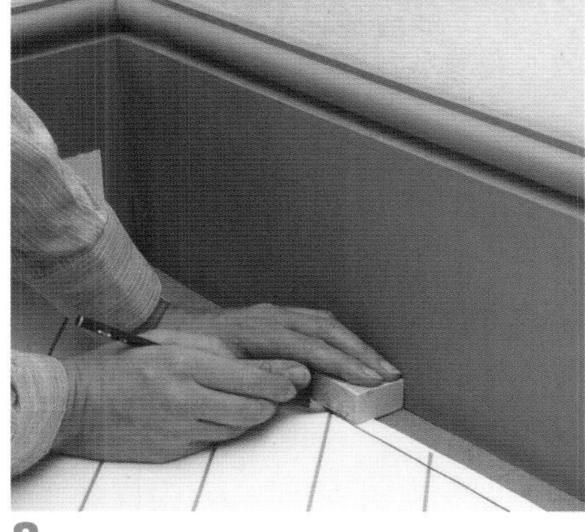

3 Place the wood against the wall, hold a pencil hard against the end and move them together along the wall, tracing its contours onto the vinyl. This technique is called 'scribing' and is also used for fitting the panels of fitted wardrobes against walls.

4 Cut the vinyl along the marked line with scissors or a trimming knife held against a straightedge (on scrap hardboard) and put the vinyl in place against the wall.

Fitting to the end walls

1 With the scribed edge against the long wall, draw a chalk line on the floor along the opposite edge. Make a crosscheck on the edge and the floor.

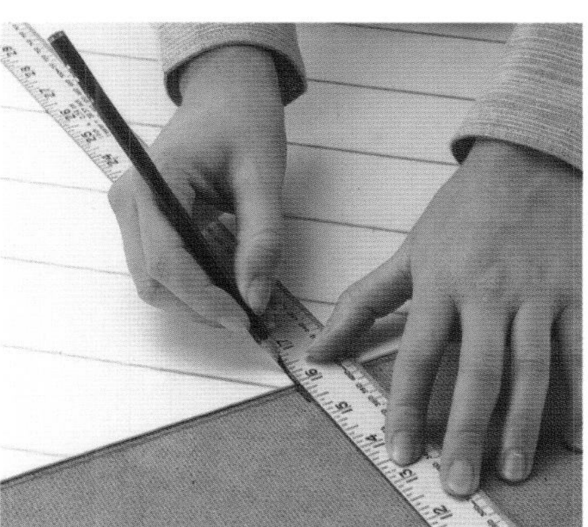

2 Pull the vinyl back from the crosscheck by the length of the second piece of wood.

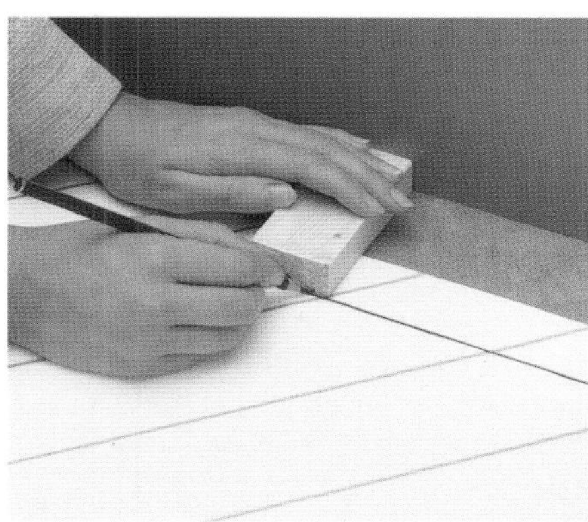

3 Keeping the outer edge of the vinyl on the chalk line, use the piece of wood and a pencil to trace the contours of the wall onto the end of the vinyl sheet.

4 Cut to this line, then use chalk line and crosscheck to position the vinyl. It should fit against the end wall. Repeat steps 2 to 4 for the opposite end of the length.

Cutting the second strip

1 The second strip will almost certainly have to be cut to width. If the excess is more than about 250mm, cut it back to that to give yourself a workable width.

2 Put the cut strip on the floor with one edge touching the wall where the wall comes nearest to the first sheet. The other edge will be overlapping the first sheet; adjust it so that the pattern matches.

3 Cut the strip at each end, to leave the trimming allowance of 75mm.

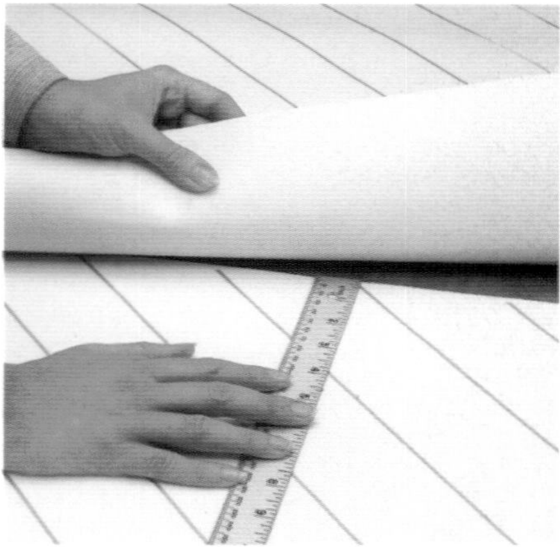

4 Make a pencil mark where the second sheet rests on the first. Lift up the second sheet and measure the amount of overlap.

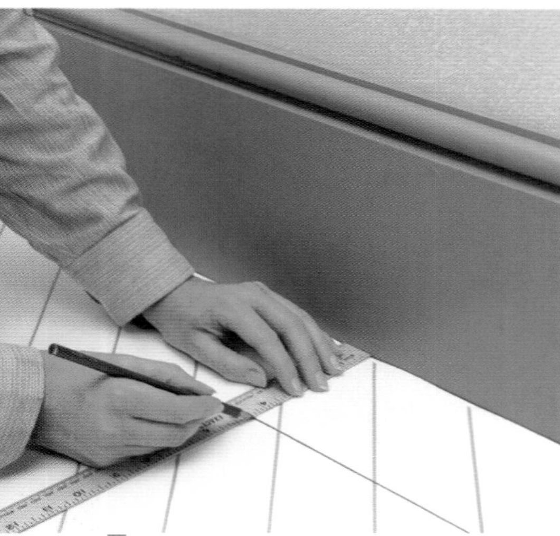

5 Place the vinyl flat on the floor again and use the ruler and pencil to scribe a line on the vinyl parallel to the wall, but half the width of the overlap away from it. Cut to this line, place the strip against the wall and scribe the ends as before.

6 Making sure the pattern on the second strip (which still overlaps the first) exactly matches, place scrap hardboard under the overlap and cut through both pieces using a trimming knife and a straightedge. They should now fit perfectly (remove the narrow cut strip from underneath).

Doorways

1 Use a profile gauge (page 112) to transfer the shape of the doorway on to the vinyl and cut the vinyl with scissors to fit.

2 If the vinyl finishes at a through doorway, cut it straight across and fit a vinyl edging strip or a threshold strip appropriate to the floorcovering in the next room.

Chimney breast alcoves

1 Measure and cut the vinyl to fit the full depth of the alcove, plus the trimming allowance of 75mm.

2 Put it on the floor and allow it to ride up the chimney breast.

3 Make a cut parallel to the side of the alcove, leaving enough for final trimming. Allow the material to lie on the alcove floor.

4 Cut off the excess material riding up the chimney breast, leaving a trimming allowance of 75mm.

5 Trim the edges as shown opposite, so that the vinyl fits the alcove, and surrounding walls. If there is a working fireplace, trim the vinyl around the hearth.

Sticking vinyl down

- Some vinyls do not need to be stuck down and will not shrink once laid.
- Other types should be glued immediately after laying. If left for any length of time – even overnight – they may shrink slightly and gaps could develop between the strips of vinyl and around the walls.
- Use the adhesive recommended by the manufacturer, and apply it to the floor with a notched spreader.
- For ordinary vinyl the floor should be glued all over.
- Cushioned vinyl needs only to be glued in a 50mm band around the room and along joins where sheets butt against each other.

Laying sheet vinyl without a seam

Most rooms can be covered with a single, seamless sheet of vinyl. This gives a neat finish, but it is hard to lay. The size of the sheet makes it cumbersome and very heavy, so you will need a helper. Trimming it to the wall also requires greater skill.

Tools *Soft broom; scissors; trimming knife; small block of wood and perhaps a metal straightedge.*

Materials *Sheet vinyl to cover the floor in one piece; adhesive and spreader (except for 'stay-flat' vinyl); cover strip for doorways.*

Before you start Work out how much vinyl you will need (page 141). To make laying as easy as possible, the sheet should be about 100mm wider than the floor on every edge – that is 200mm wider than the room in both directions. Ask your supplier to cut it to the required length and width.

Lay the sheet of vinyl flat, then re-roll it so that the shorter dimension becomes the length of the roll. This makes it easier to get into the room. Roll it with the decorative side inwards; this is the way you will need it when laying starts.

Keep the roll in the room where it will be laid for two days to reach room temperature. Have the heating on in the room in cold weather, or the vinyl will be stiff and awkward to handle.

1 Unroll the vinyl. This is hard work, and you will need help. Make sure that the longer side of the vinyl runs along the longer wall.

2 If the flooring has a pronounced pattern, adjust it so that pattern lines look to be at right angles to the wall containing the doorway by which you will most often enter the room. Sight it by eye. If it looks right, it is right.

3 For laying, the vinyl must be absolutely flat on the floor. You can ensure this by sweeping over it with a soft broom.

4 To fit the vinyl into an alcove, such as beside a chimney breast, get your helper to hold it while you make a cut running parallel to the side of the alcove. Take care to leave about 50mm surplus against each wall for final trimming.

5 Lay the material on the alcove floor, lapping up against the three sides, then cut off the excess riding up the chimney breast. Again, leave about 50mm surplus against the wall for trimming.

6 To fit into corners, cut off a small triangle at the corner of the vinyl, using scissors. When you push it down to the floor it will form a V, allowing it to hug the skirting. Be careful not to remove too much. First remove a triangle that is obviously too small, then take off more small strips until it is just right.

Trimming to fit

1 To trim to the wall, first run your knife along the vinyl lapping up the wall, taking off the excess so about 25mm remains.

2 Push the vinyl firmly against the skirting board with a small block of wood.

3 Place the point of the knife on the vinyl exactly where the skirting board meets the floor, and run it along the skirting with the blade at 45° to the wall. This will trim the material to fit snugly against the skirting, without leaving gaps.

4 To cut around a door frame, make a series of vertical cuts to the point where the vinyl meets the floor, then press it into the angle between door frame and floor. Trim off the excess. In the doorway itself, cut the vinyl so that it ends halfway under the door.

5 When the vinyl has been laid, stick it to the floor, unless it is the 'stay-flat' type which does not need sticking. Glue cushioned vinyls round the edges only. Non-cushioned types should be stuck down all over.

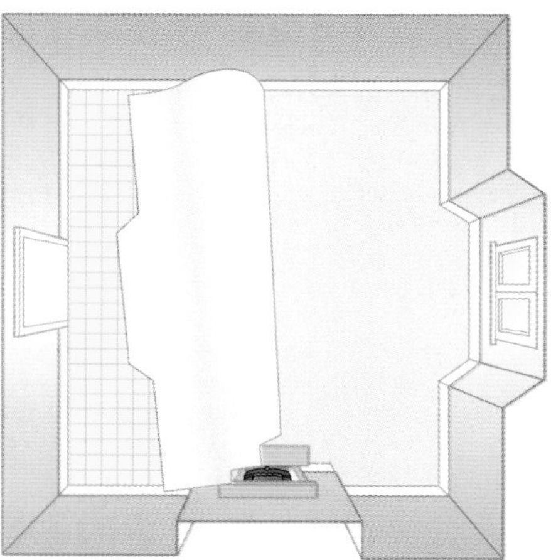

6 Roll back the sheet over half the room, and spread the adhesive on the floor.

7 Replace the sheet and press it down with the broom. Then glue the other half of the room.

8 Finish a doorway with metal cover strip.

HELPFUL TIP

Trimming vinyl that is bent up a wall is not easy and takes practice. But practising is the last thing you want to do on a large piece of expensive material. Obtain some offcuts and work on these until you get the knack. After pressing the vinyl against the wall with a block of wood, it may help to hold a metal straightedge as close to the wall as possible while you cut. Make sure the knife cuts away from the hand holding the straightedge, so if it slips you won't injure yourself.

Covering a small area with sheet vinyl

A very small room such as a lavatory can be covered by one piece of even the narrowest sheet vinyl. The best way of cutting it is to use a paper template.

Tools *Enough stiff paper (such as paper underlay) to cover the floor; perhaps adhesive tape or stapler; pencil; drawing pins or weights; scissors or knife; block of wood 40mm wide; pencil; ruler.*

Materials *Sheet vinyl; possibly adhesive and spreader.*

Make a template

1 If the paper is not big enough to cover the room, stick two pieces together.

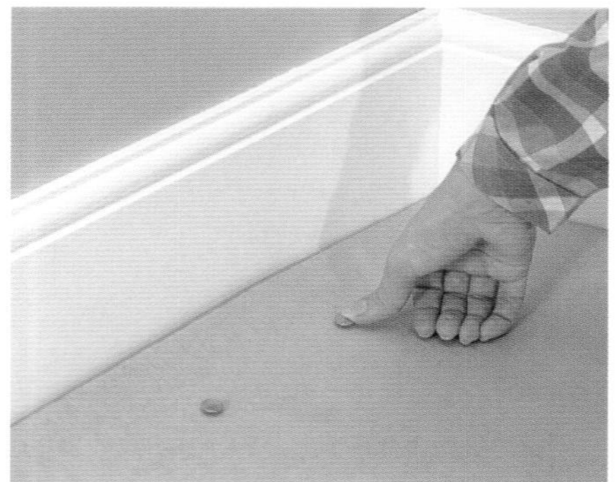

2 Put the paper on the floor with the edges folded underneath. Fix in place with drawing pins. On a solid floor use weights.

3 To fit it around obstacles such as a WC or a pipe, cut the paper from the wall inwards.

4 When the paper is laid, use scissors or a knife to trim it all the way round the room so that its edge is about 15mm from the wall or skirting board. Trim it around obstacles as well.

5 Cut a small block of wood about 40mm wide, and mark the width on it so there is no confusion later.

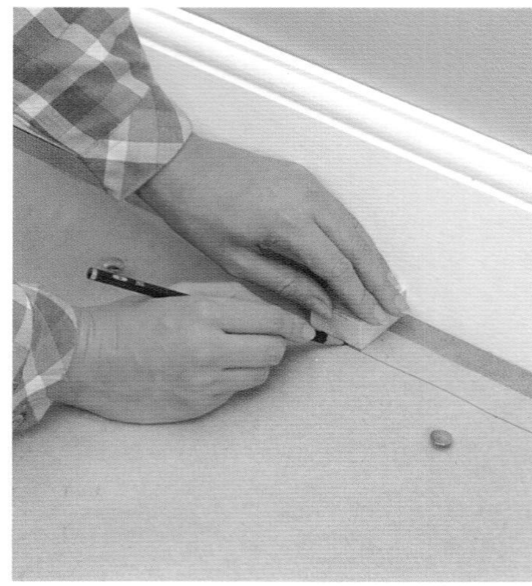

6 Put one edge against the wall and hold the pencil against the other edge. Move the block and pencil all the way around the room, tracing an outline of the room onto the paper.

7 Also trace around larger obstacles, such as the pedestal of a wash basin.

8 If a pipe comes up through the floor, put a ruler against it on four opposite faces and draw a pencil line along the outside edge of the ruler to make a square.

Cut out the vinyl

1 Lay a piece of the flooring material – right side up – on the floor of a larger room and put the template on top, fixing it in place with adhesive tape.

2 Put one edge of the wood block on the pencil line on the template. Put the pencil against the other edge and draw it along, tracing the shape of the room onto the vinyl. Do the same for large obstacles.

3 Cut the vinyl along the pencil line, using a ruler as a guide on straight lines. Put a piece of scrap vinyl or hardboard underneath to avoid damaging the floor.

4 If you have marked a square for a pipe, draw diagonal lines from the corners of the square. Where they cross is the middle.

5 Use a coin or other round object to draw a circle the diameter of the pipe. Cut out the circle with the knife. Alternatively, use a pipe offcut of the same diameter and a hammer to make a hole (page 136). Cut a slit between the hole and the nearby edge.

6 The piece of flooring will now fit the room exactly. To fit the vinyl around obstacles, make a cut from the cut-out to the nearest edge.

7 Stick down the vinyl in the normal way (page 142) unless it is a 'stay-flat' variety of cushioned vinyl which does not need to be glued.

Choosing carpet

Carpets can be soft and luxurious or practical and hardwearing. They are always the warmest choice for a floor, and modern technology means that you can buy carpet suitable for almost any area of the house.

Choosing a carpet

There are several things to consider when choosing a carpet. The first thing is the amount of wear it will get.

Durability Carpets are classified as 'light domestic' (bedrooms); 'medium domestic' (light traffic – dining room or main bedroom); 'general domestic' (living rooms); and 'heavy domestic' (hall, stairs and landings). So you need to choose a carpet hardwearing enough for its intended use.

What is it made of? The best carpets are wool, or a wool and man-made fibre blend. But many of the latest synthetics are barely distinguishable from wool, and no longer suffer from the 'static' problems that used to cause a mild static-electric shock when you touched a door handle. Synthetics are often highly stain resistant, but they will shrivel and burn quickly when exposed to intense heat.

Pile The pile determines the texture of the carpet. There are six types of pile. 'Loop' feels smooth; 'twist' is coarser; 'cord' is hard and feels ridged; 'cut' feels soft and velvety; 'velvet' is a smooth short-cut pile; 'saxony' is a long, shaggy pile.

Woven or tufted These terms are used to describe the weave of the pile. The traditional carpets like Wilton and Axminster are woven; most carpets, however, are tufted. The latter is less expensive and slightly less durable.

Integral or separate underlay Underlay increases the life of your carpet. It stops dust from rising between the floorboards and spoiling it, and cushions the floor, making it softer to walk on. Most underlay is a rippled foam rubber, although you can still buy traditional thick felt. Foam backed carpet has built in underlay, but it is a good idea to put down a separate underlay first (page 148).

Colour and pattern A carpet is a major expense, and it is not practical to replace carpet whenever fashions change or you redecorate. Therefore, plain carpets in neutral or subdued colours are a wise choice. Small repeat patterns often work well, but bold designs can be limiting in terms of what furnishings you can put with them, and unpopular with potential house buyers. Using one carpet throughout a house makes it feel more spacious.

CARPET FIXINGS

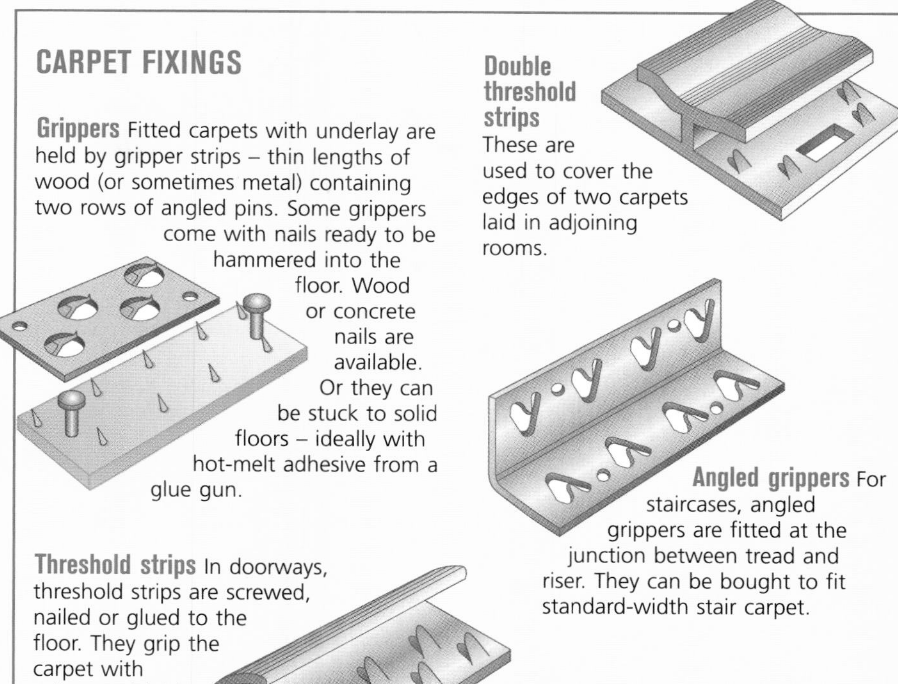

Grippers Fitted carpets with underlay are held by gripper strips – thin lengths of wood (or sometimes metal) containing two rows of angled pins. Some grippers come with nails ready to be hammered into the floor. Wood or concrete nails are available. Or they can be stuck to solid floors – ideally with hot-melt adhesive from a glue gun.

Double threshold strips These are used to cover the edges of two carpets laid in adjoining rooms.

Angled grippers For staircases, angled grippers are fitted at the junction between tread and riser. They can be bought to fit standard-width stair carpet.

Threshold strips In doorways, threshold strips are screwed, nailed or glued to the floor. They grip the carpet with spikes and fold down over the edge to protect it.

Stair rods Stair rods are again being made, and old ones can be found in antique shops or on the Internet. Make sure you have enough for your stairs. The method of fixing is usually obvious.

CARPET LAYING TOOLS

Carpet-layer's hammer This has a narrow heavy head and is useful for fixing gripper strip to a floor or stairs, as it will drive in the nails without hitting the pins on the gripper. It will probably have to be bought from a carpet shop. Or use a hammer and nail punch.

Carpet stretcher or 'knee-kicker' This has a flat sole with teeth at one end, which grips the carpet. At the other, there is a large pad, which the layer 'kicks' with his knee. Carpet stretchers are expensive to buy, but they can be hired.

Staple gun This is needed for fixing underlay to a timber floor. Manual and powered versions can be hired. Use double-sided carpet tape to fix underlay to a solid floor.

Carpet layer's hammer

Carpet stretcher

Staple gun (manual)

Foam-backed carpet

Carpet with integral foam underlay is much easier to lay than hessian-backed carpet, which needs a separate underlay. Foam-backed carpet does not have to be stretched. It is held to the floor with double-sided carpet tape, which can be stuck to wood or concrete floors.

Tools *Trimming knife; scissors.*

Materials *Carpet, 100–150mm bigger all round than the floor; double-sided carpet tape; paper underlay.*

A one piece carpet

Many DIY superstores sell inexpensive foam backed carpets for laying in small rooms such as bathrooms or box-rooms. This is a straightforward job.

1 Put down paper underlay (see box). It must stop short of the walls by the width of the carpet tape so that the tape will stick to the floor, not to the paper.

2 Fix double-sided carpet tape all round the perimeter of the room but do not peel off the tape's backing paper.

3 Place the carpet loosely in position. If the carpet has a pile, have the pile running away from the window if possible. The surface should feel smooth when you run your hand away from the window, with the pile. If you feel resistance, you are going against the pile.

HELPFUL TIP

When cutting the carpet to fit exactly against the skirting board, there is a danger that a gap will be created between the carpet and the wall. For maximum accuracy, hold the knife at an angle, with the point of the blade against the skirting and the handle leaning away from the wall.

4 If the carpet has a pattern, adjust it so that it looks true when seen from the door.

5 To lay the carpet into an alcove, make a cut at a right angle to the back of the alcove. Leave 25mm excess for trimming.

6 Trim off the excess all round the room, so that the carpet is the size of the floor plus a trimming allowance of at least 25mm on each wall.

7 Trim off the excess in the corners of the room. Cut away triangles in the corners so that you can push the carpet right into the angle between the floor and the skirting. This is easily done using the back of your trimming knife (above).

PAPER UNDERLAY FOR FOAM-BACKED CARPET

On concrete floors or smooth floorboards, paper underlay can be used (an uneven floor should be lined with hardboard to level it out. See page 126). It prevents dirt from blowing up between the boards and harming the carpet. It also stops rubber or foam-backed carpets from sticking to the floor. It is sold by the roll in carpet stores and DIY superstores.

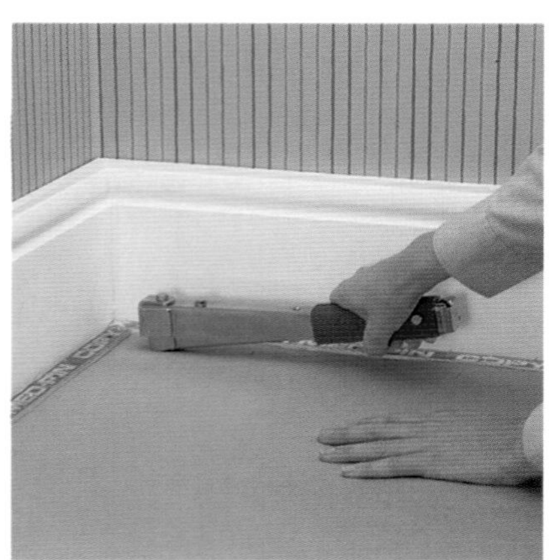

1 Beginning in a corner of the room, unroll about a metre of the paper so that it lies against the side wall and fix it in place with staple gun or double sided tape. If you plan to lay foam backed carpet, you will need to leave a border about 50mm wide right round the perimeter of the room so that the double sided carpet tape can be stuck to the floorboards.

2 Trim the end of the paper to the end wall and fix it in place.

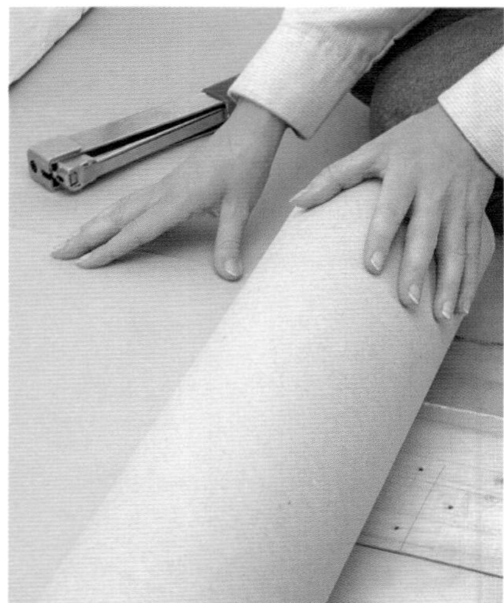

3 Roll the paper out to the far end of the room, smoothing it out as you unroll it, and fix it along both edges. Make sure the paper stays perfectly flat. Then fix and trim it at the other end.

4 Fix parallel strips of paper to cover the entire room, overlapping each length by about 25mm. The last length will probably have to be cut to width as well as to length.

8 Once the carpet is pushed well into the join between floor and skirting board, trim off the surplus with a sharp trimming knife.

9 Carefully lift up the carpet, peel off the tape's backing paper, and press the carpet firmly in place.

Foam backed carpet in two pieces

A wide room can be carpeted with two lengths of foam-backed carpet, joined together with double-sided carpet tape. The strip of floor where the two pieces of carpet will meet must be left clear of paper underlay so that the tape can be stuck directly to the floor. Make sure that the pile of both pieces lies in the same direction, or that the pattern matches.

1 Cut the first piece of carpet to length so it will run across the room with about 50mm lapping up the skirting boards at each end. Butt the machine edge of the carpet against the skirting board at one side of the room.

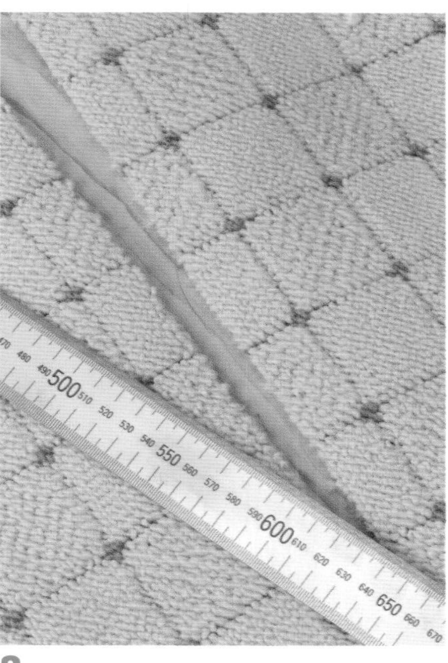

2 Cut the second piece of carpet to the same length. Cut it down in width so it is about 100mm wider than the remaining floor area of the room.

3 Position the second piece of carpet so it laps up the skirting boards by about 50mm along three sides, and overlaps the edge of the first piece by about 50mm at the meeting point. Make sure that the pattern matches – if there is one.

4 Use a sharp knife and a straightedge to cut through both layers of carpet, about 25mm from the edge of the overlapping piece.

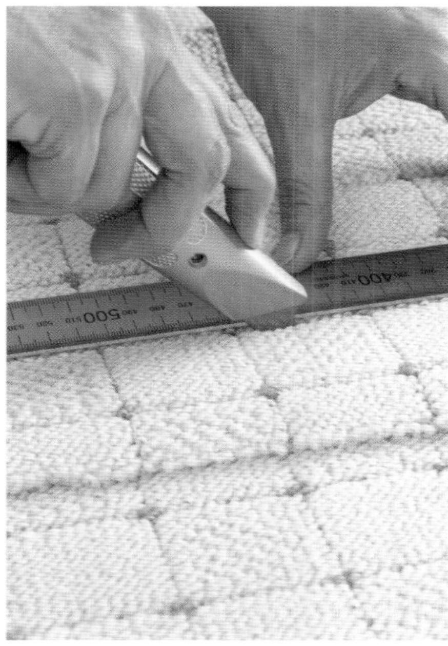

5 Turn back the edges of both pieces and stick 50mm carpet tape to the floor, centred so that both pieces of carpet will stick to it.

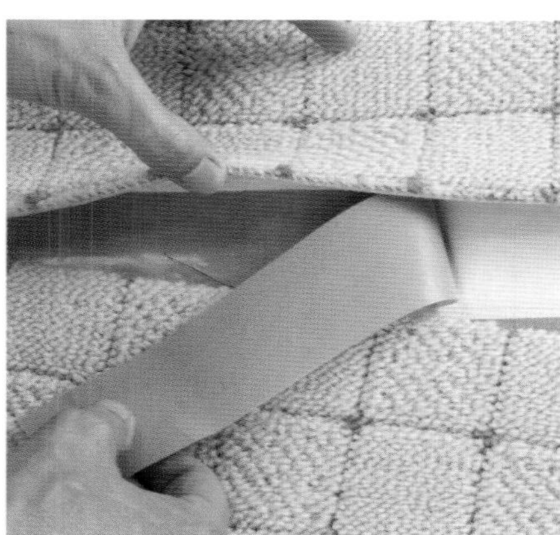

6 Lay the edge of the first piece of carpet back down over the tape and press it into place. Peel off the release paper.

7 Align the edge of the second piece of carpet with the first one and press it on to the tape, and against the edge of the first piece.

8 Trim the edges of the two pieces all round the room as for a one-piece carpet.

HELPFUL TIP

If your carpet frays very easily, you can reinforce the join with carpet adhesive. Once the first piece of carpet has been stuck to the carpet tape, apply a continuous bead of latex carpet adhesive along its edge. Than align the edge of the second piece of carpet with the first and press it into place. Wipe off any excess adhesive with a damp cloth.

Laying carpet with a separate underlay

It is not worth laying new carpet yourself: good-quality carpet is expensive and a fitting fee adds little to the overall cost. But used carpet is easier to lay as it has already been stretched once. So if you want to re-lay an existing fitted carpet, the job is worth trying.

Tools *Hammer and nail punch (or carpet-layer's hammer); tenon saw or hacksaw; vice or bench hook; protective gloves; trimming knife (preferably with a hooked blade) or scissors. Possibly also electric staple gun; carpet stretcher (from a hire shop); clean bolster chisel or wooden kitchen spatula.*

Materials *Gripper strip and nails or adhesive; threshold strip and screws or adhesive; underlay (felt or foam rubber); staples or tacks; carpet to cover the room in one piece.*

> **HELPFUL TIP**
>
> If you are laying carpet on a concrete floor, test first to make sure that central heating pipes are not lying too close to the surface. Switch the heating full on until the radiators are hot, and then walk over the floor in bare feet. If you feel heat, don't nail gripper strip; glue it instead.

Fixing grippers

1 Measure the perimeter of the room to work out how many gripper strips you will need. Gripper strips are usually sold in 1.5m lengths.

2 Put down the grippers with the pins pointing towards the wall. Leave a space slightly less than the thickness of the carpet between the gripper and the wall. This is for trimmed carpet to be tucked into later.

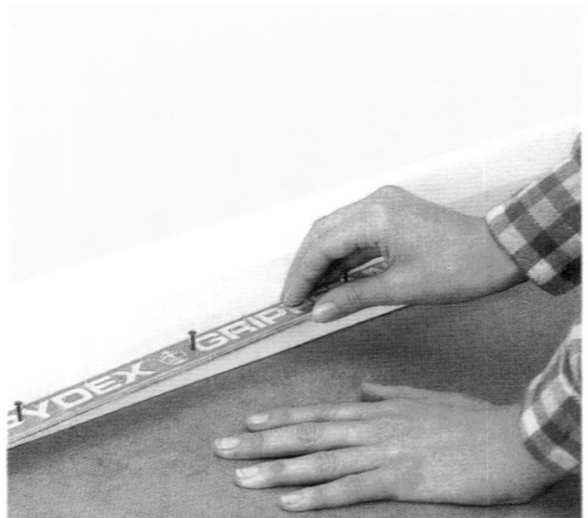

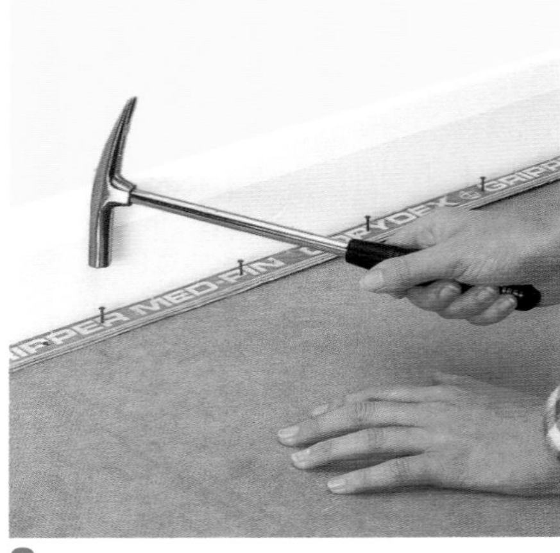

3 Nail the strips to the floor, using a small-headed carpet-layer's hammer. This will enable you to drive in the nails without hitting the pins. Alternatively, start off with a claw hammer, then use a nail punch when the nail heads get close to the pins.

4 When a radiator prevents you from getting close to the wall, fit the gripper as close as the radiator will allow.

5 When you reach a corner of the room, cut the strip to length using a tenon saw. Hold the strip in a vice or bench hook and be careful not to hurt yourself on the pins. Heavy gloves will help to protect hands. Butt-join two pieces of gripper. There is no need to cut mitre joints at the ends.

6 In a curved area, such as a bay window, cut the gripper into short pieces to follow the curve.

7 At a doorway, fit a metal threshold strip midway under the door.

Putting down underlay

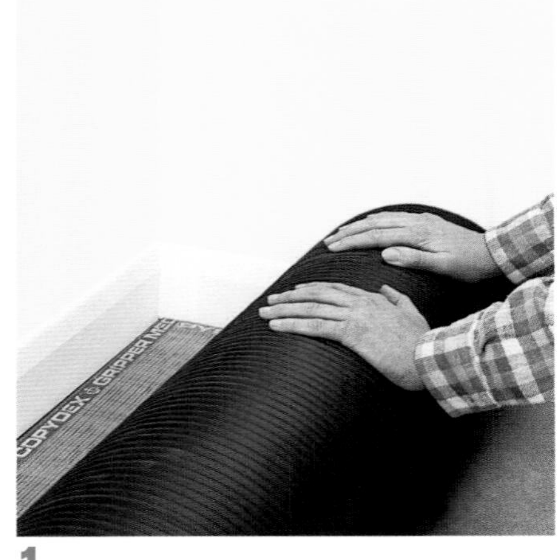

1 Unroll a short length of underlay in a corner of the room so that the end and the side lie against the gripper strip.

2 Fix the edges of the underlay to the floor with the staple gun, or with hammer and tacks. On a concrete floor, use double-sided carpet tape.

3 Roll out the underlay along the edge of the room, smoothing as you go, and fixing along both edges. Make sure it is perfectly flat on the floor. It is not necessary to stretch the underlay.

4 Where a radiator is fixed to the wall, lay the underlay up to the edge of the gripper, even if the gripper has been fitted a little way out from the wall.

5 At the end of the room trim the underlay against the gripper strip with a trimming knife or scissors.

6 When you have almost covered the room, you will have to cut the last length of underlay to width as well as to length.

Laying the carpet

1 In a larger room – or on the lawn if it is dry – cut the carpet to the size of the room to be covered. Add a trimming allowance of 150mm on all sides – even more if the carpet has a pattern. Keep the waste; it may come in handy for patching later.

2 Put the carpet in place on the floor of the room where it is to be laid. If it has a pattern, adjust it so that the pattern looks true, and does not run off line when seen from the doorway.

3 Make cuts to allow the carpet to lie flat in any alcove. Cut the carpet at a right angle to the back of the alcove and take care not to cut too far. Leave some excess for trimming around the alcove.

4 Cut off the surplus riding up the face of the chimney breast, leaving some excess for trimming.

5 Trim off the excess all round the room, leaving an allowance of about 10mm along two adjacent walls, and an allowance of about 40mm along the other two.

HELPFUL TIP

When trimming into an alcove it helps if you make vertical cuts at the corners. You can then press the carpet down on to the floor before cutting off the excess. This makes it easier to judge the appropriate allowance to be pushed down later.

6 Start the fixing in the corner of the room with the smaller allowance. Working along one wall, run your fingers along the top of the carpet so that it engages on the gripper pins farthest from the wall. Take care not to injure fingers on the spikes.

7 Do the same along the second wall with the smaller allowance.

8 Run the head of your hammer flat along the top of the carpet, pushing it onto the other row of pins and forcing the excess carpet into the space between the gripper strip and the skirting board.

9 When the first two edges have been fixed, kneel on the carpet with your back to one of the completed walls. Push the teeth of the carpet stretcher into the carpet ahead of you and 'kick' the padded end with your knee to force the carpet forwards. Move forwards and repeat once or twice until you are close to the opposite wall.

10 Hook the carpet onto the gripper pins with your hand. It will immediately contract and be firmly fixed in place.

11 Repeat this process three or four more times across the room until the carpet is fixed all along one wall. Then turn 90° and fix it along the fourth wall.

12 When the hooking is complete, excess carpet will be left lapping up the walls. Trim this off to 10mm with a sharp trimming knife.

13 Push the remainder into the space between the gripper and skirting, using a clean bolster chisel or a wooden kitchen spatula. Take care not to scratch the paintwork if you are using a bolster.

14 Check that the excess carpet on the other two walls of the room is properly pushed down, and use the bolster or spatula where necessary.

15 Finally, tap down the cover of the threshold strip at the doorway using a piece of waste wood or carpet to protect the metal from becoming dented.

CUTTING A DOOR TO CLEAR A CARPET

After fitting a carpet, the base of the door may drag on the surface. One cure is to change the hinges for rising butts (page 192).

Alternatively, the bottom of the door can be trimmed off. You can hire a door trimming saw from tool hire shops, and trim the door without removing it from its hinges. Otherwise, with the door in place, take a thin block of wood as thick as the amount of wood to be removed. Put it on the floor with a pencil on top and run it along the door to mark the cutting line.

Take off the door and either saw or plane off the base. If you use a hand saw, work slowly to avoid splintering the face. If you use a plane, hold the door upright on its long edge in a portable work bench and plane downwards. Work inwards from each side to avoid splintering the stiles at the end. Sand the bottom of the door so that it will not damage the carpet.

Laying a stair carpet

Laying fitted carpet on a straight staircase need not be too difficult – and is relatively easy if you are using a 'runner' with varnished or painted wood visible on either side. Half-landings make the job a little trickier and winder stairs are even harder if the carpet is to look good and be safe.

Tools *Tape measure; tenon saw; workbench; hammer; trimming knife and blades; straightedge; staple gun; carpet bolster chisel or clean brick bolster. Possibly also: tack lifter; spatula.*

Materials *Underlay; carpet; carpet gripper strip.*

How much carpet?

1 Measure from the front to the back of a tread (the part you walk on) and multiply the figure by the number of treads in the staircase.

2 If the stairs turn a corner on a half-landing, measure the length of half-landing and add it to the total. When you want the carpet to turn to the far end of any landing at the top of the stairs, add this measurement as well.

3 Now measure the height of a riser (the vertical part of each step) and multiply the figure by the number of risers.

4 Add this to the figure you already have. The total is the length of carpet needed to cover the stairs.

5 Measure the width of the stairs if you want full-width carpet. Carpet runners, fitted with stair rods (see opposite) come in standard sizes: 690 or 700mm is common, but you can get narrower or wider sizes.

HELPFUL TIP

When measuring carpet for a staircase that has winder treads deeper at one edge than the other (see picture opposite and on page 258), take the larger measurement. Measure the depth of each tread, at its widest point, as depths may vary. In particular, the bottom tread may be deeper than the rest.

Preparing stairs for carpeting across the width of the tread

1 If an old carpet has just been removed, inspect the staircase for defects, and repair as necessary. Remove any nails or tacks left over from the old carpet with a tack lifter.

2 Cut lengths of gripper strip to the width of the stairs less 40mm. Position a strip on a tread, with a gap of about 12mm between it and the riser above it, and nail in place, with teeth on the strip pointing backwards. Repeat for all the treads. Then position and nail the strips to the risers, again leaving a 12mm gap, with teeth pointing downwards. Alternatively, use angled grippers (page 145).

3 Cut pieces of gripper strip for the sides of the treads, so they touch the strips at the back of the treads and finish 25mm in from the front edge of each tread. Nail them in place about 12mm in from the side edge, with teeth facing the side of the tread.

4 Cut underlay into separate pads for each tread. Each pad should be long enough to fit over the tread and cover the face of the riser below it, and wide enough to fit snugly between the gripper strips at the sides. Use a staple gun to fix the pads to the treads and risers. Fit a smaller underlay pad to the last riser at the top of the stairs.

Laying a full-width carpet on a straight staircase

1 Measure the full width of the tread and cut one or more strips of carpet to this width, ensuring the pile direction runs down the stairs and not across them. (A carpet wears better if the pile faces down the stairs.) Working downwards from the top of the stairs, fit the first strip in place.

2 Starting at the top tread, use a carpet (or brick) bolster and hammer to drive the folds of carpet securely in between the gripper strips in each internal angle. Then pull the carpet taut over the front edge of the next tread and repeat the process.

SAFETY TIP

Using a staircase with only underlay pads in place is dangerous, because the pads hang loosely over the edge of the tread. Also, the pins on gripper strips are very sharp. Therefore, if the house is occupied, try not to leave the job unfinished.

3 If you have more than one carpet strip, cut the end of the first strip at the bottom of a riser with a trimming knife. Tuck the edge into the angle between the gripper strips, using the bolster and hammer.

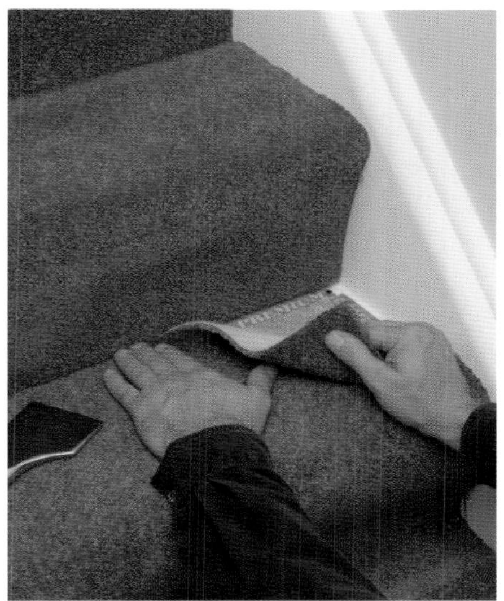

4 Tuck the top edge of the next strip of carpet into the angle between the gripper strips at the rear edge of the tread and secure it with bolster and hammer. Continue fitting the strip down the stairs. Trim it to finish at the foot of the last riser, at the angle between the riser and the hall carpet.

5 When you have finished laying the carpet, use the bolster to tuck the side edges of the carpet into the gaps between the gripper strips and strings on each tread.

Laying a stair runner

Before you start Paint or varnish the treads and risers and leave to dry.

1 Cut gripper strips 40mm less than the width of the carpet runner and nail them in place as for fitted carpet opposite. Leave out the strips on the bottom riser and on risers above winder treads (see below).

2 Cut underlay to the same width as the gripper strips and secure to treads and risers as for fitted carpet opposite. Shape the underlay to fit winder treads. On risers above winder treads, finish the underlay just below the nosing.

3 Start laying the runner at the bottom of the stairs by tacking the end of the runner to the top of the bottom riser (with its surface facing the riser).

4 Secure it at the bottom of the riser with a gripper strip nailed across it and fold it over to bring it back up the riser pressing it against the gripper strip at the bottom.

5 Work up the stairs, forcing the carpet runner into the gap between the pairs of gripper strips, until you reach the top. On winder stairs, secure the carpet to the bottom of the riser with a gripper strip as in Step 4, before making a fold as shown below which is then secured by the gripper.

6 At the top of the stairs, finish by cutting the runner to length and pushing it over the gripper strip on the top tread or taking it up the riser and tacking it above or below the nosing (depending on how the landing is to be carpeted).

USING STAIR RODS

Stair rods have made a comeback in recent years and can be a very attractive addition to a stair runner. They are, however, mainly decorative and should not be relied on to hold the carpet in place; the runner (and underlay) should first be fitted securely as described on the left.

The brackets which hold stair rods in place are fitted directly to the staircase next to the runner on each side – all you need is a bradawl and a screwdriver. You can also use rods on fitted stair carpet, with brackets secured on top of the carpet.

FITTED CARPET ON WINDER STAIRS

Laying fitted (full-width) carpet on winder stairs is a job best left to a professional carpet fitter. Not only is it difficult to get a neat finish, but poor fitting can result in the carpet slipping and causing a fall.

Carpet runner on winder stairs

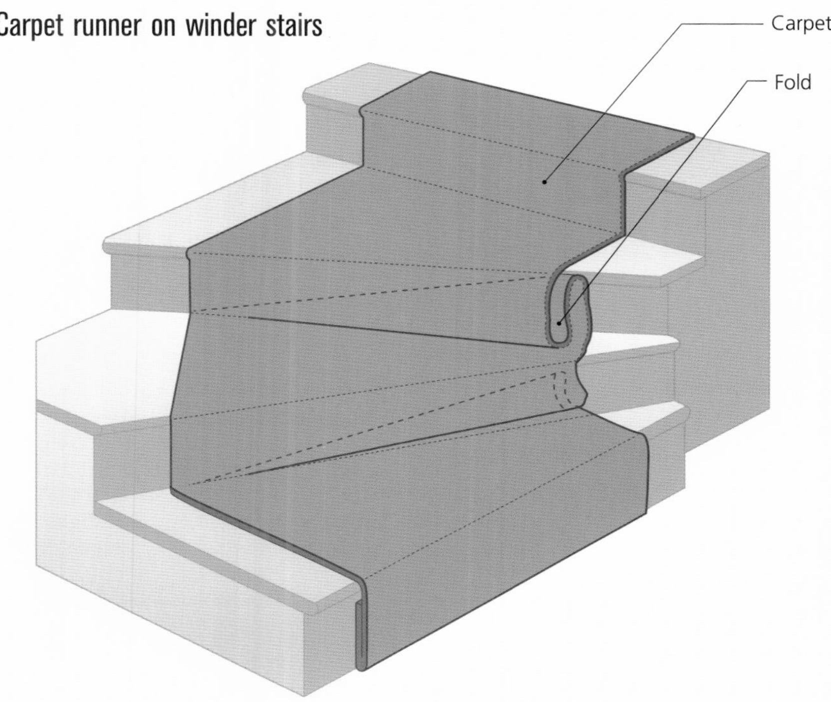

Landings

Full and half landings may be carpeted wall-to-wall, or may have a narrow runner laid across them.

If the landing is to have wall-to-wall carpet but the stairs are carpeted with a runner with gaps at either side, finish the stair carpet at the top of the last riser. Cut off any surplus, leaving about 25mm to fold under. Fix it with tacks along its top edge.

Lay the landing carpet in the same way as a room carpet, but take it over the top step and tack it to the top riser.

Put underlay beneath the landing carpet, overlapping the top riser of the staircase.

Half landings

Where a staircase makes a 90° turn, treat it as two flights of stairs. Cover the half-landing with one of the stair carpets. Butt the other one up to it, turn under the end and tack it down.

If the staircase makes a 180° turn, there will be a rectangular half-landing at the turn, which needs to be covered with carpet laid at right angles to the lengths on the stairs.

Carry on laying both stair carpets to the far edge of the landing, cut them off and tack them in place, without putting underlay beneath them. Lay a third strip of carpet across them to cover the landing.

There will be a gap under the landing carpet in the middle between the two strips of stair carpet. Fit a strip of underlay or some stair pads tacked in place and trimmed to size to make a level surface for the top layer of carpet. Take the landing carpet over the top step of the lower flight and tack it to the top riser. Tack down the landing carpet on all the other edges for a neat finish.

Carpet problems

Damaged or torn carpet can be a trip hazard, and should be dealt with promptly. At best, stains, rips and burns are unsightly. If you have some spare carpet from when it was first laid, fix the problem with a patch.

Patching a damaged carpet

To repair a hole or a frayed patch in a carpet, you need a piece of the same carpet slightly bigger than the damaged area. The piece may have been left over when the carpet was laid, or you can cut it from under a large piece of furniture that is never moved, where it will not show. The joins of the repair should not be visible. At first, there will be a colour difference between the new patch and the rest of the carpet, but in time this will become less obvious.

Tools *Trimming knife; hammer.*

Materials *Carpet patch; latex-based carpet adhesive; 50mm self-adhesive carpet tape (possibly double-sided); a piece of hessian larger than the patch (except for foam-backed carpet).*

Cut the new piece

1 Place the new piece over the damaged portion, ensuring that the pile runs in the same direction. (Run your hand over both carpets to find the direction in which they feel smoothest.)

2 Hold the patch firmly on the carpet and cut through both at the same time with a sharp knife. This ensures that the patch and hole are exactly the same size.

Take care not to cut through a separate underlay as well.

LOOSE CARPET

Do not rely on furniture to hold carpet in place in a room. Not only is a properly stretched and fitted carpet much neater, it is also far safer. In anything bigger than the smallest of rooms, loose-laid carpet can wrinkle and bunch over time, leading to folds or creases that will wear unevenly and can cause people to trip. If a carpet is not lying flat, deal with the problem as soon as possible, by re-laying it, and fixing it firmly in place with tacks, adhesive tape or gripper strips around the edges of the room and threshold strips in doorways.

Loose-laid carpet

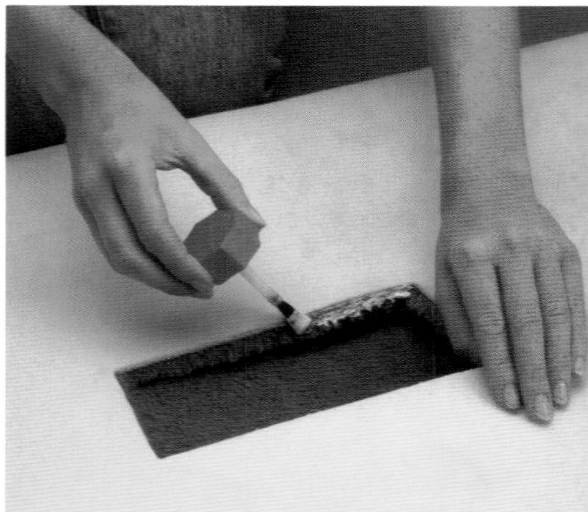

1 In the case of a loose-laid carpet, roll it back and apply a carpet adhesive round the edge of the patch to about halfway up the pile. This prevents fraying.

2 Leave the adhesive to dry, then insert the patch in position.

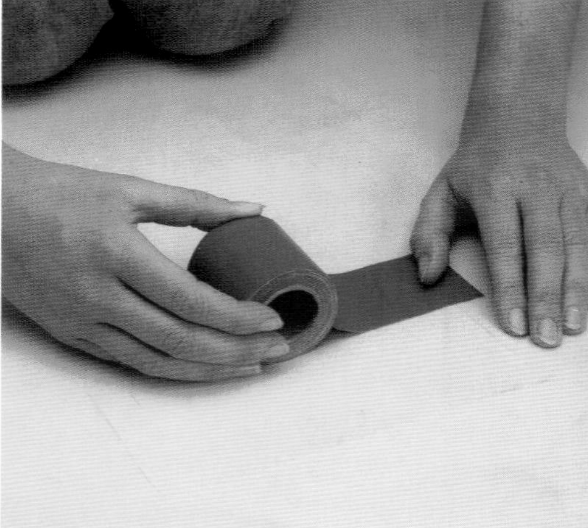

3 On a foam-backed carpet, fix the patch in place with 50mm self-adhesive carpet tape on all the edges.

With other carpets, spread carpet adhesive on a piece of hessian 50mm bigger all round than the patch. Stick it over the back of the patch and over the surrounding carpet.

4 Turn the carpet right side up and pinch the edges of the patch and the carpet between your fingers to make quite sure they stick well together.

5 Finally, tap the join all over lightly with a hammer to disguise the join as much as possible, although the colour difference will probably still be visible.

Fitted carpet

1 Apply a latex adhesive round the edges of the hole and the edge of the patch to about halfway up the pile, and leave it to dry.

2 Take four lengths of double-sided carpet tape, push them through the hole, and stick them to the floor or the underlay where the patch will join onto the main carpet. Remove the backing from the tape.

3 Place the patch in position and press it firmly down.

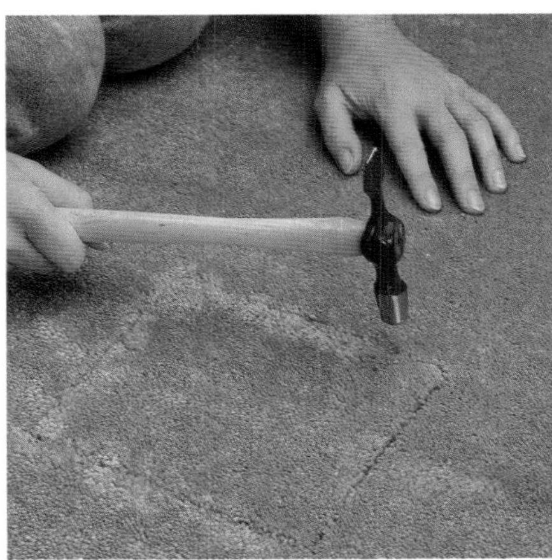

4 Push the edges together, and tap lightly with a hammer to bond the patch in place.

Removing stains on carpet

Try to treat stains as soon as they occur. The longer they are left, the more difficult they will be to remove.

Do not add extra liquid of any sort and do not rub the carpet. If you do so, you will only drive the stain deeper, or spread it.

If you are going to use dry-cleaning solvent or a proprietary carpet stain-removal product, test the cleaner on an unobtrusive patch of carpet first, to check its colour-fastness.

1 First scrape off any solid matter with a spoon or blunt knife. Mop up liquid by pressing on it with a dry towel or wad of tissues. Use different areas of the towel or tissues until no more moisture can be lifted.

2 If a stain still remains, treat it according to whether it is water-based or grease-based. A water based stain – a drink, for example – can be removed with a carpet shampoo; a grease-based stain, such as gravy or fat, can be removed with a dry-cleaning solvent.

3 When applying the shampoo or solvent, use just enough on a cloth to moisten the area. If you use a saturated cloth you are likely to drive the stain deeper. Turn the cloth to a dry side as soon as it becomes dirty. Work from the outside of the stain towards the middle to avoid spreading it.

4 Finally, cover the area with a thick wad of tissues weighed down with something flat and heavy, such as a phone book. The remaining moisture will be absorbed by the tissues, further reducing the risk of a permanent stain.

5 When the treated patch has dried out, it may be necessary to shampoo the entire carpet to ensure uniform colour. Carpet-cleaning firms will do the job for you, or you can hire carpet-cleaning equipment by the day (right).

GETTING PROFESSIONAL HELP

The National Carpet Cleaners' Association will provide lists of member companies in your area who will advise on stain removal and carry out cleaning work. The contact address is 62c London Road, Oadby, Leicester LE2 5DH (telephone 0116 271 9550). Check their web site for excellent advice on carpet care and stain removal, at www.ncca.co.uk

Using a hired carpet cleaner

Most DIY superstores and carpet warehouses hire out equipment for cleaning carpets. These are efficient and easy to use.

Book the carpet cleaner in advance. Most companies hire the machines by the day, so if you collect the cleaner first thing in the morning you can clean all your carpets for the price of a day's hire.

When you collect the cleaner, make sure that you buy enough of the recommended carpet shampoo. Most companies supply this on a sale-or-return basis. You will get a refund on any unopened bottles.

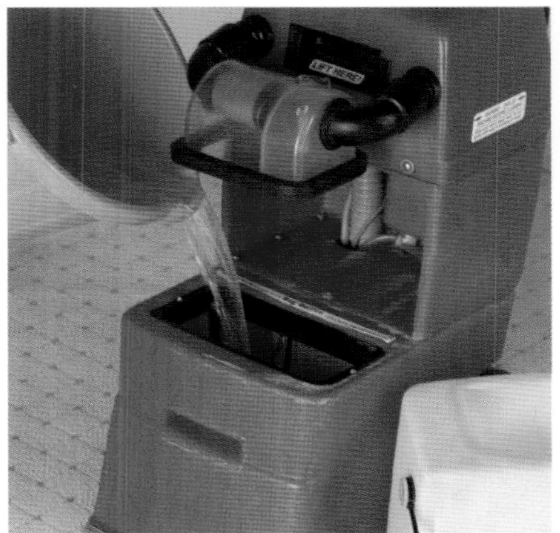

1 Read the instructions carefully. Before filling the unit make sure the switches are off and the hoses on the back are connected. To fill this machine, the upper tank is removed and a mixture of shampoo and water poured into the lower tank.

2 Replace the top tank and turn on the machine. On this model a trigger switch sprays the shampoo solution onto the carpet and activates a vibrating brush. Walking backwards, slowly, pull the machine towards you. As you clean, dirty water is sucked into the upper (clear) tank.

An A-Z of carpet stains

Spillages are inevitable at some time in the life of a carpet, but treated promptly a spill can often be cleaned up without leaving a stain. The advice given here will help you to remove a wide variety of spills from floorcoverings, but the same techniques can also be used to eradicate stains from soft furnishings.

Alcoholic spirits
Mop up with a dry towel or wad of tissues. Sponge with warm water. Allow to dry. Then clean with carpet shampoo. Treat any remaining stain with methylated spirit.

Animal stains
Remove loose solids with paper. Scrape the residue with a blunt knife or spoon. Blot dry with a cloth or wad of tissues. Lightly sponge with a carpet shampoo (add acetic acid for urine). If the stain is serious call a professional carpet cleaner. The most serious stains penetrate to the back of the carpet and the underlay.

Ball-point pen
Speedy action is essential. Dab with methylated spirit on a cotton wool bud. Take care not to spread the stain.
On vinyl upholstery or wall coverings, immediately scrub with a nail brush and warm soapy water (the ink will cause a permanent mark if left).

Beer
Blot with kitchen towel, add a little white vinegar solution (⅓ cup white vinegar with ⅔ water), blot again then clean with carpet cleaner following the bottle's instructions.

Blood
Sponge with cold water. Blot dry. Clean with carpet shampoo if necessary. Dried stains may not clean completely.

Candlewax
Scrape off as much as possible. Cover remainder with blotting paper or brown paper. Apply the point of a warm iron. Do not allow the iron to touch nylon carpet; it may cause it to melt. Move the paper about until the wax is absorbed into it.

Clear any remaining traces with a dry-cleaning solvent.

Chewing gum
Freeze the chewing gum with blocks of ice wrapped in a plastic bag, or use a proprietary aerosol chewing gum remover.

Then break it up into pieces and brush up the bits by hand – chewing gum clogs up vacuum cleaners.

Chocolate
Scrape off the chocolate with a knife, and clean the area with carpet shampoo. Treat stubborn stains with dry-cleaning solvent when the shampoo has dried.

Cocoa
Mop up the worst and dry off with a towel or wad of tissues. Clean with carpet shampoo. Treat any remaining stain with a dry-cleaning solvent when the shampoo has dried.

Coffee
Mop up the worst of the liquid. Blot dry. Treat any remaining stain with a carpet shampoo. When dry use dry-cleaning solvent to remove grease from milk or cream.

Curry
An extremely difficult stain. Large marks should be treated professionally. With small marks, scrape off the deposit and rub lightly with borax solution (15ml borax to 500ml water). Stubborn stains can sometimes be helped with a little neat glycerine rubbed into the carpet and left for about 10 minutes. Then sponge out with warm water, and blot dry.

Dyes
Have the stain treated by a carpet-cleaning firm.

Egg
Scrape off the deposit. Treat with dry-cleaning solvent or with a proprietary carpet spot-removing kit.

Eye make-up
Moisten the area, then treat with a drop of liquid detergent on a cotton wool bud. Rinse. Treat stubborn stains with dry cleaning solvent.

Fats, grease and oil
Mop up the worst. Scrape off any deposit. Apply dry-cleaning solvent.

Heavy deposits often respond to the blotting-paper-and-iron technique (see Candlewax).

Felt-tip pen
Some felt-tip pens have spirit-base ink, some have water-based ink. Methylated spirit on a cotton wool bud will remove spirit-based ink, which has a pungent smell. But do not allow it to penetrate to a foam backing. The methylated spirit may stain a light coloured carpet. For water-based ink, use carpet shampoo.

Fruit juice
Mop up with a clean cloth or paper towels. Clean with carpet shampoo.

Gravy
Mop up with paper towels. Treat with dry-cleaning solvent. Clean with carpet shampoo.

Ice cream
Scrape up and wipe with paper towels. Treat with a dry-cleaning solvent when dry. Clean with carpet shampoo.

Ink (fountain pen)
Must be tackled immediately. Blot with absorbent paper. Sponge with warm water to remove further ink. You may need more than one application. Blot well each time.

Treat remaining small stains with a proprietary carpet spot-removing kit.

Jam/marmalade
Spoon up deposits. Wipe area with cloth wrung out in warm water. Clean with carpet shampoo. Remove any remaining stains with a proprietary carpet spot-removing kit.

Ketchup
Scoop up or wipe away excess deposits. Take care not to spread the stain. Gently rub with lather made up from carpet shampoo. Wipe with cloth wrung out in warm water. Work in direction of the pile. Treat any remaining stain with a dry-cleaning solvent.

Lipstick
Scrape off with a knife, and use a dry-cleaning solvent. Alternatively, use a proprietary carpet spot-removing kit or a little paintbrush cleaner.

Metal polish
Scrape off or blot up any deposit. Treat with carpet shampoo containing a few drops of household ammonia.

Milk
Immediate action is essential to prevent milk penetrating down into the carpet where it will give off a smell for weeks. Blot dry. Clean with carpet shampoo. If a stain remains use a dry-cleaning solvent. May need professional attention to prevent smell recurring each time room warms up.

Mud
Allow to dry. Brush, then vacuum. Clean with carpet shampoo if necessary.

Mustard
Scrape off deposits. Sponge with damp cloth. Treat with carpet shampoo.

Nail varnish
Spoon up deposit; avoid spreading the stain. Moisten a pad of cotton wool with non-oily nail varnish remover and dab on affected area. First test on a hidden corner as acetone may damage man-made fibres. Use as little as possible, as over-soaking can damage the backing. Remaining traces of colour can be removed with methylated spirit. Apply a dry-cleaning solvent if necessary.

Paint

All paint spills must be dealt with immediately. Once it has dried it is almost impossible to remove. Scrape up and wipe off as much as possible, then treat according to the type of paint.

Emulsion Mop with cold water, working from the edges inwards. Large area of dried-on emulsion should be left to a professional carpet cleaner.
Acrylic Mop up with tissues. Sponge with warm water. Finish with methylated spirit or dry-cleaning solvent.

Gloss (solvent-based) paint Sponge with white spirit or a dry-cleaning solvent. If dry, soften with paintbrush cleaner. Large areas need professional attention.

Perfume
Clean with carpet shampoo, and allow to dry. Use more shampoo if the stain persists.

Plasticine
Scrape off as much as possible, then treat the remainder with a dry-cleaning solvent.

Scorch marks
Bad scorch marks are impossible to remove as the fibres are damaged. For repairing a carpet, see page 152. For slight marks trim the pile with scissors, or lightly shave with a disposable razor. Or remove loose fibres with a stiff brush, then make circular movements with a wire brush or abrasive paper to disguise the area.

Shoe polish
Scrape off and dab with dry-cleaning solvent. Finish with methylated spirit. Clean with carpet shampoo if necessary.

Soft drinks
Mop up. Treat with carpet shampoo. Stubborn marks often respond to methylated spirit.

Soot
Vacuum the area with a suction-only type cleaner, not a brush type. Or shake a rug outside. Do not brush or the mark will spread. Use a dry-cleaning solvent to remove any small marks. Get professionals to treat large areas.

Tar
Very hard to remove. Scrape away any loose deposit. Treat with a dry-cleaning solvent. If the surface is hard, scratch it to allow the solvent to penetrate. On stubborn stains try dabbing with eucalyptus oil or paintbrush cleaner.

Tea
Mop up as much as possible. Treat with carpet shampoo. Treat any left-over stain when dry with dry-cleaning solvent which will remove the grease from milk.

Toothpaste
Scrape up any deposit and treat with carpet shampoo.

Vomit
Remove the bulk of it, sponge the area with soda water, blot with kitchen towel and then clean with carpet cleaner and blot again.

Wine
Fresh spills Sponge red wine spills with white wine then blot with kitchen towel before using carpet cleaner. Do not put salt on the carpet; it may affect the colour. Blot white wine stains with kitchen towel.
Old stains May respond to glycerine solution (equal parts of water and glycerine) left for an hour, then rinsed off. Sponging with methylated spirit may reduce very old stains.

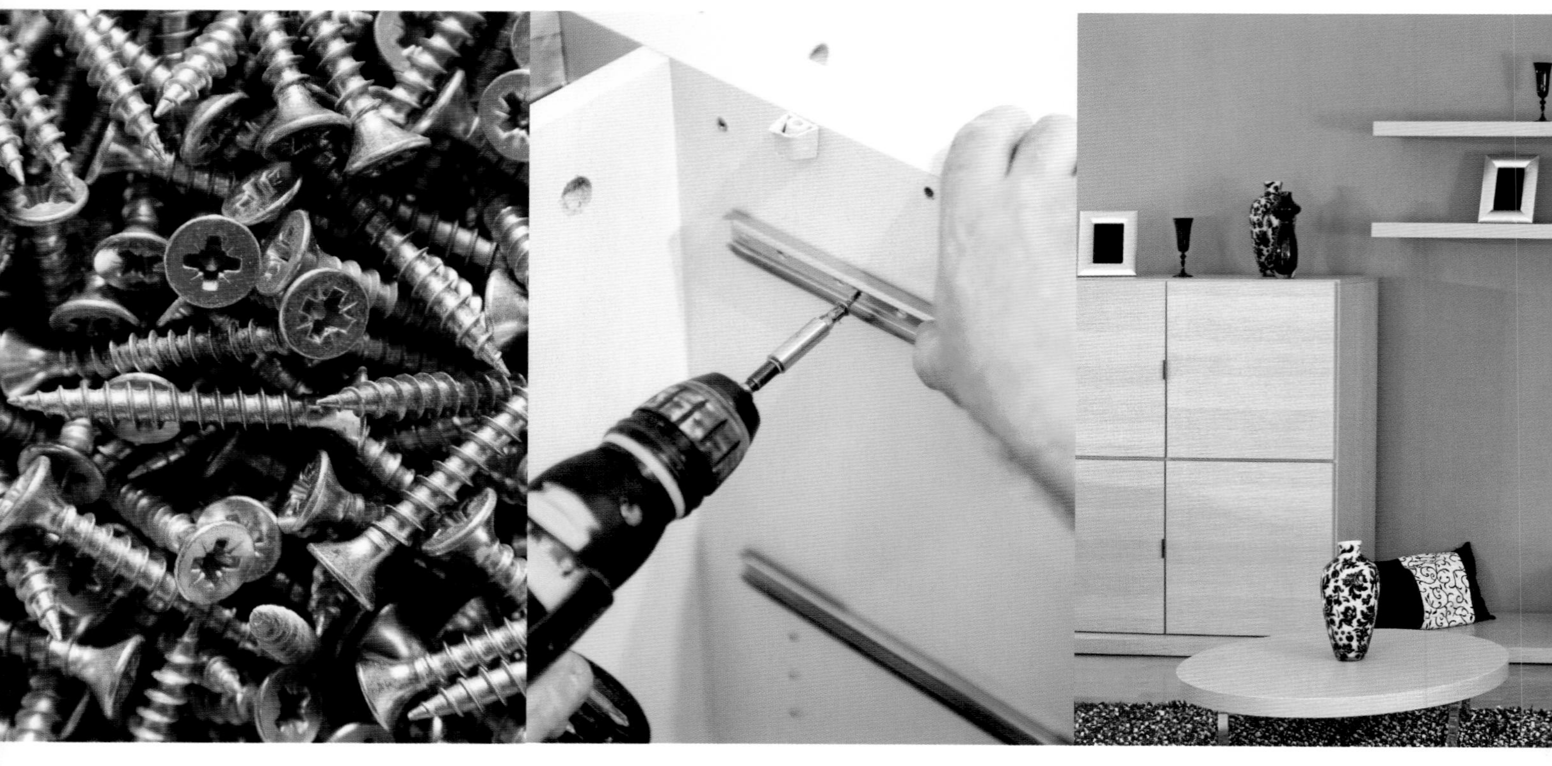

Fixtures and fittings 5

Choosing wall fixings

Whatever you are fixing to a wall – shelving or curtain rails, for example – it is always essential to provide good, strong fittings, suitable for the load.

Fixings for solid walls

For masonry walls Use screws that will penetrate the wall by a minimum of 50mm, driven into plastic wall plugs that match the screw size.

On timber-framed walls Where the screws pass directly into the framing, 40mm penetration will be adequate, unless a heavy load is to be put on the shelves, when screws should go in by 50mm. Before putting up any fixing, always use a an electronic detector (see page 34) to locate pipes, cables, studs and noggins.

STANDARD WALL PLUGS

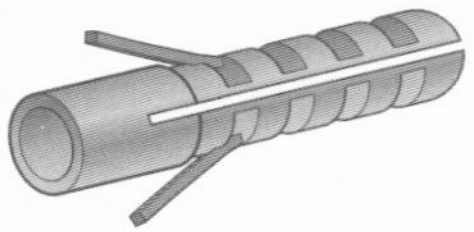

Finned plastic Tapered plug with split end to allow expansion, and either fins or lugs to prevent it turning in the hole. A rim of flexible ears prevent it being pushed in too far. Each size will accept screws of several lengths and diameters.

Ribbed plastic Has no fins or lugs, but the shallow lengthways ribs prevent it from turning in the hole. Sold in colour-coded sizes.

Strip plastic Straight-sided plug with shallow lengthways ribs. Can be bought in strips and cut to length with a trimming knife. Sold in colour-coded sizes.

Universal plug Can be used in all walls – expands in a solid wall and collapses (without spinning) in a hollow wall.

Masonry nail Hardened galvanised nail that will penetrate and grip when driven into bricks or blocks. Not suitable for use in concrete or hard stone. Lengths typically from 15mm to 100mm.

A fast way of fixing timber battens to brick walls. Choose a length that will penetrate beyond the fixing by about 15mm into bare masonry or about 25mm into a plastered wall. Hammer with short, positive strokes. Nails will not bend, and will shatter if not struck squarely. Wear eye protection.

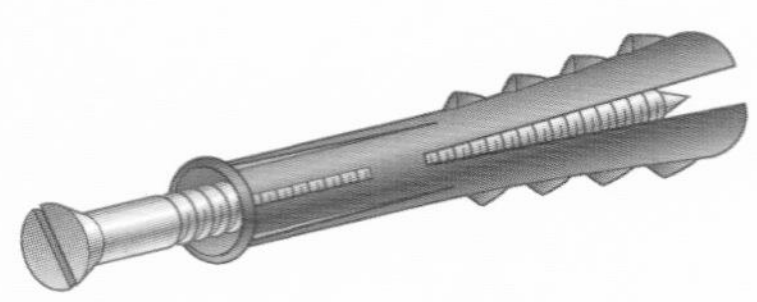

Woodscrew and wall plug The fibre or plastic plug expands to fit the hole and grip the masonry wall. Plugs are in lengths from 15mm to 90mm.

For lightweight fittings, use 4mm screws and matched plugs. For heavier fittings use 5mm or 6mm screws. The screw should be long enough to extend about 25mm into the masonry after passing through the fitting and the plaster.

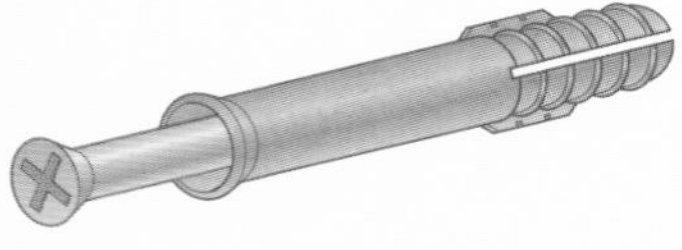

Hammer-in fixing or nail plug A screw with a special thread for easy driving, ready-fitted into a nylon sleeve. It can be tapped with a hammer into a drilled hole. Lengths typically 50mm to 160mm will fix objects from about 5mm to 110mm thick.

A strong, fast method for fixing a lot of timber battens to brick or concrete. Also suitable for lightweight fixings into building blocks. The hole should extend 5–15mm beyond the screw tip. So for a screw 50mm long fixing a 10mm thick object, make wall holes at least 45mm deep.

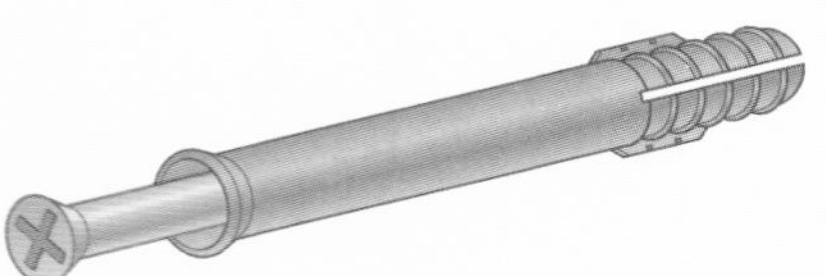

Frame fixer A long screw ready-fitted into a nylon wall plug. Drill the hole through the frame into the wall, push or lightly tap the fixing through and tighten with a screwdriver. Lengths to secure frames from about 20mm to 110mm thick. A secure and convenient method of fixing new or replacement door or window frames to walls. Useful for repairing a door frame that has worked loose. As a guide, the depth of the masonry hole should be at least five times the diameter of the plug.

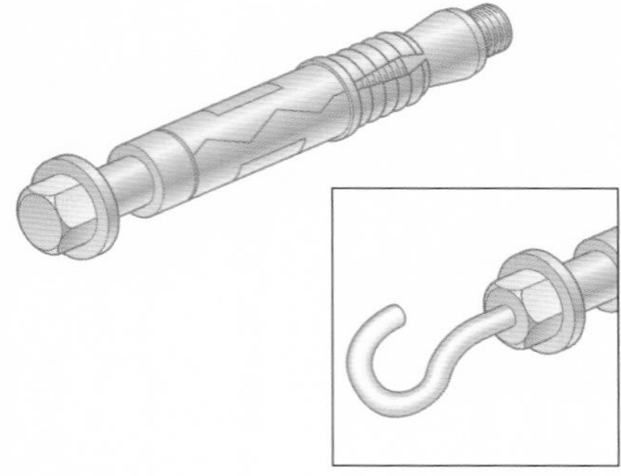

Wall anchor (masonry bolt) A bolt with a segmented metal shield. The shield fits into a drilled hole in masonry, and expands to grip the hole sides when the bolt is tightened. Bolts range from about 5mm to 25mm in diameter, in lengths to fix objects from about 10mm to 120mm thick. The bolt head may be fixed, fitted with a nut and washer, or hook or eye shaped (inset).

A very strong, heavy-duty fixing suitable for objects such as wall cupboards, garage doors, lean-to framework, or fence and gateposts fixed to masonry. A fixed-head bolt (known as a loose bolt) is pushed through the fixture before being screwed into the shield. A nut-head (or projecting) bolt is placed in the hole with the shield and the fitting is hung on it before the nut and washer are fitted. The masonry hole needs to be wider than the hole through the fitting – generally 6mm wider than the bolt diameter.

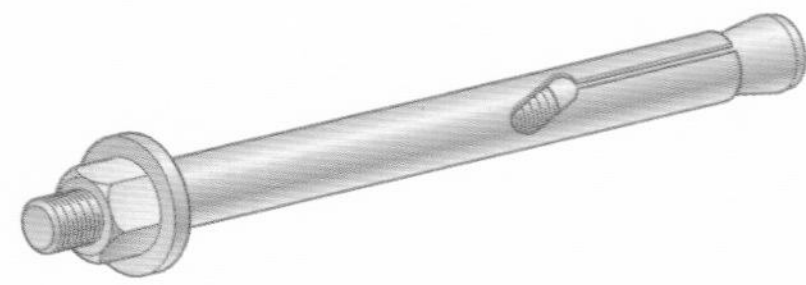

Through bolt (sleeve bolt) Steel bolts with an expanding wedge at the end for gripping against the sides of a drilled hole. Bolts have screw-on nuts and washers. Sizes are available for fixing objects ranging from about 5mm to 110mm thick.

Easy, quickly fitted heavy-duty fixing for things such as door and window frames, trunking, or hand rails. The hole can be drilled through the frame and masonry at the same time, and is the same diameter for both the fitting and the masonry. Bolt diameters are typically from 5mm to 20mm.

Plugging

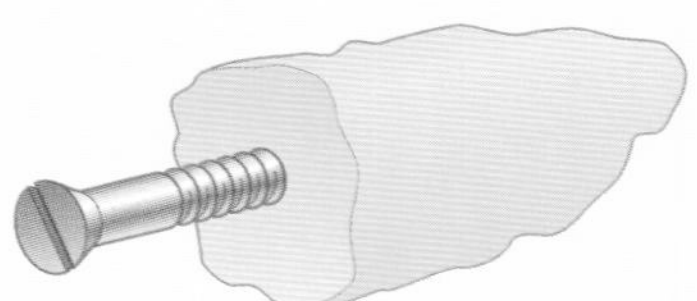

compound For making fixings in holes that have become enlarged because of the drill bit wandering or because a previous fixing has failed. It is supplied in a two-colour putty-like strip. Cut off the amount required with scissors. Take off the protective film and knead the strip. When the blue pigment turns white, it is ready.

Fixings for hollow walls, ceilings and lightweight blocks

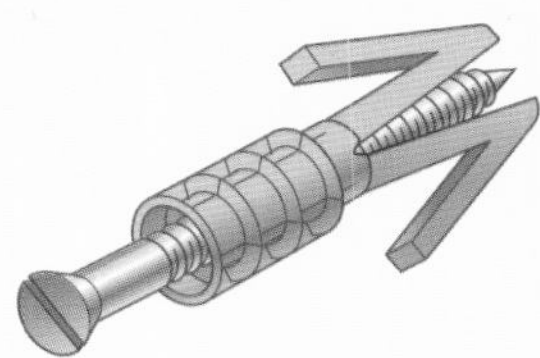

Woodscrew and plug The screw has a winged plastic plug that spreads out to grip the back of a wall or ceiling board. The plug can be re-used if the screw is withdrawn. For lightweight or medium fittings to plasterboard, hardboard or plywood (including hollow doors) up to about 25mm thick. The cavity behind the board needs to be at least 15mm deep.

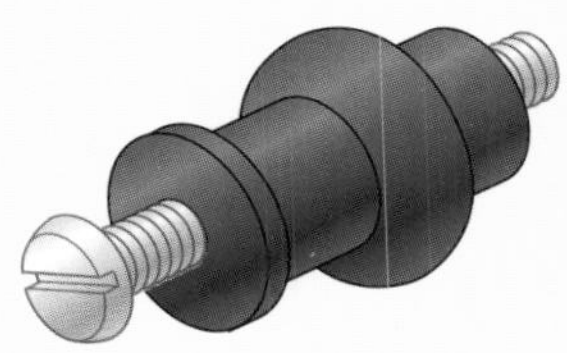

Machine screw and expanding rubber plug The screw fits into a nut in a rubber sleeve that is compressed to grip the back of the board. The plug stays in place if the screw is withdrawn. Plugs are sold with or without a screw. A strong fixing for plasterboard, plywood, hardboard, sheet metal, glass or plastic, up to about 45mm thick. The plug protects the screw from vibration and rusting. It can also be used as a wall plug in masonry where it shapes to the hole's contours.

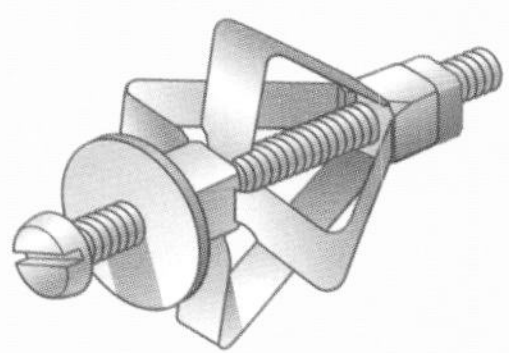

Machine screw and metal cavity fixing A metal plug with a nut welded in the end. It collapses to form metal wings that grip the back of the board. A strong fixing for heavyweight fixtures to hardboard, plasterboard, chipboard, plywood and fibreboard, up to about 35mm thick.

Gravity toggle A machine screw with a swinging metal bar (toggle) attached. When the screw is inserted, the toggle swings down and grips the back of the wall. It is lost if the screw is withdrawn.

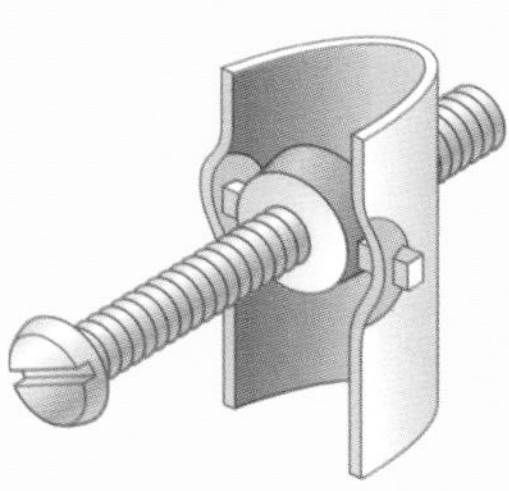

A strong fixing for plasterboard or lath-and-plaster walls. The cavity has to be at least 32mm wide, or wider for larger sizes.

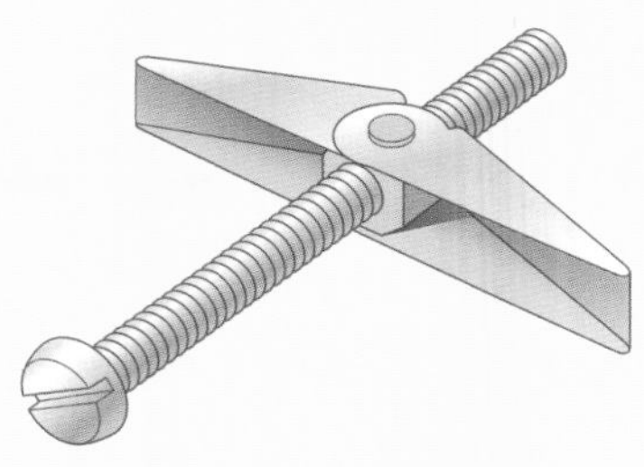

Spring toggle A machine screw fitted with a spring-operated toggle bar that folds back while it is being inserted and then springs open when it is inside the cavity. The toggle is lost if the screw is withdrawn. Typical size range is for screws 50–80mm long.

A strong fixing for plasterboard or lath-and-plaster walls and ceilings. The cavity has to be at least 45mm wide – even wider for larger sizes. The toggle can be used with a hook for hanging a light-fitting from the ceiling.

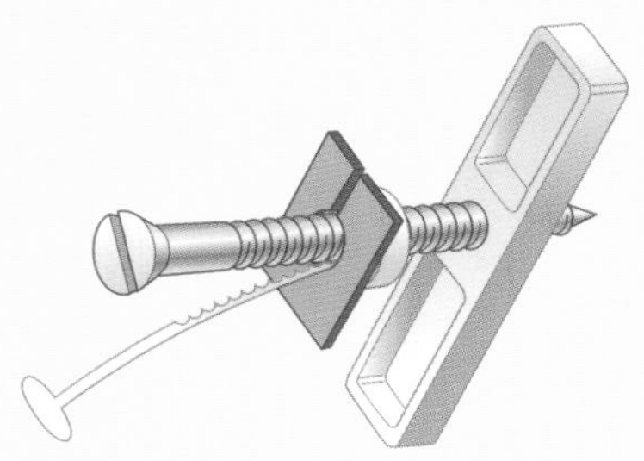

Nylon toggle and collar A nylon collar that takes a wood screw and is linked by a notched nylon strip to a toggle. After insertion, the strip is used to draw the toggle towards the collar to take the screw tip and grip the back of the board. It is then cut off. Typical size is for No. 6 woodscrews.The collar closes the drilled hole and the adjustable fitting is used for fixing to plasterboard, lath-and-plaster or suspended ceilings of different thicknesses. The toggle is retained if the screw is withdrawn.

SPECIAL TYPES OF WALL PLUG

Winged-arrow type
Light plastic plug that spreads out to grip the back of plasterboard. For use with 4mm screws and lightweight fixings. The plug can be re-used.

Nylon rivet anchor
The plug is split along most of its length and is compressed into wings. For use with 4 or 5mm screws for making fixings to plasterboard, particularly partition walls. The plug can be re-used.

Expanding-wing type
The wings are forced apart to grip the back of the board. Small-sized plugs are for use with 3.5mm screws in hollow doors.
Longer-sized plugs are for use with 4mm screws for medium-weight fixings to board. Cannot be re-used.

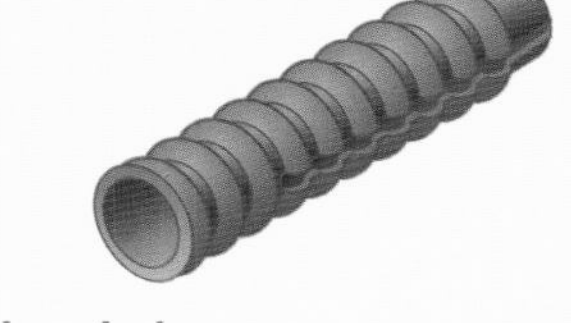

Chipboard plug
Nylon fastener with an outside thread that is hammered into a hole drilled in chipboard. It has a split end and expands to give a secure grip. For use with 3.5, 4 and 5mm screws. The plug can be re-used.

Self-drill plug
A metal or plastic device which can be screwed directly into plasterboard, cutting its own hole and threads. The screw supplied is then driven down the centre to secure the fitting.

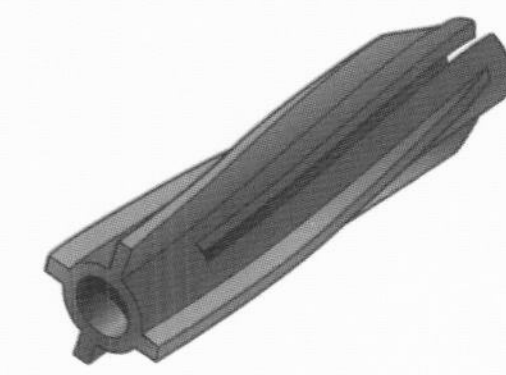

Helical wing or twist-lock type
The nylon plug has helical wings that cause it to rotate as it is tapped home with a hammer, and prevent it from coming out if the screw is ever withdrawn. For use with large diameter screws to make strong fixings into aerated blocks. Can be re-used.

Choosing shelving

Shelves can be put up just about anywhere – alcoves are a good choice, but any wall space can be used. There is a huge selection to choose from, ranging from adjustable track systems to flat-pack units or tailor made.

FIXED BRACKETS

Most right-angle brackets have one arm longer than the other. Fix the long arm to the wall, unless the instructions state otherwise. The width of a shelf should be only about 25mm greater than the length of the horizontal arm of the bracket. Large overhangs can lead to the shelf becoming overloaded, which may cause the brackets to fail. Always secure shelves by screwing them to the brackets.

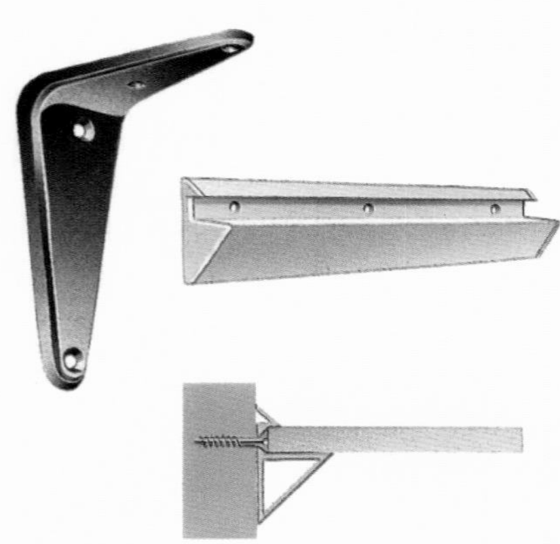

For heavy loads

- Usually made in high-strength pressed steel. One type above (right) has a continuous aluminium bracket that supports the shelf along its whole length.
- Sizes range from 75 x 50mm to 350 x 350mm. Aluminium strip comes in lengths from 600mm to 2.5m.
- Finishes include: red, black brown and white epoxy-coated; or galvanised (silvery).
- The manufacturers usually state load capacity on packaging.

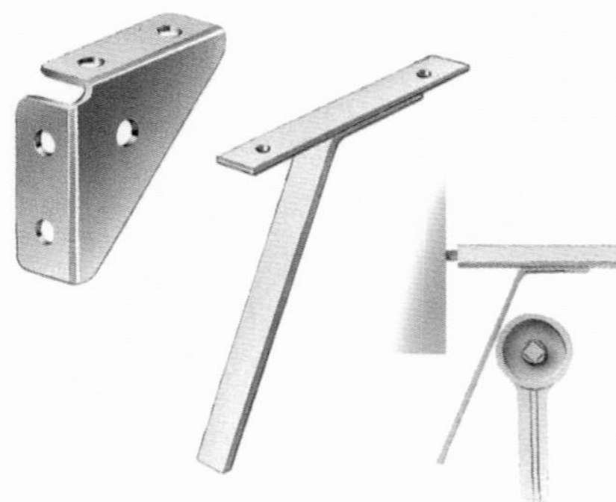

For medium/light loads

Suitable for narrow shelves where other brackets are too large. Designed for reinforcing the corners of cabinets, but suitable for shelves. Radiator shelf option wedges behind radiator and needs no wall fixings.

- Sizes: 50 x 50mm; and a radiator shelf of 125mm or 150mm.
- Finishes include: cadmium-plated and galvanised (silvery).

For medium/heavy loads

A range of styles for different types of medium to heavy loads. Includes wrought-iron, pressed steel, both with holes for screws.

- Sizes range from 100 x 75mm to 240 x 240mm.
- Finishes include: red, brown, gold, yellow, green, black and silver. Radiator shelf support is in white or brown plastic.

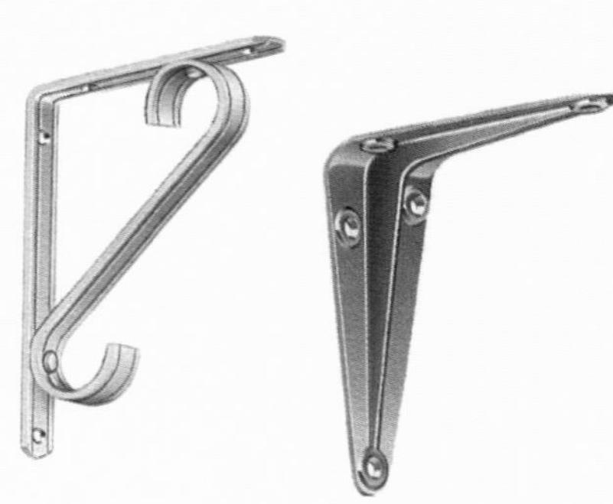

For light loads

Made in either pressed steel (right) or aluminium (left), they have holes for screws.

- Sizes from 100 x 75mm to 300 x 250mm.
- Finishes include: black or grey dip painted and anodised silver, gold and white for braced bracket.

Glass shelving brackets (not shown)

- Chrome, white or silver finish brackets with a slot to hold a glass shelf.
- Normally available for a specific thickness of glass – 6mm for example.
- Glass must be toughened and ideally bevelled or with a rounded edge.

ADJUSTABLE SHELVING

The most widely-available type of adjustable shelving consist of horizontal brackets which slot or clip into vertical uprights (standards) screwed to the wall. Consider what you will put on your shelves and choose a shelving system that is suitable – overloading is obviously very dangerous.

For heavy loads

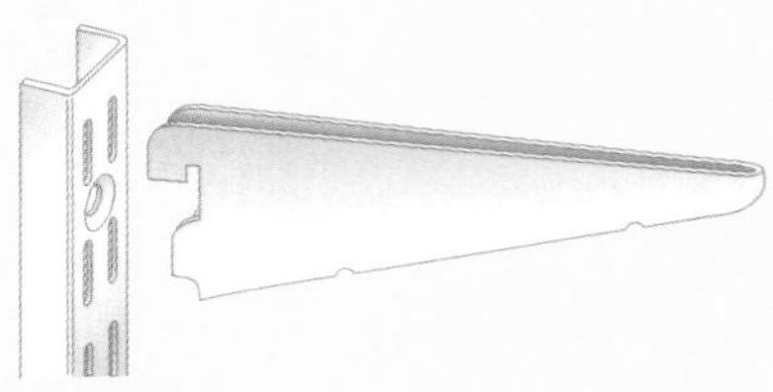

Made of steel in lengths from 430mm to 2400mm. Uses brackets from 120mm to 610mm. Available in frost white, black, cream and gloss aluminium. Look for double hooks for extra strength. Accessories may include square book ends, spring rod book supports and universal book supports.

For medium loads

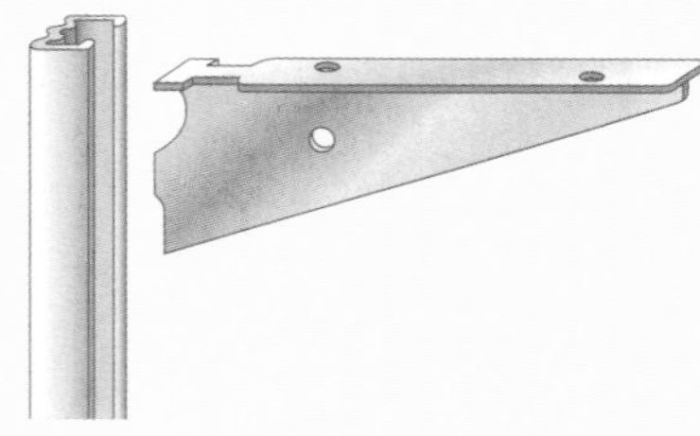

Fully adjustable slot-free systems that can be used for most work around the house. Made of steel in lengths from 188mm to 2500mm. Uses brackets from 100mm to 570mm. Finishes: silver, white, brown, black, red, magnolia, gold and gloss aluminium. Accessories may include book ends, book end shelf supports, end caps, wall plates, clip on shelving supports, a fixing pack and upright connectors.

Hanging track systems

A variant on the double-slot system shown above where all the uprights are suspended from a single horizontal hanging rail. Only the rail needs to be secured to the wall, making it an ideal choice for plasterboard partition walls.

CHOOSING SHELVES

Coated chipboard Inexpensive and needs no finishing. Choose 15mm board for light items and 18mm for heavier loads, such as books.

Medium-density fibreboard (MDF) Versatile and easy to work with but must be sealed or painted. It is relatively inexpensive. It is sold in sheets and comes in several thicknesses. Also available melamine-coated or wood-veneered.

Timber and wood-veneered chipboard More expensive than coated chipboard and needs to be sealed, with varnish or paint, for example. Solid wood shelves are normally limited to 225mm. For shelves bigger than that, use parana pine (up to 300mm, but expensive) or timberboard (up to 600mm).

Glass shelves Must be at least 6mm thick or, ideally, toughened 9mm glass. Bracket spacing must not be more than 400mm. Get the edges of glass bevelled by the supplier, and use sturdy brackets as glass is heavy.

Floating shelves These are so-named because they have no visible means of support. They look modern, clean and attractive, and are great for display purposes. However, they are suitable only for light items. Floating shelves are available in kit form and are supported by a concealed batten or rods fixed into the wall.

BRACKET INTERVALS

Buying the cheapest shelf-and-bracket system can be a false economy if you plan to fill the shelves with heavy loads, such as books. The cheapest shelving material is the weakest, and if it is to be loaded up it will require closer support. This table is a guide to the intervals at which typical shelf materials need to be supported.

Material	Interval
15mm chipboard (coated or plain); 15mm softwood (finished thickness)	Heavy loads 400mm Medium loads 600mm
18mm coated chipboard; 18mm MDF; 18mm softwood; 18mm hardwood	Heavy loads 500mm Medium loads 700mm
25mm MDF; 25mm softwood; 18mm plywood; 22mm hardwood	Heavy loads 700mm Medium loads 900mm
32mm softwood; 25mm plywood; 25mm hardwood	All loads 900mm

Strengthening shelves with battens

Shelves can be reinforced to improve their resistance to bending. The reinforcements can also be a decorative feature, perhaps hiding fixings or strip lights.

Apply a softwood or hardwood batten – a thick piece of wood – to the front or back edge of the shelf. It should run the full length and can be on the top or bottom. For extra strength, battens can be fixed to both front and back edges. The bigger the batten, the greater the strength. Fix the battens to the shelf with adhesive and screws, screwing through the shelf.

Hardwood lipping – a thin strip of wood – can be glued and pinned along the front edge. It may be the same thickness as the shelf to give a decorative finish only, or it may be much bigger, which will strengthen as well as decorate.

SAFETY TIP

Use an electronic cable detector (see page 34) to check for cables in a wall on which you plan to fix shelves. It's best to avoid areas around socket outlets and wall lights altogether.

Load test Before fixing a shelf in place, check whether it will bow under the weight you intend to put on it. Rest the shelf on bricks set at the proposed bracket spacing, load it up and lay a straightedge along its surface. If the shelf bows, either move the bricks closer together, add more bricks or increase the thickness of the shelf material.

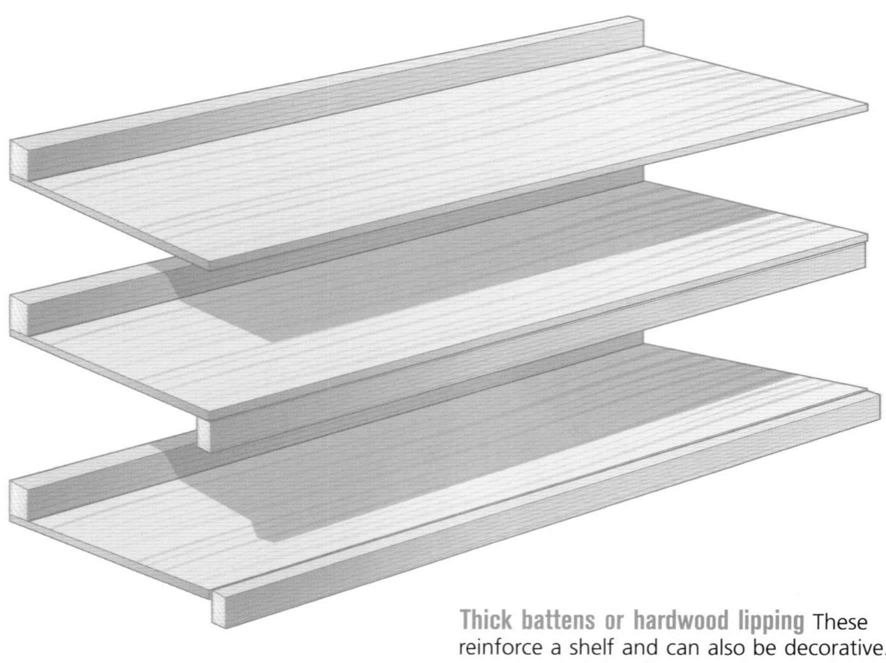

Thick battens or hardwood lipping These reinforce a shelf and can also be decorative. Keep in mind that lipping or battens that extend under the front edge will slightly restrict the height of the items you can store on the shelf below.

POSITIONING THE BRACKETS

End supports Maximum bending occurs under heavy loads.

Supports set in Loads at each end balance the central load.

The bracket positions can give shelves greater resistance to bending. If the shelves extend beyond the brackets they are less likely to bend in the middle. But they must be fixed to the brackets with screws, otherwise they will tip up if a weight is placed at one end. For a shelf with two supports, the brackets should be 2/9ths the shelf length in from the ends (3/20ths for 3 supports). On partition walls, fix shelf brackets to the studs (normally 400mm apart).

Finding your levels

When you are putting up shelves, the most important part of the job is getting the shelves horizontal and the brackets and tracks vertical.

Spirit level

Investing in a good spirit level is crucial. Levels are available in different lengths and designs, from miniature and pocket levels to long carpenter's levels and even digital levels that give a readout of a slope angle.

A spirit level has one or more clear vials filled with a liquid. When the level is truly horizontal, a bubble in the liquid floats within an area marked on the centre vial to indicate that it is exactly level (page 34).

Laser level

State-of-the-art laser levels fire a laser beam enabling horizontal or vertical guidelines to be marked quickly and accurately.

Laser levels have a wide range of uses including guaranteeing a consistent and accurate level for wall lights across a room or positioning brackets for shelves within an alcove. However, their main use is in establishing levels for setting out outdoor work, such as putting up fences or laying paving.

Using a plumb line

You can use the vial at the end of a spirit level for setting true verticals, but you will get more accurate results with a plumb line. This is simply a weight tied to a length of string. If you hold it firmly at the top, it will hang vertically, provided that the string and weight are not touching anything. You can buy a plumb line, or make your own by tying something heavy to the end of a length of string.

Tools *Plumb line; a hardback book; a long screw; pencil; a long straightedge, such as a length of track from a shelving system.*

1 When fixing adjustable shelving, mark and then drill the hole for the topmost fixing screw.

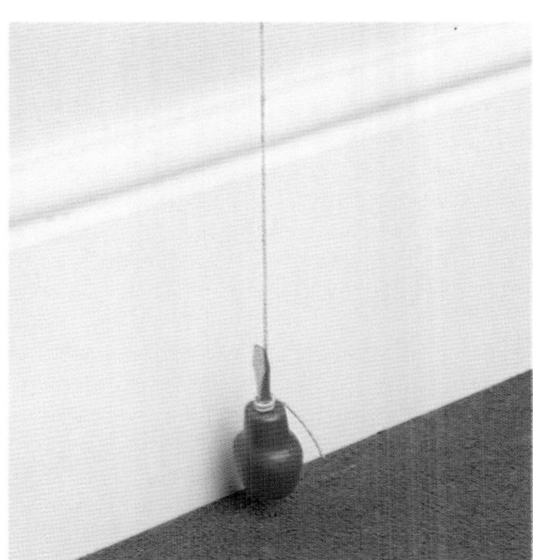

2 Plug the hole and partly drive a long screw into it.

3 Suspend the plumb line from the screw so that it hangs as close to the floor as possible.

4 Let the string become steady. Then place one edge of the book on the wall and slide it up to the string until they touch. Mark the wall where the corner of the book has come to rest. Make a second mark further down the wall.

5 Remove the book, string and screw. Using a track from the shelving system or a straight wooden batten, draw a line between the centre of the screw hole and the pencil marks. This line will be the centre line for the track or brackets to be fitted.

6 Other vertical lines on the wall can be measured from the first line, using a steel tape measure.

Putting up a fixed shelf

Whether for storage or display, fixed shelves must be sturdy, spacious and perfectly level.

Tools *Pencil; spirit level; drill; masonry or wood bit to fit wall plugs; screwdriver. Possibly a straight wooden batten.*

Materials *Brackets; screws for fixing brackets to wall; wall plugs to fit screws; shelf; small screws for fixing shelf to brackets.*

Before you start Check the walls with an electronic detector (page 34) so as not to drill through any hidden pipes or cables and also to detect the positions of the studs on a timber-framed wall.

1 Hold a spirit level against the wall at the point where you want the shelf. Check that it is level and draw a light pencil line on the wall. For a long shelf, rest the spirit level on a straight wooden batten.

2 Hold one bracket against the wall with the top against the mark. Use the spirit level to check that it is vertical, and then mark the wall through the screw holes with the pencil.

HELPFUL TIPS

- Right-angled brackets will need screws about 45mm long to fix them to the wall. The screw must go through the plaster and at least 25mm into the brickwork, or into the wood stud if it is a stud partition wall.
- Don't use winged wall plugs to fix brackets to hollow walls unless the shelf is only to be used to hold a light decorative object.
- The screws should be the biggest diameter that the holes in the bracket will take – usually 4mm on small ones and 5 or 6mm on larger ones.

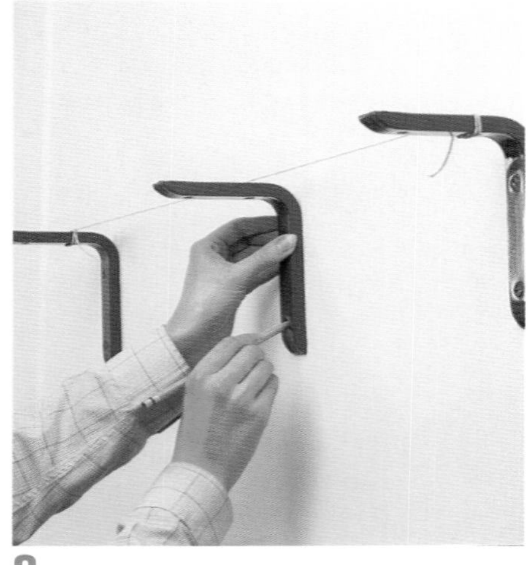

3 Repeat for the second bracket. If there are more than two brackets, it is best to fix the outside ones to the wall, and then tie a piece of string tightly between them across the tops. Then the intermediate brackets can be lined up exactly.

4 Drill holes about 45mm into the wall. Use a masonry bit (or a twist bit for wooden studs).

5 Insert plugs into masonry, and screw the brackets tightly to the wall. If the plug turns in the wall as you drive in the screw, remove it, insert a larger one and try again. Do not use plugs in wood.

6 Lay the shelf across the bracket. Using a pencil or bradawl, mark the underside of the shelf through the bracket holes.

7 Drill pilot holes for the small screws and screw the shelf into position.

Shelves in alcoves

An ideal place to fit shelves is in an alcove beside a chimney breast. This is best done using wooden battens cut and screwed to the side and rear walls of the alcove.

Positioning the battens

Tools *Tape measure; pencil; steel ruler; tenon saw; mitre box; spirit level; power drill; twist drill bits; masonry bits; countersink bit; screwdriver.*

Materials *Wood for battens 50 x 25mm; timber or MDF shelves cut to fit alcove; 63mm 4mm screws and wall plugs; wood filler.*

Before you start Cut battens to the length of the back wall and shorter ones to the depth of each shelf. Drill and countersink screw holes no more than 300mm apart through each batten. Battens are fairly unobtrusive even if left square-ended, but to make them less noticeable the ends can be angled or curved.

1 Mark the position of each shelf, checking that the spacing between them is large enough for the items you want to store there – don't forget to allow for the thickness of the shelving material, too.

2 Hold the rear batten to the mark with a spirit level on top. Mark the wall through one end hole with the twist bit. Remove batten and level, switch to a masonry bit and drill and plug the hole. Drive in a screw part way.

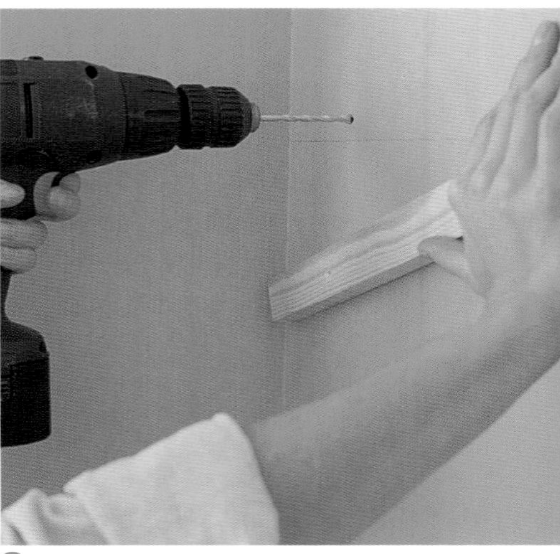

3 Hold the rear batten level and mark the other holes in the same way. Allow the batten to drop out of the way when you drill the wall, then plug the holes and drive the other screws.

4 Position the first side batten, ensuring that it is level with the rear one. Mark the wall beneath it as a guide. Mark drill holes in the same way as for the rear batten. Repeat for the other side batten.

5 Screw the side battens into position. You will be able to hide the countersunk screw heads with wood filler.

Fitting the shelves

1 Few walls are true, and your alcove is unlikely to have perfect right angles. Use a sliding bevel (page 50) to transfer the actual angles to each shelf before cutting. Be prepared to cut each shelf individually: the alcove may vary in shape and size.

2 After you have cut a shelf to fit, drill and countersink a couple of holes through each end and use woodscrews to secure the shelves to the battens.

3 You could strengthen the shelves and improve their appearance by stiffening them with battens or lipping fixed along the shelf fronts (page 162).

Adjustable shelving systems

Adjustable shelving systems consist of uprights which are fixed to a wall, plus brackets which fit on the uprights. Shelves can be raised or lowered by changing the positions of the brackets.

Putting up the tracks

Tools *Pencil; drill; masonry bit; screwdriver; straight wooden batten; spirit level; bradawl.*

Materials *Uprights and brackets; shelves; screws at least 50mm long to fix tracks to wall; wall plugs; screws to fix shelves to brackets.*

Before you start On a solid wall, you can drive the screws into wall plugs. In a hollow partition wall, locate the vertical studs using a stud detector (page 34) so you can screw directly into them.

1 Hold the first upright to the wall and mark the position of the top screw with a pencil.

2 Using a spirit level or plumb line, draw a vertical line down the wall equal in length to the upright.

3 Measure the position of the other uprights and draw similar vertical lines for each. Once the first vertical has been set, others can be measured off with a tape measure. See page 161 for the spacing needed. On timber-framed or partition walls, go with the stud spacing.

4 Use a spirit level to mark the position of the top screw hole on the other vertical lines, level with the first screw position.

Important Slotted uprights must be fixed at exactly the same height. Otherwise the shelves will not be level.

5 Drill and plug each top screw hole. Screw the uprights temporarily in position, but do not tighten. When they are all in place, check that their tops are level.

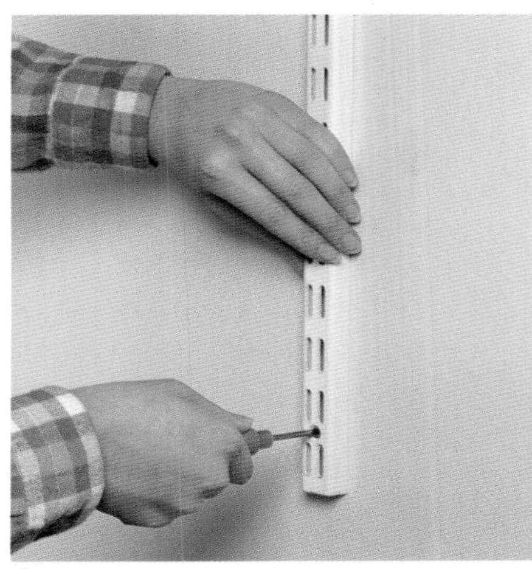

6 Use the bradawl or pencil to mark the positions of the other holes on the centre lines. Swing the uprights aside one by one, and drill and plug the holes.

7 Screw the uprights in position. As the screws tighten, watch each upright to make certain it is not bending because of an uneven wall. Pack behind the upright with hardboard or cardboard where hollows occur.

Putting on the shelves

1 Fit the uprights into the correct slots and put on the shelves. Shelves should slightly overhang the brackets, but avoid wide overhangs which could tempt you to overload the system.

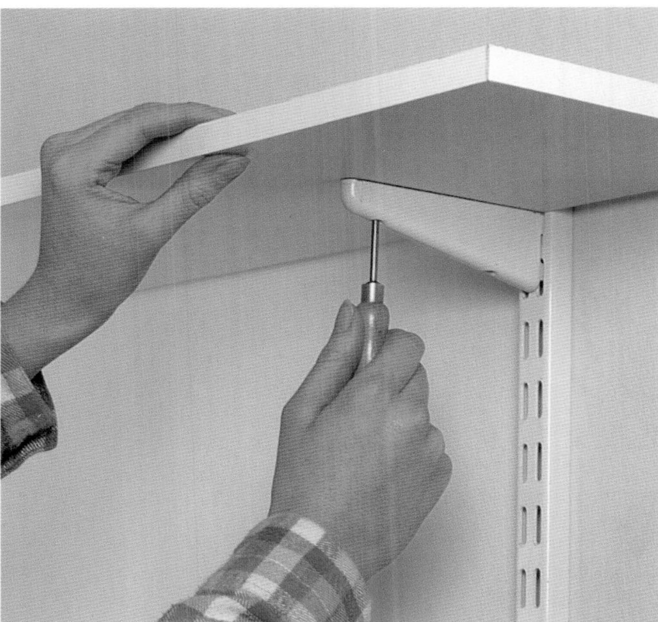

2 Line up the shelves so that their ends are above one another. Mark screw holes in the underside of the shelves by pushing the bradawl through the holes in the brackets.

3 Make pilot holes for the small screws with the bradawl, and screw the shelves in place. This improves the strength of the unit, prevents the shelves from tipping up if a heavy weight is put on one end, and stops them from sliding off if they are knocked.

THREE OR MORE UPRIGHTS FOR FLEXIBILITY

When only two uprights are used, the shelves can be adjusted for height, but each one must run the full width of the system.

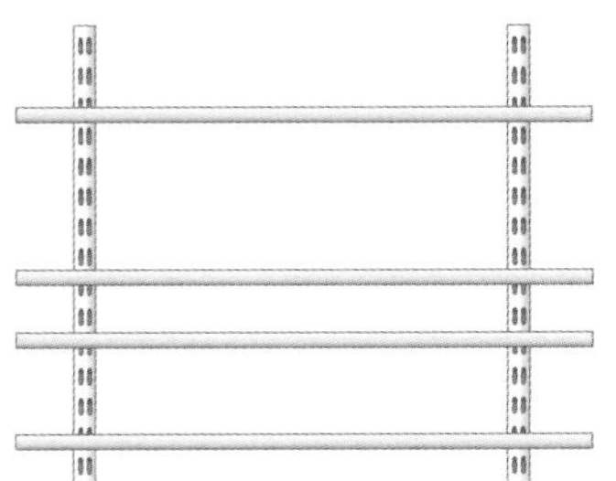

Three or more uprights enable shelves to go halfway at one height and the other half at a different height. This allows greater flexibility in storing objects of different sizes. Shelves of different depths can also be used.

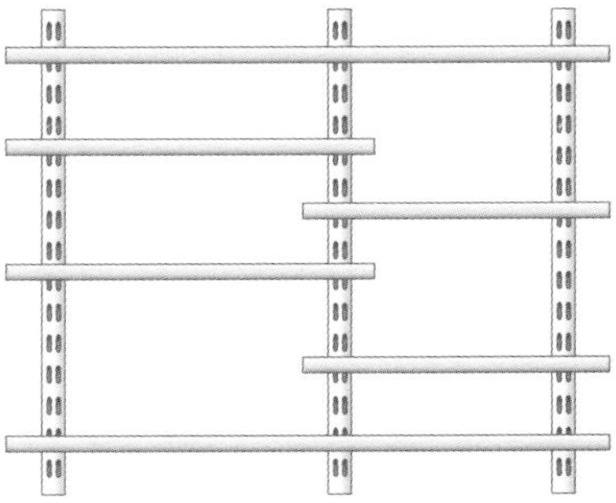

On timber-framed or partition walls, fit an upright to every stud (normally at 400mm spacing), unless you can use shelving with 800mm spacing.

Tailor-made shelving units

You can build shelf units to fit your own design anywhere you like. Compartments can be tailor-made for books, CDs, videos, a DVD or CD player, loudspeakers, or to display items like plates or ornaments.

Tailor-made shelving units use shelf supports (see right) fitted to vertical side panels. The side panels must be firmly secured.

Four situations for tailor-made units

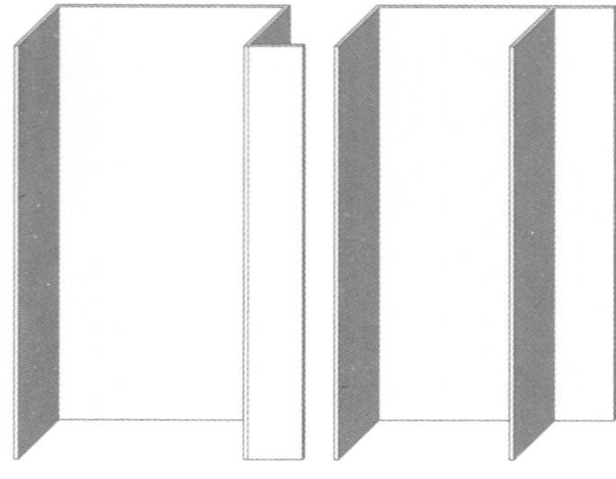

• If a unit is built within an alcove, secure the side panels to the walls (above left).

• Where one side panel is standing free, it must be secured along the whole length of its back edge to a batten screwed to the back wall (above right).

• When both side panels are free, they should each be secured to the wall with battens (above left).

• For a free-standing unit, the most effective stabiliser is a thin plywood or hardboard sheet fixed across the back (above right). If you are using white shelves, a good choice would be white-faced hardboard (see page 53).

• The front corners of any free-standing panels should be secured – see Making the corners rigid (opposite).

Choosing shelf supports

There are various ways you can support shelves fitted between side panels. Battens and nail-on supports can be used for fixed shelves; other supports can be used to give a choice of shelf positions – with peg types, you simply make more holes than you have pegs, spacing them at, say, 30 to 40mm intervals. You can buy jigs to help you get regular spacing.

Drilling the holes the correct size, to the correct depth and exactly at right angles to the side panel is vital if the pegs are to fit correctly. This is a job where a drill stand comes into its own, used with dowel drill bits for precision (see page 58).

Steel

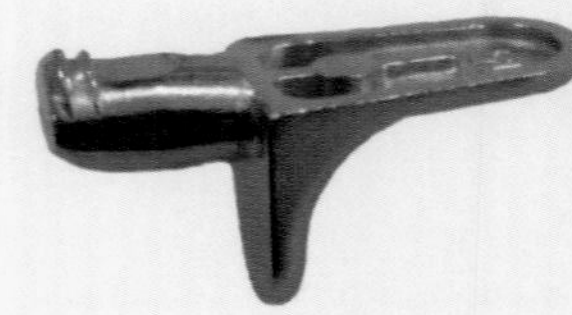

Chrome effect; pushes into 5mm hole. This type of shelf support is widely available and often supplied with kitchen units. Provides a strong support and will not distort or break.

Plastic

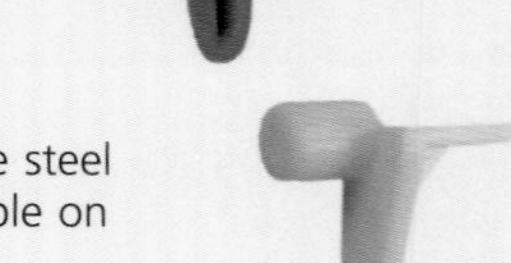

White or clear; pushes into 5mm hole. A plastic version of the steel peg (above), but not as strong. Inexpensive and readily available on the internet.

Metal flat-top

Solid brass or metal with nickel finish; pushes into a 5mm or 6mm hole – or can be used with matching sleeve that needs a slightly bigger hole. Needs to be rotated once in hole so that the flat side is uppermost, but shelf holds peg in place. Good choice for use with natural wood shelving. You'll need more sleeves than pegs if you want the shelves to be adjustable.

Plug-in

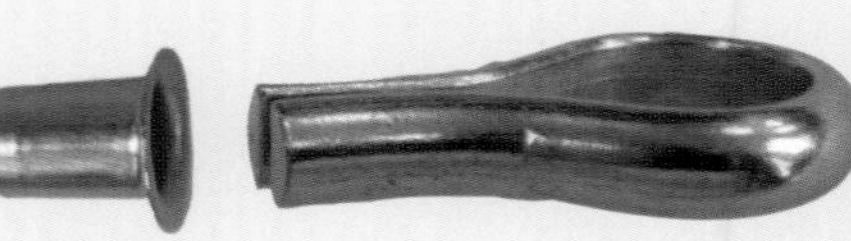

Also known as 'banjo' fitting or bookcase stud. Available from specialist suppliers in brass, nickel plate or bronze finish; normally pushes into socket that fits into 6mm hole. Traditional and provides good support; needs extra sockets for adjustability.

Dowel

Widely available in three sizes: 6, 8 and 10mm and with matching dowel drills for holes. Not particularly attractive, but can be stained or varnished to match colour of wood shelves.

Round

Metal (brass or chrome); fits into 5mm hole. Available through internet suppliers; some types can be fitted with a rubber or plastic sleeve for supporting glass shelves.

Bookcase strip

Steel with bronze, brass or zinc finish in long lengths that are screwed to side panels. Single-hook or double-hook supports clip into the strips. Two types are available: surface-mounting or recessed. With surface-mounting, there is a gap at the end of the shelf (unless you cut out a slot); with recessed strips, you need to use a router to cut the recesses in the side panels. Unobtrusive once fitted and provides excellent adjustability.

Nail-on

Plastic support supplied with nail. Readily available; no hole needed. Not the strongest, but easy to fit with pin hammer for fixed shelf positions.

Battens

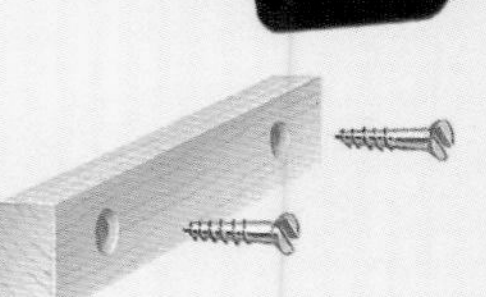

Home-made using suitably-sized wood. Obtrusive, but simple to fit and wood can be stained or varnished to match natural wood shelves. Cut wood slightly shorter than the shelf size and chamfer the front for a more pleasing appearance. Only for fixed shelves – not adjustable.

Making the corners rigid

A unit with one or more free-standing side panels should be made completely rigid with plastic corner joints screwed to the top and bottom shelves and the sides. If the unit is high, one or two of the intermediate shelves should also be secured with corner joints.

Fixing side panels to the walls of an alcove

Instead of fixing battens straight to the walls of an alcove, you can fix vertical side panels and secure the shelves to these. Side panels must be at right angles to the back wall. They must also be vertical and parallel to one another.

If, as is often the case, the walls are not flat, square or upright, the side panels will have to be mounted on spacers.

Gaps between the walls and the front of the side panels can be concealed with timber strips, scribed to the shape of the wall and pinned into place.

Shelving with vertical dividers

Vertical divisions make shelves stronger, and also provide partitions to separate one area from another – books divided from audio equipment, for example. As the divisions can help prevent long shelves from bending under heavy loads, they are particularly useful in wide shelving units.

The dividers must transfer the weight onto something solid or the shelves will still bend. There is no advantage in fitting a divider partway up a unit if you do not put more dividers below to carry the weight down to the floor or some other support.

Fixing dividers in place

- Shelf dividers can be joined to the upper and lower shelves with 38mm 4mm chipboard screws, or oval nails or panel pins, driven down through the top shelves and up through the bottom shelves. This method is fairly simple, but requires great care to ensure that the fixings enter the centre of the dividers and do not break out to one side. Drill narrow pilot holes through the shelves to guide nails or panel pins. Shelves up to 150mm from front to back need two fixings into a divider at top or bottom; bigger shelves need a further fixing for each extra 150mm.
- Fix the dividers to the shelves with dowel joints (page 169). The joints are invisible on the surfaces of the shelves and are structurally sounder than screws or nails. But they take longer to make.
- Join the divider to the shelves with two small corner blocks (page 168) top and bottom. The joints will obstruct the bottom corner on one side of the divider.
- Shelf dividers cut from thick timber – 50mm or more in diameter – need no fixing.

Fitting the dividers

The height of vertical dividers must be exactly the same as the distance between shelves. If they are too long or short the shelves will be out of true. They must also be cut perfectly square at the ends.

1 Plan the positions of the dividers and get them cut square and to exact size by a timber/board supplier who offers a cutting service. The precision that they will be able to achieve will be well worth any extra cost. Have all the other components cut to size and ready to assemble.

2 Number each of the shelves from top to bottom, using a soft pencil. Also mark each shelf 'top', 'bottom' and 'front', so there is no confusion as you build the unit.

3 If the gap between shelves varies from shelf to shelf, mark each divider with the numbers of the shelves it is to fit between.

4 Stand each pair of adjacent shelves on edge with the front edges uppermost, and the top face of the lower shelf against the bottom face of the upper shelf. Mark the positions of each divider across the two

edges with a pencil and try square. Mark two lines to indicate the thickness of the divider.

5 Open the boards out flat so that the face that meets the divider is uppermost. Using a try square, mark the positions of the dividers across the faces from the marks on the edges. The fixings must be centred between the two lines.

6 Repeat the marking process with each pair of shelves.

7 Before going any further, double-check that the height of the dividers and the thickness of the shelves measures up to what was expected. Stand the dividers and shelves on their back edges in numbered order. Then move the dividers to one end of the shelves so that an accurate measurement can be taken. Reduce the height of one or more dividers if the unit is over-height, or have a larger one cut if the unit is too small.

8 If you are making a free-standing unit, mark out the joints between the top, bottom and side panels. Assemble them and then undo the fixings.

9 Assemble the shelves and dividers in their numbered order, on the floor.

10 For free-standing units, complete the construction by rejoining the side panels to the top and bottom. Line the shelves up so that they are parallel with one another and check that the front edges are flush or set back as required. Join them to the sides with corner joints.

11 For shelves and dividers which are to fit into an alcove or between sides that are already fixed, carefully lift the assembly and slide it between the uprights. Then join the shelf ends to the upright sides with shelf supports.

SUPPORTING SHELVES ON BEAMS

If you do not want to continue vertical shelf dividers down to the floor (or the bottom shelf resting on the floor), the load imposed by dividers on upper shelves can be supported by strengthening the lowest shelf with dividers above it.

You can do this with battens as shown on page 162, fitted to both front and back of the shelf close to the front and back edges. Long shelves with a heavy imposed load require thicker battens than short shelves or shelves with light loads. Always position a batten with its longest dimension vertical.

Size of batten for average loads

Shelf length	Batten cross-section
Up to 1m	50 x 25mm
1–1.5m	75 x 25mm
Over 1.5m	100 x 25mm

Shelving with full-height vertical dividers

Using full-height vertical dividers for your tailor-made shelving unit gives you the flexibility to have shelves at different heights to suit the items you want to put on them. The shelves themselves can be fixed or adjustable in height.

Adjustable shelves

Using full-height vertical dividers allows you to design the shelving in separate 'compartments' of different heights – and allows you to have straight vertical dividers (not possible when the dividers are fitted between the shelves).

The dividers are cut to the same height as the side panels and secured to the top and bottom of the unit with glued dowels or corner joints. Drill two lines of evenly spaced holes in each side panel to take shelf supports (page 166). You can then position shelves at any height within each section of the unit and move them easily if you need to rearrange your storage.

If the shelves on either side of a vertical support are to align, you must stagger the position of the dowel holes so that the holes on opposite sides do not coincide. Drill the line of holes in one side of the dividing panel at a slightly different distance from the front and back from the holes in the other side.

Fixed shelves

To make a truly tailor-made shelf unit, assess exactly what you intend to store on the shelves and how much room it will require, then build compartments of exactly the right dimensions.

One way of making a regularly-shaped unit (such as the one illustrated below) is to use halving joints where the shelves meet the dividers, cutting a precise slot in the front of each divider and the back of each shelf, so that they fit snugly together. Or you can secure fixed shelves to the dividers with wooden battens or nail-in shelf supports.

Tailor-made units make optimum use of available space and can be specially designed to meet all your storage needs. This plinth-mounted shelving unit is fitted with display lights to create an attractive, practical feature wall in a dining room.

Self-assembly fixings for flat-pack furniture

When you buy an item of flat-pack furniture, it comes with fixing holes already drilled and special types of fixing to enable you to assemble it yourself easily and with the minimum number of tools. Often all you need is a special spanner or hex key supplied with the unit. Here are some of the most common fixings that you are likely to encounter (see also page 67).

Many of these are also available to buy separately so that you can use them when making your own units. Always use fittings in pairs and use a steel ruler, not a tape measure, when marking where to drill – it is essential for drill holes to be accurately positioned if the unit is to be square when assembled.

Two-part block fitting

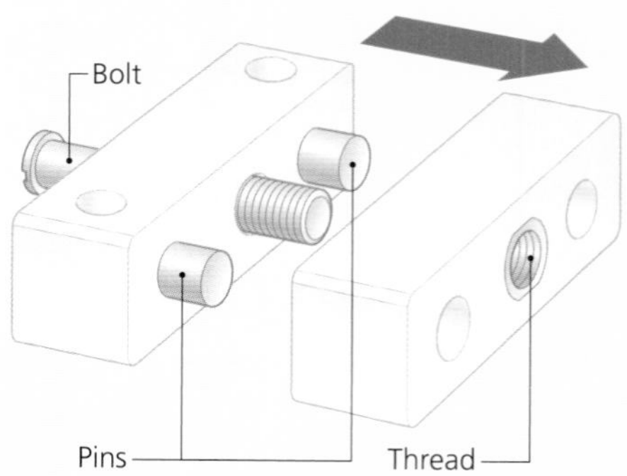

The joint consists of two plastic blocks and is normally used to join two sections of cupboard together such as a side to the base. One of the blocks is screwed to the base and the other to the side into pre-drilled holes; a bolt is then screwed in to hold the two sections firmly together. One of the advantages of this type of fixing is that it can be dismantled and reassembled whenever necessary with no loss of strength.

Plastic corner block

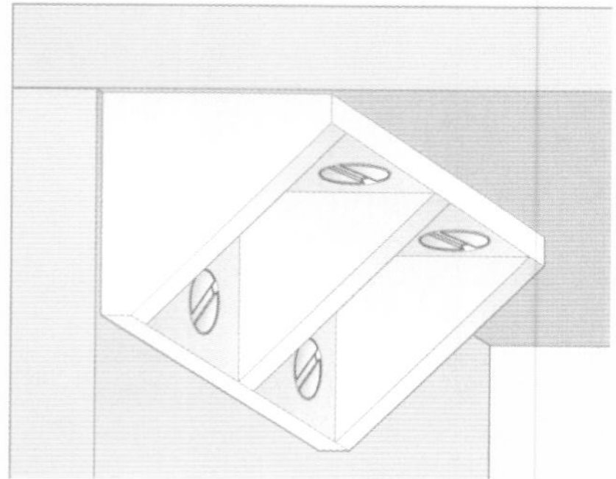

One of the simplest of the fittings and versatile in use. Plastic corner blocks hold two panels together at a perfect right angle. As screws are driven into the panel core material, this fitting cannot be taken apart and reused without compromising its strength.

Dowels

Dowels are for more permanent joints and those that are not to be taken apart once assembled. Usually about 25–30mm long, they are glued in place. Like the majority of the fixings used in flat pack furniture they are tapped into factory-made pre-drilled holes. Although simple they are very effective and give a strong concealed joint. See page 64.

Cross dowel fitting

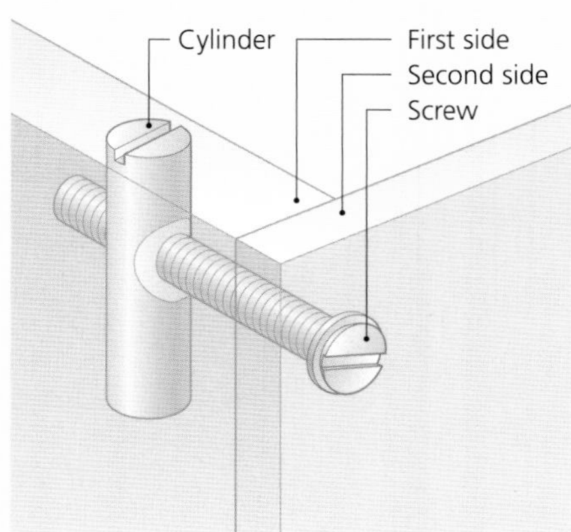

This is one of the most popular joints used in flat pack furniture. The cylinder is inserted into a factory-made pre-drilled hole in one side of the cabinet. A machine screw is then inserted into a hole in the other side until it meets the cylinder. The two components are tightened with a screwdriver until both sides of the cabinet pull together. The slot in the head of the cylinder part of the fitting allows you to align it so that it will receive the screw (below). Although it is possible to over-tighten these fittings they do hold very securely and can be repeatedly taken apart with no loss of strength.

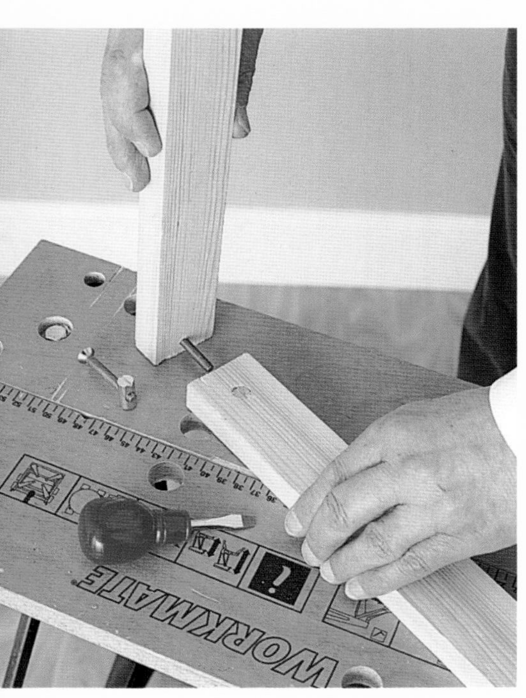

Cam lock fittings

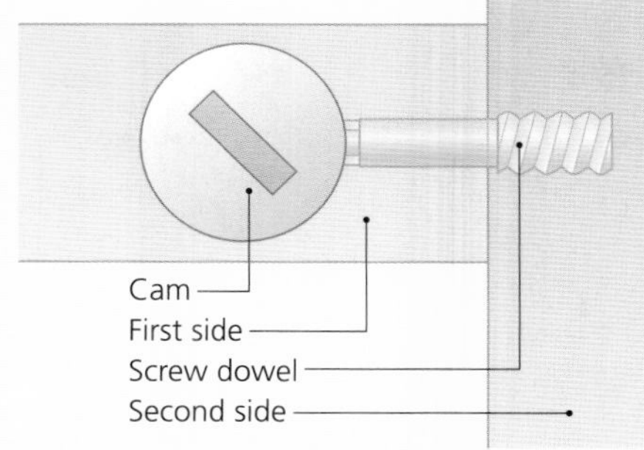

Like the cross dowel fitting, this fastening is for joining two planks or panels together. The cam is dropped into a shallow recess on the face of one part and a screw with a pronounced head or a steel screw dowel is driven into a pre-drilled hole in the other part to be joined.

The head of the screw passes through a clearance hole in the first part and into the cam. Turning the cam 90° clockwise tightens the joint. Also see page 67.

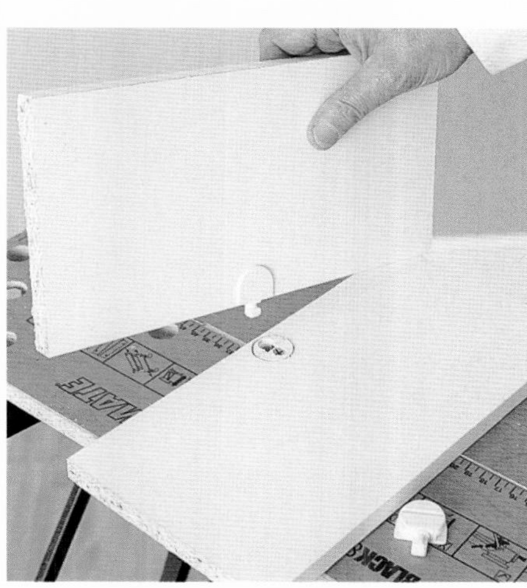

Some cam fittings come with the peg attached to a disc the same size as the cam. Both components slot into pre-drilled holes in the panels to be joined.

Another variation on this type of fitting replaces the peg with a special moulding like a wall plug. This is pushed into a hole drilled in the edge of the second board. A pin is driven into the plug and the fitting is assembled as before.

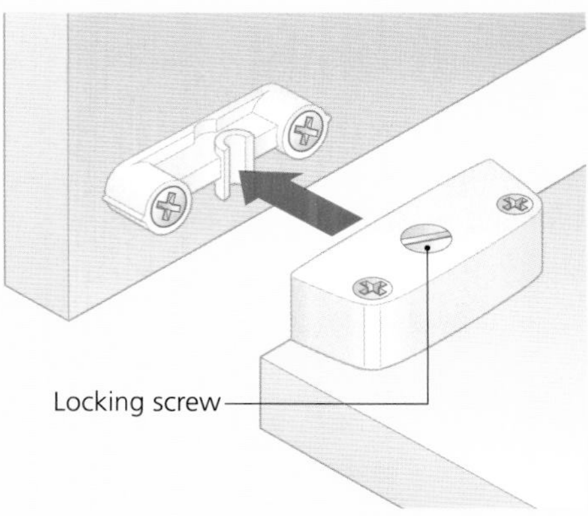

The two parts of the joint are screwed into separate panels. The two panels are then brought together and the screw is turned through 90° to lock the joint.

Dowel-and-bush-fitting

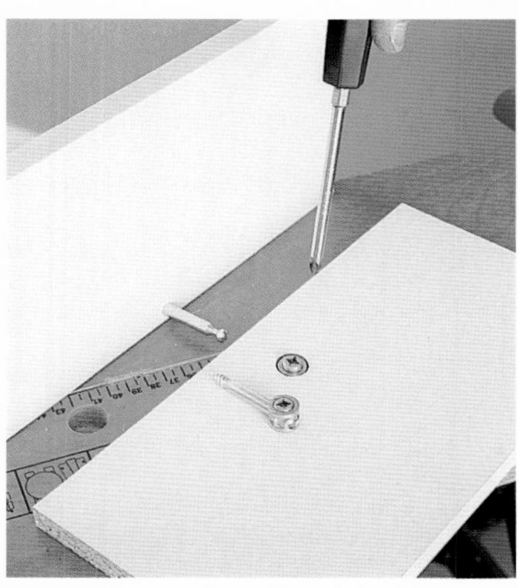

This fitting consists of a zinc alloy bush and a steel dowel. Screw the dowel into the face of one board so that when it is butt-jointed with the second board it will align with the hole drilled in the second board's edge. The dowel reaches the bush through that hole and is locked in place by turning the screw in the bush.

Housing and bolt fitting

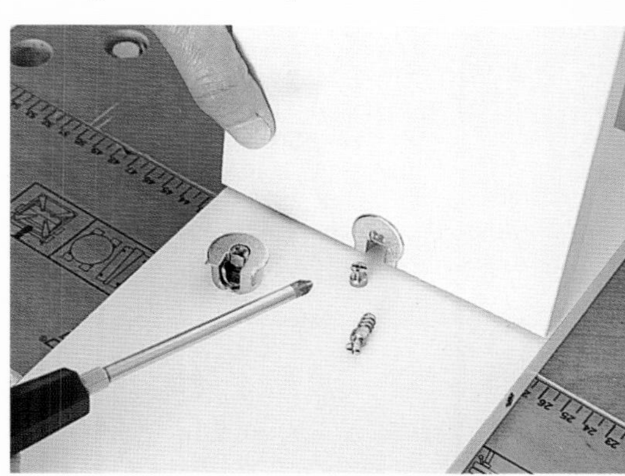

A bolt screws into the side panel of a cupboard or shelf unit and fits into the housing, which slots into a hole drilled in the underside of the shelf. These fittings are useful for strengthening shelves in an existing unit or for adding extra shelves.

Assembling flat-pack furniture

Whether you are putting together a simple bookshelf, a small bathroom cabinet or a more complex piece of flat-pack furniture, such as a computer desk with a sliding shelf, follow these steps to success.

Most flat-pack units consist of a series of panels that are fitted together to create a basic box. Extras, such as doors, shelves and internal fittings, are then added to this to complete the job. Always work in a logical order, following the instructions that came with the unit.

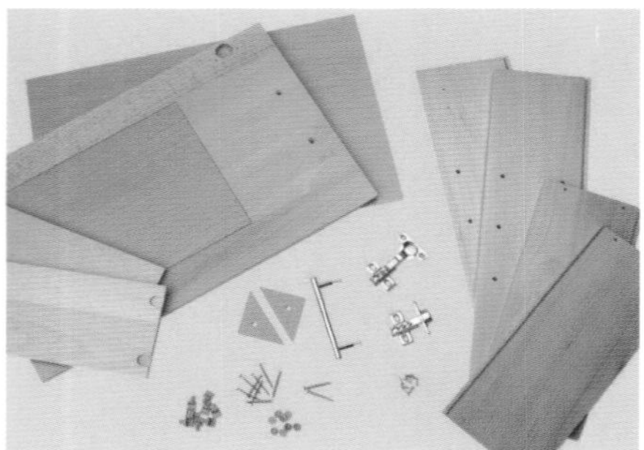

1 Unpack the kit and lay out all the components, including the assembly fittings and any other items of hardware such as hinges, handles and feet. Lay the panels on a carpet, other soft surface or the box they were supplied in to minimise scratches.

2 Identify all the parts, using the instructions, and check that you have the right number of fixings – there is usually a numbered checklist included with the instructions. If any appear to be missing, look inside the packaging to see if any are loose inside. If you still cannot locate the missing pieces, return the complete unit to the store and ask for a replacement.

3 Start with the base panel, adding any fixed feet first of all. Build tall units, such as bookshelves or wardrobes, on their backs to make the assembly manageable. If the unit has castors or wheels, fit these last or the unit will keep moving about as you try to assemble it.

SAFETY TIP

Tall pieces of furniture, such as bookshelves or wardrobes, should be secured to the wall at the top of the unit, using a bracket or restraining strap. Without them a fully loaded unit could topple over on a child climbing on it or clambering inside.

4 Connect the first side panel to the base panel. The simplest units have pre-drilled holes through which you can drive screws supplied with the furniture (above). Many units use a combination of glued dowels and cam fixings (pages 168–9). In this case, place the dowels and screwed pegs in the base unit and then offer up the side panel. Glue and locate all the dowels in the side panel, then tighten the fixings.

5 Connect the second side panel to make a three-sided box. If the unit has a back panel, locate this in the grooves in the side panels and slide it into place. Then finish the box by fixing the top panel in position.

6 Many fixings come with cover discs that match the colour of the wood or veneer of the finished item. These make a tidy job of disguising the fixings once the furniture is complete. They can be prised out of their holes if you need access to the fixings to dismantle the furniture.

HELPFUL TIP

Much flat-pack and self-assembly furniture comes with a hexagonal assembly key and every unit comes with a set of instructions. When you have finished putting the piece of furniture together, tape the key and instructions securely to the back, so that you will always have them handy if you ever have to move, dismantle or adjust your furniture.

7 Follow the instructions with the unit to add any doors. They will be hung on some form of spring-loaded hinges, and the fitting and fixing holes will all be pre-drilled in the doors and cabinet sides. Fit the hinge body to the door and the mounting plate to the cabinet sides, then connect the two with the short machine screws and adjust them so they hang squarely.

8 Add any shelves, door handles and other internal or external fittings. Double-check that all the assembly fittings are tight, and that you do not have any parts left over. Finally, fit wheels or castors if these are part of the kit.

Building a computer desk

Large items of flat-pack furniture are constructed using special fixings (pages 168–9). Follow the instructions that come with the unit, using these standard techniques to guide you.

Tools *Selection of screwdrivers; perhaps a hammer; perhaps a set of hex keys.*

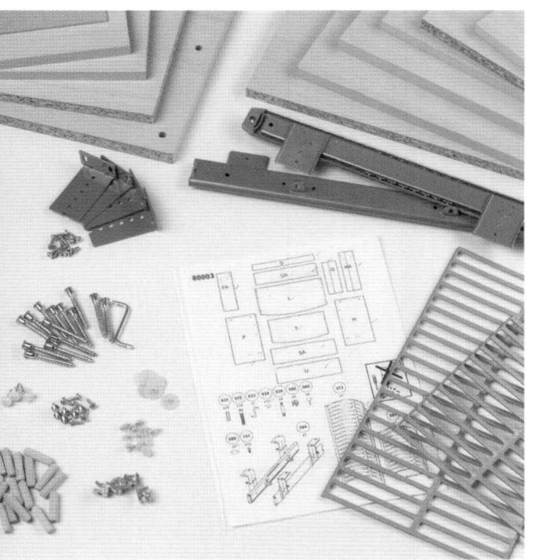

Before you start Unpack the box and lay out all the pieces and fixings. Check them against the instructions and make sure that they are all there and you know which piece is which. Often, a right and left hand piece look almost identical until you check where the fixing holes have been drilled.

1 Insert cam lock screw dowels into pre-drilled holes according to the instructions.

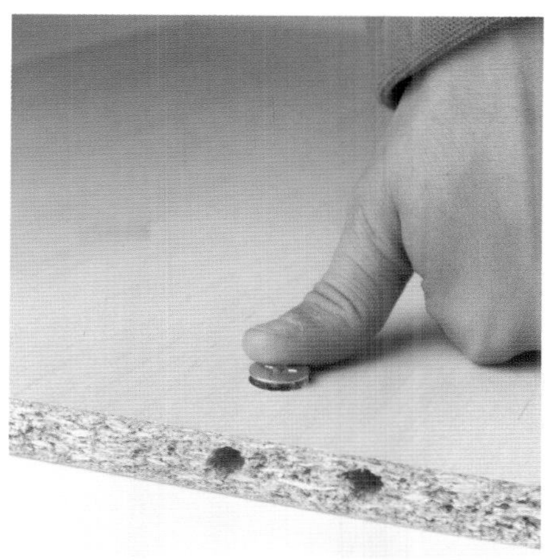

2 Use your thumb to push the cam locks into the large holes on the opposing panels, making sure that the arrow on the fitting points towards the holes on the raw outside edge of the workpiece. The cam lock pins fit into these holes, so if the locks don't face in the right direction the fixings will not work.

3 Begin to put the piece together in the order specified in the instructions. In this instance the lock pins are screwed into the cam locks using the special key supplied as part of the kit.

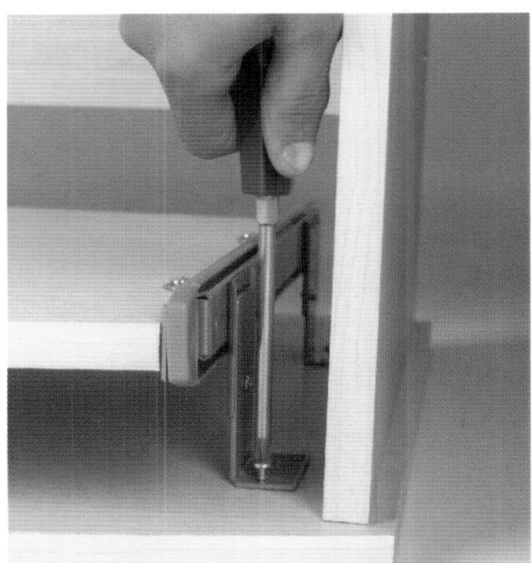

4 This workstation has a sliding keyboard table. The runners for the sliding section are fitted to the keyboard table, and then fixed to the underside of the desk. You will need to turn the desk upside down to make the fixings.

WHEN GLUING IS BEST

If you know that you will not be taking the furniture apart again at some time in the future, consider using adhesive on wood-to-wood joints for a sturdier finished piece. Ordinary white carpenters' PVA adhesive is ideal. Use a damp rag to wipe off any excess adhesive that squeezes from the joints.

5 Make up the shelf section that sits on top of the desk. This fits onto dowels that have been tapped into the desktop with a hammer. Fit the top to the base and push them together to ensure all the dowels have engaged. If you need to, hammer from above, being sure to protect the workpiece with some scrap timber.

6 Finish the item by adding any accessories. In this instance a simple plastic rack for CDs slots into the narrow stack to the left of the desk.

Choosing curtain poles and tracks

Tracks and poles come in many styles, materials and lengths. Decide on the look you wish to achieve, and then choose the components you need.

If you are not happy with the existing curtain rails or tracks in a window, or you wish to change them, there are several factors to take into account.

Privacy Is the window open to the street or overlooked by neighbours?
Light How much light comes into the room naturally, and how much more or less do you want?
Security Do you want your curtains to be open and closed automatically while you are out?
Style Is the room traditional or modern? Will old-fashioned drapes be right, or does it need minimalist blinds or sun-filters?

Once you have decided on these basic characteristics, you can set about choosing the poles and tracks to suit the window.

Bracket for wall or ceiling mounting
Endstop
Finial
Combined glider-hook

Uncorded track for mounting on brackets, and fitted with combined glider hooks

Bracketless track for top fixing
Glider
Endstop
Bracketless track for face fixing
Glider
Endstop
Bracketless track for concealed face fixing
Endstop
Glider

Brackets for ceiling fixing
Built-in cording unit
Glider
Ready-corded track for mounting on brackets
Bracket for wall fixing

Continuous track Buy all the fittings when you buy the track; the right ones could be out of stock or discontinued later. Tracks are made of steel, aluminium or plastic. Brackets to hold the track in place can be screwed into the wall or the ceiling. Some tracks fit flush to the ceiling. Bracketless tracks screw direct into a wall, ceiling or window recess. Gliders on the tracks carry the curtain hooks. Some tracks have combined glider-hooks. Endstops or finials stop the gliders running off the track ends.

Concealed track A track concealed by a pelmet or valance can be cheaper and less streamlined than one that will be on view. The brackets for holding it in place can be fixed to either wall or ceiling. The track is usually fitted in two halves with a central overlap held by a special bracket.

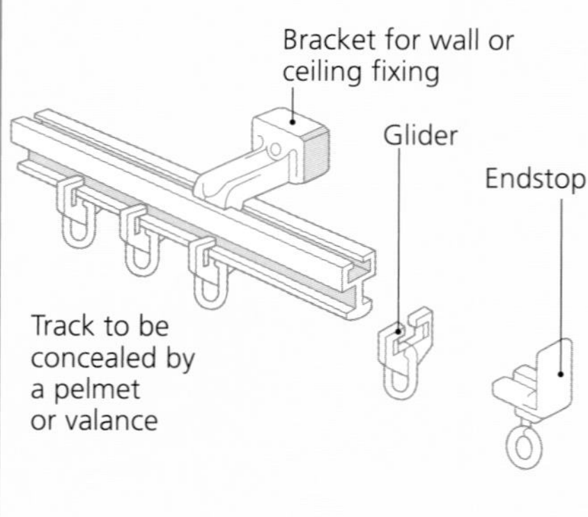

Poles Poles are generally used for straight runs. However, there are metal pole kits which are designed to fit right-angled bay windows. Standard poles are made in wood, metal and plastic. Some have rings encircling them, others have half-rings attached to gliders in a track inside the pole. Poles with glider tracks often have a built-in central overlap arm. Usually brackets are needed only at the ends, but a pole that is 2.4m or longer will need an extra bracket at the centre. Two-part brackets can hold the pole at different distances from the wall. There are side-fixed brackets for some poles. Finials on the ends of the pole act as endstops.

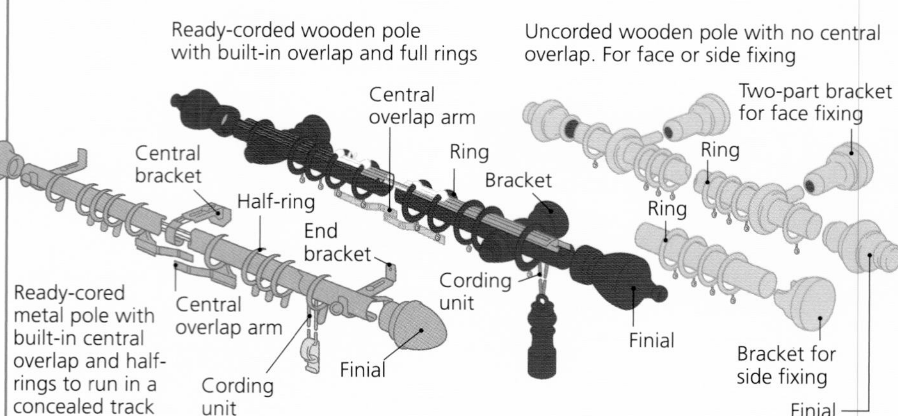

Bay window tracks Many tracks will bend round bay windows. The maker's instructions show how much each type will bend. Some shops will bend steel track for you to the perfect shape.
In a right-angled bay, you can fit three straight sections of track with connector pieces at the corners. Curtain the three sides separately.

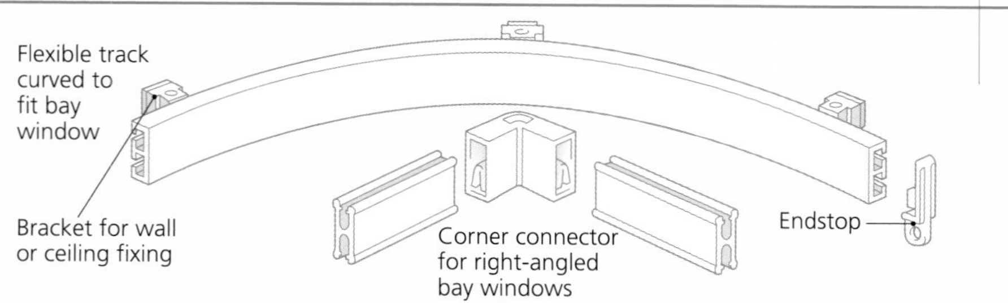

Wires and rods for nets Net and sheer curtains that are not opened and closed can be hung on a plastic-coated spring wire or on a plastic-coated extending metal rod. Café curtains can also be hung on wires or extending rods, or on slender poles with loops.

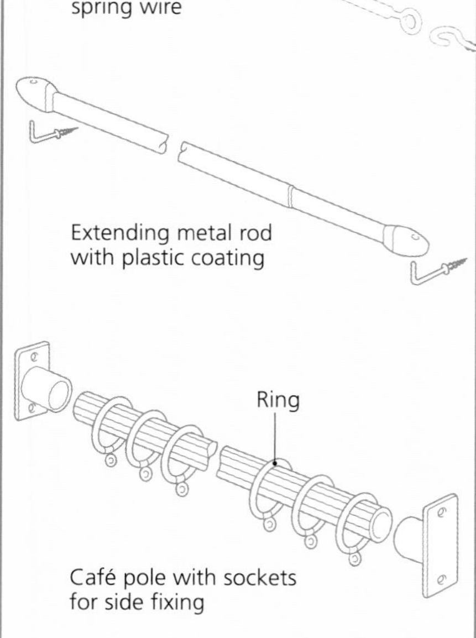

Roller blinds Blinds of various sizes and styles are available as kits which come with fitting instructions. The holding brackets are fitted to the wall or the window frame at either end of the roller, which is operated by a pulley cord. To remove a blind quickly and easily, prise it out of the snap-lock bracket with a screwdriver (below). Blinds with wooden poles and simple pins can be lifted out of their brackets.

OPTIONAL FITTINGS FOR TRACKS AND POLES

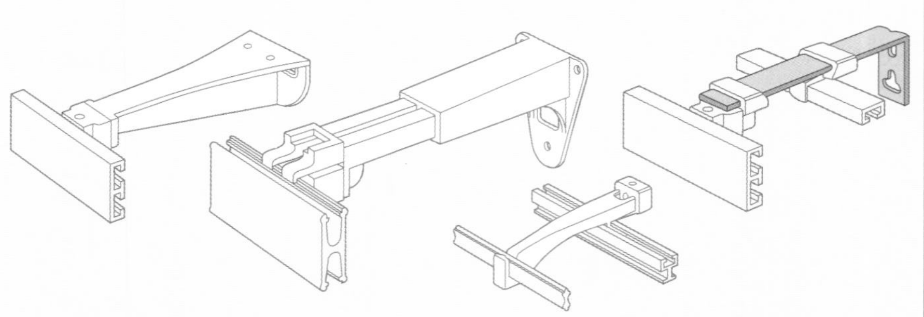

Extension bracket with fixed arm Extension brackets fitted instead of standard brackets will hold a track farther out from the wall – so that the curtains clear a projecting sill or a wooden window surround, for example.

Adjustable bracket This type of bracket has a sliding arm that you can adjust to project different amounts.

Clip-on bracket for a valance rail Secondary brackets clipped onto the main track will carry the rail for a valance.

Bracket to hold two tracks This bracket carries two tracks – one for the main curtain and another for a net curtain behind it.

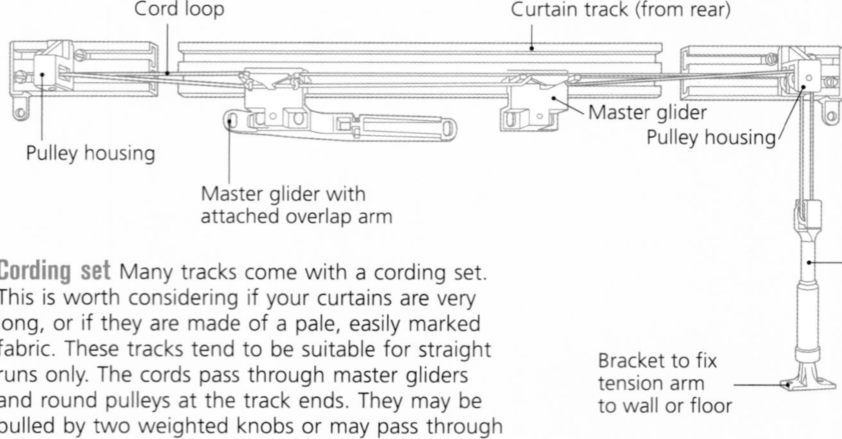

Cording set Many tracks come with a cording set. This is worth considering if your curtains are very long, or if they are made of a pale, easily marked fabric. These tracks tend to be suitable for straight runs only. The cords pass through master gliders and round pulleys at the track ends. They may be pulled by two weighted knobs or may pass through a tension arm.

Draw rods To keep curtains made of delicate fabric from being marked when handled, fit draw rods. They clip into a glider or ring at the meeting edge of each curtain. They are available in several lengths and finishes.

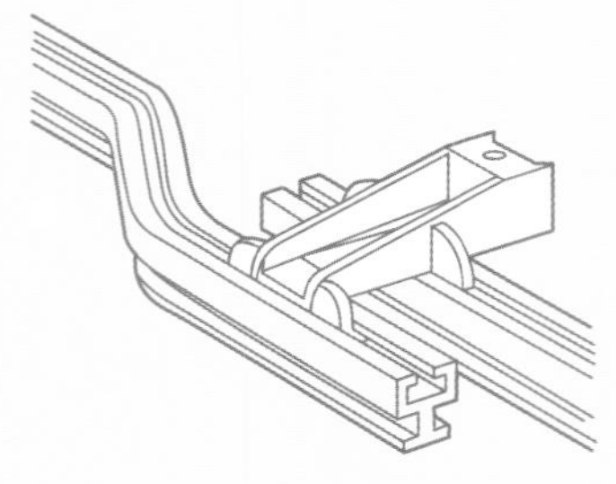

Fixed overlap arm A track behind a pelmet or valance is fitted in two halves and made to overlap by a bracket.

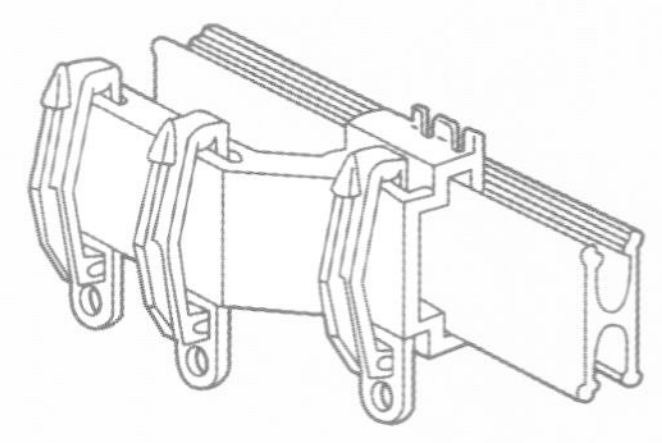

Sliding overlap arm For most continuous tracks there are overlap arms that slide along the track like gliders. The arm carries the leading edge of one curtain over the other.

How to put up a track or pole

It's important to let as much light as possible into a room, so let the track or pole extend far enough at the sides for even the bulkiest of curtains to draw back clear of the window.

Tools *Long wood or metal rule; pencil; bradawl; drill with wood or masonry bit; screwdriver.*

Materials *Track/pole. Perhaps a length of batten; wall plugs; plasterboard plugs; brackets or sockets, 38mm No. 6 screws; screw eyes; gliders or rings; end stops or finials.*

Before you start Most tracks or poles must be screwed into sound ceiling timbers or plugs in a wall; extra brackets on ceilings may be screwed into plasterboard plugs. The screws supplied with a track or pole are not always long enough to make secure fixings: replace them if necessary. Don't saw off any excess track or pole until you are certain there is enough overlap at either end.

Fixing brackets for a track on the wall

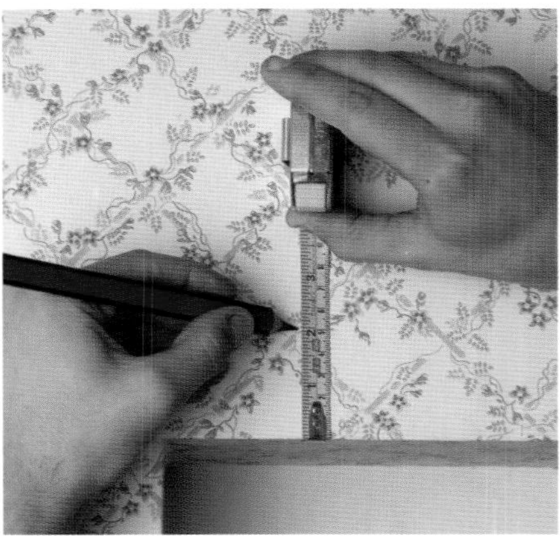

1 Mark the fixing height for the track at least 50mm above the top of the window. Brackets on which a track slots down should be at least 20mm below the ceiling to allow room for fitting the track. Brackets for clip-on tracks can be up against the ceiling.

2 Measure up from the window top every 200mm across and make pencil marks at the right height. If the track or pole is to be nearer the ceiling than the window top, measure down from the ceiling. Neither window top nor ceiling is necessarily horizontal. The track should be parallel to whichever of the two is closer or it will always look crooked.

3 Join the pencil marks with a straight line and extend it at the sides to the width of the track. Mark positions for the brackets with pencil crosses on the guide-line. Put one 50mm from each end. Space others about 300mm apart, or as specified in the manufacturer's instructions.

4 At each cross drill through the plaster into the lintel and insert a plug. On a concrete lintel, use a mains-powered electric hammer drill. Screw a bracket into each plug.

Fixing brackets on the ceiling

1 Draw a pencil guideline on the ceiling parallel with the top of the wall where you want the track to be. Locate the joists (using a stud detector, page 34) and mark them with a pencil. If they run at right angles to the window, mark spots for drilling where the pencil guideline and the joists cross, and also 50mm from the ends of the track if the ceiling is plasterboard; do not make such hollow fixings at the ends into a lath and plaster ceiling.

On a plasterboard ceiling you can mark extra drilling places between the joists if the curtains are heavy, or if the track is going to be curved and needs a bracket to hold the curve at a point where there is no joist.

Alternatively For particularly heavy curtains, skew-nail wooden struts between the joists and drill into the struts 50mm from the ends of the track and about every 300mm between them to provide extra fixing points. This method of fixing makes sure that every bracket is screwed securely into timber above the ceiling. If you cannot gain access to the loft or the floor above the window to fix wood to the joists, a wall-fixed track is safest.

2 Drill through the ceiling at the marked spots and into the timber where possible. Where you have not drilled into timber, insert a plasterboard plug through the hole.

3 Screw the brackets into the timber or plugs (unless the track has slide-in brackets; see Fitting the track, opposite).

FIXING TO JOISTS THAT RUN PARALLEL WITH THE WINDOW

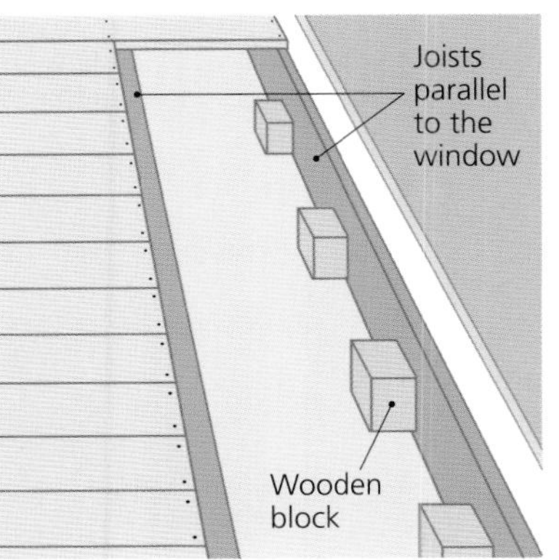

If the joists run parallel with the window and are not positioned conveniently to hold the bracket screws, you can fix wooden blocks to the side of the joist to give fixings up to 100mm away. Mark spots on the ceiling for drilling into the blocks.

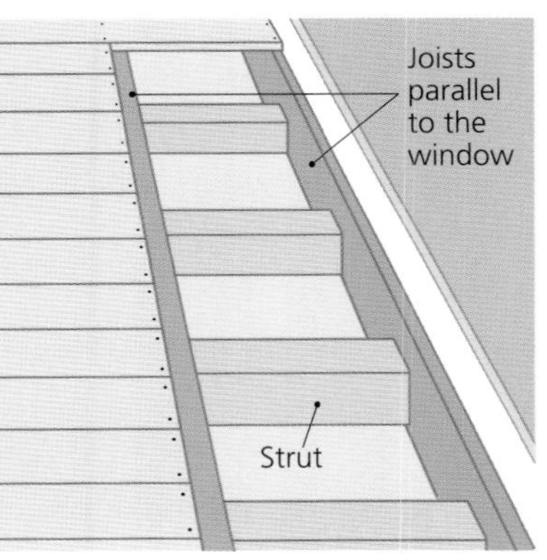

If the joists run parallel with the window and are more than 100mm away from the points where you need to make fixing, fit wooden struts between the joists. You can fit a strut wherever you need to fix a bracket. Mark spots for drilling into the struts.

Fixing to a window surround

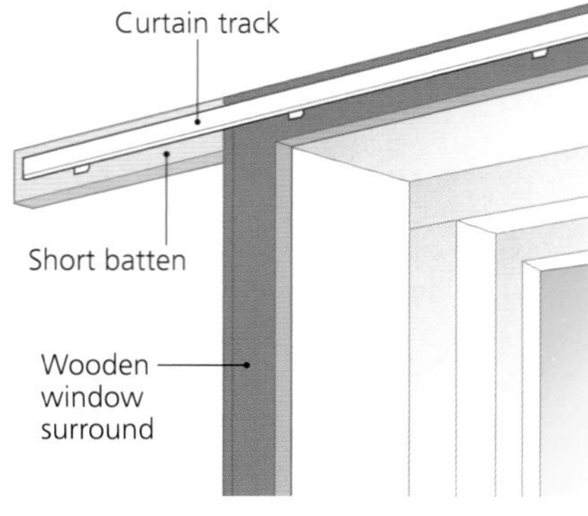

Windows with wooden surrounds on the wall surface may seem to offer easy fixing points for brackets. However, the track cannot extend beyond the sides of the window. This excludes too much daylight because the curtains cannot be drawn back to clear the glass. Fix a wooden batten at each side of the window to extend the fixing width.

Fixing brackets in a recess

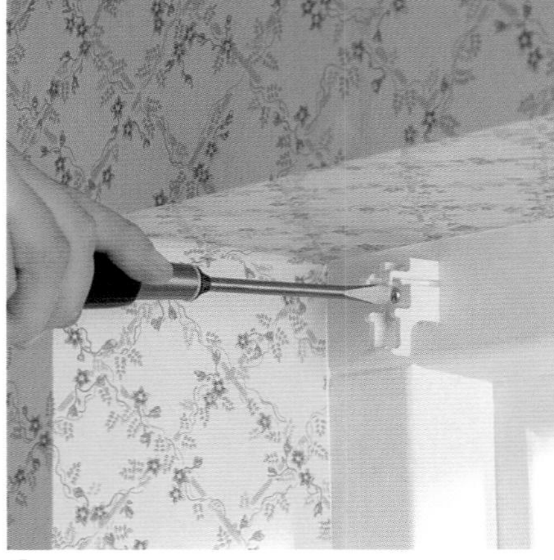

1 For tracks in a window recess, screw the brackets securely into the window frame, if it is wooden.

2 Where the frame is metal or PVC, screw the brackets upwards with 38mm 3.5mm screws into drilled, plugged holes.

Fixing a concealed track

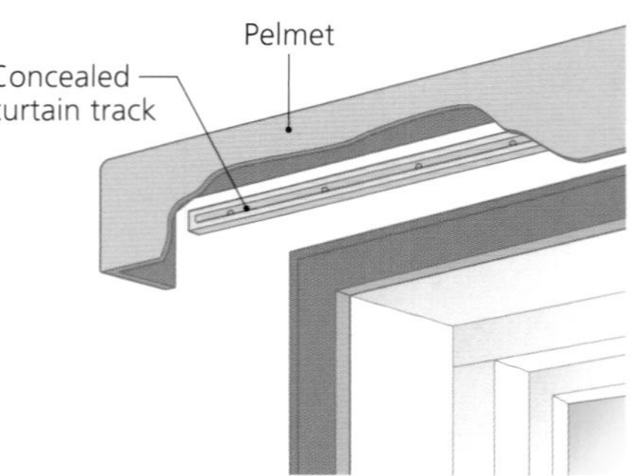

Where a pelmet or valance is going to cover the curtain track, fix a wooden batten above the window and screw the brackets for the track into the batten.

Fitting the track

- With a wall-fixed track, clip or slot it onto the brackets.
- With a ceiling-fixed track of the clip-on type, clip the track to the brackets.
- With a ceiling-fixed track that has a channel for the brackets to slide into, position the brackets on the track before screwing them into place.

Once the track is in position, slide on the gliders and fit the end stops or finials in place.

Fixing a pole to the wall

1 Draw a guideline on the wall as for fixing brackets for a track on the wall (opposite).

2 Measure how far above the centre of the bracket the screw hole is and make the drilling marks that distance above the line; 100mm from each end, and in the centre if needed.

Alternatively If the bracket is in two parts, make drilling marks on the guideline through the holes on the mounting plate.

3 Drill and plug the holes. Drive in the screws, letting the heads project; or screw in place the plates for two-part brackets. Fit the brackets in place.

4 Position the pole, centring it on the brackets, and slide on the rings. Make sure that one ring is outside each end bracket and the remainder between the brackets. Push the finials firmly into place at each end of the pole.

5 Drive the screw provided into the hole in the base of each bracket until it bites into the pole. This prevents the pole from being dislodged.

FITTING A ROLLER BLIND

If the window is in a recess, decide whether to fix the blind inside or outside the recess. If inside, measure the full width, from one side of the recess to the other. This will give you the size of the roller blind kit you require. If the blind is to go outside the recess, add 50mm.

If the exact size of roller you need is not available, buy the next size up and cut it down by sawing the pole and trimming fabric with scissors.

Hold each bracket in its position inside the recess as near the top as possible and mark the screw holes for drilling. Make sure the brackets will be level and the same distance from the sides of the recess. For a blind outside the recess, make the drilling marks 50mm above the top of the recess, and again make sure that the brackets will be level.

Drill and, if necessary, plug the holes, and screw the brackets into place. Then fit the blind by clipping it into the brackets according to the manufacturer's instructions.

Fixing wires and rods

The wires and rods for net or café curtains are held by screw hooks. Screw them to the window frame if it is made of wood; if it is metal or PVC, screw them into drilled and plugged holes in the sides of the window recess.

Some rods are held in place by sockets. One type is face-fixed; screw the sockets into wooden window frames. Another type is side-fixed for use where a window frame is not wooden; screw these into drilled and plugged holes in the sides of the recess.

Putting up plasterboard coving

Coving gives a decorative finish to the joint where the ceiling and wall meets, and also covers any unsightly gaps and cracks.

Tools *Tape measure; pencil; coving mitre box; fine-toothed saw; wide filling knife; ceiling props; hammer.*

Materials *Coving; coving adhesive; masonry nails.*

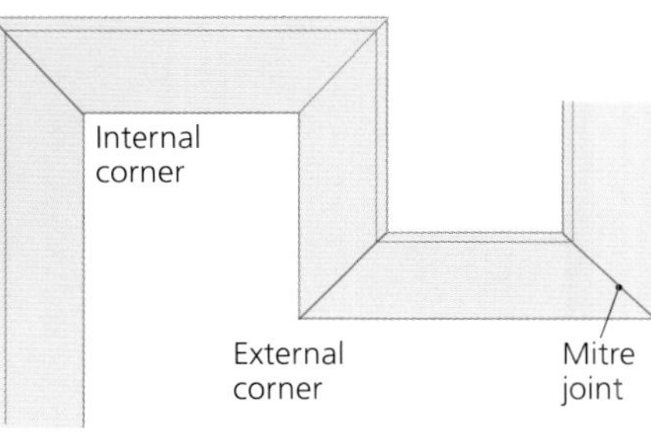

You will need to cut mitres to join pieces of coving at internal and external corners. Use the diagram above to guide you when making your cuts.

1 Begin at an internal corner. Put a full length of coving in the mitre box with the edge that will fit against the ceiling resting on the base of the box. Cut the first mitre so it will fit into a left-hand corner.

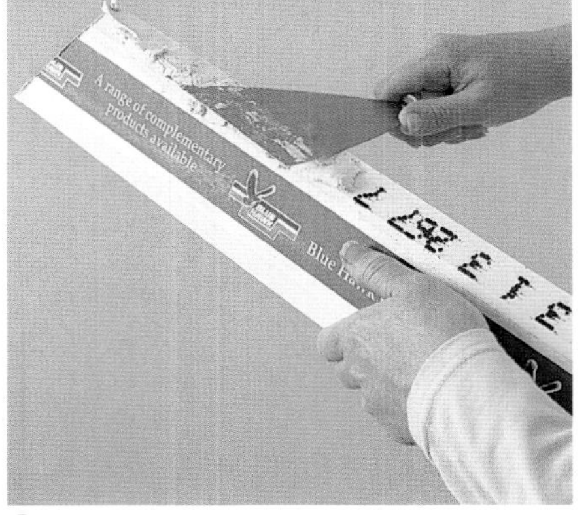

2 Use a filling knife to spread coving adhesive along both edges of the coving. Spread an even layer about 10mm thick all the way along, but do not let too much adhesive past the flat edge sections. This will not help to stick the coving in place and will be a waste.

3 Press the coving in place against the wall and ceiling, with the mitred end in the corner. Ask a helper to hold the other end until the adhesive sticks. Alternatively, prop the coving up with a length of wood. Or tack a few masonry nails through the coving and into the wall plaster only; pull them out and fill the holes once the adhesive has set. Remove extra adhesive.

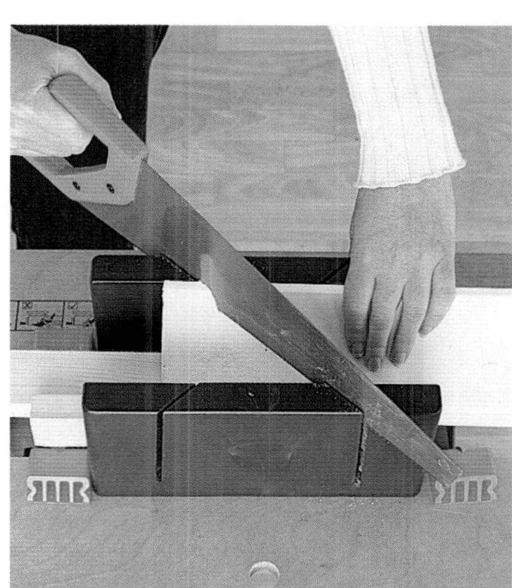

4 Cut a reverse mitre on another length of coving to join with your first cut. Position the coving so that it is facing the opposite way in the mitre box with the saw running in the other pair of guide slots.

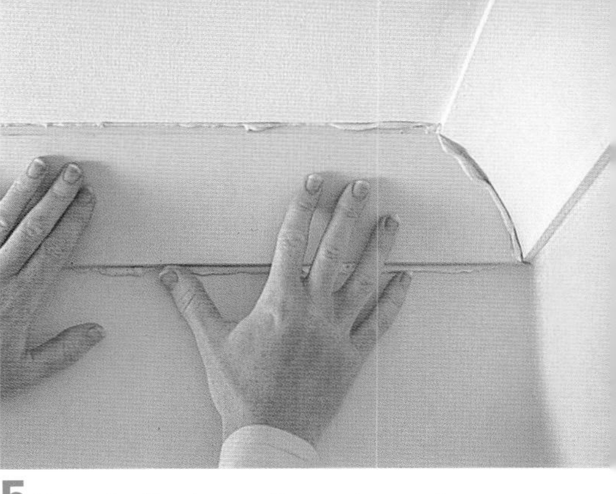

5 Spread adhesive on the coving and on the mitred end. Place it in position, pushing the mitred end against the mitred end of the length already in place. Trim off any excess adhesive along the length and from the mitre joint.

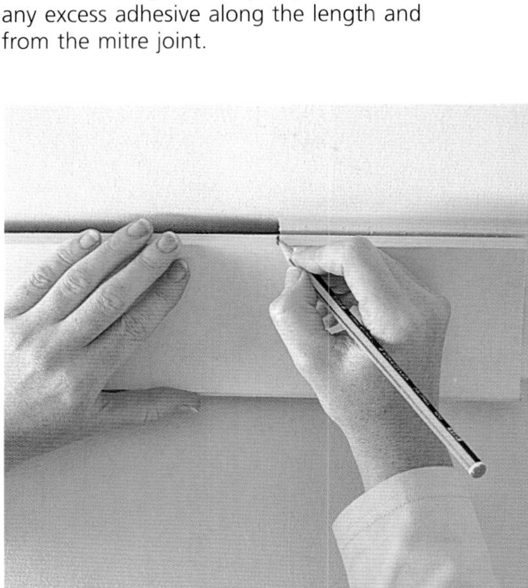

6 Repeat steps 1 to 5 for each internal corner. To make an external corner, cut coving as shown in the diagram (far left).

If a wall requires just two lengths of coving, mark and cut the second one to meet the square end of the first one partway along the wall. If the wall needs three lengths or more, fit the corner lengths at each end, then cut one or more square-ended lengths to bridge the gap between them. Fill any small gaps.

Restoring a cornice

Old cornice (ornate decorative moulding) is often clogged with paint.

1 If the cornice has been painted with a modern paint, you may have to apply paint stripper. Remove accumulations of distemper by soaking a small area at a time with warm water applied with a house-plant hand sprayer. Spray repeatedly for about half an hour until the distemper has been thoroughly soaked.

2 Pick out the paint carefully with a very small screwdriver, taking care not to damage the plasterwork.

3 Remove loose material with an old paint brush so that you can see the areas that still need cleaning.

Repairing a broken cornice

If parts of the cornice have broken away, it can often be repaired with Plaster of Paris.

1 Mix the Plaster of Paris with water to a stiff paste – only a little at a time as it sets in about 3 minutes.

2 Damp the surface of the cornice, then use Plaster of Paris to build up the moulding in layers, using a clay modelling tool or a small knife.

Alternatively Traditional cornice lengths, ceiling roses and beadings made of fibrous plaster are available from specialist firms.

Fitting picture rails and dados

These timber mouldings will break up high walls. Fix picture rails 450–600mm below ceiling level – they are often level with the top of the door surround. Dado rails were traditionally fitted to protect the wall from chair backs and are now usually positioned at about waist height.

Tools *Pencil; straightedge; spirit level; tape measure; tenon saw; abrasive paper; power drill; coping saw; twist, countersink and masonry drill bits; screwdriver; mitre box; portable workbench; filling knife.*

Materials *Mouldings to fit walls; screws and wall plugs; wood filler.*

Before you start Buy only mouldings that are dead straight and have no large knots.

1 To fit the rail, mark a pencil line along the walls at the required height using a straightedge and spirit level or laser level.

2 Begin at a corner. Cut the first piece of moulding to length if it runs up to an obstacle such as a door frame and sand down the sawn edge. Mark positions for screw holes at 600mm intervals on the rail. Countersink holes, or the bit may make a ragged hole. Drill the holes with a twist bit.

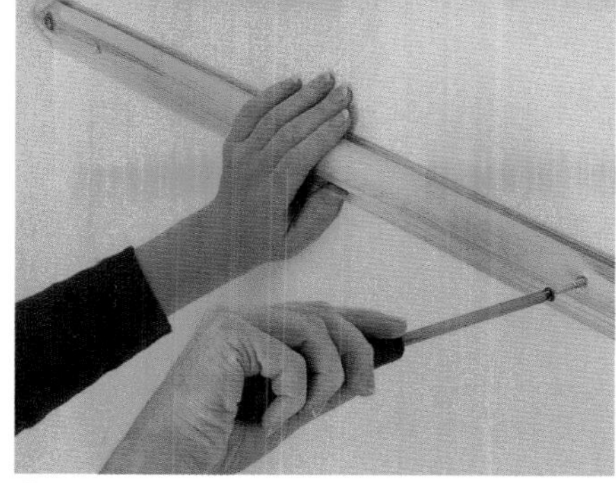

3 Line up the rail with the pencil line, and mark fixing positions on the wall through screw holes. Drill holes in the wall and plug them. Drive one end screw almost all the way in, then the other end screw. Fit the rest of the screws and tighten them all.

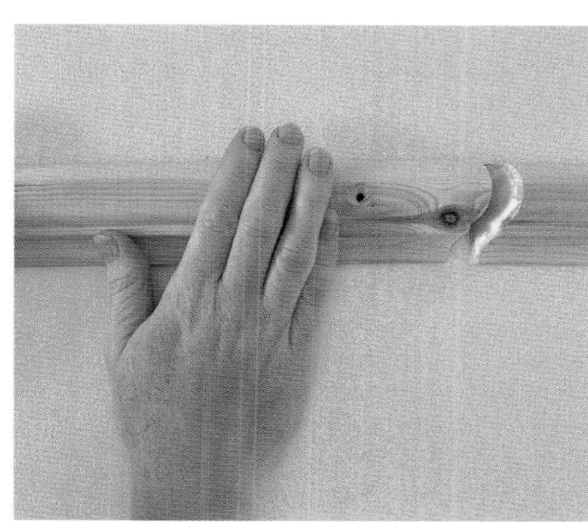

4 On long walls you will need more than one length of moulding. Avoid a gap opening up over time by cutting the ends that are to meet at a 45° angle. You can use a mitre box to do this (see page 50).

Tackling corners

1 A butt joint is the best choice at an internal corner, with the end of one rail scribed and cut to fit against the face of the next section. Draw the shape of the rail on the back of the next length, following the shape of a moulding offcut.

GLUING RAILS IN PLACE

You can fix rails to a wall by applying quick-grab adhesive and holding the moulding in place until the adhesive grips. This takes less time, but the rail cannot then be moved without damaging the plaster.

2 Use a coping saw to cut along the marked line. Sand the cut edge and make sure that it fits. Any gaps can be masked later on with wood filler.

3 Drill holes in the cut moulding, and drill and plug holes in the wall. Apply woodworking adhesive to the scribed end, place it in position and drive in the fixing screws. Remove extra adhesive with a damp cloth.

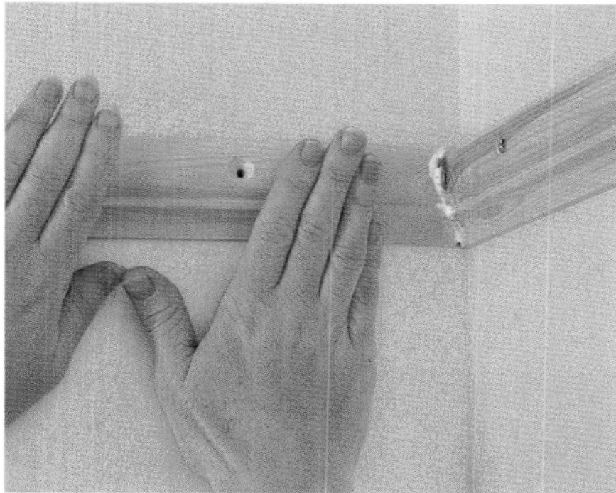

4 When taking a rail round an external corner, mitre the joint. Cut the pieces so the joint fits as closely as possible, and glue the angled pieces together as you attach the sections to the wall. If necessary, add a panel pin to the joint to secure it.

5 Make sure screw heads and nail heads are well below the surface. Cover the heads (and any gaps) with wood filler.

REMOVING A RAIL

Remove an unwanted picture rail or dado by prising it away from its backing using a mallet and an old, wide wood chisel. Start at the centre of the longest length and ease it gently away, working from both edges. Wedge between the backing and the moulding with a scrap of wood or hardboard as soon as possible.

Having removed the rail, make good any holes in the plaster or any other damage. The gap left by the rail can be difficult to disguise if the plaster above and below the rail is at different levels due to the wall having been plastered after the rail was fitted.

Putting up or replacing architraves

Architraves are strips of timber moulding used to cover a joint between woodwork and a wall, such as round a door or window frame. They can be decorative or plain.

Tools *Trimming knife; chisel; pencil; mitre saw or mitre box and tenon saw; hammer; nail punch; cartridge gun.*

Materials *Architrave moulding; scrap wood; 38mm oval wire nails; woodworking adhesive; 25mm panel pins; acrylic mastic.*

Before you start Ensure new mouldings are straight, flat and as wide as any you are replacing. If they are narrower, you will need to redecorate the wall around the door, and there will be a gap between the architrave and the skirting board. If the mouldings are wider, notch the ends of the side pieces so they fit round skirting boards.

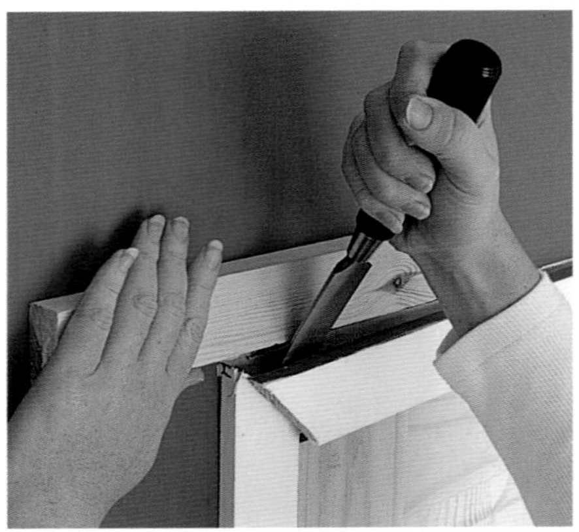

1 If you are removing an old architrave, run a knife blade between the architrave and the door frame to break the paint seal. Prise off the top section with a wide chisel while using scrap wood to protect the wall.

2 Remove the two side mouldings. Insert the blade of the chisel under a moulding from the wall edge if you can; otherwise, slide it between moulding and door frame.

3 Position a length of new moulding against the door frame, with the bottom edge of the moulding resting on the floor. Mark the position of the inside of the mitre joint on it with a pencil. Check you are sawing in the right direction, then cut the mitre, using a mitre box (page 50) and tenon saw, or a precision mitre saw.

4 Hold the moulding against the door frame, line up its inner edge with the paint line on the frame and hammer nails into the moulding. Space the nails about 450mm apart. Use a nail punch to drive the heads just below the surface. Fit the other side moulding in the same way.

PIN MITRED CORNERS

For a really thorough job, pin the mitred joints of architraves together, even though they are already glued in place. Pinning will prevent the joints from gradually opening up. This is most often a problem with door frames in stud partition walls, because the walls may move slightly if the door slams, and this loosens adhesive holding the joint in place.

5 Before fixing the top section in place, place a short length of moulding upside down across the tops of the side mouldings, and mark on it the positions of the mitre joints. Then cut the two mitres at the marks and sand the edges smooth.

6 Add a little woodworking adhesive to each end of the top section, then position the section between the side mouldings. Fix it to the door frame with two nails. Use a damp cloth to remove any visible adhesive.

FILLING THE GAPS

If plaster on the wall is uneven, there will be a gap between the architrave and the wall. Fill this gap with a flexible acrylic sealant. Fit the sealant tube into a cartridge gun and pipe a 'bead' of sealant along the joint. Obtain a smooth finish by running a wet fingertip along the sealant surface.

Removing and replacing skirting boards

An old wooden skirting board can be levered away from the wall, but this may be difficult if it has been screwed or nailed into the masonry.

Removing a skirting board

Tools *Hammer and bolster chisel; wrecking bar; thin pieces of wood for protecting the wall and for wedging. Possibly also: trimming knife; torch; hacksaw blade; screwdriver.*

Before you start Use a sharp trimming knife to cut through any wallpaper stuck to the top of the skirting board. If the top of the board is covered with plaster, chip it away carefully first.

1 Start levering at an external corner or where skirting butts against a door frame. When removing only part of the skirting, note whether the board to be removed is overlapped by another at an internal corner. If it is, remove the overlapping board first.

2 Ease the board away from the wall with a hammer and bolster chisel, until there is enough space to insert a thin piece of wood, which will protect the wall.

3 Hold the wrecking bar near its hooked end and insert the blade behind the skirting. Prise the board away from the wall, and wedge it with a piece of wood. Move along the skirting board, wedging the board as you go, and continue until the whole board is loosened.

4 When a board is difficult to loosen, wedge a gap open to look behind and check the type of fixing used.

If the fixing is a screw, probe the front of the board to find the head (it will probably be covered with filler). Unscrew it if you can, otherwise cut through it from behind with a hammer and cold chisel or hacksaw blade in a padsaw handle.

If the fixing is a large cut nail, you can pull the board away, leaving the nail behind. If you cannot prise the nail out, cut through it or break it off flush with the masonry by bending it from side to side with a series of hammer blows.

Replacing a skirting board

Plaster is rarely taken far down the wall behind skirting.

- When you are fitting new skirting, buy board of the same height as the old to avoid having to patch the plaster. To match high skirtings (Victorian, say), use square-edged board topped with architrave.
- If new skirting board is thinner than the plaster or lining above it, pack behind with an extra piece of timber to bring it out to the required thickness.
- If the plaster does reach to the floor, fix the skirting board through it into the brickwork with screws and wall plugs.

Before you start

- Coat the back of new skirting board with wood preservative to guard against rot.
- Before fitting the new skirting board, lay it flat along the floor and mark on the front the positions of any existing fixing points (see above right) so that you can nail through the marks. Fit skirting board to existing fixing points wherever this is possible.

Types of fixing points

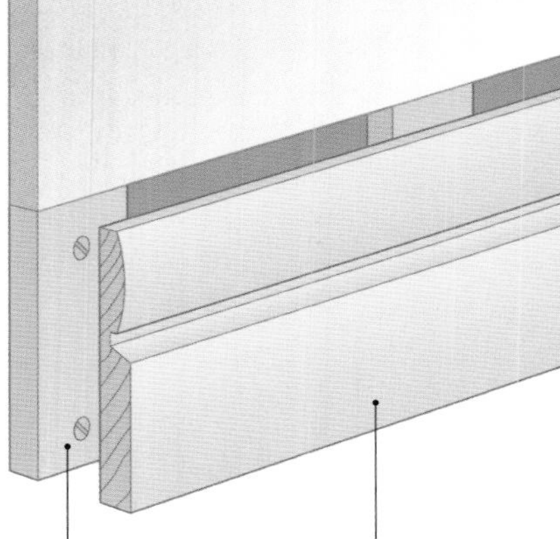

The commonest type of fixing point is a timber block. Blocks are nailed or screwed to the wall at 450–600mm intervals.

Fit new blocks if necessary, using timber treated with wood preservative. Fix the blocks with masonry nails or screws and wall plugs.

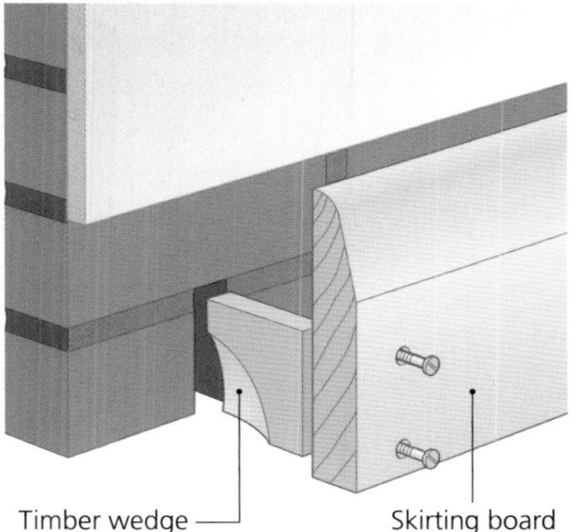

Another type of fixing point is a timber wedge. These are inserted into the mortar joints between bricks.

If a timber wedge is damaged, remove it by partially driving in a large screw, then pulling it out, together with the wedge, using a crowbar claw or claw hammer. Make and fit a new wedge.

Gluing a skirting board

Modern quick-grab adhesives are so strong that you can secure skirting boards and other mouldings with adhesive instead of using screws or masonry nails.

Apply the adhesive evenly – a zigzag pattern works well – to the back of the moulding. Press firmly against the wall and hold in position with wood offcuts while the adhesive sets. Wipe away any excess adhesive with a damp cloth.

Forming external and internal corners

Before fitting new skirting, shape the ends of the boards where there are external or internal corners.

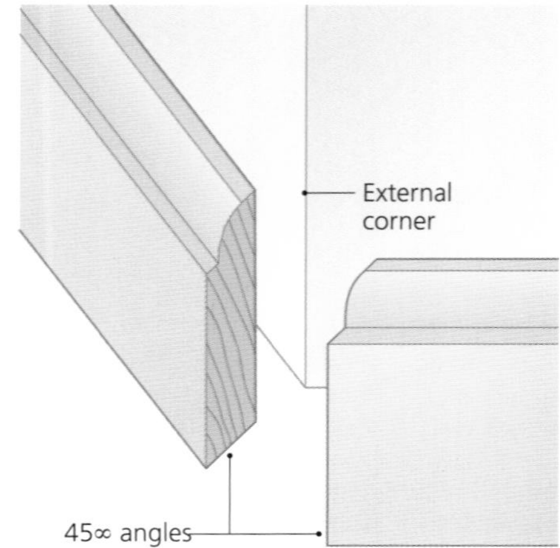

On an external corner, mitre the two boards to meet each other at an angle of 45°. On an internal corner, shape the end of one board to overlap the other, as described below.

1 Fit one board into the internal corner and temporarily nail it in position.

2 Hold the second board butted at right angles to the first and pencil its profile onto the end of the first board.

3 Remove the first board and cut away the end along the pencilled mark with a coping saw.

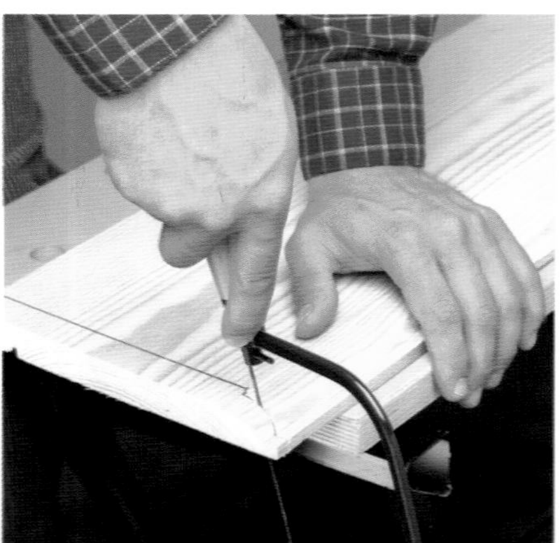

4 Refit the boards with the second, uncut board pushed into the corner and the first board lapped over it.

Joining straight lengths of skirting board

When joining two straight lengths of skirting board, do not make straight butt joints, which are impossible to hide. Instead, make a scarf joint by cutting the two ends at 45° angles.

Try to position the join where it will not be seen – behind furniture, for instance.

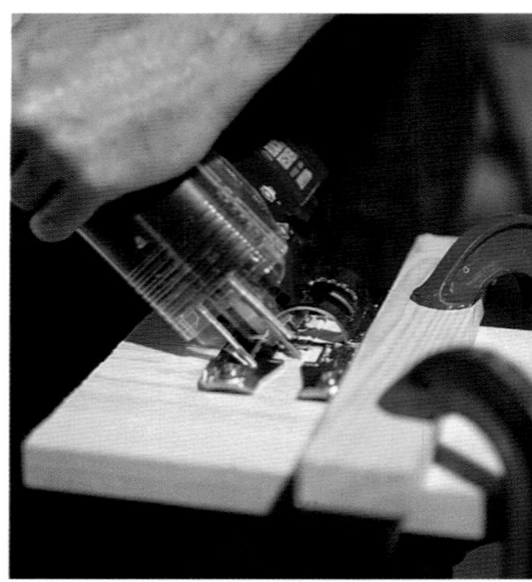

1 Make each joint with matching 45° cuts using a jigsaw with an adjustable sole plate.

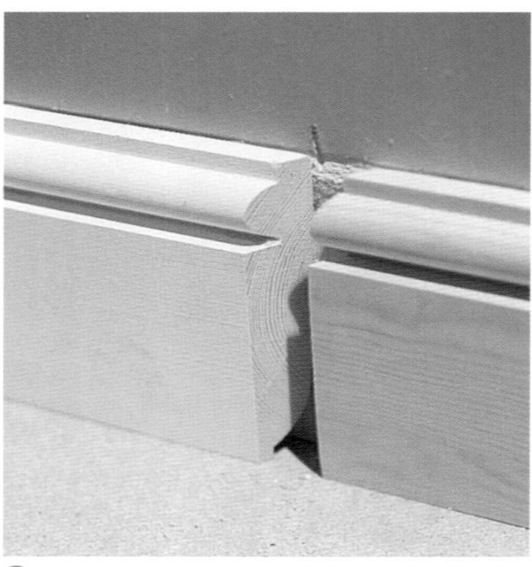

2 Fix one length of skirting board in place then position and fix the other. Apply woodworking adhesive to the cut ends and secure the joint with angled pins.

Fixing skirting to a hollow wall

Skirting board fitted to a hollow wall – a partition or a dry-lined wall – is fixed to the vertical studs and the sole plate of the framing. Locate the studs using a stud detector (page 34). Refit the board using 65mm oval nails.

Repairing moulding on a skirting board

It may be impossible to buy matching moulding to repair a damaged section of skirting board (or picture rail) in an old house. You may be able to have a similar moulding cut to order by a timber merchant. Or you can do the job yourself by cutting a matching piece with a router.

Where a small section of ornate moulding is damaged or missing, take an impression from a sound piece by pressing model-casting compound against it. Fill this mould with car-body filler. Smooth the cast and glue in place.

GAPS BELOW THE SKIRTING

A regular gap of about 5mm between the skirting board and the floor can be very useful if you want to push fitted carpet or vinyl flooring beneath it. But if uneven gaps occur below newly fitted skirting because the floor is not true, the skirting can be scribed to the floor using the technique described on page 185 for worktops, by running a thin wood block along the floor. Support the skirting so its top is horizontal and the block just covers the largest gap. Alternatively, nail quadrant or scotia moulding to the bottom of the skirting against the floor.

Do not nail moulding to the floorboards, as these expand and contract more than the skirting, and another gap could open up.

Hanging pictures and mirrors

Pictures and mirrors bring life and light into a room. It's important to use fixings strong enough to bear the weight of the item.

Lightweight or medium-weight items, including small framed mirrors, can be hung from a pin-type picture hook, driven into the wall with a hammer. Make sure the plaster is sound.

A heavy or wide picture should be fixed with two hooks positioned near the ends of the cord rather than from one central hook. Alternatively, it can be hung from a round-head screw fitted into a wall plug, or hung on battens (page 181).

When you are hanging a mirror that is heavy, use mirror chain rather than picture wire or cord.

Positioning a picture

Because of the tension on a picture cord, it is difficult to judge the right spot to fix the supporting hook if you want the top of the picture to be set at a particular level and the cord to be out of sight.

1 Hold the picture against the wall exactly where you want it to hang and lightly mark on the wall the positions of the top corners. Make another pencil mark in the centre of the top edge.

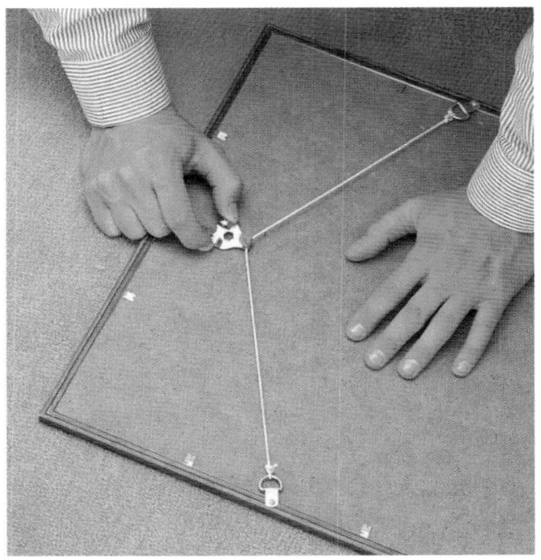

2 Lay the picture on its face, mark the top centre, and use the hook to pull the cord towards the mark until it is tight.

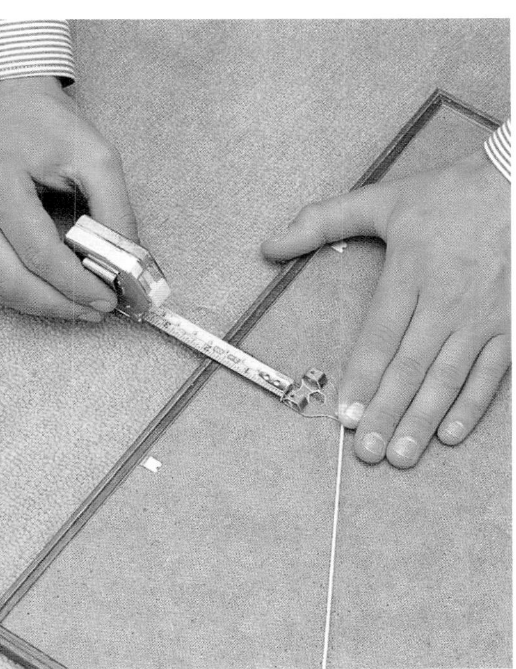

3 Measure the distance between the top of the hook and the top of the picture frame.

4 Measure down from the central pencil mark the required distance between the top of the hook and the top of the frame. Mark the spot and hammer the hook into the wall with its top against the mark.

Hanging a heavy picture on battens

Interlocking battens can be used to support a heavy picture. The battens are both cut from one piece of wood. One half is fixed to the wall, the other across the frame.

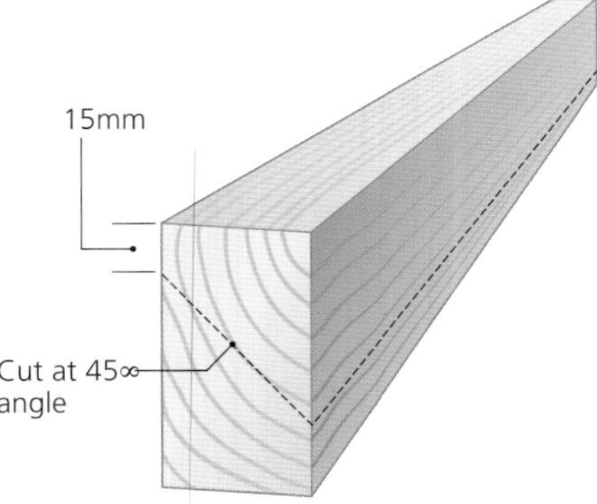

1 Use a piece of timber about 50mm by 20mm and cut it slightly shorter than the picture width. Mark a line along one face, 15mm from the edge. Cut along the line with a circular saw at a 45° angle towards the batten centre.

2 Screw one piece of batten to the back of the frame about a third of its height from the top, with the point of the angle on the outside pointing downwards.

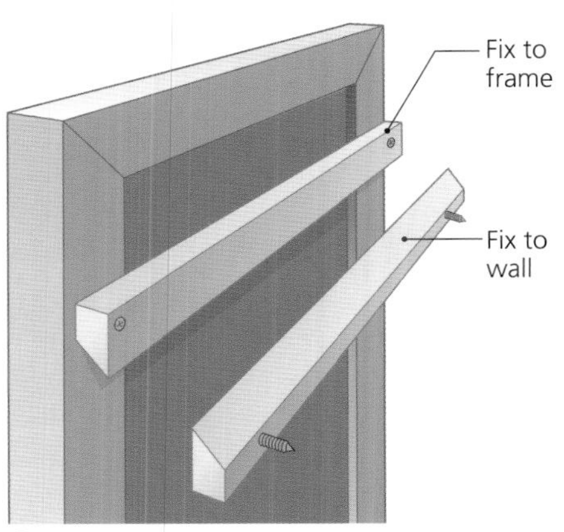

3 Screw the other piece of batten to the wall with the point of the angle uppermost and away from the wall.

4 Hook the frame batten over the batten on the wall.

Using sliding mirror clips

Unframed mirrors with holes ready drilled are fixed using mirror screws (see right). For mirrors without screw holes, use mirror clips: two fixed clips to support the bottom and two sliding clips at the top. On large mirrors, use three clips top and bottom and, on high mirrors, one or two sliding clips on each side as well.

1 Use a spirit level and straight-edge to mark where you want the bottom of the mirror to lie, then hold the mirror in position and lightly mark all four corner positions and the top edge.

2 Drill holes for the bottom clips about 50mm in from the corners. Fit the clips firmly and be sure to use the plastic washers around the screw heads to cushion the back of the mirror. The top clips are also fitted about 50mm in from the top corners. Before drilling, make sure you have allowed for the distance from the top of the clip to the top of its screw slot.

3 When you secure the top clip, position the screw at the base of the slot leaving just enough play for the clip to slide when it is pushed. Then fit the mirror into the bottom clips and hold it in position while you slide the top clips down to grip the mirror.

Using mirror screws

If you are using screws, buy 4mm mirror screws with domed chrome covers that screw into the head. Be sure to use plastic spacer washers between the back of the mirror and the wall. This allows for any slight unevenness in the wall surface, and lets air circulate behind the mirror reducing the risk of condensation.

Planning a new kitchen

The kitchen is one of the most-used rooms in the house, so if you intend to replace yours it is worth spending time planning the content and layout of your new space.

Start by drawing up a wish list of all the things you would like to incorporate and try to plan around those. Sketch out a scale plan of the room on graph paper and draw in where you would like the oven, fridge and other key appliances to go, then fit the other cabinets around this.

Don't plan your kitchen to fit exactly between two walls. It will be much easier to fit if you allow for a little tolerance at either end – walls are seldom completely flat and it is very difficult to cut down a unit by a tiny amount in order to squeeze it into a very tight space.

Planning the work

- Solid flooring, such as stone or ceramic tiles, should be fitted before the units. This is the best way to achieve a good finish, but does mean that you pay for flooring you never see, underneath the units. Vinyl can be laid after the units and tucked under the plinths at their base.
- Consider adding halogen spots or strip lights beneath wall units to illuminate the work surface. Plan the wiring before you install the units if you want the lights to run from a single switch on the main lighting circuit.
- Run any cables or pipes to their new position before you start fitting units, when you have clear access to all the walls and the floor.
- Venting extractor fans must be fitted with ducting leading to an external wall. If the ducting is more than 5m long, the fan is unlikely to be powerful enough to expel any air. In this case, choose a recirculating model, which does not need venting to the outdoors.
- Most base units are 570mm from front to back and standard worktops are 600mm, so you get an overhang of 30mm – or slightly less after you have shaped (scribed) the back of the worktop to an uneven wall.

If a worktop finishes at a 'free' end (i.e. not a wall or a tall unit or appliance), you can have a matching overhang – or cut the worktop to be flush with the unit's side.

HELPFUL TIP

If you are fitting worktops in a U shape (on three walls), try to arrange the joins so that you do not have a complete length of worktop along the central wall. Exact worktop fitting between two end walls is not easy.

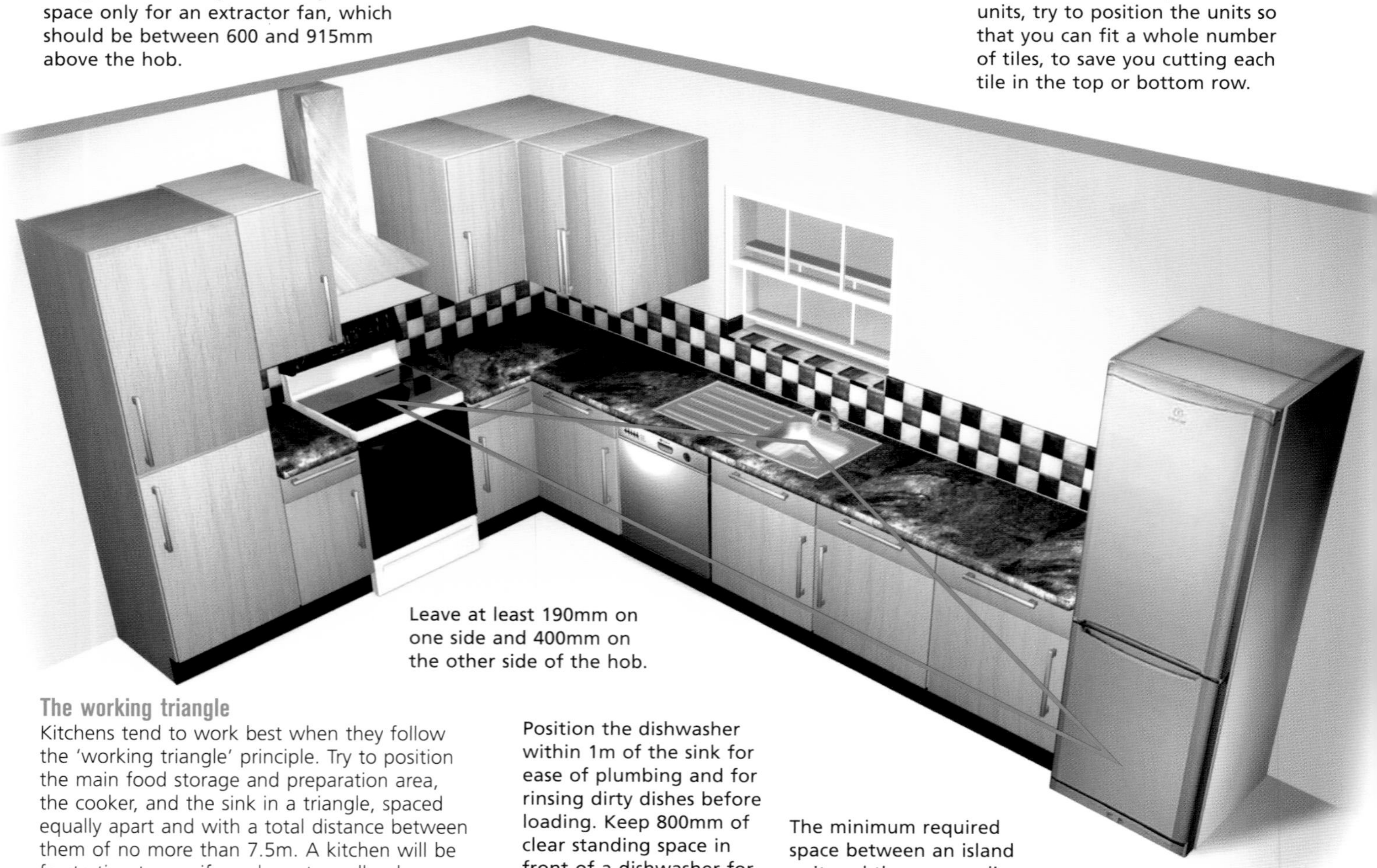

There must be at least 600mm directly above a hob, although it is best to avoid siting units here if you can. Try to use this space only for an extractor fan, which should be between 600 and 915mm above the hob.

Keep a minimum of 460mm between the worktop and the base of the wall units.

Allow at least 450mm on one side and 600mm on the other side of the sink to give room for stacking clean and dirty pans when washing up.

If you plan to tile the splashback between the worktop and the units, try to position the units so that you can fit a whole number of tiles, to save you cutting each tile in the top or bottom row.

Leave at least 190mm on one side and 400mm on the other side of the hob.

The working triangle

Kitchens tend to work best when they follow the 'working triangle' principle. Try to position the main food storage and preparation area, the cooker, and the sink in a triangle, spaced equally apart and with a total distance between them of no more than 7.5m. A kitchen will be frustrating to use if you have to walk a long way between the fridge and the cooker or double back time and again every time you so much as make a cup of tea.

Position the dishwasher within 1m of the sink for ease of plumbing and for rinsing dirty dishes before loading. Keep 800mm of clear standing space in front of a dishwasher for easy loading.

The minimum required space between an island unit and the surrounding units is 1.2m, so that cupboard doors on both sides can be open at once.

Next to the opening side of the fridge, try to leave at least 400m of worktop space.

Installing kitchen units

A methodical approach is essential when fitting a new kitchen. Take the job one step at a time and enlist some help with lifting and positioning.

Tools *Spirit level; tape measure; power drill and drill bits; screwdrivers; jigsaw; hammer; cramps.*

Materials *Kitchen units; work surface; sink; wall plugs.*

Assembling the units

Put the cabinets together one at a time, to avoid muddling parts. All the bits might look the same, but there are often subtle differences from unit to unit. Assemble and fit the wall units before the base units; this will give you better access to the wall area.

1 Take all the components out of the box and check them against the list of contents. If anything is missing, check the box and all the packaging again.

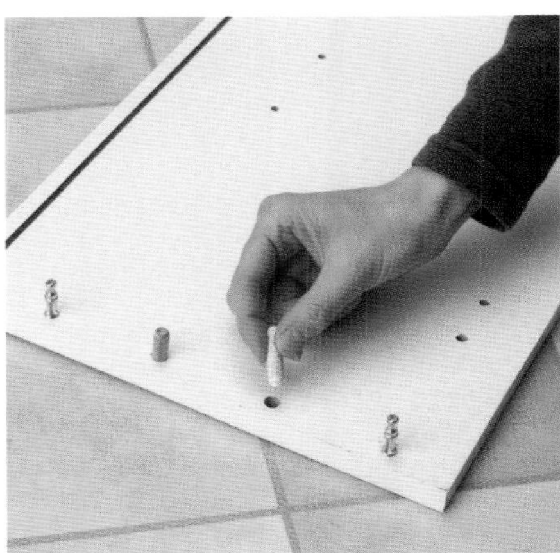

2 Screw or hammer in the fixings to the inside of the side panels. This unit is assembled using wooden dowels and cam and screw fixings (pages 67 and 169).

3 If the wall unit is to be hung from brackets, fit the cupboard section of the bracket now. Wall units are assembled fully and then screwed directly to the wall.

4 Slot the cam part of the cam and screw fixing into the adjacent panel and then slide it into place, tapping it down gently if necessary to get a tight fit.

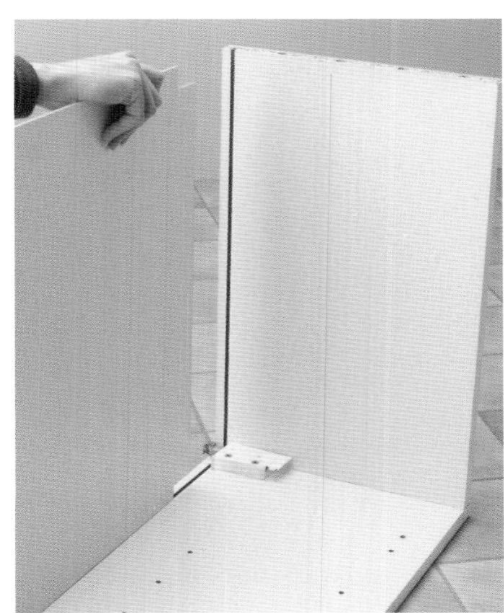

5 Slide the back panel into place (the right way round!) then complete the assembly of the other two panels.

HELPFUL TIP

Whatever the instructions might say, leave fitting the wall unit doors until they are all on the wall. Fitting them first makes installation much more difficult and they could be damaged.

Hanging wall units

1 The position of wall units is determined by any tall units you have – all the cupboard tops should line up. Work out the height (the instructions may tell you), measure up from the floor and make a mark on the wall for the bottom of a normal-height wall unit. Use a spirit level or a laser level to transfer this mark to all the walls where units are to be fitted.

2 If your wall units are to be screwed directly to the wall, fix a temporary batten to the wall at this level, to help to support the units while you fix them in place.

3 If your units hang from brackets, hold the wall-mounted part of the bracket in place against the cupboard-mounted part and measure from the bottom of the cupboard to the base of the bracket. Transfer this measurement to the wall.

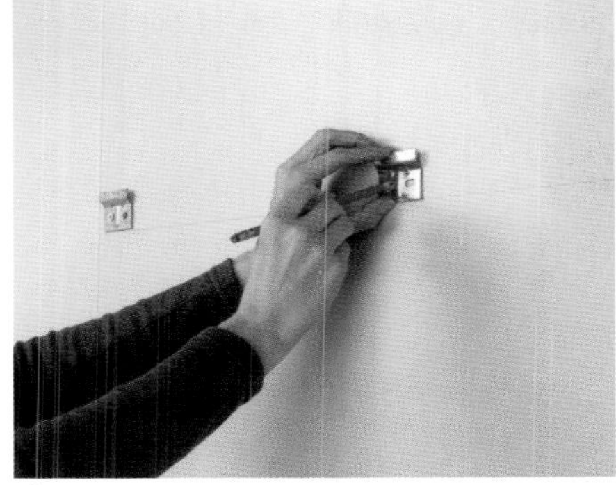

4 Starting with a corner unit if you have one, fix the first wall-plate in position then measure across the cupboard and then the wall to mark the position for the second.

5 Hang the cupboard on the brackets, check that it is level horizontally and vertically then tighten the brackets from inside to secure the unit in place.

6 Fix the two-part hinges to the cupboard and door; then hang the door and adjust the hinges as necessary for a good fit.

FIXING WALL UNITS TO STUD PARTITION WALLS

You should not rely on hollow wall fixings to secure kitchen wall units in place on stud partition or timber-framed walls. Fit a timber batten to the studs to take the load.

Mark a line on the wall at the height of the fixing screws and then two more lines above and below this to mark the edges of a 25mm thick 100mm wide batten (check its actual width first). Cut out the plasterboard between the lines using a padsaw, use a router to recess the studs to exactly the thickness of the batten, and then screw the batten to the studs.

Installing base units

As with wall units, start fitting the base units in a corner and work out from there.

1 Set the first unit in position. Set the spirit level on top of the cupboard and check it is level in each direction.

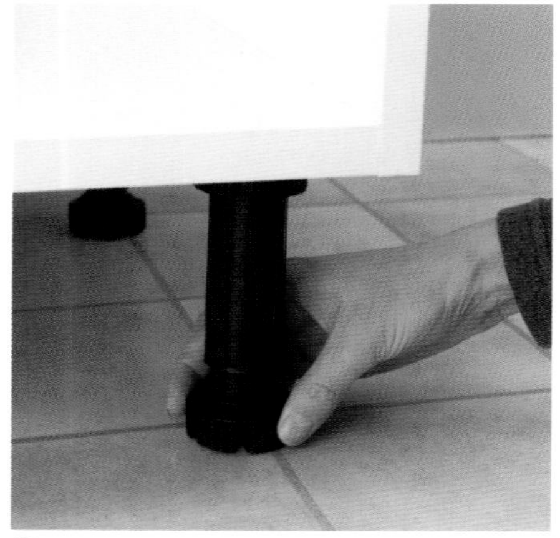

2 Adjust the leg heights until the cupboard is roughly level. Don't spend too long on it at this stage. You will need to level each complete run when all the units are in place.

3 Position the next cupboard in the run, using clamps to hold the units together while you adjust their levels.

4 Check the level of all the units around the room, adjusting their heights with the legs until they are all aligned.

SAFETY TIP

Never extend the cupboard legs to their full height, as they will lose their strength. If your floor is very uneven, pack pieces of wood beneath the legs to get the units roughly level and then use the legs for fine adjustments.

5 Screw the units back to the wall using brackets attached to the side panels or by screwing through the back panel, if this is adjacent to the wall. Then screw the units to one another, through the side panels using special connector bolts (which you can buy if not supplied with the units).

6 Where two cupboards join in a corner, you will need to fit a corner post. Position this on the side panel of one of the cupboards, 2–3mm back from the front edge to avoid the door fouling on it when it opens.

7 Position the adjacent cupboard then drill through the cupboard side into the corner post and screw through the cupboard side panel to fix it.

8 Fix handles to the cupboard doors, then hang the doors on their respective cupboards, using the adjuster screws on each hinge to get a good fit. Make sure that all the doors are flush with one another when closed and hang squarely at the same height.

9 Glue or screw the fixing clips to the inner face of the plinth that will run beneath the cupboards. Take care to position the clips to match the position of the cupboard legs they will clip onto. Fit the plinths in place.

Fitting worktops and inset sinks

The worktops in your kitchen are one of the most prominent features, so it is important to fit them as carefully and professionally as possible.

Tools *Jigsaw; plane; try square; tape measure; pencil; pair of saw horses or workbenches; screwdriver.*

Materials *Kitchen worktop; silicone sealant; PVA adhesive; contact adhesive; inset sink.*

Before you start Always measure twice and cut once when fitting a length of worktop. Cut the surface too short and you will have made an expensive mistake. Where a worktop meets an end wall at a corner, use a sliding bevel to check the angle of the corner and transfer it to the worktop before cutting – it may not be 90°. The long lengths are heavy and cumbersome, so you will need help with manoeuvring them for cutting and lifting them into place.

Fitting the worktop

1 Set the worktop on top of the base units and push it against the wall. If one end is into a corner, make sure that it is pushed up against this too.

2 Adjust the worktop until there is an even overhang at the front; this will be determined by any high spots on the wall.

3 Clamp the worktop in place, so that it does not move while you are scribing it with a block of wood or a pair of compasses as described right. Apply a strip of masking tape all along the back edge of the worktop so that the pencil line will show.

4 Lift the worktop onto a pair of saw horses or two workbenches – it will be too long to rest securely on just one bench – and use a rasp, a Surform or a small plane to shape the worktop to the marked line. If there is more than a few millimetres to remove, use a jigsaw, fitted with a downward-cutting blade to cut along your line before final shaping.

5 If the worktop finishes at a 'free' unit, mark a pencil line on the underside along the unit edge and then a second cutting line the width of the required end overhang (unless it is to be flush). Cut to the line and use a strip of matching melamine trim to cover the exposed core on the cut end. Glue it in place with contact adhesive before trimming it back with a sharp file. File towards the worktop to avoid lifting the stuck-on lipping. Some worktops come with ready-glued iron-on edging strips.

FINISHING OFF

Imperfect joins along the back of a worktop can be disguised by tiles or by moulding, fixed in the angle between the worktop and the wall and finished with a bead of sealant. Wood mouldings look particularly effective as a finishing touch to a wooden worktop.

6 Drill pilot holes in the underside of the worktop, taking care not to drill too deeply and come through the surface, and drive in 18mm long screws through the top rails of the base units to fix the worktop in place.

Alternatively Use the brackets supplied with the kitchen units or joint blocks as shown and described on page 67.

7 If worktops go around a corner use a joining strip to suit the worktop. Scribe this second section to the wall as before. Then screw the joining strip to the second length of worktop, butt it up to the first and secure it in place from below.

Fitting the sink

1 Place the upturned sink on the worktop. Sinks are sometimes handed if taps are to be positioned to one side or the other, in which case the sink may be supplied with a template for marking cutouts.

2 Carefully measure to ensure that the cut out will fall inside the face and end panels of the cupboard beneath, that the basin will not foul on any part of the cupboard and that the sink is parallel to the front of the worktop.

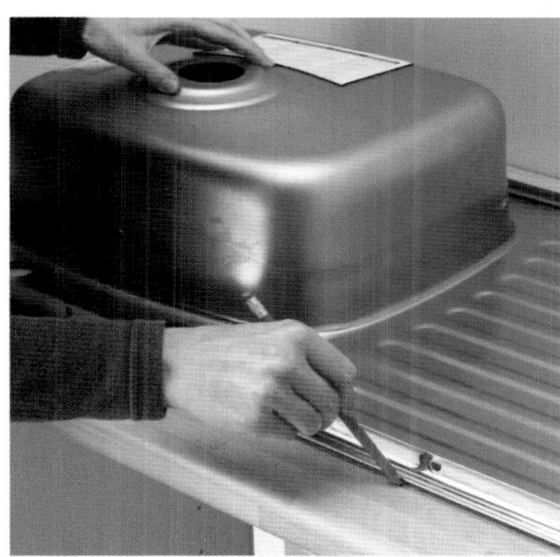

3 Use a pencil to mark the outline on the worktop.

HELPFUL TIP

Some inset sinks are supplied with a separate rubber gasket, which is sandwiched between the sink and worktop to create a water-tight seal.

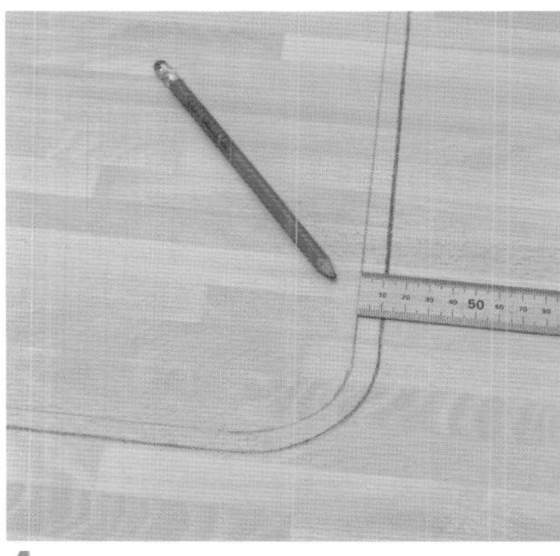

4 Copy this line 10mm in, to leave a 10mm lip for the sink to rest on. Drill a hole at each corner of the cutout, large enough for a jigsaw blade, and cut out the waste using a downward-cutting blade.

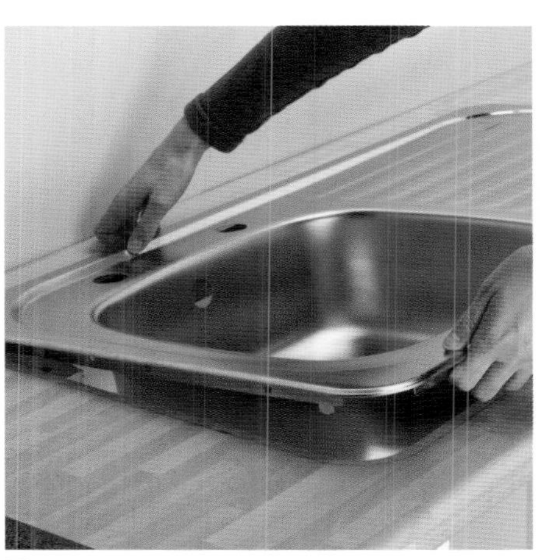

5 Run a bead of silicone mastic around the underside lip of the sink (or fit the gasket) before dropping it into place. Connect an earth wire to the tag (see page 361).

SCRIBING THE LINE OF AN UNEVEN WALL

Scribing is a very useful technique for achieving a neat finish when butting a worktop against a wall that is not completely flat.

Position the worktop against the wall, making sure that it is square and has an even overhang all the way along the front edge. Hold a thin block of wood against the wall and press a pencil up to it. Move the block of wood and pencil together along the wall, tracing the line of any lumps and bumps in the wall onto the top of the worktop. The wood should be the same size as (or slightly larger than) the largest gap between worktop and wall.

Using compasses

A pair of school compasses is a useful tool for scribing a line on a worktop. As with using a block of wood, set the worktop against the wall with an equal overhang for all units and set the compasses to the largest gap (or more if you want to reduce the amount that the worktop overhangs the units). Keep the compasses at right angles to the wall, running the point along the wall so that the pencil draws a line all along the masking tape on the back of the worktop.

After scribing the back of the worktop, cut or shape it as described in Step 4 (left) and seal all cut surfaces with polyurethane varnish.

6 Use the clips supplied with the sink to secure it from inside the cupboard.

7 Wipe off any excess silicone sealant that has squeezed out and connect up the plumbing (see page 361).

Doors

Doors and windows 6

Windows

Curing faults in doors

Most faults in doors can be cured quite easily. For some jobs you may need another person to help you, or to steady the door while you work on it.

Door binding along one side

Doors often bind (stick) in their frames because regular repainting causes a build-up of paint on the edge of the door and on the frame.

1 Strip off the paint. Do this mechanically to avoid damaging the finish on the door faces. Use either a power sander or a Surform planer file.

2 Smooth the stripped surfaces with glasspaper and check that the door opens and closes easily.

3 There should be a slight gap between the edge of the door and the frame. To check for this, run a thin knife blade all round the edge of the door when it is closed. Where the gap is insufficient, strip and then plane that edge of the door. You may have to take the door off its hinges, and perhaps remove locks and latches.

4 Prime and paint the stripped edges of the door. Then let the paint dry before closing the door.

Door binding at the bottom

If an external door binds at its lower corners, the problem is often caused by moisture being absorbed through an unpainted bottom edge.

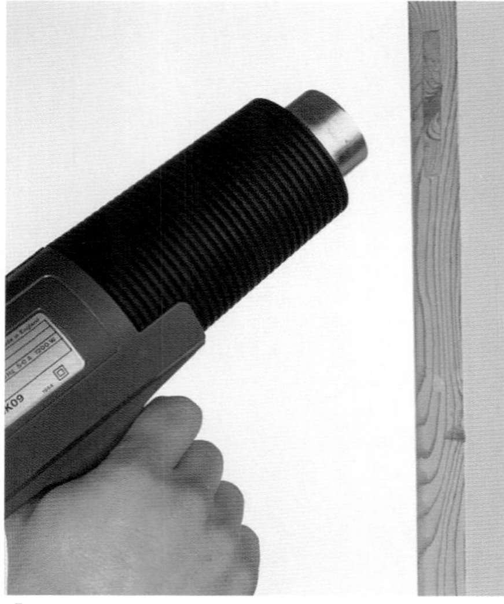

1 Take the door off its hinges and dry the bare wood thoroughly with a hot-air gun.

2 If the binding is severe, stand the door on one of its long edges between your legs and use a rasp, a Surform planer file or a sharp plane to remove wood from the bottom edge. Mark a line to work to and then work from the edge to the middle, turn the door over and work towards the middle from the other edge. Sand any rough surfaces with glass paper wrapped around a sanding block.

3 Seal the bare edge with two coats of quick-drying wood primer. Re-hang the door when the primer is touch-dry. Painting is unnecessary as the edge is out of sight.

Door binding at the top

You may be able to plane the top edge of a door (which is often unpainted) without taking it off its hinges. Prop it open with wedges while you work from a stepladder. Otherwise take it off its hinges and plane the whole edge as in step 2 above.

Door squeaks

Oil the hinge pins with an aerosol lubricant. Work the door backwards and forwards a few times to get the lubricant into the hinge, then wipe away any surplus with kitchen roll.

With rising butt hinges, lift the open door off the hinge pins and lightly smear them with grease or petroleum jelly. Wipe away the surplus after re-hanging the door.

Door tends to slam

The best solution for a slamming door is to fit a door closer, which slows down the speed at which the door shuts.

1 A template is always supplied with a door closer. Decide whether you want the door to open to 100° (straight into the room) or 180° (flat back to the hinge wall), and use a bradawl or a pencil to mark through the appropriate template spots.

2 Drill pilot holes and screw the door closer onto the door.

3 With the door closer fitted to the door, you can now mark the position of the pivot arm on the door architrave. Chisel out a recess and screw it in position.

4 Fix the pivot arm to the body of the closer and turn the adjusting screws so that the door shuts smoothly and slowly without slamming.

Door panels split

Sometimes splits develop in the panels of old doors. The solution depends on whether the door is painted or varnished.

Painted door

On a painted door, fill the crack with a wood filler and paint over it.

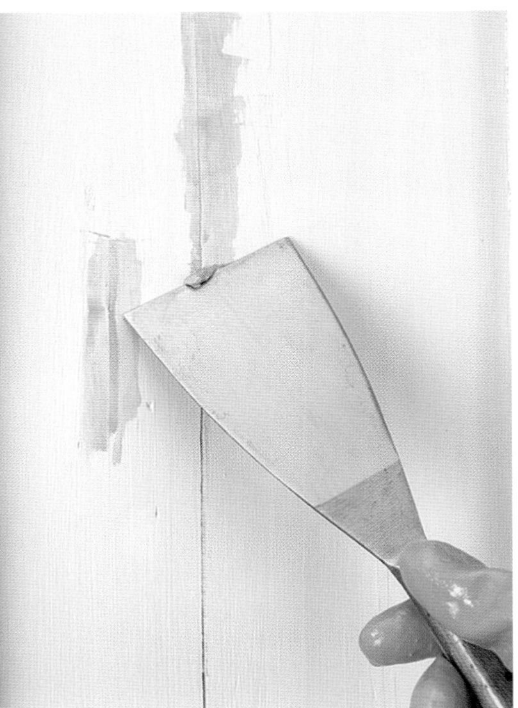

Natural wood door

On a varnished door where the filler will show, drive dowels into the edge of the door to press against the edges of the panel and close the crack.

1 First clean out old varnish or filler from the crack with a sharp knife.

2 Drill two or three 8mm diameter holes through the edge of the door to line up with the near edge of the panel. Measure the thickness of the door stile and mark the drill bit with a piece of tape to act as a depth stop.

3 Cut some 8mm dowels about 20mm longer than the width of the stiles.

4 Squirt PVA wood adhesive into the crack in the panel and into the holes in the stile. Drive the dowels into the holes so they press against the edge of the panel and close the crack.

5 Wipe off excess adhesive with a damp cloth. Leave the protruding dowel until the glue has set, then trim it off flush with the door edge. Smooth the cut end with abrasive paper.

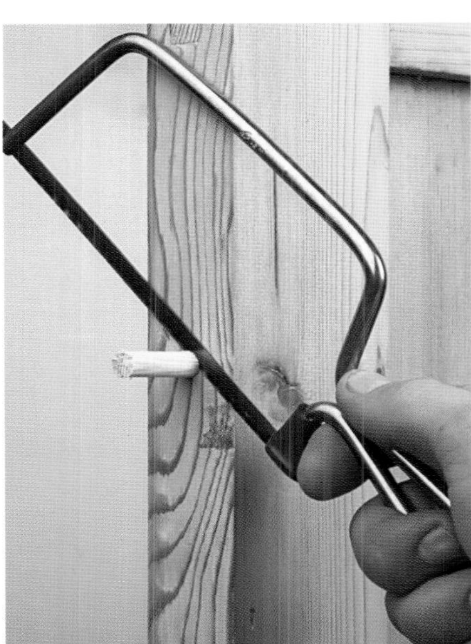

Latch will not engage

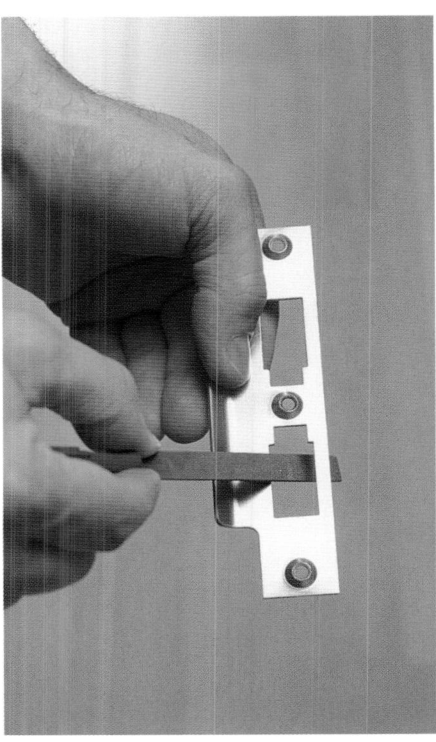

If a door sags or warps a little, the latch bolt will be out of alignment with the striking plate. First check where the latch bolt is fouling the striking plate – it could be at the bottom or at one edge. You can correct a small misalignment by unscrewing the plate and enlarging its cut-out with a small metal file.

Otherwise, remove the striking plate and re-fix it a little lower down the frame or, for a warped door, a little further away from the door stop.Use a sharp chisel and a mallet to extend the recess in which it fits. If the plate has to be moved only a small distance, drill out the old screw holes and hammer in glued dowels. Drill new pilot holes for the fixing screws.

Lock stiff to turn

1 Spray aerosol lubricant into a surface-mounted lock using the applicator tube provided. Squirt the lubricant through the latch and bolt holes and through the keyhole.

2 If this is not sufficient, remove the lock from the door, take off one side of the case, and lightly grease the mechanism. Before starting work, note the positions of the components so they can be put back if they become displaced.

Do not use oil or aerosol lubricants in Yale-type cylinder locks; they attract grit. Instead puff graphite powder or PTFE dry powder lubricant into the keyhole.

Door frame loose

Slamming a door often leads to the frame becoming loose. Make new fixings with three hammer-in fixings or frame fixers (see page 158). These come supplied with their own screws and the length you need is the thickness of the frame plus at least 60mm to go into the wall.

1 Using a masonry bit, drill through the frame and into the wall behind it to the required depth.

2 Hammer the screw and plug into the hole. Tighten with a screwdriver until the screw head is flush with the frame.

Door hard to close

A door that is difficult to close, and tends to spring open, is said to be hinge-bound. The problem is usually caused by hinge recesses cut too deep in either the door edge or in the frame. When correctly fitted, the hinge flaps should be flush with the surface of the wood.

1 Open the door fully and then put a wedge under it.

2 Clear any paint from the slots in the hinge screws, and remove the screws.

3 Get someone to steady the door while you lever the hinge flap out of its recess. Pack out the recess with one or more pieces of cardboard until the hinge is flush with the wood surface, then replace the screws. Use new screws if you damaged the slots of the old ones.

Protruding screw heads

Hinges may bind because the screws have been put in askew, or because their heads are too large to fit flush in the countersinks in the hinge flaps.

Remove the offending screws and replace them with screws with smaller heads. If they will not tighten, pack out the holes with glued-in matches.

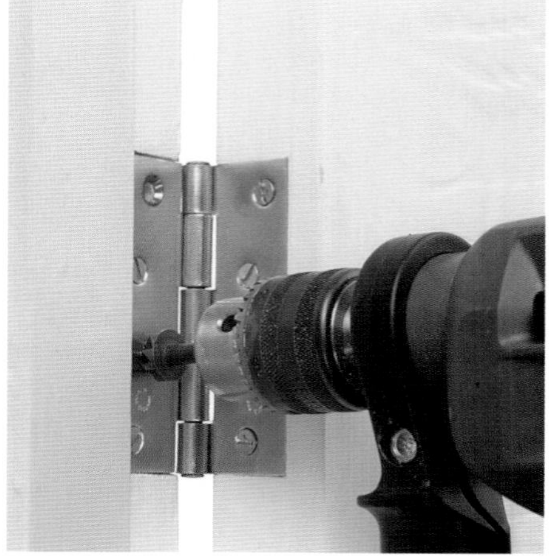

Alternatively Deepen the countersinks in the hinge flaps so that the screw heads will be flush with the surface. Use a high-speed-steel countersink bit.

If the screws were originally set in askew, drill out and plug the old screw holes with dowels (see step 1 below) and drill new pilot holes for the screws.

Badly placed hinge flaps

Binding can also be caused by hinge flaps that are set into the frame too near to the door stop. As the door is closed, the face of the door presses against the stop.

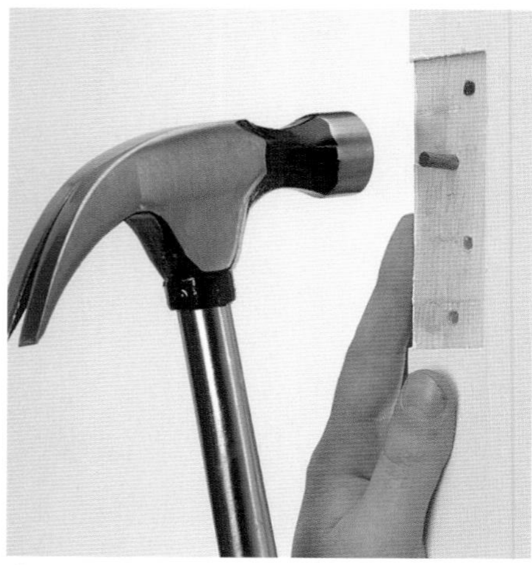

1 Remove the hinges, drill out the old screw holes and plug them with glued dowels. Chisel the dowel ends off flush with the recess.

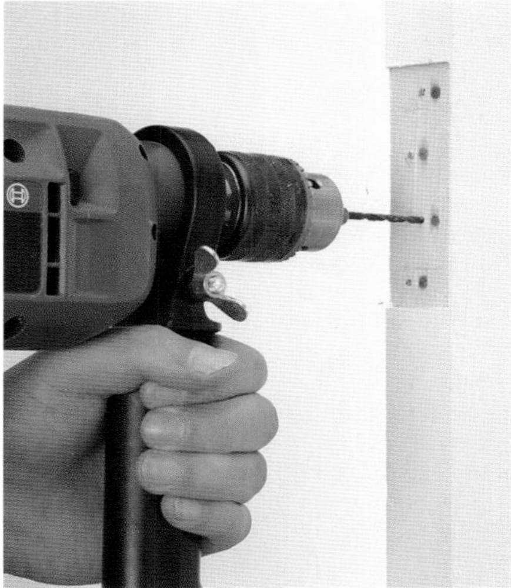

2 Drill new fixing holes so that the hinge is farther away from the door stop. The hinge pin should be just clear of the door edge. Fill the resulting gaps beside the repositioned hinges with wood filler.

Alternatively On an internal door, it may be easier to prise off and reposition the door stop, which is usually a separate piece of wood pinned to the door frame.

Door is rotting

If exterior doors have not been protected with paint or varnish, wet rot may set in, especially near the bottom and at joints. You can repair minor damage with wood hardener and high-performance exterior wood filler.

1 Chisel away the rotten wood and use a hot-air gun to dry the exposed bare wood.

2 Treat the area with the wood hardener. When this has soaked in and dried, fill the recess with the filler. Build it up slightly above the surface, and sand it flat when it has hardened.

3 Repaint the door to disguise the repair.

Frame is rotting

External door frames often rot near the sill. The only satisfactory repair is to insert a new piece of timber. Use a general-purpose saw: this is a bit like a small panel saw, but the angle between blade and handle can be adjusted and the rigid blade has strong teeth, which will not be blunted if they hit metal (a nail, say) or masonry.

1 Probe the wood with a sharp knife to reveal where the soft, rotten section ends. Make a 45° downward cut into the frame about 75mm above this point.

2 Prise the rotten part away from the wall. Its bottom end was probably tenon-jointed into the hardwood sill.

3 Cut a length of new wood to fit the gap, sloping one end to align with the saw cut. Test its fit and adjust it as necessary.

The old frame may have a door stop machined into it. Make a matching section from two or more pieces of wood glued and cramped together.

4 When the new section is a good fit, treat all its surfaces with clear wood preservative. Drill and countersink holes in it, and mark the fixing positions on the wall through these holes. Drill and plug the wall and screw the section in place.

5 Where the old and new frame section join, drill 8mm holes through the joint at right angles to it. Smear glue on 8mm hardwood dowels and hammer them into the holes.

6 Trim the dowels flush with the surface when the glue has dried. Prime and paint the repair.

Door sags

When the bottom corner of the door rubs on the floor, the cause is either faulty hinges or loose joints in the door. Partly open the door and lift it by the handle to see if there is movement at the hinges or joints.

Faulty hinges

If the hinge screws are loose, try tightening them. If they will not hold, remove them, drill out the screw holes and plug them with glued dowels. Drill new pilot holes and refit the screws.

If the movement is in the knuckle of the hinge due to a worn hinge pin, the only cure is to fit new hinges (page 192). The hinges may not be large enough to support the weight of the door. In this case fit larger, stronger hinges, and add a third hinge midway between them if you are working on an exterior front door.

Loose door joints

If the problem is that corner joints on a framed door are loose, glue and cramp them back into place.

1 Take the door off its hinges, and try to prise the loose joints apart.

2 Squirt woodworking adhesive into the joints and cramp them closed with sash cramps. Be sure to check that the door frame is square.

3 On the edge of the door, drive small wooden wedges into the ends of the tenons in order to prevent the joints from opening up again.

4 Drill through the face of the door and the tenon, and drive a glued dowel into the hole to lock the tenon in place.

5 Trim off the dowels and wedges flush with the surface of the door.

How to hang a front or back door

When buying a new door, measure the height and width of the frame and get a door that is either the right size or slightly too big. An exterior door is heavy, so get someone to help you if you can.

Panelled doors can have up to 20mm removed all round to fit, but most flush doors should have no more than about 10mm planed away, otherwise they may be seriously weakened.

Flush doors contain wooden blocks for fitting hinges and locks; their positions are marked on the edges of the door. When fitting the hinges and locks, note where the blocks are, as they will affect the way round that the door is placed in the frame. If you want to reverse the face of the door, most are reversible top to bottom.

You will need three butt hinges for an exterior door either 75mm or 100mm long. The job will be simpler if you choose a size to fit existing hinge recesses on the frame.

If a flush door is being fitted, buy pressed-steel cranked butt hinges (above right). A panelled door, which is heavier, requires cast butt hinges.

Tools *Pencil; tape measure; try square; marking gauge; 19mm or 25mm chisel; mallet; plane; panel or tenon saw; trimming knife; drill and twist bits; screwdriver; folding workbench.*

Materials *Exterior door; three hinges; screws to fit (check that the heads fit fully into the countersunk holes on the hinge).*

1 Remove the old door carefully, without damaging the hinge recesses on the frame. Put pieces of wood under the door to take the weight while you remove the screws, and get someone to hold it.

2 New panelled doors are sometimes protected with strips of timber or cork pads at the edges; remove these by prising them off with a broad scraper blade.

REMOVING STUBBORN SCREWS

When you remove your old door, the hinge screws may be difficult to get out. Scrape off any paint, particularly out of the slots. If a screw still will not shift, put a screwdriver in the slot and hit it with a mallet.

Choosing hinges to hang a door

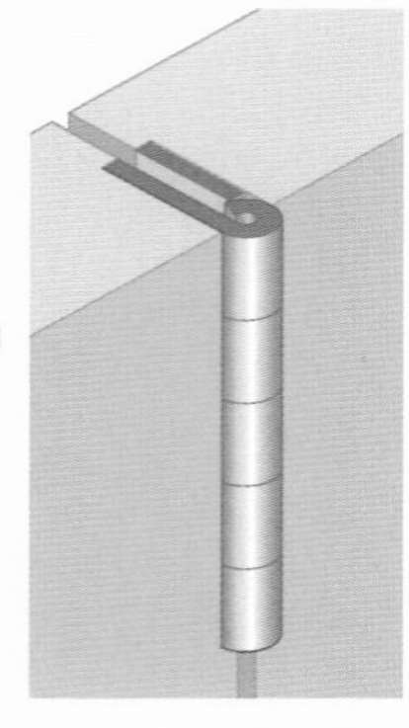

Cast butt hinge Doors usually have butt hinges – two rectangular flaps (called leaves) joined by a pin running through an interlocking knuckle. Heavy exterior doors have cast hinges 75mm or 100mm long. The centre of the knuckle is fitted in line with the face of door and frame.

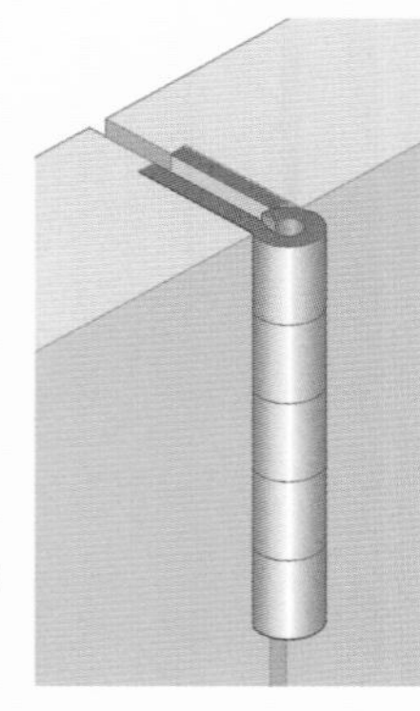

Cranked butt hinge A butt hinge that is made of folded pressed steel. It is cheaper but not as strong as other hinges, so should not be used to fix heavy exterior doors. When fitted, the whole of the large knuckle projects from the face of the door and the frame.

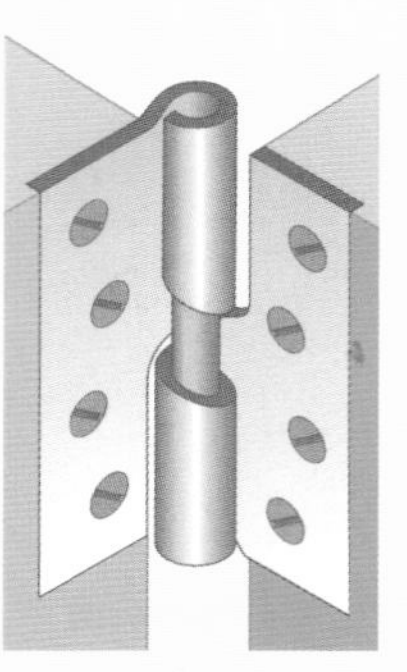

Rising butt hinge When a door opens onto a carpet, rising butt hinges are an alternative to cutting a strip off the bottom of the door. The spiral in the knuckle of the hinge lifts the door as it opens, and also tends to close it. The door can easily be lifted off the hinges. Usual sizes are 75mm

and 100mm. The hinges are sold for both right-hand and left-hand hanging.

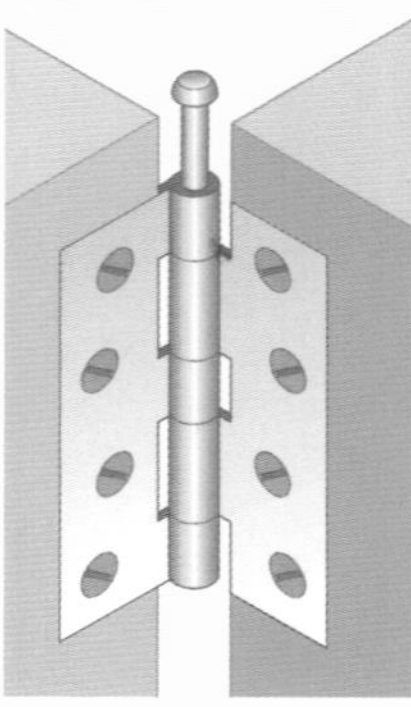

Loose-pin butt hinge The pin can be withdrawn to separate the leaves, and remove the door easily – perhaps when laying a floor covering. Decorative finials may be fitted at the top and bottom, and are unscrewed to release the pin. The hinges are usually made of brass.

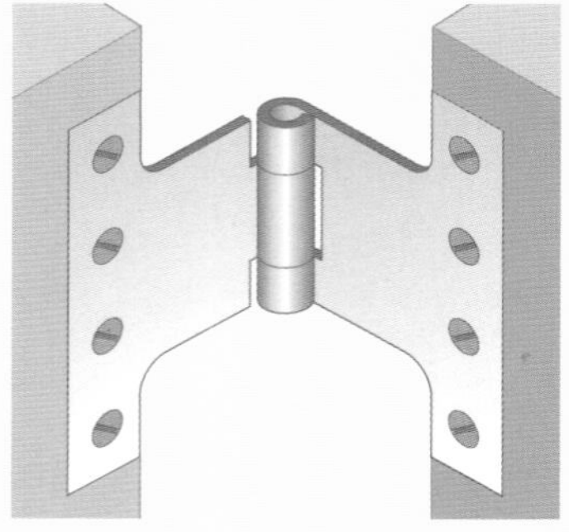

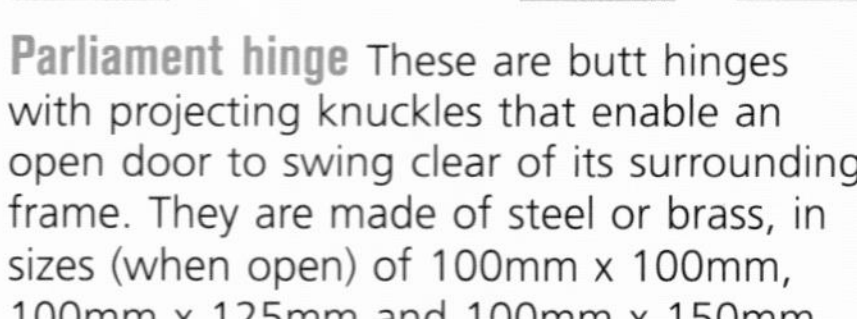

Parliament hinge These are butt hinges with projecting knuckles that enable an open door to swing clear of its surrounding frame. They are made of steel or brass, in sizes (when open) of 100mm x 100mm, 100mm x 125mm and 100mm x 150mm.

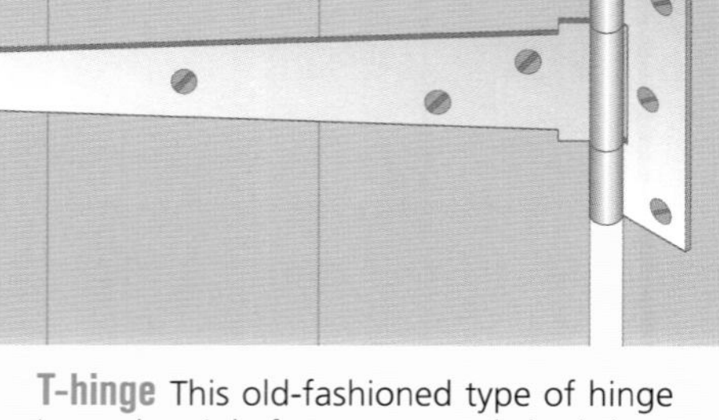

T-hinge This old-fashioned type of hinge is used mainly for garage and shed doors, but is sometimes fitted to cottage-style house doors. It is screwed to the surface of the back of the door and the frame.

Getting the fit right

1 Hold the door against the frame to mark it for trimming.

2 When the door is centrally positioned, get someone to steady it, and put wedges underneath to hold it at the correct height.

3 Lightly mark the face with a soft pencil to give the correct gap round the perimeter. A panelled door should have a gap of 3mm all round to allow the wood to swell in wet weather. A flush door should have a gap of 2mm. If the frame is straight you may not have to trim all the edges of the door.

However, if the frame is out of true, or if there is a fair amount of trimming to do, it will be necessary to trim all round.

4 If there is more than about 5mm of wood to remove, lay the door flat on boxes or trestles and saw it close to the trimming line, then finish off with a plane.

5 For planing, hold the door on its edge in the jaws of a folding adjustable workbench. Protect the bottom edge on scrap timber and then plane the top edge down to the pencilled trimming line.

6 Plane the long edges of the door in the direction of the grain. The shavings will be removed smoothly, whereas if you plane against the grain the blade may dig in.

7 Plane the top and bottom edges of the door from each side towards the centre. This will avoid splitting wood at the edge of the stiles where you will be planing across the grain.

8 Stand the door in the frame on thin wedges and check that there is the right gap all round.

9 When the fit is correct, plane a slight slope on the edges of both door stiles towards the doorstop on the frame. This will ensure that the door will close easily without binding against the frame.

Hanging the door

1 Hold the door in the frame to mark the hinge positions. If the hinge recesses in the frame are already cut to the right size, mark the top and bottom of the recesses on the edge of the door. If not, increase the size with a chisel as explained right, and then mark the top and bottom of the hinge positions on the door.

2 Hold the hinge in place on the door and mark round the edge of each hinge flap with a trimming knife. With a cranked butt hinge the whole knuckle of the hinge should project from the face of the door and from the frame. With a cast butt hinge the centre of the knuckle should be in line with the face of the door and frame.

3 Mark the thickness of the flap on the door face with a marking gauge.

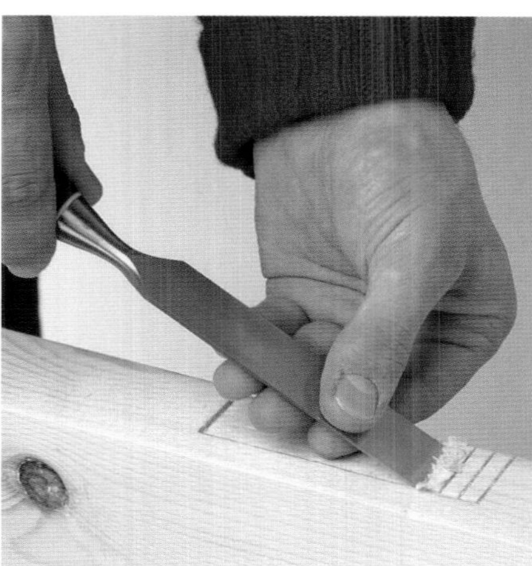

4 Cut around the perimeter of the hinge recess with a sharp chisel. Then make a series of cuts about 5mm apart across the grain of the wood, and carefully pare away the waste, using the chisel with its bevel facing down – see page 66.

5 Screw the hinge flaps into the recesses in the door, putting only one screw in each hinge for the time being.

CUTTING A REBATE FOR A WATER BAR

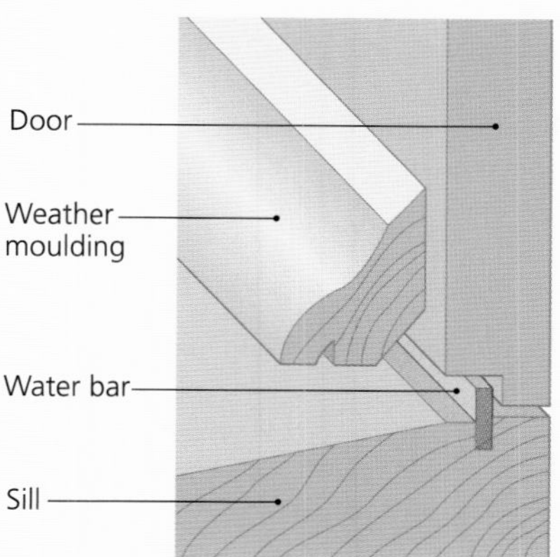

A door which is directly exposed to rain, without the protection of a porch, will close against a water bar set in a groove in the sill. Some external doors are supplied with a rebate already cut in the bottom to fit over the water bar, but if your door doesn't have one, you will need to cut it yourself.

- Draw a line across the front of the door at the bottom, a little higher than the water bar.
- Set a circular saw or router to the depth of the rebate (about half the thickness of the door) and cut right along the line, using the tool's fence.
- If you have used a circular saw, make a second cut with the saw set to the width of the rebate (again using the fence) and clean up the rebate with a sharp chisel.

6 Hold the door open on wedges and screw the hinges to the frame – again using one screw each. Each screw head should lie flush with the surface of the hinge flap.

If the screw heads protrude, they will bind and prevent the door from closing. You can either deepen the countersinks in the hinge with a high-speed-steel twist bit in a power drill (page 190), or else you could buy screws one size smaller.

If the screws do not tighten into the frame, glue pieces of dowel in the old screw holes and drill new ones.

7 Check that the door swings open and shut easily. If it does not close properly, the hinge positions may have to be adjusted (see Door hard to close, page 190).

8 When the door moves correctly, insert the remaining hinge screws and paint the hinge if required.

Re-hanging a door on the other side of the frame

Changing a door so that it hinges on the left rather than the right (or vice versa) can make better use of space in a room – or allow you to see fully into the room as you open the door.

Before you start Decide which way round the door will face. If you keep it facing the same way, you can be sure it will fit but there will be more carpentry – cut new hinge recesses on door, fully fill old recess, make new latch/lock holes, fill old latch/lock holes. Reversing it (as we have done here) means less carpentry, but it may not fit (if it has bowed) and you may have to re-paint it (if the two sides are different colours).

Tools *Wedges; screwdriver; tenon saw; vice or bench hook; plane; hammer; abrasive paper; pencil; chisel; try square; mallet; trimming knife; drill and twist bits.*

Materials *Scrap softwood, or pieces of timber to match the door; wood glue; panel pins; new screws for hinges – probably 50mm 5mm gauge.*

1 Open the door and put wooden wedges under it to take the weight.

2 Unscrew the hinges from the frame, take down the door, and remove the hinges completely.

Repositioning the hinges

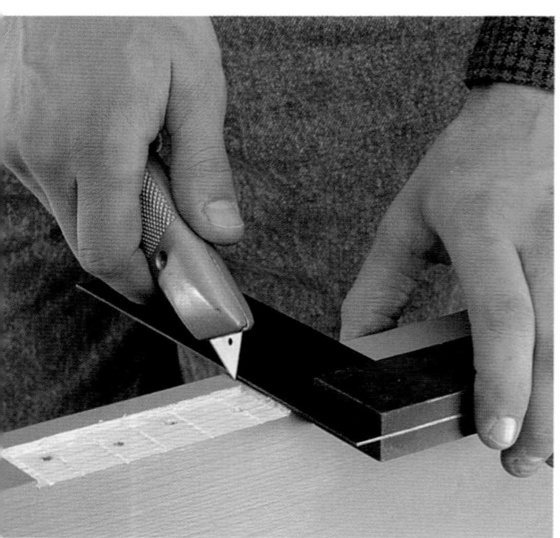

1 Use a trimming knife and try square to cut through the raised wood at the ends of the hinge recesses on the door.

RE-HANGING A DOOR TO OPEN OUTWARDS

Altering a door so that it opens outwards rather than inwards is very similar to re-hanging it to hinge on the other side of the frame – except that it is easier to keep the door facing the same way round.

After removing the door, prise away the stop bead – the strip of wood on the frame that the door rests against when it is closed. To do this, use an old chisel together with a couple of wooden wedges or a bolster chisel. When you have re-hung the door in its new position, pin the stop bead back on the frame so that it fits snugly against the inside face of the door and repaint.

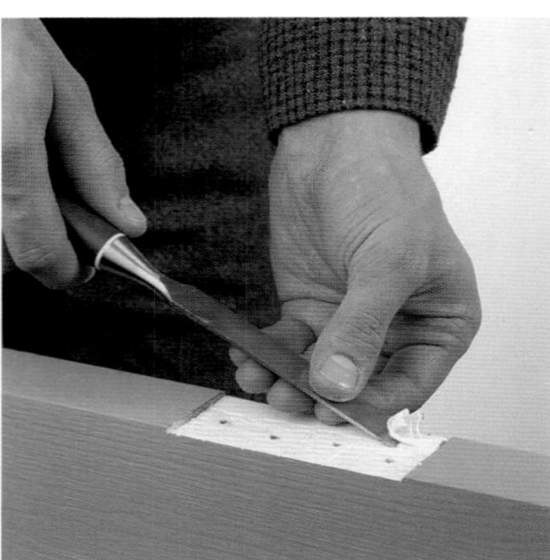

2 Remove the raised sections with a chisel (bevel facing down – see page 66), so that the recesses extend right across the door edge.

3 Hold a hinge against each recess on the opposite side from where it was originally, and cut strips of wood to fit along the other edge to fill the gaps. Use softwood if the door is painted, or matching timber if it is varnished. Cut the pieces to stand slightly raised.

4 Glue the strips in place and temporarily hold them with panel pins that are not driven right in.

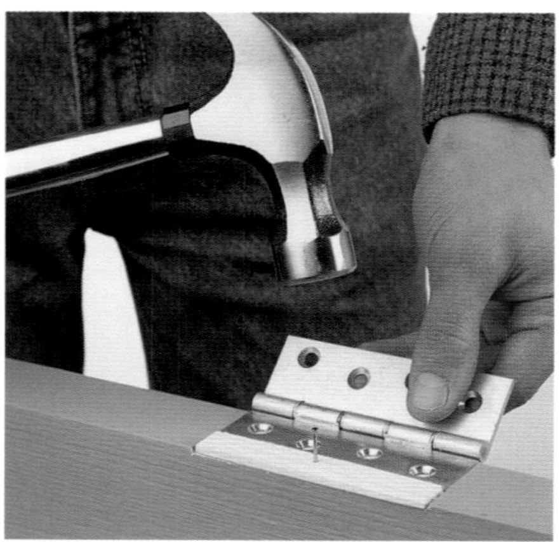

SAFETY TIP

Never hang a door so that it opens onto a corridor or landing as there is a danger of walking into the door.

5 When the adhesive has set, remove the pins and plane the filling pieces flush with the door edge. Finish with abrasive paper.

Relocating the striking plate and lock

1 Unscrew the lock striking plate from the door frame. Cut a thin piece of wood to fill the recess, and fix it in place as described in steps 3 and 4, left.

2 When you turn the door around, the side that faced out of the room will now face inwards. The latch will be facing the wrong way to engage when the striking plate is refitted.

3 Remove the lock and reverse the latch, either by turning the lock over (simple mortise latch only) or by unscrewing the side of the lock and turning the latch over.

Rehanging the door

1 Hold the door in the frame with wedges under it to support it at the right height off the floor. Check that the gap between the door and the frame is equal all the way round, and that the bottom of the door will not catch on the carpet.

2 Mark the top and bottom of the hinge positions on the edge of the frame. Remove the door.

3 Hold each hinge in place on the frame and mark round its edge with a trimming knife. If it is a cast butt hinge, the centre of the knuckle should be level with the face of the frame (and the face of the door). A cranked butt hinge should have the whole knuckle projecting.

4 Mark the thickness of the hinge flap on the edge of the frame.

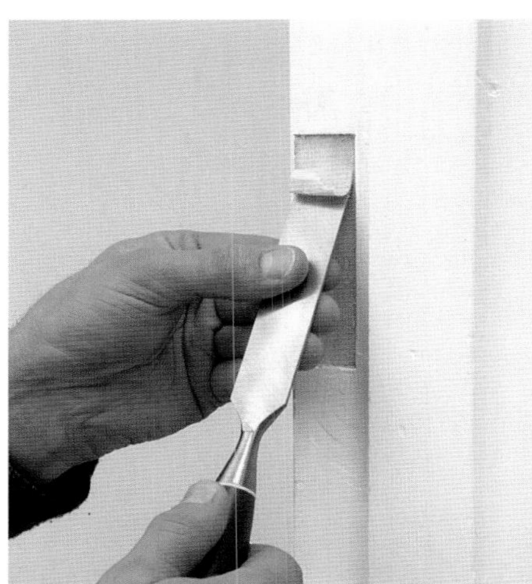

5 Cut round the scored outline with a sharp chisel. Then make a series of cuts about 5mm apart across the grain with the chisel and carefully pare away the waste.

FITTING RISING BUTT HINGES

Rising butts are available for right-hand and left-hand hanging, so make sure you buy the right type. Stand so the door will open away from you; if it is to be hinged on the left, buy left-hand hinges; if it is hinged on the right, buy right-hand hinges.

The part of the hinge with the pin is fitted (pin upwards) to the door frame, and the open spiral section is screwed to the door.

Fit them in the same way as ordinary butt hinges. It will also be necessary to plane a small slope on the inner top edge of the door on the hinge side. This prevents the door from catching on the top of the door frame as it swings open.

6 Repeat at the other hinge positions on the frame.

7 Drill pilot holes for one screw in each hinge on the door, and fix the hinges into the recesses, using one screw only.

8 Hold the door open on wedges, and screw the hinges to the frame – again with one screw in each hinge. Make sure that each screw head is flush with the surface of the hinge. If the screws protrude beyond the surface the door may not close correctly.

9 Check that the door swings open and shut easily. If it does not, the hinge positions may have to be adjusted (page 190).

10 When the movement is correct, drill the remaining pilot holes and put in the screws.

11 Close the door and turn the handle and key to indent the frame where the lock striking plates will be fitted.

HELPFUL TIP

Re-hanging a door may mean that the room light switch is now on the 'wrong' side. See page 298 for details of how to move it.

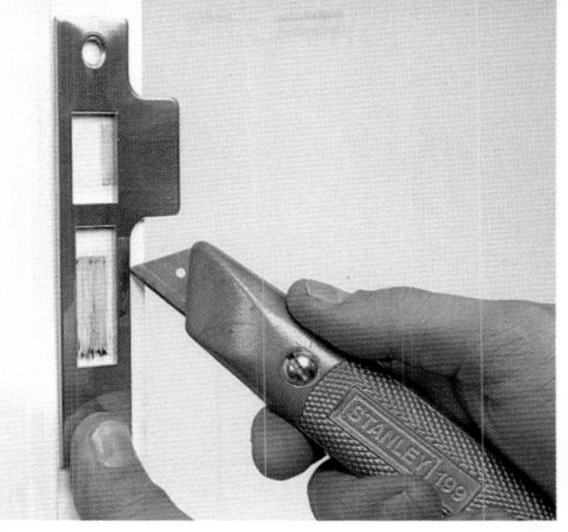

12 Mark the frame around the striking plate, and chisel out a recess. Cut out the mortises for the lock and catch. Screw the plate in place and paint bare wood.

Hanging an interior door

Normal interior doors are hung in largely the same way as exterior doors with the following differences.

Conventional hinged doors

- As interior doors are not likely to swell because of moisture, a 2mm gap between door and frame will be enough.
- When cutting the door to fit, make sure that it will open over a carpet without rubbing. It should just brush the carpet top. Alternatively, fit rising butt hinges.
- If you need to trim more than 10mm off each edge of a standard-size door, buy an interior quality panel door. The internal support-frame of a flush door is too narrow to be substantially cut down.

  Alternatively, buy a slightly undersize flush door and add timber lipping all round to make up the height and width; add no more than 10mm on each edge.
- Two hinges will be enough for hanging an interior door. Use 75mm cranked butt hinges (page 192).

Hanging bi-fold doors

Hang a bi-fold door in the same way as a conventional door, with these exceptions:

1 If the pair of doors is not already hinged together, join with three brass butt hinges.

2 Fix the door to the frame with two parliament hinges. They have projecting knuckles that let the door fold right back, clear of the architrave around the opening.

3 Where two pairs of bi-fold doors join together at the centre of the opening, glue and pin a full-height batten about 40mm x 15mm to one door to overlap the closing edge and serve as a door stop. If the meeting edges are rebated, there will be no need for the batten.

4 Fit a mortise latch (page 197) and handle to the adjacent door of the other pair.

Choosing locks and latches for your doors

Choosing an appropriate lock or latch for each door in the house is crucial for safety and security. But remember that any lock is only as strong as the frame to which it is fitted and the screws you use.

Single-point locks and latches are available in two main types.

- Rim locks are screwed to the inner face of the door; they are easy to install but not so secure as they are only held by screws, and could be forced off the door.
- Mortise locks are fitted (mortised) into the door edge; they are more difficult to install, but more secure because the door frame has to be smashed to get past them. A metal reinforcement, called a London bar, can be fitted to the frame beside a mortise lock, but must be ordered to size.

Multi-point locking systems can secure a door along its full height.

BACK AND SIDE DOORS

A deadlock (a lock with a bolt that can be opened only with a key) is essential for side and back doors, because these doors are often glazed and in secluded positions. If there is no deadlock, a burglar can break the glass and turn a latch from the inside.

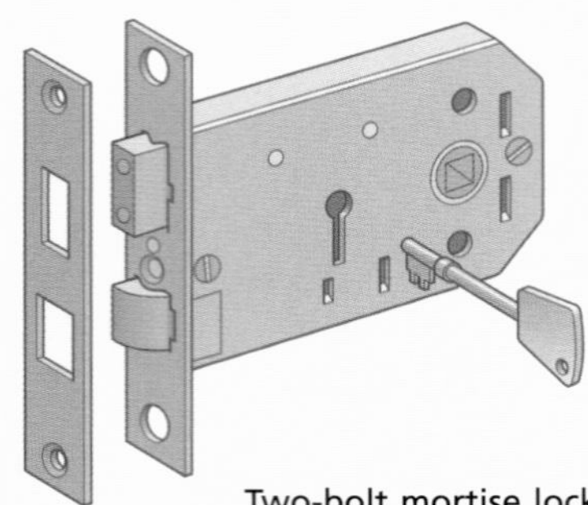

Two-bolt mortise lock

Mortise sashlock The two-bolt mortise lock is also called a mortise sashlock. The latch is operated by handles on both sides of the door and the bolt can be operated only by the key. Choose one with five levers for good security (or buy an upgrader unit) and use only locks manufactured to British Standard BS3621. Narrow models are available for doors with narrow stiles. Use with rack bolts at top and bottom of the door. Take the dimensions of the old lock when buying a new one, as sizes vary according to make.

Two-bolt rim lock Screws to the inner face of the door. Simple to install but easy to tamper with. Cheaper one, two and three-lever actions are unsuitable for external doors as the only lock. Fit additional bolts at top and bottom.

FRONT DOORS

If you have glass in your front door, buy a deadlocking cylinder rimlock. This becomes unmovable if you turn the key when you leave the house, so that a burglar will not be able to reach in through a broken pane of glass to open the door.

Cylinder rim lock The lock is fitted to the inner face of the door. The latch is turned back by a key from the outside and by a handle from the inside. A 'snib' (knob) holds the latch in place – either out or in. Less secure than a deadlocking cylinder rim lock. When choosing the lock, look for one made to British Standards Institution BS3621. To keep the door locked when you are indoors, choose a model with a lockable handle, so that it can be locked from the inside as well as the outside. But ensure that a key is kept near the door in case of fire. Use with a mortise deadlock for extra security.

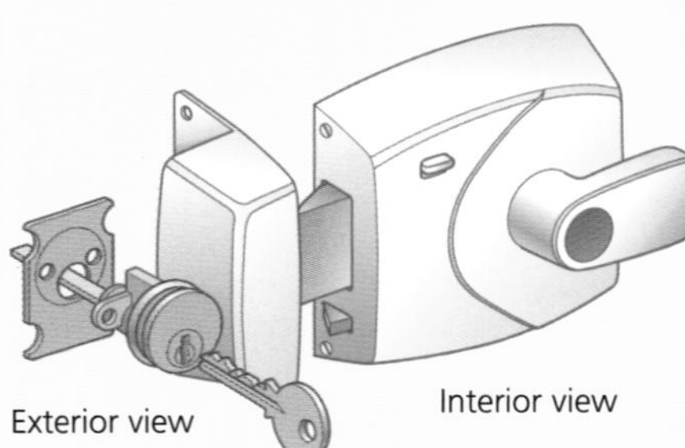

Exterior view

Interior view

Deadlocking cylinder rim lock (above) The lock is fitted to the inner face of the door. When the key is turned in the lock, the bolt cannot be forced back. On some models the main bolt automatically deadlocks when the door is closed. Bolts on standard locks are about 14mm; bolts on high-security designs are 20mm or more. A locking handle on the inside prevents an intruder from opening the door after breaking a glass panel. Use only locks manufactured to BS3621. A BS EN 1303 Grade 5 cylinder provides anti-drill and pick resistance. Some models incorporate a lock check indicator so you can see if the door is deadlocked. Use with a mortise deadlock for added security.

Mortise deadlock (above) The bolt cannot be turned back without using the key. The key operates levers, and the more levers there are, the harder the lock is to pick. A five or seven-lever lock with a box type striking plate gives the best security. Use with a rim lock for frequent coming and going. Cutting a mortise in a door will weaken it a little, so if you have a front door that is less than 44mm thick ask for a thin-pattern mortise lock.

You can get rebated mortise locks (and sashlocks) for use on French doors. Both the lock and the striking plate are shaped so that they fit the rebated edges of the doors. You should still fit a rack bolt (see right) to at least one of the doors.

PATIO AND FRENCH DOORS

Small security locks can be mounted on the inside of a wood or metal patio door. They operate a bolt which engages in a hole in the other door. For maximum security, fit locks at both top and bottom of the door. This is particularly advisable for old aluminium-framed patio doors which can sometimes be jemmied out of the sliding track and lifted out of the frame.

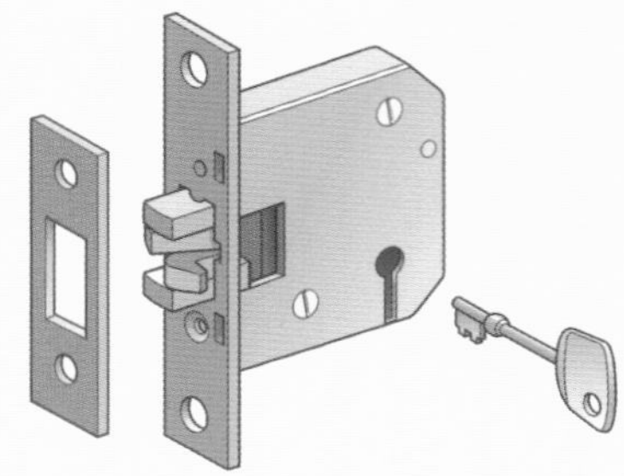

Clawbolt deadlock A pair of claws lock into the striking plate, and can only be operated by a key. The lock is mortised into the door's stile. Suitable for sliding patio doors made of wood. Metal and plastic patio doors usually come with their own lock.

Casement bolt (espagnolette bolt) The traditional way to lock French doors. A full length bolt, operated by a central handle, shoots into the frame at top and bottom. For security it should be used in conjunction with rack bolts (opposite) at the top and bottom.

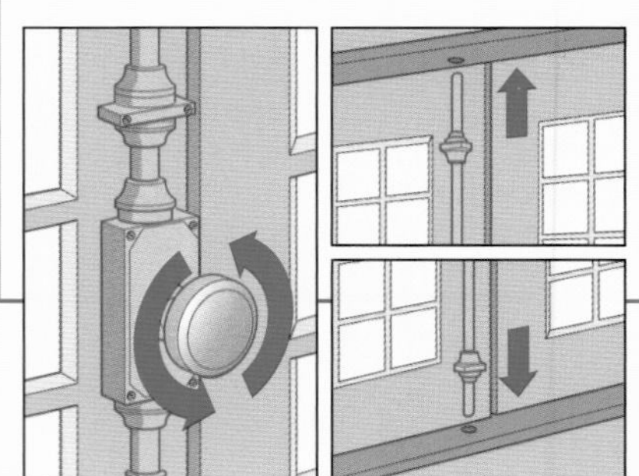

INTERNAL DOORS

Internal doors are best not locked when a house is empty. Once burglars are inside they will usually not be deterred by locked doors unless they are very strong.

When the house is occupied, ground floor doors could be locked at night. A burglar trying to get from, say, the living room to the rest of the house will probably make so much noise that he or she will wake the occupants. For this purpose, fit a two-bolt mortise lock (left), as you would for a back or side door; handles on both sides of the door will be necessary for normal use in the daytime. There are now 'lift-and-lock' sashlocks available that allow the door to be locked and unlocked from the inside simply by lifting or depressing the handle by 45°; no key is required.

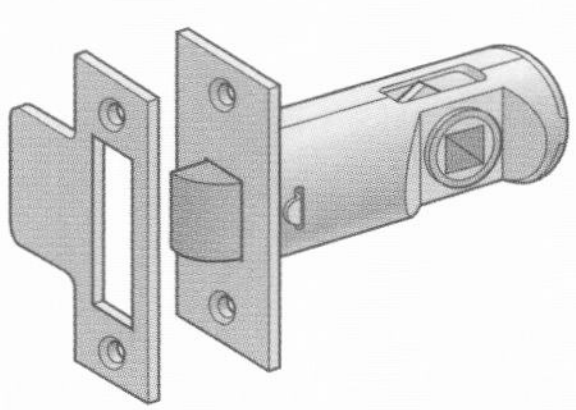

Mortise latch Only for keeping doors closed; it cannot be locked. A small model can be inserted in a circular hole. Bathroom doors normally require a latch with a 'snib', a simple locking device that can be turned from the inside for privacy. A screw slot on the outside of the door can be used to open the latch in an emergency.

Additional devices for door security

Rack bolts With every external door it is advisable to fit rack bolts to prevent forcing. The bolts are mortised into the opening edge of the door (page 200) with the key on the inside. Fit two to each door – and one at the top and bottom.

Rack bolts are an alternative method of locking a front door at night when the house is occupied.

If the glass is broken it is hard to see where the bolts are fitted. Even if the holes are found, a fluted key is needed to undo them.

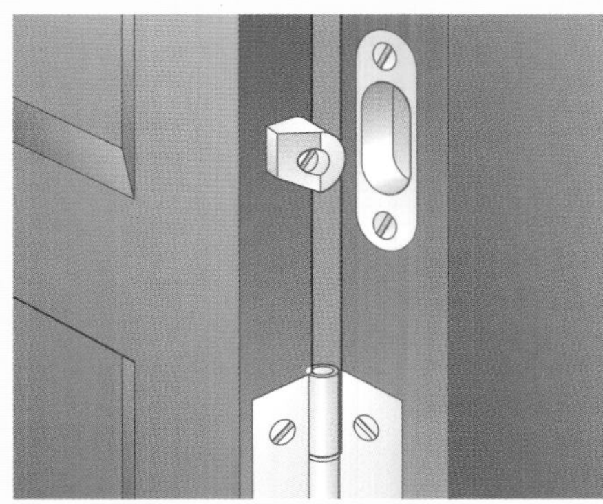

Hinge bolts It is possible to unhinge a door by using a jemmy on the hinge side. To prevent this, fit hinge bolts – two per door – about 75mm away from the hinges (page 200).

Self-locking bolts Where a door is too thin to house a rack bolt without being weakened, fit a surface mounted, self-locking bolt. It is merely screwed in place; when fitted, all screws are concealed. Pushing the bolt end slides it into the locked position, where it deadlocks and cannot be moved without the use of a key.

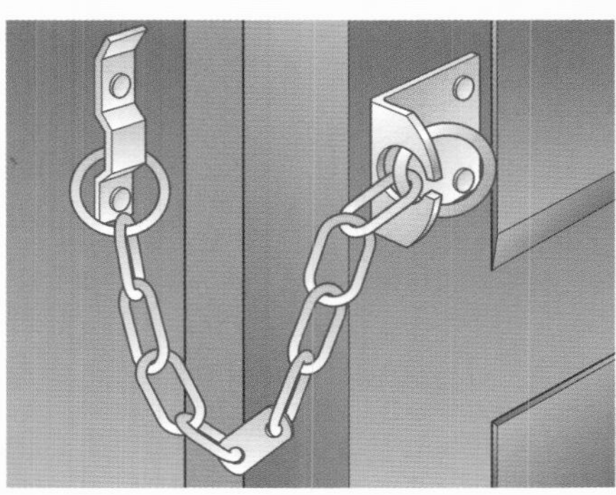

Door chains To prevent an intruder forcing his way in after ringing the doorbell, fit a chain to the front door. It allows the door to be opened just far enough to speak to a caller, but the door has to be shut again before the chain can be released to allow entry.

The strength of the device depends entirely on how well the chain is anchored to door and frame, so use the longest and largest diameter screws possible.

Various patterns are available, including a simple chain, a chain combined with a sliding bolt, a chain which can be unlocked from the outside with a key, and a chain with an in-built alarm, which is triggered by an attempt to enter.

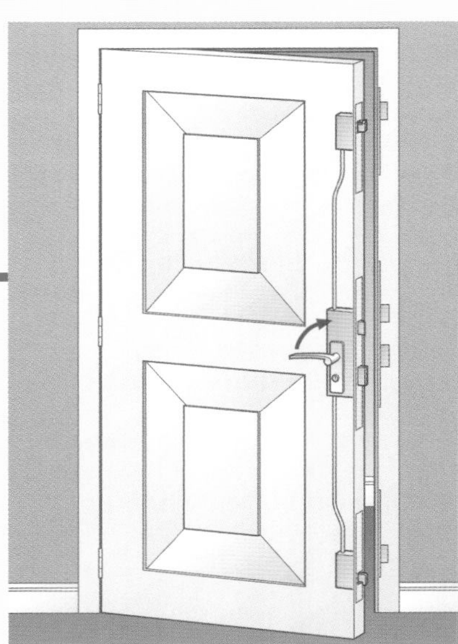

MULTI-LOCKING SYSTEMS FOR SECLUDED DOORS

External doors that are not overlooked are especially vulnerable because attempts by an intruder to gain entrance are unlikely to be spotted. To counter this, a multi-point locking system is advisable. This locking system can be used on doors 30–47mm thick, made of uPVC, composite material, timber or aluminium. Locking mechanisms can be fitted along the full length of the door. The high-security hookbolts are actuated by pulling the door handle up, and retracted by pulling the handle down. The door cannot be locked until all the bolts are thrown, and turning the key will deadlock all locking points as well as the latch bolt.

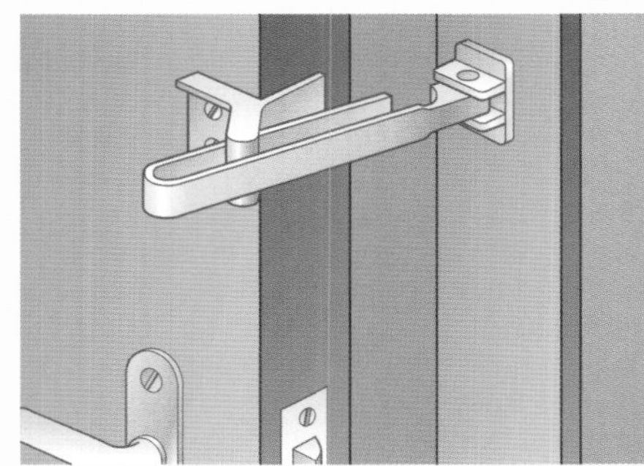

Door limiter A more substantial version of a door chain is a door limiter, with a sliding bar replacing the chain. When in place, the bar engages with the retaining part of the unit, restricting the opening of the door. The door has to be closed and the bar swung away before it can be fully opened.

Fitting door locks

Locks are vital to your security and safety, so make sure they are securely fitted and are sturdy enough to keep out intruders.

Fitting a cylinder rim lock

Tools *Pencil; tape measure; power drill and twist bits; flat wood bit (32 or 38mm); screwdriver. Perhaps chisel and mallet.*

Materials *Cylinder rim lock to British Standard BS3621.*

1 Mark the position of the key cylinder at a convenient height on the door stile, using the paper template supplied with the lock.

2 Drill the hole for the cylinder. When the point of the wood bit emerges through the door face, withdraw it and complete the hole from the other side. This will prevent the wood from splintering as the bit exits.

3 From the outside of the door, insert the cylinder throught the brass ring and into the hole. Hold the mounting plate against the inside face and fix the two together using the flat ended connecting screws supplied. The connecting bar will protrude through the plate. Align the mounting plate correctly, use a bradawl to make pilot holes and screw the mounting plate to the door.

4 The connecting bar has grooves etched into it. Offer up the lock to the connecting bar and count how many grooves disappear into the lock. In this instance it is four. The connecting bar therefore needs to be 'four grooves' long. Mark the bar and saw off the excess with a junior hacksaw.

5 If the lock has a fore-end that is recessed into the door edge (this one doesn't), temporarily fit the lock onto the mounting plate and mark where to cut the recess. Cut it out using a sharp chisel.

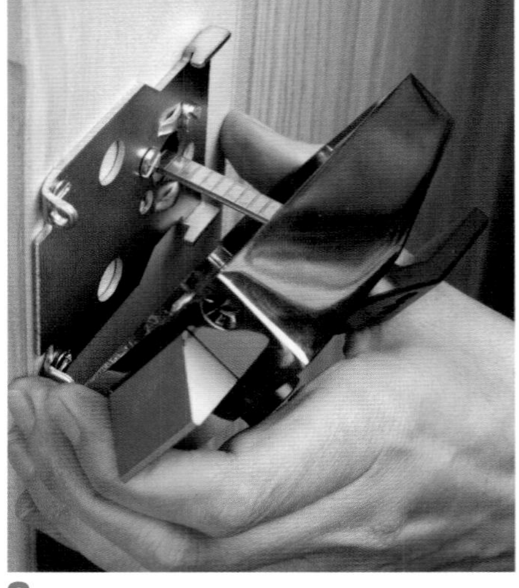

6 Use the button on the lock case to latch the lock in its 'open' position. Align the arrow on the back of the case with the arrow on the rotatable slot. Fit the lock case onto the mounting plate ensuring the connecting bar engages in the lock.

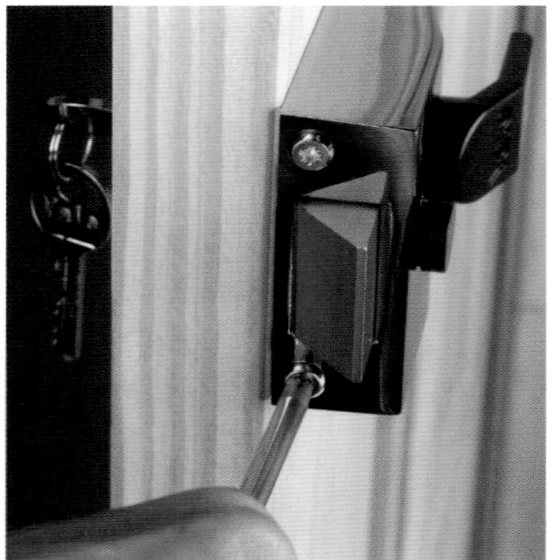

7 Push the lock case downwards firmly onto the mounting plate and slide it sideways into its final position, flush with the edge of the door. Secure to the mounting plate with the two small screws supplied.

8 Close the door and mark the position of the 'staple' on the door frame, using the lock case as a guide. Then hold the staple to the frame and mark its perimeter with a pencil.

9 Chisel a recess in the door frame to hold the staple flush with the frame, and fix it in position with the screws supplied.

Fitting a mortise lock

Tools *Pencil; try square; power drill; twist drill bits; flat wood bit to match thickness of lock body; mallet; chisels; pliers; bradawl; padsaw; screwdriver.*

Materials *Mortise lock made to British Standard BS3621.*

1 Hold the lock in place against the door face. Ideally it should line up with the door's centre rail. On new flush doors, lock fixing points are often marked on the edge. Mark the dimensions of the lock casing on the door and transfer the height marks to the edge of the door using a try square.

2 Mark the centre line of the lock mortise on the edge of the door between the height marks. Then mark the depth of the lock body on the wood bit with a strip of tape, and drill a line of holes along the centre line to the depth of the lock body. Take care to keep the bit horizontal and square on to the door edge.

3 Use a mallet and a narrow chisel to square up the top and bottom of the mortise. Then use a wider chisel to trim the sides of the mortise so that the lock body will slide snugly into it.

4 Turn out the bolt of the lock with the key, then push it into the mortise and mark the shape of the fore-end (its rectangular faceplate) on the edge of the door. Grip the bolt with pliers to withdraw the lock.

5 Chisel a recess for the fore-end so the lock will fit flush with the edge of the door.

6 Hold the lock in position against the face of the door, and with a bradawl mark the centre point of the keyhole (and the handle spindle on a mortise sashlock).

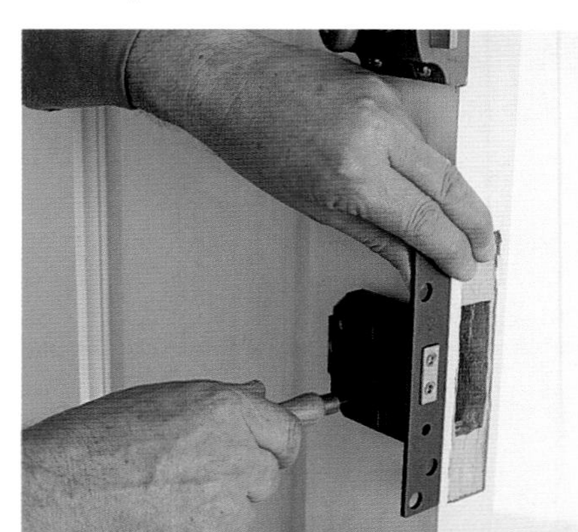

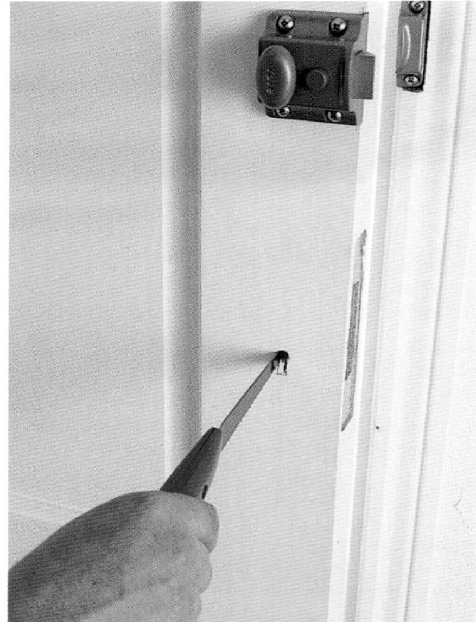

7 Using a drill and twist bit, make holes through the door to take the key (and the handle spindle for a mortise sashlock), at the positions you have marked with the bradawl. Make the keyhole the correct shape by enlarging the lower part with a padsaw. Cut out the bottom of the keyhole with a narrow chisel.

8 With the bolt of the lock sticking out, push the lock into the mortise and check that the key (and handle spindle if required) will operate freely. Drill pilot holes and drive screws through the fore-end of the lock into the edge of the door.

9 For a mortise sashlock, push the handle spindle through the lock and screw the handle plates on each side of the door.

10 For a mortise lock, screw the escutcheons on each side of the door.

11 Almost close the door and mark the positions of the deadbolt (and the latch of a sashlock) on the edge of the frame. Continue the mark onto the frame face.

12 Measure the distance from the outside face of the door to the centre of the bolt, and mark that distance on the frame, measuring from the doorstop.

13 Use the narrow chisel and mallet to cut mortises for the bolt (and latch if required). Check that the lock bolt (and latch) operate properly. If not, enlarge the mortises as much as necessary.

14 Hold the lock striker plate over the two mortises and mark the outline of its faceplate on the door frame with a pencil.

15 Cut a recess for the faceplate, fit it and check that the lock (and latch) properly. Screw the striker plate to the frame.

Fitting a new mechanism to a lock

If the keys are lost, or if you want to be sure of security when taking over a new house, it can be cheaper to replace the working part of a lock than to buy a complete new unit.

Mortise lock

Apart from possibly swapping locks with a friend or relative (if they have a front door lock of the same size), there's not much you can do if you want to change a mortise lock after you have moved house – except to buy a new one, ideally with exactly the same dimensions so that it will fit neatly into the existing hole. A locksmith may be able to help if you have lost the keys.

Cylinder rim lock

Buy a new cylinder and keys, as long as it is a straightforward lock. You cannot replace the cylinder on the type which has a locking interior handle.

Tools *Screwdriver; self-grip wrench or vice. Perhaps a junior hacksaw.*

Materials *New cylinder and keys.*

1 Unscrew the lock body from inside the door to expose the connecting screws which hold the cylinder in place.

2 Unscrew the connecting screws until the cylinder can be removed. The connecting bar will come too.

3 Hold the new connecting bar in a self-grip wrench or vice and use a junior hacksaw to cut it to the same length as the old one, so it is correctly housed in the lock case when the cylinder is in place.

The bar is divided into marked segments along its length.

4 Make sure that the connecting screws are also the right length. They can be cut to length with a junior hacksaw.

5 Insert the new cylinder into the hole. Tighten the screws and replace the lock case, making sure that the handle of the lock connects with the bar.

Replacing a mortise lock

When buying a new mortise lock, try to take the old one to ensure they are the same size and that the holes for the key and handle spindle match up.

Tools *Screwdriver; hammer; small piece of scrap wood.*

Materials *New five-lever mortise lock.*

1 Remove any handles or knobs. Unscrew the lock fore-end on the edge of the door.

2 If it is a sashlock, tap the spindle with a hammer towards the door edge to loosen the lock. Remove the spindle.

3 Lever out the lock at the top and bottom with the screwdriver, using a piece of wood under the screwdriver to protect the door.

4 Insert the new lock in the slot, ensuring it is the right way round if it is a sashlock. Screw it in place. Replace the spindle and handles or knobs.

Adding security bolts to doors

Although most door locks are secure, you may feel the need for added safety – in which case, security bolts may be your best choice.

Fitting a rack bolt

Tools *Pencil; drill and bits (sizes according to the manufacturer's instructions); pliers; 19mm chisel; screwdriver; try square.*

Materials *Rack bolt for doors (not the version sold for windows – see page 218).*

1 Mark a central point on the edge of the door where you want to fit the bolt. Use a try square and pencil to continue the mark onto the inner face of the door.

2 Drill a hole into the edge of the door to the diameter and depth of the body of the bolt.

3 Wind out the bolt and push it into the hole. Mark round the faceplate, withdraw the bolt with pliers and cut a shallow recess for the faceplate with a chisel.

4 Hold the bolt flush with the face of the door and mark the spot for the key. Drill a hole (see the manufacturer's instructions for the size) through the inside face of the door only.

5 Push the bolt back into the door and screw the faceplate to the edge of the door. Check that the bolt operates correctly. If necessary, enlarge the keyhole.

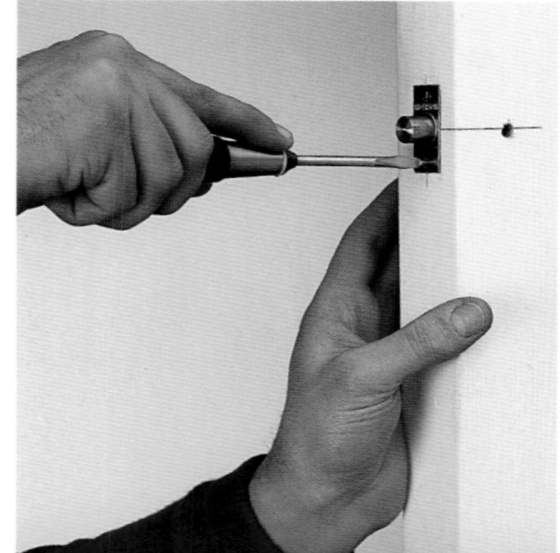

6 Screw the keyhole plate to the inside of the door aligned with the hole.

7 Close the door and wind out the bolt to mark the door jamb. There is usually a pimple on the end of the bolt to mark the wood.

8 Open the door and drill a hole to the required depth at the mark. Check that the bolt will go smoothly into this hole.

9 Hold the cover plate over the hole, draw around it, cut out a shallow recess and screw the cover plate in place. Check the operation of the bolt and make any necessary adjustments.

Fitting hinge bolts

Tools *Pencil; drill and bits (sizes according to the manufacturer's instructions); adhesive tape; mallet; chisel; screwdriver.*

Materials *A pair of hinge bolts.*

1 Open the door fully and mark the centre of the door edge about 75mm away from the hinges at the top and the bottom.

2 Drill a hole into the door edge to the diameter and depth given on the maker's instructions.

Wrap a piece of coloured adhesive tape around the bit as a guide to the depth.

3 Push the bolt into the hole. Partially close the door so that the bolt marks the frame.

4 At this spot, drill a hole into the frame to the depth of the protruding bolt, plus a bit more for clearance. Check that the door shuts easily. If necessary, enlarge the hole.

5 Open the door and hold the cover plate over the hole. Mark the edge of the plate with a pencil and chisel out a recess so the plate lies flush with the frame.

Fix the plate in place with the screws provided.

Choosing handles, knobs and other door furniture

Door furniture is available in a multitude of designs, from ornate reproductions to simple modern styles. It may be made of cast iron, brass, aluminium, steel, ceramics, glass or plastic. Whatever the design or material, each piece of door furniture has a particular function.

HANDLES

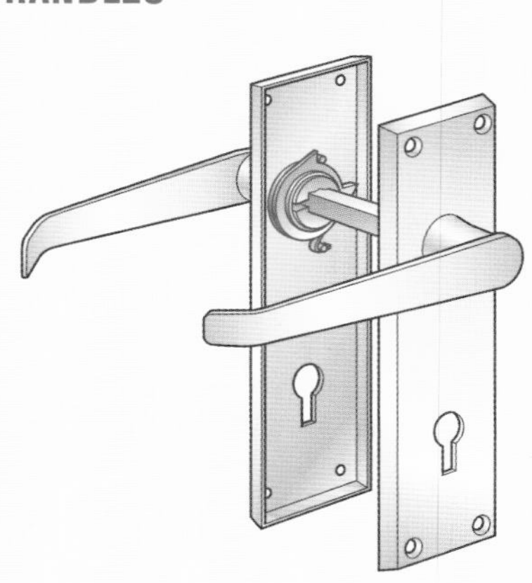

For a mortise sashlock Most commonly used for a back or side door. Also used with interior doors when privacy or security is a requirement. Each handle is handed left or right.

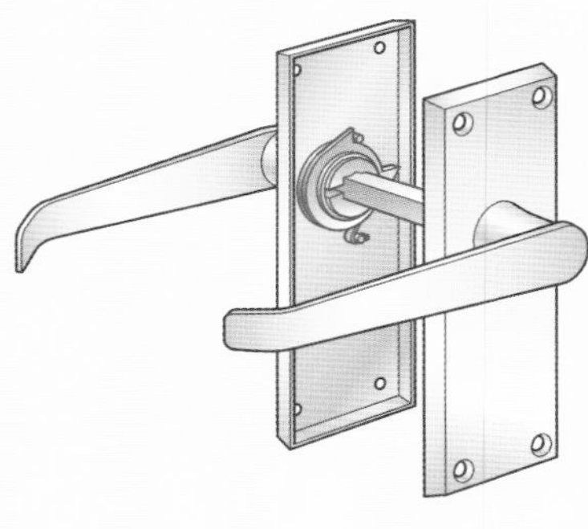

For a mortise latch The handle plate has no keyhole because a mortise latch is used on interior doors which will be left unlocked.

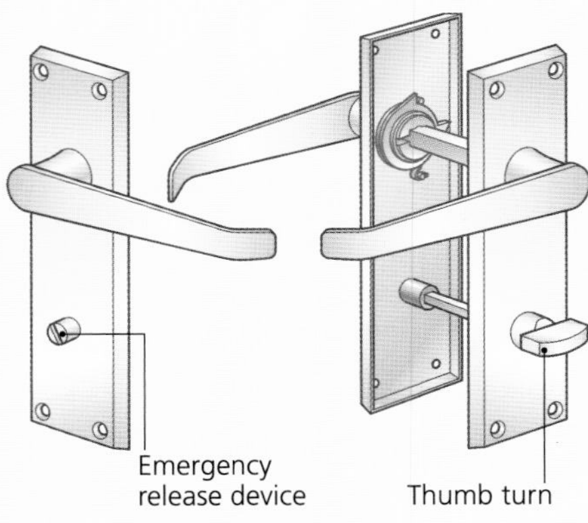

For a bathroom or WC A thumb-turn on the inside of the door prevents it from being opened. The outside of the door has an emergency release device. Buy either a right-hand or left-hand opening set, as the handles are not interchangeable.

DOOR KNOBS

Can be used on a mortise lock or latch, provided the spindle is far enough from the edge of the door to allow you to open the door without scraping your knuckles. Can be used for bathroom or WC doors with a privacy adaptor kit.

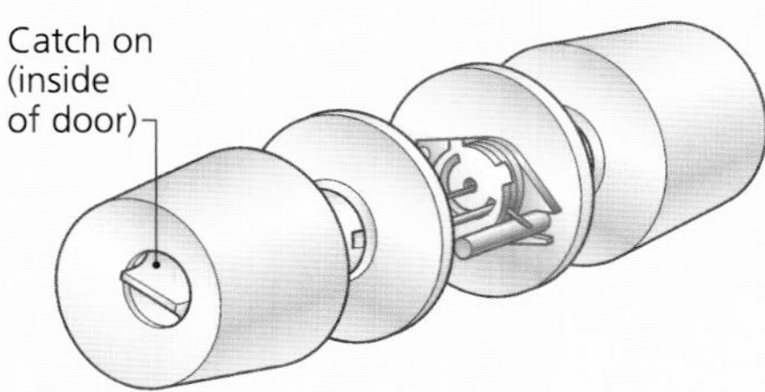

For a bathroom or WC The knob has a catch that prevents the door from being opened from the outside.

DOOR FURNITURE

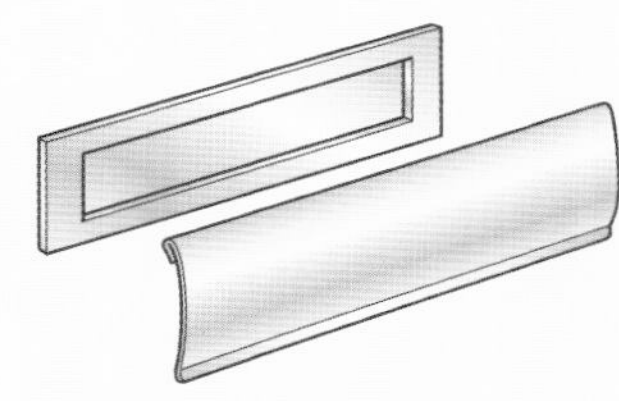

Letterplate and inner flap A standard letterplate fits on the outside of the front door. An inner flap fitted on the inside of the door gives a neat finish and helps to prevent draughts.

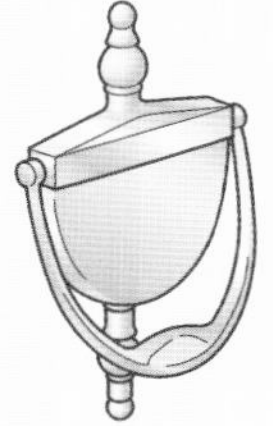

Door knocker
Fits to the front door instead of a bell. A wide range of designs is available.

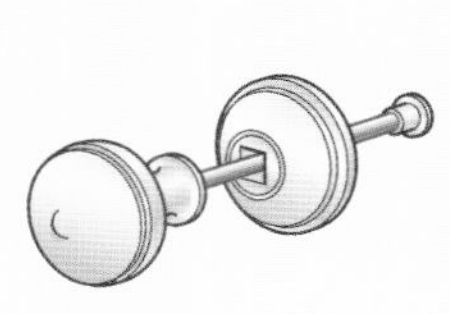

Centre knob
For closing the front door as you leave the house. It is often fitted to the door above a central letterplate.

Pull handle
Can be fitted to either the inside or outside of a front door to provide a grip while opening or closing it.

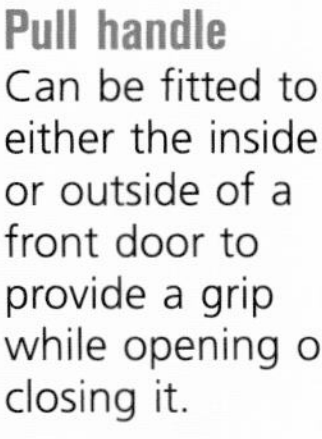

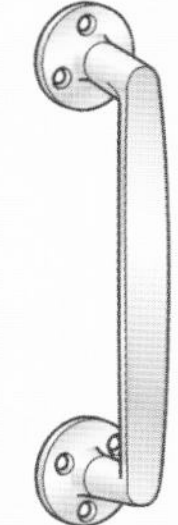

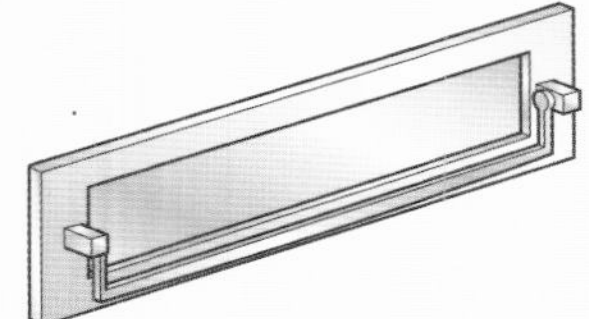

Letterplate knockers
A horizontal letterplate (above) incorporates a handle for pulling the door closed; this can also be used as a door knocker.

A vertical option fits on the lock stile of the door. The hole allows a rim lock cylinder to be set into the knocker.

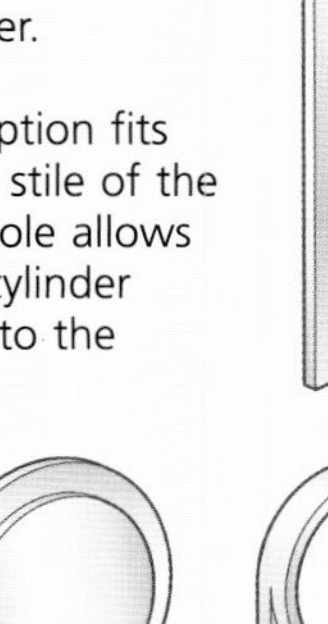

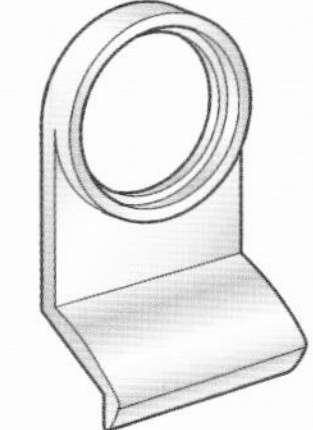

Escutcheon (open or covered) An escutcheon gives a tidy finish to the keyhole of a mortise lock. A covered escutcheon keeps out draughts.

Cylinder pull Fits under a rim lock cylinder on the outside of a front door, and is used to pull the door closed.

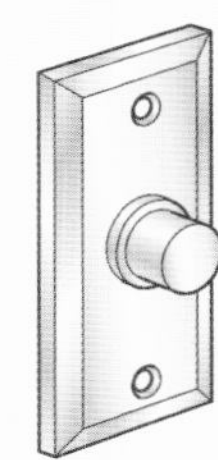

Bell push A bell push, which may be made of metal or plastic, is fitted to the door frame.

House numbers
The number of the house can be indicated with brass, black iron, plastic or porcelain numbers.

Fingerplate
Decorative plates to protect interior doors from becoming grubby with frequent use. Ceramic, brass and plastic are the most common types.

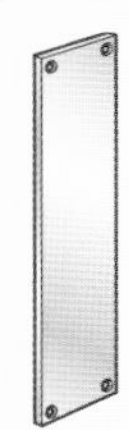

Fitting door furniture

The front door of a house usually needs a letterplate, a handle to close the door (which may be built into the letterplate), either a knocker or bellpush, and probably a house number.

Before you start A power jigsaw makes the job of cutting the letterplate opening much quicker than doing it by hand with a padsaw.

Letterplate

There are many different designs available for letterplates. Some incorporate a handle which can be used as a door-knocker.

Tools *Pencil; ruler; power drill and twist bits; 13mm flat wood bit; jigsaw or padsaw; chisel; abrasive paper; screwdriver; small adjustable spanner; hacksaw.*

Materials *Letterplate and fittings.*

1 Decide where you want the letterplate. On a panel door it can be fitted horizontally in the middle rail or vertically on the lock stile. On a flush door, fit it horizontally in the middle to coincide with the rail position that is marked on the edge of the door.

2 Measure the size of the flap and spring mechanism and lightly mark the outline of the required cut-out with a pencil.

3 Using the flat bit, drill a 13mm hole at each corner of the cut-out position and saw along the cut-out line. Preferably use a jigsaw with a long blade. Alternatively, you can make the cut-out with a padsaw, but it will be very slow work.

4 At each side of the cut-out, mark the positions of the holes for the fixing bolts.

5 Working from the front of the door, drill shallow 13mm diameter holes to accommodate the fixing lugs of the letterplate.

6 Using a twist bit the same diameter as the fixing bolts, drill from the centre of the holes right through the door.

Smooth the edges of the holes with abrasive paper.

7 Fit the letterplate to the door and then tighten the fixing nuts with an adjustable spanner.

8 If the bolts protrude, use a hacksaw to cut them off flush with the face of the nuts.

Door knocker

1 Hold the knocker in position and press it hard against the door so that the lugs leave light marks.

2 At these positions, drill holes for the lugs and the bolts.

3 Screw the bolts into the lugs on the back of the knocker, and push them through the holes.

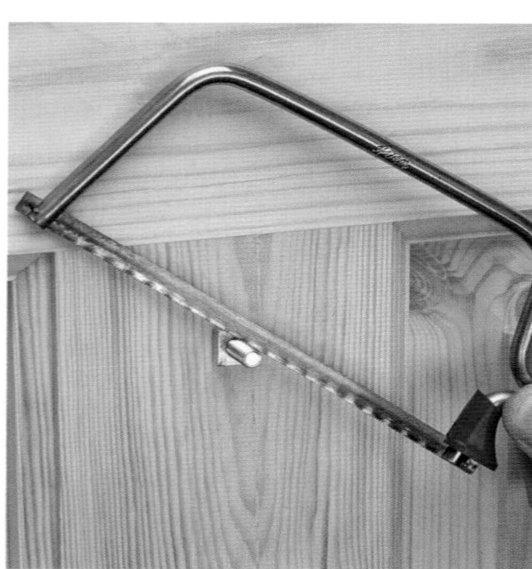

4 Tighten the fixing nuts, and if the bolts protrude cut them off flush with the face of the nuts.

Other door furniture

- A centre knob needs only a hole drilled through the door.
- A pull handle, finger plate and house numbers are screwed to the surface of the door – use a bradawl to make a pilot hole.
- A bell push is normally screwed to the surface, but some require a recess and, if wired, a through hole for the bell wire.

Wooden windows that stick

If a window will not open or close easily, examine it carefully to discover the cause. Check first for broken or loose hinges and put these right.

Build-up of paint

Layers of paint that have built up over the years are a common cause of sticking.

1 Use a plane or a rasp to strip the painted edge of the window back to bare wood.

2 Check that there is a clearance gap of about 2mm between the edge of the window and the frame before repainting.

3 If necessary, plane the window edge to give enough clearance. A casement window can be removed by unscrewing the hinges from the frame. For removing a sliding sash window, see page 206.

Swollen timber

Damp that has made the timber swell is also a cause of sticking windows.

1 Strip off the paint and let the timber dry out during fine weather.

2 When it is dry make sure there is a clearance gap of about 2mm between window and frame. If necessary, plane the edge of the window.

3 Repaint the window, ensuring that putty around the glass is well covered with paint.

Staff beads too tight

On a sliding sash window, the staff beads might have been nailed on too close to the inner sash.

1 Prise off the staff beads (see Replacing broken sash cords, page 206) and re-nail them so they lightly touch the edges of the inner sash. Before driving the nails right in, test that the sash will slide easily.

2 Rub the inside face of the staff bead with a candle to help to improve the sliding action.

3 Check that there is not a build-up of paint on the inside edge of the staff beads.

4 If necessary, loosen the old paint with a chemical paint stripper and then scrape it off. Re-coat with new paint.

Fixing loose joints on wood windows

The corner joints on both sash and casement windows often work loose. A painted window can be repaired with a steel corner plate. A window finished with varnish or wood stain must be repaired with glued dowels, or the repair will show.

A corner-plate repair

Flat L-shaped steel corner plates are available in various sizes. Choose one large enough to bridge the damaged area and give a secure fixing into sound wood. Before putting it on, repair any damage with exterior wood filler.

Tools *Small wooden wedges; trimming knife; chisel; small paintbrush; abrasive paper; sash cramp.*

Materials *Steel corner plates; 25mm 5mm countersunk zinc-plated screws; metal primer; exterior wood filler; paint.*

1 Remove a casement window from its frame by unscrewing the hinges. To remove a sash window, see page 206. Lay the window on a flat surface and fit a sash cramp to tighten the loose corner.

2 Put a plate over the joint on the inside or outside of the window – or both if it is very weak – and mark around it with a knife.

REPAIRS IN SITU

It may be possible to strengthen the corners of a window without removing it from the frame.

Make up some small wooden wedges by taking a piece of softwood about 100mm long, 20mm wide and 12mm thick. Draw a diagonal line from one corner to the other on the largest face, hold the wood in a workbench and saw along the line to make two wedges.

You can drive these in either side of the window to hold the corners tight while you repair them with a plate or dowels. On a sash window, remove the staff beads first (see page 206).

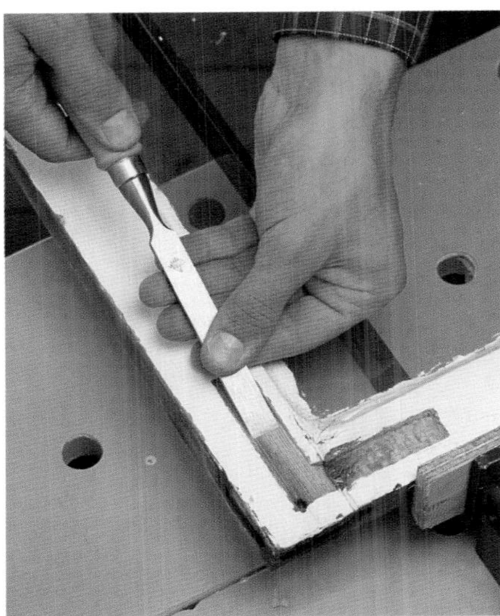

3 Cut a recess for the plate to rest slightly below the surface.

4 Fix the plate with the screws, and paint it with metal primer.

5 Cover the repair with exterior wood filler, smooth with abrasive paper, and paint with undercoat and two coats of gloss.

A dowelled joint

Glued dowels driven through the joint give an invisible and very strong repair.

Tools *Screwdriver; G-cramps or portable workbench, sash cramp or web cramp; drill and 6mm twist bit; chisel; hammer; panel saw; abrasive paper; paintbrush.*

Materials *6mm dowels; waterproof wood adhesive; varnish or preservative stain.*

1 Take out a casement window by unscrewing the hinges. To remove a sash window, see page 206.

2 Close the loose joints with a sash cramp or web cramp, then cramp the window to a workbench.

3 Drill holes for three 6mm dowels per joint. One goes through the face of the vertical stile to pin the tenon that protrudes from the end of the horizontal rail.

Two go through the side of the vertical stile into the end of the horizontal rail to reinforce both sides of the tenon.

4 Smear the dowels and the holes with wood glue, and drive in the dowels with a hammer.

5 When the glue has set, cut off the surplus dowel so that each one is flush with the surface of the wood.

6 Smooth the repair with abrasive paper, and repaint or, for bare wood, coat it with varnish or preservative wood stain.

Gaps around a window frame

Gaps around the outside of the window frames will result in damp appearing on the internal walls around the window. It will also encourage rot to attack the frames.

Using frame sealant

Cracks up to about 10mm wide can be filled with frame sealant (see panel).

Tools *Trimming knife; thin screwdriver; clean rag.*

Materials *Frame sealant and applicator. Perhaps a jar of water.*

CHOOSING FRAME SEALANT

Frame sealant is commonly available from hardware shops and DIY stores in three colours – white, brown and transparent, but other colours are sometimes available.

The sealant is sold in a cartridge which may either have a screw-down applicator or has to be fitted into a trigger-operated sealant gun. The gun is not expensive to buy and will last indefinitely.

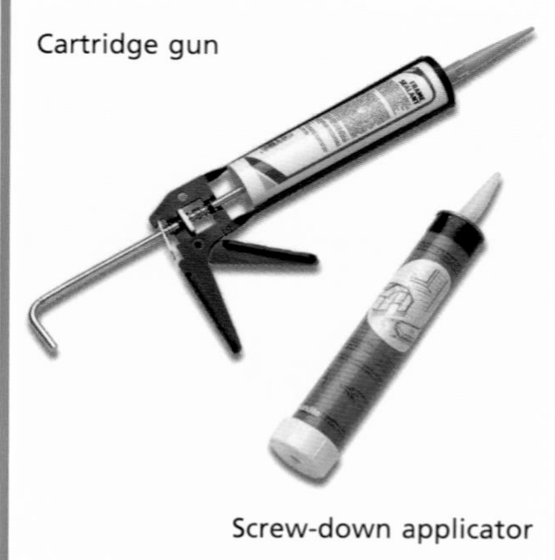

1 With a trimming knife, cut the nozzle off the sealant cartridge at an angle to give the necessary width of sealant to fill the gap. Break the foil seal or cut the sealed top of the cartridge.

2 Wipe around the frame with a clean rag, and inject a bead of sealant into the crack all round. The sealant should be placed in the angle between the window frame and the wall.

For neatness, try to inject the sealant in a single run without stopping, except at corners. Release the trigger to stop the flow.

3 If it is necessary to smooth the sealant, use a wet finger.

4 Sealant can be painted once a skin has formed (one to three weeks), but it is not necessary.

EXPANDING FOAM FILLER

For large, irregular gaps that are hard to reach, use a can of expanding foam filler. This adheres to most building materials. It is injected by nozzle at any angle, after which it expands in volume, effectively sealing even hidden areas. Once hardened, the foam is heat, cold and water resistant and rot-proof. It can be cut, sanded, plastered or painted.

Sealing with mortar

If the gap is more than about 10mm wide it should be filled with mortar, which is available in small bags – ideal for jobs of this scale.

Tools *Plant sprayer; small trowel or filling knife; trimming knife; clean rag.*

Materials *Water; mortar; sealant and applicator.*

1 Dampen the crack with water. A plant sprayer is ideal.

2 Press the mortar in place with a small trowel or filling knife, so that it is level with the surface of the brickwork.

3 When the mortar has hardened, which will take two or three days, seal all round the frame with frame sealant as described above.

Problems with metal windows

Old steel windows often rust. If the putty has been dislodged or the glass cracked, first carefully chip out the putty with an old chisel or hacking knife and remove the glass. Whether or not the glass has to be removed, the renovation process is the same.

Rust in old frames

Tools *Paint scraper or small brush, for paint stripper; small cold chisel; hammer; wire brush; safety goggles; small paintbrush; gloves.*

Materials *Rust remover; zinc-based primer; undercoat; gloss paint; white spirit. Possibly paint stripper and epoxy filler.*

1 Scrape off the paint, or remove it with a chemical paint stripper.

2 Using a small cold chisel, chip off as many of the rust flakes as possible. Then wire-brush the frame by hand, or use a wire wheel or wire-cup brush in a power drill. Wear safety goggles and gloves during this part of the job.

3 Brush over the frame to remove dust and loose particles, then fill any holes with epoxy-based filler and allow it to dry.

4 Paint the prepared frame with a coat of rust remover.

5 When the rust remover is dry, apply a zinc-based metal primer, then an undercoat and two coats of gloss paint.

6 If necessary, re-glaze the window, using metal casement putty (page 209).

Warped frames

Check whether a build-up of paint or rust on the frame is distorting it. If this is so, clean it off and repaint the frame.

If the frame is warped for no apparent reason, nothing can be done to straighten it. Seal the gap between window and frame with silicone sealant. First clean both frames with soap and water and dry them thoroughly. Then put a bead of sealant on the fixed frame, making sure that it is deep enough to fill the gap.

Cover the closing frame with soapy water, shut it tight to compress the sealant, then open it at once. Leave the sealant to set, and it will form a perfect seal. Trim off excess sealant with a knife.

Paint not adhering to galvanising

On new steel frames paint will sometimes flake off the galvanised surface soon after being applied.

1 Remove existing paint with paint stripper to get right back to the galvanising.

2 Rub the frame lightly with fine wet-and-dry abrasive paper, used wet. Wipe it with a clean damp cloth.

3 When it is dry, wipe it with a clean rag soaked in white spirit, then prime with metal primer.

4 Repaint the window frame with an undercoat and gloss paint.

Condensation

Condensation is quite a common problem with metal windows, and in serious or persistent cases it can lead to the surrounding wallpaper or plaster becoming damp.

In cold weather, windows are always colder than other parts of a room, because they are thinner than the walls, so when the warm, humid air from inside the room meets the glass, condensation forms. The problem is exaggerated with metal-framed windows, because the metal of the frames gets colder than wooden or plastic frames.

The most effective solution is to fit a replacement window and frame made of timber or plastic. Even an aluminium frame will produce an improvement, as long as it is fitted with a thermal break to insulate the outside face from the inner face.

Windows that are kept permanently closed are particularly susceptible to condensation. Fitting ventilation locks to these windows and keeping them secured slightly ajar will help.

Alternatively Fit a secondary double glazing system (page 211–13) to isolate the cold metal surfaces from the warm air inside the room.

Alternatively Installing an extractor fan will also help, by extracting the moist air from the room.

Replacing broken sash cords

When a sash cord breaks, replace all four cords on the window. The other three are probably failing, too.

Tools *Old chisel; string; trimming knife; pincers; screwdriver; hammer; small weight (a screw will do); matches. Perhaps machine oil.*

Materials *Sash cords (preferably Terylene); 25mm galvanised clout (large head) nails; 25mm oval nails; filler.*

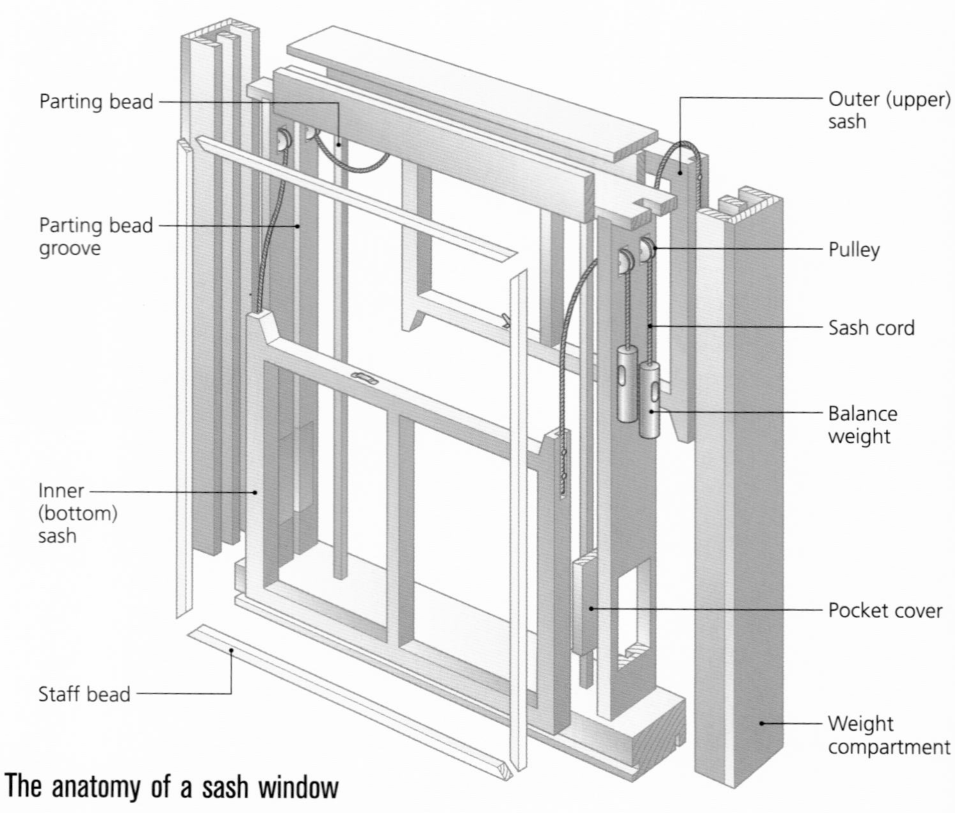

The anatomy of a sash window

Taking out the sashes

1 Working from inside the room, prise off the staff beads from the front of the window frame on each side. An old chisel or a large screwdriver is a suitable tool for the job.

Start at the centre of the staff bead to avoid damaging the mitre joints at the top and bottom. Once they have been lifted at the centre, the staff beads can be sprung out of place.

2 Lift the bottom sash out of the window as far as it will go. Rest it on a table or a portable workbench or ask someone to hold it for you.

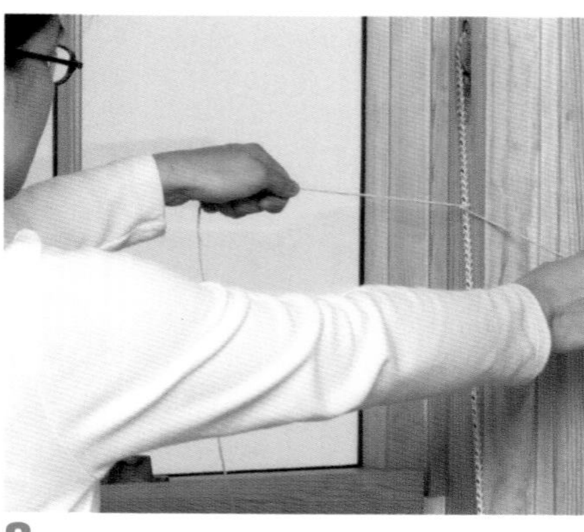

3 Tie the end of a ball of string to the upper part of each cord (if the cords are not already broken).

4 Hold each cord in turn, and cut through it with a trimming knife. Release it gently to lower the balance weight to the bottom of the box. This will draw the string over the pulley. The string will be used to thread the new cord. Set the released sash to one side.

5 Prise the narrow parting beads out of their grooves. If they have been nailed (incorrectly) rather than merely wedged in place, remove the nails with pincers, taking care not to split the beads.

If they are already split, buy new beads and cut them to length.

6 Lift the top sash into the room. If the cords are unbroken, tie string to the upper part and then cut the cords in the same way as before.

Fixing the cords to the weights

1 When measuring up for new cords, measure from the top of the window down to the sill, and add two-thirds again. This will allow enough spare cord for fixing at each end. Cut four pieces of cord to this length – one for each weight.

2 With the chisel, carefully prise the pocket covers from the weight channel at each side of the frame, towards the bottom. Usually they are just pushed in place, but sometimes they are screwed.

3 Reach into the pockets and lift the weights (two on each side) into the room. Leave the strings in place over the pulleys, ready to pull the new cords through.

4 Where cords have broken, tie a 'mouse' (any small weight – a screw will do) to a length of string and push it over the pulley, so that it drops down into the weight compartment and can be drawn out through the pocket.

5 Use a screwdriver to push the old pieces of cord out of the sash weights.

6 Remove the old cords from the grooves in the side of the window sashes. They are held with clout (large-head) nails which can be extracted with pincers.

HELPFUL TIP

To make a sash window slide up and down more smoothly, rub a candle over all the sliding surfaces and lightly oil the pulleys. You can do this at any time to ease running but make a point of doing it when the window is dismantled for repair.

7 Tie the end of the new cord to the string coming from one of the rear pulleys. Pull it over the pulley, into the weight compartment, and out through the pocket.

8 Untie the string, and tie the new cord to the balance weight, using a double knot. To prevent Terylene cord from fraying, heat the end with a match to melt the fibres into a solid lump.

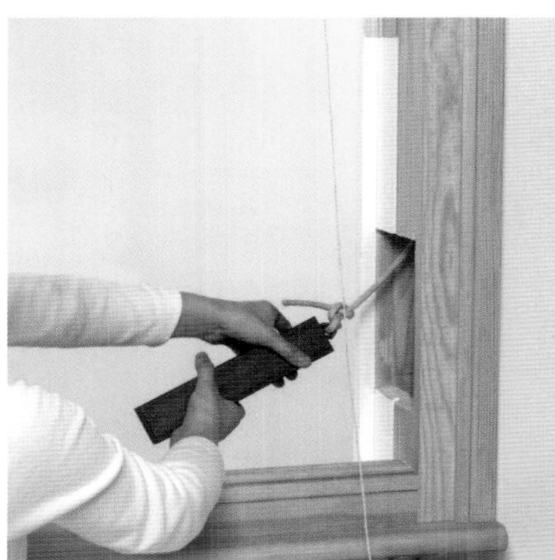

9 Replace the weight in the pocket. Repeat the process for all four weights, then fit the pocket covers in place; they should not be nailed or glued.

Fixing the cords to the sashes

1 Rest the top (outer) sash on the inside window ledge.

2 Get a helper to pull down one of the cords so that the weight is at the top of its compartment and just touching the pulley.

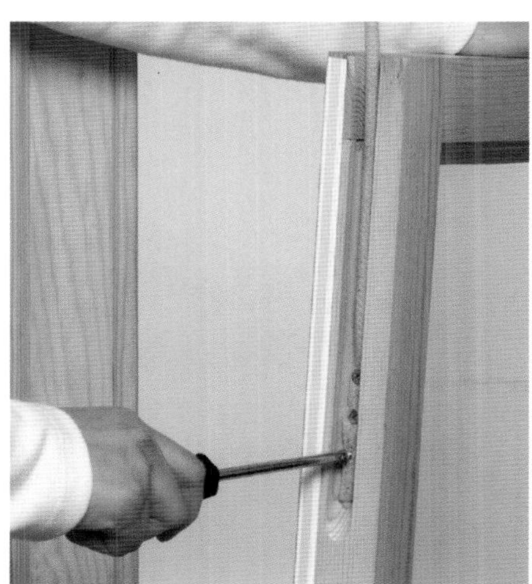

3 Screw or nail the cord into the groove at the side of the sash, using galvanised screws or clout (large-head) nails. Do not fit the screws or nails close to the top of the groove; they will prevent the sash sliding all the way up. The top screw or nail must be no higher than the distance from the mid-point of the pulley to the top of the frame.

HELPFUL TIP

If you have no one to help you nail the cord to the side of the sash, pull the weight up to the top of its compartment and wind the cord around a screwdriver. It will hold the weight while you nail the other end of the cord in place.

Alternatively Jam a wedge, such as a pencil, between the cord and the top of the pulley aperture.

4 Repeat for the second cord.

5 Put the sash in place and check that it operates smoothly before you reassemble the window.

Reassembling the window

1 Refit the parting beads between the runners on each side, tapping them into the grooves so they will not move.

2 Attach the sash cords to the lower (inner) sash in the same way as the upper sash. Then fit the sash in position in the frame.

3 Refit the staff beads on each side of the frame, checking that the mitred ends match up neatly with the beads at the top and bottom. Fix them without glue, using two or three oval nails so that they will be easy to remove in the future. Do not drive the nails fully home yet.

4 Check that the lower sash operates easily. If it rattles in its runners move the beads slightly closer to the sash. If not, drive the nails home. If the staff beads are damaged, replace them with lengths of new beading mitred at each end.

5 Repair any damaged areas around the frame with wood filler. When it is dry, smooth with abrasive paper and touch up the repairs with paint.

Renewing parting beads and staff beads

Before you can renew the beads, remove the damaged ones as described under Replacing broken sash cords (page 206).

Renewing parting beads

1 Buy new parting beads the same dimensions as the old ones or slightly larger and plane them down. Cut the beads to the height of the inner frame.

2 With a plane, take a few shavings off the length of the bead on each side, towards the edge that will fit into the groove. This slight taper will ensure that the bead is a tight fit.

3 Tap the beads into the grooves; there is no need to nail them.

Renewing staff beads

Buy new staff beads the same dimensions as the old ones. Alternatively, buy new ones as close as possible in shape, and long enough to go all round the frame. You will need slightly more than the measurement of the frame to allow a little wastage for mitres to be cut at each corner.

1 Cut a 45° mitre at one end of a length of bead, using a mitre box to ensure an accurate cut.

2 Hold the bead against the frame with the mitre pressed into a corner and mark with a pencil where the other mitre is to be cut.

3 Cut a second mitre, and repeat for each length of beading all round the frame.

4 When all the lengths have been cut, wedge them in place and examine the corner joints for fit.

5 Fix each bead in place with two or three 25mm oval nails.

Fixing a sash window that rattles

Sash windows will rattle if there is too much space around each sash.

The problem occurs more often with the lower (inner) sash and is caused by the inner (staff) bead not being fixed close enough to the sash. The remedy is to remove and re-fix the two staff beads (see left). If a top sash rattles, there is no way to reduce the width of the track, but fitting draught excluders (see right) can help.

From specialist suppliers (via the internet) you can buy replacement staff and parting beads that have draught excluders built in. These should stop window rattles.

Fitting a fitch catch

Another possible cure is to change the existing window catch for a fitch catch – a cam-shaped sash fastener which draws the sashes tightly together when closed. The two parts are screwed to the upper surfaces of the meeting rails of each sash.

Fitting a draught excluder

To cure draughts and rattles in one operation, fit a nylon brush pile draught excluder to the inside face of the staff beads so that the inner face of the lower sash presses against it. Fit another strip between the outer frame and the upper sash so its outer face presses against the strip.

Alternatively Fit the draught excluder to the inner face of one of the meeting rails. This is simpler, but is only effective in reducing rattles when the window is fully closed.

Replacing a broken window pane

There is no need to call a specialist when a window pane breaks. It is quicker and much cheaper to replace it yourself.

Before you start When buying glass, tell the supplier the size of the panes. He will advise on the thickness of glass you should use and will cut them to fit.

Use 3mm glass in very small panes, such as Georgian-style windows. For windows up to about 1m square use 4mm glass. For anything larger, use 6mm glass.

When glass is to be used over a very large area such as a picture window, or where it may be mistaken for an opening, as in a patio door, or where it will be fitted within 800mm of the floor, use safety glass.

For wooden windows use linseed oil, universal or acrylic putty; for metal windows use metal casement, universal or acrylic putty. You will need about 1kg of putty for 3.5m of frame. Brown putty is available for windows that are to be finished with preservative stain. Broken glass in doors is replaced in the same way

HELPFUL TIP

Disposing of broken glass can be difficult. The best way is to take it to your local bottle bank or recyling centre. Otherwise, wrap it thickly in newspaper and put it either beside or in your dustbin, clearly labelled 'broken glass'.

as for wooden windows, unless the door has been glazed with beads which are replaced as for square-edged double glazing units (page 210).

Tools *Leather gloves; safety goggles; glass cutter; hammer; hacking knife or old chisel; pincers; dustpan and brush; paintbrush; putty knife.*

Materials *Primer paint; putty; glazing springs; glass to fit the window.*

Removing the broken glass

1 Lay a dustsheet on the ground on both sides of the window to catch the fragments of old glass.

2 Put on leather gloves and safety goggles. Also wear thick leather shoes in case jagged pieces of glass fall to the ground.

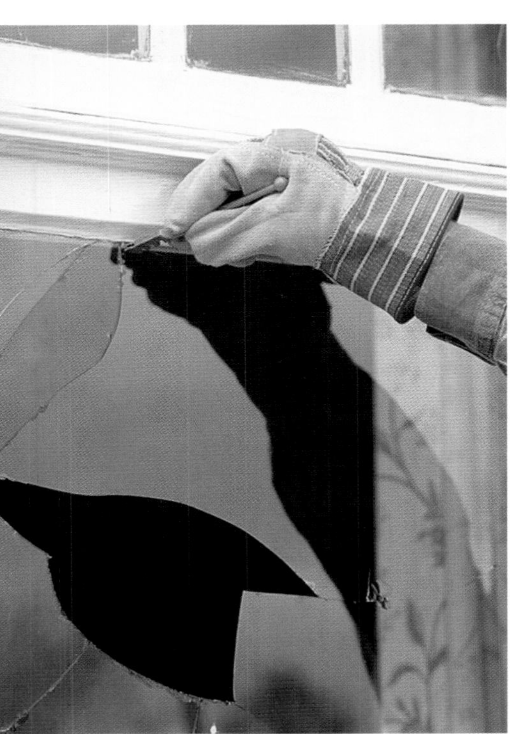

3 Using a glass cutter, score the glass all round the window, close to the putty.

4 Working from the outside, tap the glass with a hammer to break it, starting from the top. Try to keep the pieces as large as possible.

5 After breaking out as much old glass as possible, remove remaining putty and glass with a hacking knife or old chisel. Hold a hacking knife in one hand with the point against the putty and tap it on the blunt edge with a hammer. Look out for glazing sprigs embedded in the putty, or metal clips in metal frames. Pull them out with pincers. Leave the rebate in the window as clean as possible, before putting in new glass.

6 Brush all dust from the frame and paint a wooden frame with primer, which should be allowed to dry. This is not necessary on a metal window unless it is rusty (page 205). If the window has to be left overnight, cover it with a sheet of polythene or a piece of plywood (see panel, right).

Putting in the new glass

1 Mould the putty in your hands to get it soft and pliable. If it sticks to your hands, try wetting them, or take some of the oil out by rolling the putty on kitchen paper.

2 Hold the pliable putty in the palm of your hand and squeeze it out between the thumb and forefinger to form a layer about 3mm thick in the rebate all the way round the window.

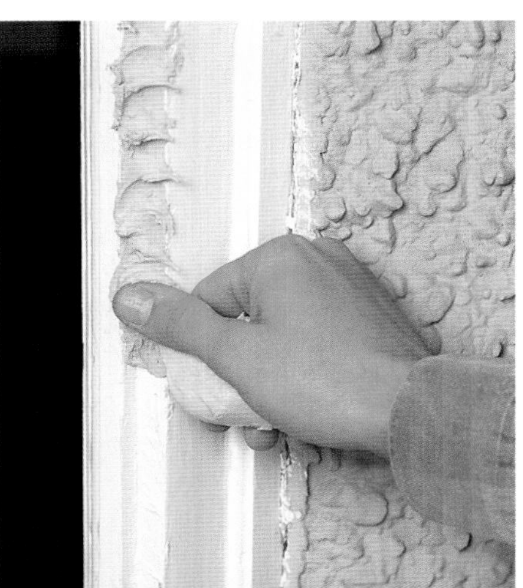

EMERGENCY COVER FOR A BROKEN WINDOW

It is often impossible to repair a broken window immediately, so carry out an emergency repair to keep out weather while you arrange to get the new glass. A cracked pane can be temporarily sealed with waterproof glazing tape, which is transparent. If the panel is smashed, cover the window with heavy-gauge polythene, secured with timber battens nailed around the edge of the frame. The battens will prevent the sheet from tearing. If security is important, cut a sheet of plywood to cover the window frame and fix it with either nails or screws.

3 Press the glass carefully into the rebate so it is well bedded on the putty. Press it round the edges only, taking care not to push too hard in one place – and never in the middle of the glass. It could break and cause injury.

4 Fix the glass in place with glazing sprigs inserted into the window about 250mm apart. Knock them in with the edge of the chisel or with the back of the hacking knife, sliding it along the face of the glass. The heads of the sprigs should protrude about 5mm from the frame. Trim off excess bedding putty on the inside of the pane.

5 Apply more putty to the front of the glass to fill the rebate, and smooth it off with a putty knife to form a neat triangular line of putty that covers the heads of the sprigs and lines up with the putty on the inside edge. Make neat mitres at corners.

6 Leave the putty for about two weeks to harden slightly before painting it. When you paint it, allow the paint to spread onto the glass by 3mm to keep out the rain.

Repairing leaded lights

Doors and windows may have leaded-light panels, consisting of small panes of glass held together with lead strips that are H-shaped in cross section.

Repairing cracked glass

It may not be necessary to fit new glass if the crack is only a minor one. You can try running a few drops of special glass bonding adhesive into the crack.

Replacing broken panes in a leaded-light panel is a difficult job best left to a glazier.

Curing bulges and buckles

Take the complete panel out of the frame. It may be held with putty, like an ordinary sheet of glass (page 209), or it may be held with both putty and an outer wood beading. You can remove the beading by unscrewing it or, if it is nailed, by prising it out very gently. Lay the panel on a flat surface and press the lead strips flat. Be very careful not to press too hard or you are likely to crack the glass panes.

If this does not work, it may be necessary to take the panel to a glazier to have it rebuilt. While this is being done, cover the opening in the door or window, as explained on page 209.

Dealing with leaks

Using polyurethane varnish

1 Mark the leaks with a wax crayon so repairs can be undertaken in fine weather.

2 Carefully scrape any dirt away from the edge of the lead strips.

3 With a small artist's brush, paint clear, exterior grade polyurethane varnish liberally along the flanges of the strips. Take great care to seal the outside of the glass.

Alternatively Inject a bead of the clear sealant used to seal leaks around car windscreens.

4 Press the flanges down, with a helper supporting them firmly from the other side. Wipe varnish off the lead and the glass with a cloth moistened with white spirit.

Using putty

If the varnish does not work, the putty in which the glass is set must be replaced. Use soft glazier's metal casement putty. You can colour the putty grey with a little black powder paint.

1 Open up the lead strips slightly on the outside of the window by levering up the edges with a chisel. To do this it may be necessary to make angled cuts at the corner joints with a trimming knife.

2 Scrape out as much of the old putty as possible and clean out the dirt.

3 Press in the new putty.

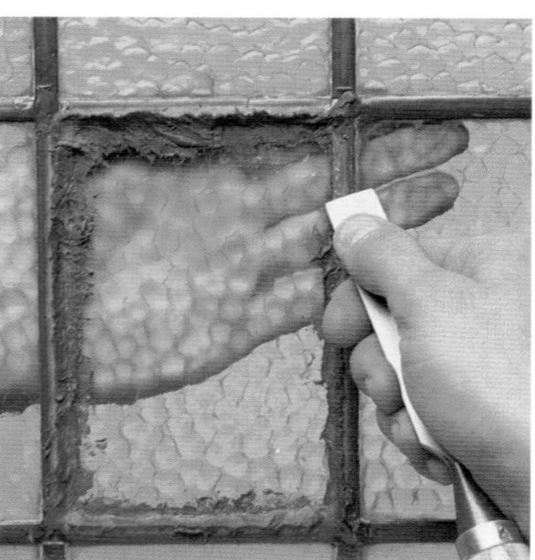

4 Press the lead strip back in place, with a helper supporting the glass from the inside.

5 If it was necessary to cut the corner joints, glue them back together with two-part acrylic adhesive.

6 Wipe the excess putty off the lead and the glass.

Replacing double-glazed sealed units

There are three main ways of replacing failed double-glazed units, depending on whether they are sealed stepped units, square-edge units, or are in aluminium or plastic windows.

Before you start Double-glazing units must be bought ready-made to the exact size of your window from a glass merchant or double-glazing supplier.

Sealed stepped units

Replacing a sealed stepped double glazing unit is similar to fitting a single sheet of glass, except that spacer blocks are fitted in the rebate of the window to keep the stepped part of the double-glazed unit clear of the frame.

Retain the old spacer blocks so they can be re-used, or buy new ones from your glass merchant if they are not supplied with the new units.

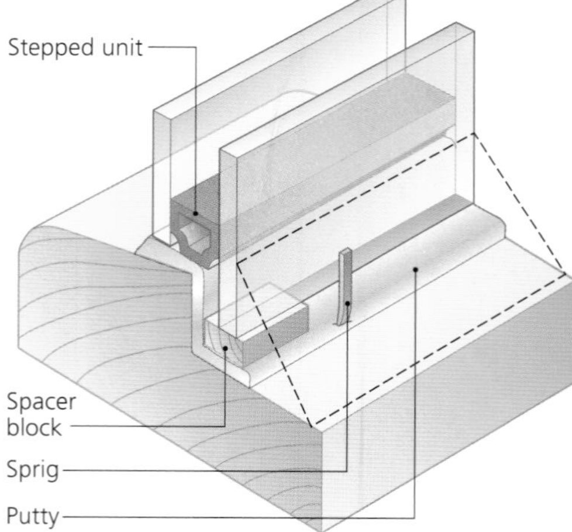

1 Place the spacer blocks in a bed of putty about 300mm apart along the bottom of the rebate.

2 Stand the double-glazed pane on the blocks and fix it in place with sprigs all round. Apply putty to the outside of the window in the normal way.

Square-edge units

Glazing beads are usually screwed into the outside of the window to hold square-edged double-glazing units in place.

1 Unscrew the glazing beads before removing the broken glass.

2 Put a bed of non-setting putty (available from glass merchants) around the rebate. Press spacer blocks into the putty (two blocks spaced well apart on each of the four sides).

3 Lift the sealed unit into place on the spacers and press it well back into the rebate.

4 Coat the glazing beads with non-setting putty on the inside face and press them tightly in place against the glazing units.

5 Fix the beads in place with brass screws and remove excess putty.

Aluminium or plastic windows

The glass is often in rubber gaskets, making replacement difficult. Call in a glazier, or ask the manufacturer for details on glass replacement for your particular model of window.

Choosing double glazing

Double glazing – having two layers of glass instead of one in a window – traps a layer of still air or inert gas between the panes. This acts as an insulator, but the warm inner pane also reduces cold down-draughts from the window and prevents condensation. Although double glazing will not save much on fuel bills, it will greatly increase indoor comfort. There are two main types of double glazing – sealed units and secondary double glazing.

How double glazing works

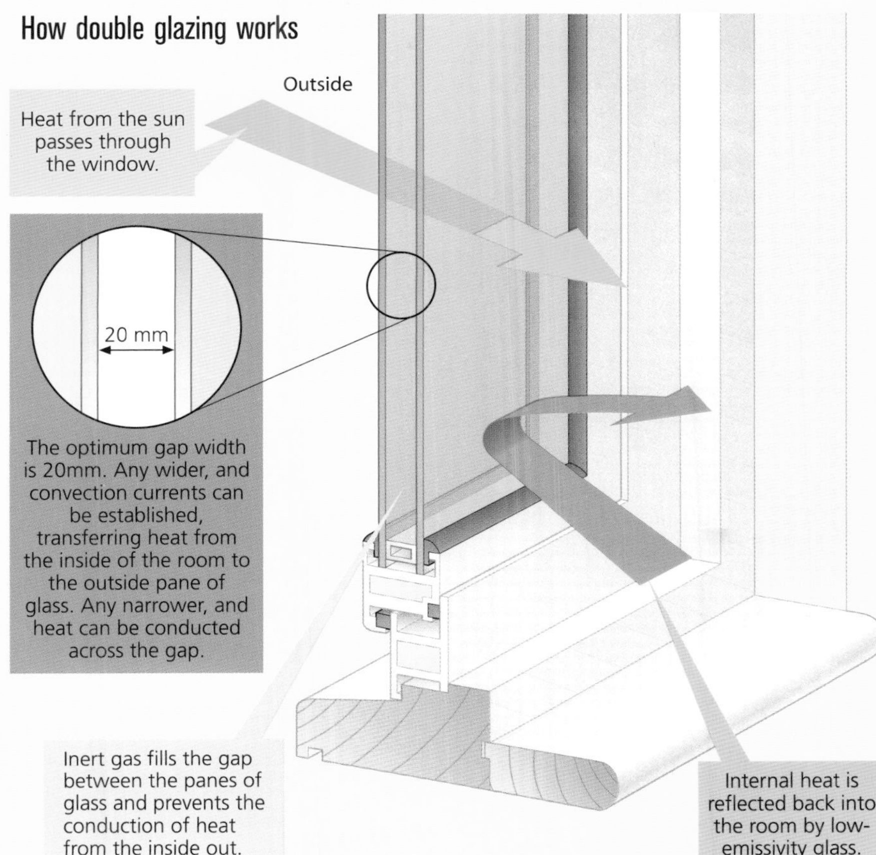

Sealed units Two panes of glass separated by a spacer are bonded together and sealed at the factory before being fitted into the window frame. The panes may be separated by between 6 and 20mm; wide gaps give better insulation than narrow ones.

Secondary double glazing A pane of glass or plastic is fixed to the window frame, leaving an air gap between it and the existing glass. This is less effective than a sealed unit unless the opening part of the window is well draught-proofed. The air gaps are generally wider than in a sealed unit, allowing the air to circulate between the panes and carry heat from the warm inner pane to the colder outer one. Condensation in the gap can be a problem in cold weather.

Triple glazing A wide air gap between panes of glass (100–200mm) insulates effectively against noise, but is too wide to retain heat. Triple glazing combines a sealed twin-pane unit with a third pane, like secondary glazing, to provide excellent heat and sound insulation.

REPLACEMENT REGULATIONS

Since 2002, all replacement windows (and replacement doors with more than 50 per cent glazing) have needed Building Regulations approval.

In order to meet the requirements of Part L (conservation of fuel and power), replacement windows need a 'U' value of 1.6 W/m²K (1.8 for glazed doors), so make sure your supplier can prove that their windows meet these requirements.

Windows also have to comply with regulations concerting structure (i.e. adequate lintels), ventilation, protection against impact (see page 14), means of escape in fire and protection from falling. If you use an installer registered under the FENSA scheme (see Chapter 14) they will be able to self-certify their work.

You do not need planning permission for replacement windows unless you live in a listed building or in a 'designated' area – see box on page 482.

Four cheap secondary double glazing systems

A house can be fitted with secondary double glazing relatively cheaply using materials that give effective results. They have to be removed in summer, and may not look very attractive. Nevertheless, the cost saving compared with having replacement windows is considerable.

Study the fitting instructions supplied with the system you choose and follow them carefully. Double-check your measurements before you order glass or rigid plastic sheet. Mistakes can be expensive.

Clean the windows, inside and out, before you start work. If you are using a system that involves adhesive tape, make sure the window frame is clean and dry. The tape will not stick to surfaces that are dirty or damp.

Existing window glass

Secondary glazing fixed to internal window frame

How secondary double glazing works
Secondary double glazing systems are fitted on the inside of an existing window. The secondary panel is usually fixed to the inside of the frame, creating a gap the depth of the frame between the exterior glass and the new inner pane. Hinged or sliding systems are available from glazing companies or in kit form, allowing you to open the window without removing the double glazing.

Insulating film

A clear plastic film is stuck to the window frame and then shrunk with gentle heat from a hair dryer to remove wrinkles. Although this is not a permanent system, you could extend its life by attaching the plastic film to a frame of timber battens. The framework could be taken down when not required and kept for later use.

Tools *Scissors; hair dryer.*

Materials *Kit containing clear film and double-sided adhesive tape.*

1 Cut a sheet of film a little larger than the window, so that it overlaps all round the window frame by about 50mm.

2 Stick the double-sided adhesive tape around the frame.

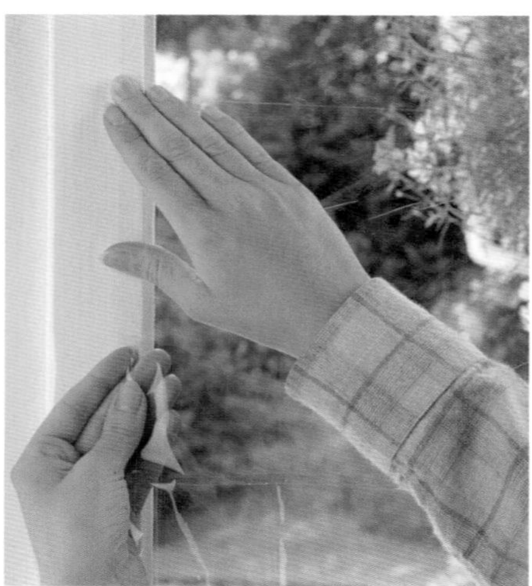

3 Remove the backing from the tape and press the film against it, working from the top downwards and keeping it as taut as possible.

4 Warm the film with a hair dryer to remove wrinkles.

5 Trim off the excess film.

Plastic channelling

Strips of plastic channelling are fitted along the edges of a sheet of glass or rigid plastic. They are then fixed to the window frame with screws and fixing clips.

Some systems have hinged channelling that allows the secondary glazing to be opened. Other types are fixed to the window frame all round and cannot be opened. They have to be taken down completely in summer before any windows can be opened.

Measure the window to allow for the glass or rigid plastic to overlap onto the frame, leaving enough space for the fixing clips to be screwed to the frame.

Tools *Trimming knife or tenon saw (depending on the type of channelling); pencil; bradawl; screwdriver. Perhaps a mitre box.*

Materials *Sheet of 4mm glass or 2–4mm rigid plastic; plastic channelling; screws; fixing clips.*

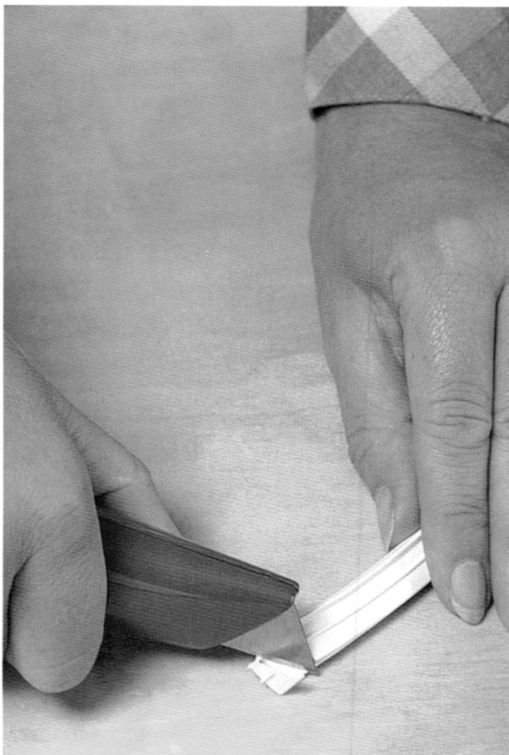

1 Cut the channelling to fit the four edges of the glass or plastic sheet. Mitre the ends to give a neat fit. If the channelling is rigid you will need a tenon saw or hacksaw and a mitre box. Push the channelling onto the glass or plastic sheet.

HELPFUL TIP

You do not need planning permission or Building Regulations approval for secondary glazing.

2 Hold the framed pane over the window while a helper marks positions for the fixing holes, following the maker's instructions for spacing.

3 Deepen the marked spots with the bradawl to provide pilot holes, and screw the fixing clips and glazing in place.

Fixing with Velcro tape

Rigid plastic sheet can be fixed with self-adhesive touch-and-close fastening tape, such as Velcro.
• When you are buying the plastic, measure it to overlap 15mm on all sides of the window frame.
• Do not use glass, because it is too heavy for the system.
• The double glazing can be removed when necessary but the loop part of the tape will have to remain in place and it may look unsightly and collect dirt.

Tools *Scissors.*

Materials *Self-adhesive touch-and-close fastening tape; 2–4mm thick clear rigid plastic; foam-strip draught excluder.*

1 Cut several pieces of tape about 40mm long. It is too expensive to use in long strips.

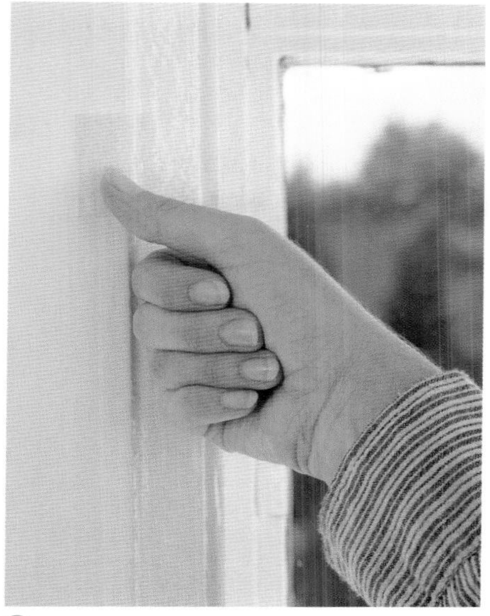

2 Peel the backing paper off the loop (soft) side of the tape and fix it in place at intervals around the window frame.

3 Leave the backing paper on the hook side of the tape, and press the pieces onto the loop strips.

4 Stick foam-strip draught excluder between the patches to prevent draughts.

5 Peel off the remaining backing paper from the tape and press the pane in place.

Magnetic fixing strip

Rigid plastic sheets can be fitted as secondary glazing using magnetic fixing strip. The strip has two self-adhesive parts, a magnetic strip that adheres to the plastic and a metal strip to go on the frame.
• The system is designed for use with plastic up to 4mm thick. Never use it with glass because it is not strong enough to hold the weight.
• Have the plastic cut slightly larger than the window so that it overlaps onto the frame by about 25mm.

Tools *Scissors or trimming knife.*

Materials *Magnetic fixing strip; 2–4mm thick clear rigid plastic.*

1 Cut the strip to fit around the plastic, mitring the corners with sharp scissors or a trimming knife.

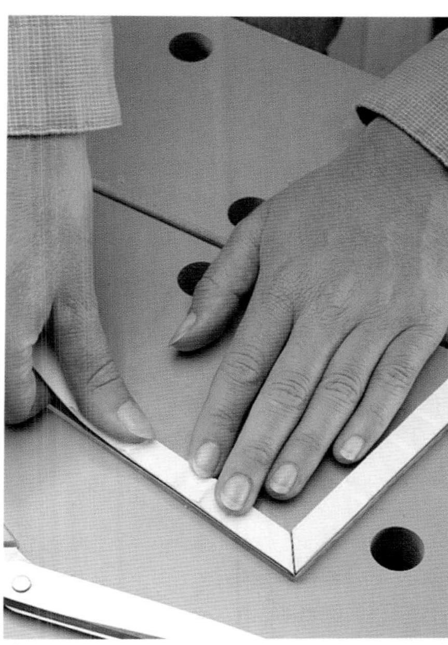

2 Stick the strip to the plastic, with the metal half upwards.

3 Press the sheet to the frame. The metal strip will stay on the frame when the plastic pane is removed.

4 The metal strip can be covered with a thin coat of paint to match the window frame. This makes it less noticeable when the sheet is removed. When redecorating, rub the surface with fine abrasive paper to prevent a build-up of paint.

Fitting a wooden casement window

Building Regulations in England and Wales require that all new windows comply with the government's thermal performance standards (page 211). If you want to fit them yourself, you need to apply to your local authority for Building Regulations approval.

What to buy

- Buy a replacement that matches the style of the other windows in the house – as far as regulations permit.
- Buy a standard size window and frame to fit the space. If that is not possible you can have one made to measure, but it will be much more expensive.

Before you start

- The most important part of the job is measuring the opening in the wall. Take measurements in several positions. Check that the diagonals are equal, which means that the opening has right-angled corners.
- With a spirit level, check that the sill and top of the frame are both level, and that the sides are vertical. If they are not, it may be best to call in a builder, or a replacement window company.
- Do not start to remove the old window until you have taken delivery of the new window.
- New windows are usually supplied without glass or double-glazed units, which are installed after the window has been fitted.
- The job is likely to last more than a day, so be prepared to cover the wall opening – or unglazed window – with polythene or hardboard overnight to keep out the weather.

Tools *Spirit level; steel tape measure; screwdriver; leather work gloves; safety goggles; claw hammer; metal container for broken glass; hacksaw blade; old wood saw; wrecking bar or lever; bolster chisel; builder's trowel; power drill; twist bits; countersink bit; masonry bit to match wall plugs; sealant gun. Possibly a plane and self-grip wrench.*

Materials *New wooden window frame; mortar (page 467); wooden wedges; 100mm No. 14 countersunk zinc-plated screws; wall plugs for screws; strip of damp-proof course the width of the window; frame sealant. Possibly also: strips of hardwood as wide as the frame's thickness; panel pins; wood mouldings to go around frame; plaster.*

Removing the existing window

1 Remove hinged windows by unscrewing the hinges. If the window is a big one, you will need a helper to support it.

2 Remove the glass from any fixed windows. Wearing the gloves and goggles, break the glass with a hammer. Remove all the pieces from the frame and put them into a metal container for safe disposal.

3 You will probably have to take the frame out in pieces. Use an old saw to cut through the vertical and horizontal timbers close to the sides, top and bottom of the frame.

4 Saw at an angle through the jamb at one side of the frame.

5 With a strong lever, such as a wrecking bar, prise the jamb that you have sawn through until it comes away from the brickwork. This will allow you to lever out the other parts of the frame – the top, the sill and finally the jamb at the other side.

If an internal window board is fitted inside the windowsill, keep it in one piece, because you will need it when you fit the new window. Try also to keep the sides of the opening intact, as you do not want to damage the wall plaster or the damp-proof strip that closes the wall cavity.

6 Clean up the sides, top and bottom of the opening with a bolster chisel to leave the bricks as smooth as possible and free from old mortar.

7 Remove any protruding screws (with a self-grip wrench) or nails (with a claw hammer). Take out any bits of timber 'horns' from the frame that may have been built into the top corners of the opening.

8 Fill any large cavities neatly with pieces of brick and mortar and wait for the repairs to dry.

TAKING OUT THE FRAME IN ONE PIECE

It might be possible to remove the old window frame in one piece.

1 Locate the screws or nails fixing the frame to the wall and clear them of mortar.

2 Cut through the screws with a hacksaw blade. Fit the blade into the handle so you can cut by pulling, not pushing.

3 Try lifting out the frame.

REMOVING STUBBORN SCREWS

Begin by using an old screwdriver to clear paint from the screw slot. Then put a well fitting screwdriver blade in the slot and strike the handle with a hammer. Press hard while turning screwdriver counter clockwise. For really stubborn screws, use an impact driver – a type of screwdriver that turns automatically when struck with a hammer. Or try heating the screw head with a large soldering iron to expand the screw temporarily and break the seal between screw and frame. As a last resort, drill out the screw head.

Installing the new window frame

The new window normally comes with a new exterior sill; if a separate sill is required it should be hardwood or moulded plastic.

Normally the frame is fitted up against the existing inside window board.

1 Hold the new frame up to the opening to see if it fits. (You will probably need a helper.) There should be a clearance of about 6mm all round.

2 If the frame is slightly too big, plane a little off it. Then treat the bare wood with clear preservative followed by primer, or with preservative wood stain.

Alternatively If the new frame is too small, pack it out by nailing strips of hardwood up to 20mm thick to the sides. After the window has been installed, moulding can be tacked around the edges of the frame to cover the packing strips.

3 Lift the frame into place and temporarily hold it with wedges. If the window is a large one, you will need a helper at this stage. Wedge it to within 6mm of the lintel to allow space for mortar at the bottom.

The frame must be vertical, and must be pushed right back against the plaster inside the room. Use a spirit level to check that its face is vertical and that both the top and bottom of the frame are horizontal.

4 Drill holes through the jambs at suitable intervals. Position the holes where they will coincide with the mid-points of bricks, not the mortar joints. Allow the drill to penetrate just far enough to mark the bricks. On most windows four fixings – at the top and bottom of each jamb – are sufficient. On windows more than 1.2m from top to bottom, put a third fixing about midway up each jamb.

5 Carefully remove the frame from the opening and check that you can see the drilling marks.

Alternatively leave the frame in place and drill holes for frame fixers as on page 190.

6 Using a masonry bit, drill the bricks at the marked points and insert wall plugs.

7 Countersink screw holes in the frame.

8 Lay a thin bed of mortar (page 467) on the sill brickwork.

9 Lay a strip of damp-proof course along the sill and then cover it with another layer of mortar.

10 Replace the frame and wedges at the sides and top, and check with a spirit level that it is level and the face is vertical.

11 Fix the frame by screwing into the wall plugs in the bricks.

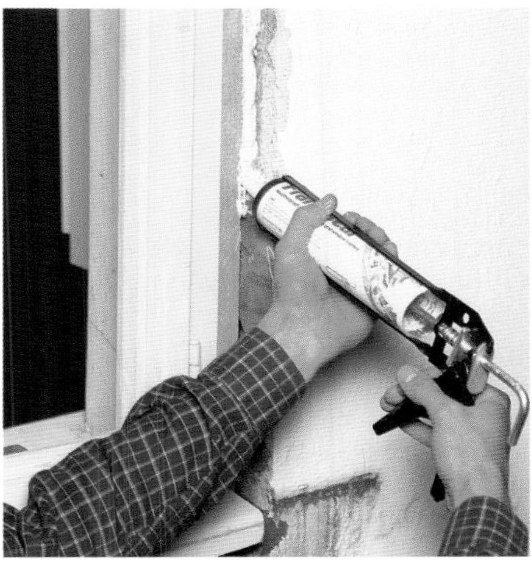

12 Use a frame sealant to fill any gaps around the frame. Inject the sealant from a cartridge with a sealant gun. Do not use mortar; it cannot accommodate movement in the wood.

13 If needed, repair damage to rendering around the outside of the opening with mortar, and make good inside with plaster. The window is then ready for glazing and final decoration if necessary.

Choosing a draught excluder

Before you buy a draught excluder, measure the width of the gaps which need to be blocked. The packaging on most draught excluders indicates how big a gap the product is intended to fill and where it can be used.

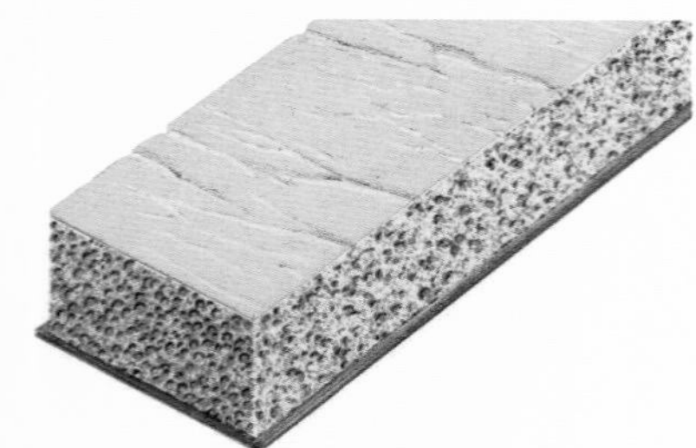

Self-adhesive foam strip Use on casement windows and exterior doors. Quality varies a lot. Some strips perish after only one or two seasons; more expensive types will last for five years or more. Cheaper versions are made of polyurethane, which hardens with age. Sizes vary according to the manufacturer but strips are usually about 6mm thick and 10mm wide. Most strips are only supplied in white. Avoid getting paint on foam – it will harden with age, unless the strip manufacturer states otherwise.

Self-adhesive rubber strip Use on casement windows and exterior doors. Available in a limited colour range and in profiles including P and E. This type of excluder is tough and will last longer than foam. Fix to the frame as for self-adhesive foam strip (above).

Brush strips Use on exterior and patio doors, and on sash and casement windows. The strips consist of siliconised nylon pile in self-adhesive strips or in a metal plastic holder that is to be tacked to the frame, not the door or window. The strip is particularly designed for surfaces which slide against each other, as on sash windows and patio doors.

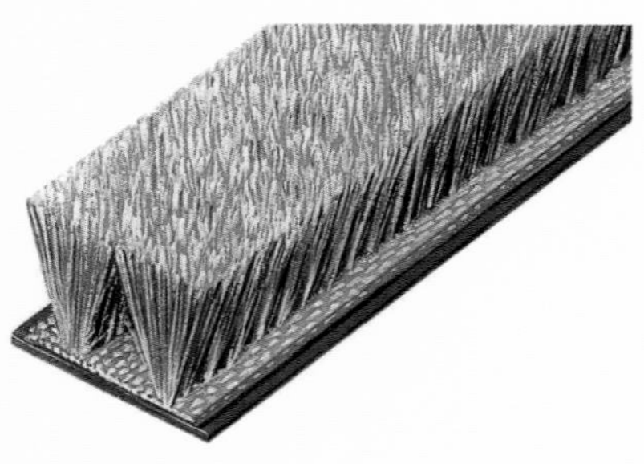

Draughtproofing a window

There are many ways to improve the seal around your windows and keep out draughts. Measure the height and width of the window to gauge how much of the draughtproofing strip you will need.

Before you start Clean the window frame with water and a little washing-up liquid to remove all grease and dirt. Rinse and wait for the surface to dry.

A casement window

Most of the draughtproofing strips shown left are suitable for use on a wooden casement window. Only strips with an adhesive backing can be used on a metal casement window.

1 Cut lengths to fit with scissors or a trimming knife.

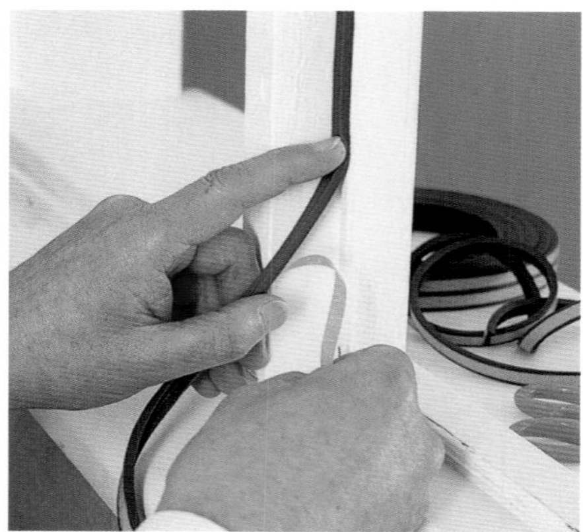

2 Peel away the protective backing as you stick down each length on the rebate. Make sure that one piece of excluder goes right into each corner.

Silicone sealant for large gaps For large or uneven gaps, a silicone sealant (also called a frame sealant) is particularly useful, but cannot be used on sash windows. It can also be used on doors – see page 205. Read any instructions before you begin.

A sash window

Rigid brush strip is the most suitable material for sealing the sides of a sash window, as the sashes slide over it easily.

1 Measure the height of the sliding sashes and cut four pieces of brush strip – two pieces for each sash.

2 Fix the strip to either side of the frame: on the inside of the inner sash and on the outside of the outer sash. Use pre-holed strip, fixing it with the pins provided and a hammer. Unless the window is not opened very often, self-adhesive strip is not suitable because it is unlikely to withstand the friction from the sashes as they slide.

3 Seal the gap at the top and bottom of the sashes with any of the more durable foam strips fixed to the frame or the sash.

4 If there is a draught between the top and bottom sashes of the window, fix nylon brush pile strip to the bottom sash at the meeting point.

HELPFUL TIP

To improve the adhesion of self-adhesive strips, apply a thin coating of clear all-purpose adhesive over the surface to which the excluder is to be fixed. Let the adhesive dry before pressing on the strips.

Draughtproofing a door

You may need to use more than one type of draught excluder on a door. Fix a foam strip around the sides and top of a door and a threshold excluder at the bottom for a snug finish.

If you are fitting one of the foam, rubber or flexible strips for the first time – or are unsure which excluder is most suitable – experiment on one door before you buy all the material you need. To calculate how much of a strip draught excluder you need to buy, measure the height and width of the door.

Some threshold excluders are designed to deflect in-blown rain as well as to stop draughts. Threshold excluders are usually sold in standard lengths for external doors and some come in two parts: one to fix to the base of the door and the other to the sill.

Adding an enclosed porch

If you put an enclosed porch around an outside door – especially if it is exposed to prevailing winds – you will greatly reduce the draughts entering the house. You will also help to reduce condensation inside if you can leave wet umbrellas and coats in a porch.

Unless you live in a listed building or in a 'designated' area (see box on page 482), you do not need planning permission to build a porch, provided that the floor area is not more than $3m^2$, and no part is higher than 3m above ground level. You must also ensure that the porch is at least 2m from the boundary between the garden and a road or public footpath. Porches also have to meet some of the requirements of the Building Regulations – see page 487.

HELPFUL TIP

If you cannot find the source of a draught, light a candle and hold it in front of the door or window. Move around the edge of the frame and the flame will flicker at the point where the draught is coming in. Take care not to set curtains alight.

Strip excluders for the frame Self-adhesive foam strips or nylon brush strip are cut to length and fitted to the frame. Some require pinning.

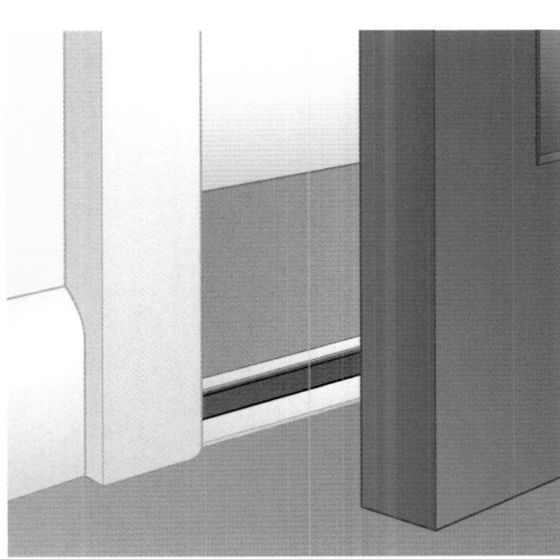

Metal or rubber seal for the sill A plastic or metal bar fitted to the sill has a rubber insert which seals the gap under the door when it is closed.

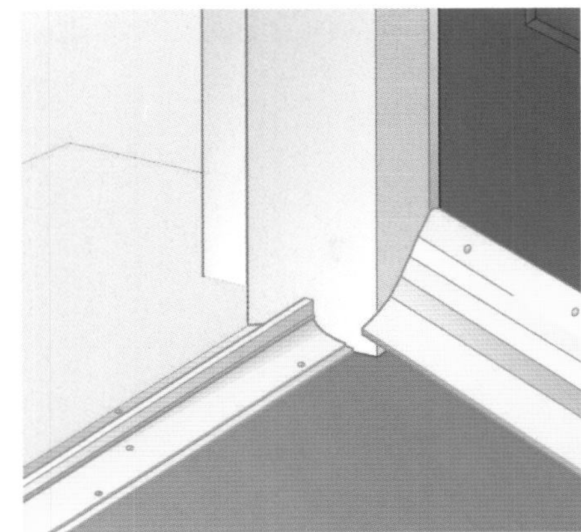

Two-piece excluders fitted to door and sill A weatherbar is attached to the sill and a deflector is attached to the base of the door. The deflector is shaped to deflect rainwater over the weatherbar when the door is closed and the weatherbar prevents rain from being blown in beneath the door.

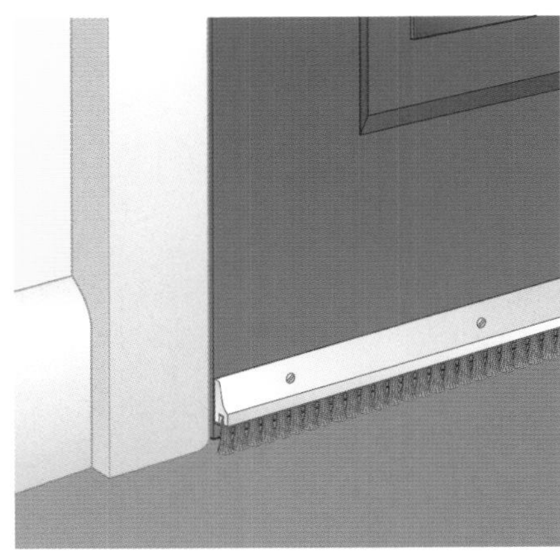

Strip excluders for the base of the door A strip of nylon, rubber or plastic bristle mounted in aluminium. The excluder is fitted to the base of the door – on the inside – and is usually adjustable for height to give a good seal.

Letterbox excluder A plastic frame with two rows of nylon bristle fits over the letterbox slot on the innerside of the door.

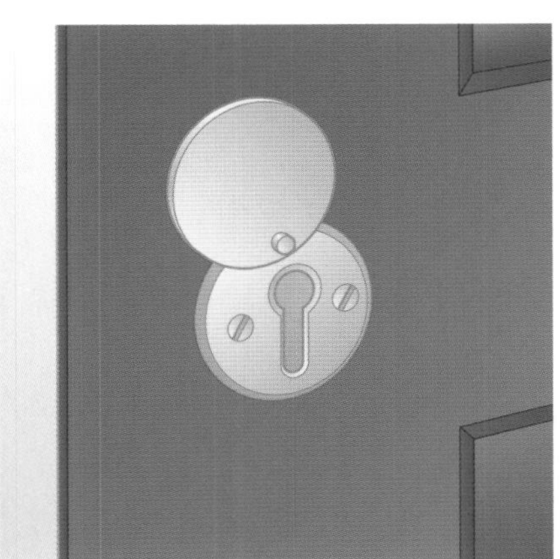

Keyhole cover A pivoted cover, or escutcheon, hangs in front of the keyhole of a mortise lock. Best fitted on the inside for security.

Choosing security locks for your windows

Windows are the main points of entry for burglars. The most common method of breaking in is to smash the glass and release the catch, but window locks will lock the frames together, make the handle immovable, or restrain the stay arm. Before buying window locks, make sure they are suitable for your windows. A lock for timber frames will come with woodscrews. Locks for metal windows will have self-tapping screws. Make sure the frames are thick enough to accommodate the device.

SASH WINDOW LOCKS

Sash stop (left) A locking nut screws into a mounting plate on the upper sash to prevent the lower sash from sliding up. They can be positioned a little higher to allow the window to be opened a little for ventilation. Fit two to large windows.

Sash window press lock (below) A two-part surface-fitted lock secures the two meeting rails together, in place of the standard interlocking sash catch. A push bolt locks the inner and outer plate together. They are released with a key.

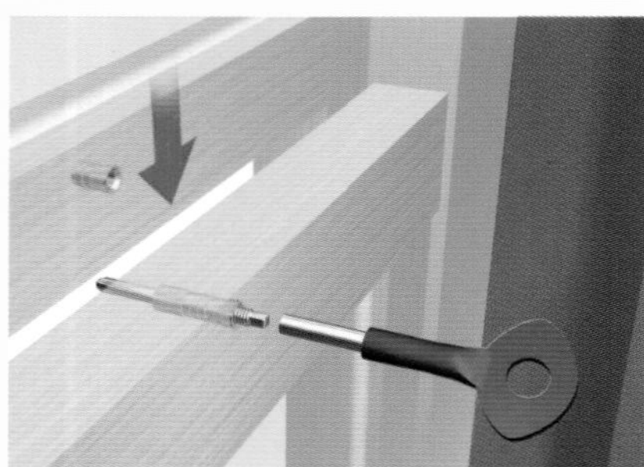

Dual screw A long, steel, key-operated screw goes through a barrel in the inner sash into a threaded sleeve in the outer sash. Fit two dual screws if the window is large.

METAL WINDOWS

Locking clamp A key shoots a bolt from the window into a bracket mounted on the frame.

Stay bolt Fits underneath the stay arm. A bolt slides under the stay retainer, preventing the arm from being lifted.

Cockspur bolt When the cockspur handle is closed, the case of the bolt is moved up on the fixed frame and locked, preventing the cockspur from opening. Alternatively, a locking cockspur handle can be fitted.

SAFETY WARNING

- When windows are locked, keep a key in the room so a window can be opened in an emergency (but out of the reach of a burglar who may have smashed the glass).
- Do not permanently screw windows closed that may be needed as an escape route in time of fire.

CASEMENT WINDOW LOCKS

For locking window to frame

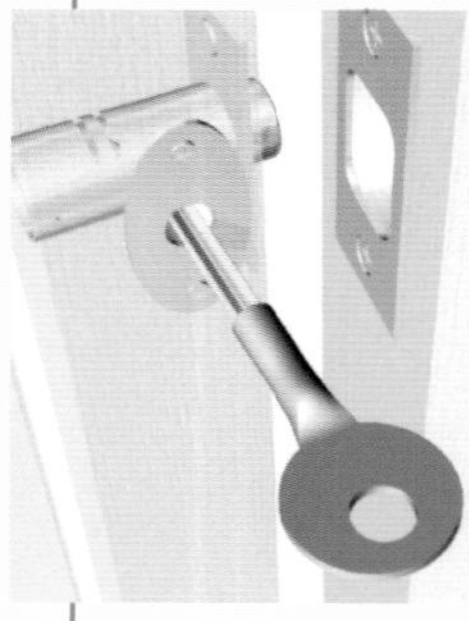

Mortise rack bolt The lock is mortised into the opening window, and the bolt slides into a hole in the fixed frame. They are suitable only for windows at least 35mm thick. Gives excellent security – fitted as for longer door rack bolt (see page 200). Fit close to the centre of the opening edge. On large windows, fit a mortise rack bolt at each end of the opening edge.

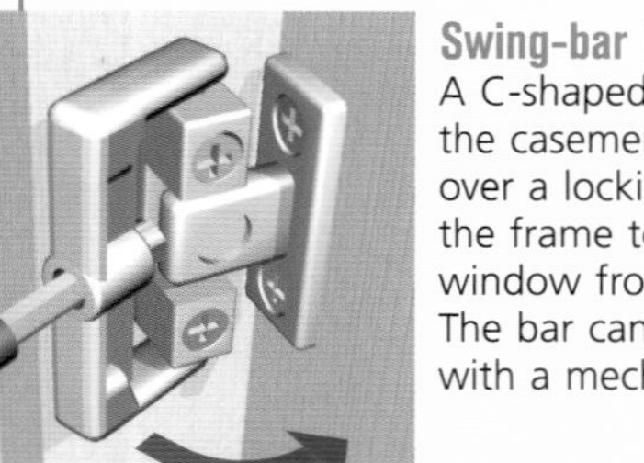

Swing-bar lock A C-shaped bar fixed to the casement swings over a locking plate on the frame to stop the window from opening. The bar can be locked with a mechanical key.

Cam lock A key turns a cam, or notched rotating shaft, into the second part of the lock, fixed to the frame, securing the two components together.

For locking the handle and stay

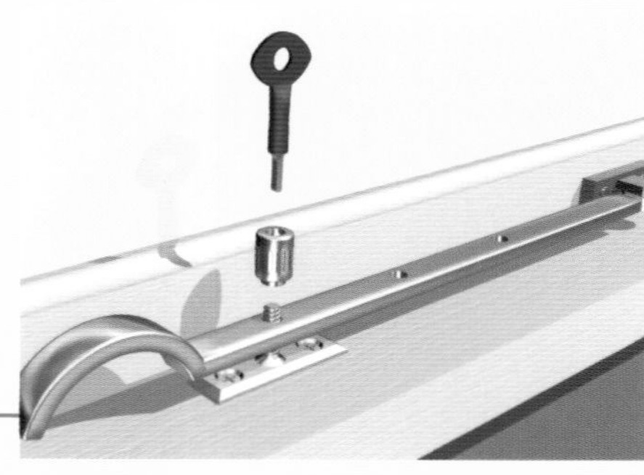

Locking handle A new handle with a lock replaces the existing cockspur handle. Once locked, it cannot be opened without the key. Make sure you buy the correct right-hand or left-hand type for your window. Some types allow the window to be locked slightly ajar for ventilation. Alternatively, a blocking bolt can be fitted to the fixed frame that prevents the cockspur handle from moving, if the cockspur is on the frame surface. The bolt is retracted with the key.

Stay lock Replaces the pegs that secure the stay when closed. The peg is threaded and is locked by screwing on a key-operated nut. Ventilation locks allow the window to be locked closed or slightly open: the peg locates in a short sliding bar fixed to the casement, so that the position can be adjusted.

Fitting locks to windows

Most locks come with their own clear fitting instructions, but these are three of the most common and effective window locks to fit yourself.

Casement window lock

Surface-mounted locks are easy to fit to casement windows, provided that the surfaces of the fixed frame and the opening casement are at right angles to each other.

- If the fixed frame is tapered, wood may have to be chiselled so the lock fits against the opening frame. Some locks are supplied with a wedge to get over this problem.
- For large windows, or for extra security, fit two locks on each frame, at top and bottom. They will withstand a jemmy attack better than a single lock.
- The technique shown below is for a swing-bar lock, but other models are installed in a similar way.

Tools *Pencil; drill and twist bits; bradawl; screwdriver. Perhaps a small chisel.*

Materials *One or two window locks, depending on size of window.*

1 Open the window and position the locking plate on the frame, 1mm from the edge. Make sure it is straight, mark the position of the holes with a bradawl and screw the plate in place.

2 Close the window and position the body of the lock behind the locking plate. Fix one screw, check the operation of the lock, then drive in the second screw.

SAFETY AND SECURITY

Laminated glass
Particular windows in a house may be at risk from burglars. They may be ground-floor windows hidden from the neighbours, or they may be upstairs windows that are accessible from an extension roof, a drainpipe or a tree. Fitting laminated glass will greatly add to the security.
It consists of a sandwich of glass with a clear plastic film between. Although the glass may be cracked by a blow, the plastic will resist efforts to break through. Do not use wired glass: it prevents fire spread, but has little security value.

Plastic windows
An increasing number of plastic windows are being used in houses, and they can pose a security problem. Most manufacturers of security devices do not recommend them for plastic windows because a thin plastic section offers no grip for screws. If a plastic window frame is known to have a timber inner frame, security devices suitable for a wooden frame can be used. If there are steel inserts within the plastic section, self-tapping screws could be used, as for metal frames. But locks cannot be fitted to hollow sections of windows filled with rigid foam. The ideal solution is to make sure your plastic replacement windows come with locking handles.

Metal-framed window lock

Locks are fitted to a steel or aluminium window frame with self-tapping screws, which should be supplied with the lock. To drill a pilot hole in the frame, use a high-speed-steel (HSS) twist bit. Most locks come with instructions giving the drill size.

If in doubt, make the hole the same diameter as the 'core' of the screw, not the shank. Use a bit that is too small rather than too big.

Tools *Bradawl or ball-point pen; electric drill; HSS twist bits; screwdriver.*

Materials *Window lock with self-tapping screws.*

1 Hold the lock in position and mark the screw hole with a bradawl or ball-point pen.

2 Drill a pilot hole just through the metal. Provided the bit is sharp, it should not skid on the metal.

3 Screw the lock to the frame. If the screw hole is too tight, re-drill the hole one size bigger.

Dual screw sash window lock

A dual screw is a very secure locking device for a sash window, but it is not suitable if the window is frequently opened.

Before you start If the window is opened often, use a surface-fitted bolt (see opposite). For large windows, fit two locks, one at each end of the centre meeting rail.

Dual screws vary in design. Some have barrels for both inner and outer frames, other have a lockplate for the outer frame.

Tools *Drill and auger bit the width of the lock barrel; hammer and piece of wood, or a large screwdriver (depending on the model). Perhaps a small screwdriver, small twist bit and chisel (depending on model).*

Materials *One or two dual screws.*

1 Drill through the inner meeting rail and on into the outer meeting rail to a depth of 15mm. Wind some tape around the bit as a guide to the depth of the hole. Take care not to catch the edge of the glass.

2 Tap the longer barrel into the inner meeting rail, using a hammer and a piece of wood to protect it from being damaged. Squeeze it into the frame using a G-cramp if the frame is old and the glass liable to shatter.

3 Reverse the sashes. Tap the shorter barrel into the outer meeting rail. Alternatively, fit the locking plate to the outer meeting rail. If the sashes clash as they pass, recess the plate with a chisel.

4 Close the window and screw the bolt into the barrel with the key. Trim the bolt with a hacksaw if it is too long.

Walls and ceilings

Walls, ceilings and fireplaces 7

Types of plaster for indoor use

Ordinary quick-setting, lightweight gypsum plaster is used by professional plasterers. For DIY users, one-coat plaster in powder or ready-mixed form is easier. Gypsum based indoor plasters are usually sold in 50kg packs, though smaller packs may be available. Choose a cement-based plaster for damp areas indoors.

Working times (the time you get to apply the plaster before it sets too solid to work) and setting times (the time the plaster takes to go hard) are given as a guide, but these are shorter in warm rooms and longer in cold.

If water is absorbed too fast from plaster, it will crack. So if you are using a standard two-coat plaster, choose the undercoat suitable for your wall – different types are made for differing wall surface absorbencies.

Browning undercoat For solid, fairly absorbent surfaces indoors, such as bricks or building blocks.
• Layers should be about 10mm thick.
• A lightweight quick-setting pink or grey undercoat, mixed with clean, cold water. Apply within 15–30 minutes of mixing.
• Sets in 1½–2 hours.
• 10kg covers about 1.5m² 10mm thick.

Bonding undercoat On dense, not very absorbent surfaces indoors – for example, concrete, engineering bricks, or surfaces treated with PVA adhesive, such as laths.
• Layers should be about 8mm thick.
• A lightweight quick-setting pink or grey undercoat, mixed with clean, cold water. Apply within 15–30 minutes of mixing.
• Sets in 1½–2 hours.
• 10kg covers about 1.5m² 8mm thick.

Finishing coat On browning or bonding undercoats.
• The layers should be about 2mm thick.
• A lightweight, quick-setting pink or grey finish plaster, mixed with clean, cold water.
• 10kg covers about 4.5m² 2mm thick.

Plasterboard finish On a plasterboard surface (ivory side).
• Layers should be about 5mm thick.
• Sets in 1–1½ hours.
• 10kg covers about 1.5m² 5mm thick.

One-coat plaster On most indoor surfaces, such as bricks, blocks or plasterboard.
• Can be applied up to about 50mm thick into cavities.
• Suitable for filling or finishing in one application.
• Mixed with clean, cold water; dries white or pink.
• Workable for 30–60 minutes.
• 8kg covers about 0.7m² 10mm thick.

Renovating plaster For use in damp conditions (but not below ground level on an unlined background), or in slow-drying places.
• Undercoat layers should be about 10mm thick, finishing layers about 2mm. Some are one-coat plasters.
• A lightweight plaster mixed with clean cold water.
• Sets in 1½–2 hours.
• Treat backgrounds with low absorbency, such as concrete or dense bricks or blocks, with a water-resisting bonding aid first.
• 10kg covers about 1.2m² 10mm thick.

Ready-mixed undercoat or one coat Used on most indoor building surfaces such as bricks, blocks, plasterboard or laths.
• Layers can be up to about 50mm thick into cavities.
• A grey paste applied straight from the container. Available in 2.5kg packs.
• Workable for about 4 hours after application.
• Slow setting – takes about 24 hours to dry.
• Can be used without a finishing coat if the surface is to be papered.
• 10kg covers about 0.75m² about 10mm thick.

Ready-mixed finishing coat On ready-mixed undercoat or other plaster surfaces.
• Layers should be about 3mm thick.
• A creamy-white paste applied straight from the container.
• Workable for about 4 hours after application.
• Sets in about 24 hours.
• 10kg covers about 2m² 3mm thick.

Accessories for use with plasterboard

Joint compound Used on plasterboard and joint tape. Sold in 10kg or 25kg packs.
• For filling and embedding joints on plasterboard by hand.
• In powder form; mixed with clean, cold water.
• Workable for up to 30 minutes.

Joint tape Used on plasterboard taper-edged joints before decorating (ivory side out).
• A 50mm wide self-adhesive tape for reinforcing plasterboard joints.

Plasterboard primer/sealer Used on ivory-coloured surface of plasterboard.
• For preparing plasterboard surface for decoration.
• Two coats will give the surface protection against moisture.
• Workable for about 30 minutes; sets in 1 hour.

Patching damaged plaster

Large cracks, holes or crumbling areas of plaster can generally be repaired quickly and cheaply with plaster.

Damage caused by damp Do not repair damage caused by damp until the cause has been remedied. If large cracks reopen after repair, get the advice of a builder or surveyor, as the cracks may be caused by structural movement of the building.

Using ready-mixed plaster

Tools *Cold chisel; club hammer; hand brush; filling knife or plasterer's trowel. Possibly also fine abrasive paper or power sander; face mask and safety goggles; large paintbrush; plastic spreader (supplied with skim-coat container).*

Materials *Ready-mixed plaster. Possibly ready-mixed skim-coat plaster.*

1 Chip away loose or crumbling plaster with a cold chisel until you reach a firm surface all round.

2 Brush away dust and debris. If bricks or building blocks are exposed, dampen the areas with water.

3 Stir the plaster and apply it to the wall with a filling knife or plasterer's trowel held at an angle.

4 Build up deep areas in layers – applied up to 50mm deep in cavities. Allow each layer to stiffen before applying the next.

5 If the surface is to be papered, fill the undercoat to the top of the damaged area. When it is thoroughly dry, smooth it with fine abrasive paper or a power sander. Wear a mask and goggles to protect you from dust.

Alternatively If the surface is to be painted, fill the top 3mm of the area with a coat of skim plaster to give smooth finish. Apply it with a large brush, in upward strokes, then spread it with light strokes. When it begins to dry, smooth it with the plastic spreader supplied.

USING ONE-COAT PLASTER

Mix the plaster according to the instructions on the packet – generally up to about 500ml cold water per 1kg of powder – until it is a smooth paste that is just stiff enough to use. Apply it in the same way as ordinary plaster (right), and finish in the same way.

Using ordinary plaster

This is the least expensive plaster, but requires skill to achieve a professional finish. It is applied in two coats and you need to work fast. It's a good idea to practise somewhere inconspicuous before beginning the job.

Tools *Cold chisel; club hammer; hand brush; large paintbrush or plant spray; clean plastic bucket; mixing stick or wooden spoon; length of wood; plasterer's trowel; carrying board (also called a hawk).*

Materials *Undercoat plaster; finishing plaster; supply of clean, cold water for mixing.*

1 Chip away loose or crumbly plaster with a cold chisel until you reach a firm surface all round.

2 Brush away dust and debris. If bricks or building blocks are exposed, dampen the areas with water.

3 Mix the undercoat plaster with cold water in a clean bucket until its consistency is between that of stiff porridge and whipped cream. Use it as quickly as possible after mixing – within 15–30 minutes.

4 Load plaster onto a carrying board. Apply it with a plasterer's trowel held at an angle of about 45° to the wall and sweep it upwards to press the plaster to the surface, flattening it slightly at the end of the stroke. Be careful not to press the trowel flat against the surface, or the plaster will pull away when you lift off the trowel.

5 If necessary, build up the damaged surface in thin layers. Wait for each successive layer to stiffen (but not to dry) before applying the next.

6 Fill the undercoat to within 3mm of the surface and while it is still wet knock off the high points by drawing a length of wood across it. Rest it on the edges of a firm surrounding surface and work upwards with a slight zigzag motion.

7 When the undercoat is dry (about 2 hours after application) mix the finishing plaster in a clean bucket to the consistency of melting ice cream.

8 Using a plasterer's trowel held at a slight angle, spread the finishing coat on top of the undercoat within about 15–30 minutes of mixing. This is a messy job, so make sure the surroundings are protected from splashes, if necessary.

9 When the finishing coat has stiffened – about 20 minutes after application – smooth the surface with a plasterer's trowel held at a slight angle, using wide backwards and forwards sweeps. While you are doing this, keep on dampening the area with water using a large paintbrush or house-plant spray.

Repairing and reinforcing corners

When filling an external corner with plaster, it can be difficult to get a level surface and a straight edge. The job is easier if it is done in two operations using a timber batten as a guide.

Tools *Cold chisel; club hammer; softwood timber batten 50 x 20mm and longer than the depth of the area to be filled; straight-edge; masonry nails; hammer; hand brush; plasterer's trowel. Possibly also carrying board; large paintbrush or plant spray; spirit level with horizontal and vertical vials; corner trowel; rubber gloves.*

Materials *Plaster. Possibly also; length of expanded metal angle beading (see panel).*

1 Cut back crumbling plaster to a firm surface and brush away debris from the damaged area.

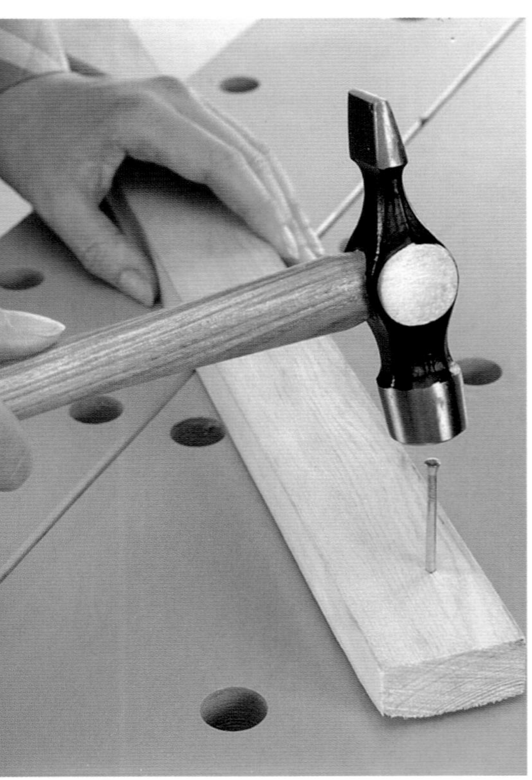

2 Drive two masonry nails through the batten, closer to one edge than the other, and position them so that they will either be driven into the mortar between bricks, or will fit into firm plaster well beyond the edges of the damaged area, to avoid cracking more plaster.

3 Hold the wood batten vertically against the damaged edge with the nails nearer to the inner side. Use a straight-edge along the adjacent wall to align the batten with the plaster surface at the top and bottom.

4 Nail the batten gently to the wall, leaving the nail heads protruding.

5 Plaster the area with a suitable undercoat or one-coat plaster to align with the edge of the batten.

6 When the plaster has dried, remove the nails and pull away the batten to avoid crumbling the edge of the new plaster.

7 Nail the batten to the other side of the corner and then plaster the remaining damaged area in the same way.

8 If using a finishing coat, use the batten in the same way to plaster both sides of the corner.

9 Finishing the edge of the corner is easier with a corner trowel. Or you could round it off with a plasterer's trowel.

Alternatively Before the plaster hardens fully, put on a rubber glove, wet it, and run your fingers down the edge to blunt it slightly.

Repairs around sockets

1 Switch off the mains supply at the consumer unit before patching round a switch or socket.

2 Disconnect the fitting, noting the wiring connections, and remove it.

3 Whether the socket is seated in plaster or plasterboard, fill small cracks or holes with an interior filler and larger holes by one of the methods described above.

4 Wait for the plaster to dry before refitting the switch or socket.

Repairs around ceiling roses and light fittings

1 Turn off the mains supply at the consumer unit when dealing with light fittings. Repairs to the edge of a ceiling rose generally do not carry any risk of electric shock.

2 For small, difficult to reach holes and breaks in the plaster, use a small amount of expanding foam filler.

3 Squirt some filler into the space.

4 Allow it to harden and then cut away the excess with a sharp knife.

REINFORCING A DAMAGED CORNER

If an external corner is prone to damage, reinforce it with expanded metal angle beading before plastering the wall. The beading is formed from two bands of galvanised steel mesh set at right angles to a rounded centre strip. It is sold in lengths and can be cut to the required size with tinsnips and a hacksaw. Treat the cut ends and any areas of the galvanised coating accidentally damaged during installation with metal primer.

1 Fit beading against the corner with dabs of plaster about 600mm apart on each side.

2 Use a straight-edge and spirit level to make sure it is vertical.

3 Press the mesh firmly against the wall and check with a straight-edge that the centre strip, or corner bead, will not protrude above the plaster surface.

4 The bead can be used as a guide to forming a straight edge when plastering, instead of using a timber batten.

Filling gaps round waste pipes

When a new dishwasher or washing machine is fitted, it may be necessary to make a hole through the wall, to accommodate the water waste pipes.

Once the pipe is fitted, it is necessary to fill the space around the pipe in order to cut down on draughts and to prevent damp from entering the property.

Squirt expanding foam filler all round the pipe and allow it to dry thoroughly before trimming off the excess with a sharp knife. The advantage of this material is that it can be removed quite easily should you wish to move the appliance to another position.

Filling holes in lath and plaster

Fill small holes and cracks in lath and plaster in the same way as for plaster (page 222). If the hole is large enough to reveal the laths, repair depends on whether the laths are intact or broken.

If the laths are intact

1 Paint the laths with a solution of PVA building adhesive to make the surface less absorbent.

2 Fill the hole with layers of plaster in the same way as patching damaged plaster (page 223). If you are using ordinary quick-setting plaster, use a bonding undercoat plaster rather than a browning undercoat plaster.

If the laths are broken

Either patch the laths or – if the hole is not more than about 75mm across – plug the gap before you fill it with plaster.

1 To patch the laths, use a piece of expanded metal mesh, cut to the size you need with tinsnips. Wrap it round the laths to bridge the gap between broken edges.

Alternatively To plug the gap, use a ball of newspaper soaked in water and then worked round in a bowl of runny plaster.

Dealing with large areas

1 Where a large area of plaster has crumbled away from the laths, cut back the damaged area to a regular shape and patch it with a piece of plasterboard (page 226).

2 Use plasterboard that is as close to the thickness of the layer of plaster as possible. Nail the plasterboard patch, ivory side outwards, to the timber framework supporting the laths.

3 Fill the gaps round the edges with interior filler (page 78) and finish the surface of the patch with a coat of skim plaster.

Repairing holes in plasterboard

Small holes in plasterboard can be repaired in the same way as in plaster. Medium-sized holes – up to about 125mm across – need to be fitted with a backing piece to block the cavity before they are filled with plaster filler. Larger holes, or a severely damaged surface, cannot be satisfactorily repaired with a filler. The damaged section must be removed and a new piece of plasterboard patched in.

Using a backing piece

Tools *Pencil and ruler; trimming knife; drill and twist bit; padsaw or mini hacksaw; filling knife; sanding block; scissors; length of wood.*

Materials *A plasterboard offcut or a piece of MDF; piece of string 150–200mm long; a long nail or wood sliver; interior or plaster filler or coving adhesive. Possibly finishing plaster (page 222).*

1 Draw a neat square around the damaged area, and drill holes at the corners so that you can get the blade of your padsaw in. Cut along the lines to create a neat, straight-sided hole.

2 Cut a backing piece from a plasterboard offcut. It should be narrow enough to go through the hole, but long enough to overlap the hole by about 25mm at the top and bottom.

3 Bore a hole in the middle of the backing piece and thread the length of string through it.

4 Knot a nail or a sliver of wood to one end of the string to anchor it against the back of the offcut. Make sure you have the ivory side (which will be covered with plaster filler) as the front if using plasterboard. Make a loop in the front end of the string so that it is easy to hold.

5 Apply coving adhesive or filler to the front of the backing piece.

6 Guide the coated backing piece through the hole, then use the string to pull it into position against the back of the hole.

7 The patch should stick fairly quickly. Cut off the string when you are sure it has stuck firmly.

8 Use quick-setting filler to cover the patch, filling the hole to about half its depth. When it has dried, put in another layer, leaving it slightly proud of the surrounding wall.

9 With a length of wood, skim off the excess filler, leaving a smooth surface level with the surrounding area.

10 When the filler has dried completely, smooth the surface with a power sander or a piece of fine abrasive paper wrapped round a sanding block.

Fitting a plasterboard patch

Tools *Trimming knife or padsaw; broad-bladed filling knife or plasterer's trowel; pencil; straight-edge; spirit level; try square; hammer; medium or fine abrasive paper; sponge; steel tape measure.*

Materials *Small sheet of plasterboard or offcut as thick as board on wall; two lengths of 50 x 25mm timber to fit tightly between uprights (studs); four 75mm oval nails; 30mm galvanised plasterboard nails; G-cramps; joint tape or scrim tape (page 222); joint compound or plasterboard finishing plaster (page 222).*

Before you start Check the thickness of the plasterboard on the wall; it will be either 9.5mm or 12.5mm thick.

1 Check that there are no pipes, cables or studs behind the board (page 34). Use a trimming knife or padsaw to cut across the plasterboard from the middle of the damaged area outwards to each side until you reach the timber studs supporting the panel.

2 Use the straight edge of a spirit level to draw the edge line of the studs vertically on the plasterboard. Then draw horizontal parallel lines across the panel between the studs, about 50mm above and below the edge of the damaged area. Make sure the lines are at right angles to the studs.

3 Cut out the squared-off section of damaged plasterboard.

4 On each side of the opening, draw a vertical line to indicate half the width of the timber stud – usually about 25mm – and score it using a straight-edge and trimming knife.

5 Cut back the sound plasterboard down the scored lines to reveal half the width of the studs.

6 Fit the two timber pieces as cross-pieces (noggins) between the studs at the top and bottom of the opening. Position them with the 50mm thick side outwards so 25mm is under the edge of the existing plasterboard as a nailing surface for the patch.

7 Hold the noggins in position with G-cramps while you drive 75mm oval nails through the noggins and into the studs at an angle.

8 Measure the area of the hole and cut plasterboard to fit. Insert it with the ivory side facing outwards so that it can be plastered or decorated.

9 Nail the plasterboard to the wood surround with plasterboard nails. Set the nails at intervals of 150mm, positioned at least 12mm from the edge of the patch. Sink them into the surface of the plasterboard so they do not protrude, but take care not to damage the outer layer of paper.

10 Lightly sand edges of the joint with abrasive paper, if necessary, to remove any burring.

11 Using a plasterboard finishing plaster or joint compound, fill the joints and sand them smooth and flat. Then decorate the surface.

MENDING DAMAGED CORNERS

Damaged external corners of plasterboard can be repaired with battens and filler in the same way as plaster corners (pages 224–5).

Reinforce the corners with joint tape bedded in joint compound. Ideally use corner tape, which is reinforced with metal strips. Crease the tape down the centre and fit it so that the metal strips lie inwards, close against the surface of the wall. The tape gives the corner a clean, sharp edge.

HELPFUL TIP

If the surface of your plasterboard wall is dented but not broken, simply cover the dent with quick-setting filler and smooth it level with a ruler. Once it is dry, sand it smooth and redecorate.

Working with plasterboard

Plasterboard is used mainly for lining internal walls or ceilings and for building partition walls.

Plasterboard can be nailed to timber battens or joists, screwed to metal supports, or fixed directly to a masonry wall with adhesive. Use 30mm plasterboard nails with boards 9.5mm thick and 40mm nails for 12.5mm board. There are different types and thicknesses of board (see panel). Common plasterboard lengths are 1800mm and 2400mm. The widths are normally 600mm, 900mm or 1200mm. Some types are fire-resistant or moisture-resistant.

Handling plasterboard

Standard plasterboard is generally supplied bound in pairs of sheets with the grey side outwards. The binding tape identifies the type of edge and the size of the boards.

Two people are needed to carry a full-length sheet of plasterboard. Carry it on edge to avoid straining the core, and handle it with care to prevent damage to the paper-covered surface or the edges.

Store boards flat. If they warp they will be difficult to fix to walls or ceilings. Stack them in a pile not more than about 1m high, on a dry, flat surface. When removing a board from a stack, avoid dragging it, as this can scuff the surface of the board beneath.

Making a footlifter

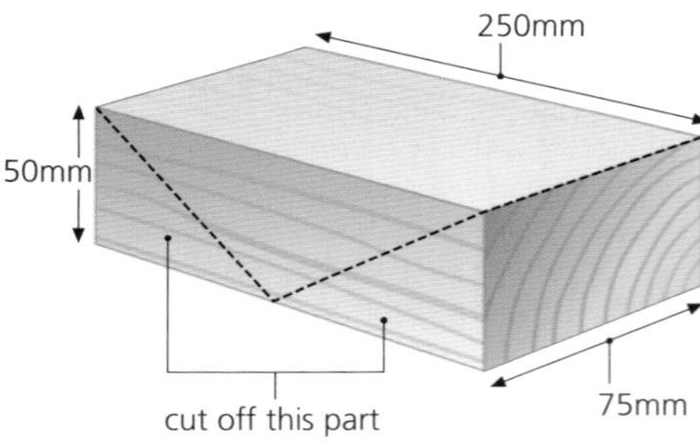

A footlifter, or rocking wedge, is needed to lift boards into position for nailing to a wall.

- You can make a footlifter from a piece of softwood 250 x 75 x 50mm.
- Draw lines from the top corners of the block to the centre of the base, and another line across the base centre.
- Cut away the two wedge-shaped pieces of waste to create a tool that works on the same principle as a see-saw.
- When a sheet of plasterboard is placed on one end, you lift it into place by pressing down with your foot on the other end.

CHOOSING PLASTERBOARD

Standard wallboard Has one ivory face intended for direct painting or wallpapering. Available with square or tapered edges. Use with tapered edge facing outwards for taped and filled joints or single-coat gypsum plaster finish. Use square edge out for single-coat plaster, textured coating or for painting or wallpapering. Available in 9.5mm and 12.5mm thicknesses in a variety of sheet sizes.

Insulating plasterboard Standard wallboard with a backing of thermal insulation. Used as an insulating lining inside an external wall or on a ceiling. 'Vapour-check' board has a water-vapour resistant membrane between the plasterboard and insulation. Many types of insulation are available, including expanded polystyrene and polyurethane foam. Thicknesses vary from 22mm up to 90mm in standard 2400 x 1200mm sheets.

Duplex plasterboard Has a metallic foil backing to resist water vapour. The backing also acts as a reflective insulator when facing into a wall cavity. Cannot be fixed with an adhesive. Available in 9.5mm and 12.5mm thicknesses as 1800 x 900mm or 2400 x 1200mm sheets.

Aquapanel Moisture-resistant 12.5mm cement-based board, designed for use behind tiled wall areas in kitchens and bathrooms. Comes in 900mm widths and 1200 and 2400 lengths. Fixed with special screws. Also available in insulated version for use on tiled floors.

Filling plasterboard joints

When lining a whole wall that will be plastered, painted or papered, the ivory side of the plasterboard should face into the room. In the past, the grey side was used for plastering, but the plasterboard makers now advise using the ivory side for everything.

Use tapered-edged boards to make the jointing as smooth as possible. If you have to cut ivory-faced board, you should joint the cut square edges in exactly the same way as you would the tapered edges. The steps opposite detail the methods for filling joints on both tapered-edged and square-edged boards.

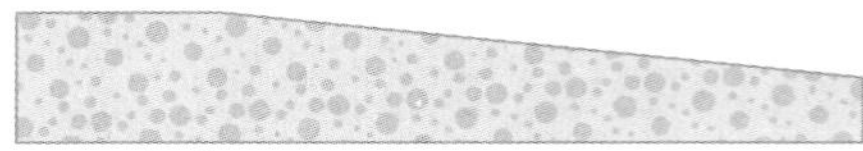

Tapered edge

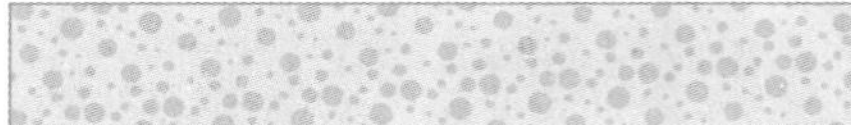

Square edge

CUTTING PLASTERBOARD

Cut plasterboard with the ivory side upwards, using either a fine-toothed saw such as a panel saw or a trimming knife. Sawing is slower and makes more mess.

On a long length, support the sawn ends to prevent the board breaking.

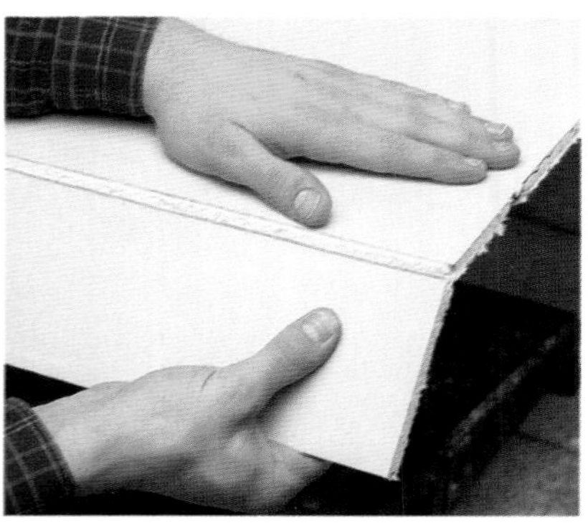

Use a straightedge when using a trimming knife and cut part way through the board with the board resting on hardboard. Snap the cut open along a timber batten and cut through the other paper backing.

Rub sawn or cut edges lightly with medium abrasive paper.

Use a padsaw (page 56) to cut holes in plasterboard to fit switches or mounting boxes.

Tapered-edged boards

Joint compound is workable for about 30 minutes after mixing. To begin with mix only a small amount so that you can gauge your working rate. If you mix only about a quarter of a bucketful, you can use it all up completing a number of joints up to the feathering stage. Self-adhesive mesh jointing tape is also now available and does not require jointing compound.

Tools *Clean bowl or bucket; mixing stick or wooden spoon; plasterer's trowel; broad-bladed filling knife; scissors or trimming knife; sponge; large paintbrush.*

Materials *Joint compound and joint tape or self-adhesive mesh jointing tape; clean, cold water; plasterboard primer/sealer.*

1 If you are using conventional joint tape, prepare the joint compound as indicated on the packet. Use a stiff mixture to cover nail heads and fill gaps wider than 3mm.

2 Use a broad-bladed filling knife or plasterer's trowel to press the compound into each joint, spreading it in a thin band just over 25mm wide on each side.

3 Cut a strip of tape to length and while the compound is still wet use the knife or trowel to press it on the joint. Press out any air bubbles, but make sure there is enough compound under the tape for it to stick.

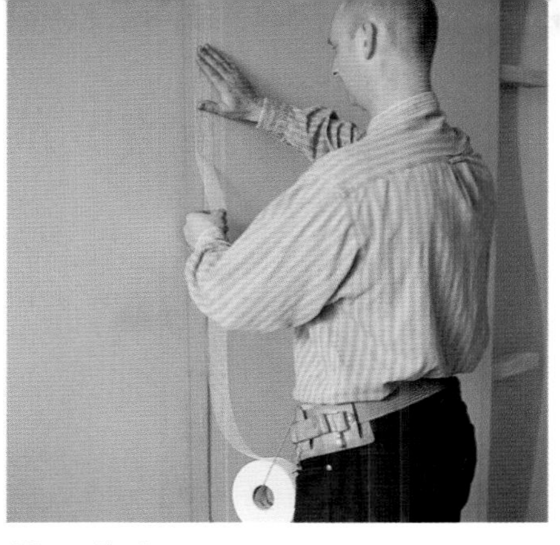

Alternatively If you are using self-adhesive tape, stick it in place along the joint without first applying jointing compound.

4 Finish the joints, whichever tape you have used, with a top layer of joint compound, spread over the tape in a wide band. Smooth it flush with the surface.

5 Before the compound begins to stiffen, moisten a sponge and use it to feather out the edges into the surrounding surface and to remove excess compound without disturbing the tape.

6 When the joint has dried, apply another layer of compound in a wider band – up to 300mm – and feather the edges smooth.

7 When the surface is dry, finish the whole board for decoration by applying one or two coats of plasterboard primer/sealer.

Square-edged boards

This should only be attempted over a small area – a repair in an old plaster wall, for example – because there is a risk that it will crack at the joints. Use scrim tape and plasterboard finishing plaster, applied in the same way as ordinary plaster (page 223).

Tools *Plasterer's trowel; scissors or trimming knife; large paintbrush or plant spray; clean plastic bucket; mixing stick.*

Materials *Plasterboard finish; scrim tape or self-adhesive jointing tape; cold water.*

1 Mix the plaster in the same way as ordinary plaster. If you are using self-adhesive tape, apply the tape first.

2 If you are using scrim tape, press the plaster into the joint with a plasterer's trowel, and spread it thinly on each side to form a band about 100mm wide.

3 Cut a strip of scrim tape to length and press it into the plastered joint with the trowel. Cut self-adhesive tape to length and tape over the bare joint.

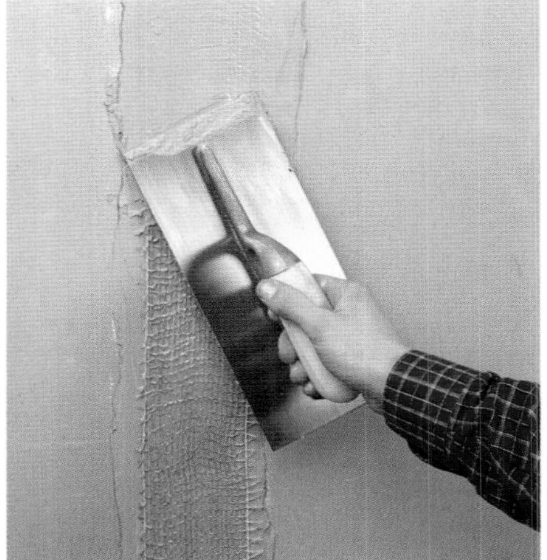

4 Apply a thin coat of plaster along the length of the tape.

5 When all the joints have been covered, apply plaster to the boarding between the joints to cover the whole area with a thin plaster coat about 5mm thick.

6 When the first coat has set, apply a second coat of the same thickness, and as it stiffens, dampen and polish it with the trowel (page 223) to make it smooth and flat.

Fitting and repairing ceilings

Modern ceilings are generally made of plasterboard, but lath-and-plaster ceilings are still found in some older houses. To reach the ceiling easily and safely, with your head about 150mm from it, use either the base section of a scaffold tower or stout scaffold boards resting on two stepladders or hired decorator's trestles.

Fitting a plasterboard ceiling

The simplest way to fit a new ceiling is to nail sheets of standard plasterboard to the ceiling joists. A new ceiling can be fitted over an existing one as long as it is only cracked, not crumbling or sagging.

If the ceiling is covered with polystyrene tiles, they can be left in place for extra insulation under the plasterboard. But you will have to locate and mark the joists in the ceiling (page 235), and use nails long enough to go through all the ceiling material and at least 25mm into the joists.

Tools *Hired panel lifter (see below) or a T-shaped floor-to-ceiling prop (known as a dead-man); hammer; saw.*

Materials *Plasterboard; nails (see Before you start, right).*

HELPFUL TIP

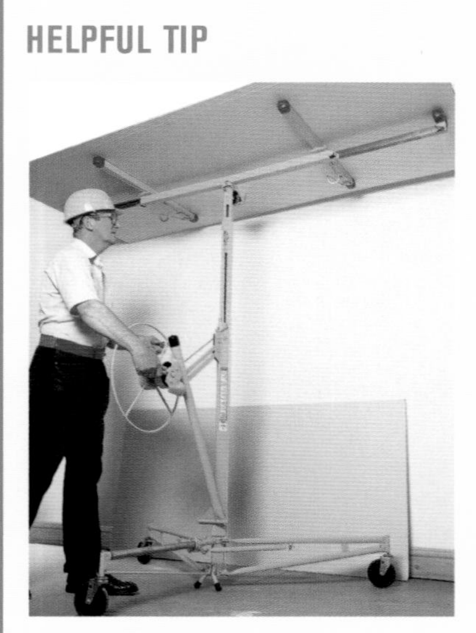

Plasterboard is too heavy to fix to a ceiling by yourself. Hire a panel lifter to raise the boards into place and hold them there while you drive in the fixing nails. The machine can support panels while they are fixed to walls and sloping ceilings, too.

Before you start Establish how far apart the joists are (see page 235).

- For joists up to 400mm apart, use plasterboard 9.5mm thick with 30mm galvanised plasterboard nails.
- For joists up to 600mm apart, use plasterboard 12.5mm thick with 40mm plasterboard nails.
- Make a 'dead-man' from a length of 38mm square timber the height of the room, with a piece of flat timber about 600mm long – such as a floorboard offcut – nailed to the ceiling end (see step 4).

1 Take down the old ceiling, if you can (see panel, right). You can then nail direct to the joists, and see any pipes and electric cables. It puts less weight on the joists and also enables you to treat the joists against woodworm if necessary.

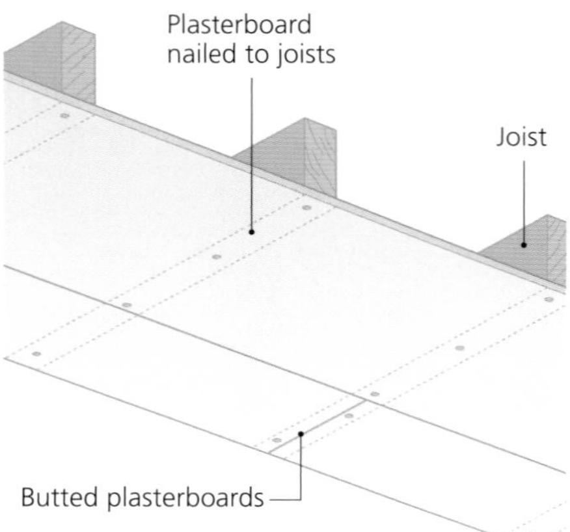

2 Fix boards with their long edges at right angles to the joists, with board ends butted centrally on a joist – ivory side facing downwards.

3 Stagger the rows so that adjacent boards do not butt on the same joist, cutting boards as necessary. Boards along the edge of the ceiling may need scribing to fit if the wall is not true.

4 You will need a helper to lift each board into place at one end. To support the board at your end while you nail it, use a T-shaped floor-to-ceiling prop, known as a dead-man. Or hire a panel lifter (left).

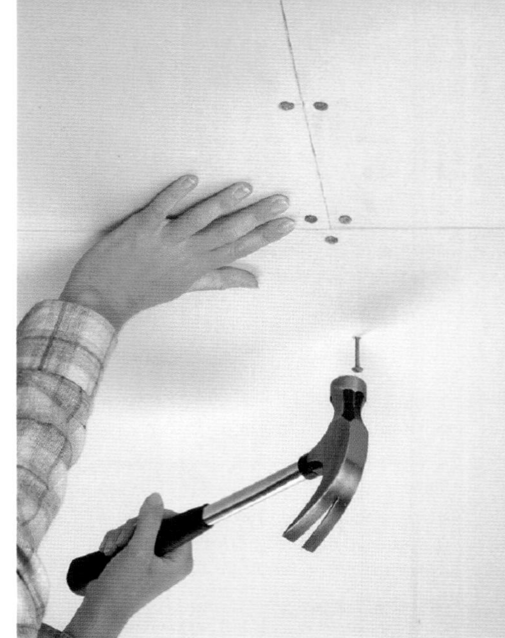

5 Nail the boards in the same way as for lining a stud partition wall (page 239).

6 When all the boards have been nailed to the joists, fill the joints between them (page 229) and finish the surface for decoration.

Gaps where wall and ceiling meet

The simplest way to cover gaps between the wall and ceiling is to fit coving – decorative moulding designed for wall and ceiling joints (page 176). A less effective alternative is to seal the gap with acrylic decorator's sealant.

Dealing with a bulge in the ceiling

On a lath-and-plaster ceiling, an area of plaster sometimes sags away from the laths to form a distinct bulge. If you can get at the ceiling from above you may be able to repair it.

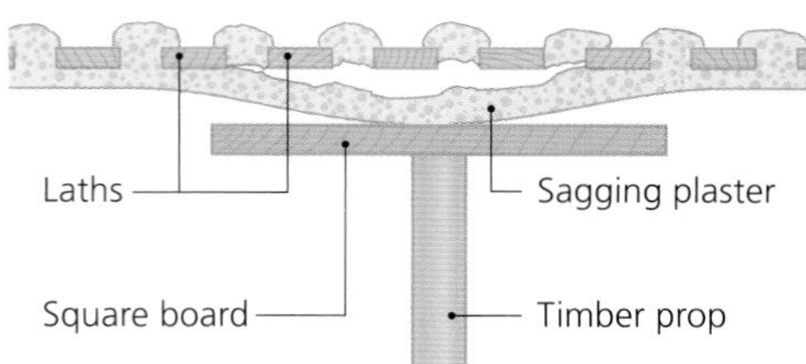

1 Try to push the bulge back into position using a square of chipboard or plywood nailed to a floor-to-ceiling timber prop (known as a dead-man).

2 To re-fix the plaster, you need to reach it from above – either from the loft or by lifting the floorboards in the room above.

3 Remove all the old loose nibs and vacuum clean the area between the joists at the back of the ceiling bulge.

PULLING DOWN AN OLD CEILING

It is best to replace an old lath-and-plaster ceiling with a plasterboard one if it needs more than small localised repairs. If the plaster key has failed in one place already, it is sure to fail in others as time goes by. However, this is an extremely dusty and unpleasant job.

Prepare by clearing the room of all furniture and fittings, and lift any carpet and its underlay. Remove ceiling-mounted light fittings and insert the cable conductors into plastic terminal blocks before pushing the cable up into the ceiling void. Hire enough heavy-duty dust sheets to cover the entire floor, and invest in safety goggles, strong work gloves, a supply of disposable face masks and a cap. Wear old clothes or a disposable one-piece work suit. Set up a work platform spanning the room, using stepladders or trestles and scaffold boards. Tape up the room door to keep the dust in, and open all the windows. Put on your safety gear.

It is best to pull down the old ceiling from below, even if you have access from above via a loft, because this way you can keep the demolition under better control.

Start by making a hole in the old ceiling with a club hammer, and tear down the old plaster and the laths section by section, working parallel to the joists. A small crowbar is an ideal tool to use for this. Try to pile the debris in one corner of the room as you work.

When you have pulled down as much of the ceiling as possible, work along each joist in turn, removing any remaining pieces of lath and pulling out all the old nails. Then finish by brushing the sides and bottom of each joist with a stiff brush to remove any remaining debris.

4 Pour fairly runny bonding plaster (page 222) over the area. This should bond the ceiling plaster back to the laths, replacing the 'nibs' of holding plaster that have been broken or dislodged.

5 Leave the supporting prop in place until the plaster has dried.

If this method does not work, remove the sagging area and patch it with plasterboard. A ceiling that sags over a large area should be pulled down and replaced with new plasterboard.

Moving switches, sockets and ceiling lights

When a wall (or ceiling) lining such as plasterboard or timber cladding is fixed to timber battens (see overleaf), switches or sockets on the wall have to be moved forward and remounted (or ceiling lights need to be moved).

Before you start Always switch off the power supply at the consumer unit before disconnecting and moving any electrical fitting.

- If you are moving a single socket, it is a good time to replace it with a double or triple fitting, if required (page 278) – or to add an extra socket on a spur of cable (page 285).

Switches and sockets

Most light switches and socket outlets are flush mounted over a metal mounting box that is recessed into the wall. They must be brought forward before the wall lining is completed. The way you do this depends on whether you want the accessory to be flush or surface mounted in its new position. In either case, first disconnect the accessory faceplate and abandon the existing mounting box in the wall.

Flush-mounting Buy a new 35mm deep metal mounting box in single or double format to match the accessory faceplate. With cladding (or plasterboard) approximately 10mm thick fixed to 25mm thick battens, the lip of this box will be flush with the face of the cladding if it is mounted on the existing wall surface.

Remove a metal knock-out disc from one side of the box and fit a rubber grommet in the hole. Screw the box to the wall beside the old box position and feed the circuit cable(s) into it through the hole, ready for reconnection to the faceplate once the wall cladding has been completed. Then you can screw the faceplate to the lugs of the new box to complete the job.

Surface mounting Buy a plastic mounting box deep enough for the accessory (usually 17mm for a switch and 25mm or 30mm for a socket outlet). Fix wall battens to the wall above and below the existing mounting box and draw the cable out of the box between them. As you fix the wall cladding, make a hole in it and pass the cable through it. Then feed it into the plastic mounting box via a knockout, and screw the box to the battens behind the

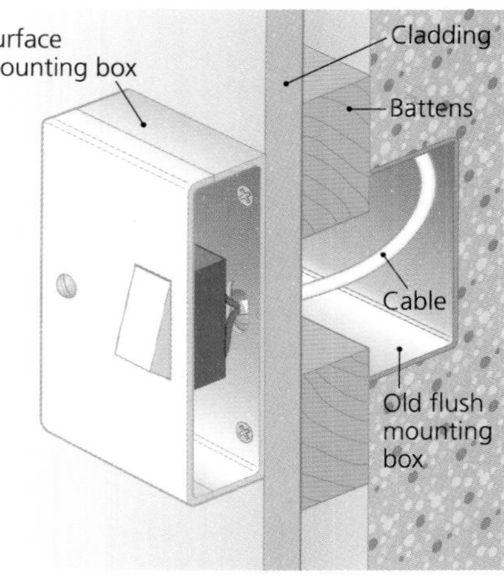

cladding. Connect the cable(s) to the faceplate terminals and screw the faceplate to the box.

If the accessory was originally surface mounted and you are happy to retain this arrangement, unscrew the old mounting box from the wall and set it aside. Follow the instructions above to reposition the old box on the surface of the new cladding and reconnect the cable(s) to it.

HELPFUL TIP

If the cable is not long enough to reach the terminals of the repositioned faceplate, extend it by connecting a short length of new cable to it using a strip of terminal connector blocks.

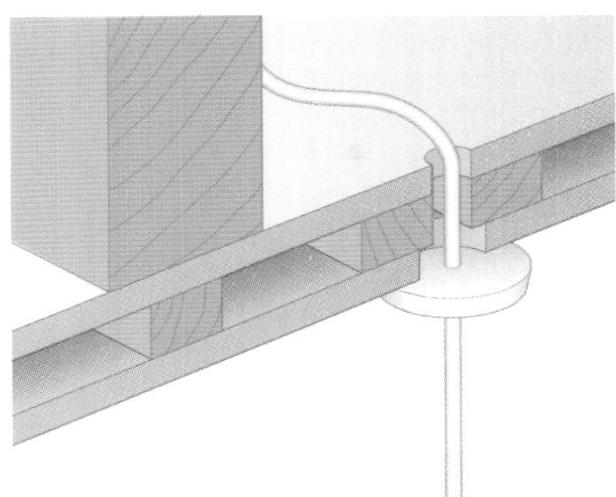

Ceiling fittings

A ceiling light can be dealt with in the same way as a surface-mounted wall socket, with the rose back-plate remounted on top of the new panelling and screwed to battens fixed on each side of the cable outlet.

The rose position can be altered slightly as long as the cable will not be too stretched and the connections strained. If the cable will not reach the new position, fit a junction box and an extension cable as for adding a new lighting point on a spur (page 300).

Dry-lining a wall with plasterboard

Dry lining is a good way of covering poor plaster, concealing pipework, or providing additional insulation – either with insulation material or by using insulating plasterboard.

Dry lining usually involves nailing standard wallboard to a timber framework fixed to the wall (with insulation, if required, within the timber framework). Insulating plasterboard (see page 228) can be secured directly to flat walls with special adhesive and nailable plugs designed for the purpose.

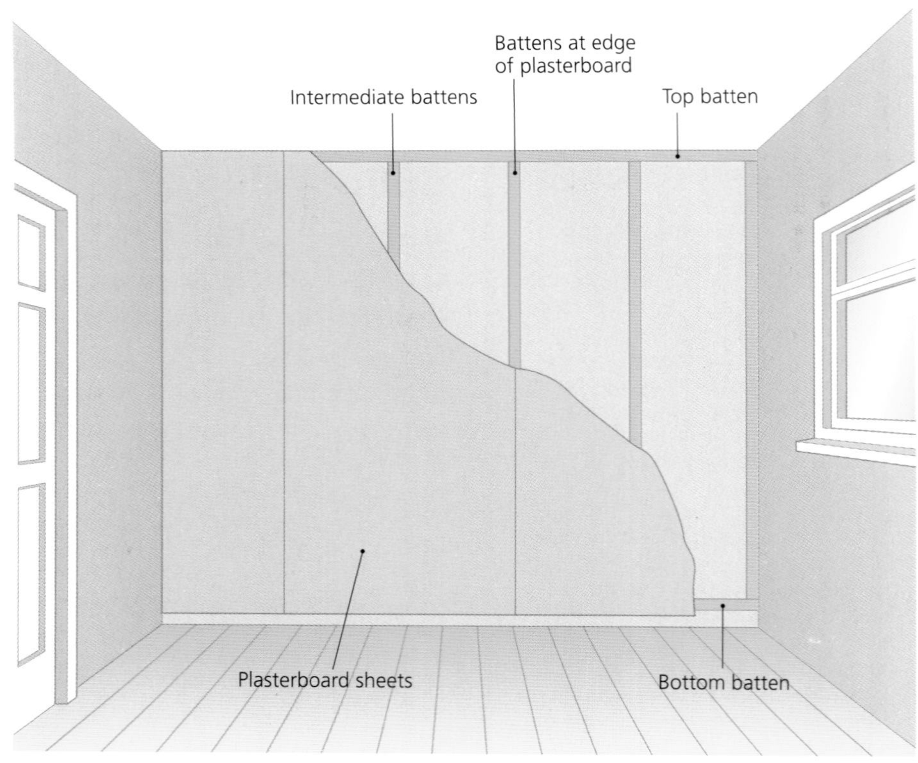

How many boards do I need?

The boards do not have to fit the height of the wall exactly – a gap of up to 25mm is usually left at the bottom for expansion, and may be covered by the skirting board. Boards need not be fitted vertically. They can be fitted horizontally if this is more convenient for the wall measurements.

1 Measure the height of the wall at each end (heights may be slightly different – use the highest figure). Also measure the width at the top and bottom.

2 From these measurements work out how many boards you need. If the widths will not fit exactly, plan to place the boards so that narrow widths will fit equally at each end of the wall.

3 Allow for separate pieces of board above door frames and above and below windows.

4 If the wall height is considerably more than the board length, fit the boards in staggered long and short upper and lower panels. Or fix the boards horizontally.

Fixing battens to the walls

Remove wall fittings such as picture rails and skirting boards (page 179) for later replacement. All switches and sockets will have to be moved forward (page 231). Take down architraves (page 178) and refit them on the lining. If the wall is plastered, leave the plaster in position if it is sound; use a hammer and cold chisel to chip off slight humps. But if plaster is broken or coming away from the wall, chip it away.

Before you start Check the wall surface to see if it is true and straight. If not, find and mark the most protuberant part of the wall surface so that the timber framework can be made to accommodate it.

Tools *Pencil or chalk; plumb line; steel tape measure; hammer or screwdriver; hand-saw; padsaw; drill and twist bits; portable workbench. Possibly also; trimming knife; countersink bit; masonry bit.*

Materials *Sawn timber battens 25 x 50mm – all treated with wood preservative; masonry nails or hammer-in fixings at least 10mm longer than the combined thickness of the batten and plaster (if any); hardboard slivers for packing pieces; plasterboard; plasterboard nails. Possibly also: insulation material and tacks, drawing pins or adhesive.*

1 Lay a framing batten on its side flat against the base of the wall and mark its thickness, with pencil or chalk, along the floor for the whole length of the wall to be lined.

2 Take a batten of the same height as the wall and hold it vertical, flat against one end of the wall to be lined.

3 Using a spirit level or plumb line to keep the batten vertical, move it along the wall and mark any position where its base is outside the line marked on the floor.

On a plastered wall, any obvious plaster humps can be chipped away.

4 At the outermost floor mark, draw a second line along the floor parallel with the first.

5 Using a plumb line and timber batten, mark a line along the ceiling in line with the second floor line.

6 Use masonry nails or countersunk hammer-in fixings at about 500mm intervals to fix a horizontal batten to the base of the wall 25mm above the floor.

7 Align the outer edge of the batten with the second floor line, placing hardboard packing pieces between the batten and the wall where necessary.

8 Fit a horizontal batten to the top of the wall, against the ceiling, in the same way.

9 Use a plumb line to check that the two horizontal battens are in line. Adjust the position of the top batten if necessary.

Fixing the vertical battens

1 Measure and draw lines down the wall where the edges of boards will meet. Vertical battens will be fixed centrally on these lines.

2 Mark the positions of the intermediate vertical battens (which will lie at board centres) midway between the edge battens.

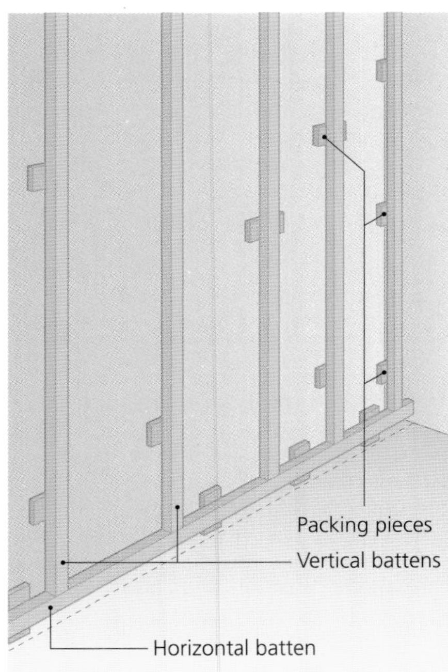

3 Cut vertical battens to length to fit snugly between the horizontal battens.

4 Fit the vertical battens for the plasterboard edges in the positions marked. Before driving the fixings fully home, use a plumb line to check that each batten is vertical and in line with the horizontal top and bottom battens. Pack behind the batten where necessary (see below left).

5 When you are satisfied, drive the fixings fully home.

6 Fit the intermediate vertical battens in the same way as the board-edge battens, using packing wherever necessary.

7 Fix battens all round window and door openings. Make sure they align horizontally and vertically with the other battens.

8 If necessary, put a short length of batten round electrical outlets to support board edges (see Moving switches and sockets, page 231).

9 If there are to be any fixtures such as wall cupboards, fix extra battens at anchor points in the required positions. Mark a horizontal line along the centre of the batten and the adjoining studs as a guide for fixings. Transfer it to the plasterboard when fitting. This needs to be positioned at exactly the right height (for kitchen cupboards, say). If you cannot be certain, use a larger batten for this – 75mm or 100mm rather than 50mm.

10 If insulation materials, such as rigid polystyrene sheets or mineral fibre batts (page 243), are being fitted, wedge them in place between the battens.

Fixing plasterboard to the frame

1 Cut the plasterboard to leave a gap of 13mm between the base and the floor – the board will hang 12mm below the horizontal batten.

2 Nail the board to the battens with plasterboard nails in the same way as for building a stud partition (page 238). Then fill in the joints between boards (page 229).

Creating an archway

A door that is always left open can be removed and the space turned into an eye-catching archway with an expanded metal arch-former kit.

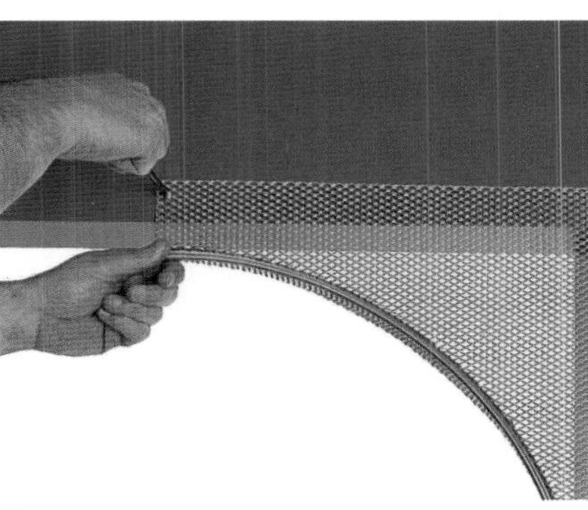

1 Fix the first section of arch-former to the opening. Use galvanised screws on a timber-frame partition. On brick, cut back the plaster to just past where the metal reaches, and fix the arch-form to the masonry with short masonry nails.

2 Fix the other side of the arch in the same way. Then go to the other side of the opening and fix two arch-formers there.

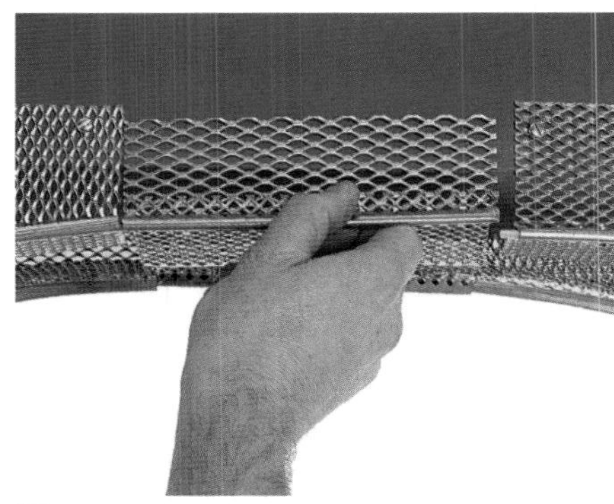

3 Cut a bridging section with tinsnips to about 6mm less than the gap. Push a corner bead connector into the open end of the corner bead at each end and slip the bridging section over them.

4 Cut a strip of mesh to form the curved underside of the arch and fix it to the curved sections with small loops of wire. Tighten the loops and snip off the excess.

5 Plaster the inside curve first, working from the bottom up. Then plaster the two wall faces, feathering the edges.

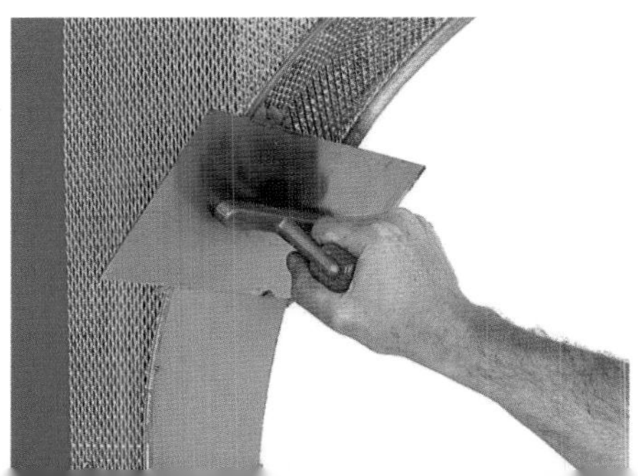

Preparing to timber-clad a wall or ceiling

Think carefully before completely cladding a small room – the effect could be overpowering. If you plan to line the ceiling and one or more walls, tackle the ceiling first.

Fitting boards along the length of a ceiling makes a room appear longer; across the width makes it look wider.

Similarly, horizontal boards on a wall make a room look longer, and vertical boards make a ceiling look higher.

Buying and preparing boards

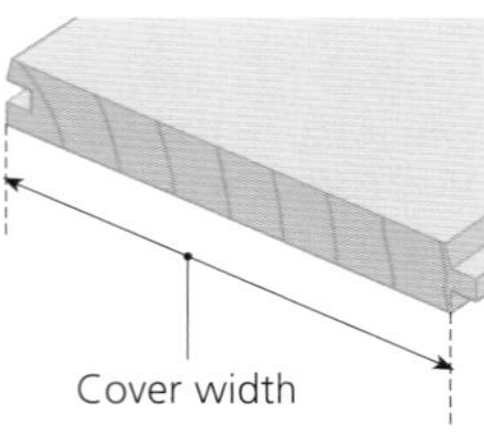

Work out how many boards you need in the same way as for plasterboard (page 232), but remember that because the boards interlock, the width of a board is greater than the width it will cover. Buy them all at the same time and check that they are of a similar appearance – characteristics such as knots and grain pattern can vary from pack to pack. Buy boards about three weeks before you intend to put them up, and stack them flat in the room to be lined. This allows the moisture content to even out and lessens the risk of joints being pulled apart by boards shrinking.

Fixing battens to the ceiling

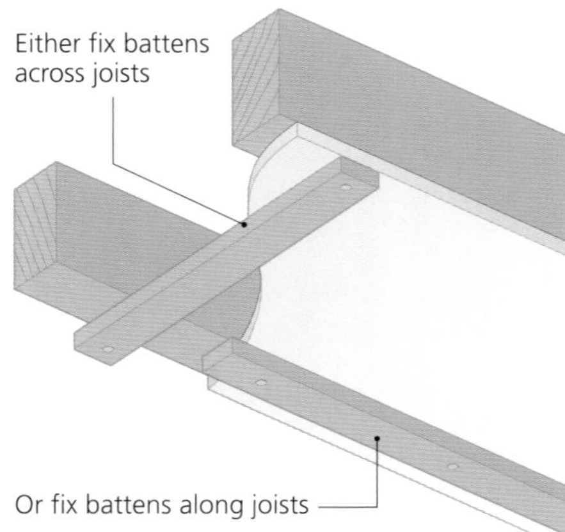

Use sawn timber battens 40mm wide and 25mm thick, treated with wood preservative (page 439). Screw them flat against the ceiling, into the ceiling joists, using countersunk screws. The fixing should be long enough to penetrate at least 25mm into the joist (see locating joists, opposite).

If, however, you want the boards to fit at right angles to the joists, position the battens along the centres of the joists.

- Fit the battens at 400–600mm intervals. Use a builder's square (page 467) to check whether the ceiling corners are true.
- If they are not, use a chalked string line to mark true lines across the ceiling as a guide to positioning the end battens.

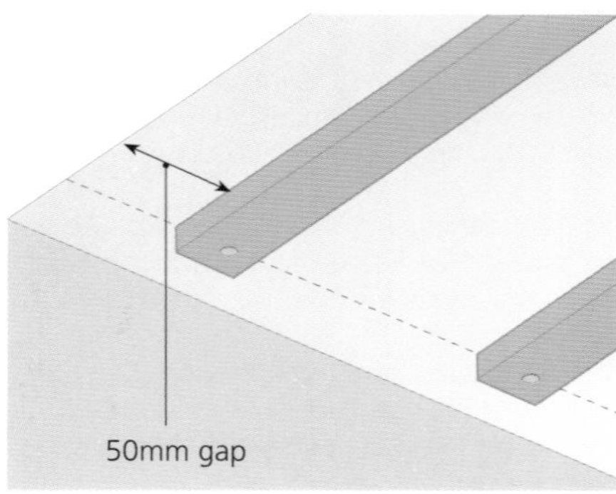

- Do not position the end battens right against the wall, as it makes nailing the boards to them difficult. Leave a gap of about 50mm.
- After fitting the first batten, hold a spirit level along it to check that it is horizontal. If necessary, pack hardboard pieces behind to level it.

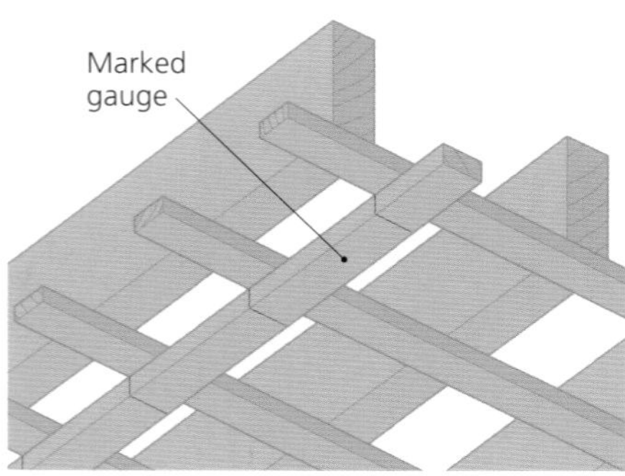

- When fitting succeeding battens, use a tape measure, or make a marked gauge with another batten, to ensure that battens are parallel and are correctly spaced. Hold a spirit level across the two battens to check they are level, and pack out as necessary.

Fixing battens to a wall

Use sawn timber battens 40mm wide and 20mm thick, treated with wood preservative (page 439). Fix them to the wall with hammer-in fixings (page 158) or countersunk screws and wall plugs. For vertical boarding, fix the battens horizontally. For horizontal boarding, fix the battens vertically. The skirting board can be left in place unless you want to remove it.

- Place battens at intervals of 400–500mm for 9mm thick boards, or at 500–600mm intervals for 12mm thick boards.
- The fixing should be long enough to penetrate at least 25mm into the wall.
- To ensure a level surface for the cladding, find the most protruberant point of the wall as for dry-lining (page 232), and mark a guideline on the floor or skirting board for the batten surface.
- Fit vertical battens in the same way as for dry-lining (page 233). When fitting battens horizontally, use a spirit level to ensure that each is horizontal.
- Check that the batten surfaces are all level with each other using either a spirit level or a plumb line dropped to the marked guideline. Pack behind battens with hardboard pieces where necessary to maintain a level surface.

ALLOWING FOR VENTILATION

In kitchens and bathrooms, where condensation is likely, allow for airflow behind the cladding.

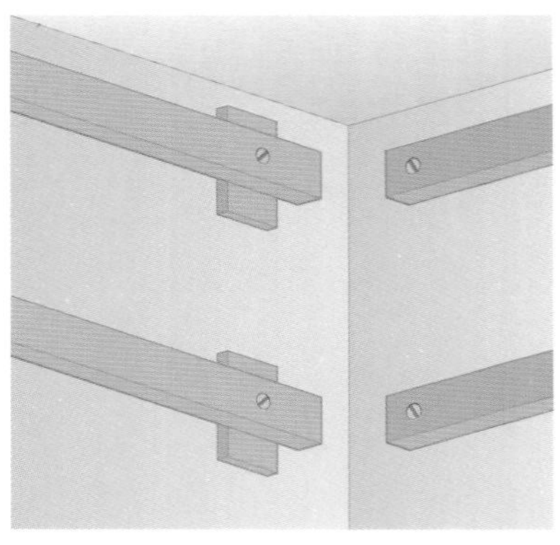

Pack behind horizontal battens with hardboard or thin plywood to lift them away from the wall. Also leave a gap at the top and bottom of the cladding. With vertical battens there is an automatic airflow if a 3mm gap is left at the top and bottom of the cladding. Use only vertical cladding on horizontal battens in kitchens and bathrooms because water can collect in the channelling of horizontal boards.

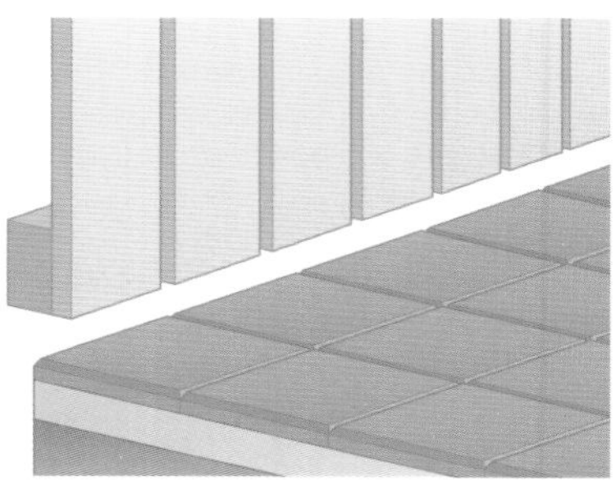

Stop the cladding slightly clear of a kitchen work surface, to prevent it getting wet, and 25mm or more clear of the top of a bath. Ceiling cladding can be stopped short to give a small gap on all edges, allowing for board expansion and ventilation. Or leave a gap at the long edges of the cladding only to give airflow between battens.

HOW BOARDS FIT TOGETHER

Boards for timber cladding are long and narrow, and are mostly jointed together on their long edges. Solid timber cladding is usually varnished to keep it clean and prevent it from darkening.

Tongued-and-grooved with narrow V The commonest type; generally 95–100mm wide, with a cover width of about 90mm. When the tongue is fitted into the groove of the adjoining board a narrow V-shaped channel is visible between boards.

Tongued-and-grooved with wide V The channel formed between the boards is slightly wider than for the narrow V type, but the size and cover width of the board is generally the same.

Tongued-and-grooved with double V The board has a wide V-joint and an extra groove cut down its centre to give the appearance of narrower panelling. The board is wider than other tongued-and-grooved types – generally 120mm with a cover width of 110mm.

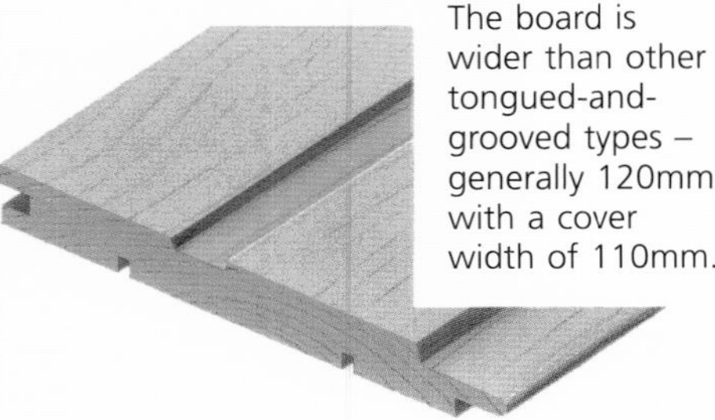

Shiplap Each board has an L-shaped edge and a curved edge. The boards fit together with the overlap over the curve, forming a channel curved along one side. When fitting boards horizontally, place the curved edge at the top. Boards may be wider than average: 120mm with a 110mm cover width.

Square-edged Square-edged boards can be overlapped louvre fashion or they can be spaced with narrow channels that reveal the wall behind. Thick boards are normally used and they can be fitted without using a batten framework.

Locating joists in a floor or ceiling

Timber framework for supporting a partition wall or a ceiling lining must be fixed to solid timber joists in the floor or ceiling.

Joists are parallel timbers about 50mm thick stretched across from wall to wall to support the floorboards or ceiling. They are usually 400–600mm apart, but on a top floor, ceiling joists may be 350mm apart.

Locating floor joists

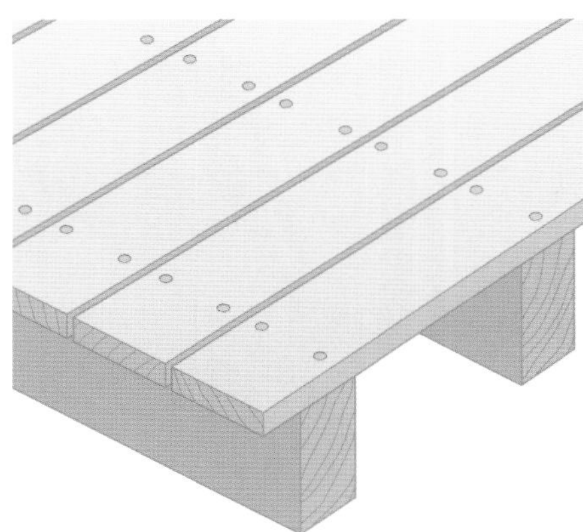

Find the position of joists by noting the lines of nails where the floorboards are fixed to them. The joists are always at right angles to the floorboards.

Locating ceiling joists from above

One way to find ceiling joists in an upstairs room is to get into the loft above and mark their positions through the ceiling.

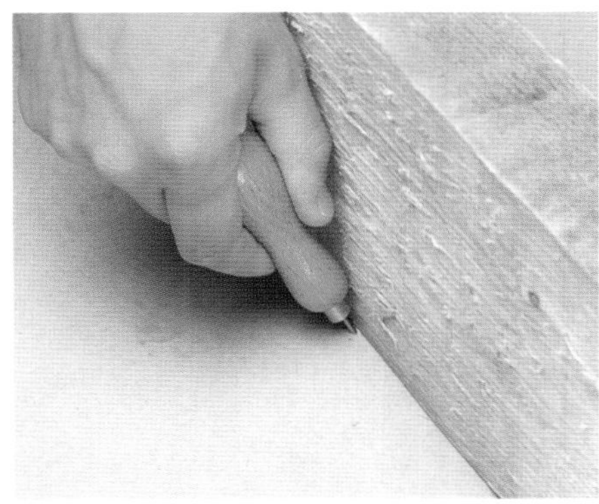

Use a bradawl to poke down through the ceiling on each side of a joist, at both ends. Measure the width of a joist and the distance between joists, and mark the position of another joist at the far side of the area through the ceiling.

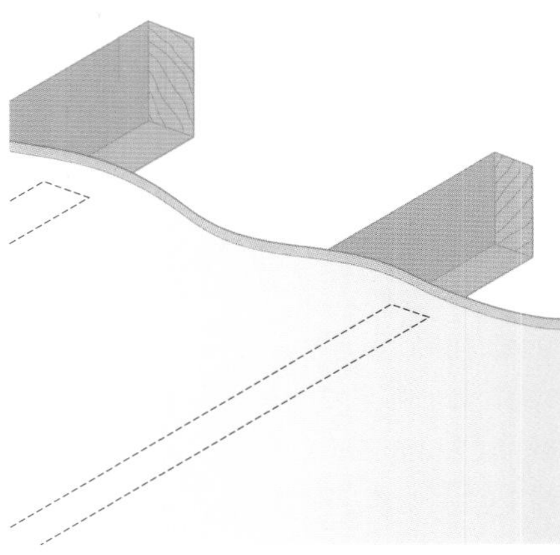

From below, you can join up the marks to show the joist positions, then measure and mark the positions of the other joists. A quick method of marking the position is with a chalked string line (page 109).

Locating ceiling joists from below

In a downstairs room you will have to find the ceiling joists from below, unless you are prepared to lift the floorboards in the room above. You can get an idea of their positions (and the direction in which they run) by lifting the upstairs floor covering and looking at the nails or screws securing floorboards or chipboard floors.

You can locate the joists precisely by using a stud detector (page 33), which detects the change in density when there is wood behind the plasterboard. A pipe/cable detector (or a multi-function detector) will help you find any electric cables or metal pipes above the ceiling.

To find the joists without a detector, tap the ceiling lightly to detect a solid area, then probe with a bradawl. Use the bradawl to trace the position of one joist, and mark it with a chalked string line. From this, you can measure and mark the other joists, testing each surface with the bradawl.

Lining a wall or ceiling with timber cladding

Do not fit boards right up to wall or ceiling edges. Leave a small gap of about 3mm to allow for board expansion. If ventilation is not required, any gaps can be covered with a strip of moulding.

Stop cladding several centimetres short of a fireplace or a boiler, if you can, and use tiles or plasterboard as a surround. If you cannot stop the cladding short, protect the board edges with a metal edging strip. When fitting cladding to the wall horizontally, start at the bottom.

Tools *Spirit level; steel straightedge; steel tape measure; hammer; tongued-and-grooved board off-cut; mallet. Possibly also power saw; screwdriver; nail punch; plane; gauge made from a batten marked with the width of two or three fitted boards; try-square; push-pin magnetic nail holder.*

Materials *Cladding boards; nails, clips, screws or panel adhesive. Possibly moulding; wood filler.*

Before you start Move electrical fittings forward if necessary (page 231), or leave them in position and line round them so that they are recessed within the cladding.

Decide which of the following methods you will use to fix the boards:

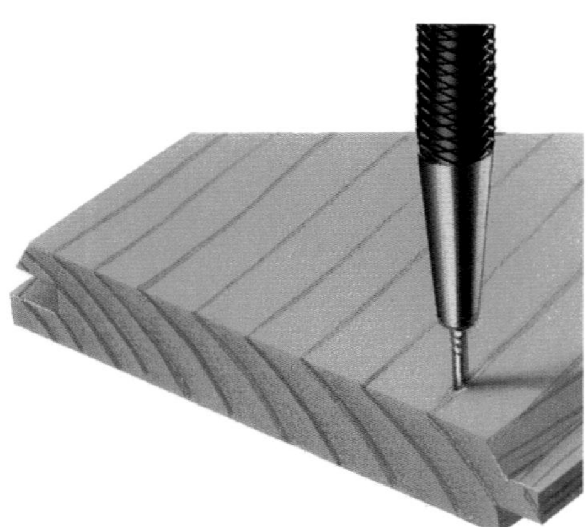

Face-nailing Suitable for all types of board. Use 30mm thin lost-head or oval nails or panel pins. Position them at least 15mm in from the board edge. Drive them straight in, using a nail punch. Leave the head either flush with the surface or just below it. Nails with the head left exposed should be arranged in a uniform pattern. Where nails are punched just below the surface, fill the holes with matching wood filler.

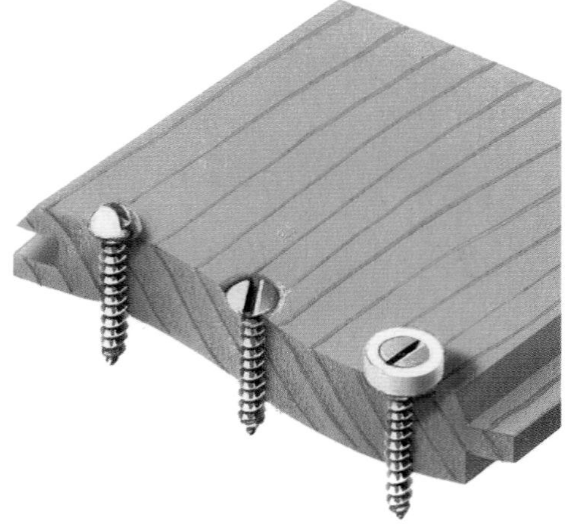

Screwing Usually used only for fixing square-edged boards, but advisable where any type of board may have to be removed to get at a covered-in fitting. Use 30mm roundhead or countersunk screws. Drill holes through boards before screwing.

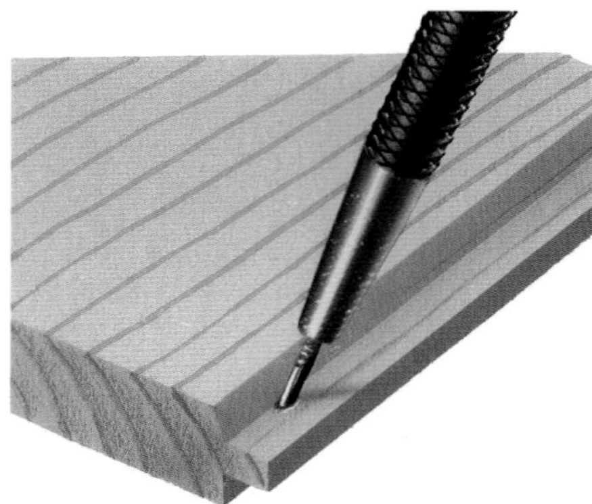

Secret nailing A method of nailing so that nails holding the cladding cannot be seen. Suitable for tongued-and-grooved boards only. Use 30mm thin lost-head or oval nails or panel pins. Hammer the nails in at an angle through the tongue of the board. Use a thin nail punch when the head gets near to the board, and drive the nail in until the corner of the head just protrudes. If the nail is driven in too far, the tongue is likely to split. The nail head is hidden when the groove of the next board is fitted over the tongue. Nail vertical boards with the tongue on the right if you are right handed, on the left if left-handed. Nail horizontal boards with the tongue upwards. Some face-nailing is needed for boards fitted at the edge of the panelling.

HELPFUL TIPS

- When secret nailing thin dry boards such as pine, drill a pilot hole right through the board to avoid splitting the tongue.
- If a tongued-and-grooved board is difficult to slot in straight, hammer it lightly with a mallet, using a board offcut between the board and the mallet. Slot the offcut groove over the tongue of the board that you are fitting.
- Avoid fitting boards together too tightly in kitchens and bathrooms, because humidity will cause the wood to swell and expand.

Fixing boards to wall or ceiling battens

1 Position the first board at right angles to the wall or ceiling battens and about 3mm from the edge of the adjoining wall. Fit the grooved edge of a tongued-and-grooved board or the straight lip of a shiplap board facing the adjoining wall.

2 Use a spirit level to check that the board is vertical or horizontal. For a board fitted to a ceiling, use a try-square to ensure that it is at right angles to the batten.

3 Fix the board to the battens using the chosen method (left).

4 Fix the second board, using a straight-edge to check the ends are aligned with the first board, and a spirit level to make sure that it is vertical or horizontal.

5 On a ceiling, use a marked gauge (page 234) to check near each end that the first and second boards are parallel.

6 Continue fitting boards in the same way. The last board may have to be trimmed to fit the remaining space. When trimming, allow for a 3mm gap against the wall. If using secret nailing, secure the last board either with panel adhesive or by face nailing.

Fitting boards round doors and windows

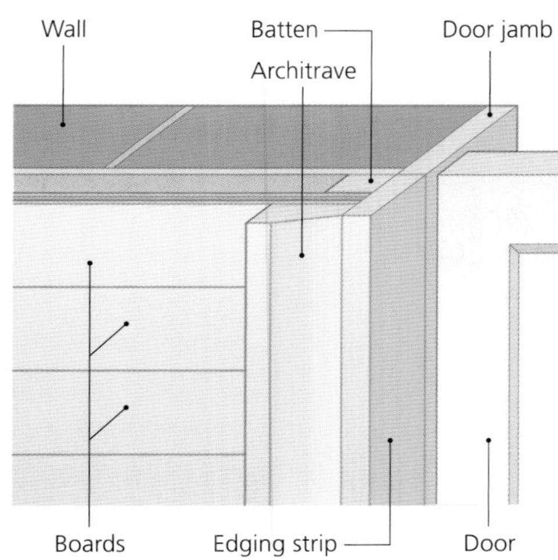

At doors and windows, remove any architraves (page 178). Fit vertical battens alongside a door jamb, leaving enough room for an edging strip to cover the batten and the edge of the end board.

- Architrave can then be fitted over the edging or, if desired, the edging can project in front of cladding and give an edge to which the architrave can be refitted.
- Line a deep window recess with cladding boards, with the external corners joined using one of the methods described below.
- Windowsill boards are difficult to remove. If the edges of a sill project, it is best to cut the cladding to shape to fit round them.

Joining boards at corners

How you join boards at corners will depend on whether the corner is internal or external (at a chimney breast, for example).

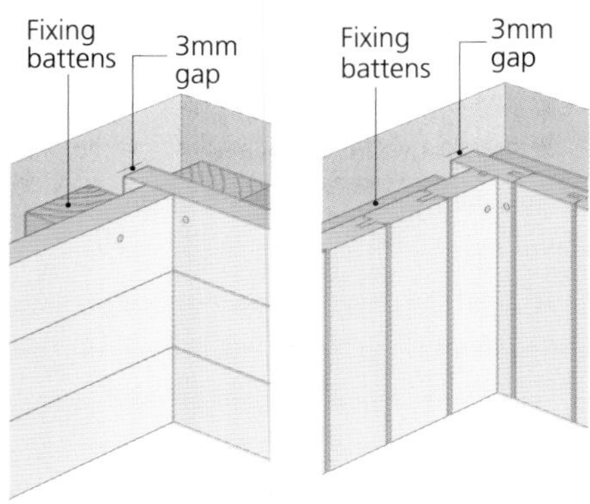

Internal corners

For horizontal boarding, fit one line of cladding into the corner, leaving a gap of about 3mm at the wall. Butt the cladding on the adjoining wall against it. Joints can be covered with quadrant moulding if desired.

Vertical boarding is fitted into the corner in the same way as horizontal, with the cladding butted.

External corners

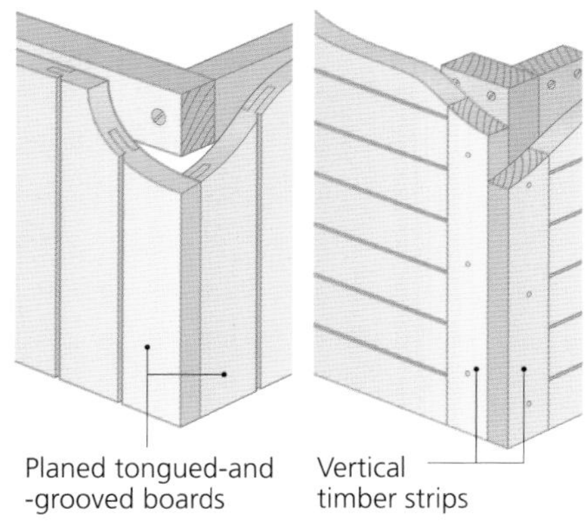

Vertical boards can be planed to remove the tongue and groove and then butted at right angles. Alternatively, you can butt the grooved edges of two boards and cover the joint with right-angled corner moulding.

For horizontal boards, fit vertical timber strips at the corner and butt the cladding boards against them.

Cladding a wall with brick slips

Brick slips (or stone cladding) are stuck in rows in a brick-bond pattern. The joints between are filled in with mortar and pointed in the same way as for brick walls, or left open and painted later.

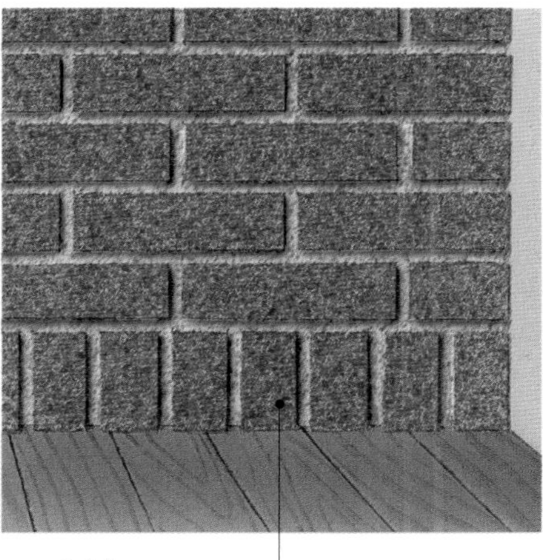

Before you start Work out how many slips will fit across the wall, and how many rows you will need to create.

Do this by marking a wooden batten with lines 222mm apart – this allows a 10mm joint between each slip. Hold the batten horizontally against the wall and count the number of slips. Decide how to arrange any part bricks.

Now mark the other side of the batten every 75mm to see how many rows you will get. If the height fit is not exact, allow a small gap at the bottom, or insert a 'soldier course' (see below left).

Tools *Spirit level; steel tape measure; plumb line; tile cutter or saw (as recommended by the slip manufacturer); filling knife; pointing trowel.*

Materials *Brick cladding adhesive; water; wooden spacers; pointing mortar (page 467).*

1 Remove skirting boards (page 179) and prepare the walls as for decorating.

2 Use the primer recommended by the slip manufacturer on absorbent surfaces such as plaster or plasterboard.

3 Secure a horizontal batten to the wall as for wall tiling (page 115) and apply brick cladding adhesive to a strip above it.

4 Press the first row of slips into place, using your 10mm spacers and making sure the surfaces are level. Continue with the other rows, using your chosen pattern.

5 When the all the slips are in place and the adhesive has dried, mix up the recommended pointing mortar (grey, cream or white) and apply to the joints. Leave to dry and brush away any excess.

PLASTIC CLADDING

Cladding made from uPVC consists of narrow, white, hollow boards similar in appearance to timber cladding, usually with tongued-and-grooved or shiplap joints. They are particularly suitable for walls and ceilings in bathrooms or kitchens, where high moisture levels can damage wood panelling. The cellular structure of the cladding traps air inside that acts as insulation, so the wall feels warm to the touch and resists condensation. The cladding can be simply wiped clean with a damp cloth.

Boards can be cut with a fine-toothed saw and trimmed with a sharp knife. Measure the length of cladding needed and then subtract 3mm to allow for expansion.

The cut boards are then fitted to a framework of timber battens screwed to the wall at 600mm intervals, at 90° to the direction in which the cladding is to run. The uPVC boards are attached to the battens with concealed clips, following the manufacturer's instructions. The cladding is added length by length, each one sliding into place against the previous board. Use matching trim strips for a neat finish.

Building a stud partition

A non-load-bearing stud partition is made from plasterboards that are fixed to each side of a timber frame made from uprights (studs) fitted between top and bottom rails (head and sole plates).

These instructions are for 12.5mm thick plasterboard on a partition no more than 2.4m high. To improve sound insulation, fit a layer of glass-fibre blanket or batts (page 243) at least 75mm thick between the lining boards.

For even better insulation, build the partition with two layers of plasterboard on each side, with the joints between boards staggered. This will prevent voices at normal speaking level penetrating the partition.

Tools *Plumb line; pencil; 75 x 50mm timber offcut; bradawl; hammer; screwdriver; spirit level; power drill and twist bits; portable workbench; straight-edge; panel saw or trimming knife; footlifter (page 228); plasterboard jointing tools; medium abrasive paper. Possibly also: padsaw.*

Materials *Plasterboards 12.5mm thick and 1200mm wide; glass-fibre insulation blanket or batts at least 75mm thick; sawn timber 75 x 50mm sufficient for head and sole plates, uprights at 600mm intervals, and cross-pieces; 100mm nails; 100mm 5mm screws; 100mm frame fixings (pages 158–9) or screws and wall plugs; 40mm plasterboard nails; plasterboard joint tape (page 222). Possibly also ceiling noggins 100 x 50mm; screws and wall plugs for fixing to a solid floor; packing such as hardboard or vinyl tile pieces; timber door casing about 100 x 25mm; skirting board; architrave moulding; 50mm panel pins or oval nails.*

Before you start Buy the interior door and casing first, because there are various door widths. Measure the height from the floor, not the sole plate. If possible, avoid positioning a door right beside an adjoining wall, against an end stud.

Finding solid fixing points

The partition must be fitted so that the head and sole plates can be securely fixed to solid floor and ceiling timbers (see Locating joists, page 235).

Position the partition in line with the floorboards, if possible, so that it can be fixed across the joists supporting the floor. If the partition has to be at right angles to the floorboards, try to position it along the line of a joist.

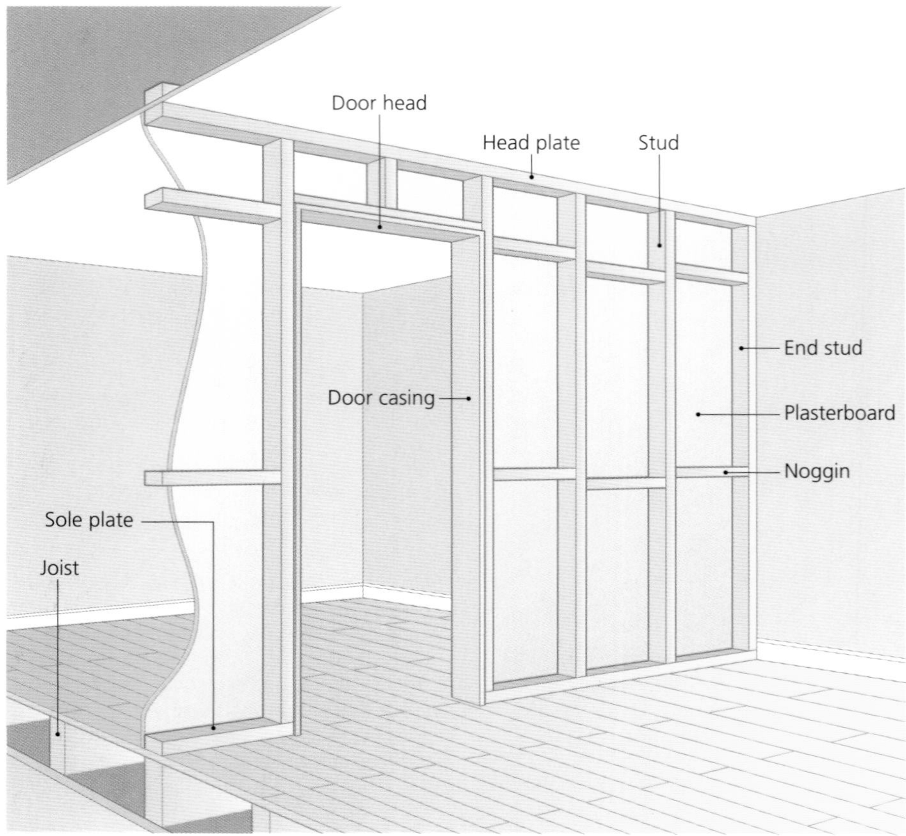

The sole plate can be fixed along a joist, as shown here, or alternatively, it can go across the joists in line with the floorboards.

Where the partition cannot be positioned along a floor joist, skew-nail 100 x 50mm cross-pieces (noggins) between the joists at intervals of 1 metre to support it.

Position the head plate in the same way, so that it can be fixed either across the ceiling joists or parallel with one. If the plate has to be positioned between two parallel joists, fit noggins between them in the same way as for floor joists, working from the loft or from the room above.

Putting up the timber frame

1 Use a 75mm offcut to mark each end of the head-plate position on the located fixing points. Place the offcut at right angles across a joist, or centred along it.

2 Drop a plumb line from each of the marked edges and get a helper to mark each point on the floor as a guide to positioning the sole plate.

3 Temporarily fix the sole plate at about 600mm intervals, but do not drive the fixings fully home yet. Use 100mm nails for a wooden floor, driven into the joists where possible. Use 90mm 5mm screws for fixings to a solid floor.

4 Drill through the ceiling into joists (or noggins) and screw the head plate to them temporarily, using 100mm 5mm screws.

5 Use a plumb line to check the alignment of the two plates near each end and adjust their positioning if necessary. Then drive the fixings fully home. Mark one side of the sole plate with stud positions at 400 or 600mm centres, taking into account the width and position of any doorway and how the plasterboard sheets will fall at the ends – avoid narrow strips.

6 Mark a centre line on the 50mm thick side of the timber offcut. Place the offcut squarely across the sole plate with the two marks aligned, and pencil in the edge positions for each stud.

7 Measure and cut the studs. They should be a tight push fit between the head and sole plates. If necessary, recess the studs to fit over skirting (or coving) on the adjoining walls.

8 Push each end stud into place against the wall, using a spirit level to ensure each one is vertical. If a wall is not true, pack any gaps with hardboard or pieces of vinyl tile.

9 Fix each end stud to the wall using either 100mm frame fixings or 5mm screws and wall plugs.

10 Get a helper to hold each of the other studs in position, while you temporarily nail an offcut to the sole plate on one side to hold the stud in place for nailing.

11 Use a spirit level to ensure that the stud is vertical on both the 75mm and 50mm sides.

MAKING A DOORWAY

1 Fit studs on each side of the doorway, far enough apart to allow 2–3mm for the hanging of the door (page 195) and for the thickness of the casing round the opening.

2 Fix a noggin across to form the door head, again allowing for the casing. The door casing should be the same width as the studs plus the thickness of the plasterboard on each side – usually 100mm overall.

3 If fitting a glass pane above the door, line this opening also.

4 To complete the doorway, saw through and remove the section of sole plate at the base of the opening.

SKEW-NAILING A JOINT

Mark the position of the join on the sole plate and temporarily nail a block of wood in place, with one edge butting up to the line. Hold the stud against the block, and drive the first nail diagonally down into the sole plate a third of the way in from one side. Remove the block and nail from the other side in the same way.

12 Nail each stud on the head and sole plates by skew-nailing (see box above). Use three 100mm nails – two one side and one on the other. Temporarily mark the stud positions on the floor as a guide when nailing the plasterboard on later.

13 Brace the studs with horizontal noggins positioned halfway between the floor and ceiling. Either skew-nail them in place, or stagger the position of adjacent noggins so you can drive the nails through the stud into the end of each noggin.

14 Fit any extra noggins needed for supporting fixtures such as wall cupboards, and mark the noggin position on the stud edges for transfer to the board.

15 Run any necessary cables through the framework (see page 283).

Lining the frame with plasterboard

1 Cut each board (page 228) so it is 15mm shorter than the floor-to-ceiling height.

2 Fit whole-width boards first, working from one side to the other. Leave narrow-width boards that need trimming to fit a side wall or at a doorway until last.

3 Fit each board with the ivory face outwards, holding it in position resting on the footlifter (page 228).

4 Align each edge of the board midway over a stud, using the edge of the stud as a guide to make sure it is vertical.

5 Press the board tight against the ceiling with the footlifter while you nail it to the timber framework all round the edges and into the noggins between the studs.

6 Fix plasterboard nails at least 15mm in from the edge of the board, spaced at 150mm intervals. Drive them home until the head dimples the board surface but does not burst the paper lining.

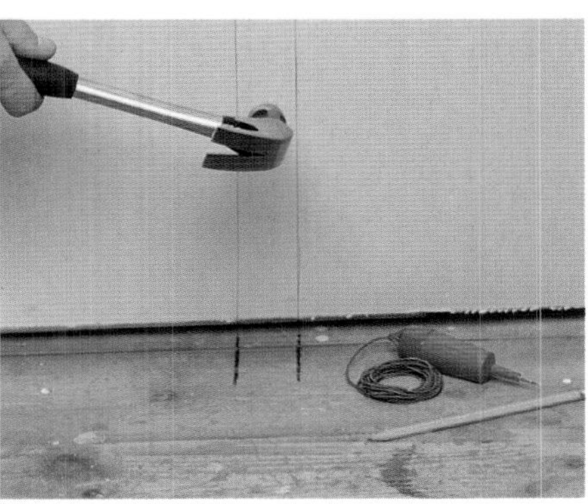

7 Use floor marks and a plumb line and straight-edge to pencil in the position of the stud at the board centre. Nail the board to it at 150mm intervals.

8 Butt end boards against the wall to cover end studs and any packing. If the wall against which the board fits is out of true, scribe the board and cut it to fit the wall contours.

9 Line the other side of the stud partition framework with plasterboard in the same way. Then fill the joints between boards (page 228).

10 Fit skirting board round the room (page 179) and an architrave (page 178) round the door frame, if necessary, to match other mouldings in adjoining rooms.

Building a metal-framed stud wall

Instead of the traditional timber-framed stud wall, a steel frame is lighter and thinner and can be positioned anywhere without danger of overloading the floor.

A metal stud partition wall will be only about 75mm thick when complete. It is ideal for dividing rooms where sound penetration is not a problem.

Tools *Portable workbench; gloves; pencil; tape measure; hacksaw; plumb line; screwdriver or power drill with screwdriver bit; masonry drill bit; spirit level; trimming knife; straightedge; filling knife.*

Materials *Metal profiles; sealing tape; 50mm wood screws; wallplugs or cavity fixings; 12.5mm plasterboard; 25mm drywall screws; joint tape; filler.*

1 Cut the head profile to size. If the new wall is to run at right angles to the ceiling joists, screw the profile to each joist. If it is to run parallel with the joists, locate a suitable joist and fix the profile to it.

2 Drop a plumbline from the head profile and mark the floor. This will be where the sole profile is placed. Cut it to length, stick double-sided adhesive tape to its underside and screw it to the floor.

3 Measure the distance between the head and sole profiles, and cut your first vertical stud to length, less about 5mm to allow for clearance at the top.

4 Hold the stud in place, mark the fixing holes with a pencil and drill and plug the holes.

5 Screw the stud to the wall. Repeat for the stud at the other end.

6 Work out the intermediate stud spacing such that you can use as many full-width sheets of plasterboard as possible without too narrow strips at the ends. Mark the position of the first intermediate stud so that your end cut sheet will be exactly in the middle of it. Cut the first stud to length and put it in place. The intermediate studs are not screwed to the head and sole plate – they push-fit into them.

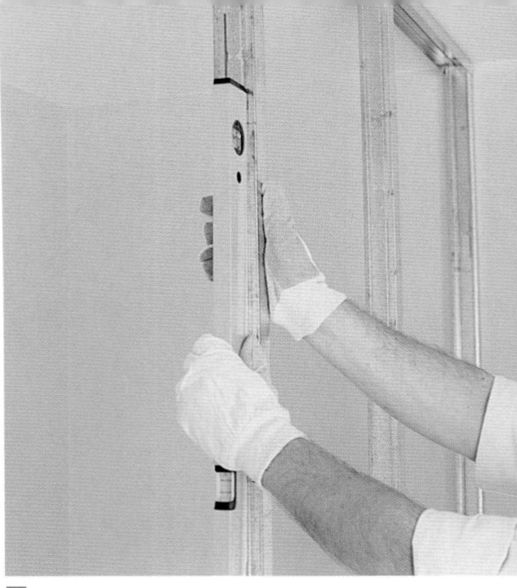

7 Fit the rest of the studs at 600mm centres measuring carefully and checking that they are all vertical. If there is to be a door, the kit will contain the necessary components to make a lintel and the door linings.

8 Cut the plasterboard sheets 6mm shorter than the floor-to-ceiling height, and hold them up against the ceiling. Secure them to the studs with drywall screws, about 10mm in from the edge of the board, and at 300mm centres.

9 Clad one side of the wall first, then run in any cables for wiring accessories before finishing off the other side.

HELPFUL TIPS

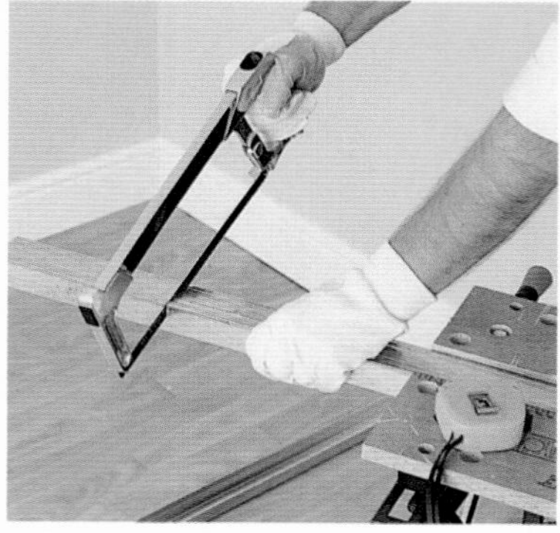

- If you have to cut the metal lengths, use a hacksaw.
- When cutting studs, always remove the excess from the same end, so that the internal service slots remain aligned once the wall is assembled.
- Remember to wear gloves – the profiles have very sharp edges.
- The wall relies on the plasterboard for its strength and rigidity so try to arrange that the edges of boards on the two sides meet at different studs.
- If something heavy, such as a cupboard, has to be fixed to the wall, you can support it by screwing a flat steel plate to the faces of the studs. The plate is provided as part of the partition system and is fixed in place with pan-head screws.

Insulating the walls of a house

A lot of heat can be lost through un-insulated walls. Both cavity and solid walls can be improved: you do not need to add insulation to the walls of timber-framed houses.

Cavity walls

Insulating cavity walls saves heat loss from a house, but it is not a DIY job. To check if the cavities have already been filled, drill a hole into the cavity from the outside and feel with a probe. If it is empty, call in a contractor specialising in cavity insulation (see Chapter 14).

Note that walls to be insulated must show no sign of penetrating damp. The cause of any damp must be cured first and the walls allowed to dry out. The contractor should thoroughly examine the walls to make sure they are fit for filling, with no evidence of damp, or damage that may let in damp.

There are two main insulation systems to choose from:

Mineral-wool fibres or polystyrene beads

The dry system consists of mineral-wool fibres or expanded polystyrene beads being blown through holes drilled in the outer leaf of the wall until the cavity is filled.

Expanding foam

With the second system, the cavities are filled with foam. This is produced on site and pumped through holes drilled in the outer brick leaf. The foam normally dries after a few days and becomes firm.

Solid walls

Any extra width of insulation on the inside of a house wall may bring the wall out beyond skirting boards, picture rails and architraves. Often lights, wall sockets, light switches and radiators will have to be repositioned.

You can insulate solid external walls with insulating plasterboard (page 228), either applied directly to the wall with adhesive and nailable plugs or secured to a timber dry-lining frame with additional insulation fitted within the frame (page 232).

INSULATION SAVINGS

Installing cavity wall insulation can reduce your home's heat loss by up to a third. Cavity wall insulation will pay for itself in four years or less. Solid walls lose even more heat than cavity walls and though internal insulation savings are harder to calculate, they are considerable. Wall insulation makes your home more energy efficient and helps to lower your rating should you need to apply for an Energy Performance Certificate (pages 26–27).

Soundproofing a room

Noise pollution can be distressing. Fortunately it is possible to cut down on the amount of sound that enters – and leaves – a room.

Depending on where you live, you may suffer from airborne noise created by nearby road, rail or air traffic, by local industry or other commercial activity, or simply by noisy neighbours with a taste for loud music and unruly dogs. If you live in a terraced or semi-detached property, or a flat, you also have the problem of sharing the building with other occupants, whose activities create noise that travels through each separating (party) wall into your home.

Cutting airborne sound

Acoustic double glazing

The single biggest improvement you can make is to have acoustic double glazing installed. This takes the form of secondary glazing, creating a gap of at least 100mm between the new glazing and the existing window glass. For the best results:

- the existing windows must be efficiently draught-proofed to prevent sound transmission through air gaps;
- the secondary glazing should use glass thicker than that in the existing windows;
- the window reveal should be lined with acoustic tiles.

It is essential that the secondary glazing is kept closed for maximum effect, but make sure that a window can be opened easily to offer an escape route in the event of a fire. It may be necessary to provide the room with alternative means of ventilation if the window is the only source of fresh air.

External doors

To improve the sound insulation of an external door:

- replace a glazed or lightweight door with a solid one;
- ensure a door is well draught-proofed;
- fit secondary glazing to a porch or hall window.

Seal all gaps

Use non-setting flexible sealant to fill gaps round door and window frames.

Cutting transmitted sound with an insulated lining

You can significantly reduce the sound transmitted through a party wall by building an insulated lining – similar to a timber-framed stud partition wall (page 238) – parallel to but separated from the party wall. If the wall contains a chimney breast, the lining can be built in front of it if you can afford to lose the floor space. If you cannot, erect the lining in the alcoves. If the fireplace is not in use, this should be bricked up (see page 249) and plastered over as part of the work.

Tools *Tape measure; plumb line; hand or power saw; hammer. Possibly also power drill and drill bits; wide filling knife or plasterer's trowel; cartridge gun.*

Materials *75 x 50mm sawn softwood; 100mm round wire nails; 100mm thick loft insulation blanket; 12.5mm plasterboard; 40mm plasterboard nails; self-adhesive joint tape; joint filler; non-setting mastic.*

1 Draw a line on the ceiling parallel with the party wall and 100mm away from it. Cut the head plate to length, position its front edge on the line and nail it to the ceiling joists if it runs at right angles to them. Fix it with expanding metal cavity anchors if it is parallel to them.

2 Drop a plumb line from the head plate to the floor and make another mark. Cut the sole plate to length and nail it to the floor. Use masonry nails on a concrete floor.

3 Cut and fit studs at each side of the wall and at 600mm centres in between. Skew-nail them to the head and sole plates.

4 Cut lengths of loft insulation and hang them between the studs, tucking their ends and sides behind the framework.

5 Cut the first sheet of plasterboard to match the ceiling height. Offer it up and nail it to the framework. Fix further sheets to complete the first layer.

6 Cut and fit a second layer of plasterboard over the first layer, with the joint positions staggered. Tape and fill the joints, and seal the perimeter of the wall with non-setting flexible sealant. Fit a new skirting board and decorate the wall.

HELPFUL TIPS

- If you live near an airport or major road, you may be able to get a local authority grant towards the costs of soundproofing your home.
- For professional advice on further means of sound insulation in the home, look up Acoustic Engineers in your local *Yellow Pages* directory.

Preventing condensation

Condensation occurs in a room when warm air filled with moisture meets a cold surface, such as an external wall or a pane of glass. It has become a more common problem in the home as draughtproofing has improved.

Insulating walls (page 241) and adding secondary double glazing to windows (page 212) will increase the temperature of the wall and window surfaces facing the room and both will reduce condensation.

There are two other measures you can take: reduce the amount of water vapour produced in the home and increase the amount of ventilation by fitting extractor fans in the kitchen and bathroom.

Only in extreme cases will you need a permanent dehumidifier – these are normally used as temporary measures when a room needs to be dried out.

Reducing water vapour

Large amounts of water vapour are produced by cooking, laundry and bathing. Try to reduce the amount of moisture released into the air.

- In the kitchen, a hood over the cooker will reduce condensation by removing steam.
- Cover saucepans with lids when you are cooking, and use an automatic kettle that will switch itself off as soon as the water has boiled.
- If you have a tumble dryer, make sure that it is vented to the outside unless it is of the condenser type that needs no vent.
- Condensation often occurs in bathrooms, especially on cold tiled surfaces. A heated towel rail will help to raise the temperature of the room.
- Less water vapour will form if you run a little cold water into the bath before turning on the hot water. Keep the bathroom door shut to prevent moisture from spreading to other parts of the house.

HELPFUL TIP

Use anti-condensation paint (page 83) instead of standard emulsion in very steamy areas. The paint insulates the surface (making it warmer) and some types absorb moisture during periods of high humidity and allow it to evaporate later on. The paint also contains a fungicide that reduces the risk of mould.

Installing an extractor fan

The most effective way to improve ventilation is to install an extractor fan. Position it opposite a door for best results.

Axial-flow fan

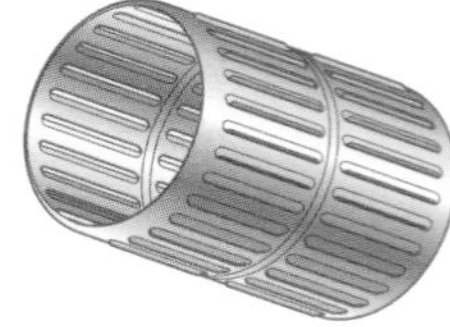

Centrifugal impeller

Axial-flow fans contain flat, propeller-like blades, and include models for mounting in a window. Centrifugal fans have a long, cylindrical impeller.

Wall-mounted fans discharge to the outside through a hole. Ceiling-mounted fans discharge along a duct above the ceiling to a hole in an external wall.

Window-mounted fans are normally cheap and easy to install, but as they tend to have smaller motors, they are more likely to be affected by strong winds than wall-mounted types. All types are driven electrically and controlled by a pull-cord switch on the fan or a separate wall switch.

A pull-cord fan is the best choice for a bathroom – a wall switch would have to be sited outside the room to comply with regulations for electrical bathroom fittings.

Fans with two or three speeds have complex electrical wiring. You may need to get the wiring work done by an electrician.

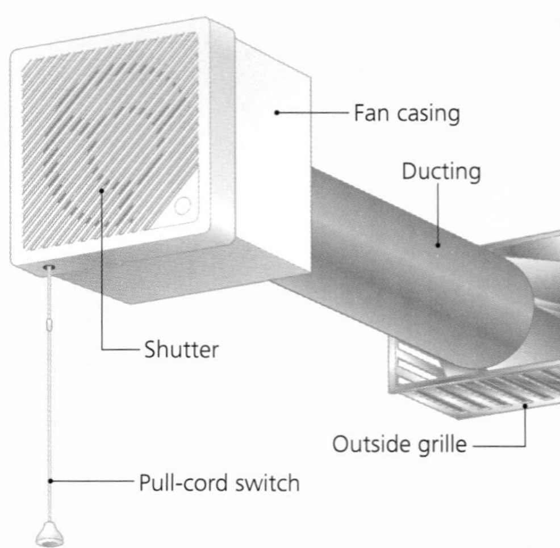

Wall-mounted fan
A shutter fits onto the fan inside the room, and a grille fits on the outside wall. The two are connected by plastic ducting. This is essential in a cavity wall, but useful in a solid wall too, as it makes cleaning easier. The fan may have a pull-cord switch or a separate wall switch.

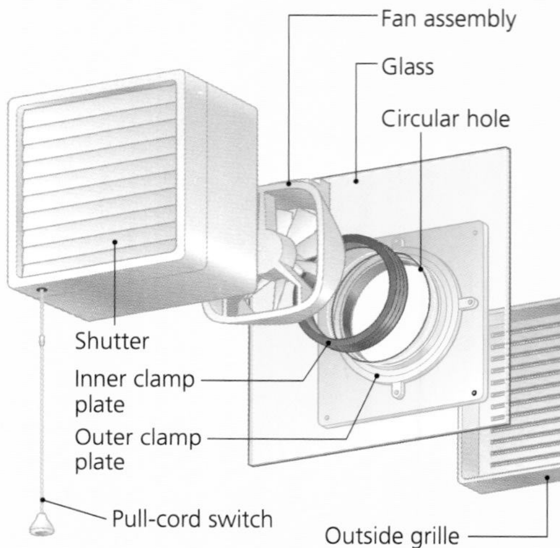

Window-mounted fan
The fan is fitted around a circular hole cut in the glass and outer parts are screwed together with clamp plates on each side of the window.

Fitting a wall or window-mounted fan

1 Position the fan as high in the wall or window as possible, opposite the door or main air entry point so that air is drawn right across the room.

2 If there is a boiler or gas heater in the room, make sure it is independently ventilated. Otherwise, when doors and windows are shut the extractor fan could allow fumes to be drawn into the room.

3 Make a hole in the wall (page 410) at the chosen position. Fit the external clamp plate and grille and the inner clamp plate and fan assembly. Holes for window-mounted fans are best left to a glazier (or specified when double glazed sealed units or safety glass are ordered).

4 Prepare a cable route (page 282) to a spot within reach of the fan's flex. At the end of the route fit a mounting box for a flex outlet plate in a bathroom, or for a switched FCU elsewhere (pages 286–7).

5 Following the maker's instructions, make any electrical connections necessary to the fan assembly before fitting the internal grille and shutter. Some models are wired to a plug-in block. Use the flex recommended by the manufacturer.

6 Fit the grille and the shutter on the inside of the room.

7 Connect the fan into its electrical supply circuit.
- In a bathroom, follow the method described in Installing a heated towel rail (page 287).
- Elsewhere, follow the method described under Fitting a fused connection unit for a stationary appliance (page 286).

CHOOSING A FAN OF THE RIGHT CAPACITY

Before buying a fan, find out how much air it can move. Airflow capacity is given in either cubic metres per hour, or litres per second.

The fan extract rates required by the Building Regulations vary from room to room. They are:
- kitchens 60 litres per second (216m³ per hour); 30 litres per second (110 m³ per hour) for cooker hoods
- utility rooms 30 litres per second (108m³ per hour)
- bathrooms 15 litres per second (54m³ per hour)
- separate WCs 6 litres per second (22m³ per hour).

As an example, a typical 150mm diameter wall or window fan has an extract rate of about 280m³ per hour, which is more than enough to meet the Building Regulations requirements for a kitchen.

Fitting a ceiling-mounted fan

The fan is fixed into a hole in the ceiling between joists (or into a false ceiling) in the same way as a wall fan, except that a hole has to be made in the ceiling.

Fit a length of ducting from the ceiling intake to a wall outlet. Ducting, made up of slotted-together sections of metal or plastic piping, should be ordered with the fan. If it goes through a wall, it terminates with a wall grille; if it goes through the roof it is covered with a roof cowl.

From an upstairs room, ducting can pass through the loft. On the ground floor, a false ceiling may be necessary to hide it.

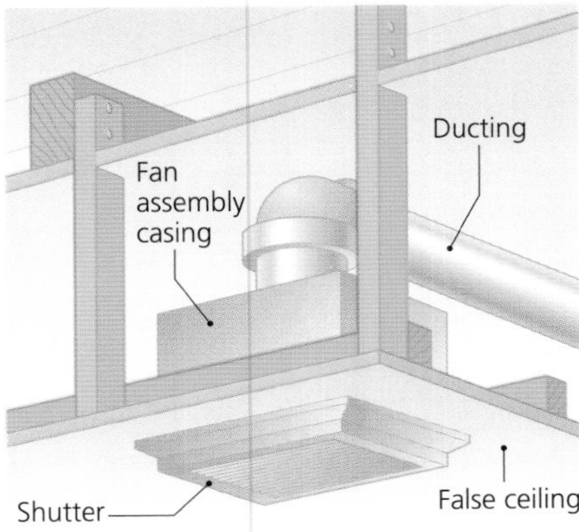

A long length of ducting reduces the airflow capacity of the fan – probably by about 10 per cent for each metre of run. An elbow bend will reduce it even more.

Take this into account when working out the size of the extractor fan required (top).

Choosing loft insulation

You can insulate a loft yourself with blanket, loose fill or sheet insulation or pay a specialist company to blow loose-fill insulation between the joists. If you do it, lay or top up to at least 270mm of insulation: the minimum recommended in the current Building Regulations. A thicker layer will prevent even more heat loss. You may be eligible for a grant – ask your local council or Citizens Advice Bureau for details.

Before you buy Find out if a supplier will deliver the insulation. Blanket rolls and sacks of loose-fill are very bulky for their weight. Most cars will only hold a fraction of the amount needed for most lofts.

How much material do I need? Calculate the size of your loft before buying the insulation material. Measure the overall length and width of your house and multiply the two figures. Most suppliers will advise on how much material is needed for a given area.

Blanket rolls Mineral fibre blanket is sold in single 370mm rolls or in 'combi' rolls 1140 or 1160mm wide that can be cut into two or three widths. Either plain or 'encapsulated' (sleeved in plastic) and in 100, 170 and 200mm thicknesses.

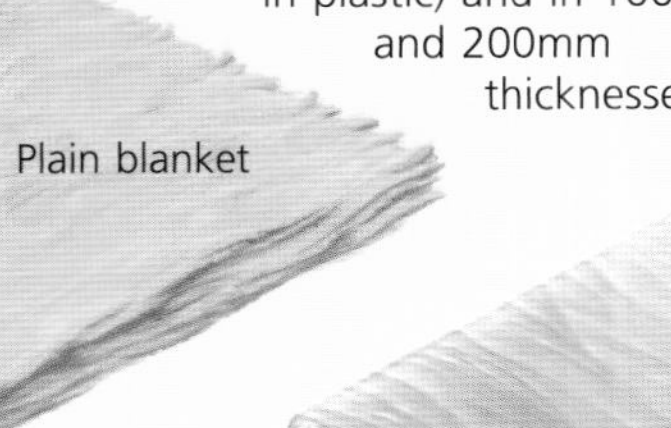

- Use a panel saw to cut through the roll while it is still in its wrapper, or cut through single widths with scissors.
- Fibre blanket is cheap and effective, but tends to compress as it ages.
- Sleeved blanket is much more pleasant to handle.
- Insulation is not effective if water condenses in the material. Use a reflective foil vapour barrier if laying plain (unsleeved) blanket.

Mineral fibre batts Multipurpose semi-rigid batts can be used instead of fibre blanket in any insulation job. They are available from 25mm to 150mm thick so two or more batts are needed to meet the minimum depth required for insulating a floor. Batts are 1200mm long and 600mm wide, making them easy to handle and ideal for roofs (page 245).

HELPFUL TIP

If you're laying blanket insulation to a minimum of 270mm you may need two layers – one between the joists and one to lay crossways over the top. Take this into account when calculating and ordering quantities.

Loose fill This is supplied in sacks and is simply poured between the joists.
- Common loose-fill materials are mineral wool and cellulose fibre (recycled newspaper), though you can still buy vermiculite loose fill.
- Allow for joists when estimating quantities – or there will be too much left over.
- Current regulations require a depth of insulation greater than the depth of standard joists. If you want to top up to 270mm, use blanket rolls over the loose fill.

Polystyrene sheets Useful for sliding into areas which have been boarded over or are difficult to reach – the flat roof over an extension, for example. It can also be used to insulate a cold-water cistern, but is too expensive for a whole loft.
- Expanded polystyrene is available in 25, 50 and 100mm thicknesses in 2.4m lengths and 600mm or 1.2m widths, but is easy to cut to the width you want.
- Extruded polystyrene 'space' boards are 52.5mm thick and come in 500mm x 1.2m sizes to make an insulated loft floor, laid over the joists or existing boards.

Reflective foil building paper Acts as a vapour barrier so that moisture cannot condense in the insulation material. Heat reflects off the shiny surface – either back into the house in winter or back into the loft in summer.
- Lay the foil between joists or drape it over them. If using it between joists to stop loose granules blowing about, pin the paper in position. There is no need to pin it if it is laid on the floor beneath roll or sheet insulation.
- Supplied in 25m or 50m rolls 900mm wide by builders' merchants.

Insulating a loft

If the loft space is used only for storage then insulate the floor. But if the loft is to be turned into a room – insulate the roof slope.

If you put down flooring-grade chipboard or extruded polystyrene boards (page 243) after you have insulated between the joists, you will have a useful storage area. But remember the joists are only ceiling joists for the room below, not floor joists, so you cannot use the space as a room or store too many heavy things there.

Before you start Clear the floor space as much as possible and vacuum-clean the loft. At the same time, check for woodworm and rot, and, if necessary, call in a specialist contractor to treat it.

If the loft has no lighting, connect an inspection lamp to a socket downstairs or run a table lamp off an extension cable.

The instructions on this page are for plain blanket. If you use sleeved blanket, you will not need a vapour barrier and should not need to wear gloves.

Fixing a vapour barrier on the floor

Tools *Scissors.*

Materials *Rolls of reflective foil building paper or sheets of polythene; masking tape.*

1 Cut the material with scissors so that it is about 50–75mm wider than the gap between the joists.

2 Lay the material in the gap. Remember that reflective foil paper must be laid foil-side down.

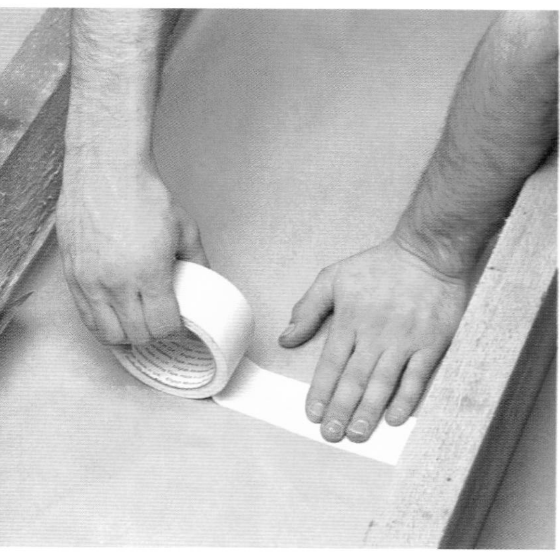

3 Seal any overlaps in the material with 50mm masking tape.

Laying insulation blanket on the floor

The spacing between joists varies but about 350mm is average. Do not cut the excess off a 400mm blanket – let it curl up on each side to make a snug fit.

Tools *Scissors; face mask; protective gloves.*

Materials *Rolls of glass fibre or mineral wool blanket.*

PROTECTING YOURSELF

Insulating products can be very irritating. Only open the packaging in the loft and keep the hatch closed while you are working. Wear protective gloves and overalls or a long-sleeved shirt, and tuck sleeves and trouser legs into gloves and socks. If fibres do get into the gloves, they will cause more irritation than if you wore no gloves at all. Wear a suitable face mask and throw it away after use. It is also a good idea to wear a safety helmet to protect your head against the rafters.

1 Start unrolling the blanket between two joists at the eaves at one end of the loft.

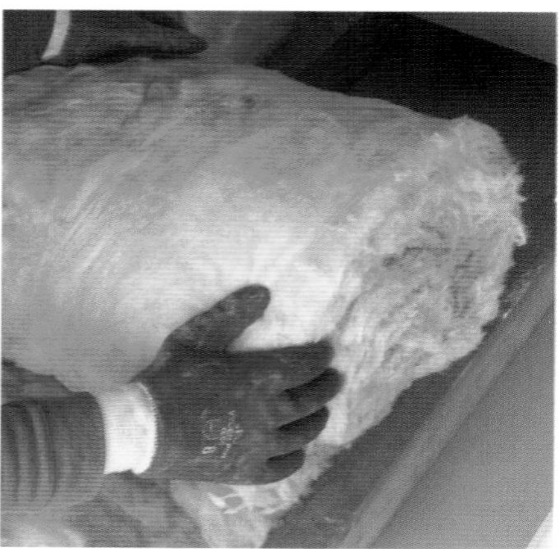

2 Do not take the material right into the eaves; you must leave a gap of about 50mm so that air can come in through the soffit and flow through the loft. If the air cannot circulate, condensation may form.

3 Press the blanket down lightly as you unroll it so that it lies flat but do not squash it so that it becomes compressed.

4 When you reach the other side of the loft, cut the blanket with scissors, again taking care not to block where essential ventilation comes in under the eaves.

5 Continue to lay insulation between the other joists.

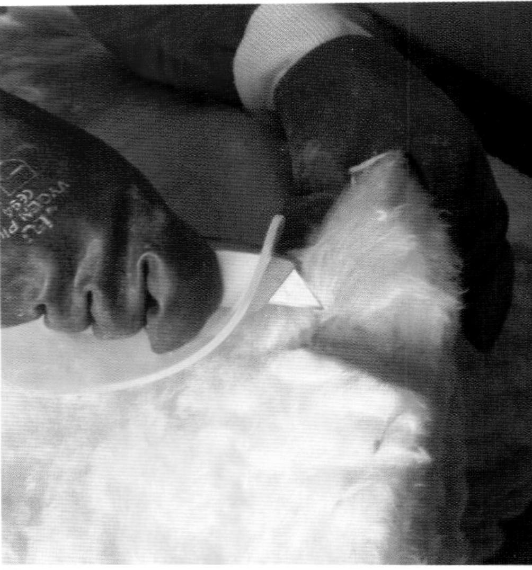

6 When joining two rolls, make a butt join, pressing the ends close to each other. Cut the insulation so that it fits tightly around pipes.

7 Try to slip insulation under loose electric cables to prevent them overheating. Where practicable, fix cables to the sides of the joists to keep them out of the way.

8 Never insulate under the cold water cistern. Leave a gap in the insulation so that warm air from below will keep the chill off the base of the cistern and help to prevent the water from freezing.

Insulating with loose-fill

Loose-fill material is easy to use – just pour it between the joists and level out. But as most ceiling joists are 100–150mm deep, filling level with the top of the joists will fall short of the recommended insulation depth of 270mm. You can raise the joists by nailing wooden battens to each of them, but this is costly in terms of time and money and will add considerable weight to the existing joists. The best solution is to top up loose fill with blanket insulation laid at right angles to the joists. If you want to use the loft for storage, use extruded polystyrene 'space' board, which can be secured to the joists.

HELPFUL TIP

If the loft does not have a boarded floor, you must keep your weight on the joists. Do not step on the plaster or plasterboard – your foot will probably go through. Find a stout board thick enough to take your weight and long enough to be laid across at least two joists. It may be easier if you have two or three boards so you don't have to keep moving the one you are on.

LAGGING A LOFT-HATCH DOOR

• Cut a piece of plain mineral fibre blanket or thick expanded polystyrene sheet to fit above the loft hatch.
• Cut a piece of polythene sheet large enough to cover the blanket. Fix the sheet over the blanket, holding the edges in place with drawing pins.
• Alternatively, use sleeved ('encapsulated') insulation blanket.
• If you are using expanded polystyrene sheet, stick it to the door with polystyrene ceiling tile adhesive.
• Make sure that the hatch door is a tight fit. Fix a foam, rubber or flexible draught excluder to the rebate so that damp air cannot pass through into the cold loft above and possibly cause condensation problems.

Alternatively Buy a pre-insulated loft-hatch door and use it to replace the existing door.

HELPFUL TIP

When laying insulation blanket, use a broom to push the blanket into the areas that are hard to reach.

THE IMPORTANCE OF VENTILATION

A good flow of air across the loft is important for keeping the roof timbers dry. In old lofts without roofing felt under the tiles or slates, air blows in and out through the gaps. If the roof has a layer of felt under the battens, then this prevents air coming in. Some modern roofs have ventilation around the eaves and also often at high level. Any insulation laid under the felt on the underside of the roof slope must allow ventilation to continue in order to clear any moisture from the surface of the felt. A gap of 50mm behind the insulation is usually enough to ensure good ventilation, provided there is room at the ridge for the air to escape and room at the eaves for it to enter. If you are in any doubt about the best way of carrying out the insulation work, consult your local building control officer.

Insulating a roof

If you want to use your loft for storing items that need to be kept warm and dry it is advisable to insulate the underside of the roof. This will also keep the loft cooler in summer.

Tools *Knife or large pair of scissors; staple gun. Possibly power drill.*

Materials *Mineral-fibre insulation batts or polystyrene sheets; garden netting. Building paper, hardboard sheets or foil-faced plasterboard; drywall screws.*

1 If using polystyrene sheet, hold the sheet against the rafters to mark the position of the rafter gaps on it.

2 Using scissors or knife, cut the polystyrene to fit between the rafters. Mineral-fibre batts should already be the correct width to push into the gaps.

3 Do not hammer anything into the rafter because you could dislodge a tile or slate. Use a staple gun and nylon garden netting to hold the insulation in place. You may need a helper with this part of the task.

4 For a quick, simple finish, staple sheets of building paper to the rafters. Where two strips of building paper join, make sure they overlap by at least 100mm and tape along the join with waterproof adhesive tape. Alternatively, screw hardboard sheets to the rafters.

5 For an even better finish, you can screw foil-faced plasterboard to the rafters, as shown. The foil should face the roof. Use plasterboard drywall screws, which can be put in with a power drill.

Coping with a flat roof

Flat roofs should be insulated at the time they are built. If you are having an extension added to your house, make sure that insulation is incorporated when the roof is constructed.

Flat roofs must be ventilated above the insulation to prevent condensation on the timbers. You can do this by drilling small holes in the fascia or soffit board to take ventilator insect screens.
• If an existing roof lacks insulation, remove a fascia board so that you can see into the space between the roof lining and ceiling. The fascia board will either be nailed or screwed to the ends of the ceiling joists.
• Slide sheets of expanded polystyrene – preferably 75mm thick – into the gap. If you cannot take off a fascia board, line the ceiling below, preferably with insulating plasterboard (page 228).
• Alternatively, you can place insulation above the roof decking if access to the roof void is not possible. There are several ways of doing this, but the simplest involves laying sheets of rigid polystyrene or other exanded foam insulation on the roof decking, covering it with a permeable geotextile membrane and placing a layer of ballast on top to keep the membrane and insulation in place on the roof surface.

Diagnosing the causes of damp

Damp problems can be due to a number of causes – rain getting through the walls or roof, moisture being absorbed from the ground, condensation settling on cold surfaces, or a mixture of these. Make sure you know what the cause of dampness is before you try to cure it. Otherwise, you may be dealing only with part of the problem, or worse still adopting the wrong remedy for the sort of damp involved.

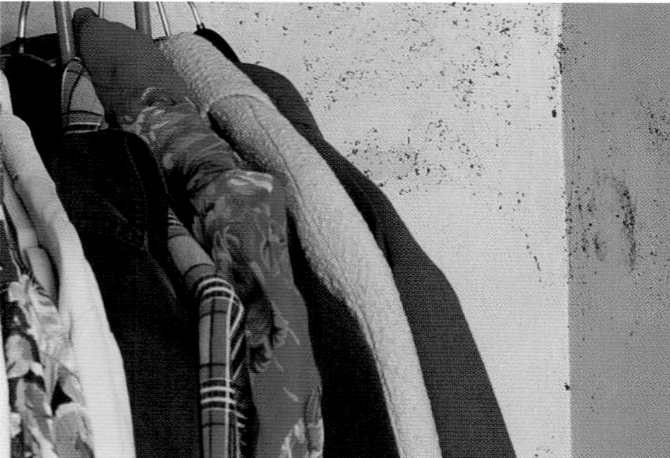

Damp can seep through gaps around windows (above) or lead to mould growth in a built-in wardrobe (right).

Spot the tell-tale signs
In an old house with a slate damp-proof course (DPC) slight movement of the building can crack the slates, allowing damp from the ground to rise into the masonry above the crack. A single point of failure will cause a patch of damp that can be up to 1m across, while multiple cracks will lead to an almost continuous band across the affected wall.

Prod the paintwork
Use a bradawl to test the soundness of skirting boards if there are signs of rising damp in downstairs walls or the underfloor space. The backs of skirting boards are usually left unpainted, and as a result they readily absorb moisture from the masonry. However, severe deterioration is often not apparent because of layers of paint on their face sides.

Crossing the bridge
If you think you have rising damp, locate the DPC and make sure it isn't covered by a flowerbed, path, drive or patio. Look for rendering that has been applied over the DPC. Check whether there is a vertical DPC sandwiched between the house wall and a garden wall built up against it. Curing these common causes of rising damp will solve the problem at little or no cost.

Try the foil test
If you aren't sure of the cause of a damp patch, try the foil test. Dry the surface of the wall with a fan heater, then tape some kitchen foil tightly over the damp area. If the surface of the foil is wet after 24 hours you have condensation. If the foil is dry but the wall surface beneath it is damp, you have rising or penetrating damp. Discount rising damp if moisture is more than 1m above outside ground level.

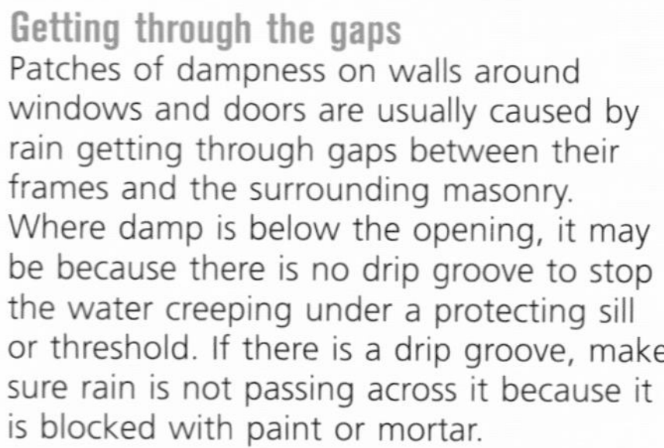

Getting through the gaps
Patches of dampness on walls around windows and doors are usually caused by rain getting through gaps between their frames and the surrounding masonry. Where damp is below the opening, it may be because there is no drip groove to stop the water creeping under a protecting sill or threshold. If there is a drip groove, make sure rain is not passing across it because it is blocked with paint or mortar.

HELPFUL TIP
Some specialist companies offer a free survey to check for rot and insect attack. If they find a problem, they will quote for treating the infestation or curing the damp, or they can supply you with the chemicals you need if you want to do the job yourself.

Looking for a leak in the roof
Discovering exactly where a pitched roof is leaking can be difficult. Rain can trickle down the underside and along the sides of the rafters before it drips onto the loft floor. Clues such as dampness on a party wall or chimney stack in the loft may indicate that flashings are defective or missing. Getting someone to play a hose on the roof area by area while you remain inside the loft can also help to reveal where water is getting in.

Check the plumbing
Leaks in plumbing and central heating pipework can cause damp patches which could be misinterpreted as rising or penetrating damp. This is especially common where pipes run beneath a floor or are buried in wall plaster. A pinhole leak in buried pipework can release a lot of water over time. You can either expose the fault and replace the affected pipes, which will cause a lot of disruption. Or you can leave them in situ and bypass them by installing new ones.

Suspect condensation
If the roof isn't leaking but the loft timbers and insulation are damp, the culprit is probably condensation. This is caused by warm, moisture-laden air rising into the loft from the rooms below and condensing on cold surfaces within the loft space. This could cause rot in the roof timbers and staining to ceilings.

Deal with water vapour
The kitchen and bathroom are the main sources of condensation in the home. Bathing, cooking, washing-up and washing and drying clothes pour a lot of water vapour into the air. Portable gas heaters and paraffin stoves also create lots of moisture. Poor room ventilation and efficient draught-proofing stop the moist air being replaced with cooler drier air from outside. Unventilated cupboards built against outside walls can suffer badly from condensation. This can lead to unsightly mould growth that will quickly spoil clothes stored there.

Treating rot, woodworm and mould

If walls and constructional timber become damp and do not dry out – perhaps because of a lack of ventilation – wet rot and woodworm can develop in timber, dry rot can attack anywhere and you may get mould forming on walls. Major attacks may mean calling in a specialist firm to deal with them.

Preventing damp problems

- Deal with any damp as soon as you find it and ensure that the ventilation in the house is adequate.
- Check regularly that the airbricks round the outside of the house are clean and free from obstruction.
- A suspended timber floor needs to be thoroughly ventilated with approximately one airbrick for every 30m² of floor.
- If you discover a damaged airbrick or if you find that an airbrick is missing, put one in (page 410). There should also be an airbrick indoors if a fireplace has been closed up (page 249) and at the top of a chimney if this has been capped.

Wet rot

Several different species of fungi attack very wet wood causing wet rot. It is most likely to occur outside at the bottom of a door or window frame, for example, but even inside it is much more common than dry rot, and easier to eradicate since it can only spread over damp timber surfaces.

- If wood turns dark and shrinks, and sparse dark or white strands become visible on the surface, wet rot may have set in. The wood will crack along the grain. Test the wood by prodding it with a sharp screwdriver, bradawl or knife. If the wood is soft and pulpy, it needs treatment.
- Deal with the cause of the damp. When the wood has dried out, the wet rot will die. Treat damaged wood with wood repair products (page 412) or replace with some well-seasoned wood.

Dry rot

Damp, unventilated conditions indoors are perfect for dry rot. It does not occur outside. This is a much more serious condition than wet rot, and the timber need not be wet before the fungus takes hold. Early growth forms white fluffy strands which later thicken and resemble dirty cotton wool. The fruiting body which develops resembles large, pancake-like lichen, and is rusty-coloured with a grey-white rim.

The fluffy strands will spread across masonry or metalwork seeking out timber. They can extend 12m or more. Dry rot can spread rapidly, and it is very difficult to eradicate; every strand must be traced and killed to prevent the risk of a new outbreak. If they are not killed, strands can remain dormant for several years and then start into growth again.

- Affected wood becomes dry, soft and brittle, cracking across the grain. Dry rot smells musty and is often hidden from view – behind skirting boards, under floorboards, or behind paint.
- Treating dry rot is not a DIY job. Call in a specialist company.

Woodworm

When you see the tell-tale flight holes, you can treat small attacks of woodworm (on furniture, say) with woodworm killer yourself, but get a specialist firm in for anything major – in flooring, for example.

Mould

In damp, warm conditions, mould may affect paint and wallpaper and sometimes grout – perhaps if a waterproof grout has not been used to fix tiles in a bathroom or kitchen.

- Never use bleach to treat mould. Although this will kill the mould flowers, it will not harm the root and the problem will recur within a few weeks.
- If mould has ruined a wall covering, strip the covering off. If paintwork is affected, wash the surface with warm soap or detergent and water. Treat the wall with a proprietary fungicide. Wear gloves as protection and brush on two or three coats.
- When putting up new wallpaper, use a paste containing fungicide. Most pastes for vinyls are suitable.

Damp-proofing basements and cellars

Rooms below ground level are prone to damp, especially if the house is in a hollow. Some damp problems can be solved with DIY methods, but if the walls have been treated and they still weep, seek advice from a surveyor.

Treating slight damp

If the damp is slight, treat the walls with a bituminous waterproofing compound.

1 Prepare the surface so that it is clean and free from old paint or wallpaper.

2 Apply two coats of the treatment, following the manufacturer's instructions.

Providing a tougher barrier against damp

Use a moisture-curing polyurethane sealant. The urethane resin in this liquid sets by the action of moisture upon it and forms a water resistant film.

1 Prepare and clean the surface thoroughly. If you have soaked off old wallpaper, wait for the walls to dry and then apply three coats.

2 Wait about two or three hours between coats – the previous coat should have lost its tacky feel before you brush on the next.

Dealing with damp in a concrete floor

Damp rising through a concrete basement floor indicates that there is no damp-proof membrane in the floor, or that if there is, it has failed or been punctured at some point. It is difficult to locate such failures.

1 If the damp is not severe, remove dust and other loose material from the surface and repair any cracks or small potholes.

2 Dry the floor surface as much as possible, for example by playing warm air from a fan heater across it.

3 Brush on three coats of moisture-curing polyurethane sealant, allowing each to become touch-dry before applying the next. No more than four hours should elapse between coats.

4 If you plan to lay a self-levelling compound over the treated floor surface to provide a new, flat surface for laying floor coverings (page 125), scatter dry sand over the final coat of sealant while it is still damp. Leave for three days, then brush off excess sand. Lay the self-smoothing compound following the manufacturer's instructions.

HELPFUL TIP

If a mortgage lender's survey reveals trouble – perhaps dry rot or woodworm – the lender will usually insist that the work is carried out by a professional who will give a guarantee. Banks and building societies will not accept DIY work.

Removing an old fireplace

An unwanted fireplace opening can be permanently bricked up, or it can be boarded up in case you want to reopen it later. Or you can keep the fireplace opening as a wall recess by sealing off the bottom of the flue. Before sealing off a fireplace, get the chimney swept and then have the stack capped by a builder.

SAFETY TIP

Removing a chimney breast is not a DIY task and can have disastrous results if carried out incorrectly. The chimney breast may be load-bearing and removing it could destabilise the floor (and fireplace) above. If you want to remove a chimney breast, have it done professionally.

A cast-iron surround

Cast-iron surrounds generally enhance the value of a property – people like to have an open fire, or to fit a fuel effect gas fire into an existing opening. Think carefully before removing an original feature like this. If you decide to go ahead, remove the fireplace surround carefully, as you may be able to sell it.

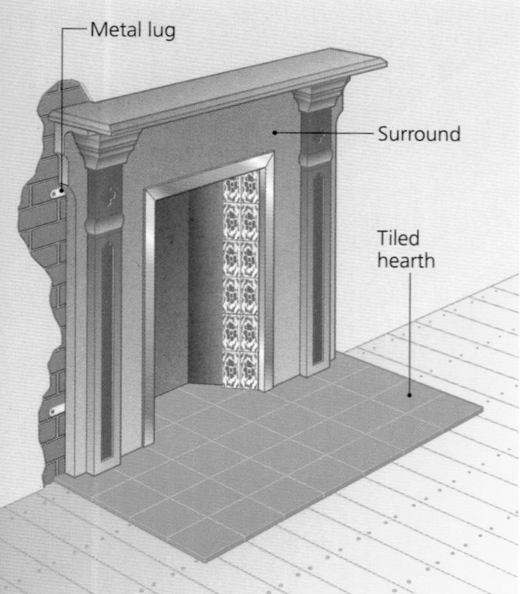

Cast-iron surround Old cast-iron surrounds can be valuable. They are usually fixed to the wall through lugs hidden underneath the plaster. Often there is an inner surround of tiles.

REMOVING OLD BOLTS OR SCREWS

- If you want to separate a cast-iron surround from its grate, you may have to soak bolts or screws with penetrating oil before you can undo them. Make several applications of oil over about 24 hours, if necessary.
- If they are still difficult to undo, use a nut splitter, which can be hired, to cut through the nuts. The splitter clamps round the nut or the bolt head and cuts it off as it is tightened.
- Drill out screw heads with a high-speed steel twist bit of about the same diameter as the screw shank (compare the screw head with loose screws to estimate the size). If necessary for resale, drill screw or bolt stubs from the surround and use a tap wrench to cut new threads.

1 Remove the wall covering and carefully chip away the plaster to expose the lugs at each side of the fire surround.

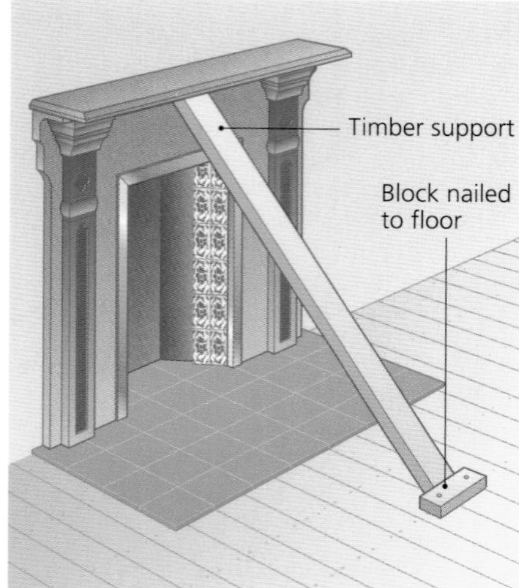

2 Support the surround by wedging a length of timber between the top and the floor. Cast-iron surrounds, particularly, are often top heavy. Without support the surround may fall forward when you undo the fixing screws.

3 Remove the fixing screws if possible. Otherwise, prise the lugs away from the wall, but be very careful as they are brittle and will break easily (this lowers the value of the surround).

4 The grate may be fixed to the surround with screws or bolts, and will come away with it. There is no need to separate them unless you are planning to sell the fireplace surround only.

A timber surround

A timber fireplace surround is usually screwed to battens fixed to the wall behind. There may be a tiled inner surround, which has to be removed separately.

1 Scan the timber surface to find filler covering the screw heads. If necessary, strip off the surface with paint or varnish remover to reveal the screw heads.

2 Dig out the filler to clear the screw slots, and undo the screws.

3 Lift away the surround and remove from the wall the battens used for fixing points.

4 Remove an inner tiled surround in the same way as a tiled surround (below). It is usually much lighter, however, and can be handled by one person.

A tiled surround

A tiled surround normally has a concrete backing that is screwed to the chimney breast through metal lugs, in the same way as a cast-iron surround. It is usually very heavy, and you will need a helper to hold it steady and help to lift it away. If a raised hearth is resting against the front of the surround, move the hearth first (right).

1 Remove the wall covering and plaster at the sides, near the top, to reveal the lugs. Either undo the fixings or prise the lugs away from the wall with a crowbar.

2 Get a helper to steady the surround as it comes away from the wall. If it does not come away easily, there may be another set of lugs lower down on each side.

3 Lower the surround with the aid of a helper. If possible, take it outside for breaking up. Lay the surround face downwards and cover it with sacking. Put on safety goggles and protective gloves before breaking it up with a sledgehammer.

A brick or stone surround

Before you start, check that the surround is not imitation brick or stone with facings bonded to a concrete backing. If it is, remove it in the same way as a tiled surround.

1 Begin removing bricks or stones at the top course, loosening them by chipping away the mortar with a hammer and cold chisel. Make sure you protect your eyes.

2 There may be metal ties or nails in the mortar joints, linked into the wall behind. Chip into the wall to remove them, and make good with filler afterwards.

Alternatively An expanded metal key may link the bricks to the wall.

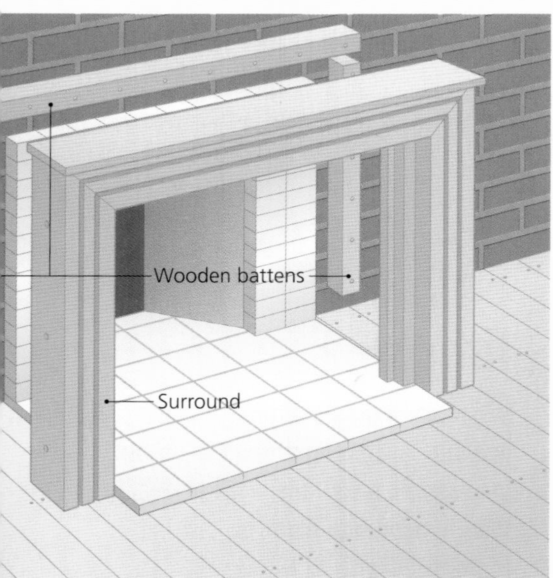

Timber surround The surround is usually screwed to wooden battens fixed to the brickwork behind.

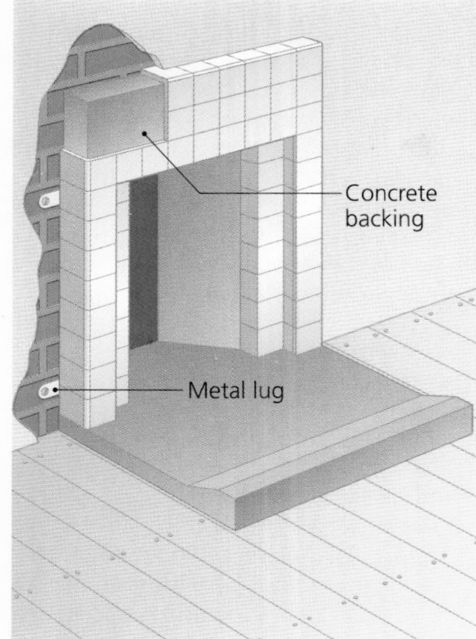

Tiled surround There is usually a concrete backing, making the surround very heavy.

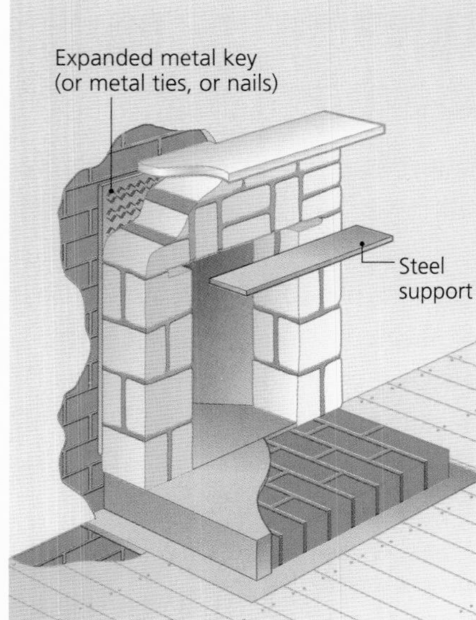

Stone surround The stones (or bricks) over the opening stand on a steel support.

Removing a raised hearth

A raised hearth may be a tiled slab of concrete or a number of stone slabs or bricks. The raised hearth is bonded to a concrete layer flush with the floor (known as the constructional hearth) with mortar.

1 Chip away the mortar with a hammer and cold chisel and prise out stones or bricks individually. Alternatively, use a crowbar to prise up a solid slab hearth.

2 Leave the constructional hearth in place. Smooth it with self-levelling compound before laying the floor covering.

Bricking up the opening

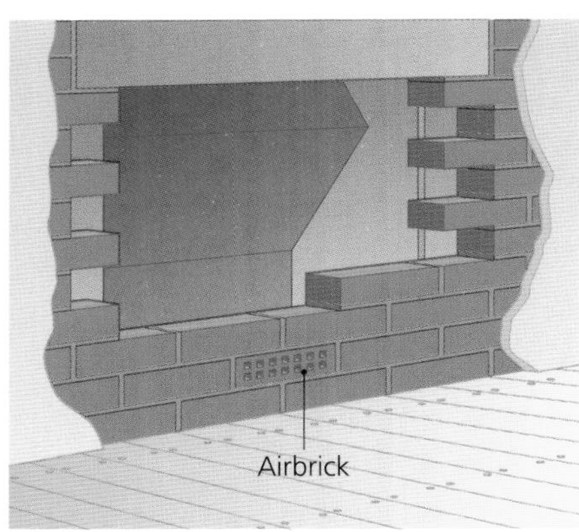

Use bricks or blocks and mortar (page 466) to block the opening, building them up in courses. The face should be level with the surrounding brickwork – that is, set back slightly from a layer of plaster.

Unless the opening is wider than about 1.2m, there is no need to tooth-in the bricks (that is, remove surrounding half bricks so that new bricks can be linked in).

1 Insert an airbrick (page 410) in the centre of the second or third course, to keep the chimney dry. If you are left with a gap about 25mm or more deep at the top of the opening, fill it in with a course of slates or part tiles.

2 Cover the brickwork with plaster to bring the surface flush with the surrounding wall. Fit a grille into the plaster in front of the airbrick.

Boarding up the opening

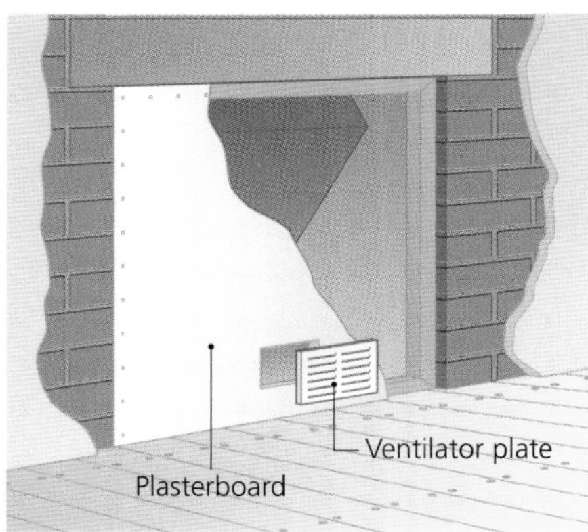

Use a piece of plasterboard or non-combustible building board cut to fit snugly into the opening.

1 Fit a frame of 50 x 50mm timber battens all round the edge of the opening, set back to allow for the board thickness.

2 If the opening is more than about 600mm wide, fit a central vertical batten to give extra rigidity.

3 Nail or screw the board to the battens so it lies flush with the surrounding wall.

4 Cut a hole near the bottom at the centre and fit in a ventilator plate.

5 Tape the top and side joints of the board to reinforce them (page 229).

6 Cover the board with ready-mixed skim-coat plaster, if necessary, to match the surrounding wall.

SAFETY PRECAUTION

If the opening to be blocked is linked to a common flue serving a fireplace still in use, do not fit a ventilator plate, through which hot soot may fall. When boarding up such an opening, you should use non-combustible building board.

Creating a wall recess

Screw a horizontal framework of 50 x 50mm timber battens to the inside of the opening, just above the crosspiece supporting the mouth of the flue.

1 Cut a panel of non-combustible building board to fit to the frame.

2 Make a hole in the centre of the board, and fit through it a length of 68mm diameter rainwater downpipe with a bend of about 90° at the top. Secure it in position with duct tape. The pipe keeps the flue ventilated, and the panel prevents soot and debris falling into the recess.

3 Secure the board, with the pipe facing up, to the frame using galvanised screws.

Opening up an old fireplace

In most cases a fireplace and grate will have been blocked off using sound building practices, but in some homes this may not be the case. It is always advisable to get expert advice from a surveyor or architect before you begin work.

Tools *Club hammer; bolster chisel; crowbar; saw; tape measure; pencil; pointing trowel. Possibly also trimming knife; wrecking bar.*

Materials *Lime mortar; new skirting board.*

Before you start Every home is different, and the way that the fireplace was blocked up will vary too. Some fireplaces will have been filled in with brick or blockwork while others may have a very simple board wedged into the opening. This is likely to be a messy job, so fold back the carpet or lay down lots of dustsheets to protect your furnishings.

1 Examine the chimney breast. If the chimney has been blocked up correctly, there will be a vent in the wall just above the skirting board. Remove this vent and use a torch to look inside the opening. This will give you some idea of the size of the fireplace opening.

2 Remove the skirting board in front of the fireplace. If this is in one long length, you will either have to remove the complete length, or make a cut on either side of the fireplace and remove a section of the skirting board.

3 Uncover the hearth. This is the solid section of floor in front of the chimney breast. It is usually a concrete slab set into the surrounding floorboards. This gives a further indication of the size of the original fireplace.

4 Tap the wall: a hollow sound indicates that the fireplace was probably blocked up with a board. If you can find the edge, which sometimes shows up as a bump under the wallpaper or paint, cut around this with a trimming knife and try to prise out the board with a wrecking bar. If this is difficult, drill a hole in the board to see whether it is plasterboard or timber. Break out a plasterboard sheet, using a club hammer, or use a padsaw or jigsaw to cut around the edge of a timber board. Unscrew or lever off any supporting battens.

Alternatively If the wall is brickwork, start from the vent and slowly knock out a few bricks at a time with a club hammer and bolster chisel. You may find it easier to remove the plaster from the area first and then go back to chip out the bricks, one by one, once you can see where the mortar joints are. Work left and right and upwards, gradually opening up the hole.

5 Cut the bricks back to the edge of the original opening before making good any joints in the brickwork at the side and back of the fireplace. Use a lime mortar specially formulated for fireplaces; you can buy this in small bags from fireplace suppliers. Regular sand and cement mortar will crack with the heat.

6 Once the fireplace is revealed you will be able to see whether the original fireback is still in place and in good condition. The fireback is a shaped section, often made from iron or fireclay, at the back of the fireplace. It is designed to reflect heat from the fire into the room, rather than allowing it to rise straight up the chimney (page 24).

7 A cracked fireback can be repaired with fire cement. Brush the area clean and spray the cracks with water to wet them, then fill them with cement. Let the cement dry for three days before using the fireplace.

8 Check the draught of the chimney by holding a lighted candle just in front of the fire opening. If the chimney is working, smoke and flame should be drawn up the chimney; if it does not happen, the chimney may well be blocked or capped off. Remove blocking within the flue. Get professional help if the flue has been capped at the top.

9 Get the chimney swept before installing a new grate and fireback (below). A professional sweep will be able to advise on the condition of the flue and will remove any build-up of soot and tar from the inside of the chimney.

CHECKING THE FLUE

Fires give off toxic fumes, which can kill. In a well designed and correctly working fireplace, these are exhausted up the chimney and pose no threat to occupants of the house.

Be aware of the dangers and get a professional to examine your chimney before you light a fire for the first time, whether you have opened up an old fireplace or installed a new one. Find a qualified chimney engineer in your area by contacting the National Association of Chimney Engineers (NACE). Regular maintenance is also important. Contact the National Association of Chimney Sweeps (NACS) for a list of registered sweeps in your area. See Chapter 14 for more details.

Fitting a new fireplace

Installing a fireplace in an existing opening is a straightforward job but, for safety's sake, any work involving the chimney flue must be tackled by a professional.

Tools *Club hammer; bolster chisel; brick trowel.*

Materials *Fibre cement board; 75 x 25mm planed timber boards; concrete; fireback; fire-proof rope; lime mortar; corrugated cardboard; brick rubble; fire cement; fireplace surround.*

Installing a fireback

If you revealed an empty fireplace opening when you unblocked your fireplace and plan to use the fireplace for a solid fuel or fuel-effect gas fire, you will need to install a fireback.

1 Measure the width of the opening. Firebacks are sold in standard widths of 400 and 450mm, but can be made in other sizes if necessary.

2 Tap along the cutting line with a club hammer and bolster chisel to split the fireback in two.

3 Lay a bed of lime mortar where the fireback will sit. Position the fireback then move it forwards slightly and sandwich lengths of fire-proof rope between it and the edges of the fireplace opening.

4 Slot two lengths of corrugated cardboard the height of the fireback behind it, mortaring them in place. When you first use the fire this cardboard will burn and leave a crucial expansion gap to allow the fireback to expand in the heat.

5 Use the broken rubble created by opening up the fireplace and mortar to fill the space behind the fireback.

6 Once you have filled to the level of the lower section of the fireback, use mortar to fix the upper section in place. Remove any excess mortar from the joint and continue filling behind the fireback.

7 Finish the fireback with a sloped line of mortar around the top edge, chamfering the join with the rear face of the flue. This will help to encourage smoke to rise up the chimney.

Installing a new fire surround and hearth

1 The hearth must be at least 200mm wider on each side than the fireplace opening, and must extend out into the room to a distance of at least 500mm from the face of the chimney breast.

2 You can make a hearth from a concrete mixture. Begin by screwing two layers of fibre cement board to the floorboards and extending these back into the fireplace opening. Screw 75 x 25mm planed timber boards together at the corners to make a formwork around the edge of the fibre cement board where it sticks out into the room. Use blocks of wood to hold it tightly in place.

3 Mix concrete from one part cement, two parts sand and three parts aggregate, and pour this into the form. Level it off with a wooden float and leave for 24 hours before removing the formwork.

Alternatively Buy a slate, granite or marble hearth at the same time as your new fire surround. Ask the fireplace supplier to cut this to size for you. It may come in two pieces: one to extend into the back of the opening and a rectangular piece to sit in front of the fireplace.

Bed the hearth on several blobs of mortar, check that it is perfectly level in all directions and wipe away any excess mortar that has seeped out at the edges from the weight of the hearth.

4 Carefully lift the fireplace surround into place. This may come as one piece, with a decorative surround and mantelpiece in one, or as separate components.

5 Use a spirit level to check the surround for level. Fit wooden shims on either side if the surround needs to be adjusted. Then screw the surround to the wall through the lugs provided. Use fire cement to seal the surround to the edges of the fireback.

6 Make good the plaster on each side of the surround. When this is dry, fit skirting boards to match those already in the room. Butt them up tightly to either side of the fireplace surround.

7 Tile or paint the hearth if it is concrete, then refit the carpet or other floor covering.

Choosing a fireplace surround and fire

A fireplace is the focus of the room but should not over-dominate. It is important to select a surround that looks right for the style of the room and house. The choice has never been wider: genuine antiques, Victorian reproductions, wood, marble, Art Deco, chrome and modern combinations of pebbles and stainless steel.

Choosing a fireplace surround

Cast-iron Victorian fireplaces were often made of cast iron, sometimes incorporating decorative tiles. Antiques and modern reproductions are available in a wide range of sizes, from slim all-in-one fireplaces, surrounds and mantelpieces to cast-iron insets that require a separate surround.

The traditional choices of cast iron grate and stone surround have a classic appeal. Many grates can be adapted to accommodate a gas fire if you prefer.

Stone The classic, clean lines of stone have an appeal that is timeless. Marble and limestone are popular choices, but many other options are also available.

Brick The warm colour and texture of a brick surround gives a room the cosy appeal of a cottage or farmhouse.

Tile Popular in the early and mid 20th century, tiled surrounds suit rooms decorated in the styles of those times and often have an Art Deco design. You can use new tiles to change the look of an existing surround or hearth – but check first that they will withstand the heat.

Wood A wood surround can be simple or ornate, traditional or modern, stained or painted, as you wish.

Choosing a grate

Cast iron The traditional choice for an open fire. Usually has a tray beneath the grate for collecting ash and easy cleaning. Cast-iron fronts are available to disguise the workings of a fuel-effect gas fire.

Concrete or stone For a more modern look, the clean lines of a stone grate can be complemented by a simple surround in a colour to match the rest of the room.

Stainless steel An ultra-modern alternative to the traditional Victorian grate is a stainless steel bowl filled with fire-resistant stones or pebbles. A gas flame provides the heat, which is retained by the stones to create a more intense warmth.

Clean lines suit a minimalist setting. Here, gas burns through heat-retaining stones.

Floors and staircases 8

Lifting and replacing a floorboard

You may need to lift a floorboard in order to access pipes or cables beneath the floor for repairs.

Tools *Thin-bladed knife; drill and twist drill bits; jigsaw; bolster chisel; hammer; screwdriver. Also for tongue-and-groove boards: circular saw (or panel saw or flooring saw).*

Materials *50 or 75mm floorboard nails; 75mm 4mm screws; pieces of timber about 40mm square and 100mm longer than the width of the boards.*

Before you start First find out whether the boards are tongue-and-groove or square edge by poking a thin-bladed knife between them. If they are square edge, the blade will pass right through.

Removing a square-edge board

Before lifting the board, you must cut across it at each end just before it meets a joist. Lines of nails indicate joist centres.

1 Drill a 10mm starting hole near the edge of the board you want to remove, and complete the cut across it with a jigsaw.

> **HELPFUL TIP**
>
> Whenever you do not need access below the floor, put the board back loosely in position, even if only for a few minutes, to stop the risk of someone stepping into the hole.

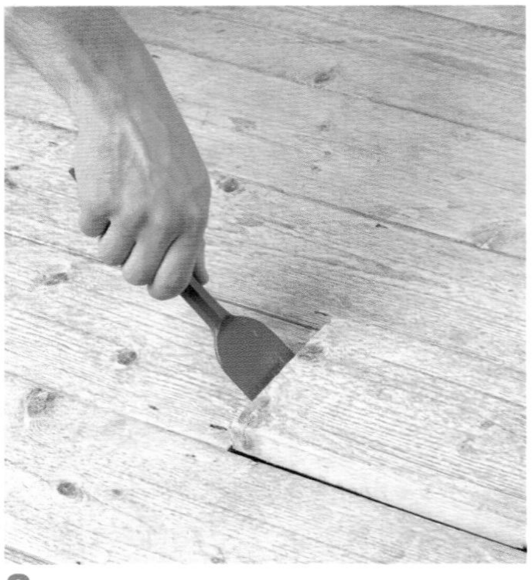

2 Starting at one end, prise out fixing nails by levering up the board with a bolster chisel.

3 Once you have loosened one or two sets of nails, push the handle of a hammer under the board as far from the loose end as possible, and try to prise the board up. This sends a shock wave along the whole length, loosening nails farther along, which you can then remove.

4 Push the hammer farther forward, and repeat the process, until the board is free.

How to remove tongues

On tongue-and-groove boards, the tongues on each side of the board must be removed. If adjoining boards are to be lifted, only the tongues at the outer edges of the group need cutting.

1 Adjust the depth of cut on a circular saw so that the blade just protrudes below the underside of the tongue. Since floorboards are usually 19mm thick, the underside of the tongue will be about 13mm below the surface. This will avoid pipes and cables. If you do not have a circular saw, use a panel or flooring saw. Cut at a shallow angle.

2 Place the blade between the boards, switch on the power, and move the saw along the length of board.

3 With the tongues removed you should be able to see the joists between the boards. Remove the board in the same way as a square-edge board.

Replacing the board

Use new nails and proper floorboard brads. You will not be able to nail the board to a joist at its ends as it has been sawn off before the joists.

1 Screw a short batten to the side of each joist, its top edge jammed hard up against the underside of adjacent floorboards still in position. Nail the board to the batten.

Alternatively If you have old ceilings, it may be wise to screw the boards down. Vibration from heavy hammering can cause ceiling damage. Screws are also useful if access may be needed to pipes or cables beneath the floor in future.

CURING LOOSE AND SQUEAKING BOARDS

A floorboard squeaks because it is not firmly held to its joist. When someone steps on it, it springs under the weight, rubbing against a neighbouring board. A squeak can be temporarily cured by dusting talc down the side of the board.

Not all loose boards squeak – there may be too big a gap around them – but even so they should be properly secured before a floor covering is laid, otherwise you will feel (and hear) the movement under new flooring.

A board becomes loose when one or more of its fixing nails loses its grip due to vibration or the movement of the joist below. Prise out the nail if it is still there and refix the board with a screw big enough to fill the hole left by the nail. A 50mm 4mm screw should be suitable.

The screw will hold the board securely in place, and as it goes exactly into the same hole as the nail there should be no danger of striking a cable or pipe.

Replacing a damaged floorboard

Follow the instructions opposite to lift the damaged board. It is then a simple job to cut and fit a replacement.

Tools *Saw; hammer; perhaps a chisel; perhaps an electric drill and 2mm twist bit.*

Materials *Floorboards exactly the same thickness and width as the old ones – you may need to have these specially cut and planed at a timber yard; 50 or 75mm floorboard nails; perhaps scraps of hardboard or plywood and panel pins.*

Laying square-edge boards

1 Cut the timber to the same length as the old boards.

2 Lay the new boards in place and nail them to each joist with floorboard nails.

Laying tongue-and-groove boards

1 Cut the first board to length, and shave off its tongue with a chisel or plane.

2 Lay it in position, butting its former tongued edge to the grooved edge of an existing board, which may still have the remains of the cut-off tongue in it.

3 If a second board is needed, cut it to length, lay it on the joists and tap it into place so that its tongue locates in the groove of the first new board. Continue with the other boards.

4 When you come to the final board, you will probably have to shave off its tongue, as you will not be able to manoeuvre it into place with the tongue attached.

Alternatively Shave off the underside of the groove of the second to last board. It may be possible to tap the last board into place with tongue intact.

5 Fix the boards to the joists with floorboard nails. You will be able to see the positions of the joists from the lines of nails in the existing floorboards.

6 If nails have to be driven in near the end of a board, first drill pilot holes smaller than the nails to avoid splitting the wood.

Replacing a floor with chipboard

If a floor is beyond repair, it can be replaced more cheaply with chipboard than with new floorboards.

Flooring-grade chipboard is sold in two thicknesses – 19 and 22mm. For joists up to 460mm apart, use 19mm board. Chipboard is heavy, so use the smallest sheets available unless you have someone to help you. You can use square-edge boards, but sheets with tongue-and-groove edges make a more stable floor, and edge joints do not need any support battens.

Lay boards flat in a pile inside the house as soon as they are delivered or they may distort. At least 24 hours before you begin work, loose-lay them so they can adjust to the moisture content of the room.

Tools *Circular saw; panel saw or flooring saw; hammer; brush for applying adhesive; rag; pencil.*

Materials *Chipboard; 5mm gauge annular ring nails – 55mm nails for 19mm sheets, 60mm for 22mm sheets; lengths of 50mm square timber; 75mm oval nails; PVA wood adhesive.*

1 Start by taking up enough of the old floorboards to give space for the first row of chipboard sheets.

2 If there is not enough space between skirting board and joist to push in the chipboard, the skirting board will have to be removed from the wall (page 179).

3 Lay the first sheet of chipboard in one corner of the room.

4 A gap of 10mm must be left around the edge of the room to allow the chipboard to expand in damp weather. If you have removed the skirting, you can see this easily; if not, then push the sheet of chipboard hard against the wall beneath the skirting board, draw a line where it meets the skirting and then pull it out by 10mm.

HELPFUL TIPS

- If access may be needed in future to a cable or central heating pipe, fix the sheet above it with screws, which are much easier to remove than nails. Or create a removable access panel.
- If you are flooring an upstairs room or loft, and the ceiling below is weak, drill pilot holes in the chipboard for the nails. This reduces vibration when you hammer them in.

JOIST ALERT

The wall on one side of the room may be a hollow partition erected after the floor was installed. It is likely to cover the top of a joist. If so, you must nail a length of 50mm square timber to the side of the joist to provide a fixing point for the chipboard.

You can see the position of the joists by the rows of nails in the floorboards. If the partition wall has been built between joists, no fixing point for the chipboard will be available and a new joist must be installed. This is a job for a builder.

Square edge sheets

1 Lay square-edge sheets with the long edge parallel with the joists. They must be supported on every edge, so the long sides should rest on the centre of a joist, and the ends should rest on a nogging.

2 Make the nogging from a piece of 50mm square-section wood placed between the joists and fixed with 75mm oval nails driven down at an angle through the nogging and into the joist.

3 If the width of the sheet does not suit your joists, cut the sheet to fit. However, if this involves too much waste it may be a better idea to use tongue-and-groove sheets which are laid across the joists and so do not have to be cut to width.

4 Nail the sheets at 300mm intervals all the way round, putting the nails 10mm in from the edge. On intermediate joists put nails about 600mm apart.

Tongue-and-groove sheets

1 Position tongue-and-groove sheets with the long edge across the joists and nail them down. Drive four nails into each joist, one 10mm from each edge and the others at equal distances.

2 Normally the sheet edges should meet at the centre of a joist, but if one overhangs, saw it off close to the side of the joist.

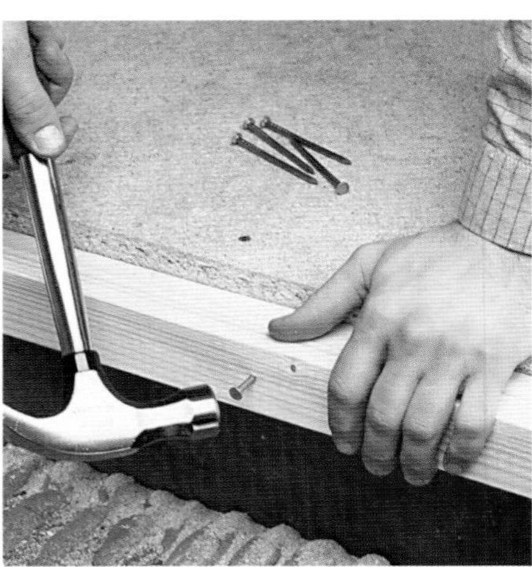

3 Nail a 50mm square batten to the joist side, flush with the top, and nail the next board to it after planing off the tongue.

If you need to hammer tongue-and-groove sheets together, use a block of wood to protect the edge from damage.

Completing the job

- Coat the meeting edges of all boards with PVA wood adhesive, then push them firmly together. The adhesive will prevent the floor from squeaking. Wipe any glue from the surface with a damp cloth.
- When you come to the end of a row, cut the sheet to fit. Use the offcut to begin the next row so that the joins do not coincide.

Draughtproofing a timber ground floor

Air can come up into the room if the boards are merely butted together, particularly in older properties.

Draughtproofing a floor depends on the size of the gaps. Fill large gaps (wider than 6mm) with wood. Smaller gaps can be filled with a flooring filler applied via a sealant gun. The colour does not matter if you are laying a new floor covering. If you intend to sand the boards, choose a filler close to the desired colour, or use a filler that will absorb stain when you apply it to the boards.

Large gaps

Tools *Mallet; plane; power sander or flap-wheel attachment on a power drill.*

Materials *Thin strips of softwood planed to a wedge section; PVA wood adhesive.*

1 Apply adhesive to the two long sides of a wedged strip of wood.

2 Tap the wood into place with a mallet, aiming to make its top edge flush with the floor surface.

3 When the adhesive has set, use a power sander, a plane or a flap-wheel attachment for an electric drill to level any raised parts of the strip. If you are sanding the floor, stain the strip to match the floorboards.

Small gaps

Tools *Sealant gun; filling knife for removing excess.*

Materials *Flooring filler cartridges; lining paper or similar for wiping excess filler from knife (newspaper will cause black stains).*

1 Check the width of the largest gap between the boards, and cut the cartridge nozzle off at an angle to give a bead of the correct width.

2 Load the cartridge into the sealant gun and squeeze the trigger to start the flow of filler.

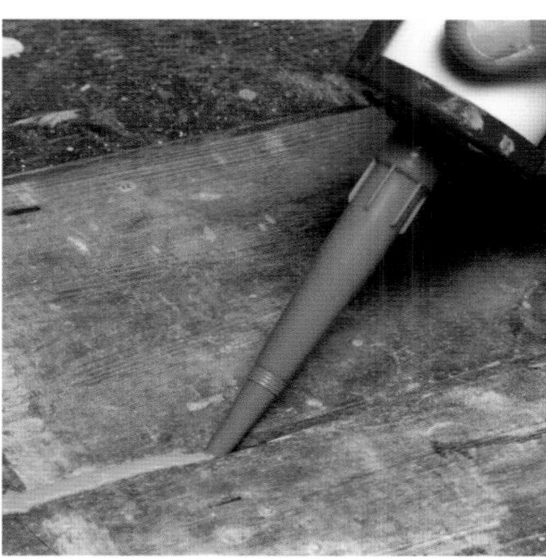

3 Draw the nozzle along each joint in turn, allowing the filler to sink in.

4 As you complete each joint, use the filling knife to remove excess filler and wipe the blade on some lining paper or similar material. Repeat the process to fill each joint in turn.

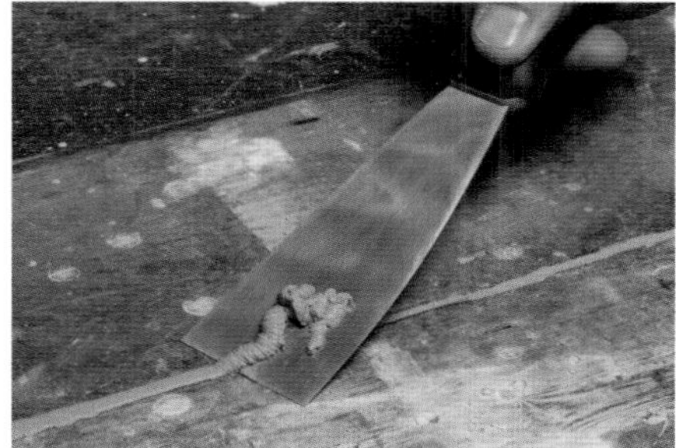

WHEN THE FLOOR IS TO BE COVERED

If you are laying a floor covering, you do not need to fill the gaps between the floorboards. Instead, lay sheets of hardboard over the whole floor (page 125). This will provide a flat surface for the new floor covering as well as draughtproofing the floor. If the cracks are small and the floorboards are level, lay foil-coated building paper – foil side up – under a carpet. This is cheaper than hardboard, and will stop draughts and also reflect some warmth back into the room.

SEALING THE GAP BELOW A SKIRTING BOARD

A skirting board is often fitted so there is a gap between it and the floor. If carpet has not been pushed into this gap, draughts may come up from below a timber floor. To seal a gap, use panel pins to fix quadrant beading (see picture) to the base of the skirting board, pressing it tight to the floor. Do not pin beading to the floor, or the boards will not be able to expand and contract, as they normally do when the weather varies from damp to dry. Quadrant beading secured like this is also ideal for covering the expansion gaps at the edge of laminate flooring (page 131). For a different effect you can also use scotia moulding, which is concave rather than convex.

INSULATING TIMBER FLOORS

If all the floorboards in a downstairs room have to be lifted (page 256), take the opportunity to fit underfloor insulation.

One way is to staple nylon garden netting across the joists and place lengths of loft insulation blanket between them. Draw the netting up tight so the blanket does not sag between the joists.

The other way is to cut rigid foam insulation boards into strips to match the joist spacing and support them on battens nailed to the joist sides.

How a staircase is built

Stairs consist of treads (the part you walk on) and risers (the vertical pieces in between). The treads may be nailed to the risers, or the risers may have tongues slotted into a groove in the treads.

At each side the treads are supported by a piece of timber called a string. A closed string has its top and bottom edges parallel, and the treads and risers slot into grooves. A cut string has a zigzag profile with the treads resting on the horizontal section.

A wall-side string is always closed, but the outer string may be either type. Staircases with cut strings are easier to repair than ones with closed strings.

On the open side of the staircase balusters are attached to the string at the bottom and the handrail at the top.

Many houses have a cupboard below the staircase, with the underside of the stairs left exposed. This is convenient for repairs. However, the underside may be covered with plaster, which has to be removed before repairs can be done.

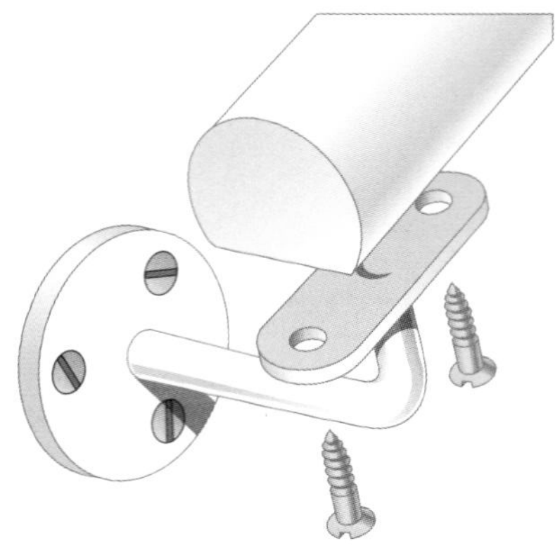

Wall handrail A handrail can be fixed to a wall on a bracket (above), or a specially shaped rail can be screwed directly to the wall (below).

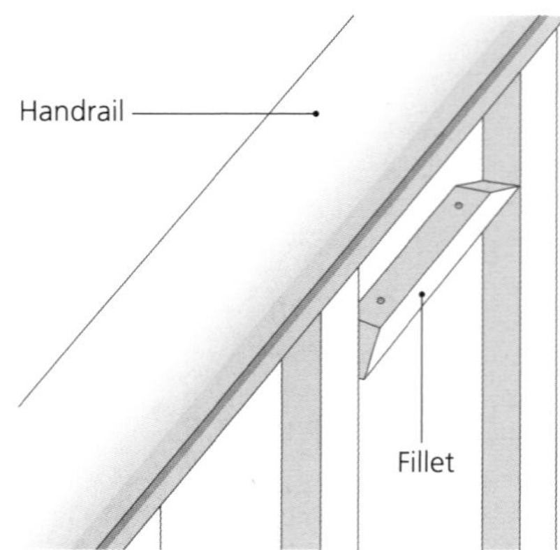

Handrail fillet On some staircases the balustrades are fitted to the handrail between wooden fillets. On others they are simply nailed.

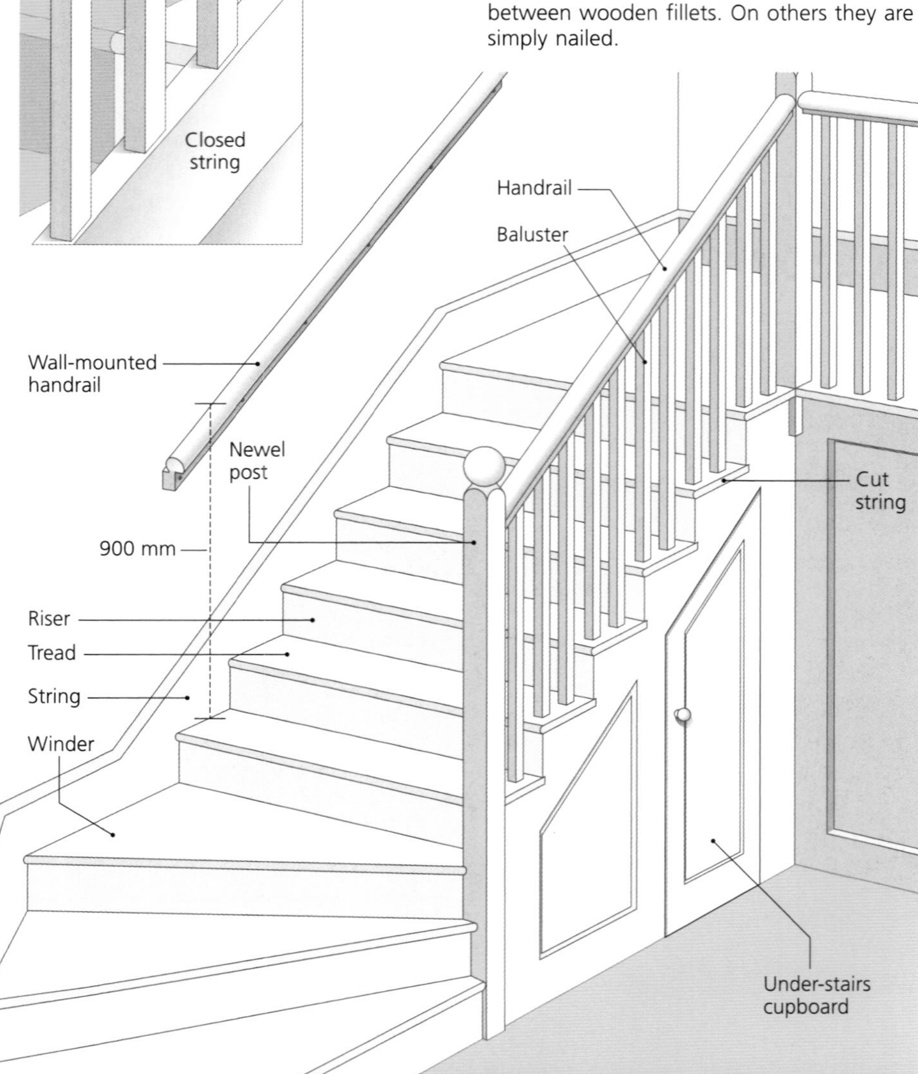

Fixing creaking stairs

Stairs creak when a tread or riser is not securely fixed and rubs against an adjacent piece of wood. The cure is straightforward if the underside of the staircase is accessible.

Determine which tread is creaking. If you have a cupboard under the stairs, ask someone to walk slowly up the stairs: you should be able to see which treads are flexing as well as hear the creak.

Working from underneath

The best remedy is to add extra wood angle blocks, screwed and glued to the tread and riser from underneath.

Tools *Saw; bradawl; drill and twist bits; screwdriver.*

Materials *Blocks of wood about 40mm triangular or square in section and about 75mm long; PVA adhesive; four 4mm screws per block (choose a length that will not break through the face of the stair).*

1 Drill four clearance holes in each block – one pair at right angles to the other.

2 Apply PVA adhesive to the blocks and push them in place.

3 Secure the blocks to the tread and riser with four screws.

4 You can strengthen the join between the bottom of the riser and the tread below by squeezing PVA adhesive into the join. Then drive three evenly spaced screws horizontally through the riser and into the tread. Position the screws 12mm up from the bottom of the riser.

Working from above

You will have to lift the stair carpet to work on the treads. Try brushing some talcum powder into the squeaking join to act as a lubricant. If the squeak continues, screw down the front of the tread onto the riser.

Tools *Old chisel; drill and twist bits; countersink bit; screwdriver; filling knife; abrasive paper.*

Materials *PVA adhesive; 38mm 4mm countersunk screws; filler.*

1 Using a chisel, force apart the top of the riser and the tread above, and insert some adhesive in the space: this is only possible if the treads and risers are not jointed together.

2 Drill clearance holes every 250mm through the tread and pilot holes into the top of the riser. Countersink the clearance holes so screws will sit below surface level. Insert the screws and screw down tight.

3 Cover screw heads with filler and smooth with abrasive paper. If the stairs are varnished, use a matching wood filler.

Repairing broken balusters

If you still have all the pieces, it may be possible to mend a damaged baluster. If the damage is severe, you will have to replace it.

Tools *Mallet; old chisel; handsaw; hammer; vice clamp.*

Materials *New baluster if needed; nails (same length as the old ones).*

Before you start Examine the broken baluster: if it has split or a piece has broken off, apply PVA adhesive to the two surfaces and bind them with insulating tape. Clamp the baluster between two blocks of wood until the adhesive has dried. Then remove the tape and smooth off any hardened adhesive with fine abrasive paper.

Square section balusters are easy to match, but you may have to pay a wood turner to reproduce a fancy one for you.

1 Free the baluster at the bottom. If the outer string is cut (see opposite) prise off the cover moulding on the side of the tread. Then gently tap the bottom end of the baluster out of its slot with a mallet.

If the outer string is 'closed' (its top and bottom edges are parallel and the tread and riser slot into grooves), a baluster on an old staircase may be held in a mortise or it may be pinned. Scrape away the paint to check. If it is mortised use a handsaw to cut through it at the bottom following the line of the string. If it is pinned, knock it out with the mallet.

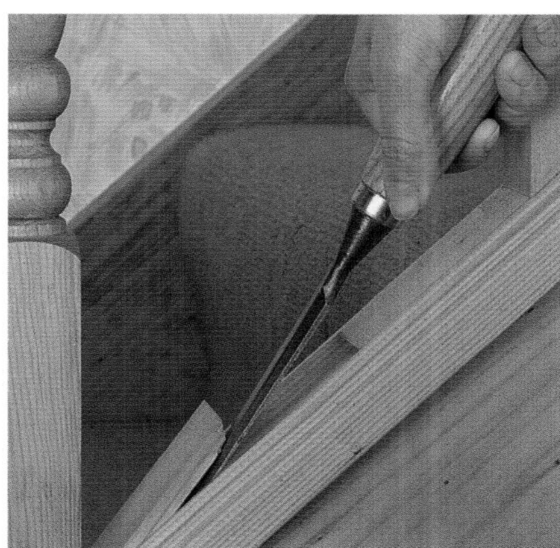

Alternatively On a modern staircase it may be held at the bottom between fillets of wood. Lift out the broken baluster, and lever out the lower fillet.

2 Remove the top part of the broken baluster by tapping it with a mallet so it is freed from the rail. If there is no space between the balusters to wield the mallet, place the end of a piece of wood against the baluster and tap the other end with the mallet. Or pull out the baluster by hand.

3 Use the broken baluster as a pattern to mark the correct slope on the top of the new one. Before you cut it to length, make sure that you have got the measurement right.

4 Hold the new baluster in a vice and cut along the marked line.

5 On a cut string, fit it back in place in its notch on the tread and nail the baluster to the handrail at the top.

On a closed string, use the old baluster to cut the angle at the bottom and fit the new one in place, top and bottom. If the baluster was originally mortised into the string, it will have to be nailed in place. The repair will not be as strong as the original.

If you have to replace a fillet, tack it in place. A nail punch will help you to work in an awkward space.

FIXING LOOSE BALUSTERS

Balusters are usually fixed to the handrail by nails driven through them at an angle, and into the underside of the rail. Sometimes they are fitted between fillets of wood.

Nailing the baluster If a nail works loose, try to remove it with pincers, and insert a longer, slightly thicker nail in its place. If you can't remove it, drive another one in at a different place. On slender balusters drill a fine pilot hole first. Do not use glue. The baluster may have to be removed at some time in the future.

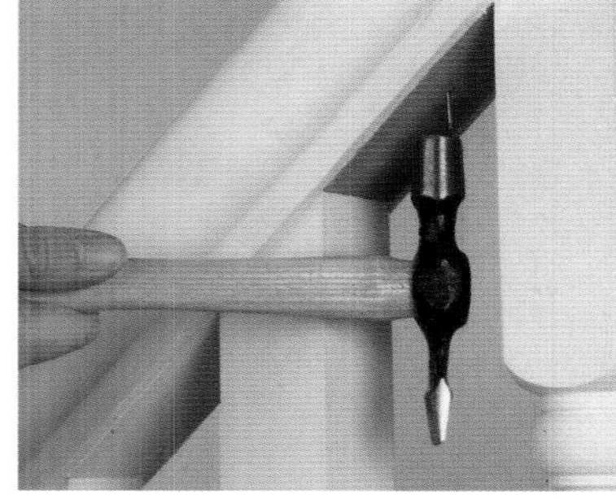

Replacing a fillet The balusters must be fitted into a groove in the underside of the rail, with the spaces between balusters filled with fillets of wood. If a fillet has dropped out, cut a new piece of wood to the right size and nail it in place. Do not use glue. A nail punch will help to drive the nail in. Baluster fillets can be bought at some DIY stores, but they may not fit your staircase.

Wall-mounted handrails

Re-fixing a handrail

A stairway with a wall on both sides usually has a wall-mounted hand-rail instead of a baluster rail. Often, the fixings come loose.

1 Take the rail down from the wall and find out why it is loose.

2 If the handrail is on a metal bracket, fill the existing screw holes with a plugging compound. Re-drill the holes, insert wall plugs and refit the handrail with screws the same size as the old ones. Make sure the fixing is secure; if not, you must reposition the brackets and make new holes.

Alternatively If the rail is screwed directly to the wall, use a longer, thicker screw than the original. You may have to drill a slightly larger hole in the bracket.

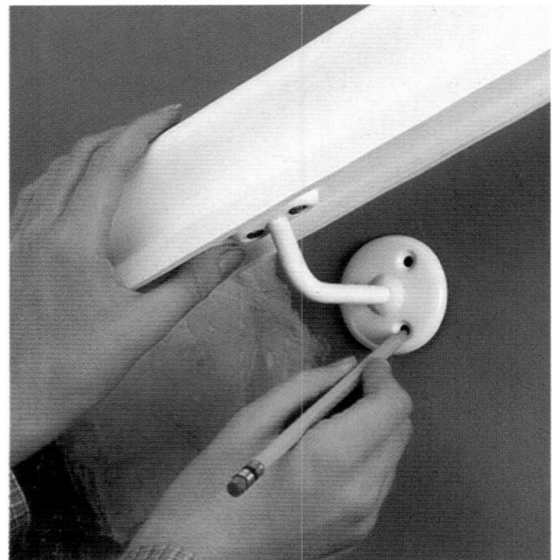

3 If the wall around the plug has become damaged, make a new fixing in a slightly different place. The brackets will also have to be repositioned on the rail. Fill any visible holes with interior filler.

Fitting a new handrail

If you are putting up a new wall-mounted handrail, it must run parallel with the string (the diagonal line of the stairs).

1 Measure 900mm up from the front of each tread and join the marks with a straightedge.

2 Fit the brackets to the rail, then get a helper to align the top of the rail with the line while you mark the fixings for the top bracket.

3 Drill and plug the wall and fix the top bracket with one screw only. Hold the bottom of the rail at the correct height and mark the positions of the other fixings.

Replacing a balustrade

Balustrade parts are available that should make fitting a new balustrade straightforward. Replacing the newel posts is often optional.

Tools *Tape measure; saw; screwdriver; wood chisel; nail punch; pin hammer; portable workbench.*

Materials *New handrail, base rail, balusters and spacer fillets; 75mm 5mm woodscrews or angled handrail brackets; socket set to remove and fit handrail brackets; 50mm oval wire nails; panel pins.*

Before you start Measure the lengths of handrail and base rail you will need, and calculate the number of balusters. To comply with Building Regulations, balusters must be spaced no more than 100mm apart, and a handrail must be at least 900mm above the string. It may be that your old balustrade did not comply with these regulations.

1 Saw through each old baluster in turn and pull it away from the rails. Prise out the spacing fillets, and lever off the old base rail.

2 Undo any screws connecting the handrail to the newel post at each end.

Alternatively Look for a metal bracket attaching rail and newel post by prising out the handrail fillet. If you find a bracket but can't unscrew it, look for a wooden plug on the opposite side of the post and prise it out to see if there is a nut. Use a socket set to undo the nut and free the bracket.

3 Cut the new base rail to length, using the old base rail as a template. The ends are angled so they fit against both newel posts. Place it in position and secure it with 50mm wire nails about 300mm apart.

4 Use the old handrail as a template to cut the new one. Attach it to the upper and lower newels, with a helper supporting the other end in each case. Secure it to the newel with 75mm long woodscrews, or with special angled handrail brackets.

5 Use an old baluster as a pattern for cutting new ones to size. Pin fillets into the grooves in the handrail and base rail next to the top newel post, then fit the first baluster and nail it to both rails. Repeat for the other balusters.

HELPFUL TIPS

- Apply primer, paint, stain or varnish to balusters before fitting them; touch up later if necessary.
- The easiest way to fit a new newel post is to cut off the old post about 100mm above the string, and use a large dowel (from a staircase parts supplier) to join on the new post.

Fitting a loft ladder

Most houses have a loft or attic which in many cases is accessed through a hatch in the upper floor ceiling. The installation of a loft ladder makes the roof space more easily accessible, for storage or as a hobbies room.

There is a wide variety of styles available in both aluminium and wood. Most if not all will fit between the width of the joists, but often the length of the existing opening is too short to accommodate a ladder. Altering the length of the hatch opening is often the trickiest part of the installation. This will normally involve removing one of the trimmers – short lengths of timber fitted at right angles to the joists to create the opening – and fitting a new trimmer.

Tools *Hammer; screwdrivers; try square; pencil; panel saw; crowbar.*

Materials *Loft ladder; 18mm MDF; trim for opening; timber the same size as existing ceiling joists.*

Before you start Pull back loft insulation from between the joists while you carry out the work and replace it when you have finished. Lofts are often dark so unless you have a light already installed you will need a portable light or head torch to illuminate the work area.

1 Remove the existing hatch, pull off the architrave moulding from around the opening and remove the stops on which the hatch sits or against which it closes.

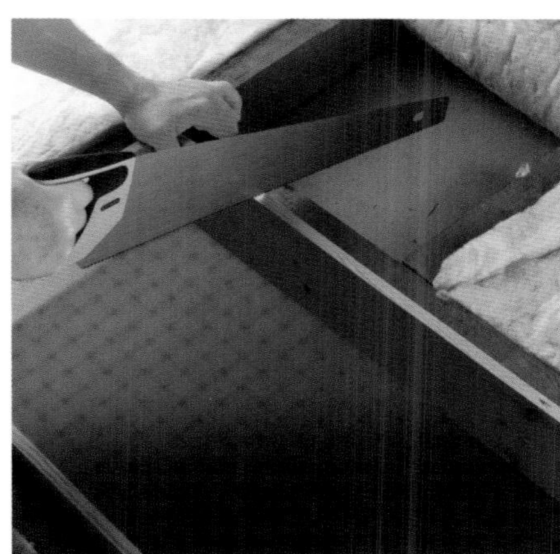

2 Completely remove any lining where this is fitted inside the opening. You may have to use a panel saw to cut through the centre of the wood before levering it out.

3 Cut through the centre of the existing trimmer that you are removing before knocking it out with the hammer.
Be careful to avoid damaging the ceiling.

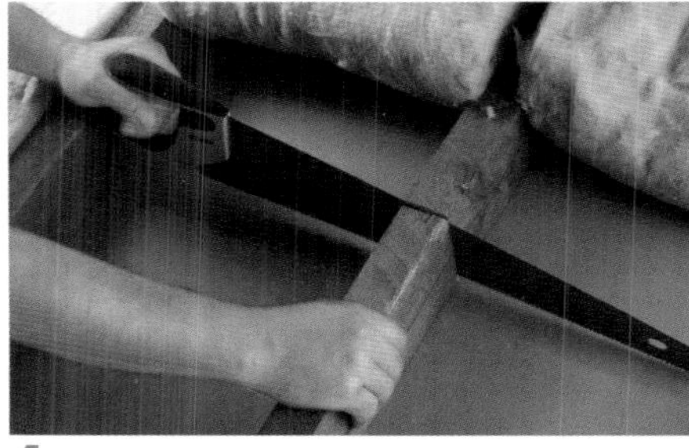

4 Refer to the manufacturer's instructions and mark the length of the opening from the remaining trimmer. Square down the line on the inside faces of the joists

5 Cut a new trimmer to fit snugly between the joists. Position with reference to the pencil marks and nail in place.

6 Fix the ceiling below to the new trimmer with plasterboard screws before cutting back the ceiling flush with the edge of the new trimmer.

7 Cut and fit a new lining to the hatch opening and nail this into place.

8 Attach the loft ladder pivots to the top or face of the trimmer as indicated in the manufacturer's instructions.

9 Attach the ladder to the pivots and check the movement and action of the ladder.

10 Fit new architrave to cover the joint between the lining and ceiling, mitring it carefully at the corners for a neat finish.

11 Cut a new hatch cover from 18mm MDF and fit this, following the instructions that came with the ladder. In some cases the cover is attached to the underside of the ladder and will automatically close when the ladder is retracted. With others, a touch latch is provided, the case of which is fitted on to the hatch lining. One push closes the loft hatch; another push opens it. Fit this, add new stops for the hatch to close against and paint or varnish visible bare wood as required.

MEASURING UP FOR A LADDER

- Before buying a ladder, you will need to take several measurements. It is advisable to get makers' leaflets that show the pivoting height needed by the ladder inside the loft (marked A below). This is usually 1.1m above the loft floor. If there is not enough room, collapsible ladders are available.
- The leaflets will also show the minimum length of the hatch (B) and the minimum width (C).
- For easy access to the loft, the hatch should be about 760mm long and 510mm wide. Ladders can be installed in smaller openings, but you may have difficulty carrying things into the loft.
- A standard loft ladder will fit a height of up to 2.6m, measured from the floor of the room or landing below to the top of the loft joists.

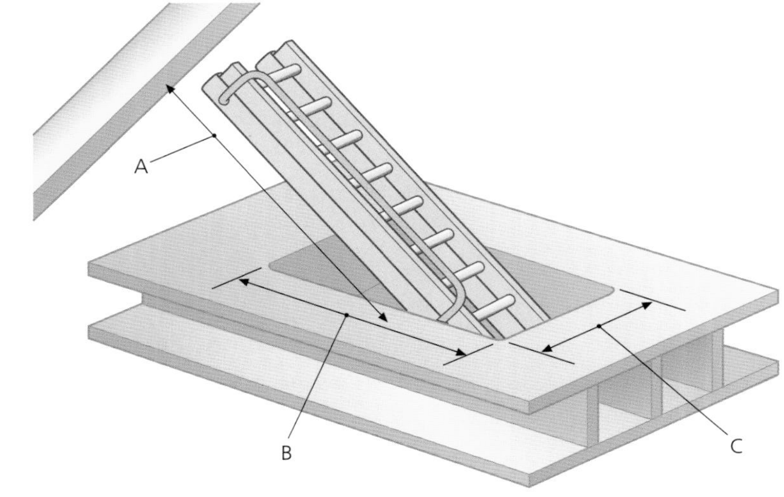

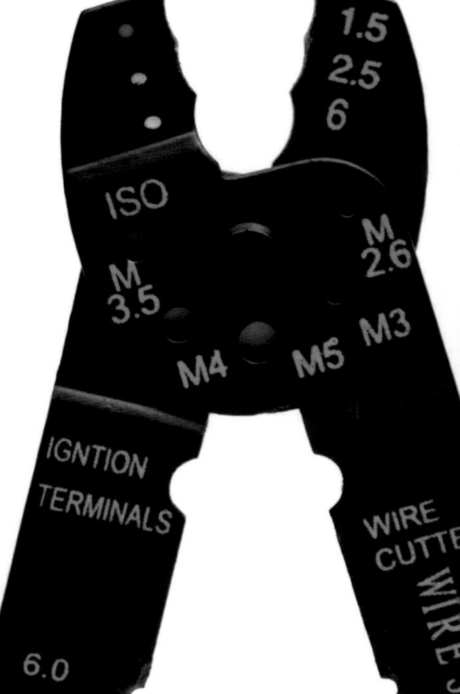
1.5
2.5
6
ISO
M 2.6
M 3.5
M4
M5
M3
IGNTION
TERMINALS
WIRE
6.0

Wiring and lighting 9

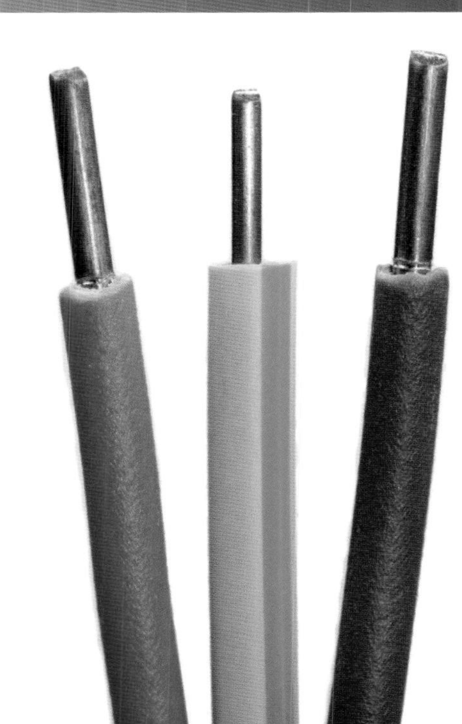

Electrical emergencies

Warning: the main on-off switch on your consumer unit disconnects only the fuses or MCBs and the cables leading out from it to the household circuits. It does NOT disconnect the cables entering via the meter from the service cable. Do not tamper with these cables. They are always live at mains voltage.

Electric shock

Warning If you get a minor shock from an electrical appliance, a plug or other wiring accessory, stop using it immediately.
- Get a repair expert to check the appliance for earth safety, and replace damaged plugs and wiring accessories as soon as possible. Only use PVC insulating tape to make a temporary repair.
- If someone receives a major shock, DO NOT touch bare flesh while the person is in contact with the source of the current. If you do, the current will pass through you as well, giving you an electric shock.

1 Immediately turn off the source of the current if you can.

2 If you cannot do this, grab the person's clothing and drag him or her away from the source of the current, or stand on some insulating material such as a book, and use a broom or a similar wooden object to move the person or the current source.

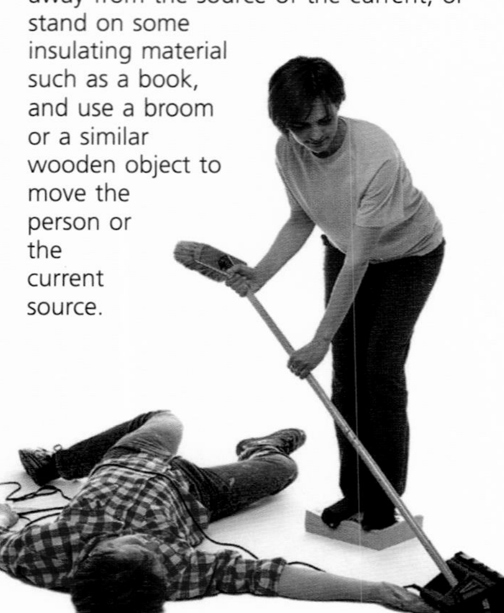

3 Lay a conscious but visibly shocked person flat on their back with their legs raised slightly and cover with a blanket. Do not give food, drink or cigarettes. Cool visible burns with cold water, then cover them with a dry sterile dressing. Do not apply ointments. Call an ambulance.

Before you start

Electricity can kill – and doing your own electrical wiring work has obvious dangers.
- Always turn off at the main consumer unit and remove the fuse or switch off the MCB for the circuit you are working on.
- Make sure you know what you are doing – if in any doubt, employ an electrician.
- Remember that all wiring work is now covered by the Building Regulations – so make sure you have sought approval from your local authority if you need it.
- Regulations in Scotland and Northern Ireland may differ. For Northern Ireland, check with the Building Control department at your local council; for Scotland, the Building Standards Services of your local council.
- United Kindom rules do not apply in the Republic of Ireland where electrical installations must comply with Ireland's National Rules for Electrical Installations. For information contact your local government or the Electro-Technical Council of Ireland: www.etci.ie

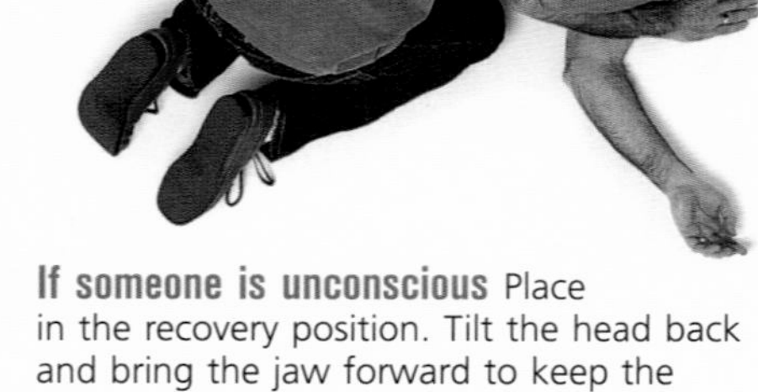

If someone is unconscious Place in the recovery position. Tilt the head back and bring the jaw forward to keep the airway clear. Cover them with a blanket and call an ambulance.

Check breathing Monitor breathing and heartbeat continuously until the ambulance arrives. If either stops, give artificial ventilation or external chest compression as necessary, if you are trained to do so.

Fire in an appliance

1 If a plug-in appliance is on fire, switch it off at the socket outlet and pull out the plug.

2 If a fixed appliance with no plug is on fire, turn it off at the wall switch, or at the main switch on the consumer unit.

3 Do not use water on an electrical fire. Smother the fire with a rug or blanket, or use a dry-powder fire extinguisher.

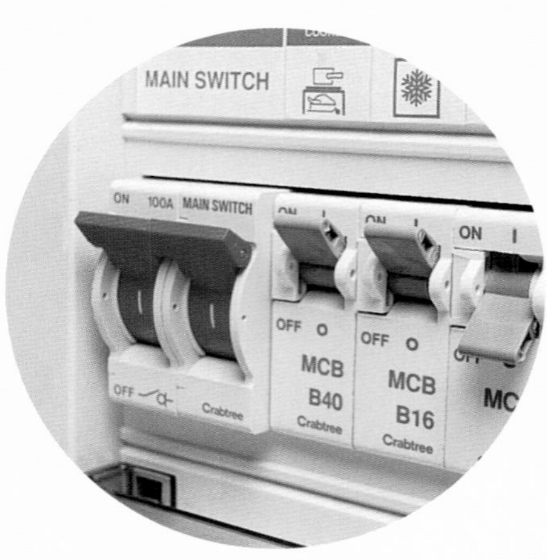

Smell of overheating

1 If you smell burning from an appliance, turn off the switch at the socket and pull out the plug. If it is a fixed appliance with no plug, turn off its wall switch or the main switch at the consumer unit. Turn off the appliance switch. Check flex connections and re-connect if necessary; if they are sound, have the appliance checked by an expert.

2 If the smell comes from a socket outlet or plug, turn off the main switch at the consumer unit. Allow hot plugs to cool, then unplug. Check connections including the fuse contacts, and examine the flex for damage. Replace as necessary (page 274). If the socket is hot, check for faulty connections and renew as necessary (page 278).

No electricity

1 If power throughout your house fails and neighbouring houses are also without power, there is a mains supply failure. Report it to the 24-hour emergency number under 'Electricity' in the phone book.

2 If your system is protected by a whole-house residual current device (RCD), check whether it has switched itself off. Try to switch it on again if it has.

3 If it will not switch on, the fault that tripped it off is still present on the system. Call an electrician to rectify it.

4 If you do not have an RCD and your house is the only one without power, there may be a fault in your supply cable or your main supply fuse may have blown. Do not touch it. Report the failure as above.

Minor emergencies

1 If one appliance fails to work, unplug it and check its plug, fuse and flex; renew them as necessary. If the appliance still fails to work, plug it in a different socket outlet to test it. If it works, the problem is with the original socket; if not, take the appliance to an expert for repair.

2 If all lights or appliances on one circuit stop working, switch off at the consumer unit and check the circuit fuse or MCB (page 270). If it is sound, there may be a fault in the circuit cable: call an electrician.

Understanding the consumer unit

Modern fuse boards – called consumer units – may look different from home to home, but the basic components are the same.

Consumer unit The householder's responsibility for the system begins here. It houses the main on-off switch, the main earthing terminal block for all the house circuits, and individual MCBs for each one. Some modern consumer units have blanked out spaces for additional MCBs to be installed at a later date.

- Circuits vary according to a household's needs, but always include separate lighting and power circuits.
- Label the MCBs to show which circuit each one protects. To identify the circuits, turn off the main switch and switch off one MCB at a time. Turn the main switch back on and check which lights or appliances are *not* working.

OLD FUSE BOXES

In older systems, each circuit is protected by a fuse, not an MCB. Each fuseholder is marked with the rating in amps (A) of the fuse if contains. A lighting circuit is protected by a 5amp fuse, and a ring main circuit by a 30amp fuse.

If the current demanded by the circuit exceeds these ratings, the fuse melts ('blows') and the circuit is disconnected.

The fuse link inside a carrier may be a wire or a sealed cartridge.

Miniature circuit breakers (MCBs) Modern consumer units have MCBs instead of fuses. If too much current is demanded, the circuit is disconnected instantly and a switch moves to the 'off' position or a button pops out. Reset the switch or button to restore power to the circuit.

MCB CURRENT RATINGS

As part of a move towards European standardisation, the ratings marked on new MCBs are being changed.

5amp	becomes	6amp
15amp	becomes	16amp
30amp	becomes	32amp
45amp	becomes	40amp (or 50amp)

Circuit cables Individual circuits are supplied by cables running out from the consumer unit. The live conductor in each circuit cable is connected to a terminal on its MCB. The neutral conductor connects to the main neutral terminal block in the consumer unit, and the earth conductor to the main earthing terminal block.

Residual current device (RCD) An RCD monitors the balance of the live and neutral current flows. An imbalance occurs if current leaks from a circuit because of faulty insulation, or because someone has touched a live part and received an electric shock. If the RCD detects an imbalance (of just 30mA) it switches off the supply fast enough to prevent an electric shock from being fatal.

- An existing consumer unit may have a single 30mA RCD (with a current rating of 80A or 100A) protecting all circuits, but is more likely to be 'split' with RCD protection only for at-risk circuits such as those to socket outlets. This prevents a single fault taking all the circuits out. An RCD in its own enclosure may have been added to an existing installation to protect at-risk circuits.
- Wiring Regulations require 30mA RCD protection on most new circuits, which can be achieved by having more than one RCD or by using RCBOs (RCDs combined with an MCB).

METER TAILS

Houses wired after April 2006 will have brown and blue meter tails.

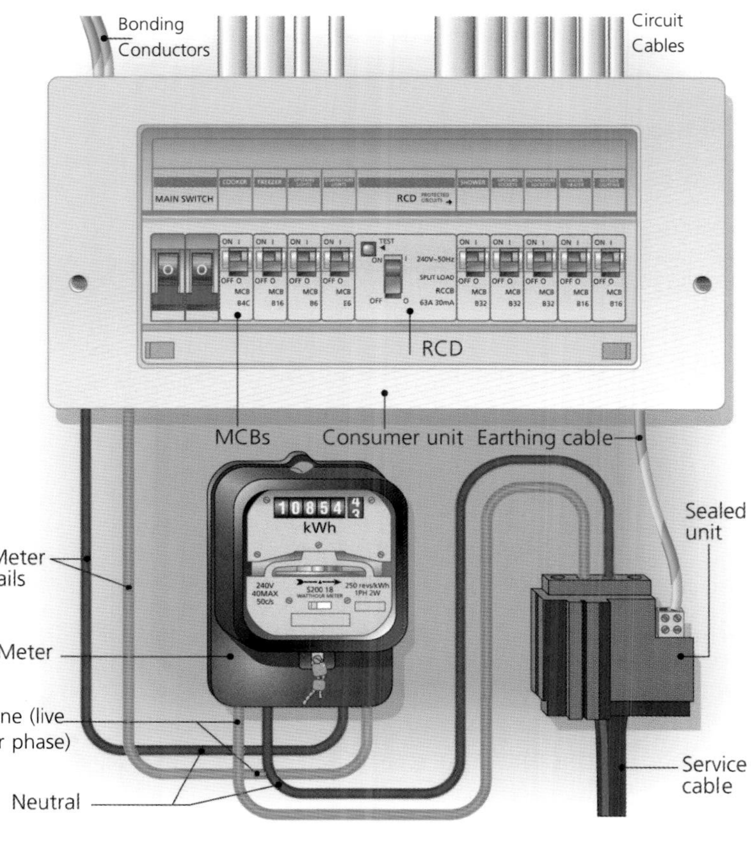

Service cable Electricity enters the home through the service (supply) cable – usually buried underground in urban areas, but may be run overhead in rural areas. It carries electricity at 230 volts. The current flows along the live conductor and returns along the neutral conductor. Never interfere with the service cable, which is the property of your electricity supply company.

The term 'live' has been replaced by 'line' or 'phase' in the electrical industry. Live and neutral imply that current flows only in the live conductor, whereas both carry current at all times. The terms live and neutral are used throughout this book for clarity.

Sealed unit/service cut-out The service cable ends here. Its neutral conductor is connected to a solid terminal. Its live conductor is connected to a fuse (the service cut-out), which is usually rated at 60amps or, in modern installations, at 100amps. It is a deliberate weak link that will melt and disconnect the supply to the house if more current is demanded than the service cable can safely supply.

Do not tamper with the sealed unit.

Meter tails The cables (live and neutral) link the sealed unit to the meter and the meter to the consumer unit.

- The live cable is covered with red insulation and the neutral cable with black. Homes with new wiring dating from 2006 and after will have a brown live cable and a blue neutral cable.
- The outer sheaths may be grey or match the insulation.
- The electricity supply company must disconnect the supply before work can be done on the meter tails.

Earthing cable This connects the main earthing terminal block in the consumer unit (to which all the circuit cables are connected) to the earthing point provided by the electricity supplier – usually on the service cut-out or the service cable. Bonding conductors connect metal gas and water supply pipework to the main earthing terminal block.

Meter A two-tariff meter with two displays may be installed to make use of off-peak electricity for storage heaters.

Understanding your electrical system

Before you do any electrical work, you need to understand some technical terms and get to grips with the different types of circuit you will find in your home.

Technical terms

Watts Electric power consumed is measured in watts (W for short). Every electrical appliance has a wattage rating marked on its rating plate. The higher the wattage rating, the more electricity the appliance consumes when it is in use.

Amps The amount of current flowing in a conductor is measured in amperes (amps or A for short). With a cable or flex, the greater the number of amps it carries, the thicker its conductors must be. Its current-carrying capacity also depends on its length and whether it is running through thermal insulation.

Volts The electrical pressure that drives current through a conductor is measured in volts (V for short). The pressure of the public supply in Britain has been standardised at 230 volts. The supply voltage may vary by plus 10 per cent (23V) or minus 6 per cent (14V) and a further drop of 6V is permitted on individual circuits.

Voltage-sensitive equipment, such as a personal computer, can be protected from voltage variations by a surge suppressor.

Batteries and some portable generators and transformers supply other voltages for lighting and appliances that have been designed to operate on them.

17TH EDITION RULES

All new electric wiring in homes should meet the requirements of the Wiring Regulations (BS7671): Requirements for Electrical Installations (see Rules and regulations, page 280).

The current edition – the 17th – was first published in 2008 and, among other things, requires much greater use of residual current devices (RCDs – see page 281), especially on new socket outlet and bathroom circuits.

The Wiring Regulations are being modified as this book goes to press (and the modifications are likely to relax the requirements on cables run at a depth of less than 50mm in walls – see page 282). Check our website (www.readersdigest.co.uk) for the latest information.

Basic circuit types

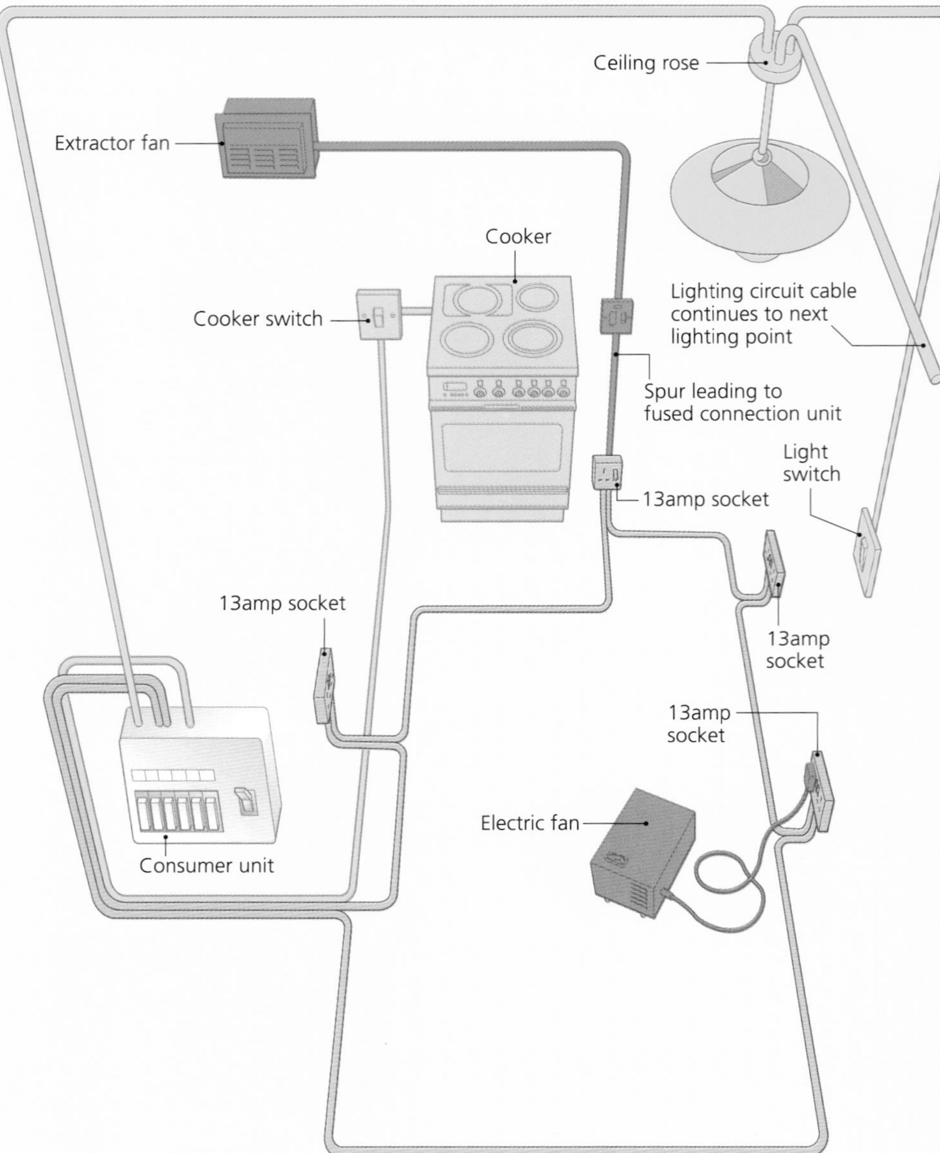

Lighting circuit The circuit runs out from the consumer unit, linking a chain of lighting points. Cables run from each lighting point to its switch. The circuit is protected by a 5 or 6amp circuit fuse or MCB. It can safely supply up to a maximum of about 1200 watts, but in practice should not serve more than ten lighting points. The circuit would be overloaded if each of the lighting points had high-wattage lights.

Ring main circuit The circuit is wired as a ring that starts from the consumer unit and returns to it, allowing current to flow to socket outlets either way round the ring. It can serve a floor area of up to 100m². It is protected by a 30 or 32amp circuit fuse or MCB. It can have any number of sockets or fused connection units on it, but its maximum total load is about 7000 watts. For larger total loads and larger floor areas, additional ring circuits are needed.

Socket outlet The maximum load that can be supplied by a socket outlet taking a 13amp plug is 3000 watts. The plug is fitted with a 13amp or a 3amp fuse, according to the wattage rating of the appliance connected to it.

Spur on a ring circuit Extra socket outlets can be added to an existing ring main circuit via spurs branching off the ring at a socket outlet or junction box. In theory, each outlet on the ring could supply a spur to a single or double socket or a fused connection unit. However, the circuit including any spurs must not serve rooms with a floor area of more than 100m² – and its maximum load is still 7000 watts.

Single-appliance circuit An appliance that is a large consumer of electricity and in constant or frequent use – a cooker, a fixed water heater, or a shower heater unit, for example – has its own circuit running from the consumer unit. It would take too large a proportion of the power available on a shared circuit and would be likely to cause an overload.

A safe earthing system

The jobs described on the following pages are suitable only for modern wiring systems. **Proper earthing of metal parts you can touch on electrical equipment and appliances provides vital protection from the risk of electric shock.**

The earth conductor in each circuit cable is connected to the main earth terminal block in the consumer unit. This is connected in turn to an earthing point provided by the electricity supply company.

Modern installations have protective multiple earthing (PME). This is earthed via the electricity supply cable's neutral connector to the 'star point' at the local electricity supply transformer, which is connected to a permanent earth at the substation.

Non-electrical metal fittings such as plumbing pipework that might come into accidental contact with the electrical system also need earth 'bonding' – see right.

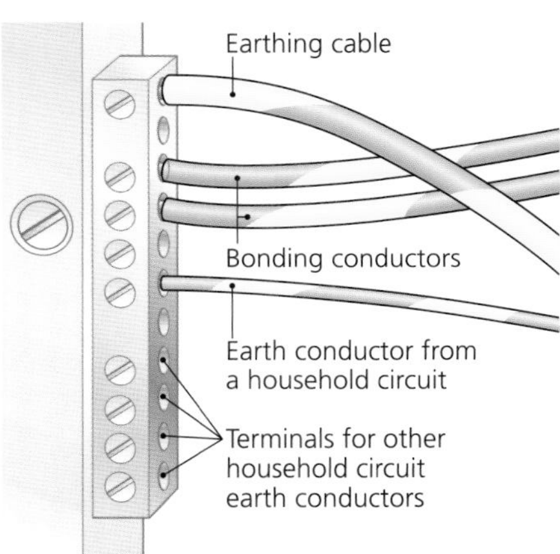

The main earth terminal block in the consumer unit has terminals for the earth conductors in all the house circuit cables. One terminal is for the main earthing cable running to the main house earthing point. Other terminals take the main bonding conductors.

A house in a rural area with an overhead power supply may have no earth connection via the supply cable. The house is earthed by an earth electrode (a metal spike) driven deep into the ground close to the house. This 'TT' earthing needs additional protection, provided by a residual current device (RCD).

The house wiring is connected to the earthing system via the earth conductors in the circuit cables. The casing of electrical equipment is either earthed or insulated by the manufacturer. Check that any metal items that you install yourself, or have installed for you, are safely earthed.

Bonding metal pipes and fittings

Certain non-electrical metal items – like pipes and bathroom radiators – must be linked to the earthing system. This is known as 'bonding' and is done with single-core earth cable.

Main bonding

One or more green-and-yellow insulated cables called main bonding conductors should run from the main earth terminal block in the consumer unit to incoming metal water, gas and oil service pipes (but not to telephone or television cables). The size of the cable should not be less than 10mm².

Supplementary bonding

In rooms containing a bath or a shower, most homes will have supplementary 'equipotential' bonding where all metal items – such as radiators, towel rails, supply pipes and metal baths – are linked together by earth cables and are also linked to the earth conductors in circuits supplying the bathroom (for a shower or heated towel rail, for example). This prevents you getting an electrical shock if you were to touch one of these items while in contact with faulty electrical equipment.

Additions to such circuits should follow these rules as shown below and described on the next page. There is no need to run a separate earth cable all the way from the consumer unit.

New bathroom circuits – that is those wired to the 17th Edition of the Wiring Regulations – do not require supplementary bonding provided they are RCD protected.

Main bonding

The main bonding conductors should be connected at one end to terminals on the main earth block in the consumer unit and at the other to water, gas and oil pipes.

Clamps must fit tightly and be in contact with bare metal, not paint. They must be free from corrosion and should be easily accessible for inspection.

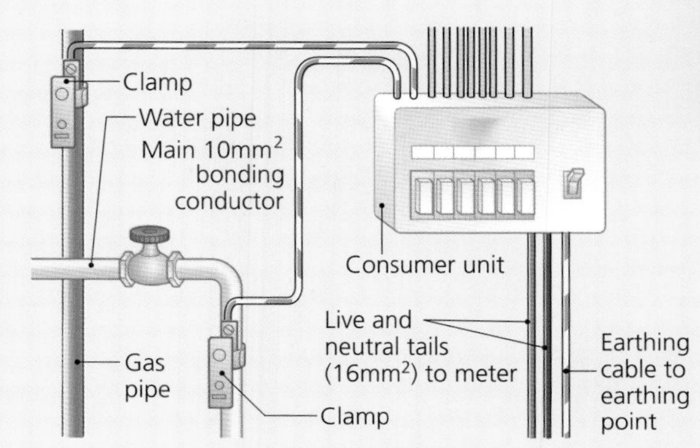

Supplementary bonding

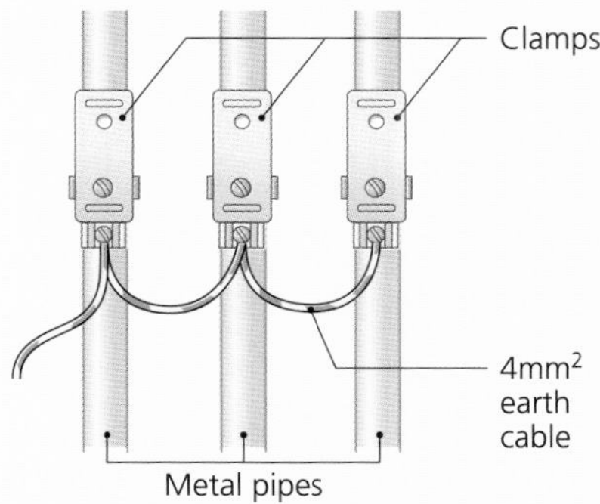

Link airing cupboard pipes to ensure the pipework offers an unbroken metal earth route.

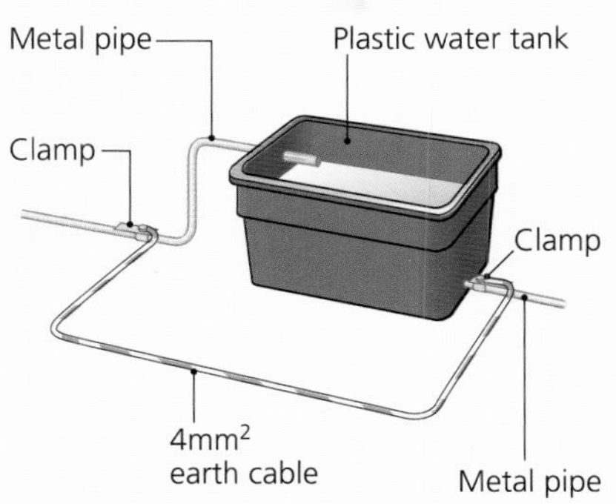

Bridge across a plastic water tank from metal pipe to metal pipe with 4mm² earth cable.

Link together non-electrical metal fittings in bathrooms or shower rooms with 4mm² earth cable. Such fittings might include inlet pipes to taps on the basin, bath and bidet, towel rails and the metal cradles of plastic baths. Connect the earth cable to the metal with clamps. Hide cable behind fittings and under the floor.

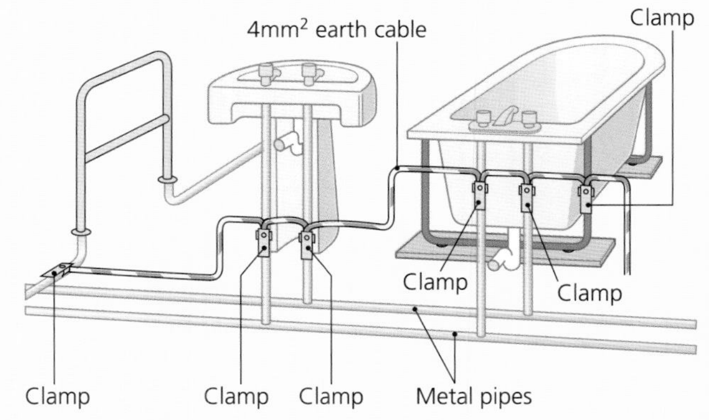

Installing supplementary bonding conductors

Use 4mm² green-and-yellow insulated earth cable. To connect it to metal pipes, use clamps complying with British Standard BS951.

Plan the route of the bonding cable. You can lead the earth cable from the metal item either to the earth terminal in a socket outlet or to metal pipework which has been bonded.

If you are connecting it to a socket outlet, first turn off the main switch at the consumer unit and remove the fuse for the circuit the socket outlet is on. If you are going to connect to a pipe, make sure that all of the pipe will be bonded. The bonding continuity will be interrupted by plastic water tanks, plastic push-fit fittings and by replacement sections of plastic pipe and all of these must be bridged with 4mm² green-and-yellow insulated cable – see page 267.

The connections of supplementary bonds should be accessible for inspection and checking. Connections to the earth terminals of socket outlets are easy to inspect. Connections to pipework can be made in cupboards, behind removable panels or under the floor. If they have to be made under the floor, the section of floorboard above should be fixed with screws so that it can easily be lifted if necessary.

Metal baths are fitted with an earth tag. Connect the bonding cable by winding the bared end of the conductor round a bolt passed through the tag. Trap it with a metal washer secured under the nut. Make sure that the tag is clean and free of paint or enamel.

An earth clamp Use a clamp to connect the earth cable to metal pipework. Clean the pipe with wire wool first. If the pipe has been painted, strip off an area of paintwork. Screw the core of the earth cable tightly into the terminal. The clamp should already be fitted with a permanent metal label that says SAFETY ELECTRICAL CONNECTION – DO NOT REMOVE. Make sure this is in place.

Wiring in bathrooms

Correct earthing and supplementary bonding are particularly important in bathrooms, where the combination of water, electricity and bare skin spell danger. In addition to this, the Wiring Regulations define areas (called zones) in bathrooms where specific safety rules must be followed. These describe what electrical equipment can be installed in each zone.

All new wiring work in bathrooms is notifiable to your local Building Control Department as are any modifications or additions to bathroom wiring. Because of the changes in the 17th Edition of the Wiring Regulations (see next column), it might be better to leave all bathroom wiring to a qualified electrician.

Bathroom zones

Any room that contains a bath or shower is divided up into three zones.

Zone 0 is the inside of the bath or shower tray. No electrical equipment is permitted here. The space beneath the bath is outside any zone if the bath panel is secured with screws and cannot be removed without the use of a screwdriver. This makes it a suitable place for the installation of equipment such as a shower pump. However, if there is no panel, or if the panel can be removed without the use of tools, the area beneath the bath is designated as zone 1.

Zone 1 is the space immediately above the bath or shower tray, and extends to a height of 2.25m above the floor. Within this zone you can install: an instantaneous shower or water heater; an all-in-one power shower unit with a waterproof integral pump, a shower pump, a towel rail, a whirlpool unit, ventilation equipment and suitable light fittings. All of these must have suitable IP ratings (see Box), especially if a power shower is fitted, which may require a minimum of IPX5 equipment.

Zone 2 extends horizontally to 600mm from the edge of zone 1 (that is, the edge of the bath or shower tray), and vertically to a height of 2.25m above floor level. Within Zone 2, you are allowed any of the equipment allowed in Zone 1 plus a shaver unit that complies with BS EN 61558-2-5.

Outside the zones you are in theory allowed to have any equipment with the exception of socket outlets that must be at least 3m away from the boundaries of Zone 1 (which rules out sockets in all but the largest bathrooms). Most people would probably be happier to follow the previous Wiring Regulations and not have any sockets in a bathroom at all – see 17th Edition Rules.

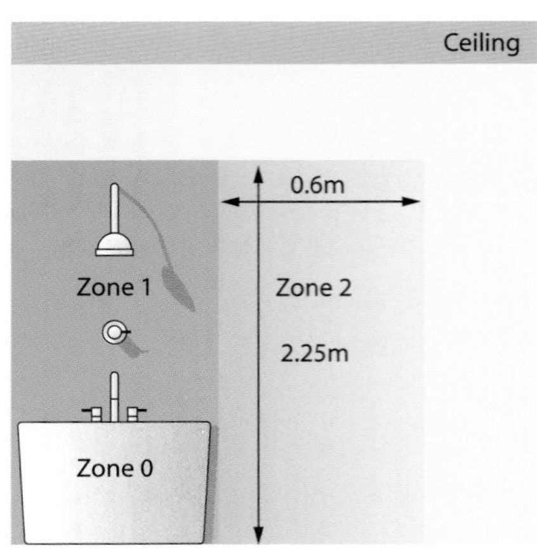

Bathroom switches
Wall-mounted light switches and double-pole switches (as part of a fused connection unit or for a shower unit) are not allowed within the Zones. Switches here must be the ceiling-mounted type, with an insulated pull-cord.

17TH EDITION RULES

The latest Wiring Regulations have introduced significant changes for wiring in bathrooms – some less stringent than before, some more. The main changes are:

- All new bathroom circuits must now be RCD protected. These include a shower circuit, the bathroom lighting circuit and the ring circuit that supplies power to an extractor fan, shower pump or towel rail;
- Supplementary equipotential bonding (see page 267) is no longer required (provided the circuits are RCD protected and all main services are bonded – see page 267);
- Socket outlets are now allowed, but only if they are at least 3m from the Zone 1 boundary, so cannot be touched by anyone using the bath or shower.

These changes are not retrospective, but do apply to 'extensions and modifications' to existing installations.

IP RATINGS

Any equipment installed in Zones 1 or 2 must have suitable protection against water splashes. IP ratings consist of two digits. The first describes the level of physical protection the equipment provides against contact with live (or moving) parts. The second describes the level of protection against water penetration. The higher the number, the greater the protection provided. An X is used where the protection is not relevant. The minimum ratings for bathrooms are IPX7 (protection against immersion) for Zone 0 and IPX4 (protection from splashed water) for Zones 1 and 2 except for shaver units properly installed.

Tools for wiring work

Many of the jobs involved in wiring are non-electrical in nature – lifting floorboards, say. But for the electrical work, some special tools are essential.

Wire cutters A pair of 125mm or 160mm side wire cutters will cut cable and flex, and trim conductors to length.

Torch Choose one with a sturdy stand, or clip-on fitting. A powerful torch will light up work under floors and in lofts. Have a supply of spare batteries available or ideally choose a torch with a rechargeable battery.

Circuit continuity tester With a simple battery-powered tester you can check the continuity of circuits and whether a socket outlet is on a ring main circuit or on a spur.

Wire strippers The adjustable blades will strip the insulation from cores of different sizes in cable and flex without damaging the conductors inside.

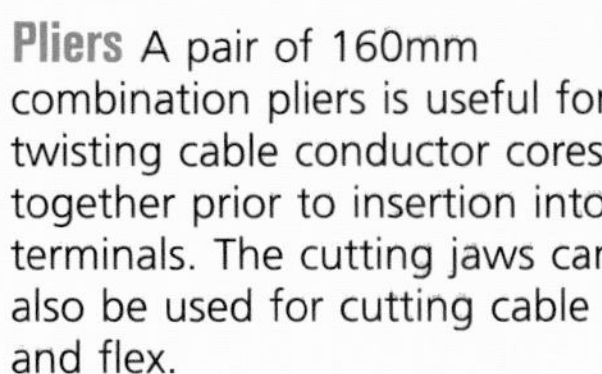

Pliers A pair of 160mm combination pliers is useful for twisting cable conductor cores together prior to insertion into terminals. The cutting jaws can also be used for cutting cable and flex.

Tester screwdriver An insulated screwdriver with a 3mm blade is used for tightening terminal screws in plugs and other wiring accessories. A bulb in the handle lights up if the tip touches a live terminal or conductor.

Trimming knife A sharp trimming knife will cut through the outer sheath of cable and flex.

Insulated screwdriver A larger screwdriver with an insulating sleeve on the shaft is useful for undoing and tightening plug screws and the screws fixing accessory faceplates to their mounting boxes.

Changing a fuse in the consumer unit

If you have circuit fuses, keep spare cartridge fuses or fuse wire to hand for instant repairs if a fuse 'blows'.

Mending a rewirable fuse

1 Turn off the main on-off switch in the consumer unit. On an older system it may be in a separate enclosure near the meter. Remove or open the cover over the fuse carriers.

2 Pull out each fuse carrier in turn to find out which has blown. Scorch marks often show this, or simply a break in the wire.

3 If a power circuit is affected, switch off and unplug all the appliances on the circuit. If it is a lighting circuit, turn off all the light switches. If you do not switch everything off, the mended fuse is likely to blow again immediately you turn the main switch back on. Replace the fuse wire (below).

TYPES OF REWIRABLE FUSE CARRIER

Bridged fuse The wire runs from one terminal to the other over a plug of white arc-damping material. The carrier is ceramic.

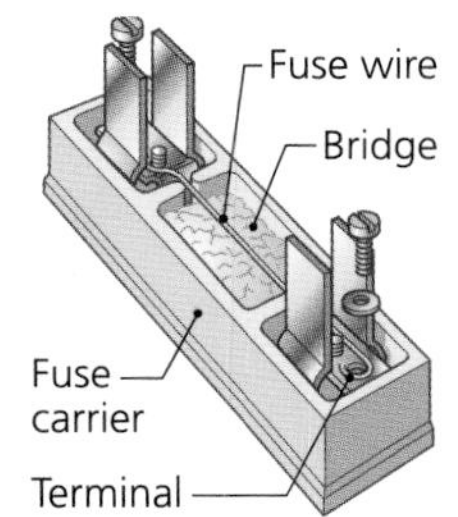

Protected fuse Between the terminals the wire runs through a porcelain arc-damping tube. The carrier is tough plastic.

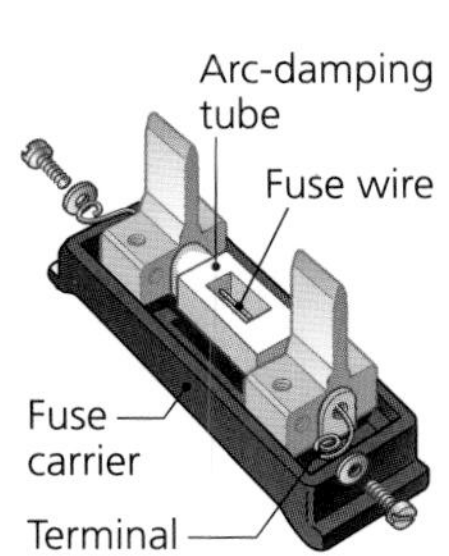

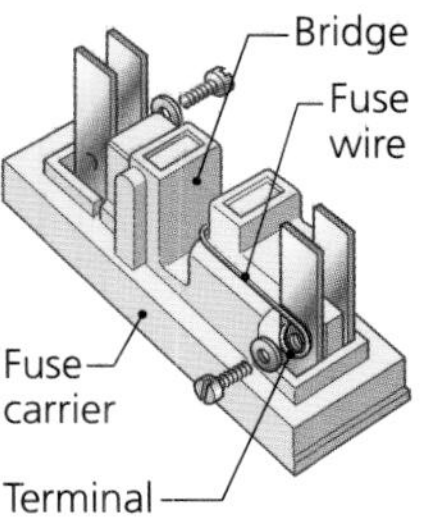

Fuse between humps The unprotected wire passes round humps between one terminal and the other. The carrier is ceramic.

Replacing the fuse wire

1 Loosen the two terminal screws and remove any pieces of old wire. Cut a new piece of fuse wire of the correct amp rating, long enough to cross the carrier and go round both screws.

2 Wind the wire clockwise round one screw and tighten the screw.

3 Pass the wire across the bridge or thread it through the holder. If you are unsure about how the wire runs in the carrier, examine one of the intact fuses.

4 Wind the wire clockwise round the second screw. Make sure there is a little slack in the wire so that it will not snap and then tighten the screw. Cut off loose wire.

5 Replace the fuse carrier in the consumer unit. Close the cover and restore the power by turning on the main switch.

Checking the circuit

Look for damage on the appliances, lights and flexes that were in use on the circuit when it failed. Make repairs if necessary, then switch on the appliances or lights one at a time. Check that you are not overloading the circuit with too many high-wattage appliances. Overloading is the likeliest cause of the blown fuse. If the fuse blows again, call an electrician.

Replacing a cartridge fuse

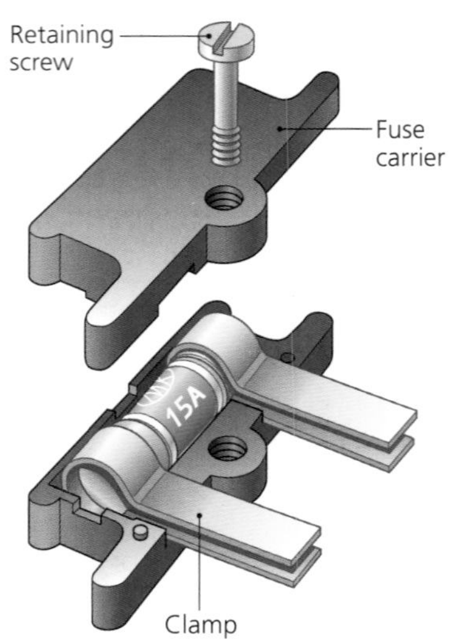

Tools *Insulated screwdriver; fuse tester.*
Materials *Cartridge fuses.*

1 Turn off the main switch on the consumer unit.

2 Find out which fuse has blown – unless you already know: take out each fuse carrier in turn so you can test the cartridge.

3 Prise the cartridge gently from the clamps. Some carriers are in two halves and the screw holding them together has to be removed to give access to the cartridge.

4 Test the cartridge with a fuse tester (see below). Remove only one carrier at a time. Test its cartridge and replace the carrier before removing the next one for inspection and testing.

5 When you have traced the blown fuse, replace the cartridge with a new one of the amp rating shown on the carrier.

6 As with a rewirable fuse, switch off all appliances or lights on the affected circuit. Replace the fuse carrier, close the box and turn on the main switch. Check the circuit in the same way as for rewirable fuses.

Checking a miniature circuit breaker

If the consumer unit is fitted with miniature circuit breakers (MCBs) instead of circuit fuses, it is immediately clear which circuit is affected. The switch will be in the 'off' position or the button will have popped out.

1 Turn off the main switch on the consumer unit.

2 Switch off all appliances or light switches on the affected circuit. If you do not do this, the MCB may trip off again when you reset it.

3 Push the MCB switch to the 'on' position or push in the button. Then turn the main switch back on.

4 Check the circuit in the same way as for a rewirable fuse (left).

TESTING A FUSE

You can buy an inexpensive tester that will tell you if a cartridge fuse has blown. Some types can also check flat batteries and blown light bulbs.

Choosing the right fuse

Always use the correct fuse for the job in hand. NEVER use any other metallic object or material in place of a blown fuse in order to restore power to a circuit or appliance. Doing so would remove the protection the fuse provides, and could allow an electrical fire to start or result in someone receiving a potentially fatal electric shock.

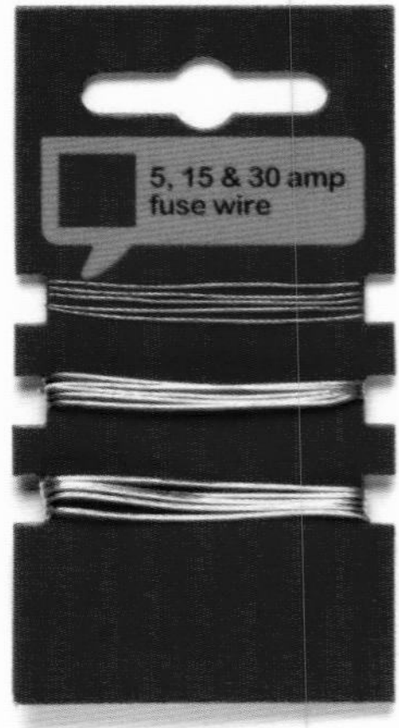

Fuse wires
If your consumer unit has rewirable fuses, use 5amp wire for a lighting circuit, 15amp wire for an immersion heater circuit, and 30amp wire for a ring main circuit or a circuit to a cooker rated at up to 12kW.

Cartridge fuses

5A Use for a lighting circuit

15A Use for a storage heater or immersion heater circuit.

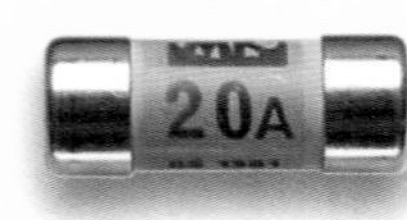

20A Use for a 20amp radial power circuit and storage heater.

30A Use for a ring main circuit or a 30amp radial power circuit.

45A Use for a cooker or shower circuit.

Choosing flexes

Most flex is round in cross-section and has a white PVC outer sheath that contains colour-coded insulated conductors. The live conductor is brown, the neutral blue and the earth green-and-yellow. Each conductor (called a core) is a bundle of thin wires, which is why it is so flexible. The thicker the core, the more strands it has and the more current it can carry.

Ordinary PVC-sheathed flex will withstand temperatures of up to 60°C. Heat-resistant rubber-sheathed flex will withstand temperatures of up to 85°C. Non-kink flex has a rubber sheath with an outer cover of braided fabric. Flex with an orange sheath is used outdoors to make it easy to see.

Metal light fittings and most appliances need three-core flex. Two-core flex with no earth core is used on double-insulated power tools and appliances (marked ⧈), and for wiring non-metallic light fittings.

Key to flex colours
L – Live (brown)
E – Earth (green and yellow)
N – Neutral (blue)

2-core flex For non-metallic light fittings and double-insulated appliances. Available with flat or round PVC sheath. Use 0.5mm² for up to 700W with a pendant weight of 2kg; 0.75mm² for up to 1.4kW and 3kg; and 1mm² for up to 2.3kW and pendant weight of 5kg.

3-core flex Used for all other appliances and for metallic light fittings and pendant lampholders requiring earthing. Has a round PVC sheath. Use 0.75mm² flex for up to 1.4kW, 1mm² for up to 2.3kW, 1.25mm² for up to 3kW; 1.5mm² for up to 3.7kW. Use 1.5mm² heat-resisting flex for immersion heaters.

3-core braided flex Used for portable appliances, such as irons, toasters and room heaters, with hot parts that could damage PVC-sheathed flex. Use sizes as for 3-core PVC flex.

3-core curly flex Useful for worktop appliances such as kettles, to keep flex safe and tidy. Use sizes as for 3-core flex.

Preparing flex for connection

The cores inside flex must be exposed before they can be connected to the terminals of a plug, appliance or ceiling rose.

Tools *Trimming knife; wire cutters and strippers; pliers.*

Materials *Flex. Possibly also PVC insulating tape or a rubber sleeve.*

Stripping the outer sheath

Most flex has an outer sheath of tough PVC. Remove enough to make sure that the cores can reach the terminals easily or they may be pulled out. For most connections you need to remove about 40mm of the sheath. Take care not to cut or nick the insulation on the cores as you cut the outer sheath.

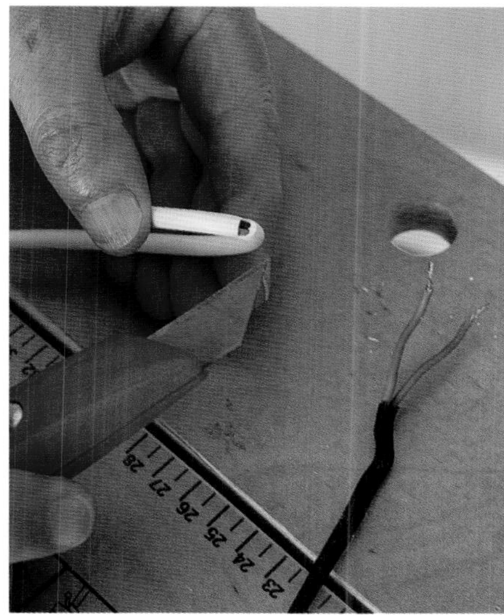

Bend the flex over and cut the sheath lightly with a trimming knife. The tension at the fold will open up a split halfway round the sheath. Fold the flex the other way and repeat. Then pull off the unwanted length of sheath.

Cutting and stripping the cores

1 Cut the individual cores to the right length to reach their terminals.

2 Set the wire strippers to match the thickness of the cores you are stripping. The core should just be able to slide out of the opening in the tool.

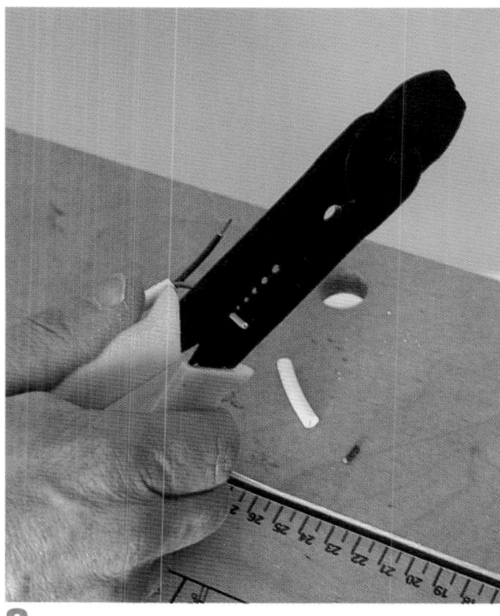

3 Press the handles together to cut the core insulation about 15mm from the tip. Rotate the strippers half a turn and pull them towards the tip of the core. The insulation will slide off.

4 Twist the strands of wire together.

Alternatively If you are preparing very thin flex for connection, strip off 30mm of insulation from each core, rather than 15mm. Twist the wire strands together, then fold the bare core over on itself in a tight U-shape. This makes it easier to insert into the terminal and provides a better electrical contact.

Fabric-covered flex

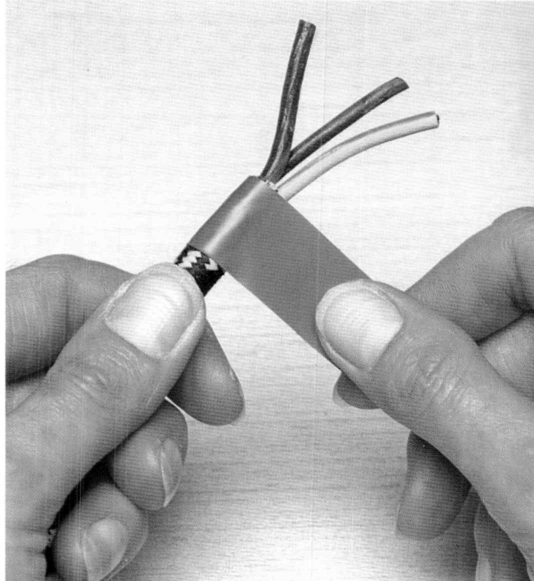

The outer cover of braided fabric on non-kink flex is likely to fray where it is cut. Wrap a strip of PVC insulating tape two or three times round the cut end of the fabric to seal down the loose threads.

Alternatively Cover the cut with a purpose-made rubber sleeve. This will be held by the cord grip of the plug. Remember to put it on before inserting the flex in the plug.

Extending a flex

Never join lengths of flex by twisting together the cores and binding the join with insulating tape. It may overheat and start a fire.

If you have to extend a flex, use a one-piece connector to make a permanent joint, or use a two-part connector if you want to be able to separate the joint. This must have three pins for connecting appliances that use three-core flex. Two-pin connectors are used mainly for connecting double-insulated garden power tools (marked with the symbol ⧈) to extension leads.

Tools *Insulated screwdrivers; trimming knife; wire cutters and strippers; pliers.*

Materials *Flex connector; length of flex fitted with a plug.*

EXTENSION LEADS AND ADAPTORS

Trailing socket adaptor This provides three or more outlets and is normally fitted with a fuse and neon indicator. It plugs into an existing socket and can supply a total wattage of up to 3kW. Use for low wattage appliances like computer equipment.

Plug-in adaptor Allows two or three plugs to fit into a single socket outlet. The total wattage for the adaptor is 3kW and it should be fitted with a 13A fuse. Do not plug one adaptor into another; the pin contacts will be poor and overheating could result.

Wire-in adaptor Makes a permanent connection for up to four low-wattage appliances and supplies total wattage of up to 3kW. Mount on the wall near the socket. Use for hi-fi or other equipment that is always kept in the same place.

A one-piece connector

1 Unscrew the connector cover and remove it. Prepare the ends of both flexes for connection. Check that the cores (the wires) are long enough to reach the brass terminals when each flex sheath is held over its cord grip.

2 Lift out the brass barrel terminals and loosen all the terminal screws.

3 Push the cores into the terminals so that they match – brown to brown in one terminal, green-and-yellow to green-and-yellow in the second, and blue to blue in the third. Tighten all the terminal screws.

4 Loosen one screw and remove the other from each cord grip so you can swing the bar aside.

5 Fit the brass barrel terminals in their slots and position each flex sheath beneath its cord grip.

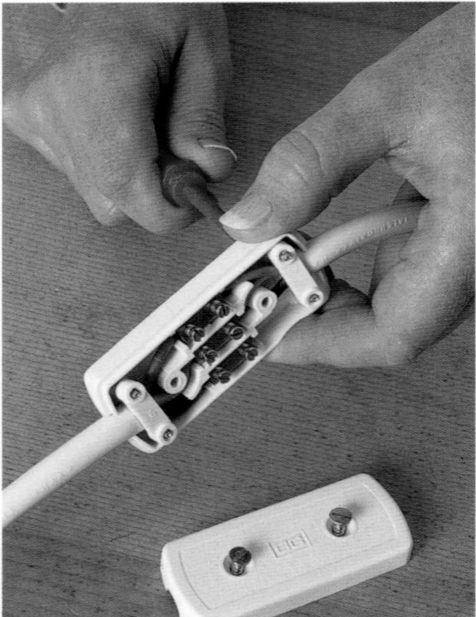

6 Replace the cord grip screws and tighten them to grip the flex sheaths securely. Fit and screw on the cover.

A two-part connector

You must fit the flex from the appliance to the part of the connector with the pins, and the flex from the mains supply to the part with the sockets.

If you fit the flexes the other way round, you will have live pins exposed if the two parts of the connector become separated while the power is switched on.

1 Prepare the ends of both flexes. Separate the two halves of the connector. Remove the screw holding the terminal block inside each cover and push it out. Undo the cord grips.

2 Slide the outer covers onto the two prepared flexes.

3 Connect the cores to each terminal block with the green-and-yellow core in the middle. Make sure that the brown and blue cores in each part of the connector are opposite each other so they will connect when the parts are joined.

4 Fit each flex sheath in its cord grip and tighten the screws to hold it securely. Push each terminal block back into its cover and replace the fixing screw.

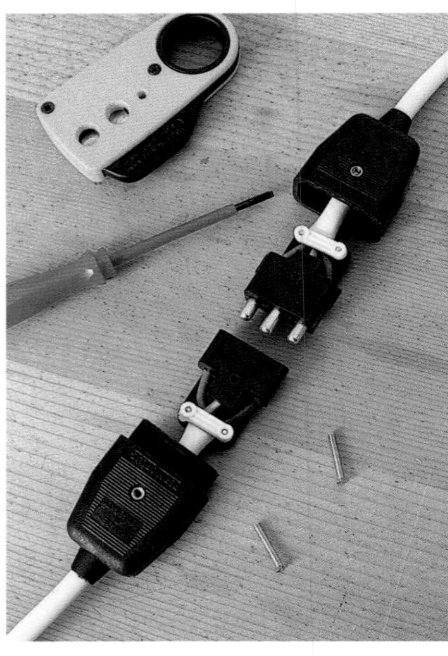

Choosing an extension reel

Even if you have furnished your home with a sufficient number of socket outlets (see page 292), there will be many times when you need to use an extension reel. This allows you to have power down the garden, up on the roof, in the garage, up in the loft; anywhere, in fact, where there is not a convenient socket outlet.

Many power tools have flexes so short that you will need some kind of extension lead almost every time you use them; even with a decent length of flex, you will often need to use an extension lead. A cable reel has the advantage that you get two, three or four sockets on the reel – but note that the total load for all the sockets is equal to the load current rating of the reel.

An extension reel has two ratings – one for the cable fully wound up and the other for it fully unwound. For most DIY uses, it's best to have a 13amp (13A) reel (the highest rating) and always to use it fully unwound – it's quite possible to 'cook' a lower-rated reel if you use it unwound. There are three main types of reel: cassette reels, 'handbag' reels and heavy-duty stand-alone open reels.

Cassette reels These are the cheapest type and come in lengths up to 15m, with typical ratings of 6A, 10A and 13A. Better suited to use inside the house: look for reels with a thermal cut-out (see Reel safety above), a built-in hand grip and a rotating knob for easier winding.

'Handbag' reels A cassette reel in a plastic case (with a handle) that can be stood up, making the reel suitable for use outside. Mostly 13A, with lengths from 15m to 50m. Some reels fitted with RCD plug (see Reel safety, above) as well as thermal cut-out. Again look for rotating knobs; some handbag reels have a place for storing the plug and some have ON indicator lights.

REEL SAFETY

Thermal cut-out Many extension reels are fitted with a thermal cut-out that operates if the flex on the reel gets too hot. You have to wait until the reel has cooled down before re-setting the cut-out.

RCD protection It is essential that an extension reel should always be used with an RCD, which cuts off the power at once if you sever the flex and touch a live core.

Unless the socket outlet into which you plug the extension lead is on a circuit that is RCD protected (see page 265) or the socket outlet itself has an RCD built in (see page 317 for an example), you should always use an RCD adaptor (left) between the plug and the socket outlet. Some extension reels are fitted with an RCD plug that can safely be plugged into any socket outlet.

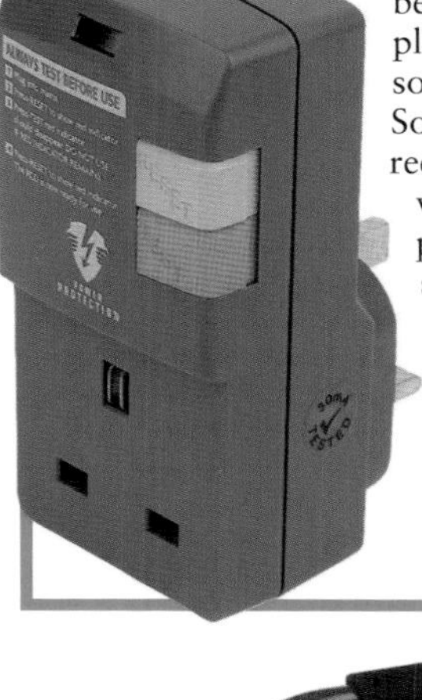

Open reels An open plastic drum on a galvanised steel frame with a rubber carrying handle. Lengths from 20m to 50m, mostly fitted with thermal cut-outs and some with RCD plug (see Reel safety, above). On some stand-alone reels, the sockets do not turn with the reel, so the reel can be extended with the plugs in place. Look for locking brakes, cable tidies and ON indicator lights.

Choosing plugs and fuses

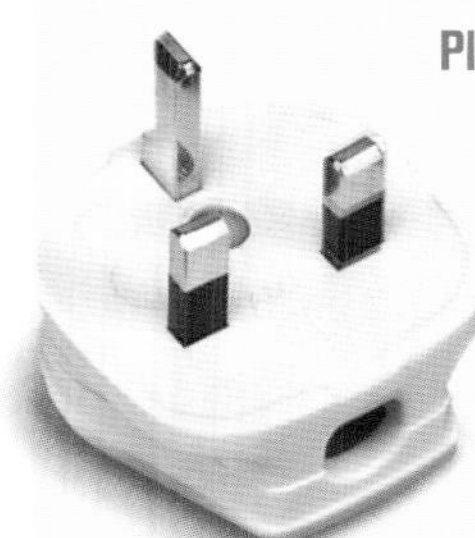

Plastic plug Moulded plastic plugs are the commonest type. They are usually white, but other colours are available. All new plugs have plastic sleeves on the live and neutral pins, to prevent accidental finger-tip contact with live metal as you pull the plug out of its socket outlet.

Rubber plug Tough rubber plugs are intended for use on power tools. Rubber will not crack if the plug is knocked or dropped in use. You have to thread the flex through the rubber cover before connecting it to the plug terminals.

Moulded-on plug All new appliances should have a one-piece factory-fitted plug. These cannot be opened, so must be cut off and replaced if damaged. Hammer the pins out of line before you throw it away so it cannot be plugged into a socket outlet if found by a child. The cut end of the flex would give a shock if touched.

3amp cartridge fuse Use in plugs and fused connection units for appliances rated at up to 700 watts. Check the wattage on the rating plate of the appliance. Low wattage appliances include table or standard lamps, hi-fi equipment, home computers and ancillaries, and electric blankets.

13amp cartridge fuse Use in plugs and fused connection units for appliances between 700 and 3000 watts such as most TV sets, vacuum cleaners, large power tools, room heaters and all domestic appliances that contain a heating element.

Fitting a new plug

All electrical appliances sold in the UK must have a factory-fitted plug. This has greatly improved household electrical safety, by eliminating the need for the consumer to fit a plug to every new appliance – a task that many found difficult to carry out correctly.

However, you will need to fit a replacement plug if the factory-fitted one is damaged. Many older appliances in the home will still have hand-wired plugs, which may also need replacing over time.

All three-pin plugs are fitted with a cartridge fuse. Many contain a 13amp fuse when you buy them, but you should fit a lower-rated fuse if the appliance rating is below 700 watts (see Choosing plugs and fuses, page 273).

Tools *Insulated screwdrivers; trimming knife; wire cutters and strippers; pliers.*

Materials *Plug; cartridge fuse (either 3amp or 13amp).*

1 Unscrew the cover of the new plug and remove it.

OLD COLOUR, NEW COLOUR

The colours of the plastic insulation on the cores in flex were changed to brown (live), blue (neutral) and green-and-yellow (earth) in 1968. Any appliance with flex cores coloured red (live) and black (neutral) should be checked for electrical safety.

Old colours	New colours
E ⏚ N L	E ⏚ N L
Black to N Green to earth (E or ⏚) Red to L	Blue to N Green-and-yellow to earth (E or ⏚) Brown to L

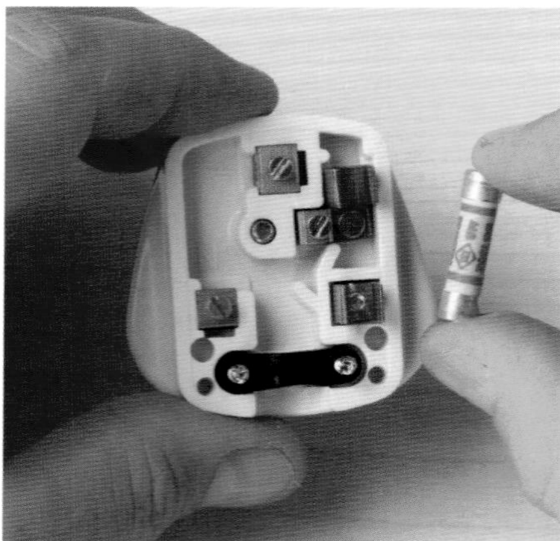

2 Prise out the cartridge fuse if necessary to reveal the terminal. Loosen the screw-down bar that secures the flex if there is one. Nylon jaws grip the flex in some plugs.

3 If you are replacing a hand-wired plug, remove its cover and loosen the terminal screws to release the flex cores from their terminals. Release the flex from the cord grip. Inspect the bare cores. If they appear damaged, cut them off and strip off some core insulation to expose undamaged wires ready for reconnection to the new plug.

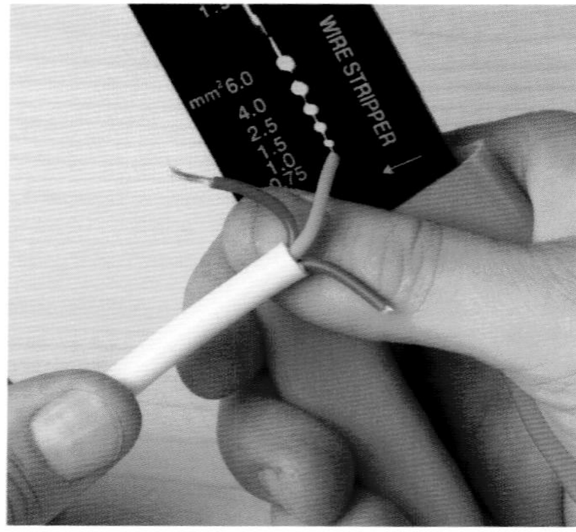

4 If you are replacing a factory-fitted plug, cut through the flex close to the plug body. Prepare the end of the cut flex (page 271). For some plugs all the cores have to be the same length, for others they have to be different lengths. Check that the prepared cores are long enough to reach their terminals with the flex sheath held in the flex grip.

5 Tough rubber plugs designed for use on power tools have a hole in the plug cover through which the flex passes before being connected to the plug terminals.

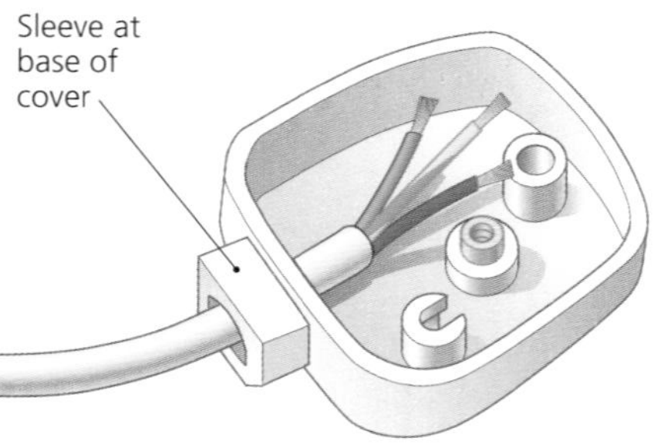

6 Connect each flex core to its correct terminal. The **BR**own (live) core goes to the **B**ottom **R**ight terminal, the **BL**ue (neutral) core to the **B**ottom **L**eft terminal, and the earth core in three-core flex (green-and-yellow) to the top terminal.

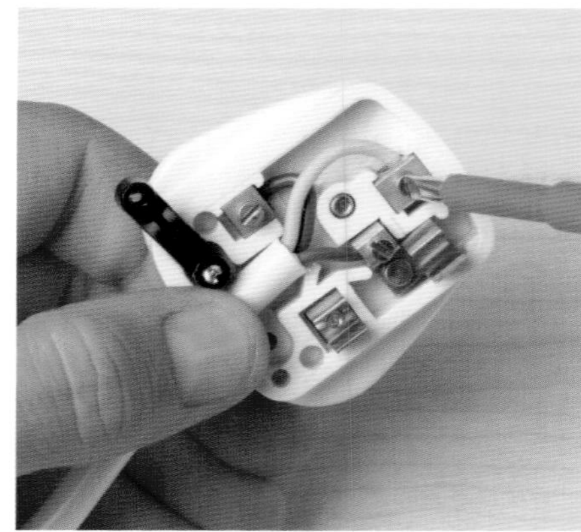

7 With pillar-type terminals, loosen the terminal screw and insert the bare end of the core in the hole. Tighten the screw to trap it in place. Plugs with this type of terminal often have loose pins; remove these from the plug first if it makes connecting the cores easier.

Alternatively With screw-down stud terminals, remove the stud and wind the bare end of the core clockwise round the threaded peg. Screw the stud down to trap the wires in place.

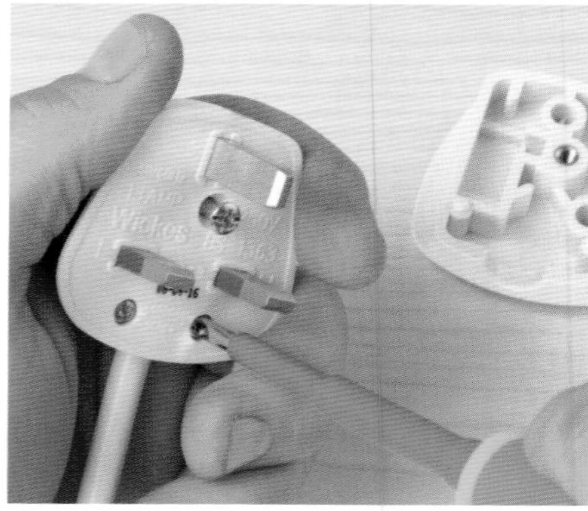

8 Arrange the cores in their channels in the plug body and place the flex sheath in the cord grip. If the plug has nylon jaws, press the flex in between them. If it has a screw-down bar, undo one screw, position the flex in the grip, swing the bar back over it and screw it down securely. Fit the fuse.

9 Replace the plug cover and make sure that it is firmly screwed together.

Reconnecting flex to a lampholder

The flex connections within a pendant lampholder may pull away from their terminals in time and stop the light working, but it is a simple matter to reconnect them.

- You will also need to reconnect the cores if you are shortening the flex, perhaps to fit a new lampshade that needs to be higher.
- If the lampholder is a metal one without an earth terminal, replace it with an earthed one – or with a plastic lampholder if the flex has no earth core. You must use three-core flex with a metal lampholder or metal lampshade.
- If the flex is discoloured or cracked, replace it with new flex.

Tools *Insulated screwdrivers, one with a small, fine tip; trimming knife; wire cutters and strippers; pliers.*

Materials *Replacement flex. Perhaps a new lampholder.*

1 Turn off the power at the consumer unit and remove the fuse or switch off the MCB protecting the circuit that you will be working on.

2 Remove the light bulb and unscrew the ring that holds the lampshade. With a very old lampholder, you may have to break the ring by crushing it with pliers; some shops sell the new rings separately. Remove the shade.

The parts of a lampholder

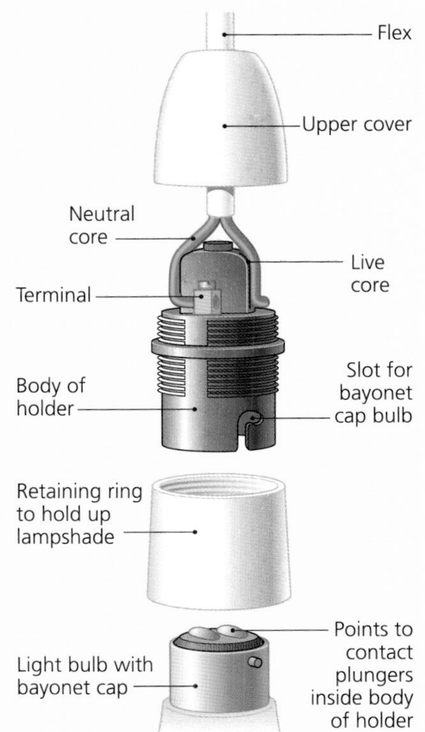

3 Unscrew the upper cover of the lampholder and push it up the flex to reveal the flex connections. Unhook the flex cores from the lugs on the body of the lampholder.

4 With the fine-tipped screwdriver, undo the terminal screws enough for you to draw out the flex cores.

5 The light bulb makes its connection via the two spring-loaded plungers in the base of the lampholder. Push these in to see whether they return to their original positions when released. If they do not, or if the lampholder is damaged or scorched, fit a new one.

6 Prepare the ends of the flex cores for connection (page 271).

7 If you are fitting a new lampholder, thread the new cover onto the flex.

8 Screw the brown and blue cores tightly into the lampholder terminals. It does not matter which each goes to. In a metal lampholder you must connect the green-and-yellow earth conductor to the earth terminal.

9 Hook the flex cores over the support lugs. Screw the lampholder cover on, taking care not to cross-thread it.

10 Insert the lampholder into the lampshade and screw the retaining ring in place to secure the shade. Fit the light bulb.

11 Replace the circuit fuse or switch on the MCB and restore the power at the consumer unit.

Connecting flex to a ceiling rose

If a light flex has discoloured or become brittle, it is easy to connect a new one between the ceiling rose and the lampholder.

Before you start Inside a modern ceiling rose on a loop-in wiring system (page 306) is a row of terminals in three groups. The live and neutral conductors of the circuit and switch cables are connected to these. A separate terminal is marked E or ⏚ for the earth conductors.

Use the right type and size of flex for the installation (page 271). If it connects with a metal lampholder or light fitting it must have an earth core.

Tools *Insulated screwdrivers, one with a small, fine tip; trimming knife; wire cutters and strippers; pliers.*

Materials *Replacement flex.*

Disconnecting the old flex

1 At the consumer unit, turn off the power and remove the fuse or switch off the MCB protecting the circuit you will be working on. It is not enough simply to turn off the light switch; the cables in the ceiling rose will still be live.

2 Remove the light bulb and shade to avoid the risk of dropping them.

3 Unscrew the cover of the ceiling rose and slide it down the flex.

4 Using the small screwdriver, loosen the terminal screws connecting the flex cores at each end of the row of terminals. Withdraw the cores from the terminals and unhook them from the lugs.

5 If the flex has an earth core, unscrew the earth terminal enough to withdraw it. Do not dislodge the other cable earths.

Connecting the new flex

1 Connect the new flex first to the lampholder (page 275).

2 Thread the new flex through the cover of the ceiling rose.

3 Prepare the new flex for connection (page 271). Take care not to strip off too much of the outer sheath. The cores have to reach the terminals without strain, but they must not show below the ceiling-rose cover; the outer sheath of the flex must enter the hole in the cover.

4 Slip the end of the green-and-yellow insulated earth core into the earth terminal in the ceiling rose. Make sure before you tighten the screw that the other cable earth cores from the circuit and switch cables have not been dislodged from under the terminal screw.

5 Connect the blue flex core to the terminal where the circuit cable neutral (black) cores are connected.

6 Connect the brown flex core to the terminal at the other end of the row where the switch cable neutral core is connected. This core is usually identified with a strip of red PVC insulating tape, to show that it is, in fact, live.

7 Hook the flex cores over the support lugs at each side of the rose baseplate.

JUNCTION BOX SYSTEM

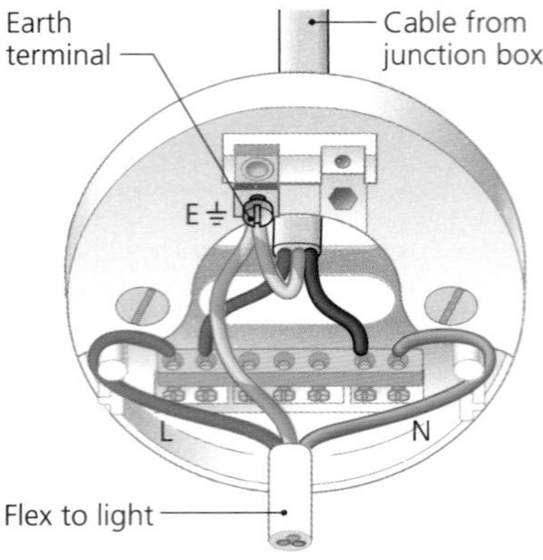

A loop-in ceiling rose might have been used on a junction box system (page 306). There will be only one cable entering the base of the rose. The flex connection is the same as for a loop-in system (steps 5–7, left).

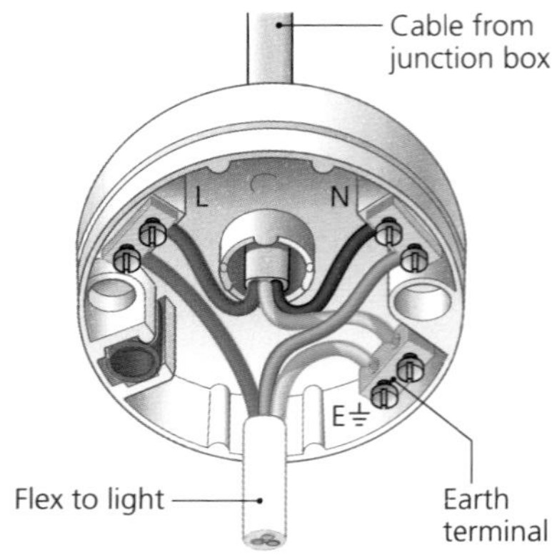

Another type of ceiling rose, used on a junction box system (above), has three sets of separate terminals, not in line.

1 Connect the blue flex core to the same set of terminals as the black cable core.

2 Connect the brown core from the flex to the same set of terminals as the red core from the cable.

3 Connect the green-and-yellow earth core from the flex to the same set of terminals as the earth core from the cable.

If the earth from the cable has not already been sleeved with green-and-yellow insulation, disconnect it and sleeve it before connecting it – with the flex earth – to the terminal.

8 Slide the rose cover up and screw it onto the baseplate. Replace the shade and bulb.

9 Replace the circuit fuse or switch on the MCB and restore the power.

Rewiring a table lamp or standard lamp

To fit a new flex to a table or standard lamp with no exposed metal parts, or for a double insulated lamp (marked ⧈), use two-core flex without an earth core. For a lamp with metal parts, use three-core flex.

- If the lamp has a brass lampholder without an earth terminal, you must fit a new brass lampholder with an earth terminal, or a plastic lampholder. If it is not possible to fit a new lampholder, do not use the lamp.
- The flex must be threaded up inside the lamp base. The hole to thread it through is often on the side of the lamp near the bottom.
- If the hole is underneath, the lamp base should have small feet to raise it and keep its weight off the flex.
- Most lamps have a push-through switch in the lampholder. If there is no integral switch, fit an in-line switch in the flex.

Tools *Insulated screwdrivers; trimming knife; wire cutters and strippers; pliers.*
Materials *Lamp; suitable flex. Perhaps also an in-line flex switch.*

1 Unplug the lamp and remove the bulb.

2 With a plastic lampholder, unscrew the upper cover to release the lampshade. With a brass lampholder, unscrew the narrow ring.

3 With a plastic lampholder, unscrew the body from the base, then screw down the lower cover to reveal the terminals.

With a brass lampholder, unscrew and remove the second wide ring so that you can lift off the outer lampholder section and then pull out the inner section which has the flex connected beneath it.

4 Release the flex cores from the terminals. Wind the cores securely round the end of the new flex and tape the two together.

5 Gently pull out the old flex from below, using it to pull the new flex through the lamp base.

Plastic lampholder

Upper cover
Flex grip
Switch
Terminal
Lower cover

Brass lampholder

Narrow ring
Wide ring
Inner section
Outer section
Terminal
Switch
Earth terminal
Lower cover

6 Prepare the flex for connection (page 271) and then finish drawing it through the lamp base until only about 40mm is protruding.

7 Connect the brown flex core to one lampholder terminal and the blue flex core to the other.

For a brass lampholder, connect the green-and-yellow earth core to the terminal marked E (or ⏚) on the lower cover.

8 With a plastic lampholder, screw the lower cover over the terminals and screw the lampholder body onto the lamp base. As you do so, turn the flex or it will become twisted. With a brass lampholder, lower the inner section of the lampholder back into place. Fit the outer section on top and secure it with the wide screw-on ring.

9 Replace the lampshade and secure it with the upper narrow ring or plastic upper cover. Fit the light bulb.

Fitting an in-line flex switch

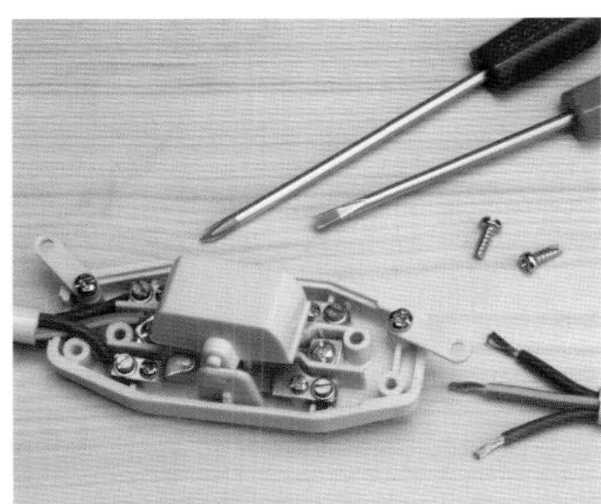

- If you are using three-core flex, use an in-line switch with an earth terminal.
- For a two-core flex on a double-insulated lamp, no earth terminal is necessary.

1 Switch off and unplug the lamp. Cut the flex where the switch is to go and prepare the ends for connection (page 271).

2 Unscrew and remove the cover of the in-line switch.

3 Take out a screw from each flex clamp so that you can swivel the clamps aside.

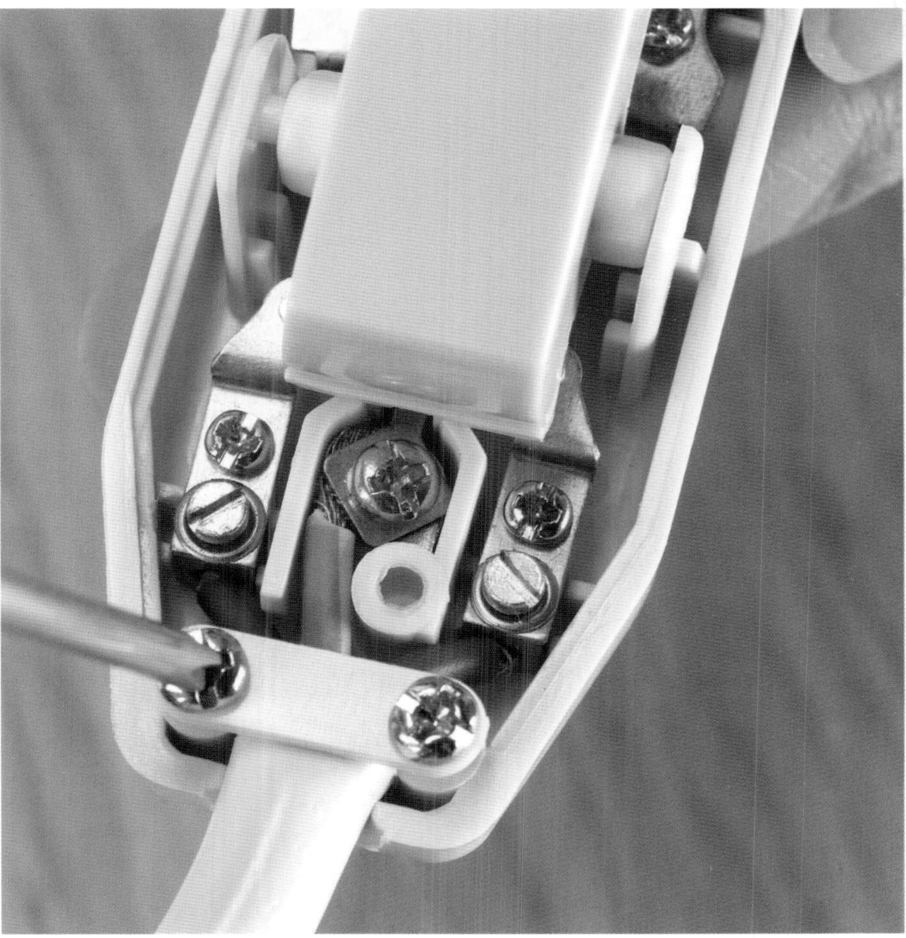

4 Release the terminal screws and connect each flex core – brown (live) to the terminals marked L, blue (neutral) to the terminals marked N, and green-and-yellow to the terminals marked E (or ⏚). Replace the flex clamps and tighten the screws.

Alternatively For a two-core flex on a double-insulated lamp, connect the two brown cores to one pair of terminals and the two blue cores to the other pair. Ignore the earth terminals.

5 Screw the switch cover back into place.

Fitting a plug to the new flex

Connect the plug as described in *Fitting a new plug*, page 274.

● Cable core colours have changed – see page 281

Replacing sockets

Electric shock or fire could be caused by contact with the conductors in a damaged socket. Replace it as soon as possible.

Replacing a faceplate

If a socket outlet faceplate is burnt or cracked by an impact, do not use the socket until you have replaced the faceplate. If the socket outlet is surface-mounted, replace the mounting box as well if it is damaged. You could take the opportunity to replace a single socket with a double one at the same time.

Tools *Large and small insulated screwdriver; perhaps also a trimming knife; wire cutters and strippers; pliers.*

Materials *New socket outlet. Perhaps a new plastic mounting box, with fixing screws; green-and-yellow earth sleeving.*

1 Turn off the power at the consumer unit and switch off the MCB that protects the circuit you want to work on (or remove the appropriate fuse if you have an old-style fuse box). Plug in and switch on a lamp you know to be working to check that the socket outlet is dead.

2 Undo the screws that hold the faceplate in place and pull it away from the wall. Keep the screws; you may find that the ones supplied with your new socket outlet will not fit the lugs in the existing mounting box. In that case, use the old screws.

3 Loosen the three terminal screws on the back of the faceplate to release the conductors. Note how many conductors are connected to each terminal; there may be one, two or three depending on whether the outlet is on a spur, is on the ring circuit or is supplying power to an extra outlet on a spur. The new outlet must be connected in the same way as the damaged one.

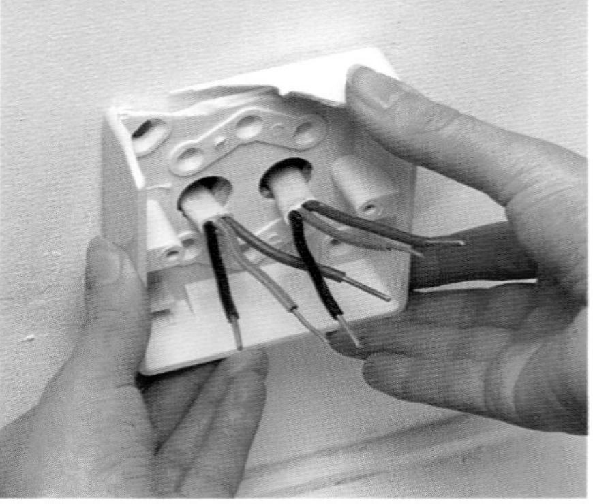

4 If there is damage to the plastic mounting box of a surface-mounted socket, undo the screws holding it to the wall and remove it. Pass the cable or cables through one of the knock-outs of a new surface-mounting box and screw the box in place.

5 Check that the cable cores will reach the terminals on the new faceplate. If necessary, cut back the cable sheath with a trimming knife to expose longer cores, taking care not to nick the core insulation. If the earth cores are bare, cover them with green-and-yellow plastic sleeving, leaving only the metal ends exposed.

6 Insert the cores into their terminals and tighten the terminal screws firmly. Connect the red core(s) to the terminal marked L, the black core(s) to the terminal marked N, and the earth cores to the terminal marked E or ⏚. Tug each core to check that it is securely held by its terminal screw.

7 Place the faceplate over the mounting box, folding the cables carefully into it.

8 Screw the faceplate to the box. Do not over-tighten the screws or the plastic may crack.

9 Turn on the MCB for the circuit you have been working on, or replace the fuse you removed. Restore the power and check that the new socket outlet works – by plugging in a lamp, for example. If it does not, switch off again at the mains and check and tighten the connections.

Replacing a single socket outlet with a double

If the single socket outlet is surface-mounted, use a double surface-mounted replacement. If it is flush-mounted (or recessed), you can fit a plastic surface-mounted box called a pattress over it. Alternatively, you can remove the existing metal mounting box, enlarge the recess and fit a larger box. Flush-mounted fittings are neater, and safer because they are less likely to be damaged by knocks from furniture. You will have to cut into the wall to fit a new double or triple flush mounting box.

Tools *Suitable tools for enlarging the recess (page 282); insulated screwdriver; trimming knife; wire cutters and strippers; pliers.*

Materials *Double or triple mounting box (or pattress, see opposite); new socket outlet; rubber grommet; screws and wall plugs. Perhaps earth sleeving.*

Removing the single outlet

1 Turn off the main switch on the consumer unit and switch off the MCB that protects the circuit you will be working on. Remove the appropriate fuse if you have an old-style fuse box. Check that the socket outlet is dead by plugging in a lamp you know to be working.

2 Unscrew the faceplate and ease it away from the mounting box. Then disconnect the cable cores from their terminals and set the old faceplate aside.

Fitting the mounting box

Flush-mounted boxes

1 Take out the screw or screws holding the old box in place and ease the box out of its recess.

2 Enlarge the hole for the new double mounting box (page 282).

3 Remove a knock-out (a pre-cut entry disc) from the new box. Fit a grommet in the hole to prevent the cable sheath from chafing on its edges, then feed the cable into the box and fix the box in place.

Surface-mounted boxes/pattresses

1 If you are replacing a surface-mounted box, take out its fixing screws and remove it. If you are fitting a pattress, leave the old flush metal mounting box in place.

2 Hold the mounting box in place, check with a spirit level that it is horizontal, and use a bradawl to pierce the wall through the fixing holes.

3 Drill holes at the marked spots and insert wallplugs in them.

4 Feed the cable through a knockout in the back of the box or the hole in the pattress. Screw the box to the wall or the pattress to the old flush metal mounting box.

Connecting the double outlet

1 Use pliers to straighten the ends of the cable cores. Cover the earth cores with green-and-yellow sleeving if they are bare.

2 Screw the live (red) cores into the terminal marked L. Screw the neutral (black) cores into the terminal marked N. Screw the earth conductors into the terminal marked E or ⏚.

3 If the mounting box is metal, fit a short length of earth core (taken from a cable offcut and covered with green-and-yellow sleeving) between the faceplate earth terminal and the earth terminal in the box. This so-called flying earth ensures that the metal box is safely connected to earth.

4 Fold the cables neatly into the mounting box and push the faceplate back into position over the box.

5 Screw the faceplate to the box or pattress. Do not overtighten the screws if fixing to a plastic box, or it may crack.

6 At the consumer unit, replace the fuse or switch on the MCB to restore power to the circuit you have been working on.

Choosing socket outlets and mounting boxes

There is a wide variety of socket outlets and mounting boxes to choose from. When increasing the number of outlets you have, or replacing old outlets, try to ensure that what you choose will supply enough power and sockets for any future use of electric appliances.

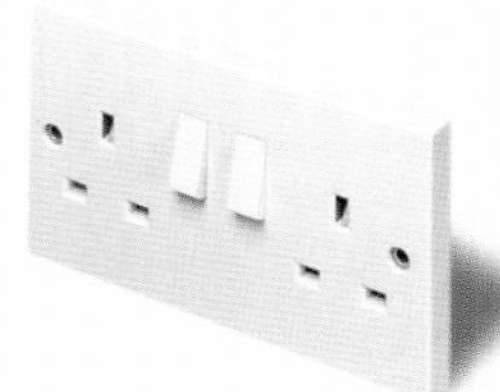

Plastic socket outlets
Socket outlets are available in single, double and triple configurations, with or without switches. Holes for the plug pins have spring-loaded shutters to prevent children from poking anything into them. Most sockets fit into a 32mm deep white plastic surface box or a 25mm steel flush-mounted box; deeper (35mm) flush boxes allow more space for the wiring.

Metal socket outlets
Single and double brass, chrome and stainless-steel sockets are available in a variety of styles. There are plastic inserts round the shuttered pin holes and switches. Metal sockets fit on a flush steel box or a matching metal surface box.

Socket outlets with indicators
Both plastic and metal sockets are available with a neon indicator above each outlet. The indicator lights up to show when the socket outlet is switched on. Take care not to dislodge the small neon bulb clipped behind the coloured window when handling the faceplate.

Fused connection units
Fixed appliances, such as wall-mounted heaters and fans, should be connected to a ring circuit by a fused connection unit (FCU) with a direct flex connection, rather than by a plug. The flex from the appliance can enter the FCU through the edge or a hole in the front. The FCU may have a switch and a neon indicator, and is fitted with a fuse to match the appliance wattage.

Flex-outlet plates
In bathrooms where socket outlets are not permitted, a fixed appliance such as a towel rail is wired into a flex-outlet plate. The cable (from a fused connection unit) goes into the back of the mounting box and the flex enters through the front of the plate and is connected to terminals on the back of it. There is no switch.

Boxes for flush mounting
Metal boxes for single, double and triple socket outlets have pre-cut discs to allow cables to enter. Knock out a disc and fit a grommet in the hole to protect the cable. The earth terminal in the box must be linked to the earth terminal on the accessory faceplate with sleeved earth core.

Single and double plastic 'drylining' boxes are available for use in plasterboard walls. They also have knock-out cable entry points, but do not need grommets.

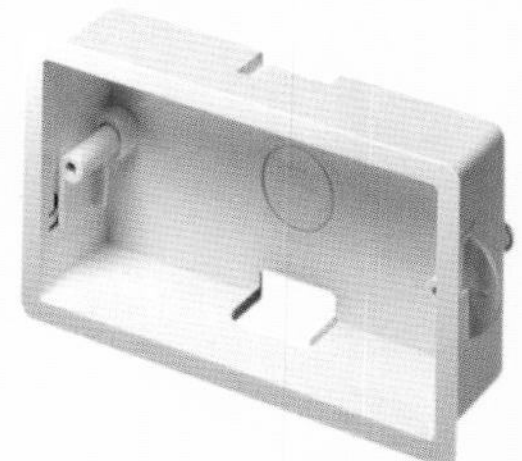

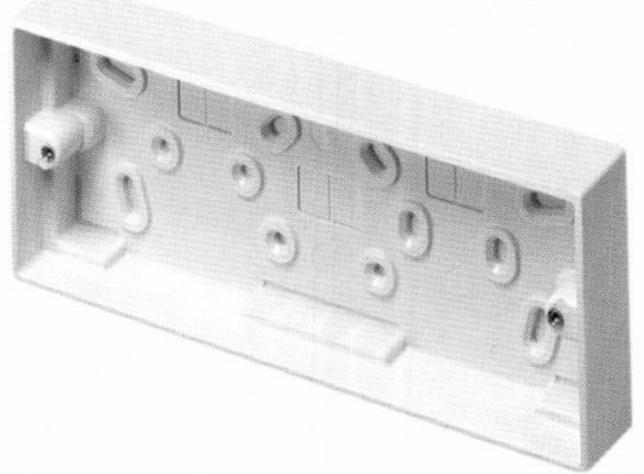

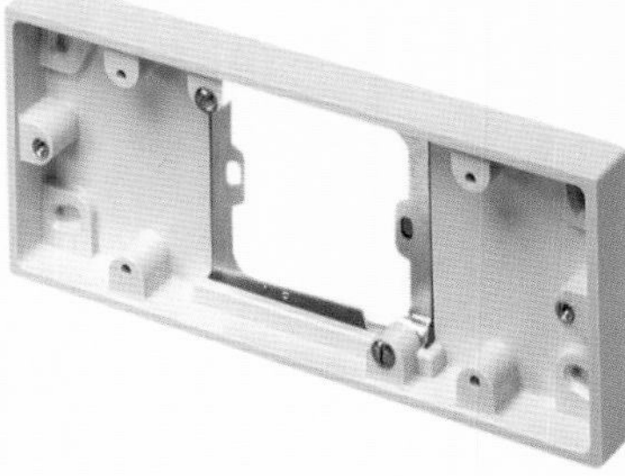

Boxes for surface mounting
Single, double and triple surface boxes are made in plastic. They have knock-out cable entry points, but do not need grommets. Metal surface boxes are also available; they are used mainly in outbuildings.

Pattress for converting a socket outlet
A mounting frame called a pattress allows a surface-mounted double or triple socket outlet to be fitted over a single flush-mounted metal box.

All projects carrying this symbol are notifiable (see below)

Cable core colours have changed – see page 281

Working on electrical circuits

Many electrical jobs and projects involve working on the house's electrical circuits – either extending an existing circuit in some way, or adding an entirely new one. Whatever the task, the most important skill required for safety and success is the ability to plan the job carefully and carry out the work methodically.

A typical project will involve running cable from one point to another, either from the main consumer unit or from a point on an existing circuit. This new cable is used for installing new wiring accessories or light fittings, and making connections to them and to the existing circuit wiring.

To minimise disruption, do all the new installation work as far as possible while leaving the power supply on. You can bury new cables in walls, run them beneath floorboards or through lengths of plastic trunking and create recesses for new mounting boxes for sockets all with the power live – in fact you may need power for some of the jobs. Leave the new cables sticking out where they terminate at a new socket outlet or light fitting and where they link to the existing circuit and turn off the power supply only when you are ready to make the final connections.

Rules and regulations

Since April 2006, electrical installation work has been covered by Part P of the Building Regulations. As with other work covered by the Building Regulations, you need to inform the Building Control Department of your local authority if you are planning to carry out 'notifiable' work (see below) which will then be subject to inspection and testing (page 483). Part P-registered electricians are able to self-certify their own work.

- Simple replacements of socket outlets, switches and ceiling roses are not notifiable and you can replace the cable for a single circuit if it is damaged or upgrade bonding without telling your local authority.
- Adding socket outlets, fused spurs and lighting points to existing circuits is not notifiable provided the work is not in a kitchen or bathroom or outside.
- Virtually all other electrical jobs are notifiable, including new circuits back to the consumer unit, extensions to circuits in kitchens and bathrooms and new outdoor wiring. A new consumer unit is notifiable, but not work in conservatories or attached garages unless it is a new circuit.
- If you are in any doubt, ask your local Building Control Department for advice. Note that non-notifiable work must still meet the requirements of the Building Regulations which, in practice, means that it must be done to the IEE Wiring Regulations BS7671 (page 497).

Extending circuits

Jobs such as adding extra socket outlets in a room, installing a cooker hood or shaver socket or providing new lighting points all involve adding branch lines (called spurs) to existing circuits. A spur from a ring main circuit can supply one single, double or triple socket outlet or a single fused connection unit providing a sub-circuit to a cooker hood, extractor fan, waste disposal unit, wall heater or central heating control. Before you add a spur to a lighting circuit, check that adding the extra lighting point will not overload the circuit, which can supply lights with a maximum total of 1200 watts. The first thing you have to decide is where and how to connect the spur to the wiring that is already in place.

1 You can extend a ring main circuit in two ways. The spur cable can be connected into the terminals of any socket outlet or fused connection unit (FCU) that is on the main circuit. This is often the most practicable solution. Note that only one spur can be connected to each outlet or FCU.

Alternatively Make a connection via a three-terminal junction box inserted in the main circuit cable. This means locating cable below floorboards but may offer a more convenient connection point if boards have to be lifted anyway to route the spur cable to its destination.

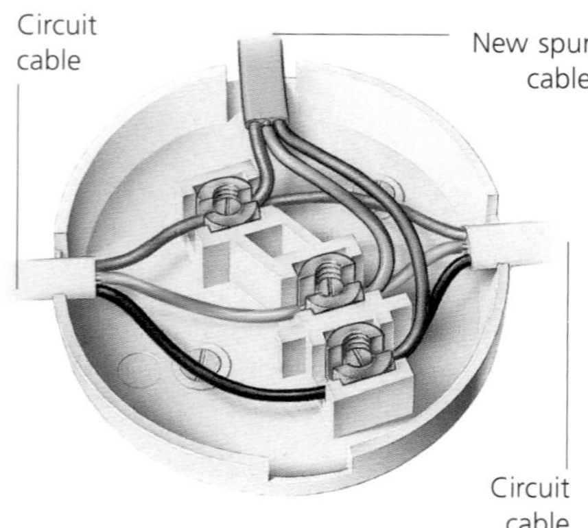

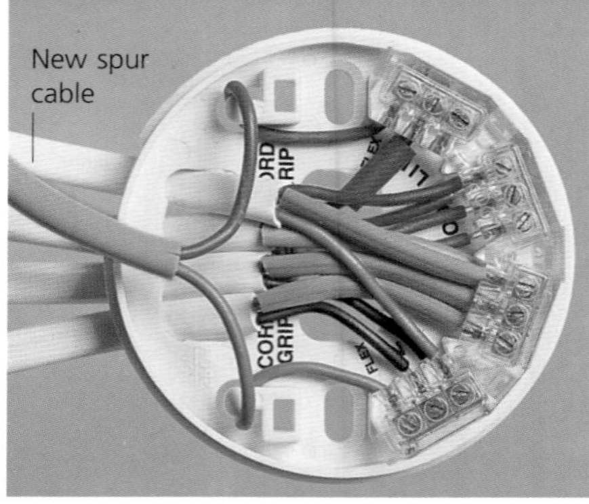

2 You can extend a lighting circuit in three ways. All three connection options require access to ceiling voids or the loft space. The spur cable can be connected directly into the terminals of an existing loop-in ceiling rose (above), or into a four-terminal junction box that is already supplying an existing lighting point (below).

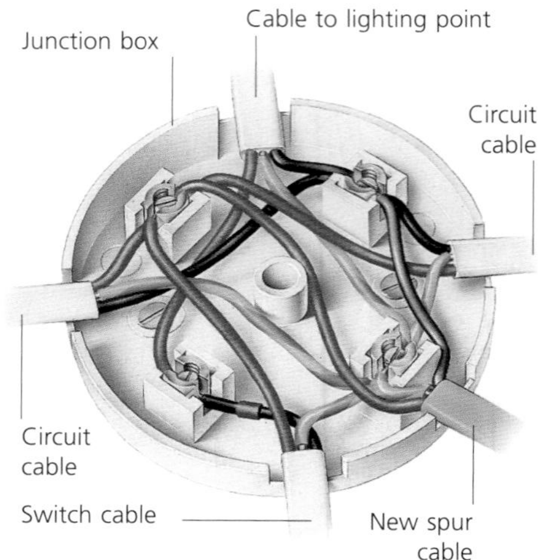

Alternatively You can make the connection via a four-terminal junction box inserted in the main lighting circuit cable. This box will supply the new light fitting and its switch. Care must be taken with this method to identify the circuit cable correctly.

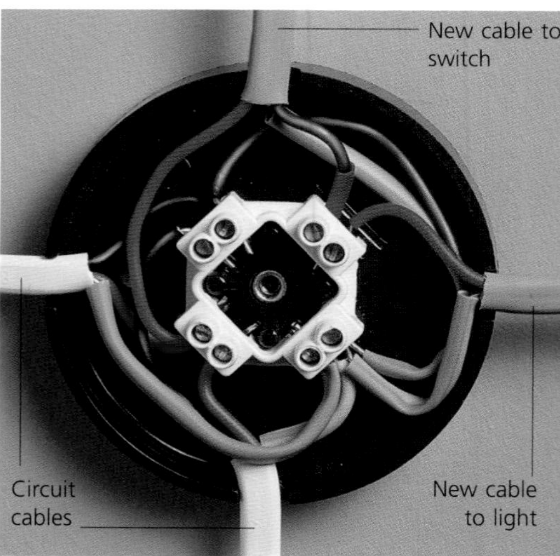

HELPFUL TIP

The Wiring Regulations allow an individual socket to be provided on its own non RCD-protected circuit, provided it is suitably labelled. Examples are dedicated freezer or computer sockets.

Adding circuits

Jobs such as installing an electric shower or cooker require an entirely new circuit, run from the consumer unit. The circuit cable runs first to a double-pole (DP) isolating switch, then on to the appliance. For an electric shower, the double-pole isolating switch is usually ceiling-mounted and must be cord-operated for safety. The circuit runs from here on to the shower unit, where it is connected to the appliance's terminal block.

In most situations there will not be a spare fuseway available for the new circuit cable, so one will have to be provided. There are two options for doing this, bearing in mind that the new circuit will almost certainly have to be RCD protected – all new bathroom circuits (page 268 and 287), all new socket outlet circuits (page 279) and any other circuits where the wiring in walls is not mechanically protected (page 282).

1 Fit a four-way enclosure with a 63amp/30mA RCD and two MCBs (the current rating of the RCD should equal the sum of the MCB ratings) so that you can add another circuit later on. In either case, you can install the new unit alongside the existing fusebox or consumer unit and connect the new circuit cable to it (see page 318). Call in your electricity supply company or a qualified electrician to connect the new unit to the main incoming power supply; you are not allowed to do this yourself.

2 Replace the existing fusebox or consumer unit with a new, larger consumer unit to which existing and new circuit cables can be connected. This has several advantages. The new unit will provide a single main on-off switch, RCD protection for any circuit and can include some spare MCBs for future extensions to the system.

Replacing a consumer unit is a job for a qualified electrician, who will specify its contents correctly for your requirements and reconnect the unit to the incoming supply.

Choosing cable for indoor circuits

Cable is used to wire up the circuits to ceiling roses, light switches, socket outlets and fixed appliances. It has a flattened oval cross-section, with a white or grey PVC outer sheath to protect the conductors inside.

• The most commonly used type has two conductors insulated in coloured PVC and a bare earth conductor, and is known as two-core-and-earth or twin-and-earth cable. Cable with three insulated conductors plus a bare earth is used solely for wiring between two-way switches (see page 297).
• Cable is made in several sizes, each identified by the cross-sectional area of the conductors in square millimetres (mm^2). Each circuit is wired in cable sized to match its current demand.

The conductors carrying the current in cable are colour-coded so they can be connected up correctly. In existing two-core-and-earth cable (see below right), the core coloured red is used as the live conductor, and the core coloured black as the neutral conductor. Since April 2006, cable with the old core colours has not been available. All new wiring work in the home must now be done using cable with new core colours (see below left). In two-core-and-earth cable, the live core is brown and the neutral core blue – the same as the colours used on flex cores, which were changed in 1968. The cores in three-core-and-earth cable are brown, grey and black.

There is no requirement to change existing wiring. Take care when making connections to existing wiring to link new brown cores to old red ones, and new blue cores to existing black ones. A warning notice must be fixed close to the consumer unit with the following wording: CAUTION This installation has wiring colours to two versions of BS7671. Great care should be taken before undertaking extension, alteration or repair that all conductors are correctly identified.

New cable colour key (effective April 2006)
Live (brown), Earth (bare wire), Neutral (blue)

Old cable colour key
Live (red), Earth (bare wire), Neutral (black)

1.0mm² Two-core-and-earth, used for lighting circuits.

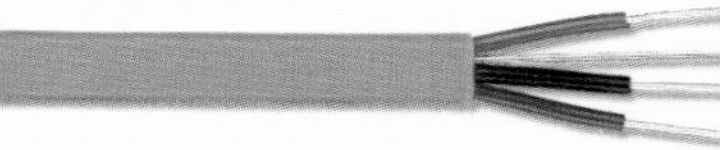

1.0mm² Three-core-and-earth, used for wiring between two-way switches. Cores are colour-coded for identification.

2.5mm² Two-core-and-earth, used for ring main circuits, 20amp radial socket outlet circuits for immersion heater, or storage heaters up to 20amp.

4mm² Two-core-and-earth, for radial power circuit with 30amp fuse.

6mm² Two-core-and-earth, used for 30amp circuit for cooker up to 12kW, or 45amp circuit for shower up to 8kW.

10mm² Two-core-and-earth, used for circuit for cooker above 12kW or shower rated above 8kW.

Sleeving for earth conductors When you strip off the outer sheath of a cable and prepare its conductors for connection, you must always cover the bare earth conductor with a length of green-and-yellow PVC sleeving of the appropriate size.

Preparing the circuit route

New cable can be run under floorboards and up and down walls – either buried in a 'chase' cut into the plaster, or hidden behind plasterboard or in surface-mounted trunking.

• You will have to lift floorboards to run cables in floor or ceiling voids. If the floor is solid, you will have to run it in trunking. Do not attempt to cut chases in a concrete floor; you are likely to damage the damp-proof membrane in the structure.
• Cable buried in plaster must be protected against penetration by screws or nails – at least by oval PVC conduit, but preferably by metal conduit or galvanised capping. See *17th Edition Rules* for more details.

Tools *Electronic detector (page 33); power drill; masonry drill bits; flat wood bits; twist drill bits; club hammer; brick bolster; cold chisel; claw hammer; pencil; trimming knife; hacksaw; chisel; spirit level; bradawl; filling knife; wire cutters and strippers; pliers; screwdrivers.*

Materials *Cable; cable clips; oval PVC conduit or metal capping; galvanised nails for fixing conduit; mounting boxes with screws; wallplugs and grommets; ceiling roses; plaster or interior filler; timber offcuts; nails.*

Fitting a flush mounting box

1 Hold the mounting box in position. For a socket outlet it should be at least 450mm above the floor or 150mm above worktop level. For a light switch, it should be at about shoulder height. Check with a spirit level that the box is horizontal and draw a line round it as a guide for drilling.

2 Using a masonry bit, drill holes all round the marked outline to the depth of the box. If the drill has no depth gauge, mark the bit with adhesive tape at the required depth and drill until the tape reaches the wall. Drill more holes within the marked area.

17TH EDITION RULES

The 17th Edition Wiring Regulations have new rules for cables in walls at a depth of less than 50mm. Even if they are run in the 'safe zones' (within 150mm of the top of the wall or the junction between walls or vertically/horizontally to an accessory), cables must either be physically protected or the circuit of which they are part be protected by a 30mA RCD. This requirement (which is likely to be modified in 2011) has serious implications for any electrician (amateur or professional) working on circuits that are not already RCD-protected (lighting circuits, for example). Existing RCD-protected socket outlet circuits are not affected, but other circuits being extended (or added) may need a new RCD in or near the consumer unit. See page 281.

It is not a good idea to have all circuits protected by a single RCD (one fault and everything goes out); new "17th Edition" consumer units are fitted with two RCDs and the circuits are shared between them.

3 Cut out the recess to the required depth with a brick bolster and club hammer. Brush out the recess, fit the mounting box and make marks with a pencil or bradawl through the fixing holes at the back of the box. Take out the box, drill holes at the marks and insert wallplugs.

4 Knock out one of the discs stamped in the back or sides of the box for the cable to enter. Fit a grommet in the hole. Do not fix the box until the cable has been run.

Laying cable under a floor

The cable can run alongside one joist or it can cross several at right angles.

1 Where the cable is to be at right angles to the joists, lift one or two boards to get access to the joists. Drill holes through the joists at least 50mm down from the top edge and big enough for the cable to pass through easily. If necessary, drill the holes at a shallow angle.

2 Thread the cable through the drilled holes. Leave a little slack between the joists.

3 Where the cable runs alongside a joist, lift a floorboard (or a section of one) about every 500mm along the joist. Feed the cable beneath the boards and secure it with clips to the side of the joist. Run it 50mm below the top edge of the joist and hammer in a clip where the cable is exposed.

Burying a cable in plaster

1 Plan the route for the cable. It should run vertically above or below a socket outlet or switch. A horizontal run should be close to the ceiling or between sockets. Never run it diagonally.

2 Mark the route with two lines 25mm apart. Avoid making sharp bends, wherever possible.

3 Check with an electronic detector along the route to make sure that you are not

going to interfere with any cables or pipes buried in the wall. If you are at all uncertain whether there is live wiring near the spot where you are working, switch off at the mains until you have made sure.

4 When you know that the route is safe, use a trimming knife to score along both edges of the chase.

5 Use a cold chisel and club hammer to cut out the plaster. Protect your eyes with safety goggles.

Alternatively Hire an electric chasing machine to cut out the chase. This creates a great deal of dust which spreads everywhere, so shut all doors.

6 Use a long masonry drill bit to make a hole behind the skirting board where cable is being taken down to run under the floor. Enlarge it with a cold chisel if necessary.

7 Cut a 3m length of oval PVC conduit to size and check that the chase is deep enough for it to fit easily. If it is too near the surface, only a skim of plaster or filler will cover it when you make good and it will probably crack. A covering of 5mm of plaster or filler over the conduit should be thick enough to prevent cracking.

Alternatively Use galvanised steel capping to protect cable. This is sold in 2m lengths, cut with a hacksaw and secured with galvanised nails. It needs a wider chase.

8 Feed the cable into the conduit and secure it in the chase with galvanised nails on each side. When the cable comes up behind a skirting, feed it into the conduit so that the end of the conduit is below the top of the skirting.

9 Leave enough spare cable at each end of the run to reach the mounting boxes easily. Ease the end of the cable or cables through the grommet into the mounting box. Slide the box into the recess and screw it into the wall behind.

Routes in stud partition walls

Cutting the route

With walls of plasterboard fixed to both sides of a timber frame, the cable can be run in the cavity behind the plasterboard. You will have to cut notches in the frame.

1 Use a bradawl or a stud detector to locate the frame, or a pipe/cable detector

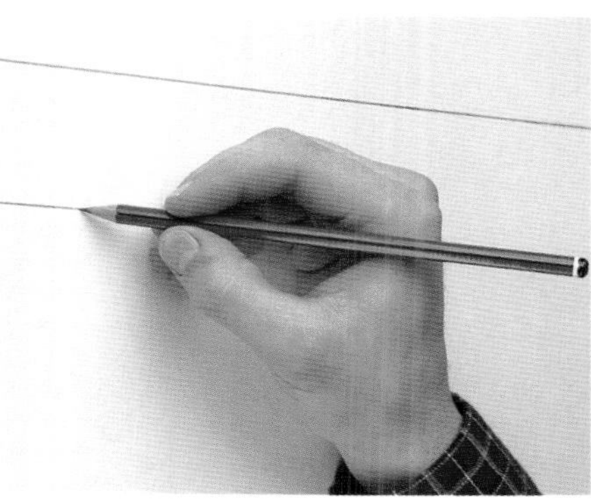

to locate the rows of nails holding the plasterboard to the frame. Draw pencil lines to show where the timbers are.

2 With a trimming knife, cut away a section of plasterboard about 120mm square wherever your planned route crosses a frame member.

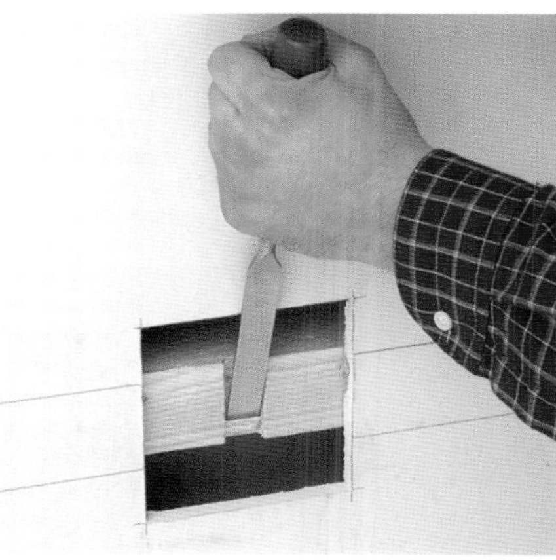

3 Chisel a groove in the exposed frame to hold the cable easily.

CABLE IN TRUNKING

Where it is not possible to lead cable under a floor or bury it in plaster, or if you want to reduce the labour, run the cable in surface-mounted mini-trunking. This protects the cable from damage as well as concealing it. The trunking is screwed or glued in place; the plastic cover clips on once the cables have been put in place.

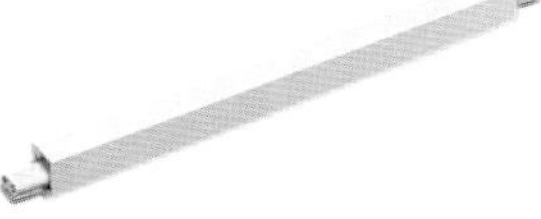

Mini-trunking is usually fitted along the top edge of skirting boards and alongside architraves. It is made in several sizes, some with two separate compartments.

Feeding in cable from above

1 Cut out a square of the plasterboard to reveal the top of the timber frame and drill a hole through it large enough to take the cable. You can use a long drill bit and drill at a slight angle, or fit a right-angle adaptor and drill vertically.

2 Thread the cable down through the drilled hole. Feed it down, ease it over each crosspiece of the frame and position it in the groove, allowing plenty of slack.

Feeding in cable from below

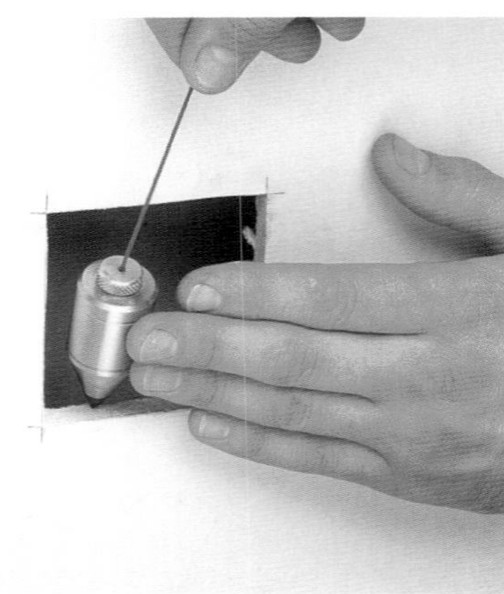

1 Cut out a square of plasterboard near floor level to reveal the base of the frame. Drill a hole through it for the cable, using a long bit and drilling at an angle or fitting a right-angle adaptor and drilling vertically. Feed a weighted cord down from the hole in the wall for the accessory.

2 Tie the cord to the cable and draw it up carefully, easing it over each crosspiece of the frame, and position it in the prepared grooves. Leave plenty of slack in the cable.

Feeding in cable sideways

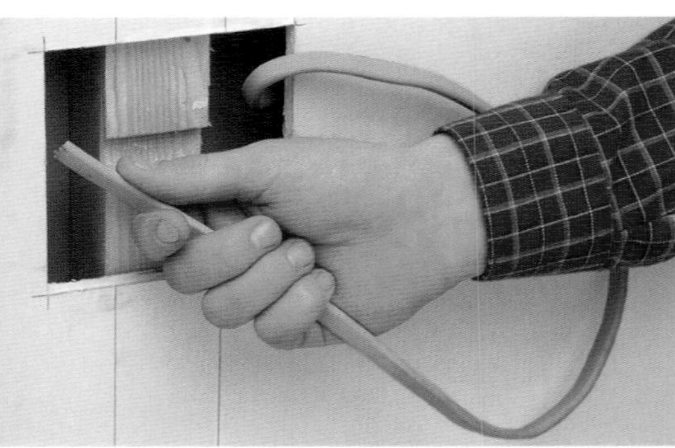

1 Push the cable along between the plasterboard panels. At each upright, draw out a loop of cable long enough to reach the next upright. Feed it along and set it in the prepared groove. When the cable is in the required position, cover the groove with a metal plate, pinned to the wood above and below, to prevent accidental damage from a nail or picture hook.

2 Cut new squares of plasterboard to replace the sections cut away. Tack them securely to the timbers at top and bottom, keeping the tacks well clear of the cable. Fill in round the edges of the squares with interior filler.

Fitting a plastic drylining box

Cut out the most convenient holes for the cable or cables to enter the mounting box. Hold the box in position, check with a spirit level that it is horizontal and draw a line round it. Cut away the marked section of plasterboard with a trimming knife. Feed the cable or cables into the box. Push the mounting box into the hole. Some boxes have spring-loaded fixing clips which simply snap into place as you push the box in; others have retractable lugs which you push out to hold the box. Prepare the conductors (page 271) and connect them to the terminals on the accessory faceplate. Screw the faceplate to the box.

Fitting a ceiling rose

A ceiling rose has to be screwed securely into wood above the plasterboard of the ceiling. It is not sufficient to screw it through plasterboard into a cavity fixing device. Plasterboard (or lath and plaster) is not strong enough to bear the weight of the light fitting and lampshade. The rose must be screwed to a joist or to a batten secured between the joists.

1 Mark the spot on the ceiling where you want the light fitting to hang.

2 Drill up through the ceiling at the marked spot. If the drill strikes a joist, probe with a bradawl about 50mm round the hole until you find space above the plasterboard. Insert a piece of spare cable through the hole to stick up above the ceiling as a marker.

3 Examine the ceiling from above, lifting a floorboard if necessary, and locate the hole with its piece of spare cable identifying it.

4 If the hole for the cables is between joists, cut a batten to length to fit between the joists.

5 Lay the batten between the joists with its edge touching the hole for the cables and mark the edge just beside the hole.

6 Drill through the centre of the batten, aligning the drill bit with the mark at the edge. The hole must be large enough to admit up to three or four cables.

Alternatively If the hole for the cables is immediately below a joist, chisel out a groove in the bottom of the joist to fit the cables. You may need to nail a block of wood to the side of the joist to widen it so you can screw the ceiling rose exactly where you wish. Chisel a groove down the side of the block that will fit against the joist. The groove must be large enough to hold three or four cables easily.

7 Thread the cables through the hole in the batten and then on through the hole in the ceiling.

8 Secure the batten to the joists with a nail hammered in at an angle at each end.

Alternatively Thread the cables through the prepared groove at the bottom of the joist and down through the hole in the ceiling. Fit the cables into the groove in the side of the prepared block of wood. Hold the block beside the joist and nail it in place, keeping the nails well clear of the cables.

9 Knock out the entry hole for the cables in the ceiling rose baseplate and thread the cables through the hole.

10 Hold the baseplate in place and insert a bradawl through the screw holes to penetrate through the plasterboard and pierce the timber above (see opposite).

11 Screw the baseplate into place.

Making good

Do not connect any sockets or switches until the walls or ceilings are made good or the connections are likely to be dislodged as you make the necessary repairs.

1 Fill all the chases cut in the plaster with new plaster or interior filler and leave it to dry completely. For the best finish, fill them in two stages and sand the repair smooth when the filler has set hard.

2 Replace any floorboards you have lifted. If any board is likely to pinch a cable where it starts to run up a wall from below the floor, cut a notch in the end of the board before you replace it. Boards, or sections of boards, that you may need to lift again in the future – to add a junction box in a lighting circuit, for example – should be screwed down, not nailed. They can then be lifted without being damaged.

Adding a spur to a ring main circuit

The easiest way of adding a socket outlet to your wiring system is to run a spur from an existing outlet on the circuit.

- The spur is wired from the back of the outlet and can supply one new single, double or triple socket outlet, or one fused connection unit (FCU).
- Care is needed to find a suitable socket outlet for the spur connection. You must not use one that is already supplying a spur or is itself supplied as a spur.
- Make sure that the spur will not increase the floor area of the rooms served by the circuit to more than 100m^2.

Tools *Suitable tools for preparing the route (page 282): insulated screwdrivers; circuit tester; trimming knife; wire cutters and strippers; pliers.*

Materials *2.5mm^2 three-core cable; cable clips; green-and-yellow earth sleeving; mounting box with grommets and fixing screws; socket with switch.*

Finding a supply socket

1 Turn off the power at the consumer unit and take out the fuse or switch off the MCB protecting the circuit you want to work on. Check that the socket outlet is dead – for example, by plugging in a lamp that you know to be working.

2 Unscrew the faceplate of the socket outlet you plan to use for the spur. Ease it away from its mounting box until you can see the cables. If there is only one, the outlet is on a spur. If there are three, it is supplying a spur. Neither can be used to supply another spur.

3 A socket outlet with two cables may be suitable, but check with a circuit tester (see right) before you go ahead. It could be the first outlet on a two-outlet spur installed earlier (but no longer permitted).

Preparation

When you have found a suitable socket outlet, ease its faceplate out and undo the terminal screws. Release the cores so that you can remove the faceplate. Remove the screws that hold the mounting box in place and carefully draw it out of its recess.

Prepare the route (page 282) for the cable from the supply socket to the new socket. Feed the cable ends into the mounting boxes for the new and the supply sockets after fitting grommets in the knock-out cable entry holes.

Fix the cable and the boxes in place (page 282) and make good the wall damage. When the plaster has set, prepare the new cable ends for connection (page 271). Put green-and-yellow sleeving on the bare earth cores.

Connecting at the supply socket

1 Match the cores on the new spur cable with those on the existing circuit cables – brown to red, blue to black, and green-and-yellow to green-and-yellow.

2 Connect the cores securely to the terminals on the faceplate. The red and brown cores go to the terminal marked L, the black and blue cores to the one marked N, and the green-and-yellow sleeved earth cores to the one marked E or ⏚.

3 Fold the cables carefully into the mounting box and position the faceplate over the box.

4 Screw the faceplate to the mounting box. Do not overtighten the screws or you may crack the faceplate.

Connecting at the new socket

1 Connect the new cable cores to the terminals – brown at L, blue at N and green-and-yellow at E (or ⏚).

2 Fold the cables carefully into the mounting box and position the faceplate over the box. Screw it in place.

3 At the consumer unit, replace the circuit fuse or switch on the MCB and restore the power supply.

USING A CONTINUITY TESTER TO CHECK A SPUR

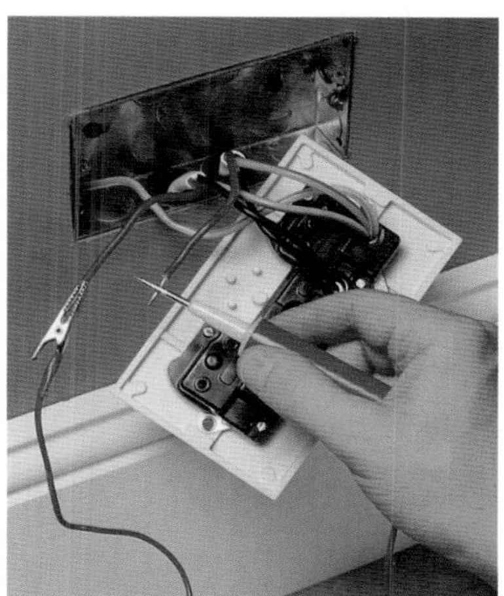

Use a continuity tester to check whether a socket outlet with two cables connected to it is on a ring main circuit.

1 Turn off the power at the consumer unit, remove the fuse or switch off the MCB protecting the circuit you will be working on, and unplug all appliances on the circuit.

2 At the socket outlet, disconnect the two red cores.

3 Attach the tester's clip to one end of each core and touch the probe to the other. If the socket is part of a ring circuit, the bulb on the tester will light up because you have completed the circuit; this is a suitable supply outlet for a spur.

If the tester does not light up, the outlet is itself on a spur and cannot be used to supply one.

Fitting a fused connection unit

A fused connection unit (FCU) connects wall heaters, extractor fans, cooker hoods and central-heating timers to the power supply.

- An FCU is the only kind of power supply point (except for a shaver socket) that is allowed in most bathrooms. It can supply an extractor fan or a wall-mounted heater, both of which must be out of reach of a person using the bath or shower (see page 268 for more details).
- The FCU can be installed as part of a new ring circuit, as a replacement for one of the socket outlets on an existing circuit, or can be installed on a spur (see page 285).
- A cartridge fuse is housed in a small fuseholder in the FCU faceplate. The fuseholder can be removed by undoing a screw or can be prised open with a screwdriver to give access to the fuse. This should be a 3amp fuse for appliances rated up to 700watts and a 13amp one for higher-wattage appliances.
- All FCUs fit a standard single mounting box. They may be switched or unswitched, and may have a neon indicator light. An unswitched FCU is suitable only for an appliance that has its own on/off switch. Do not use a switched FCU in a bathroom.
- For most appliances, choose an FCU that has a flex outlet at the front or side. In cases where the wiring from the FCU goes to a flex-outlet plate (see page 279), you do not need an entry hole: the wiring from the FCU to the flex outlet plate is done in two-core-and-earth cable, which can be buried in plaster or otherwise concealed.

Tools *Trimming knife; wire cutters and strippers; pliers; insulated screwdriver. Perhaps tools for preparing the route (page 282).*

Materials *Appliance in place with flex fitted; appropriate fuse.*

1 Turn off the power at the consumer unit and take out the fuse or switch off the MCB protecting the circuit you will be working on.

2 If the FCU is replacing an existing socket outlet, unscrew the faceplate and disconnect the cable cores from their terminals.

3 If the FCU is on a new spur, install the spur (page 285) up to the point where the mounting box and spur cable are in place. Remember that for many of the appliances connected to an FCU, the FCU should be above worktop height so that the switch and fuse are easily accessible.

4 Prepare the ends of the cable and the flex for connection (page 271). Remember to sleeve the bare earth conductor of the cable.

5 Feed the flex from the appliance to the back of the FCU. If there is a flex grip, release it sufficiently to let the flex through and then tighten it securely.

6 Connect the brown (live) core of the appliance flex into the terminal marked L and Load (or Out).

7 Connect the blue (neutral) core to the terminal marked N and Load (or Out).

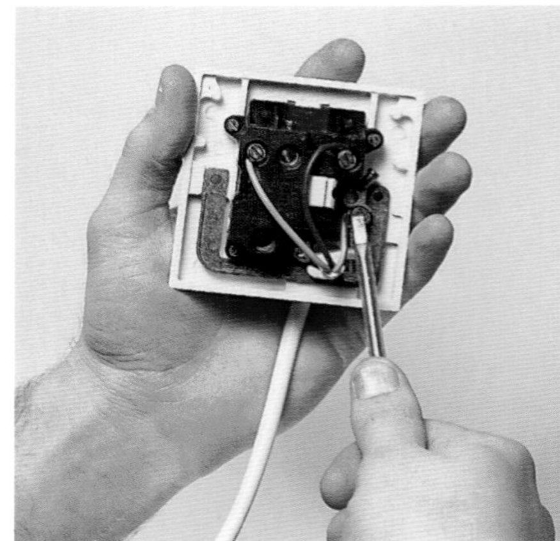

8 Connect the green-and-yellow earth core to one of the terminals marked E or ⏚. If the FCU has only one earth terminal, do not connect the core yet. It will share the earth terminal with the spur cable earth core and you should insert them both together when you are connecting the cable to the FCU.

Connecting a spur cable to the FCU

1 Connect the brown (live) spur cable core to the terminal marked L and Mains (or Feed or Supply or In).

2 Connect the blue (neutral) spur cable core to the terminal marked N and Mains (or Feed or Supply or In).

3 Connect the green-and-yellow sleeved earth core of the spur cable to the second terminal marked E or ⏚.

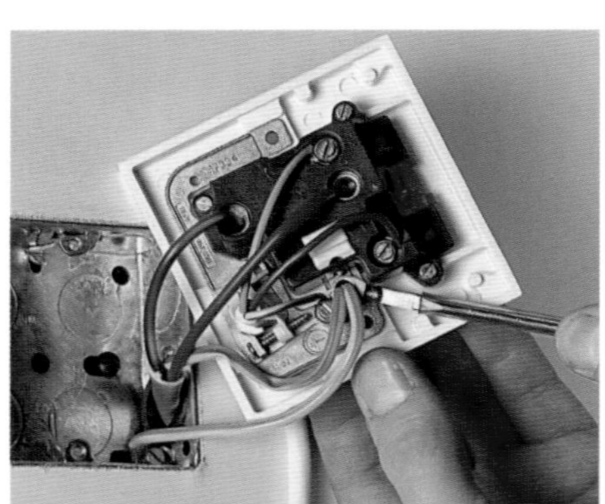

CONNECTING AN FCU AS PART OF A RING CIRCUIT

Connect the flex cores as for an FCU on a spur.

Connect the existing circuit cable cores into the terminals marked Mains (or Feed or Supply or In) as for an FCU on a spur – red to L, black to N, green-and-yellow to E or ⏚. There will be two conductors to screw into each terminal.

Screw the FCU to the mounting box as for one on a spur.

Alternatively If there is only one earth terminal, connect the earth cores from both flex and cable to it.

4 Add a flying earth link between the earth terminals on the faceplate and in a metal mounting box (see page 279).

5 Fit the correct cartridge fuse into the fuseholder in the FCU faceplate.

6 Fold the cable and flex neatly into the mounting box and press the faceplate against it.

7 Screw the faceplate into place. Do not over-tighten the screws or the plastic may crack.

Wiring electrical appliances in a bathroom

For safety, any electrical appliances installed in a bathroom should be run from a fused connection unit outside the room. Follow these instructions for preparing the wiring for an electrically heated towel rail or oil-filled radiator, an extractor fan or a shaver socket.

For a towel rail, radiator or extractor fan (page 242) cable runs from the back of the flex-outlet plate (page 279) to a switched fused connection unit (FCU) outside the bathroom. The FCU is fitted on a spur led from a socket outlet on the ring main circuit, as shown.

Tools *Suitable tools for preparing the route (page 282); trimming knife; pliers; insulated screwdrivers; wire cutters and strippers.*

Materials *Two standard single mounting boxes; 2.5mm² two-core-and-earth cable, cable clips; green-and-yellow sleeving for the earth cores; FCU; 13amp cartridge fuse; flex-outlet plate; towel rail, radiator or extractor fan (or shaver socket).*

Wiring outside the bathroom

Cable from fused connection unit to flex outlet plates (or shaver socket)

Switched fused connection unit, flush fitted on a spur from the ring circuit

Spur cable to fused connection unit from ring circuit, chased into wall

Supply socket on ring circuit for spur cable

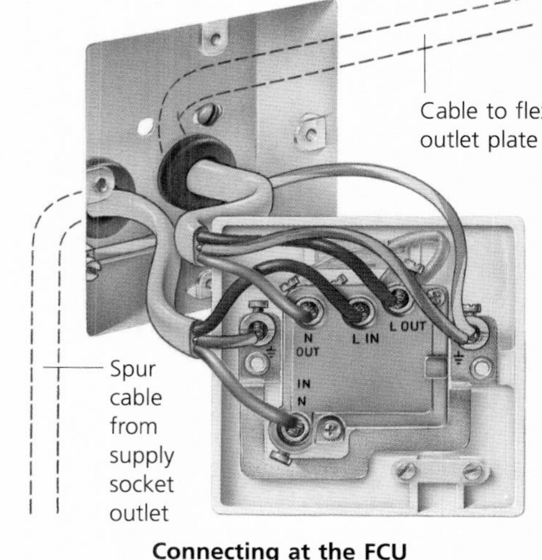

Connecting at the FCU

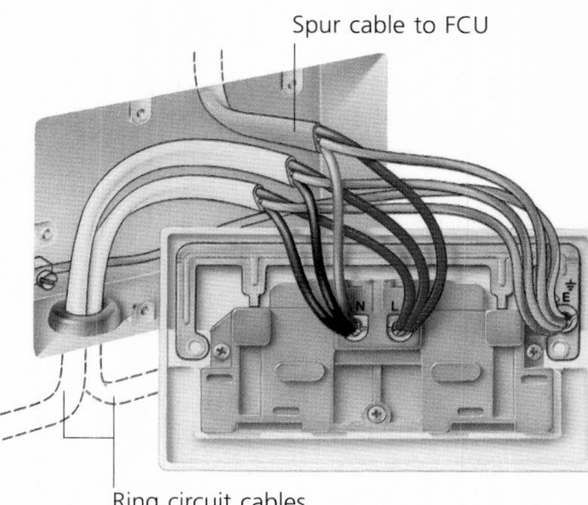

Connecting at the supply socket

Preparation

1 Check the earthing and bonding (page 267) and remedy any defects. All the metallic parts in the room must be cross-bonded to one another and to earth.

2 Turn off the power at the consumer unit and remove the fuse or switch off the MCB protecting the circuit you want to work on.

3 Find a suitable supply socket outlet from which to run the spur (page 285). Remove the faceplate and undo the terminal screws to release the conductors.

4 Prepare the route (page 282). Lead the spur cable from the supply socket outlet to the wall outside the bathroom where the FCU will be sited, and from there to the bathroom wall where the flex outlet plate is to be fixed.

5 Prepare recesses for the mounting boxes for the FCU and the flex outlet plate.

6 Fix two lengths of cable in place, one from the supply socket to the FCU, the other from the FCU to the flex outlet plate.

7 Feed the ends of the cables into the mounting boxes after fitting grommets in the knock-out holes. Screw the boxes into place. Feed the end of the appliance flex through to the back of the flex outlet plate. Prepare the new cable and the flex cores for connection (page 271).

8 Repair the plaster and wait for it to dry. Replace any floorboards.

Connecting at the socket outlet

1 Connect the cores of the new spur cable – brown with red, blue with black and green-and-yellow with green-and-yellow.

2 Add a flying earth link between the earth terminals on the faceplate and in a metal mounting box (see page 279).

3 Press the socket onto the mounting box without disturbing the conductors and screw it in place.

> **17TH EDITION RULES**
>
> There are new rules about wiring within bathrooms – see box on page 268.

Connecting at the FCU

1 Connect the spur cable from the supply socket to the FCU. The brown (live) core goes to the terminal marked L and Mains (or Supply, Feed or In). The blue (neutral) core goes to N and Mains (or Supply, Feed or In). The green-and-yellow earth core goes to the nearer of the two terminals marked E or ⏚. If the FCU has only one earth terminal, do not connect it yet.

2 Connect the cable leading from the FCU to the flex outlet plate. The brown (live) core goes to the terminal marked L and Load (or Out), the blue core to N and Load (or Out), and the green-and-yellow sleeved earth core to the second terminal marked E or ⏚. If there is only one earth terminal, connect both earth cores to it.

3 Add a flying earth link between the earth terminals on the faceplate and in a metal mounting box (see page 279).

4 Fit the 13amp fuse in the fuseholder in the FCU faceplate and screw the faceplate to the mounting box.

5 Then connect the cable that runs from the FCU to the flex outlet plate or shaver socket in the bathroom (overleaf).

Connecting a heated towel rail or electric radiator

The flex for an electrical appliance in a bathroom is normally wired into a flex outlet plate that does not have a switch.

1 Run a cable from a fused connection unit (FCU) outside the bathroom (page 287) to the position of the flex outlet plate. Fit a recessed mounting box into the wall and feed the cable into it then connect the new cable at the FCU and the flex outlet plate.

2 Connect the flex cores to one set of terminals – brown to L, blue to N, and green-and-yellow to E or ⏚.

3 Connect the cable cores to the other set of terminals – brown to L, blue to N and green-and-yellow to E or ⏚.

4 Add a flying earth link between the earth terminals on the faceplate and in the metal mounting box (see page 279).

5 Screw the faceplate to the mounting box.

Wiring inside the bathroom

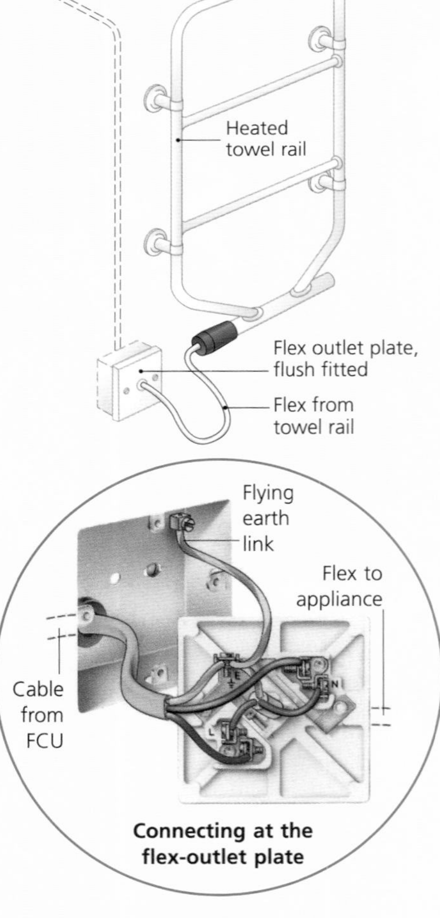

Connecting at the flex-outlet plate

Fitting a shaver point

The only electric socket outlet permitted in most bathrooms is a shaver point. Connect it to the main power supply via an FCU outside the bathroom (page 287).

- There are purpose-made mounting boxes for shaver supply units. Surface-mounted boxes are available but it is safer to fit a flush-mounted metal box into the wall.
- You can install the unit on a spur led from a suitable existing socket outlet on a ring main circuit.
- The preparation and general principles of installing a shaver supply unit on a spur from a ring-main circuit are the same as those described for connecting heated towel rails or radiators at the supply socket or FCU (page 287). In the bathroom, connect the cable run from the FCU to the shaver socket (below).

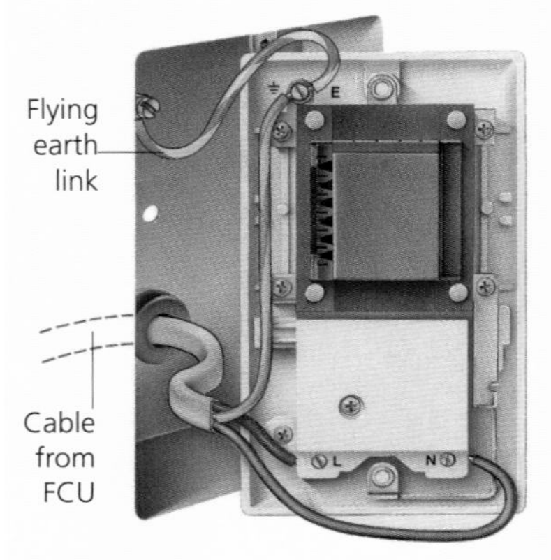

Connecting at the shaver point

Installing a shaver point on a lighting spur

It is also common to install a shaver socket on a spur led from a junction box inserted in the lighting circuit above the bathroom (see page 300).

1 Lead the spur cable from the lighting circuit to the shaver supply unit position, using 1mm² twin-core-and-earth cable.

2 Fit the mounting box for the shaver supply unit at about shoulder height on the wall. Feed in the cable through a grommet.

3 Prepare the end of the cable and connect the cores into the terminals on the shaver supply unit faceplate – brown to L, blue to N, and green-and-yellow to E or ⏚.

4 Fold the cable neatly into the mounting box and screw on the faceplate. Restore the power supply to the lighting circuit.

Installing an electric shower

An electric shower uses a lot of power in short bursts. It must have its own circuit leading from the consumer unit, protected by an RCD.

- For electric showers up to 7.2kW, the circuit can be run in 6mm² two-core-and-earth cable protected by a 32A MCB; up to 9.2kW, you will need 10mm² cable and a 40A MCB; up to 10kW, you would need to go to a 50A MCB.
- Under the latest Wiring Regulations (see Box on page 268), the shower circuit must be RCD protected, which means either using a spare RCD-protected 32A or 40A MCB in the existing consumer unit or replacing a spare MCB with an RCBO (a combined MCB and RCD) or fitting an extra enclosure as described on page 281.
- The circuit cable runs first to a pull-cord switch with neon and mechanical indicators.
- From the switch, the cable runs to the back or base of the shower heater unit, where it is connected to a terminal connector block inside the unit.
- Follow the maker's instructions on fitting the unit to the wall and plumbing it in.

Tools *Suitable tools for preparing the route (page 282); insulated screwdrivers; trimming knife; wire strippers and cutters; pliers.*

Materials *Two-core-and-earth cable of appropriate size; green-and-yellow plastic sleeving for earth conductors; cable clips; 45amp double-pole pull-cord switch with neon warning light and mechanical on/off indicator; shower heater unit.*

Preparation

1 Plumb the unit over the bath or in a shower cubicle (see page 360).

2 Take off the front cover of the shower heater and hold the back plate against the wall. Mark the wall through the cable entry point so that you know where to lead the cable, and also through the screw fixing points. Drill and plug the screw fixing points.

3 Check the main and supplementary bonding (page 267).

4 Prepare the route for the cable (page 282). There is no need to switch off the electricity until you are ready to make the final connection at the consumer unit. Make the route from the consumer unit to the pull-cord switch position on the ceiling of the bathroom or shower room. Continue the route from the switch to a point on the ceiling above the shower and then vertically down the wall to the position of the shower heater unit.

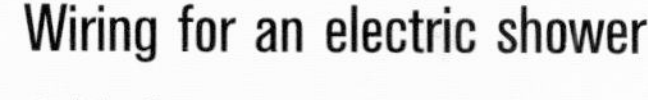

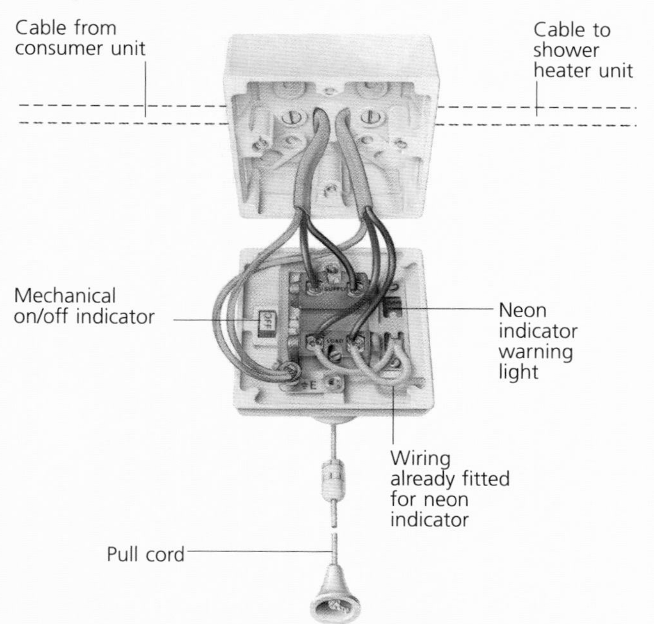

Connecting at the ceiling switch

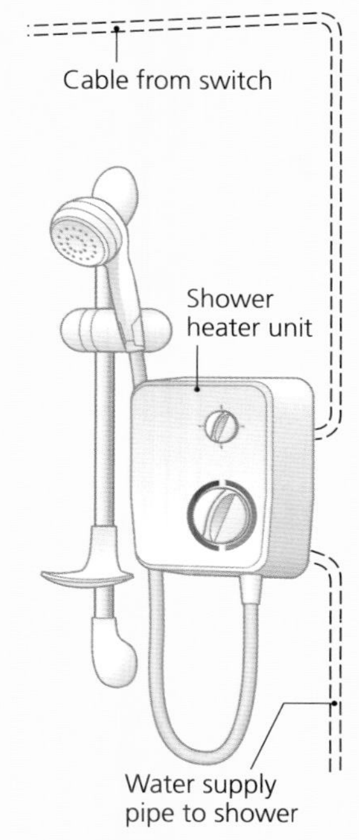

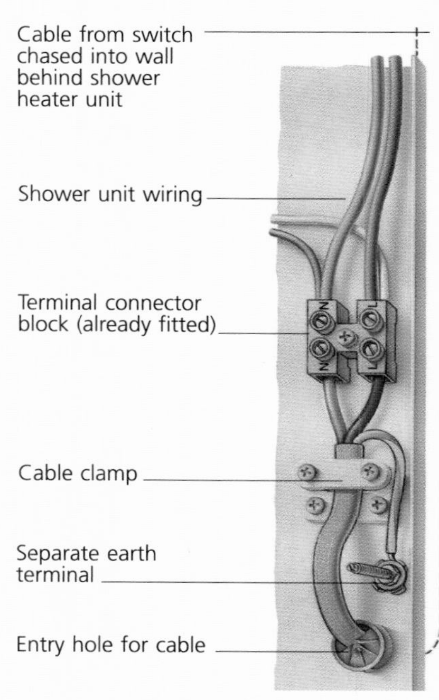

Connecting at the shower heater unit

5 Fit the baseplate for the switch to the ceiling (page 284), making sure that the fixing is secure enough to withstand the switch cord being pulled. Before you screw it in place, knock out two of the stamped circles for the cables to enter.

6 Lay the cable along the route, from the consumer unit to the double-pole switch and from the switch to the cable entry point on the shower heater unit. Allow sufficient cable at each end to reach all the terminals comfortably.

7 Feed the cable ends into the switch. Then feed the cable through the entry hole of the shower heater. Screw the unit to the wall.

8 Prepare all the cable ends for connection (page 271). Fit green-and-yellow sleeving on all the bare earth conductors.

9 If there is no spare suitable MCB on the consumer unit, fit a separate enclosure as described on page 281. You can get special 'shower protection' units that contain a double-pole 40amp RCBO or a (63amp/30mA) RCD feeding a 50amp MCB.

10 Complete the plumbing connections.

EARTH SAFETY

Cross-bond the shower supply pipework to earth by fitting an earth clamp to the pipe and connecting 4mm² single-core earth cable to it. Run this cable to the earth terminal on either the ceiling-mounted switch or the shower unit, whichever is the more convenient.

Connecting the ceiling switch

1 Insert the two green-and-yellow sleeved earth cores into the terminal marked E or ⏚ and connect them tightly in place.

2 Connect the brown and blue cores of the cable from the ceiling switch to the shower unit. The brown core goes to the terminal marked L and Load (or Out) and the blue core to the terminal marked N and Load (or Out). Check the neon indicator cores at the same time, one (it does not matter which) to the same terminal as the brown cable core and the other to the same as the blue core. Do not dislodge the bulb.

3 Connect the brown and blue cores of the cable from the consumer unit to the other terminals (marked Supply, Feed or In). Connect the brown core to the terminal marked L and the blue core to the terminal marked N. Fit the switch cover over the baseplate and screw the cover in place.

Connecting at the heater unit

Do not disturb the internal wiring already fitted in the shower unit.

1 Release the screws of the cable clamp, lead the cable under the clamp and screw the clamp back in place.

2 Connect the cores of the cable to the terminal connector block incorporated in the shower heater unit. Flex cores will already be connected at one side of the block. Connect the brown cable core to the terminal opposite the brown flex core, and the blue cable core to the terminal opposite the blue flex core.

3 Instead of a pair of earth terminals on the connector block, there may be a single separate earth terminal marked E or ⏚. Connect the green-and-yellow sleeved cable earth core to this terminal.

Alternatively If the connector block has a third terminal for the earth core, connect the sleeved core to it opposite the green-and-yellow flex core already connected there.

Connecting the circuit at the consumer unit

1 Turn off the power at the consumer unit and switch off the RCD-protected MCB you will be using for the new circuit.

2 Unscrew the cover of the consumer unit. If the unit has a wooden frame, drill a hole through it and feed in the new cable.

Alternatively On a metal unit, knock out the entry hole immediately above the MCB you will be using. Fit a rubber grommet into the hole and feed in the cable.

3 Check that you have stripped off enough outer sheath from the cable for the cores to reach their terminals easily.

4 Connect the cores tightly to their terminals: brown to the terminal at the top of the MCB; blue to a free terminal on the neutral terminal block; sleeved green-and-yellow earth core to a free terminal on the earth terminal block.

5 Replace the cover of the consumer unit. If you have fitted a separate enclosure to provide RCD protection, ask your electricity supplier to connect this up.

Understanding an electric cooker circuit

An electric cooker uses so much electricity that it must have its own circuit. If it shared a circuit with other appliances the circuit would frequently be overloaded.

At the consumer unit The cooker circuit is protected by a 30amp fuse or 32amp MCB for a cooker rated at up to 12kW.

- A 45amp fuse or 40amp MCB is needed for a cooker rated at above 12kW.
- A separate oven and hob operating on the same circuit may have a higher rating than 12kW.
- A circuit protected by a 30amp fuse or a 32amp MCB needs to be run in $6mm^2$ two-core-and-earth cable; a circuit protected by a 45amp fuse or 40amp MCB needs larger $10mm^2$ two-core-and-earth cable.

The cable runs from the consumer unit to a cooker switch This is mounted above worktop height on the kitchen wall – beside the cooker, not above it.

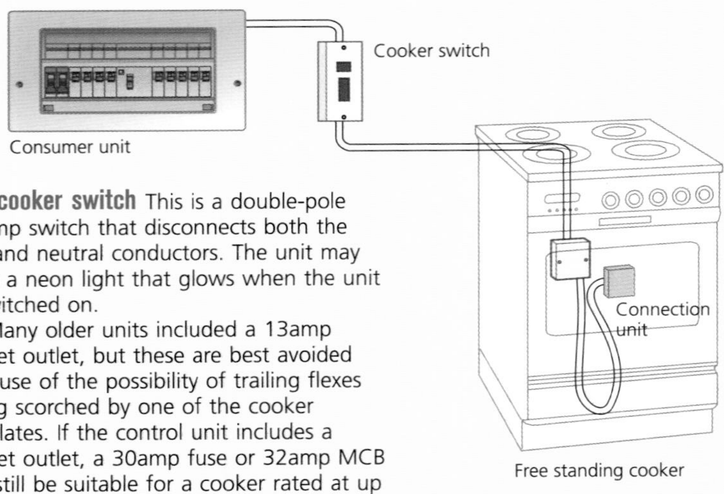

The cooker switch This is a double-pole 45amp switch that disconnects both the live and neutral conductors. The unit may have a neon light that glows when the unit is switched on.

Many older units included a 13amp socket outlet, but these are best avoided because of the possibility of trailing flexes being scorched by one of the cooker hotplates. If the control unit includes a socket outlet, a 30amp fuse or 32amp MCB will still be suitable for a cooker rated at up to 10kW.

For a free-standing cooker A second length of cable is buried in the wall to run from the cooker switch to a cooker connection unit fitted on the wall about 600mm above floor level behind the cooker. A 2m length of cable (not flex) runs from the connection unit to the cooker, so that the cooker can be drawn away from the wall when necessary. Use the same size of cable for this as for the rest of the circuit.

For a separate oven and hob These can be connected to one cooker switch provided that neither the hob nor the oven is more than 2m away from the switch.

- You can make the connection by running two cables from the switch, one to the oven and the other to the hob.
- Alternatively, you can run one length of cable from the switch to one part of the cooker and a second length of cable from there to the second part of the cooker.
- It is possible to connect the cable directly into the oven and the hob (as they are permanently built-in, but it is much better practice to install a cooker connection unit (or two cooker connection units) as for a free-standing cooker.
- If either oven and hob would be more than 2m away from a single cooker switch, you will need two switches, but both can be connected to the same cooker circuit.

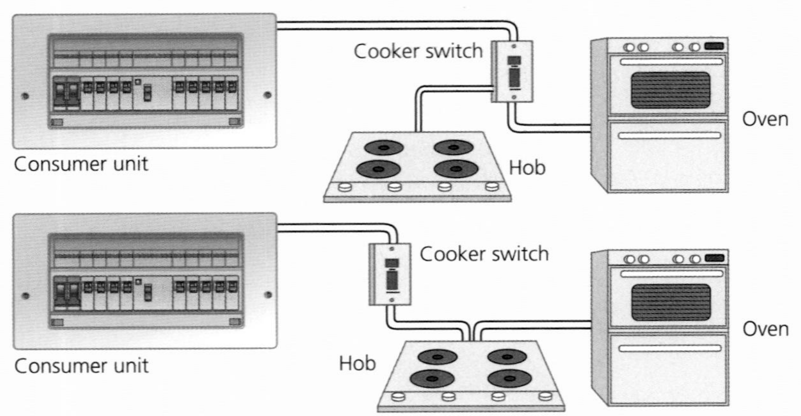

Installing a new cooker circuit

Plan the cable route (page 282) from the cooker switch back to the consumer unit. To meet Wiring Regulations, a new cooker circuit must be RCD-protected. If there is not an RCD-protected MCB to connect to, either fit an RCBO as for a shower (page 288) or fit a new enclosure (page 281).

Tools *Suitable tools for preparing the route (page 282); trimming knife; insulated screwdrivers; wire cutters and strippers; pliers.*

Materials *45amp cooker switch with mounting box; cooker connection unit(s) with mounting box(es); grommets; fixing screws and wallplugs; two-core-and-earth cable and green-and-yellow plastic sleeving of the correct size; cable clips; free-standing cooker or separate oven and hob; available MCB of the correct rating.*

Putting in the cables

There is no need to switch off at the mains until you are ready to connect the new circuit cable to the consumer unit.

1 Prepare the route (page 282), leading it from near the consumer unit to the cooker switch. From there lead it to the cooker connection unit behind a free-standing cooker, or to connection units behind a separate oven and hob.

2 Fit the mounting box for the cooker switch and fit the mounting box(es) for the connection unit(s). Remember to remove knock-outs from the mounting boxes for the cables to enter, and to fit grommets in the holes.

3 Fit lengths of cable along the route from the consumer unit to the switch, and from the switch to the connection units. Do not feed the cable into the consumer unit but feed the other cable ends into the mounting boxes. Allow enough spare cable at the ends to reach all the terminals easily. Prepare the cable ends for connection (page 271), remembering to sleeve the earth conductors.

4 Repair the plaster and wait for it to dry. Replace any floorboards you have lifted.

Connecting at the switch

1 Connect the cable from the consumer unit to the terminals of the cooker switch. Connect the brown core to the terminal marked L and In. Connect the blue core to the terminal marked N and In. Connect the green-and-yellow-sleeved earth core to the nearer of the terminals marked E or ⏚.

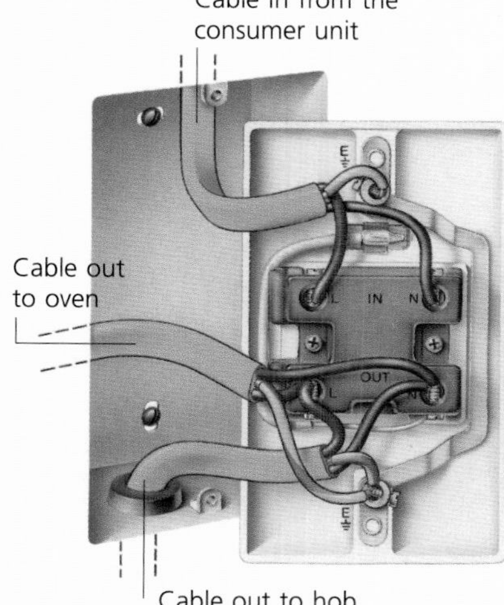

Connecting at the cooker switch
Two cables lead to a separate oven and hob. Only one goes to a free-standing cooker or to the oven and hob if they are to one side of the control unit.

2 Connect the cable leading out to the connection unit(s) to the terminals behind the switch plate. Take the brown core to the terminal marked L and Out, and the blue core to the terminal marked N and Out. Connect the green-and-yellow sleeved earth core to the nearer of the terminals marked E or ⏚.

If you are leading separate cables to an oven and hob, there will be two outgoing sets of cores. Match the cores in pairs – brown with brown, blue with blue and green-and-yellow with green-and-yellow. Insert the pairs of cores into the correct terminals and screw them in place.

Connecting a free-standing cooker at the connection unit

1 Remove the screws holding the cover to the metal frame. Then unscrew and remove the cable clamp at the bottom of the frame.

Wiring at the connection unit

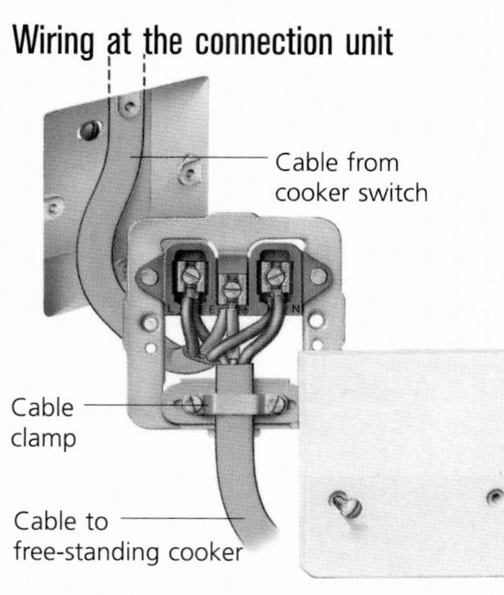

2 Pair the cable cores from the cooker switch and to the cooker – brown with brown, blue with blue, and green-and-yellow with green-and-yellow. Screw the pairs into the terminal block on the frame – brown to L, blue to N and green-and-yellow to E or ⏚.

3 Screw the frame to the mounting box and screw on the cable clamp.

4 Screw the cover of the connection unit in place.

Connecting to a free-standing cooker

1 Remove the metal plate covering the terminals on the back of the cooker. Release the cable clamp.

2 Connect the supply cable cores to their terminals – brown to L and blue to N. Sometimes the cores have to be bent round a pillar and held down with brass washers and nuts. Make sure enough insulation has been removed for the bare wire to wind round the pillars. Connect the green-and-yellow sleeved earth core to E or ⏚.

3 Screw the clamp over the cable. Screw the plate back over the terminals.

Connecting to the consumer unit

1 Turn off the main switch at the consumer unit and switch off the MCB for the cooker circuit. Make sure the cooker switch and all cooker controls are off. Replace MCB with an RCBO if necessary.

2 Remove the screws of the consumer unit cover and take it off.

3 Drill through the frame of the consumer unit if it is wooden, or knock out an entry hole and fit a grommet if it is a metal or plastic one. Feed in the cable. Make sure that you have removed enough outer sheath for the cores to reach the terminals.

4 Connect the blue core to a spare terminal at the neutral terminal block and connect the brown core to the terminal on the MCB or RCBO.

5 Connect the green-and-yellow sleeved earth core to a spare terminal at the earth terminal block.

6 Switch on the MCB or RCBO.

7 Screw on the cover of the consumer unit and turn the main switch back on.

CONNECTING A SEPARATE OVEN AND HOB

If you have led two cables from the control unit, one each for the oven and hob, connect each cable in the same way as a free-standing cooker (left) and secure under the clamp.

Alternatively, if you have led one cable from the cooker switch to the first component (via a connection unit), you will have two cables to connect and clamp there – one from the cooker switch and one to the second component.

Match the cores – brown with brown, blue with blue, and green-and-yellow with green-and-yellow. Connect them to the terminals – brown to L, blue to N, and green-and-yellow to E or ⏚.

Connect the ongoing cable to the second component as for a free-standing cooker.

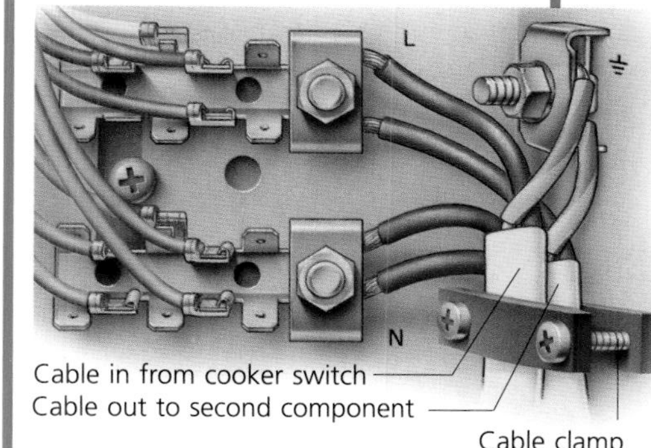

Installing a new ring main circuit

A ring main circuit to supply socket outlets starts at the consumer unit. A 2.5mm² two-core-and-earth cable runs round the rooms supplied by the circuit, looping into and out of each socket outlet before returning to the consumer unit to complete the ring. All new socket outlet circuits must now be provided with RCD protection.

If you have a modern consumer unit, fitted with a 30mA RCD and with a spare RCD-protected 32amp MCB, and are installing a new ring circuit – perhaps to serve an extension – you can connect the new circuit to the consumer unit. If your consumer unit has spare non RCD-protected MCBs, you may be able to replace one with a 32A RCBO (combined RCD and MCB) as for an electric shower circuit (page 288). For older consumer units, fit a new enclosure (page 281) or have a new consumer unit fitted.

- Any number of single, double or triple socket outlets can be installed on the new ring main circuit, but the floor area of the rooms served by the circuit must not exceed 100m².
- If a socket outlet is needed in a position that is not on the most convenient route for the ring circuit, you can run a non-fused spur to it from one of the socket outlets on the ring, but this will reduce the possibility of adding spurs later.
- The number of non-fused spurs must not exceed the number of outlets on the ring.

Tools *Suitable tools for preparing the route (page 282); trimming knife; insulated screwdrivers; wire strippers and cutters; pliers.*

Materials *Mounting boxes; screws and wallplugs; grommets; socket outlets (and perhaps FCUs); 2.5mm² two-core-and-earth cable; green-and-yellow plastic sleeving for bare earth cores; cable clips; fuses for FCUs; available 32amp MCB in the consumer unit.*

Preparation

1 Prepare the route (page 282), leading it from the consumer unit to the nearest socket outlet position on the new ring main circuit, and on from there to each socket outlet position in turn. Prepare the route for any spurs branching off the ring main circuit. Lead the route back from the final socket outlet position to the consumer unit.

2 Prepare recesses for the mounting boxes of the new socket outlets.

3 Fit the mounting boxes in position, remembering to knock out the most convenient cable entry holes, and fit grommets in metal boxes.

4 Lay the cable along the route (page 283). Start above the consumer unit, leaving plenty of spare cable for the cores to reach the terminals in the unit easily. Do not interfere with the consumer unit at this stage. Continue along the route, taking the cable in and out of the most convenient entry holes at each mounting box. Cut the cable at each box, leaving 100mm spare at each cut. Fit branch cables along the route to any spurs. Again leave 100mm spare at each end of the cable. Lead the cable back from the last socket outlet on the circuit to the consumer unit.

5 Prepare all the cable ends (page 271) for connection at the socket outlets.

6 Repair the plaster and wait for it to dry completely. Replace any floorboards you have lifted. Do not fix them down if you will be removing old wiring from under them later.

Connecting the socket outlets

1 At each socket outlet, pair the two sets of cable cores – brown with brown, blue with blue, and green-and-yellow with green-and-yellow.

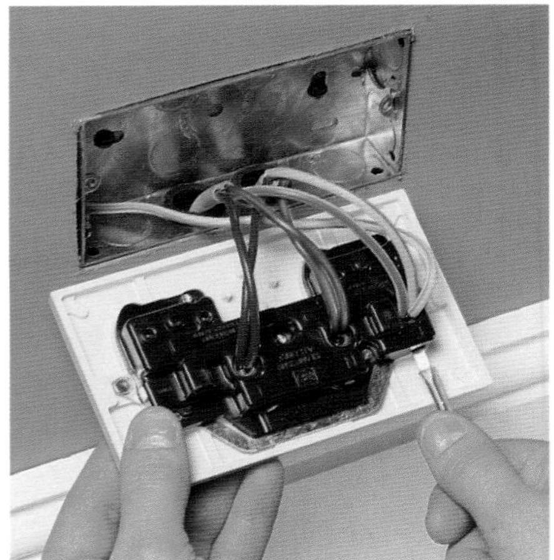

2 Connect the cores into the terminals on the rear of the faceplate – browns to L, blues to N, and green-and-yellows to E or ⏚. Add a flying earth link (see step 3 on page 279) between the earth terminal on the faceplate and the earth terminal in the mounting box if the latter is metal.

3 Fold the two cables neatly back into the mounting box and press the faceplate into position over the box. Screw it in place until there is no gap between the faceplate and the mounting box. Do not overtighten the screws or the plastic may crack.

Planning a ring circuit

1 Draw a plan of the rooms that the ring circuit will supply. The new circuit might serve the kitchen only, all the other ground floor rooms, all the upper floor rooms or the socket outlets in an extension.

2 Mark on the plan where socket outlets are needed – and where they might be needed in the future. Most rooms will need sockets on at least two sides. Large rooms may need them on three sides and at two places along the sides. A choice of socket positions does away with flexes trailing across rooms.

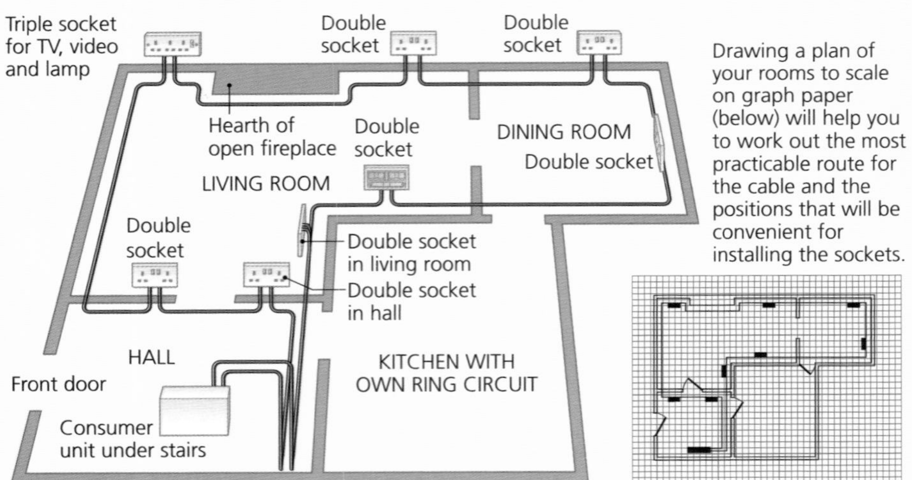

Drawing a plan of your rooms to scale on graph paper (below) will help you to work out the most practicable route for the cable and the positions that will be convenient for installing the sockets.

3 Install a double socket at each new outlet. In a kitchen or living room, triple sockets may be wiser. At some positions you may want to fit a fused connection unit (FCU) rather than a socket for a built-in appliance, such as an extractor fan or cooker hood (page 286).

4 The recommended number of double socket outlets is: kitchen and living room 6 to 10 (each); bedrooms 4 to 6 (each); dining room 3; hall, garage and utility room 2; study/home office 6; landing/stairs and loft 1.

Connecting spur socket outlets

1 At socket outlets supplying spurs, there will be three sets of cable cores – one from the previous outlet on the circuit, one going to the next outlet, and one for the spur. Match the cores in threes, then follow steps 2 and 3 from the previous section.

2 The socket outlet at the end of a spur has only one set of cores to connect. Follow steps 2 and 3 from the previous section.

Connecting FCUs

The appliance should be fitted in place, complete with its flex.

1 Feed the flex through the entry hole to the back of the fused connection unit (FCU) and prepare the end of the flex for connection (page 271).

2 Connect the flex cores – brown to L and Load (or Out), blue to N and Load (or Out), and green-and-yellow to the nearer of the two terminals marked E or ⏚.

3 Pair the cores from the two cables, brown with brown, blue with blue, and green-and-yellow with green-and-yellow. (If the FCU has been fitted at the end of a spur there will be only one cable.)

4 Connect the cable cores to their terminals – brown cores to the one marked L and Mains (or Supply or Feed or In), blue cores to the one marked N and Mains (or Supply or Feed or In) and green-and-yellow cores to the nearer of the two terminals marked E or ⏚. Add a flying earth link to the earth terminal in a metal box (page 279).

5 Fit a 3amp or 13amp cartridge fuse in the fuseholder to suit the wattage rating of the appliance.

6 Fold the cable(s) and flex neatly into the mounting box and press the FCU faceplate into position. Screw it to the mounting box.

Testing the new circuit

Test the continuity of each conductor in the circuit (see panel, below). Check and tighten all connections, if necessary.

Connecting at the consumer unit

1 Turn off the main switch on the consumer unit. Remove the retaining screws and the cover of the consumer unit.

SAFETY WARNING

The main switch disconnects only the MCBs and the cables leading out from the consumer unit to the household circuits. It does not disconnect the cables entering via the meter from the service cable. Do not interfere with these cables. They are always live at mains voltage.

2 Drill though the top of the consumer unit or knock out an entry hole and fit a grommet. Feed in the cables and make sure that enough sheath has been removed for the cores to reach the terminals easily.

3 Match the cores of the circuit cables – brown with brown, blue with blue, and prepare cable ends green-and-yellow with green-and-yellow.

4 Connect the cores to their terminals – brown cores to the terminal on the spare 32amp MCB, blue cores to the neutral terminal block, and green-and-yellow sleeved earth cores to the earth terminal.

5 Switch on the MCB. Replace the cover of the consumer unit.

6 Turn on the main switch and test the circuit by connecting a table lamp you know to be working to each socket outlet in turn or use a plug-in socket tester.

Having a consumer unit installed

If you do not have a modern consumer unit, arrange with your electricity supply company (or another approved electrical contractor) to install one. The installer will connect it to the meter and reconnect the new and existing circuit cables to it.

Disconnecting the old wiring

1 At the fuse board, turn off the main switch or switches that controlled the superseded circuits and remove any fuses. You can arrange for your energy supplier to disconnect the old system from their meter.

2 Trace the cables leading from the switch to the old socket outlets down to the floor or up to the ceiling. Cut them off there.

3 At each of the old socket outlets, unscrew the faceplate and release the cable cores from the terminals. Unscrew and prise out the mounting box.

4 To remove all the old wiring you may have to lift several floorboards. Remove as much as you can and wherever possible any junction boxes, but leave any conduits in the wall. Repair the walls as necessary, and replace any floorboards you lifted.

5 Remove the old main switch and old fuse box once they have been disconnected by the supply company. Remove the cables that lead from them. If the old system has not been disconnected, do not remove the switch or fuse box. Keep the switch off and the fuse out.

TESTING A NEW RING CIRCUIT

When you install a new ring circuit, use a circuit tester to check that all the connections are sound *before* you connect it at the consumer unit. Where the two cable ends approach the consumer unit, clip the tester to the end of one brown core and put the probe on the other. If the tester fails to light, tighten the connections all round the circuit. Carry out the same checking procedure with the blue and earth cores.

If the tester lights when it is linking two *different* cores there is a serious wiring fault and you should call in a qualified electrician.

Choosing light switches

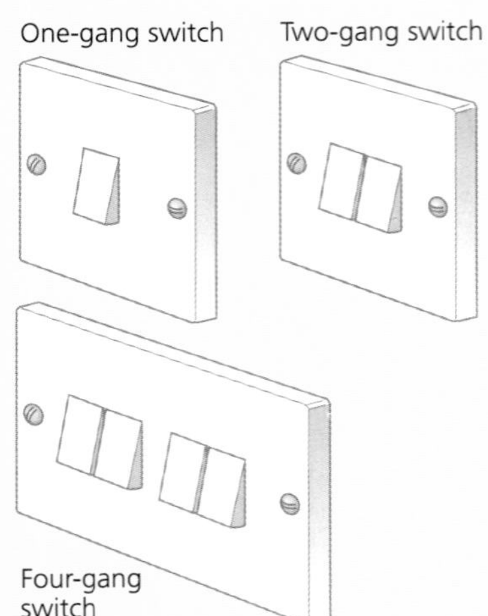

Plastic switches The most common are white plastic, designed to blend with light-coloured paintwork. There is no earth terminal for the cable behind plastic light switches; it is in the mounting box.

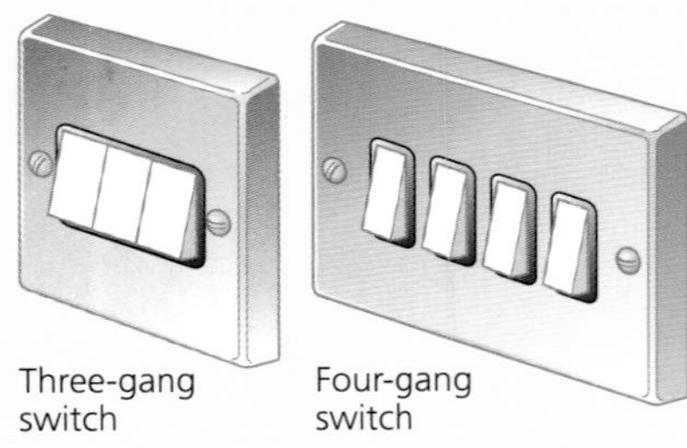

Metal switches Metal switches are made in satin finish or shiny brass, chrome or stainless steel; some brass switches have decorative scrolling at the edge. All metal switches must have an earth terminal on the rear of the faceplate. The switch rockers are fixed in plastic inserts.

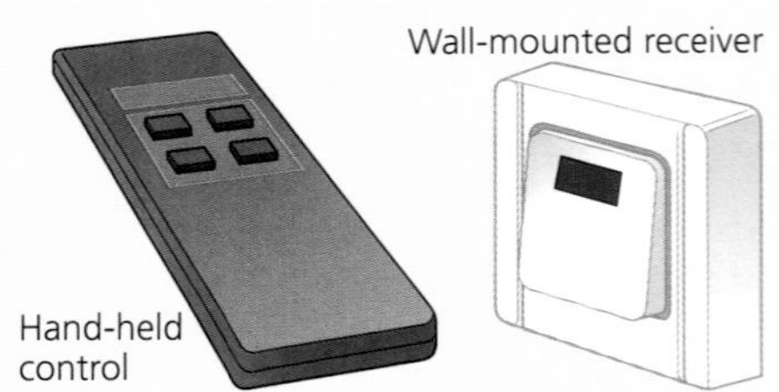

Remote control switches Remote control switches are operated by an infra-red signal from a control unit; this triggers a wall-mounted receiver which acts as the switch. The receiver must be in sight of the control unit but can be up to 8m away. The switch can also be operated by hand.

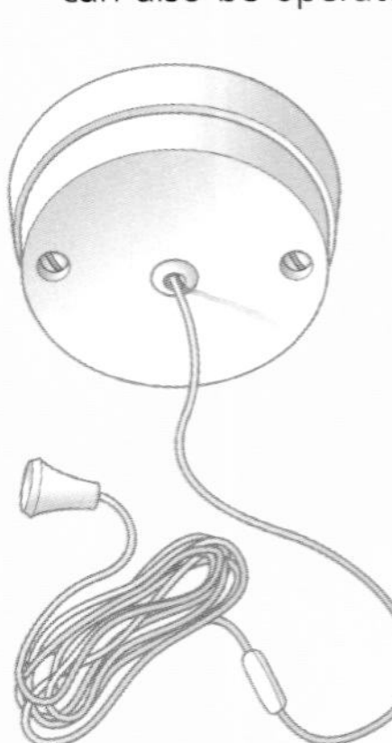

Pull-cord switches
If a pull-cord switch is fitted in a bathroom the mechanism must be well out of reach of anyone who is using the bath or shower. Pull-cord switches are useful in bedrooms, too.

MOUNTING BOXES

Boxes for surface mounting can be metal or plastic, but flush-fitting boxes for solid walls are only of metal. A single mounting box will take a faceplate with one, two or three switches (gangs); a double box is needed for a faceplate with four or six switches. All metal boxes must have an earth terminal for the earth core of the switch cable; many plastic boxes also have one.

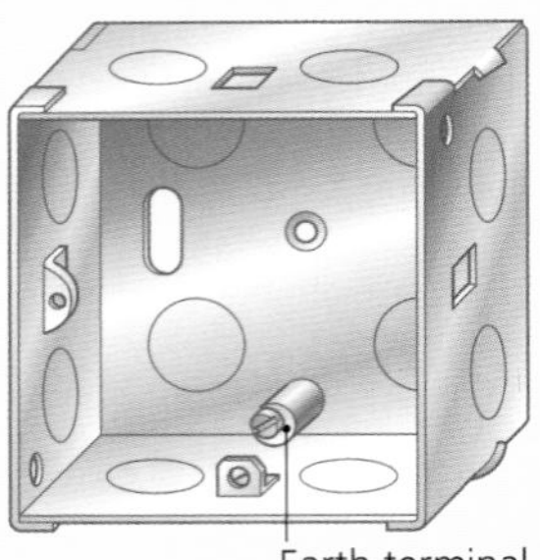

25mm metal box

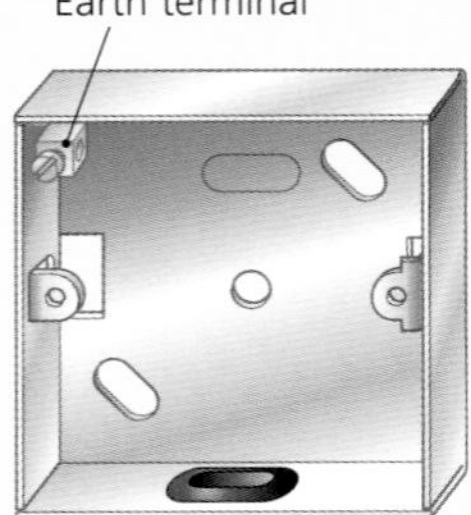

16mm metal box

Flush-mounting metal boxes A standard mounting box for a flush-fitted switch is made of metal and is 25mm deep. It is set in a recess in the wall and is screwed in place at the back. A plaster-depth box 16mm deep is also made and can be used for normal switches. Deeper (35mm) flush-mounting boxes may be required for some dimmer switches.

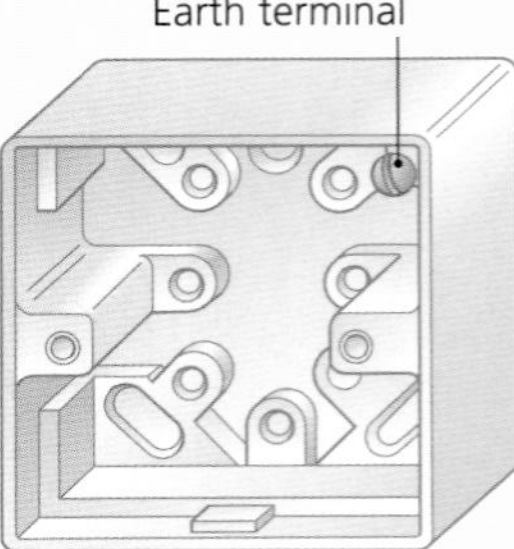

16 mm plastic box

Surface-mounting boxes Surface-mounting boxes for light switches are normally plastic, but metal boxes are available to match metal light switches. Depths range from 16mm to 47mm; no recess is needed in the wall.

Boxes for architrave switches
Metal boxes for flush-mounted architrave switches are 30mm deep; plastic boxes for surface mounting are 16–18mm deep. Both types are available for mounting one-gang and two-gang switches.

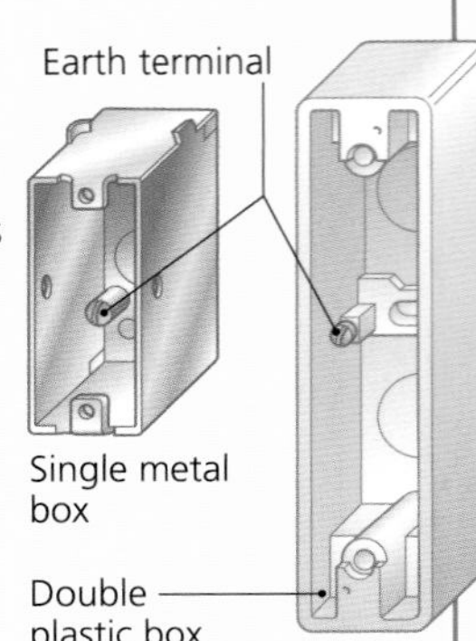

Boxes for stud partition walls Plastic 'drylining' boxes are made for flush-fitting switches (and socket outlets) in plasterboard walls. They fit in a hole cut in the board, and have spring-loaded or rotating lugs at each side which grip the inner face of the board when the box is fully inserted. Single and double boxes are available.

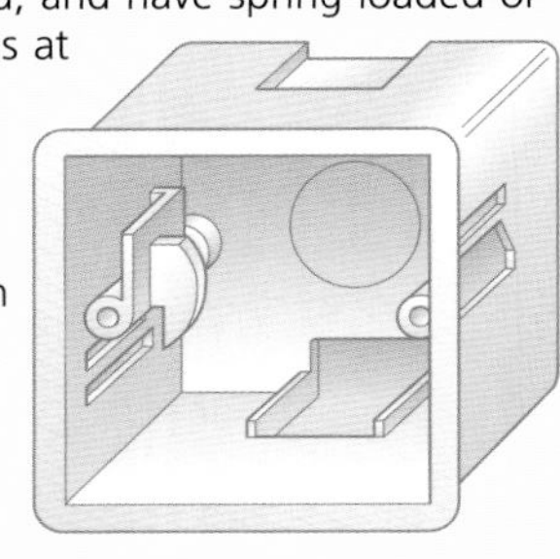

Plastic drylining box with rotating lugs

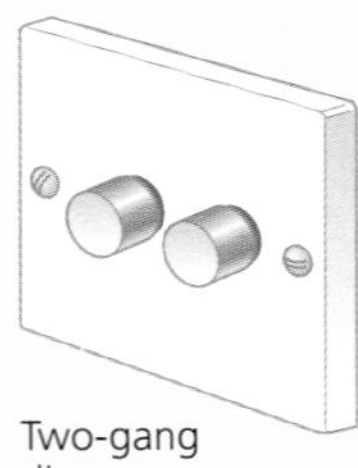

Two-gang dimmer

Dimmer switches Dimmer switches control the amount of light a lamp gives out. Dimmer switches can have push, sliding or rotary control; others have a touchplate. Ordinary dimmers cannot be used with fluorescent lights, but some can be used with low-voltage halogen lights.

One-gang switch

Two-gang switch

One-gang switch

Architrave switches Architrave switches can be fitted where there is limited wall space – for example, where two door frames are so close together that there is not enough space between them for a standard switch. Mounting boxes are made to suit them (see above).

Standard light fittings

A ceiling rose is the connection point for the flex of a pendant light and the cables of the lighting circuit. The terminals on the rose baseplate are hidden by the screw-on cover.

The body of a lampholder is concealed inside a two-part heat-resistant cover. The top part conceals the terminals to which the pendant flex is connected. The lampshade ring secures the lamp-shade. You can buy pendant sets with the ceiling rose and lampholder pre-wired.

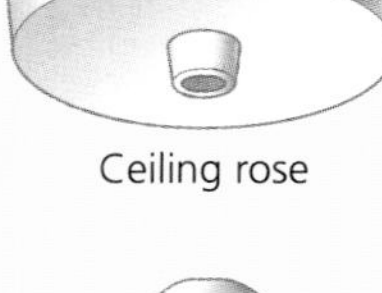
Ceiling rose

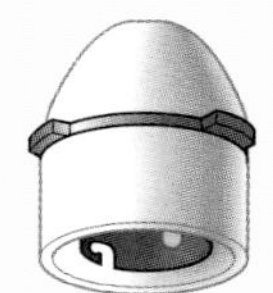
Lampholder

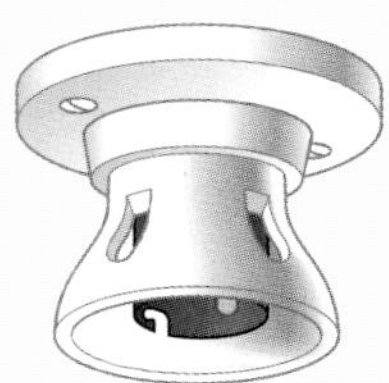
Batten holder

A batten lampholder is a ceiling rose and lampholder combined. Some batten lampholders have a deep shield over the metal bulb holder; they are for use in bathrooms to prevent accidental contact with the metal. Angled batten lampholders carry the lampholder at an angle to the base, and are intended for wall mounting – in an under-stairs cupboard, for example.

Low-voltage fittings For essential information about low voltage lighting, see page 302.

WALL LIGHT FITTINGS

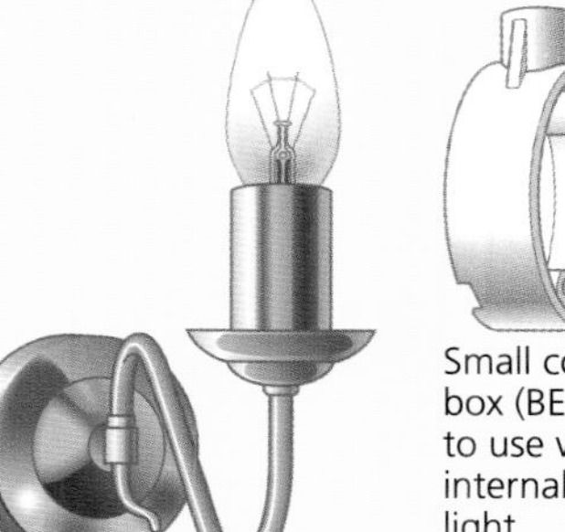
Small conduit box (BESA box) to use with internal wall light

Most wall lights have a circular backing plate which can be secured direct to a small conduit box (known to electricians as a BESA box), recessed into the wall. The wiring is then done inside the box, using a terminal connector block cut from a strip of terminal connectors.

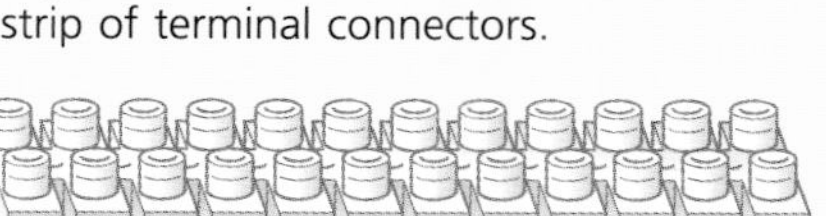
Terminal connector strip

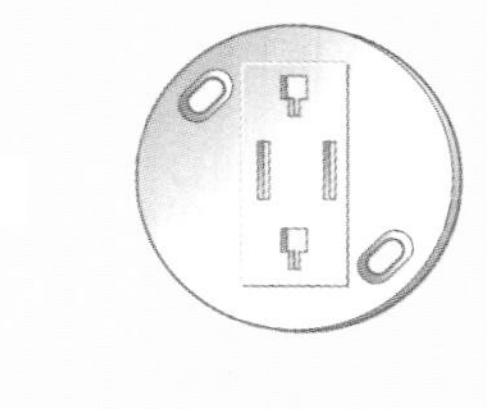

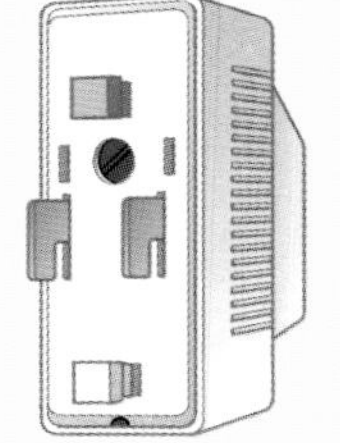

The alternative is to use a fitting known as an LSC (luminaire supporting coupler) which comes in two parts: the 'socket' is attached to a conduit box in the wall; the 'plug' is on the light fitting.

Uplighters are secured direct to the wall; again, the wiring connection can be done in a conduit box recessed into the wall.

Track lighting Mains-voltage track lighting can be wall or ceiling mounted and lengths of straight or curved track can be joined. Several types of small, neat light fittings are made to clip into the track. You can mount track over an existing lighting point, or lead flex to it from a lighting point a short distance away. Make sure that you will not overload the circuit if you fit a multi-spot track. If low-voltage halogen bulbs are used, the transformer can be built into the track, so no extra wiring is needed.

DECORATIVE LIGHT FITTINGS

There is a wide range of decorative light fittings available that are designed to be fitted flush to the ceiling surface or recessed into it.

- Light fittings with a flush baseplate must be installed over an enclosure recessed into the ceiling to contain the terminal connector block that joins the fitting to the lighting circuit cables.
- Recessed light fittings are set in a hole cut in the ceiling surface. The connections to the lighting circuit cables are made within the ceiling void.
- Spotlights may be surface-fixed or recessed, and direct light in one direction only. 'Eyeball' lights are recessed and swivel to beam light at any angle. They vary in diameter but all need 100 to 125mm of clear space above the ceiling.
- Spotlights and recessed lights can use reflector and halogen bulbs (page 296).
- The most economical but least attractive ceiling fitting is a fluorescent tube, covered with a diffuser.
- Heavier lights, such as chandeliers, must be supported by a chain secured via a hook to a ceiling joist.

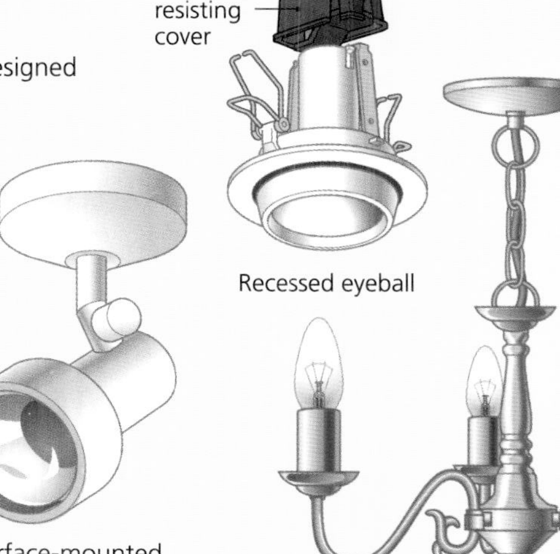

Recessed eyeball

Surface-mounted spotlight

Decorative light with supporting chain

CHOOSING LIGHTS FOR A BATHROOM

Strict regulations govern the use of electric light fittings in wet areas. When choosing lights for a bathroom, think about the position of the fitting and choose a light with an IP rating (indicating how waterproof it is) suitable for the appropriate zone (see page 268). If water jets are likely to be used for cleaning purposes in any of these zones, a fitting rated to a minimum of IPX5 must be used.

Zone 1	IPX4, protected by an RCD if mains voltage (240V)
Zone 2	IPX4

Choosing light bulbs

The most usual source of lighting for the home, commonly called a light bulb, is more properly called a lamp. Up until 2010, most light bulbs were incandescent with a white-hot tungsten filament but this inefficient type of bulb has now largely been phased out, both in the UK and all across Europe, and replaced by low-energy (compact fluorescent and LED) and low-voltage lamps (see page 302).

- Most light bulbs have a bayonet cap (BC) fitting to push and twist into a BC lampholder. Some have Edison screw (ES) caps that screw into an ES lampholder. There are small versions of both – called SBC and SES.
- Halogen lamps give a brighter, whiter light than tungsten filament lamps.
- See page 302 for details of fluorescent tubes, which are still available.

Reflector bulbs Used in spotlights and recessed lights, reflector bulbs direct light in a wide cone. They come in three main sizes: R50, R63 and R80, usually with an ES fitting.

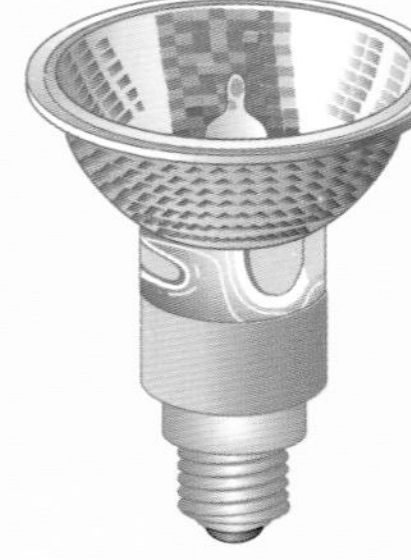

Halogen spots Some mains voltage halogen spots can replace normal reflector bulbs; others need their own fitting with a 'twist-and-lock' action. For more information on low-voltage lighting, see page 302.

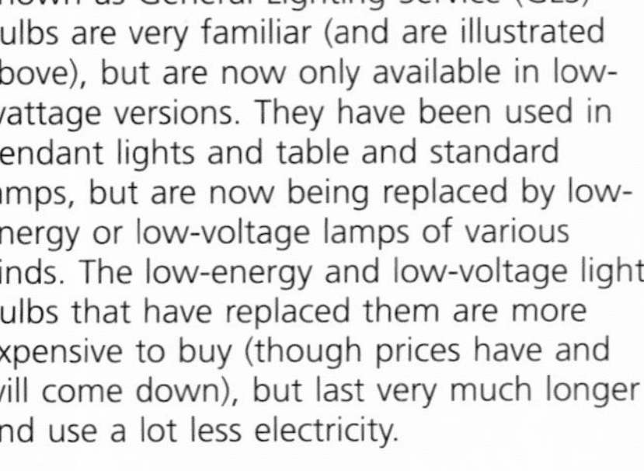

Standard light bulbs The light bulbs known as General Lighting Service (GLS) bulbs are very familiar (and are illustrated above), but are now only available in low-wattage versions. They have been used in pendant lights and table and standard lamps, but are now being replaced by low-energy or low-voltage lamps of various kinds. The low-energy and low-voltage light bulbs that have replaced them are more expensive to buy (though prices have and will come down), but last very much longer and use a lot less electricity.

Halogen lamps These bulbs can directly replace standard bulbs, and give a clean, crisp white light. They are more expensive, but last twice as long. They are also available as candle bulbs for use in reflectors and uplighters.

Shaped bulbs Used in wall and ceiling fittings, and available in a wide range of shapes, these lamps may have small bayonet caps (SBC) or small Edison screws (SES).

LOW-ENERGY BULBS

Compact fluorescent lamps are designed to replace conventional light bulbs. They fit into standard bayonet or screw-in fittings, can use just a fifth of the energy of a normal filament bulb and last eight to ten times as long. They are more expensive to buy, but will save you a lot of money over time. (See page 302 for more details.)

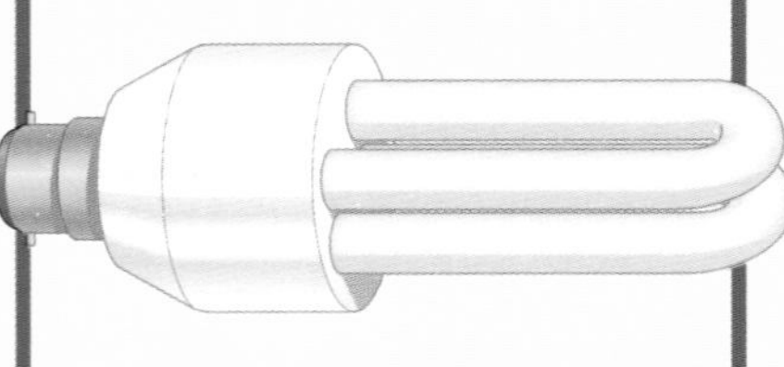

Striplights Tungsten filament striplights are ideal for use under shelves, inside cupboards and above mirrors. To avoid glare they can be used with a baffle.

Replacing a one-way switch or fitting a new dimmer switch

If a switch faceplate is cracked, you must replace it at once to prevent the risk of users touching live parts.

Before you start If you want to fit a metal switch, the switch cable must have an earth core connected to an earth terminal in the switch mounting box.

- Most light switches control just one light, and are one-way switches with two terminals on the back. Switches with three terminals are needed only for two-way switching arrangements (page 297).
- You may want to replace an existing switch with a dimmer switch. Choose one that will fit the depth of the existing mounting box, and is suitable for the light(s) it will control.

Tools *Insulated screwdrivers (one with a small, fine tip).*

Materials *Light switch or dimmer switch.*

1 Turn off the main switch at the consumer unit and remove the fuse or switch off the MCB for the circuit you are working on.

2 Remove the screws securing the switch faceplate and ease it away from the mounting box. Keep the screws; the ones provided with the new switch may be metric and will not fit the lugs in an old pre-metric mounting box.

3 Use the fine-tipped screwdriver to release the switch cable cores from their terminals (see step 2, right). Connect the red and black cable cores to the new faceplate. If there is an earth core in the cable, it will be connected to an earth terminal in the mounting box.

4 If you are fitting a metal faceplate to a metal mounting box, add a flying earth link (page 279) between the earth terminal on the faceplate and the one in the box. On a plastic mounting box, disconnect the switch cable earth core from the terminal in the mounting box and connect it to the faceplate earth terminals.

5 Fold the switch cable back into the mounting box and screw the faceplate to it, making sure that TOP is uppermost. Use the old screws again if necessary.

6 At the consumer unit, replace the circuit fuse or switch on the MCB and restore the power.

Replacing a one-way with a two-way switch

Two-way switches allow you to turn a light on and off from two switch positions. This is necessary for stairs and rooms with two doorways.

Before you start A length of three-core-and-earth cable has to be run between the two switches. A two-way switch has three terminals, usually marked L1 and L2 (or just 1 and 2) and COM (or COMMON). All two-gang switches are two-way types, but you can use them on a one-way system (using the common and L2 terminals.

- In three-core-and-earth cable, the cores are colour-coded brown, black and grey, and the earth core is bare as in other cables. There are no regulations about which terminals the three coloured cores should go to as long as the connections are the same in both switches. Usually the brown core is connected to the common terminals of each switch, the black cores to L1 and the grey cores to the L2 terminals.
- It is essential to tag the black and grey cores with brown sleeving or brown PVC insulating tape to show they can be live.

Tools *Suitable tools for preparing the route (page 282); insulated screwdrivers (one with a fine tip); trimming knife; wire cutters and strippers; pliers; pipe and cable detector.*

Materials *Two two-way switches; one new mounting box; screws and wallplugs; grommet; 1mm² three-core-and-earth cable; green-and-yellow plastic sleeving; brown plastic sleeving or brown PVC insulating tape; small and large oval conduit; galvanised nails.*

1 Turn off the switch at the consumer unit and remove the fuse or switch off the MCB protecting the circuit you are working on.

2 Undo the retaining screws that hold the existing one-way switch in place. Ease the faceplate away from the mounting box. Disconnect the two switch cable cores from their terminals and the earth core from its terminal in the mounting box. If the switch cable has no earth core, you must use only plastic switches and plastic mounting boxes.

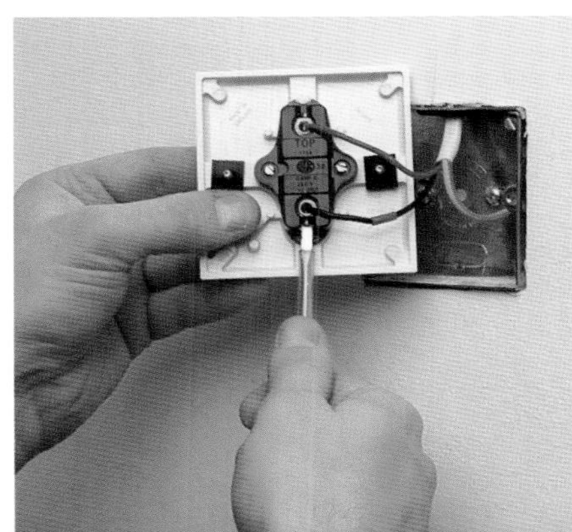

3 Prepare the route (page 282) from the new switch position, up the wall, through the ceiling void and down the wall to the original switch position. In solid walls, cut a chase for the new cable and a recess for the new switch mounting box. Cut oval conduit to fit in the new chase, and feed one end of the three-core-and-earth cable into it. Run the cable through the ceiling void to a point above the existing switch.

4 Use a pipe/cable detector to locate the position of the cable running down to the original switch. Enlarge the chase between switch and ceiling level without damaging the cable. Cut a length of large oval conduit to fit in the chase.

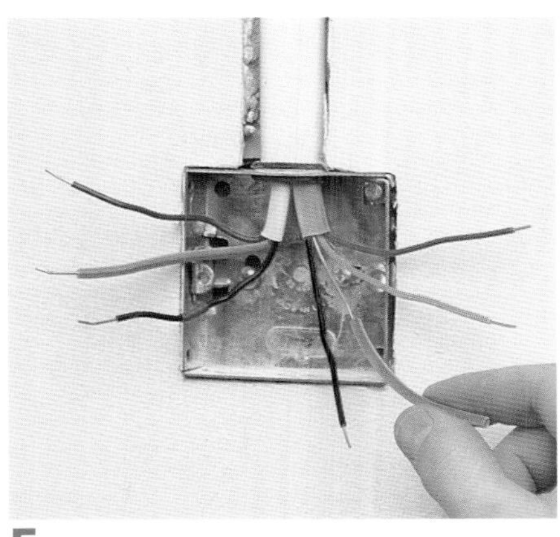

5 Pull the existing switch cable away from the mounting box and out of the newly widened chase. Feed it and the new three-core-and-earth cable into the conduit and on into the existing mounting box. Fix the conduit in the chase with galvanised nails.

6 Feed the three-core-and-earth cable into the new switch mounting box and fix the box in its recess.

7 Make good the wall around the new switch mounting box, and plaster over the two wall chases.

8 Prepare the cable for connection (page 271); remember to sleeve the bare earth cores. Use pliers to straighten the original cores.

9 At the original switch position, connect the red core from the original cable and the new black core to the terminal marked L1 on the new switch faceplate. Connect the

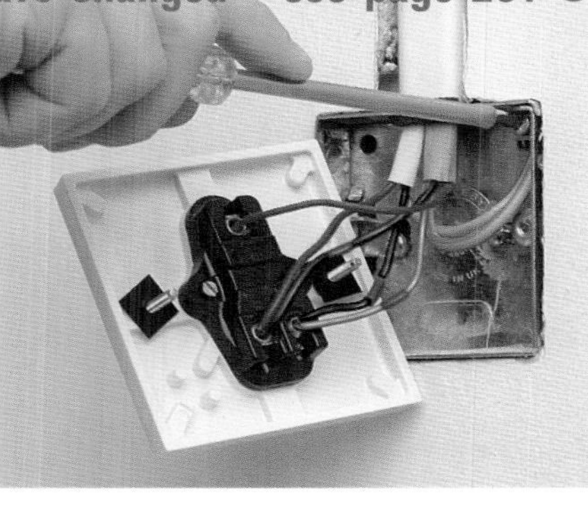

red-tagged black core from the original cable and the new grey core to the terminal marked L2. Connect the new brown core to the terminal marked COM. Screw the two green-and-yellow-sleeved earth cores into the terminal at the back of the mounting box.

10 If the new faceplate is metal, add a flying earth link (page 279) between the earth terminal in the mounting box and the earth terminal on the switch faceplate.

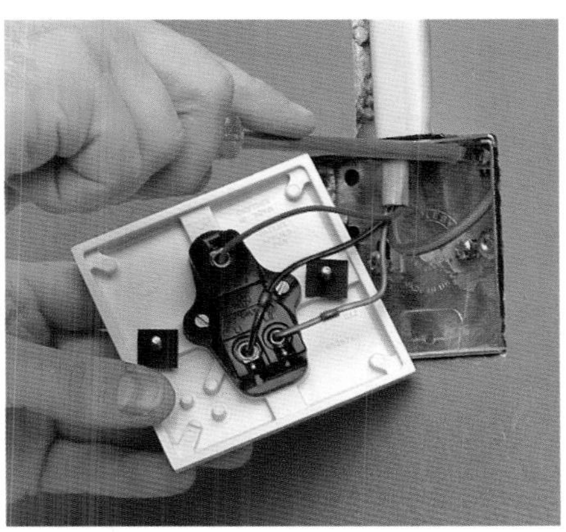

11 Fold the cables neatly into the mounting box and screw on the faceplate.

12 At the new switch position, connect the brown core to the terminal marked COM, the black core to L1, the grey core to L2, and the green-and-yellow sleeved earth core to the terminal in the mounting box. Again add a flying earth link if the new switch is metal.

13 Screw the new switch faceplate to its mounting box.

14 At the consumer unit, replace the circuit fuse or switch on the MCB, then restore the power and test the switches.

PLASTERBOARD WALLS

Running the wiring for two-way switching in hollow stud partition walls is much easier than for solid walls – as is cutting the hole to take the new flush drylining mounting box. See pages 283 and 294 for more details. Flying earth links are not needed, but metal switch plates should be earthed.

Moving a light switch

When you re-hang a door on the other side of a doorframe (see page 194), the light switch will now be on the 'wrong' side. It's not too difficult to move it to the other side of the door.

Before you start Lift the floorboards in the room above the existing light switch to identify the cable that runs from the ceiling rose (or wiring junction box) and then down the wall to the switch. For an upstairs room, go into the loft – you may need to make a hole in the ceiling and poke a thin wooden stick through to identify the position.

Tools *Suitable tools for preparing the route (page 282), insulated screwdrivers (one with a fine tip), trimming knife, wire cutters and strippers, pliers.*

Materials *New plaster-depth mounting box, two short M4 screws, 5A four-terminal junction box, green-and-yellow earth sleeving, screws, red and brown sleeving (or insulating tape) oval conduit, galvanised nails, blanking plate (or wall filler).*

1 Turn off the main switch at the consumer unit. Remove the fuse or switch off the MCB of the lighting circuit you are working on.

2 Undo the retaining screws that hold the existing light switch in place. Ease the faceplate away from the mounting box, disconnect the cable cores from the switch and the earth core from the mounting box.

3 Go into the room above (or the loft) to the position where the switch cable comes through the ceiling. If the switch is mounted on a plasterboard partition wall, you should be able to pull it up through the ceiling. For solid walls, cut off the cable where it passes through the ceiling.

4 Prepare the free end of this cable (page 271) and connect the cores to three of the terminals of a 5A four-terminal junction box screwed to the side of a joist – make sure that the outer sheath of the cable finishes inside the junction box, tag the black core with red sleeving and cover the earth core with green-and-yellow sleeving.

5 Prepare the route (page 282) from the new switch position, fit a new mounting box and run a length of 1mm² two-core-and-earth cable from the new switch position to the new junction box position in the same way as described for replacing a one-way switch on page 297.

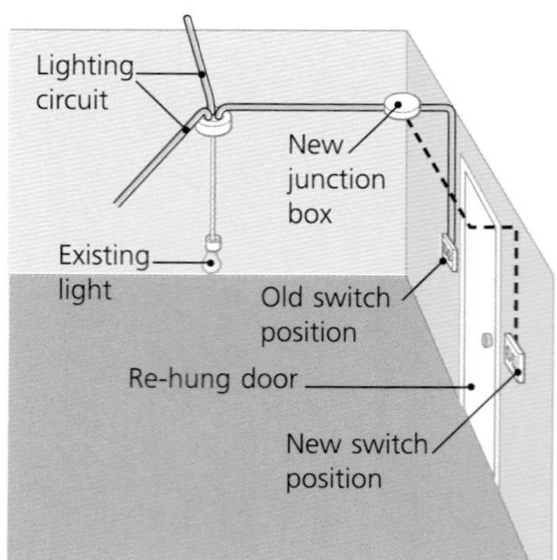

6 Curl the cable inside the mounting box, make good the plaster round it and plaster over the wall chase.

7 At the junction box, prepare the end of the cable (page 271) and connect the brown core to the terminal with the existing red core, blue core (tagged with brown sleeving) to existing black and earth (covered with green-and-yellow sleeving) to the matching earth. The fourth terminal is left empty.

8 When the plaster repairs have dried, prepare the end of the cable at the new switch position, connect the brown core to the terminal marked COM and the blue core (tagged with brown sleeving) to the terminal marked L2 and the green-and-yellow sleeved earth to the terminal in the mounting box.

9 Fold the switch cable back into the mounting box and screw the faceplate to it, using new metric screws..

10 At the old switch position, cut off the cable. Unless you are prepared to fill the whole recess with wall filler (removing the old box if it protrudes) and redecorate, simply fit a blanking plate, using the old securing screws. With partition walls, you could remove the box and repair the plasterboard as described on page 226.

11 At the consumer unit, replace the circuit fuse or switch on the MCB, then restore the power and test the switch.

> **HELPFUL TIP**
>
> If the old ceiling switch has been painted over, run a trimming knife around the join between the ceiling and the switch before you remove it.

Fitting or replacing a ceiling switch

A ceiling-mounted pull-cord switch is the only type you are normally allowed in bathrooms, but is often fitted in bedrooms for two-way switching.

You will have to notify your local Building Control Department if you want to fit a new ceiling-mounted pull-cord switch in a bathroom (perhaps to replace a wall switch), but you do not need approval to install one in a bedroom.

For a lighting circuit, you need a 6amp pull-cord switch, available in both one-way and two-way versions. You will need a two-way version for two-way switching in a bedroom, but you could use it in place of a one-way switch if you needed to. The switch comes with its own plastic mounting box, which is secured to the ceiling.

Tools *Suitable tools for preparing the route (page 282), insulated screwdrivers (one with a fine tip), trimming knife, wire cutters and strippers, pliers.*

Materials *Ceiling-mounted light switch, 1mm² two-(or three-)core-and-earth cable, green-and-yellow earth sleeving, screws, spare piece of timber, red (or brown) sleeving.*

1 Turn off the main switch at the consumer unit and remove the fuse or switch off the MCB protecting the circuit you are working on – in this case, one of the lighting circuits.

2 Choose the position for the new pull-cord switch – if you are replacing a wall switch, make this more-or-less immediately above the existing wall switch. Make a hole in the ceiling large enough to pass cable through.

3 If you are replacing a wall switch with a ceiling switch, follow Steps 2, 3 and 4 for Moving a light switch (left), then go to Step 6 below. It is possible you may not need the junction box in Step 4 if there is sufficient cable to take through the ceiling to the pull-cord switch.

4 If you are replacing an existing ceiling switch, remove its cover, disconnect the wires and remove the base from the ceiling. Then go to Step 6 below.

5 If you are fitting a new two-way ceiling-mounted switch in a bedroom, follow the instructions on page 297, but take the new cable from the existing switch to the position of the new ceiling-mounted switch.

6 Make sure that there is adequate support for the ceiling light switch, using a timber batten as described on page 284.

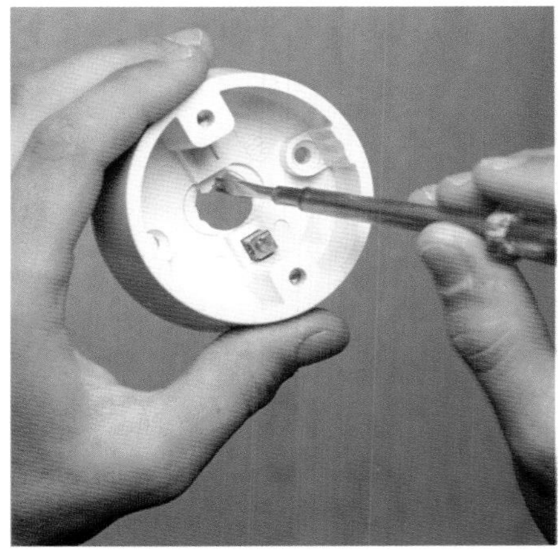

7 Use a screwdriver to remove the knock-out in the base of the mounting box to make an entry for the cable.

8 Secure the mounting block for the switch to the ceiling, making sure that the screws go right through the ceiling into the timber block (and joist if appropriate).

9 Feed the end of the switch cable down through the hole and prepare the cores if necessary. Slip a length of brown sleeving over the blue wire.

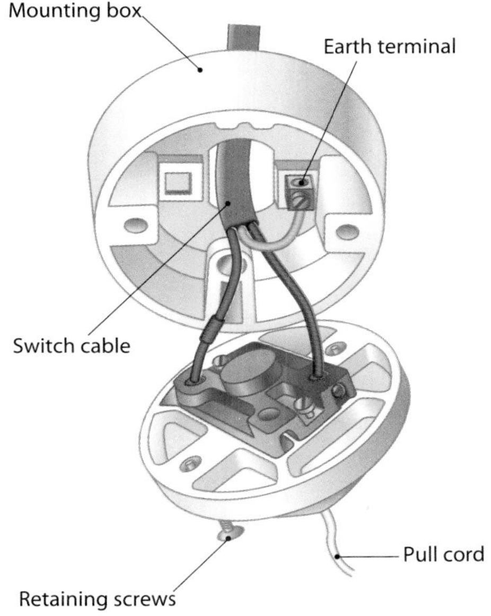

10 Connect the cores to the terminals in the switch – brown to COM and blue to L1 or L2 for one-way switching, brown to COM, black to L1 and grey to L2 for two-way switching. If using the original cable (for straight replacement), it's red core to COM and red-tagged black to L1 or L2. Sleeve the earth core and connect it to the earth terminal in the mounting box.

11 Push the switch gently back into its mounting block and screw it in place. Do not overtighten the screws.

12 At the consumer unit, replace the circuit fuse or switch on the MCB, then restore the power and test the switch.

Installing a new ceiling light fitting

Replacing a ceiling rose and pendant lampholder with a new light fitting gives your room an instant update.

Tools *Screwdriver; electrician's insulated screwdriver; bradawl.*

Materials *New light fitting; 5amp connector strip. Possibly green-and-yellow earth sleeving.*

1 Turn off the power to the lighting circuit at the consumer unit. Take down the bulb and lampshade, then undo the ceiling rose cover and unscrew the rose baseplate. Disconnect the single cable from the terminals – if there are two or three cables, see Loop-in wiring right. If the existing wiring has no earth core, you can only use double-insulated fittings.

2 After making sure that there is adequate support for the light (as for Fitting a ceiling rose on page 284), hold the baseplate in position and mark the positions of fixing holes on the ceiling, using a bradawl.

3 Remove the terminal connector block from the baseplate. The fitting shown here is double-insulated and needs no earth connection, so the circuit cable earth core should be terminated in a 5amp strip connector. Wire the circuit cable live and neutral cores into the terminal connector block.

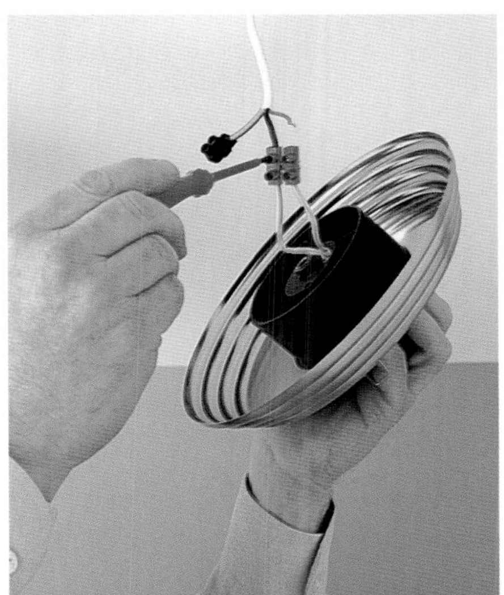

4 Put the main terminal block and the strip connector containing the earth terminal back into the baseplate. Push the excess circuit cable up into the ceiling void.

5 While holding the baseplate and surround in their final position, locate the fixing screws in the holes you have already marked, and fix screws in place to secure the fitting to the ceiling. Add a light bulb and diffuser. Switch on the power supply.

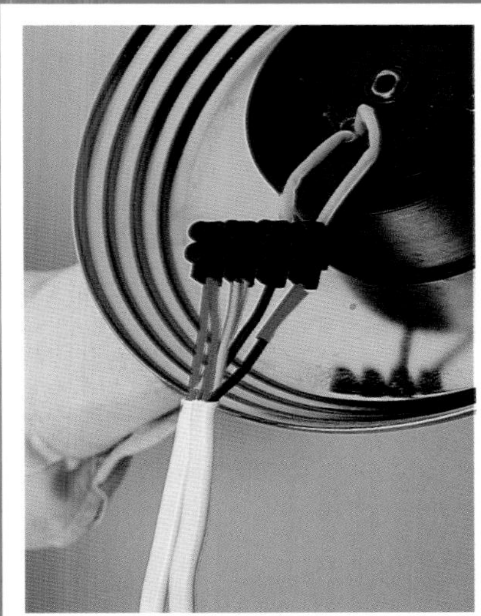

LOOP-IN WIRING

Two or three cables present at the existing ceiling rose indicates loop-in wiring, where the switch cable is wired into the ceiling rose. If this is the case, identify and mark the cables (using the photograph at the bottom of page 276 as a guide). If there is sufficient space, use four strip connectors wired up as above: the circuit neutral core and the switch return core linked to the light's flex tails; the circuit lives in the third terminal and all the sleeved earths in the fourth. If there is not space in the light fitting, you will have to re-connect all the cable wires in a junction box above the ceiling – as shown on page 280 (ignore the spur cable), taking a single cable back through the ceiling to the light.

Adding an extra light

You can run a spur cable from a lighting circuit to supply an extra lighting point.

There are three places where the spur can start: at any ceiling rose on a loop-in system (page 306), but easiest at the last one; at any box on a junction-box system (page 306); or at a new junction box inserted into the lighting circuit, whether it is a loop-in or a junction-box system.

Tools *Insulated screwdriver, tools for preparing the route (page 282); wire cutters and strippers; trimming knife; pliers.*

Materials *1mm² two-core-and-earth cable; green-and-yellow plastic sleeving; cable clips. Perhaps a three-terminal junction box to connect the spur cable.*

Preparation Turn off the main switch at the consumer unit and remove the fuse or switch off the MCB protecting the circuit you are working on. Prepare the route (page 282) and lay the new cable.

Adding to the last loop-in ceiling rose on the circuit

1 Unscrew the loop-in ceiling-rose cover and slide it down the flex. Then loosen the screws holding the rose baseplate to the ceiling. This will make it possible to work the new spur cable carefully through the ceiling in the same hole as the existing circuit and switch cables and through the entry hole in the ceiling rose.

2 Prepare the new cable for connection (page 271). Screw the rose baseplate back to the ceiling.

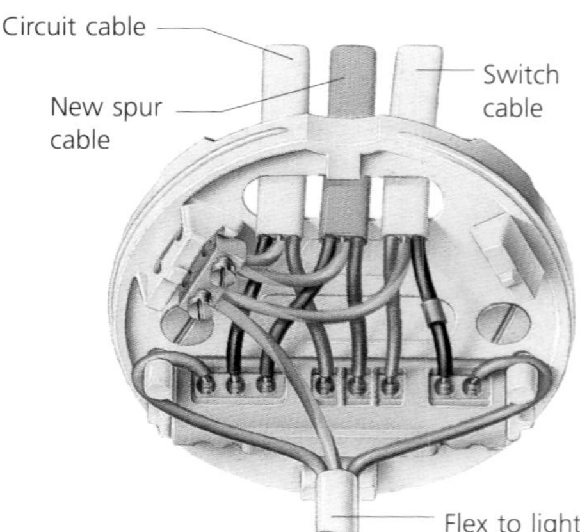

3 Connect the brown core of the spur cable to the spare terminal in the central terminal block, which already holds two red cores. Next, connect the blue core to the spare terminal in the outer terminal block to which the existing circuit cable black core is connected. Finally, connect the green-and-yellow sleeved earth core to the separate earth terminal.

4 Screw the ceiling rose cover back in place.

Adding a spur to a junction box wiring system

1 Remove the cover of the junction box where the spur will start. You can cut out an entry hole in it for the spur, or let the spur share the same entry hole as an existing cable.

2 Prepare the new spur cable for connection (page 271). Feed it into the box.

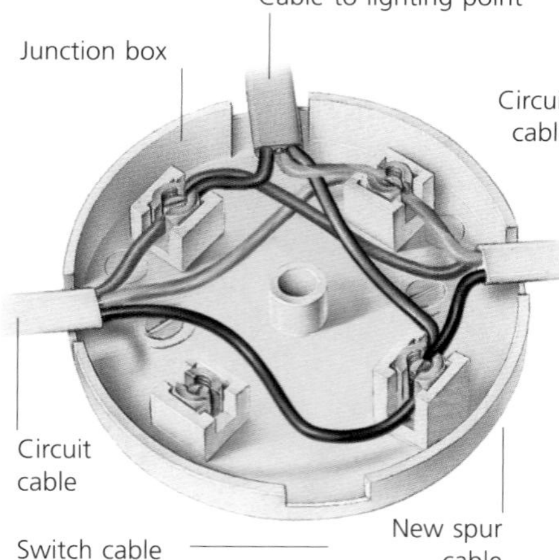

3 Connect the brown core of the new spur cable to the terminal where two or three red cores are already connected. Connect the blue core to the terminal where two or three black cores are already connected. Connect the green-and-yellow sleeved earth core to the terminal where the other earth conductors are already connected.

4 Screw the cover on the junction box.

Leading a spur from a new junction box in the circuit

1 Trace the cable to which you plan to connect the spur, to make sure that it is not a switch cable but the circuit cable running from one loop-in rose or junction box to the next.

2 Screw the baseplate of the new junction box to the side of a joist so that the circuit cable runs across it.

3 Cut the cable over the centre of the box, then strip back enough of the outer sheath to allow the cores to reach their terminals with the sheath still within the box. Then strip about 15mm of the core insulation from the live and neutral cores.

4 Sleeve the bare earth cores with green-and-yellow sleeving.

5 Prepare the ends of the spur cable for connection.

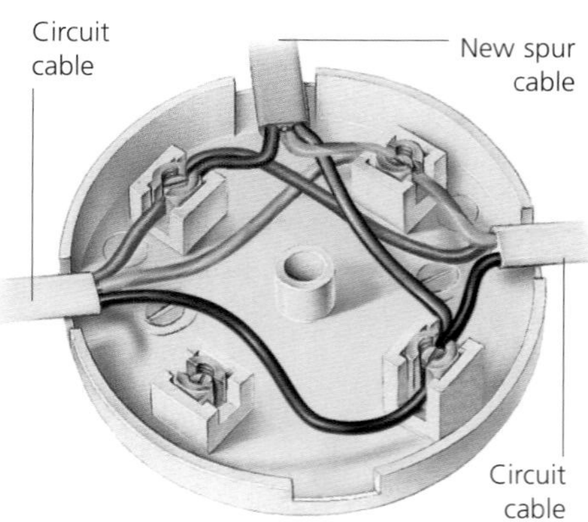

6 Connect the circuit and the new spur cable cores to the terminals as shown here. Then screw the cover back onto the junction box.

At the new lighting point

At the new loop-in ceiling rose, connect in the spur cable cores – the brown core to the central terminal, the blue core to one of the outer terminals and the sleeved earth core to the earth terminal. Connect the flex cores to the outer terminals. Run the switch cable to the new switch position and connect it to the switch terminals.

Next, connect the new switch cable at the rose. The brown core goes to the centre terminal, the blue core to the outer terminal where the brown flex core is connected and the earth core to the earth terminal. Identify the blue core as live by wrapping some brown PVC tape around it.

Adding a spur for a wall light

You can add a wall light by leading a spur from an existing lighting circuit.

Before you start The wall light may incorporate its own switch; if it does not, or if you want to be able to switch the wall light from the door, you can fit an extra junction box in the spur cable to connect a new switch cable.

- You should fit a mounting box in the wall for making the wiring connections.
- If the base of the light fitting is too small to conceal a square box, use a round, plastic or metal conduit box or a slim architrave mounting box. Use a round dry-lining box in a timber-framed partition wall.
- Choose a light wired with an earth conductor or double-insulated (marked ▣).

Wiring to a wall light

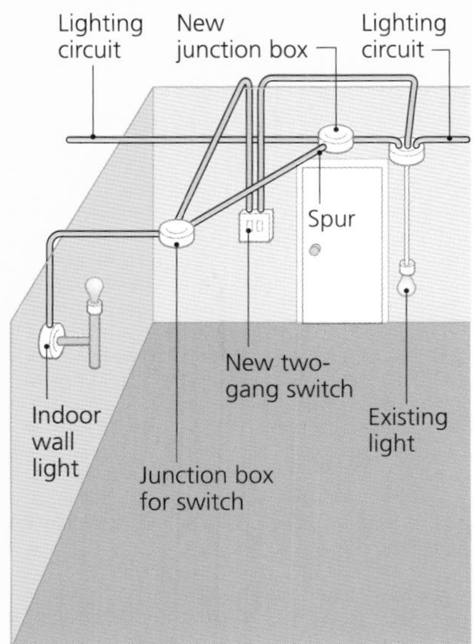

Tools *Suitable tools for preparing the route (page 282); insulated screwdrivers; trimming knife; wire cutters and strippers; pliers. Perhaps a circuit tester.*

Materials *Wall light; 1mm² two-core-and-earth cable; green-and-yellow earth sleeving; metal mounting box or slim architrave box or round dry-lining box; short length of green-and-yellow insulated earth conductor; connector block with three pairs of terminals (cut from a strip). Junction boxes for connecting the spur and switch; brown plastic sleeving; two-gang light switch.*

Preparation Turn off the power at the main switch in the consumer unit, and remove the fuse or switch off the MCB protecting the circuit you will be working on. Prepare the route for the spur cable. You will need to lead it above the ceiling from a convenient spot on the lighting circuit to a point immediately above the wall light position, and then down the wall.

The wall light should be about 1.8m above floor level. Make a recess there for the mounting box or slim architrave box, or cut a round hole in a plasterboard wall for a dry-lining box.

In order to incorporate a switch, lead the spur cable route above the ceiling to a spot halfway between the wall light position and the switch position and fit the four-way junction box there. Continue the cable run from there to the wall light position and run another cable from the junction box to a point directly above the switch. You should be able to complete the route by enlarging the recess in the plaster leading down the wall to the existing switch. Take great care not to damage the existing switch cable. Unscrew and disconnect the switch. You can use the single mounting box already fitted and fit a two-gang switch over it when you are ready to make the connections. Alternatively, you could fit a new switch next to the existing one.

1 Lay the spur cable along the route from the circuit to the junction box for the switch, and from there to the wall light position and also to the switch position. Secure the cable along the route.

2 At the wall light, feed the cable into its mounting box. At the switch, feed the switch cable into its mounting box.

3 Prepare the new cable ends for connection. Slide a piece of brown sleeving on the switch cable's blue core at each end.

4 Connect the spur to the lighting circuit (see opposite page).

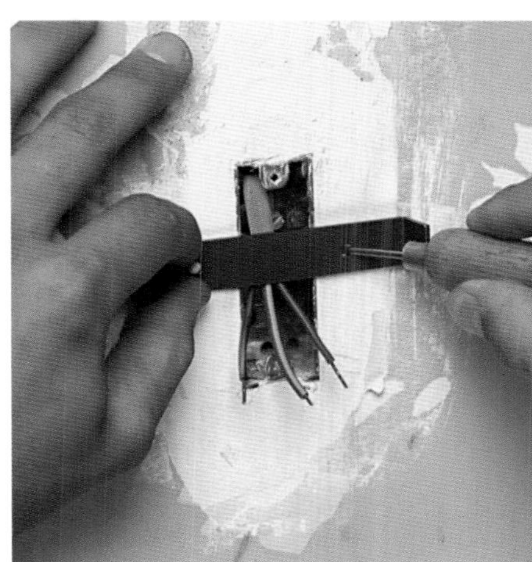

5 Hold the wall light or its bracket in place and push the bradawl through its fixing holes to see if they match up with the screwed holes of the mounting box. If they do not align – or if you are using an architrave box – make drilling marks with the bradawl. Drill at the marks and plug the holes.

6 Make good any plaster damage.

Connections at the wall light

1 Connect the brown and blue spur cable cores to the two outer terminals on one side of the terminal connector block.

2 At the central terminal, connect the spur cable earth core. If you are using a metal mounting box, connect a flying earth core (page 279) to the central terminal, on the same side. Connect the other end of this earth core to the earth terminal in the box.

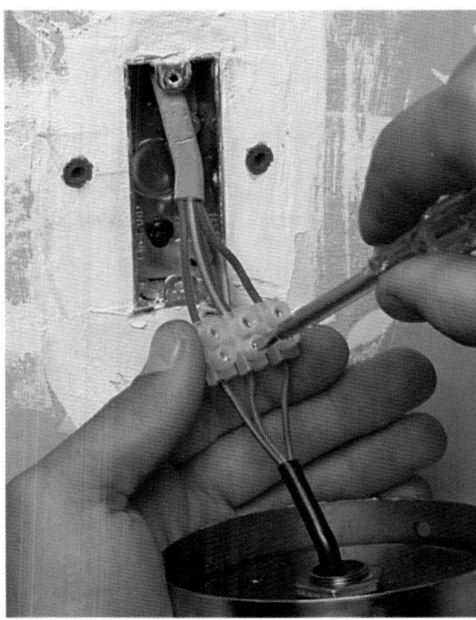

3 Connect the flex cores from the wall light to the terminal connector block with brown, blue and green-and-yellow cores opposite the brown, blue, and green-and-yellow cable cores respectively.

4 Screw the wall light into place to or over the mounting box.

Connections at the switch

1 Make the connections behind the new two-gang switch. All two-gang switches are designed to operate as two-way switches. When you use one as part of a one-way system, you must use the Common terminal and one of the other two terminals. Connect the new brown and brown-sleeved blue cores to the first switch gang using the terminals marked Common and L2.

Connect the cores from the original cable to the second switch gang in the same way.

Connect both the green-and-yellow sleeved cores into the earth terminal at the back of the box.

2 Fold the cables neatly and screw the switch faceplate to the mounting box.

3 At the junction box for the switch, connect the brown cores from the spur and switch cables to one terminal.

4 Connect the blue cores from the spur cable and the cable leading to the wall light to another terminal.

5 Connect the brown core from the wall light cable and the brown-sleeved blue core from the switch cable to a third terminal.

6 Finally, connect all the green-and-yellow sleeved earth cores to the fourth terminal.

7 At the consumer unit, replace the circuit fuse or switch on the MCB and restore the power.

Choosing low-voltage lighting

Low-voltage lighting uses a transformer to step down mains electricity to just 12 volts. A transformer can be attached to each individual light, or one transformer can supply several lights. A transformer can be large and heavy, so mounting it away from the lights often makes sense. One major advantage of low- voltage lighting is that the risk of electric shock is minimal – it is quite safe to touch the terminals on the low voltage side of the transformer.

Separate transformers Having a separate transformer makes the light fitting compact and easily fitted into a confined space. A single transformer can run several lights, or each light may have its own box. The transformer can be mounted near the mains power supply, allowing unobtrusive cables to run to the light fitting or it can be slotted into the ceiling void alongside the light. Compact and maintenance free, transformers are a fit-and-forget item that can be hidden away on top of a kitchen cupboard or in a ceiling or wall space.

Integral transformers The outward appearance of these lights is similar to those that have a separate transformer, but there is a transformer built in to each light fitting. They are generally more expensive than those with a remote transformer as not only are you paying for the cost of the fitting but also the cost of a transformer for each light source. Also, while each light fitting may be small, its transformer may be fairly bulky and this must be taken into account when siting lights.

Choosing LED lighting

Light emitting diodes (LEDs) are familiar enough in electronic equipment, but are now being produced in a wide range suitable for use in the home. Although very expensive to buy, they use very little electricity and last for a very long time (up to ten years). LEDs are available to replace most types of light bulb and come in a range of exciting colours as well as white. Most can be used in standard light fittings. LEDs have several advantages: they are virtually everlasting; they don't emit heat; and they consume very little electricity.

You can also fit walk-over LEDs into floors, both indoors and out. Because these lights remain cool to the touch, they are safe for use in playrooms.

Dimming If low-voltage lights are to be dimmed then the dimming control must be mounted on the primary or 230 volt side of the circuit (not the transformer side). Dimming increases lamp life for low-voltage lighting, as it does for regular light bulbs.

Colour All light has what is known as a colour temperature. The higher the number, the whiter the light appears. Many low-voltage lights used in shops for display purposes use halogen bulbs, which appear too white and stark for domestic use. For room lighting, low-voltage bulbs give a warmer and more relaxing light.

ENERGY SAVING LIGHTING

Although more expensive at the outset, low voltage lights use only around a third of the electricity used by conventional lights and last much longer – typically 2-3,000 hours.

Choosing fluorescent lamps

A fluorescent lamp uses electronic discharge to illuminate the coating of a tube. It gives roughly five times as much light per watt as a tungsten light bulb and lasts at least ten times as long.

Fluorescent tubes Long white tubes, for use in fluorescent light fittings with a starter, are a fixture of many homes. However, they now come in a range of sizes and colours, including warmer tones than the traditional clinical white. The most common sizes are 26mm diameter (labelled T8) and 16mm (T5). Less efficient 38mm (T12) tubes are still sold for older fittings. Power output depends on length: 600mm is 18W, 1200mm is 36W and 1500m is 58W, for example. The most efficient type is the triphosphor fluorescent tube, which also has improved colour rendering and a life of up to 20,000 hours. These cannot normally be used with a dimmer switch.

Compact fluorescent lamps Also known as low energy and energy-saving lamps. These work in the same way as fluorescent lights, but the tube is bent back on itself and the control gear is built in, so they can be used to replace normal light bulbs with a screw or bayonet fitting.

- An 11W CFL replaces a 60W light bulb
- A 20W CFL replaces a 100W light bulb
- Many types dimmable

Other options Fluorescent lamps are available in a range of shapes, including pencil shapes, bent tube shapes and glass covered lamps, which look similar to the standard light bulbs they are meant to replace. Low-energy replacements are also available for R50, R63 and R80 reflector bulbs – see page 296. Flat square (2-D) lamps have their own range of special fittings including porch lights, bulkhead lights and ceiling lights.

Fitting plug-in under-cupboard lighting

The simplest way to illuminate your worktops is with a chain of linked fluorescent strip lights that are plugged in to an electric socket.

This job does not involve any mains wiring, so can be done without notifying the Building Control Officer even though it is in a kitchen. Once the lights are in position, you simply plug the master light (the first in the run) into a nearby mains socket, which powers all the lights. Each light has its own rocker switch. Make sure the plug has a 3amp (red) fuse, not a 13amp (brown) one.

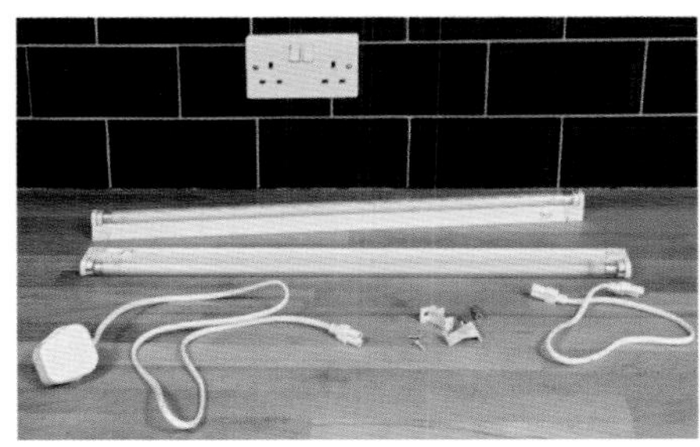

The striplights are sold in kit form – together with fixing clips, screws, cable clips and two-core connecting flexes that simply plug in to link the run of lights together.

1 Allow one fitting for every 500mm of worktop. Lay the kit out along the worktop to plan exactly where you will fit the lights, making sure that there is a socket outlet within reach of the master light.

2 Position the fixing clips and screw them to the underside of the wall units.

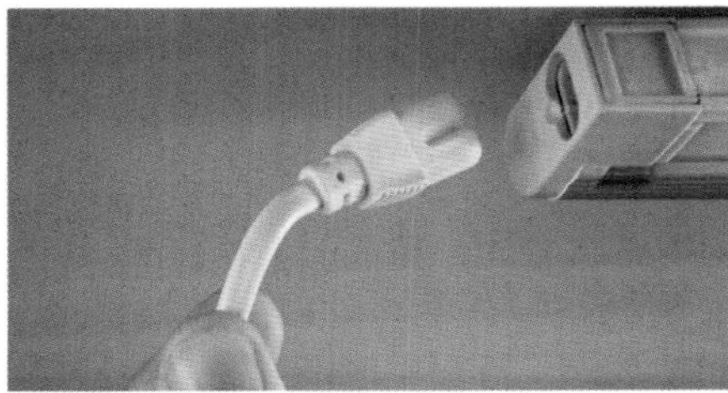

3 Plug in the connecting cables to link all the lights together. Each linking cable has a plug at one end and a socket at the other, so it will be obvious how to fit them.

4 Lift the lights into position and secure them in their fixing clips. Neaten any excess flex by pinning it to the underside of the cupboards using plastic cable clips.

5 Plug in and switch on at the mains socket, and test each light in turn.

Wiring in under-cupboard kitchen lights

When refurbishing a kitchen, it is possible to connect under-cupboard lights permanently to the kitchen ring circuit. You can use fluorescent or tungsten striplights or special low-voltage spotlights.

Low-voltage spotlights for use under kitchen cupboards need a separate transformer. This can run more than one light – a 60 volt-amp (60VA) transformer, for example, can power three 20W lights. The transformer can be wired to a switched fused connection unit (FCU) wired into the kitchen ring circuit. The switch turns the lights on and off.

Tools *Suitable tools for preparing the route (page 282), insulated screwdrivers (one with a fine tip), trimming knife, wire cutters and strippers, pliers.*

Materials *Switched fused connection unit, flex outlet plate, mounting boxes, 2.5mm² and 1.5mm² two-core-and-earth cable, 0.75mm² flex, green-and-yellow plastic sleeving, screws, low-voltage light fittings; 12V transformer.*

1 Turn off the main switch at the consumer unit and remove the fuse or switch off the MCB protecting the circuit you are working on – in this case, the kitchen ring circuit.

2 The FCU can be wired into the kitchen ring circuit (page 273) or wired as a spur from a kitchen socket outlet (page 286).

3 Prepare the cable route for the 2.5mm² cable running to the position of the switched FCU. Fix the switch mounting box in place and run the cable from the socket outlet.

4 A good place to put the transformer is on top of the kitchen cupboard. Prepare a cable route for the 1.5mm² cable from the FCU to a position above the cupboard and fit a mounting box for the flex outlet plate (page 279). Repair all wall damage.

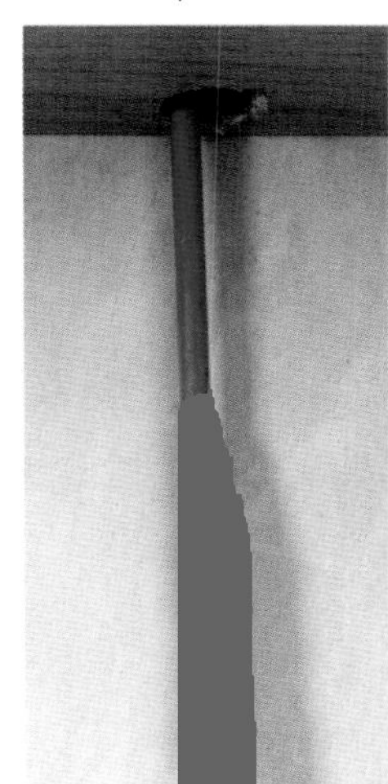

5 To run the wires from a light fitting to the transformer, drill a hole in the base and top of the cupboard at the light position and feed a length of stiff wire or a flexible rod up through the two holes to the top of the cupboard. Pass the fitting over the end of the stiff wire (or rod) and tape the cable of the light to the end of the stiff wire (or rod) and pull it though to the transformer position. Repeat for the other light fittings.

6 Screw each light fitting to the underside of the cupboard and position the lampholder in the light fitting.

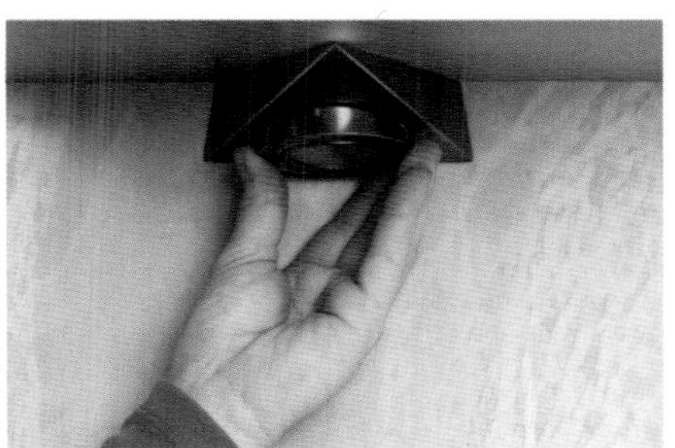

7 At the transformer, connect the cables from the lights to the output terminals and connect the 0.75mm² flex to the input terminals, following the instructions provided.

8 Make the connections at the socket outlet for the spur cable to the FCU (page 280), at the FCU for the spur cable and cable leading to the flex outlet plate (page 286) and at the flex outlet plate for the cable from the FCU and the flex leading to the transformer (page 288).

9 Secure all faceplates back to their mounting boxes, taking care to fold the cables neatly into the mounting boxes.

10 Turn the electricity back on at the consumer unit and test the lights.

Wiring in fluorescent lights

It is not always feasible or desirable to fit a lighting kit that runs from a mains socket or an FCU. You may need to wire a fluorescent lamp fitting into the mains lighting circuit. If you are in any doubt about tackling this type of work, then hire a qualified electrician.

Fluorescent lights make good task lighting: a lamp above a desk or a dressing table, for example. They can also be used as accent lights, to illuminate a picture or another feature in a room. In all these instances, you will want to hide the wiring. The light itself can be operated with a pull-cord or rocker switch, or a wall-mounted light switch, usually sited near the door.

Tools *Bradawl; tools for preparing the route (page 282); trimming knife; wire cutters and strippers; insulated screwdrivers; pliers.*

Materials *Light fitting; two-core-and-earth 1mm² cable; green-and-yellow earth sleeving; cable clips. Perhaps also four-way junction box; one-way light switch with mounting box, fixing screws; grommet; brown plastic sleeving; insulating tape.*

Before you start To connect the fitting to the electricity supply, you will need to lead a spur to it from the lighting circuit (page 300). Remove any baffle and end covers from the fitting. Hold the base plate against the wall (or shelf) and mark the fixing points and, if necessary, the cable entry hole. Drill holes at the marks and screw the base plate of the light fitting firmly in place.

Fitting a light with a built-in switch

1 Turn off the main switch at the consumer unit and remove the fuse or switch off the MCB protecting the circuit you are working on.

2 Lead a spur from the lighting circuit (page 300) to the position of the light fitting, burying it in the wall plaster or hiding it behind plasterboard (page 292).

3 When plaster repairs have dried, thread the 1mm² spur cable through the entry hole of the light fitting. Prepare the cable ends (page 271) and connect the cable cores to the terminals of the terminal connector block in the light fitting. Connect the brown core opposite the brown flex core, the blue core opposite the blue flex core, and the green-and-yellow sleeved core to the terminal marked E or ⏚. If the fitting is double-insulated (marked ⧈) and has no earth terminal, cut the earth conductor of the cable and seal it with insulating tape or fit a single plastic terminal block (cut from a strip) to the end of the sleeved earth core.

4 Screw the end covers in place and fit the baffle or shade.

5 Turn the electricity back on at the consumer unit and test the light fitting.

Fitting a light with a separate switch

1 Turn off the main switch at the consumer unit and remove the fuse or switch off the MCB protecting the circuit you are working on.

2 Lead a spur from the lighting circuit (page 300) to a junction box in the ceiling space or loft above the position for the light.

3 Prepare the cable routes. You will need one cable run from the junction box to the light fitting and another from the junction box to the switch position. Fit a mounting box for the switch.

4 Lay 1mm² cable from the junction box to the light. Feed it into the light fitting through the entry hole.

5 Then lay 1mm² cable from the junction box to the light switch position and feed it into the mounting box. Repair plaster.

6 Prepare all the cable ends for connection. Remember to put a piece of brown plastic sleeving over the blue core of the switch cable at both ends to show that it is live.

7 Connect the cable to the terminal block in the light fitting (left, step 3).

8 At the light switch, connect the brown core to one of the terminals and the brown-sleeved blue core to the other terminal. Connect the green-and-yellow sleeved earth core to the earth terminal in the mounting box. Screw the switch faceplate to its mounting box, folding the cable neatly into the box.

9 At one terminal in the junction box, connect the brown cores of the spur cable and the switch cable. At another terminal connect the blue cores of the spur cable and the cable from the light. At a third terminal connect the brown core of the cable from the light and the brown-sleeved blue core of the switch cable. At the fourth terminal, connect all the green-and-yellow sleeved earth cores.

Fitting low-voltage recessed spotlights

Brilliant, low-voltage lights are ideal for kitchens. Because they are small, it is possible to site lights directly above where they are needed, thus avoiding the shadows and dark areas that can arise with more traditional centrally mounted lighting.

The following instructions relate to a typical installation of ceiling-mounted recessed lights to replace an existing single light. Not all lights are identical, so be sure to read the installation instructions that come with your particular lights, as there may be differences from those described here. In order to fit these lights, you will need access to the ceiling from above.

Tools *Pencil; padsaw, or power drill with holesaw attachment, probably 57mm in diameter; compasses; insulated screwdriver; trimming knife; wire cutters and strippers.*

Materials *Low-voltage lights with individual transformers; 1mm² two-core-and-earth cable; junction boxes.*

Before you start Although low-voltage lighting is very safe, the transformers connect to the 230-volt mains circuit and must be treated accordingly.

1 Decide on where you want to site the lights and draw circles on the ceiling the same diameter as the light fittings. Then use a holesaw of this diameter – usually 57mm – fitted to a power drill, to cut perfect holes fast and accurately.

Alternatively Drill a hole just inside each circle large enough to admit a padsaw blade and cut the holes by hand.

2 Switch off the power at the mains and remove the fuse or switch off the MCB for the circuit you are working on. Examine the wiring to the present light fitting. If there is just one cable leading into a ceiling rose or the light fitting, disconnect this and re-connect the cores into three of the four terminals of a 5A junction box secured to the side of a joist. If you have a loop-in ceiling rose, identify the cables (page 275), label them with a ball-point pen and re-connect them in a 15A junction box, secured to a joist, using all four terminals (central picture on page 300 ignoring the spur cable).

3 Remove the old light fitting and make good the damage to the ceiling plaster.

4 Connect a new length of 1mm² two-core-and-earth cable to the terminals in the junction box – blue core to black circuit cables and brown core to red sleeved black core in switch cable (or, for a single cable, blue to black and brown to red). Run the new cable to the nearest new light position. Terminate it at a junction box together with a new length of 1mm² two-core-and-earth cable. Run the new cable to the next light in the sequence and so on until each hole has wiring to it and a junction box to connect into. Working from above, use a cordless drill with a 12mm wood bit if you have to make cable holes through any joists.

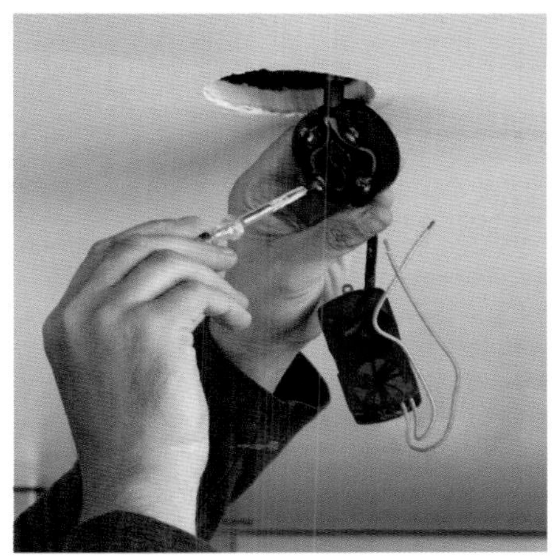

5 At each location, wire in the transformer supply lead to the junction box.

HELPFUL TIP

Use a stud detector to check the positions of ceiling joists in the area that you wish to place the lights. Ideally, lights should be placed centrally between the joists. If you position most of the lights between the same two joists, you will have less trouble running cables, as you will not need to drill through joists.

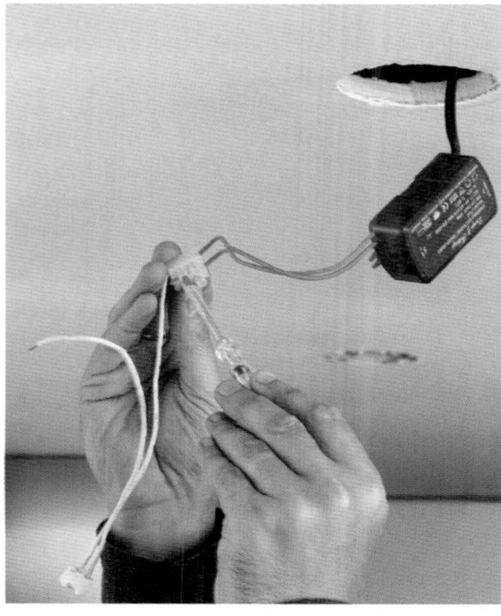

6 Connect each light to its transformer, using the plastic strip connectors supplied. Then push each transformer and junction box up into the ceiling void, leaving the bulb connectors hanging down.

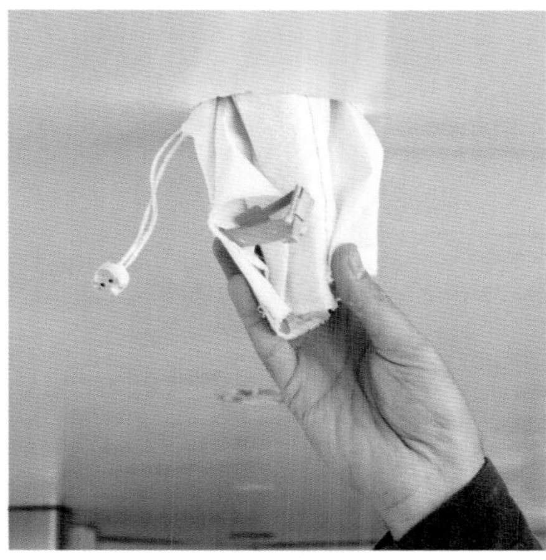

7 Push the smoke hoods up into the ceiling void, taking care not to push the bulb connectors with them.

8 Insert the light fittings into the holes until you hear them click: as you push the light up, the shorter arms on the clips force the longer arms to flatten against the upper surface of the ceiling.

SAFETY WARNING

Each recessed spotlight should be fitted within a smoke hood. This sits in the ceiling void above each spotlight and prevents smoke from the kitchen rising through gaps in the ceiling and floorboards to the upper floors, in the event of a fire.

9 Fit a halogen bulb into each light fitting. Push the bulbs into place and snap on the metal ring clip to hold them. Turn on the power at the main switch to check the operation of the lights. If you need to change a bulb at a later date, gently squeeze the ends of the metal ring clip together so you can remove it and take out the bulb. Be sure to replace it with one of the same wattage.

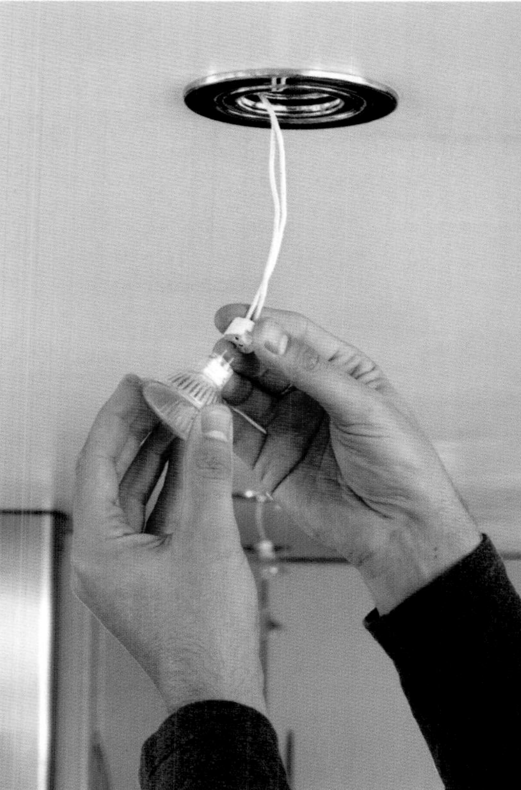

 **All projects carrying this symbol are notifiable – see page 280**

Wiring a new lighting circuit

Lighting circuits are wired with 1mm² two-core-and-earth cable. A house usually has two lighting circuits, one serving the downstairs and the other upstairs. You may need an extra circuit if you want to install a lot of extra lighting, or if you build an extension.

A lighting circuit is protected by a 5amp fuse or a 6amp MCB at the consumer unit. The maximum load that one circuit can supply is 1200 watts.

For each lighting point on the circuit, the cable passes through either a loop-in ceiling rose or a junction box and is connected to terminals there. From the rose or junction box, wiring leads off to the light and to the light switch. In many houses, a light circuit will include both loop-in ceiling roses and junction boxes.

In order to meet the Wiring Regulations, a new lighting circuit with cable run in walls will have to be protected by a 30mA RCD. Unless you have a spare 6A MCB that can be RCD-protected (or can be replaced with a 6A RCBO – see page 288), install a 30mA RCD and a 6A MCB in a new four-way enclosure as described on page 281.

Loop-in system

A loop-in ceiling rose has a row of terminals to connect in three cables – the two circuit cables, and the switch cable – and the flex that goes to the lampholder. If the rose is the last one on the circuit, there will be only one main circuit cable.

All the connections, except the earths, are made to a single row of terminals. All can be reached simply by unscrewing the rose cover. There is no need to lift floorboards in the room above to reach them, as with junction boxes.

Junction box system

The circuit cable is not led to the lighting point but to a junction box between the lighting point and the switch position. The junction box has four terminals for connecting four cables – two circuit cables, the switch cable and the cable to the lighting point.

- This system is seldom used for a whole lighting circuit because of the extra work involved in installing a junction box for each lighting point, and the fact that once the wiring is completed the connections are not accessible without lifting a floorboard. But there are some situations where it is needed for individual lighting points. For example, strip lights, spotlight tracks, recessed lights and some other special fittings are not designed for loop-in wiring; instead they incorporate a terminal connection block for connection to a single cable from a junction box.

Planning the circuit

Consider whether each lighting point will be better suited to loop-in or junction box wiring. Position any junction boxes in a ceiling space or loft where you can screw them to joists.

- Cables to light switches must run from the rose or junction box to a spot directly above the switch and then be chased in plaster, or led inside a stud partition wall, or in trunking vertically down the wall. Never run cables diagonally across walls; there is a danger of piercing them later with fixings for pictures or built-in furniture.

Loop-in wiring system

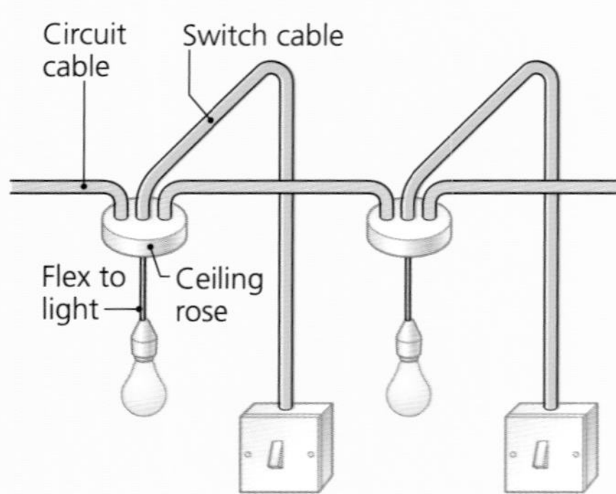

Junction box wiring system

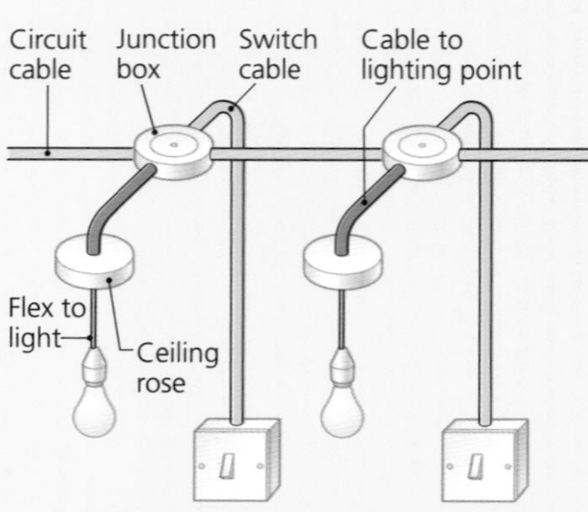

Installing the circuit

Tools *Suitable tools for preparing the route (page 282); trimming knife; wire cutters and strippers; insulated screwdrivers; pliers.*

Materials *1mm² two-core-and-earth cable; green-and-yellow sleeving; brown sleeving; ceiling roses; flex; lampholders; light switches with mounting boxes, screws and grommets; available 5amp fuseway or 6amp MCB in consumer unit. Perhaps 1mm² three-core-and-earth cable for two-way switches; special light fittings.*

1 Prepare the route for the circuit cable (page 282). Leave one end at the consumer unit for connection later, and run the cable up to ceiling level. If it is to go above the ceiling, you will have to lift floorboards to run it along and through joists.

2 Prepare the routes for the switch cables which will run from every loop-in-ceiling rose or junction box to the switch positions. If a light is to be controlled by two-way switches (page 297), prepare a route to the second switch position.

3 For lights that will be wired on the junction box system, prepare routes from the junction boxes to the light positions.

4 Fit ceiling roses securely (page 284) where there are to be pendant lights.

5 Fit junction boxes where necessary for special light fittings, screwing the bases of each to the side of a joist.

6 Fit mounting boxes for all the switches.

7 Lay lengths of cable from above the consumer unit to the first ceiling rose or junction box, from there to the next rose or box, and so on. Leave enough cable at the ends of each length for the cores to reach all the terminals easily. Secure the cable by threading it through joists or by fixing clips to hold it to the sides of joists.

8 Lay and secure switch cables from each loop-in ceiling rose or junction box to each switch. For any two-way switches, also lay three-core-and-earth cable to connect the two switches. Allow enough cable to reach all the terminals easily.

9 Feed the cable ends into ceiling roses or junction boxes and into the light switches. Repair all plaster damage.

10 Prepare the cable ends for connection. Sleeve the earth conductors and on all switch cables put brown sleeving over the blue conductor at both ends.

11 For each ceiling rose, cut a length of flex that will allow the lampholder to hang at the desired height. Connect the flex to the lampholder first, then slide the cover of the ceiling rose onto the flex and connect it to the rose (see page 275).

Connecting at switches

Connect one-way switches as described on page 296 and connect two-way switches as described on page 297.

Loop-in connections at a ceiling rose

At each ceiling rose except the last one on the circuit, two circuit cables have to be connected; at the last there is only one circuit cable. There is also a switch cable and a light flex to connect at each rose.

1 In the central group of three terminals, connect the brown cores from the two circuit cables and switch cable. Connect the blue cores from the circuit cables to one of the outer terminals. Leave the outermost one clear for connecting the blue flex core.

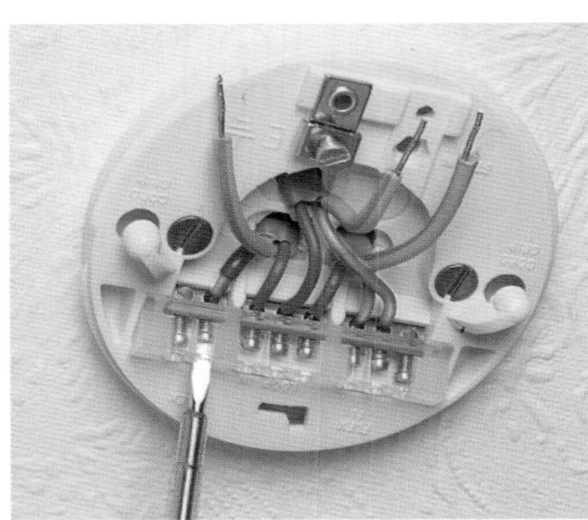

2 At the other outer terminal, connect the brown-sleeved blue switch core. Connect the brown and blue flex cores to the outer terminals and pass the flex cores over the hooks to take the lampshade's weight.

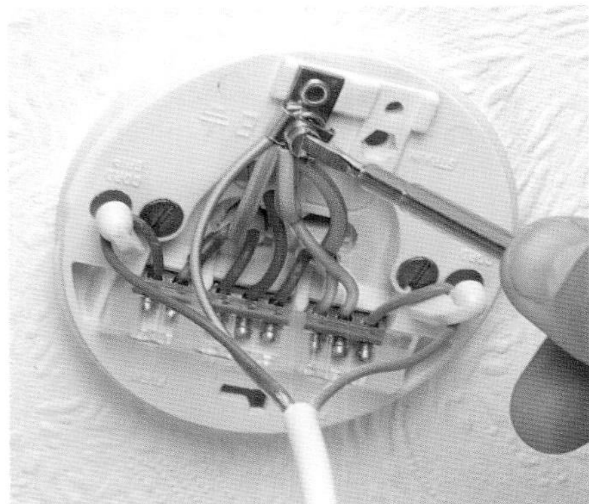

3 Finally, connect all the green-and-yellow sleeved earth cores to the terminal marked E or ⏚. Fit the ceiling-rose cover.

Connections at a junction box

At each junction box except the last on the circuit there will be two circuit cables, a switch cable and a cable to the lighting point. At the last box there will be one circuit cable instead of two.

1 At one of the terminals, connect the brown cores from the two circuit cables and the switch cable. At another terminal, connect the blue cores from the two circuit cables and from the cable to the lighting point.

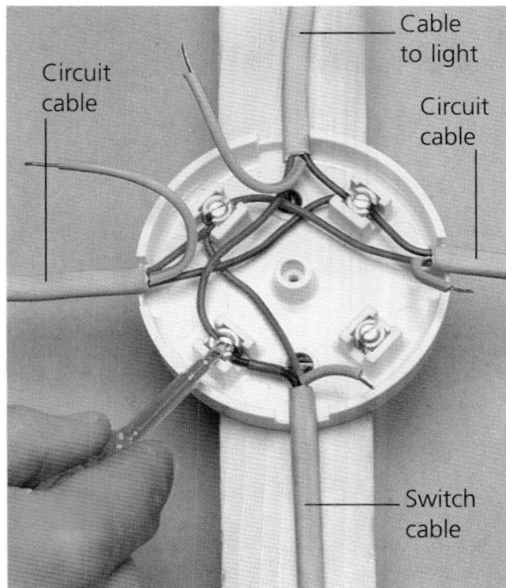

2 At a third terminal, connect the brown core from the cable to the lighting point and the brown-sleeved blue switch core.

3 At the fourth terminal, connect all the sleeved earth cores.

4 Screw on the junction box cover.

Connecting light fittings to a junction box system

Single spotlights, multi-spotlight tracks, recessed lights and fluorescent strip lights are among the special light fittings that are best connected to a junction box system.

1 Fix the light fitting to the ceiling. The mounting plates to hold tracks and strips should be screwed through the plasterboard or plaster into joists or into battens nailed between the joists to give a secure fixing (see page 284).

2 The light fitting may have a terminal block already holding the flex cores and ready to receive the cores from the light cable. Connect the brown cable core to the terminal opposite the brown flex core. Connect the blue core to the terminal opposite the blue flex core. Connect the green-and-yellow-sleeved earth core to the third terminal. If the light fitting is double-insulated (marked ⧈) there will be no earth terminal; cut short the cable earth core and seal it with insulating tape to make sure that it cannot touch any terminals.

Alternatively The light fitting may not have a terminal connector block – and no space to fit your own. If this is the case, install a circular drylining box in the ceiling and make the connections between cable and flex inside that, using your own terminal connector block cut from a strip.

Connecting at the consumer unit

1 Turn off the main switch on the consumer unit, if you have not already.

> **WARNING**
>
> The main switch disconnects only the fuses or MCBs and the cables leading out from the consumer unit to the household circuits. It does NOT disconnect the cables entering via the meter from the service cable. Do not interfere with these cables. They are always live at mains voltage.

2 Remove the screws from the consumer unit cover and open it. Feed the circuit cable into the top of the consumer unit. Use an existing hole if there is room.

3 Check that you have stripped off enough outer sheath for the cores to reach the terminals easily, but make sure that the sheath enters the consumer unit.

4 Connect the new cable's brown core to the terminal at the top of the spare 6amp MCB or RCBO you are using.

Alternatively Connect the brown core to the top of the 6A MCB in the four-way enclosure as shown on page 281. The other MCB in this enclosure could be used for a new cooker circuit (page 290), a new shower circuit (page 288) or a new socket outlet circuit (page 292).

5 Connect the new cable's blue core to the neutral terminal block. Then connect the green-and-yellow sleeved earth core to the earth terminal block. Switch on MCB or RCBO.

Alternatively Connect the blue core to the neutral terminal block in the four-way enclosure and the green-and-yellow sleeved earth core to the earth block.

6 Fix the cover of the consumer unit back in place, refit the cover over the fuse carriers and turn the main switch back on.

Testing and making good

Fit bulbs or fluorescent lamps into the lampholders and fittings and turn on each light in turn to make sure that it is working. If not, check and tighten the connections, remembering to turn off the electricity at the consumer unit before you do so.

Adding an aerial socket outlet for a second TV set

You can connect more than one TV set to your aerial by leading the aerial cable into a splitter unit, which has one input and two outputs.

Run coaxial cable from each output on the splitter to a coaxial socket outlet near each TV set. Link each set to a socket with coaxial cable fitted with a coaxial plug at each end. Plugs vary in design but have the same basic features. There are male and female plugs to suit different socket outlets.

The aerial cable may be run outside the house and brought inside through a hole drilled in a wall or window frame. Position the splitter where the cable enters the house. The cables between splitter and sockets are normally run as surface wiring, typically along the tops of skirting boards, held in place with matching cable clips or hidden inside mini-trunking.

Where the coaxial cable runs into the house from outside, you can use flush-fitting socket outlets over standard single mounting boxes recessed into the wall; for surface wiring, use surface-mounted sockets and boxes screwed to the wall.

Tools *Suitable tools for preparing the route (page 282); trimming knife; wire cutters and strippers; insulated screwdrivers; pliers.*

Materials *Coaxial TV cable; cable clips or trunking; splitter unit; two flush-fitting coaxial socket outlets with mounting boxes and grommets, or two surface-mounting coaxial sockets; coaxial plugs.*

1 Prepare cable routes from the position for the splitter to the position for the sockets and, if necessary, from where the cable enters the house to the splitter.

2 If you are using flush-fitting socket outlets, fit mounting boxes for them. Knock out a convenient entry hole in each box, fit a grommet and screw the boxes in place. Feed the aerial cable out through the wall to the chosen position for the splitter.

3 Lay cable along each route from the splitter position to the socket outlet positions. Use cable clips or trunking to secure it. Avoid bending it sharply.

4 If you are fitting flush socket outlets, feed the cable end for each outlet through the grommet into the mounting box. Make good the plaster and wait for it to dry.

Alternatively For surface-mounted sockets, feed the cable end up through the floor at the base of the skirting. You will have to cut a notch or drill a hole in the floorboard to prevent it from chafing the cable. If the cable is not under the floor, feed it from the skirting or trunking to the spot where the base of the socket will be.

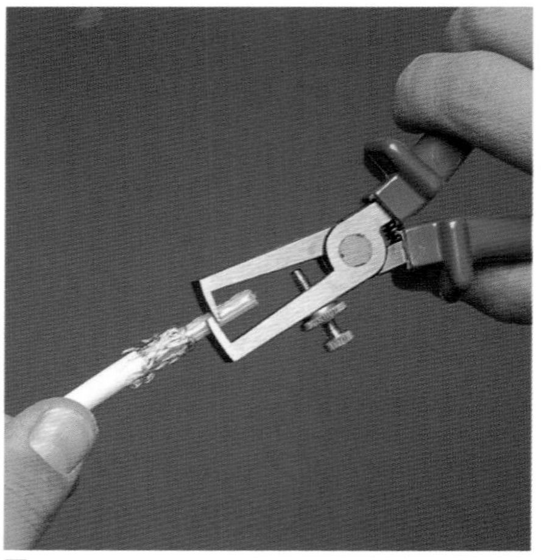

5 Prepare all the cables ends for connection. Make a 30mm slit with a trimming knife lengthways at the end of the outer sheath. Fold back the sheath and cut it off. Loosen the wire mesh and press or fold it back to leave 20mm of inner insulation. Use wire strippers to remove 15mm of the inner insulation.

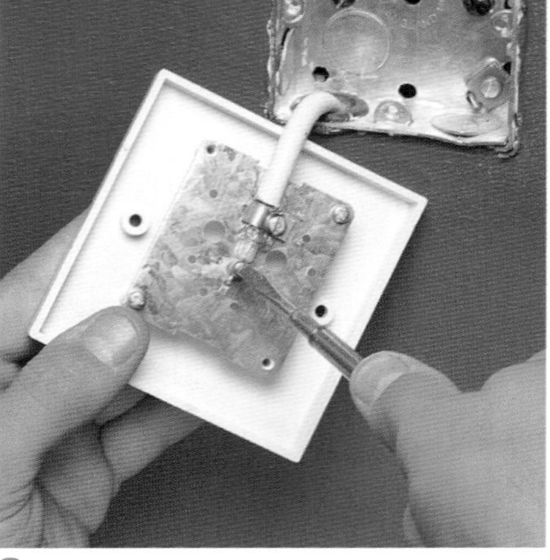

6 To connect at a flush socket outlet, secure the inner wire tightly in place at the terminal. Loosen the adjoining clamp, secure the wire mesh and cable under it and screw the clamp tight. The strands of the mesh must not touch the inner wire. Screw the socket outlet over the mounting box.

Alternatively With a surface-mounted socket, secure the inner wire to the central terminal and the wire mesh and cable itself under the clamp and screw the socket to the skirting board behind the TV set.

7 Secure the splitter to a joist or to the skirting and push the aerial cable plug into the correct socket on the splitter.

8 Plug the cables that run to the sockets into the splitter outlets, and the other two cables into the socket at one end and the TV set at the other end.

Choosing connectors for aerials

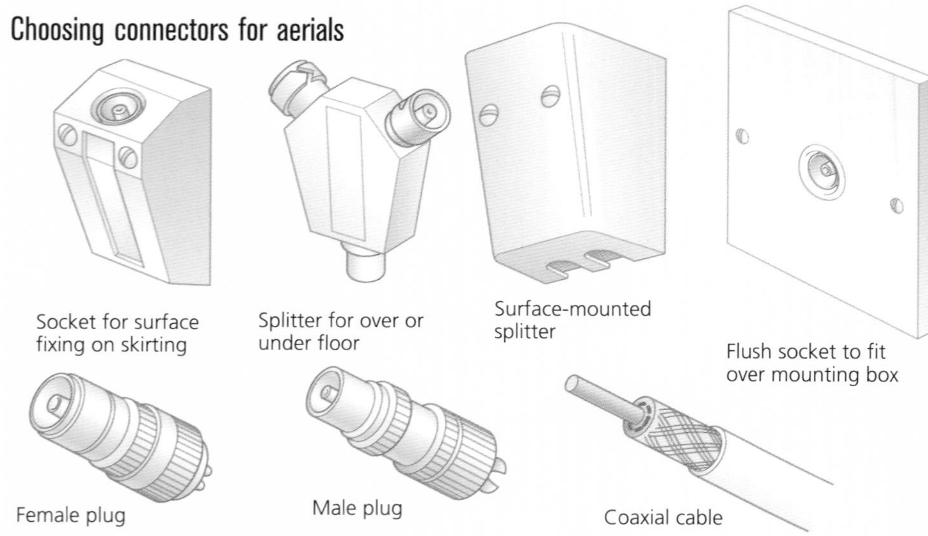

Wiring a coaxial plug

Aerial connectors can work loose over time, or you may need to extend the length of the cable to reach from the socket to your television. You can wire a new plug to a coaxial cable or repair a broken connection.

Tools *Trimming knife; pliers.*
Materials *Required length of coaxial cable; pair of coaxial plugs.*

COMPONENTS OF A COAXIAL PLUG

Coaxial plugs come in several parts, which must be separated for fitting. The wire at the centre of the cable carries the signal and connects with the pin in the male plug.

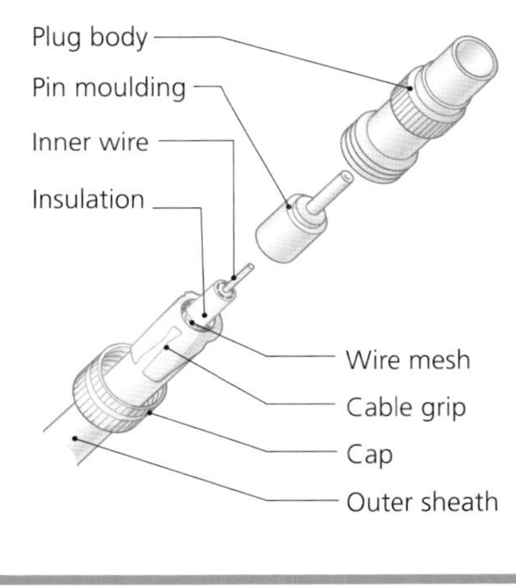

1 Strip away a 30mm length of the outer sheath to expose the wire mesh beneath. Fold back 20mm of the wire mesh to expose the inner insulation.

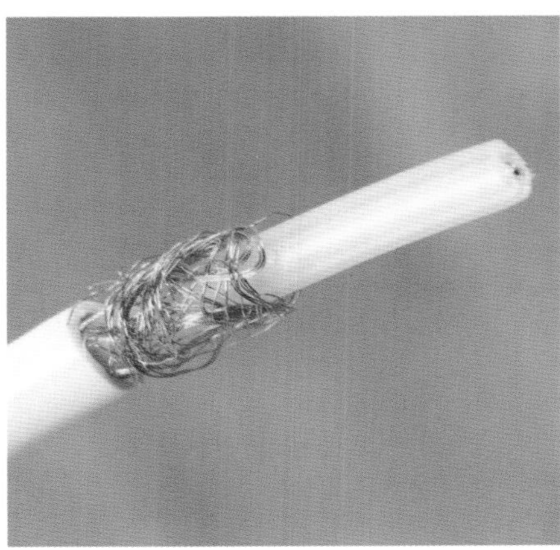

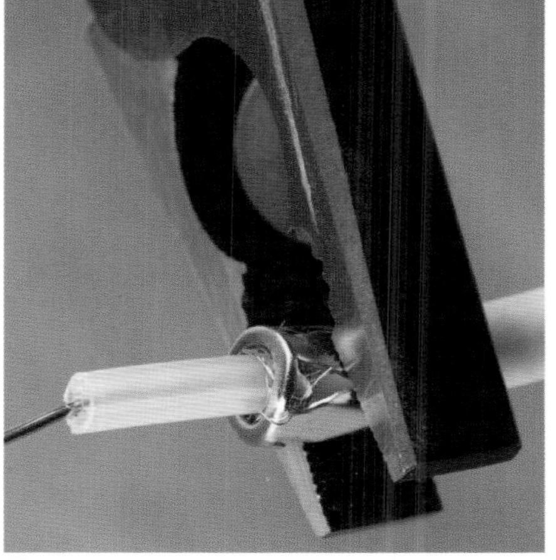

2 Use wire strippers to remove 15mm of the inner insulation (see opposite), leaving the central inner wire exposed. Slide the cap down the cable and fit the cable grip over the exposed mesh and cable. The strands of the mesh must not touch the inner wire. You will have to open the jaws of the grip to cover the mesh and then squeeze them together with a pair of pliers.

3 Feed the inner wire into the pin moulding and fit the moulding in the plug body. Slide the cap over the cable grip and screw it to the plug body. (For a really secure connection, solder the inner wire into the pin moulding.)

4 Connect all the plugs in the same way, fitting a male or female plug as necessary to suit the connection on the socket outlet or splitter and the television set.

Splitting and combining signals for TV and audio

If you have a standard television aerial, a satellite dish and maybe an FM aerial as well, you can combine the signals to run just one cable from the roof to the living room and then split them again to route to individual television and audio components.

1 Fit a TV/FM diplexer, or triplexer if you have three signals to combine, in the loft or wherever your television and FM aerials are mounted. This simple socket allows two or three cables to be fed in and one single cable to run out, carrying multiple signals at slightly different frequencies.

2 Run this cable to the point where you need the signals to diverge once more and fit a TV/FM diplexed twin socket (or a triple, if required) in the room.

BOOSTING THE SIGNAL

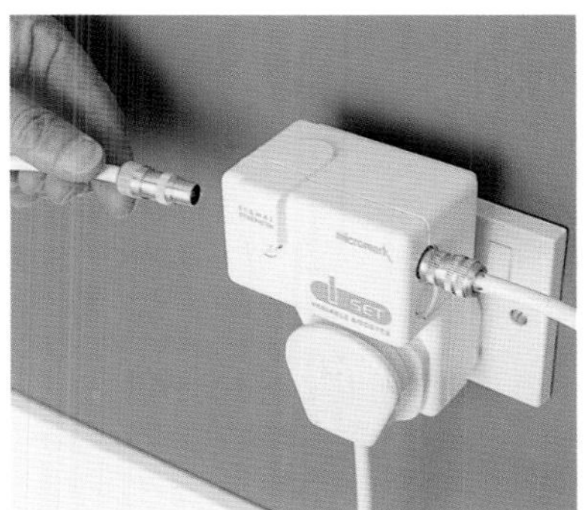

If the television signal where you live is weak, a simple plug-in amplifier can make a big difference to your picture quality. Plug the amplifier into the socket that powers your television then connect the lead from the aerial and the lead going out to the television.

Every time you split a signal to supply an additional television set, the signal to all the sets is weakened. Using a combined splitter and amplifier unit solves this problem, by boosting the signal where it first enters the house. Plug in the main 'in' cable from the aerial and take out separate feeds for each set in the house.

Installing your own telephone extensions

You can install telephone extensions easily by using kits sold in electrical shops, DIY centres and phone shops.

The law requires a master socket to be fitted by the company that provides the service. You should already have one; it is a square white socket. An old-style box will not accept the new plugs.

• Once you have a modern master socket you can install extensions throughout the house, provided there is no more than 100m of cable between the master socket, and the farthest extension socket, and no more than 50m between the master socket and the first extension socket.

• Extensions should not be fitted in damp areas such as bathrooms or toilets, or close to swimming pools.

• For safety reasons, telephone wiring must be kept at least 50mm from mains electric cables. The wiring works on a safe voltage, but it is advisable not to plug it into the master socket while doing the installation. If you need to join lengths of cable, use a joint box (see right).

These instructions use British Telecom fittings; others may vary slightly.

Tools *Wire cutters; electrical screwdriver; trimming knife; bradawl or pencil; drill and masonry bit to fit wallplug provided with kit; screwdriver; small hammer; insertion tool (provided with kit).*

Materials *Telephone socket for each extension; socket converter attached to cable; cable clips; two or more telephone sets fitted with plugs. Possibly extra cable (without converter) and clips, depending on the number of extensions.*

Main telephone and extensions

The square white master socket must be installed by the company that provides the telephone service. This socket is the starting point for all extensions, which can be fitted anywhere in the house. A converter plugs into the master socket, and its cable runs to the first extension socket where the other end is wired in. Another cable runs to the next extension. Telephones are plugged into the converter and the sockets.

HELPFUL TIP

You will probably find it easier to wire the socket before fixing it to the wall (as described).

Wiring one extension

1 Decide where the extension socket is to be placed, and plan a route for the cable. It can be fitted along walls or skirting boards, or can run above ceilings and under floors.

2 Run the cable from the master socket to the point where the extension socket will be fitted. The converter on the cable goes at the master socket end, but do not connect it yet.

3 Fix the cable by hammering in the cable clips every 300mm, but leave the last few clips at the extension end until later.

4 Cut the cable where it reaches the extension-socket position, leaving about 75mm to spare.

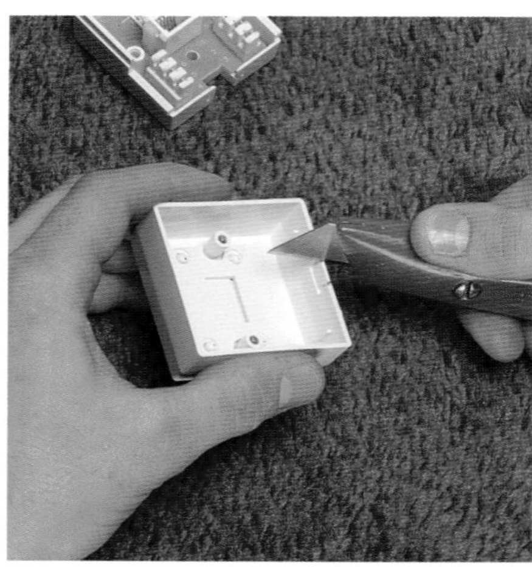

5 Unscrew the front plate from the extension socket and use a trimming knife to cut away the entrance hole which is marked on the inside of the plate at the bottom.

6 Using the trimming knife, strip about 30mm from the cable's outer sheath.

7 When there are six conductors, use the insertion tool to connect them to the socket, pushing them firmly into the grooves. Hold the tools as shown top right and push the green conductor with white

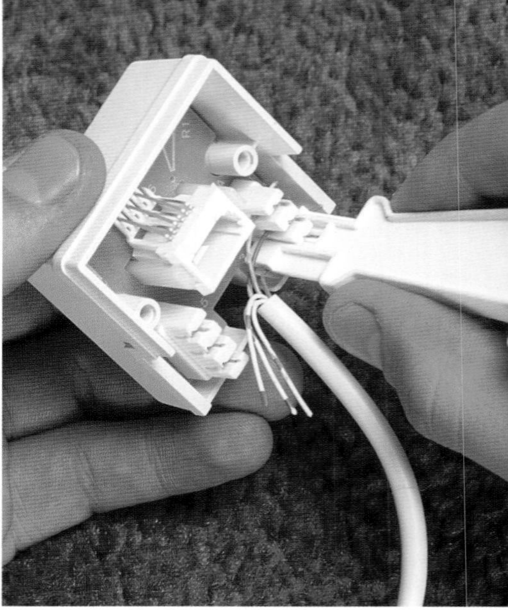

rings into the connection marked 1; blue with white rings into connection 2; orange with white rings into connection 3.

Now rotate the tool to push in the others, but be careful; the numbers 4, 5 and 6 run from bottom to top. Push the white conductor with orange rings into connection 4, white with blue rings into connection 5, and white with green rings into connection 6.

8 Hold the back plate on the wall in the chosen position and mark the wall through the middle hole with a bradawl or pencil. Drill a hole in the wall to the depth of the wallplug. Insert the wallplug and screw the box to the wall.

9 Fit the front plate onto the back plate with the two screws.

10 Plug the converter into the master socket.

11 Fit the plug from the master telephone into the socket on the face of the converter.

12 Plug the extension telephone into its own socket.

Fewer than six conductors

If there are fewer than six conductors, leave connectors 1 and 6 empty or choose a four-connector extension socket.

Wiring extra extensions

You can install a second extension socket by running another cable from the first extension socket. No converter is needed. A third extension socket can be installed by running cable from the second, and so on.

1 Unplug the converter from the master socket and unscrew the front plate from the first extension socket.

2 Connect the conductors of the new cable in the same order as previously, on top of the existing ones. This can be done with the socket on the wall or, if you prefer, the socket can be temporarily removed.

3 Wire the other end of the cable to the second extension socket. Continue in this way for any further extensions. Fit the new conductors on top of those already there.

4 Screw the front plates on the sockets and plug in the converter and the telephones.

What if it fails to work?

If a newly installed telephone fails to work, carry out this fault-finding procedure:

- Unplug the converter from the master socket, plug in the telephone and make a call. Test each extension telephone by plugging it into the master socket as well.
- If none of them works, the fault is in the wiring installed by the telephone company.
- If one of the phones fails to work, it is probably faulty. Return it to the supplier.
- If they all work, the fault lies in your new wiring, so check each socket to make sure that you have wired the coloured conductors to the correct numbers and pushed them right in. If the conductors are wrongly connected, pull them out one at a time with long-nosed pliers, cut off the used core and re-make the connection.
- If the sockets are properly connected, check that the cable is not kinked, cut or squashed. If it is, replace it.
- If the phones still do not work, return the sockets, joint box converter and cable to the suppliers and ask for a replacement.

More than one extension from a single point

There are some situations where you may want to run more than one extension from a single point. In this case, run cable from the converter at the master socket to a telephone joint box which will take that cable plus as many as three extensions.

1 Fit cable between the master socket and the position for the joint box. Do not plug in the converter yet.

2 Unscrew the front plate from the joint box and cut out the plastic for the cable at the top of both plates.

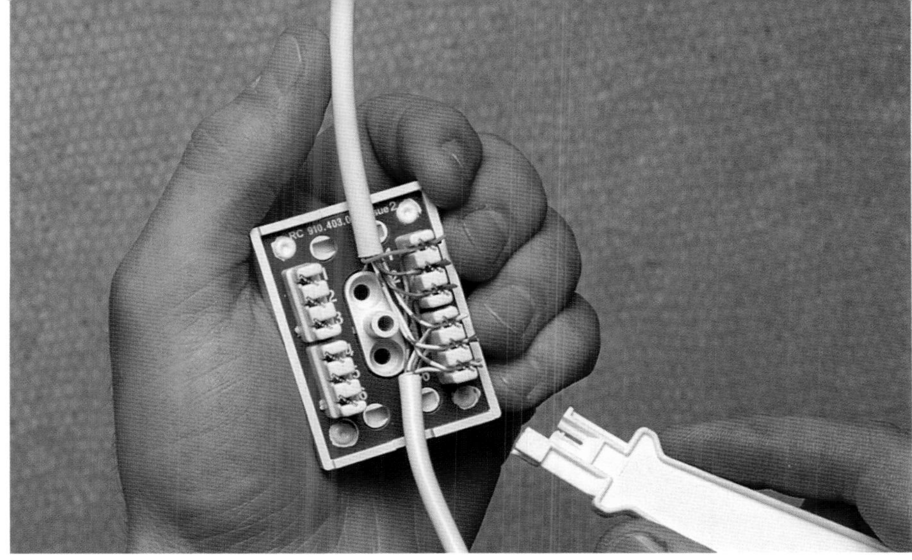

3 Fit the conductors into the joint box in the same way and the same order as in an ordinary socket. The one difference is that the six connectors are in two linked lines down the sides rather than to the left and right, so strip off about 40mm of the cable sheath to fix them. Fit one of the extension cables.

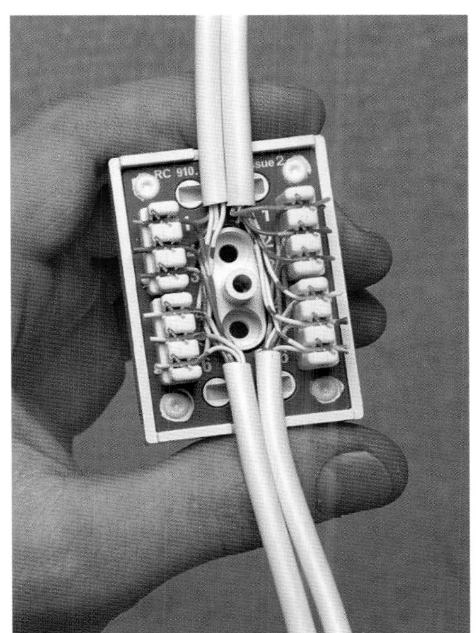

4 Fit the remaining extension cables in the same way, feeding them in from the top or the bottom.

5 Push the cable straps under the pairs of cables and through the holes at the top and bottom of the back plate, and pull them tight. Then cut off the tails.

6 Fix the back plate to the wall with the two wallplugs and screws provided.

7 Fit the extension cables to their sockets in the normal way.

8 Screw the front plates on all the sockets, then plug in the converter and all the new telephones.

COMPONENTS FOR DIY TELEPHONE WIRING

Extension sockets are smaller than the master socket that is installed by the telephone company. They are wired up with a plastic insertion tool supplied with the extension kit. A converter is supplied already attached to a long length of cable that is fixed in place with cable clips. A telephone joint box can be used to take up to three extensions from one point, as well as the cable. It can also be used to join two lengths of cable together if necessary.

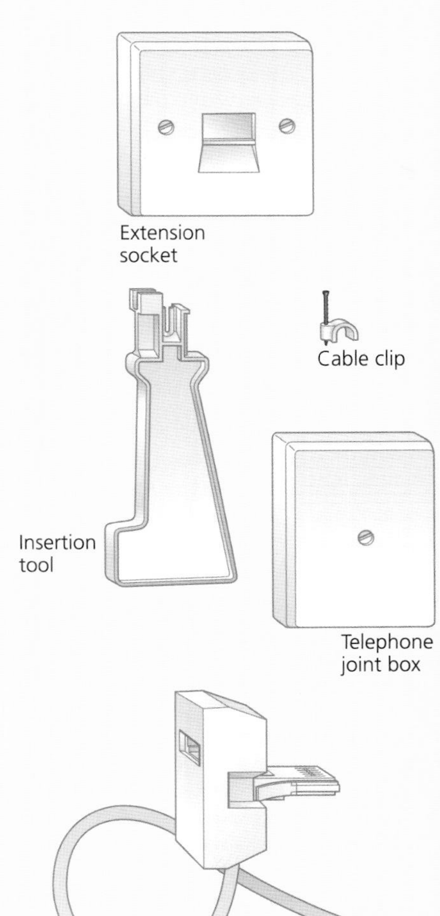

Wiring options for home computers

Many homes now routinely have more than one computer. Linking these together as a network allows the individual workstations to share a printer or internet connection or to transfer files from one to another automatically.

Benefits of a home network

Linking all the computers in the house on a single network makes it easy to transfer files from one to another. If you have one computer with a significantly larger hard drive than the others, you can also use that computer as a file server for the additional machines or as a back-up for the information stored on the individual PCs.

Another major benefit of a home network is the ability to share peripherals, such as printers, scanners or Webcams and to access the internet from any of the computers on the network via a single connection. Having just one computer 'live' online is a more secure option than having several computers simultaneously connected to the internet. With a high-speed broadband connection, more than one computer can be connected and online at any one time – or permanently.

Home network options

A home network system or LAN (Local Area Network) brings together all the systems that transmit electronic information around the house. This means that it is possible to integrate other services and systems into the network such as cable television, home entertainment systems, security systems and phone lines. The older traditional method is the peer-to-peer wiring method, where various jack sockets or connectors are installed along a single loop running throughout the house – in much the same way as telephone extensions are wired. Although simple to install, this kind of primitive network cannot handle voice and data signals at the same time. In addition, the more devices such as computers that are placed on the line, the more the network signal is weakened.

Wired or wireless? A hard-wired network of Ethernet cables linking computer to computer is the cheapest and most reliable option, whichever network design you choose to use (below). Transfer of information is often faster than with a wireless signal, but the initial set-up will cause greater disruption to the house and you will have to find ways of concealing cables or making them safe. A wireless network does away with trailing cables and fixed workstations. It offers flexibility that a wired network cannot match and is particularly well-suited to lap-top computer users. However, the hardware is more expensive than that required for a wired system and the connection will be less reliable, and often also slower.

Peer-to-peer networks The very simplest and oldest type of network is a loop-in system (above) where computers are linked in a string, known as a peer-to-peer system. In a home with only two computers, the workstations can be fitted with a network card and wired together with a single Ethernet cable. This system can also be used for more computers, but the quality of the signal is likely to be poor and if a problem develops with just one of the outlets in the string, the entire network will be affected.

Star networks Newer network systems resolve these problems by using what is called star topology in which all the cables are distributed from a central point. With this arrangement, if one connection fails it is unlikely to affect all the rest of the computers or other devices on the system. The ideal is to install all the cables when a house is built or replastered, burying them beneath floorboards or within the wall and terminating in sockets around the house. However, it is also possible to install these in existing properties, running cables beneath floorboards and above ceilings.

The central distribution point of the network may be a hub, wired Ethernet switch or wireless router (below), depending on your requirements. A hub will connect up to four computers in an average home network reliably and cost-effectively. If you have more than four computers to link, or if you often transfer very large files, such as music or video files or want the facility for high-speed online gaming, then a wired switch may be a faster and more reliable option.

WHAT IS ADSL?

ADSL stands for asymmetric digital subscriber line. What this means is that digital signals are sent over phone lines to and from your home computer. Even though you may only have one line into your home the ADSL recognises the difference between voice and data so you are able to be online and talk on the telephone at the same time. Using an ADSL connection, files downloaded from the internet are faster than those that are uploaded, in other words sent. If you will be sending files regularly then consider investing in an SDSL connection, or symmetric digital subscriber line. With this, data can be sent with the same speed in either direction.

CAT5 wiring If you are building a new house or completely renovating an existing property, it is worth considering installing CAT5 data cabling throughout. This is a more powerful Ethernet cable than the standard linking cable used in most wired networks, and is capable of carrying more data, much faster.

Even if you currently only use your home network for computer file-sharing, fitting a CAT5 network will give you the options of running telephone, computer, music or audiovisual signals throughout the house at a later date. The network also has the potential for upgrading to more sophisticated household electronics, such as room-to-room intercoms or door entry systems, touch-sensitive heating and lighting controls in each room, internet access from terminals other than home computers and much more.

Connecting computers in a star network

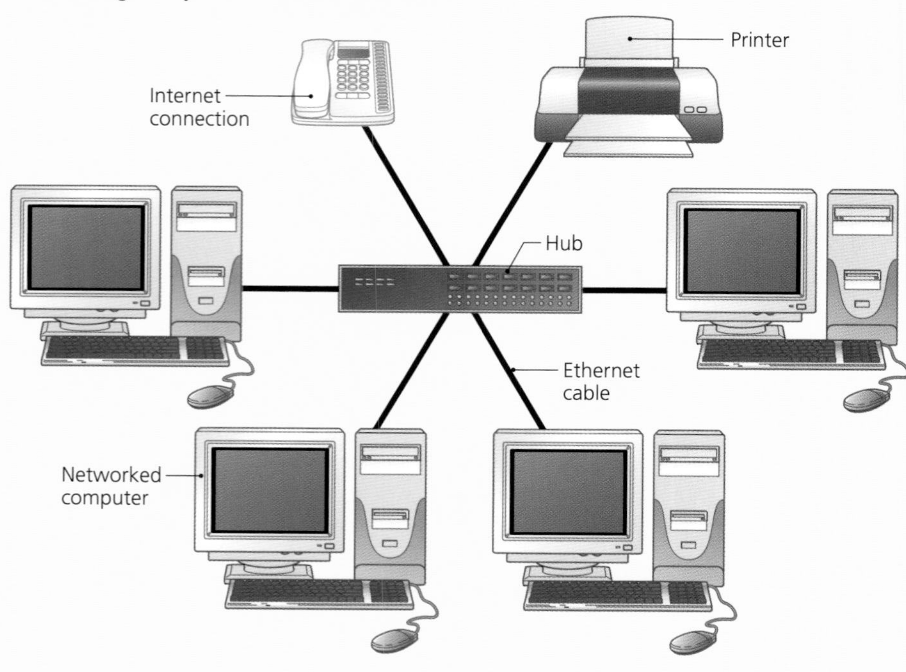

Wireless networks A wireless, or 'WiFi' network works from a hub called a router, which is wired into the internet connection, if you have one, and communicates with the computers on the network via a radio signal. Each computer is fitted with a Network Interface card: a credit card sized transmitter, and receiver that communicates with the base station, although most wireless routers allow for a combination of wired and wireless connections with computers on the network. Either the router or one of the terminals on the network may be connected to peripheral devices, such as a scanner, that each of the network computers can access.

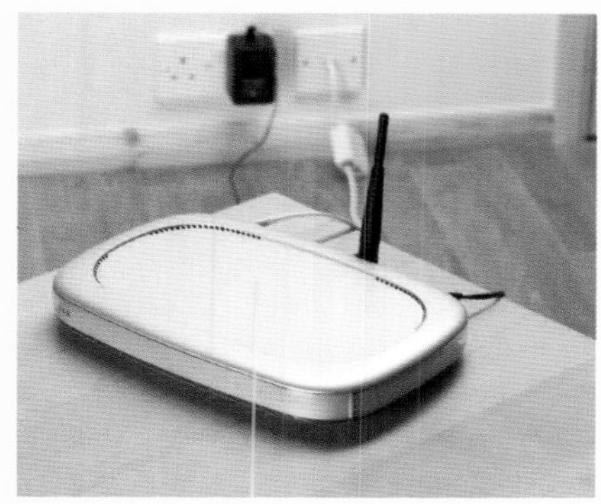

Most wireless routers have a range of up to 45m, but this is reduced if the signal has to pass through walls, particularly solid brick walls. To get the best connection to all the computers on the network, position the router high up in the house and as central as possible. A badly placed base station will lead to the signal dropping off and one or more of the computers becoming disconnected. Follow the instructions that come with the router for more specific advice on positioning.

Wireless routers are prone to interference from other household devices, such as microwave ovens, cordless telephones and automatic garage door openers. Consider this when deciding where to position your base station – putting it too close to the main cordless telephone in the house may affect the reliability of the network signal.

SHARING AN INTERNET CONNECTION

For several networked computers to access the internet through a single dial-up connection, the PC fitted with the modem must have enabled Internet Connection Sharing. Broadband routers make the connection themselves, eliminating the need for a designated internet 'host' computer. They also have the added benefit that they often come with built-in firewall support.

Installing a home computer network

Installing a home network allows you to link several computers together to access a single Internet connection, transfer or back up files, or share peripheral devices, such as a printer or scanner.

Tools *Drill; screwdriver; possibly also wire strippers and trimming knife.*

Materials *Network router; required lengths of Ethernet cable; required length of telephone or modem cable; broadband microfilter, if appropriate; possibly also lengths of plastic trunking to conceal cables.*

1 Mount the network router on the wall in a convenient location close to the incoming internet cable (telephone socket) and to a mains socket outlet. Follow the manufacturer's instructions: you may need to fit a wall bracket, or simply fix two screws protruding from the wall, on which the router will hang.

2 Decide on the route the network cables will have to take to reach the computers the router is to feed. Either prepare the route for burying the cables in the wall (page 282) or cut and fit lengths of plastic trunking along the skirting boards and door architraves. Connect the modem cable from the telephone socket to the router (above), running via a broadband micro filter if you use an ADSL internet connection (see opposite).

3 Run Ethernet cables out from the router to the computers it will serve. Tack the cables to the skirting board, bury them in the wall, or conceal them in plastic trunking to keep them out of the way.

4 Plug in the router to the socket outlet and follow the manufacturer's set-up instructions to establish the connection for each computer on the network.

Choosing a burglar alarm

Most thieves are likely to be deterred by locks on windows and doors, but you may decide to install an alarm system as an extra defence against a burglar who tries to force his way in. A noisy alarm may deter him from entering the house, or greatly reduce the time he stays there.

Before buying a system, check that the alarm is loud enough. Anything below 95 decibels has little effect and cannot be heard over any distance. Most alarms sound for about 20 minutes and then reset to avoid nuisance to neighbours. Notify your local police and your neighbours that an alarm has been fitted, and give a trusted neighbour a spare key to the system or the code number. A valuable addition to a system is a panic button, which can be used to trigger the alarm at any time. Some burglar-alarm systems are designed for DIY installation; others need to be professionally fitted.

WHOLE-HOUSE SYSTEMS THAT WARN OF A BREAK-IN

The most common alarm systems are designed to set off a bell or siren if a burglar tries to break in. Before buying one, ensure that the alarm has a 'closed' electrical circuit. This means that when the system is turned on the circuit is completed. If there is any interference – such as the wires being cut – the alarm will go off. Each system has three main components – the switches and detectors, the control unit and the alarm.

Control unit The 'brain' of the system is the control unit, which receives signals from the switches and sends an electric current to activate the alarm. The system is turned on or off with a key or a push-button panel to which a code number is first keyed in.

Connected with the control unit will be some form of power supply, either mains or battery. In most systems mains power will feed the system under normal conditions, but if the power is cut off for any reason, a battery will take over. The battery is automatically recharged when power is restored.

Passive infra-red (PIR) motion detectors These are small units, fitted at ceiling height, which sense movement through changes of temperature within their field of detection.

Panic button A manually operated switch can be fitted as a panic button – at the bedside or by the front door. It is usually wired so that it will trigger the alarm whether or not the rest of the system is switched on. Panic buttons can be very sensitive; the slightest pressure will set off the alarm.

External alarm The alarm has a bell or siren that should be loud enough to frighten off potential intruders and alert neighbours. Some external sirens also incorporate a bright, flashing strobe light; others feature flashing LEDs to indicate that the system is active and to add to the visual deterrent. The external alarm box should be tamper-proof and should contain its own battery, so that it will still sound if the cable to it is cut.

Magnetic door and window contacts A magnetic switch can be fitted to a door or window that opens. One part is secured to the frame, the other to the door or casement. If the magnet is moved (by opening the door or window) the circuit is broken and the alarm is triggered.

Door alarm This unit can be fitted to an external door and will set off an alarm if the door is opened. It is battery operated, so no wiring is needed. The alarm is turned off with a push-button code that you set yourself, or with a key. A delay switch allows several seconds for you to enter or leave the house without triggering the alarm.

Shed alarm This type of self-contained battery-powered alarm can be fixed in a shed, garage, caravan or greenhouse. It will pick up movement within its field of detection and activate its own alarm.

Wireless alarm systems Passive infra-red sensors and magnetic door contacts are independently battery powered and transmit a radio signal to the control unit when they sense movement; this in turn triggers the alarm. These 'wirefree' systems can be set using a remote key fob switch which doubles as a mobile panic alarm. Because the kits remove the need to run cables, they are much quicker to install. Some systems offer a repeater unit which increases the transmission range so that outbuildings may also be protected.

Closed-circuit television (CCTV) systems CCTV systems are now within the budget of most ordinary householders. Cameras are compact and systems that you can install yourself are widely available. You can choose whether to have the camera tied to its own dedicated monitor, or to utilise your own TV and video set-up. Some cameras incorporate passive infra-red (PIR) detectors to start recording only when movement is detected. When used to see who is at the front door, the sensor will automatically switch from the channel you are watching, to the surveillance camera.

PROTECTION FROM FIRE: SMOKE ALARMS

Building Regulations require mains-powered smoke alarms to be fitted in new properties and existing homes that are extended or where the loft has been converted. The Government recommends that at least two alarms approved to British Standard BS5446 Part 1 are fitted in an average two-storey house – one downstairs in the hall and the other on the landing.

Smoke alarms should be fitted within 7.5m of the door to every habitable room – living rooms, kitchens and bedrooms. An alarm fitted to the ceiling should be at least 300mm away from a wall or ceiling light fitting. Some alarms have an escape light fitted; some can be linked – so that if one detects smoke, all are activated.

Smoke alarms for existing homes can be battery-operated, wired to the mains with a back-up battery or plugged into a ceiling light fitting (below).

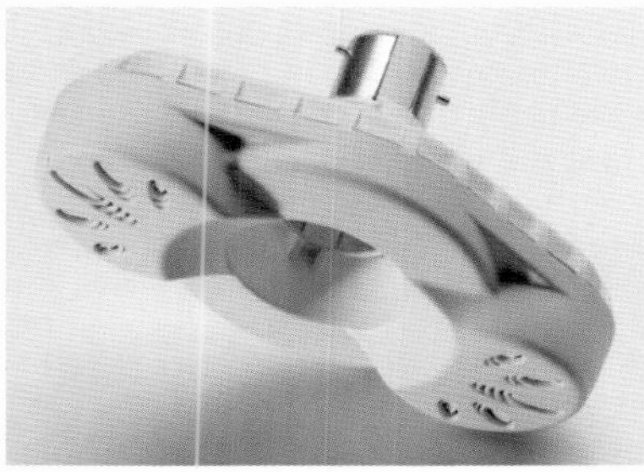

There are two basic types, ionisation and photoelectric. For good, all round protection use one of each.

- The ionisation alarm works by detecting invisible smoke particles in the air and responds quickly to fast, flaming fires, so it is a good choice for a bedroom, hall or landing. It is not suitable in or near a kitchen because it will be set off by cooking fumes.
- The photoelectric alarm 'sees' smoke and is more sensitive to smouldering fires which usually occur in furniture.

Some battery-powered alarms have indicators to show that the battery is still working; others give an audible warning when the battery is low. Plug-in alarms recharge when the light is switched on. Accumulated dust impairs performance, so clean alarms regularly using a vacuum cleaner nozzle.

Choosing time controls for security

A dark, silent house can arouse the interest of burglars. If you make the house appear occupied, by day or night, a prowler is likely to move on to an easier target.

Voices, music and lights after dark can suggest you are in – but only if used with discretion; a single light in the hall left on all evening, or a radio playing all day are more likely to betray that you are out. The illusion that you are there is given by a change in the house – music stopping, or a light going off in one room and on in another. Sockets and switches operated by timers help to create the illusion. Some sophisticated controls will memorise your schedule of switching lights on and off and reproduce it.

Light-switch timers

Time-controlled light switches are connected to the lighting circuit in place of normal switches and are wired in the same way (page 296). Some will switch on and off many times. Others switch on only once – at dusk – so there is no danger of the light shining in the daytime because a power cut has interfered with the setting.

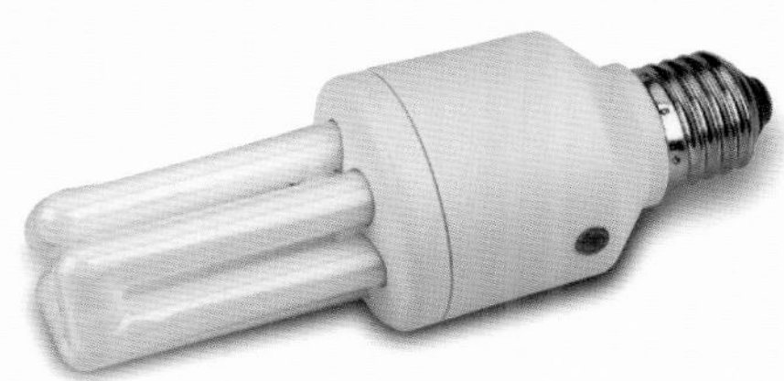

Sensor lamp and light sensor switch

Sensors automatically switch a low-energy bulb on and off at sunset and sunrise; the lamp has a 10,000 hour life. Alternatively, a light sensor switch can be used with tungsten lighting, or fluorescent or low-energy fittings. The switch is controlled by a light-sensitive photocell that activates it when daylight fades. The switch-off time is set at 1 to 8 hours after the light comes on.

Programmable switch Digitally controlled, these switches offer a sophisticated combination of on/off switching and are programmable to come on at different times during the week. Features may include light sensor settings and an over-ride. Most can only be used with tungsten lighting, but others are adapted to use low-voltage or fluorescent lighting.

Automatic outdoor light An infra-red sensor activates the light when anyone – visitor or burglar – comes within its field of vision. The sensor can be incorporated in either the light or a separate unit operating a number of lights. Once on, the light shines for a period chosen by the user.

Plug-in timers

A plug-in timer will control any appliance that plugs into a 13amp socket outlet – a radio or a lamp, to give the impression that the house is occupied, or a heater or electric blanket for convenience.

Set the required programme on the timer, plug it into a switched-on outlet, plug the appliance into the timer and switch on the appliance. It will not actually come on until the programmed time. You can override the set programme manually. There are 24-hour and seven-day timers. They vary in the number of times they will switch on and off, and in the shortest possible 'on' period.

24-hour timer Some plug-in timers allow you to design a pattern of switching on and off over a 24 hour period. Some models allow up to 48 changes in a day. Markers on a dial trigger the timer to switch on or off as the dial turns. The shortest 'on' period is usually 15 to 30 minutes. The pattern will be repeated every day until it is switched off or the markers are changed.

Seven-day timer These work in the same way as 24-hour timers, but switching patterns can be varied from day to day over a period of seven days; some will allow up to 84 switchings a week. The on/off pattern will then be repeated each week until altered. The minimum period for which it can be switched on is 2 hours.

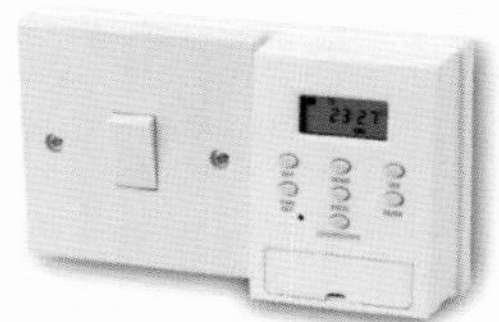

Electronic digital timer These timers offer a number of setting programmes and may allow up to 84 switchings a week. A random setting will switch lights or a radio on or off during the power-on period, to give the impression that a house is occupied. It can be used as a daily or weekly timer and will automatically repeat programmes.

 All projects carrying this symbol are notifiable – see page 280

Wiring to an outbuilding

An electricity supply to a detached garage, greenhouse, garden shed or other outbuilding must be run as a permanently fixed cable from the consumer unit in the house. A long flex run to the outbuilding from a socket inside the house is not acceptable.

The circuit to an outbuilding can be run overhead or underground.

• It is best to bury the cable despite the work involved. Cable underground does not mar the view, and with careful planning the length of the underground section can be kept to a minimum. Run the cable through the house to reach the point nearest the outbuilding to save work. If this is difficult, run the cable along the outside wall of the house to reach the point nearest the outbuilding. You can also run it along a boundary wall, but not along a fence.

• You can take the cable overhead, but it is unsightly to have it hanging immediately outside the house. It should be fixed at least 3.5m above the ground, which frequently entails fitting a timber post securely to the outbuilding to achieve the clearance. If it is more than 3m long, the cable span must be supported along its length by a metal wire (called a catenary) and must have a drip loop at each end.

• For underground cable, make the route of the trench as short as possible, well clear of obstacles such as rockeries, inspection chambers or trees. Allow some extra cable when you calculate the length needed in case you meet unexpected obstacles.

A professional electrician is likely to install armoured cable (see Cables and fittings for outdoor wiring, right), but this is fairly expensive and needs special connecting glands, which require some skill to use. It is easier to use ordinary two-core-and-earth cable for the entire sub-circuit between house and outbuilding, but the outdoor section of the circuit cable must be run in protective PVC conduit fixed to the walls of the buildings and laid in the trench. The run is made up using lengths of conduit linked with solvent-welded straight and elbow connectors.

• A 20A radial circuit can be run from a spare RCD-protected 20amp MCB in the consumer unit, but if this is not available, fit a new enclosure as described on page 281 with a 63amp/30mA RCD and one or two MCBs.

• Call in your electricity supply company to connect a new unit to the meter once you have installed the new circuit wiring. You are not allowed to do this yourself.

• Inside the outbuilding, the cable can be run to a socket outlet. A switched fused connection unit (FCU) can be run from this to provide a starting point for a fused lighting sub-circuit.

Tools *Tape measure; side cutters; wire strippers; power drill; long 20mm masonry bit; hammer; spade; hacksaw; trimming knife; hacksaw; screwdrivers.*

Materials *2.5mm² two-core-and-earth cable; cable clips; green-and-yellow PVC earth sleeving; brown PVC insulating tape; 20mm PVC conduit; wall clips; straight connectors and elbows; solvent-weld adhesive; sand; bricks; paving slabs; warning tape; enclosure with 30mA RCD and one or two MCBs; metal-clad double socket outlet and mounting box; metal-clad FCU and mounting box; 1mm² two-core-and-earth cable; batten lampholder; metal-clad light switch and mounting box; grommets; wood-screws; wallplugs.*

Cables and fittings for outdoor wiring

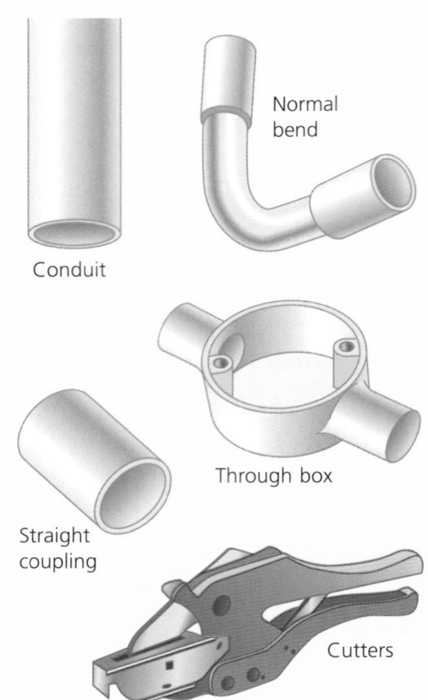

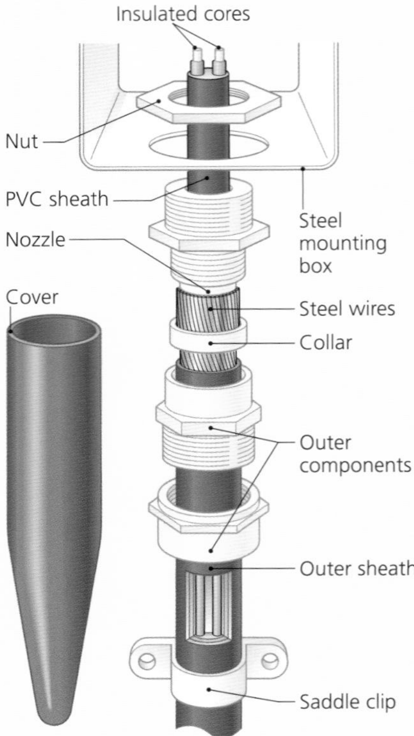

Plastic conduit

Plastic (PVCu) conduit can be used for protecting cable run in solid walls (page 282), to protect surface wiring run in an outbuilding and for underground wiring as described on these two pages. It comes in black or white, in various sizes (from 16mm to 50mm) and in two grades – make sure you use the high-impact (heavy gauge) grade underground. You can get straight couplers, curved connectors (bends and elbows), T-connectors and a whole range of special boxes and support clips. The conduit itself comes in 3m lengths, but can easily be cut with a hacksaw or special cutters; joining to fittings is done by solvent welding.

Armoured cable

Two insulated conductors are in a PVC sheath inside steel wires that serve as the earth conductor. There is a PVC outer sheath. Three-core armoured cable has three insulated cores, coloured brown, grey and black – the grey core can be used for the earth covered at the ends with green-and-yellow sleeving. Armoured cable needs no further mechanical protection, making it ideal for use outside and in outbuildings.

Use the right size and type of gland to seal the cable into a deep steel mounting box. On the two-core cable, be sure to tighten the gland nut hard to complete the earth continuity. Use galvanised, copper or plastic clips to hold the cable.

Work inside the house

1 Plan and prepare the cable route from the consumer unit or new enclosure to the point where it will leave the house. With suspended timber floors, run it beneath the floorboards.

2 Where the circuit cable will leave the house, locate a mortar course in the wall at least 150mm above the level of the damp-proof course. Use a long 20mm diameter masonry drill bit to drill from the outside, sloping the hole slightly upwards to discourage rainwater from entering and mortar in a short length of conduit.

3 Mount the new RCD unit on a board close to the meter. Remove knockouts from the base of the unit to admit the incoming meter tails and circuit cable. Clip the RCD and the MCB(s) onto the metal busbar, ready for connection later.

Outside work

1 Plan the cable route between the house and the outbuilding, and excavate the trench along the marked route. Avoid cultivated ground if possible; a route running close to a path or boundary wall is often the ideal choice.

2 Check the depth of the trench. In open ground, it should be at least 500mm deep.

3 Remove any sharp stones from the trench and put in a layer of dry sand about 50mm deep to protect the cable.

4 Measure the conduit run and work out how many lengths of conduit you will need. Conduit is available in 3m lengths.

5 At the house end of the run, feed the end of the circuit cable into the conduit in the wall. Pull enough cable through the conduit to make up the run inside the house from the entry point in the wall to the meter position and then unroll enough cable to complete the run.

6 Use a short length of conduit with an elbow solvent welded (page 347) on one end to connect to the conduit in the house wall and a large-radius elbow to connect to the conduit underground. Secure this to the house wall with clips. Assemble the conduit run by solvent-welding lengths of conduit together with straight joints. Brush a little of the special adhesive onto the pipe end, taking care not to get any on the cable sheath. Push the fitting onto the pipe and rotate it slightly to ensure a waterproof joint. Feed the whole cable run through the next length of conduit before joining it to the previous one. Continue adding lengths of conduit one by one in the same way.

7 Use a hacksaw to cut the last section of conduit to length as necessary. Smooth off any roughness using fine abrasive paper before joining it to the previous length of conduit.

8 When you have joined all the lengths of conduit together, lower the completed run into the base of the trench. Use a large-radius bend and a short length of conduit to take the run up to the point where it enters the outbuilding.

9 Pass a short length of conduit through the outbuilding wall and connect it to the underground run with a standard elbow. Secure exposed conduit with clips. Feed enough cable into the outbuilding to allow it to be connected to the wiring accessories that will complete the sub-circuit.

WEATHERPROOF SOCKETS

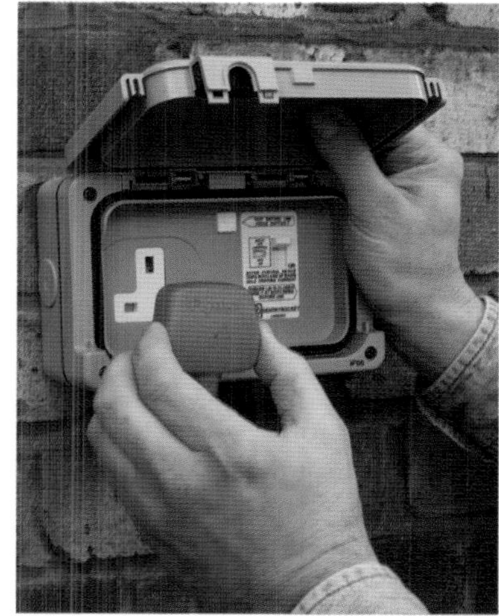

Sockets and light switches that are fitted outdoors must be weatherproof. Socket outlets on the house wall can be wired as spurs from an indoor power circuit (page 285), but must be protected by a high sensitivity (30mA) RCD (see page 318).

10 When you have completed the conduit run and laid it in the trench, place a line of bricks on the sand bed at each side of the conduit and lay narrow paving slabs over the bricks. This ensures that any future digging cannot damage the conduit or the cable inside it. Lay lengths of special yellow-and-black plastic warning tape over the slabs.

11 Back-fill the trench with the soil you excavated earlier, and tamp it down firmly.

Work in the outbuilding

1 Decide where in the outbuilding you want to position the various wiring accessories. Because the sub-circuit is controlled and protected by the RCD and MCB at the house end of the circuit, the simplest way of wiring up the accessories is to create a radial circuit. Run the incoming cable to the first socket, then on to any other sockets you want to install. At a convenient point in this radial circuit, include a fused connection unit (FCU) fitted with a 3amp fuse. From here a length of 1mm² cable is run to supply one or more light fittings and a separate light switch.

2 Screw the metal mounting boxes for the various wall-mounted accessories to the wall of the outbuilding. Use woodscrews driven direct into timber walls or frame members, and into wallplugs in drilled holes in masonry walls.

3 To protect the cable within the outbuilding, fit plastic conduit, supported by saddles, between the mounting boxes. The conduit is connected to the boxes by glands that fit into the box knock-out holes.

4 Feed the incoming cable into the first mounting box and cut it to leave about 150mm of cable within the box. Then run cable from this box to the next one, cutting it to length as before. Carry on adding lengths of cable one by one to connect all the wiring accessories. If you have difficulty pushing the cable through the PVC conduit, you can get draw tape to help.

5 Prepare all the cable ends for connection by stripping about 75mm of insulation from each conductor. Cover the bare earth cores with lengths of green-and-yellow PVC sleeving.

6 There will be two sets of conductors to connect to the socket faceplate at each socket (except at the last one on the circuit, which will have just one set). Connect the two brown conductors to the terminal marked L and the two blue conductors to the terminal marked N. Connect the sleeved earth conductors to the earth terminal on the faceplate. Add a short length of sleeved earth core (taken from a cable offcut) between this terminal and the earth terminal in the mounting box to earth the mounting box.

7 Check that all the connections are secure. Fold the conductors back into the mounting box and screw the faceplate to it. Repeat this process to connect up the other sockets on the sub-circuit.

8 At the fused connection unit (FCU), connect the conductors of the incoming cable to the terminals marked FEED or IN. The brown conductor goes to the terminal marked L, the blue conductor to the terminal marked N and the sleeved earth conductor to E or ⏚. Add an earth link between the earth terminals on the faceplate and the mounting box as before. Connect the 1mm² cable that will supply the light fitting in the same way, but to the terminals marked LOAD or OUT. Run this cable up to the position of the batten holder or light fitting you are installing. Fit a 3amp fuse in the fuseholder and screw the faceplate to the mounting box.

9 At the batten holder or light fitting, connect in the 1mm² cable from the FCU and another 1mm² cable to run onto the light switch. The two brown conductors go to the centre bank of terminals, and the blue conductors to the end terminals; it does not matter which way round these two are connected. Connect the two earth conductors to the earth terminal. Screw the cover on to the batten holder.

Connecting at the RCD unit

At the new MCB/RCD unit in the house, connect the brown conductor of the circuit cable to the top terminal of one of the MCBs. Connect the neutral and earth cores to their respective terminal blocks. The second MCB shown here is already wired to supply another sub-circuit. Your electricity supply company will fit the meter tails to the RCD and add the main earth cable shown.

Fitting an outdoor socket

Using power tools in the garden doesn't have to mean trailing extension leads out of a window. Run a spur from an indoor socket outlet circuit and install a weatherproof outdoor socket. If the circuit is not already RCD protected, use an outdoor socket with its own RCD.

1 A neat way to fit an outdoor socket is to drill through the back of an existing indoor outlet and locate the new one on the other side of the wall.

Alternatively, run a cable along the inside wall and drill through to the outside where you want the new socket.

2 Turn off the mains power and remove the faceplate and mounting box of the socket you will be working from. Drill a pilot hole then switch to a 10mm masonry bit at least 300mm long to drill through the wall. With the power switched off, you will need a cordless drill with a hammer action, to get through the wall.

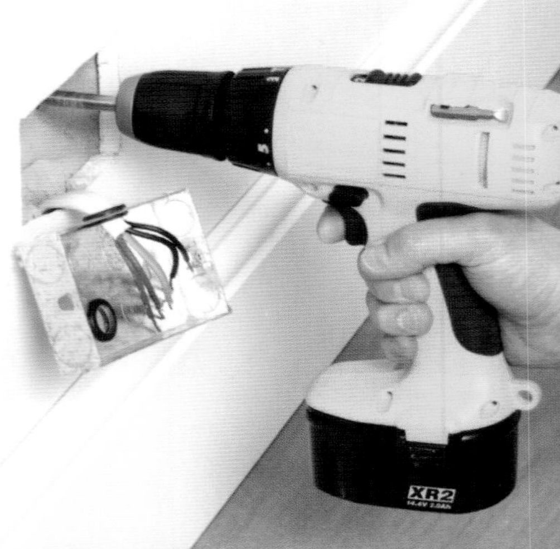

3 Screw back the mounting box and feed the new cable through the wall. Connect the old and new cores to the faceplate. There will be three cores in each terminal: the ring main cores coming in and going out, and the new spur. Reconnect the 'flying earth' cable to the box earth terminal and replace the faceplate.

4 For safety, use an outside socket with an entry point through the back. Any exposed cable on an outdoor wall should be armoured or protected in a conduit (see page 317). Use the grommet supplied to make the cable hole watertight, drill out any drainage holes indicated and screw the box to the wall, after first running some silicone sealant round the box/wall junction.

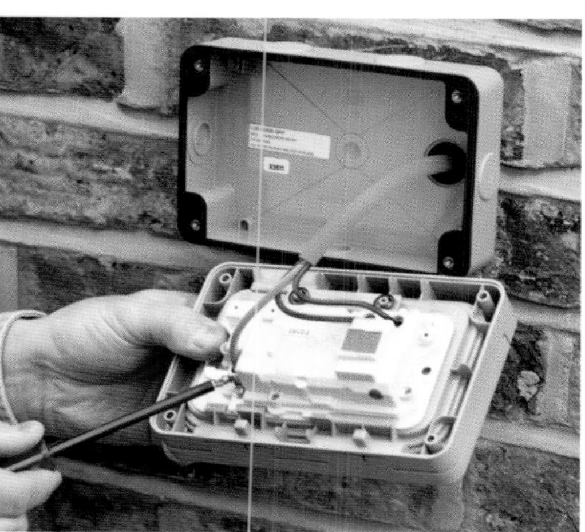

5 Cover the bare earth core with PVC sleeving and connect the cores to the terminals on the faceplate. There is no need to earth a plastic mounting box. Screw the faceplate to the box. Restore the power and test both sockets before use.

> **SAFETY TIP**
>
> Test the RCD before you start work every time you use your outdoor outlet by pressing the TEST button. If the RCD trips off, press RESET: the outlet is ready to use. If it does not, there is a fault, and you should call an electrician.

Fitting an outdoor wall light

To install a light on an outside wall under a porch or over a patio, follow the same method as for an inside wall light. Choose a weatherproof light fitting designed for use outside.

If the light is on a bracket, not a flush-fitting baseplate, you will need waterproof sealant or a rubber gasket to fit the bracket's base.

It is safest to have the switch indoors. You can take the cables for the light and the switch along the same route over the ceiling and down the indoor surface of the external wall on which you are going to install the light.

At the right height for the wall fitting – about 1.8m above ground level – drill from the back of the chase through the inner and outer leaves of the external wall to make a hole to lead the cable outside. Feed the light cable out through the hole.

Install and connect the junction boxes and the switch in the same way as for an indoor wall light (see page 300).

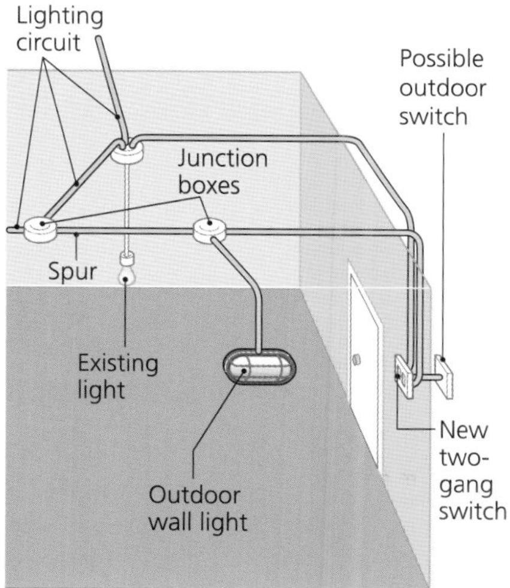

Wiring for an outdoor wall light

Light on a baseplate

1 Hold the baseplate of the light fitting against the wall and probe with a bradawl through the fixing holes to mark drilling spots on the wall. Drill holes at the marks and insert wallplugs in them.

2 Feed the cable through the baseplate and screw the plate to the wall. Prepare the cable for connection (see page 271).

3 Connect the brown and blue cores to the terminals of the lampholder; it does not matter which core goes to which terminal. Connect the green-and-yellow sleeved earth core to the terminal marked E or ⏚.

Light on a bracket

1 If your light is on a bracket, not a baseplate, you cannot reach the lampholder. Flex will have been connected to it already and the flex end will stick out from the bracket. Prepare the flex cores and connect them to a terminal connector block.

At the terminals on opposite sides of the block, connect the cores of the light cable. Link brown to brown, blue to blue and sleeved earth to earth.

Coat the rim of the bracket's baseplate with sealant, or fit a rubber gasket.

2 Screw the light fitting into the drilled and plugged holes. Make sure that any sealant or gasket is squeezed tight against the wall to make a weatherproof seal.

Fitting an outside switch

If you want a switch outdoors as well as inside for a new light, use a two-way sealed splashproof design. Put it on the outside wall back to back with a two-way indoor switch. You will need an additional short length of three-core-and-earth 1mm^2 lighting cable for the connection between the two switches. Drill a hole between the switches and feed the three-core-and-earth cable through it. Connect the cable as described on page 297.

The water system

Repairs

Pipes and fittings

Appliances

Plumbing and heating 10

Plumbing emergencies – what to do if:

Water pours from the loft

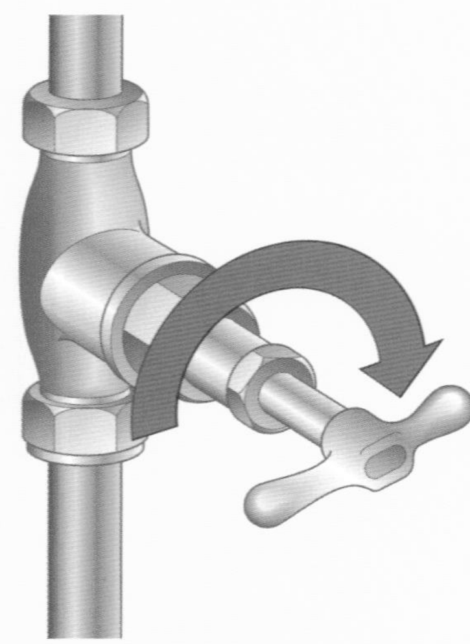

1 Turn the main stoptap off (clockwise). It is usually close to the kitchen sink (if you can't, see right). Put buckets under the leaks, then turn on all the cold taps in the house and flush all the WCs to drain the cold water storage cistern.

2 Find the cause of the trouble. It may be a burst pipe in the loft or a cistern overflow caused by a blocked overflow pipe.

No water comes from a tap

1 If no water flows from the kitchen sink cold tap, check that the main stoptap is open. If it is, call your water supply company. You will find their emergency number on your water bill.

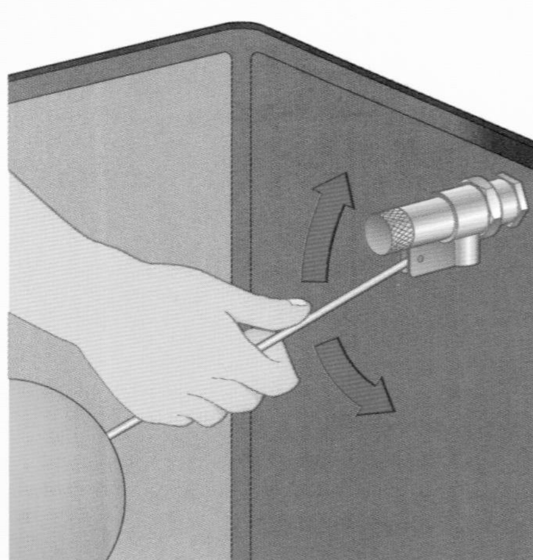

2 If no water flows from other taps, check the cold water tank. It may have emptied because of a jammed or blocked ball valve. If it is empty, move the float arm sharply up and down to free the valve, then clean the valve (page 339).

Alternatively In frosty weather there may be an ice plug blocking a supply pipe. If the kitchen cold tap is working, check the flow into the cold water tank by pressing down the ball valve. If there is no inflow, the rising main is frozen, probably between the ceiling and the cistern inlet.

3 If the tank is filling, check the bathroom taps. If there is no flow from one tap, its supply pipe from the cistern is frozen.

4 To thaw a pipe, strip off any lagging from the affected part and apply hot water bottles. If a pipe is difficult to get at, blow warm air onto it with a hair dryer.

WARNING Do not use a blowtorch to defrost a frozen pipe. It may cause a fire, or melt the solder in a pipe joint and cause another leak.

Hot water cylinder leaks

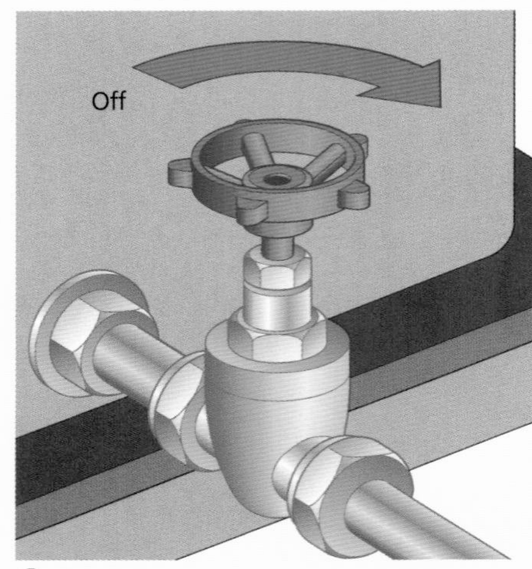

1 Turn off the gatevalve (clockwise) on the supply pipe from the cold water cistern to the hot water cylinder.

If there is no gate valve, turn off the main stoptap and turn on all the taps to empty the tank. (This will not empty the hot water cylinder, but will stop water from flowing into it.)

2 Switch off the immersion heater, if there is one.

3 Switch off the boiler, or put out the boiler fire.

4 Connect a hose to the cylinder drain valve, which is located near the base of the cylinder where the supply pipe from the cold water tank enters. Put the other end of the hose into an outside drain.

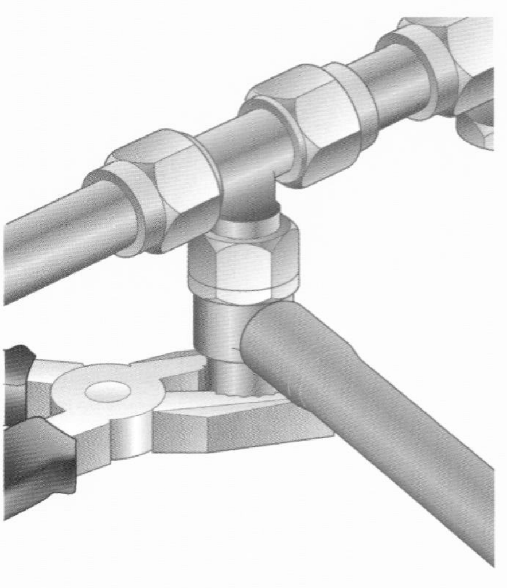

5 Open up the drain valve with a drain valve key or pliers.

6 Get the hot water cylinder repaired or replaced by a plumber.

You cannot turn off the water

If the problem is on the tank fed hot or cold supplies, you can tie up the float valve in the tank, then run the taps and flush the WCs to empty the pipes. If the problem is on the mains fed cold supply, or hot supply through an unvented cylinder or combination boiler, you need to turn off the rising main either at the stoptap inside your home or the outdoor stoptap in the ground (page 323). You will probably need a key to do this. If you don't have one, call your water company for assistance.

Other plumbing problems

Central heating radiator leaking page 375
Cistern water level high or low page 339
Drain or gully blocked page 407
Gutter overflowing page 400
Pipe has burst page 330
Sink blocked or slow to empty page 331
Tap dripping page 332
Tap flow poor page 330 (Airlocks)
Rainwater downpipe blocked page 402
WC cistern not flushing page 336
WC pan will not empty page 342

How water is supplied to the home

Whether for home improvements, or for tackling emergencies, it is important to know what type of water system you have, and where to find all the relevant system controls.

The cold water supply

There are two types of cold water supply in British homes: direct and indirect.

In a direct cold water supply, branch pipes from the rising main lead directly to all the cold taps and WC cisterns in the house. This means that you can drink cold water from any tap. A pipe from the rising main will usually feed a storage cistern in the loft – the reservoir that feeds the hot water cylinder.

A direct cold water system is simpler and cheaper to install than an indirect system. Most British homes have an indirect system. The rising main feeds the cold tap at the kitchen sink (and possibly pipes to a washing machine and an outside tap).

BE PREPARED

Make sure that you and others in the house know where the indoor and outdoor stoptaps are, as well as the gate valves on the supply pipes to the hot water cylinder and cold taps, and label them.

This water is clean drinking water. It then continues up to a cold water storage tank in the loft, which supplies all other taps, the WCs and the hot water cylinder.

There are advantages to an indirect system: water from a cold water storage cistern gives even water pressure, which produces quieter plumbing and less wear and tear on washers and valves. Leaks are also less likely, and any leak that does occur will be less damaging than one from a pipe under mains pressure.

Water from a cistern is warmer than mains water, so less hot water is needed for washing and bathing. It also reduces condensation on WC cisterns. And if the house supply is temporarily cut off, there is a supply of stored water available for use.

SAFETY NOTE

If your house has an indirect system, do not drink water from any tap other than the kitchen one. Water from a tank may not be clean.

5 Rising main The service pipe enters the house and leads to the indoor stoptap, usually close to the kitchen sink (but sometimes under the stairs or in a garage). From there, the rising main leads to the cold water storage cistern (tank) in the loft and/or direct draw-off points. New houses have a 25mm MDPE (plastic) service pipe to allow for the use of unvented cylinders or combination boilers. If you have a lead service pipe contact your water supply company to ask about their lead replacement programme.

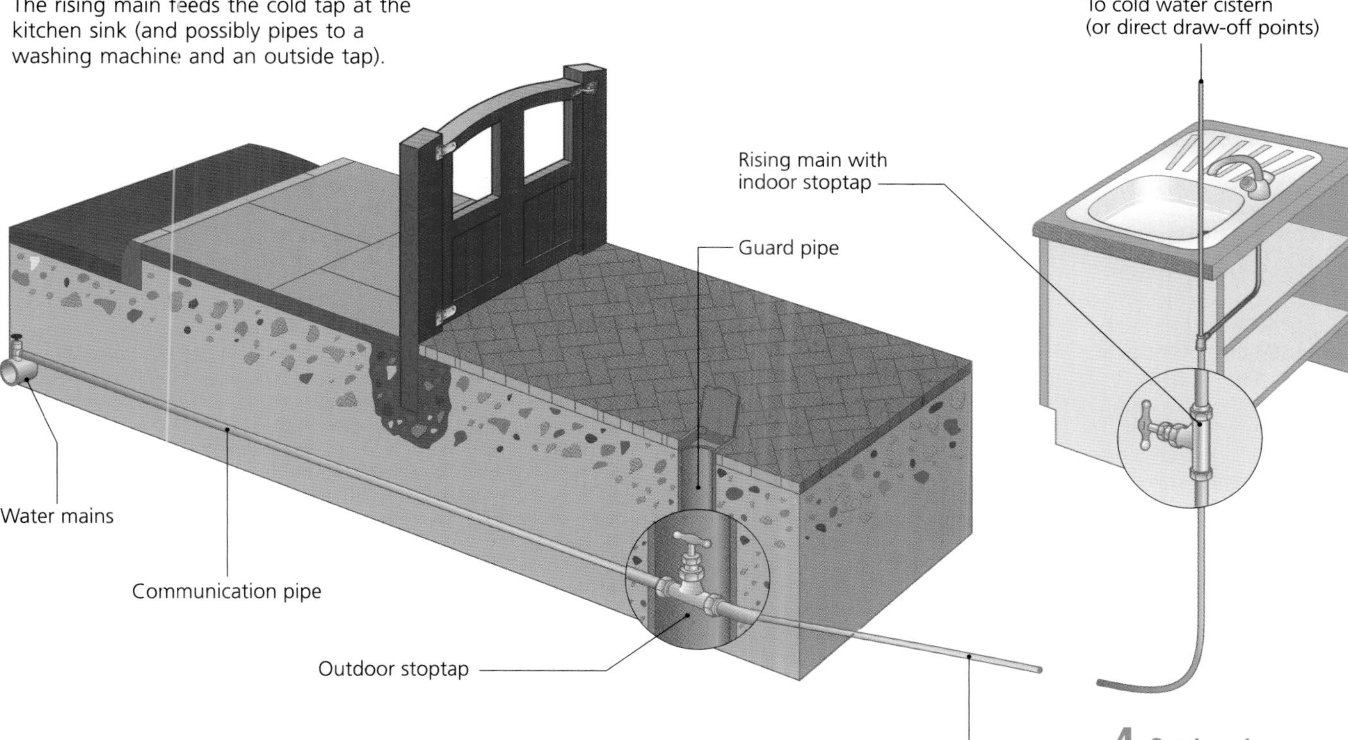

1 Water mains The water supply to most British homes is provided by the local water supply company, through iron or heavy plastic water mains.

2 Communication pipe From the mains, a pipe known as a communication pipe takes the water to the water company's outdoor stoptap – a control valve about 1m below the ground at or near the boundary of each property.

3 Outdoor stoptap The stoptap, which is turned with a long key, is at the bottom of an earthenware guard pipe under a small metal cover, set into the surface of the garden or the public footpath outside. In older properties, this may be the only place where the water can be turned off.

4 Service pipe From the water company's stoptap, a service pipe carries water into the house. The pipe should meander slightly in the trench to allow for ground movement, which would otherwise pull on the fittings at each end. To avoid frost damage, it should be at least 750mm and not more than 1.35m below ground.

Hot water supply

There are two main ways of providing hot water in the modern home: storage systems and instantaneous systems. Most homes will have one system or the other; some homes may have both. What you have will depend on the size and age of your home and the type of cold water supply you have.

Homes with an indirect cold water supply (where cold water is supplied from a large storage tank in the loft) are most likely to have a storage hot water system, with the hot water coming from a hot water cylinder.

Homes with a direct cold water supply (all cold taps fed directly from the rising main) are more likely to have an instantaneous hot water system with hot water being supplied either by a gas multipoint water heater or by a combination boiler.

Few homes these days are likely to have back boilers or boilers which heat only the hot water and not a circuit of radiators. These 'direct' boiler systems suffered badly from scale and should be replaced where possible.

Storage hot water systems

The central feature of a hot water storage system is the hot water cylinder, normally fed by cold water at its bottom by a pipe leading from the cold water storage tank and with a pipe (the vent pipe) coming out of its top which leads back up to the cold water storage tank, curving up and over the top of it with the end passing through the lid and finishing just above the water level. A branch pipe just above the hot water cylinder takes hot water to all the house hot taps: the vent pipe is there as a safety measure to allow an escape route for air or if the water in the cylinder overheats.

The water in the cylinder can be heated in one or both of two ways: immersion heater or heating coil.

Immersion heater An immersion heater is a bit like the element in a kettle. It has its own electric supply circuit (with an on/off switch close to the cylinder) and when it is turned on it heats the water in the cylinder. An immersion heater may be the only method of heating the hot water (in an all-electric house or one with warm-air heating) as shown on this page or it may be in addition to a heating coil as shown opposite. See page 364 for more details.

Heating coil This is a coil of pipework fitted within the hot water cylinder through which water heated by the central heating boiler passes – see drawing on opposite page. Heat is transferred through the walls of the pipe coil to the water in the cylinder, but the water from the boiler (in the 'primary' circuit) does not mix with the water coming from the cold water tank and going (after it's heated) to the hot taps – known as the 'secondary' circuit.

Unvented hot water systems These are the latest systems available for domestic hot water heating. What makes them different from normal systems is that the cold water supply to the cylinder comes directly from the rising main – so if all the cold taps in the house are also fed from the rising main, there is no need for a cold water storage tank in the loft.

Special cylinders are needed (because of the higher pressure) plus a whole host of safety devices (which makes their installation a job for a plumber), but they can have either immersion heaters or heating coils just like normal ('vented') systems.

If the central heating boiler uses a 'sealed' system (see page 382), there is no need for a header tank in the loft either.

Instantaneous hot water systems

A whole-house instantaneous hot water system will use either a gas multi-point water heater or a combination ('combi') boiler. Both take water directly from the rising main and heat it as it is needed, distributing it around the house to the hot water taps. The combination boiler (see drawing below left) also heats the radiators. In a large house, you might use a gas multi-point in addition to a storage system for providing hot water to rooms that are a long way from the hot water cylinder.

There are also point-of-use instantaneous water heaters for heating water where it is needed – gas or electric water heaters over a kitchen sink, for example - or powerful electric heaters for showers.

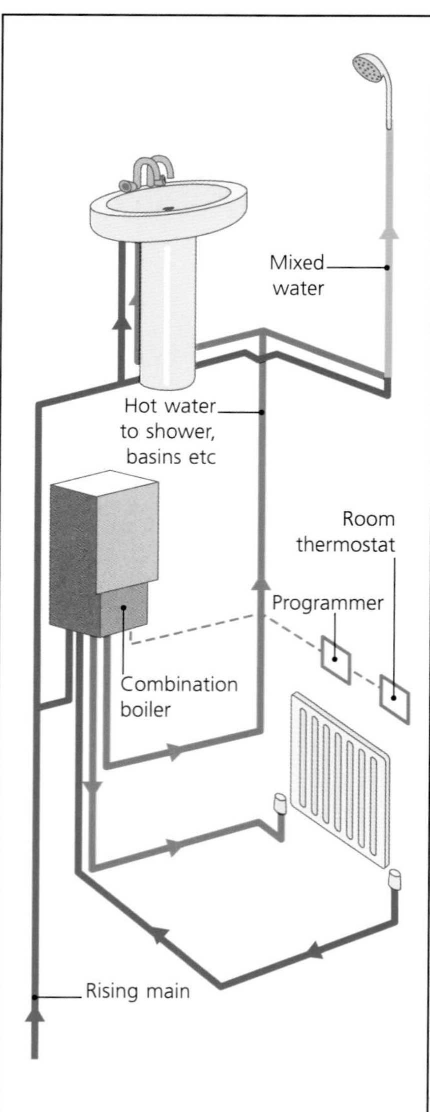

Instantaneous hot water The combination boiler shown here heats cold water directly from the rising main and also supplies heated water to radiators.

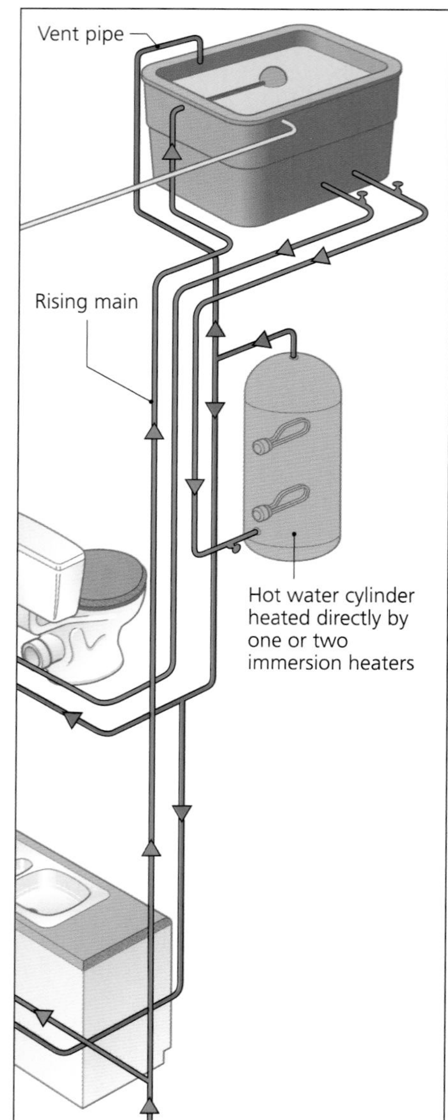

Storage hot water The hot water cylinder here is fitted with immersion heaters to heat water up from cold, but is not connected to a central heating boiler.

A typical household plumbing system

1 The rising main feeds the kitchen cold tap and kitchen appliances before it rises to the cold water storage cistern and the central heating header tank. It also feeds an electric (instantaneous) shower.

2 The cold water cistern is filled from the rising main, and the inflow of water is controlled by a float-operated ball valve. The capacity of the average household cistern is 230 litres, and it has an overflow pipe to carry water out to the eaves if the cistern overfills through a failure of the ball valve.

3 Water regulations require new cold water storage cisterns and header tanks (feed and expansion tanks) to have dust-proof and insect-proof (but not airtight) covers and to be insulated against frost. The storage cistern must supply drinkable water.

4 Water from the cistern is distributed by at least two 22mm (or 28mm) diameter pipes fitted about 75mm from the bottom. One supplies WCs and cold taps – except for the kitchen cold tap. Normally the 22mm pipe goes direct to the bath cold tap, and 15mm branches feed washbasins and WC cisterns.

5 The other distribution pipe feeds cold water to the bottom of the hot water cylinder – usually a copper cylinder of about 140 litres capacity. In a typical modern house with a central heating boiler, there are two water circuits through the hot water cylinder – the primary circuit that heats the water, and the secondary circuit that distributes it (see facing page).

6 Hot water stored in the cylinder is heated indirectly by the primary water circuit through the boiler, and sometimes by an immersion heater as well. This system can also heat radiators.

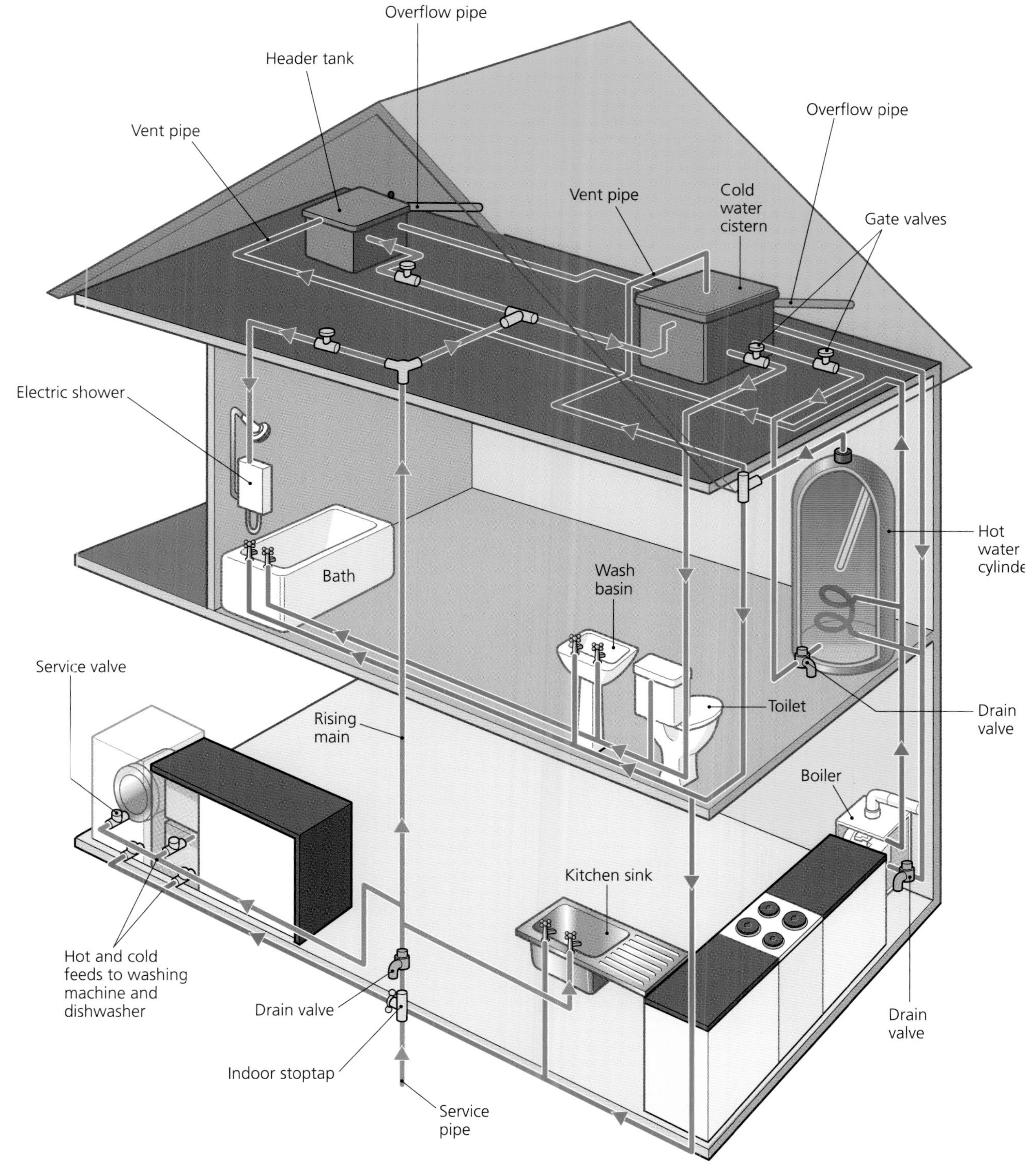

Where the waste water goes

All waste water is channelled out of the house into the main underground drain system. If you live in a house built before the mid-1960s, you probably have a two pipe drainage system; newer houses have one soil pipe – a single stack system.

Whatever the drainage system, every bath, basin or sink in the house is fitted with a trap – a bend in the outlet pipe below the plughole. This holds sufficient water to stop gases from the drains entering the house and causing an unpleasant smell. The trap has some means of access for clearing blockages. All WC pans have built-in traps.

Below ground, the household soil and waste pipes are channelled through an inspection chamber near the house to form the main drain, which runs into the water company's sewer (see page 22).

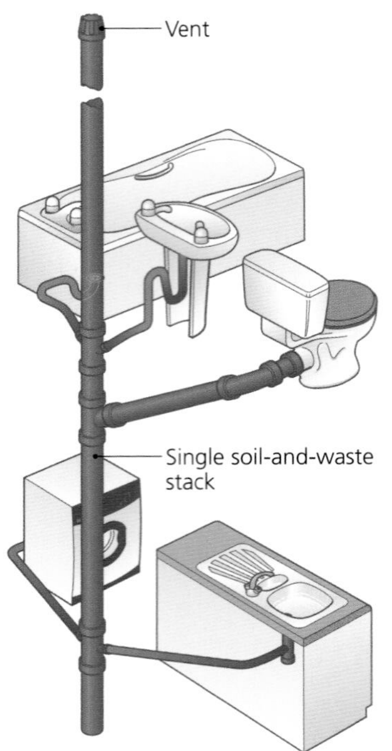

Single stack system

Modern houses have a single stack drainage system. Waste from all sinks and WCs is carried underground by a single vertical pipe known as a soil stack. This pipe may be installed inside the house and its vented top extends above the roof.

Two pipe system

Most houses built before the mid-1960s have what is known as a two pipe drainage system for waste water disposal.

1 A vertical soil stack fixed to an outside wall carries waste from upstairs WCs to an underground drain.

2 The open top of the soil stack – the vent – extends above the eaves and allows the escape of sewer gases. It is protected from birds with a plastic terminal guard.

3 Ground floor WCs usually have an outlet direct into the underground drain.

4 A second outside pipe – the waste pipe – takes used water from upstairs baths, basins and showers via an open hopper head to empty into a ground-level gully. Water from the kitchen sink also runs into a gully.

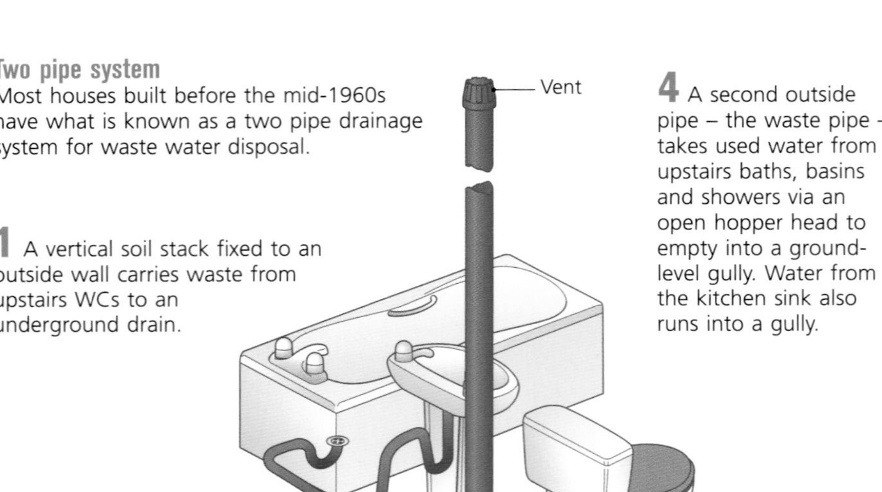

The tools for the job

You will probably have most of the basic tools needed for plumbing – such as spanners and pliers – in your toolkit. For more specialist jobs, tools and equipment can be bought or hired.

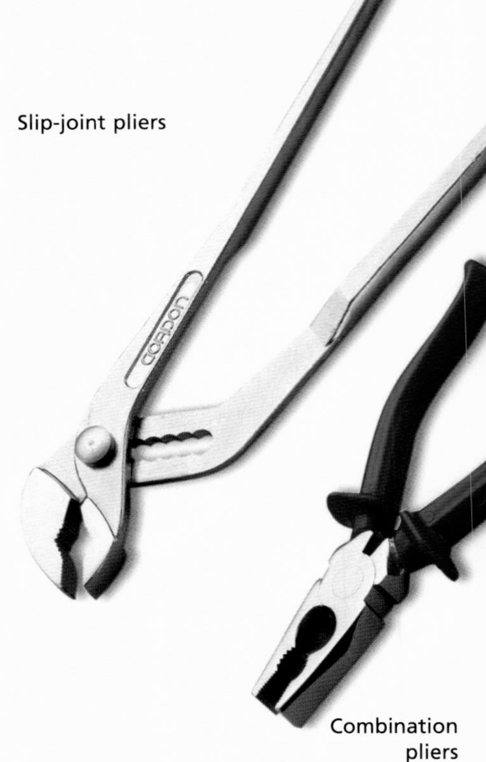

Pliers A pair of 180mm standard combination pliers is useful for jobs such as removing split pins from ball valves, and long-nose pliers will grip a sink or washbasin outlet grid. Slip-joint pliers have adjustable jaws and are useful for a wide range of gripping jobs.

PTFE tape Makes threaded fittings watertight. Wrap the tape around the thread before screwing the joint together.

Radiator key An essential tool for bleeding air from the central heating system.

Pipe wrenches For gripping pipes, circular fittings or hexagonal nuts that have been rounded off at the edges. Two wrenches are needed for some jobs. Some pipe wrenches, such as Footprint wrenches, are operated by squeezing the handles together, but the Stillson type has an adjuster nut for altering the jaw size. Useful Stillson wrench sizes are 250mm and 360mm, with jaw openings up to 25mm and 38mm.

When using a wrench, always push or pull in the direction of the jaw opening. Pad the jaws with cloth if they are likely to damage the fitting – if it is plastic, for example.

Plunger Inexpensive tool used to clear blockages from a sink, basin or bath. Pump it up and down over the plughole.

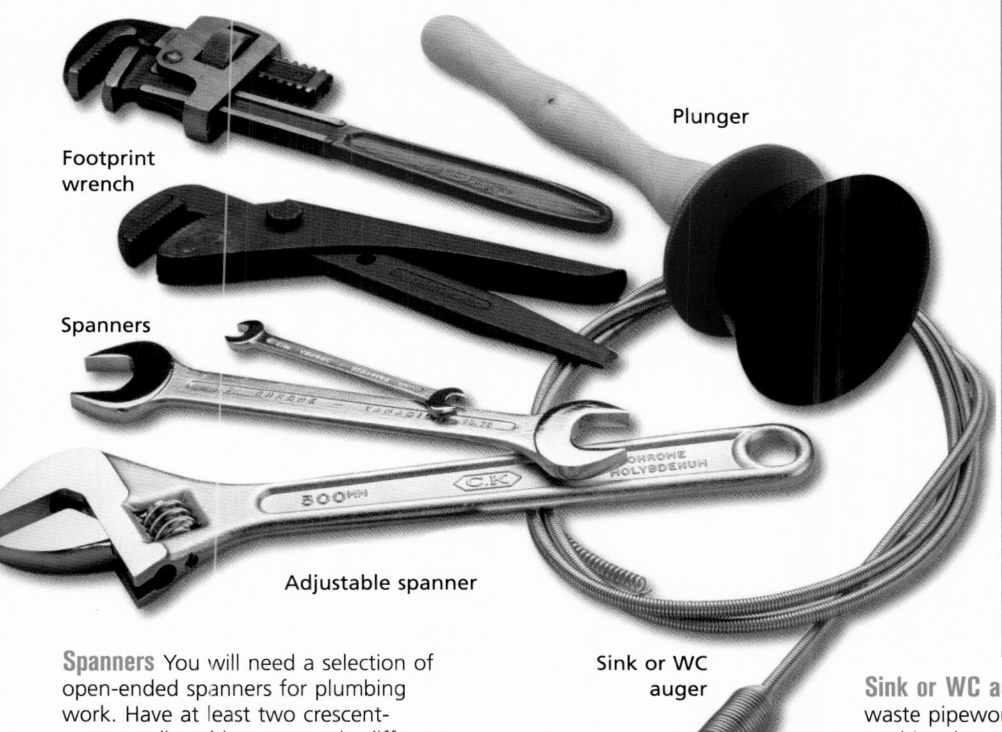

Spanners You will need a selection of open-ended spanners for plumbing work. Have at least two crescent-pattern adjustable spanners in different sizes up to 60mm.

Sink or WC auger Used to dislodge blockages from waste pipework. Some augers have a rotating handle to drive the wire into the blockage and break it up; others work just by pushing the wire manually into the blocked pipe.

OTHER USEFUL TOOLS

Screwdrivers A cross-head (Phillips) screwdriver and two flat-bladed screwdrivers – one large, one small – are sufficient for most plumbing jobs.

Vice and workbench Not essential, but useful for some jobs, such as dismantling a ball valve. Use a grooved jaw lining in an engineers vice. Some portable workbenches incorporate grooves for holding a pipe.

Ladder Plumbing emergencies usually occur in the loft. A retractable loft ladder is the safest means of access. Alternatively, use a ladder that reaches right into the loft.

Torch Plumbing is often in dark places. Keep a powerful torch (and spare batteries) handy – preferably one in a square casing so that it will stand up, or one designed to strap to your head.

Pipe repair clamp For an instant, though temporary, repair to a leaking pipe. The clamp is a two-part collar lined in rubber that you screw together around the pipe.

Plumbing putty An epoxy putty useful for patching slow leaks.

Blowtorch A torch flame is necessary for joining copper pipes with soldered capillary fittings.

TOOLS FOR ADVANCED WORK

Pipe-bending machine A lightweight machine is useful if you have a number of bends to make in a 15mm, 22mm or 28mm diameter pipe, and can be hired. It incorporates a curved former for shaping the bend, and separate guide blocks for each pipe size.

Hacksaw Use a large or small (junior) hacksaw to cut metal or plastic pipes.

Half-round metal file Use for smoothing the burred edge of a cut pipe.

Pipe-bending springs Steel bending springs support the inside of copper pipe while bending it by hand. Springs are sold in 15mm and 22mm sizes.

Basin wrench This wrench (also known as a crowsfoot spanner) is used for tightening or loosening the backnuts of taps.

Wire wool Use to clean inside pipe ends before making joints, and to remove rust.

Pipe cutter Quicker and more accurate than a hacksaw for cutting copper pipe. It may have an adjustable slide for cutting tubes of different diameters, and a fixed cutting wheel. Some have a tapered reamer on the front for removing the burr from the inside of the pipe. A small circular cutter known as a pipe slice is useful for cutting pipes in situ. It is fitted round the pipe and rotated to make the cut.

Immersion heater spanner This large spanner is specially designed for removing and fitting the electrical element of an immersion heater. Hire one if you need it.

Cutting off the water supply

In many homes, only the kitchen tap is fed from the rising main; others are fed from the cold water cistern. It depends whether the plumbing system is direct or indirect (page 323).

Taps fed from the cistern

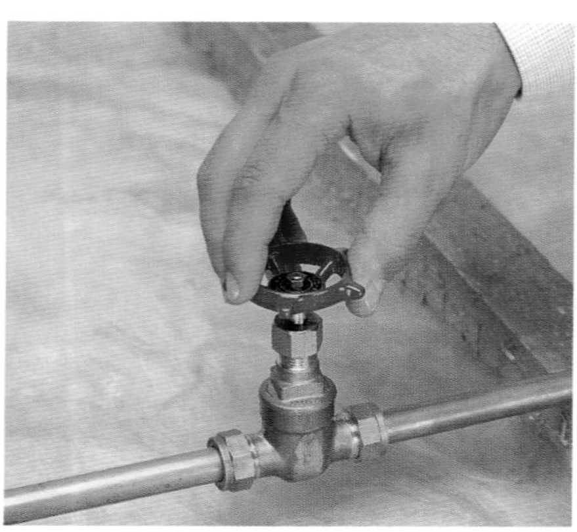

1 To isolate a hot or cold tap supplied from the cistern, turn off the gatevalve on the supply pipe from the cistern. If a service valve (see right) is fitted in the pipe to the tap, turn it off with a screwdriver.

2 Turn on the tap until the water has stopped flowing.

Alternatively If there is no gatevalve or service valve on the pipe, you will have to drain the cistern.

Draining the cistern

1 Tie the ball valve arm to a piece of wood laid across the cistern (see opposite). This stops the flow from the mains.

2 Turn on the bathroom cold taps until the water stops flowing, then turn on the hot taps – very little water will flow from them. (You need not turn off the boiler, as the hot water cylinder will not have to be drained.)

HELPFUL TIP

A stoptap that has been open for a long time may be jammed. To guard against this, close and open the stoptap fully twice a year. After opening it, give the handle a quarter turn towards closure. This prevents jamming without affecting water flow. If the indoor stoptap is difficult to turn, don't try to force it. Isolate it by turning off the stoptap outside the house. Then the indoor one can be dismantled and serviced.

TYPES OF STOPTAP AND ISOLATING VALVE

Stoptap A tap with a valve and washer that is inserted into a mains-pressure supply pipe to control the water flow through it. A stoptap is usually kept turned on, being turned off only when necessary to cut off the supply. It must be fitted the right way round (an arrow mark shows the flow direction). Most stoptaps have a crutch handle.

Gate valve An isolating valve with a wheel handle, through which the water flow is controlled by raising or lowering a metal plate (or gate). It can be fitted either way round and is normally used in low-pressure pipes such as supply pipes from a storage cistern. With the gate open, the flow is completely unrestricted. When it is closed, the seal is not as watertight as a stoptap.

Drain valve A tap without a handle, opened by turning the spindle with a drain valve key. It is normally kept closed, but has a ribbed outlet for attaching a hose when draining is necessary. A drain valve is fitted in those parts of the plumbing system that cannot be drained through household taps – for instance, in the boiler or central-heating systems and on the rising main.

Service valve A small isolating valve operated with a screwdriver. This turns a pierced plug inside the valve to stop or restore the water flow. Normally used in a low-pressure supply pipe to a tap or ball valve to cut off the water for repairs. A similar valve with a small lever handle and a threaded outlet is used to control the flow to the flexible supply hoses of a washing machine or dishwasher.

Taps fed from the rising main

Turn off the main indoor stoptap, then turn on the mains-fed tap until the water stops.

Draining the rising main

You may want to drain the rising main to take a branch pipe from it or to repair the main stoptap. Find the drain valve above the stoptap, fit a short piece of hose to its outlet and open it with a drain valve key or pliers. Catch the water, usually only a litre or two, in a bucket.

Turning off the outdoor stoptap

You may need to turn off the outdoor stoptap if the indoor one is broken, jammed or has a leak from the spindle.

Stoptap keys can be bought from plumbers' merchants, but first check the type needed – the tap may have a crutch handle or a square spindle.

Alternatively If you have no stoptap key, make your own. Take a piece of strong wood about 1m long and in one end cut a V-shaped slot about 25mm wide at the opening and 75mm deep. Securely fix a piece of wood as a cross-bar handle at the other end. Slip the slot over the stoptap handle to turn it. This tool will not turn a stoptap with a square spindle.

1 Locate the stoptap, which is under a cover, about 100mm across, just inside or just outside the boundary of your property. If you cannot find the outdoor stoptap, call your water supply company.

2 Raise the cover. This may be difficult if it has not been raised for some time.

3 Insert the stoptap key into the guard pipe and engage the stoptap handle at the bottom. Turn it clockwise to close.

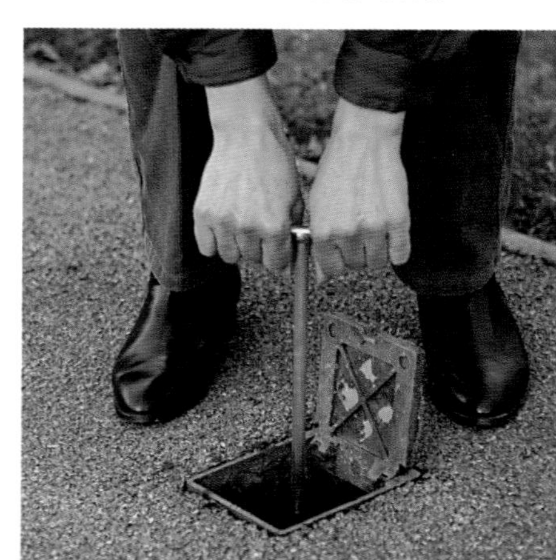

Draining down the heating system

Central heating systems sometimes have to be drained down – to repair a leak, for example. The following method is for an open-vented system, the most common type.

1 Switch off the boiler at the programmer. After a few minutes switch off the main electricity supply to the heating system. This is usually a fused spur located near the programmer.

2 If there is a solid fuel fire serving as a boiler, make sure the fire is out and the boiler is cold.

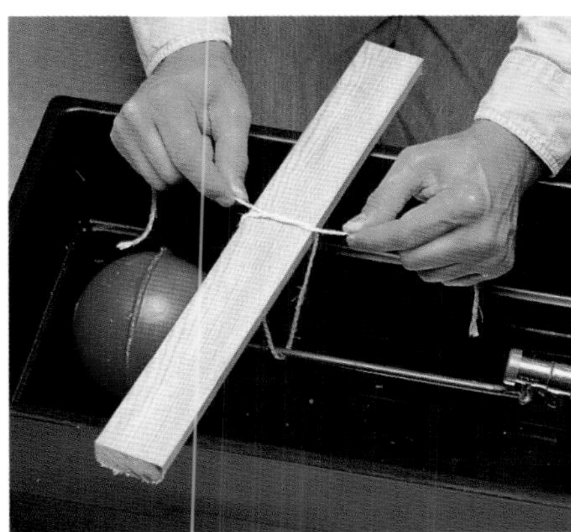

3 Shut off the water supply to the feed-and-expansion cistern. There should be a separate stoptap for this on the branch pipe from the rising main connected to the cistern's ball valve. If there is no separate stoptap, or it is jammed and cannot be turned, stop the water flow into the cistern by tying up the ball valve to a piece of wood laid across the top of the cistern.

4 Locate the drain valve, which may be near the bottom of the boiler. There may be more than one drainage point on the system. Clip a garden hose onto the outlet and run the hose to a drain outside. Open the drain valve so the water starts to flow.

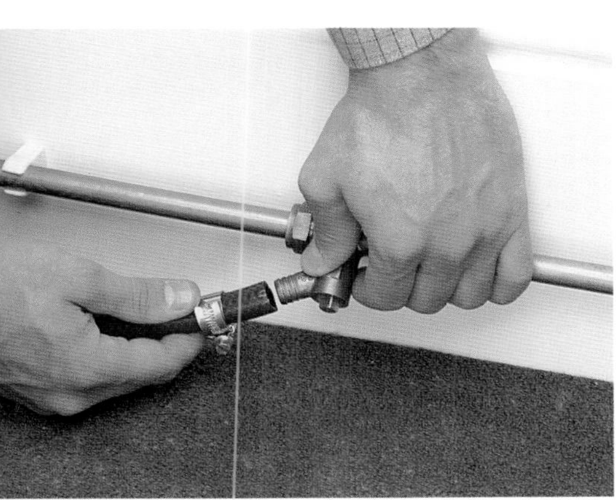

5 Locate all the points at which air is vented from the central heating system. There will be radiator vents, a vent on the primary flow near the hot water cylinder in fully pumped systems, and manual or automatic vents in the loft if circulating pipes run there. There could be additional vents at other points as well.

6 Open the drain valve with a spanner, pliers or an Isle of Man key, turning counter-clockwise. Water will then start to flow out of the hose at a fairly slow rate.

7 Start opening the venting points at the top of the system. This will greatly speed up the flow from the drain valve. As the water level drops further, open the lower venting points until they are all open.

Refilling the system

1 Close all the drain valves and all the air vents in the system. Then check that all work on the system is finished.

2 Turn on the stoptap to the header tank, or untie the ball valve, in order to let water back into the system.

3 Open one of the lowest air vents until water starts to flow out, then close it. Repeat with the lower air vents until the bottom of the central heating system is full of water. Then do the upper vents, and close them when the system is full.

4 Make sure that the ball valve to the header tank has closed. The water level should be around 100mm above the outlet: the rest of the cistern space is to take up the expansion of the water in the system as it heats up.

5 If the water level is too high, close off the mains water supply to the cistern and open the drain valve to let some out. Adjust the arm on the ball valve so that it closes the valve at the correct water level. Check that the cistern's lid and insulating jacket are in place.

6 Switch on the electricity and turn on the gas. Re-light the pilot light in a gas boiler. Turn on the system at the programmer or timeswitch. Turn up the room thermostat.

7 Re-light the boiler, following the manufacturer's instructions.

8 As the system heats up, more venting will be necessary in order to release air driven off from the water. Minor venting will be required for a few days.

9 Check for leaks.

HELPFUL TIP

When you open a drain valve it is always a good idea to check the condition of the washer. If it looks worn or perished, replace it. While the system is drained down it is also an excellent time to fit isolating service valves to various sections to save you draining down the whole system in the future.

If your system contained corrosion inhibitor, this needs to be replaced.

COMBINATION BOILER OR SEALED HEATING SYSTEM

If you have a combination boiler or a boiler running with a sealed system (see page 382), the water in the system is 'topped up' by a special flexible filling loop connected to the rising main. This is fitted with control valves and is normally connected (to the heating return pipe) only when needed. A pressure gauge is fitted so that you know how much water to let in.

Repairing a burst pipe

Metal pipes are more likely to suffer frost damage than plastic pipes. Copper and stainless steel pipes are less vulnerable than softer lead pipes.

As an ice plug forms, it expands and may split the pipe or force open a joint. When the ice melts, the pipe or fitting starts to leak. A split copper or plastic pipe can be temporarily repaired with a proprietary burst-pipe repair clamp.

Cut off the water supply (page 328), drain the pipe and replace the damaged length. For a split less than 90mm long in a copper pipe, you can make a permanent repair with a slip coupling.

For lead piping, use a tape-repair kit for a strong repair that will allow you to restore the water supply until a plumber can make a permanent repair (working on lead pipework is best left to a professional).

Using a slip coupling

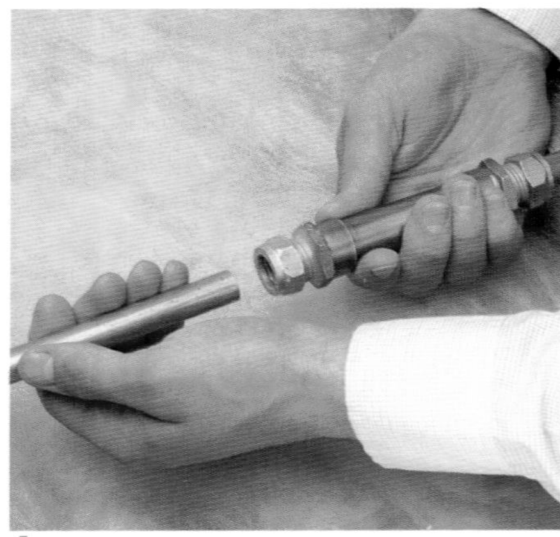

1 Cut out the damaged part and slide the slip end of the coupling (with no pipe stop) onto a pipe end. Then push it onto the other end. If it will not go in, unscrew the back nuts and slide the nuts and olives at each end along the pipe first.

2 Refit the nuts and olives and screw them up hand-tight. Then tighten the nuts for one and a quarter turns with a spanner.

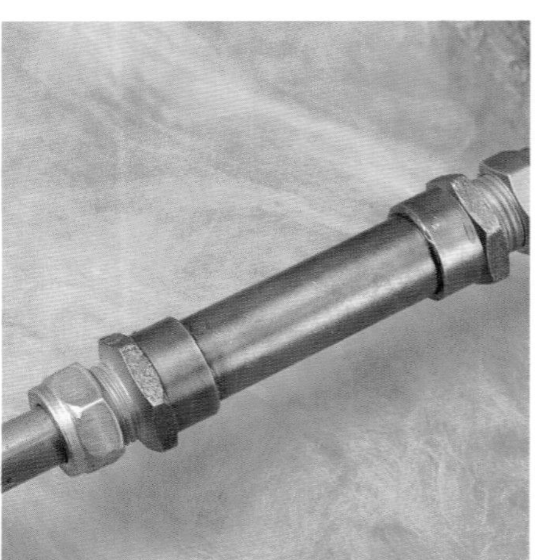

3 Alternatively Fit an emergency pipe repair clamp and tighten the screws fully with a screwdriver.

Lead pipe emergency

If you have a burst on a lead pipe and can't turn off the water, flatten the pipe with a hammer to stem the flood of water. The pipe can be replaced with plastic or copper at a later date, using adaptors.

Compression tape

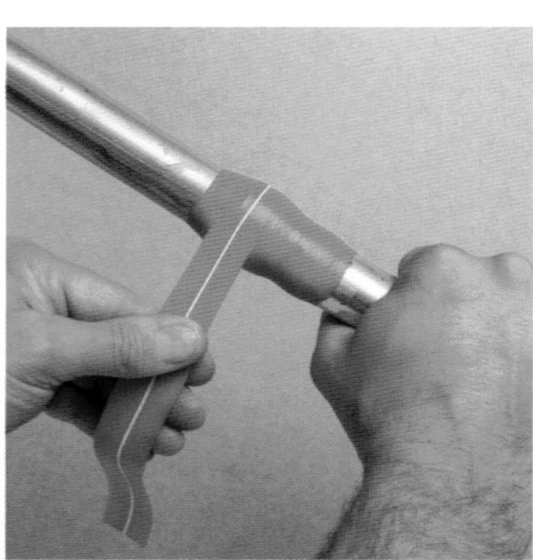

Compression tape, known as Alfa tape, is a quick way of repairing any hot or cold water pipe. The tape forms a permanent repair and can withstand high pressure and heat.

Dealing with an airlock

If the water flow from a tap (usually a hot tap) is poor when fully turned on, then hisses and bubbles and stops altogether, there is an airlock in the supply pipe.

Tools *Length of hose with a push-fit tap adaptor at each end. Possibly also dishcloth; screwdriver.*

1 Connect one end of the hose to the tap giving the trouble. If it is a bath tap and the hose is difficult to fit, connect to the nearby washbasin hot tap instead.

2 Connect the other end of the hose to the kitchen cold tap or to another mains-fed tap. Turn on the faulty tap first, then the mains-fed tap. The pressure of the mains water should blow the air bubble out of the pipe.

Important When applying mains pressure to a pipe in a stored-water circuit, there is a very slight risk of water from the system contaminating the mains water supply. Therefore you should do the job quickly and disconnect the hose immediately afterwards.

Airlock in a kitchen mixer

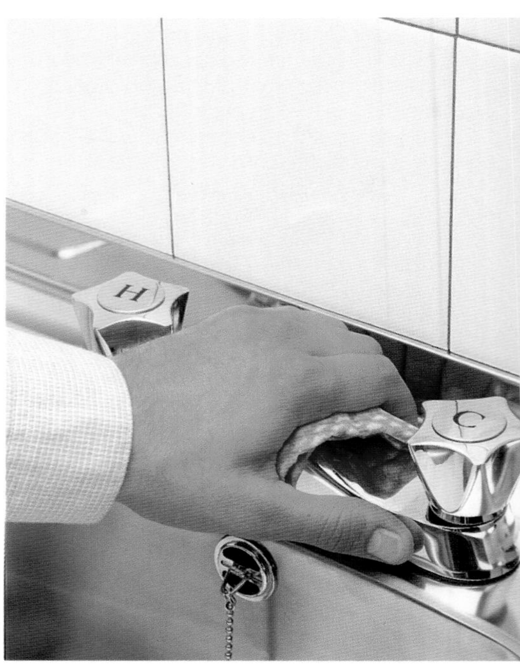

If the hot tap will not work, remove the swivel spout (page 335) and hold a cloth firmly over the spout hole while you turn on first the hot tap then the cold tap.

If airlocks keep occurring

There are many ways that air can be drawn into the water system and cause airlocks. Check these possibilities:

- Is the cold water cistern too small for the household's needs? If it is smaller than the standard 230 litres, replace it with one of standard size.
- Is the ball valve in the cold water cistern sluggish? Watch the cistern emptying while the bath fills. If the valve does not open wide enough as water is drawn off, there will be a slow inflow and the cistern will empty before the bath is filled, allowing air to be drawn into the supply pipe. Dismantle and clean the ball valve (page 339).
- Is the supply pipe from the cold water cistern to the hot water cylinder obstructed or too narrow? Check that any gate valve is fully open, and replace the pipe if it is narrower than 22mm in diameter. If hot water drawn for a bath is not replaced quickly enough, the water level in the vent pipe will fall below the level of the hot water branch pipe, and air will enter.

> **HELPFUL TIP**
>
> When additions are made to the hot water plumbing, make sure that all horizontal lengths of supply pipe are laid so that they fall away slightly from the main vent pipe. Any air bubbles entering the system will then be able to escape via the vent pipe.

Dealing with a blocked sink

Grease may have built up in the trap and waste pipe, trapping food particles and other debris. Alternatively, an object may be obstructing the waste pipe.

Tools *Possibly a length of wire; sink-waste plunger; sink auger or a length of expanding curtain wire; bucket.*

Materials *Possibly caustic soda or proprietary chemical or enzyme cleaner; petroleum jelly.*

Sink slow to empty

- If a sink is slow to empty, smear petroleum jelly on the rim of the plughole to protect it, and then apply proprietary chemical or enzyme cleaner according to the manufacturer's instructions.

Sink completely blocked

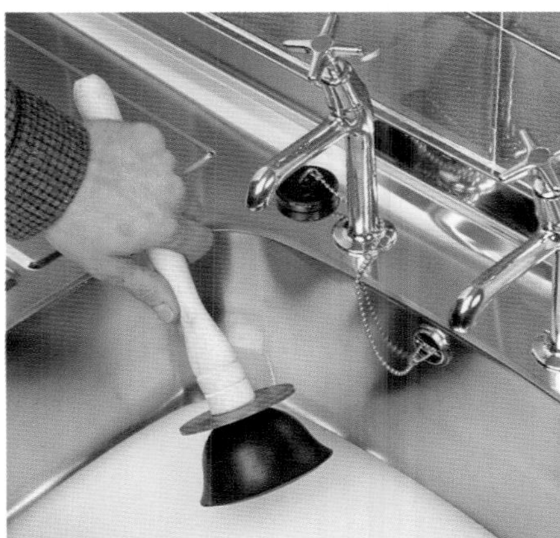

1 If the water will not run away at all, place the sink plunger cup squarely over the plughole.

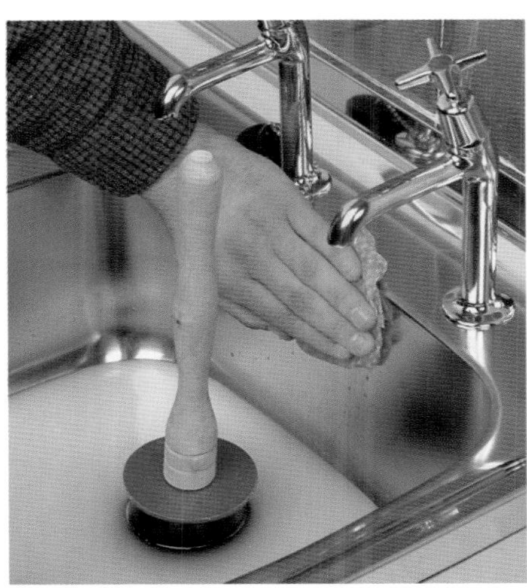

2 Stuff a damp cloth firmly into the overflow opening and hold it there. This stops air escaping through the hole and dissipating the force you build up by plunging.

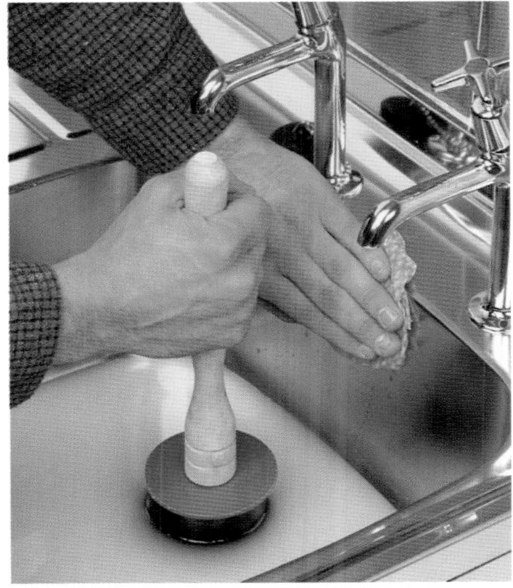

3 Pump the plunger sharply up and down. If the blockage does not clear, repeat the operation.

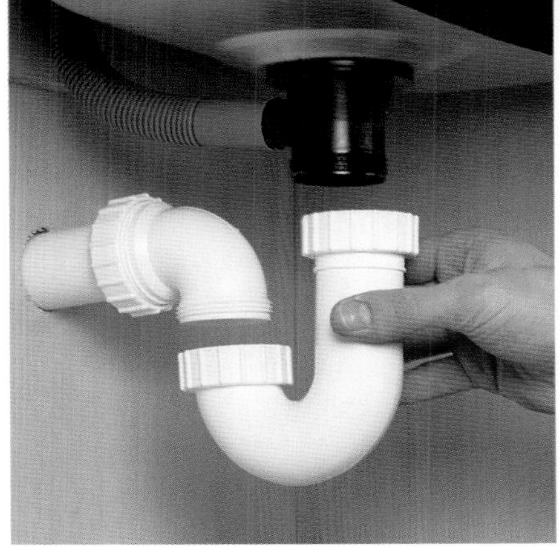

4 If plunging fails, replace the sink plug. Put a bucket under the sink and disconnect the trap. Wash it out thoroughly if it is blocked with debris.

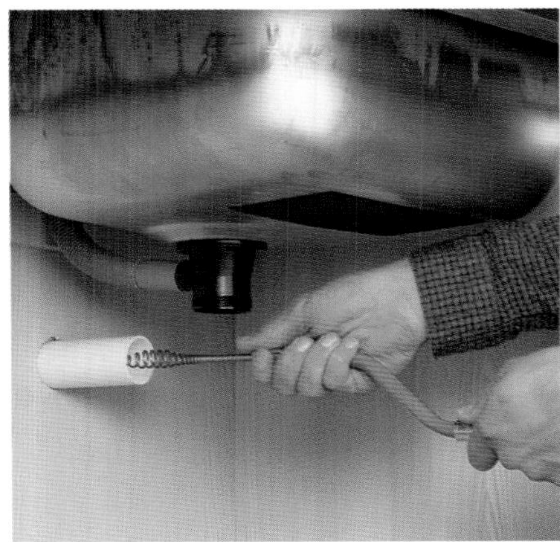

5 If the obstruction is not in the trap, try using a sink auger. It is a spiral device that can be hired or bought. Disconnect the blocked pipe from its trap and feed the wire into it. Then turn the handle to rotate the spiral. This drives its cutting head into the blockage and breaks it up.

Alternatively If you have a vacuum cleaner that is designed to cope with liquids, you can use it to try to dislodge a blockage in a sink trap. Press a cloth over the overflow in the sink. Then place the suction tube of the vacuum over the plughole and switch on. This will probably loosen the blockage sufficiently to allow it to be carried away by the water flow through the trap.

Alternatively If you have poured fat into the sink and it has hardened, try warming the pipe with a hair dryer, to melt the grease. Flush plenty of hot water after it.

Other pipe blockages

The waste pipes from washing machines and dishwashers are often connected to the under-sink waste trap. Alternatively, they may join the main waste pipe at a T-junction away from the sink. If all your appliances feed into the one trap, you may need to disconnect all the pipes in turn and then clean each one to clear a blockage.

If cleaning the trap and waste pipe does not work, the blockage may be in the gully outside (page 406) or in the underground drains (page 407).

Repairing a dripping tap

A dripping tap usually means that the tap washer needs renewing, but can also be caused by a damaged valve seating. If the drip is from a mixer spout, renew both tap washers.

Tools *One large open-ended spanner, normally 20mm for a 12mm tap or 24mm for a 19mm tap (or use an adjustable spanner); old screwdriver (for prising). Possibly also one small spanner (normally 8mm); one or two pipe wrenches; cloth for padding jaws; one 5mm, one 10mm screwdriver.*

Materials *Replacement washer or a washer-and-jumper valve unit; alternatively, a washer-and-seating set; petroleum jelly. Possibly also penetrating oil.*

Removing the headgear

1 Cut off the water supply (page 328). Make sure the tap is turned fully on, and put the plug into the plughole to stop any small parts falling down the waste pipe.

2 Unscrew or lever off the cover of a non-rising spindle tap to expose the retaining screw. Remove the screw and put it in a safe place. Remove the head.

Alternatively With a rising spindle tap, prise off the index disc (if necessary) and remove the retaining screw to release the capstan head from the spindle. Use a wrench wrapped in cloth to unscrew the metal shroud and lift it away from the headgear nut.

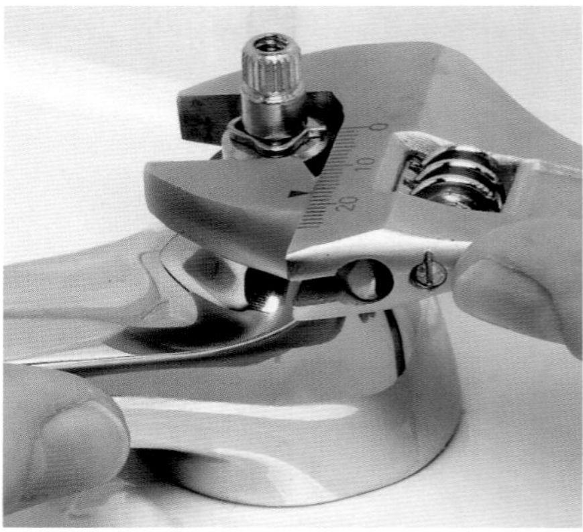

3 Undo the headgear nut with a spanner. Do not force the nut, if it is stiff. Brace the tap body by hand or with a pipe wrench wrapped in a cloth, to prevent the tap from turning and fracturing a ceramic basin or bidet.

4 If the nut is still difficult to turn, apply penetrating oil round the joint, wait about 10 minutes to give it time to soak in, then try again. You may have to make several applications.

Rising spindle The jumper valve is in the shape of a rod and plate, and the washer is attached to the base of the plate. When changing a washer, the handle is lifted off with the headgear. When adjusting the gland nut, the handle has to be removed so that the bell-shaped shroud can be pulled off out of the way.

Non-rising spindle The jumper valve and washer are the same as in a traditional rising spindle tap, but the spindle is sealed by an O-ring nut rather than a gland nut. The tap handle and headgear have to be removed to change a washer or to renew an O-ring.

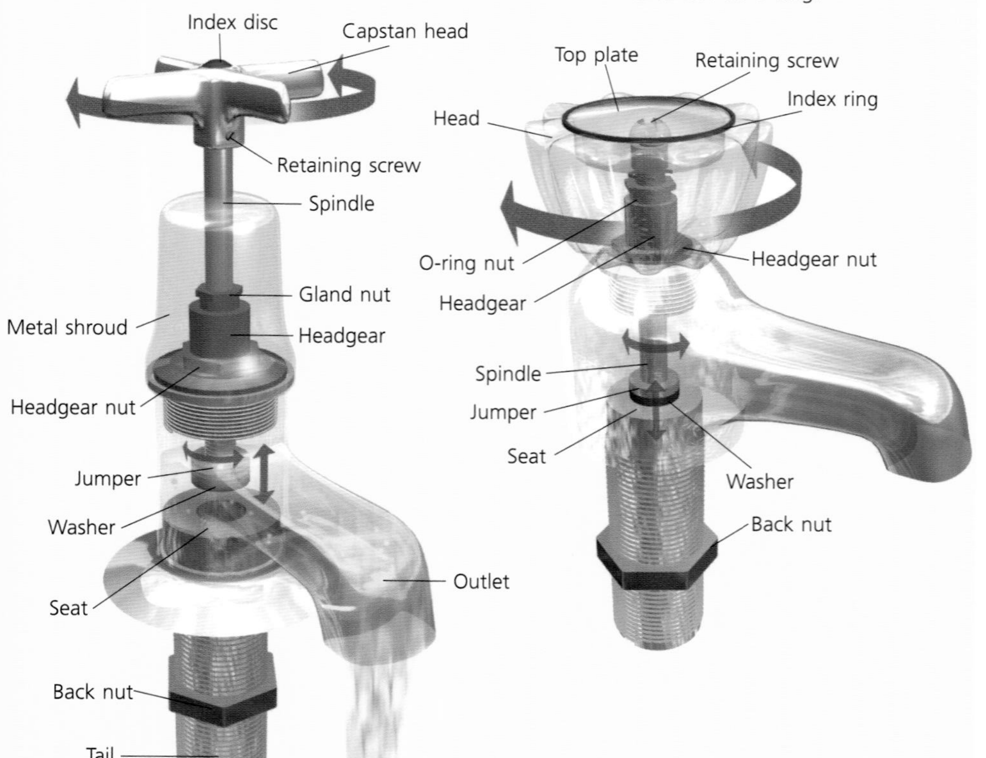

Fitting the washer

1 Prise off the washer with a screwdriver. If there is a small nut holding it in place, unscrew it with a spanner (normally 8mm). If it is difficult to undo, put penetrating oil round it and try again when it has soaked in. Then prise off the washer.

Alternatively If the nut is impossible to remove, you can replace both the jumper valve and washer in one unit.

2 After fitting a new washer or washer and jumper, grease the threads on the base of the tap before reassembling.

STOP DRIPS AND SAVE WATER

Just one dripping tap can waste thousands of litres of water a year. If you can't repair the tap yourself, contact your water supplier to see if they run a tap re-washering service to prevent such unnecessary leakage. They may offer a special discount on this service for pensioners.

Repairing the valve seating

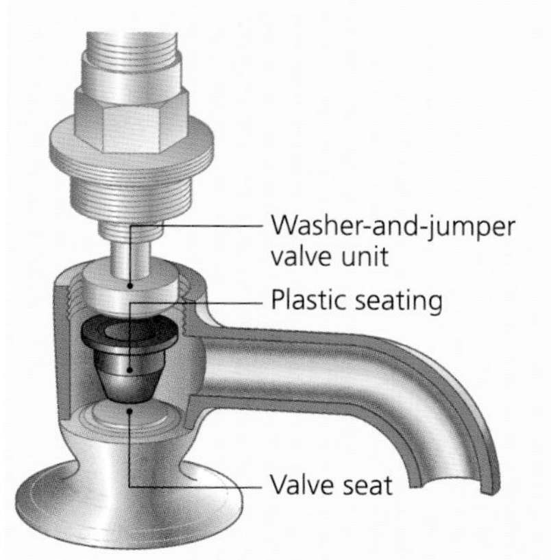

When renewing a washer, inspect the valve seat inside the tap body. If it is scaled or scored by grit, the seal between washer and seat will not be effective even with a new washer.

The simplest repair is with a washer-and-seating set. This has a plastic seat to fit into the valve seat, and a washer-and-jumper valve unit to fit into the headgear.

When the tap is turned off, the plastic seating is forced firmly into place. It may take a few days for the new seating to give a completely watertight fit.

An alternative repair is to buy or hire a tap reseating tool and grind the seat smooth yourself.

Tap conversion kit

You may be able to get a tap conversion kit to change the style of taps and replace worn or broken mechanisms. Newer heads can be changed back to Victorian brass heads, or a tap with a crutch or capstan handle can be given a newer look. The spout and body of the tap remain in place.

Some kits have bushes to fit different tap sizes. The kits are available from most DIY stores and fitting instructions are included.

AVOIDING HARD-WATER DAMAGE TO TAPS

If you live in a hard-water area, you should check your taps for damage, once a year.

Turn off the mains water supply. One at a time check that the headgear on each tap unscrews easily. Use penetrating oil to release stiff nuts and use a spanner and a wrench wrapped in a cloth to hold the body of the tap as you turn.

If limescale has built up, remove and soak small parts in vinegar or limescale remover. Smear the thread with lubricant before reassembling.

Cleaning or replacing ceramic discs

Ceramic disc taps operate on a different principle from conventional taps that have washers and spindles. Positioned in the body of the tap is a cartridge containing a pair of ceramic discs, each with two holes in it.

One disc is fixed in position; the other rotates when the handle is turned. As the movable disc rotates, the holes in it line up with the holes in the fixed disc and water flows through them. When the tap is turned off the movable disc rotates so that the holes no longer align. Ceramic discs are hardwearing and more resistant to damage than washers, and they are especially good for hard water areas as they are less susceptible to water corrosion.

Dealing with a dripping tap

If a scratched ceramic disc is causing the leak, the entire cartridge needs to be replaced: left-handed for a hot tap or right-handed for a cold tap. Remove the old cartridge and take it with you when buying a replacement to make sure it is the correct size and 'hand'.

Mixer taps can also drip at the base of the spout if the O-ring seal has perished. Replace it if necessary.

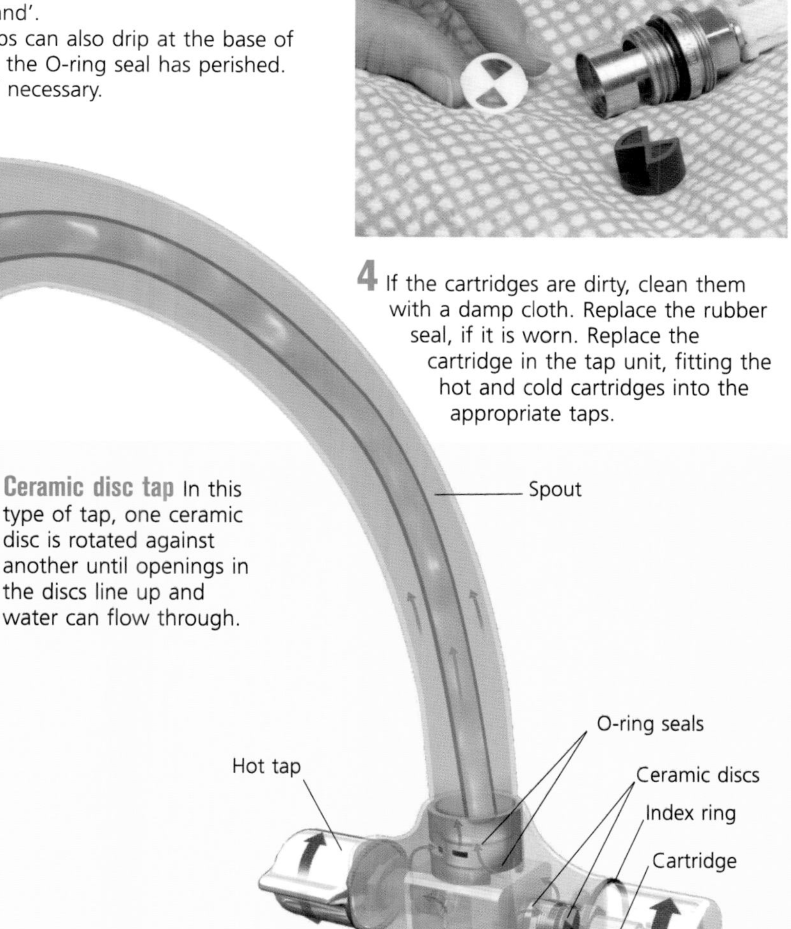

Ceramic disc tap In this type of tap, one ceramic disc is rotated against another until openings in the discs line up and water can flow through.

Checking discs in a ceramic disc mixer tap

1 Turn off the water supply. Pull off the tap handles (it may be necessary to unscrew a small retaining screw on each) and use a spanner to unscrew the headgear section.

2 Carefully remove the ceramic cartridges, keeping hot and cold separate. Check both cartridges for dirt and wear and tear.

3 If the cartridges are worn, replace with identical parts for the tap unit. Make sure that the hot and cold cartridges are fitted into the correct taps.

4 If the cartridges are dirty, clean them with a damp cloth. Replace the rubber seal, if it is worn. Replace the cartridge in the tap unit, fitting the hot and cold cartridges into the appropriate taps.

Curing a leak from a spindle or spout

Leakage from the body of the tap – from round the spindle, the base of a swivel spout, or the diverter knob on a shower mixer tap – may indicate a faulty gland or O-ring seal.

Possible causes This sort of leak is most likely to occur on a kitchen cold tap with a bell-shaped cover and visible spindle. Soapy water from wet hands may have run down the spindle and washed the grease out of the gland that makes a watertight joint round the spindle. If the tap is used with a hose for watering the garden, back pressure from the hose connection will also weaken the gland.

On a modern tap, especially one with a shrouded head, there is an O-ring seal instead of a gland, and it rarely needs replacing. However, an O-ring seal may occasionally become worn.

Tools *Small spanner (normally 12mm) or adjustable spanner. Possibly also one 5mm and one 10mm screwdriver; penknife or screwdriver for prising; two small wooden blocks about 10mm deep (such as spring clothes pegs).*

Materials *Packing materials (gland-packing string or PTFE tape). Possibly also silicone grease; O-rings (and possibly washers) of the correct size – take the old ones with you when buying, or give the make of tap.*

Adjusting the gland

There is no need to cut off the water supply to the tap.

1 With the tap turned off, undo the small screw that secures the capstan handle and put it in a safe place (it is very easily lost), then remove the handle. If there is no screw, the handle should pull off.

2 Remove the bell-shaped cover to reveal the gland nut – the highest nut on the spindle. Tighten the nut about half a turn with a spanner.

3 Turn the tap on by temporarily slipping the handle back on, then check whether there is still a leak from the spindle. If there is not, turn the gland nut another quarter turn and reassemble the tap. Do not overtighten the gland nut, or the tap will be hard to turn off.

4 If there is still a leak, give another half turn and check again.

5 If the gland continues leaking after you have adjusted it as far as possible, repack the gland.

Replacing the packing

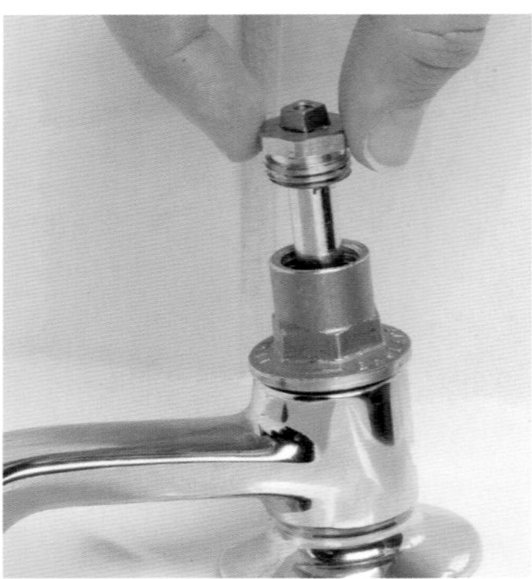

1 With the tap turned off and the handle and cover removed, use a spanner to remove the gland nut and lift it out.

2 Pick out the old packing with a small screwdriver. Replace it with packing string from a plumbers' merchant or with PTFE tape pulled into a thin string. Pack it in with a screwdriver, then replace the gland nut and reassemble the tap.

Renewing the O-ring on a shrouded-head tap

1 Cut off the water supply to the tap (page 328) and remove the tap handle and headgear in the same way as for renewing a washer.

2 Hold the headgear between your fingers and turn the spindle clockwise to unscrew and remove the washer unit.

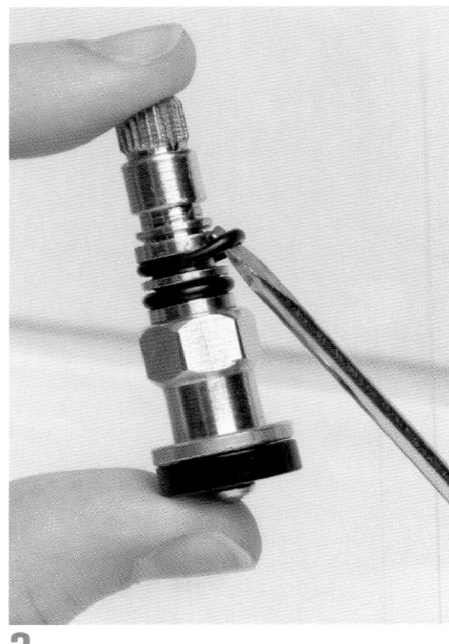

3 Prise out the O-ring at the top of the washer unit with a screwdriver or penknife.

4 Smear the new O-ring with silicone grease, fit it in position, and reassemble the tap.

RELEASING THE SPINDLE

A non-rising spindle tap may have a circlip keeping the spindle in place. When you have removed the headgear, lever out the circlip so that you can gain access to the worn O-rings.

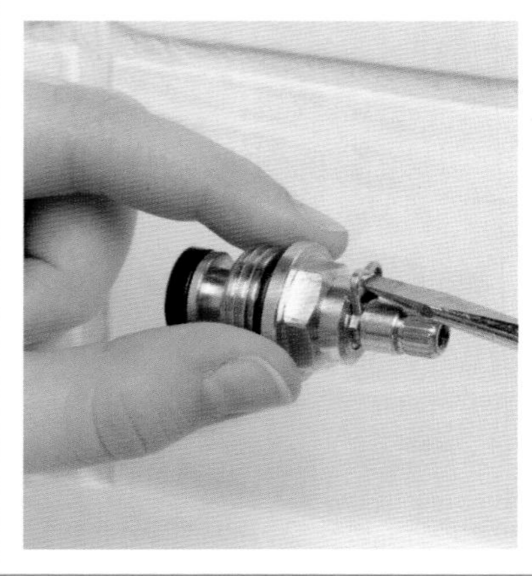

Renewing O-rings on a kitchen mixer tap

1 With both taps turned off, remove any retaining screw found behind the spout. If there is no screw, turn the spout to line up with the tap body and pull upwards sharply.

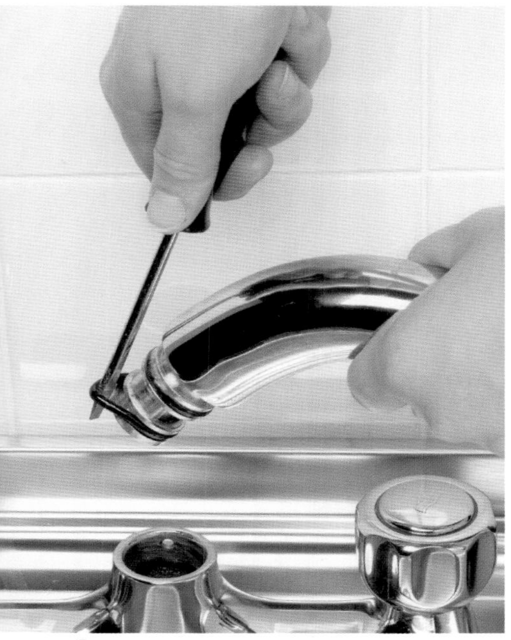

2 Note the position of the O-rings (probably two) and remove them.

3 Coat new O-rings of the correct size with silicone grease and fit them in position.

4 Smear a little petroleum jelly onto the end of the spout and refit it to the tap body.

Replacing shower-diverter O-rings

Diverters vary in design, but most have a sprung rod and plate attached to the diverter knob. When the knob is lifted, the plate opens the shower outlet and seals the tap outlet for as long as the shower is on.

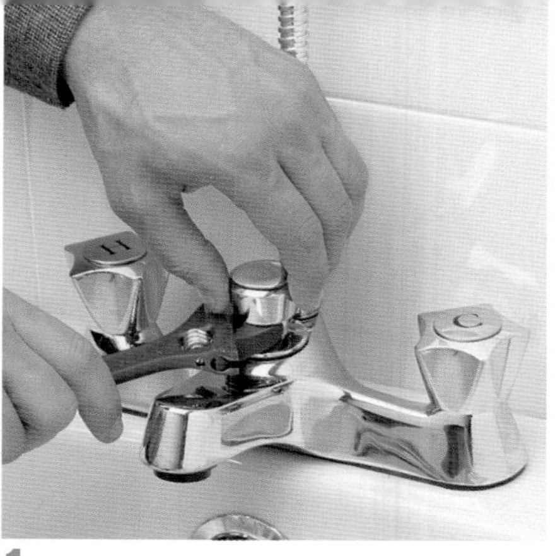

1 With the bath taps turned off, lift the shower-diverter knob and undo the headgear nut with a spanner (probably 12mm size or use an adjustable spanner).

2 Lift out the diverter body and note the position of the washers and O-rings.

3 Remove the knob from the diverter body by turning it anticlockwise. You may need to grip it with a wrench.

4 Withdraw the rod and plate from the diverter body and remove the small O-ring at the top of the rod.

5 Grease a new O-ring of the correct size with silicone grease and fit it in place.

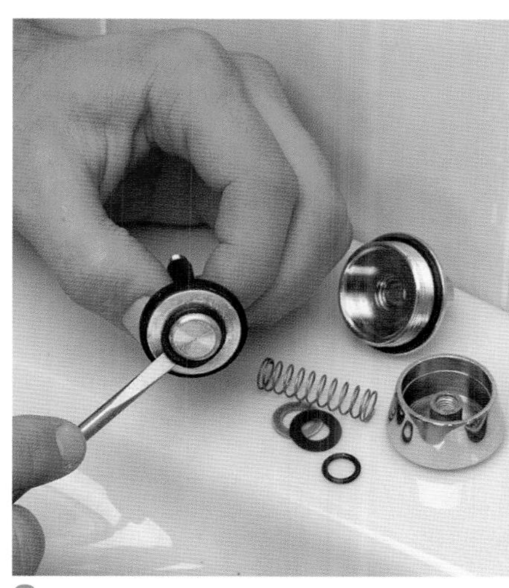

6 Replace all other rubber washers and O-rings on the base of the rod and plate. Old ones may have to be prised out.

REPACKING A STOPTAP WITH FIBRE STRING

The gland on a capstan-handle stoptap is the type most likely to need repacking. Use fibre string (from a plumbers' merchant) or PTFE tape.

1 Turn off the stoptap. Undo the gland nut, slide it up the spindle and remove it.

2 Rake out the gland packing with a penknife or similar tool.

3 To repack the gland with fibre string, steep a length in petroleum jelly and wind and stuff it into the gland with a screwdriver blade. Wind and push the string in until it is caulked down hard, then reassemble the tap.

Repairing a faulty WC cistern

An overflowing or continuously flushing WC is often caused by a faulty ball valve, which governs the water level in the cistern. Modern cisterns no longer have an external overflow so the excess water from a faulty ball valve will flow into the WC bowl.

Before you start Failure to flush properly is caused by either a low water level, or a worn or damaged flap valve. To determine the cause, first check the water level.

The plastic lever arm linking the spindle of the flush control to the siphon lift rod may eventually wear out and break. Replacement lever arms can be bought and are easily fitted.

Checking the water level to find out if the ball valve is at fault

1 Remove the cistern lid (it may lift off or be held by one or more screws). When the cistern is full, the water level should be about 25mm below the overflow outlet, or level with the water line marked on the inside wall of the cistern.

2 If the level is above this and the cistern is overflowing, either through the external pipe or into the bowl, turn off the water supply, flush the WC, then repair or adjust the ball valve.

3 Often it is quicker and easier to fit a new valve. If the level is correct and water is still pouring into the pan, then the problem probably lies with the flush valve. Modern two-part flush valves are now replacing siphons. They have a rubber washer at the bottom which may have either perished, or picked up foreign matter. It is usually possible to just clean them off and put them back.

4 If you have an older-style siphon (shown right) which needs to be pumped by the flush lever before it delivers water into the pan, there are two possible problems. Either the water level is below the internal water line, in which case you need to adjust it on the ball valve, or the internal polythene flap has disintegrated and needs to be replaced.

The flap valve is an inexpensive part, but you need to remove the siphon in order to replace it. A newer (turbo) siphon will have a pin holding the top half and this is easy to lift out. If it is an older one-piece siphon then it needs to be removed to access the polythene flap valve.

Renewing the flap valve in a standard siphon

The flap valve for a standard siphon may be sold under the names siphon washer or cistern diaphragm. If you do not know the size you want, buy the largest available and cut it down.

Tools *Screwdriver; wooden batten slightly longer than the cistern width; string; pipe wrench with a jaw opening of about 65mm; bowl or bucket. Possibly also sharp coloured pencil; scissors; container for bailing, or tube for siphoning.*

Materials *Plastic flap valve. Possibly also O-ring for ring-seal joint.*

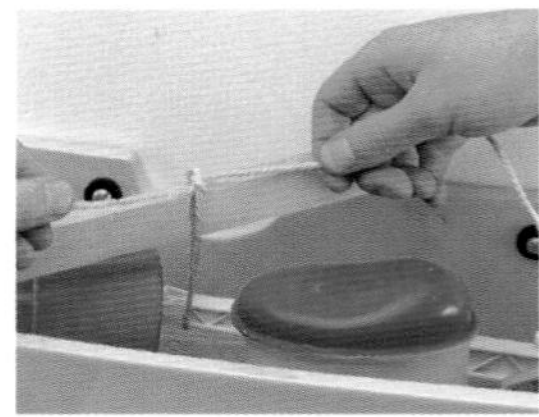

1 Turn off the water. If you can't do this easily, then hold the ball valve up with string and a length of wood.

2 Empty the cistern. If it cannot be flushed at all, bail or siphon the water out.

3 Use a large pipe wrench to undo the lower of the two large nuts underneath the cistern, then disconnect the flush pipe and push it to one side.

4 Put a bowl or bucket underneath the cistern and undo the large nut immediately under the cistern (this is the siphon-retaining nut). Water will flow out as you loosen the nut.

5 Unhook the lift rod from the flushing lever, lift the inverted U-pipe (the siphon) out from the cistern and lay it on its side.

6 Pull out the lift rod and plate and remove the worn flap valve. If the new valve is too big, cut it down with scissors using the old valve as a pattern. It should touch, but not drag on, the dome sides.

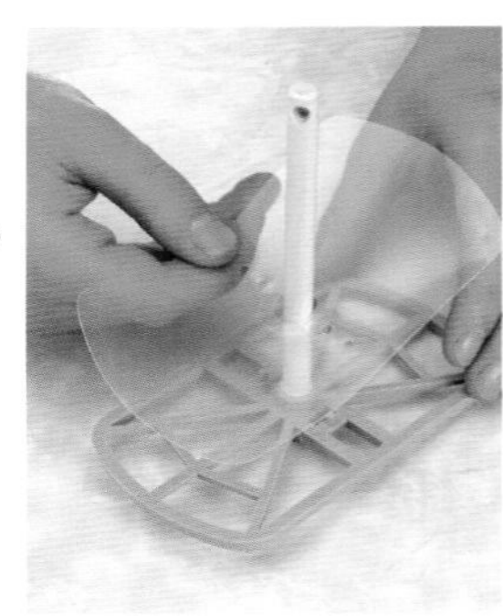

7 Fit the new valve over the lift rod and onto the plate, then reassemble the flushing mechanism and reconnect it to the cistern.

FLUSHING PROBLEMS

The most common problems with WCs are that the WC will not flush, that water runs continuously into the pan or that water runs continuously into the cistern and out through the overflow pipe. Most of these problems are easily fixed.

WC will not flush Check that the flushing lever is still attached to the internal workings of the cistern. Reattach the link or improvise a replacement from a length of thick wire. If the link is still in place, the flap valve may need replacing – this is often the cause if you need to operate the lever several times before the WC will flush.

Continuous flushing When water keeps running into the pan, the siphon may have split or the sealing washer at the base of the siphon may have perished. Both can be replaced. Alternatively, the cistern may be filling too fast, so that the siphoning action of the flush mechanism cannot be interrupted. Fit a restrictor in the float valve to reduce the water flow.

Overflowing cistern Continuous filling may be caused by a faulty ball valve or a badly adjusted float arm. Try adjusting the float arm before you replace the valve.

Renewing the flap valve on a close-coupled suite

On some close-coupled suites, the siphon is held by two or more bolts inside the cistern rather than by a large nut underneath. Except for this difference, the flap valve is renewed in the same way as on a standard suite.

On others, the cistern must be lifted off in order to disconnect the siphon. The flap valve can then be renewed in the same way as on a standard suite. Lift off the cistern as follows:

1 Cut off the water supply to the cistern in the same way as for a tap. Empty the cistern by flushing, bailing or siphoning out the water.

2 Disconnect the overflow pipe and water supply pipe from the cistern. They generally have screw fittings with a back nut.

3 Undo the screws holding the cistern to the wall, and the wing nuts securing it to the rear platform of the pan.

4 Lift off the cistern from the pan and unhook the lift rod. Turn the cistern over, unscrew the retaining nut, remove the siphon and plate, and renew the valve as left.

Renewing the flap valve on a two-part siphon

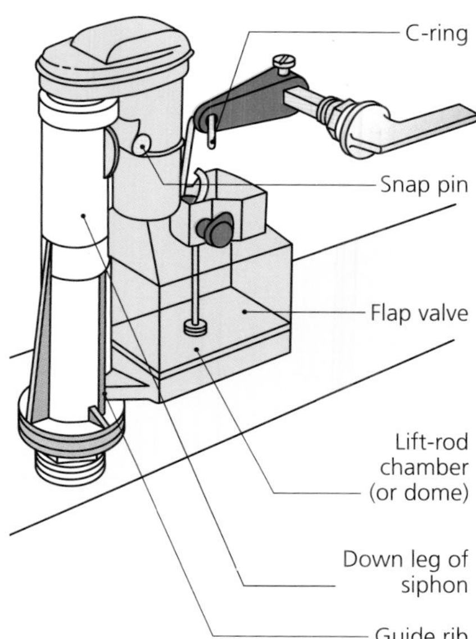

If a cistern is fitted with a two-part plastic siphon, there is no need to stop the inflow or, with a close-coupled suite, to remove the cistern.

A two-part siphon can be fitted to most types of WC cistern. The initial fitting does involve cutting off the water supply and, if necessary, lifting off the cistern (see left). After that, maintenance is as below.

Tools *Screwdriver.*

Materials *Spares pack for size of siphon (containing flap valve); washers. Possibly also O-ring-seal.*

1 With the cistern lid removed, unhook the flush lever from the lift-rod C-ring. Remove a lever-type flush handle, as it may be in the way later.

2 Withdraw the snap pin about 30mm to disconnect the lift-rod chamber from the down leg of the siphon.

3 Slide the chamber upwards to disengage it from the guide rib on the down leg.

4 Remove the C-ring and washer from the top of the lift rod and slide the lift rod from the bottom of the chamber.

5 Take off the lift-rod washers and weight so that you can remove the old flap valve and fit a new one.

6 Before reassembling, check if the O-ring seal at the top of the chamber section is worn. Renew it if necessary.

HOW A PUSH-BUTTON FLUSH WORKS

Many modern slimline WC cisterns are too small to accommodate a traditional ball float-operated inlet valve and siphon flush mechanism, operated by a lever and float arm.

Instead, the inlet valve is either a modified diaphragm type with a very short float arm and miniature float, or an ingenious vertical valve with a float cup that fits round the central column of the valve body. Both are very quiet in operation, although the float-cup valve can be slow to refill the cistern if it is supplied with water from a storage tank, rather than being plumbed in directly to the mains.

In these slimline mechanisms, the traditional siphon flushing method (page 354) is replaced by a plastic valve-operated flush mechanism that is activated by a top-mounted push button in the cistern lid. The mechanism also incorporates an integral overflow. The push button is in two parts: you depress one part for a low-volume flush, and both sections of the button for a full-volume flush. The push button is linked to a plunger to operate the flush, rather than the conventional wire link and lift rod of a traditional flushing mechanism.

Repair and maintenance
The float-cup inlet valve contains a rubber ring seal at the base of the cistern, which may need replacing in time, and these may not be widely available. Be sure to keep the installation instructions after you have installed the valve so that you have a record of where to obtain any spare parts in the future.

How a ball valve works

In a cold water storage cistern or WC cistern, the water level is regulated by a ball valve that is opened and closed by a lever arm attached to a float.

Understanding the system

A cold water storage cistern, or a WC cistern where the supply is direct from the mains, needs a high-pressure valve.
A WC cistern supplied from the cold water storage cistern needs a low-pressure valve. Check the packaging when you buy as the two versions look similar. Equilibrium valves can be adapted for high or low pressure. Low-pressure valves have wider inlet nozzles than high-pressure valves. If a high-pressure valve is fitted where a low-pressure valve is needed, the cistern will fill much too slowly. If a low-pressure valve is fitted in a cistern supplied from the mains, water will leak past the valve.

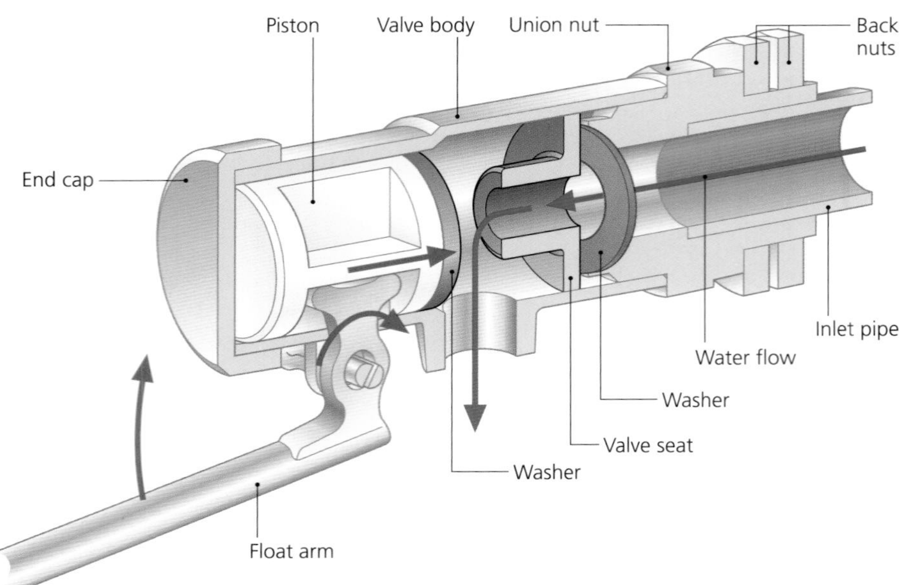

Most modern valves can be changed from high-pressure to low-pressure operation either by inserting a different fitting into the inlet nozzle or by changing a detachable inlet nozzle. Some types are suitable for high or low water pressure without any alteration.

1 When the cistern is at normal level, the float (or ball) holds the arm horizontal and the valve is closed.

2 When the water level drops, the float lowers the arm and the valve opens to let more water in.

BALL VALVES IN COMMON USE

The name ball valve is from the early type of copper ball float. Modern floats are not always balls, they are invariably plastic and ball valves are often called float valves. Ball valves may be made from brass, gunmetal or plastic, or may be metal with some plastic parts. The size is measured by the inlet shank diameter; 15mm or 22mm sizes are usually needed for domestic cisterns.

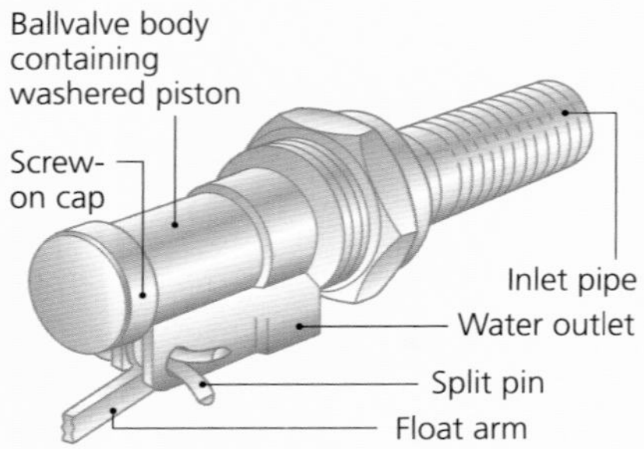

Portsmouth valve The most common type in British homes, although no longer allowed on WC cisterns unless a double-check valve is fitted immediately before the valve. Known as Part 1 valves, Portsmouth valves are sturdy and long-lasting. However, they can be noisy and require regular maintenance. Water hammer – vibration of the rising main – can result from the valve bouncing in its seating. The bouncing is caused by ripples on the water surface when the cistern is almost full, making the float arm shake; sometimes also by the pressure of incoming water against the valve. Scale or corrosion can prevent the valve from operating properly. These valves have now been superseded by diaphragm valves. There must be a method of water adjustment other than bending the float arm.

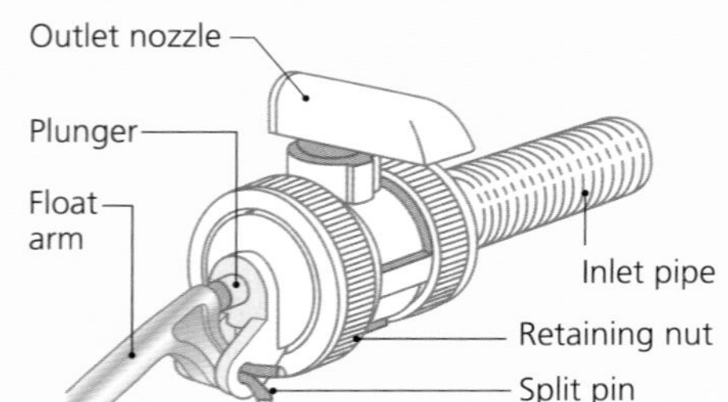

Diaphragm valve (also known as BRE, BRS or Garston) The water inlet is closed by a large rubber or synthetic diaphragm pushed against it by a plunger attached to the float arm. A detachable nylon overhead outlet nozzle discharges water in a gentle shower. Available with either a metal body (Part 2 valve) or a plastic body (Part 3 valve) and in high-pressure or low-pressure versions. The discharge spray cuts down filling noise and rippling, and the diaphragm keeps the plunger and float arm from contact with water, so they are not affected by scale and corrosion. The diaphragm can become worn, and grit can block the inlet chamber. The valve can be dismantled by hand for cleaning or replacement by undoing a large knurled retaining nut.

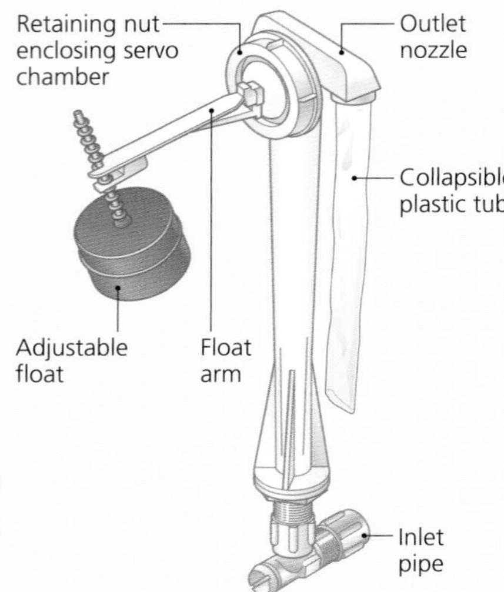

Equilibrium valve (also Torbeck, Part 4 or 'quiet' valve) A plastic valve with small float and short float arm for use only in a WC cistern. Behind a diaphragm covering the inlet is a water chamber fed via a metering pin. Equal water pressure on each side of the diaphragm keeps it closed. When the float arm drops it opens a pilot hole in the back of the chamber, covered by a sealing washer. This reduces pressure in the water chamber, and the diaphragm opens the inlet. The outlet is overhead and via a collapsible plastic tube. Can cope with a range of water pressures: available in bottom and side entry versions. Delivery is rapid and silent. The valve can be fitted with a filter, which collects grit that might otherwise obstruct the metering pin and pilot hole.

Adjusting the cistern level

The normal level of a full cistern, or cold water tank, is about 25mm below the overflow outlet. The level can be raised by raising the float, or lowered by lowering the float.

Adjusting a ball valve

Before you start If the cistern overflows, the water level is too high because the float either needs adjusting or is leaking and failing to rise to close the valve (or the valve itself may be faulty, right).

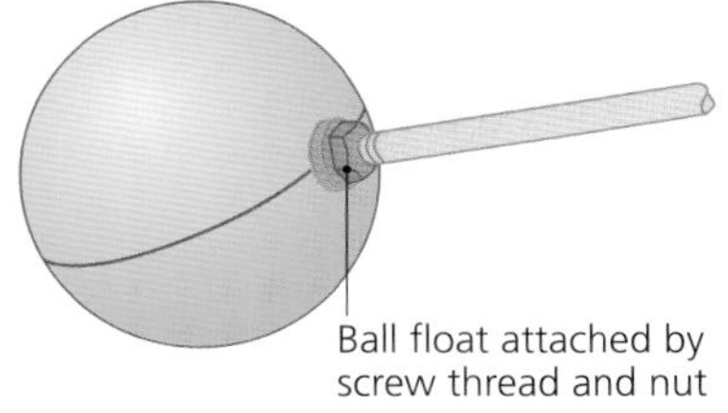

Tools *Possibly small spanner; vice.*

On a Portsmouth-pattern valve with a ball float, unscrew and remove the float from the arm. To lower the level, hold the arm firmly in both hands and bend it slightly downwards. Then refit the float. If the arm is too stiff to bend in position, remove it from the cistern and grip it in a vice.

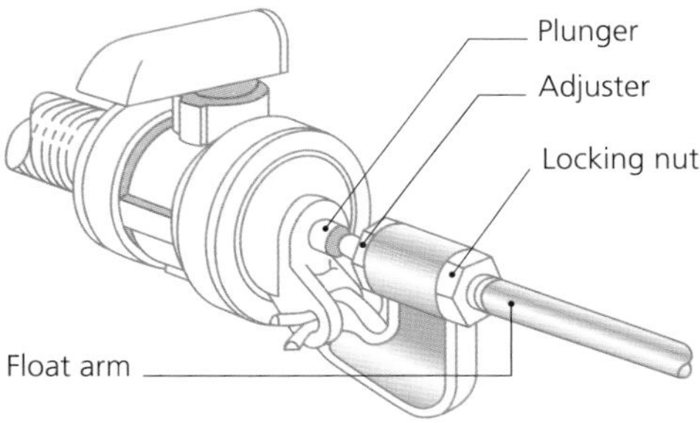

On a diaphragm valve with an adjuster at the top of the float arm, adjust the level by loosening the locking nut and screwing the adjuster forward, nearer to the plunger.

Alternatively Use an adjuster nut or clip near the float to move the float farther away from the valve along a horizontal arm, or to a lower position if it is linked to the arm by a vertical rod.

SAVE WATER – USE A HIPPO

Hippos are durable plastic bags designed for use in older-style WC cisterns to help save water. The bag sits in the cistern, and every time you flush, some water remains in the bag.

Repairing a faulty ball valve

When a ball valve does not open or close fully, it can cause airlocks and supply problems.

Portsmouth valves

Before you start If a ball valve does not open fully, the cistern (WC or cold water storage) will be slow to fill and airlocks will occur. If the ball valve does not close fully, the water level in the cistern becomes too high and causes a constant flow from the overflow pipe.

The water inlet of a Portsmouth valve is opened and closed by a washered piston that moves horizontally. The piston is slotted onto a float arm which is secured with a split pin. Some types have a screw-on cap at the end of the piston. The water outlet is on the bottom of the valve in front of the float arm. The detachable inlet nozzle can be changed to suit the water pressure.

The valve will not work efficiently if the washer is worn or moving parts are clogged by limescale or corrosion.

Tools *Combination pliers; small screwdriver; fine abrasive paper; pencil. Possibly also penknife.*

Materials *Split pin (cotter pin); washer; petroleum jelly. Possibly also penetrating oil.*

1 Turn off the main stoptap if you are working on the cold water cistern, or close the gate valve or service valve to the WC cistern.

2 Use a pipe wrench to loosen the ball valve end cap, if there is one, then unscrew and remove it.

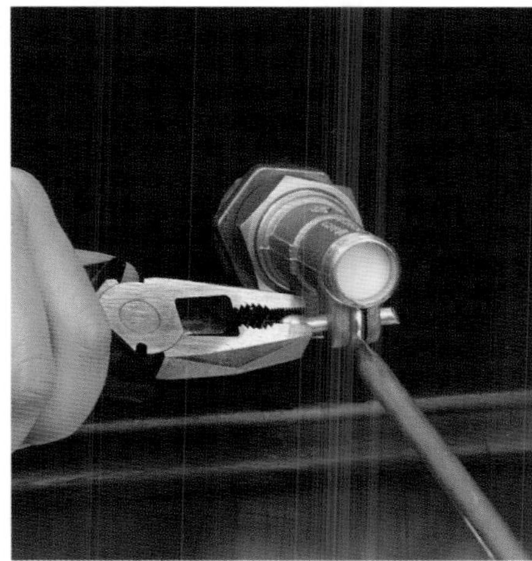

3 Use pliers to close the end of the split pin securing the float arm, then withdraw the pin. Remove the float arm and put it to one side.

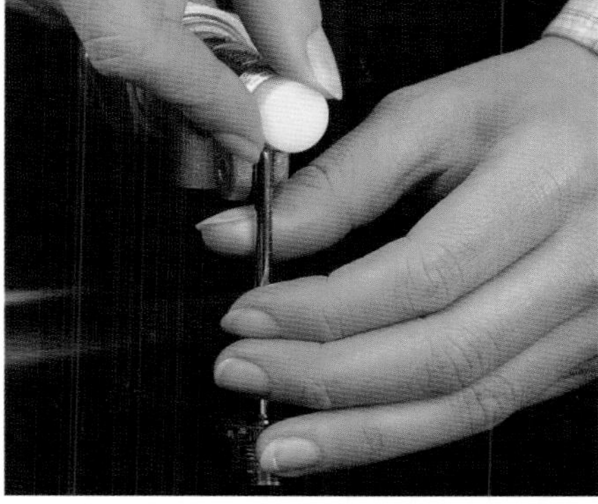

4 Insert a small screwdriver blade into the slot where the float arm was seated. Use it to push the piston from the end of the casing. Catch the piston with your other hand as it comes out.

5 Clean the outside of a metal piston (but not a plastic one) with fine abrasive paper. Wrap fine abrasive paper round a pencil shaft and clean the inside of the metal valve casing.

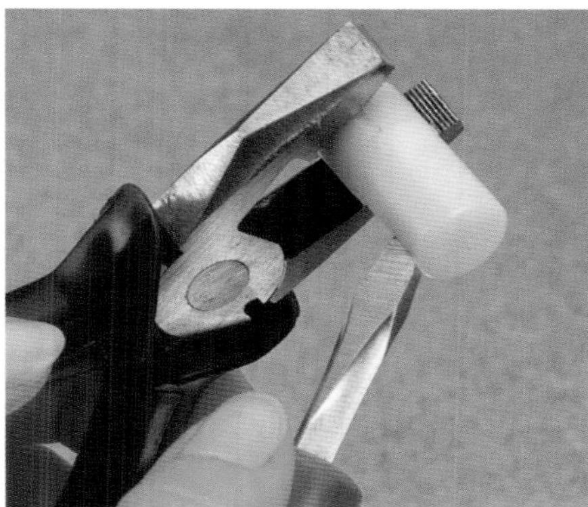

6 To renew the washer, hold the piston with a screwdriver thrust into the slot and use pliers to unscrew its washer-retaining cap. Do not force it or you may damage the piston. If a metal cap is difficult to undo, smear penetrating oil round the cap edge and try again after about 10 minutes.

7 With the cap removed, use a screwdriver to prise out the washer from the inside. (If you were unable to remove the cap, try to pick out the old washer with a penknife through the cap's open centre.)

8 Fit the new washer and screw the cap back on. Tighten with pliers. (If the cap is still on, try to force the new washer through the centre hole and push it flat with your finger.) Before refitting the piston, turn on the water supply briefly to flush out dirt from the valve casing still attached to the cistern. Lightly smear the piston with petroleum jelly before reassembling the valve and float arm. Use a new split pin to secure the arm. Restore the water supply.

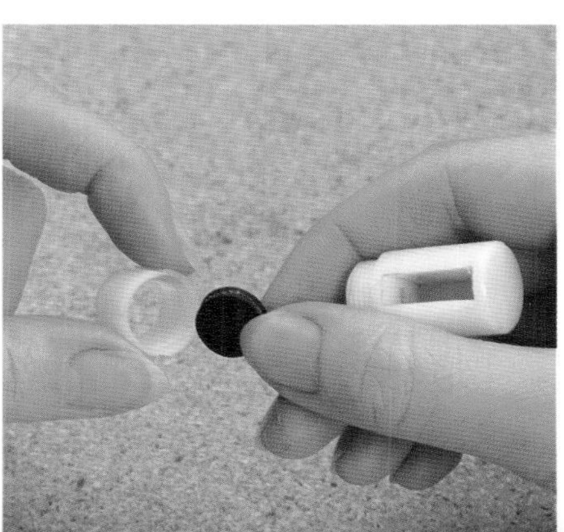

Diaphragm-type valves

The water inlet of a diaphragm-type valve is closed by a large rubber or synthetic diaphragm pushed against it by a plunger attached to the float arm. The cistern will be slow to refill if the inlet gets clogged or the diaphragm gets jammed against it.

Tools *Screwdriver. Possibly also pipe wrench; cloth for padding wrench jaws.*

Materials *Lint free rag; warm soapy water in container; clear water for rinsing. Possibly also replacement diaphragm.*

1 Turn off the main stoptap if you are working on the cold water cistern, or the gate valve or service valve on the pipe to the WC cistern (page 328).

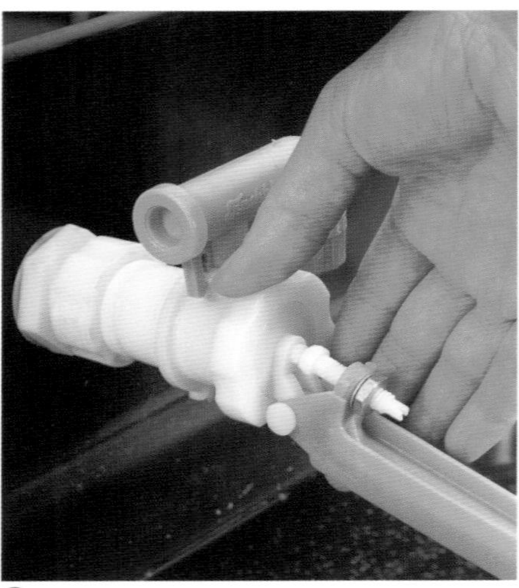

2 Unscrew the large knurled retaining nut by hand. If it is stiff, use a padded pipe wrench.

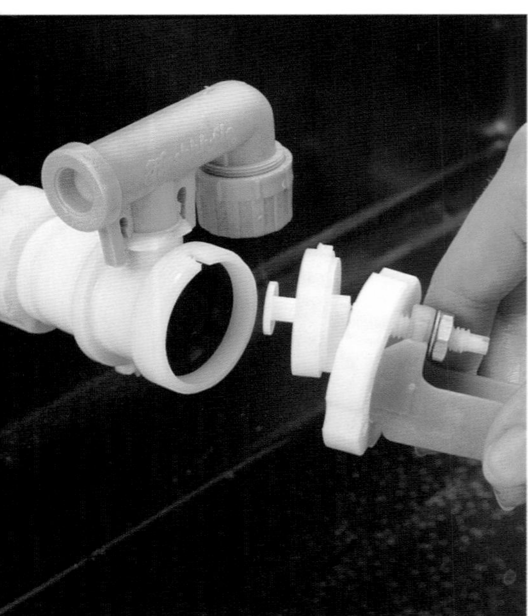

3 With the nut removed, the end of the float arm and plunger will come away. Put them to one side.

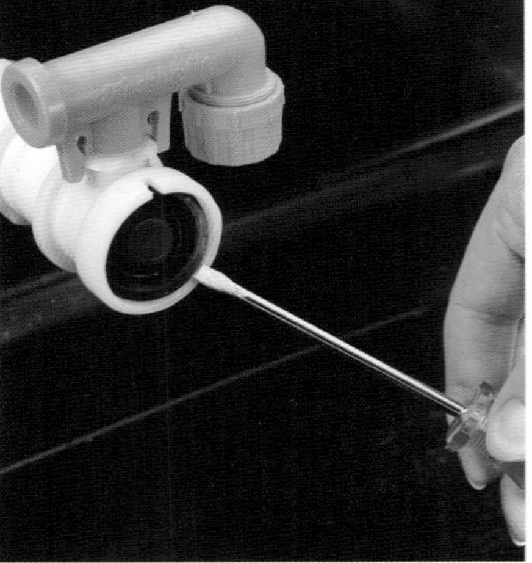

4 Use a screwdriver blade to free the diaphragm from the inlet pipe, taking care not to damage it. Note which way round it is fitted.

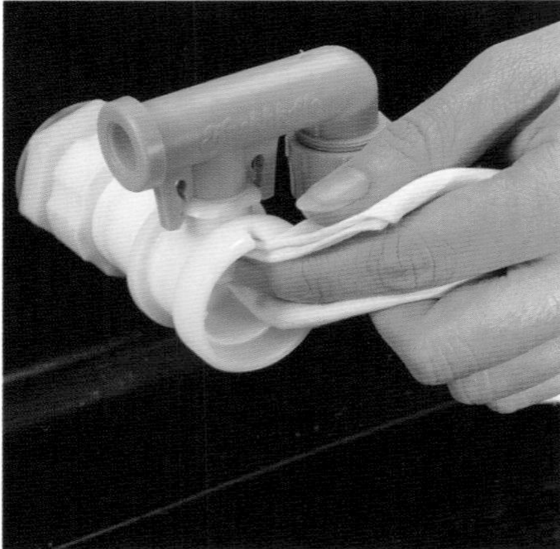

5 Use a piece of clean, lint-free rag to clean out any dirt and debris from the inlet pipe.

6 Wash the diaphragm in warm soapy water, then rinse it. If it is pitted or damaged, replace it. Fit with the rim inwards.

Alternatively If the valve is a servo type with a filter fitted, remove the filter and wash it in warm soapy water, then rinse it. If the servo valve has no filter, flush the part attached to the float arm under the tap.

GETTING RID OF WATER HAMMER

Banging or humming from the rising main is due to the pipe vibrating when the cistern ballvalve bounces on its seating. This occurs when the float is shaken by ripples on the water as the cistern fills. Cut down the bouncing by fitting the float with a stabiliser made from a plastic pot. Hang the pot on a loop of galvanised wire from the float arm. It should trail underwater just below the float.

Ensure that the rising main is securely clipped to the roof timbers near its entry to the cistern. Also, check that a metal bracing plate is fitted on a plastic cistern to reduce distortion of the cistern wall.

The surest way to reduce water hammer is to replace a Portsmouth valve with an equilibrium valve – a type less affected by water pressure.

7 Before reassembling the valve, turn on the water supply briefly to flush dirt or debris out of the casing. Then refit the parts and restore the water supply.

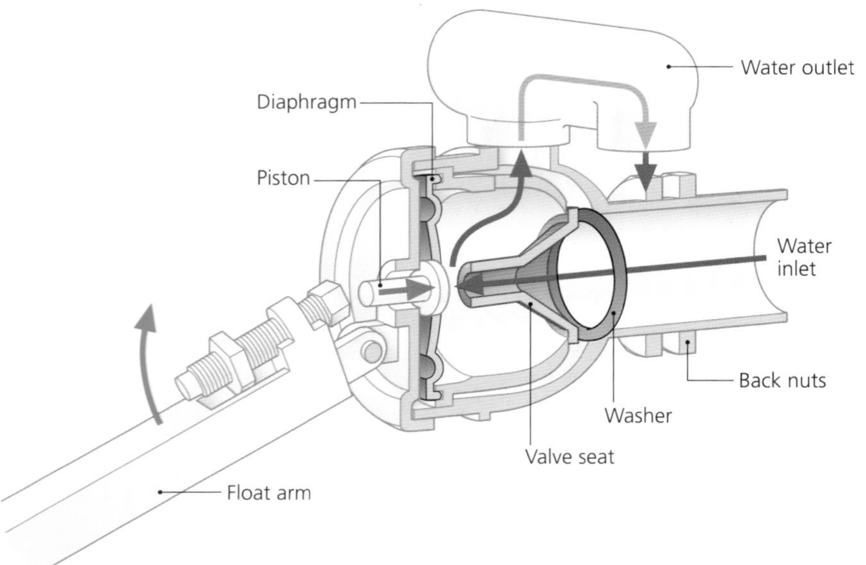

Fitting a new ball valve

Fit a new ball valve if the old one gets damaged or broken, or if you decide to change the type of valve to get rid of noise and vibration.

Tools *Two adjustable spanners.*
Materials *Ball valve with float (of same size as existing valve); service valve (page 328) with compression fitting inlet and tap connector outlet.*

1 Turn off the main stoptap to cut off the cistern water supply.

2 Use a spanner to undo the tap connector securing the supply pipe to the valve tail. You may need to hold the valve body or any securing nut inside the cistern steady with a second spanner.

3 Disconnect the supply pipe.

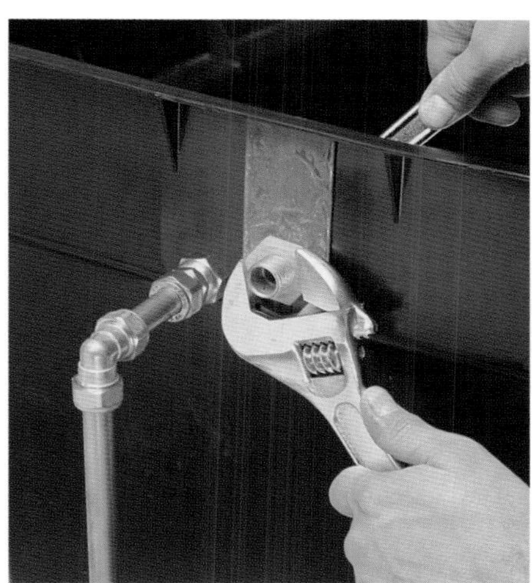

4 Undo the backnut securing the ball valve to the cistern. Remove the valve.

5 Take off the backnut from the new ballvalve and put it aside.

6 Slip the inner securing nut over the new valve tail and push the tail through the cistern and the bracing plate from the inside.

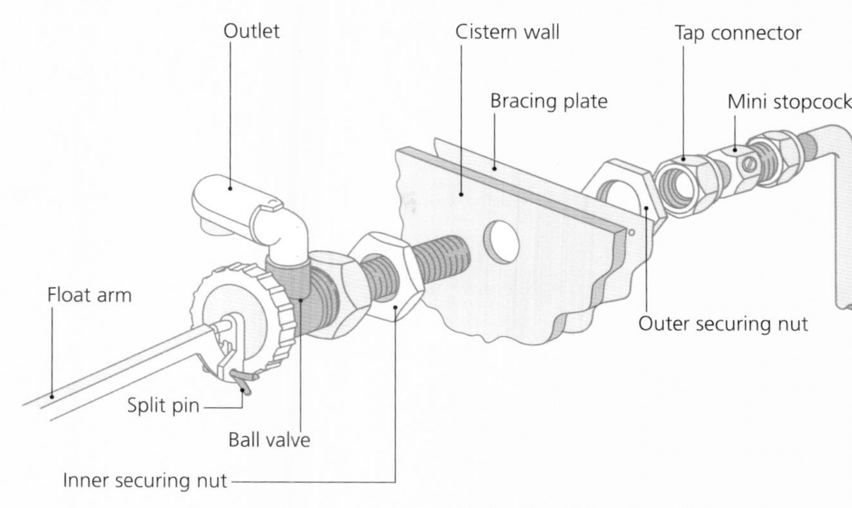

Ball valve fixing to cistern The valve is held against the wall of the cistern by two backnuts on its threaded inlet tail.

7 Screw on the backnut by hand. Tighten it by half a turn with a spanner.

8 Remove the existing tap connector and fit the service valve. Screw the connector nut to the new valve tail.

9 Restore the water supply, making sure the service valve is fully open. Adjust the cistern water level (page 339).

REPAIRING A LEAKING FLOAT

For a permanent repair, a new ball float must be fitted. But to get the valve back in action again until a new float is obtained, the old one can be temporarily repaired.

Tools *Small spanner; sharp knife or old-fashioned bladed tin opener; piece of wood to go across cistern.*
Materials *Plastic bag; string.*

1 Raise the float arm to close the valve and cut off the flow of the water. Then tie the arm to a length of wood laid across the top of the cistern.

2 Unscrew and remove the ball float from the float arm.

3 Find the hole through which the water is leaking and enlarge it with either a sharp knife or tin opener.

4 Drain the water from the float, then screw it back in position on the float arm.

5 Slip the plastic bag over the float and tie it securely to the float arm with string.

6 Release the arm and lower it into position to refill the cistern.

Clearing a blocked WC

The usual faults with a WC pan are blockages or leaks. A leak from the pan outlet is not difficult to repair, but a cracked pan will have to be replaced.

Clearing a washdown pan

When a washdown bowl is flushed, the two streams of water, one from each side of the rim, should flow equally to meet at the front. The water should leave the pan smoothly, not eddying like a whirlpool. If the cistern is working properly but the bowl fails to clear, something is obstructing either the flush inlet or the pan outlet.

If the flush water rises almost to the pan rim, then ebbs away very slowly, there is probably a blockage in the pan outlet (or possibly in the soil stack or drain into which it discharges).

Tools *WC plunger. Possibly also flexible drain auger; bucket; mirror; a pair of rubber gloves.*

1 To clear the pan, take the plunger and push it sharply onto the bottom of the pan to cover the outlet. Then pump the handle up and down two or three times.

2 If this does not clear the pan, use a flexible drain auger to probe the outlet and trap.

3 If the blockage persists, check and clear the underground drain (page 407).

4 Flush the cistern to check that water is entering the pan properly, with streams from each side of the rim flowing equally to meet at the front.

5 If the flow into the pan is poor or uneven, use a mirror to examine the flushing rim. Probe the rim with your fingers for flakes of limescale or debris from the cistern that may be obstructing the flush water.

Alternatively If you have no WC plunger, use a mop, or stand on a stool and tip in a bucket of water all in one go.

Clearing a siphonic pan

Blockages are more common in siphonic pans because of the double trap and the delicate pressure reducing pipe seal (also known as the atomiser seal). Do not use a plunger on a blocked siphonic pan because this can dislodge the seal.

A blockage can usually be cleared with an auger or by pouring several buckets of warm water into the pan. But if, after clearing the blockage, the water still rises in the pan as it is flushed, renew the seal.

Tools *Screwdriver; adjustable spanner; container for bailing or a tube for siphoning; silicone grease.*

Materials *Pressure reducing pipe seal.*

1 Remove the cistern (page 336) and locate the pipe protruding from the bottom of the siphon.

2 Remove the rubber mushroom-shaped seal and fit a replacement. Lubricate the new seal with silicone grease so that it will slide down the pipe.

3 Refit the cistern and test the flush. The water should be removed from the bowl with a sucking noise before the clean water comes in from the rim of the bowl.

Repairing a leaking pan outlet

A putty joint may leak when the putty gets old and cracked. To replace a putty joint with a push-fit connector (page 355), the pan must be moved forward then refitted. Alternatively, repair the joint using waterproof building tape or non-setting mastic filler.

Chip and rake out the old putty with an old chisel and bind two or three turns of tape round the pan outlet. Then poke more tape firmly into the rim of the soil-pipe inlet. Fill the space between the rim and pan outlet with mastic. Bind two more turns of tape round the joint.

Choosing pipes and fittings

Copper and plastic are the two most common materials used in household pipework. Stainless-steel piping can be used in the same way as copper. Although it is more expensive and harder to work with, it can be used safely with galvanised steel pipes, without the corrosive reaction that copper produces. Lead and iron pipes are no longer used, although they may still be found in older buildings.

Pipe sizes Domestic water supply pipes are made in metric sizes. Copper pipe is measured by the outside diameter. Standard sizes are 15mm, 22mm and 28mm. Older supply pipes were made in imperial sizes and were measured by the inside diameter. Imperial and metric piping can be joined, but an adaptor is needed for some sizes, depending on the type of joint and connector used.

Plastic supply pipes are made in the same nominal sizes as copper pipes, but have thicker walls. Medium-density polyethylene (MDPE) pipe is now widely used for underground supply pipes, and is coloured blue. Semi-flexible polybutylene (PB) and cross-linked polyethylene (PEX) pipes can both be used for indoor hot and cold supply pipes. They come in white or grey, but can be painted. Long lengths (in rolls) are available.

PLUMBING AND EARTHING

All metal pipework must be joined to the house's main earth bonding system so that it is impossible for someone touching exposed metalwork to be electrocuted if it becomes live. See page 267. Plastic pipe and fittings are non-conducting so if either has been used in a run of metal pipe, a 'bridging' earth wire must be fitted between the metal sections. When installing a metal bath or sink, follow the instructions on page 361.

If your house earthing system still relies upon a connection to the rising main for an earthing point, this must be changed to a common earthing point near the meter. Contact a qualified electrician for advice.

Types of pipe

Copper

For hot and cold supply pipework indoors. Sold in three sizes (15, 22 and 28mm) in 2m and 3m lengths. Join with compression joints, with soldered capillary joints or with push-fit joints. Cut with a hacksaw or pipe cutter.
Advantages Withstands high temperatures. Bends easily round corners, so neat and economical to use. Can be painted. Widely available. Rigid, so needs few supports: 15mm pipe every 1.2m horizontally, 1.8m vertically; 22mm and 28mm pipe every 1.8m horizontally, 2.4m vertically.
Disadvantages Pipes hot to touch. May split or burst if water freezes. Brings about the corrosion of galvanised (zinc-coated) steel if joined directly to it.

Semi-flexible plastic For hot and cold pipework indoors. Sold in 15mm, 22mm and 28mm sizes in straight 2m and 3m lengths and in rolls up to 100m long. Join with plastic push-fit joints or brass compression joints (always with a metal supporting insert). Cut with a trimming knife or with special pipe cutters shaped like secateurs.
Advantages Easy to cut and to bend in gentle curves or round corners (metal bend supports available) and can be run through holes cut in floor joists. Joints easy to make (and re-make) and allow pipe to be twisted in fitting (important for tee joints). Long lengths minimise number of fittings needed. Can be painted with water-based or solvent-based (but not cellulose) paints. Widely available with full range of fittings. Insulates well – pipes not too hot to touch. Pipes less likely to freeze in cold weather but cannot withstand too high temperatures – so must not be used close (within 1m) to boiler for central heating pipe runs. Does not corrode or support scale formation.
Disadvantages Needs more support to prevent sagging: 15mm pipe every 0.3m horizontally and 0.5m vertically; 22mm pipe every 0.5m horizontally and 0.8m vertically. Pipe cheaper than copper; fittings cost about the same as compression fittings for copper (though fewer needed). Extra earthing needed if replacing length of copper pipe.

BRASS IN ACID WATER

In areas where the water supply is particularly acid, check with the regional water company before using brass joints – especially if you are using copper piping. Brass is an alloy of zinc and copper, and in highly acid water a reaction between the two metals can cause the zinc to dissolve and the joint to fail. This process is known as dezincification. Use joints made of gunmetal or DR (dezincification-resistant) metal instead.

CHOOSING THE TYPE OF JOINT

There are several different joint types available. Some can be used for more than one pipe type. All the joints are available as straight couplers, elbows and tees for joining pipework, and as threaded joints for connecting pipes to taps, ball valves, storage cisterns and hot water cylinders.

Compression joint

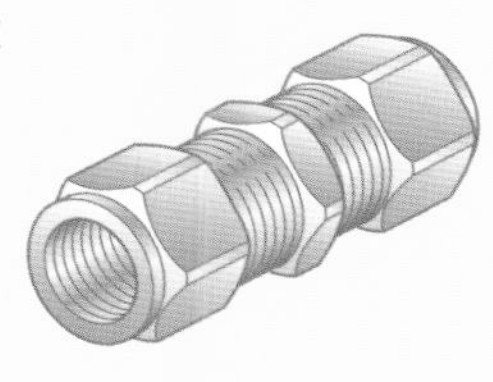

A brass joint with screw-on cap nuts at each end. A soft metal compression ring (known as an olive) fits over each pipe. When the cap nuts are tightened with a spanner, the olives are pressed against the pipe and the joint to form a watertight seal. When used with plastic pipes, a metal insert is fitted inside the pipe ends to support the pipe walls.
Advantages Widely available. Can be re-used if dismantled (with a new olive).
Disadvantages More expensive than a capillary joint. Looks clumsy. Tightening can be difficult in awkward places.

Capillary joint

A copper joint with internal pipe stops, inside which copper pipe ends are sealed with solder heated by a blowtorch.
There are two types:

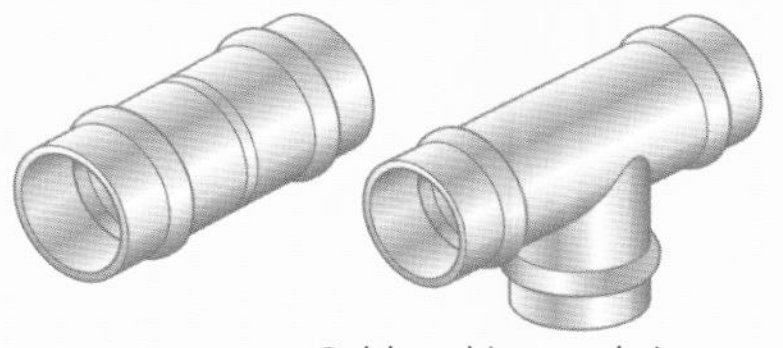

Soldered integral-ring type

Solder-ring joint Has a built-in ring of solid solder near each end. This is melted and flows round the pipe by capillary action as the joint is heated. Also known as a integral-ring, pre-soldered or Yorkshire joint.

End-feed joint

End-feed joint Contains no solder. Wire solder is fed into each end of the fitting as the joint is heated, and is drawn in by capillary action. Cheaper than solder-ring joints.
Advantages Widely available. Cheaper than all the other joints (especially end-feed). Neat appearance.
Disadvantages Only for copper pipe. Cannot be re-used if dismantled. Tricky to use successfully. Special joints needed to link new metric and old imperial pipe sizes.

Plastic push-fit collet joint

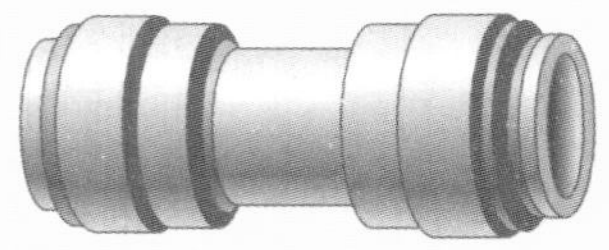

A plastic joint with a toothed ring (called a collet) to grip the pipe and an O-ring seal. The pipe end is pushed into the joint, and can be released by holding the collet against the joint as the pipe is withdrawn. Suitable for both copper and plastic pipe.
Advantages Quick and easy to use. Extremely reliable. Can be dismantled easily and re-used. Pipe can be rotated in joint for branch alignment. Fitting unobtrusive in appearance.
Disadvantages Not suitable for connection directly to boiler. More expensive than capillary fittings.

Plastic grab-ring push-fit joint

A plastic joint with an internal grab ring and O-ring seal. The pipe end is pushed into the joint, and can be released by undoing the cap nuts and prising open the grab ring with a special tool. Suitable for both copper and plastic pipe.
Advantages Quick and easy to use. Can be undone and re-used if new grab ring is fitted. Pipe can be rotated in joint for branch alignment.
Disadvantages More expensive than compression fittings. Bulky.

Metal push-fit

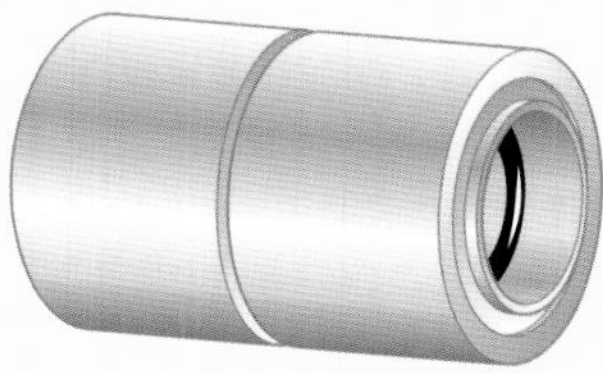

A sleek copper or brass fitting with an internal seal. Can be released with special tool. Suitable for use with copper and plastic pipe (with pipe insert).
Advantages No tools needed to make fitting. Maintains earth continuity when used with copper. Neat in appearance.
Disadvantage Fairly expensive.

Threaded joints

Joints for connecting pipes to taps, cylinders and cisterns have a screw thread at one end which may be internal (female) or external (male). Threaded joints must be matched male to female. Made water-tight by binding PTFE thread-sealing tape round the male thread.

Ways of joining pipes

Preparing the pipe ends

Before two pipe lengths of any material can be joined, the ends must be cut square and left smooth. Copper pipe needs careful cutting and finishing to ensure watertight joints. You can cut plastic pipes with special cutter or with a sharp trimming knife.

Tools *Pipe cutter or hacksaw; half-round file. Possibly also vice or portable workbench.*

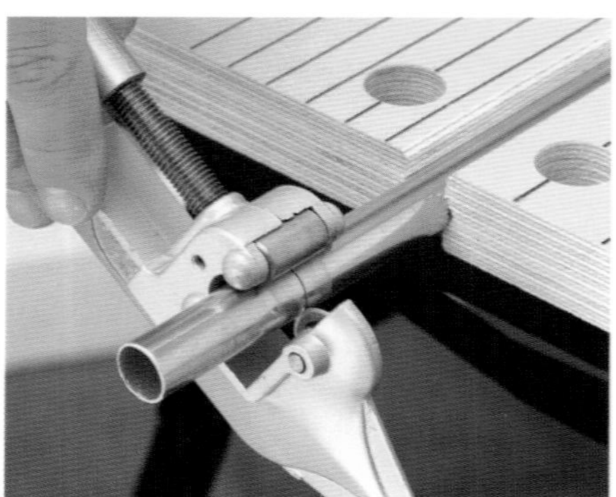

1 Cut the pipe ends square using a pipe cutter or hacksaw (not on plastic pipe). Holding the pipe in a vice while sawing helps to ensure a square cut.

2 Smooth away burrs inside the cut ends of copper pipe with the reamer on the pipe cutter. Use a file to smooth the end and the outside of the pipe.

Making a compression joint

This is a strong and easy method of joining copper and plastic pipes. Tightening the nuts correctly is critical – the joint will leak if they are not tight enough or if they are over-tightened.

Tools *Two adjustable spanners (with jaw openings up to 38mm wide for fittings on 28mm piping); or, if you have any that fit, two open-ended spanners – cap nut sizes on different makes of fittings vary.*

Materials *Compression fitting.*

1 Unscrew and remove one cap nut from the fitting. If the olive has two sloping faces rather than a convex one, note which way round it is fitted as you remove it.

2 Take one pipe and slide the cap nut over it, then the olive. Make sure the olive is the correct way round if it has two sloping faces. Fit a pipe support sleeve to plastic pipe.

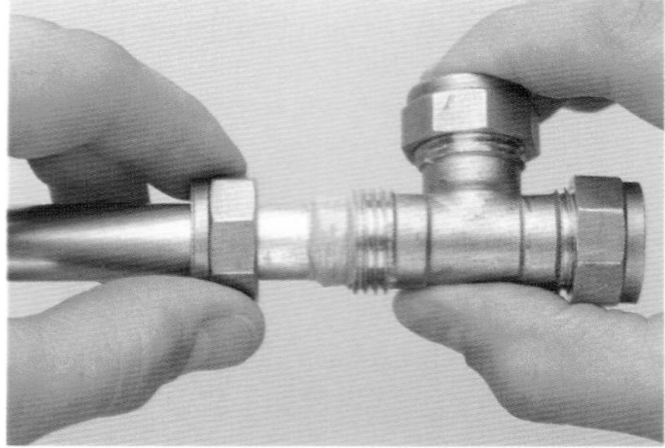

3 Push the pipe into one end of the fitting up to the internal pipe stop. Then slide the olive and nut up to the fitting and hand-tighten the cap nut.

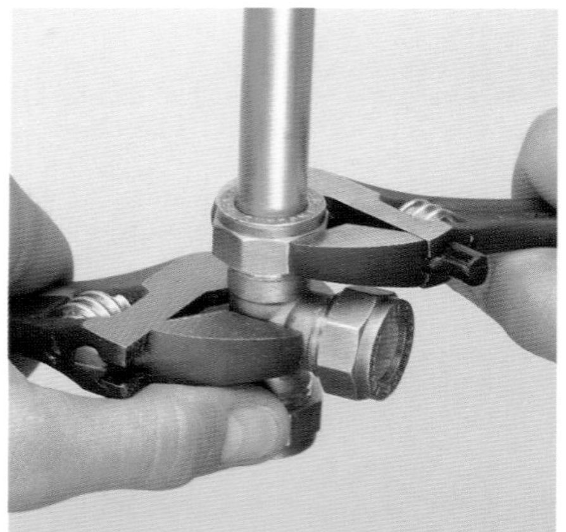

4 Hold the body of the fitting securely with one spanner while you give the cap nut one and a quarter turns with the other. Do not overtighten it further. Fit pipes into other openings of the fitting in the same way.

HELPFUL TIPS

Until you have had some practice in making compression joints, take care not to over-tighten the cap nuts. One way to do this is to make a scratch on the fitting and the cap nut before dismantling it. When you refit and tighten the nut, you will have made a complete turn when the marks meet.

When connecting a fitting into a vertical pipe, use spring-clip clothes pegs to stop the olives and cap nuts slipping down the pipe while you insert the fitting.

Making a soldered joint

This is a more difficult joint for the amateur plumber to make successfully. Too little heat will fail to make a complete solder seal inside the fitting, while too much heat will make all the solder run out.

Tools *Wire wool or fine emery paper; blowtorch; clean rag.*

Materials *Tin of flux; soft lead-free solder wire for end feed joints only. Possibly also sheet of glass fibre or other fire-proof material for placing between the joint and any nearby flammable material.*

1 Clean the ends of the pipes and the inside of the fitting thoroughly with wire wool or fine emery paper. They must show clean, bright metal to make a successful joint.

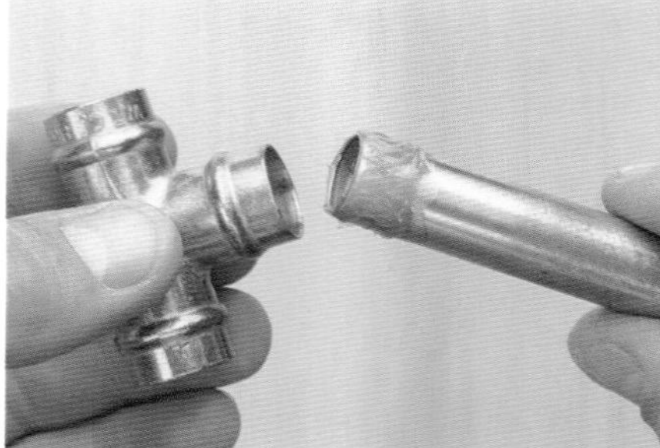

2 Smear the cleaned surfaces with flux, which will ensure a clean bond with the solder. Push the pipe into the fitting as far as the pipe stop. For an integral-ring fitting, push pipes into all the openings because all the solder rings will melt once heat is applied to the fitting. Wipe off excess flux with a clean rag, otherwise the solder will spread along the pipe surface.

3 Fix the pipe run securely in position with pipe clips and position fire-proof mat.

4 For an integral-ring fitting, heat the joint with a blowtorch until a silver ring of solder appears all round the mouths of the joints. Solder all the joints on the fitting in the same operation.

Alternatively For an end feed fitting, heat the joint until you see flux vapour escaping. Then remove the heat (otherwise the solder will melt too fast and drip) and apply soft solder wire round the mouth of the fitting and heat again until a silver ring of solder appears all round. If you have to leave some joints of the fitting until later, wrap a damp cloth round those already made to stop the solder re-melting.

5 Leave the joint undisturbed for about 5 minutes while it cools.

Making a push-fit joint

This is a simple method that can be used to join both copper and plastic pipes. The only tools needed are those used to cut and smooth the pipe ends.

Both plastic and metal push-fit fittings can be used on either copper or plastic pipe – with plastic pipe, pipe inserts must be used. You will also need adaptors for joining to old-size (imperial) copper pipe.

Tools *Pencil; measuring tape, pipe cutters (or hacksaw for copper pipe), trimming knife (for plastic pipe).*

Materials *Push-fit joint.*

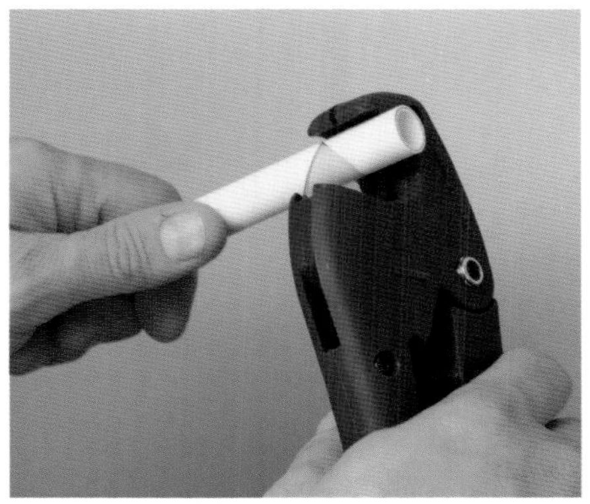

1 Cut plastic pipe using the special pipe cutters (secateurs) available – some plastic pipe is marked with insertion distances and you cut it at an insertion mark. Cut copper pipe as shown opposite.

2 Check that the cut pipe end is smooth, otherwise sharp edges could damage the O-ring seal in the fitting and cause the joint to leak. Use a file on copper pipe and a trimming knife on plastic pipe.

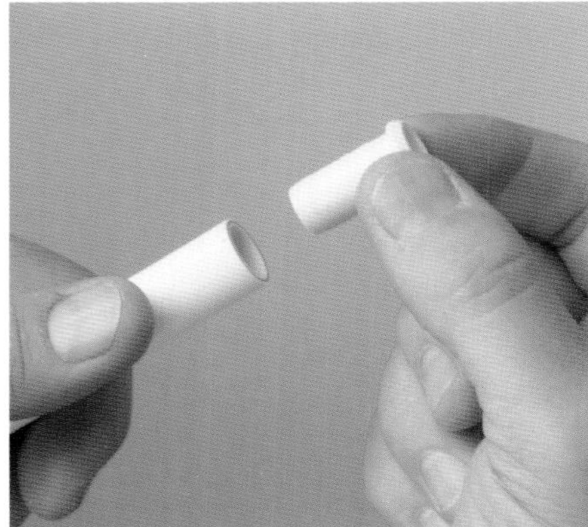

3 For plastic piping, push the support sleeve into the pipe end with a twisting motion.

4 Unless you have cut plastic pipe at an insertion mark, use a pencil to make a mark on the pipe for the correct insertion distance (check instructions supplied with the fitting).

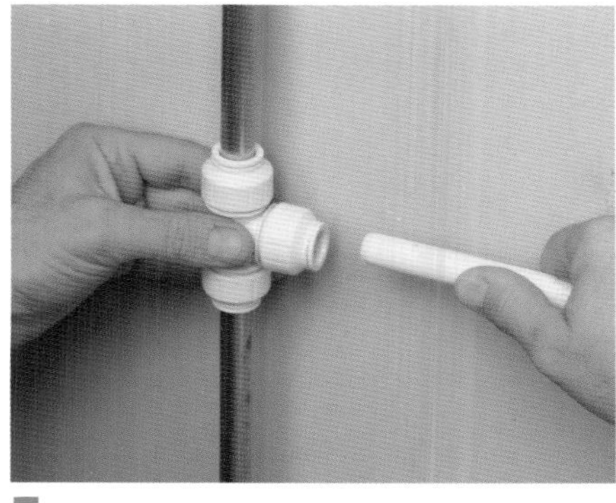

5 Push the pipe into the fitting up to the insertion mark. If it is not pushed fully home the pipe will blow out under pressure. Check that the pipe is properly home by tugging gently on it. Fit abridging earth wire (see page 267) if you have used a plastic push-fit fitting in a run of copper pipework.

Re-using fittting Check which method is needed to de-mount a push-fit fitting so it can be remade. With some slimline fittings, you just push in the collet; with others you need some kind of de-mounting tool or collar. With grab-ring fittings, you unscrew the large retaining cap, lever out the old grab ring and fit a new one. Take care – it's sharp.

Bending copper pipe

Never try to bend rigid copper pipe by hand without a spring to support the pipe walls – the pipe will kink at the bend if it is not supported.

Tools *Bending springs of the required diameter (15mm or 22mm); or pipe-bending machine with pipe formers and guide blocks; screwdriver; length of string.*

Materials *Petroleum jelly.*

Bending with a spring

1 If the pipe is longer than the spring, tie string to the spring end.

2 Grease the spring well with petroleum jelly and push it into the pipe.

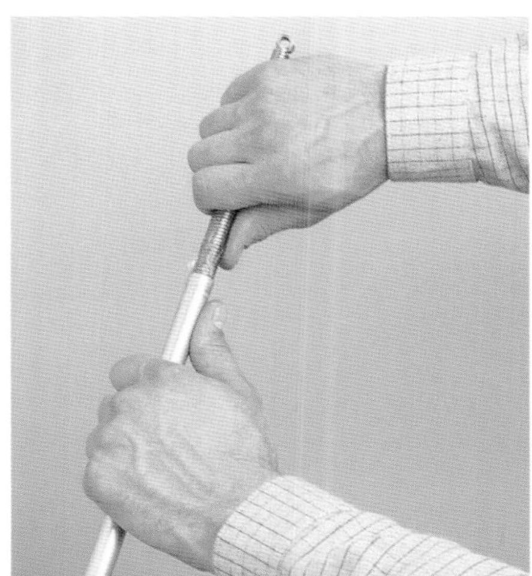

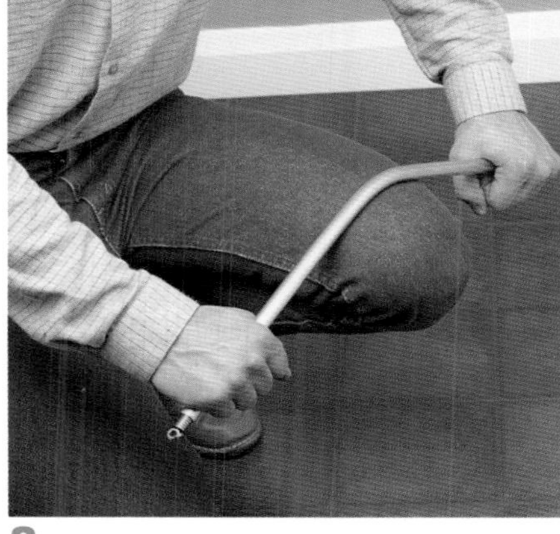

3 Bend the pipe across your knee with gentle hand pressure to the required angle.

4 Overbend the pipe a little more, then ease it gently back again. This action helps to free the spring and makes it easier to withdraw.

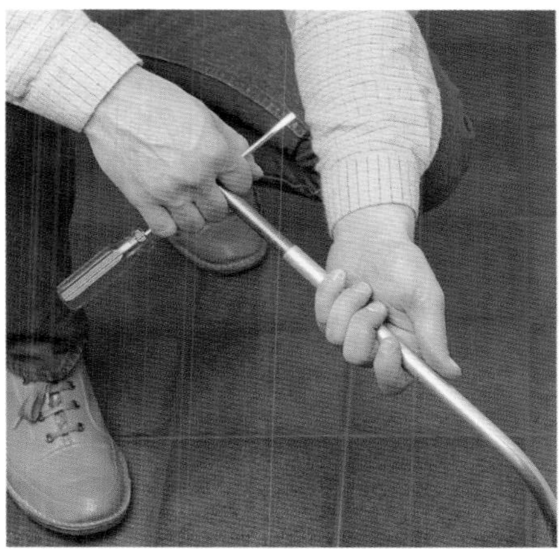

5 Insert a screwdriver blade through the spring loop or string. Twist the spring (if you can) to reduce its diameter, then pull it out.

Bending with a machine

1 Clamp the pipe against the correct-sized semicircular former.

2 Place the guide block of the correct diameter between the pipe and the movable handle.

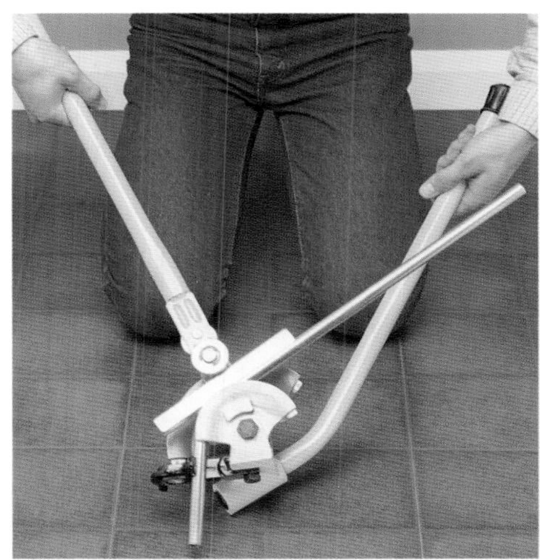

3 Squeeze the handles together until the pipe is curved to the required angle round the semicircular former.

Choosing waste pipes and traps

All waste water outlets are fitted with a trap – a bend in the piping that retains water and stops foul air from the drain getting back into the room.

Plastic waste pipes are made in 40mm and 50mm diameter for sinks, baths and shower trays, 32mm for washbasins and 22mm for overflow pipes from cisterns. Pipes and fittings from different makers are not always interchangeable.

PVCu (or PVC) For cold water overflow pipes from WC and storage cisterns. Joined by push-fit or ring-seal joints or by solvent welding. White, grey, brown, sometimes black. Sold in 3m and 4m lengths.

PVCmu (modified un-plasticised polyvinyl chloride) For hot waste from sinks, baths, washbasins and washing machines. Joined by push-fit or ring-seal joints, or by solvent welding (see opposite). Ring-seals for connection to main stack. Grey, white, sometimes black. Sold in 4m lengths.

Polypropylene For cold-water overflow pipes and hot waste from sinks, baths, washbasins and washing machines. Joined by push-fit or ring-seal joints only. White and black. Has slightly waxy surface. Sold in 3m and 4m lengths.

FITTINGS FOR WASTE PIPES

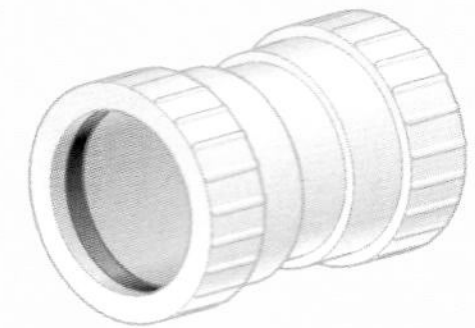

Locking push-fit (ring-seal) joint
Polypropylene joint with screw-down retaining capnuts. The sealing ring is usually ready-fitted.

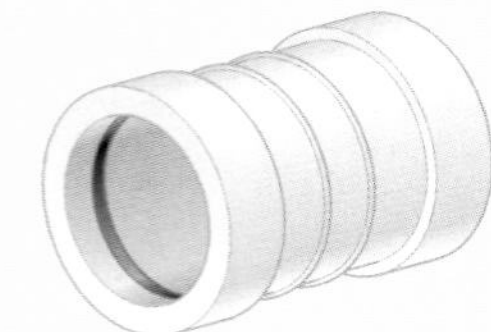

Push-fit (ring-seal) joint
Rigid polypropylene sleeve with a push-fit connection. Cannot be connected to any existing copper, steel or plastic system unless a locking ring fitting is interposed.

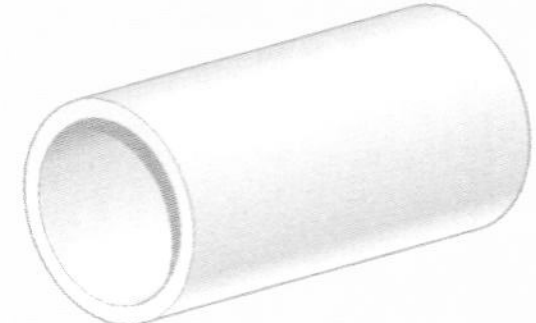

Solvent-weld joint
A plastic sleeve with a built-in pipe stop at each end. Used with PVC piping, which is secured in the sleeve by means of a strong adhesive, recommended by the joint manufacturer.

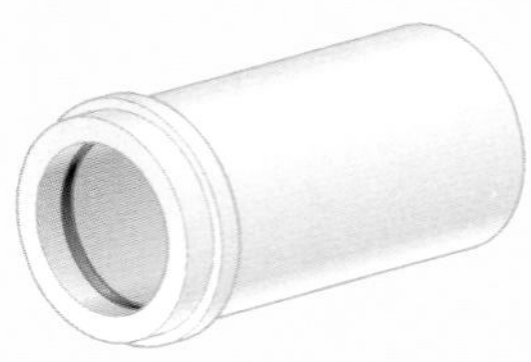

Expansion coupling
PVCmu joint designed for a solvent-weld joint at one end and a ring-seal joint at the other. Because solvent-weld joints do not allow for heat expansion, the coupling should be inserted every 1.8m in a long run of solvent-welded waste pipe.

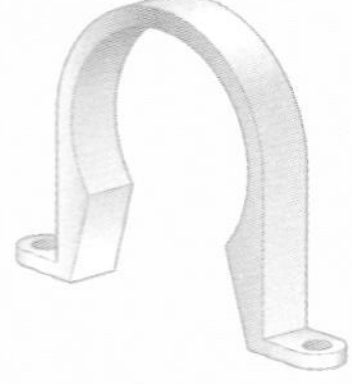

Pipe strap
Straps or clips for supporting waste pipes are available in compatible sizes. For sloping pipes they should be fixed about every 500mm. The slope must be at least 20mm per 1m run (page 351). For vertical pipes, fix clips every 1.2m.

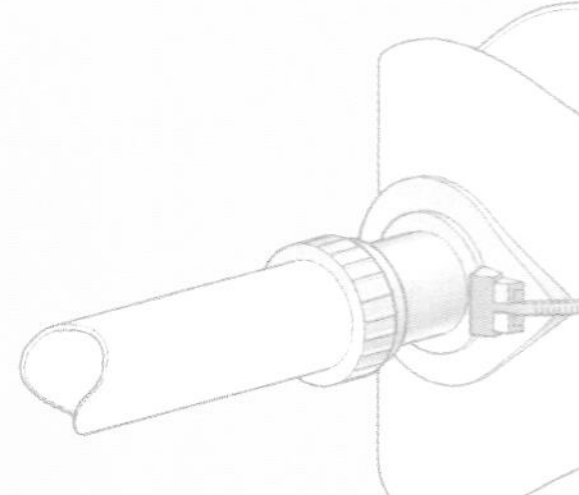

Stack connector
A clip-on polypropylene boss for fitting a new waste pipe into the stack, in which a hole has to be cut.

CHOOSING A TRAP

There are different types of trap for different situations. There may also be different outlet types (vertical or horizontal) and different seal depths. The seal – the depth of water maintained in the trap – is normally 38mm, but a trap with a deep seal of 75mm must, by law, be fitted to any appliance connected to a single-stack drainage pipe (see page 326). This guards against the seal being destroyed by an outflow of water, allowing foul air from the stack to enter the house.

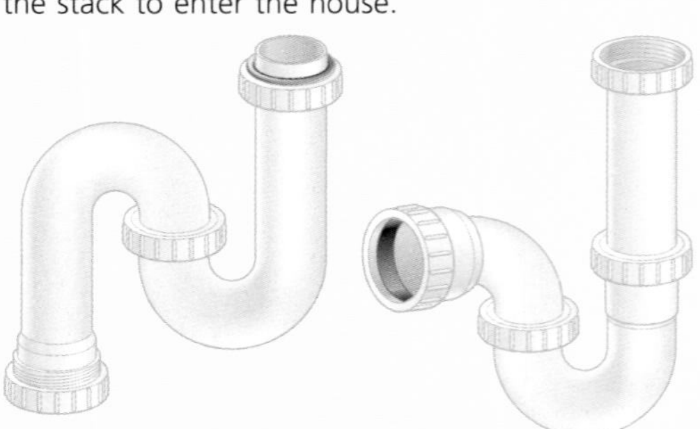

Tubular traps
A two-piece trap for a sink or basin, with an S (down-pointing) outlet (above left). Traps are also available with a P (horizontal) outlet (above right) and an adjustable inlet to allow an existing pipe to be linked to a new sink at a different height. Tubular traps are cleaned by unscrewing the part connected to the sink waste outlet.

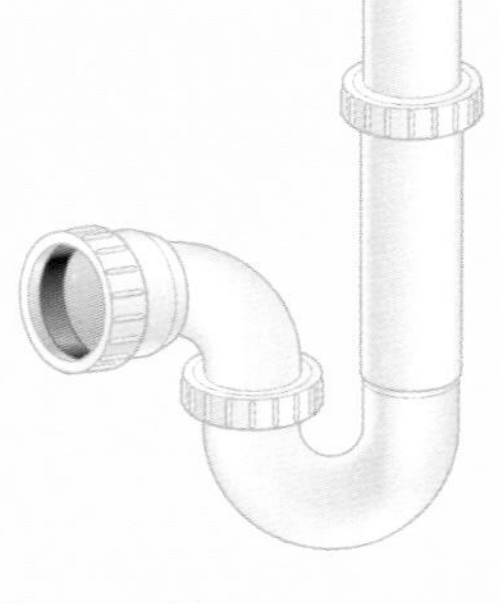

Washing-machine trap
A tubular trap with a tall stand-pipe for the washing-machine waste hose, and an outlet to link to the waste pipe.

Standard bottle trap
Normally used only for washbasins, which have a small outflow.
Most have a P outlet, but an S converter may be available. Some have a telescopic tube to adjust to different heights.

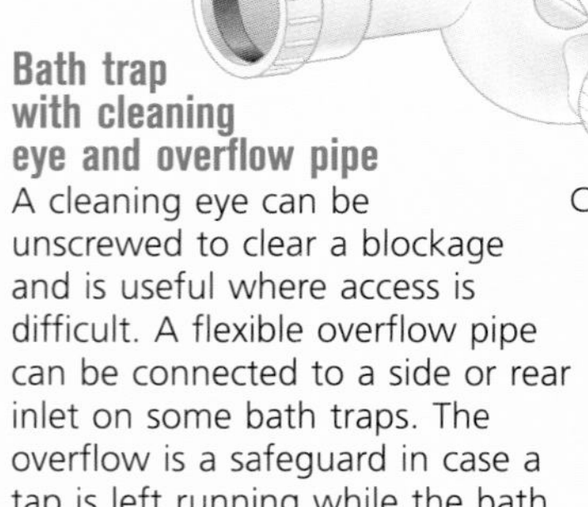

Bath trap with cleaning eye and overflow pipe
A cleaning eye can be unscrewed to clear a blockage and is useful where access is difficult. A flexible overflow pipe can be connected to a side or rear inlet on some bath traps. The overflow is a safeguard in case a tap is left running while the bath plug is in.

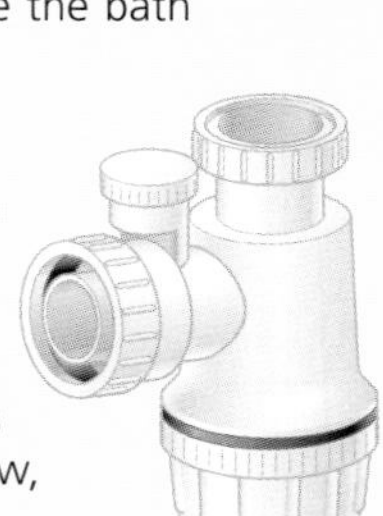

Anti-siphon bottle trap
Designed to allow air to enter the trap and prevent the seal being lost. Use where there is an occasional heavy flow, or long, steep pipe run.

Fitting a waste pipe and trap

Before 1939, waste and overflow pipes for sinks, washbasins, baths and cisterns were made of lead or galvanised steel. After that, copper was used until about 1960. Since then plastic has been in general use.

Joints for joining waste pipes come in broadly the same configurations as those for joining supply pipes; some additional joints are shown opposite.

If you plan to fit a new pipe that has to be connected into a soil stack (page 326), get the approval of your local authority Building Control Officer.

Making a push-fit joint

Push-fit or ring-seal joints must be used to connect polypropylene waste pipes, as these cannot be solvent-welded. Joints can be re-used with a new seal.

Tools *Hacksaw; sharp knife; clean rag; newspaper; adhesive tape; pencil.*

Materials *Push-fit joint; silicone grease.*

1 Wrap a sheet of paper round the pipe as a saw guide. Cut the pipe square with a hacksaw.

2 Use a sharp knife to remove fine shavings of polypropylene and any rough edges from the pipe.

3 Wipe dust from inside the fitting and the outside of the pipe.

4 On a locking-ring connector, loosen the locking ring.

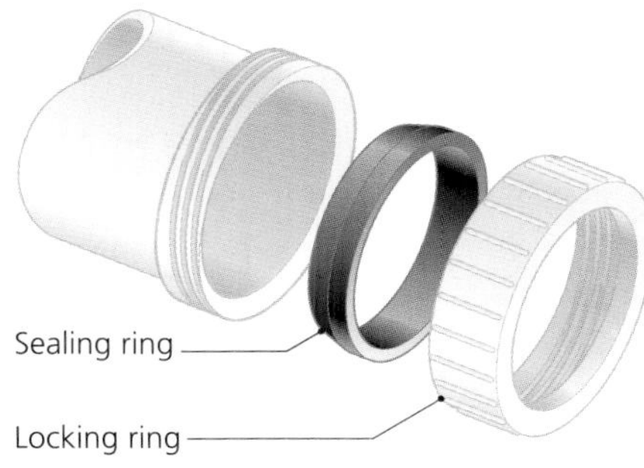

5 Make sure that the sealing ring is properly in place, with any taper pointing inwards. If necessary, remove the nut to check.

6 Lubricate the end of the pipe with silicone grease.

7 Push the pipe into the socket as far as the stop – a slight inner ridge about 25mm from the end. This allows a gap of about 10mm at the pipe end for heat expansion.

Alternatively If there is no stop, push the pipe in as far as it will go, mark the insertion depth with a pencil, then withdraw the pipe 10mm to leave an expansion gap.

8 Tighten the locking ring.

Making a solvent-welded joint

Because solvent-welded joints are neat they are suitable for exposed MuPVC pipework. However, they are permanent and should be used only where they will not need to be disturbed. Push-fit connections are used at traps, where the joint may need to be undone occasionally.

Tools *Hacksaw; half-round file; cloth.*

Materials *Solvent-weld cement; appropriate connector (see page 346); appropriate pipe.*

1 Cut the pipes to the required length with a hacksaw, remove the burrs inside and out with a half-round file, and wipe thoroughly with a clean cloth.

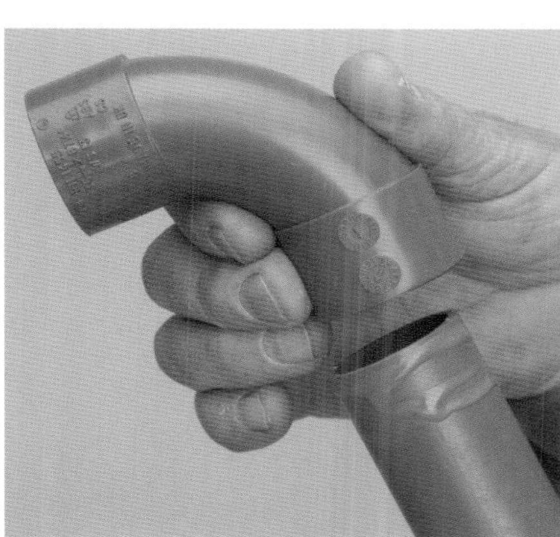

2 Apply solvent-weld cement around the end of the pipe and push it into the joint.

3 Wipe off excess cement with the cloth and allow the joint to dry before moving on to the next joint.

HELPFUL TIP

When running waste pipes along a wall, hold them in place with waste pipe clips.

Use wallplugs and screws to attach the clips to a masonry wall, or hollow-wall fixings on plasterboard.

Remember to check for pipes and cables before you drill.

Fitting a trap

Traps are either tubular or bottle-shaped (see Choosing a trap, left), and are made in suitable sizes to fit between a sink, bath or washbasin waste outlet and its waste pipe.

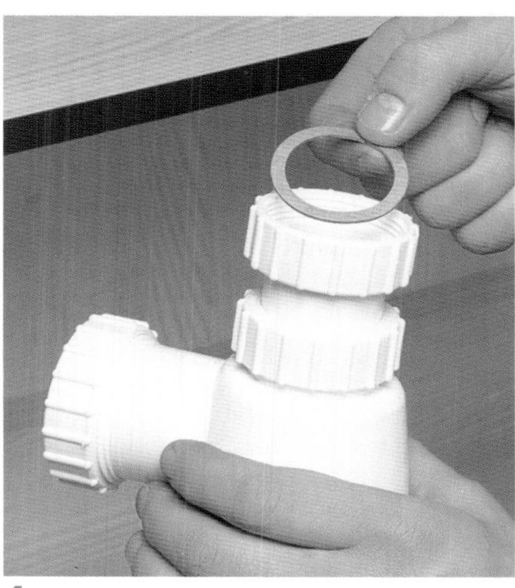

1 Check that the locking nut on the trap inlet is unscrewed and the rubber washer in position.

2 Push the trap inlet into the waste outlet and screw the nut onto the waste outlet thread.

3 Connect the trap outlet to the waste pipe with a push-fit joint.

Choosing a tap

Most taps work in the same way – turning the handle opens or closes a valve that fits into a valve seat. The valve – a rod and plate known as a jumper valve – is fitted with a washer that is replaced when it is worn and the tap drips.

Mixed measurements

New plumbing fittings come in metric sizes, but if the plumbing in your house dates from before the mid 1970s, your pipework is in imperial sizes (½in, ¾in and 1in inner diameter). Modern copper pipe comes in outer diameters of 10mm, 15mm, 22mm and 28mm. Choose 15mm pipe to join to existing ½in pipework and 28mm for 1in pipework. You will need special connectors for joining 22mm pipe to ¾in pipework.

High-neck taps The spout on an ordinary tap is about 22mm above its base, whereas the spout on a high-neck tap will be at least 95mm above its base. With a shallow sink this allows a bucket to be filled or large pans to be rinsed with ease. High neck taps are available with capstan, handwheel and lever handles.

CERAMIC WASHERS

The latest tap designs incorporate hardwearing ceramic discs – one fixed, one moving – instead of washers, and when the tap is turned on, openings in the discs line up so that water flows through. They open or close with only a quarter turn (through 90°) of the handle.

The discs become smoother and more watertight with wear, so should never need replacing but, in hard water areas, performance may eventually be affected by limescale.

Pillar tap The type still often used in bathrooms, with a vertical inlet that fits through a hole in the sanitaryware. The conventional tap has a bell-shaped cover – generally known as an easy-clean cover – and a capstan (cross-top) handle.

Lever handle Another type of shrouded head has a lever handle, which is easy for elderly or disabled people to use as it can be pushed rather than gripped. Most lever-handle taps have ceramic discs so require only a quarter turn of the handle.

WATER-SAVING TAPS

Many modern taps have a reduced rate of flow so that they use less water. You can slow the flow rate of an older tap by fitting a service valve. This valve can then be adjusted to give the flow rate you require.

Handwheel handle On modern taps, the cover and handle are replaced by a shrouded head that forms a handwheel. Shrouded heads not only give a neater appearance but also prevent water from wet hands going down the spindle and allowing detergent to wash the grease out of the tap mechanism.

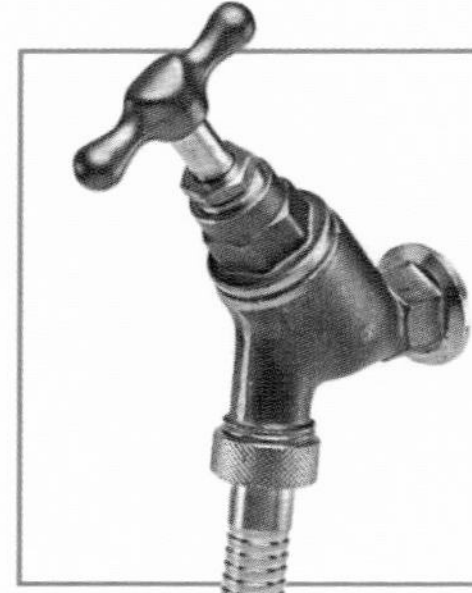

Hose union bib cock A tap with a horizontal inlet now used mainly outdoors or in the garage. Most bib taps have an angled head and threaded nozzle, suitable for use with a garden hose.

MIXER TAPS

Two taps with a common spout are known as a mixer. The taps are linked either by a deck block (flat against the surface) or a pillar block (raised). Most mixers are two-hole types that fit into a standard two-hole sink: one for the hot tap and one for the cold. Some mixers, however, need three holes (a centre hole for the spout) and some (monobloc types) only one.

Bath or basin mixer Hot and cold water merge within the mixer body, as both taps are usually fed from a cistern. It is illegal to fit this type of mixer on a fitting where cold water is supplied from the rising main and hot water comes from a cylinder. This is because, if mains pressure alters, differences in pressure might result in stored water being sucked back into the mains, and create the possible risk of contaminating drinking water supplies.

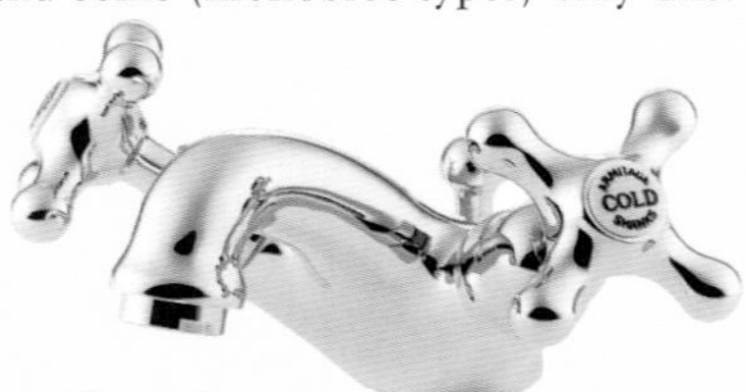

Monobloc mixer A single-hole monobloc mixer tap has a compact body with the handles and spout close together. Some designs have very narrow inlet pipes. There are monobloc designs for kitchens and bathrooms. Some kitchen monobloc mixers include a hot-rinse spray and brush fed from the hot water pipe by a flexible hose, so that the spray can be lifted from its socket for use.

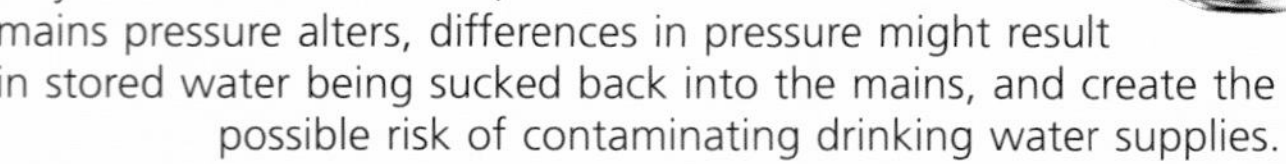

Kitchen mixer The spout has separate channels for hot and cold water. This is because the kitchen cold tap is fed direct from the mains, and it is illegal to mix cold water from the mains and hot water from a storage cistern in one fitting. The spout usually swivels and should be able to reach both of the bowls in a double sink. Kitchen mixers are available with capstan, handwheel and lever handles.

Bath/shower mixer Bath/shower mixer taps have a control knob that diverts the water flow from the spout to the shower handset. It will not provide a forceful spray but is a convenient addition to a bath.

Choosing a washbasin and bidet

There is a huge choice of washbasins available, from a traditional ceramic pedestal to an ultra-modern polished limestone bowl. Pedestals hide pipework and give some support to the weight of the bowl. Wall mounted sanitaryware can look sleek, but needs a solid wall and strong fixings.

There is no standard size for basins – most are around 550 x 400mm and 125mm deep. Order taps when you order the basin or bidet to ensure that your chosen unit has the right type of holes for the fittings.

Countertop basin These are often made in acrylic or enamelled pressed steel. They usually rest on the edge of a cutout or recessed ledge in the worktop and may have a rubber sealing ring and securing clips or be secured with mastic or sealant. Undermounted basins are screwfixed to a solid worktop from beneath.

Pedestal basin Usually made of vitreous china but glass versions with stainless-steel pedestals are also available. Luxury models can be much bigger. The pedestal hides the plumbing and helps to support the basin, but it is not the basin's sole support: the back of the basin must be screwed or bracketed to the wall. The basin may be joined to its pedestal with fixing clips or mastic. The pedestal is screwed to the floor through holes at the back. The basin's height – usually 800mm – is not adjustable.

Washstand basin Wall-mounted washstand basins are usually of generous proportions and come with a surround supported on two legs so they appear freestanding. They are usually made of vitreous china or glass, with stands made of wood or chrome. The plumbing is not concealed.

Standalone basin These are designed to look like old-fashioned washbowls. They can be made of vitreous china, glass, stainless steel, wood and limestone. Plumbing for the basin is concealed in the unit on which it stands. Taps are fixed to the bowl or to the wall behind the basin.

Semi-pedestal basin Usually made of vitreous china but glass versions with stainless-steel pedestals are also available. The semi pedestal hides the plumbing but leaves the floor free and makes cleaning easier. The bowl is fixed in the same way as a pedestal basin.

Wall-hung basin Usually made of vitreous china, glass and stainless steel, wall hung basins are available as small as 400 x 350mm or as compact corner basins and space-saving short projection designs. They can be fixed at any height (low in a nursery, for example). Plumbing is visible unless boxed in.

TYPICAL WALL-HUNG BASIN FIXINGS

The brackets for wall-hung basins bear a heavy load and should only be fixed to a solid wall. If you have a stud wall, spread the weight with a countertop, washstand or pedestal type instead. Specialist fixings are usually supplied with the basin.

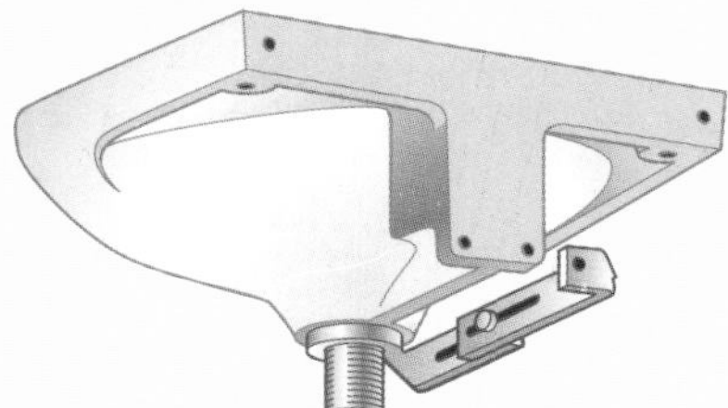

Wall plate and waste bracket The waste outlet of the wall-hung basin fits through the bracket, with its back nut below the bracket.

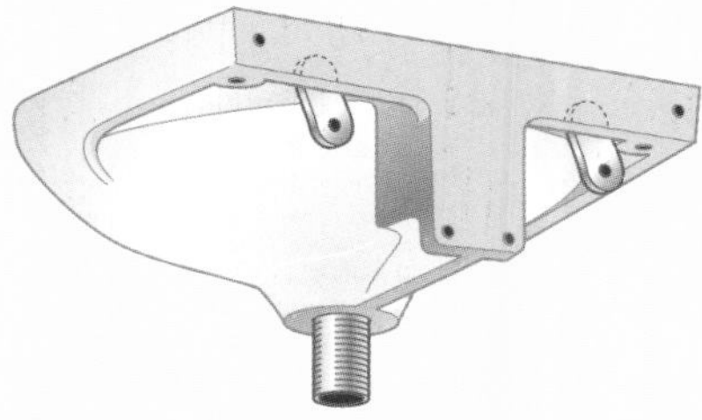

Concealed wall hangers A pair of hangers for a wall-hung basin is screwed to the wall. They fit into slots in the back of the basin to support it.

Over-rim bidet Usually vitreous china and typically 560–600mm deep and 350–395mm wide. The rim height of floorstanding models is about 400mm. Wall-hung designs are also available and are especially suitable for wet rooms. Screwed to the floor inside the rear of pedestal. Wall-hung types (for concealed plumbing) are bolted at the rear through the wall to metal support brackets.

Rim-supply bidet Water enters under rim, so warm water warms the rim; a control diverts water to an ascending spray. This is more expensive than an over-rim bidet, and must be installed in accordance with Water Authority requirements. It is not suitable for DIY installation.

Replacing a bidet or washbasin

The operations involved in replacing a washbasin or bidet are very similar. You may need to make slight adaptations to the existing plumbing to accommodate the new appliance.

Before you start You need to turn off the water supplies to the taps (page 328), and disconnect (or cut through) the supply and waste pipes. Then you can remove the fixings holding the basin (and its pedestal, if one is fitted) or bidet in place. Fit taps, wastes and overflows to the new basin or bidet before installing it.

Tools *Basin wrench; spanner; long-nose pliers; steel tape measure; spirit level; damp cloth; screwdriver; bucket. Possibly also hacksaw.*

Materials *Basin or bidet; taps or mixer with washers; deep seal or anti-siphon bottle trap (page 346); waste outlet with two flat plastic washers, plug and chain; silicone sealant; fixing screws for wall (and floor if required); rubber washers to fit between screws and appliance. Possibly also flexible pipe with tap connectors.*

1 Fit the new taps or mixer. Place the sealing washer on the tap tail first, position the tap and screw on the backnut to secure the tap in place. Tighten it with a spanner. Check that single taps are correctly aligned.

2 If you cut the supply pipes, fit flexible pipes (corrugated copper, braided hose or plastic) to each tap. These have tap connectors on one end and may include a service valve.

3 Attach the new waste outlet. Fit one sealing washer between the outlet and the appliance, then insert the outlet in its hole. Fit the second sealing washer from below and tighten the backnut. Use pliers to hold the outlet grid and stop the waste outlet from rotating as you do this. Ensure that the slots in the outlet tail line up with the outlet of the built-in overflow duct.

4 Fit the bottle trap to the tail of the waste outlet.

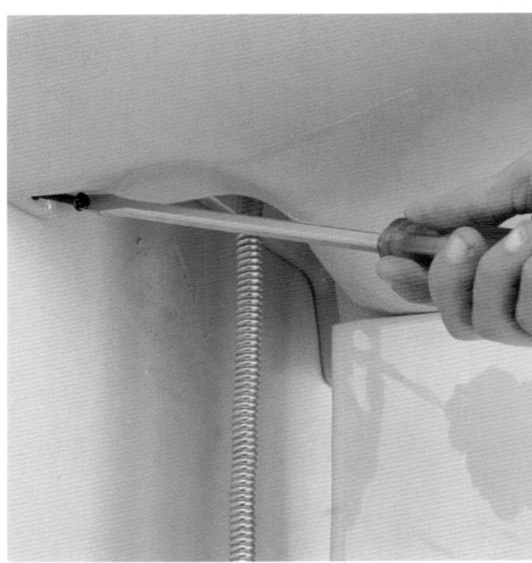

5 Set the new appliance in position and mark where new wall and floor fixings will be needed. Drill and plug the wall (and drill pilot holes in the floor too if necessary) and fix it in position.

6 Connect the taps or mixer to the supply pipes. If you disconnected the old tap connectors, there may be enough play in the pipes for you to reattach them directly to the new tap tails. If there is just a small gap, fit a tap tail adaptor to each tap and attach the old tap connectors to the adapters. If you severed the supply pipes, link the flexible connectors you attached to the taps in step 2 to the supply pipes using compression fittings. Include a service valve on each pipe (see right) if none is fitted.

7 Connect the outlet at the base of the bottle trap to the waste pipe.

8 Restore the water supply and check all joints for leaks. If necessary, tighten them.

9 Run a bead of silicone sealant around the appliance where it touches the wall.

Connecting a washbasin If it is difficult to disconnect the water supplies to the taps on the old basin, cut through the pipes lower down and use flexible connectors to connect the new taps to the supply pipes. Fit a service valve between the connectors and the pipes at the same time so that you can isolate the taps easily for future maintenance.

An over-rim supply bidet is connected to the supply pipes in the same way as a basin. You will need adapters to connect the narrow tails of a monobloc mixer to 15mm diameter water supply pipes.

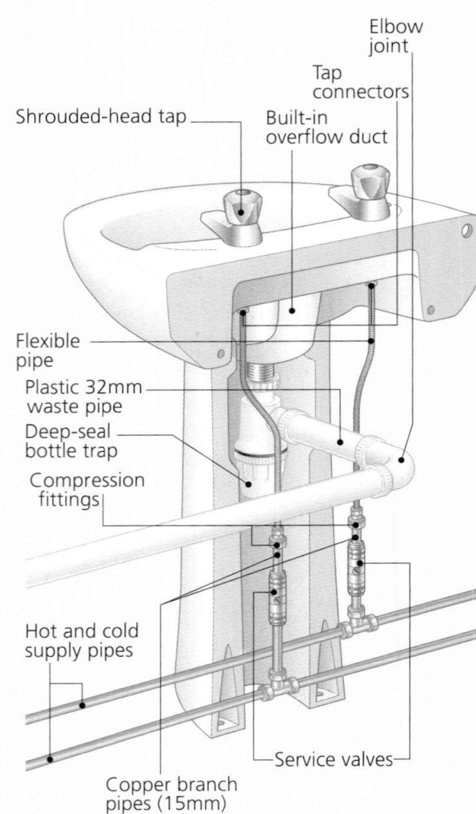

HELPFUL TIP

If you want to renew the taps on an existing basin, it is often easier to cut through the supply and waste pipes and remove the basin from its supports. Even with a basin wrench, the back nuts can be extremely difficult to undo. With the basin upside down on the floor, it is easier to apply penetrating oil, and also to exert enough force without damaging the basin.

If removing the basin is not practicable, the tap handles and headgear can be replaced with a tap conversion kit, sold in packs with fitting instructions.

Installing a new countertop basin

Washbasins, particularly countertop basins on a vanity unit, are very often installed in a bedroom to ease the demand on a family bathroom.

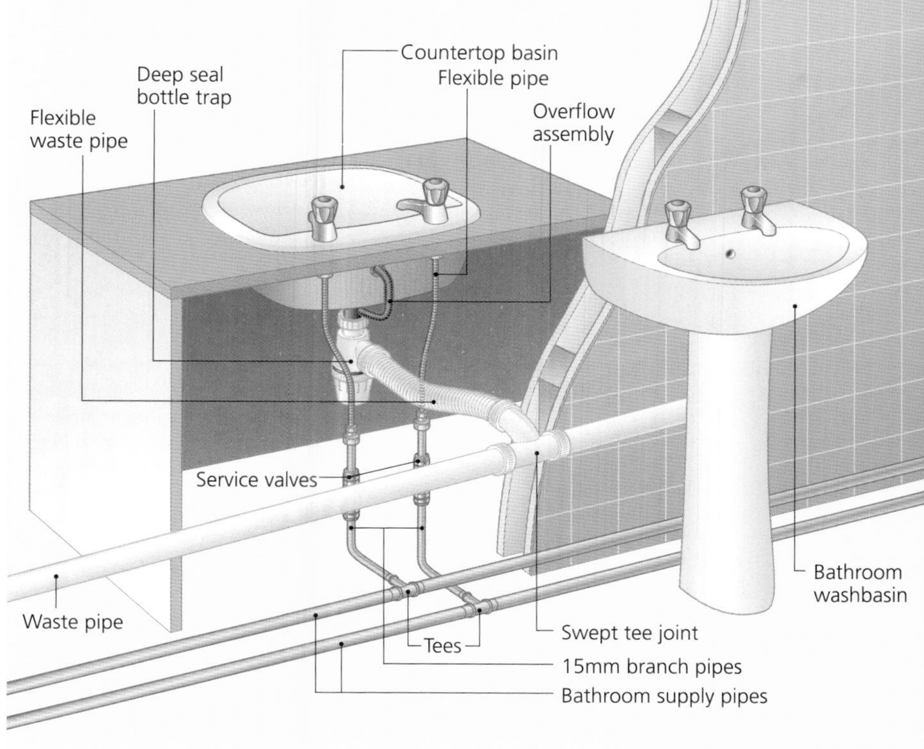

Before you start Give the local authority Building Control Officer details of your proposed arrangements for the new waste pipe connections.

1 Choose a site for the basin as near as possible to the bathroom waste pipe and supply pipes – ideally against a wall adjoining the bathroom.

2 Work out how to route the waste water from the basin to an existing waste pipe or direct to an outside drain (see below right). Trace the routes of existing hot and cold supply pipes and work out the shortest route possible for the new pipe.

3 Check that the basin position will allow sufficient space for a person to use it. Generally, allow at least 640mm bending room in front of the basin, and at least 300mm elbow room at either side.

4 Check that the installation of the basin will not interfere with any electric cables, gas pipes or other fittings, especially where you need to make a hole in a wall.

5 Fit the taps, waste outlet and trap to the new washbasin as described in Replacing a bidet or washbasin (left). Use a deep-seal trap (or an anti-siphon trap, if required).

6 Cut off the water supply (page 328) and use tee connectors to run hot and cold-water pipes to the basin site as 15mm branch pipes from the supply pipes to the bathroom. Do not tee into the pipes supplying a shower, unless it has a thermostatic mixer (page 359). If you find you have to tee into a 22mm distribution pipe, you will need an unequal tee with two 22mm ends and a 15mm branch.

7 Fit the waste pipe in position. If you have to make a hole through the wall, do it as for Installing an outside tap (page 363). If you plan to connect the new waste pipe into an existing one, insert a swept tee joint and link the new pipe to it.

8 Fit the basin or basin unit to the wall and connect it to the supply pipes and waste pipe (see left).

Routeing the waste pipe

The waste pipe run should be no more than 1.7m long. It must slope enough for the water to run away – not less than 20mm for each 1m of run – but the depth of fall to the pipe outlet should be no greater than about 50mm for a pipe under 1m long, or about 25mm for a longer pipe. If you cannot avoid a pipe run longer than 1.7m, prevent self-siphonage by fitting an anti-siphon bottle trap (page 346).

Alternatively Use a waste pipe of larger diameter – 40mm instead of 32mm. This pipe run should be no longer than 3m, and you will need a reducer fitting to connect 40mm pipe to the 32mm trap outlet. If you need a run longer than 3m, ask the advice of your local authority Building Control Officer.

Linking to an outside drain

How the waste pipe is linked to a drain depends on the household drainage system. If you are unable to link into the waste pipe from the bathroom basin, fit a separate waste pipe through an outside wall to link with a household drain (see page 410).

If the bedroom is on the ground floor, direct the waste pipe to an outside gully, if possible, such as the kitchen drain. The pipe must go below the grid.

Where the bedroom is on an upper floor, the method of connecting the waste pipe depends on whether you have a two-pipe or single-stack system (page 326).

With a two-pipe system, you may be able to direct the waste pipe into an existing hopper head. Alternatively, you can connect the waste pipe to the waste downpipe (not the soil-pipe) using a stack connector.

In a house with a single stack system, the waste pipe will have to be connected to the soil stack. For this you need the approval of the local authority Building Control Officer. There are regulations concerning the position of the connection in relation to WC inlets, and the length and slope of the pipe is particularly critical. The connection is made by fitting a new boss, which is a job best left to a plumber.

HELPFUL TIPS

If you tee into an old water pipe, it is likely to be an imperial size of ¾in internal diameter. There is no way of recognising an imperial size, except by measuring the internal diameter of the pipe once you have cut into it.

On ¾ in copper pipe, you can fit 22mm compression joints straight onto it provided that you substitute the olives for ¾in olives, available at a plumbers' merchant. You can get metric/imperial adaptors for most types of plastic push-fit fittings.

On soldered capillary joints, use adapters, which are available from a plumbers' merchant, that convert ¾in piping to 22mm, before inserting the tee.

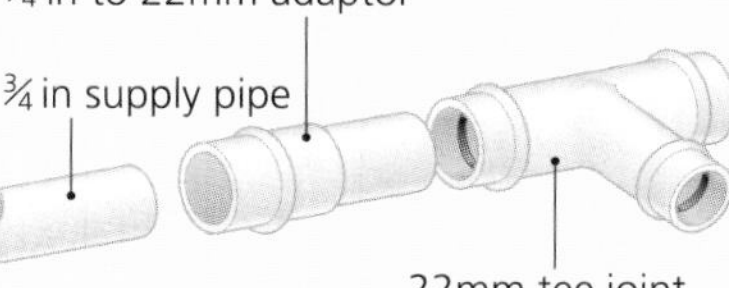

Flexible plastic push-fit joints are useful for fitting between the trap and waste pipe where alignment is difficult – for example, round a timber stud in a partition wall.

Renovating and repairing a bath

Major bath renovation is best done by professional firms. They take a day or two and will repair cracks or chips and apply a new coating, available in a range of colours. You can do smaller repair jobs yourself, using a DIY kit.

Repairing bath enamel

Before you start Remove every trace of grease or flaky enamel from the surface of the bath. Once clean, do not touch the surface again with your fingers.

1 Fill small surface chips with an epoxy resin filler (such as car-body filler) or use one of the proprietary bath repair kits available on the market.

2 Rub the surface smooth with fine abrasive paper, then coat the repaired area with two coats of matching bath enamel, following the instructions on the pack. Touch-up sticks are available in a variety of colours to cover small repairs.

Changing the colour

Changing an entire bathroom suite because you hate the colour can be expensive. A short-term solution is to resurface the suite using a proprietary colour-changing pack. These are available in DIY stores, and they offer a wide range of soft colours. Follow the instructions carefully (they vary) and bear in mind it will be about five days before you can use the bath again.

Repairing a plastic bath

Burns on an acrylic surface cannot be repaired. However, chips can be filled with a special acrylic repair paste available as a kit. You can polish out scratches with metal-polish wadding because the colour goes right through the material.

However, glass-reinforced plastic (GRP) can be damaged by abrasive cleaners as only the top layer of material is coloured.

Changing bath taps

Because of the cramped space at the end of a bath, fitting new taps to an existing bath can be difficult. It is often easier to disconnect and pull out the bath (see right) so that you have room to apply enough force to undo the back nuts of the old taps.

The alternative to disrupting the bathroom is to fit new tap headgear only, using a tap conversion kit.

Removing an old cast-iron bath

A cast-iron bath may weigh around 100kg, so you will need helpers to move it. A pressed-steel bath is lighter. It can usually be moved intact.

Before you start Unless you want to keep a cast-iron bath intact, it is easier to break it up after disconnecting it than to remove it whole. Be careful when you break it up, as the pieces are often jagged and very sharp.

Tools *Torch; adjustable spanner; safety goggles; ear defenders; club hammer; blanket; protective gloves. Possibly also padded pipe wrench; screwdriver; hacksaw.*

1 Cut off the water supply (page 328).

2 Remove any bath panelling. It is often secured with dome-head screws, which have caps that cover the screw slot.

3 With a torch, look into the space at the end of the bath to locate the supply pipes connected to the tap tails, and the overflow pipe. In older baths, the overflow pipe is rigid and leads straight out through the wall. In more modern types the overflow is flexible and connected to the waste trap.

4 Check the position of the hot supply pipe: it is normally on the left as you face the taps. Use an adjustable spanner to unscrew the tap connectors from the supply pipes and pull the pipes to one side. If unscrewing is difficult, saw through the pipes near the ends of the tap tails.

5 Saw through a rigid overflow pipe flush with the wall.

6 Disconnect the waste trap from the waste outlet. For an old-style U-bend, use an adjustable spanner. A plastic trap can normally be unscrewed by hand, but use a padded pipe wrench if it proves difficult. Pull the trap to one side. Disconnect a flexible overflow pipe from the overflow outlet.

7 If the bath has adjustable legs – normally brackets with adjustable screws and locking nuts – lower it to lessen the risk of damaging wall tiles when you pull it out. But if the adjusters on the far side are difficult to reach, lowering may not be worth the effort.

8 Pull the bath into the middle of the room ready for removal or break-up.

9 To break up the bath, drape a blanket over it to stop fragments flying out, and hit the sides with a club hammer to crack the material into pieces.

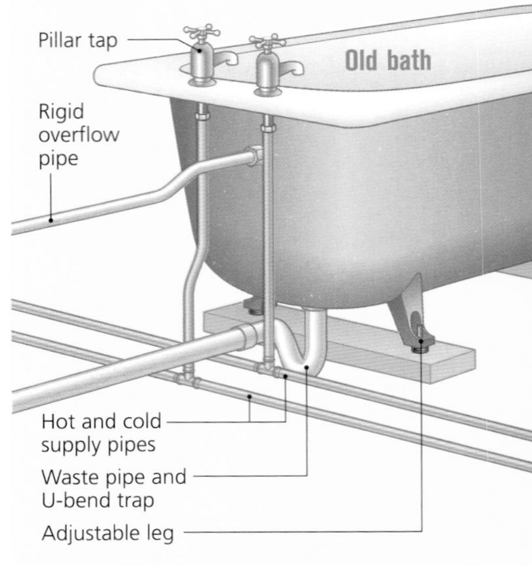

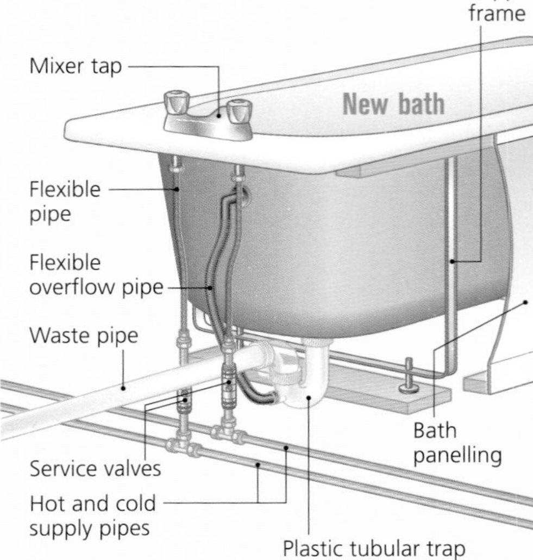

Connections to an old and new bath
As when replacing a washbasin or bidet (page 350), add a service valve on each of the supply pipes before connecting them to the new taps. This allows them to be isolated easily for future maintenance.

Installing a new bath

This is a good time to re-think your bathroom: you can fit the new bath in a different position and take advantage of the latest designs.

Before you start Assemble as many fittings as possible onto the new bath before you remove the old one. Not only will fitting be easier before the bath is in position, but the water will not be cut off for as long.

Use flexible connectors and a flexible waste joint. If you want to put the bath in a different position, you will have to work out how to re-route the waste pipe, as well as adapting the supply pipes.

Tools *Two adjustable spanners; spirit level; damp cloth. Possibly also long nose pliers; small spanner; hacksaw; screwdriver.*

Materials *Bath; two 25mm thick boards to support its feet; two new taps or a mixer tap (with washers); two 22mm flexible pipe connectors; 40mm waste outlet with plug and two flat plastic washers; bath trap (deep-seal if the waste pipe links to a single stack) with flexible overflow assembly; silicone sealant; PTFE tape.*

1 Fit the supporting frame following the maker's instructions. It is usually done with the bath placed upside down.

2 Fit the taps or mixer and the tap joints in the same way as for a washbasin. Deck mixers come with a rubber gasket to fit between the deck and the bath. On a plastic bath, fit a reinforcing plate under the taps to prevent strain on the bath deck.

3 Fit the waste outlet. This may be a tailed grid fitted in the same way as for a sink. Or it may be a flanged grid only, fitted over the outlet hole (with washers on each side of the bath surface) and fixed with a screw to a tail formed at one end of the flexible overflow pipe.

4 Fit the top end of the overflow pipe into the back of the overflow hole and screw the overflow outlet, backed by a washer, in position.

5 Slot the banjo overflow, if supplied, onto the threaded waste outlet and fit the bottom washer and back nut. Attach the trap, then fit the bath into position with a flat board under each pair of feet in order to spread the load.

6 Place a spirit level on each of the four sides of the bath to check that it is horizontal. If necessary, adjust the legs until the bath is perfectly level. Then tighten the locking nuts on the adjustable legs.

7 Fit the flexible connector on the farthest tap to its supply pipe, making a compression joint. If the supply pipe is too high, cut it back to a convenient length, leaving it too long rather than too short, as the connector can be bent slightly to fit.

8 Connect the second tap tail in the same way as the first. Then connect the trap outlet to the waste pipe (normally a push-fit joint). Restore the water supply and check the joints for leaks. Tighten if necessary, but not too much.

9 Fix the bath panels according to the maker's instructions. They may screw or clip to a wooden frame, or be fixed to a batten screwed to the floor. Fill the bath with water before sealing the joints between the bath sides and walls with silicone sealant. This ensures that the bath will not settle in use and pull the sealant away.

HELPFUL TIPS

If, on a mixer, the hot and cold indicators are on different sides from the appropriate supply pipes, reverse the discs on the tops of the taps, if possible. Alternatively, cross the flexible pipe connectors to join the taps to the correct pipes. The hot tap should always be on the left.

Choosing a new bath

The style and shape of the bath you choose is based on personal preference. But it helps to have a clear idea of what you are looking for when you go to choose one.

Type Many people are happy with a standard, traditional bath, but there are exciting new types of bath available that are worth considering.
- Whirlpool systems have water jets in the side of the bath, which give the bather an invigorating massage.
- Spa baths have air nozzles in the base of the bath, forcing bubbles upwards and creating a stimulating wave action.
- Hydro baths combine whirlpool side jets with spa nozzles in the base. In addition they may offer jets to stimulate the neck and shoulders and the feet.

Material Most modern baths are made from acrylic or glass-reinforced plastic (GRP) in various colours, and are light and quite easy to install. They are usually cradled in a support frame to avoid distortion when filled.
- Vitreous-enamelled pressed-steel baths are lighter and cheaper than old-style, porcelain-enamelled cast-iron baths.

Quality Cheaper baths are thinner and tend to need more support to prevent sagging and creaking when occupied. A good-quality plastic bath should be at least 6mm thick.
- Pressed-steel and cast-iron baths are strong and firm, but can feel cold, often initially lowering the temperature of the water until they warm up. Enamel is easily chipped, and often requires special cleaning materials.

Shape Bath shapes may also include two-person, corner-fitting and circular. They can be free-standing, with ornate legs, or fitted into a panelled framework. Sunken baths are glamorous but can be rather difficult to clean.

Types of WC suite

A WC suite consists of a cistern and a pan. The cistern can be low or high level, joined by a flush pipe to the pan, or close-coupled with a direct connection. Modern suites are designed to use less water than old ones – 6 litres rather than 7.5 or 9 litres. When siting a WC suite, allow for at least 530mm of space in front of the pan, and for about 760mm overall space from side to side.

Types of cistern

Cisterns are made of plastic or vitreous china (ceramic), and screwed to the wall from inside, through the back. The flushing control is a central push button or a side lever (fitted to right or left of the cistern).

For the flushing action to be correct, the cistern must be at the height given by the manufacturer – usually with the base about 600mm above the floor. Water flow into the cistern is controlled by a ball valve. An older cistern fed from a cold water tank is quieter than one fed from the rising mains.

WC cisterns installed before 1991 will have a 9 litre flush (dual flush 9/4.5 litre). This was reduced by water regulations to 7.5 litres in 1992 and to 6 litres in 2001.

The standard cistern A direct-action cistern installed at a low level is the standard option. It can also be used at high level, and is quieter than the chain-pull type. If a suite is converted from high to low-level, the standard size cistern – about 200mm from front to back – is too deep to go behind the pan, so a slimline type is needed.

A slimline cistern Measures the same as a standard cistern from side to side but as little as 115mm from front to back. However, it still provides a full flush. It may be concealed behind panelling.

Dual-flush type A variation on the direct-action cistern is the dual-flush type, which provides either a water-saving small flush, or a double-sized flush for solid waste.

Push-button or 'European' cistern Part 1 (piston-type) ball valves are no longer allowed on WC cisterns (unless a double-check valve is fitted immediately before them). The best type to fit in modern compact cisterns is an equilibrium ball valve (see page 338) or a vertical valve with a float cup that fits round the central column of the valve body. Both are quiet in operation, although the float-cup valve can be slow to refill the cistern if it is supplied with water from a storage tank. The traditional siphon flushing method is replaced by a plastic valve-operated flush mechanism that is activated by a top-mounted push button in the cistern lid. The mechanism incorporates an integral overflow. The push button is in two parts and is linked to a plunger to operate the flush. One part of the button activates a low-volume flush and the other (or both, on some models) gives a full-volume flush.

Low-level suite designs
In a low-level suite, the cistern is either linked to the pan by a short flush pipe or is close-coupled, with the cistern and pan joined together in one unit.

Standard cistern

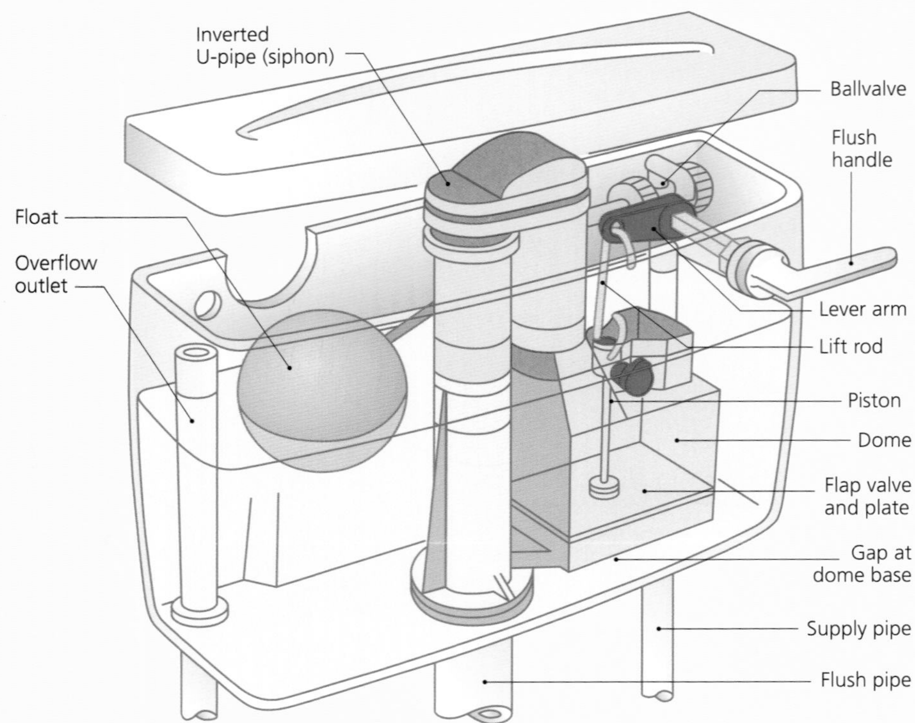

HOW A CISTERN WORKS

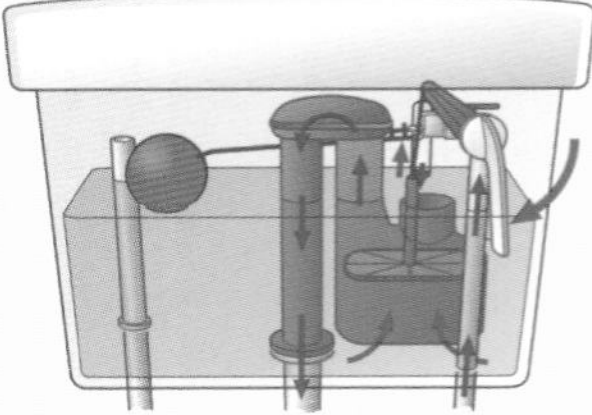

1 An inverted U-pipe in the cistern is linked to the flush pipe into the pan, and at the other end opens out into a dome (siphon). When the flush is operated, a lift rod raises a plate in the dome and throws water into the crown of the U-bend.

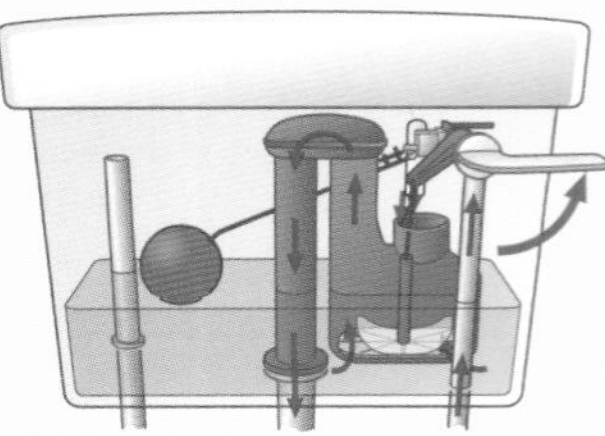

2 Openings in the plate are covered by a plastic flap valve held flat by the weight of the water. As water falls down the flush pipe, it creates a partial vacuum, causing water to be sucked up through the plate openings and to raise the flap valve.

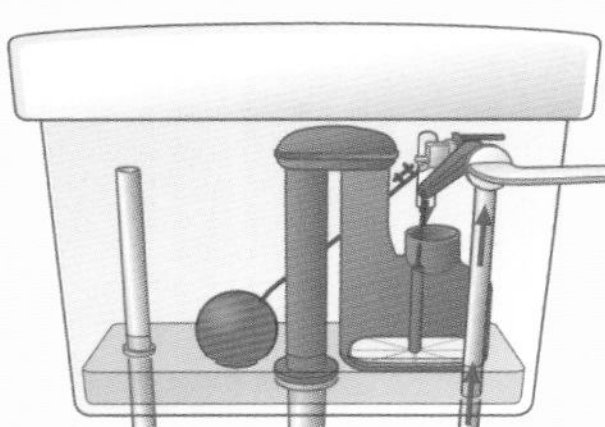

3 The base of the dome is about 10mm above the cistern base. When the water level falls below the dome base, air drawn in breaks the siphonic action and stops the flush.

DUAL SAVINGS

Modern WCs are usually configured for use as dual flush. The two-part button allows the user to select a reduced amount of water, depending on what they need to flush away. This system works by means of a hole in the side of the dome. If the flush control is released immediately, the hole lets in air to break the siphonic action after approximately 4 litres of water has been siphoned. When the control is held down for a few seconds, it operates a device that temporarily plugs the air hole, allowing a double flush.

Types of WC pan

Pans are normally made from vitreous china and are screwed to the floor through holes in the base of the pedestal. Some are designed to fit flush to the wall with their plumbing concealed, and some can be wall-hung.

Unless connected directly to an internal soil stack, the outlet pipe of the pan needs to be connected to a soil pipe that passes out more or less horizontally through the wall (usual for upstairs WCs) or passes vertically through the floor (common for downstairs WCs).

There are two types of pan: wash-down pans and double-trap siphonic pans.

Wash-down pan

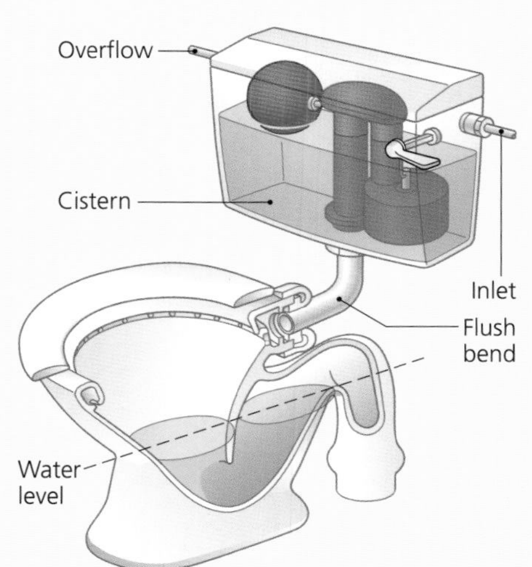

All new pans sold today are of the wash-down pan type, where the pan is cleared by water from the cistern splashing on the sides of the pan and forcing the contents of the pan through the trap, leaving clean water in the bottom of the pan.

Three designs of pan are made: horizontal outlet; P-trap (just below the horizontal) and S-trap (vertical). The vast majority of pans now being sold have a horizontal outlet, but this can be connected to a soil pipe formerly fitted to a vertical outlet using an angled connector (below).

Double-trap siphonic pan

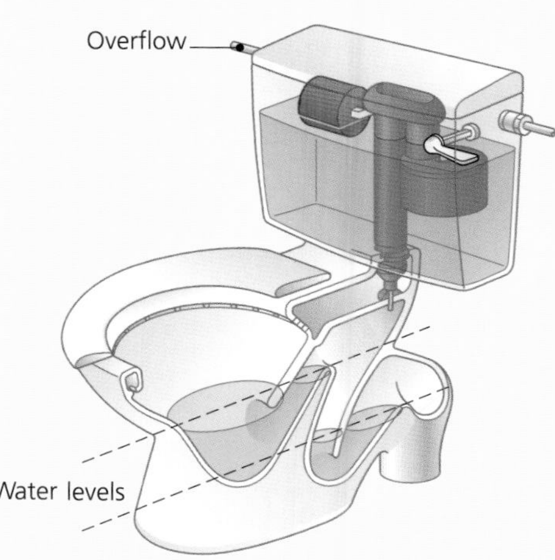

Some existing pans are the double-trap siphonic type; these are no longer made, though spares should still be available. When the cistern is flushed, the pan starts to empty by suction before the flush water reaches it, making it very silent and efficient in operation.

MACERATOR UNITS

A macerator unit allows you to put a WC in a room distant from the main soil stack. It takes waste from the WC pan and passes it through a shredder so that it can be carried away through a small-bore (22mm or 32mm) plastic pipe. The WC pan can be 20–50m from the soil stack if the pipe is horizontal, but pumping distance and height are interlinked, so pumping vertically would restrict the horizontal distance.

The installation of a macerator unit needs to meet the Building Regulations requirements, so you should inform your local Building Control Officer if you intend to install one.

You will also need an electrical connection to drive the shredding motor and this must be via a fused connection unit (unswitched or via a flex outlet if within reach of anyone using the bath or shower).

There are a wide variety of macerator units available: the simplest is for use only with a WC; the most complex will take a whole bathroom suite (WC, wash basin, bidet and bath or shower). High-capacity units are available to take the output from a power shower. There are also macerator units designed for kitchen waste (sink, washing machine and dishwasher).

Macerator units can be bulky, but there are slimline units available that fit neatly behind a conventional WC pan, below the cistern.

TYPES OF WC PAN JOINTS

Plastic push-fit joints are now universally used and come in a variety of shapes to allow connection of virtually any pan to any soil pipe. Most joints are either straight or 90° (for horizontal or vertical soil pipes), but offset joints, extension joints and even fully flexible joints are also available.

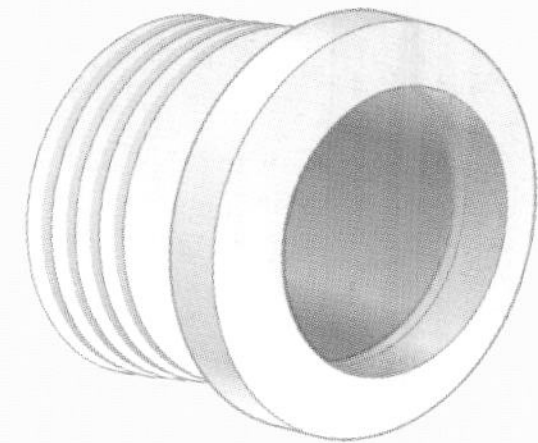

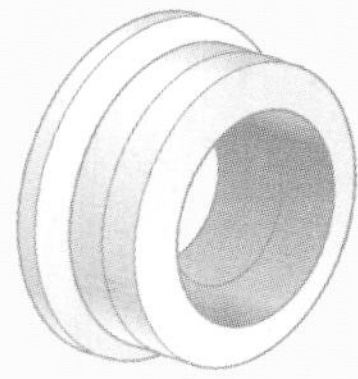

Rubber cone joint For linking the flush pipe from the WC cistern to the flush horn of the pan.

Angled push-fit pan joint A 90° joint for converting a horizontal (P-trap) pan outlet to a down-pointing (S-trap) outlet for a floor-exit pipe. It can also be used to link a horizontal outlet to a wall-exit pipe situated at right angles to the pan.

Straight push-fit pan joint For a straight link between the pan outlet and the inlet branch to the soil pipe. The cupped end fits over the pan outlet, and the narrow (spigot) end inside the soil-pipe inlet. Different diameters and lengths are made. Before buying, check the outside diameter of the pan outlet, the inside diameter of the soil-pipe inlet, and the distance to be bridged. Joints have watertight seals at each end. Offset types can be used where the alignment is not exact.

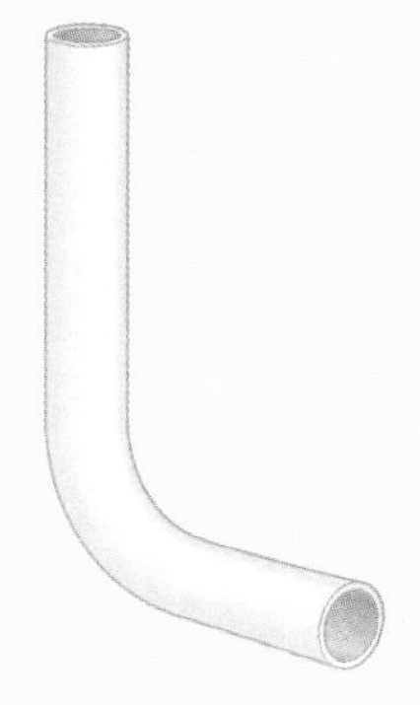

Flush pipe Angled plastic pipe linking a separate cistern to the WC pan. Pipes for high-level suites are normally 32mm in diameter, and pipes for low-level suites have 38mm diameters.

Replacing a WC pan

At one time WC pans were always cemented to a solid floor, but the setting of the mortar often put a strain on the pan and caused the china to crack. Now they are usually screwed down to a wooden or a solid floor.

Before you start An old or cracked WC pan with a down-pointing outlet cemented to a floor-exit metal soil pipe is the most difficult type to remove. Examine yours carefully before attempting to remove it.

Tools *Screwdriver; spirit level. Possibly drill and wood or masonry bits; safety goggles; club hammer; cold chisel; rags; old chisel; thin pen, pencil or nail; trimming knife.*

Materials *WC pan and seat; pan fixing kit; rubber cone connector; suitable push-fit pan connector. Possibly also wall plugs (for a solid floor); packing (to steady the pan) such as wood slivers, vinyl tile strips or silicone sealant.*

Removing a pan with a horizontal outlet

1 Disconnect the flush pipe by peeling back the cone connector. Alternatively, chip away a rag-and-putty joint with an old chisel. Protect your eyes.

2 Undo any screws used to secure the pan to the floor.

3 Pull the pan forward slowly, moving it from side to side, to free it from the soil-pipe inlet. It should come away easily. If you have any difficulty, break the pan outlet in the same way as for a down-pointing outlet (right).

4 If the outlet joint was cemented with putty or mastic filler, chip it off the soil pipe inlet.

Removing a pan with a down-pointing outlet

1 Disconnect the flush pipe in the same way as for a horizontal-outlet pan.

2 Undo the floor screws, or break cement with a hammer and cold chisel.

3 To free the pan outlet, put on safety goggles and use a club hammer to break the outlet pipe just above its joint with the drain socket in the floor. Then pull the pan forward, away from the jagged remains protruding from the soil pipe socket.

4 Stuff rags into the socket to stop debris falling in, then chip away the rest of the pan outlet with a hammer and cold chisel. Work with the chisel blade pointing inwards, and break the china right down to the socket at one point. The rest of the china should then come out easily.

5 The new push-fit connector fits directly into the pipe so the collar is redundant. Break out the collar gently by tapping it outwards and remove the pieces so the pipe finishes flush with the floor level. Alternatively cut it off with an angle grinder.

Fitting a separate pan

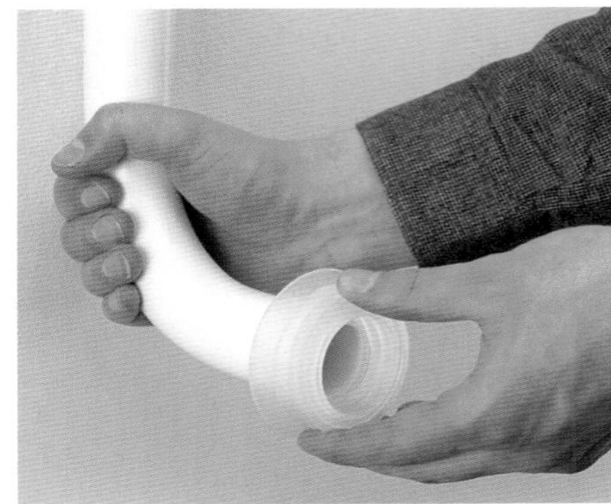

1 Fit a rubber or plastic cone connector to the flush-pipe outlet, unless one has already been fitted.

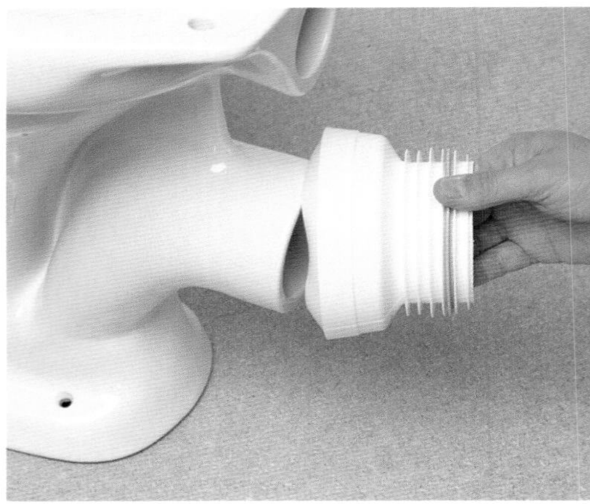

2 Fit a plastic push-on connector to the pan outlet. If the soil pipe socket for the pan is in the floor, use an angled 90° connector to link a horizontal pan outlet to the vertical inlet to the soil pipe.

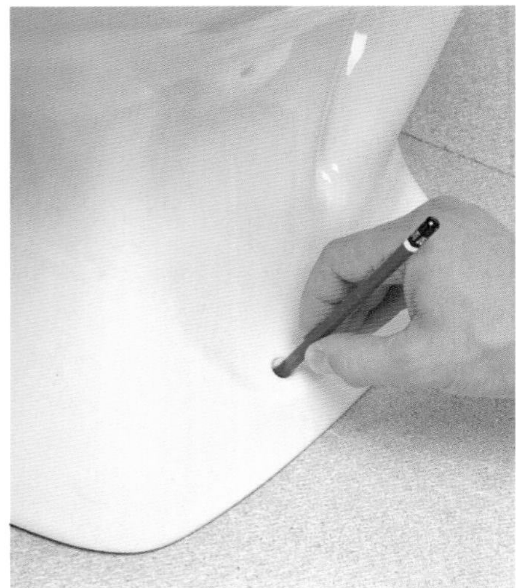

3 Mark the position of the holes in the pan on the floor, using a slim marker such as a ballpoint pen or a pencil.

4 With the pan still in position, draw a line round its base so that it can be put back in place accurately. Then remove it.

5 You need rust-proof screws to secure a WC pan to the floor. You can buy 'kits' which have the screws, wall plugs, plastic bushes and caps to cover the screw heads.

On wooden floors, drill a pilot hole for the screws; on a solid concrete floor, use a masonry drill bit to make holes in the concrete and insert wall plugs.

6 If the soil pipe inlet is a floor socket, remove the rags, taking care not to spill any of the debris into the inlet.

7 Carefully lift the pan into position using the previously marked outline to guide you, and at the same time positioning it so that you can push the flexible connector into the soil pipe inlet. Fold back the cone connector and slip it over the flushing horn of the pan.

8 Put in the screws to hold the pan firmly in position. However, do not tighten them fully yet.

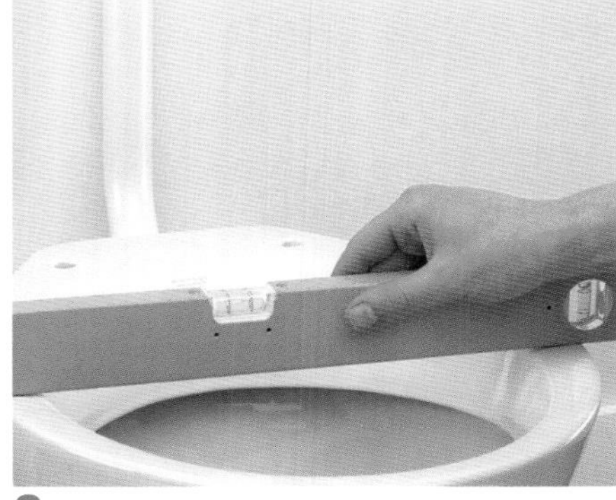

9 Use a spirit level placed across the top of the pan to check that it is level from side to side and from front to back.

10 To level the pan, loosen the plastic nuts and pack under the pedestal with strips of vinyl tile, or use a bead of silicone sealant to steady the pan and provide an even bed. Once you are sure that the pan is level, screw it down firmly.

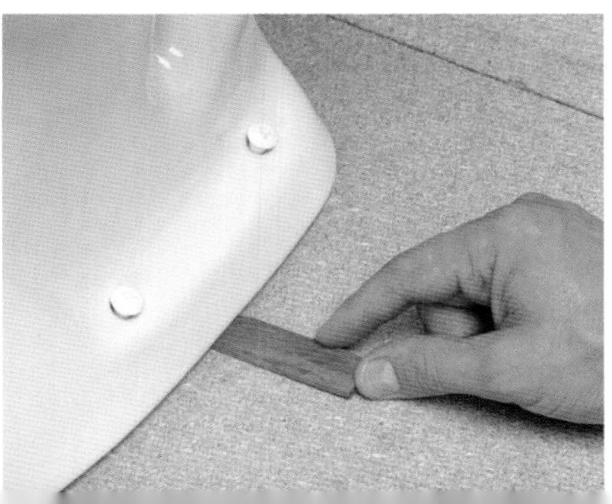

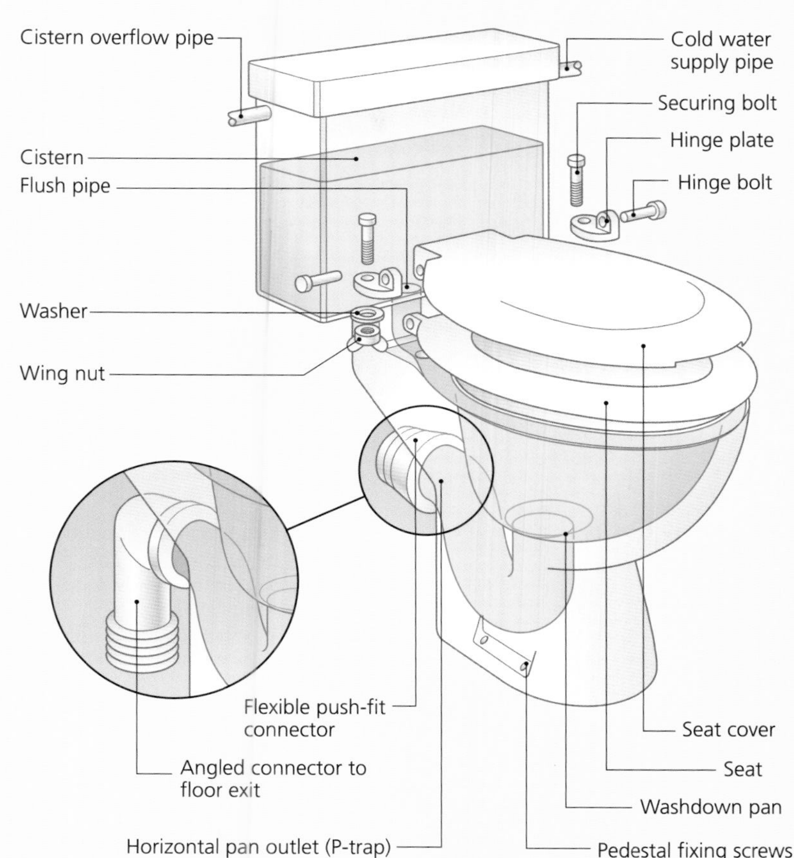

Fittings for a separate low-level suite Most modern WC pans have a horizontal outlet. If the replacement pan has to be fitted to a soil pipe on a ground floor, connect the P-trap outlet of the pan to the soil-pipe inlet using an angled push-fit joint (page 355). After fitting a WC suite, you may find that condensation – particularly apparent on a ceramic cistern – is a nuisance and leads to damp walls and floors. Make sure the WC or bathroom is properly ventilated (page 242). In a bathroom, avoid drip-drying washing over the bath, as this contributes to condensation.

Checking the fitting

When fitting a new WC pan, make sure that it is level and that the connections to the flush pipe and soil pipe are true. Otherwise slow pan clearance or a blockage could result.

On an existing WC pan with old-style joints rather than flexible connectors, blockages can occur because the openings are out of true or partially obstructed by the jointing material. Putty from an old rag-and-putty joint between the flush pipe and horn may have squeezed into the flush inlet and be impeding the inflow of water.

Putty or other jointing material could be obstructing the joint between the pan outlet and the soil-pipe inlet. This is evident if the water rises slowly in the pan before it flows away.

Make sure the pan is firmly fixed and that the fixing screws have not worked loose. Check that the pan is horizontal when fixing it in place.

FITTING A NEW WC SEAT

A WC pan seat and cover are usually fixed onto hinge bolts or a rod at the back. These fit into hinge plates or covers at each side of the pan.

Hinge plates or covers are each held in place by a securing bolt that fits through a fixing hole in the back of the pan and is secured by a wing nut.

Make sure that you insert washers to shield the pan from the head of the securing bolt and the wing nut. Washers shaped to the pattern of hinge covers are often supplied. Screw the wing nuts firmly finger-tight.

A WC seat breaks easily if misused – such as if you stand on it to close a window. If you simply have to stand on something, lift the seat and balance yourself on the rim of the pan.

Planning a shower

A shower is a useful addition to any home, but you need to think about where and how to install it.

There are four main types of shower – bath/shower mixers, shower mixer valves, instantaneous electric showers and 'power' showers. All can be installed over an existing bath and all (except bath/shower mixers) in a separate cubicle.

Electric showers are connected directly to the rising main, so can be fitted in any house; power showers can only be fitted to stored hot and cold water supplies. For mixer showers, the ideal is to have both hot and cold water supplies at the same pressure – either stored or from the mains.

Water supply

The plumbing needed depends on the type of shower you fit and your water supply.

Bath/shower mixer No extra plumbing is normally required for a bath/shower mixer: it simply replaces the bath taps.

Shower mixer If you are installing a shower mixer valve with stored hot and cold water, a separate pipe should be taken from the cold water tank for the cold supply and the hot supply should also be a separate pipe run as the first connection to the vent pipe above the hot water cylinder. These connections avoid the shower running hot (or cold) when water is drawn off elsewhere in the house (can also be avoided with a thermostatic mixer shower).

Where you have different pressures (cold from storage tank, hot from combi boiler, for example), the cold needs its own supply from the cold water tank and you must use a pressure-balanced shower mixer valve.

Note that you should inform your water supply company if you are making connections to mains-fed water pipes.

Electric shower This needs only a connection to the cold water rising main.

Power showers Because of the high volumes of water used, the cold supply should be direct from the cold water tank and the hot supply may need a special connection to a hot water cylinder.

Drainage

Showers fitted over a bath need no extra drainage, though you might need a different trap with high-volume showers.

A separate cubicle will need its own drainage arrangements and you may need approval for this from your local authority Building Control Officer.

Achieving adequate pressure

For a mixer supplied from the household's stored hot and cold supplies, the bottom of the cold-water cistern needs to be at least 900mm – and preferably 1.5m – above the showerhead for pressure to be adequate. If you do not have sufficient water pressure to supply a shower at the required position, there are two ways to increase it: you can either raise the height of the cistern or have a booster pump installed. Or you could fit a power shower.

Raising the cistern The cold water cistern can be raised by fitting a strong wooden platform beneath it, constructed from timber struts and blockboard or plywood. You will also have to lengthen the rising main to reach the cistern, as well as the distribution pipes from the cistern.

Booster pumps These incorporate an electric motor and must be wired into the power supply. There are two main types. A single pump is fitted between the mixer control and the spray and boosts the mixed supply to the spray. A dual pump is fitted to the supply pipes and boosts the hot and cold supplies separately before they reach the mixer. Depending on the model, a booster pump will provide sufficient pressure with as little as 150mm height difference between the water level in the cistern and the spray head.

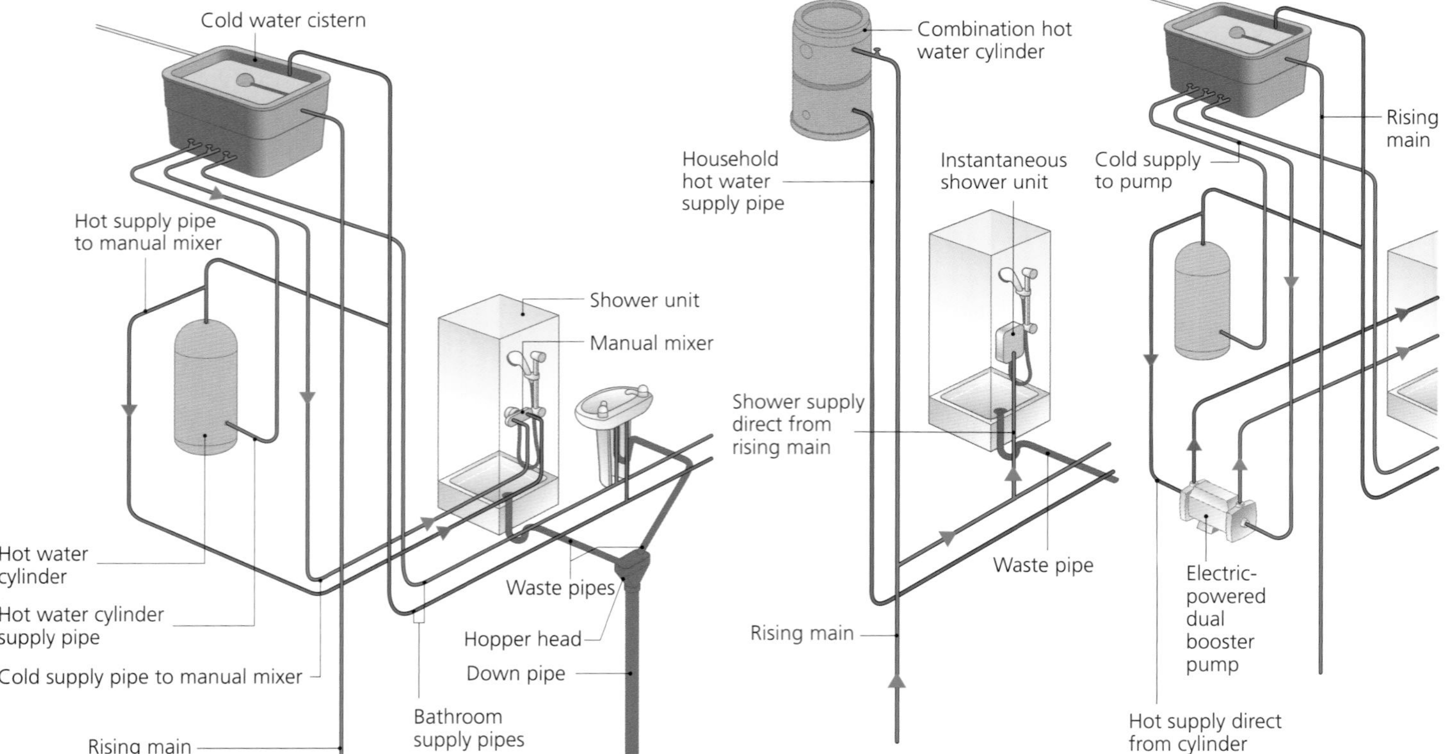

Pipework for a shower mixer For a shower mixer, take the cold supply pipe direct from the cold water cistern to avoid risk of scalding when other cold taps are turned on. Take the hot supply from the hot water cylinder distribution pipe – tee in above cylinder height. For a thermostatic mixer, which has a temperature stabiliser, you can tee in to bathroom supply pipes.

Pipework for an instantaneous shower Here, only a cold supply, direct from the rising main, is needed. This is useful where there is no cold water storage cistern, as shown here with a combination hot water cylinder (see page 364 for details).

Boosting water pressure with a dual pump This boosts hot and cold water supplies separately. Some types of pump have a hot supply pipe direct from the cylinder casing, some from the vent pipe. A dual booster pump should be fitted by a plumber.

Choosing a shower

As described opposite, the type of shower that can be installed depends in part on your water supply system – and also on the strength of shower spray you like to have. But there are still choices to be made within each type.

Bath/shower mixer A shower spray combined with a bath mixer tap provides a shower for little more than the cost of the bath taps, and no extra plumbing is involved. The temperature is controlled through the bath taps, which may not be convenient, and will be affected by water being drawn off elsewhere in the home, unless you fit an (expensive) thermostatic type of bath/shower mixer. Pressure-balanced types also available. No extra drainage required.

Power shower An all-in-one shower which incorporates a powerful electric pump that boosts the rate that hot and cold water are supplied to the shower head from the storage cistern and the hot water cylinder. A power shower is unsuitable where water is supplied from a combination boiler under mains pressure. Removing waste water from a power shower fast enough can be a problem. The shower tray must cope with up to 20 litres a minute, so it may be worth fitting a 40mm (or even 50mm) waste pipe. Not normally suitable for fitting over a bath, unless it has a very good shower screen.

Shower tower or shower panel A wall unit that incorporates a thermostatic mixer shower with a number of adjustable body jets. Tower units also have a fixed showerhead and a hand-held spray, and may be designed to fit into a corner or on a flat wall. Some can be installed over a bath while others are made for cubicles or wet rooms. A pump is usually needed to boost water pressure.

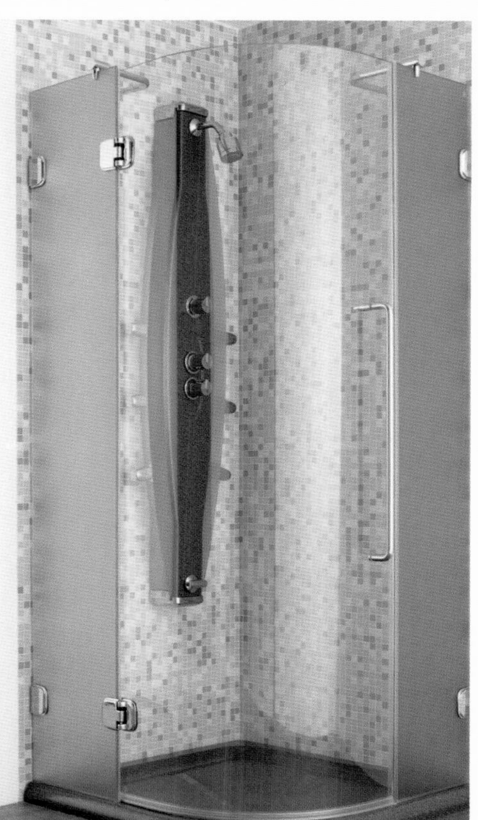

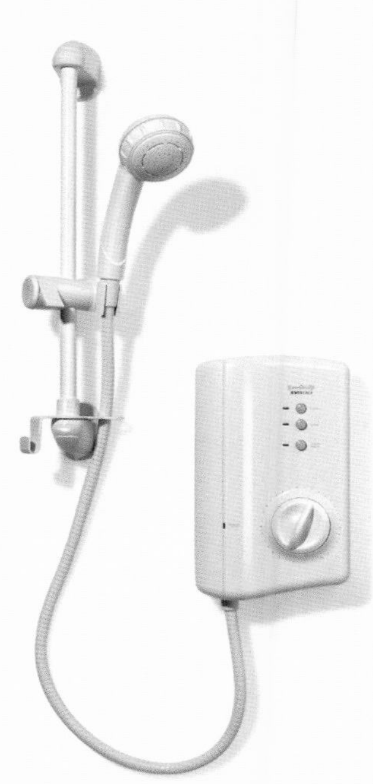

Instantaneous electric shower A wall unit plumbed in to a mains cold water supply, and heated by an electric element. Controls allow less water at a higher temperature or more at a lower temperature, so the spray is weaker in winter when mains water is colder. The unit must be wired to an electric power supply meeting Wiring Regulations requirements (page 288). This type of shower can be installed with any plumbing system and wattages up to 10.8kW available.

CHAMPAGNE SHOWER

Showerheads can be purchased with a number of different spray patterns or a head with several spray options. A low-volume high-pressure shower produces a mist or 'champagne' effect which gives an effective shower using less water than a conventional system. They are particularly useful with unvented mains-fed hot water systems.

SAFETY WARNING

The hose to a showerhead must be fed through a retaining ring on the shower wall. This prevents the showerhead hanging in standing water in the bath or shower tray, avoiding potential contamination of the mains supply.

SHOWER FITTINGS

Spray roses Showerheads may be fixed or part of a handset on a flexible hose. The simplest have a single spray; multi-spray showerheads offer a choice of spray patterns selected by rotating the outer ring on the rose. Large diameter single spray showerheads offering a rain-style shower are also available.

Shower trays GRP-reinforced acrylic trays are light to handle and not easily damaged. A reconstituted stone or resin shower tray is heavy, stable and durable, but the floor must be level before it is installed. Shower trays come in sizes from 700mm square and are usually 110–185mm high; low level 35mm trays are available for 'walk-in' showers. Quarter circle and pentangle trays help to save space.

WETROOMS

A wetroom consists of a WC, basin and shower area. No shower tray or enclosure is fitted and water drains through a central drain set in a sloping floor, so the whole room must be waterproofed. This is not a DIY job. Wetrooms may have a powerful thermostatic mixer shower and body jets or a shower tower.

Manual and thermostatic mixers These are wall-mounted units with hot and cold water supplies linked to a single valve. In a manual mixer, temperature and volume are controlled by one dial or separately. Thermostatic mixers are more expensive: their temperature control has a built-in stabiliser so water cannot run too hot or too cold.

Computerised models have a control panel to programme temperature and flow rates and can store the data for each user. Pressure-balanced models are available for use when either hot or cold supply is at mains pressure; mains-fed mixers can be linked to a pump to improve performance.

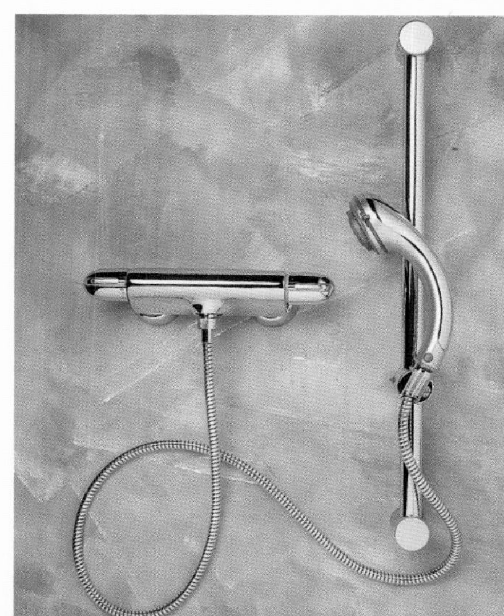

Installing a mixer (or electric) shower

Most types of shower can be fitted either over a bath or in a cubicle. The fixings and pipe routes vary according to the shower type, the bathroom layout and the shower location, but the method of installation is basically the same.

Before you start Decide on the type of shower you want, bearing in mind that the shower head must either be fitted so as to prevent it coming into contact with water in the bath or shower tray, or it must have double-check valves fitted in the hot and cold pipes leading to the shower.

1 Mark the required positions of the spray head and shower control.

2 Plan the pipework to the shower control and how the waste water will be routed to the drainage system.

3 If you are fitting an instantaneous electric shower, work out the positions of the cable route and the switch (page 288).

4 Fit the shower control. Some shower mixers are available as either surface-mounted or recessed fittings, and come with fixings and instructions.

When fitting a recessed mixer, if possible mount it on a removable panel flush with the wall so that you have easy access to the controls.

5 Cut off the water supply and fit the water supply pipes. You can recess the pipes into the wall and then replaster or tile over them. However, they must be protected with a waterproof covering and have service valves fitted.

6 Fit the shower head and spray. For a separate cubicle, fit the base tray and waste fittings.

7 Connect the supply pipes to the shower control. An adaptor with a female screw thread (copper to iron) may be needed.

8 Restore the water supply and check the piping for leaks. Tighten any joints as necessary.

9 For an electric shower, turn off the electric supply at the consumer unit (fuse box). Make the necessary electrical connections (page 288), following the shower manufacturer's instructions. Restore the power supply.

10 Fit screening panels and seal the joints between the wall and screening, and the tray.

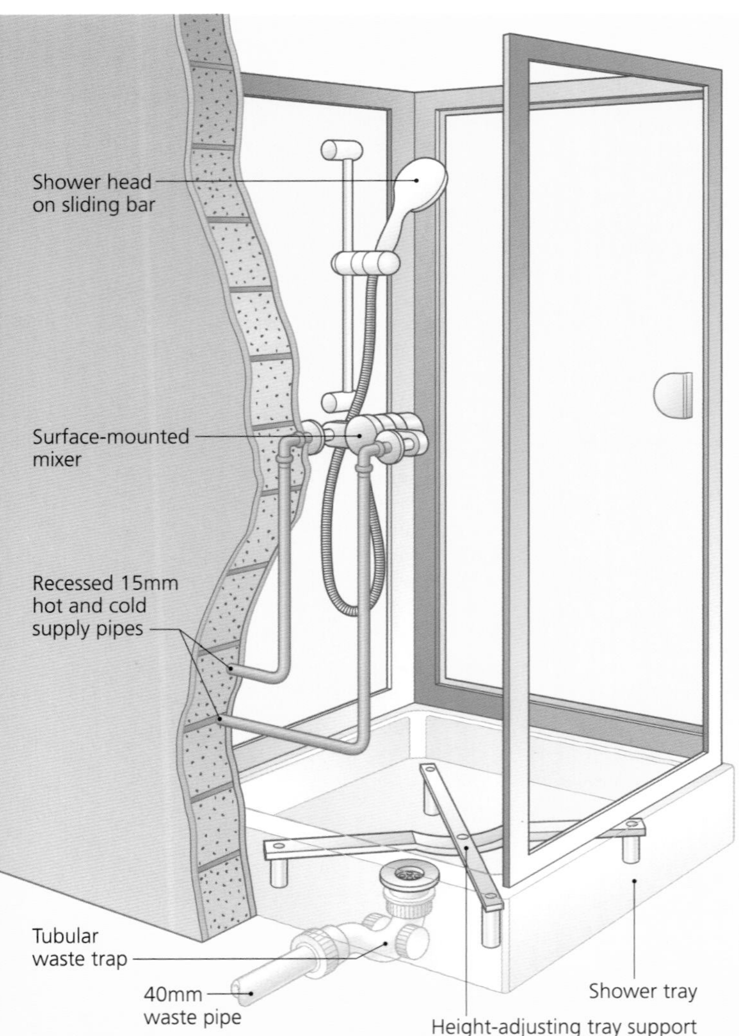

A typical cubicle installation
Screens are usually about 1.8m high. Panel widths can usually be adjusted by 25–50mm to allow for walls that are out of true. Doors may be hinged, folded (with panels shaped to keep water in), sliding with corner entry, or pivoted to give a wide entry without taking a lot of opening space. Some shower trays have an adjustable support by which the height can be altered so that the waste pipe and trap can be positioned either above or below the floorboards.

Replacing a sink

You have several options if you plan to replace an old sink. A range of styles and bowl configurations is now available.

Some sinks have two tap holes, or holes for a two-hole mixer. Others have only one hole for a monobloc mixer. All have an outlet hole – either a 38mm hole for fitting a standard waste outlet, or a 89mm hole for fitting a waste disposal unit.

There are two basic sink designs: lay-on and inset. Lay-on sinks rest on a base unit of the same size as the sink rim. They are being replaced by inset types, which fit into a cut-out in the worktop and may be one unit or a separate bowl and drainer.

Sinks are available in a range of sizes and patterns. They are typically about 500mm wide and vary in length from about 780mm to 1.5m. Patterns vary from one bowl and a drainer in one unit, to combinations of one-and-a-half, two and two-and-a-half bowls with a drainer, two drainers, or no drainer at all. Drainers can be to the right or left side of the unit. Think about which will suit you best.

Stainless steel is the most common sink material. Enamelled pressed steel and more expensive polycarbonate are available in a range of colours. Easy-to-clean ceramic sinks are the toughest and most expensive, but china banged against them may chip.

Checking the waste outlet

Before choosing a sink, check the height of the waste outlet of the existing sink. The new sink may be higher or lower depending on bowl depth or the height of a new support unit. A typical waste-outlet height from a bowl 180mm deep in a unit 870mm high would be 690mm.

If the new outlet will be higher than the old one, use a telescopic trap. If the new outlet will be lower, reposition the waste pipe.

If the pipe runs into an outside drain, you may need a new exit hole in the wall. If the pipe links to a single soil stack, make a new connection. The downward slope should be about 20mm for every 1m of run. Connecting the waste pipe to a single stack should be left to a plumber.

Fitting an inset sink

Most new sinks are inset into the worktop, and are designed for use with a monobloc mixer tap rather than two separate pillar taps. The sink may have one or two bowls.

The rim of the sink is sealed in its cut-out to stop water seeping beneath it, and is held in place by locking clips underneath. The monobloc mixer tap fits into a 35mm diameter hole in the sink unit, and has two flexible 10mm pipe tails projecting from its back nut. These are linked to the existing hot and cold water supplies with reducing joints. Fit an in-line service valve to each pipe before connecting it to the tap.

Tools *Two adjustable spanners for compression joints; long-nose pliers; screwdriver; jigsaw; power drill and twist drill bits; pencil; masking tape. Possibly also pipe cutter.*

Materials *Inset sink; monobloc kitchen mixer with top and bottom washers; two compression joints (probably reducers); two in-line service valves; silicone sealant; PTFE tape; varnish.*

1 Mark the cut out shape on the worktop according to the sink manufacturer's instructions. Check that the cut will not interfere with any structural parts of the base unit. Run masking tape around the cut line to prevent accidental scratches from the saw's sole plate, then cut out the hole with a jigsaw. Seal cut edges with varnish.

Alternatively Make the cut-out from the back (to avoid splintering) or use a downward-cutting jigsaw blade (page 185).

2 With the sink on its face, seal round the rim and fit the earthing tag (page 267) into the slot marked E on the rim.

3 Fit the securing clips to the sink, following the instructions. They are commonly hinged clips that are screwed to the sink rim and can be adjusted to fit worktops 27–43mm thick.

4 Fit the mixer tap, the waste outlet and any overflow pipes to the sink. Take care to position all sealing washers correctly.

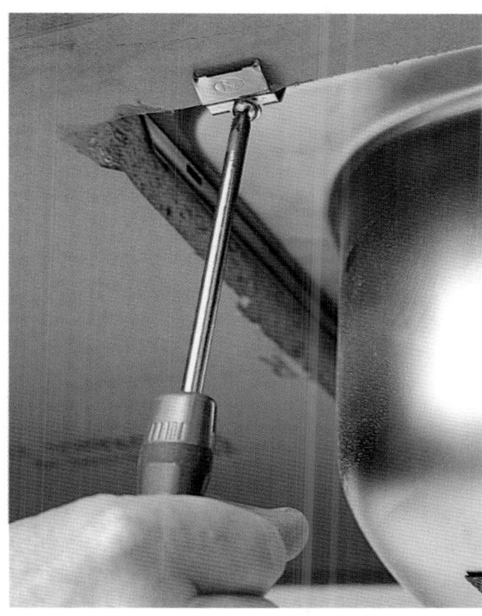

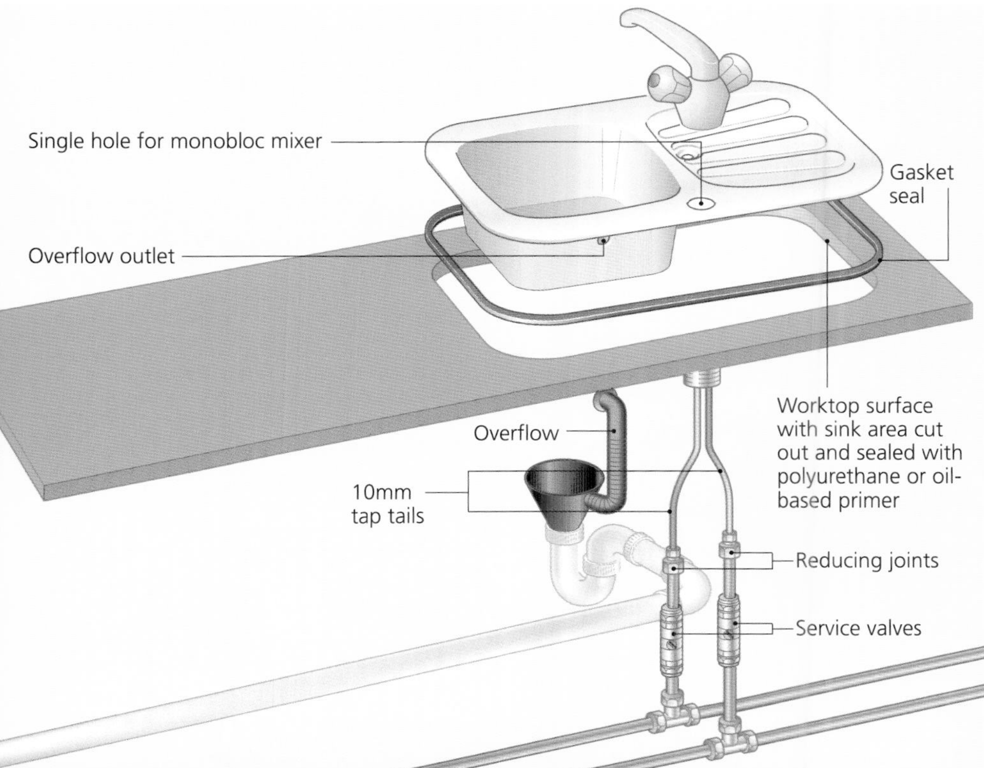

5 Fit the sink into the worktop, tightening the clips gradually in sequence.

6 Connect the trap to the waste outlet and add any overflow pipework as instructed. Then modify and connect the supply pipework.

CONNECTING A MONOBLOC MIXER TAP

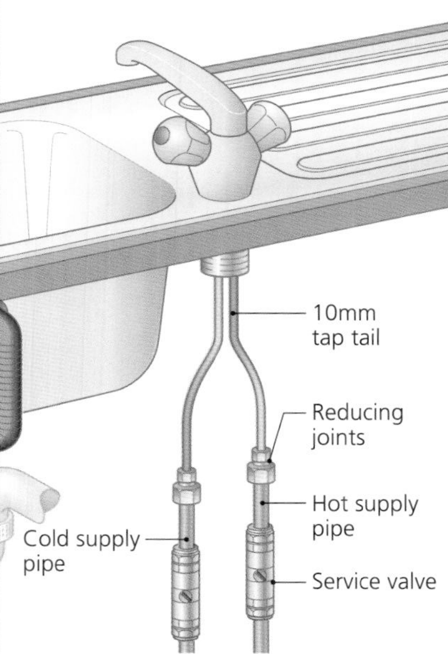

1 Check that the supply pipes are the right height for connecting to the tap tails. Cut the pipes if they are too high, and save the offcuts to link the new service valves to the tap tails. Label the pipes 'hot' and 'cold' so that you connect them correctly.

2 Fit a service valve to each supply pipe and turn it off with a screwdriver. Then add a short length of 15mm copper pipe to the outlet of each valve.

3 Connect the 15mm end of a reducing joint to each tap tail.

4 Connect the narrower end of each reducing joint to its tap tail. You can bend the tap tails slightly to line up the connections, but take care not to kink them.

5 Screw up each capnut until it is finger-tight at both ends of each fitting. Hold each fitting steady with one spanner while you give each nut $1\frac{1}{4}$ turns with the other spanner.

6 Open each service valve and check each fitting for leaks. Tighten any weeping capnuts by another quarter turn.

Plumbing in a washing machine or dishwasher

How you connect up the plumbing and drainage for a washing machine or dishwasher depends partly on how far away from the kitchen sink it is – the closer the easier.

Before you start Check the machine's instructions to see what the requirements are – especially for arranging the drainage. Some methods may not be allowed.

Tools *Hacksaw or pipe slice; pipe cutters; half-round file; two adjustable spanners; medium-sized screwdriver; measuring tape; soft pencil; two spring-clip clothes pegs; spirit level. Possibly also shallow pan.*

Materials *15mm copper or plastic pipe, one or two washing machine valves, one or two 15mm equal compression or push-fit tees, 15mm pipe clips, 40mm P trap, 40mm waste pipe and elbows, waste pipe clips.*

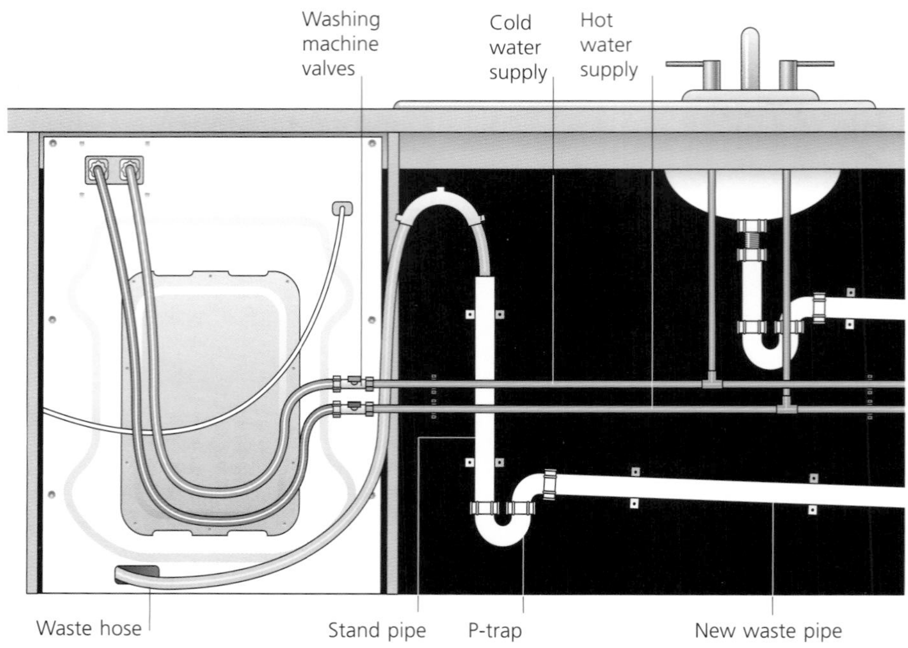

Washing machine connections The washing machine is shown connected to the hot and cold supply pipes under the kitchen sink via tee joints, with pipe leading to two washing machine valves. The waste hose is hooked into a stand pipe and new waste pipe is taken, via a P-trap, to the outside drains.

Connecting up the water

1 Turn off the water supply to the kitchen sink cold tap at the main stoptap.

2 It will often be easiest to connect directly to the rising main. Mark this at a convenient point (above the stoptap) with two pencil lines 20mm apart. Alternatively, remove the elbow on the pipe leading to the sink cold tap and replace it with a tee.

3 If connecting to the rising main, cut through the pipe squarely with a hacksaw or pipe slice at the lowest point marked. A small amount of water will run out as you cut the pipe. Cut at the second mark on the pipe and remove the section of pipe. File the pipe ends smooth.

4 Use spring-clip clothes pegs to stop the caps and olives slipping down the pipe. Fit a tee joint to the pipe with the branch outlet pointing towards the machine.

5 Cut a length of 15mm pipe sufficient to get close to the machine and fit it into the tee. Use a pipe support for plastic pipes.

6 At the other end, fit the compression (or push-fit) joint end of a cold (blue) washing machine valve, fit pipe clips to support the pipe, and connect the cold-water hose.

7 For a washing machine, turn off the water supply to the hot tap over the kitchen sink (page 328). Cut the pipe and fit a tee joint, new pipe and (red) washing machine valve as above. Connect the machine's hot-water hose to the valve and restore the hot and cold water supplies.

Alternatively If the machine is close to the sink, you may be able to use self-cutting washing machine valves, which can be connected directly to the supply pipes.

Connecting the waste

1 Most washing machines require the use of a stand pipe into which the machine's hose is hooked. Install this, following the machines' instructions, on the wall close to the machine, securing it with clips.

2 Fit a P trap, followed by more 40mm waste pipe, leading to a convenient place on an outside wall through which it can be taken to the drains.

3 Make a hole through the wall (page 410) and pass a length of waste pipe through it, connecting it with an elbow to the pipe from the trap on the inside and to the drains on the outside (see page 351). Make good the hole in the wall.

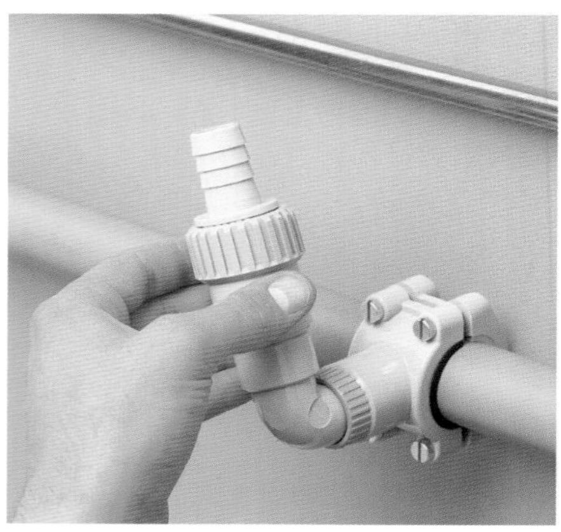

Alternatively:

1 If the machine's instructions allow and the machine is positioned close enough, you may be able to connect directly to the nozzle of a 'washing machine' trap fitted under the kitchen sink.

2 With some machines, you may be able to use a self-cutting washing machine drain kit which is simply secured to the waste pipe leading from the kitchen sink.

Installing an outside tap

Bib taps have a threaded nozzle which is suitable for fitting a garden hose. A tap installed against an outside wall should have an angled head; otherwise you will graze your knuckles when you turn the handle.

What you must do You do not need to inform your water company that you are fitting an outside tap – unless it is to be connected to some kind of mechanical or automatic watering system.

You do, however, need to fit a double-check valve in the installation – either in the new pipe leading to the tap or built-in to the tap itself – to prevent possible contamination of the mains supply.

About the installation This job involves running a branch pipe from the rising main through the wall to the tap position.

The instructions given here are for fitting copper pipe run from a 15mm rising main with compression fittings; other pipe materials or fittings could be used.

- You should fit a stoptap into the branch pipe.This allows you to do the job in two stages, and in winter you can cut the water supply to the tap and drain it to prevent frost damage.
- As an alternative to making up the pipe run yourself, outside tap kits are available from most DIY stores.
- The best way to make a hole through the brick wall of a house is with a heavy-duty power drill and masonry bit, both of which can be hired. Choose a bit at least 325mm long and 20mm in diameter to allow the pipe to be passed through the wall easily.

Tools *Two adjustable spanners; hacksaw or pipe slice; pipe cutters; half-round file; power drill with masonry bits; screwdriver; two spring-clip clothes pegs; soft pencil; measuring tape; spirit level.*

Materials *Angled bib tap with threaded nozzle; 15mm stoptap; 15mm double check valve; 15mm copper or plastic pipe; plastic pipe clips; 15mm equal tee; two 15mm elbows; wall-plate elbow; PTFE tape; wall filler; weatherproof pipe insulation.*

Positioning the tap

1 Mark the required position on the outside wall of the kitchen, as near as possible to the rising main.

2 Check that the mark is high enough for a bucket to be placed underneath the tap quite easily, and is at least 250mm above the damp-proof course in the house wall.

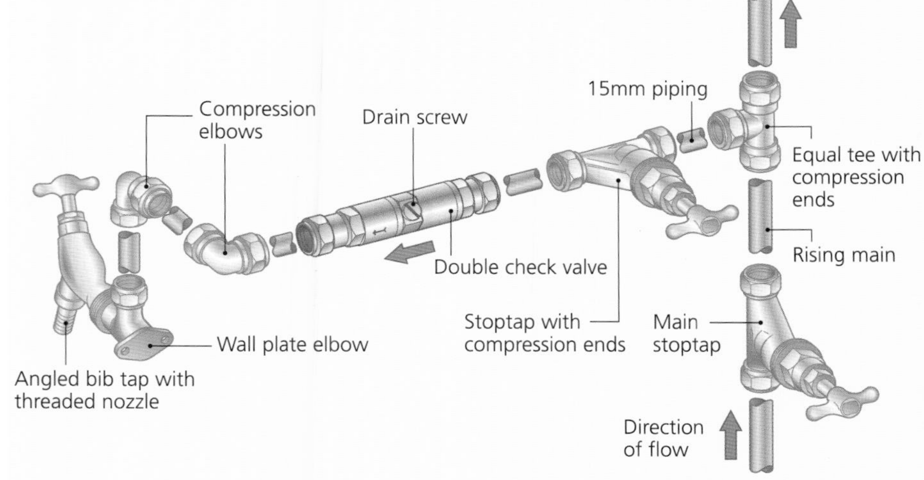

Pipework and fittings An outside tap is supplied by a branch pipe, commonly run from a tee joint fitted into the rising main. Instead of a tee joint, you can use a self-boring tap, which can be fitted to the pipe without turning off the water. No separate stoptap is then needed in the branch pipe.

3 Make another mark for the hole through the wall about 150mm above the tap mark.

4 Take measurements from the hole mark to a point such as a window, so that you can locate and check the corresponding hole position inside.

5 Mark the position of the hole on the inside of the wall. Check that it will not interfere with any inside fitting and will be above the position of the main stoptap on the rising main.

Fitting the branch pipe inside

1 Turn off the main stoptap, then turn on the kitchen cold tap to drain the pipe.

2 If there is a drain valve above the stoptap, turn it on to drain the rising main, and prepare to collect the water that runs out in a container.

3 Mark the rising main at a point level with the hole mark on the inside wall. Make a second mark 20mm higher.

4 Cut through the rising main squarely with a hacksaw or pipe slice at the lower point marked. If there was not a drain valve above the main stoptap, be prepared for a small amount of water to run out as you cut through the pipe.

5 Cut the pipe at the second mark and remove the section of pipe. Use a file to smooth the pipe ends and remove burrs, and to square the ends if necessary.

6 Fit a cap nut and olive over each cut pipe end. Use spring-clip clothes pegs to stop the nuts and olives slipping down the pipes. Fit the tee into the rising main with the branch outlet pointing towards the hole mark.

7 Cut a short length of pipe and connect it to the branch of the tee.

8 Connect the stoptap to the pipe, with its arrow mark pointing away from the rising main. Angle the stoptap so its handle leans away from the wall.

9 Close the new stoptap by turning its handle clockwise. You can now turn on the main stoptap and restore the water supply to the rest of the house.

10 Cut another short length of pipe and connect it to the outlet of the stoptap.

11 Connect the check valve to the pipe, making sure that its arrow mark points in the same direction as the stoptap arrow. Then complete the pipe run (see overleaf).

Connecting the outside tap

1 Use a long, slim masonry drill bit to drill through the wall from the inside first, making sure to keep the drill at right angles to the wall. Withdraw the bit at intervals to cool it and to pull out dust. Then use a 20mm masonry bit, working from both sides of the wall, to make a hole wide enough for the pipe to fit through easily.

2 Cut a length of 15mm copper (or plastic) pipe to fit through the wall with at least 50mm to spare.

3 With the pipe in position through the wall, slip on an elbow and measure the length of pipe needed to join the elbow to the double-check valve, allowing for the depth of pipe in each fitting.

4 Cut the pipe to the required length and smooth the cut ends.

5 Make the connections indoors.

6 Outside the house, cut the projecting pipe to leave only 25mm sticking out from the wall.

7 Fit another elbow to the projecting pipe, making sure that the free end of the elbow points towards the tap position mark.

8 Measure from the elbow to the tap mark and cut another length of pipe to fit the distance.

9 Fit the pipe to the inlet of the wall-plate elbow.

10 Fit the other end of the pipe temporarily into the elbow above, then hold the wall plate against the wall and mark the position of the screw holes.

11 Put aside the wall-plate elbow and pipe end, and drill and plug the wall.

12 Join the pipe to the projecting elbow and fix the wall-plate elbow to the wall.

Fitting the tap

1 Bind PTFE tape round the tail thread.

2 Screw the tap fully into the outlet of the wall-plate elbow.

3 If the tap is not upright when screwed home, take if off again, put one or two thin fibre washers over the inlet and refit. Keep on adjusting in this way until it is tight and upright.

4 Open up the new stoptap inside, and check all the pipe joints for leaks. Tighten if necessary.

5 Turn on the newly fitted outside tap and check that it is working properly.

6 Use wall filler or polyurethane foam filler inside and silicone sealant outside to seal round the pipe hole in the wall. Add weatherproof insulation to outside pipes.

Ways of heating water

The average household uses 220–320 litres of hot water a day. Finding the best way of heating water for your home deserves some thought.

The commonest type of water-heating system is a hot water storage cylinder heated by a boiler (pages 382–3), probably combined with the central heating system. Various kinds of gas or electric heater can also be used to supplement the system, or as a complete system in themselves. They may be fed either by a low-pressure supply from the cold water cistern, or by a high-pressure supply direct from the mains.

Hot water cylinders

There are five main kinds of hot water cylinder to choose from – direct, indirect, combination, Economy 7, and unvented. All are sold pre-fitted with insulation.

• Direct cylinders are used where an immersion heater (see below) is the only way of heating the hot water – in an all-electric house or one with gas warm air central heating (or no central heating!). They have just two pipe connections – one for cold water coming in, one for hot water out – plus one or two immersion heater 'bosses'. Standard sizes are 450mm diameter and 900mm high (120 litre capacity) or 1050mm high (140 litre).

• Indirect cylinders are used where a boiler is used to heat the water (see page 325). It has two additional connections for the boiler pipes. Same sizes as direct cylinders.

• A combination cylinder is used where there is no main cold water storage tank and cold taps are fed directly from the rising main – it has its own cold water cistern fitted above the main cylinder. Can be direct or indirect (may have two cisterns).

• Economy 7 cylinders are larger versions of normal cylinders (up to 210 litres) and are fitted with two horizontal immersion heaters – the lower one to heat the water at night, the upper one to top up during the day. Can be direct, indirect or combination.

• Unvented hot water cylinders are designed to take their cold water supply directly from the rising main. They come with various safety devices and must be installed by a qualified plumber. Can be direct or indirect.

Immersion heaters

Electric elements fitted into hot water cylinders to heat water. Sold in various sizes to suit different sizes of cylinder and horizontal/vertical application. All 3kW. Special versions available for hard water.

• There are three types: top-entry with one element extending almost to the cylinder bottom; top-entry with two

elements – a long one for cheap night electricity and a short one for heating a small amount of water as needed; side-entry – usually a pair, one at the bottom to heat the entire cylinder at night and one at the top for heating small amounts.
• All types have thermostats. Can be fitted into a copper hot water cylinder as the sole means of heating, or as a supplement to a boiler. Can be renewed if the element burns out. Modern cylinders usually have 32mm or 57mm bosses in the dome or low in a side wall (or both) for heater fitting. Only water above the level of the element is heated. Expensive to use unless the storage cylinder is well insulated.

Instantaneous gas heater

The water is heated by gas as it flows through small-bore copper tubing. When the hot tap is turned on, the gas jets are ignited by a pilot light that burns continuously. The jets go out when the tap is turned off.
• Large multipoint heaters can supply all household hot taps; smaller single-point types supply one tap only. The water supply is normally direct from the rising main. The heater can be fed from a cold water cistern if it is high enough – usually at least 2m above the highest tap – to give enough pressure.
• Useful where there is no cold water storage cistern. Only the water used is heated – there is no slow cooling of unused water. But the delivery rate is slower than from a cylinder, and the flow from one hot tap is interrupted if another is turned on. It is designed to raise water temperature by about 26°C, so in cold weather – when mains water can be near freezing – the heated water is either cool or slow running. In summer it may be too hot. Some have a winter/summer setting to vary the heat.
• The heater has a flue and must be fitted against an outside wall.

Instantaneous open-outlet electric heater

Small heater, supplied direct from the rising main, in which the water is heated as it passes through. Heaters with 10.8kW elements are designed for showers (page 359) or for a shower plus a basin, those with a 3kW element are designed for washing hands.
• The water emerges through a spray nozzle. Useful for providing a shower where there is no suitable storage cistern supply or for hot water for washing hands in a cloakroom that has no hot water supply pipes.
• As with instantaneous gas heaters, these electric heaters usually raise the temperature by about 26°C, so water heat varies according to mains water temperature, but some types have a winter/summer setting. Also, the flow may be interrupted when other taps are used, unless a compensating valve is fitted.

WAYS OF SAVING HEAT

Money is wasted if water is heated and then not used. Inefficiencies in the plumbing system, or inefficient use of heaters, can also waste heat.

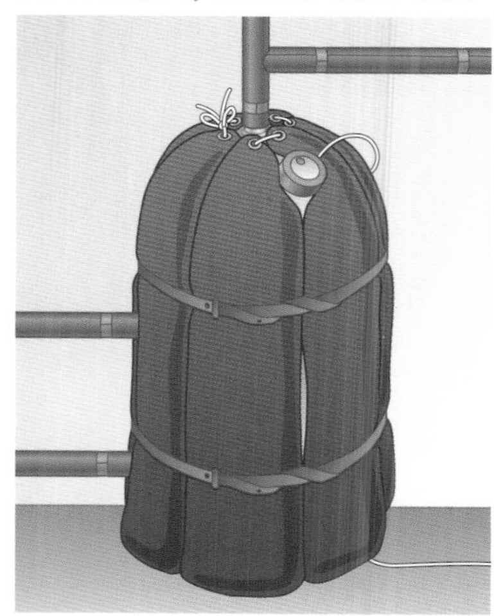

Insulate the hot water cylinder

A 75mm thick lagging jacket on a hot water cylinder cuts down heat loss by about 70 per cent. A 140 litre cylinder without a jacket, maintained at a temperature of 60°C, loses enough heat every week to heat about 20 baths. All modern cylinders are foam-lagged by the manufacturer.

Keep hot water pipes short

The length of pipe between the hot water cylinder and a hot tap is known as a dead leg, because hot water left in the pipe after each use of the tap cools and is wasted. The longer the pipe, the more the waste.

Water at 60°C travelling through a 15mm copper pipe loses heat equivalent to more than 1 unit of electricity for roughly each 300mm of run a week – enough to heat about 45 litres of water.

Where a hot water supply pipe to a basin or shower would involve a dead leg of piping of more than 6m long, it is wiser to use an instantaneous heater instead.

If you have an electric storage heater installed, position it as near as possible to the hot tap most often used – usually the one over the kitchen sink.

Avoid secondary hot-water circulation

At one time, if a shower or tap was some distance from the hot water cylinder, there was a constant circulation of hot water to it by means of a return pipe back to the cylinder. This ensured that there was no delay in the arrival of hot water to the tap. Because of the heat lost, avoid such secondary circulation, particularly with electric heating.

Install a shower Use a shower for daily cleansing and keep the bath for relaxed soaking. A bath uses about six times as much water as a normal shower.

Heat water only as needed A thermostat gives economical heating by controlling temperature, but even a well-lagged cylinder will lose heat (generally the equivalent of about 6 units of electricity a week). This adds considerably to costs if the heater is left on all the time.

Savings can be made by switching on an immersion heater or boiler for about an hour before hot water is needed, and switching it off when it is not wanted. The most convenient way to do this is to fit the heater with a time switch set to turn it on for times of peak household use. Time switches have a manual override to allow use of the heater at other than the set times.

You can buy special immersion heater timers allowing several on/off periods a day (both 24-hour and 7-day version available). If you are on an electricity tariff offering cheap off-peak electricity, invest in an Economy 7 controller, which can be wired to control 2 immersion heaters bringing on one automatically at night and allows the other one to be used during the day when required. Both timers and controllers are wired between the fused connection unit (or double-pole switch) on the immersion heater circuit and the immersion heater(s).

Prevent scale formation in water pipes and appliances About 65 per cent of British homes – chiefly those in the south-east and Midlands – have hard or moderately hard water. This is caused by a high concentration of dissolved calcium and magnesium salts, and is evident when, for example, soap does not dissolve properly and scale forms inside the kettle and around a tap nozzle.

Hard water drying on any surface leaves a crust of salts behind, and at high temperatures the salts solidify into scale. When scale forms inside a domestic boiler or hot water cylinder, it insulates the water from the heat and wastes fuel, and pipes become blocked.

Scale can be prevented or limited by a number of methods:

1 Controlling hot water temperature – scale starts to form above 60°C.

2 Suspending scale-inhibiting chemicals in crystal form in the cold water cistern. They need changing every six months.

3 More expensively, by plumbing a water softener into the rising main – beyond the kitchen tap and a branch to an outside tap. This leaves hard water, which most people prefer, for drinking.

Replacing an immersion heater

An immersion heater element can burn out after long use or if it becomes coated with scale. Water that takes longer than usual to heat up may indicate scaling. Some immersion heaters are designed for use in hard water.

Before you start Although modern heaters have a thermostat and can be prevented from heating above 60°C – the temperature at which scale starts to form – they may be used as a supplement to a boiler that does not have the same degree of heat control.

To fit a replacement immersion heater to a combination cylinder (page 364), check the cylinder manufacturer's instructions. The heater may be on a plate assembly that can be withdrawn without draining the water chamber.

Tools *Immersion heater spanner – box-type for deep lagging; electrician's screwdriver; adjustable spanner; hose clip.*

Materials *Immersion heater; PTFE tape. Possibly also 1.5mm² three-core heat-resisting flex (page 271); penetrating oil.*

1 If the cylinder is heated by a boiler, switch the boiler off. Then switch off the electricity supply at the consumer unit (fuse box).

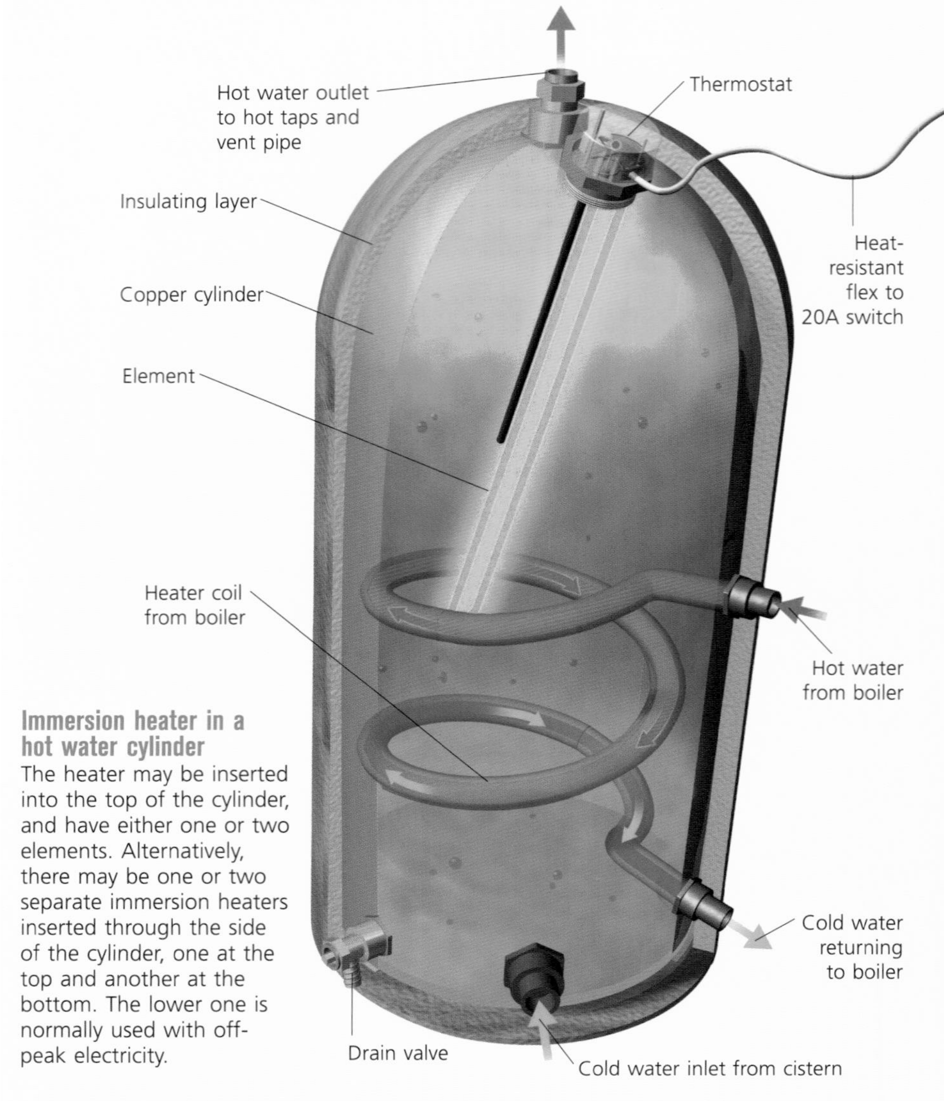

Immersion heater in a hot water cylinder
The heater may be inserted into the top of the cylinder, and have either one or two elements. Alternatively, there may be one or two separate immersion heaters inserted through the side of the cylinder, one at the top and another at the bottom. The lower one is normally used with off-peak electricity.

2 Stop the water supply to the cylinder. Turn off the gate valve on the supply pipe, if there is one, or drain the cold water cistern (page 328).

3 Turn on the bathroom hot taps to draw off any water in the supply pipe.

4 Locate the cylinder drain valve. For an indirect cylinder (or a direct cylinder heated solely by an immersion heater) it is on the supply pipe where it runs into the base of the cistern.

5 Drain water from the cylinder as necessary – about 4.5 litres for a top-entry or high side-entry heater, or the whole cylinder for a low side-entry heater. Close the drain valve.

6 Unscrew and remove the immersion heater cover. Note which of the three conductors is connected to which terminal, then disconnect them using an electrical screwdriver.

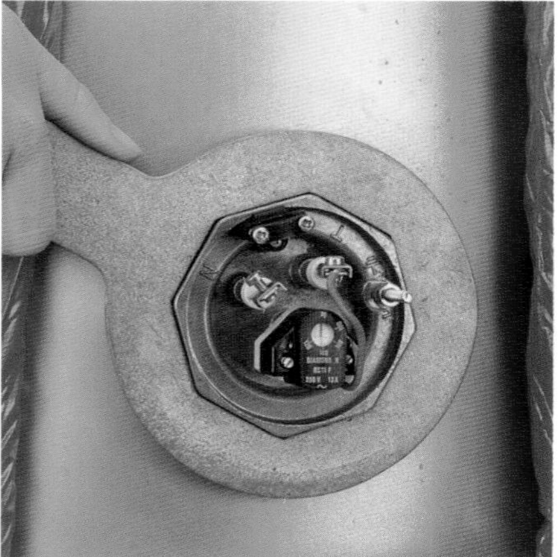

7 Use an immersion heater spanner to unscrew the old immersion heater and withdraw it from its boss. A flat spanner is suitable only if there is no deep lagging.

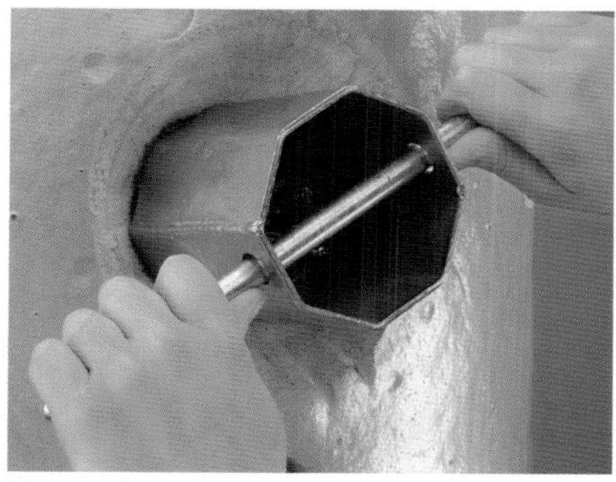

Alternatively For a deep-lagged cylinder, you will need a box-type immersion heater spanner, turned with a tommy bar.

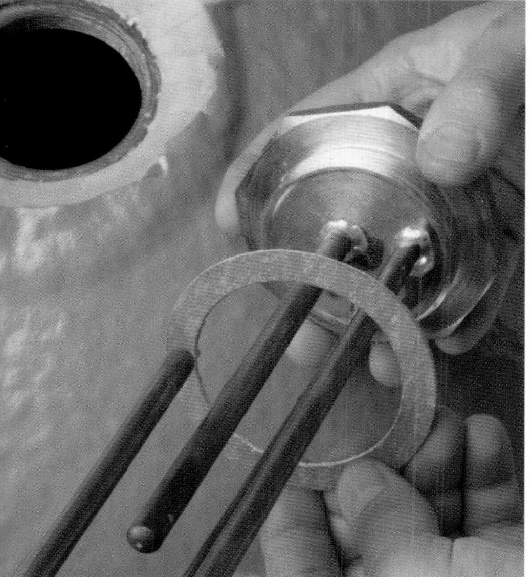

8 Fit the heat-resistant fibre washer or rubber washer if supplied.

9 Fit the new immersion heater into the boss taking care to position it so it doesn't foul any internal heat exchanger coil.

10 Tighten the heater into the boss. At this point you should fill the cylinder and check very carefully for signs of water seepage. If the mating surfaces are clean and the immersion heater is tight then you may need to tighten it a little more. Take care not to over tighten as you may damage the cylinder.

11 Re-connect the heat-resistant flex conductors to the terminals – normally brown (live) to the thermostat, blue (neutral) to the heater and earth (green/yellow) to the earth terminal.

12 Set the heater thermostat (see right). Set a single thermostat (or the cheap-rate thermostat on an off-peak system) no higher than 60°C in a hard-water area (to prevent scale forming), or up to 65–70°C in a soft-water area. Where two thermostats are fitted, set the one for day-time operation to 50–55°C.

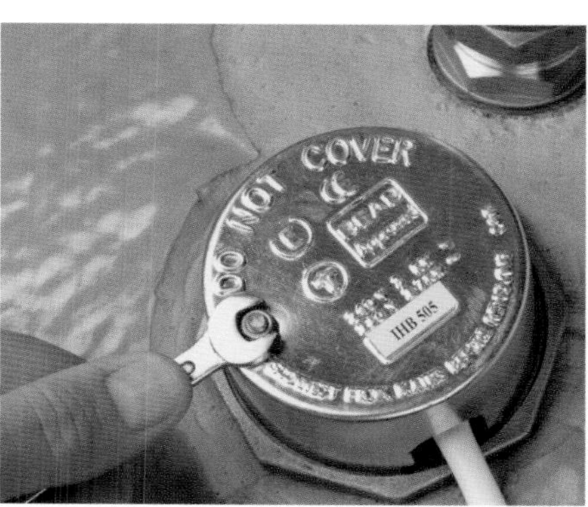

13 Replace the cover that protects the terminals and tighten the nut or screw that holds it in place. Do not cover the immersion heater to prevent heat loss because the cable will overheat.

SETTING THE THERMOSTAT

The temperature control can normally be adjusted with a screwdriver – the settings are marked round the screw. Some two-element heaters have one thermostat, some have two.

Choosing pipe insulation material

Insulating pipes is critical to prevent them from freezing and bursting in very cold weather, and to minimise heat lost as hot water travels around the system.

Self-adhesive foam wrap Thin foam insulating wrap, 50mm wide, is supplied in rolls usually 5m or 10m long. Some types have a metallic finish.

There is no formula for estimating how much wrap to buy – it depends on the size of the pipes and how large you make the overlaps. Buy and use one or two packs, then work out how much more you will need to complete the job.

Before you fix the lagging, make sure that the pipes are clean and dry. Peel off the backing paper and wind the material round the pipes. Overlap the tape as you wind, especially at bends.

This flexible lagging is also useful for insulating awkward fittings, such as multiple joints and stoptaps.

Plastic foam tubes Easy-to-fit plastic foam tubes are split down one side and have to be eased open to fit them round the pipe. They are secured with adhesive tape wrapped round at intervals, or with purpose-made clips. Tubes are available to fit 15mm, 22mm and 28mm pipes. Plastic foam tube is slightly more expensive than self-adhesive foam wrap, but is much easier to fit.

Foam tubes are available in two wall thicknesses. In most cases the standard grade is sufficient, but if you live in an area that often experiences severe frosts or if your pipes are particularly exposed, it is worth investing in the thicker material.

Glass fibre blanket Pipes that are boxed in can be insulated by stuffing glass fibre blanket around the pipes.

COLD-WEATHER CHECKS

- Make sure no tap is left dripping. If that is not possible, put a plug in the bath or basin overnight. Drips cause ice to block waste pipes.
- Never allow cisterns to overfill. Water in overflow pipes can freeze, causing the cistern to overspill.
- In a long cold spell, open the loft hatch occasionally, to let in warmth from the house.
- If you leave the house for short periods, keep the central heating switched on, but turned down to the minimum setting.
- For long periods, drain the plumbing system by closing the main stoptap and opening all the taps. When the water stops running, open the drain valve near the stoptap. For central heating, see page 379.

Insulating hot and cold water pipes

Hot and cold water pipes that are exposed to the cold should be lagged to prevent winter freeze-ups.

Before you start Concentrate first on pipes that run across a loft, above an insulated floor, and those that run along outside walls in unheated rooms. Overflow and vent pipes that are exposed to the cold should also be lagged. Some pipes are boxed in. To lag them, unscrew the box and stuff pieces of glass fibre insulation all round the pipes. Make sure all pipes are clean and dry before you start.

Lagging pipes with self-adhesive foam wrap

Tools *Scissors.*

Materials *Rolls of self-adhesive foam wrap.*

Self-adhesive foam wrap is useful where there are many bends in the pipes and it would be difficult to use flexible foam tubes.

1 For pipes in the loft, begin work at the cistern. Cut pieces of foam wrap to a workable length with scissors.

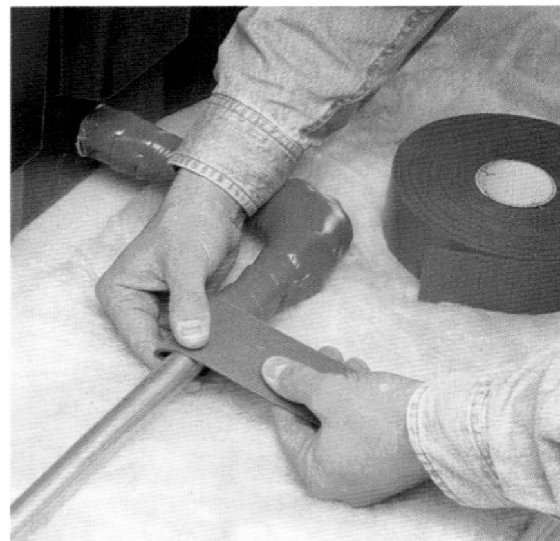

2 Wrap foam round the pipe, making generous overlaps of about one-third of the width of the wrap. Take care to cover the pipe well at bends – these are the vulnerable areas most likely to freeze.

3 Take the wrap around any valves or stoptaps as you meet them, leaving only the handle exposed.

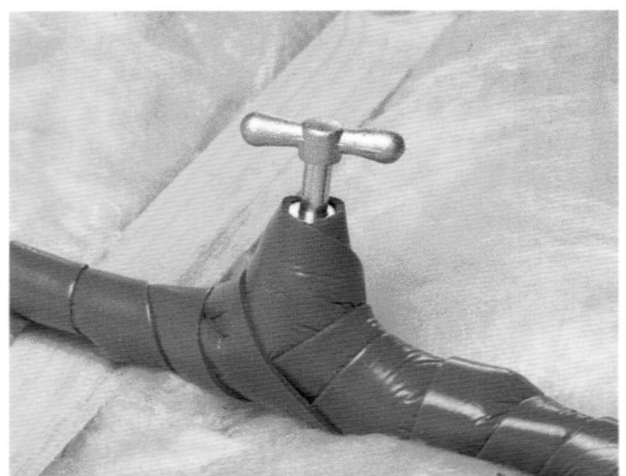

Lagging pipes with flexible foam tube

Tools *Scissors; serrated knife.*

Materials *Foam tube to match pipe size; adhesive tape; plastic clips.*

1 Lag the pipes leading from the cistern first, if you are insulating pipes in the loft. Wrap plastic adhesive tape around the first tube to hold it in place, even if the tube is one of the self-locking types. Push it up tight against the cistern so that the tank connector joint is covered.

2 Butt-join the tubes where they meet and wrap around the join to hold them tight. Cut the tube at 45° to fit it round elbows and tee fittings, and tape the joints. Alternatively secure joints with plastic clips.

3 Cut the tube to fit around the body of a gatevalve as closely as possible.

Lagging a cold-water cistern

Never lay lagging under a cold water cistern. Heat rising through the ceiling will help to prevent a freeze-up.

Before you start Purpose-made jackets are available to insulate most cisterns. Measure the cistern's diameter and height, if it is round, and its height, length and width if it is rectangular.

It does not matter if the jacket you buy is too large, since the sections can be overlapped. If the cistern is an odd size or shape, or you want to provide extra insulation, use plastic-sleeved glass fibre loft insulation blanket. This is easier to handle than unsleeved blanket and will not release fibres into the air as you handle it.

Using glass fibre blanket

Tools *Steel tape measure; scissors.*

Materials *150mm thick wrapped glass fibre blanket; string.*

1 Wrap the cistern in a continuous length of blanket, which you have cut with scissors so that the edges will meet. Tie a length of string round the blanket.

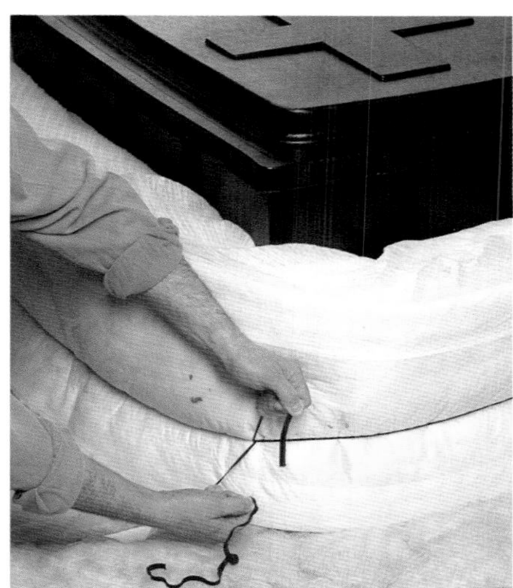

2 If necessary, wrap a second length of blanket round the tank. Cut it to length and tie it on the same way as the first layer.

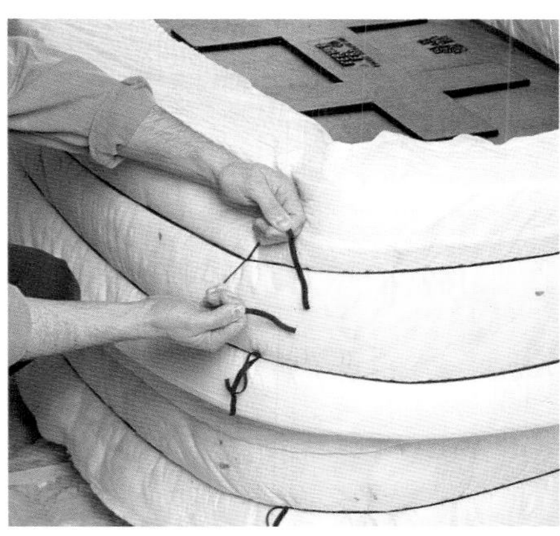

3 Extend the top layer beyond the top of the tank, to create a small rim to hold the tank's lid in place.

4 Measure the size of the tank lid. Cut a length of blanket to match and staple the ends closed. If the blanket is too wide, squeeze it up tightly to fit. Do not cut the blanket along its length.

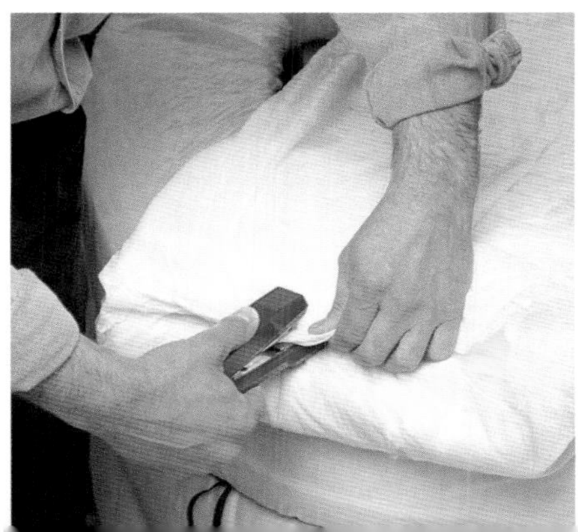

Insulating a high-level cistern

High-level tanks in roof spaces are more at risk from freezing than tanks sitting on the loft floor. This is because the heat rising from the house is not trapped under the tank.

For the same reason, the pipes leading up to the tanks are also at risk. If these pipes freeze, then there is a chance that the central heating boiler could explode. The most vulnerable pipe to freezing and bursting is the cold mains supply to the central heating tank, because the water in this pipe rarely moves so it has plenty of time to freeze.

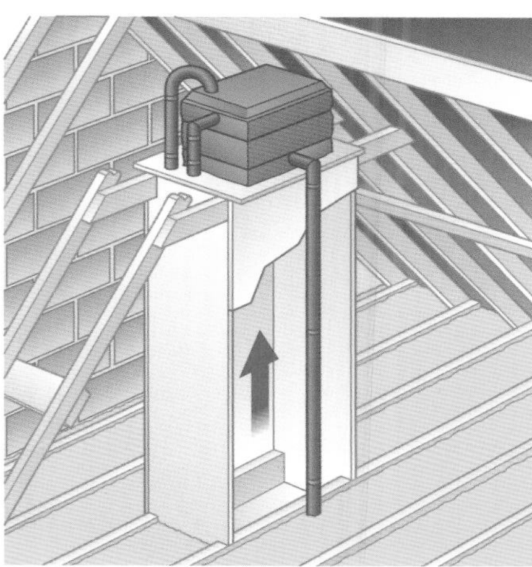

The best way to solve this problem is to build an enclosure directly under the tank in order to funnel heat upwards from the house and give added protection to the pipes. You can do this from any insulation material but the easiest to work with is fire-retardant polystyrene. It is lightweight, easy to cut and self-supporting. You can buy sheets of it very cheaply from builders' merchants. You may find even cheaper sheets with corners broken off.

Tools *Fine-toothed saw, hacksaw blade or serrated bread knife; tape measure; plumbline or spirit level.*

Materials *Sheets of polystyrene; polystyrene tile adhesive; 100mm wire nails or wooden meat skewers; adhesive tape.*

1 Use a plumbline to drop a vertical position from the edges of the high level tank down to the ceiling below. Cut and peel back the loft insulation at this point so that you have a clear area of ceiling corresponding to the shape of the cylinder.

2 Lay a piece of polythene over the ceiling at this point, cut to the same size as the base of the enclosure. This is to stop vapour from the house, which evaporates through the ceiling, from entering the new enclosure and condensing on the underside of the tank.

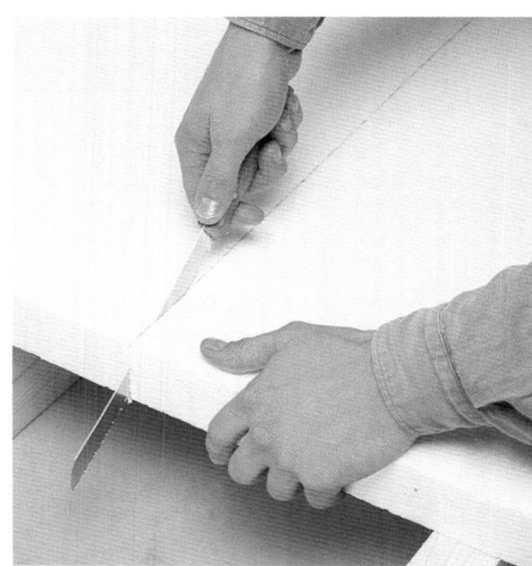

3 Using the saw blade or knife, cut the polystyrene sheet to form walls from the ceiling to the tank sides. Stick the edges together with a small amount of tile adhesive and push the nails or skewers through the corners to hold the sheets in place while the adhesive dries.

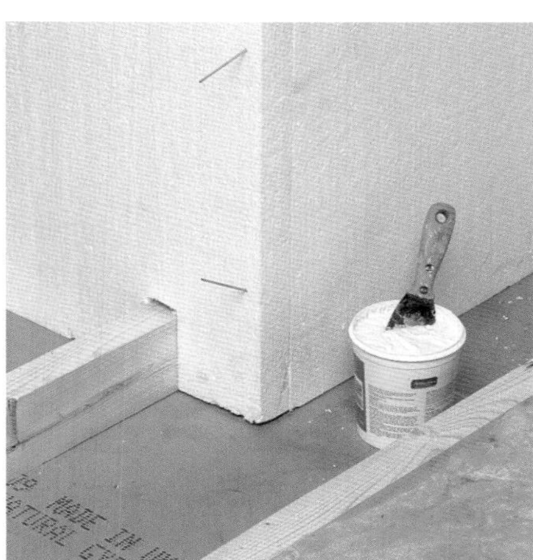

4 Use a little adhesive on the ceiling around the polystyrene to seal any gaps and hold the sheets in place. Remember that lofts can be quite draughty in high winds and polystyrene can be blown around if it is not fixed.

5 Bring the polystyrene right up to the underside of the tank. The tank must be supported on an independent structure. Tape the top of the polystyrene to the sides of the tank support.

6 The tank or tanks must be very well insulated. A thin jacket is not sufficient if the tank is near the slope of the roof. Use glass fibre blanket over the top of existing insulation to increase protection.

7 Make sure that the vent pipe, which goes over the tank, has an open passage to the tank to discharge any water. The vent pipe outlet must be above the water line.

How central heating works

The type of central heating system you have may depend on the age of your house. It is important to understand how it works.

A typical fully-pumped system

Most central heating systems warm the rooms of a house by passing hot water through radiators. There are many ways of heating the water, but it is usually through a boiler, which switches on automatically at certain times of day.

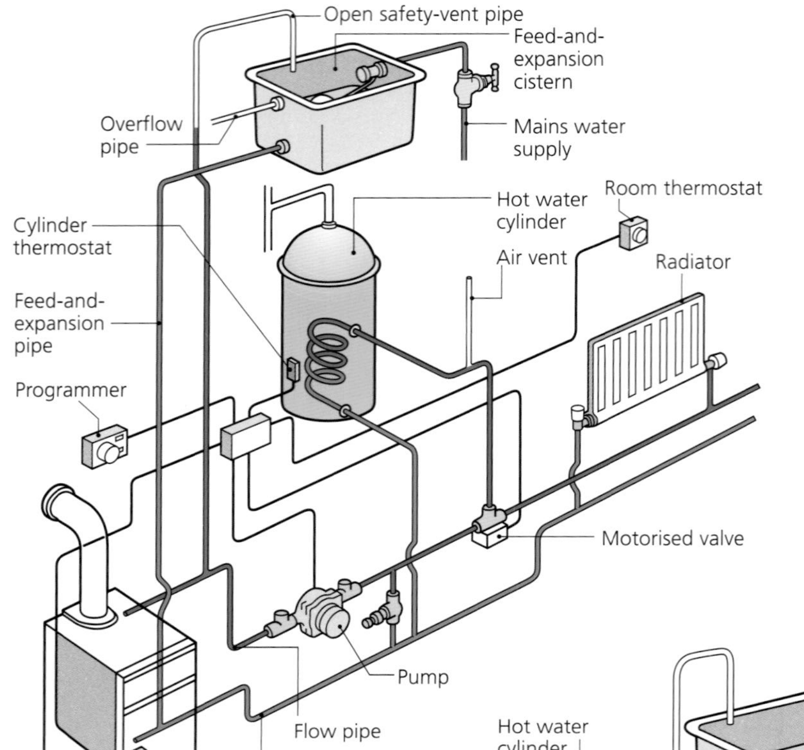

1 The 'central' in central heating is the boiler – but it is the programmer that is in charge. This has two channels – one for heating and one for hot water – which provide the electrical energy at pre-set times of day to switch the boiler and the pump on to send heated water round the radiator and hot water circuits.

2 The room thermostat responds to the air temperature and the cylinder thermostat to the water temperature in the hot water cylinder; if either is 'calling' for heat, electric current flows in the wiring to switch on the boiler and the pump and also to actuate the motorised valve – to send water round whichever circuit needs it. Some motorised valves allow flow round both circuits simultaneously; others give priority to the hot water. When the air (or water) is up to the temperature pre-set on the room (or cylinder) thermostat, the boiler and pump shut down.

3 The same water is constantly circulated around the system. In an open vented system, in case of leakage or evaporation, the water is topped up from a feed-and-expansion cistern. This cistern also takes up the expansion that occurs when the water heats up from cold.

4 An open-ended pipe, called the open safety-vent pipe, provides an escape route for steam and excess pressure if the boiler overheats.

Gravity hot water circulation

In some older central heating systems and in solid fuel systems, the heated water going to the hot water cylinder is circulated by gravity. When water is heated it expands, and hot water weighs less than cold water.

1 Hot water rises up a large pipe from the boiler to the hot water cylinder. Cooled water descends down the return pipe, pushing the lighter hot water up the flow pipe. Gravity circulation is reliable as it needs no mechanical assistance, but it requires larger 28mm pipes. The system is most efficient if the cylinder is directly above the boiler.

2 A pump, controlled by a programmer and room thermostat, drives water around the radiators and is controlled by a programmer and room thermostat as for a fully-pumped system.

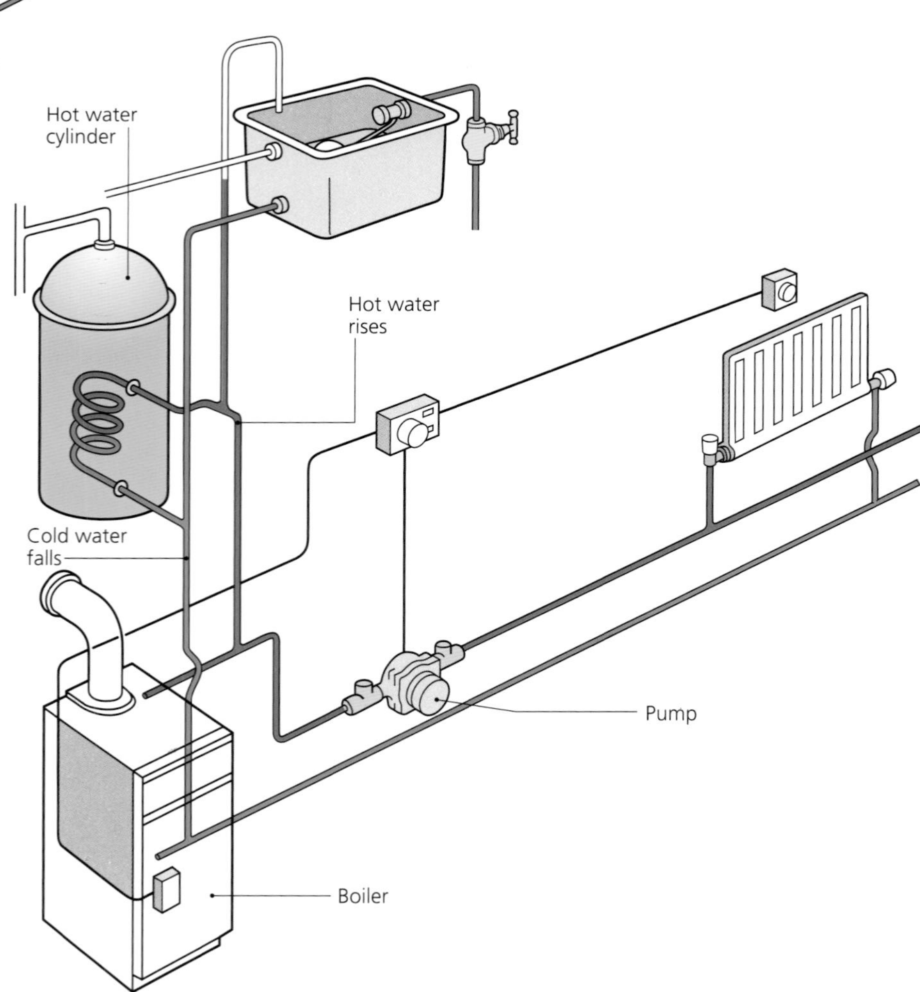

A sealed system

A sealed central heating system has an expansion vessel instead of an expansion cistern, and a pressure relief valve instead of a safety-vent pipe. The valve should be set permanently to 3 bar. Any water lost over time through minor leaks is topped up manually from the mains supply.

1 The system is controlled by a programmer as for a full-pumped system.

2 A room thermostat starts the boiler and pump to send water round the radiator circuit and a cylinder thermostat does the same for the hot water circuit (except for combination boilers – see below).

3 The boiler has an over-heat cut-out to prevent the system boiling should the standard thermostat fail, and on no account must a boiler without over-heat protection be fitted to a sealed system. A 'system' boiler used in sealed systems has many of the necessary components housed within the boiler casing.

Combination boilers All combination boilers – see page 324 – utilise sealed systems. As well as saving space because of the lack of a feed-and-expansion cistern, a combination boiler also has the advantage that no hot water cylinder is needed as the boiler heats mains water and delivers hot water directly to the taps at mains pressure.

Controlling your central heating

Efficient temperature and time controls can save a great deal of money on fuel bills.

Room thermostat This temperature-sensitive switch is set to a pre-selected room temperature. It sends an electrical signal to switch the heating on when the air temperature falls below the pre-set level, and off when it rises above the level.

On fully pumped systems the room and hot water cylinder thermostats operate motorised valves. When these are opened they in turn switch on the boiler and pump.

On gravity hot water systems the room thermostat operates the pump and the boiler is switched on and off by the programmer.

A room thermostat is best placed in a draught-free spot on an inside wall away from direct sunlight, about 1.5m above floor level, and away from any heat sources.

Thermostatic radiator valve The best means of controlling the temperature in each room is to fit a thermostatic radiator valve (TRV) to each radiator. The valve opens and closes according to the temperature in the room. If the room is cold, a full flow is allowed through to the radiator. As the room warms up, the valve closes to reduce the hot water flow through the radiator.

Rooms facing south and rooms with open fires or other heat producing appliances, such as an oven, benefit most from TRVs.

Most systems are suitable for use with thermostatic radiator valves. Seek expert advice on which ones to buy.

Leave one or two radiators without TRVs to act as a bypass, in order to maintain open circulation in the system. Alternatively, a bypass pipe can be installed just after the pump. The best type of bypass is a pressure-operated valve which opens progressively as the TRVs close the radiators down. It also helps to cut surging noises.

TRVs do not control the central heating pump and boiler, so they must be combined with a room thermostat or a boiler energy manager.

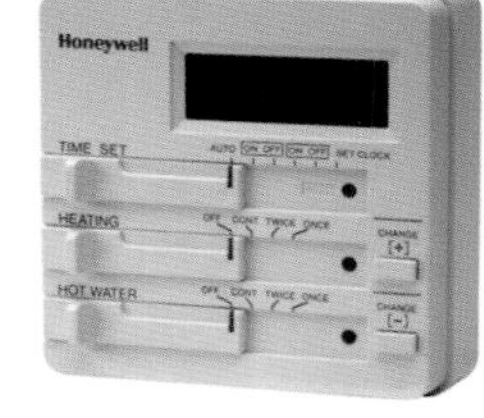

Programmers Time controls range from simple switches to complex electronic programmers. The most useful time room heating and domestic hot water separately, so water heating can be turned on and off at the same times of day all year round, while space heating times can vary with the season. Electronic types can give you three control periods a day and different settings for every day of the week.

Water-heating control The hot water temperature is often controlled only by the boiler thermostat. So hot water to the taps is the same temperature as the water supplied to the radiators. This is probably hotter than necessary. An electric thermostat that is fitted on the outside of the hot water cylinder will restrict the temperature of the water inside. It switches a motorised valve on and off to control the flow of water passing through the heating coil inside the cylinder.

Boiler energy management Sophisticated devices make sure that the boiler works only when needed. A boiler energy manager reduces wasteful short cycling on a boiler – that is, when 'hot water only' is selected on a conventional central heating programmer, the boiler will continually switch on and off to keep the water at the selected temperature. It will do this even though the cylinder is already full of hot water. This 'short cycling' can add as much as 30 per cent to fuel bills. The boiler energy manager will also take account of outside temperatures, and will regulate the central heating system accordingly.

ECO CONTROL

If you have more control over your heating system, you can save money and reduce carbon output. Larger houses can be divided into two zones (upstairs and downstairs). Each zone can then be programmed so that it is heated at a specific, possibly different time. Programmable room thermostats can give you six different temperature periods over 24 hours. Rooms can be programmed to be cooler in the morning when people are moving around the house and warmer in the evening, when there is less activity and it is cooler outside.

Updating your central heating programmer

An old-style programmer can be replaced quite easily with a more modern one.

Before you start It is now very easy to update your central heating programmer because all new programmers have an industry standard backplate. This allows you to swap one for another with more settings such as 'weekend' settings and 'one hour boost'. If you have an old-style programmer you will need to rewire the backplate to suit the new programmer. Full instructions will be supplied with the new model.

Tools *Electrician's screwdriver.*

Materials *New programmer. Possibly also pencil; paper; masking tape.*

1 Turn off the power supply to the heating system and remove the fuse.

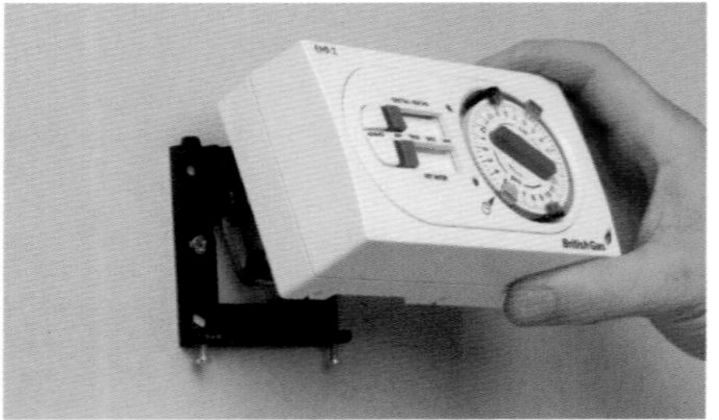

2 An old-style mechanical programmer with very limited time settings and options can be removed from the backplate by undoing the retaining screws.

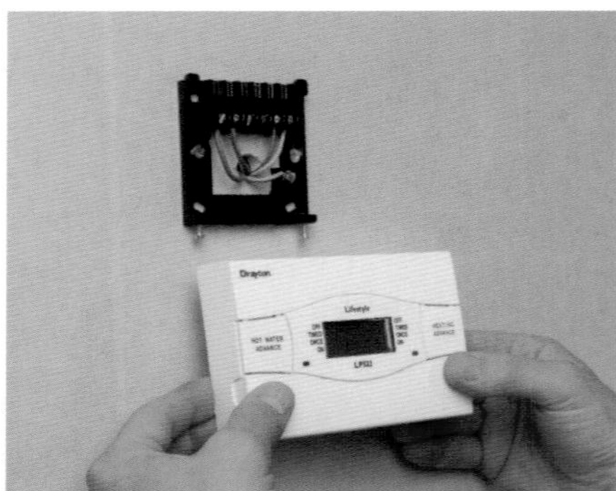

3 If your backplate looks like the example shown above, you can fit a new programmer directly to it. You may need to change the settings on the switch at the back to suit your heating system.

An older style gravity hot water system which only allows the heating to operate if the hot water is switched on is known as a ten position programme. If you can turn the heating on without the hot water then you can leave the slide switch set to 16 positions.

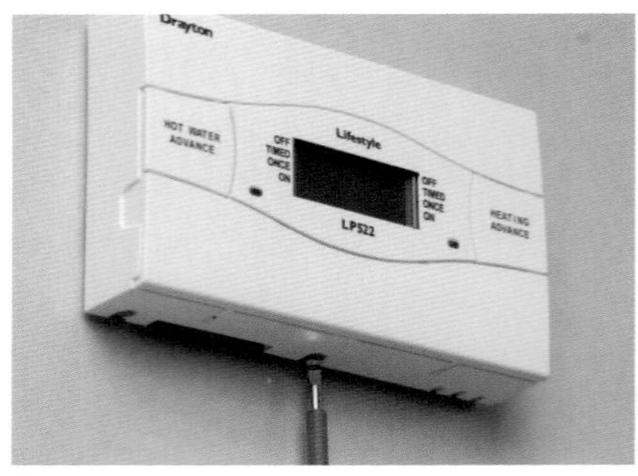

4 The new programmer must be tightened onto the backplate so the pushfit terminals are secure. You can then switch on the power and set the on-off times.

5 If the new faceplate does not fit the old backplate, study the wiring carefully and label each wire clearly. Sketch the old connections, then disconnect the cable cores from their terminals.

6 Remove the old backplate and attach the new one, using the manufacturer's instructions and your sketch of the old programmer to wire it up.

7 Push the new faceplate into position and restore the power to the wiring centre.

Central heating problems: what to do

If the hot water or heating stops working, there are some useful checks that could save you a call-out fee, or help you to give a plumber information about the nature of the problem.

No central heating or hot water

- Check that the programmer is set to 'on'. It may have been turned off in error.
- Check that the thermostats are turned up to the correct level.
- Check that the electricity supply is switched on and that the fuse has not blown. If the power is on and the fuse is working, but the programmer is not receiving power, there may be a loose wiring connection. Call an electrician to check the wiring and trace the fault.
- If a motorised valve is fitted, check that it is working properly. Slide the manual lever to open the valve. If there is resistance, the valve is not opening. This could indicate a burnt-out motor. Call a heating engineer.
- If the pump is not working, you can try to start it manually. Turn off the central heating system and wait until the pump is cold. Remove the screw in the middle of the pump and turn the impeller (the pump's manual starter). On some models this is a small screw that is turned with a screwdriver, on others there is a small handle attached.
- If this does not work, try tapping the pump casing sharply, but gently, with a mallet two or three times.
- If this does not work, remove the pump (page 378), and flush clean water through it with a hosepipe. Do not submerge it in water.
- If this does not work, replace the pump (page 378).
- If the pump is running, but the boiler does not light, check that the pilot light is on and that the gas supply is turned on at the meter. If you have an oil boiler, check that the fuel is turned on and that there is oil in the tank. Check that the filter is clear.
- If the pilot light is not lit, follow the procedure in the handbook or on the boiler casing to relight it. If the flame will not stay lit, the flame failure device probably needs renewing. Call a central heating engineer.
- If a combination boiler will not light, check on the pressure gauge that the water pressure is at least 0.5 bar. If it is above this, call a central heating engineer. If it is below, top it up via the mains filling point.
- If the mains pressure to the entire house has dropped (check by running the taps), call your water supply company for advice.

The central heating is working but there is no hot water

- Make sure that the thermostat on the hot water cylinder is set to 60°C.
- Check that the motorised valve (if fitted) to the cylinder is open (see No central heating or hot water, left).
- Bleed the air-release valve beside the hot water cylinder (if there is one). The valve is usually located on the pipe which enters the heating coil.

Hot water working but all radiators cold

- Make sure room thermostat has not been altered – it should be set to 21°C.
- Check that the motorised valve is opening properly (see No central heating of hot water, left).
- Check that the pump is working – it should be warm to the touch and you should be able to feel if it is running. If not, try to re-start it – see No central heating of hot water, left.

Noise in a central heating system

Unusual noises in a central heating system should not be ignored. The cause may be something quite easy to rectify.

Creaking in the floors and walls

Pipes expand as they heat up and contract as they cool. If the pipe is gripped tight by timber or a wall, or if it is in contact with another pipe, a creaking noise will occur when it gets hot or cold.

1 Pack some felt or pipe lagging around the pipes where they come up through the floorboards.

2 If that does not work, take up the floorboards around the source of the noise.

3 If one or two pipes are lying in a notch in a joist, and there is no room for movement, make the notch slightly wider by cutting down with a tenon saw and chiselling away the waste. Do not make the notch deeper; you may weaken the joist. Ease a piece of felt or pipe lagging under and between the pipes.

4 With the floorboards up, use a rasp to enlarge the holes through which the pipes rise to the radiator, if they are tight. Cover the pipes with pipe lagging where they pass through the boards.

5 Where pipes run the same way as the joists, make sure they do not sag or touch. Hold up sagging pipes with pipe clips fitted on struts between the joists. Put lagging between any pipes that touch.

6 If the pipes go through a wall, sleeve them with fire-resistant material, such as glass-fibre matting, or pack it in around them, tamping it fairly hard with a screwdriver.

Boiler noise

- Loud banging noises or sounds like a kettle boiling coming from a boiler indicate the presence of corrosion in the heating system and possible scale build up within the boiler's heat exchanger. Both can be removed by adding a central heating system cleaner to the feed-and-expansion cistern (or injecting it into a radiator for a sealed system – see page 379) and then running the system hot for at least an hour. After this, drain the system and flush through with clean water until it runs clear.
- To prevent future corrosion and scale formation, add a corrosion inhibitor (system protector) to the final water fill.
- Noise may occur if the water flow through the boiler is insufficient. With modern lightweight gas boilers, water flow rate is particularly important.

Banging in the pipes

- Banging noises in the pipes may be due to overheating. To find the cause of the fault, start by checking that the boiler thermostat is working properly. Turn the boiler off but leave the pump running to help to cool the system down. Then turn the boiler on and turn up the thermostat. If you do not hear a click, turn everything off again and call a central heating engineer.
- You can cut down on the amount of noise transmitted along copper pipework by cutting out a section and inserting one or two plastic push-fit fittings into the run. If the noise persists, replacing troublesome sections of copper pipework with semi-flexible plastic pipe may be the answer.

Sound of rushing water in the pipes

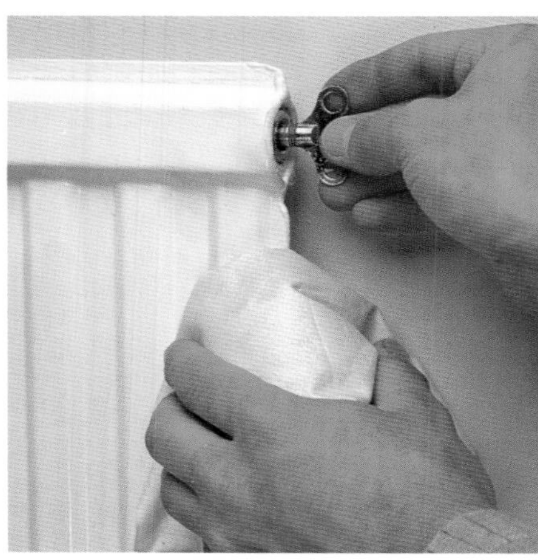

Air that has entered the system, or gas that has formed as a result of internal corrosion, can cause a noise in central heating pipes like the sound of rushing water.

Try releasing the air from the air vents on the radiators, and any other venting points in the system. If the noise continues, it may be a symptom of serious faults that could eventually damage the whole system. Poor positioning of the open safety-vent pipe (page 370–1) could be the cause. Get expert help.

Humming in the pipes

An annoying humming sound usually comes from the pump. Call in an expert to find the cause.

- Anti-vibration pump brackets can be fitted that may help to reduce the problem.
- Pipes may vibrate if they are too small for the amount of water they have to carry.
- The pump speed may be set too high. Try turning down the speed control knob on the pump body by one setting. If this fails to cut the noise and also makes the radiators take longer to heat up, call in a central heating engineer. He may suggest relocating the pump.

Balancing a radiator circuit

Hot water is carried from the boiler to the radiators by a flow pipe, which branches off to supply each radiator. Cool water leaves each radiator at the opposite end and joins a return pipe carrying it back to the boiler.

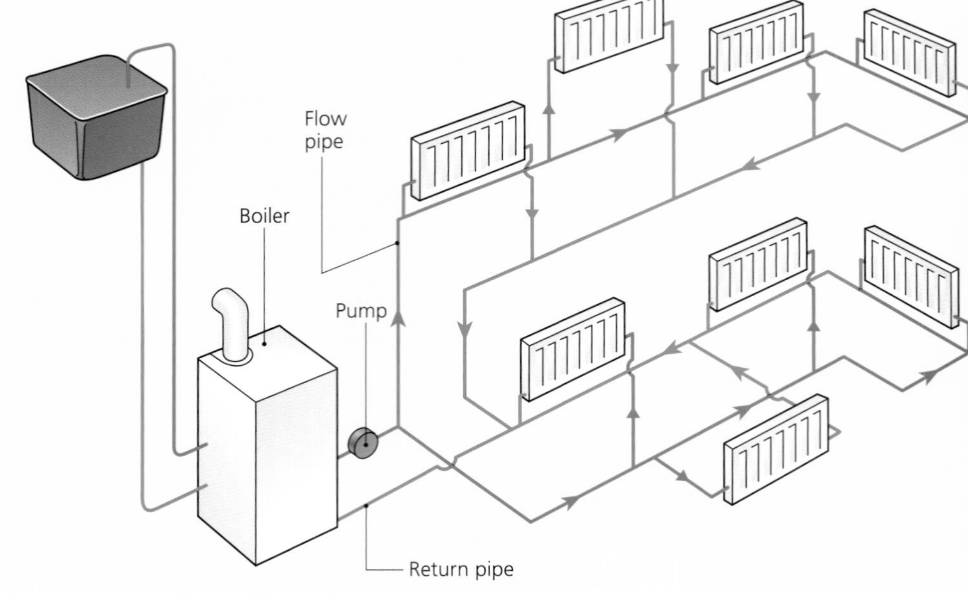

As water flows round the radiator circuit, it cools down, so the radiators nearest to the boiler receive hotter water than those furthest away. This is dealt with by adjusting the water flow through each radiator, so that the less-hot ones get more water through them. Adjustment is carried out using the lockshield valve on the radiator: the one with a plain cover.

Tools *Two clip-on radiator thermometers; spanner; small screwdriver.*

Materials *Sticky labels; pencil.*

1 Two or three hours before you intend to start work on the radiators, turn off the central heating system to allow the water in the radiators to cool down.

2 Open all lockshield valves and handwheel valves fully.

3 Turn on the central heating system. Work out the order in which the radiators heat up, and label them accordingly.

4 Clip a radiator thermometer onto the flow pipe bringing water into the first radiator, and one onto the return pipe.

5 Turn down the lockshield valve until it is closed, then open it slightly. Adjust the flow until the temperature of the flow pipe is roughly 11°C higher than that of the return pipe.

6 Repeat for all radiators in the circuit, working in the order as labelled. The lockshield valve on the last radiator will probably need to be fully open.

Leaks in a central heating system

Never ignore leaks in a central heating system. Fresh water that is drawn in to replace the lost water contains free oxygen which can cause radiators and cast-iron boilers to rust and scale to form.

Before you start Internal leak sealants similar to the radiator 'weld' used in cars can be used in central heating systems to seal very minor leaks. Pour the sealant in through the feed-and-expansion tank.

A leaking pipe joint

Most leaking pipe joints are compression fittings, which can be tightened with a spanner. Tighten the joint slightly, no more than a quarter turn. If this does not stop the leak, do not tighten any further as this will damage the joint.

1 Drain the system to below the level of the leak. Undo the nut on the leaking joint and pull the pipe out slightly.

2 Wrap two or three turns of PTFE tape around the face of the olive where it meets the joint. Tighten the nut.

3 If the leaking joint is soldered, drain the system. Heat the joint with a blowtorch and take it apart, then replace it (see page 344).

A leaking radiator valve

If the leak is from the compression joint below the valve, drain down the system to below the joint. Then call a plumber or repair the joint yourself. Use PTFE tape to cure a leak from the union nut connecting the valve to the radiator.

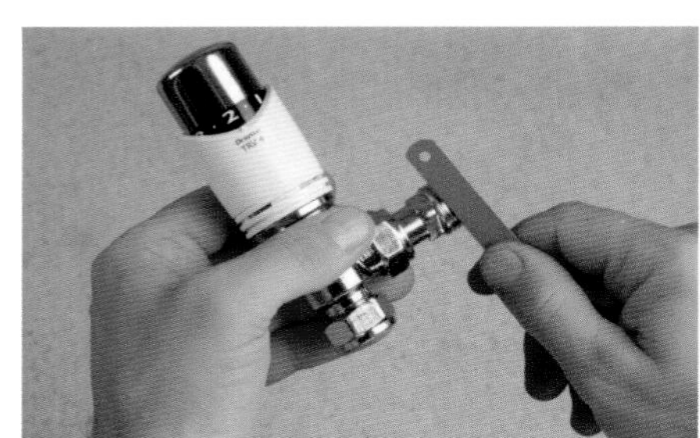

1 The most common cause of leaks on radiator valves is where the PTFE sealant tape has run up the shiny chrome as the valve is screwed into the radiator. This leaves no sealant on the thread. Use a hacksaw blade to 'break in' the thread by striking it across as if you were striking a match. The small barbs will hold the tape in place. Some threads come ready broken.

2 The valve seal to the tail is made at the olive and not around the thread, as many believe. Improve the seal by wrapping some PTFE tape around the olive face.

3 When you tighten or loosen a radiator valve always counter the force with another spanner to prevent any strain on the pipe.

Thermostatic valves

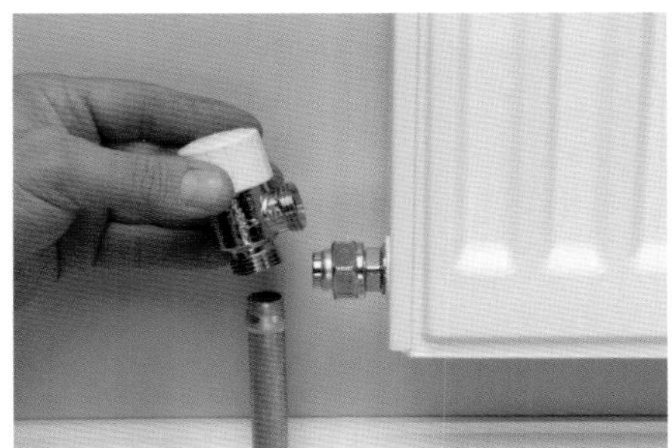

1 Modern thermostatic valves (TRVs) use a 15mm compression fitting on each port and are bi-directional so you can fit them on the flow or the return.

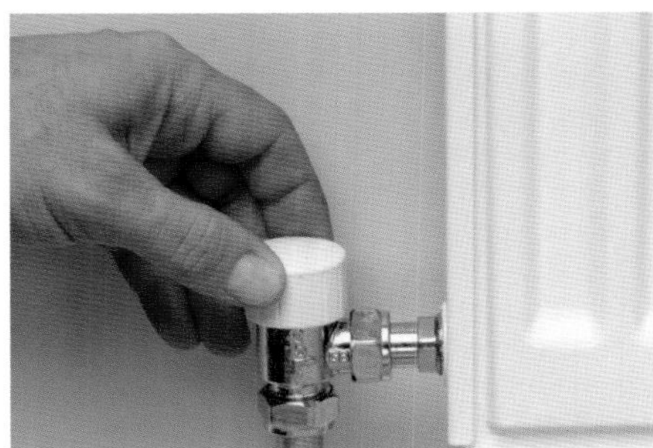

2 TRVs have closing off caps to allow you to remove the radiator safely. Never rely on the thermostatic valve closing the water off. They can open suddenly as the temperature drops in the night.

3 Remove the closing off cap and fit the thermostatic head. To enable you to screw it down fully, the head must be screwed onto the body with the setting on 'maximum'.

A leaking valve tail

The leak may be from the valve tail screwed into the radiator. Use a radiator spanner to remove it. Cover the male thread on the valve tail with PTFE tape and replace the tail.

A leaking radiator vent

If the radiator air vent leaks, drain the system to below the vent. Remove the air-vent fitting using a radiator spanner. Bind the screw joint with PTFE tape, and replace the fitting.

A leaking radiator

A small jet of water from the body of the radiator is called a pinhole leak. It is caused by internal corrosion and can happen within a few weeks of the system being fitted if the debris that collects during installation has not been removed, or if air is being drawn in.

Turn off the valves at each end to relieve the pressure. Then remove the radiator and leave the rest of the system running. Before fitting a new radiator, flush out and clean the system using a non-acidic cleaner.

Repacking a radiator gland

If a radiator valve weeps water from under the cap, the packing gland is worn. You can replace the packing with PTFE tape or thread-sealing fibre, sold by plumbers' merchants. Some radiator valves cannot be repacked; instead they have renewable O-rings which can be replaced with a kit.

Tools *Small adjustable spanner; small screwdriver; PTFE tape; silicone grease.*

1 Turn off the valve. If it continues to leak, close the lockshield valve at the other end of the radiator.

2 Remove the cap from the leaking valve and undo the small gland nut. Slide it up out of the way.

3 Pull a length of PTFE tape into a string and wrap this around the spindle several times.

4 Use a small screwdriver to push the tape down into the valve body. Smear on silicone grease and re-tighten the gland nut. Replace the head and turn the valve back on.

Replacing a radiator valve

Before you start Drain the heating system (page 329). As it drains, open the vents on the upstairs, then downstairs radiators.

Tools *Two adjustable spanners. Perhaps hexagonal radiator spanner.*

Materials *New radiator valve; wire wool; PTFE tape.*

1 Undo the nut that connects the valve to the radiator by turning it counter-clockwise. To stop the valve rotating, hold the body of the valve upright with a second spanner.

2 Undo the cap nut that connects the pipework to the valve body by turning it clockwise (as seen from above). Lift the valve away. Let the cap nut slip down the pipe.

3 Separate the new valve from its tail piece and check whether the valve will fit the old tail piece. If not, use the radiator spanner to remove the old tail and clean the threads in the radiator with wire wool.

4 Fit the new tail piece to the radiator if necessary after first wrapping PTFE tape clockwise around its threads to make a watertight seal. Tighten it with the radiator spanner. Check that the valve lines up with both the tail piece and the pipework.

5 Place the valve over the pipe, slide up the cap nut and screw it up finger-tight. Finger tighten the nut securing the valve to the tail piece before tightening both nuts with a spanner – use a second spanner to brace the valve when tightening the nuts.

6 Re-fill the system and bleed each radiator to get rid of trapped air. Close the radiator air vents one by one and check the valve for leaks – tighten nuts if necessary.

Removing and replacing a radiator

It may be necessary to remove a radiator in order to flush out sludge that has built up inside, replace it or decorate behind it. This can be done without draining the whole system.

Tools *Polythene sheets; old towels; rags; two bowls; pliers; two large adjustable spanners; absorbent paper; hammer; hexagonal radiator spanner.*

Materials *PTFE tape. For replacement: new radiator the same size as the old one; new radiator air vent; radiator plug.*

1 Lay a polythene sheet and old towels on the floor around the radiator. This could be messy.

2 Shut the control valve by hand. Then remove the cover from the lockshield valve and use pliers or a small spanner to shut it too. Count the number of turns that this takes and write it down.

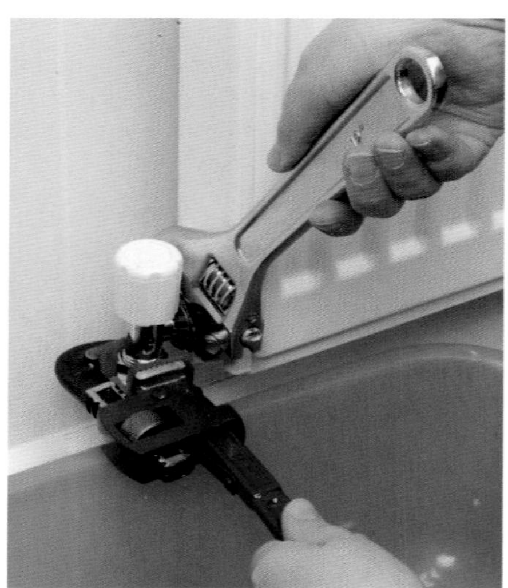

3 Put a bowl under the control valve and disconnect the union nut. Take care not to distort the pipe. Water will flow out (there may be a lot, so have bowls ready).

4 Open the air vent to increase the flow of water.

5 When it has stopped, undo the union nut on the lockshield valve. Some more water may come out.

6 Block the open ends of the radiator with twists of absorbent paper.

7 Lift the radiator off its brackets and carry it outside. You may need help.

Replacing the radiator

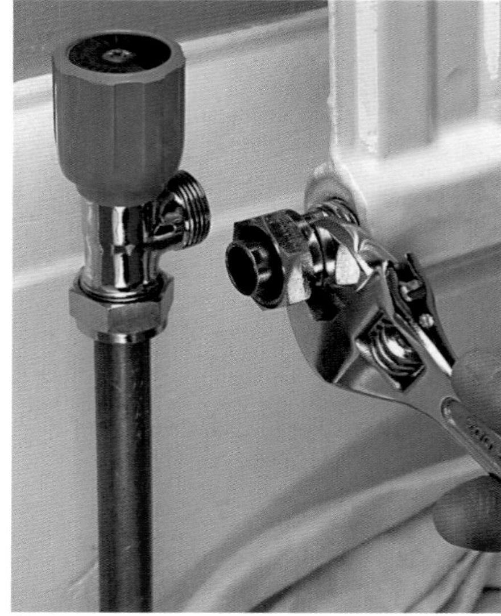

1 If you are replacing a radiator, but keeping the valves, remove the valve tail pieces from the old radiator. Turn the valve tail counter-clockwise (when looking at the end of the radiator).

2 Hold the new radiator in position to check if the wall brackets need repositioning.

3 Wind PTFE tape round the thread of the valve tail pieces. Screw the tail pieces in place.

4 Fit a new air vent at the same end of the radiator as before, using PTFE tape as for the valve tail. Use the radiator spanner to tighten it in. Fit a new plug if there is an open tapping in the other top end.

5 Lift the radiator onto the wall brackets and reconnect the valve union nuts.

6 Open the valves to fill the radiator with water. Let air out through the air vent, and check for leaks. Reset the lockshield valve to its original position.

> **WARNING**
>
> If there is a thermostatic radiator valve on a radiator, turn it down to zero before disconnecting the tail pieces and removing the radiator. Otherwise there is a risk that the valve will open, flooding the room, if the temperature drops.
>
> Alternatively, fit the special screw-down cap, supplied with the valves, in place of the sensor to shut off the valve while the radiator is out of use.

Relocating a radiator

Changing the position of a radiator can free up valuable wall space when you change the layout of a room.

Before you start Drain the heating system (page 329). As it drains, open the vents on the upstairs, then downstairs radiators. Remove the radiator, as described left, but leave the valves in place.

With the floorboards raised, cut back the pipes leading to the radiator from the main flow and return pipes: either fit a stop-end to each pipe below floor level or fit a blanking plug to the compression tee fitting. Extend the central heating pipework as appropriate so that you will be able to have two new pipes coming up through the floor at the new radiator position, but don't fit the final new pipes yet.

Tools *Tape measure; pencil; power drill; masonry drill bit; screwdriver; spirit level; hacksaw or pipe cutter; spanners.*

Materials *Radiator; wall mounting brackets; 50mm screws; wall plugs; 15mm copper pipe or 6mm plastic pipe; compression or push-fit plumbing fittings; PTFE tape.*

1 Before removing the old brackets from the wall, measure their spacing and distance above the floor – and use these measurements to mark the bracket positions at the new radiator location. If the wall at the new location is a stud wall, make sure the brackets will be secured into studs – or fit horizontal battens across the studs to take the bracket screws.

2 Drill holes for wallplugs in a solid wall (pilot holes on a stud wall) and screw the brackets to the wall or to your two new battens (use new screws if necessary).

3 Use a spirit level to check that each bracket is vertical and that they are aligned horizontally – if anything, there should be a very slight rise towards the end where the air vent is fitted. The brackets are designed to allow adjustment.

4 Hang the radiator on the brackets, check that it is level, and fit the new pipes from the main flow and return so that they align with the two radiator valves. You may find plastic pipe easier to use – see page 343.

5 Connect the pipes to the valves, re-fill the system and bleed each radiator to get rid of trapped air. Close the radiator air vents one by one and check for leaks at all connections at the old and new radiator locations – tighten nuts if necessary.

Boxing in pipes

Exposed pipework can be concealed in boxes – but remember to insulate hot water and heating pipes before covering them.

Tools *Bradawl; screwdriver; pencil; drill bit with twist, masonry and countersink bits; panel pins; hammer; nail punch; spirit level; plane.*

Materials *Timber battens; one-piece joint blocks (often used to assemble flat-pack furniture); screws and wall plugs; hardboard or 3mm thick MDF; foam pipe insulation.*

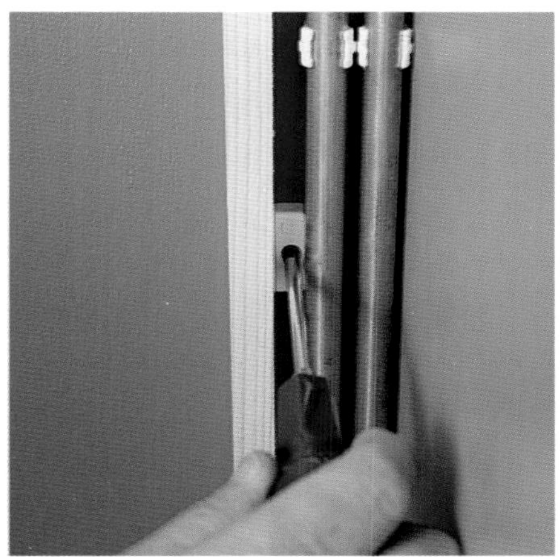

1 To box in a group of pipes in a corner, fix a batten a little wider than the depth of the pipes to the wall, using one-piece plastic joint blocks at 1m intervals.

Fix a second batten on the other side of the pipes if they are not in a corner.

2 Insulate pipes if necessary. Cut a strip of hardboard or MDF wide enough to cover the batten and the pipes and pin it to the batten with panel pins or screw it home.

3 Where pipes run along a skirting board, fit a horizontal batten above the pipes, then fit a slimmer one at floor level, and finish off with a cover strip, ready for painting or papering.

Radiators that do not heat up correctly

If your radiators are not giving out enough heat, check them all and make a note of which are cool and which (if any) are hot. Some may be cooler at the top or bottom.

Radiator cool at the top

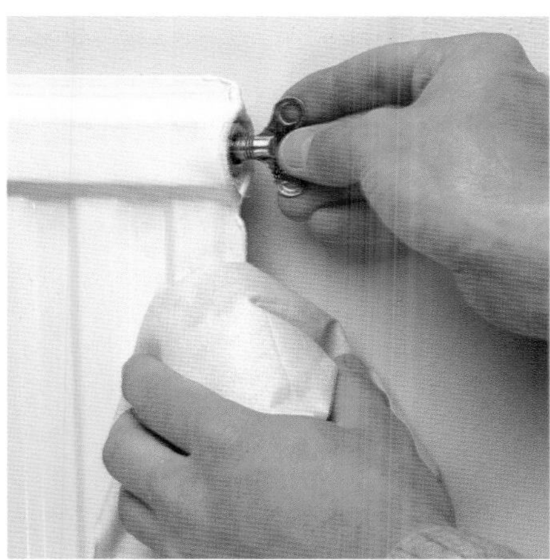

Air is trapped at the top of the radiator. Turn off the central heating. Then use a radiator bleed key to open the air vent at one end of the radiator. Air should start to hiss out. When water appears, close the vent. Hold a rag under the vent to catch the water escaping from it. Turn the heating on again.

If radiators need bleeding more than once a year, air is entering the system and this can cause corrosion. There may be a serious fault that needs expert attention. Some systems have one or more extra bleed points on the pipes either upstairs or in the loft. Manual bleed points are opened with a screwdriver.

On an automatic air valve the small, red plastic cap must be loose in order for air to escape. If it is tight, unscrew it.

Radiator cool at the bottom and hot at the top

Sludge (black iron oxide) produced by internal corrosion can build up at the bottom of a radiator and stop the circulation. Remove the radiator, take it outside and flush it through with a hose. If more than one radiator is affected, drain and flush the whole system before adding a system cleaner to the feed-and-expansion cistern as described on page 373. After final flushing, add a corrosion inhibitor to the final water fill.

Top-floor radiators cold

Cold radiators upstairs only, often indicate that the feed-and-expansion cistern is empty. The ballvalve may be faulty (page 339).

Refill the feed-and-expansion cistern so that there is just enough water to float the ball when the water in the system is cold. The extra space accommodates expansion of the water in the system as it heats up.

After re-filling the system, bleed all the top floor radiators (left).

Top-floor radiators hot, lower radiators cold

This is almost certainly due to pump failure (see Changing a central heating pump, page 378).

Cold radiators throughout the house

Most likely to be a wrongly-set room thermostat, a faulty motorised valve or a faulty pump – see Hot water working but radiators all cold on page 372.

Radiators farthest from the boiler are cool

The system is not properly balanced (page 374).

Top radiators heat up when hot water only is selected on programmer

Hot water naturally rises above cooler water. On a gravity driven system, hot water for the hot water cylinder is prevented from creeping into upstairs radiators when the heating is switched off by a mechanical valve, called the gravity-check valve. It is situated on the flow pipe to the upstairs radiators.

If the gravity-check valve is stuck in the open position, the pipe on either side of the valve will be warm. Call a central heating engineer to replace it.

Changing a central heating pump

You can change a central heating pump without first draining down the whole central heating system, provided that there are service valves fitted on each side of the pump.

Before you start Domestic pumps are now a standard size, but if the old pump was longer than the new one, you may need adapters to fill the gaps.

When you go to buy a replacement from a plumbers' merchant take all the details of the old pump with you. Measure the length of the old pump, and the diameter and type of the connections. Most domestic pumps have 1½in BSP threaded connections.

Also make a note of the type of pump and the setting of its output regulator (domestic pumps are available with different ratings).

Tools *Electrician's screwdriver; bowl; towels; pipe wrench or adjustable spanner; pencil and paper.*

Materials *New pump.*

1 Switch off the electrical supply to the central heating at the fused connection unit – or at the consumer unit.

2 Make a note and sketch of how the electrical wiring on the old pump is connected. It may be helpful to label each conductor. Then disconnect the conductors with a screwdriver.

3 Close down the service valves on each side of the pump using the valve handle or an adjustable spanner. If there are no isolating valves, drain down the system (page 329).

HELPFUL TIPS

The central heating pump is designed to run full of clean water. Any air or sludge that gets into the water can damage the pump, so keeping the system full of water and limiting corrosion are essential. Never run the pump unless it is full of water.

If your pump is out of use in summer, as is usually the case with a combined gravity and pump-driven system, run it for a minute once a month to keep its impeller free.

4 Put a bowl and towels under the pump ready to catch any water that escapes when you remove it.

5 Unscrew the union nuts holding the pump in place. Turn them counter-clockwise (facing along the pipe towards the pump). Remove the old pump.

6 Fit the new pump in position with the new sealing washers in the unions to prevent leaks.

7 Open the isolating valves (or refill the system) and check that the unions are watertight.

8 Dry the pump carefully to remove any traces of moisture; reconnect the wiring.

9 Test the newly installed pump by switching on the electricity supply and turning on the central heating system at the programmer or time switch. You may also need to turn up the room thermostat to get the system going.

10 Once the central heating system has started up, check that the open safety-vent pipe over the feed-and-expansion cistern does not discharge water when the pump starts or stops. If it does discharge water, seek expert advice.

11 If you have had to add much fresh water to the cistern, bleed any air out of the system in order to guard against future corrosion and to protect the new pump.

Repairing a motorised valve

If a motorised valve ceases to open, its electric motor may have failed.

Use a mains tester to check whether the valve is receiving power. If it is, you will need a new motor. You should be able to buy one from a plumbers' merchant. There is no need to drain the system, but you must switch off the electricity supply to the central heating system. Just turning off the programmer is not enough, because a motorised valve has a permanent live feed.

Take off the valve cover and undo the retaining screw that holds the motor in place. Push the lever to open the valve, and lift out the motor. Cut off the connectors to disconnect the two motor wires.

Insert the new motor, then let the manual lever spring back to a closed position. Fit the retaining screw and tighten. Strip the ends and connect the wires, using the two connectors supplied with the new motor. Put back the cover. Check the new motor by turning on the power and running the system.

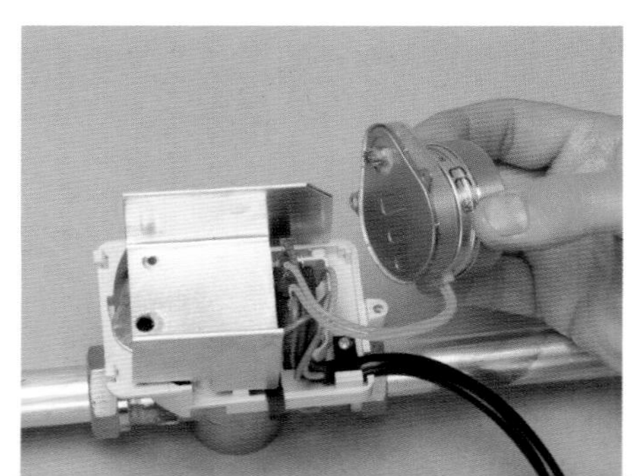

Preventing a freeze-up

If you turn off your central heating while you go on a winter holiday, there is a danger that the system will freeze and a pipe will burst.

Lagging only reduces the speed of heat loss, so eventually the temperature of an unused system will drop to the level of the surrounding air. With a gas-fired or oil-fired system, leave the heating on and turn the room thermostat down to its minimum setting if you will only be away a few days.

Using a frost thermostat

For a long holiday, you could have a frost thermostat installed (it is also called a low-limit thermostat). It overrides the controls and turns on the system when the temperature approaches freezing point. Rising air temperature makes it turn the system off again.

Adding antifreeze

You can also add antifreeze to the water in the central heating system. Tie up the ballvalve arm in the feed-and-expansion cistern and pour in antifreeze according to the maker's instructions. Then drain off enough water via a drain valve for the antifreeze to be drawn into the system. After restoring the water level in the cistern to the correct level, turn the central heating on for a few minutes in order to thoroughly mix the antifreeze with the water.

Protecting a system against corrosion

The life and efficiency of a central heating system can be increased by adding a corrosion and scale inhibitor.

Before you start Test the water in the system every year or so to see how corrosive it is. To do this, drain a sample of the heating system water into a jar and place two bright (not galvanised) wire nails in the jar. Screw the lid on. Wait for a week.

If the nails rust and the water turns a rusty orange, the water is seriously corrosive (or has no corrosion inhibitor) and you must take immediate action. If the water remains fairly clear and the nails do not rust, then no further action is necessary, since the water in the system has lost its free oxygen. A few black deposits are acceptable.

Finding out where air is entering the system

The most common cause of corrosion is fresh air in the system. If the radiators need bleeding more than once or twice a year then too much air is being drawn into the system and this must be eliminated.

The most common areas where air gets into the system are a leaking joint on the suction side of the pump, or through the feed-and-expansion cistern.

Leaks around pumps can be repaired in the same way as other leaking joints. But if air is entering through the feed-and-expansion cistern you will need expert help.

You can find out if the feed-and-expansion cistern is the source of the problem by running the programmer through its functions and checking for any swirling movement of water in the cistern. To find out whether the vent pipe is sucking in air, submerge the end of the pipe in a cup of water. If the pipe draws up water from the cup, then air is entering the system through the pipe and causing corrosion. You will need to call a central heating engineer to rectify the problem.

CLEANER IS GREENER

Corrosion and a build-up of scale will dramatically reduce the efficiency of a boiler. Adding a specialised system cleanser and then a corrosion inhibitor will save fuel as the system will work so much more effectively.

Adding a corrosion inhibitor

Corrosion inhibitors are available in liquid form. In an open-vented system the liquid is added to the system through the feed-and-expansion cistern in the loft.

In a sealed system, you can inject the corrosion inhibitor into a radiator through the air vent.

If there is sludge in the system (see page 377), add a system cleaner and flush the system out before adding inhibitor.

Replacing a hot water cylinder

Hot water cylinders are mostly trouble-free, but do sometimes develop leaks or become so clogged with limescale in hard water areas that they have to be replaced.

Most domestic hot water cylinders hold around 140 litres of water, so a leak should be dealt with swiftly, before it destroys the ceiling or floor below.

Tools *Pipe grips; open-ended spanners; screwdrivers; hose; pipe clips; immersion heater spanner.*

Materials *New pre-lagged copper cylinder; PTFE tape; immersion heater fibre washer.*

Before you start Older cylinders were often lagged with a jacket, which you will need to remove. New cylinders usually come prelagged. You may have to alter the plumbing if the existing connections do not line up with those on the new cylinder.

1 Turn off the power to the immersion heater, remove the round top cover and disconnect the flex from the terminals.

2 Shut down the boiler and turn off the cold water feed to the cylinder. This pipe enters the cylinder at the bottom. If there is no gate valve, tie the ball valve up in the cold water tank to stop the cylinder from refilling.

3 Open the hot and cold bath taps to drain the supply pipes, but note that this does not drain the water from the cylinder.

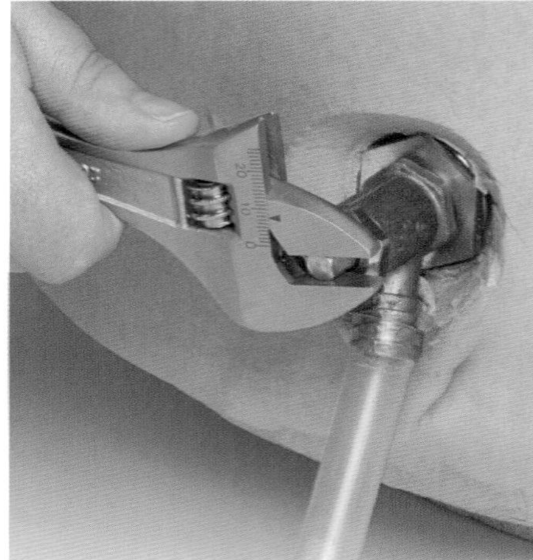

4 Attach a length of hose to the drain valve on the bottom of the cylinder. Put the other end into a drain, open the small square nut on the drain valve two turns and let the water drain from the cylinder.

5 Remove the immersion heater from the top of the cylinder by unscrewing it with a special immersion heater spanner then withdrawing it (pages 366–7).

6 Disconnect the pipes from the cylinder. Use two spanners: one to hold the securing nut on the cylinder and the other to undo the outer union nut. If you have a round ribbed style nut use a pipe wrench instead. You will need to disconnect the cold water inlet, the hot water outlet at the top of the cylinder and the connections to and from the heater coil if the water in the cylinder is indirectly heated (see artwork below).

7 Lift out the old cylinder, being careful not to damage the ends of the disconnected pipework.

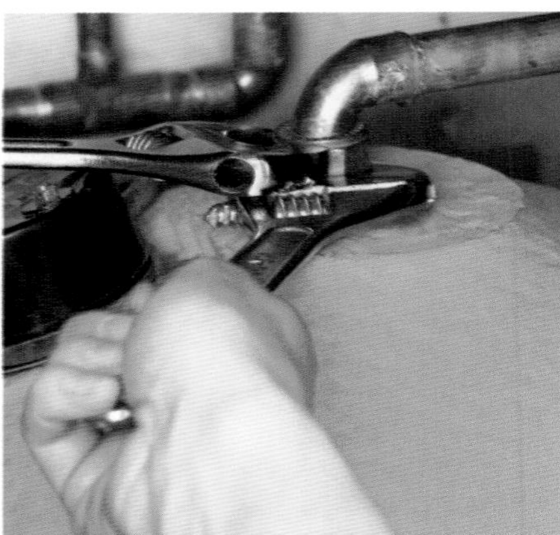

8 Wrap three layers of PTFE tape around the connection spigots on the new cylinder. Lift it back into place and reconnect the pipes, using two spanners to tighten the joint as you did when undoing the old connection.

9 Refit the immersion heater (pages 366–7). If it was fitted with a fibre washer then replace the washer or wrap PTFE tape around the threads before you refit it. Tighten with the immersion heater spanner but do not over tighten, cylinders are thin and can crease easily.

10 Reconnect the flex to the immersion heater terminals and install the cover.

11 Close the drain valve, then turn on the water supply to the cylinder. Close both taps and check for leaks as the cylinder fills. If all is well, relight the boiler.

Connections to the hot water cylinder

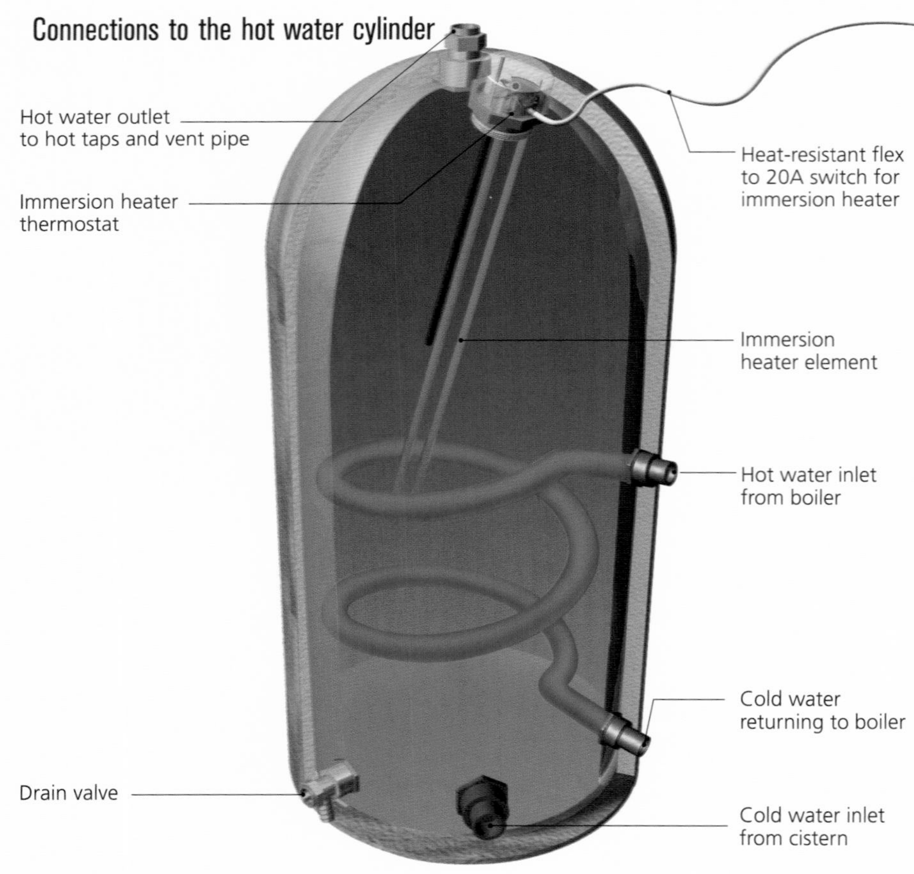

Having a central heating system installed or replaced

If you are planning to have central heating installed in your house, first read as much about heating as you can so that you can discuss your wants and needs with the heating contractors.

Boilers, heat emitters and controls

Read pages 382–3 first, and then gather further information on boilers and heat emitters. You can get additional information from the advisory bodies and trade associations listed on page 502 and in Chapter 14. It is also worth paying a visit to your local plumbers' merchant and picking up brochures on the latest boilers and heat emitters.

Many of the larger DIY stores now sell a full range of central heating equipment – and you can find product details widely available on the Internet.

Getting quotations

Find three Gas Safe-registered contractors in your area and ask them to quote for the job. Give them all the same outline brief, including where you would like radiators positioned, and what temperatures you wish to achieve in the rooms. A living room temperature of 21°C when the temperature outside is –1°C is normal. If you need a margin built in for extra cold weather you should say so. Make a list of any other requirements you feel are important.

1 Be wary of paying a deposit. The first payment should be made when the materials are delivered. Retain a small amount of the balance (2 per cent) for any faults you find that need fixing after the job's completion.

2 Ask the contractor to give start and completion dates.

3 Before the job starts, decide where pipes are to run and in what order they will be laid so that you can clear the room. If you want pipes to be concealed, state this plainly before any of the the work starts. It will cost you more than surface-mounting, but is well worth the expense.

4 If several rooms will be affected, ask the contractor to finish in one room before starting in the next one.

5 Your home should be left clean and tidy at the end of each day and should be respected – for example, there should be no loud music or smoking by any of the contractors.

6 Work should comply with statutory requirements such as water supply regulations, the Building Regulations and all relevant codes of practice. Materials must meet the requirements of CEN (European) or British Standards where applicable.

7 'Making good' means filling in holes and replacing panels. Floorboards should be screwed back down to prevent creaking. Damaged boards should be replaced. Normally, however, making good does not include decoration.

8 Establish what other contractors will be required to help to complete the work – electricians, for example.

Where to install radiators

Naturally you want to get the maximum heat from the minimum number of radiators, so siting them correctly is essential:

1 Radiators should be fitted in the coldest part of the room, preferably under the windows if they are single glazed. The heat rising from the radiator will counteract the cold air falling from the glass. This produces a flow of air across the room, as illustrated above.

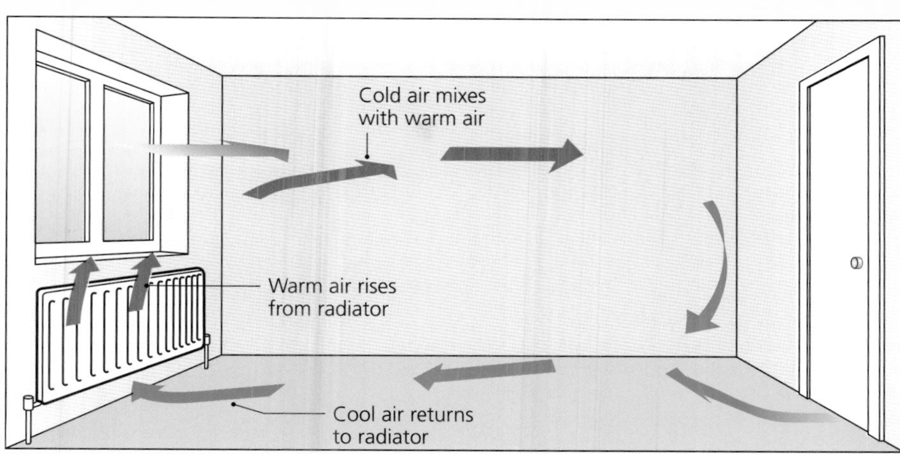

2 Radiators placed on inside walls opposite a window can accentuate the flow of cold air down a window and can produce a cool draught across the floor.

3 Make sure that there is at least 100mm of space between the bottom of a radiator and the floor to allow a good circulation of air and so that the floor below the radiator can be cleaned.

4 At least 40mm should be left between the wall – or the skirting board – and the back of the radiator to allow air to circulate.

5 A shelf should not be placed any closer than 50mm to the top of a radiator for the same reason.

6 A radiator installed inside a decorative casing can lose a quarter or more of its output unless the casing permits a full flow of air over all of the radiator's surfaces.

When the work is finished

The contractor must flush out the new central heating system in order to remove debris which could corrode and clog it in the future. He should then run the system to full heat and check that all the radiators heat up. The contractor must leave you all instructions and technical leaflets, and fill out guarantee cards.

Choosing a boiler

Choosing an appropriate boiler for your household needs is crucial. Consider whether you need it to supply heating and hot water, the size of your household and how many bathrooms you have – see opposite page.

When choosing a boiler

- Its proposed position affects whether you need a wall-hung or floor-standing model. The boiler's distance from an outside wall or the roof will affect the type of flue you have.
- Boilers are available for all types of fuel (oil, gas, LPG, solid fuel and even electricity). Gas is the most common, followed by oil and LPG for homes with no gas supply.

Oil and gas have similar running costs and are cheaper than LPG. Oil and LPG require storage tanks.

- Consider the space available – not just for the boiler, but also for a hot water cylinder and cold water tanks, and what the demands on the system are likely to be.
- Look for energy rating labels to compare running costs. Remember that some boilers need more maintenance than others.
- All boilers must be serviced regularly and faults dealt with by an expert. A new or replacement boiler must now meet Building Regulation requirements. This demands a minimum efficiency (of 78 per cent for gas boilers, 80 per cent for LPG and 85 per cent for oil) and should be installed by a Gas Safe or OFTEC engineer. Programmers and thermostats must be installed, too.

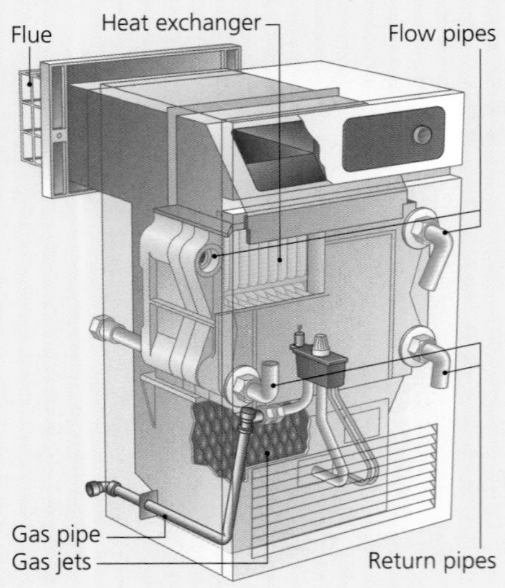

Conventional boiler The gas or oil-burner heats water in a heat exchanger, rather like a gas-ring under an old-fashioned kettle. Traditionally, heat exchangers have been made from cast iron, but lighter aluminium and stainless steel are more commonly used now. Most modern, conventional boilers are wall-hung with balanced flues, but floor-standing models with conventional flues are still available. Most conventional boilers are designed for use on fully-pumped open-vented systems; a few will work with existing gravity hot-water systems.

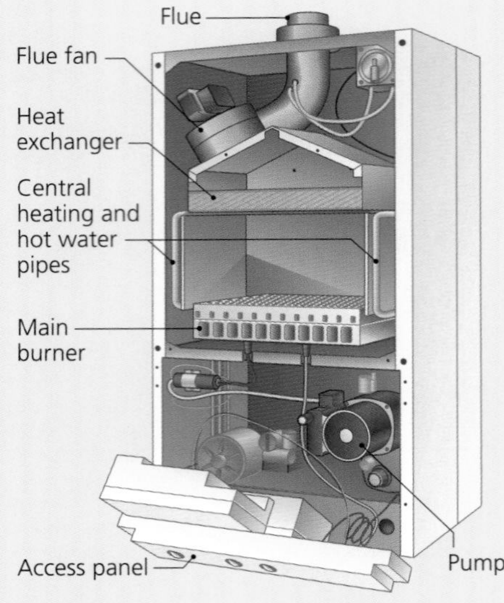

Combination boiler Also known as a 'combi' boiler, this is a central-heating boiler and multi-point water heater all in one. Hot water for the radiators is heated in its own sealed circuit, but the boiler also heats cold water from the mains, delivering it on demand to the hot water taps around the house. The main advantages are the savings in space – no hot water cylinder or cold water tanks – a constant supply of hot water and better water pressure at showers. By altering the cold-water plumbing, there can also be drinking water at all cold taps. The disadvantages are the cost of the boiler and low flow-rates if more than one hot tap is being used. Some combi boilers store a little hot water so that it is immediately ready for use. Most can be used with gas or LPG, though oil-fired options are also available.

Back boiler This is a heat exchanger located behind a gas fire. Although many still exist in older houses, they are no longer fitted new. They work in much the same way as a conventional boiler, sending hot water to radiators on a central heating circuit and to a hot water cylinder, but need a conventional open flue, suitably lined for the fuel being used. A back boiler can be used with a fully pumped system, or with gravity hot water circulation. The firefront may be inset into a fireplace or may protrude into the room.

GREENER BOILERS

It is now a legal requirement (in all but very rare cases) to fit a condensing boiler (also called an HE boiler) when installing a central heating system. The fuel savings can be substantial – as much as 30 per cent – when compared with older types of boiler. It will also reduce carbon emissions.

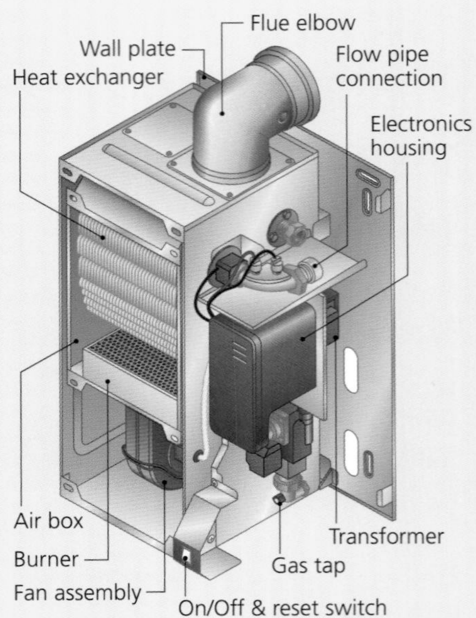

Condensing boiler With a larger heat-exchanger than a conventional boiler, a condensing boiler is designed so that the water returning from the heating system is used to cool the flue gases, extracting extra heat that is normally lost through the flue. Often known as 'high efficiency' boilers, they are meant to be used with a fan-assisted balanced flue and in a fully pumped system. When the flue gases are cooled, water vapour will condense and so a pipe has to be installed to drain this water away.

Condensing boilers work best with lower system water temperatures, but even with normal radiator temperatures, the efficiency will be significantly greater than with a conventional system; this means the extra cost of the boiler is soon recovered in the saving in fuel costs, after which you continue to save money and reduce carbon dioxide emissions. Condensing boilers are available for use with either gas, LPG or oil. Combination condensing boilers are available, too.

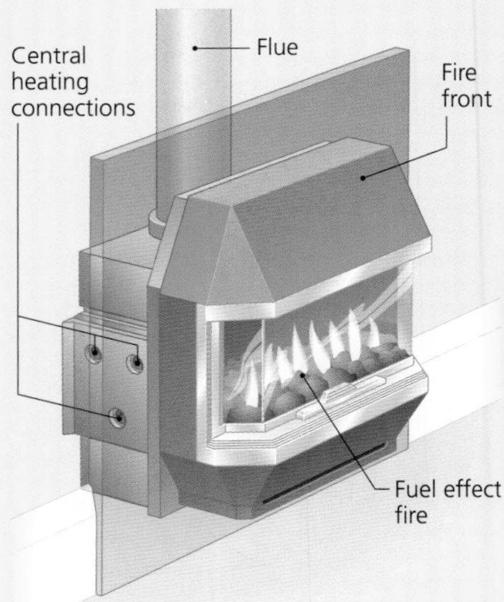

Back boiler

THE TWO TYPES OF FLUE

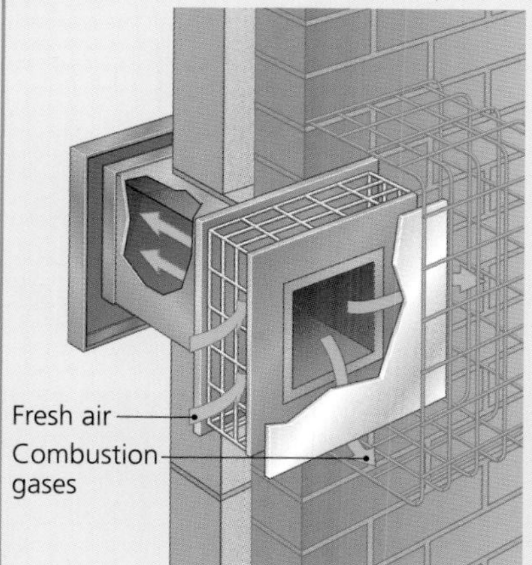

Balanced flue In order to work properly, this two-part duct allows the combustion gases to escape and fresh air to enter. The flue is sealed so that no combustion gases can enter the room where it is installed – its other name is a 'room-sealed flue'. With a natural-draught balanced flue (as above) the boiler must be installed on an outside wall, so that the flue passes directly through the wall. With a fan-assisted balanced flue, the boiler (which contains an electric fan) can be mounted on any wall, and is connected by a duct to a flue that can be on an outside wall or pass through the roof. Fan-assisted balanced flues are more efficient, but noisier, than natural-draught flues.

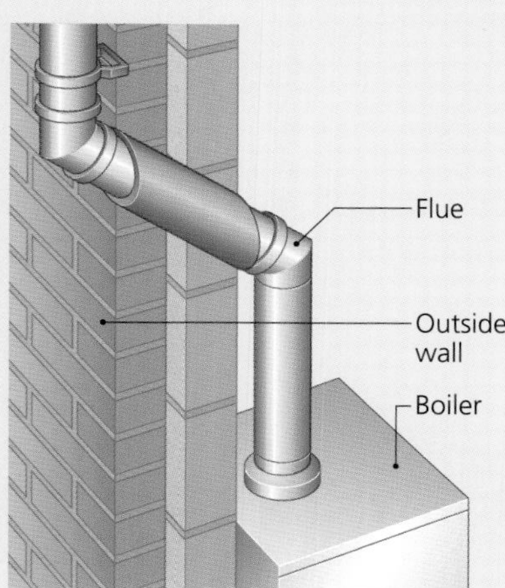

Open flue This can be either a lined existing chimney or a new circular duct installed in an outside wall. The flue will take only the combustion gases, so the fresh air supply for the burner must come from the room. Consequently, special ventilators or grilles will need to be installed on outside walls.

Choosing radiators and other heat emitters

Though most people's first choice is a radiator, there are many other heat emitters that can be connected to central-heating pipes.

These include fan convectors, trench-duct heaters, skirting heaters and under-floor heaters. When mixing different types of heat emitter on the same system, fit thermostatic valves to each in order to allow full, individual control.

Radiators Despite the name, only a tiny proportion of heat given off by a radiator is emitted from the front through radiation. If you put your hand just a few inches from the front the heat is negligible. Most of the heat is given out from the top by convection.

To work properly a radiator must have a good flow of air passing from the bottom on the front and back surfaces. There must be at least 100mm clearance from the floor for air to enter and 40mm at the top.

Old-style plain panel radiators have now been almost completely superseded by convector radiators, which have metal boxed fins welded to the hidden faces of the panels. They act as chimneys for hot air, almost doubling the heat output and making it possible to fit smaller radiators. There are many different styles of tubular radiator available, from modern interpretations of a traditional Victorian style (above left) to quirky wall-mounted spirals (above right).

Trench-duct heaters If windows go down to the floor, trench heaters can be installed. A pipe fitted with fins runs along one side of a trench in the floor. A dividing plate along the centre of the trench separates the hot air rising from the pipe from the cooler air returning to be reheated.

Underfloor heaters Burying pipes under concrete floors has gained in popularity. Plastic pipe is laid in a continuous loop and carries hot water under the floor. The pipes must be fitted on top of under-floor insulation and are normally covered with a sand-and-cement screed which helps to spread the heat evenly. This is an ideal system for use with a condensing boiler, because it works well at low temperatures.

Skirting heaters

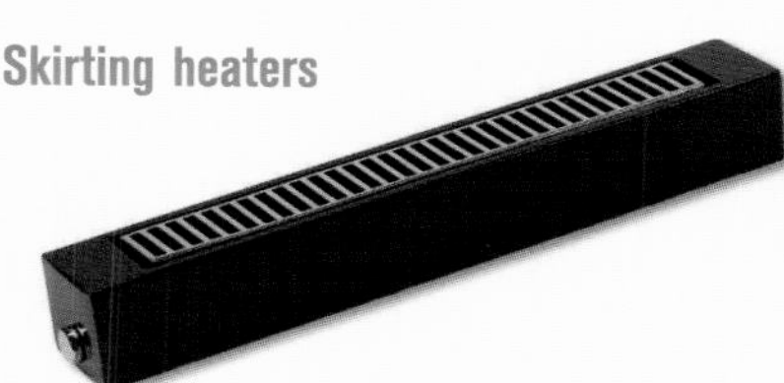

Small metal convectors run round the room just above or in place of a skirting board. This system is good for background heating and it gives an even spread of heat, which can help to prevent condensation on walls. However, it is not usually powerful enough to heat a room in very cold weather.

Fan convectors Use a fan convector where there is not enough wall space for a radiator. Special kick-space models are made to go under kitchen base units (below). Low-voltage versions are available for bathrooms. Air curtain models can be installed above doors and wall units, and some models sink into the floor.

An electrical fan blows air across copper fins, which are heated by hot water from the central-heating circuit. A filter in the air intake traps dirt. This should be regularly cleaned to maintain maximum performance and to prevent noise.

Roofs

Drainage

Outdoor maintenance 11

What can go wrong on the roof

You may discover that the roof needs to be repaired only when stains appear on the ceiling from rain seeping into the loft.

Making regular checks in the loft for damp timber and checking the roof from the outside for signs of damage could help you to discover the problem earlier. Repair damage as soon as possible after its discovery.

To examine the roof thoroughly, set up a ladder which is at least three rungs above the gutter. If you move onto the roof, use a proper roof ladder which hooks over the ridge (see opposite).

Flat roofs

The main problem with a flat roof is that instead of draining off, water may collect on the surface and seep through even very small cracks. This can lead to rot in timbers as well as damp patches appearing on ceilings.

Felt is generally built up in layers on larger roofs, and often the top layer will blister. To repair the damage, see page 396. Bitumen felt roofs on sheds are usually only a single sheet of felt. If this starts to break up, strip it off and replace it (page 428).

Corrugated plastic sheeting may leak at overlaps or where screws or nails pass through the sheets. Seal gaps with silicone sealant or replace the sheet (see page 398).

Glass roofing may leak if the seal fails along glazing bars and rain may be driven up overlaps by strong winds. Use adhesive tape – preferably the foil type, rather than the black – to seal a glazing bar. If a poor overlap cannot be increased, seal the outer gap with silicone sealant.

WHEN SHOULD A WHOLE ROOF BE REPLACED?

It is hard to judge whether a roof should be completely re-surfaced. If a large number of the tiles or slates are broken, this is obviously needed. Faults in the structure are harder to diagnose. Bumps and hollows may have been caused by movement in the roof timbers years earlier, but it may have stabilised and be perfectly sound and weatherproof. If movement is recent, however, it may need professional attention.

If you have doubts about the soundness of your roof, pay an architect or surveyor to give an unbiased report on it; a builder's report may not be so impartial.

Ridge tiles The mortar holding these tiles in place may fail with age or if it is soaked with rain that freezes; high winds may then dislodge tiles. To replace a ridge tile, see page 391.

Roof tiles Tiles are usually nailed in place or held by the nibs that project behind each tile and hook over roofing battens. If the nibs are damaged or if the nails rust away, tiles will slide down the roof. Tiles may also be blown off by strong winds or pushed out of place by the weight of a build-up of snow that turns to ice. To replace a roof tile, see page 389.

Slates There are no nibs on slates, so they need nails to hold them. They may slip out of position if the nails rust. To replace a slate, see page 390.

Flashings When a roof surface meets a wall or chimney stack, the gap between them is sealed with flashing. Lead flashing is the most durable type; felt and mortar flashings do not last quite as long.

Flashings can become displaced when mortar joints fail (the flashing strip is pushed into the joint between bricks or pieces of masonry and sealed with mortar). Cracked mortar flashing is usually caused by slight movement in the building or between neighbouring buildings. This movement is common and depends on the water content in the soil.

For how to repair flashings, see page 394. Check all the flashings – around chimney stacks, dormer windows and adjoining flat roofs – when making a repair.

Chimney stacks Because of its position and the potential danger, few DIY jobs can be done on a chimney stack – special scaffolding must be erected around the stack so work can be done in safety. However, you can keep an eye on the condition of the chimney stack and have any repairs carried out quickly to prevent damp.

If a flue is not in use, rain which gets onto the flue lining can cause damp problems. Have the chimney capped with a half-round tile or a cowl to keep rain out. You can only see the edge of the flaunching (the mortar which holds the pots in place) but have it checked if any deterioration is visible. If you notice faults in the brickwork, get expert advice.

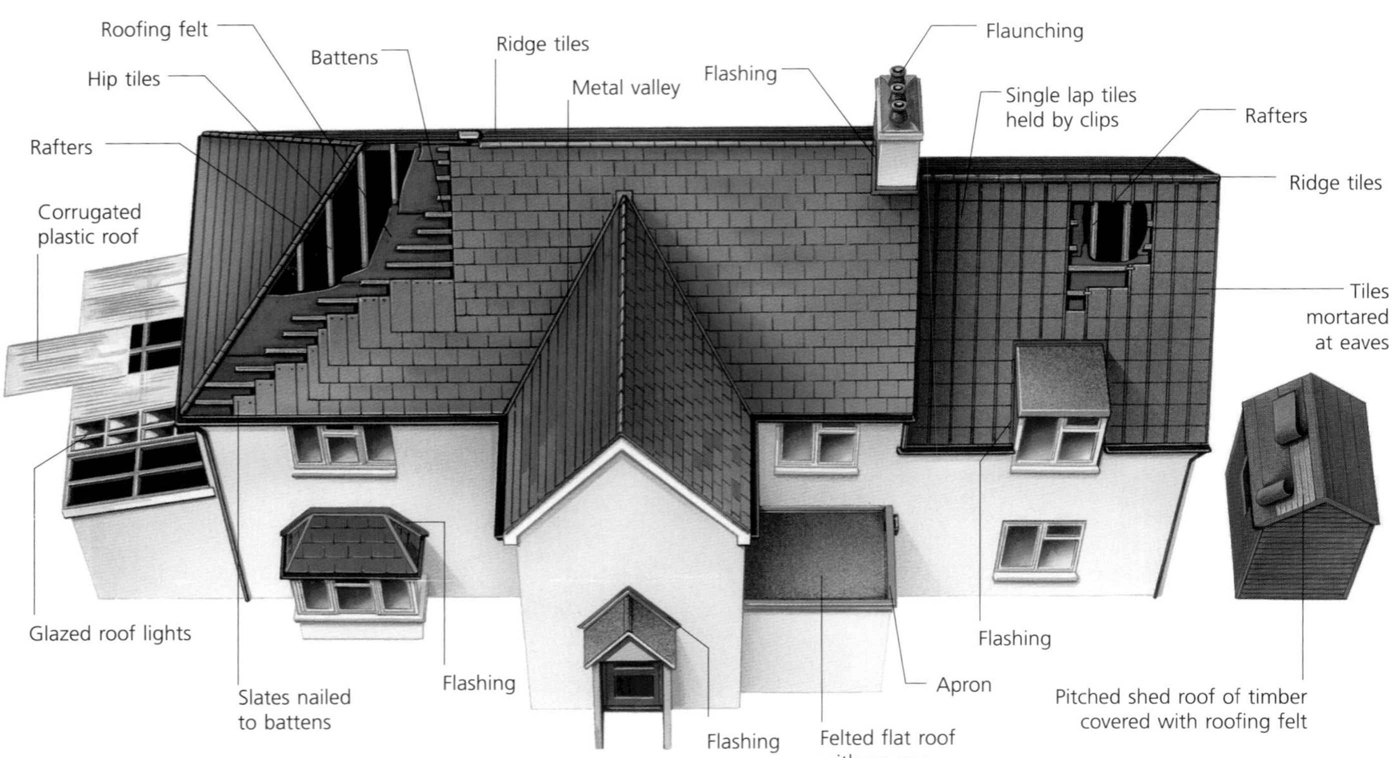

Roof repairs: tools for the job

It is possible to make minor repairs to your roof, but you should always have a helper and be safety-conscious when working at height.

HOW TO WORK SAFELY AT ROOF LEVEL

- Always have a helper to hand when you are working at a height. Ask them to steady the weight at the bottom of the ladder when you are carrying up heavy items.
- Have a safe place to put your tools. Fix a tray to a ladder or hold tools in a bag or pouch slung across your chest, or a tool belt.
- Wear a purpose-made safety harness with a tape attached to a firm point – such as a properly secured roof ladder.
- Lower debris to the ground in a stout sack or bucket attached to a rope. Take care not to drop anything; it could cause serious injury to someone below.

Roof ladder Never venture onto a roof without a purpose-made roof ladder fitted at one end with rubber wheels and a large hook. Using the wheels, you can push the ladder up the roof without dislodging slates or tiles. When the top of the ladder reaches the roof ridge, turn it over so that the hook lodges on the ridge securely. The ladder must reach all the way from the roof ridge to the gutter to allow you to transfer easily from the ordinary ladder on which you have climbed to gutter level. Extension pieces can be added to a roof ladder if necessary.
Hire a roof ladder rather than buy one; or buy the wheels-and-hook section for fitting onto a conventional ladder.

Plugging chisel The plugging chisel, also called a seam chisel, is designed to remove mortar from between bricks or pieces of masonry. It can be used when replacing flashing. The fluted face of the blade allows debris to be cleared quickly.

Slate cutter When the handles are squeezed together, the steel blades meet and shear off the edge of the slate. Useful for cutting an oversized slate to the right size.

Slate ripper The steel blade is about 280–380mm long. It is slipped under the tile or slate to be removed until one of the barbs of its arrow-shaped tip can be hooked round a nail that is driven into the roof batten. A sharp tug, or a hammer blow on the curve of the handle, jerks the barb down, and it cuts through the nail. The ripper is then moved to the other edge of the tile or slate to cut the second nail. Slate rippers can be hired.

Scaffold towers If you have to work all along the gutter, hire a scaffold tower with locking wheels, guard rail and a firm platform.

Tinsnips The scissor-action will cut through lead, zinc or other sheet metals used for roof valleys. Snips are made in several sizes – from 200–360mm long.

Soft-faced mallet A mallet with a head made of rubber, plastic or rawhide is used to tap sheet metal into shape – when renewing a valley, for example.

Ladders Always make sure that the ladder is set up at the correct angle: 1m away from the wall for every 4m up the wall.

The ladder or scaffold tower should be long enough or high enough to reach at least 600mm beyond the working point to avoid the need to stretch.

Fit a stand-off bracket to the top of a ladder to make sure it presses against the wall, not against an insecure gutter.

For extra security, you can screw an eye bolt into the fascia board and tie the ladder to it. Always move the ladder or scaffold tower along the wall to take you within easy reach of the working point. Never lean sideways to reach the work.

Choosing roof tiles

There are four important considerations when choosing roof tiles: the type of tile used on neighbouring or adjoining houses; the cost in relation to the appearance; the weight of new tiles on existing timbers; and the slope of the roof.

Tiles or slates? Roof tiles are made of concrete, or occasionally clay, in a range of red, brown, grey and greenish shades. Shapes are available to cover different parts of the roof (see below). Because slates are comparatively expensive, a deteriorating slate roof is often replaced with cheaper tiles. However, consider whether tiles will spoil the appearance of your house. In a terrace, for instance, it looks better if all the roofs are in the same material.

Simulated slates are much less expensive than real slates and may be a better option. Or you may be able to cut costs by finding secondhand slates from roofing companies or builders' merchants. Check that they are the right size, thickness and colour.

Tiles and many simulated slates are heavier than real slates, so the roof timbers may need strengthening. Ask a surveyor or builder for advice.

Roof pitch The pitch (slope) a tile needs varies with its profile and finish. Rainwater runs freely off a smooth finish, so smooth tiles need not be as sloped as grainy ones. Makers recommend a minimum angle of pitch for each style of tile that they make.

SINGLE LAP TILES

These are also known as interlocking tiles. Usually the tile surface undulates from side to side so that one or more channels run down the tile. Courses are overlapped, with the tiles in one course aligned exactly with the tiles in the courses above and below so that the channels run all down the roof slope. Each tile in a course interlocks with the tiles on both sides. A few styles have no channels.

Some styles of single lap tiles hang from the roofing battens on nibs with alternate courses nailed to the battens through holes at the top of the tiles. Others are fixed at the sides with aluminium-alloy tile clips which are nailed to the roofing battens.

There are no single lap bonnet hip tiles but some firms make trough valley tiles (rectangular valley tiles that are set below the level of the main foot tiles).

Full-size tiles are used for the top course and there is no underlayer at the eaves. Gaps left under the undulating profile at the ridge or hip of the roof are sealed with mortar or by purpose-made profile fillers.

Single lap tiles Most are 380–430mm long and 330mm wide. They are used with standard ridge and hip tiles.

Pantiles S-shaped tiles 381mm long and 227mm wide resemble the original clay tiles characteristic of some areas of the country. They are usually made of concrete now.

PLAIN TILES

The tile surface is slightly convex and there are two nibs behind the top edge to hook over the roofing battens. Nail holes allow every third or fourth course of tiles to be nailed in place for extra stability. Courses of plain tiles are staggered so each tile overlaps the gap between two tiles in the course below.

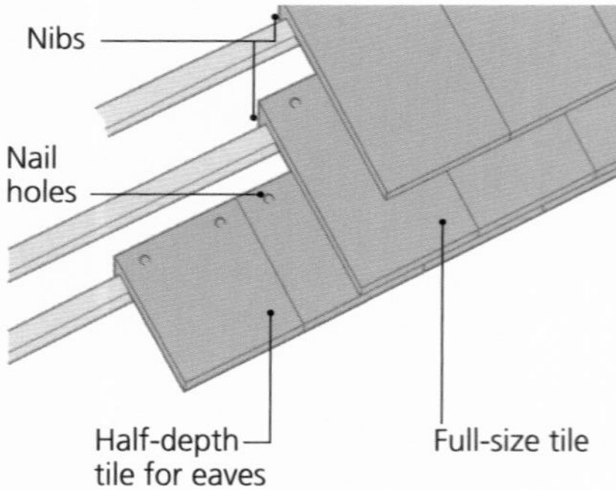

Half-depth tiles are made for the top course and for the under layer at the eaves. Half-width and one-and-a-half width tiles are made for starting and finishing courses at the gable ends.

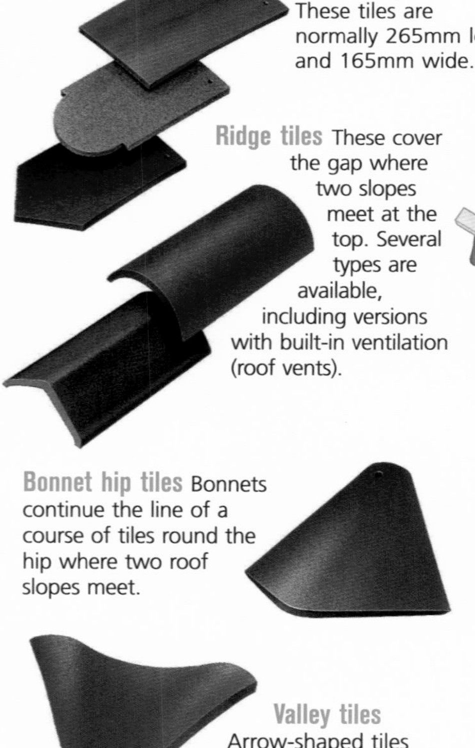

Standard plain tiles These tiles are normally 265mm long and 165mm wide.

Ridge tiles These cover the gap where two slopes meet at the top. Several types are available, including versions with built-in ventilation (roof vents).

Bonnet hip tiles Bonnets continue the line of a course of tiles round the hip where two roof slopes meet.

Valley tiles Arrow-shaped tiles bridge the gap where two roof slopes meet at an internal angle (called a valley).

(centre) nail hole

Traditional slates There are still some older houses roofed with traditional natural slates. These are nailed in place on the roof battens through holes cut in the slate on site, either in the centre or in the head of the slate. Buying new slates is expensive, but second-hand ones are available for replacements and there are many simulated or reconstituted slates available in the form of single lap tiles (also called interlocking tiles), and with 'deckled' edges so that the tiles look like slate.

Roof repairs

Missing or broken slates or tiles can quickly become a problem, allowing water to penetrate the roof space and wind to lift more of the neighbouring tiles. Act promptly to fix the problem.

Making a temporary repair to a cracked tile or slate

If rainwater is coming in through a cracked tile or slate and it is not possible to get a replacement immediately, you can use flashing strip to make a temporary repair to minimise the damage done by damp. Alternatively, bituminous sealant in an applicator gun seals a fine crack with very little work: prop up the surrounding tiles and brush the crack as for flashing strip, and then inject the sealant.

Tools *Ladder with a stand-off bracket; roof ladder; wooden wedges (see box, right); wire brush; paintbrush; sharp knife; old wallpaper seam roller.*

Materials *Flashing strip primer; self-adhesive flashing strip.*

1 Raise the one or two tiles or slates that overlap the cracked one, to give you better access. Prop them up with small wooden wedges (see right). Use the wire brush to clean the surface round the crack.

2 Brush a coat of flashing strip primer into and round the crack, making a strip as wide as the flashing strip. The primer ensures a good bond between tile or slate and flashing strip.

3 Cut a piece of flashing strip from the roll with a sharp knife. Make it long enough to cover the whole crack.

4 Press the strip into place and bed it down well. Run a small wallpaper seam roller to and fro over it to firm it down.

Replacing a broken plain tile

If you don't have a spare tile of the same size and style as the broken one, a builders' yard or salvage merchant may have one or be able to obtain one for you.

Before you start Beware of matching the replacement tile to the colour your tiles were when new. The tiles may have changed colour considerably, so try to match the replacement to the colour they are now. If you can't find a good match, 'steal' a tile from an unobtrusive place on the roof – such as a side porch. A tile near the end of the bottom course will be easy to reach. Put the poor match in its place.

Tools *Ladder with stand-off bracket; roof ladder; wooden wedges; large builder's trowel. Perhaps a slate ripper.*

Materials *Replacement tile.*

WEDGES TO PROP TILES UP

To prop up tiles you need to prepare two or more wedges from 20mm thick wood. Cut them 200mm long and make them taper from 30mm at one end to a point at the other.

1 Lift the two tiles that overlap the broken tile from the course above. Tap a wooden wedge under each to hold it up.

2 Slip the large builder's trowel under the broken tile. Lift up the whole tile until its nibs are clear of the batten and you can draw it out towards you.

Alternatively If the broken tile is one that has been nailed to the batten, try to free it by wiggling it from side to side until the nail breaks or comes away.

If this does not free it, you will have to use a slate ripper (page 387) to cut through the nails. Slate rippers can be hired.

3 Lay the replacement tile on the trowel and slide it up under the two wedged tiles until the nibs hook over the batten. There is no need to nail it, even if the original was nailed. Take out the wedges.

Replacing a group of plain tiles

If you need to replace a group of tiles and have no spares, buy replacements of the same size and style. See advice for a single tile, left.

Tools *Ladder with stand-off bracket; roof ladder; wooden wedges (above); large builder's trowel; claw hammer; bucket on a long rope. Perhaps a slate ripper.*

Materials *Replacement tiles; 40mm aluminium-alloy roofing nails.*

1 Lift the tiles in the course immediately above the highest ones to be replaced. Lift them two at a time and slide the wooden wedges under their outer edges to hold them up. This will allow you access to the tile they overlap in the course below.

2 As each tile is exposed, slide the trowel under it and lift it until its nibs clear the batten. Then draw it out. Lower it to the ground in the bucket.

If a tile is nailed to the batten, see-saw it from side to side to try to dislodge the nails. If you cannot, use a slate ripper (page 387) to cut through the nails.

3 Work along the top course of tiles to be removed and then along the course below that, and so on until all the tiles have been removed. Once the highest course of tiles has been removed, you can lift the others without using the wedges or the trowel.

4 Fit the replacement tiles onto the battens along the bottom course first. Hook each tile over the batten by its nibs and make sure that it is centred over the gap between the two tiles below it. Then work along the courses above.

5 Nail each tile in every third or fourth course to the batten with two nails.

6 To fit the top course, hold up the tiles in the course above in pairs with wedges. Work along the row, lifting each new tile on the trowel and sliding it into place.

Replacing broken single lap tiles

Tools *Ladder with a stand-off bracket; roof ladder; wooden wedges (page 389). Perhaps a slate ripper; hammer; bucket on a rope.*

Materials *Replacement tiles. Perhaps tile clips and 40mm roofing aluminium-alloy roofing nails.*

1 Slide up the tiles that overlap onto the broken tile. Alternatively, use wedges to raise the tiles to the left and right of the broken one, but in the course above.

2 To remove the broken tile, tilt it sideways to separate it from the tiles which are interlocked with it. You will be able to free it without disturbing them. Lever the tile upwards to release it from any clip that holds it to the batten. If the clip stays in place, the new tile may slip into it. If the clip is dislodged, there is no need to replace it; a few unclipped tiles will not matter. Sometimes alternate courses are nailed in place. If your repair is to a nailed tile, use a slate ripper to cut the nails before you remove the tile.

3 Lower the broken tile in a bucket on a rope to a helper on the ground.

4 To fit the replacement tile, slide it up into place. You will not be able to nail it or clip it. Pull back into place any tiles that you pushed out of place. Remove any wedges.

Replacing a group of tiles

Remove the highest tiles as for a single tile. Lower tiles simply need tilting to free them. Remove the clips wherever you can.

When replacing the tiles, fit the lowest course first and work from right to left.

Fit a clip for each tile wherever you are able to nail it to the batten.

Lodge the hook of the clip over the ridge at the side of the tile and hammer the nail through the hole in the clip into the top edge of the batten near the bottom edge of the tile you are fitting.

You can also nail alternate courses to the battens. The highest course cannot be nailed and the last tile of all cannot be fitted with a clip because the batten will be covered.

Making repairs to slate roofs

Slates will last a century or more, but the nails holding them to battens can corrode and break, allowing the slates to slip out of position.

Before you start The two problems most likely to affect a slate roof are nail-sickness and delamination. Corrosion, or nail-sickness, can affect a large area of a roof within a few years as the nails are the same age and corrode at the same rate. The slates can be re-nailed provided that they are sound.

A more serious problem is delamination, when the surface of the slate becomes flaky or powdery and you can see many cracks and splits. Replacement is the usual solution.

Fixing slates For fixing a group of replacement slates in several courses you can use 38mm aluminium-alloy or copper roofing nails.

If these are hard to find and you only have a small group of slates to nail into place, 40mm large-head galvanised clout nails will do.

When you are replacing single slates, you will not be able to nail them because the batten will be covered by the course of slates above. You can secure each slate with a strip of metal cut from lead, zinc, or copper that is thin enough to bend. It is fixed between the slates (see opposite).

Slates can also be fixed with adhesive expanding foam, which can be applied under a loose slate from outside, or (if the slate is visible) from inside the loft.

How to make holes New slates will not have fixing holes in them; you will have to make the holes.

A secondhand slate may have its holes in the wrong place and need drilling. Use the old slate as a pattern to mark drilling spots. The holes are usually about half-way down the sides.

Drill the holes with an electric drill fitted with a 4.5mm masonry bit; or make the hole by tapping a nail through the slate with steady, not-too-hard hammer blows.

Work from the underside, that is the side without the bevelled edges.

Replacing a broken slate

Slates may become cracked with age, or by someone clambering on the roof without using proper access equipment.

Before you start You may not be able to obtain a matching replacement slate immediately. If so, make a temporary repair to prevent water from penetrating. You can make it as for a tile (page 389).

Alternatively, you can coat the slate with mastic. Cover this with a piece of roofing felt or cooking foil cut to fit and spread another layer of mastic on top.

Replace the slate when you can obtain one that is a good match.

Tools *Ladder with a stand-off bracket; roof ladder; slate ripper; a bucket on a long rope; hammer or screwdriver. Perhaps a power drill fitted with No. 6 masonry bit, or nail and hammer.*

Materials *Replacement slate; strip of lead, zinc, aluminium or copper 25mm wide, and long enough to reach from the hole in the slate to the bottom plus 100mm; 40mm large-head galvanised clout nails.*

1 Cut through the nails that are holding the slate, using the slate ripper.

CUTTING A SLATE TO SIZE

Place the slate on a flat board and use a ceramic tile cutter and a metal rule to score a deep cutting line. To complete the cut, use a wide bolster chisel. Tap it along the scored line with gentle hammer blows. Or you can place the slate on a table with the scored line over the table edge and press down to break the slate cleanly.

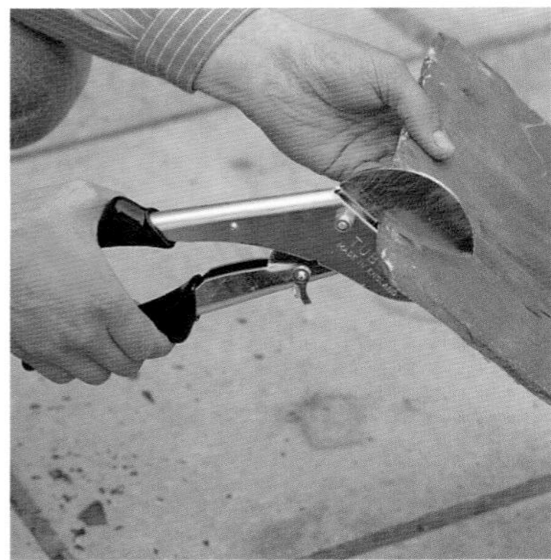

If you have many slates to cut, hire a slate cutter. Cut with the top surface of the slate downwards. On a second-hand slate in particular this ensures that weathering and cutting marks match the other slates.

Alternatively, you can hire an electric tile cutter.

2 Draw the slate towards you, wiggling it from side to side to ease it from under the slates overlapping it. Take care not to let any broken pieces slide off the roof. They are sharp and can cause damage or injury. Put the pieces in a bucket and take it to the ground or lower it down to a helper.

3 Nail the metal strip to the batten, which will just be visible in the gap between the two slates the replacement is going to lap onto. Put the nail in a ready-made hole about 25mm down from the top of the strip.

4 Carry the new slate up to the roof in a bucket or put it into a bucket and haul it up with a rope.

5 Slip the new slate, with bevelled edges upwards, under the two slates in the course above. Wiggle it a little to right and left to work it upwards until its lower edge aligns with the slates on each side. Its top edge should now be over the batten to which the course above is nailed.

6 Turn up the end of the metal strip over the lower edge of the slate, then bend it double and press it down flat against the slate. The double thickness prevents snow and ice from forcing the clip open.

Replacing a group of slates

You will be able to nail the lower courses of slates in place, but the top course and the course below that will have to be fixed with metal strips because the battens to which they should be nailed will be covered by slates (see Replacing a broken slate, facing page). If necessary, cut the slates to size and drill holes in them.

Tools *Ladder with a stand-off bracket; roof ladder; slate ripper; hammer; a bucket on a long rope; screwdriver.*

Materials *Replacement slates; 40mm aluminium-alloy or copper roofing nails; strips of lead, zinc, aluminium or copper 25mm wide and long enough to reach from the hole in the slate to the bottom plus 100mm.*

1 Cut through the nails securing the damaged slates, using a slate ripper. Deal first with the highest course to be removed. Ease each slate out in turn from the overlapping slates and lower it in a bucket to a helper or take it to the ground. Do not let a slate slide from the roof; it is sharp and can cause damage or injury.

Work down course by course, removing the slates. The lower ones will not be overlapped and are easier to remove.

2 Fix the bottom course of replacement slates first. Butt neighbouring slates closely and fit them with the bevelled edges upwards. Nail the slates through the holes to the batten.

3 Work upwards, course by course, nailing the slates in place. When you can no longer see the battens to nail the slates to, cut metal strips to secure the slates and fit them as described in Replacing a broken slate (left).

Replacing ridge, hip and bonnet tiles

Both tiled and slate roofs have the gaps at the ridge and hips covered by specially designed tiles. The tiles are most often curved, but may be angled.

Replacing a bonnet hip tile

Some tiled roofs have bonnet hip tiles to cover the gap at the hip (page 388).

Bonnet hip tiles are nailed to the hip timber as well as being bedded in mortar.

1 Remove a bonnet hip tile by chipping away the mortar above and below it with a cold chisel and club hammer and then sliding a slate ripper under the tile and giving a sharp hammer blow on the handle to cut through the nail. You can then draw out the tile towards you.

If you are removing several tiles down the hip, start at the highest one and work downwards. Clean the tiles of old mortar.

2 Brush away all dust from around the repair, then brush the area with water and with PVA adhesive.

3 If you are replacing a single tile, spread mortar to bed it on. Spread mortar also under the bonnet in the course above. Set the bonnet in place and tap it into alignment with the other tiles in the course before you smooth the mortar and clean away any excess.

4 If you are replacing several bonnets, work from the bottom upwards. Nail each, except the top one, to the timber with an aluminium nail after you have set it on the mortar. Then smooth the mortar and clean away any excess.

Replacing ridge or hip tiles

The most common problem at the roof ridge or hip is that the mortar between tiles cracks and crumbles away. Sometimes a tile may then be pushed out of place by a build-up of ice, or occasionally by strong winds. If you spot cracks early, while they are narrow, you can fill them with roof-and-gutter sealant. There are coloured sealants which make the repair scarcely noticeable.

If the mortar is crumbling or the tile itself has cracked, you will have to remove the tile and re-fix it or put a new one in its place. If it is the end ridge tile that needs a repair, you must seal up the opening left at the end. Use small pieces of slate or tile bedded in mortar. If the main roof tiles are S-shaped there will be a hollow to seal where the ridge or hip tile meets them.

Tools *Ladder with a stand-off bracket; roof ladder; cold chisel; club hammer; brush; paintbrush; small builder's trowel.*

Materials *Dry mortar mix, or cement and sharp sand; PVA adhesive; bucket of water. Perhaps replacement tiles, narrow pieces of tile or slate.*

1 With the chisel and hammer, carefully chip away all cracked or crumbling mortar until the ridge or hip tile is freed and you can lift it off. Make sure that any surrounding mortar you leave in place is sound. Clean the tile.

2 Prepare the mortar (page 466) from a bag of dry mixed material or make your own from one part cement to four parts sharp sand. To improve adhesion, add some PVA adhesive to the water, following the manufacturer's instructions. Do not make the mortar too wet; a firmer mix is easier to work with. Mix enough to half-fill a bucket.

3 Brush all dust away from the area round the repair.

4 Use the paintbrush and water to wet the roof and the existing mortar round the repair. This is especially necessary on a hot day when the mortar would lose its moisture too quickly and crack.

5 Brush PVA adhesive liberally all round the area of the repair to ensure good adhesion between the roof tiles at the ridge or hip and the ridge or hip tile itself.

6 Use the trowel to spread mortar on the roof on both sides of the ridge or hip. Cover the areas where the bottom edges of the tile to be fixed will lie.

Do not use too much mortar; there must be a gap under the ridge or hip tiles so that air can circulate to keep the timber below dry. If you lay too much mortar on the tiles, it could squeeze into the gap and fill it in when you are setting the ridge or hip tile into place.

7 The butt joints where two of the ridge or hip tiles meet can either be pointed with mortar or given a solid bedding of mortar. It is probably best to follow the method already used on the roof.

If you make a solid bedding, place a piece of slate or tile across the gap between the two sides of the ridge or hip to prevent mortar falling through.

8 Ridge or hip tiles must be dipped in water before they are set in place. Do this before you go up on the roof. Settle the tile on the mortar carefully so that it makes a smooth line with the neighbouring tiles.

Alternatively If the roof tiles have a curved profile, fill the gap between the down-curve and the ridge or hip tiles with pieces of tile or slate embedded in mortar.

Specially designed 'dentil slips' can be bought for this purpose.

9 Smooth the mortar between tiles and along the bottom edges. There must be no hollows in the mortar between the tiles because they could retain small pockets of rainwater.

10 If the re-fixed tile is at an end of the roof ridge, seal the open end with thin slips of tile or slate bedded in mortar. Smooth the end so that rainwater will flow off readily.

11 If you have been replacing the lowest tile on the hip, make sure the protecting hip iron has not been dislodged; remake its fixings if necessary. Then fill the end of the tile with mortar.

Repairs to verges

A roof with only two main slopes is usually sealed with mortar where the slopes meet the gable ends of the house – these are the verges.

Before you start You can seal any minor cracks in the mortar with roof-and-gutter sealant injected with an applicator gun (page 400).

If you choose a sealant to match the mortar, the repair will not be noticeable. For larger cracks you will have to make the repair with mortar.

Tools *Ladder with a stand-off bracket; cold chisel; club hammer; brush; paintbrush; small trowel.*

Materials *Dry mortar mix, or cement and sharp sand; PVA adhesive; bucket of water. Perhaps narrow slips of tile.*

1 With the chisel and hammer, chip away all cracked and crumbling mortar, leaving only sound mortar in place.

2 Prepare the mortar (page 466) from a bag of dry mixed material or from one part cement to four parts sharp sand. To improve adhesion, add PVA adhesive to the water, following the manufacturer's instructions. Avoid making the mixture too wet. Make enough mortar to half-fill a bucket.

3 Brush all dust away, then dampen the area with some water using a paintbrush before brushing on a covering of PVA adhesive.

4 Use the trowel to press the mortar firmly into the areas that have been prepared. Knock it in with the side of the trowel to make sure that there are no pockets of air in it.

5 Smooth the surface of the mortar and clean away any excess. Do not leave any ledges or hollows in the mortar that could retain rainwater.

Repairs to metal valleys

Where two roof slopes meet at the bottom, the long narrow gap between them is sealed – frequently by a tray of aluminium alloy, lead or zinc. This metal valley is overlapped by the tiles or slates, which drain rainwater into it to be carried down to the gutters at the eaves.

Since valleys are likely to carry a gushing stream of water in heavy rain, they must be kept waterproof and clear of obstructions. If moss, leaves or other debris accumulates, rainwater will build up at the obstruction and spill over the edges of the valley onto the timbers and into the roof space.

If a metal valley has developed a fine crack or is showing the first signs of corrosion, it can be repaired with a liquid bitumen compound. Liquid bitumen can also be used to make a temporary repair if you are waiting for a convenient time to replace the valley.

Holes or splits in a metal valley can be covered with a self-adhesive metal-backed flashing strip. If slight corrosion has set in over a large area, flashing strip can be used to cover the entire valley.

Repairing with liquid bitumen

Stir the waterproofing compound before you apply it. You can use it on a damp, but not wet, surface. Do not use it, however, if rain or frost are expected within about 24 hours.

Tools *Ladder with a stand-off bracket; roof ladder; wire brush; a spreader for the roof-and-gutter sealant; sharp knife or scissors; soft brush or broom.*

Materials *Roof-and-gutter sealant; roofing felt or cooking foil; liquid bitumen waterproofing compound; bucket of water.*

1 Use the wire brush to clean away dirt and loose metal fragments from the area of the valley that is going to be repaired.

2 Spread roof-and-gutter sealant over the damaged area and at least 50mm beyond it.

3 Cut out a piece of roofing felt or cooking foil to cover the damage and extend at least 50mm beyond it. Press the felt or foil down over the sealant.

4 Spread another layer of sealant on top of the felt or foil.

5 Brush the liquid bitumen waterproofing compound over the repair. As a precaution against leaks, you can brush it over the whole valley. Apply it with a soft brush or broom, dipping the brush in water and shaking it each time before you load it with the waterproofer. Brush the compound on with even strokes, working in the same direction all the time. Throw the brush away when you have finished.

Making repairs with flashing strip

Tools *Ladder with a stand-off bracket; roof ladder; wire brush; damp cloth; paintbrush; sharp knife or strong scissors; old wallpaper seam roller.*

Materials *Medium-coarse abrasive paper; flashing-strip primer; self-adhesive metal-backed flashing strip.*

1 Use the wire brush to clean away dirt and loose metal fragments from round the crack or hole.

2 Rub over the area with the abrasive paper.

3 Wipe the surface clean with the damp cloth and allow it to dry completely.

4 Use the paintbrush to apply a coat of flashing-strip primer to the area of the repair, extending it at least 50mm beyond the damage. Leave it to dry for the time recommended by the manufacturer – usually about 30 minutes.

5 Cut out a piece of flashing strip to extend at least 50mm beyond the crack or hole all round. Cut it with a knife or pair of scissors, then peel off the backing.

6 Press the flashing strip firmly into position, using the wallpaper seam roller to bed it down smoothly.

Repairs to flashings

Where a tile or slate roof meets a wall, there is a flashing to seal the join – for example at the meeting of a roof with a chimney stack and the meeting of a bay window or porch roof with the house wall.

Flashings fitted when the house is built are usually strips of lead which can deteriorate with age. Depending on the extent of the deterioration, it may not be necessary to replace the flashing. Small repairs are quite easily achieved.

Fine cracks To repair a fine crack, inject some bituminous sealant or other roof-and-gutter sealant into it with an applicator gun and cartridge. Some sealants are available in different colours so you can choose one that will make the repair less noticeable.

Small holes or slight corrosion A patch of self-adhesive flashing strip will make a sound repair over a small hole or where there are the first signs of corrosion.

Use the method described for a roof valley under Making repairs with flashing strip (page 393).

Renewing flashing mortar The top edge of a flashing is sandwiched into the mortar between two courses of bricks. Sometimes it works loose and lets in water.

Repoint the joint (page 408), but first push the edge of the flashing back into the gap between courses of bricks.

If the flashing springs out, wedge it with blocks of wood until the pointing has hardened. Then withdraw the blocks and fill the holes with mortar.

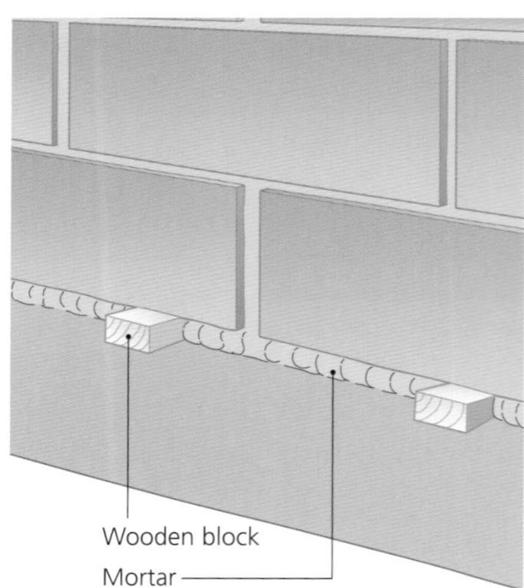

Replacing a flashing

If a flashing is badly cracked or corroded, replace it with a self-adhesive metal-backed flashing strip. Unlike lead flashing, adhesive flashing is not tucked into the mortar joints.

Tools *Ladder with a stand-off bracket; roof ladder; plugging chisel and club hammer; pointing trowel; wire brush; paintbrush; sharp craft knife; old wallpaper seam roller.*

Materials *Mortar for repointing (page 466); flashing-strip primer; self-adhesive metal-backed flashing-strip.*

1 Chip out any mortar that is still holding the flashing in the joints between bricks or masonry. Use the plugging chisel and hammer. Protect your hands and eyes.

2 Strip away the old flashing.

3 Use the wire brush to clean away loose mortar and dirt from the area to be repaired.

4 Repoint the joints between the courses of bricks or masonry (page 408). Let the new pointing dry out overnight.

5 Paint a coat of flashing primer on the wall (or chimney) and roof where the strip is to go. Let it dry for 30 minutes to an hour, according to the manufacturer's instructions.

6 Cut two lengths of flashing strip, each the full length of the area to be sealed.

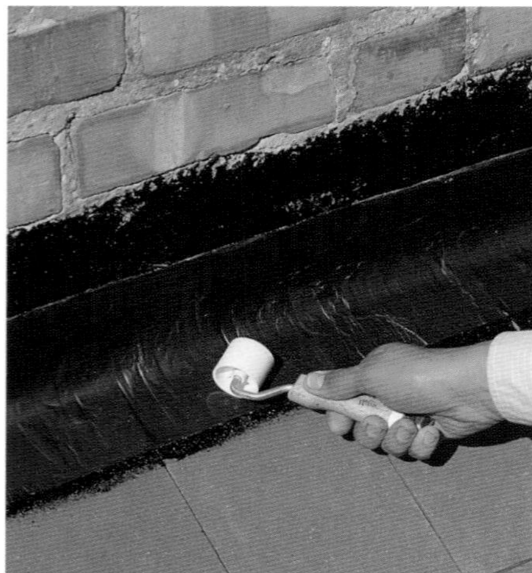

7 Peel off the backing of the first strip and put the strip in position, letting the width lie equally on the roof and the wall (or chimney stack). Roll the strip with the wallpaper seam roller to smooth it out and ensure that it is well stuck.

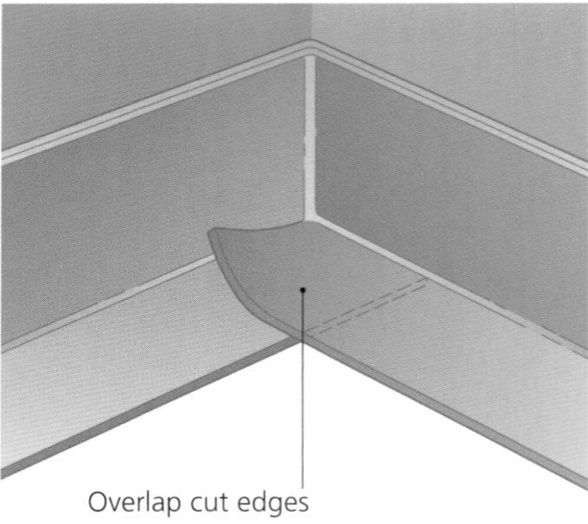

8 At internal corners, make a snip in the lower edge of the strip and overlap the cut edges.

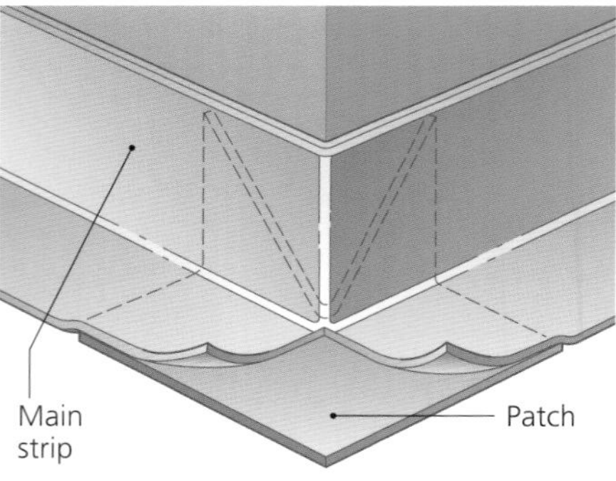

9 At external corners, fit a square patch before the main strip; make a cut from one corner of the patch to the middle. Set the patch with the centre at the point where the wall angle meets the roof and the cut running upwards. Let the cut edges splay out round the angle. In the main strip make a cut in the bottom edge and let the cut edges splay apart over the patch. Trim off any excess at the points.

10 Peel the backing off the second strip and apply it so that its top edge is 50mm above the top edge of the first layer. Treat any corners as in the first strip. Again smooth the strip out and bed it down well with the wallpaper seam roller.

HOW A FLAT ROOF WITH APRONS IS MADE

1 Timber deck Flat roofs on house extensions or garages are usually made by nailing planks of tongued-and-grooved softwood or sheets of exterior grade plywood, chipboard or strawboard to the roof joists and covering them with three layers of roofing felt.

2 Drip batten Along the top edge of the fascia at the gutter end there is a drip batten that holds the apron away from the board, so that any drips of water fall into the gutter.

3 Aprons Edges of the roof that do not meet a house wall are sealed with strips of felt taken over the fascia board. These strips are called aprons and are designed to keep the fascia dry.

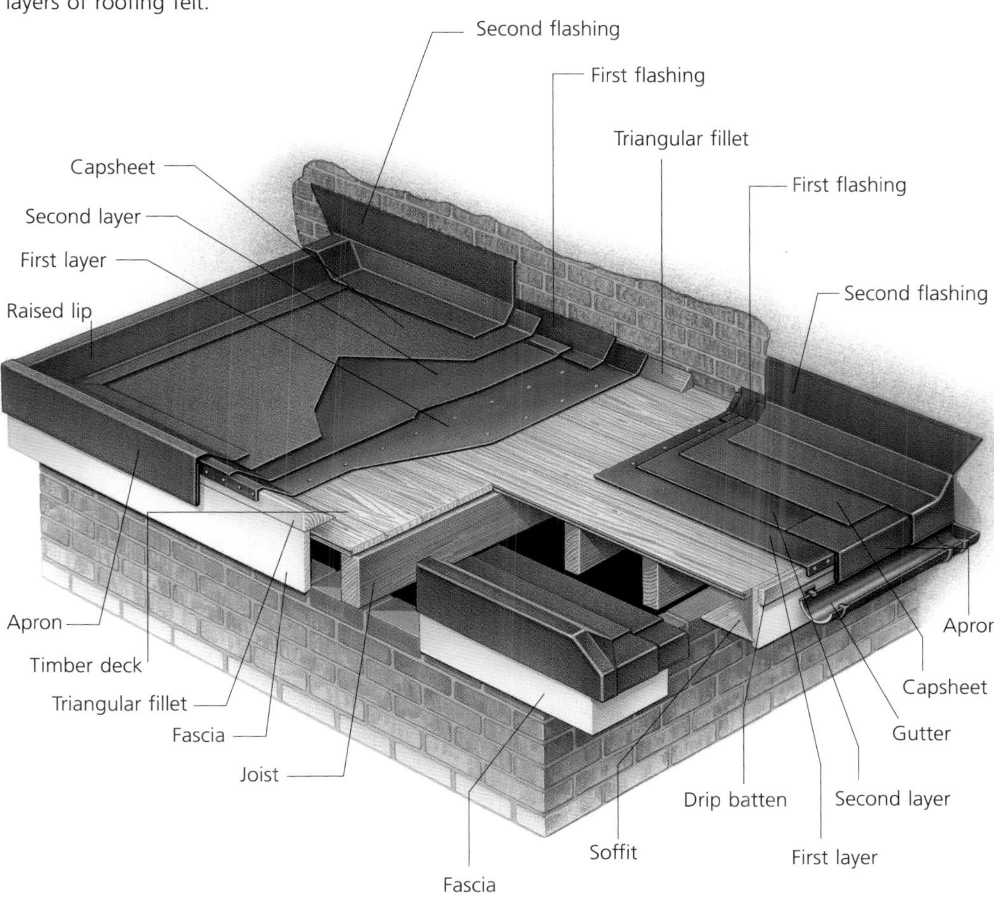

4 Gutter edge The roof has a slight fall to drain water into a gutter along one edge. The other edges should have a fillet sloping up to a raised lip so that water cannot spill off.

5 Flashing If the roof meets the house walls, there is a flashing at the join.

6 Chippings In a sunny place, the felt may be spread with chippings of limestone, granite, gravel or flint over a chipping compound. The chippings are to keep direct sun off the felt, and are not necessary in shade.

Choosing materials for a flat roof or shed

Garages and home extensions often have felted flat roofs. Felted roofs, also found on many timber garages and garden sheds, need repairing or replacing from time to time. Roofing felt is generally sold in rolls 1m wide and 10m long. Modern polyester and glass fibre felts last longer than traditional fibre-based bituminous felts. Repair products range from simple patch repair mastics to whole roof treatments that can last 20 years or more.

Roofing felt

Fibre-based roofing felt For roofs of timber garages and garden sheds; use alone or with underlay; secure with roofing nails and roofing-felt adhesive.

Polyester/glass fibre roofing felt For roofs of extensions and garages, or on sheds for longer life; combine with underlay for two-layer or three-layer system; use cold adhesive or hot bitumen.

Torch-on roofing felt For roofs of extensions and garages; use as single remedial layer or two-layer with underlay; applied by professionals with a gas torch.

Roof treatments

Aluminium paint Apply to any felted roof to reduce degradation by sunlight.

Chippings of limestone, granite, gravel or flint For flat roofs in sunny positions; sprinkle over roof surface.

Liquid rubber/elastomeric waterproofing emulsion For flat roofs covered with asphalt, asbestos or corrugated iron; use alone or with primer, according to manufacturer's instructions; brush on.

Roof repair

Bitumen waterproofing solution For repairs to felted roofs; use alone or with reinforcing mesh; brush on.

Acrylic coating For isolated repairs or whole roof cover; use brush or roller.

Repair bitumen mastic For localised repair on felted or flat roofs; trowel on wet or dry roof (aerosol also available).

Roof-and-gutter sealant Repairs cracks in flashing, felt, asphalt or guttering; applied from cartridge gun or with a filling knife.

Roof-and-gutter repair tape Repairs cracks in flashing, felt, asphalt or guttering; self-adhesive – press on.

Self-adhesive flashing Repairs cracks in flashing, felt, asphalt or guttering; use alone or with special primer; self-adhesive – press on.

Minor repairs to flat roofs

Small blisters or cracks are the most common minor defects in felt-covered flat roofs.

Before you start Scrape off any chippings carefully with an old wallpaper scraper. You can repair small blisters or cracks with a roof-and-gutter sealant (below), with self-adhesive flashing strip (see Making a temporary repair to a cracked tile or slate, page 389), or with brush-on liquid rubber (right). Repair damaged flashings as described on page 394.

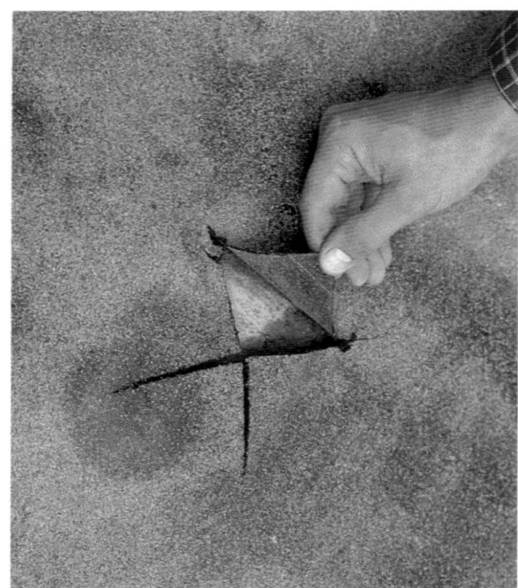

Curing bubbles A bubble may form in the felt where moisture has seeped under it and swollen in the heat of the sun. Cut a cross in the blister with a sharp knife and fold back the four flaps of felt.

Let them dry, then stick them down with a cold felt adhesive before patching the damaged area with a piece of self-adhesive flashing strip or a bitumen mastic repair compound.

Replace any roof chippings when the repairs are complete.

Bituminous sealant Apply sealant from an applicator gun to mend small cracks in roofing felt and roof tiles.

Repairing a cracked flashing

Changes in temperature and normal house movement put the flashings under stress and may cause cracks where water can seep in. The resulting wet patch indoors, however, can be several feet away from the crack because the water may run along the roof beams before dripping onto the ceiling. The crack may be difficult to spot. When you have located it, repair it with self-adhesive flashing strip (see Making repairs with flashing strip, page 393).

Repairing a hole or crack with liquid rubber

If cracks develop on a flat roof that is covered with felt or asphalt, treat the whole area with brush-on liquid rubber.

Calculate the area of the roof in square metres and buy the amount of liquid rubber recommended by the manufacturer. Liquid rubber is sold in containers ranging from 1kg to 20kg.

Tools *Ladder; stiff brush and shovel; an old 100mm paintbrush or a small broom for the liquid rubber. Perhaps a paintbrush for primer.*

Materials *Liquid rubber. Perhaps primer for liquid rubber.*

1 Use the stiff brush and shovel to clear the area of loose chippings and dirt.

2 If the area has previously been treated with a tar-bitumen coating – which gives a black, slightly rough covering – brush on a coat of primer for liquid rubber. Leave it to dry overnight.

3 Brush on a coat of liquid rubber, using all the recommended amount for the area. Leave it to dry thoroughly for 48 hours. After an hour it will be sufficiently dry not to be affected by rain.

4 Brush on a second coat of rubber, using the same amount as before.

A replacement flashing

If the flashing has cracked or corroded so much that an adhesive patch may not be able to make firm contact all over the damaged area, strip away all the flashing and plan to replace it with self-adhesive flashing strip as described in Replacing a flashing (page 394).

Seal the joint between roof and parapet (or house wall) with roof-and-gutter sealant before you apply the primer.

If your parapet is only one course of brickwork or masonry high, let the second layer of flashing overlap onto the top.

HIGH-LEVEL SAFETY

No matter how small the task, any DIY work done on a roof carries an element of danger.

- If you are working on a roof, make sure the ladder you use is securely supported. If possible have a helper with you to keep the ladder steady; if this is impossible, secure the ladder to the roof or to the building (page 387).
- Never lean over to reach a patch of roof – move the ladder, instead.

Re-covering a parapet roof with reinforced bitumen

A reinforced bitumen covering consists of a layer of open-meshed reinforcing fabric between layers of a liquid-bitumen waterproofing solution. Both are sold by builders' merchants.

Before you start When estimating how much you will need, remember that there is no need to overlap the strips. Wear old shoes which you can throw away when you have finished, or Wellington boots which can remain dirty. When leaving the roof, change into clean shoes at the parapet, before stepping onto the ladder.

Tools *Ladder; stiff brush and shovel; filling knife; paintbrush; sharp knife; wallpaper seam roller; soft broom or large cheap paintbrush for the liquid bitumen.*

Materials *Roof-and-gutter sealant; flashing strip primer; self adhesive flashing strip; bitumen solution; reinforcing fabric, such as Aquaseal glass-fibre membrane.*

1 Brush the surface clean of any loose dirt and debris.

2 Press roof-and-gutter sealant into any cracks or holes, using a filling knife to force it well in.

3 Apply a coat of flashing-strip primer to a 150mm strip at the roof edge and a similar strip of the parapet or house wall adjoining. Let it dry for 30 minutes to an hour.

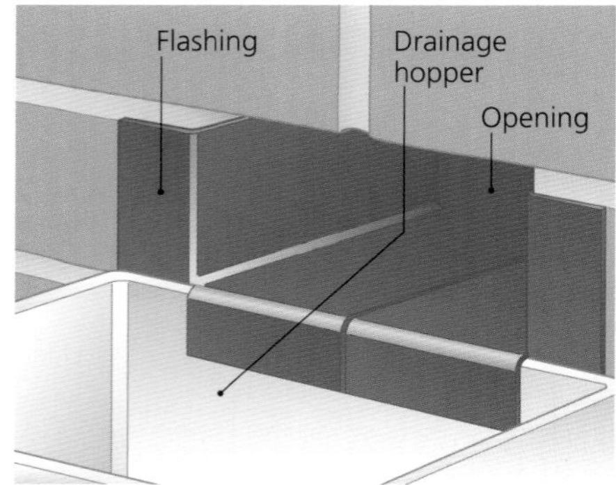

4 Cut and fit lengths of flashing strip as described in Replacing a flashing (page 394). Continue the flashing round the sides of the opening for the drainage hopper and let it lap onto the surface of the brick or stonework. Fit a patch under the external angles as shown on page 394.

5 Cut strips of reinforcing fabric to length, allowing for them to extend 150mm up the wall at each edge. Do not lay them yet.

6 Apply a coat of liquid-bitumen waterproofing solution to the roof using a soft broom or paintbrush. The coat should be applied about 150mm up any walls that enclose the roof as well and should cover the whole flat surface and the opening to the hopper.

7 Leave for a few minutes, until the surface is tacky. Then lay the fabric strips side by side over the whole flat area and to the top of the tacky rim round all the walls. At the corners of the parapet fold the excess fabric into a neat pleat and press it flat.

8 Brush a second coat of the liquid bitumen waterproofing solution over the whole area. Apply the solution generously, especially at the parapet corners, so that you avoid dislodging the reinforcing fabric as much as possible. Then leave the surface to dry. After about two hours the roof should be dry enough not to be harmed by rain.

9 Brush a final coat of the liquid bitumen waterproofing solution all over the flat area and 150mm up the enclosing walls.

HOW A PARAPET FLAT ROOF IS MADE

Where a flat roof is the main house roof, it is usually of the parapet type. A parapet roof may also be given to a one or two-storey extension or to a detached garage, as an alternative to the more usual flat roof with aprons (page 395).

Repairs Eventually, cracks may develop in the asphalt or felt covering. You can repair minor damage as described on the facing page. If the roof lets in water in several spots, it is wisest to re-cover the whole area to prevent further damage to the roof timbers or to the rooms below. Layers of rubberised liquid bitumen reinforced with a mesh fabric will make a strong new cover over both the unsound surface and the flashings (see Re-covering a flat roof with reinforced bitumen, opposite).

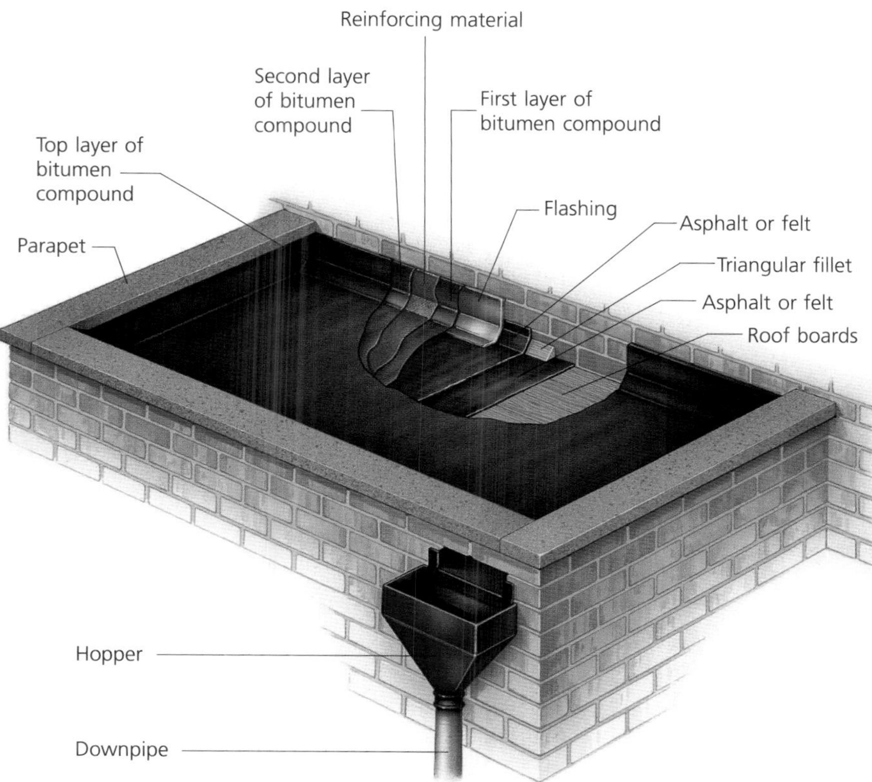

Raised edges
In a parapet flat roof, the walls continue above the roof level. The parapet may be only one course of brickwork or masonry or it may be several courses.

Wooden deck
The flat area consists of softwood planks or sheets of outdoor-grade plywood or chipboard nailed to roof beams and covered with asphalt or roofing felt.

Drainage
The roof usually has a slight fall towards an opening in one side with a drainage hopper outside it connected to a downpipe that carries away rainwater. The drainage hole to the hopper must be kept clear of leaves or rubbish that could block it.

Flashing
Where the roof meets the house wall or parapet there is a triangular wooden fillet and a flashing of lead, zinc, aluminium or felt. A cracked or displaced flashing is a frequent source of trouble.

Mending a corrugated plastic roof

A corrugated plastic roof is ideal where extra light is required, but it can become brittle and need repairing.

Before you start Measure the profile of the existing plastic on the roof before you go to buy new sheeting. The sheets may have a round or a box profile and the difference between the lowest and highest points of the profile can vary from 38 to 150mm.

If the new plastic does not exactly match the old in profile, it will not make snug overlaps. The length of the screws you use must be the difference between the low and high points of the profile plus at least 25mm to penetrate the wood.

To reduce the cost of the repair, you can fit a patch. However, the patch will have to be the width of a full sheet and extend over a roof timber at top and bottom to be screwed in place.

Temporary repairs to a corrugated plastic roof can be made using clear waterproof tape. Ensure surfaces are clean and dry before pressing the tape into place.

Tools *Sharp knife; tack lifter; screwdriver; fine-toothed saw; hand drill with blunt twist bit, or electric soldering iron with 5mm bit; steel measuring tape.*

Materials *Enough corrugated plastic sheeting to make the repair with adequate overlaps; 4mm galvanised screws of appropriate length; protective screw caps; transparent waterproof glazing tape.*

Fitting a patch

1 Use a felt pen to mark cutting lines on the damaged panel showing the area for removal. Make the top line just below a timber support and the bottom line just above a timber support.

2 Prise off the screw caps with the tack lifter and take out all the screws that were securing the panel. Carefully remove the whole panel.

3 Cut the patch to overlap the guidelines on the old panel by 75mm at top and bottom. Then cut along the guidelines on the old panel to remove the damaged part. Hold the saw at a shallow angle and support the sheet on both sides of the cut. If you have to cut to the sheet to width, cut along the valleys of the sheeting.

4 Lay the plastic for the bottom of the slope in place first. Make screw holes through the peaks that are over timbers. Make the holes at intervals of about 450mm across the panel immediately above the cross timbers. You can melt the holes with a fine soldering iron, start them with a bradawl, or use a blunt bit in a drill. Drive in the screws across the bottom edge. Do not overtighten.

5 Lay the next piece of plastic up the slope; let its bottom edge overlap 75mm onto the piece below.

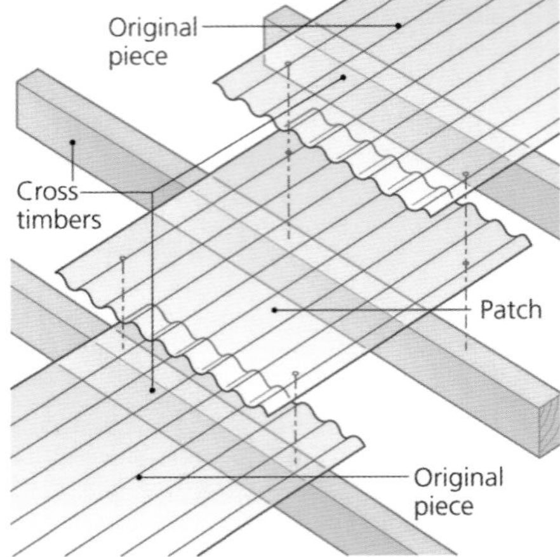

6 Drill screw holes through peaks on the overlap at 450mm intervals. Drive screws through into the timbers but do not overtighten them.

7 Lay the top piece of plastic sheet in place overlapping the previous piece by 75mm.

8 Drill and screw the bottom edge as for the previous piece.

9 Drill holes if necessary at the top edge and screw it in place.

10 Push caps on all the screws.

11 Fit new flashing strip (page 394) where the plastic sheet meets the wall. Press it down well into the valleys.

12 Seal the edges where the layers of plastic sheeting overlap at the sides with strips of the glazing tape.

HELPFUL TIPS

Overlaps at the sides should finish in a 'valley' of the corrugation, not a 'peak'. This prevents water from entering at an overlap. If you are renewing a complete panel on the roof, allow the same overlaps as on the rest of the roof.

Cut sheets to size indoors in cold weather. Plastic becomes brittle in low temperatures and could crack.

Do not walk on the roof. Kneel on scaffold boards secured with sandbags so that they will not slide.

Fitting a whole panel

1 Cut away any flashing at the top of the damaged panel.

2 Prise off the screw caps with the tack lifter and take out all the screws that were securing the panel, then remove the panel.

3 Cut the new panel if necessary to match the length of the old one. Keep the saw at a shallow angle and take care to support the sheet on both sides of the cut. If you have to cut to the sheet to width, cut along valleys.

4 Place the new panel in position on the roof, overlapping onto the old ones at either side. If there is another panel above or below the new one, make sure that the bottom edge of the panel higher up the slope laps onto the panel below.

5 Make screw holes across the bottom if necessary. Make the holes at intervals of about 450mm across the panel immediately above the cross timbers. Melt the holes with a fine soldering iron, start them with a bradawl, or use a blunt bit in a drill.

6 Drive in the screws; do not over tighten them or the plastic may split.

7 When the screws are fixed, push on screw caps. They will click into place.

8 Fit a new flashing strip (page 394) and press it down well into the valleys.

9 Seal the edges where the layers overlap with transparent waterproof glazing tape.

What can go wrong with the house exterior

Cladding Timber cladding, which forms part of an exterior wall, must be protected by preservative or paint if it is not to be affected by damp, otherwise wet rot may set in (page 246–7). Plastic cladding is not affected by damp but gaps surrounding the cladding must be tightly sealed. Follow the same procedure as for sealing gaps round window frames (page 204).

External walls Rain beating upon an external wall will be partially absorbed. Water from a dripping overflow pipe may splash onto a wall.

Faults in a damp-proof course may allow water to rise from the ground and soak the wall. To install a damp-proof course, see page 411. Soil heaped over a damp-proof course can also cause damp.

Defective pointing will allow water to penetrate the outer leaf (the outer skin of bricks). For repointing, see page 408.

Excessive damp in an external wall should be dealt with as soon as possible before it can damage the interior. You can usually see the damp patch because the wet brickwork or masonry is a different colour from the dry parts.

Window and door frames Make sure there are no gaps around window and door frames (page 204). If rain soaks between the masonry and the frame, rot may set into the timber and must be removed (pages 412–13). Maintain the paintwork also (page 414–15) to prevent rot.

Renderings Cracks and gaps in a rendered surface may allow damp to penetrate and be held in the wall. In extreme cases, this can lead to blisters which must be cut away before the rendering is repaired. For repairing cracks, and patching rendering, see pages 408–9.

Brick walls Facing brick naturally absorbs a certain amount of rainwater, which penetrates partly into the wall. When the weather dries up, the moisture evaporates and no harm is done. In older houses, some bricks may have become over porous so that they do not dry completely. This could lead to efflorescence or 'spalling' (see page 408 for details).

Gutters A gutter may leak at the joints between sections; it may become blocked and overflow; or it may sag so that water does not run away properly. In each case water may soak into the wall and penetrate to the inside, causing damp and damage to the decoration. Even on a cavity wall, water may find a way from the outer to the inner leaf of brickwork.

Cast-iron gutter sections are usually sealed with putty at joints and bolted together. The putty may disintegrate in time and, in extreme cases, bolts may rust and drop out. A plastic gutter may leak because the clip which seals two sections together has become loose, or because the neoprene gasket has perished, or because the gutter has an incorrect fall, and water spills over.

Sometimes screws holding gutter brackets to the fascia board rust away or the fascia board itself might rot, causing the brackets to move and the gutter sections to sag. For cleaning, aligning and repairing roof gutters, see pages 400–401.

Downpipes The most common problem with downpipes is that they become blocked – and if they (or the gutters leading to them) overflow or leak, damp may start in the walls.

Most downpipes first get blocked at the top and then are often obstructed farther down as the blockage sinks down the pipe under pressure of rain. For clearing blockages, see page 402.

Cast-iron pipes may crack if damp material stuck inside freezes. When they thaw the pipes can crack and the leaks may cause damage.

Cavity walls Problems arise with cavity walls when the wall ties which link the outer and inner leaves are bridged by a mortar dropped during construction of the house. It acts as a wick, carrying moisture across the cavity to the interior wall. Cavity walls should be free of all damp before you have the cavity insulated.

Treating the external face of the wall with a silicone water repellent will cure the damp.

Mortar between bricks may become highly porous and carry water into the wall. This fault often becomes apparent after a freeze – as the water expands, it breaks up the mortar, which will crumble and fall out of joints. For how to repair the damage, see page 408.

Re-aligning a gutter

If water forms a pool, even in a cleaned gutter, instead of running away to the downpipe, the fixing screw holding the support bracket or the gutter itself at that point may be loose.

Remove the screw, tap a wall plug into the screw hole and re-screw the bracket or gutter with a new zinc-plated screw. If, when you check, you find that no screws are loose, or conversely that several are loose, the fall of the gutter may need correcting. You may have to remove a section of gutter to reach the screws.

Tools *Ladder with a stand-off bracket; hammer; screwdriver; drill with wood bit or high-speed-steel bit, or both.*

Materials *Wall plugs; zinc-plated 4mm or 5mm screws; two or more 150mm nails; string and nails.*

1 Drive a long, strong nail into the fascia board near each end of the loose section of gutter, immediately below it, to support it. If the loose section is longer than 2m or the gutter is iron, drive in more nails to give it sufficient support.

2 Remove the screws that hold the gutter or its supporting brackets.

3 Fix a string line along the length of the fascia board as described in Replacing cast-iron guttering with plastic (page 404–5), but put it immediately under the guttering. Give it a fall towards the downpipe of 15–20mm in every 3m.

4 If the gutter is on brackets, as most gutters are, unscrew those that are letting the gutter sag and move them left or right slightly to new positions so that you can screw into solid wood; make sure the new screw positions align with the string line to give the correct fall.

Alternatively If the gutter is screwed direct to the fascia, raise it to align correctly with the string line and drill new holes through the gutter and into the fascia, about 50mm to the side of the original holes. Refit the gutter using new zinc-plated screws.

Alternatively If the screws through the gutter have been driven into the ends of the roof rafters, not into a fascia board, fix a string line and adjust the position of the screws to bring the gutter to the correct fall. You may have to remove a tile or slate temporarily so that you can reach the screws (pages 389 and 391).

Treating rusted gutters

Treat rust as soon as you are aware of its presence. The longer it is left, the more damage will be done and the greater the size of the repair job.

Before you start Make sure you have safety goggles to protect your eyes from flying particles when removing rust. Do not rub the metal too vigorously – it does not have to shine – just remove the rust. If the inside of the gutter cannot be seen from any upstairs window, you can use up left-over gloss paint of any colour instead of buying bitumen paint.

Tools *Ladder with a stand-off bracket; safety goggles; strong work gloves; wire brush or electric drill fitted with wire cup brush or wheel; emery cloth; paintbrush. Perhaps filling knife.*

Materials *Rust-neutralising primer; black bitumen paint or left-over gloss paint. Perhaps roof-and-gutter sealant or glass-fibre filler.*

1 Rub off smaller rust spots with the emery cloth.

2 Remove larger patches of rust with the wire brush or brush wheel fitted in the drill.

3 Apply a coat of rust-neutralising primer to the cleaned parts; and to the rest of the inside of the gutter as well, if you wish.

4 Seal any small cracks in the gutter with roof-and-gutter sealant.

5 If there is a larger crack or hole, use gutter repair tape or a fibreglass repair kit sold for car body repairs. Be sure to smooth the filling thoroughly so there is no roughness to hold water or silt.

6 Apply a coat of black bitumen or gloss paint. Allow it to dry and apply a second.

Cleaning an overflowing gutter

Gutters should be cleaned out and checked for damage each year. The job is best done in late autumn after all the leaves have fallen.

Before you start Wear sturdy work gloves to avoid scraping your hands on rough or rusty edges or on tiles or slates.

Tools *Ladder with a stand-off bracket; protective gloves; small trowel; bucket; piece of hardboard or a large rag. Possibly a hosepipe.*

1 Put the piece of hardboard at the bottom of the downpipe to prevent debris from getting into the gully or the drain, where it could cause a blockage.

Alternatively If the downpipe goes direct into the ground, stuff the rag in the top of it.

2 Scoop out any silt, grit or other debris with the trowel and put it into the bucket. Take care not to let anything drop into the downpipe. Take care not to let any debris fall down the walls because it may cause stains that are hard to remove.

3 Unblock the downpipe and pour three or four buckets of water slowly into the gutter at the end farthest from the pipe.

Alternatively Use a hosepipe to lead water there. The water should flow quickly and smoothly to the downpipe, leaving the gutter empty.
- If a pool of water remains, the gutter needs realigning (see left).
- If the water leaks through cracks or bad joints, repair the gutter (facing page).
- If the water starts to overflow at the downpipe, the pipe needs cleaning out (page 402).

Repairing leaking gutter joints

Sometimes you can spot a dripping gutter from indoors, but occasionally walk round the house during heavy rain to check on all your gutters.

Rainwater dripping through gutters and splashing the house walls will cause a water stain on the outside wall and, after a time, moss and algae will grow, disfiguring the wall. If the leak is not cured, damp will penetrate the walls, causing damage indoors. Damp quickly ruins decorations and eventually causes rot in timbers.

Leaking metal gutters

A metal gutter is difficult to take apart if the nuts and bolts have corroded, so try to seal the leak by injecting roof-and-gutter sealant into the joint with an applicator gun. First scrape the joint clean and dry it with a hot-air gun. If the leak persists, you will have to dismantle and reseal the joint. Wear strong gloves to protect your hands from rough metal.

Tools *Ladder with a stand-off bracket; gloves; safety goggles; spanner; hammer; wire brush; old chisel; small trowel; paintbrush; narrow-bladed filing knife. Perhaps a junior hacksaw and nail punch.*

Materials *Metal primer; roof-and-gutter sealant; nut and bolt of correct size.*

1 Undo the nut securing the bolt in the joint piece.

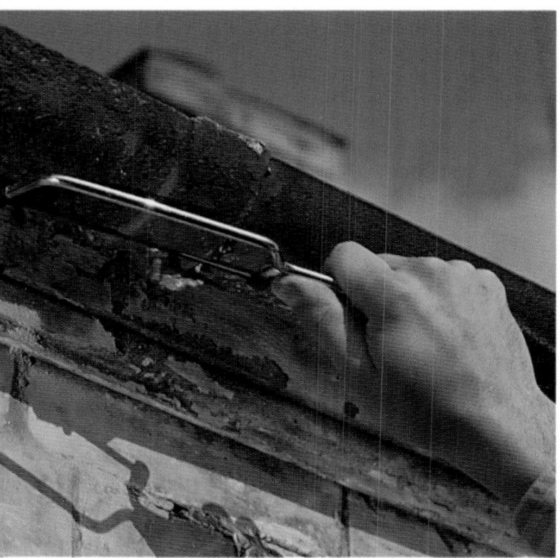

Alternatively If the nut will not move, cut through the bolt with a hacksaw and take out the shank with nail punch and hammer.

2 Gently hammer the joint piece to separate it from the gutter sections.

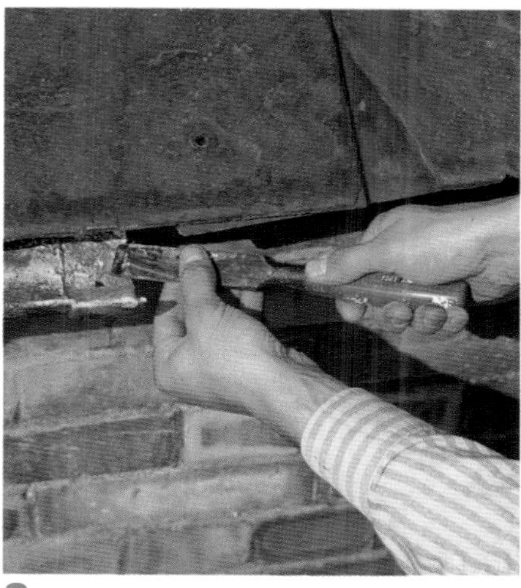

3 With the joint dismantled, chisel away the putty and clean rust from the whole joint area with the wire brush. Scoop away the debris with the trowel.

4 Apply a coat of metal primer to the gutter ends and the joint piece and leave it to dry.

5 Spread roof-and-gutter sealant onto the joint piece and reposition the gutter sections on it.

6 Secure the joint with the new nut and bolt.

Leaking plastic gutters

Where pieces of gutter join, or connect with a downpipe, they are clipped to a connector or union piece which has gaskets in it to make the union watertight.

Leakages caused by dirt forcing the seal slightly apart can be cured by cleaning. Squeeze the sides of the gutter inwards to release it from the union piece. If there is no dirt, the gaskets may need renewing.

Tools *Ladder with a stand-off bracket; filling knife.*

Materials *New gaskets or roof-and-gutter sealant.*

1 Squeeze the sides of the gutter sections in order to release them from the clips of the union piece.

2 Gently raise the end of each section of gutter in turn until you can see the gasket in the union piece. Peel the gasket away.

3 Fit the new gaskets, pressing them well into place.

Alternatively Fill the grooves for the gaskets with sealant.

4 Gently squeeze each gutter section in at sides to ease it back into the union piece clips.

Plastic guttering parts

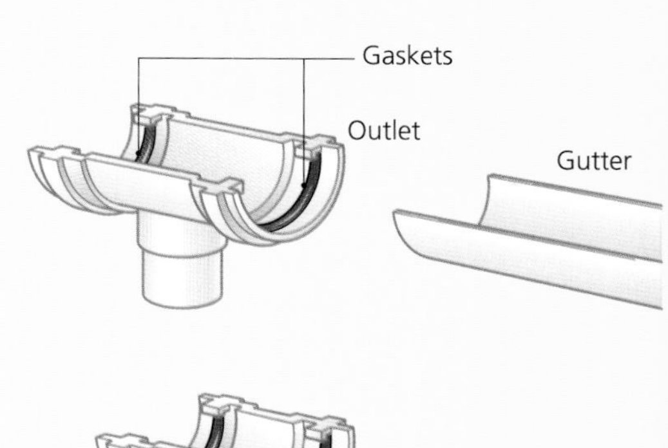

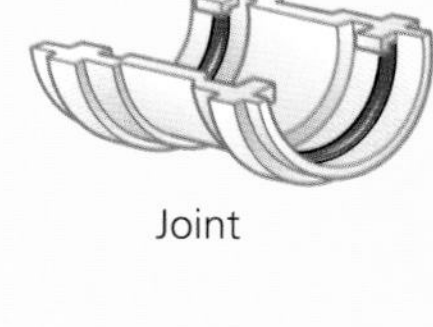

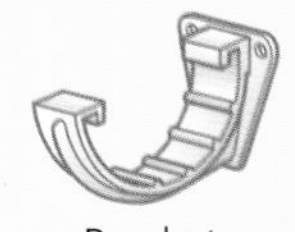

Securing loose downpipes

The screws or nails that hold rainwater downpipes to the house walls can work loose. They need to be secured to prevent leaks.

If the pipe is not firmly held, it vibrates in strong winds, and this can loosen its joints. The sections of downpipe slot loosely one into another; do not seal them together.

Cast-iron pipes

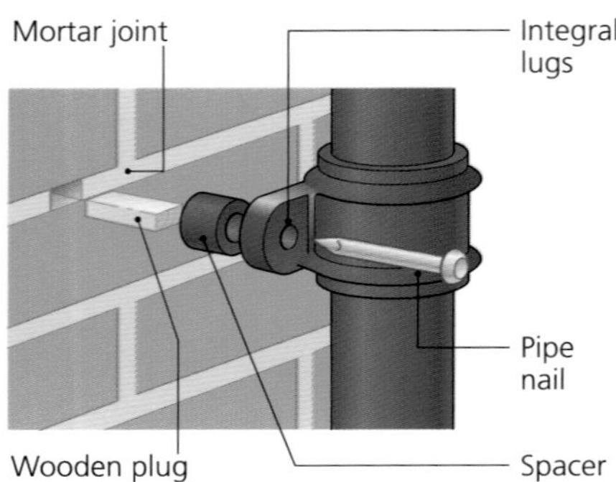

The lugs that hold cast-iron pipes are an integral part of the pipe and are fixed with large nails called pipe nails to wooden plugs inserted in the mortar joints. If only the nails are loose, take them out and fill the hole with wood filler or insert a wall plug into it. Drive the pipe nails back in, or drive in 38mm 5mm galvanised screws instead.

If the wooden plugs in the wall have come loose or rotted; you will have to remove them and fix new ones.

Tools *Ladder with stand-off bracket; pliers; saw; hammer. Perhaps a screwdriver.*

Materials *Softwood plugs slightly larger than the old ones; wood preservative. Perhaps 38mm No. 10 galvanised screws.*

1 Pull out the old pipe nails with pliers. You can use the nails again if they come out undamaged.

2 Remove the spacers that hold the downpipe away from the wall and keep them on one side.

3 Remove one or more sections of pipe to give access to the plugs. Sections are slotted together. Raise one as high as it will go on the section above to free the lower end from the section below.

4 Take out and discard the plugs.

5 Cut new plugs, sawing and planing or chiselling them until they almost fit the holes. Treat plugs with wood preservative and tap them into place with a hammer.

6 Put back the piece or pieces of downpipe that you have removed.

7 Set the spacers in position behind each pair of lugs and drive the pipe nails through the holes to hold the downpipe securely.

Alternatively Set the spacers in position and secure the lugs by driving galvanised screws through the holes.

Plastic downpipes

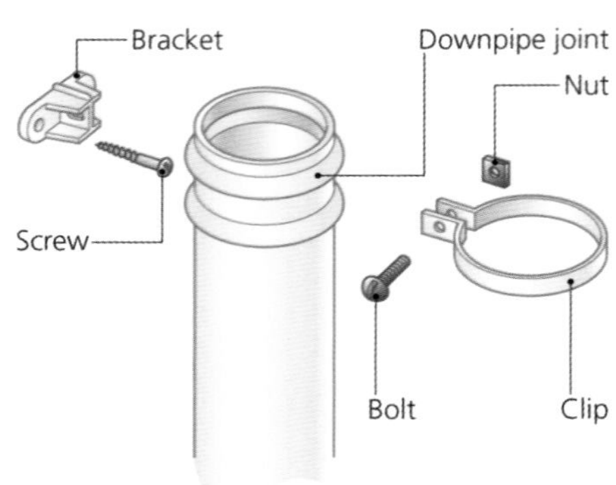

If a plastic downpipe comes loose from the wall, check the screws and the plastic or fibre wall plugs to see if they need renewing to give a better fixing. Use 40mm 5mm galvanised screws.

It might be easier to reposition the bracket slightly higher or lower, drilling new holes and fitting new wallplugs to get a firm fixing. Repair the old holes with mortar or exterior filler. Match the colour of the rest of the mortar to make the repair discreet.

Do not move a clip fixed at a joint in the downpipe system because it strengthens the joint. You could exchange a one-piece clip for a two-piece clip, or vice-versa, to give different fixing positions for screws.

Unblocking a downpipe

Overflow from a gutter may be caused by a blocked downpipe.

Before you start Check what is causing the blockage. It could be a ball, a bird's nest or some other object that you can simply lift out. But the most likely obstruction is a collection of wind-blown leaves lodged in the mouth of the downpipe.

A pipe with a swan-necked section at the top is more likely to become blocked than a straight downpipe.

Another indication of a blocked downpipe is water seeping out during heavy rain from a joint where sections of downpipe connect. Because the joints are loose, not sealed, you can tell straight away where the blockage is; it is in the section immediately below the leaking joint.

Obstructions near the top

If the downpipe is blocked near the top, you can usually clear it by probing with a length of wire. Cover the drain at the bottom of the pipe to prevent any debris from falling into it. Hook out debris if you can; if you cannot, probe until it becomes loose. Flush away remaining loose debris by pouring buckets of water down the pipe or playing a strong jet of water down it from a hose. If the pipe is straight, not swan-necked, tie rags firmly to the end of a stick (such as a bamboo garden cane) to form a ball and push the obstruction loose with it.

Obstructions out of reach

Hire a flexible drain rod to clear an obstruction lower down a pipe or in a swan-necked pipe. Or, as a last resort, dismantle the lower part of the downpipe.

Tools *Ladder with a stand-off bracket; screwdriver or pliers or box spanner; long stick. Perhaps a cold chisel and claw hammer.*

1 On a plastic downpipe, remove the screws that hold the pipe clips to the wall. Work from the bottom and remove the screws and clips up to the point it leaks. If the pipe is held by two-part brackets, undo the bolts holding the rings to the back plates; leave the back plates in place.

If the pipe is cast-iron, use pliers to pull out the large pipe nails that hold the lugs to the wall. If they are rusted, use a cold chisel and claw hammer to prise the lugs from the wall; keep the nails for re-use.

2 As you free the clips or lugs that hold it, free each section of pipe from the section below and lift it away from the wall.

3 Use a long stick to push out any obstructions inside the sections.

4 Replace the pipe section by section, working from the top down, and screw or bolt back in place the clips (or nail the lugs) that hold the section to the wall.

Preventing blockages

Wire or plastic covers are sold in different sizes for fitting in mouths of downpipes.

- If there is a hopper head at the top of the downpipe, fit fine-mesh wire netting over the top, securing it with fine galvanised wire.
- If there are large deciduous trees nearby, it is worth covering gutters. Lay a strip of plastic netting over a gutter to overlap the top by about 50mm at each side. About every 1m along it, thread a length of twine through the overlaps from the underside of the gutter and tie it firmly to hold the mesh taut. Check the netting surface regularly during autumn; if leaves coat it, rain cannot enter the gutter and will spill over it.

Planning a plastic gutter system

Several similar systems of black, white, brown or grey plastic guttering are made; they differ mainly in the shape (profile) of the gutter.

The two most common profiles of plastic gutter are round – typically 112mm wide and connected to 68mm circular downpipes and 'square', normally 114mm across and connected to 65mm square downpipes.

There are deeper versions of both for use on large houses and in areas of heavy rainfall (these have words like "deepflow" and "storm" in their descriptions); there is a smaller 'mini' version of round guttering for use on sheds (page 428). Plastic ogee gutters (below) are available to mimic cast iron.

Manufacturer's literature gives guidance on the type of gutter you need for your house: the size of the guttering you are replacing will be a good guide.

To work out how much guttering you need, measure round the house at ground level (most guttering comes in 2m, 3m and 4m lengths) and count the number of brick courses to work out the amount of downpipe necessary (each brick is 75mm; downpipes come in 2m and 3m lengths).

Fittings As well as gutters and pipes, you will need a variety of fittings, shown below: stopends, gutter joints (or joint brackets), gutter brackets, elbows, outlets, offsets, downpipe clips, downpipe connectors (not illustrated) and downpipe shoes.

Adaptors Adaptors will link plastic guttering to cast-iron, larger plastic guttering to smaller sizes, and rounded to square section guttering. However, it is not always possible to link one manufacturer's guttering to another's.

Stopend
Round gutter
Gaskets
Stopend
Joint
Bracket
Stopend outlet
Gaskets
Square gutter
90° elbow
Downpipe offset
Bracket
Joint
Running outlet
90° elbow
Hopper head for downpipe
One-piece clip
Two-piece clip
One-piece clip
Two-piece clip
Square section downpipe
Round downpipe
Downpipe shoe
Downpipe shoe

End piece
Plastic ogee gutter
Bracket

CONNECTING TO THE DRAINS

The downpipe shoes shown above are used when the rainwater downpipe discharges over the grid of a gully. If the downpipe is connected directly to the drains, you will need the correct size and shape of drain connector for this.

COLLECTING RAINWATER

Water butts designed to collect and store run-off rainwater for garden use can help to ease the demand on piped, purified water throughout the year. You can position them beneath downpipes from the gutters on your house, outbuildings and greenhouse, and even link them for maximum storage. Always choose covered water butts as these help to prevent the growth of algae and are safer as they don't put children and animals at risk.

DIY water butts connect to the guttering system by means of a rainwater diverter kit. These contain a pipe that diverts the rain from the downpipe into the water butt and an integral overflow pipe to take the water back into the downpipe and to the drain once the water butt is full.

To install, move the water butt into position and decide where in the downpipe the diverter kit needs to be to flow into the top of the butt. Mark the position on the downpipe, then cut away a slice of downpipe with a hacksaw to slot the diverter in.

Alternatively, stop the downpipe above the level of the water butt and use angled downpipe connectors and short straight sections as necessary to drop the pipe down through a

hole in the lid. Most lids have holes marked for this purpose on the inside and you will need to knock, drill or cut them out. With this method you'll need an overflow kit – a narrower bore flexible pipe that fits into the side of the water butt near the top and can be run into a drain or soakaway.

If you collect and use a large amount of run-off water, rainwater tanks are a more practical solution. They come in plastic, metal and glass fibre, with concrete an option if you want to site the tank underground. Manufacturers can advise on the best system for your needs.

Replacing cast-iron guttering with plastic

When a cast-iron guttering and downpipe system becomes too rusty to repair, you will have to replace it.

Before you start Plastic guttering is easy and cheap to fit and needs no painting. Wear strong work gloves to handle the cast-iron; rusty edges can cause nasty cuts. Follow the rules for using a ladder safely given on page 387.

Tools *Ladder with a stand-off bracket; gloves; spanner; hacksaw; nail punch; claw hammer; rope; large screwdriver; small blowtorch; slim masonry chisel; pliers; wrecking bar; string line and nails; plumb line; steel measuring tape; file; cordless drill with masonry bit; pointing trowel; filling knife; paintbrush; chalk.*

Materials *Plastic gutter; joints; brackets with 25mm 4mm galvanised screws; stopends; gutter outlet section; downpipe; offset bends; silicone lubricant; pipe clips with 40mm 5mm galvanised screws; wall plugs; mortar for pointing; filler and paint for fascia board; downpipe shoe or drain connector; perhaps gutter elbows.*

Removing the old system

Cast-iron sections, which may be 2–3m long, are very heavy and difficult to handle when standing on a ladder. If possible, have a helper to support each section and help you to lower it to the ground by rope.

1 Use a spanner to undo the bolts holding the gutter sections together. If you cannot, cut through each bolt with the hacksaw, then tap its shank upwards with a nail punch and hammer to free it.

2 Give sharp hammer taps at the joints where the sections meet. They will be sealed together with old putty or mastic.

3 Tie a rope round the middle of each gutter section as you free it. Lift it off the brackets and lower it to a helper who can steer it clear of windows and walls below.

4 Try with a screwdriver to undo the screws holding the brackets to the fascia board. If they are rusted in, heat the heads with a narrow blowtorch flame to expand the metal and break the grip of the rust. If the screws still will not turn, prise the brackets away from the board and pull the screws out with them. Use a slim masonry chisel and claw hammer to prise them off.

5 Take out the pipe nails holding the downpipe lugs to the wall. Use pliers or, if the nails are rusted, a wrecking bar to prise the lugs away from the wall. Work down the wall and, as you free each pair of lugs, lift out the section of downpipe from the section below. Use the masonry chisel and hammer to take out the wooden blocks from the wall.

6 If the downpipe goes straight into the ground to connect with a gully, break up the concrete or other surround to free it.

TAKING DOWN OGEE GUTTERING

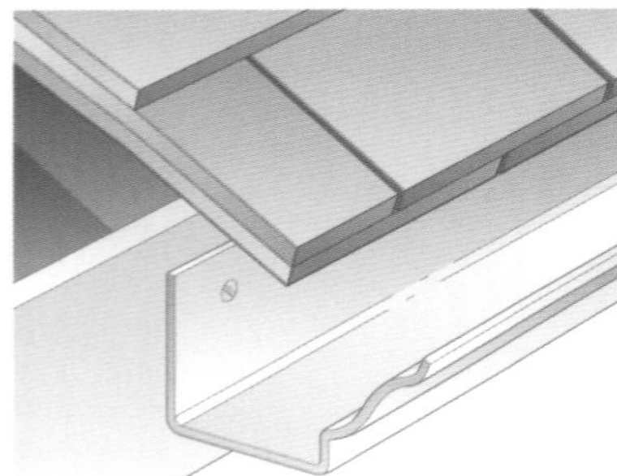

Ogee guttering does not rest on brackets but is screwed direct to the fascia board through its straight back. It is unwise to take it down without a helper. Once you take out the screws from one end, the gutter is unsupported and its weight will unbalance you. Even with a helper to support the gutter section, it is best to work from a well-anchored scaffold tower, which you can hire. Drive some 150mm nails into the fascia board to support the gutter, and then separate the gutter joints and remove the screws as for other types of cast-iron guttering.

Repairs and preparations

1 Repair the fascia board with exterior filler if necessary, before repainting it (pages 414–15). Repair damaged pointing where necessary (page 408).

2 Nail a plumb line to drop from the fascia to the gully where the downpipe will discharge. Mark its position with chalk on the fascia and wall, then remove it.

3 Fix a taut string line as a guide for positioning the brackets. Fit it as close up to the tiles or slates as you can. The top of the gutter should end up within 30mm of the bottom of the tiles or slates. Run it from the downpipe position to the farthest point of the guttering that will drain into it. This may be at the end of the fascia board or at an angle in the guttering.

Check with a spirit level that the string is horizontal, and mark its level at the downpipe position with chalk.

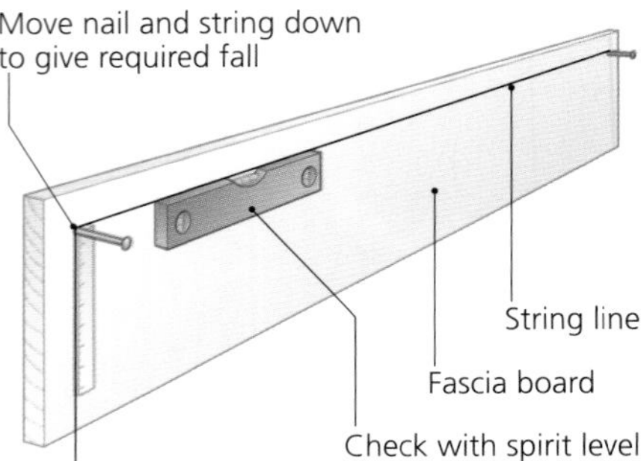

4 Then lower the string at the chalk-mark end by the amount needed to give the correct fall and fix it taut with a nail. The fall should be 6-9mm for every 3m.

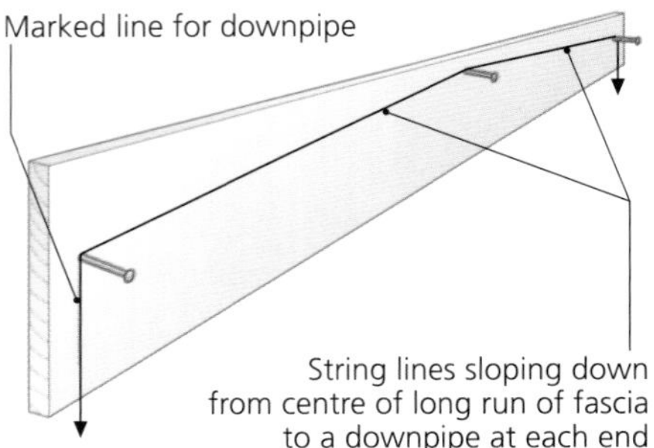

5 A long stretch of gutter may have a downpipe at each end. Fix the string line with its highest point in the centre and a fall towards each downpipe.

Fitting the new guttering

1 Start by fixing the bracket furthest from the outlet, positioning its top up against the string line at around 50-75mm from the end of the fascia. Use 25mm 4mm zinc-plated galvanised or stainless steel screws.

2 Now position the outlet at the other end (using the same size and type of screw) and check that you have the correct fall and that the outlet is directly over the drain.

3 Fit joint brackets where the ends of gutter length will come (working from the outlet), allowing for expansion (see box below) and fit intermediate brackets at 1m intervals (750mm if you get heavy snow).

4 Starting at the outlet, clip the gutter lengths into place one by one. Place the back edge under the lip of the bracket (or joint bracket) and then secure the front clip. A little silicone lubricant will help get the gutter past the joint seals on a joint bracket. Make sure any roofing felt is draped securely into the gutter.

5 The final section of gutter will have to be cut. Cut it on the ground after measuring off a piece of the right length: normally extending 50mm beyond the end of the fascia unless it is to be joined to an elbow to go round the corner (in which case it finishes short). Cut it with a hacksaw and smooth the cut with a file.

6 Fit the stopend (or elbow if going round the corner) and clip to the brackets. At a corner, fit a bracket to support the gutter at the other end of the elbow and continue the run of guttering along the next fascia board.

7 If there is guttering at both sides of a running outlet (page 404), fit the second run in the same way as the first.

Fitting the new downpipe

Most houses will have projecting eaves, so you will need an offset pipe to join the outlet to the downpipe. You can get special fittings for small offsets, but otherwise use two offset bends and a length of downpipe.

1 Measure the length of pipe needed to slope inwards from the gutter outlet to the wall. Cut pipe to this length.

2 Push the offset bends onto the pipe ends and hold this zigzag unit in position at the gutter outlet to test the fit. The lower offset bend should have its outlet the right distance from the wall to accommodate the pipe clip. Saw off more pipe if necessary to achieve the right fit.

3 With the top of the offset pushed onto the outlet, push the first length of downpipe into the bottom of the offset. Place a downpipe clip either over the lower offset bend or over the downpipe immediately below it and mark the positions of the clip screw holes on the wall.

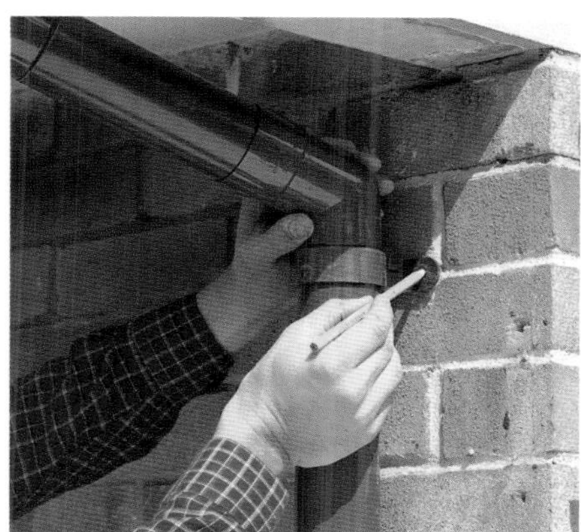

4 Make sure that everything is aligned correctly and then remove the offset and downpipe and use a cordless hammer drill with a masonry bit to make holes in the wall bricks (not mortar joints) to fit wallplugs.

5 Fit the pipe clip using 40mm 5mm zinc-plated, galvanized or stainless steel screws.

6 Align the first length of downpipe and fit a downpipe connector to its lower end. The pipe connector must be clipped to the wall – some square connectors have screw lugs.

7 Allowing a 6-10mm gap for expansion (see box below), push the downpipe connector onto the downpipe and mark the screw holes on the wall. Drill and plug holes as before and screw the clip in place.

8 If there is more than 1.8m of downpipe between the two wall clips, fit a third clip centrally in between.

9 Fit more lengths of downpipe in the same way – pushed over the bottom of the pipe connector above and into the pipe connector below (with an expansion gap).

10 At the bottom, cut the pipe so that the shoe will be about 50mm clear of the gully. You may need to lift out the drain grid while you fit the shoe. If the pipe goes direct into the ground, allow enough pipe to do this.

Alternatively Fit the final length of downpipe into a suitable connector to take it directly through the ground into the drains.

THERMAL EXPANSION

When installing plastic guttering and downpipes, you have to allow for them to expand in hot weather.

Gutter joints usually have an insertion mark against which you position the gutter end; when fitting downpipes, you need to allow a gap at each downpipe joint – check the manufacturer's instructions.

Cleaning and maintaining gullies

A gully has an underground U-trap that prevents bulky waste from flowing into the drains. It is prone to blockage.

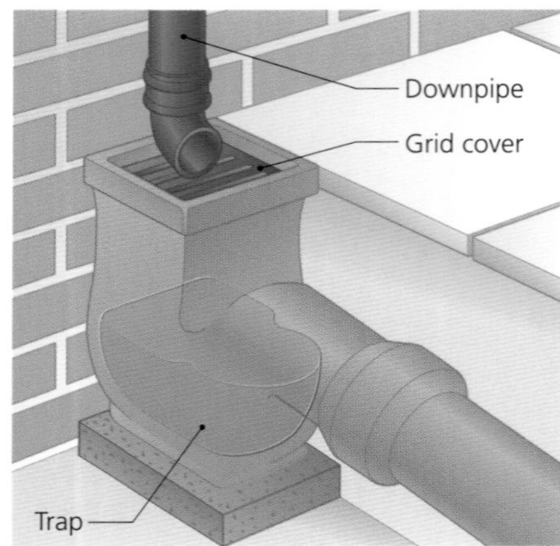

A gully is fitted at the point where a downpipe or waste pipe discharges at ground level, and is then connected to the underground drains. A yard gully is similar, but is sited away from the house and collects surface water via an open grating. The trap in the gully will collect solid waste material, preventing it from entering the drains and causing a blockage that would be difficult to remove.

In older properties, the water discharges into a gully above a grid fitted over the trap. This grid can become blocked with leaves and other debris, resulting in waste water splashing over the surrounding area instead of passing into the trap.

In newer properties, waste pipes discharge into soil stacks, and rainwater downpipes discharge into back-inlet gullies. Here the downpipe passes directly through the grating and into the trap, so avoiding overflow problems. If the gully does not have to act as a yard gully, a screw-down cover provides access to the trap.

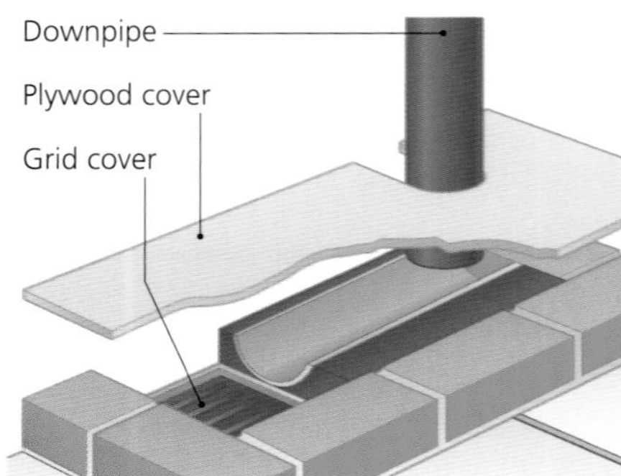

Channel gullies taking waste water via a half-round channel are especially prone to grid blockages. Prevent these by putting a cover on the gully. Cut it from outdoor-grade plywood 13–19mm thick. Make a hole for the waste pipe to pass through.

Clearing a blockage

1 Clear all debris from the gully grating. If necessary, prise out the grating and scrub it in hot soapy water.

2 If the blockage is deeper, remove the grating. Wear long rubber gloves or put your arm in a plastic bag. Reach into the trap, which may be up to 600mm deep, and scoop out as much debris as you can.

3 If the obstruction is too solid to scoop out, break it down with a garden trowel.

4 When the gully is cleared, scrub the sides with a nylon pot scourer and hose them down with a fierce jet of water. Disinfect all gloves and tools afterwards.

5 If you cannot find an obstruction in the gully, the blockage may be farther down the drain; see Clearing blocked drains, opposite.

Repairing a channel gully

A channel sometimes runs parallel with the house wall to lead water into a gully entrance or to hold water that comes too fast for the gully to take. The channel can crack or become loose. The rendering around it can also crack or develop hollows where water lodges and stagnates.

Repair damaged rendering with a mix of one part cement to four parts soft sand, with PVA building adhesive added for a better bond. Alternatively, buy a small bag of dry-mix sand-cement mortar to use instead, but add PVA adhesive to improve adhesion. Give the repair a smooth finish so that water does not collect.

Renewing a damaged channel

You will have to chip out the old one and the surrounding brick and rendering. You can buy ready-made vitrified clay channels from builders' merchants. Use the same mortar mix as for rendering repairs.

Tools *Chalk; cold chisel; club hammer; offcut of hardboard or thick card; trowel.*
Materials *Bricks; length of channel; mortar.*

1 To cut the channel to length, first measure and mark the length at several points round the pipe and join the marks with a chalk line. Lay the channel on a heap of sand and use the chisel and hammer to chip round the marked line until the channel breaks along it. Alternatively, use an angle grinder if you have one to cut the channel. Wear goggles to protect your eyes from flying dust and chippings.

2 Put a piece of hardboard over the gully inlet to prevent debris from getting in.

3 Chip out the damaged channel and the mortar and any bricks round it. If the bricks round the gully entrance are damaged, chip these out as well. Brush up the debris.

> **HELPFUL TIP**
>
> If there is no brick surround to the gully entry, it is worth making one (see Laying bricks or walling blocks, page 468). It will retain small amounts of water if there is a minor blockage, and will prevent splashing or flooding of the surrounding area.

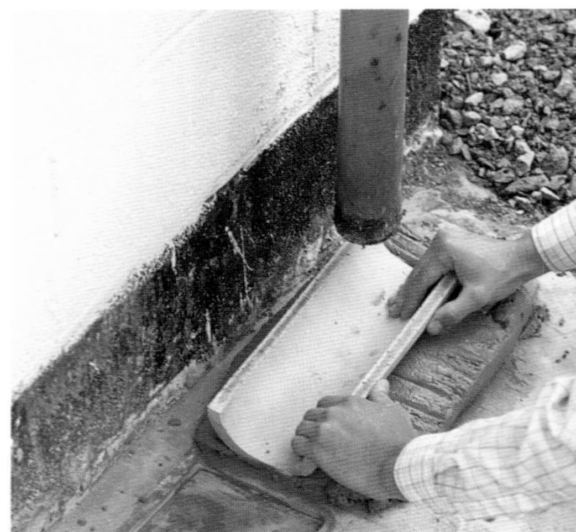

4 Mix the mortar and spread a thick layer where the channel will lie. Bed down the channel on it, setting it so that it slopes slightly towards the gully.

5 Lay a course of bricks (page 468) on edge to make a low retaining wall round the channel and gully. Set them on a bed of mortar and leave a gap of at least 25mm between the channel and the bricks alongside it. Nearer the gully the gap may need to be wider.

6 Fill the gap between the channel and the bricks with mortar.

7 Slope the mortar smoothly up to the brick surround and make sure there are no hollows to trap water.

Clearing blocked drains

Below ground, pipes carry water and waste from the house to the main drain outside the boundary of the property, or to a cesspool or septic tank. Rainwater may be led separately into the drain or into a soakaway.

Before you start Remember that the pipes below ground are laid in straight lines for as much of their route as possible. Where a change of direction is needed, the bend should be less than a right angle and there should be an inspection chamber there. A manhole cover identifies the chambers. An older property may have an interceptor chamber near the boundary before the house drain joins the main drain (see right).

The first sign of a blocked drain may be the failure of WCs and baths to drain quickly and efficiently, or an overflowing inspection chamber or gully. A gully may be cleared by cleaning (facing page). Otherwise you will have to clear the drain with rods. You can hire rods and various heads. Wear rubber gloves for the work.

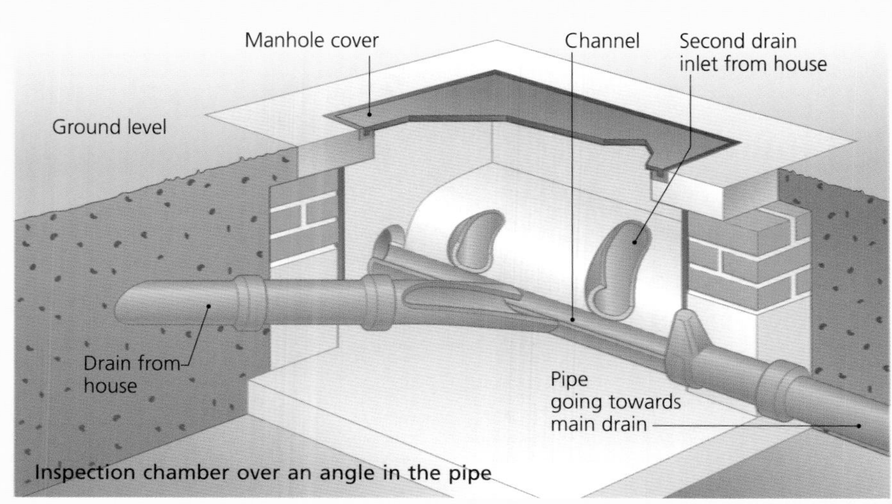

Inspection chamber over an angle in the pipe

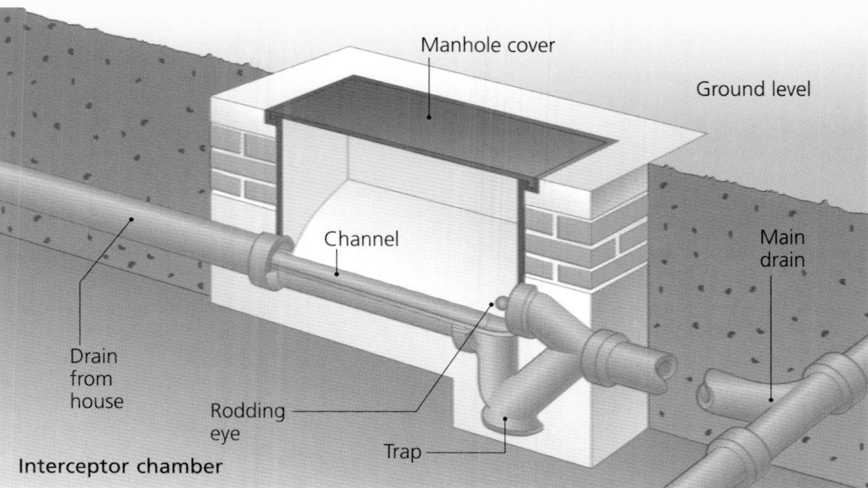

Interceptor chamber

Interceptor chambers In older properties, you may find an interceptor chamber built as the last inspection chamber between your underground drainage systems and the main sewer. It is different from other inspection chambers in that it contains a trap to prevent foul air (and rats) getting into your underground drainage system from the main drain or sewer. It may also be fitted with an above-ground ventilator, which is frequently damaged.

The trap in the chamber prevents the use of drain rods, so there is a rodding eye fitted above it, with a stopper you can remove to push the drain rods in. The common problem is that this stopper falls out on its own, drops down into the trap and causes a blockage – the first sign of which is a strong smell at or near the inspection chamber. The blockage causes the chamber to half-fill and, because of the regularity of this happening, the rodding eye may have been covered with a piece of slate mortared in place, which you have to smash if you want to use the eye. Interceptor chambers are no longer used.

Tools *Drain rods fitted with a 100mm diameter rubber plunger; pair of long rubber gloves; strong garden spade; hose; disinfectant; watering can.*

1 Locate the blockage. You will have to lift the manhole covers; a strong garden spade will raise the edge enough for you to grasp the cover. Inspect the chamber that is nearer to the main drain, septic tank or cesspool than the overflowing chamber or gully. If it is empty, the blockage is in the drain between this chamber and the higher one or the gully. If the chamber is full, inspect the chamber next nearest to the main drain or septic tank. If the chamber nearest the main drain is full, the blockage is between it and the main drain. If the drain leads to a septic tank and the last chamber is full, have the tank emptied.

2 To clear the blockage in a main drain system, insert the rod fitted with the plunger into a chamber at one end of the blocked section; it does not matter which of the two. If it is the empty chamber, you can see where the mouth of the pipe is, but if you work from the full chamber, you will have to probe with the plunger until you find the mouth.

3 Add more rods as necessary to work the plunger along the pipe to the blockage. Always turn the rods clockwise as you work; if you turn them counter-clockwise, they may unscrew and be left in the drain to cause a greater problem. Keep pushing against the obstruction and then withdrawing the plunger a little way.

If this will not shift the blockage, withdraw the rods and exchange the plunger for a corkscrew attachment, which will break up a tightly packed obstruction.

4 Complete the clearance by directing a strong jet of water down the drain from a hosepipe, or by filling the bath and sink and releasing the water in one gush.

5 Hose down the rods and gloves thoroughly and drench them with diluted disinfectant poured from a watering can.

Testing drains

If the drains are not blocked, but a persistent foul smell or unexpectedly wet ground make you suspect that there is a leak somewhere, arrange for the environmental health department to test the drains. You can get in touch with the department at your local authority offices.

Minor repairs to walls

Cracks, deteriorating mortar, damp and damaged brickwork are all easily repaired when the problem is small.

Repointing a wall

Where mortar joints in a wall are cracked or crumbling, they can be repointed with fresh mortar, but first of all you have to remove the old mortar to a depth of around 15mm. There are various ways to do this.

The simplest is to use a plugging chisel (page 387) with a club hammer and just knock out the old mortar by hand. If you own a router, you can buy a special cutter for removing mortar from old joints and if you own an angle grinder, a special diamond cutting wheel does the trick.

For large areas of damaged wall, hire a powered mortar rake. When using any of these power tools, wear suitable safety equipment – gloves, masks and goggles.

Before you start One problem when you are patching a number of joints, is to match the colour of the mortar with that of the surrounding joints. The only way to do this is to experiment with a few different mortar mixes (page 467), using varying amounts of sand and lime. Take a note of each mix and repoint a few joints at a time. Wait a week or two for the mortar to dry thoroughly and show its final colour before you decide on the best mix to complete the job.

Carry out repointing as in pointing (page 470), matching the shape with the surrounding joints. Before you apply new mortar, clean any dust from the joints then brush water into them. If you do not wet them, the joints will soak up moisture from the mortar and it will dry out too fast.

Dealing with a crack

Mortar is meant to be weaker than bricks or masonry so that it offers less resistance if movement beneath the foundations causes any strain on the wall. The mortar will crack before the bricks or masonry.

A single crack confined to a mortar joint, even through several courses, usually indicates limited amount of soil settlement. A repair can be made by repointing.

A brick may be cracked by minor settlement. You can replace it yourself. If a crack runs through more than the odd brick, there is a more serious strain on the foundations. Get a professional builder to deal with it as soon as possible.

We show in the next column how to replace a single brick. If this is in an obvious place, it may be worth taking a large fragment of the old brick to an architectural salvage yard to see if you can get a brick to match the wall.

Replacing a damaged brick

Remove a damaged brick by chipping away the surrounding mortar with a club hammer and cold or plugging chisel.

You can speed up the process by drilling a series of holes into the mortar first. Drill to a depth of about 100mm, then cut into the mortar all round to release the damaged brick. Chop as much mortar out of the resulting cavity as you can, ready for the new brick to be fitted. Dampen the cavity very well. Spread mortar on the base of the cavity and on the top and sides of the new brick. Tap the brick into the cavity with the trowel handle. When it is properly seated, trim away the excess mortar. Point the joints to match the others on the wall.

Dealing with efflorescence

The white powdery deposit called efflorescence is caused by dampness, which draws chemical salts from the bricks or mortar to the surface. It is harmless, and will disappear from a newly built wall once it has dried out.

You can discourage efflorescence by coating a wall with a silicone-based water repellent (below). If efflorescence does form, brush it off or treat it with a chemical masonry cleaner available from a builders' merchant. Do not wash off efflorescence; the water aggravates the problem.

Keeping out damp with silicone water repellent

Silicone water repellent will normally cure damp problems on external walls. It stops rain from getting into the brick but it lets the wall 'breathe' so that moisture already in the material can evaporate.

If damp patches persist, you should get professional advice.

Tools *Bucket of water; wire brush; a clean old paintbrush, 100–150mm wide; paint kettle. Perhaps a ladder.*

Materials *Silicone water repellent; white spirit for cleaning brush.*

1 Clean the surface with water and the wire brush. Wait until the surface has dried.

2 Tape paper over the window glass, frame and ledges. You will not be able to remove splashes of silicone from them. Cover any part of a drive or path adjoining the wall you are treating. The silicone could otherwise cause blotches.

3 Pour the repellent into the paint kettle and apply a generous amount of the liquid with an old paintbrush, so that you can see it flowing down the wall.

4 If the surface soaks up all the liquid – because it is very porous – apply a second coat before the first coat dries.

5 Use white spirit to clean the paintbrush and the paint kettle when the job is finished.

Repairing cracks on a rendered wall

Before you start Hairline crazing on the surface of rendering does not need filling. Cracks that go deeper than the surface do need filling to keep the wall weatherproof. Fill the cracks with exterior filler or with new rendering. Filler is convenient but uneconomical for more than one or two cracks. You can buy dry-mixed rendering in small quantities or you can make your own. The repair will show until the wall is repainted; an invisible repair is impossible to achieve.

Tools *Filling knife; brush; wet sponge or cloth; old paintbrush. Perhaps a bolster chisel and club hammer and a ladder.*

Materials *PVA adhesive; rendering or exterior filler.*

1 Draw the edge of a filling knife through the crack to form it into a V with the point of the V at the surface of the rendering and the wider part against the wall.

You can use a bolster chisel and club hammer instead of the filling knife if you find it easier.

The shape will anchor the filler below the surface and the crack is unlikely to open again.

2 Brush out the fragments and dust from the cavity to leave it as clean as possible.

3 Wet the cavity with a sponge or cloth dipped in water.

4 Paint all the inside of the cavity with PVA adhesive to improve adhesion of the filler.

5 Press the filler or rendering into the crack with the filling knife. Prod the knife into the cavity to make sure there are no air pockets in it. Smooth the filling level with the wall surface. Redecorate the wall when the filler has dried.

Patching large holes

Before you start When large slabs of rendering fall away from the wall, it is usually because a weak rendering mix has been used and become porous, or because damp has penetrated behind the layer of rendering, perhaps through a crack.

Sometimes the rendering may appear intact, when in fact it has separated from the wall behind. Check the rendering from time to time, tapping it lightly with a hammer; undamaged areas will make dead sound while defective areas give a hollow sound or fall away.

Carry out rendering work in mild weather. Frost can freeze the water in the rendering, which may cause premature cracking.

Preparing the rendering Mix the rendering from six parts plastering sand, one part cement and one part hydrated lime. Do not use builders' sand or the rendering will crack when it dries out. Use enough water to make the mixture easy to work with – not too stiff, not too sloppy.

Mix up small batches at a time. The rendering will become too stiff to spread after about 20 minutes. It is applied in two coats – a thick undercoat called the floating coat, and a thinner finishing coat.

Tools *Bolster chisel; club hammer; brush; wet sponge or cloth; steel plastering trowel; old pointed trowel or square of wood with nails driven through to project at about 38mm intervals; straight edged length of wood longer than the width of the patch; damp sponge or clean wooden float. Perhaps a ladder and a plugging chisel.*

Materials *Rendering.*

1 Use the bolster chisel and hammer to cut away any loose rendering to leave a sound edge round the patch.

2 Clean out any crumbling joints in the brickwork or masonry. Clean them out to a depth of 15mm with the plugging chisel and club hammer. Brush out all debris.

3 Thoroughly wet the area to be repaired with a sponge or cloth soaked in water. This prevents rendering from losing moisture into the wall and drying too quickly, which could cause crumbling later.

4 Apply the first coat of rendering. Take some of the mixture on the steel trowel with the handle downwards. Spread it onto the wall, starting from the bottom of the patch and pressing the lower edge of the trowel hard against the wall as you sweep it smoothly upwards. Continue until the rendering is smooth and about 5mm below the level of the wall surface.

5 As the rendering begins to stiffen after about 20 minutes – scratch a criss-cross of lines in it with the old trowel or spiked wood to make a key for the top coat.

6 Leave the first coat to dry for at least 14 hours, then apply the finishing coat. Use the same rendering mixture as for the floating coat. This time, start at the top left of the patch. Sweep the trowel lightly across from left to right to spread the rendering over the area, leaving it standing slightly proud of the surface.

7 Continue applying trowel loads from top to bottom down the patch spreading them from left to right. Mix more small batches of rendering as necessary, but work quickly.

8 Just before the rendering begins to set – about 15 minutes after it has been applied – draw the straight-edged piece of wood upwards over the rendering to level it with the wall. Hold the wood horizontally and make sure that you are pressing its ends firmly against the wall on either side of the patch. If any hollows are showing after levelling off, fill them quickly with more rendering and level them with the straight-edged piece of wood. As the rendering starts to set, smooth its surface gently with damp sponge or a damp wooden float.

Repairing pebbledash

It is simple enough to repair damaged pebbledash, but the repair will be visible unless the wall is to be painted because the new chippings and the rendering beneath will not match the original colour. You will need about 5kg of chippings to cover a square metre.

Tools *Cold chisel; club hammer; brush; wet sponge or cloth; steel trowel; sheet of polythene; small scoop; wooden float. Perhaps a ladder.*

Materials *Soft sand and cement or dry ready-mix rendering mortar; PVA building adhesive; water; chippings.*

1 Prepare the area for repair as for Patching large holes (left) and mix and lay on a first coat of rendering in the same way, but leave it about 15mm below the level of the wall surface.

2 Wash the chippings and drain them in a garden sieve.

3 Mix the rendering for the top coat, known as the butter coat. Use five parts of sand to one cement and add some PVA building adhesive.

Mix it to a slightly softer consistency than the first coat to make sure that it is still soft when you apply the chippings.

Apply the top coat; if you have a large area to repair, work on a section which you can complete within 20 minutes before the coat starts to set.

4 Spread a sheet of polythene on the ground below the repair. Throw small scoops of pebbles hard at the rendering until it is evenly covered. Gather up and re-use the chippings that fall to the ground.

Alternatively Lift batches of pebbles up to the wall on a hawk and use a float to push them off the hawk and into the wet mortar.

5 When you have pebbledashed the patched area, press the wooden float lightly all over it to bed the chippings into the surface. Continue in the same way until the repair is complete.

Making a hole in an external wall

When fitting a fan or an airbrick in a cavity wall, you will have to bridge the cavity with ducting or a sleeve liner. You may also have to cut through insulation material in the cavity.

Drill a guide hole right through the wall. You may need to hire extra-long masonry drill bits for this – a bit 260mm long for a solid wall, or 300mm long for a cavity wall.

Tools *Heavy-duty hammer-action power drill; long and standard length masonry drill bits; club hammer; sharp cold chisel and bolster chisel; pencil or chalk; work gloves; safety goggles; pointing trowel.*

Materials *Bag of dry ready-mixed bricklaying mortar. For a cavity wall: ducting or sleeve liner.*

1 Mark the outline of the hole on the inside wall at the required position.

2 Make sure there are no pipes or cables in the way. If the inner leaf of a cavity wall is timber-framed, make sure you will not cut through a stud (see Internal walls, pages 12–13). Adjust the position of the outline if necessary.

3 Transpose the outline to the outside wall. Drill the guide hole through the wall from inside, and mark the outside wall from where the drill tip emerges. For a circular hole, drill through the centre of the marked area. For a square or rectangular hole, drill through at each corner of the marked area. Withdraw the drill bit from time to time to cool it and remove dust.

4 Wear safety goggles to protect your eyes from flying dust and debris. Cut away the plaster at the marked area inside, using a club hammer and bolster chisel. Then switch to a cold chisel and chip away the mortar between the bricks so you can dislodge them whole if possible. Work from both sides of the wall.

5 In an uninsulated cavity wall, plug the lower section of the cavity with rags to stop debris falling into it as you cut through. If the cavity is filled with foam insulation material, cut through it with a knife.

6 When the hole is complete, fit the ducting. If it is a cavity wall, fit a liner across the wall cavity. Make good round it with mortar.

Installing an airbrick

An airbrick ventilates a room or under-floor space, and is either up near a ceiling or low down under the floorboards. Underfloor airbricks are usually sited at least 150mm above ground level, and if possible below the level of the damp-proof course.

Some airbricks are made of clay, others are made of galvanised steel or plastic. All are either one, two or three bricks deep.

The amount of air a brick lets through depends on the type of holes that it has. A single brick with a square grid has roughly 1500mm^2 of opening compared with the 5500mm^2 of a steel vent with vertical slots.

A damaged airbrick provides a way for vermin to get into the house under the floorboards. Replace it as soon as you can; do not block it temporarily as this decreases ventilation under the floor, and can lead to rot in the joists and floorboards.

> **HELPFUL TIP**
>
> If the hole is square, check that it coincides with as many whole bricks as possible to make their removal easier – adjust the outline to do so if necessary. If the hole is circular, position it round a whole brick that can be removed from the centre of the area. If you need to make a round hole for an extractor fan or a new waste pipe, you can make a hole up to 150mm in diameter with a hired combi-hammer and a core drill. This will cut a neat round hole ready for the fan duct or waste pipe to be fitted. See box (right).

1 To fit a new airbrick for extra ventilation, make a hole of the required size through the wall. If the brick is to be sited below the floorboards, you will be able to work only from the outside.

2 To replace a damaged airbrick, remove the old one by chipping out the mortar round it with a hammer and cold chisel (see page 408).

3 Check the liner behind the airbrick in a cavity wall, and replace if in poor condition.

4 Before fitting the airbrick, dampen the edges of the hole with water. Spread mortar in the base of the hole and on the top and sides of the new airbrick.

5 Push the airbrick into place, or tap it in with the brick trowel handle. Trim off excess mortar from the joint and point it to match the surrounding mortar joints.

6 Poke a stick or a piece of wire through the openings in the new airbrick to make sure no mortar is caught inside them that might obstruct the flow of air.

7 If the hole goes into a room, make good the inside of the hole with a filler if necessary. Then fit a plastic grille over the opening, using either a contact adhesive or screws and wall plugs.

Choosing a cavity-wall liner

In a cavity wall, a liner behind the airbrick stops the airflow being lost in the cavity. Special terracotta liners are available from builders' merchants. Straight liners are used for an airbrick fitted below a damp-proof course. For an airbrick above the course, use an inclined liner, which raises the inside hole and stops rain blowing through. Fitting an inclined liner is a job for a builder.

> **USING A CORE DRILL**
>
> A core drill looks a bit like a hole saw, but has diamond cutting teeth. It needs a powerful SDS hammer drill which you can hire along with the drilling bit. You will also need eye protectors, a face mask, ear defenders, gloves, a safety helmet and sturdy shoes.
>
> Make sure you know how to use the drill properly (the hire shop should be able to give you instructions). Before you start, use a detector (page 34) to check for any pipes or cables in the wall. To get the neatest result, drill through the wall until the pilot drill emerges from the other side and then finish off the hole by drilling from that side.

Recognising and treating damp

Damp patches at skirting-board level on an interior wall, or a tidemark as high as a metre above floor level, are two signs of damp rising from the ground.

Damp prevention

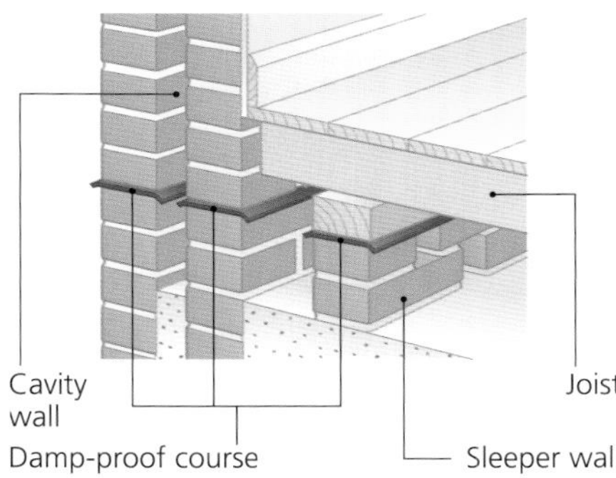

To prevent damp from rising, houses are built with a damp-proof course (DPC). This is an impermeable plastic strip in modern houses, or a layer of slates or hard engineering bricks in older properties.

In most houses (except very old ones built without a DPC), you will see a thicker than usual horizontal line of pointing about 150mm above ground level, running right round the external walls. This line indicates the position of the DPC.

Defects in the damp-proofing

If the DPC deteriorates or becomes damaged, or if there is no DPC, damp is able to rise through the house walls. Rising damp will also occur if the DPC is bridged by damp material reaching above it against the outside wall – a rockery, for example, a flowerbed or even a temporary pile of building sand.

Rising damp may occur because a path or drive is too close to, or is higher than, the level of the DPC. Paths and drives must be at least 150mm below the DPC so that rainwater cannot splash above it. Where necessary, lower the path or drive surface if at all possible.

Alternatively, dig a 300mm wide channel alongside the outside wall of the house and fill it with gravel to stop rainwater splashing the wall above the DPC.

If such alterations are not practicable, build a concrete skirting against the foot of the outside wall. Use a waterproofing agent in the concrete to make it impervious to water. Make the skirting reach at least 150mm higher than the path or drive and ensure there is no gap between the wall and skirting, into which water could run. Make the top of the skirting slope down from the wall so that water will run off it readily.

Installing a chemical damp-proof course

If you live in (or have moved into) an old house with a serious rising damp problem, you will need a specialist firm to install a new DPC for you, consisting of a silicone-based water-repellent fluid that is injected into the masonry until it is saturated. It then becomes impervious to water and acts as a damp-proof barrier.

The job may also involve hacking off and replacing internal plaster.

You may, however, be able to treat small areas of rising damp yourself by hiring a DPC injection machine. The hire shop will supply the injection fluid, power drill and masonry drill bits of the right length and diameter. Ask for an instruction leaflet when you hire the machine, and get advice on the amount of fluid. You will need roughly 3 litres per metre of wall.

To minimise disruption to the house, the injection process is carried out entirely from the outside of the building.

Tools *Heavy-duty hammer-action power drill; masonry drill bits with depth stop; extension lead and plug-in RCD; safety goggles; work gloves; face mask; damp-proof injection machine.*

Materials *injection fluid; paraffin for cleaning machine; mortar (page 467).*

1 Drill a horizontal row of holes 75mm deep into the course of bricks or stones immediately above the existing DPC. Use a depth stop or mark the bit with tape to ensure that you drill to the correct depth. Space the holes about 120mm apart – two into each stretcher (side-on brick) and one into every header (end-on brick, only found in solid walls). If the bricks are extremely difficult to drill through – or if the walls are made of stone – make the holes in the mortar joints.

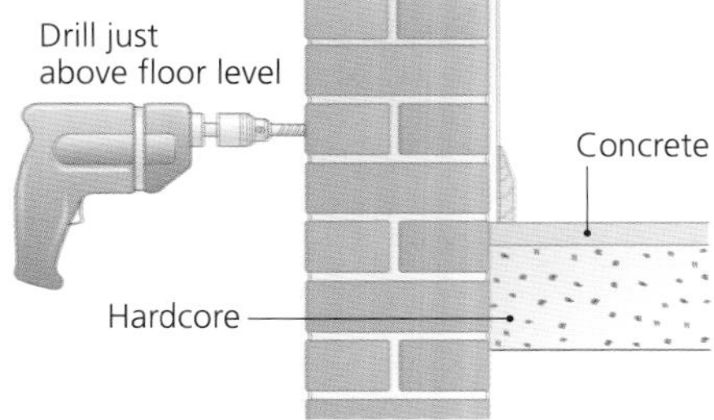

With a concrete floor, drill just above it (see above). With a suspended timber floor, drill just below it. For cavity walls, just drill into the outer leaf for the first stage of the process.

2 When all the holes have been drilled, inject the damp-proofing fluid into them. Follow the instructions supplied with the machine.

Most damp-proof injection machines consist of a pump, a suction nozzle and six injecting nozzles.

3 Insert all but one of the short injection nozzles into the prepared holes and tighten the wing nuts to hold them in place.

4 Hold the free nozzle over the container and turn on the pump. When fluid begins to ooze from the nozzle, turn off the pump.

5 Insert the free nozzle into a hole and tighten its wing nut. Turn on the pump. When the bricks or stones joints are saturated, fluid will 'sweat' from the surface. As soon as this happens, turn off the pump and close the nozzles.

6 Undo the wing nuts, move the nozzles to the next set of holes and repeat the procedure. Continue until you have treated every affected wall.

7 On solid walls, drill through the original holes to a new depth of 150mm. Repeat the treatment cycle, this time using the longer nozzles supplied with the machine.

8 On cavity walls, drill through the original holes into the inner leaf to a total depth of 200mm. Repeat the injection process.

9 When you have finished injecting all the holes, empty the machine and clean it with paraffin.

10 Wait for the fluid to dry; it may take two days or more. When the injected course is the same colour as the rest of the wall, fill the holes with mortar.

HOW TO DIAGNOSE DAMP

If damp patches appear in mild, wet weather, water is getting in from outside. If patches appear in cold, dry spells, condensation is more likely.

To get a more accurate diagnosis, stick a ring of Blu-tack on the suspect surface. Press a piece of glass onto the ring so that the glass is within 5mm of the surface. Alternatively, put a piece of aluminium foil directly on the surface and seal down its edges with adhesive tape.

After about 24 hours, lift the glass or foil. If moisture has formed on the underside, damp is coming from outside. If the top side is moist, the problem is condensation.

Repairing rot with wood-repair products

The easiest way to repair rot in a wooden window is to use a combination of wood repairing products, including liquid wood hardener and high-performance wood filler.

Before you start Make sure the item you are repairing is made of painted wood – because the repair will show up on stained or varnished wood.

Tools *Old chisel, about 13mm wide; paint scraper; hot-air gun; paintbrush for applying wood hardener; filling knife; power drill; 10mm twist drill bit; hand or power sander; paintbrush for applying finishing coats to the window.*

Materials *Wood repair products (as listed above); clear wood preservative; primer, undercoat and gloss paint.*

1 Use a hot-air gun or chemical paint stripper to soften old paint, then scrape it off to reveal the extent of the rotten wood.

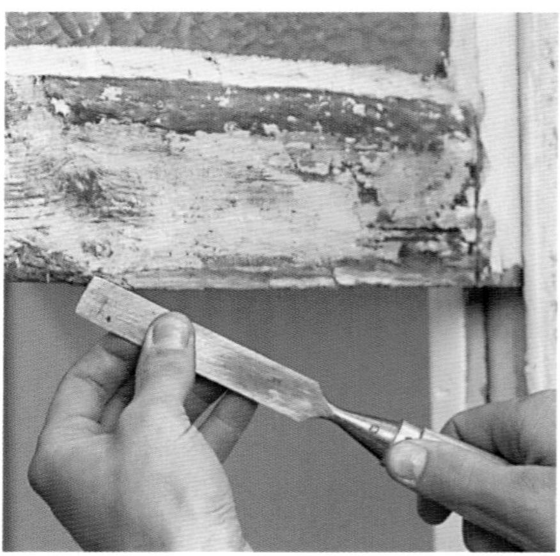

2 Dig away the worst of the rot with an old chisel. There is no need to cut back right into sound timber.

HELPFUL TIP

If the rot is close to a joint in the window, strengthen it with a flat steel L-shaped corner plate. Recess the corner plate to lie flush with the surface of the wood so that it is not noticeable after it is painted. See Fixing loose joints on windows, page 203.

3 If the timber is wet it must be dried out. Saturated wood can be covered with a flap of plastic, taped along the top, so that it dries out naturally over a couple of weeks. If it is only damp, dry it rapidly with a hot-air gun. Take care to keep the air flow away from the glass, or you might crack it.

4 When the wood is thoroughly dry, flood the rotten area with brush-loads of wood hardener. The liquid penetrates the wood, and hardens it as it dries, to give a firm base for the filler. Pay particular attention to exposed end grain. Keep flooding on the hardener until it stops soaking readily into the wood and begins to stay on the surface. Let it harden overnight.

5 Mix a small amount of the high-performance wood filler according to the instructions on the container and apply it as quickly as you can to the hole. The filler will start to harden in about five minutes – even quicker in hot weather.

6 Fill in deep cavities with a succession of layers. Because the filler hardens so quickly, even deep holes can be filled in a very short time.

7 Leave the surface of the filled hole as level as you can. After about 30 minutes it can be smoothed level with the surrounding wood with a hand or power sander. This will show up any areas where the filler is still too low.

8 Push one of the wood preservative pellets into each hole and then seal it with the wood filler. While the wood is dry, the pellets will remain inactive, but as soon as it becomes wet the pellets will release a fungicide which will prevent wood rot.

9 Coat any bare wood with clear wood preservative.

10 Paint the bare wood with primer and undercoat. Then give the whole window at least two coats of exterior gloss paint.

WOODWORM AND DRY ROT

If you see the tell-tale flight holes left by wood-boring insects as they leave the wood, you may be able to prevent further attack by using woodworm killer.

But for major attacks of woodworm (especially on flooring) and for any attack of dry rot (see page 247), call in a specialist firm.

Repairing rot with new wood

Where wet rot damage is too extensive to be rectified with wood repair products, you may be able to cut out damaged wood from window frames, window sills and even the window itself, then replace it with new wood.

The traditional way of repairing rot in a window is to cut back the rotten part to sound wood and to insert a new piece.

Before you start Wood used for the repair should match original wood in the window if it has a stained or varnished finish.

Replacing a section of sill or frame

Tools *Pencil; combination square; tenon saw or general-purpose saw; chisel, about 20mm wide; mallet; vice; power drill and twist drill bits; paintbrush; plane.*

Materials *Wood to suit size of rotten section; clear wood preservative; zinc-plated 5mm screws about 50mm long; wood dowels (same diameter as screw heads); waterproof wood adhesive; paint, varnish or preservative wood stain.*

1 Mark cutting lines on the frame about 50mm beyond signs of rot. Draw two right-angled lines on the face of the frame and then mark two more lines at about 45° to the face to form a wedge shape.

2 Using the tenon saw or general-purpose saw (page 191), cut along the lines as far as possible. Brickwork may prevent you from sawing too far into a sill.

3 Complete the cut with a sharp chisel. Try to leave straight flat sides that will form a tight joint with the new wood.

4 Hold a piece of new wood against the cut-out and mark the edges of the cut-out on it with a pencil to give a cutting line.

PREVENTING WET ROT

Outdoor woodwork is prone to wet rot. The wood darkens and starts to crumble as the fungus that causes the condition attacks damp wood.

The best prevention is to ensure that any new timber is treated with wood preservative (page 439), and to apply regular fresh coats of wood preservative, varnish or paint. Seal round frames with a frame sealant (page 204) to prevent moisture from penetrating.

5 Cut out the new piece with a saw and trim it with the saw or a plane until it is a good fit in the cut-out. It is better if its faces stand slightly proud of the surrounding surface.

6 Treat the cut surfaces of the frame and the new wood with clear wood preservative and allow it to dry.

7 Glue the new wood in place, holding it with G-cramps until the glue is dry.

8 Drill pilot and clearance holes for fixing screws, about 125mm apart.

9 Drill out the holes about 15mm deep to the same diameter as the screw heads so that the heads will be sunk well below the wood surface.

10 Insert the screws and plug the holes with pieces of glued wood dowel. Drive them firmly home with the mallet.

11 Plane the faces of the insert so they are flush with the surrounding surface. Smooth with abrasive paper, and fill any gaps with exterior grade filler.

12 Finish the repair by applying paint, varnish or a preservative wood stain.

Repairing a rotten window edge

Tools *Screwdriver; panel saw; portable workbench; plane; power drill and 6mm twist drill bit; depth stop; paintbrush.*

Materials *Piece of wood to suit the size of the rotten section; clear wood preservative; waterproof wood adhesive; sash cramps; 6mm dowels; paint, varnish or preservative wood stain.*

1 If the rot is on the edge of an opening casement or sash, remove it so you can work on it on your workbench. A casement window is taken off by unscrewing the hinges from the frame. For removing a sliding sash window, see page 206.

2 Saw off the rotten part by cutting right along the edge. Cut a replacement length of wood that is slightly oversize.

3 Treat the new wood and the cut surface of the window with clear wood preservative

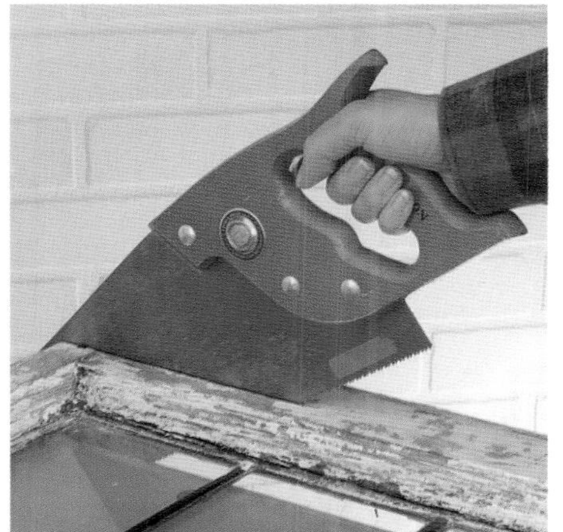

and allow it to dry. Put newspaper on the bench, and ventilate the room.

4 Apply adhesive to the new wood and fix it in position. Hold the repair together with a pair of sash cramps until the glue has set. Wipe away any excess adhesive.

5 Reinforce the repair by drilling through the new and old wood, and driving in glued dowels. Use a 6mm twist drill bit and dowels of the same size. Before drilling, mark the correct depth of the hole on the drill bit with a depth stop, or wrap a piece of coloured adhesive tape round it.

6 When the adhesive has set, cut off the protruding lengths of dowel and plane the timber to the exact width and thickness of the existing wood.

7 Fill any minor gaps with exterior wood filler. Finish bare wood with paint, varnish or preservative wood stain, depending on how the rest of the window is treated.

Decorating the outside of a house

Exterior paintwork needs repainting every five years or so. Paint deteriorates at different rates, depending on how much it is exposed to wind and rain and the direct heat of the sun and how thoroughly the surface was prepared. Check the whole house from time to time for the first signs of deterioration – usually when gloss paint loses its shine, or when wall paint becomes over-powdery to the touch.

Before you start Surfaces should be clean, stable, and stripped if the paintwork is not sound (page 72). Repair damaged areas of a rendered wall and fix gutters if they are not firmly attached to the fascia board. Some weeks before you intend to start painting, check that putty around windows is sound and, if not, replace it (page 209).

When to paint The best time to decorate is after a dry spell because paint will not take to a damp surface. Never paint in frosty conditions or rain, and do not paint on a very windy day – or dust and dirt will be blown onto the new paint. If it starts raining, stop painting at once and wait until the surface has completely dried out.

Safe access is most important: your ladder or scaffold tower must be secure and in good condition. A hired scaffold tower (plus a proper roof ladder) also gives you the opportunity to make checks and minor repairs to roof faults.

Before you buy the paint If you are going to change your colour scheme, make sure that the new colours will fit in with the surrounding and neighbouring buildings, especially if the house is semidetached or in a terrace.

Calculate how much paint you need in the same way as for interior decorating (page 82). Rendered surfaces require more paint than smooth ones. If all the walls are to be painted, estimate the total outside area of the house by multiplying the length of the walls by the height.

The easiest way to measure the height is to climb a ladder against the wall of the house, drop a ball of string from the eaves to the ground, and then measure the length of the string. Work out the combined area of the doors and windows and deduct this figure from the total.

If you are going to paint the pipes and the outside of gutters, multiply their circumference in centimetres by their length. Divide this figure by 10,000 to give an area in square metres.

Which paint to use In general, use exterior grade gloss paint on wood and metal – gutters, downpipes, windows and doors – and use masonry paint on walls. Treat natural wood with preservative wood stain.

Alternatively, on bare wood you can use microporous paint, which needs no primer or undercoat. This paint allows trapped air or moisture to evaporate, reducing the risk of flaking associated with hardwoods.

You do not have to use a paint similar to the one previously used, but never put gloss paint over surfaces (mainly pipes and guttering) that are coated with bituminous paint. This tends to be less shiny than gloss and often looks thicker and softer than other paint. If you are doubtful about whether old paint contains bitumen, rub a rag soaked with petrol over the surface. If the rag picks up a brownish stain, the paint is bituminous. Either continue to use bituminous paint or, providing the surface is sound, coat it with aluminium primer-sealer, then paint with undercoat and gloss.

DEALING WITH PLANTS

Protect climbing plants growing up a wall from any drips or splashes of paint by untying them and covering them with paper or dust sheets. Take care not to weigh down delicate plants with heavy sheets. It is easier to paint exterior walls covered by a well-established climber or creeper after you have pruned the plant, so that you do not have to cope with masses of foliage. Ideally, fix plants to trellis, not direct to the walls.

Paint the house in this order

Before you start Exterior decoration is time-consuming. It may make sense to work on one side of the house at a time. Complete all the preparatory work before you do any painting – but never leave a surface exposed. Protect it with at least a primer and, if possible, an undercoat before you stop work at the end of a session.

Always decorate from the top of the house downwards so that the newly painted surfaces cannot be spoilt. Paint doors and windows last. Most professional decorators work in the following order, but if you are working from a scaffold tower you may wish to paint all the surfaces you can reach before moving the tower to another site. Try to keep on painting a wall until you reach a natural break.

1 Bargeboards, fascias and soffits

All these surfaces are painted in the same way, but not necessarily at the same time. Metal gutters are usually painted the same colour as fascias so it is easiest to paint them immediately afterwards – before soffits, which are often painted to match the walls or windows.

- Apply knotting, if necessary, and primer to bare wood. Put on an undercoat and leave to dry. Use two undercoats if there is to be a colour change.
- Lightly sand with fine abrasive paper to remove any rough bits.
- Apply a coat of gloss with a 75mm paintbrush, finishing with the grain. Leave it to dry for at least 12 hours.
- Apply a second coat of gloss.

2 Gutters and downpipes

Whether you paint metal gutters and pipes together or at different times, follow the same painting procedure for both.

- Clean out debris and wash with water and detergent.
- Remove rust from the insides of metal gutters with a wire brush. Wipe the surface with a dry cloth and apply rust inhibitor or metal primer. Paint the inside of gutters with any left-over gloss paint.
- Paint gutters and pipes with exterior gloss using a 50mm brush. If there is to be a colour change, apply one or more undercoats first. If the surface is coated with bituminous paint see Choosing paints for every purpose (page 83).
- Hold a piece of cardboard behind pipes as you paint them, to protect the wall.
- Apply a second coat of paint when the first is completely dry.

Plastic gutters and pipes do not have to be painted, but if you want them to match a colour scheme, apply two coats of exterior grade gloss. Do not use a primer or undercoat. Manufacturers usually advise against painting new plastic because the paint will not adhere perfectly to it. After about a year it is safe to do so.

If you are leaving plastic gutters unpainted, unclip and remove them while you are painting the fascia boards.

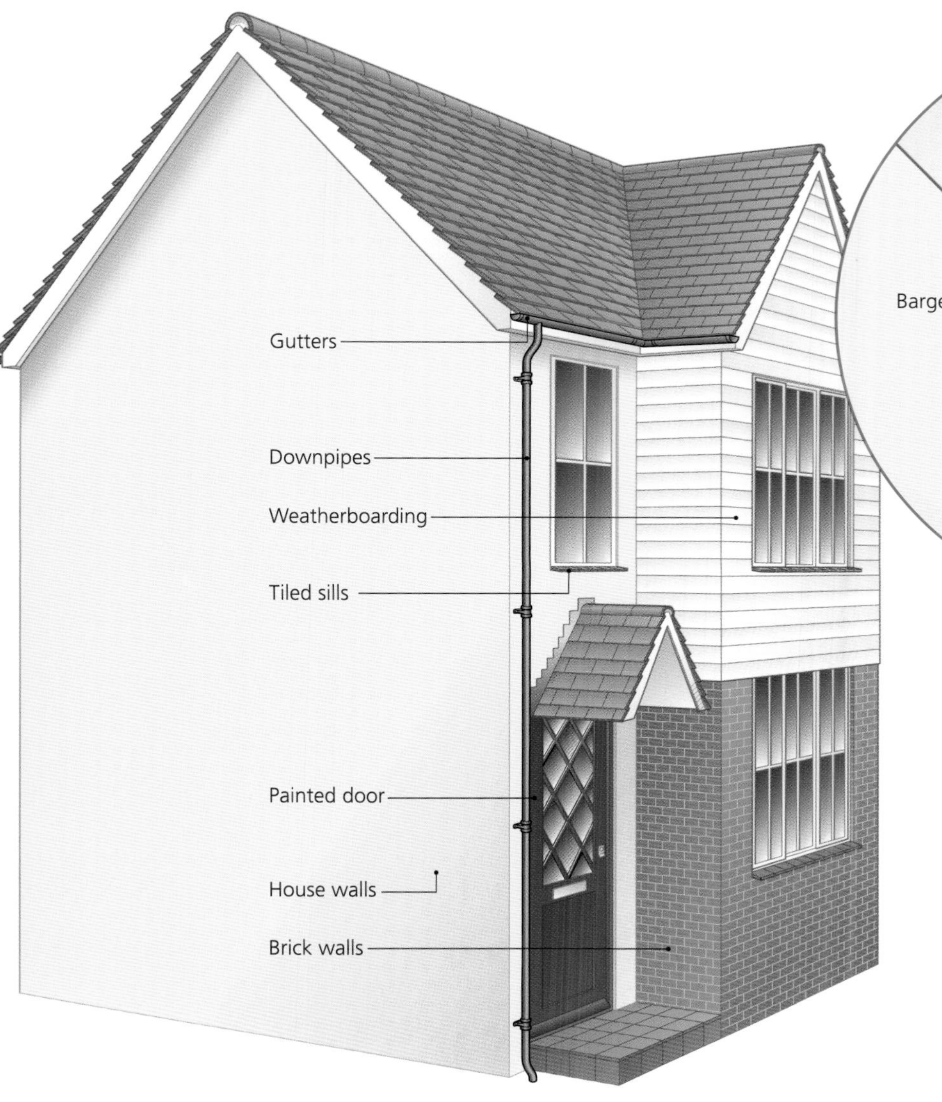

3 House walls

• Treat new rendering which has not been painted before with a stabilising solution or a primer recommended for such a surface by the manufacturer.
• On painted rendering – such as pebbledash or a textured surface – no undercoat is necessary. Apply two coats of masonry paint with a 100mm or 150mm paintbrush or an exterior grade shaggy pile roller. If you use a brush, work the paint into the surface with the tip of the bristles.
• Paint the area close to door and window frames with a 50 or 75mm brush.
• Do not try to paint the whole width of a wall along a house in one go. Instead, divide each wall into sections and paint one section at a time. If you cannot finish painting a wall in one session, stop at a corner of a feature – a window, for instance – so that joins will be less noticeable. Never stop in the middle of a wall. It will leave a noticeable mark.
• Wrap a collar of paper as protection around a newly painted pipe if you are painting the wall behind it. Move the paper down the pipe as you paint.
• Remember to work safely at high levels, ideally with a helper to steady ladders and to pass tools.

4 Brick walls

• Avoid painting good facing brickwork – it is difficult to achieve a satisfactory finish, it cannot be successfully cleaned off later and rarely looks attractive.
• If you really want to paint it, use masonry paint and a rough surface paintbrush. Apply at least two coats.
• To clean dirty bricks, scrub them with a hard bristle brush and plenty of water. Never use soap or detergent because they create permanent white stains.

5 Painted windows

If a concrete sill is damaged, repair it before painting the window frame.
• Strip paint off wooden sills and make them good, filling holes and uneven areas with exterior grade wood stopping or epoxy-based filler.
• Prepare wood and metal frames as for an equivalent inside frame (page 73).
• Apply knotting to knots and resinous patches in bare wood. Then apply primer, undercoat and exterior grade gloss with a 25mm, 50mm or angled cutting-in brush.
• Paint each type of frame following the sequence on page 97.
• Take special care to seal the joint between putty and glass with new paint. This will prevent rain seeping through the window.

6 Tiled sills

• Clean window sills made of clay tiles with a fine wire brush; wash away the dirt with water and dry with a cloth.

Alternatively Clay tiles can be painted with special tile paint which is available in a limited colour range. No primer or undercoat is needed. Apply two coats with a 50mm paintbrush. The mortar joints may be painted or left natural.

7 Painted doors

• Remove metal handles, knockers and other furniture before painting.
• Replace damaged putty in a glass panelled door (page 209).
• Prepare the surface as for interior doors (page 73).
Use exterior grade gloss to finish; again follow the same sequence and method as for painting a door inside (page 95).

8 Hardwood doors and windows

Many homes now have hardwood front doors and windows. When the finish on these starts to go, you can use a preservative woodstain, either solvent-based or quick-drying water-based.

These also come in clear finishes (so as not to darken the wood) or you could use a (flexible) exterior varnish. Treat doors and windows in the same order as for painting. You should not need to strip previous finishes – except cracked or peeling varnish.

9 Painted weatherboarding

• Prepare as for interior painted wood (page 73). Apply knotting, if needed, then wood primer, undercoat and two coats of exterior gloss paint.
• Work from the top down, and from left to right if you are right-handed and from right to left if you are left handed.
• Paint sections about 1m long at a time, using a brush just narrower than the width of one board.
• Paint the edge of the timber first, then paint the face, finishing with strokes that go with the grain.

DIY in the garden 12

Planning an area of decking

Decking has become very popular as a surface for garden terraces. Fairly easy to lay, it is a light job compared to alternatives such as paving and concrete patios. Specialised tools are not required but the work will go faster if you can arrange a helper, especially when setting posts and handling the joists.

Decking materials

If a deck is to last for a substantial period of time, it is essential that any timber used in the construction be treated to stave off fungal attack and general deterioration caused by repeated wetting and drying. Timber can be bought pressure-treated: in other words, preservative has been forced into the grain using specialised equipment at the sawmill. This type of treatment gives the most protection, especially for timber that is in contact with, or close to, the ground (though always re-treat freshly cut surfaces). Alternatively, brush or spray on preservative during or after installation.

MASONRY BOLTS

A secure way to attach decking to a house wall or similar structure is to use masonry bolts (wall anchors – page 158). Each bolt has an expanding sleeve that grips the brickwork when the bolt is tightened.

It is possible to order certain types of wood from timber merchants and decking specialists. Here are some of the types of wood available:

Softwood

Western red cedar Straight grained with an attractive smell; but has a tendency to split and dent; can be used without any treatment; very durable but soft.
Spruce Straight grained with few knots; use for out-of-ground components only.
European redwood Clearly visible grain; avoid the lower grades because they have lots of knots.
North American Douglas fir Yellow in colour with prominent grain; heavy and durable especially when treated.
British/European larch Avoid boards with lots of knots; can be expensive.
Southern yellow pine Visible grain with few knots.

Hardwood

Hardwoods are generally more expensive but will often be durable without the benefit of pressure treatment.
Teak Very durable with high strength; mid-brown colour; the king of woods for decking but very expensive.
Iroko Coarse grain, but not very visible; similar in appearance to teak but not quite so durable; brown to beige colour.
European oak Broad, straight to wavy grains; durable but expensive.

Although these three woods are common, you will find many other hardwoods being offered, depending on what manufacturers can obtain. Make sure you look at a sample before buying unseen.

Decking boards and tiles

Decking boards should be thick enough to combat the twisting and warping caused by fluctuating temperatures and changing moisture levels brought about by the wood being rained on and drying out. Softwood decking boards are normally 28 or 38mm thick; hardwood boards can be thinner (typically around 20mm). Lengths vary from 2.4m up to 4.2m.

Ready-made wooden 'tiles' are a good alternative. Up to 1m square, they can be laid on a supporting framework to form a surface deck.

Planning permission

You do not need planning permission (or Building Regulations approval) for a deck in the garden, provided the deck is no more than 30cm high and, taken with other extensions and outbuildings, it covers no more than 50 per cent of the garden area.

Points to consider

Decking boards come in widths ranging from 90mm to 145mm. Wider boards are faster to lay because fewer are needed. They often have a grooved surface that provides grip underfoot in wet weather and helps surface water to drain away.

Building a deck is generally straightforward, providing a methodical approach is adopted and you plan properly before starting work. Construction techniques vary little, whether a deck is free standing or attached to some other element in the garden. Often decks are attached to the back of the house.

Look at the planned site for your deck in relation to the rest of the landscaping in the garden and take into account any other elements that may influence the design. Look at magazines, web sites and other gardens for ideas. Consider the neighbours: will the deck be so high that you overlook your neighbour's garden? Will you have privacy when you use your deck?

MEASURING UP

To work out the amount of timber required for the job, begin by measuring the width and length of the area to be decked. Then plan the layout of the supporting framework on paper.

You need to form a straight-sided frame around the perimeter and fix joists across it – every 400mm if using standard decking boards, or every 600mm for thicker (38mm) boards. For joists over 3m long, fix cross braces every 2m to prevent warping. Work out the number of joists you need to cover the area, and calculate the amount of timber you will need for the whole framework.

For the decking boards, find out the width and length of the boards available, then calculate the number of boards you require.

Building a deck over paving

The simplest type of decking is built directly on top of an existing area of paving. This must be flat and mainly level, with a very slight drainage slope away from the house.

Tools *Measuring tape; pencil; panel or circular saw; paintbrush; cordless drill with twist drill bits and screwdriver bits; spirit level; string line; mitre saw.*

Materials *75 x 50mm timber joists; clear wood preservative; 100mm nails; 63mm zinc-plated countersunk screws (decking screws can be bought); 100mm masonry bolts; washers; packing materials such as pieces of wood or slate; decking boards; decking sealer or stain.*

1 Cut the timber into lengths to create the supporting framework. Brush cut ends with preservative and butt together in position. Drill pilot holes, then secure each butt joint using two 100mm nails driven in at an angle ('skew' nailing). Check that the sides of the frame are level and that it has an overall slope for drainage (as it should have if the paving has been laid correctly).

HIGH DENSITY DECKING

Some manufacturers now produce a hard and durable alternative to wood decking made from recycled hardwood and/or softwood, sometimes with recycled plastic included. Some manufacturers will take back and recycle unwanted offcuts. With no painting, staining or weatherproofing required, it offers a genuinely green alternative to sustainable wood.

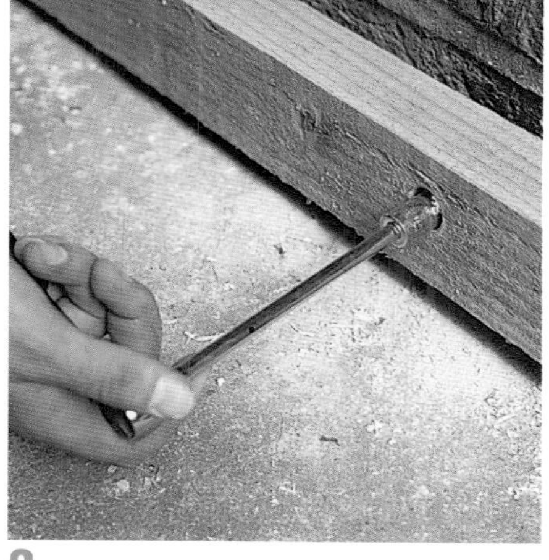

2 If you need to secure the frame to the house wall, use 100mm masonry bolts every 600mm. Fit a couple of galvanised washers on each bolt between the bearer and the wall to allow free air circulation.

3 Nail the joists in position (see Measuring up, left, for how to space them). Wedge packing material under any part of the frame that is unsupported due to unevenness in the existing paving.

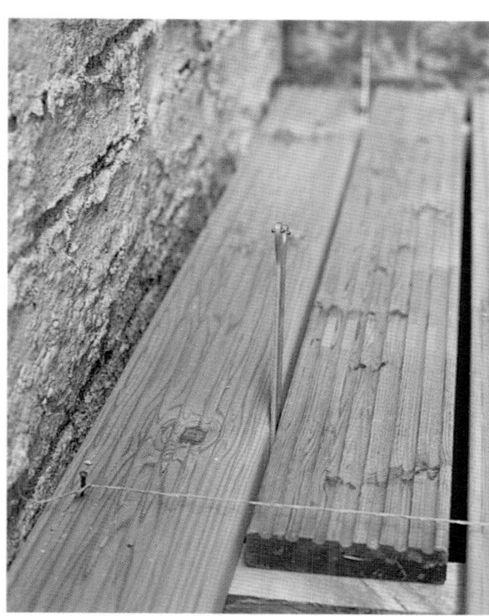

4 Cut the first decking board to length and lay it in place across the supporting framework and joists, aligning it with one long edge. To improve drainage and ensure even spacing between the boards, use metal or plywood spacers to leave a 5-6mm gap between boards, removing and re-using the spacers as you fix each board in place.

5 Using a cordless drill, screw two 63mm screws through the board over each joist and into every section of the outer framework. Use a string line to help you to align the screws across the deck's width and drill pilot holes for the screws first. Cut the remaining boards, varying the lengths if you wish to stagger the ends, and fix in place in the same way.

6 You may have to cut the final board down in width to fit it in position. Set a circular saw to match the width required. If sawing by hand, clamp the board to your workbench and tackle a metre at a time. Get a helper to support the end of the board as you work your way along it. Fix the board to the frame in the usual way. Seal or stain the deck if needed or desired.

Building a raised deck

A raised deck is useful where you have sloping ground, but note you will need planning permission (and Building Regulations approval) if it is more than 300mm high.

Before you start Nothing spoils the sight of a new deck more than weeds growing up through the cracks between its boards. Therefore, before constructing the deck all vegetation, including turf, must be cleared. Compact and level the ground, leaving a gentle slope towards the outer edge of the deck to allow for drainage. Then lay a weed-suppressing membrane over the surface and cover with gravel.

Tools *Cordless drill; saw; screwdriver; try square; spade; spirit level; tape measure. Power tools such as screwdrivers and saws will reduce the workload with some of the repetitive tasks.*

Materials *Concrete blocks for posts to rest on; cement, sand and aggregate; joist hangers and galvanised nails; stainless steel screws, countersunk; 12 x 175mm galvanised coach bolts, nuts and washers; wooden joists, 150 x 50mm, length depending on size of deck; wooden posts, 100 x 100mm, length depending on height of deck; decking boards.*

1 Use string lines pulled tightly between wooden pegs driven into the ground to mark out the edge of the site that will be covered by the deck. If the deck is to be oblong or square, use a 3:4:5 builder's square (page 467) to set out the corners.

2 If the deck is going to be attached to the house, bolt the wall plate to the house wall (page 419), ensuring that the top surface is at least 150mm below the level of the damp-proof course.

3 Mark out the centres of the joists at 400mm intervals from each end on the wall plate and nail on the joist hangers. You may need to alter the spacing slightly if the length is not divisible by 400.

4 Dig out holes 600mm deep and 300mm square where the posts are going to go. There should be a post at each corner and one no more than every 1.8m across the deck. Place hardcore (page 432) in the bottom of each hole and rest the base of a 100 x 100mm post on it.

Alternatively If you are using a double-sided supporting beam made from the same size of timber as the joists (as in the drawing below), position the outer posts in from the ends of the beam. Beam spacing can be 3m, but the supporting posts need to be no more than 1.8m apart.

5 Use a spirit level to ensure the posts are upright, nail temporary braces to the posts as support, then fill the holes with concrete, packing it tightly around the base of the posts. The concrete should be foundation mix (see page 459) or use pre-mixed post fixing concrete. Double check that the posts are vertical and in line with your setting-out string, then leave them for 48 hours for the concrete to harden before continuing with the job.

6 6 Connect one end of each outside joist to the ends of the wallplate using a corner bracket (or nails and a supporting timber block) and secure the other end to the outside of the corner posts with two galvanised coach bolts (nuts and washers on the inner side of the posts).

You may find it easier to leave the joists a little too long and then cut them flush with the outside of the deck posts when you have fixed them in place.

Alternatively Bolt the two pieces of timber that make up the supporting beam to the posts such that the outer joists rest on them with the correct drainage fall. Secure the joists to the beam by skew nailing (drill pilot holes first) or with special brackets.

7 Fix the trimmer in place. Securely bolt it to the deck posts before trimming it flush with the outside faces of the outer side joists.

8 Nail joist hangers (above) to the inside of the trimmer at identical spacing to those that you used on the wall plate.

9 Cut all the joists to length, then drop them into the joist hangers and nail them in place.

Alternatively Secure the joists to the support beam (skew nail or use brackets as above) and screw the trimmer in place on the ends of the joists.

10 Cut and fit the decking boards at right angles to the joists, using two screws where each board passes over a joist. Using a power screwdriver or a cordless drill/driver, make pilot holes and screw the boards down, 25mm in from each edge. Use a try square to make sure that each piece of decking is accurately positioned at right angles to the joists.

11 Start adjacent to the house leaving a 5-6mm gap between each board. Use metal or plywood spacers between the boards, removing and re-using the spacers as you fix each board in space.

12 To finish off, cut lengths of decking board and nail them to the edges so that they cover the cut ends of the main boards.

13 You will need a handrail (and a balustrade) on a raised deck. Buy this when you buy the decking and fit the posts before you fit the decking boards. Steps leading to the garden are an optional extra.

Anatomy of a raised deck

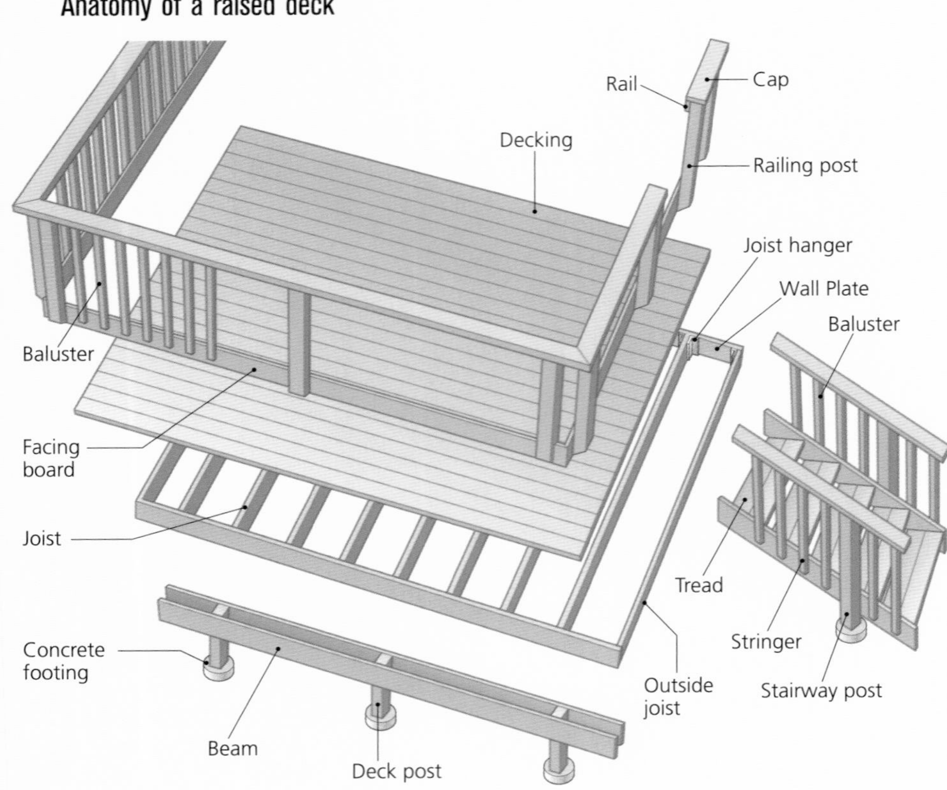

Choosing a pergola, arch or arbour

Pergolas and related garden structures may be large or small, simple or elaborate, sturdy or delicate. Often positioned against a wall or used to cover a path or link two areas of the garden, they tend to become a visual focus and therefore must be sited with care as well as soundly built.

Types of structures

Pergola A general term for a series of arches spaced at regular intervals and joined at the top by beams. It may stand alone or be a lean-to structure against a wall. It is usually intended as a support for climbing plants.

Arcade A type of pergola, either free-standing or attached to a wall, which is open to the elements.

Colonnade An arcade that covers a path linking one building to another.

Loggia A type of pergola, built against the side of a house and usually glazed or roofed overhead. It sometimes has glazed sides as well.

Arbour A structure enclosing a seat but open at the front. It is basically a pergola or arch that is closed in on three sides and typically decked with plants.

Arch A structure consisting of a pair of upright posts or pillars joined at the top by an overhead cross-beam; it is generally used to frame a path or gateway.

Site and situation

- A pergola that covers a path may entice you to explore or lead you to another area within the garden.
- Straight pergolas extend vistas and frame views, whereas a curving structure is intriguing, its end hidden from sight.
- When sited as a lean-to structure against a wall, a pergola can make an elegant transition from indoors to outdoors, especially if designed to harmonise with the style of house.
- A pergola can simply cover a patio to make an intimate outdoor sitting and eating area.

Design tips

- If lavishly decked with plants, a pergola can become an airy, colourful tunnel. Keep the design simple if the emphasis is to be on the plants.
- Left bare, a pergola or arch can have the ornamental quality of sculpture.
- For a balanced appearance, try to plan the length of a pergola so that the distance between each arch is the same as the span across the entrance.
- Slope the top of a lean-to pergola downwards, in case you decide later on to glaze or roof it in as a loggia.
- For a more decorative finish, pitch the roof beams upwards to produce a pointed central apex, or you can tilt, curve or shape the ends to give an oriental look.

- A height of 2.2–2.5m under the roof beams, and an entrance width of 1.5m between posts, is the minimum for comfortable passage, especially if the pergola is covered with plants.
- Err on the side of strength when choosing materials and dimensions, so the structure can withstand the force of strong winds and the heavy weight of wet foliage.

Materials

Timber The most popular material is planed timber, treated with preservative. Pressure-treated wood is preferred because it resists rotting and requires no additional treatment to preserve it. However, pressure-treated wood does not take stain and paint well; therefore, it's best to use regular untreated wood if you intend to apply your own finish.

Rustic poles are an attractive alternative to prepared timber. Use natural poles complete with their bark for a truly rustic appearance, or choose stripped, treated poles for longer life.

Plastic A long-lasting composite material made from recycled plastic is available. It looks and behaves like timber but is synthetic. Garden centres supply kits made almost entirely from plastic, with parts that clip together. This could be a good option if you do not feel up to making your own pergola from scratch.

Brick or stone For large, substantial, free-standing pergolas use square pillars of brick or stone to support heavy overhead timber cross beams.

Metal Tubular metal arches, with a flat, rounded or pointed profile are modern and unobtrusive; galvanised or plastic-sheathed arches last longer than wood.

Structural hints

- Use a spirit level and plumb line for accurate positioning of posts and beams.
- Make sure right angles on squares and rectangles are true by checking that both diagonals measure exactly the same.
- The greater the distance between posts, the thicker they and the bearers must be.
- For increased strength reinforce all joints with T-shaped brackets or angle brackets.
- Diagonal reinforcing poles or corner braces also add strength, especially on rustic pole structures.
- With lean-to structures, support one end of the cross beams on a 100 x 50mm wall plate screwed or bolted to the wall. Either half-joint the ends or rest them in metal joist hangers.
- Strengthen the joints on planed timber with waterproof adhesive.
- One option for joining sections together is to use halving joints (right). Timber joined in this way makes a strong and sturdy joint with the top of both pieces flush with one another. Mark out the joint, make a saw cut down each side, then chisel out the waste.

- Hurricane clips make strong joints where the beams attach to the cross members and avoid the need for complicated joinery.

Building a pergola

A simple wooden pergola with a flat top sturdy enough to carry the weight of climbing plants can be easily assembled, though the task is made easier if two people are working together.

Tools *Sledgehammer; spirit level; saw; chisel; mallet; spanner; drill.*

Materials *For a pergola 4m long, 2m wide and 2.2m high, 50 x 100mm timber treated with preservative, as follows: 6 upright 75mm posts 2.7m long; 2 bearers (main beams) 4m long; 5 cross beams 2.2m long; 80mm screws; 200mm screws or carriage bolts; 6 metal post spikes.*

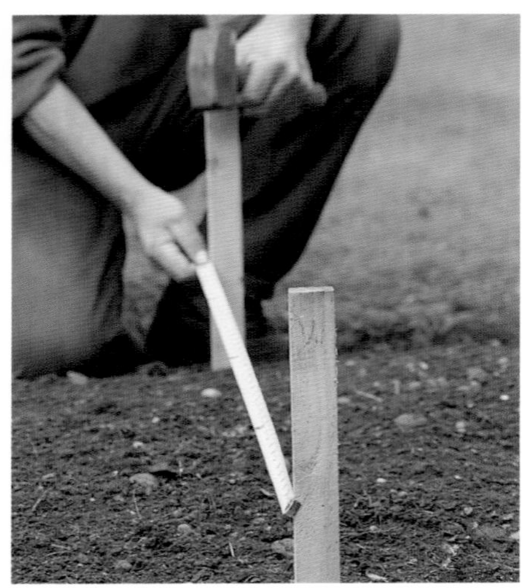

1 Mark out the area where the pergola is to be sited. Using short lengths of timber, mark positions for the posts, three on each side, and spaced 1.5m apart each way.

2 Drive metal post spikes into the ground to support the squared timber uprights. Use a sledgehammer and protect the top of the spike with a wooden 'dolly' (which can be bought) or a suitably sized offcut of timber.

3 Wedge the posts in the metal spikes and tighten the two bolts on either side to secure each one; check they are vertical.

4 Position a bearer along the top of the posts on one side of the pergola with an equal amount overhanging at each end. Using a spirit level check that it is horizontal. Mark the position of three posts on the bearer and the two midway points between the posts.

5 The cross beams can sit on top of the bearers, but will look better if you use halving joints (page 63) in the bearer and/or the cross beam. Use a saw and a chisel (with a mallet) to make these 50mm wide and 50mm deep. For our pergola, we have made a halving joint only in the cross beam.

6 Set the bearers in position, together with the three cross beams that join them, over the tops of the posts (we have made a 75mm wide halving joint in the bearer to fit over the post). Drill through the joints and use 200mm screws or carriage bolts to fix them to the posts. Join the intervening two cross beams to the bearers with 80mm screws.

7 Finally treat the completed pergola with your choice of finish, making certain that it is not poisonous to plants and animals. You may also want to add some screw-in vine eyes and plastic covered wire to encourage plants to grow over the completed structure.

ANCHORING POSTS WITH CONCRETE

If you are building a heavy structure, or erecting a pergola on a light soil, where it might be loosened in high winds, it will need a firm foundation. Bed the upright posts in concrete footings rather than using metal spikes.

1 Dig a hole for each post with a narrow spade. Make the holes about 300mm square and 600mm deep.

2 Place a layer of gravel 100mm deep in the bottom of each hole to aid drainage and prevent the bottom of each post from rotting.

3 Mix up concrete using foundation mix (page 459) or use pre-mixed post-fixing concrete (one bag per post), in a wheelbarrow or electric mixer. Aim for a slightly dry mix that will support the posts better than very wet concrete until the concrete hardens.

4 Set the posts in the holes and get a helper to shovel in the concrete while you check with a spirit level that the posts are vertical. Work the wet concrete around the posts with a wooden stake to compact the wet concrete and work out any air bubbles.

5 Always use temporary braces to support posts set in concrete to keep them vertical (and with their tops correctly spaced) whilst the concrete sets.

6 After 2 to 3 days remove the temporary braces. Ensure the concrete has set hard before continuing with the construction of the pergola.

Building an arbour

If you have room to build one, creating an arbour can provide a shady seat with a completely different view of the garden. Traditionally, the sides are covered with latticework to support climbing plants.

Tools *Tape measure; hand or power saw; power drill plus twist drill bits; try square; screwdriver; hammer; nail punch; trimming knife; sanding block and abrasive paper; pencil and string; paintbrush.*

Materials *For an arbour about 1.5m wide, 600mm deep and 2.4m high, preservative-treated softwood as listed, right. Also countersunk wood screws; panel pins; roofing felt and clout nails; exterior PVA woodworking adhesive; preservative wood stain.*

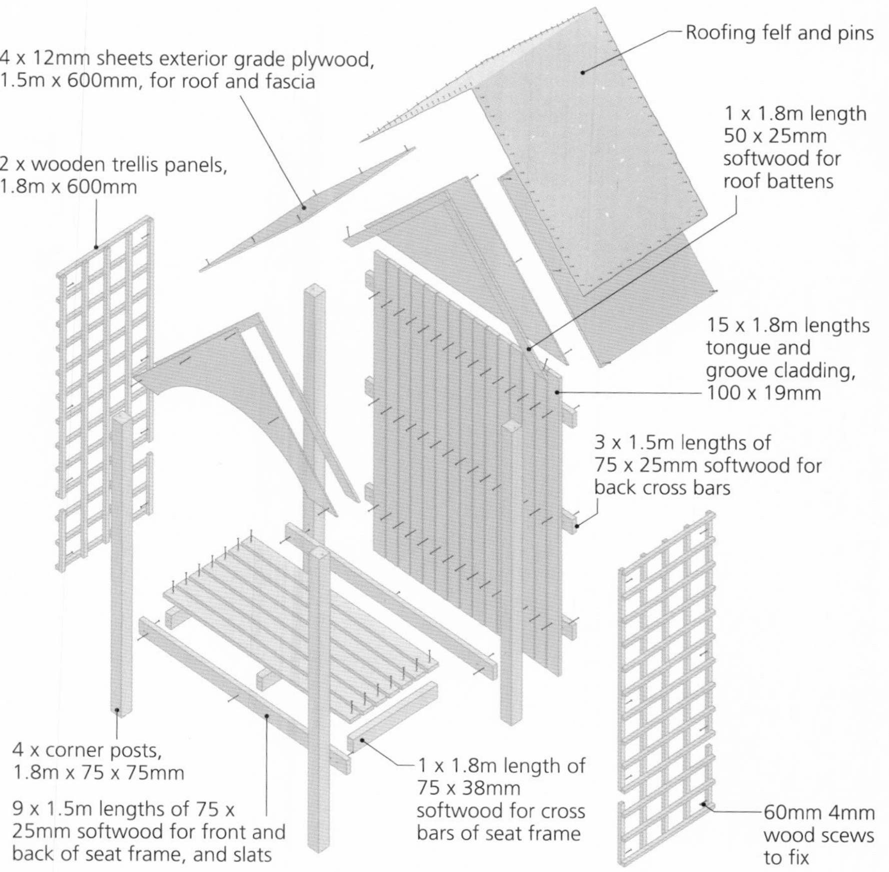

What you will need This diagram shows all the components you will need to build an arbour 1.5m wide, 600mm deep and 2.4m high – large enough for two people to sit comfortably side by side.

Making the frame

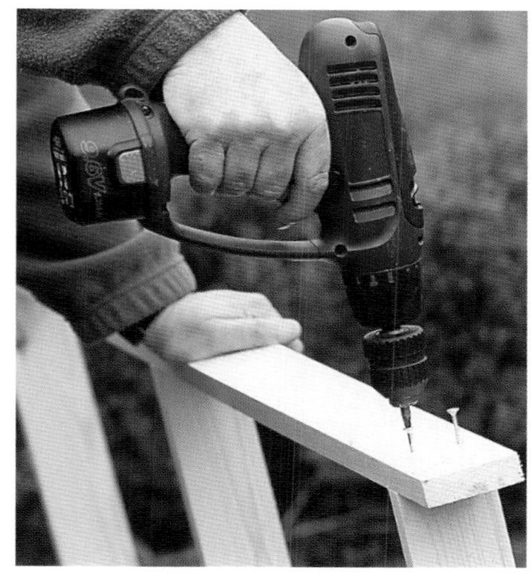

1 Cut the 75 x 25mm front and back seat rails and the three 75 x 38mm linking seat rails to length. Glue and screw them together to make the seat frame.

2 Screw the seat frame to the posts so the top of the frame is about 450mm above ground level. Attach two posts first, then get a helper to support the frame while you attach the other two posts. Check that the frame is square to the posts.

3 Stand the assembly upright and nail offcuts to the tops of the posts to keep it square. Screw the three cladding support rails to the rear faces of the back posts – one at the top, one about 300mm above ground level and the third in between.

USING POST BASES

If you are erecting your arbour on a paved surface or a concrete base, you can use bolt-down post bases to support it. Once you have completed the basic framework (step 3), set each post in the shoe of its base and get the whole assembly perfectly square. Drill and plug the fixing holes, insert masonry bolts and bolt each base down. Then replace the frame and secure each post in its shoe.

Cladding the frame

1 Fix the cladding to the back crossbars plank by plank. Slide the grooved edge of each one over its neighbour's tongue and tamp it down from the top to get it level.

2 Pin the first plank to the rails through its face and punch in the pin heads. Pin subsequent planks through their tongues so the fixings are concealed when the next plank is fitted.

3 Cut and fit the seven seat slats. Fit the front and rear slats against the corner posts, then space the others out evenly using a home-made spacer. Fix the slats to each rail with two countersunk screws.

4 Complete the arbour frame by adding a 1800 x 600mm lattice trellis panel at each end of the structure. Set each panel between its posts, drill clearance holes through its sides and screw it to the posts.

Adding the roof

1 Cut each gable end from a 1500 x 600mm rectangle of 12mm plywood and sand the cut edges. Draw a curve on the front panel (below) and cut it out.

DRAWING A CURVE

To draw a curve 1200mm wide and 280mm high, mark the apex of the curve (A) 280mm above the baseline. Measure 600mm from A to the baseline to find the two foci of the ellipse (B). Drive in a small screw at each focus and tie a loop of string round them so a pencil held in the loop rests at A when the string is taut. Move the pencil round the loop to draw the outline of the ellipse.

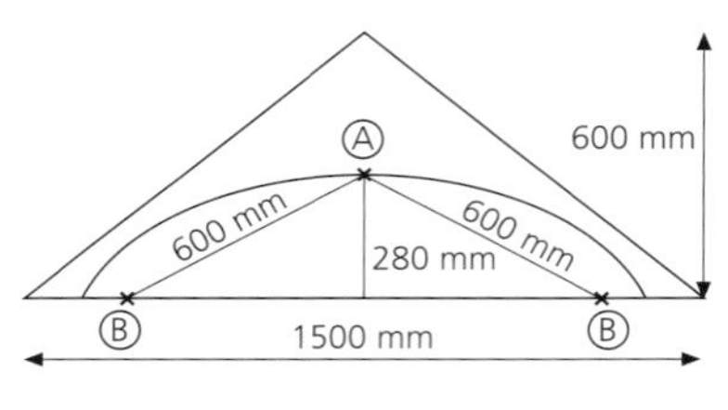

2 Glue and screw 50 x 25mm bearers to the top edges of the inner face of each gable. Cut two plywood roof slopes and glue and screw them to the top edges of the gables to complete the roof structure. Sit the roof assembly on top of the posts and drive a long screw vertically down through the roof into the top of each upright.

3 Cut a piece of roofing felt to cover the roof and fix it in place with clout nails. Add bargeboards to conceal the felt edges on the gables if you wish.

Children's play areas

Creating a safe play space in your back garden is a good idea if you have children. Take a look at the garden and see which parts you could incorporate into play areas – trees for tree houses or a sturdy branch from which to hang a swing.

You do not have to spend a fortune for your child to have a play area in the garden. If your child is old enough, involve him or her in the planning of the play area.

A secure space

One of the most versatile play areas is also one of the cheapest – a flat open area where children can run, ride bikes and generally let off steam. If there are trees, so much the better: these provide shade and encourage inventive and imaginative play.

To keep your children in one place, it is wise to have a fence or wall around the play area. Although many gardens already have walls and fences, consider a supplementary fence if your garden is large. You must also fence in pools and ponds.

Play equipment

You can buy a wide range of garden toys in wood, metal and plastic. Don't buy anything too large for your garden, and follow any assembly instructions carefully. Check all fastenings from time to time to make sure that everything is secure.

Young children love playhouses. You can spend a lot on elaborate playhouses, but a child will get just as much fun from a simple plywood box with windows cut into it. Or turn a small tool shed into a temporary den: it can revert to its former use when the children grow out of it.

Laying a safe play surface

You can minimise the risk of bumps and bruises by creating a soft surface underneath a swing, or on which to stand a climbing frame. The simplest surface is a thick layer of forest bark chips.

Tools *Scissors or sharp trimming knife; mallet; perhaps a saw; screwdriver.*

Materials *Weed membrane large enough to cover play area; edging material (such as fixed log edging, available in DIY stores); stainless steel screws; bark chips (the number of bags needed depends on area).*

1 Determine the shape and size of the area you wish to create and lay out your chosen edging. Make sure that it extends far enough around the climbing frame to break the fall of a child falling off.

2 Once you are happy with the layout, fix the edging in place. Hammer posts straight into the lawn then join the sections of edging using stainless steel screws. Lay out the weed membrane within the play area. It does not need pegging as the bark will keep it in place.

3 Rake bark chips in a thick layer (at least 50mm) over the membrane. This surface is low maintenance – all it needs is raking occasionally, and topping up with bark.

Making a sandpit

All children love sand. Here is an alternative to the bright plastic versions sold in toy shops. It has a lid to keep out rain and animals when not in use. Be sure to use playpit sand – builders' sand will stain clothes and is usually too coarse for play.

Tools *Hammer; drill with wood bits; saw; string and pegs; border edging tool; spade; screwdriver; tape measure; pencil; staple gun (or hammer and clout nails); abrasive paper.*

Materials *Eight decking boards; four 50 x 50mm sawn timber posts (about 350mm long with pointed ends) for corners; decking screws; two-half sheets of weatherproof 12mm ply for lid and corner seats; three lengths of 25 x 50mm timber for lid lip; 2 x 2m sheet of butyl pond liner; six or more bags of playpit sand.*

This sandpit is two decking boards high: make it 1170mm square so that the lid can be made from a half-sheet of plywood.

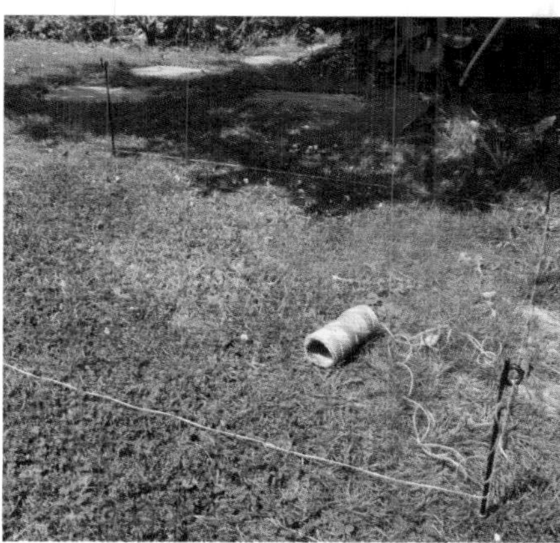

1 Decide on the position of the sandpit. Try to site it out of direct sunlight as the sand will reflect UV light, increasing the risk of sunburn. Push in a peg at each corner and stretch string all the way round. Then use an edging tool to cut through the turf along the lines to a depth of about 50mm.

2 Use a sharp spade to cut away the turf and remove the soil to a depth of about 50mm. Make the bottom as level as possible, digging out roots and stones.

3 Hammer the corner posts into the ground to the height of two decking boards from the bottom of the excavation.

4 Cut the decking boards to fit the posts – one pair to exactly cover the posts; the other to cover the post plus the thickness of the first pair. Drill pilot holes in the decking boards and, using decking screws, fix the boards to the posts as shown.

5 Tip half a bag of sand into the hole and level it to make a smooth surface for the pond liner. Lay the pond liner in the sandpit and fill it with sand *before* trimming it to size – the weight of the sand will pull the liner further into the hole.

6 Trim the liner allowing an overhang of about 50mm all round. Then fold this under to make a neat hem and staple it to the exterior of the decking boards. Don't worry about all the creases in the corners – these will be hidden by the corner seats.

7 Cut four right-angled triangles from 12mm ply with the short sides about 350mm long. Sand the cut edges to get rid of splinters; drill pilot holes and screw them onto the corners of the sandpit.

8 If you have made your sandpit 1170mm square, the lid can be an exact half-sheet of plywood (1220mm square). Cut the 25 x 50mm timber to size and glue and screw it – edge-on – along three sides of the lid. This will allow you to slide the heavy lid on and off rather than lifting it: fit handles to the side you pull to make this easier.

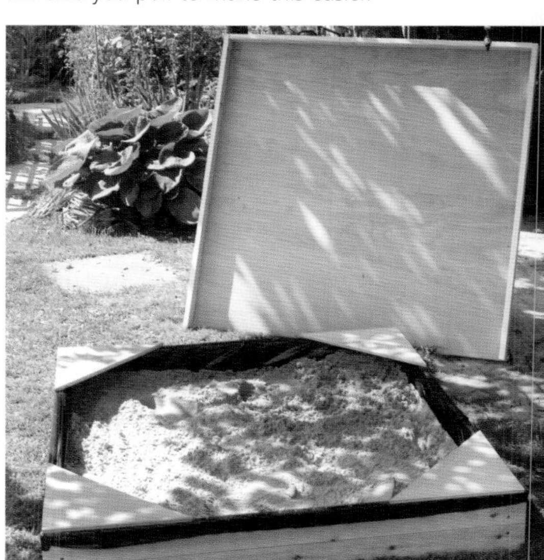

Choosing outbuildings

An outbuilding is any structure that is not attached to the main house but still forms part of the property. Outbuildings include functional sheds and workshops, decorative summerhouses and gazebos, and greenhouses and potting sheds. Factors to be taken into account when deciding between them include usage, style, permanence, size and budget.

Usage

Often you may simply require a garden shed which serves as a store for garden tools. Look at how many tools you have and wish to store – not just now but also in the future. Make a list of the things that you want to put into the shed and try to visualise how much space they will take up. Consider, too, the other things you may have that could be kept in a shed, such as bicycles and children's garden toys. A shed or outbuilding that is too small will lead to frustration and will probably not be used as it should. If you are thinking of keeping plants in an outbuilding – in a potting shed or greenhouse, for instance – consider whether you intend to keep them in the building during winter; also, whether you will need to use the building for general storage too.

Style

Garden outbuildings vary widely in style. Try to choose one which is sympathetic to its surroundings, both in style and size. For example, a good choice of greenhouse for a small garden is probably a lean-to style that can be placed against a sunny wall. A bigger garden, however, may well be able to accommodate a much larger and grander structure.

Permanence

Sheds and other outbuildings that are small in size can often be taken apart if you move, whereas more substantial buildings become permanent structures. Although this may make your house easier to sell or increase the value, you will have to start again at your new house if that does not have the sort of outbuilding you need.

Size and budget

- Free-standing garden sheds in kit form start at 1.8 x 1.2m, going up to 4.5 x 3.8m. A good minimum size, with room for a bench so you can use it for potting or as a workshop, is 2.4 x 1.8m.
- Summerhouses can be rectangular, square or octagonal. They range in size from 1.8 x 1.2m up to a massive 6.3 x 4m, complete with veranda.
- There are lots of small greenhouses that you just reach into – plus lean-to greenhouses and free-standing greenhouses similar in size to sheds.

Materials to choose from

Sheds and workshops need to be lockable and secure, and of sturdy construction; greenhouses and potting sheds must let in as much light as possible but should be strong enough to withstand the worst weather – even so, try to avoid windy sites.

Brick and block A good choice for permanent outbuildings and those that will be used as workshops and hobbies rooms where you will be spending more time than just storing things. Cavity wall construction means that the building can be properly insulated to the same standard or even higher than the main house and the installation of internal fixtures and fittings is easier. These are slower to build and more expensive than a kit-built timber framed building but will last for many years.

Wood The most popular type of garden shed comes as a ready-to-assemble kit, with either feather-edged or shiplap treated wood panels. Only the more expensive greenhouses are made of wood; the wood used for these is traditionally cedar, which is virtually maintenance-free.

Plastic The latest material for garden shed construction is plastic – either resin panels or PVC cladding on a galvanised steel frame. Plastic sheds can have translucent roofs and an integral plastic floor and are maintenance free.

Aluminium and other metals Metal buildings and greenhouses (see opposite) are lightweight so require attachment to a secure base, usually concrete, pavers or posts sunk into concrete in the ground. Other styles have their own galvanised base onto which the frame fits. They require little in the way of maintenance and, because they simply bolt together, make a good choice if you wish to move in the future.

Glazing Glass is the traditional glazing material for windows in greenhouses. Horticultural glass is 3mm thick and is rather fragile. Toughened glass is available, but is more expensive. When choosing glass, look at it edge-on: the greener it looks, the poorer its light transmission.

Rigid plastics are an alternative. They can be curved, are less likely to break and offer about 90 per cent light transmission. They are more expensive than glass, however, and attract dirt because of the build-up of static electricity. The windows in most timber kit sheds are made from plastic.

Services

The versatility of many outbuildings can be extended by the supply of electricity (page 316) and water. This makes it possible to see when it is dark, to heat the building, and to provide water for gardening or washing the car. Your local Building Control department should be notified if you plan to install a new electric circuit (page 497).

Planning permission

Unless you live in a listed building or a 'designated' area (see box on page 482), outbuildings do not need planning permission, provided they meet the rules listed on page 486. Building Regulations approval is needed only for electric wiring.

Metal is a durable and low-maintenance option for a garden shed. It does not require regular treatment against rot, like wood does and is also very secure. Panels usually bolt together, so the shed can be dismantled if you need to move it.

Installing a greenhouse

Position your greenhouse away from overhanging branches and where it will get the greatest amount of sunlight, particularly during winter.

Mark out where the greenhouse will stand, making sure you have a firm foundation of the correct size and type. It is important that the foundation will be able to support the structure you have chosen, and is dry and level. You may need to lay a brick or concrete foundation (page 460). Some greenhouse kits come with their own base, which must be anchored to the ground through pins set in concrete. Have the holes dug and concrete ready.

Tools *Spirit level; ratchet or spanner.*

Materials *Greenhouse kit; ready-mixed concrete. Possibly washing-up liquid.*

1 Lay out the base frame and bolt it together on the firm, level area where the greenhouse will stand. Make sure the frame is square and sink the metal anchors into the concrete-filled holes.

2 Identify and lay out on the ground the two ends of the greenhouse framework, before bolting them together.

> **HELPFUL TIP**
>
> When assembling a structure such as a greenhouse framework, it is wise to bolt the sections loosely to start with, and tighten them only when the glass has been fitted. As most glass is cut to right angles, it will help you to make sure the structure will fit squarely round it.

3 Next, lay out and assemble the sides of the greenhouse framework, bolting them together loosely. With a helper, lift the back and one side of the greenhouse onto the base and hold them in position while you bolt them together, making sure the corner is square.

4 Bolt the second side and the front of the greenhouse onto the first two sections, with a helper holding them steady. Then fasten the sides and ends onto the base.

5 Fix the ridge bar of the roof into place and slot in all the roof bars.

6 Now that the structure has been erected, slide the rubber glazing strips into position along the glazing bars to cushion the glass. A small amount of washing-up liquid applied to the glazing bars helps the strips to slip into place.

7 Start glazing the structure with the glass or plastic sheets supplied. It is easier and safer to work on the roof first, before doing the sides. Fasten the glass to the glazing bars using the W-shaped glazing clips supplied.

8 Finally, assemble and glaze the door, checking that it will open and close smoothly. Once this is done, tighten the bolts of the entire structure.

Putting up a shed

A garden shed can have a variety of uses, from simply being a place to store garden tools to acting as a hobbies room or workshop. Sizes vary so choose one that is large enough to cover future as well as present needs. Consider the siting of the shed carefully, particularly if you plan to run electricity to it.

Putting up a kit shed

Putting up a shed is often achievable in a few hours, but all but the smallest tool stores come in large sections, so you may need to enlist some help putting it together. The most strenuous and time-consuming part of the job is likely to be laying the base – so make sure this is all completed before the shed is delivered.

If the shed is to be used as a workshop or hobbies room consider installing insulation within the interior timber framework and cladding the inside with plywood or hardboard for a smooth finish. All sheds should come with preservative-treated timber (usually pressure-treated), but it will do no harm to add some extra treatment after you have put it up.

Tools *Tape measure; cordless screwdriver; power drill with twist and countersink bits; pencil; spirit level; try square; trimming knife; straightedge; hammer.*

Materials *Shed kit. Possibly also additional preservative.*

1 Unless you are erecting your shed on a level hardstanding, you will need to create a firm and level base for the structure before you start. The sturdiest option is to lay an area of concrete (page 460), slightly smaller all round than the footprint of the shed, so that rainwater running off the shed will drain away into the ground.

Alternatively A dry base can be created by laying several paving slabs on the site of the shed. Make sure that all the slabs are level so that the shed will sit squarely on its base.

2 Start by lifting the gable end into position and propping it upright with a post. The bottom batten of each panel should sit on the shed base, so that the panel boarding extends beyond the base.

3 Lift a side panel into place and screw it to the gable end where the frames meet. Put three fixings at each joint, at the top, middle and bottom of the panel.

4 Complete the walls by fitting the two remaining sides. The shed should balance on the base, with the panels lipping over the floor and the battens resting on it. Do not screw the walls down to the floor yet.

5 If the shed kit includes a beam to support the roof, fix it across the shed from gable end to gable end. This will also help to brace the structure.

6 Fit the door into its opening and check that it opens and closes easily. If it doesn't, the shed may not be quite square. Loosen the roof beam and check each corner with a try square. Hammer the corners to square them up if necessary, using an offcut of timber to protect the panels of the shed.

7 Lift the roof panels into place and secure them to the roof beam, if there is one. Screw through the roof into the sides and gable ends to hold it firmly in position.

8 Nail the completed structure to the floor of the shed.

9 Cut the roofing felt supplied with the shed into three equal pieces: one for each slope of the roof and a third to lay over the apex, overlapping each side panel by at least 75mm. Allow for an overhang of 50mm at either end.

10 Use felting nails to tack the felt in place, starting with the side panels. Space the tacks 300mm apart along the top edge of the felt and 100mm apart along the gable ends and the eaves. Lay the middle length of felt over the apex and nail it in position all round.

11 Make neat folds at the corners (see Re-felting a pitched shed roof, right) then hammer the fascia boards into place. Nail decorative fillets, if supplied, to the apex of each gable end.

12 Nail strips of corner trim onto each corner of the shed to finish the structure, then fix a sliding bolt or hasp and staple to make the door secure.

13 If desired, fit 'mini' guttering as described on page 405, along with a downpipe leading to a water butt.

WINDOWS IN SHEDS

Most kit sheds are supplied with plastic windows, which are easy to fit into the frames that are also part of the kit. Working from the outside, fix the plastic or metal sills provided into place and secure them by nailing wooden strips (or cloaks) to the frames between windows. Move inside the shed and slide the windows into their frames. Nail beading round the frames on the inside to hold the windows in position and make them secure.

Re-felting a pitched shed roof

If there is visible damage at several spots on a shed roof, or if water leaks through in places even though you can see no damage, the bituminous felt covering needs replacing.

Before you start Bituminous felt is sold in green, black and red, and in various grades; the heavier the felt, the longer it lasts.

You will usually be able to reach the top of the roof working from a stepladder and moving it along as necessary. If the roof has been fitted with eaves battens or fascia boards to cover the felt, lever these off.

Tools *Stepladder; claw hammer; sharp knife; wooden batten about 1m long; old paintbrush. Possibly also a chisel, plane and screwdriver.*

Materials *Wood preservative; bituminous roofing felt; 13mm galvanised clout nails; chalk; cold felt adhesive. Possibly some new softwood boarding or some outdoor grade plywood or chipboard; fascia boards, ridge board or eaves battens with galvanised nails or screws for fixing.*

Preparation

1 Tear off all the old felt. Prise out any old nails with the claw hammer. If any heads break off, hammer the shanks down flush so that there are no sharp projections to damage the new felt.

2 Check the timber covering of the roof for damage or rot, and replace it where necessary. Saturate any replacement wood with preservative and let it dry before use.

If a plywood or chipboard sheet needs replacing, unscrew it and screw a new one in its place with galvanised screws.

If a tongued-and-grooved board needs replacing, cut through the tongue with hammer and chisel so you can ease the board out. You will not be able to fit a tongued and grooved replacement, unless you remove the tongue. Alternatively, you can plane down a piece of softwood to fit the gap exactly. Nail it in place with galvanised nails.

3 Where a fascia board, ridge board or eaves batten is damaged or missing, fit a new one. Treat it first with preservative and fix it with galvanised screws or nails.

4 Treat the remaining roof timber with preservative and let it dry.

5 Cut the felt into strips of the right length with a sharp knife. The strips should run parallel to the ridge and overlap the roof by 25mm at each end.

Fixing the felt in place

1 Position the first strip with its lower edge overlapping the eaves by 25mm and its ends overlapping the roof by 25mm at each end. Run the wooden batten along it – from the centre towards the ends – to smooth out wrinkles. Using the 13mm galvanised nails, nail the top edge of the felt to the roof timber at 150mm intervals and the bottom edge to the outside face of the eaves at 50mm intervals. Nail the ends of the felt strip to the ends of the roof at 50mm intervals.

2 At the corners where the eaves and the ends meet, fold the surplus felt into a neat triangle, bend it flat and drive a nail through it.

3 Chalk a line along the length of the felt strip 75mm below its top edge.

4 Brush a strip of adhesive onto the top edge of the felt, taking it down to the chalk line. Take care not to let it spread below the line or a black smear will show on the felt. Leave the adhesive for about 30 minutes to become tacky.

5 Position the next strip of felt carefully over the adhesive. Run the batten over the felt from the middle to the ends to smooth it out. Press down the overlap firmly.

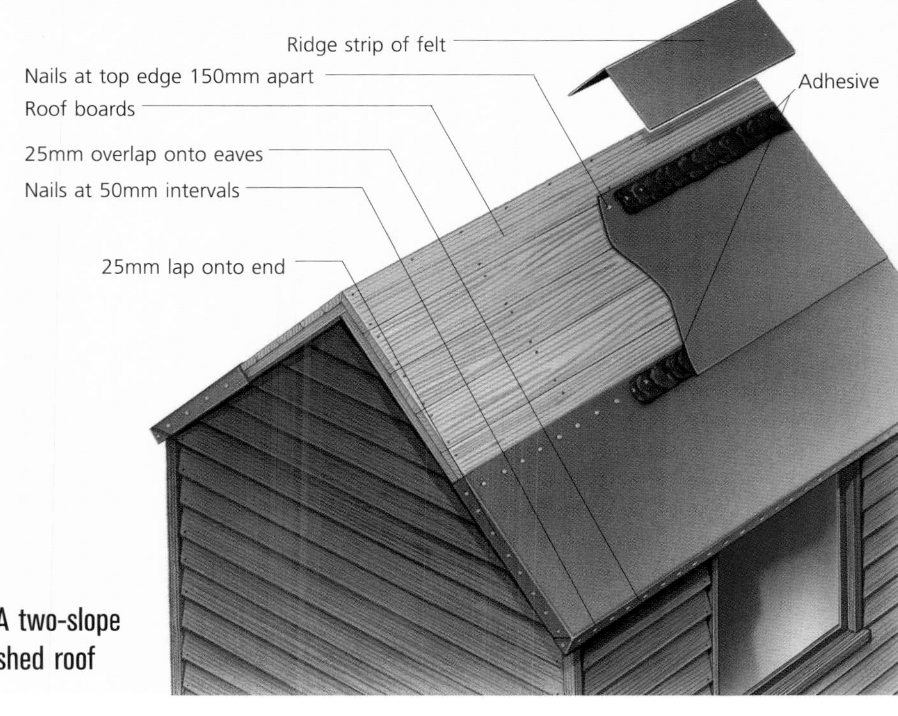

A two-slope shed roof

6 Nail the top edge at 150mm intervals and the ends at 50mm intervals.

7 Repeat steps 1–6 to felt the other slope of the roof.

8 Measure the gap from the top of the felt on one side over the ridge to the top of the felt on the other side. Measure in several places. Take the highest figure, add on 150mm and cut a strip of felt this width and the length of the ridge plus 50mm.

9 Lay the felt in place, centred over the ridge, and make a chalk line along each edge to show where to put adhesive. Put the felt to one side.

10 Brush strips of adhesive about 75mm wide along each slope. Do not let adhesive spread below the chalk lines. Leave the adhesive to become tacky.

11 Lay the felt in place on the adhesive on one slope. Press it down firmly, then smooth it over the ridge and press the other edge in place. Run the batten over the felt on both slopes from the centre outwards to drive out air.

12 Nail the ends to the fascia boards at 50mm intervals. At the top angle, fold the surplus felt over neatly and drive a nail through the fold.

13 If the shed has eaves battens and fascia boards, re-fit these as before – or replace them with new preservative-treated timber if they are missing or damaged.

One-slope roofs

Pent-style sheds – in which the roof consists of a single slope – can be felted by the same method. At the top of the slope, trim the felt to overlap 25mm onto the outside face of the eaves batten and nail it there at 50mm intervals.

PATCHING DAMAGED FELT

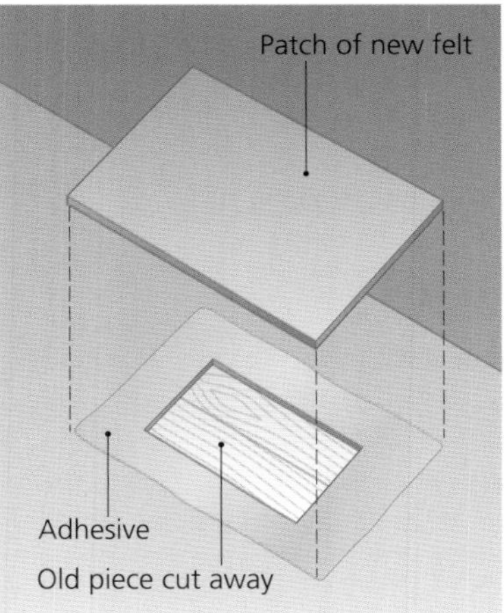

If a small area of felt is damaged, you can patch it with a felt off-cut and cold felt adhesive.

1 Cut out a rectangle of felt that will cover the damage and extend beyond it by at least 75mm all round.

2 Position the patch over the damage and run a piece of chalk around the edge to mark the area for the adhesive.

3 Brush the adhesive over the marked area with an old paintbrush. Do not let it spread outside the chalked area or smears will show on the roof. Leave the adhesive for 30 minutes to become tacky.

4 Lay the felt patch in position and press it down firmly from the centre to the edges to make sure no air bubbles are trapped under it.

Planning a fence

• In a windy spot, an open fence such as post and rails would offer little wind resistance. However, a solid fence would need to be very sturdy. Any solid fence higher than 1.2m is at risk of being blown down, no matter how well it is constructed, so it would be best to use open trellis to add any extra height.

• If the level of the neighbouring garden is higher and so the outside of a fence would be in contact with earth (which rots timber), consider building a fence on a low brick or block retaining wall, with gaps for concrete spurs to support timber fence posts.

Closeboarded vertical Upright, overlapping feather-edged boards (tapered on one side) nailed to horizontal arris rails. Boards are about 150mm shorter than the post height above ground, to allow for a horizontal gravel board. Posts are usually 2.4m apart. Excellent for screening or security, but expensive. Wood needs regular preservative treatment (page 439) to prevent shrinking or rotting. Fence has to be buillt up from separate timber components.

Closeboarded horizontal Horizontal boards nailed between posts. The boards are either feather-edged overlapping, or shiplap (with a step-shaped overlap). No arris rails or gravel boards are used. Posts are usually about 1.2m apart, with 2.4m boards butt-jointed on alternate posts. More posts are needed to give the fence strength than with vertical closeboard, making the fence very solid but a more expensive choice.

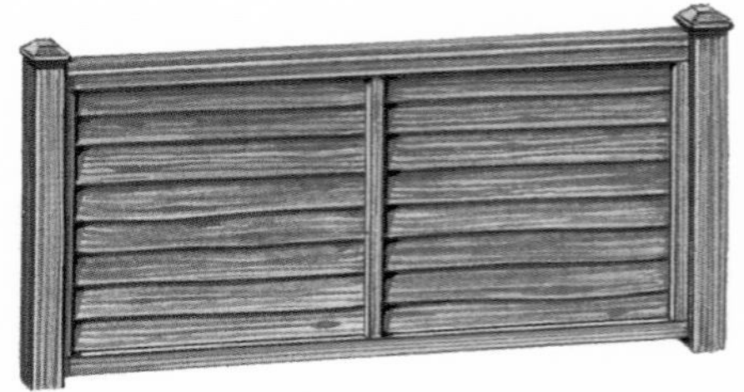

Panel Ready-made panels fixed between posts. Panels may be thin interwoven slats, overlapped horizontal boards, or vertical closeboard. Panels are normally 1.8m wide; narrower sizes are made to order. Height range: 600mm–1.8m. Easy to put up, and good for screening or security. The timber needs regular preservative treatment to prevent shrinkage or rotting. Quality varies – poorly made panels are likely to distort.

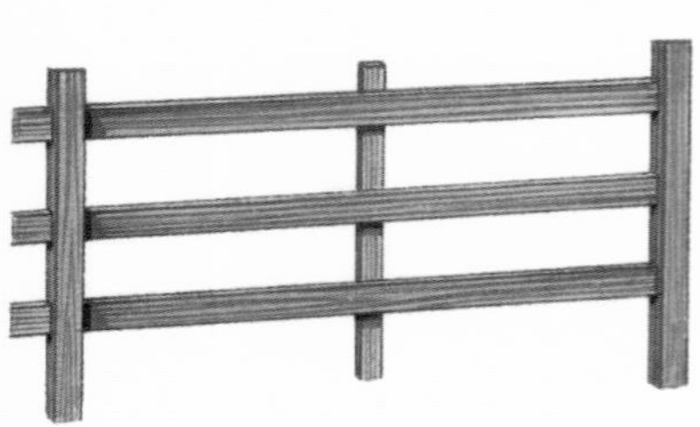

Post-and-rail (or ranch-style or railboard) Spaced horizontal rails secured to posts. Rails may be square sawn, half round, or rustic (poles, often with the bark intact). Rails (usually three) can be nailed or slotted into posts, which are usually about 1.8m apart. Height range from 300mm to 1.8m, but normally about 900mm – three rails. Suitable for a boundary or for decoration. Not as expensive as closeboard or panel fencing, and not much affected by wind. Timber needs regular painting or preservative treatment; plastic also available.

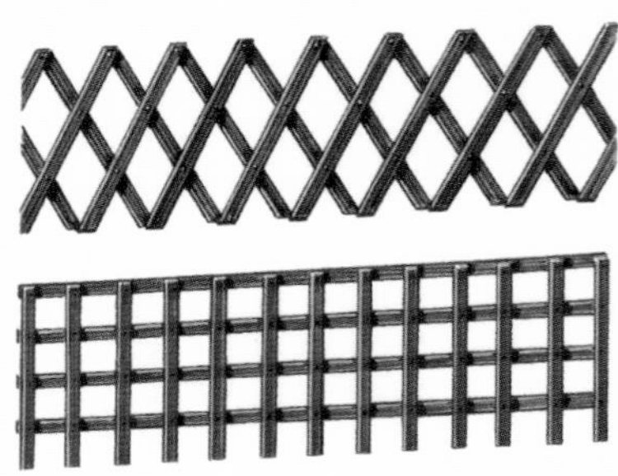

Square or diamond trellis Square trellis is usually made from hardwood battens forming squares of about 150mm, and can be bought in ready-made sections about 2m wide and 300mm–2m high, or as panel fencing. Diamond trellis is often expanding, and sold in 1.8m lengths with a height range of 300mm–1.2m. Sections can be fixed above each other. Half-round rustic diamond trellis is also available.

WIRE FENCES

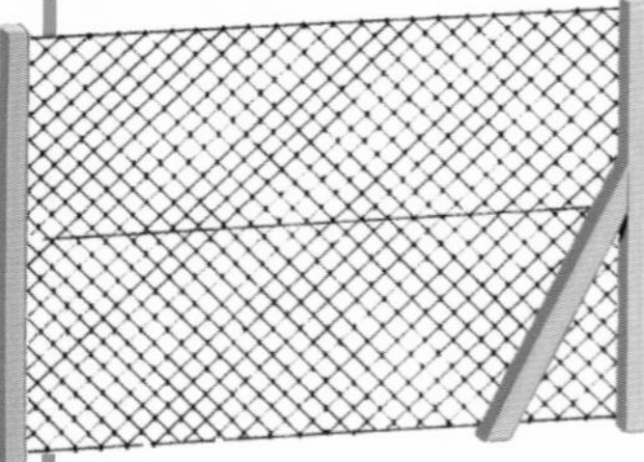

Chain link A mesh of thick, interlinked galvanised wire – plain (silver finish) or plastic coated – stretched between concrete or timber end posts by means of metal stretcher bars. The mesh is tied to two or three horizontal wires and also tied or stapled to intermediate posts. Standard height is 1.2m, but available up to 1.8m high. Sold in rolls, mesh size is normally 50mm. Good for security (especially keeping animals in or out) or boundary fencing. Fairly easy to put up, but will sag unless properly tensioned. Little maintenance is needed, except for painting timber posts, or treating them with wood preservative (page 439).

Wire or plastic netting A mesh of galvanised wire or plastic stretched between posts. It is either stapled or wired to posts, or – for greater strength – stretched on horizontal wires. Height range normally 300mm to 1.2m, with mesh 13–75mm wide. Suitable for boundary or security fencing, and cheaper than chain link, but not as strong or durable. Plastic is longer lasting than wire.

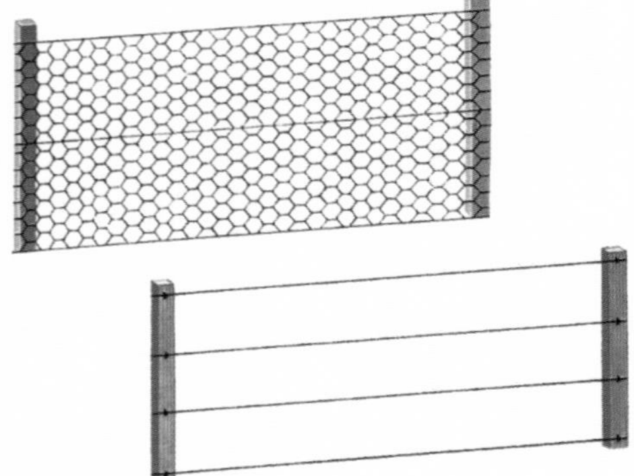

Decorative wire Straight or crimped plastic-coated wire welded or interwoven in squares or patterns. The top is usually hooped and the base spiked for sticking into the ground. Taller fencing can be stapled to timber posts. Sold either in rolls or rigid sections, with a height range of about 300–900mm, it is used mainly as decorative edging to flower borders. Easy to put up, cheap and needs no maintenance. Rolls are cheaper than rigid sections, and can be curved, but rigid sections are stronger.

Post and wire Plain or stranded galvanised wire stretched between posts. Wire is usually sold in coils by weight – from 5 to 25kg. Coil length depends on gauge. A 5kg coil of 10g (3.15mm) plain wire is 82m long, a 10kg coil twice as long. Suitable for temporary boundary fencing, it is ideal for enclosing a large area.

PLANNING PERMISSION

You must have planning permission to put up a fence more than 1m high if it fronts on a public road, or to put up any fence more than 2m high.

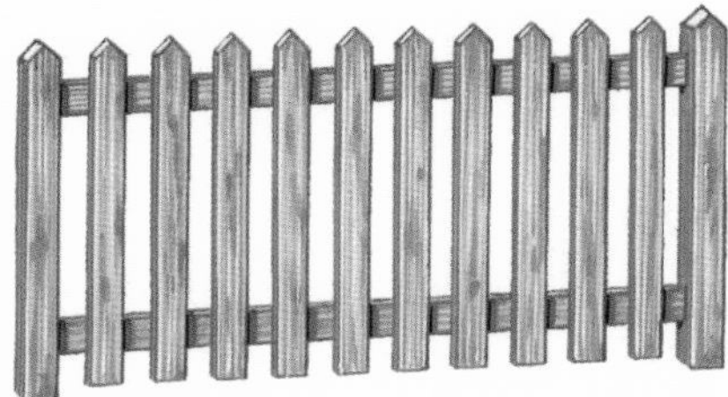

Palisade or picket Spaced, upright stakes nailed to horizontal rails slotted into posts. Posts are usually about 2.4m apart, and the height range is about 900mm–1.2m. Fencing can be bought in ready-made sections about 1.8m long, with brackets supplied for fitting sections to posts. Suitable for a boundary fence. Comparatively cheap. Can be painted or treated with wood preservative (page 439).

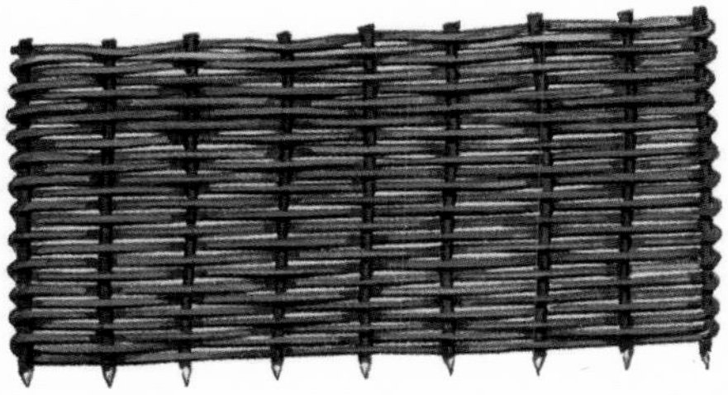

Hurdle or wattle Thin or half-round interwoven rods formed into 1.8m wide panels that can be supported on stakes or between posts. Osier (willow) rods form hurdles, hazel rods form wattles. Height range is about 600mm–2.1m. Not very long-lasting, but useful as a temporary screen for protecting growing plants. Hurdles are more expensive than wattles.

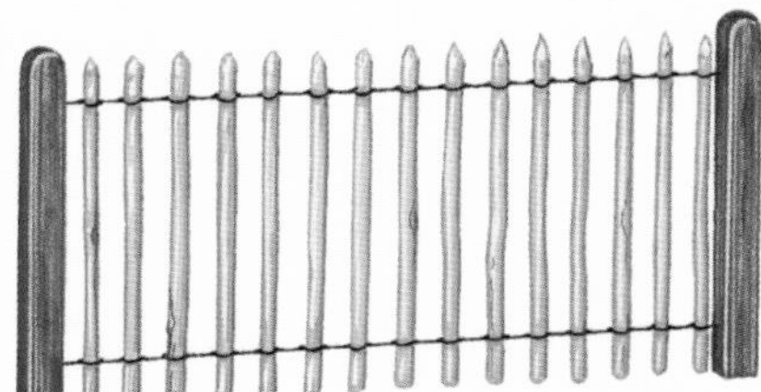

Cleft chestnut paling Stakes wired together and stretched between posts. End and corner posts are usually braced with stays. Posts are usually about 2.7m apart, and the height range is 750mm–1.8m. Suitable for a temporary boundary – while a hedge is growing, for example. Easy to put up and take down. Needs no maintenance but wires must be tensioned if the fence is to stay taut.

FENCE POSTS AND ACCESSORIES

Concrete post Heavier and more expensive than a timber post, but longer lasting and will not rot in the ground. A post 1.4m long weighs about 26kg. Posts are available with ready-made bolt holes, mortises or slots. They are generally 100mm square.

Concrete spur Short concrete post with ready-drilled bolt holes – usually 13mm across – used to support a damaged timber post. Spurs may be 75 or 100mm square. Lengths range from about 1.1 to 1.5m.

Post spike A spiked steel support (below right) driven into the ground as a base for a timber post. The post rests in a square cup above the ground. In some types the post is clamped into the cup. Concreting post spikes (right) are not pointed, but have a steel support, for anchoring into concrete. A post spike driven into soil is an unsuitable method of erecting fencing in areas subject to high winds.

Bolt-down post base A square metal cup for supporting a timber post. It has a projecting rim containing holes for bolting the base to a solid surface. It is suitable for fixing to concrete or paving slabs fully and firmly bedded in mortar, but not slabs bedded in sand.

Driving tool Fits into a metal post spike to protect it as it's being driven in. Side 'handles' allow the spike to be re-aligned if it has twisted.

Gravel board clip A galvanised bracket nailed to the inner side of the post to support the gravel board. The clip is nailed at the top and at the bottom (except where a post spike is used).

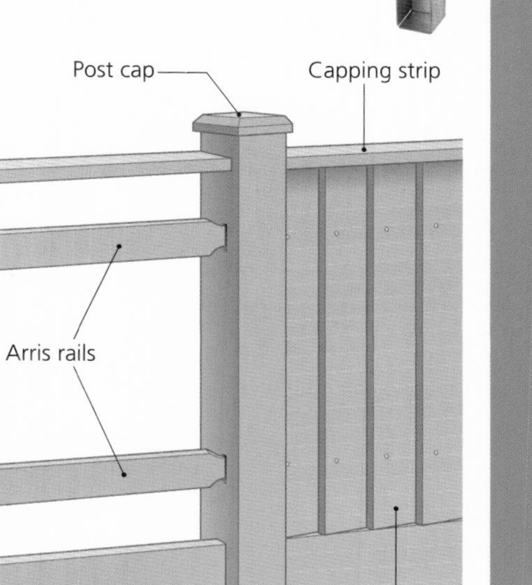

Timber post Usually softwood such as larch or pine. Buy posts ready-treated with preservative, preferably by vacuum/pressure impregnation although this is more expensive. Posts are available with ready-cut mortises for arris rails. Post sizes are normally 75 or 100mm square.

Timber post cap Flat or bevelled timber cap that is necessary for shedding rainwater and preventing rot.

Capping strip Wooden strip nailed across the top of vertical closeboard fencing to protect the vulnerable end-grain from rot.

Gravel board Board, usually made of wood or concrete, that is fitted across the base of a fence to protect the rest of the fence from rot caused by contact with damp ground.

STOP POSTS ROTTING

Even pre-treated posts will benefit from some extra protection. Soak the part of each fence post that will be buried in the soil, in wood preservative (page 439) for 24 hours. Lean the posts against a wall in separate containers, or in an improvised trough, such as a shallow pit lined with a thick sheet of polythene. Pour wood preservative into the bottom of each container. It is not usually practicable to immerse the full 460 or 610mm of the post, so brush the preservative up onto the posts from time to time. Allow posts to dry for 24 hours before using them.

Putting up fence posts

Most timber fences, posts and panels (or rails) are put up in sequence to get the spacing right; post, followed by panel (or rail), followed by post and so on. With wire and other fences, you can usually put all the posts up first.

- It is advisable to buy new posts that have been pre-treated with preservative.
- Timber posts can either be concreted in or held in post spikes. Concreting ensures a more solid and durable fixing, especially on soft ground, but may slightly increase the risk of rotting.
- Concrete posts must be concreted into place.

Preparation

- For fences over 1.2m high, sink the bottom of the post at least 600mm below ground – or 750mm for tall concrete posts.
- For lower fences, sink timber posts 450mm, and concrete posts 600mm.
- Timber posts should have about 150mm of hardcore below them to provide drainage and lessen the risk of rotting.

The distance between posts depends on the type of fence (see pages 430–1). If the new fence replaces an old one and you want to put the posts in the same positions, you will have to dig out the stumps of the old posts, and possibly the concrete surrounding them. Alternatively, you can install a half panel or short section of fencing at each end of the fence so that the new posts fall midway between the old positions.

Tools *Post-hole borer or narrow spade – unless using spikes; string and pegs; spirit level; one timber length longer than the distance between posts; one timber length as long as the distance between posts; timber lengths for temporary post supports; mallet; hammer; timber length or earth rammer (page 451). Possibly also demolition hammer or pickaxe; sledgehammer; chalk.*

Materials *Posts of treated timber or concrete; hardcore (page 450); 50mm or 75mm fence nails; post spikes or concrete foundation mix (page 459) – about one bucketful per hole; bolt-down post base.*

1 Mark the inside line of the fence by stretching the pegged string along its length.

2 On the longer length of timber, make pencil marks to show the post spacing (for a panel fence, panel length + one post width) and use these to mark out where each post should be. Then cut out the shape of each hole with a spade. Make a chalk mark instead if the fence crosses a solid surface.

3 Fix the first post to the wall, if necessary (see opposite).

4 If a hole has to be made in a patio, either take up a slab or the bricks, or break a concrete surface with a demolition hammer, and dig below.

Alternatively For a solid surface use a bolt-down fence base (page 431).

5 Using a post-hole borer or narrow spade, dig each hole to the required depth; remember to include an extra 150mm for hardcore beneath a timber post. Keep the hole as narrow as possible for the size of the post.

> **CONCRETE SHORT CUT**
>
> To secure a fence post quickly, use dry pre-mixed post-fixing concrete, which just needs to be added to water in the hole, after which it sets in around 10 minutes or less. It comes in 20 or 25kg bags, one of which is needed for each post.

6 For a timber post, fill the base of the hole to a depth of 150mm with hardcore, well rammed down.

7 Insert a post so that one side is against the string guideline, and pack some hardcore round the base to ensure that it stays upright.

8 Lay a length of timber across the top of each pair of consecutive posts and use a spirit level to check that the tops are level.

9 Use a spirit level to check that the post is vertical, then pack in more hardcore to support it.

10 To give a stronger temporary support, drive a nail into the post and wedge a length of timber under the nail as a brace.

11 Fill in the hole as soon as the fence has been erected. Either fill it with layers of hardcore and a mixture of soil and gravel, ramming the surface well down, or fill the hole with alternate layers of hardcore and concrete rammed well down. Slope the top layer of concrete round a timber post so that any rainwater can run off away from the post.

Fixing a support stay

A post support stay – chiefly used on wire and chain-link fences fixed to timber posts – can be fitted against the post in line with the fence, see page 430. Use either a spare fence post or a length of timber 75 x 50mm that has been treated with wood preservative.

The stay should be about three quarters of the length of the post it supports. Cut it so that it is at an angle of 35–40° to the vertical post. Bury the stay to about the same depth as the post, but you will have to dig a wider hole to allow for the angle of the stay. Place a brick or large piece of stone under the angled bottom of the stay to support it. Secure the stay to the post with 60 or 75mm galvanised nails.

Using post spikes

Make sure the cup of the spike is the right size for the post. You can trim the bottom of a post to fit into a smaller-sized cup, but this is not advisable as it weakens the post. The post length should be about 50mm longer than the height of the fence boards or panelling – none of it will be buried below ground.

Fit the driving tool, or dolly, into the cup, press the spike into the earth at the marked spot beside the pegged line, and drive it down using a sledgehammer.

Stop at regular intervals and check with a spirit level that the spike is vertical, otherwise the post will be out of true when fitted. Use the handles of the driving tool to twist or level the spike as necessary to straighten or align it.

The spike will break through small stones, but if you hit a rock, stop and dig it out, or the spike will be pushed out of true. Take care if you are driving a spike where you know there are service pipes. Pipes are normally more than 610mm below ground, so should not be in your way.

Continue driving the spike until the bottom of the cup is level with the ground surface. Then fit a post in the cup. Secure the post in the cup either by driving nails into it through the pre-drilled holes, or by tightening the collar with a spanner.

Fixing posts on a slope

On a pronounced slope, use vertical close-boarded or post-and-rail fencing which can follow the slope and are more easily stepped in sections than panel fencing.

To make even steps, you may have to shape the ground by digging out or building up areas so that there is not too small or too large a gap under each section.

To set each pair of posts, use a wooden block on the lower post to raise the levelling timber to the height of the higher post. How long the block should be depends on the slope – the steeper the slope, the longer it will need to be.

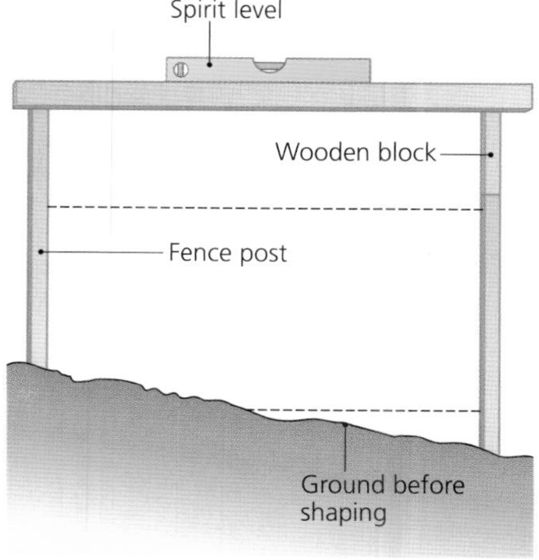

By using the same block on each post, you will ensure that all the post tops are uniformly stepped.

Fixing a timber post to a wall

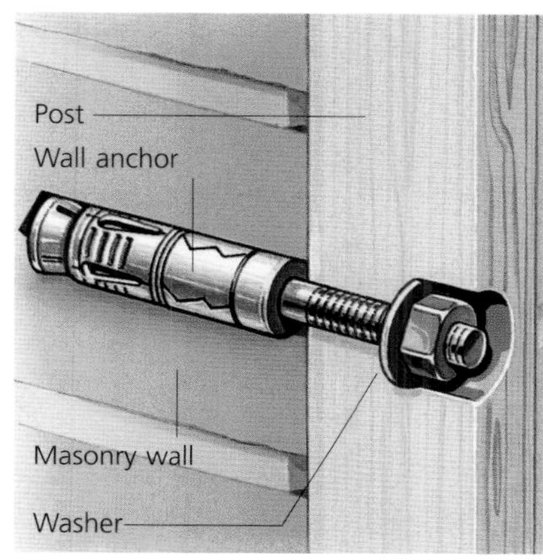

A post fixed against a wall usually rests on the surface of a path or patio, so should be cut shorter than the other fence posts by the amount they are to be buried below ground. Soak the sawn end with wood preservative overnight (page 431).

Secure a post over 1.2m high to the wall with three equally spaced wall anchor bolts at the top, middle and bottom. For shorter posts use two bolts. Each bolt should be twice as long as the width of the post, as half will be sunk into the brickwork. For panel fencing, the bolt heads must be recessed to lie flush with the edge of the post. On any type of fence, it is neater and safer if they are recessed.

Tools *Steel tape measure; chalk; power drill and two auger bits – one of the bolt-hole diameter, one wide enough for the nut recess, allowing for use of a spanner (or use a flat bit for the recess); masonry bit of the recommended diameter for the expansion bolt shield; spirit level; 100mm nail; hammer; box or socket spanner to fit bolt nut.*

Materials *Sawn post; two or three projecting-type expansion bolts – for fixing about 60mm thickness.*

1 Use a steel tape measure and chalk to mark the hole positions on the post.

2 Use the larger auger bit (or flat bit) first to make the recess for the nut and washer about 15mm deep. Then use the smaller auger to make the hole for the bolt.

3 Hold the post in position against the wall and use the spirit level to check that it is vertical. Then insert a 100mm nail through each hole and tap it with a hammer in order to mark the hole position on the wall. Avoid mortar joints.

4 Remove the post and drill holes in the wall of the correct diameter for the bolt shield, and to the depth the bolt will be sunk into the masonry. Remove debris from the hole.

5 Insert the sleeves and bolts (with nuts and washers removed) into the wall holes. Hang the post on the bolts and replace the washers and nuts. Tighten the heads with a box or socket spanner.

AN ALTERNATIVE WAY OF DIGGING POST HOLES

If you have a lot of post holes to dig, consider hiring a post-hole borer. Borers come in different sizes and styles but are, in essence, like a large corkscrew on a long handle. They save the hard work of digging, but are less effective where the ground is very stony.

To use a manual borer, twist it in and out of the ground and keep depositing the soil that gathers on the blades on the ground nearby.

Motorised borers are available to hire in one-man and two-man models, and make quick work of digging many holes.

Even faster, and more efficient, is the one-man, lightweight hydraulic auger. It is on wheels, and can be positioned easily. Use a hydraulic auger if you have more than ten post holes to dig.

Other means of digging post holes include a post-driver – a closed cylinder that fits over the post and is hammered to ram the post into the ground. This is useful where the ground is reasonably easy to work.

The one-man shovel holer is like a large pair of tongs with two sharp-edged shovels, face to face, at the end of its arms. It 'bites' out a shovel-load of soil at a time.

All these post hole borers, augers and holers can be hired from firms listed in *Yellow Pages* under Hire Services – Tools and Equipment (or on Yell.com). To hire the borer for the shortest possible period, plan to dig all the holes in one go, even if the posts are to be put up later.

Fixing panel fencing to posts

Put up posts as described on page 432. You will need a helper to lift and support large panels.

Before you start With panel fencing, the spacing of posts is crucial – each gap must be exactly the width of a panel (normally 1.83m, which is exactly 6ft) at both top and bottom. The best answer is to fix the first post securely and then work from there. The height of the post needs to allow for the height of the fencing plus a 150mm gap at the bottom to fit a gravel board to prevent the bottom of the fence rotting. Never fit fence panels resting on the ground.

Tools *Cordless drill; wood bits; hammer. Possibly also screwdriver; two or three bricks; timber lengths for supporting panels; G-cramp.*

Materials *75mm square posts – one more than the number of panels; panels; either nails (twelve 50mm or 75mm galvanised or alloy nails per panel) or fence clips (six per panel, with sufficient screws or nails for each clip). Annular (ring-shank) nails give the best grip; One gravel board for each panel; post caps (page 431).*

Nailing panels direct to posts

1 Drill pilot holes for the nails in each panel. Make three holes each end through the inner face of the panel frame at the top, middle and bottom. Drill the holes right through.

2 Put the panel in position against the first post. Rest the panel on bricks to give the correct spacing for a 150mm gravel board (two bricks plus a piece of gravel board laid flat will be about right) and have your helper hold it firmly against the first post (use a G-cramp if working alone).

3 Nail the panel to the first post, driving the nails in at a slightly upward or downward angle so that they will not be able to pull straight out.

4 Use the edge of the panel as a guide to drive in a post spike or position the second post hard against the panel, nail the panel to the post and then fill in the post hole with concrete. Make sure post tops are level.

When all posts and panels are in place, fit gravel boards and post caps.

Using fence clips

Drill pilot holes for nails or screws that are to be driven into the panel frame, otherwise the wood could split.

L-shaped clips have a screw welded to them. Fit three of these on the post (top middle and bottom) into pilot holes drilled into the post with the flat face facing away you. Position the panel as for nailing and nail through the clips into the panel edges.

U-shaped clips (above) need extra screws to secure them to the post, while Z-clips (below) slot on to the panel frame edge before you nail them to the post.

Once all the panels and posts are fixed, add gravel boards and post caps.

USING CONCRETE POSTS

Slot the gravel board into the first post, then the panel. Support the panel with a prop while you position the second post so that it slots onto the other end of the panel and board.

Fixing closeboard vertical fencing to posts

Closeboard fencing is stronger and more secure than panel fencing, but takes longer to put up as it is all assembled on site.

Before you start Posts can be timber or concrete, and are available with ready-made slots (mortises) for arris rails. Some concrete posts may also have holes for securing gravel board cleats (opposite).

- Put up posts (page 432) fitting arris rails between them as you go. Closeboard fences facing the road are usually put up with the 'good' side (the feather-edged pales) facing the road; on boundaries between houses, you will probably want to fit the good side facing you, which means you can do all the fencing from your side.
- Use 100mm square posts for closeboard fencing – 75mm posts would be too weakened by the arris rail slots.
- Arris rails come in 1.8m and 2.4m lengths.
- Use two arris rails for fencing up to 1.2m high, and a third central rail for a higher fence.
- For 2.4m arris rails, use a 'centre stump', made from 50mm square timber shaped to fit underneath the bottom arris rail. These are sold by fencing suppliers.

Tools *Spirit level; hammer; block of wood about 85mm wide as a width gauge. Possibly also panel saw; wood plane or shaping tool; power drill with wood bits.*

Materials *Posts – one for each 2.4m section and one extra; two or three arris rails for each section; four 50mm galvanised or alloy nails for each rail; feather-edged boards treated with preservative (probably 27–29 between posts); two 50mm galvanised or alloy nails per board; one 2.4m gravel board and a centre stump for each section. Possibly also capping strip and nails (page 431); clips for fixing gravel boards.*

SHAPING AN ARRIS RAIL

You can buy arris rails with their ends already correctly shaped, but you may need to shape the ends of rails you have had to shorten.

Use a panel saw to make three cuts as shown below and a rasp or Surform to do the final shaping so that the rail fits snugly into its slot.

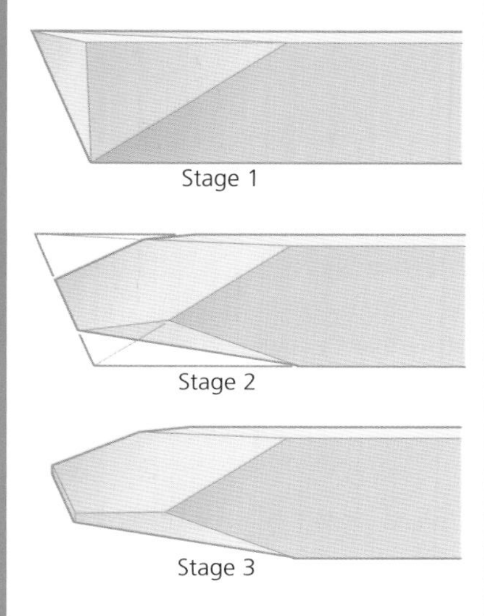

Fitting arris rails

1 With the first post in position (page 432), insert one shaped end of each rail into the post to the full depth of the slot.

2 Hold the second post in position while you fit the other ends of the rails into its post slots to half the depth of the slot (for intermediate posts, there will be a rail fitted in from each side). For long arris rails (and high fences), you will need a helper for this.

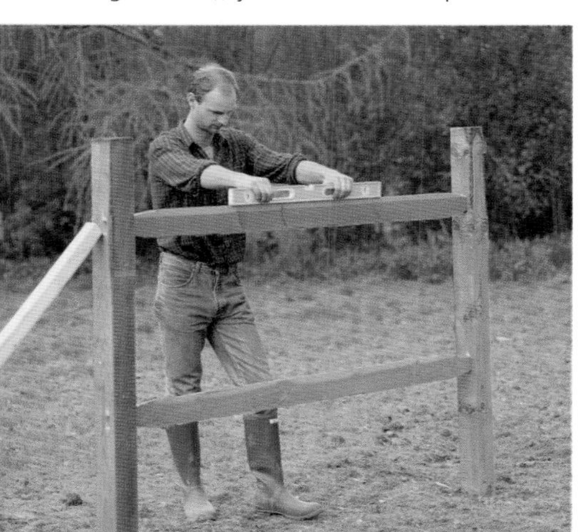

3 Support the post temporarily with timber braces while you align it with the first post and check also that the arris rails are horizontal.

4 Adjust the post as necessary before concreting it in.

5 Nail the arris rails to the posts, driving one nail at an angle through the top of each rail and the other at an angle through the bottom of the rail.

6 Continue fitting posts and rails in the same way until the main skeleton of the fence is complete.

7 With long (2.4m) arris rails, dig a hole halfway between posts and fit a centre stump with its angled end nailed to the bottom arris rail. Backfill the hole.

Fitting gravel boards

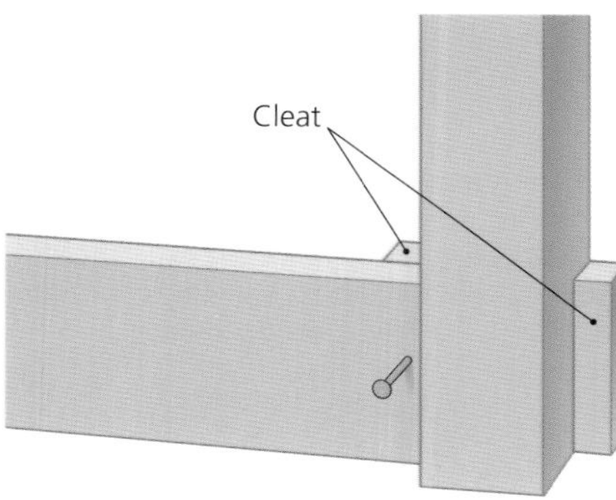

- Using a panel saw, cut the gravel board to fit between the posts and treat the cut ends with preservative (page 439).
- With wooden posts in concrete, the simplest way to fix them is to nail small pieces of timber (150 x 50 x 25), known as cleats, to the sides of the post and then nail the gravel boards to the cleats. Also nail the gravel board to the centre stump.
- Metal cleats are sold for use with concrete posts (provided they have suitable holes).

Alternatively Nail gravel board clips (page 431) to the sides of the posts and drop the gravel board into place. This method works well with posts in spikes.

Fitting feather-edged boards

1 Fit the first board resting on the gravel board with its thicker end butted against the post. Nail it to the centre of each rail around 20mm from the thick edge. If you need to cut boards, treat the cut ends with preservative.

2 Place the width gauge on the first board, aligned with the thick edge, and fit the second board against it. The thick edge of the second board should then overlap the thin edge of the first board by 15mm.

3 Nail the second board to the top rail, making sure the nail misses the board underneath. Use a spirit level to get the board vertical and nail to the other rail(s).

4 Continue fixing boards in the same way, checking continually that they are vertical.

5 Before fitting the last three or four boards, measure the gap still remaining to see whether you need to decrease or increase the overlap to fill the rail.

Alternatively Maintain the 15mm overlap and fill the last gap with a board fitted with its thick end butted to the end post.

FENCING ON A SLOPE

Fencing is normally put up level – except on sloping ground.

- Panel fencing is 'terraced', with all panels horizontal, but each panel higher than one of its neighbours. You need longer posts for this.
- Closeboard fencing can follow the slope with gravel boards cut at a slight angle so they fit snugly.

Fitting a capping strip

A wooden capping strip is nailed across the top of vertical closeboard fencing to improve appearance and to keep rain off the end grain of the feather-edged boards. If the posts have sloped ('weathered') tops or are to be fitted with post caps, the capping strip is fitted between them. Alternatively (as described below), long lengths of capping strip are fitted across the posts, butted up against each other.

1 Saw off the fence posts level with the top of the fence boards.

2 Treat the cut ends with wood preservative (page 439).

3 Nail the capping strip to the top of the first post and the next post if it covers that, with 50mm galvanised or alloy nails. Drill pilot holes and use two nails per post.

4 Use 25mm nails to nail the strip to board tops at each end, and at one or two places in between. Take care not to split the boards. If you find that the nails are splitting the wood, drill a pilot hole for each nail.

Fixing other types of fencing

Timber posts and rails

For rails slotted into posts, put up posts (page 432) and fit the rails between. Nail the rails in the same way as arris rails (page 435), using 50mm galvanised or alloy nails.

For rails nailed to posts, put up a line of posts before fixing the rails. Allow two posts for each stretch of rails, and one for the end of the run. Butt the rail ends on alternate posts, and stagger the centre rails so they butt on to the posts that the other two rails run across. Use 75mm galvanised or alloy nails.

Palisade or picket fencing

1 Put up posts and arris rails in the manner described for closeboard fencing (pages 434–5).

2 Treat any cut parts with wood preservative (page 439).

3 Use 50mm galvanised or alloy nails to fix the pales – preferably cut with pointed or rounded tops to shed the rain – to the arris rails.

4 With 75mm spaces between 75mm pales, you should need 15 pales to fill a 2.325m run of rail between 75mm posts.

5 If you are unsure that the pales will fit evenly into your run of rail, mark out their prospective positions against the rail, adjusting the space between pales so that they appear evenly spaced when seen from a few paces away.

Chain-link fencing

Concrete straining posts with ready-made holes (usually 15mm diameter) for eyebolts are normally used for chain-link fencing. Narrower intermediate posts have holes of about 9mm for fixing line wires.

Put up straining posts (page 432) at ends and corners, with intermediate posts between them at 2m intervals. End posts should each have a support stay (page 432), and corner posts two support stays. Fences of up to about 1.2m have a line wire at the top and bottom, higher fences an extra wire in the centre.

With timber posts, you can either fit the mesh with stretcher bars as described here, or use eyebolts for line wires only and staple the mesh to the posts. You may have to drill holes for the eyebolts. Corner posts need two sets of bolt holes at right angles to each other, one set slightly higher than the other.

Tools *Spanner; pliers. Possibly also drill with 13mm wood bit.*

Materials *Straining posts and intermediate posts; chain-link mesh together with galvanised line and tie wires; stretcher-bars (one for each end post and two for a corner post), together with eyebolts and angle cleats.*

1 With the posts in place, thread a stretcher bar through one end of the chain-link roll. Bolt angle cleats to the stretcher bar, and fix each to the first post with an eyebolt (loop end inwards). Leave the roll of mesh standing on end.

2 Thread a line wire through each of the eyebolt loops, securing the wire by twisting it with pliers.

3 Run the line wires to the next straining post, and secure them to the post with eyebolts. Do not make the wires taut yet.

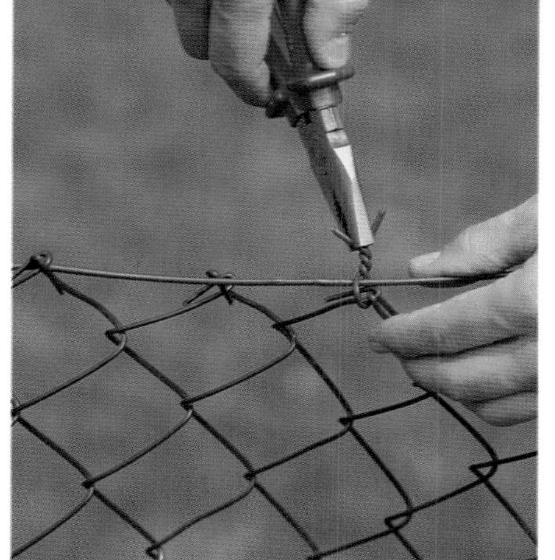

4 Unroll the chain-link mesh along the line wires, keeping it as taut as possible. Secure the mesh to the line wire with tie wires as you go along. Use tie wires at 150mm intervals on the top wire and at 450mm intervals on the bottom (and middle) wire.

5 When you reach the straining post, untwist two linked wires at the top and bottom of the mesh and unthread them to separate the secured fencing from the roll.

6 Thread a stretcher bar through the last row of meshes. Undo the eyebolts holding the line wires to the post, fit the bolts through the angle cleats of the stretcher bar, and fasten the bar to the post with the eyebolts.

7 Tauten the line wires by tightening the eyebolt nuts with a spanner as necessary. Do not overtighten, or the line wires may snap and whiplash dangerously.

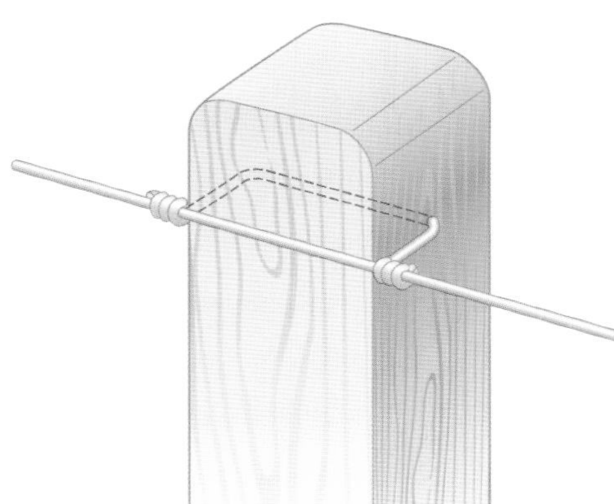

8 Use lengths of wire threaded through the intermediate post holes to secure the line wire stirrup fashion to the post.

Wire netting

Put up posts at about 1.8m or 2.4m intervals (page 432).

Use eyebolts through the posts to stretch line wires between end and corner posts in the same way as for chain-link fencing (above). The netting can be stapled to timber posts, or tied to concrete posts stirrup fashion. Use tie wires to tie the mesh to the line wires.

To keep out rabbits, bury wire mesh 150–300mm below ground. Mesh of 38 or 32mm is suitable.

Post-and-wire fencing

Put up straining and intermediate posts (page 432) in the same way as for chain-link fencing, and use eyebolts to stretch line wired between the straining posts.

The line wires can either be threaded through or tied to the bolt holes on intermediate concrete posts, or stapled to intermediate timber posts.

Fence repair and maintenance

All wood is susceptible to rot and attack by wood-boring insects, so treat fences and other garden woodwork with wood preservative regularly to prolong their life.

Timber rots in contact with earth, so whenever possible keep it from direct contact with the ground. Never pile soil against a wooden fence. Timber fence posts are most likely to rot at the bottom below ground, and will eventually collapse and bring down part of the fence unless reinforced in good time. To prevent a post rotting from the top downwards, slope the top or fit a post cap (page 431).

Featheredged boards often get brittle and start to crack if they are not kept well protected with wood preservative. So do arris rails, which take a lot of strain in supporting featheredged boards or palings, and will quickly get worse unless repaired.

Reinforcing a fence post

If the main part of a rotting post is still sound, it can be supported with a concrete spur (page 431). Alternatively, it can be cut short and refitted with its base in a metal repair spike – a shorter version of the normal post spike (page 431), which is driven in around the rotted base of the post. If the rot extends higher than the top of the gravel board, you will have to free the fencing from the post on either side before you can cut the rot out. It may be simpler to replace the post.

Tools *Handsaw; old paintbrush; timber lengths for fence supports; timber length for compacting concrete; spade; hammer; drill and 13mm auger bit; spirit level with horizontal and vertical vials; spanner; hacksaw.*

Materials *Wood preservative (page 439); concrete spur; two 10mm diameter coach bolts about 200mm long; nut and washer for each bolt; concrete foundation mix (page 459).*

1 Temporarily support the fence on each side of the post with pieces of timber.

2 Remove the gravel board and cut off the rotting part of the post back to sound wood.

3 Coat the whole post, especially the bottom and end grain, with wood preservative.

4 Dig out a hole alongside the damaged post to a depth of about 450–600mm. Make the hole at least 300mm square.

5 Put the spur in the hole, fitted snugly against the post.

6 Slip coach bolts through the holes in the spur and strike them firmly with a hammer to mark their positions on the post.

7 Remove the spur and bore holes through the post at the marked spot.

8 Push the bolts through the post and spur so that the tails are on the spur side. Slip on the washers and nuts and tighten the nuts with a spanner.

9 Use a spirit level to check that the post is vertical, pushing it upright as necessary. Then brace it firmly with lengths of timber.

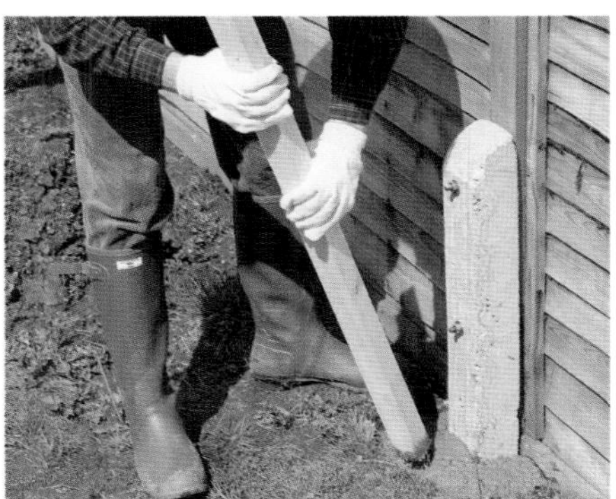

10 Ram hardcore into the bottom of the spur hole, then pour in the mixed concrete, pressing it well down with the end of a piece of timber.

11 Wait 24 hours before moving the timber supports, to give the concrete time to set. Use a hacksaw to cut off protruding bolt threads slightly proud of the nuts.

Replacing a timber fence post

Tools *Pincers or claw hammer; narrow spade; spirit level; length of timber longer than distance between posts; timber lengths for supporting post; earth rammer (page 451). Possibly also timber length; nails; strong rope; pile of about five or six bricks.*

Materials *Treated fence post the same size as the old one; hardcore (page 450) – probably 3–6 bucketfuls; two or three arris-rail brackets (see right); 50mm galvanised nails.*

1 Support the fence on each side of the post with lengths of timber, wedged under the panel top or upper arris rail.

HELPFUL TIP

If a post is difficult to remove, or if it breaks off and leaves a stump, lever it out using a length of timber and a large stone or a pile of bricks about 300mm high. Lash one end of the timber length to the post or stump, and lay the timber across the stone or brick pile as a fulcrum (balancing point).

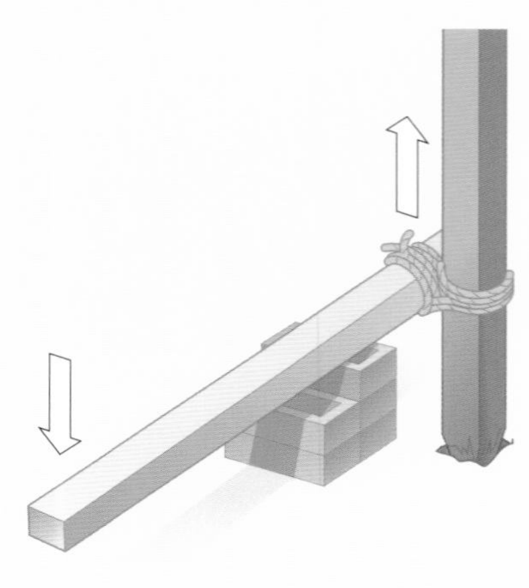

2 Free the post from the fencing. Undo panels by removing the nails or clips on each side. For vertical closeboard fencing, remove the first board on one side and saw through the arris rails. Remove nails holding the rails to the other side of the post so that they can be pulled out when the post is moved.

3 Dig down beside the post to free it at the bottom. Then remove the post and clear the hole.

4 Fit the replacement post in the same way as putting up a new post (page 432), but on a closeboard fence, fit the shaped arris rails on one side into the slots as you put the post in. Before you fill in and firm the hole, make sure the fencing will fit flush on both sides.

5 Refit sawn off arris rails to the post using metal arris-rail brackets (right), but nail shaped arris rail ends (page 435). Refit panels with nails or clips (page 434).

6 If the post top is square cut, either cut it to a slope or fit a post cap (see below). Treat sawn areas with wood preservative.

Repairing a post top

Before repairing the post, probe the top with a sharp knife to find out the extent of the rot. Saw off the rotten area back to sound wood.

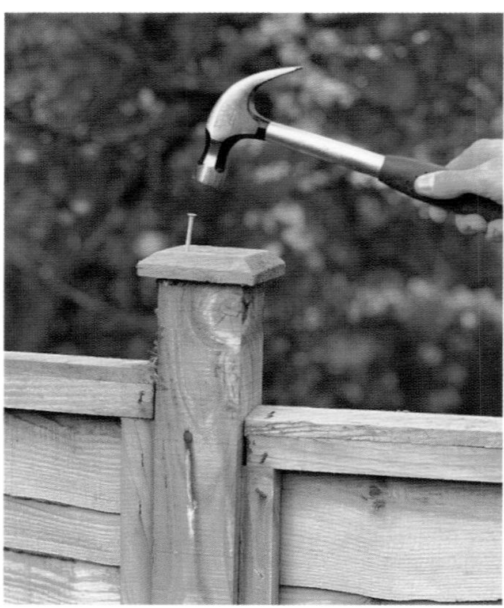

Timber or metal post caps are sold ready made. Soak a home-made wooden cap in wood preservative for 24 hours before fitting. The cap should be about 15mm wider than the post top all round. Drill two pilot holes then nail it to the post with ring nails driven in on the skew – at an angle from each side. Check wooden caps periodically, and replace any with signs of rot.

A metal post cap can be home-made from a sheet of zinc or aluminium cut about 25mm wider than the post top and turned down round the edges.

Mending a cracked arris rail

Strengthen a rail cracked in the middle with a straight arris-rail bracket – a metal bracket about 300mm long, shaped to fit the rail, with ready-made holes for screws or nails. Fasten it with galvanised or alloy 25mm screws or 50mm nails.

If the crack is near a post, use a flanged arris-rail bracket. The two flanges – projecting lugs at right angles to the bracket – are fastened to the post. If the post is concrete, use screws and wall plugs to fasten the flange to the post.

Tighten a loose arris rail by pinning it with a 10mm grooved hardwood dowel about 50mm long. Drill a hole for the dowel through the front of the post about 20mm from the edge where the loose rail fits.

Before inserting the dowel, coat it all over with waterproof adhesive. The grooves release excess glue and trapped air.

Replacing a broken arris rail

If the fence posts are concrete, the rails may be bolted to recesses in them, and are easy to replace. Or they may be fitted into mortises in the same way as timber posts, and can be repaired as described here.

Tools *Panel saw; hammer; plane or shaping tool; pencil.*

Materials *Arris rail, normally 2.4m long, treated with wood preservative; flanged arris-rail bracket (see above); 50mm galvanised or alloy nails.*

1 Hammer the boards or palings away from the damaged rail.

2 Withdraw the nails if possible and pull the damaged rail from the slots at each end. Otherwise, saw through the rail flush with the post at one end.

3 Shape one end of the new rail to fit into the post slot (page 435). Fit the new rail into the slot, mark where it will fit flush against the post at the other end, then saw it to length.

4 Refit the rail into the slot, and fix the other end to the post using the flanged bracket. Refit the boards or pales to the rail, making sure they are vertical.

Replacing a gravel board

Gravel boards should always be fitted so that they are easily replaceable. That's the point of them: they are the 'sacrificial' part of the fence.

The easiest gravel boards to remove are timber boards fitted to timber cleats (page 435) which can be knocked out (or unscrewed if screws have been used). Similar cleats may have been used for gravel boards on concrete posts.

More difficult to replace are gravel boards held by clips (page 431). You will have to drill and saw the boards out and remove the clips before fitting new boards with cleats as best you can (this may mean drilling a hole through a post spike).

Most difficult of all to replace are gravel boards held in slotted concrete posts beneath panel fencing. Unless you are prepared (with a helper) to lift the panel out vertically (in which case, replace it with a concrete gravel board), you will have to drill and saw it out and fashion supports from timber battens driven into the ground or fit gravel board clips to timber shaped to fit into the concrete post slots to hold the new board. You will need to support the panel on bricks while you are working.

Replacing a panel

Fence panels are made in standard sizes, so removing a damaged panel and fitting a new one in the same way (page 434) is not usually difficult.

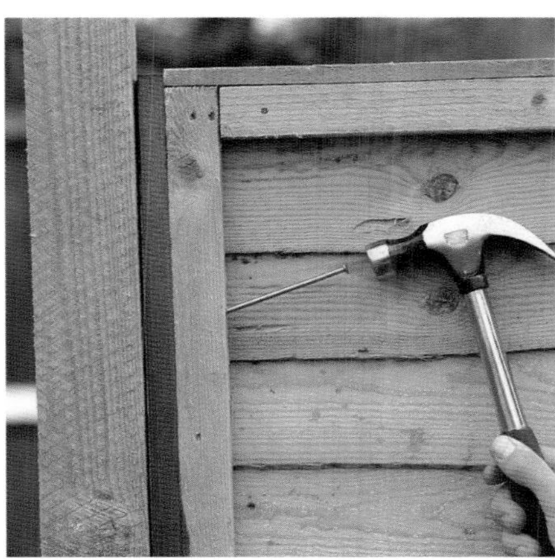

If the new panel is slightly too wide, plane off a small amount of the frame on each side. If, however, it is not wide enough, close the gap with a narrow fillet of wood inserted between the post and the panel frame. Remember to treat the wood fillet with preservative before fixing it.

Repairing feather-edged boarding

Replace damaged or rotten boards with new boards that have been treated with wood preservative (see right).

One nail secures two overlapped boards, so to remove a board you will have to loosen the overlapping boards as well and pull out the common nail. Fit the new boards as on page 435.

Undamaged boards sometimes become loose because their nails have rusted. Refit the boards using 50mm galvanised or alloy nails that will not rust.

If feather-edged boards are rotting at the bottom where there is no gravel board, saw them off along the base to leave a gap of at least 150mm. Then cut and fit a gravel board (page 435).

APPLYING WOOD PRESERVATIVE

To maintain your fences' natural colour and prevent the wood fading to grey, coat with wood preservative regularly, paying particular attention to joints and end grain.

Choices

Most modern preservatives are either solvent-based or water-based, and contain chemicals or salts that destroy fungi and insects. Clear water-repellent finishes contain UV absorbers; these only delay the wood's natural weathering, whereas products with colour will maintain the wood's fresh appearance for longer. Solvent-based types give off flammable fumes, and naked flames should be kept away until the preservative is quite dry – until at least 12 hours after application. Look for a warning on the container. Water-based types have no smell. Neither type is harmful to plants once dry, but guard against splashing any on plants while you are painting.

Application

The period between treatments depends on the type of wood preservative used and how exposed the fence is. Most modern preservatives will last 2 or 3 years.

Even if timber for a new fence has been pre-treated with preservative by the manufacturer, coat it with more preservative before you fix it in place and thoroughly soak cut ends.

The best time to apply preservative is when the wood is thoroughly dry but the sun not too hot – probably in late summer after a dry spell, with no rain expected for a day or two. Damp wood will not absorb the preservative well.

Most fence treatments can be applied with a paint brush – the bigger the better. But some are specifically designed for use with a hand-pumped or cordless sprayer, which is faster. Always follow any safety precautions given on the container.

Coverage is generally around 4–10m^2 per litre, but varies with the type of preservative and the porosity of the wood.

ECO PRESERVATIVES

Environmentally friendly wood preservatives offer an alternative to solvent-based protective stains. Based on linseed oil, they come in a range of shades, including natural woods, blues, greys and greens.

Choosing gates, hinges and fasteners

There are many different designs of gate available, including matching designs for most types of fencing. Some typical styles are shown below. Most of the types shown are also available as double gates. Before choosing a gate, consider from which side of the opening you want it to hang, and whether it opens over flat or rising ground.

Open-boarded (palisade) Paling tops may be square, rounded, pointed or some other shape.

Open-boarded (framed) With spaced vertical paling that do not protrude above the top bar.

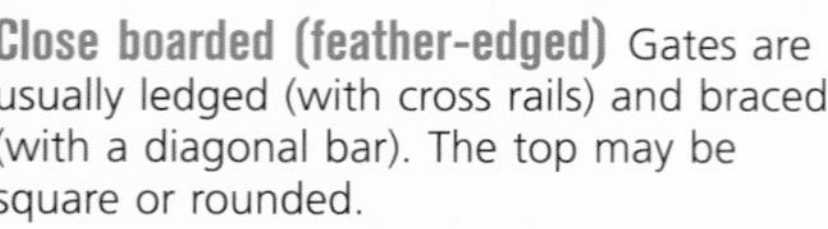

Close boarded (feather-edged) Gates are usually ledged (with cross rails) and braced (with a diagonal bar). The top may be square or rounded.

Frame and panel A timber frame with plywood panels.

Panel In various designs to match panel fencing. Generally 910mm wide and 50mm shorter than the fence height.

Wrought iron (single) Decorative tall or small gates. Hinge and latch fittings are usually built in, or are on separate metal struts for fitting to gate supports.

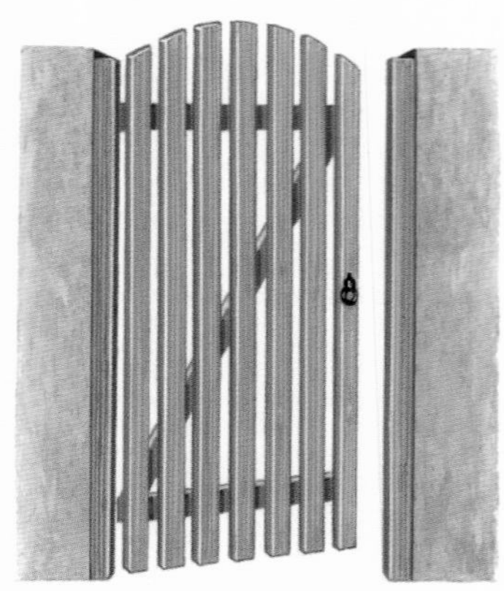

Open-boarded (palisade) With spaced vertical palings that project above the upper cross rail. Gates may be tall or short.

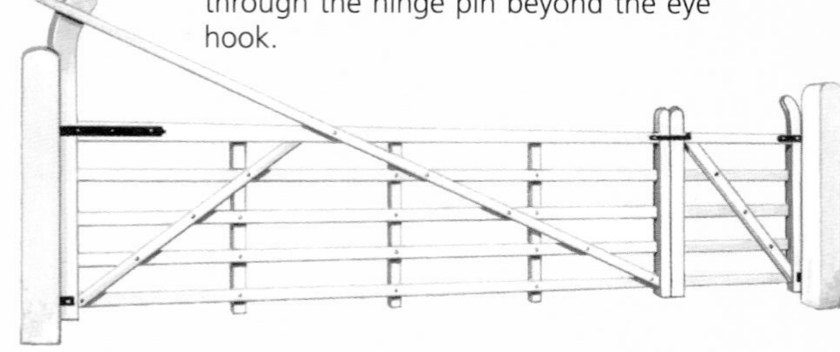

Barred (field or country gate) Usually with five or seven bars and one or more diagonal braces. Available as narrow garden gates or wide single gates suitable for driveways. Some types have a swinging stile with a curved heel at the top. A narrow hunting gate is often partnered with a wide driveway gate.

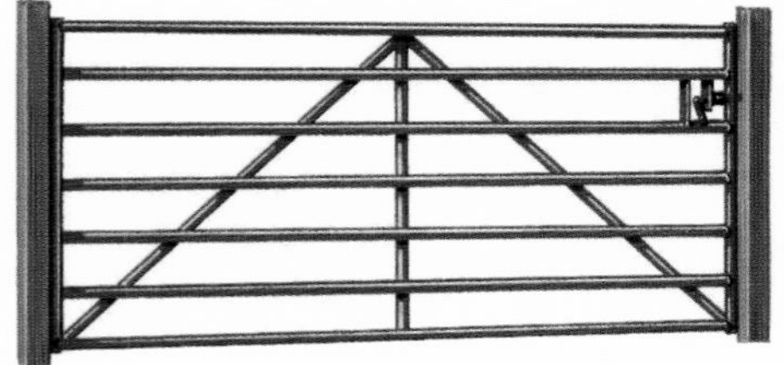

Tubular steel Usually barred gates, with adjustable built-in forged eye hooks for hinge pins, and a spring-loaded bolt fastening.

BUYING GATES AND GATEPOSTS

Do not buy a gate until you are sure how wide you want it and how you are going to hang it. The width and fitting method are interdependent. Check also that the gate is designed to hang on whichever side you require – either right or left. If it is to hang across a sloping driveway, it will need to accommodate rising hinges – some types are self-closing.

Gates are made in both metric and imperial sizes. Be sure you know the exact width, because conversions are inaccurate. The width range for both systems is generally similar.

Single gates range in width from about 900mm to about 3.7m, increasing by increments of 300mm or 600mm. Double gates may range from about 4m to 6m wide. The height range is typically from about 1 to 1.75m, but gates as high as 2m and 2.5m are available.

If you are buying gateposts as well, make sure timber posts are treated with preservative (page 439). They are generally 1.8–2.4m long, and range from 100mm square to 200mm square for wide, heavy gates.

Concrete posts may be available with ready-drilled holes for centred gate fittings, or may have top and bottom holes to which a strip of timber can be bolted as a fixing point for fitting. Do not use post spikes for putting up gateposts; they do not give enough support.

Wrought iron (double) Hinge pins may be down-pointing on the gate or upright on the support. To deter thieves, fit a split pin through the hinge pin beyond the eye hook.

CHOOSING GATE HINGES

Tee Commonly used for hanging light or medium-weight gates flush between posts. Usually painted black.

Hook and band For hanging light or medium-weight timber gates. The band goes on the gate and the hook on the post. From 300 to 914mm long.

Heavy reversible Strong hinge for heavy gates flush between posts. Can be used either way up. Hook held to pin by cups at each end. Galvanised or black.

Cranked A cranked strap hinge for smaller gates hung flush between posts. Hinge pin (see below) fits on the post and the strap is screwed or bolted to the back of the gate. Usually galvanised.

Standard hanging set For wooden gates. A double strap is bolted to the top of the gate and its eye hooks over an adjustable hinge pin. The eye of the bottom bracket fits over the eye of a fixed, drive-in pin. The whole gate can be lifted off its hinges, if required. For pairs of gates, an adjustable bottom bracket is recommended, so that the gates can be aligned where they meet. For sloping ground, rising hinges with offset pins can be used.

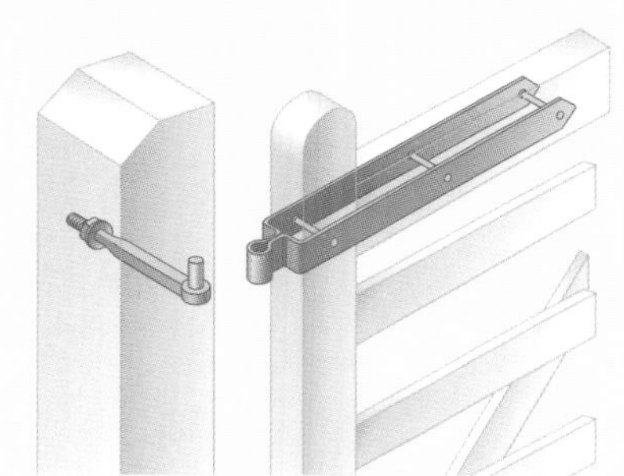

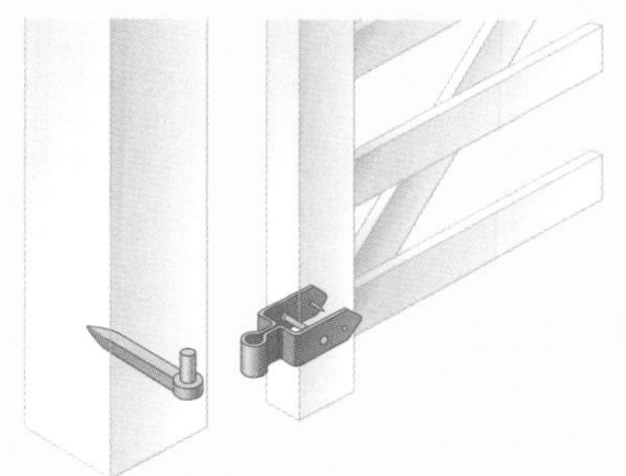

HINGE PINS FOR GATES

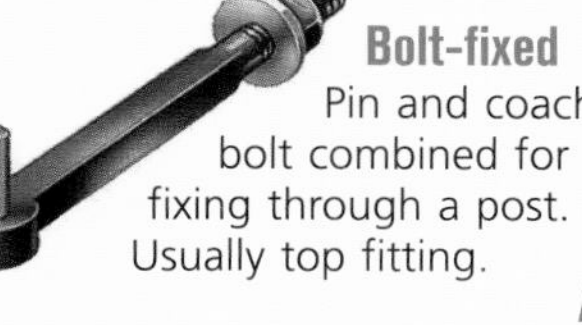

Drive-in With pointed single prong for fitting into drill hole in post. Usually bottom fitting.

Bolt-fixed Pin and coach bolt combined for fixing through a post. Usually top fitting.

Adjustable Allows pin to be moved in and out while staying upright.

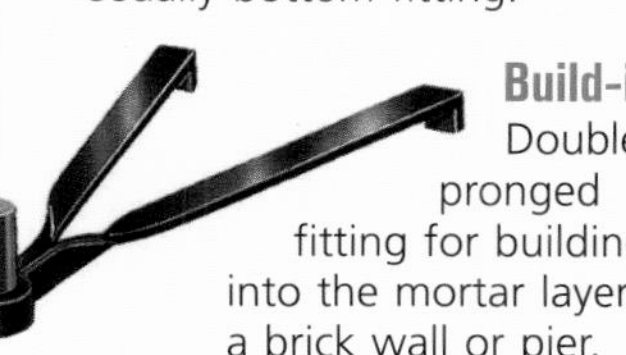

Build-in Double-pronged fitting for building into the mortar layer of a brick wall or pier.

Flat plate With broad or narrow fixing plates for screwing onto gateposts or brick piers.

CHOOSING GATE FASTENERS

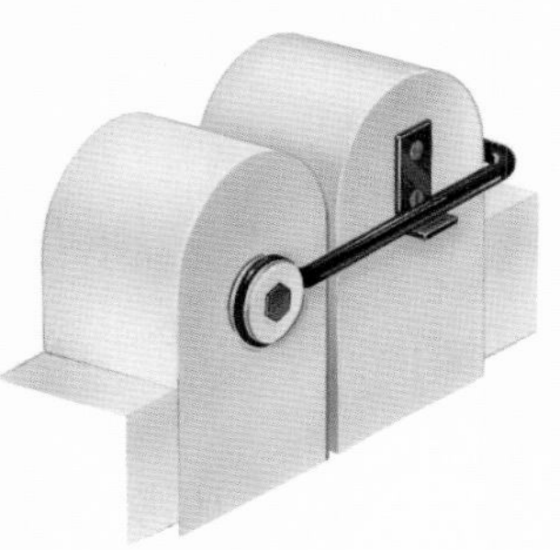

Super loop Loop-over fastener for double gates. Made for 50 or 75mm thick gates.

Pad bolt Can be padlocked. 200–250mm long, usually galvanised.

Oval pad bolt 100mm long bolt plate.

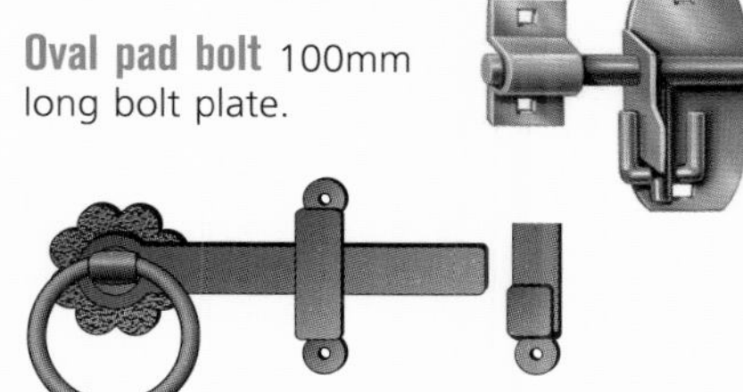

Ring latch set Traditional style for courtyard gates. Can be operated from either side. Usually black. About 150mm wide.

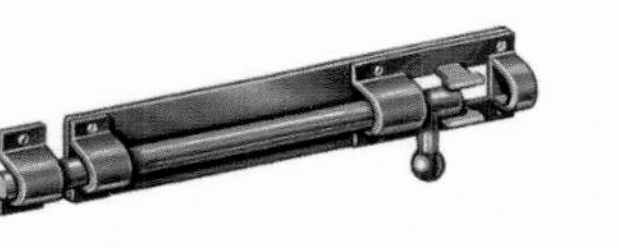

Locking bar with hasp and staple For padlock fastening. 100–305mm.

Tower bolt 150–200mm long.

Automatic catch Fits onto a gatepost to receive a cranked bar fitted to the swinging stile of the gate.

For gates centred on posts

Chelsea catch A bracket-held hook on the swinging stile fits into a catch on the inside of the gatepost.

Slim catch Fits on the inside of the gatepost to catch a striker bolt on a centred or flush-fitting gate.

Double-handed catch With a prong for fixing into the mortar of a brick pier. Suitable for built-in latch on wrought-iron gate. Has a stop to prevent the gate swinging outwards.

For gates hung behind posts

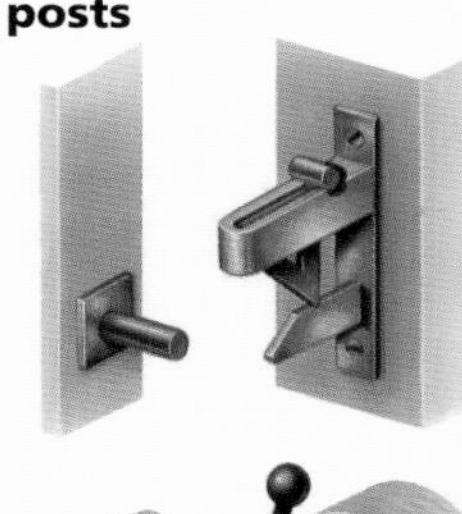

Automatic catch Fits onto the back of the gatepost to receive a striker bolt on the swinging stile of the gate.

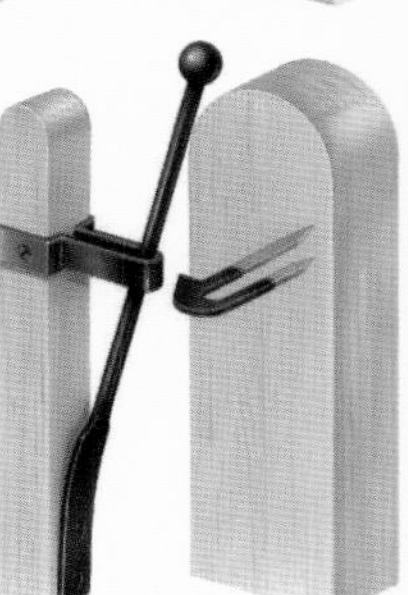

Spring fastener set A flexible bar on the swinging stile that catches in a hook on the back of the gatepost. The fastener may have a knob handle for pedestrian use (as shown), or a longer, hooked handle for horse riders.

Methods of hanging a gate

There are three main ways in which a gate can be hung from timber gateposts. The method depends on the types of fitting used.

Flush between posts

The gate is hung between the posts, with the back of the gate flush with the back of the posts.

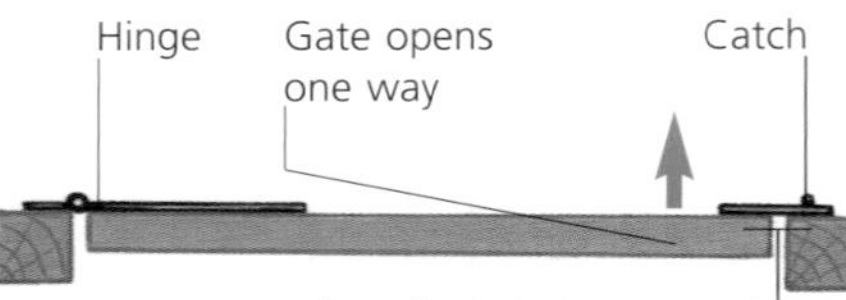

This is the usual method of hanging a timber garden gate with flush-fitting tee hinges. The gate opens one way only. The clearance for fittings on each side of the gate needs to be about 5mm.

Centred on posts

The gate is hung between posts, with the gate width centred on the gatepost width.

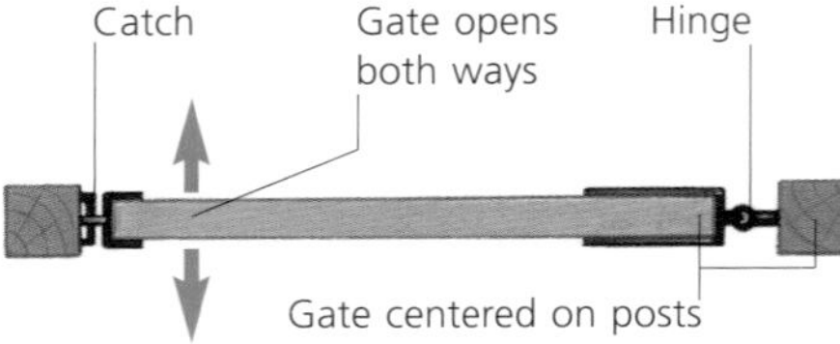

This method is common with wrought-iron gates, which usually hook onto a pin, and with double-strap hinges on timber gates. The gate will swing both ways unless there is a stop on the fastener. Depending on the type of catch, the clearance on the hinge side may need to be as much as 100mm, and on the catch side about 55mm.

Hung behind posts

The gate is hung on the back of the posts with an overlap of 15–25mm on each side. This method can be used for a pair of gates, or a wide single gate, hung with a standard hanging set.

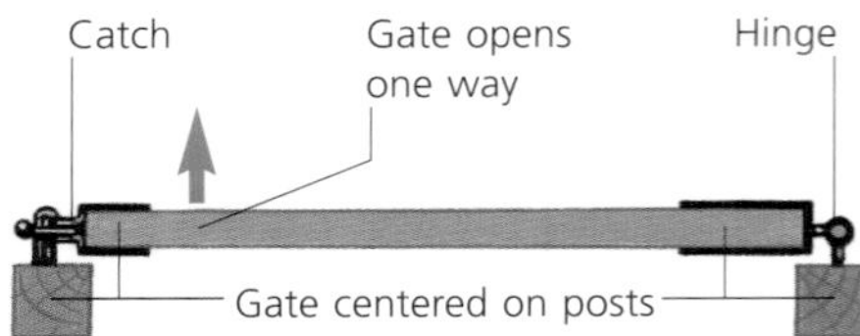

The gates can swing inwards only, and slam shut against a post. The types of fastener that can be used are limited (page 441).

Checking the design

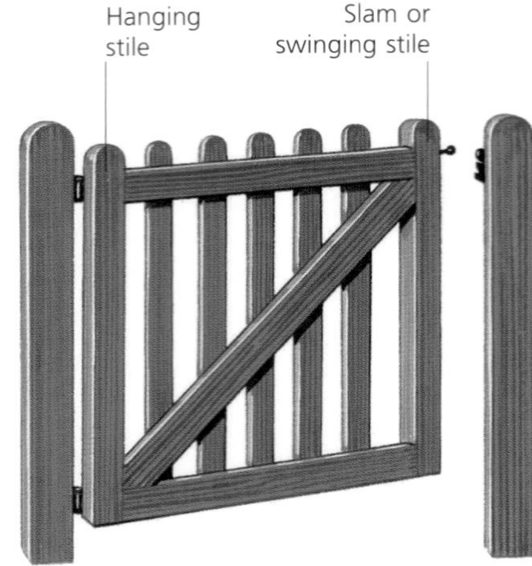

Many garden gates, especially wooden ones, have a front side and a back side. The back side has the supporting framework and should be hung facing the garden even if the gate itself opens outwards.

Gates are often also designed for either right or left hanging. The hanging stile may be wider than the slam or swinging stile, to give a strong fixing for the hinges.

Wooden gates should be braced – by fixing a diagonal strut between the top and bottom rails of the frame – or they will sag over time. Where there is only one diagonal brace, the gate must be hung with the top of the brace on the closing side and the bottom of the brace on the hanging side. You can follow this convention when working out whether a gate is designed to be hung on the right or left.

Double gates must be a matched pair, designed for left and right hanging.

Fitting a gate between existing supports

1 If you can, buy a gate that is exactly the same width as the old one. Fix the hinges to the back of the new gate before you fit it. Wedge the replacement gate between the existing posts, raising it off the ground with a couple of offcuts of wood to ensure adequate ground clearance.

2 Check that the clearances are equal on both sides of the gate then mark the position of the hinges on the post. Screw the hinges to the post.

3 Hold the latch bar horizontal and screw the latch hook to the gate post and the latch

4 Remove the wedges that are holding the gate in position and check that it swings freely and that the latch works smoothly. Adjust the positioning if necessary.

If you cannot buy a gate to fit

If you are not able to find a new gate in the exact size you need, you will need to adjust the size of the gate or the gap between the posts.

If the distance between the existing timber posts or brick piers is too wide for the gate and fittings, narrow the gap by fitting timber battens on one or both sides. The gate fixings (page 441) can then be fitted to the timber battens. Make sure that the battens allow sufficient clearance for the fittings. The gate can then be hung in the way described above. Fixings are also available for fitting gates directly to a masonry pier (page 444).

If you cannot find a gate narrow enough to fit the gap between existing supports, you may be able to trim a little off both stiles of a timber gate to reduce its width. Otherwise you will either have to have a gate specially made or remove the existing gate supports and put up new ones, spaced farther apart.

Fitting a gate and posts from scratch

For a gate to hang snugly between the posts with its base at least 50mm above the ground, the width between posts must be measured accurately.

Before you start Make sure that the bottom of a diagonal brace is on the hinge side, for strength (see left).

For small, light gates, gateposts should be about 100mm square and about 700mm longer than the gate height. For bigger, heavier gates – more than 1.2m high or wide – posts should be up to 200mm square and at least 900mm longer than the gate height. Post tops should be sloped or fitted with caps to prevent rotting. Buy fittings that are either japanned (black painted) or galvanised to resist rust.

Tools *Length of timber longer than the width of gate and posts; tape measure; pencil; spade or post-hole borer; spirit level; builder's square (page 467); six timber pieces for temporary post-support stays; pegs to hold stays; timber length for ramming hardcore; about six timber wedges to allow for width of gate fittings; drill and twist bits.*

Materials *Gate; two gateposts treated with timber preservative; two hinges; gate fastener; galvanised or alloy screws for hinges and fastener; two bricks or blocks; rubble or hardcore; concrete – foundation mix or 25kg bag of coarse dry concrete mix to make about one bucket per hole.*

Positioning the posts

1 Lay the gateposts parallel on flat ground with the gate face down between them. For flush fitting, raise it as necessary to line up with the back of the posts.

2 Position the gate about 50mm below the tops of the posts.

3 Use the timber length and builder's square to align the ends of the posts and ensure they are a uniform distance apart. You need a gap of 6mm between the gate and post on each side – use plywood offcuts as spacers to achieve this.

4 Place the hinges and catches in position. Adjust the posts as necessary to give clearance for the fastenings to operate.

5 Lay the length of timber at right angles across the posts about 50–75mm below the bottom of the gate, and use it as a straightedge to mark a line across each post. This is the depth to which the posts should be sunk.

6 Check that the marked lines are at the same distance from the top of each post.

7 Mark the timber length with the position of each side of each post.

HELPFUL TIP

Once you have got the post spacing correct, nail three temporary battens across the posts – two square and one at an angle – to keep the spacing while you are concreting them into the ground.

They will still need to be propped up so that they are vertical; the temporary battens should be left in place until the concrete has set.

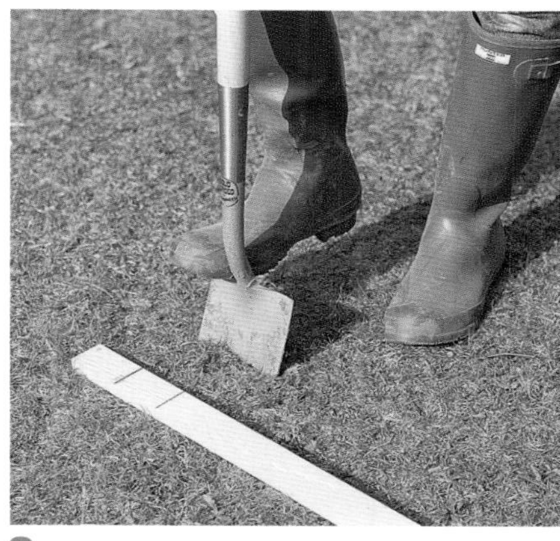

8 Use the timber length as a gauge to mark the post positions on the ground. Dig holes about 300mm square and 75mm deeper than the depth marked on the post. Drop removed soil onto a plastic sheet for easy removal.

9 Place hardcore in the bottom of each hole.

10 Lay the timber gauge across the holes as a guide to positioning the posts. Place each post in the hole on top of the brick and get a helper to hold it upright while you temporarily support it with timber stays wedged with pegs. Check with a spirit level that each post is vertical.

11 Use a flat piece of timber and a spirit level across the top of the gateposts to check that they are level.

12 Anchor each post by ramming in rubble or hardcore. Leave the top 100mm for concrete. Add the concrete and leave it to set for 48 hours, then remove the post supports and hang the gate (overleaf). If your ground is soft, anchor the posts more securely (overleaf).

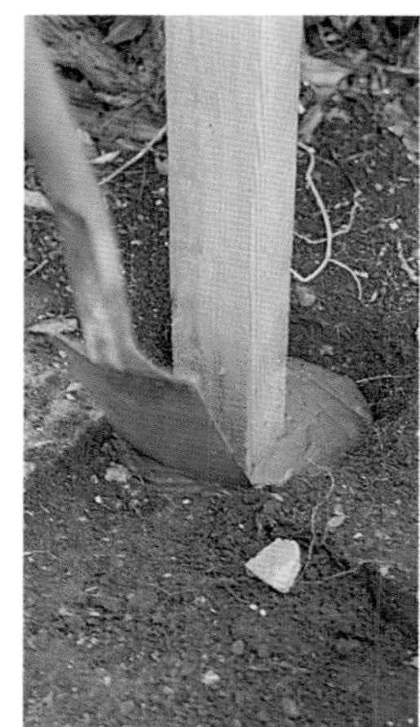

Setting posts in soft ground

On soft ground, gateposts may be pulled inwards by the movement of the gate. To prevent this, dig a trench about 300mm wide and 200mm deep between the posts and fill it with concrete.

Hanging the gate

1 Place two blocks or bricks between the gateposts and stand the gate on them. For flush hinges, line up the back of the gate with the backs of the posts. For pin fittings, centre the gate on the posts.

2 Use timber wedges to hold the sides of the gate in position with the correct clearance gaps for the fittings. Check with a spirit level that the top rail is horizontal.

3 Hold each hinge in place with the strap along the gate rail while you mark the position of the fixing holes on the post (see below). Drill pilot holes for two screws on each part of each hinge and partially fix each hinge. Then open and close the gate and check that it is level and swinging properly before you finish fitting the hinges. Partially fix the fastener on the gate and post. Then check that it closes properly before you secure the fittings.

4 Fit a post cap to each gatepost unless the post top is sloped or rounded to shed rain. If you cut a square top to a slope, make sure it is protected with wood preservative.

Hanging a gate on masonry piers

Masonry piers are usually made of large blocks of cut or ashlar stone, or bricks. Although rough stone may be used this makes hanging a gate much harder. Drilling for the hinges will be easier if you start with a pilot hole.

Tools *Hammer; drill; masonry drill bits; spirit level.*

Materials *Eyebolt hinges; gate latch; gate.*

Before you start Check the piers to make sure that they are in good order before hanging your gate and make any necessary repairs to the masonry. Special hinges are needed for hanging a gate on masonry, so don't use hinges meant for wooden posts.

1 Place the gate between the two piers. When viewed from above the gate should bisect the centre line of each pier. Sit the gate on temporary packing so that it is about 50 to 60mm above ground level.

2 Place wedges on either side of the gate so that the gate is held firmly. Use the spirit level to make sure that the top rail is level.

3 Measure down 175mm from the top rail and 250mm up from the bottom of the gate on the hanging side and put a pencil mark at these points. Transfer these pencil marks to the masonry piers then remove the gate.

4 Drill a pilot hole, then a larger hole, for the hinge: the size is dependent on the hinges that you are using. Hammer in the plug and screw in the hinge.

5 Attach the other half of the hinge to the gate, check to make sure that it swings properly and that the gap is even. If it is not, screw the hinges in or out of the piers a little to adjust their position.

6 Finally attach the latch to the other side of the gate and the striker to the pier.

Alternatively If you are building a pier to take a gate, set the gate hangers into the masonry as you work.

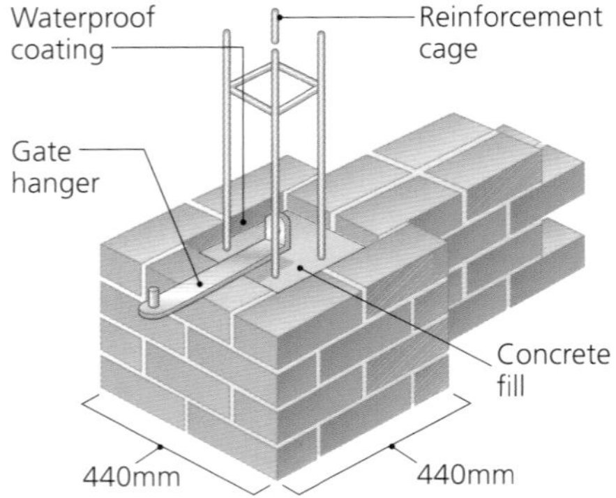

Choosing gate accessories

Apart from hinges and catches a gate may need other fittings. Double gates usually need a central ground socket of some sort to fit against, and a hook to hold the gate open is also generally necessary.

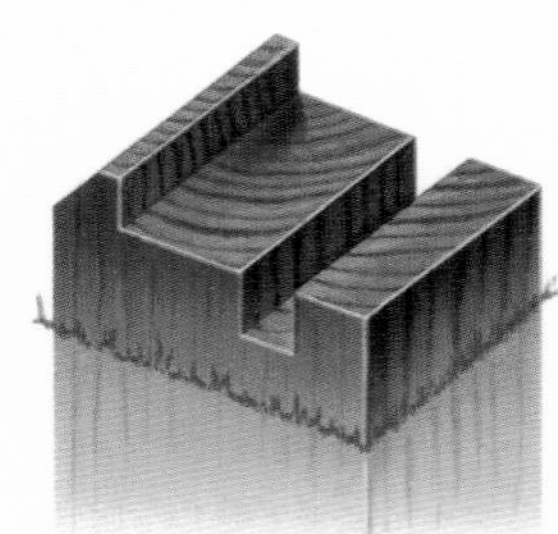

Centre stop block
Sunk into the ground at the meeting point of a pair of gates to stop them from swinging outwards, and to provide a locking point.

Drop bolts
For use with a centre stop block or a receiver socket or staple. A monkey-tail bolt (left) is easy to grasp. A heavy-duty bolt (right) is best for double gates.

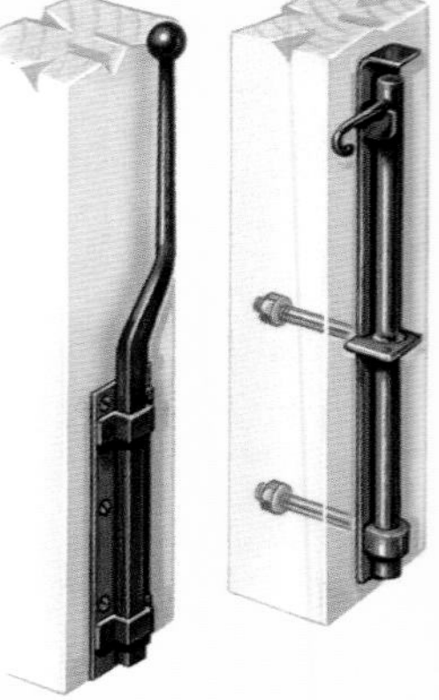

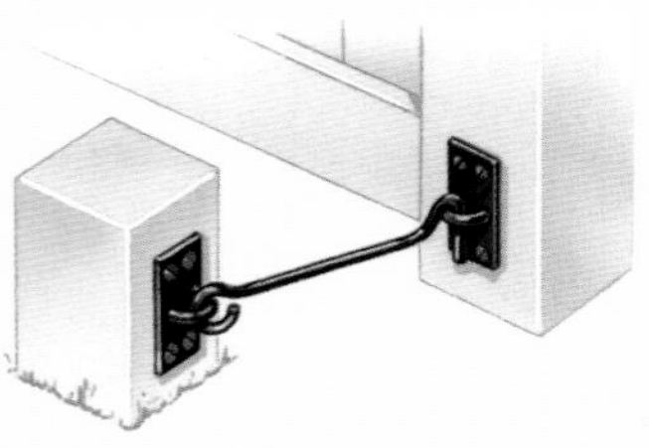

Hook-type holdback Has to be fastened and unfastened by hand.

Counter-weighted hook Stops a gate from swinging too far when it is opened, and also holds it open.

FIXING A GATE POST TO A WALL

You can buy fixing brackets for securing a gate post to a wall or a masonry pier. They comprise right-angled brackets with bolts that are anchored in the wall and plugs that are anchored in the post. A post secured in this way will support the hanging or closing side of the gate.

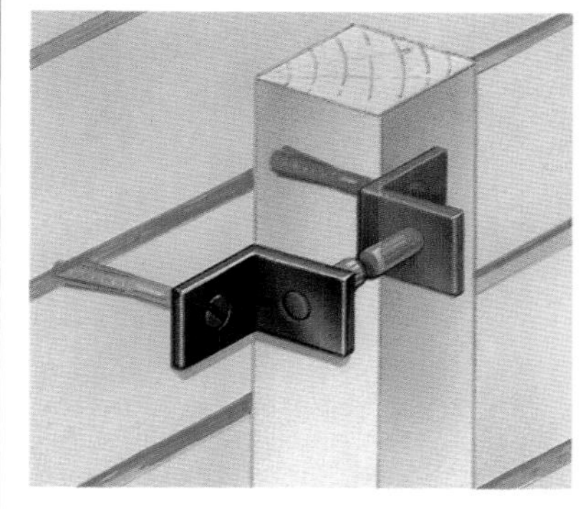

Hanging a pair of gates

Cramp double gates together and hang them in the same way as a single gate, but with a clearance gap between them.
Use a strip of wood 15mm wide down the centre, and pack it out at the top to be 20mm wide, so that the gap is wider at the top. This allows for initial wear on the hinges, which would otherwise cause the gates to drop at the centre. Use two or three large G-cramps to hold the stiles together, making sure the two gates are level with each other.

If the gates are cross-braced, make sure that the bottom of each diagonal is on the hinge side, so that the tops of the two diagonals meet in the middle.

Looking after a gate

Keep gates well treated with timber preservative or paint to prevent rotting or rusting. Hinges can be smeared with oil or grease to guard against rust, but for latches, which are constantly handled, paint is preferable, unless they are galvanised or japanned metal.

Repairing rotten timber

Cut out small areas of rot on the gate back to sound wood and fill the cavity with a two-part wood-repair filler of the epoxy-resin type. This sets after about 15 minutes and can be sanded down with medium-grade abrasive paper or a power sander to a smooth finish. The repair will not be visible after repainting.

Rotting timber parts such as pales or braces can be replaced. Treat new timber with a wood preservative (page 439), using a clear coating if it is to be painted later, or buy pre-treated timber, which will last longer. A rotting or damaged gatepost should be replaced or repaired in the same way as a fence post (page 437); but do not use a post spike. Repair a rotting post top in the same way as you would a fence post top (page 438).

Dealing with rust

Keep a lookout for rust spots appearing on fittings or metal gates, and remove them with abrasive paper. Repaint the area you have rubbed down immediately – rust can recur overnight. Remove severe rusting by scrubbing with a wire brush (wear safety goggles). Do not use a proprietary remover if you are going to repaint with a rust-inhibiting paint. Once the rust is removed, you can either repaint the area with a rust-neutralising primer followed by an undercoat and gloss coat, or use a one-coat paint such as Hammerite, which is both a rust-inhibitor and a finishing paint.

Repairing a sagging gate

The most common cause of a sagging gate is hinges that have worked loose through years of use, so check the condition of the hinges first. Replace loose hinge screws with longer, galvanised screws if possible. If not, tap wooden dowels (or fibre wall plugs) into the holes and use screws of the same size.

Alternatively, if possible, refit the hinges slightiy higher or lower so that the screws will be biting into firm wood. Replace worn or broken hinges.

If the hinges are in good condition, the timber joints of the gate may be loose. An isolated loose joint can be repaired by fixing a metal plate – tee, corner or straight – or an angle bracket to the joint. Try to force a waterproof adhesive up into the loose joint, then hold it together while you screw the bracket in place.

A very rickety gate should be either replaced or taken apart and remade. Clean away all old adhesive from the joints and reassemble using a waterproof adhesive. Reinforce mortise-and-tenon joints by drilling into the stile and through the tongue of the tenon, then insert a glued dowel. After reassembling the gate, clamp it together while the adhesive dries.

A gate may sag because it has no diagonal brace, or because the brace is not strong enough (or the gate may have been hung on the wrong side). Make a new brace from planed preservative-treated 25 x 75mm softwood. Use a sliding bevel (page 50) to set the angles at the ends before sawing and filing it to exactly the right shape so that it fits tightly. Screw and glue the brace in place with its top end on the non-hinge side. Paint or stain it to match the gate. Lift and wedge the gate into its proper position and make sure that it is a good fit before fixing the brace with waterproof adhesive and galvanised screws.

Choosing garage doors

In addition to closing off the garage, providing security and keeping the weather out of your garage, the doors are often one of the first things that most visitors to your house notice. Until the 1970s nearly all garage doors were made of wood that had to be painted on a regular basis. Modern doors are made from a wide range of durable and low-maintenance materials, including steel, plastic and glass-reinforced plastic (GRP). These are often stronger and lighter, making it possible to fit larger one-piece doors, with differing opening arrangements, such as up-and-over doors and roller doors.

Side hung doors on hinges

This is the traditional method for hanging wooden garage doors (above). The doors are hung on large hinges attached to a wooden frame screwed or bolted to the brickwork of the garage. Normally the doors are made as a pair and meet in the middle. They should be hung in the same way as hanging a pair of gates (page 442), but be sure to buy hinges that are suitable for the weight of the large doors. The doors are commonly secured using a combination of internal and external bolts and padlocks.

Wooden garage doors require regular maintenance, such as repainting, to prevent them from rotting.

Side-hung, hinged doors must open outwards for access, which prevents you from parking too close to the doors. Of all the garage door options, this one demands most clearance in front of the garage.

Up-and-over doors

Retractable door

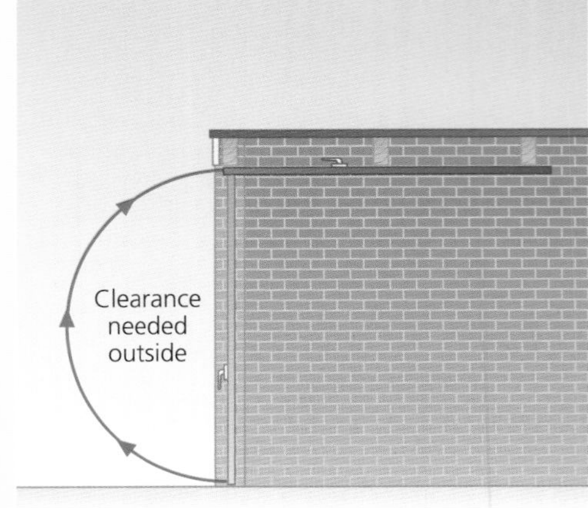

The door is swung on pivots and runs on rails fixed to the inside of the garage roof when opened. This style of door requires a large clearance in front of it for opening. Can be made in almost any material and hangs on a 75 x 75mm wooden frame attached to the inside of the opening. Suitable for use with automatic door openers.

Canopy door

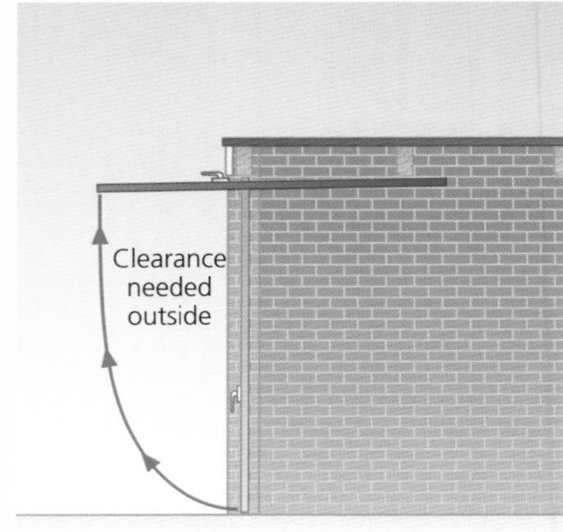

So called because, when open, a section of the door protrudes beyond the front face of the garage. The mechanism is slightly different from the retractable door and takes up less room inside the garage. The door also requires less clearance in front of the garage for opening. Not ideal for use with automatic door openers.

Sectional door One of the easiest to automate with electric openers (opposite). The door is made up of horizontal panels, wider than those in a roller door (right), which allow it to retract into the roof without protruding in front of the garage. It does not roll up. Does not require a wooden frame, as the door runs in rollers in a metal channel fitted inside the garage. The door closes against a lip seal to prevent draughts.

Roller door Made from slim sections that roll around a metal pole attached to the inside top of the door opening. Provides a very secure door, which takes up less space than any of the other types, does not need the roof inside the garage to be kept clear and requires no opening clearance in front of the garage. The door fits behind the opening in the brickwork, so this is a good choice if the opening is an unusual shape. Designs are limited but doors are available in a wide range of colours. Suitable for use with automatic door openers (right).

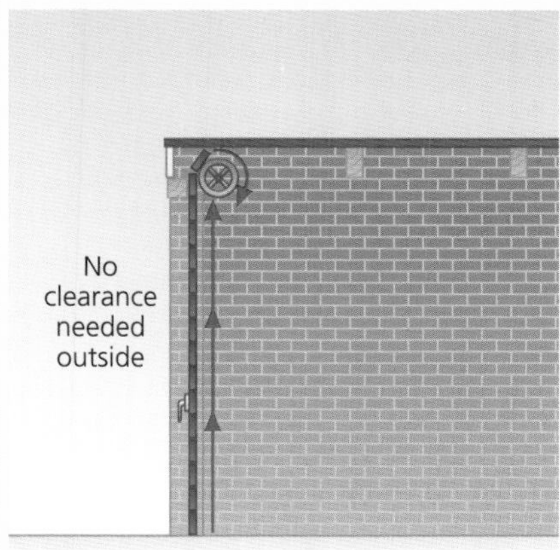

DOOR INSULATION

Single skinned garage doors are a weak point in terms of your home's energy loss. Double-skinned foam insulated garage doors are an effective energy-saving alternative, providing extra heat and sound insulation. Although the initial outlay may be more, double-skinned doors are cost-effective in the long run.

Installing an up-and-over garage door

Garage doors can be made in almost any size to fit the opening of an existing garage. If you are buying a made-to-measure door, take very careful and accurate measurements from your garage door opening before placing the order.

Before you start Despite their size, installing an up-and-over door is an easy job, provided the wooden sub-frame that you are attaching it to is in good order and square. If you are replacing an existing door, it makes good sense to replace the frame at the same time, as it is prone to rot at the bottom of the uprights.

Tools *Hammer; screwdriver; socket spanners; power drill and drill bits; tape measure; spirit level.*

Materials *Garage door; wooden shims; 75 x 75mm prepared timber door frame; 125mm hammer-in fixings or frame fixers (page 158).*

1 Install the wooden frame into the door opening. Place shims under each leg to keep the bottoms 10mm above the level of the ground.

2 Use a spirit level to make sure that both sides of the wooden frame are plumb and the head is level. Drill through the legs 250mm up from the bottom into the brickwork of the garage wall and insert a hammer-in fixing or a frame fixer so that 50mm of it is in the brickwork.

3 Check again that the frame is plumb and level and put in two more screws each side 250mm down from the top and one in the centre of each upright.

4 Attach the fixing lugs on the metal frame of the door into the predrilled and tapped holes using the screws provided. Tighten them just enough to hold them in place but do not over-tighten them.

5 From inside the garage, lift the door into place with a helper so that the metal lugs rest against the inside of the wooden sub-frame.

6 Place 10mm spacer blocks of wood under the bottom of the door and screw the metal angle brackets to the wooden frame. Check that the door is level.

7 Attach the spring clamps to the bottom of the wooden door frame, taking the measurements from the instructions that came with the door.

8 Clip the springs onto the brackets on the door frame, then pass a long screwdriver through the top loop of the spring before pulling it up and hooking it onto the metal pegs on either side of the door.

9 Attach the top rails at one end to the inside of the wooden frame and at the other end to the ceiling rafters, using the angle brackets that are supplied with the kit. If your ceiling is unusually high, you may have to extend these brackets with slotted steel or wooden extenders.

10 Attach the lock mechanism if this is not already fitted.

11 Lightly grease the rollers and latches, then check that the door opens and closes smoothly. Make any adjustments necessary and make sure that all the fixing bolts are firmly tightened.

Installing an automatic garage door opener

It is often seen as a luxury, but a simple remote-controlled motor allows you to open your garage from inside the car. Not only does this mean that you do not have to get wet in the rain, it is seen by many people as a safety feature, as they do not have to leave the car to open or close the door.

Automatic door openers are suitable for retractable sectional or roller garage doors (left). For roller doors, a motor turns a drum, which rolls the door up into a compact box fitted above the door opening.

Automatic door openers are straightforward to fit and simply require a power supply to be run to the motor. Connect the motor to a flex outlet plate run from a fused connection unit on a spur from the main garage circuit (see Fitting a fused connection unit, page 286 and Wiring electrical appliances into a bathroom, page 287). Follow the manufacturer's fitting instructions that are supplied with the kit.

Most automatic doors come with a manual override for use in the event of a power failure.

Choosing a path, drive or patio

When choosing material for a path or drive, take into account the amount of wear it is likely to get, as well as the appearance – whether it will blend in with the house exterior and garden surroundings. Consider also the amount of work that will be involved in laying the material.

The cheapest materials are often those that are quickest and easiest to lay. It may be cost-effective to mix materials, such as paving slabs and bricks or gravel.

In estimating the cost, do not forget to include materials such as mortar, hardcore or sand, as well as the surface material. Also allow for the cost of any equipment you may need to hire, such as a plate vibrator.

Paving slabs

Large, flat, pre-cast concrete slabs laid on mortar. Hydraulically pressed types are strongest and should be used for a drive, which has to take the weight of one or more vehicles. Surfaces may be smooth (non-slip), polished or patterned to appear like cobbles, bricks or tiles in straight or curved designs. Reasonably quick and easy to lay on a straight site, but difficult to form into curves. Careful planning is needed on a slope or an awkwardly shaped site. Can look monotonous in large areas unless colours, shapes or textures are used to enliven the surface. Colours include grey, buff and red. Square, rectangular and hexagonal shapes available.

Coverage
450 x 450mm – 4.9 slabs per m²
600 x 450mm – 3.7 slabs per m²
600 x 600mm – 2.8 slabs per m².

Sub-base For a drive: 100mm of compacted hardcore topped by 125mm of concrete. For a path or patio: 100mm of hardcore, or firm, well-rolled ground.

A patio laid with slabs of different sizes has an informal appearance and the appeal of traditional stone paving.

Paving blocks

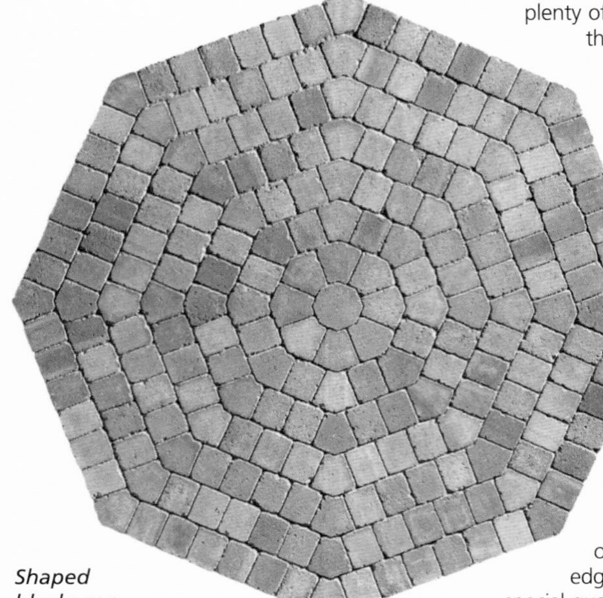

Shaped blocks can define an area or add interest to a patio.

Brick-like concrete blocks laid on a bed of thick sand, and held in place between existing walls, edging blocks or kerbing. Commonly rectangular, but interlocking decorative shapes are also available. Colours include grey, red, charcoal, brown, buff, marigold and red-grey mixtures. Blocks can be laid like brick in various bond patterns (page 465), or patterns such as basket-weave or herringbone. A herringbone pattern is best for drives because it gives blocks the stability to withstand tyre movements when vehicles are manoeuvring. Blocks take longer to lay than slabs, but look good and are easier to fit into awkwardly shaped areas. They can easily be lifted to get at underground pipes. You will need to hire a plate vibrator (pages 451, 456) to lay blocks over a large area such as a drive or patio, and a block splitter (page 456) for cutting to size where necessary.

Coverage Rectangular blocks, 200 x 100 x 60mm – 50 blocks cover 1m².

Sub-base For a drive: 100mm compacted hardcore topped with 75mm of sand compacted to 50mm when the blocks are laid. For a path or patio: firm, well-compacted ground and sand bed.

Crazy paving

Slabs of irregular shape fitted together on a bed of mortar. Broken stone or concrete slabs can be bought by the tonne or square metre. Collect your own if you can, so that you can choose your own mixture of colours, shapes and sizes, preferably mostly large and medium pieces because small pieces involve more work. Ideal for making a lively looking drive. More difficult to lay than regular slabs because the shapes have to be fitted to a pattern. Also, they may not be all the same thickness, and so may need different amounts of mortar to level them. Allow plenty of time for the job. When filling in the joints, a good way of bringing out the shapes is to draw a well-defined groove in the mortar round each slab using the tip of a brick trowel.

Coverage 1 tonne covers about 9–10m².

Sub-base For a drive: 100mm of compacted hardcore topped by 125mm of concrete. For a path or patio: 100mm of hardcore, or firm, well-rolled ground.

Bricks

Clay bricks or brick pavers laid on a bed of sand between fixed edging, or on a bed of mortar. Use special-quality F grade bricks (page 465) that withstand hard weather, especially frost. Brick pavers are normally thinner than bricks and are available in square or interlocking shapes. The colour range is very wide, in browns, reds, brindles and yellows. Bricks can be laid in walling bond patterns (page 465) or others – typically herringbone and basket weave – and used flat or on edge. Paving is also available resembling old hand-made bricks in traditional basket-weave style. They are a little more difficult to lay than blocks, if bedded on mortar, but similarly flexible and suitable for almost any setting. Bricks bedded in sand have to be tapped down by hand, as they are likely to crack under a plate vibrator.

Coverage
Bricks, 215 x 102.5 x 65mm, laid on sand, 45 bricks per m², laid on mortar (with joint) 40 bricks per m².
Pavers, 215 x 102.5 x 50mm (coverage as bricks) or 200 x 100 x 60 (as blocks).

Sub-base
As for paving blocks if laid on sand (except with 55mm sand layer); as for paving slabs if laid on mortar.

PAVING RULES

You may need planning permission for a new (or replacement) front drive or if paving over your front garden. See page 487 for details.

Concrete

Sand and coarse aggregate (crushed gravel or stone) bound together with cement and water in certain proportions (page 459) and laid, while soft, between temporary edgings. Hardens to a tough, stone-like surface. Can be mixed as you go along, or delivered in loads for large areas. The surface layer should be 100–150mm thick for a drive or 50–75mm thick for a path. Very strong, cheaper than paving slabs or blocks, and straightforward to lay. Edging formwork has to be set up in preparation. Mixing to the right consistency is critical, and mixing can be hard work. Hire a small mixer (page 460) if laying about 0.5m³ or more. Concrete hardens in about 2 hours – faster in hot weather. The surface can be given various patterned finishes.

Colouring pigments can be stirred into the mixture – the shade varies with the amount applied, and it is difficult to get a uniform colour.

Coverage Available as separate ingredients, bagged dry mix or in ready-mixed loads. Quantities per m³ are given on page 459.

Sub-base For a drive: 100mm of well-compacted hardcore and 25–50mm of ballast to fill the gaps. For a path: firm, well-rolled soil, with hardcore in soft patches or hollows.

Cold asphalt

A mixture of bitumen and finely crushed gravel or stone (macadam) spread on top of a thin coat of bitumen emulsion to 'tack' it in place, then compacted between temporary or permanent edging to form a tough, waterproof surface. Normally used to re-surface an existing drive, or for covering worn and pitted concrete or paving slabs. It is not suitable for making a new drive, but can be used for a new path provided that the hardcore base can be firmly compacted, generally by using a plate vibrator (page 451). Cheaper than paving and simple to lay, but sticky to work with. Wear protective shoes and clothing, and protect floor coverings if any is likely to be tramped into the house. The ground needs to be treated with weedkiller two weeks before the surface is laid. Supplied in bags and available in red and black. Decorative stone chippings may be provided with each bag. It tends to look monotonous in large areas, and the surface can be dented by the weight of a car on a pillar jack.

Coverage One 25kg bag covers about 0.9m² laid 20mm deep and rolled to 15mm deep. A 5kg can of emulsion covers about 7m² on a firm surface.

Sub-base For a drive: an existing surface such as concrete, paving slabs or old asphalt. For a path: well-compacted hardcore as for stone chippings (right).

Stone chippings

Can be scattered on cold asphalt as a decorative dressing, or used alone as a surface dressing, bound together with a thick coat of bitumen emulsion, to give a firm, waterproof surface, suitable for light traffic, but loose chippings may be thrown up by tyres. Normally used to re-surface an existing drive, but may be suitable for a new drive provided the hardcore base can be well compacted, generally by a plate vibrator (pages 451, 456). Colours include greyish-white, pink and grey-green. Cheap and easy to lay. The ground needs to be treated with weedkiller two weeks before the chippings are laid.

Coverage One 25kg bag covers about 2.5m². A 25kg can of bitumen emulsion covers 35m² on a hard surface, 13.5m² on a firm, dense surface or 6.5m² on a loose, open surface.

Sub-base For a drive: existing surface or 100–150mm compacted ballast. For a path: 75–100mm hardcore topped with ballast.

Gravel

A mixture of small stones laid loose on a firm surface, usually between anchored edgings. The stones are normally well-rounded pea gravel of a single size, either 10mm or 20mm. Available in white or various shades of brown. Cheap, easy and quick to lay, but can be a difficult surface for walking on or pushing a pram or bicycle across. Stones may be carried into the house on shoes. Needs regular raking or rolling. Not suitable for a drive with a pronounced slope.

Coverage A tonne covers about 15m² if laid about 25mm deep.

Sub-base For a drive or path: 100mm of well-compacted hardcore topped with 25mm of sand.

ALTERNATIVE GROUND COVER

A new and ecologically sound form of ground cover for drives and paths is a honeycombed grid made from recycled plastic. The grid is laid in easy-to-handle square or rectangular interlocking tiles 30 to 50mm thick, laid on a bed of sand. Each hole in the grid can be filled with sand or gravel. Alternatively, you can fill the grid with a soil and fertiliser mixture that can be then sown with grass seed to create a very hard-wearing grass surface.

Sub-base For a drive: 200–300mm compressed gravel or ballast mixture, or the same depth of ballast and sand mixture.

Edging and kerbing

For providing fixed edging to an area of paving blocks laid on a sand bed, or to confine loose or soft surfaces such as gravel or asphalt. Paving blocks can be edged with a header course of the same blocks used for the paving (page 457). Path edging is usually available in straight lengths only; standard kerbing, which is thicker and deeper, is also sold in curved lengths. Tops may be flat, chamfered, rounded, bullnosed or scalloped. Kerbing can be laid to finish above the paved surface (to check surface water or stop cars going onto the garden), flush with the paved surface, or just below the paved surface so that it is covered by grass or soil and only the paving shows. Has to be carefully set up in position on its concrete bed to finish at the correct height in relation to the surface, and with the correct crossfall and alignment if laid above or flush with the paving.

Coverage Edging: available in a wide range of sizes and shapes. Standard kerb: 600–900mm long, 100–150mm wide and 250mm or 300mm deep.

Sub-base Hardcore from base topped by a 70mm layer of concrete wide enough for the kerb thickness and a generous haunching of bedding mortar (for edging) or concrete (for standard kerbing).

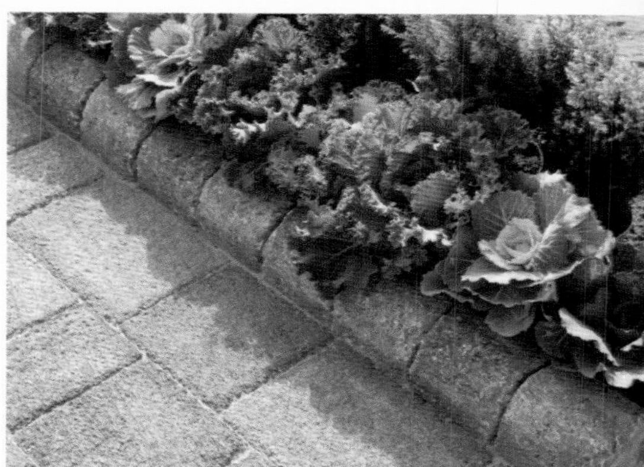

Kerbstones and edging can be chosen to match a path or driveway (above) or may be used to separate a planted border from an area of gravel (top).

Preparing the sub-base for a drive, path or patio

How well a surface will support heavy loads depends to a great extent on the strength of the sub-base. A drive that has to take the weight of one or more cars needs a stronger sub-base than a path.

Before you start Some paving materials need a sub-base of hardcore only, others need hardcore topped with a layer of concrete (pages 448–9). On soft ground or where heavy traffic is likely, the sub-base may need to be even deeper.

- A drive needs to be at least 3m wide for car doors to be opened or for people to walk past a parked car.
- All drives need to be sloped from side to side (a cross-fall) so that rainwater will not lie on the surface. A cross-fall of about 1 in 40 is suitable for a drive.
- A drive should also slope away from the house, so may need a lengthways slope of 1 in 100. It can be steeper, if necessary, to follow the natural slope of the ground.
- Consult your local authority if a new driveway needs access onto a main road.

Tools *Pegs and string lines; builder's square; mallet; spade; shovel; steel tape measure; timber pegs 25mm square and 460mm long; chalk or paint; wheelbarrow; spirit level; wooden shims; earth rammer, garden roller or plate vibrator. Possibly also sledgehammer; concreting tools.*

Materials *Hardcore (below); sand or ballast (page 458). Possibly concrete (page 460).*

THE SUB-BASE MATERIAL

Hardcore is made up of well-broken bricks, blocks or stone and can be bought from builders' merchants. A tonne of hardcore covers roughly $6m^2$ if it is laid 100mm deep.

Some hardcore may contain demolition rubble, which includes unsuitable material such as wood and plaster. Such hardcore will not bed down well.

Gaps in the hardcore surface are filled with a thin layer of ballast (sand and shingle) – a process known as blinding.

Hoggin is a more expensive form of hardcore, made up of gravel and sandy clay, and will bed down well.

Taut string line To mark the edges of the area

Blinding layer Sand or ballast to fill in gaps in the hardcore

Marker pegs Showing depths of materials

Concrete sub-base Needed for some paving materials on drives carrying heavy loads

Surface material May be paving slabs or blocks or concrete. Leave sufficient depth according to the thickness of the material

Crossfall A built-in slope from side to side to allow for surface water drainage

Hardcore The base material

Four layers of a drive The depth of the sub-base material depends on the surface it is supporting, the weight that will have to be carried, and the nature of the ground (pages 448–9). This illustration shows a drive in cross-section.

1 Use taut pegged string lines to mark the edges of the drive area, allowing for permanent edging such as a kerb. Check with a steel tape measure that the width of the site is uniform, and use a builder's square (page 467) to ensure that right angles are true. For making a curve, see opposite.

2 Decide on the direction of the crossfall. The drive should slope away from the house or garage wall. If the ground slopes naturally towards the house, build up the hardcore base to reverse the slope, if possible. Otherwise build a drainage channel and soakaway (page 452).

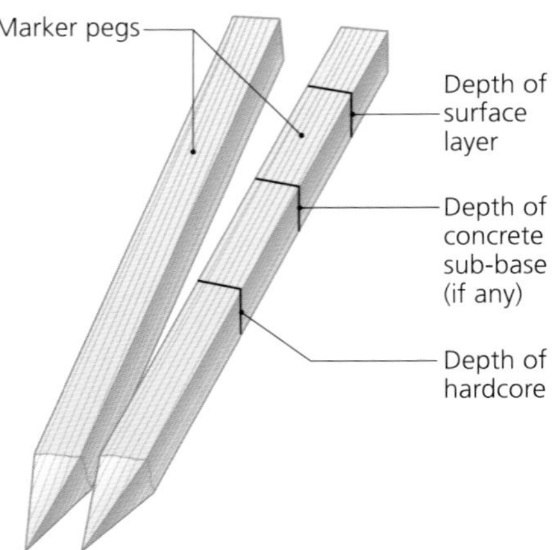

3 Mark the timber pegs from the top to show the depths of the various layers, allowing for any bedding sand or mortar.

4 Drive a marked peg into the ground in the top corner (nearest to the house) of the area to be excavated. Set it with its top at the right level for the drive surface.

5 Drive in a row of pegs at about 1.5m intervals across the top of the site, using a spirit level between pairs of pegs to ensure a crossfall of 1 in 40 (see panel, far right).

6 Drive in a second row of pegs 1.5m farther down the drive. Set the top of each to allow for any lengthways slope necessary from the first rows – for a fall of 1 in 100 use a 16mm shim.

7 Continue with rows of pegs down the drive in this way at similar intervals, adjusting the distances of the last rows as necessary so that the final row is at the bottom edge of the site.

8 Dig out the area within the string lines to the lowest peg mark (the base of the hardcore layer). Spread the topsoil on other parts of the garden. Leave any clayey subsoil in a heap for later disposal.

9 Spread hardcore in the excavated area. Ram it down well – using an earth rammer or, for larger areas, a garden roller or plate vibrator – until it is at the marked level for the hardcore surface. If laying concrete paving blocks (page 456), break up the hardcore as small as possible with a sledgehammer before compacting it with a vibrator.

10 Add a thin layer of sand or ballast to fill in the gaps. Ram it down well.

11 If the base material includes a layer of concrete, spread the concrete over the hardcore and blinding layer and tamp it down to the marked level.

12 Remove the pegs and fill in the holes with hardcore or hardcore and concrete before laying the paving material.

Preparing the sub-base for a path

A path that will be subject to heavy loads or that is on soft ground will need a well-compacted hardcore sub-base. Prepare it in the same way as for the sub-base for a drive, except that fewer surface marker pegs will be needed.

The path need not slope along its length, but it should have a crossfall of about 1 in 80 away from the wall if it is alongside a house (see Making a sloped surface, right).

If a hardcore sub-base is necessary, set up string lines and marker pegs and dig out the site only to the depth of the surface material and any bedding needed, such as a mortar or sand layer (pages 448–9). Slope the bottom of the excavation to one side and use a spirit level and shim across the bottom to get the required slope. Fill in any depression in the surface with well-broken hardcore. Use a garden roller to compact the surface until it is firm and even.

Marking out a curved path

Use a garden hosepipe or lengths of rope to mark the outline of the curve on each side by eye.

It is usually necessary to allow extra width between the curving sides. If they are the same width apart as the straight sides, an optical illusion will occur, making the path appear to be narrow at the curve when viewed from a short distance away.

Set up a peg and string line to follow the shape of the marked curve. The pegs will need to be closer together than when using straight string lines.

Preparing the sub-base for a patio

Do this in the same way as for a drive, but with hardcore only below the surface material. A slope of 1 in 60 away from the house or towards a drain is normally enough for drainage, but not so steep as to affect the levels of chairs and tables.

KEEPING CLEAR OF THE DAMP-PROOF COURSE

If the drive is against a house wall, make sure the base is dug deep enough for the drive surface to be at least 150mm below the damp-proof course, commonly visible as a thick line of mortar usually two or three brick courses up the wall.

Where it is not possible for the drive surface to be low enough, one alternative is to slope the drive towards the house and build a gully and soakaway. Alternatively, you may be able to build concrete skirting (see Defects in the damp-proofing, page 411) between the drive edge and wall.

MAKING A SLOPED SURFACE

Place a spirit level – on a length of timber, if necessary – across the pegs marking the surface level. Use a thin piece of wood (known as a shim) under the spirit level, or its support, on the lower-side pegs. Tap down the lower-side peg until the spirit level is set level with the shim in position.

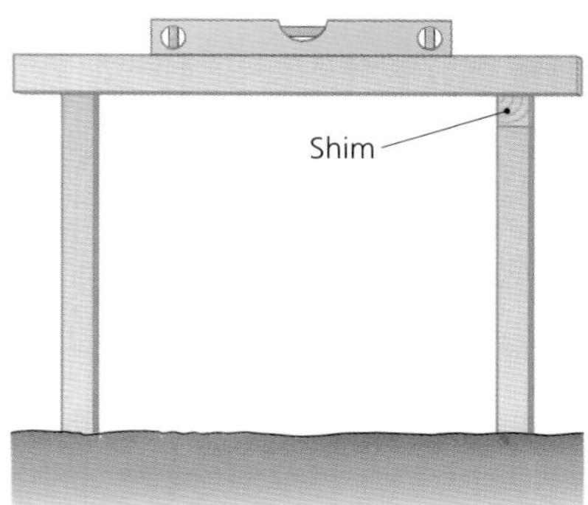

The thickness of the shim depends on the slope required and the width between pegs. For example, on a path 1m wide, you need a 13mm shim for a crossfall of 1 in 80, 16mm for 1 in 60, or 25mm for 1 in 40. For a crossfall of 1 in 40 on a drive with marker pegs spaced at 1.5m intervals, you need a 40mm shim. The calculation of the shim size need not be precise.

TOOLS FOR A SUB-BASE

Many compacting or demolition tools can be hired. Hire firms are listed in *Yellow Pages* under Hire Services – Tools and Equipment.

Earth rammer A steel handle with a heavy club end for ramming down hardcore.

Garden roller A sand or water-filled roller 100kg or heavier to be used instead of an earth rammer for compacting large areas of hardcore (or for rolling cold asphalt).

Plate vibrator Instead of a roller, you can hire a petrol-driven plate vibrator (also known as a power compactor) for ramming down large areas of hardcore. It is also used for bedding down concrete paving blocks.

Demolition or breaker hammer The easiest way to break up a concrete surface before laying a new path or drive is with an electric-powered hammer. It is fitted like a drill with a chisel or point for cutting, and can also be used with a masonry bit for drilling fixing holes into or through concrete. Hire a lightweight tool for concrete up to 100mm thick, or a heavyweight one for thicker concrete. Wear safety goggles and, if possible, steel-tipped boots when using the hammer.

Other useful tools Pegs and a string line are needed for marking the outline of an area to be excavated. The stretched string line, held taut between the pegs, is also a guide for keeping straight edges.

A garden spade is necessary for digging out soil from the sub-base area and a shovel for moving building materials. A sledgehammer may be useful for breaking up hardcore, a pickaxe for breaking hard ground or small areas and a shovel for moving building materials. old concrete. Both can be hired.

You will also need concreting tools (page 457) if the sub-base needed includes a layer of concrete above the hardcore.

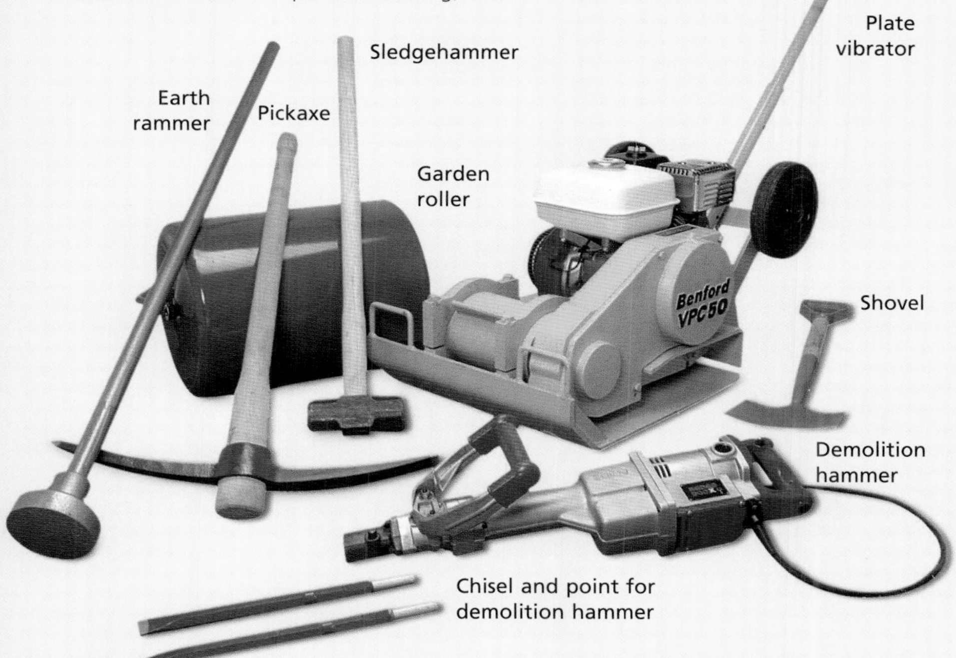

Masking or raising a manhole cover

When you build a drive or patio, the ground level is often slightly raised, which means that a manhole cover on an inspection chamber within the paving must be either masked with paving or the existing cover can be raised to paving level.

To mask the existing manhole cover, a double seal cover is used. These are sold by DIY superstores and builders' merchants in various sizes – commonly 600 X 450mm.

Two types are available. The most useful for paving is designed specifically to take standard-sized concrete paving blocks, so all you see is the narrow framework. Less deep versions can be used for other types of paving and are also suitable for fitting indoors where you have a manhole cover surrounded by, say, floor tiles.

To raise the height of a manhole cover, first remove the lid and lay a sheet of polythene in the base of the chamber to prevent debris falling into the drains.

Then chip away the mortar surrounding the cast-iron frame with a club hammer and cold chisel. Take care not to strike the frame, which shatters easily.

When you have released the frame, clean away the mortar covering the top surface of the brick walls of the chamber.

The material you use to add height to the chamber walls depends on the increase in height required. If the amount is less than the height of a brick – 75mm including the mortar – use clay pavers, brick slips or strips cut from 13mm thick concrete roofing tiles, laid in courses in the same way as bricks.

Reset the frame on a bed of sand-cement mortar – three parts sand to one part cement. Tap it gently into position using a block of wood and a club hammer. Use a spirit level to check that it is level across its width and length.

Slope the mortar round the outside downwards away from the frame to carry away rainwater.

Dealing with an airbrick

The drive or patio surface must not cover an airbrick low down in the house wall. If, however, there is no way of keeping the paved surface below the airbrick, one solution is to stop the edge of the paving short, leaving a pit at least 300mm wide in front of it. Keep the pit clear of leaves and debris.

An alternative solution is to run a duct under the surface from the airbrick to an open edge such as a retaining wall.

To fit a duct, remove the airbrick (page 408) and cement a length of 100mm diameter plastic piping for underground drainage into the hole. Use bagged sand-and-cement mortar (page 458) or a 1:4 cement-sand mix. Run the piping through the hardcore base and then mortar it to a new airbrick at the other end.

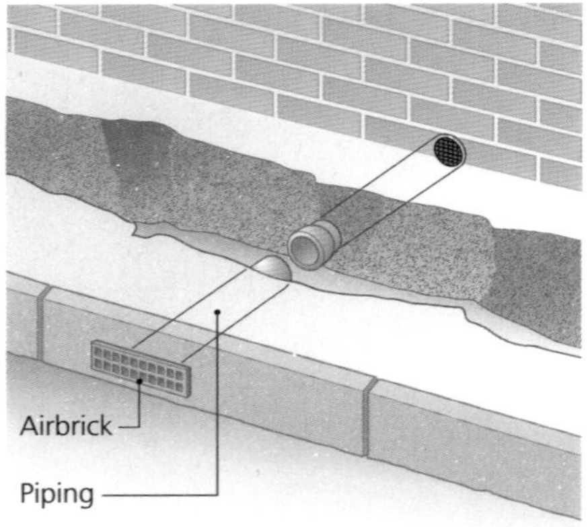

Building a drainage channel

If you build a drive that follows a natural slope of the ground towards the house, you will have to build a channel at the lowest edge of the drive to carry away rainwater.

Before you start Design the channel so that it runs into either an existing drain or a soakaway – a drainage pit sited at least 3m from the house.

The channel should be lined with concrete and should have a fall of about 1 in 40 towards the soakaway. Make the channel using a concrete paving mix (page 459) and shape it about 25mm deep using a length of drainpipe. Make sure there are no ridges.

Alternatively Use ready-made concrete channelling, mortared into the hardcore base. It is available from builders' merchants in about 900mm lengths. Enclosed types (as above) are about 250mm deep and 300mm wide with a narrow slot or metal grid in the top. Or you can buy dish channel with a 25mm deep dish.

Making a soakaway

Any type of soakaway is for dispersing rainwater or surface water only. It must not be used for household drainage water. Get advice from your local authority in case they have specific regulations.

A home-made soakaway

1 To make a home-made soakaway, dig a pit about 1.2m round or square and at least the same depth. If you hit a pan of clay that is so hard you cannot dig through it, make the soakaway larger than 1.2m to compensate for the lack of depth.

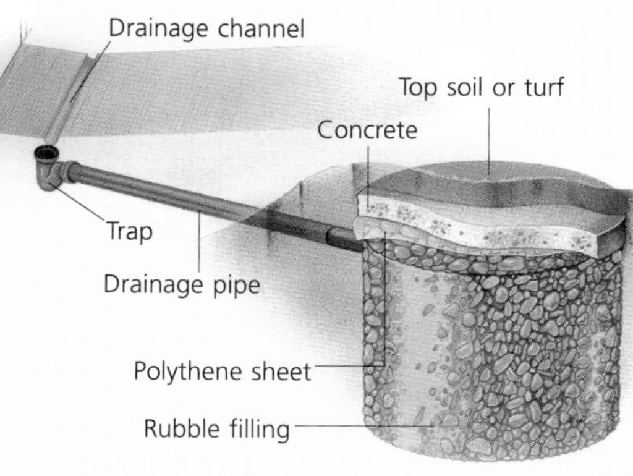

2 Break up the bottom of the pit with a fork before you fill it to within about 100mm of the top with rubble, coarser at the bottom. A pit 1.2m across and 1.2m deep needs about 1.8m³ of rubble, which is roughly 25–30 wheelbarrow loads.

3 Direct the drainpipe from the channel into the rubble at a gentle slope. Fit a gully trap at the top end.

4 Cover the rubble with a sheet of heavy-gauge polythene, then add a layer of concrete (page 460) 75mm thick. Finally, cover with a layer of soil or turf.

A ready-made soakaway

You can buy a ready-made soakaway with instructions for installation. It consists of pierced plastic or concrete segments which build up into rings (see below). They are laid on a strip foundation. Water entering the soakaway seeps out through the rings and through a wrap-round separation membrane into a surrounding layer, at least 150mm thick, of granular back-fill material.

Ready-made soakaway

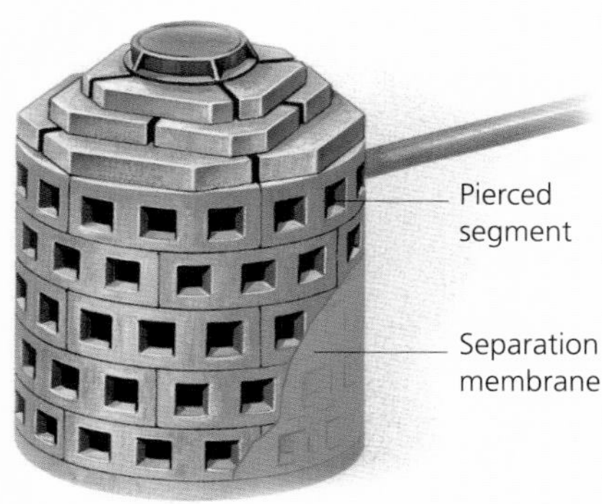

Laying slabs for a drive or patio

Covering your drive or patio with slabs is quick and easy, but careful planning beforehand is necessary.

Before you start Plan the size of the site so that it can be divided exactly by the dimensions of the slabs to be used, if possible. It will save you having to cut too many slabs. Allow for a gap of 9-10mm between slabs for mortar joints.

Make a scale plan of the site on graph paper, showing the positions and numbers of the slabs – especially if you are mixing different sizes, colours and textures. Where necessary, take up odd dimensions either by using 25mm wide mortar joints, or fill in with a small-sized unit such as a brick. Use mortar to fill small irregular areas.

Some slab manufacturers supply leaflets showing patterns that can be made using their slabs, and give an estimate of the numbers needed for different patterns.

The method of laying paving slabs on five 'spots' of mortar (one in the centre and one at each corner) can lead to a whole host of problems and is no longer recommended.

Tools *Brick trowel; straightedge about 1.8m long; steel tape measure; marker pegs; builder's square (page 467); spirit level; wooden shim (page 451); club hammer; length of timber 100 x 50mm; brick bolster or angle grinder/masonry cutter; pencil; try square; wood or plywood spacers 9 or 10mm thick (probably three or four per slab); two shovels; bucket; fine-rose watering can; mixing platform (page 457); damp sponge.*

Materials *Paving slabs – use hydraulically pressed 50mm thick slabs for a drive; bedding mortar mix (page 459) or bagged dry sand-and-cement mortar (page 458) for small areas.*

HELPFUL TIP

Store paving slabs upright, leaning against a wall. Raise them off the ground on two lengths of wood to keep the bottom edges clean.

Preparing the base

1 For a drive, prepare a hardcore and concrete base (page 450), and wait until the concrete is hard (about three days).

Alternatively For a patio, prepare a hardcore base only, with a blinding layer of sand.

2 Adjust the pegged string lines at the edge of the site as a guide to slab alignment. Drive in marker pegs as a guide to the height of the slab surface, taking into account the 25mm depth of bedding mortar, the crossfall, and any lengthways slope. Site the pegs at suitable intervals to be bridged with a spirit level, placed on a straightedge if necessary.

3 Check the marker peg levels with a spirit level and wooden shims (see Making a sloped surface, page 451). Check that the corner lines are true with a builder's square.

4 Mix the bedding mortar on a firm surface in the same way as mixing concrete (page 460), but using sharp sand and cement only. Keep one shovel solely for dry cement. Make the mortar to a fairly dry consistency to support the weight of the slab.

5 Use a brick trowel to spread mortar about 35–40mm thick for the first slab at one corner of the site. Roughen the mortar surface with the point of the trowel.

Laying the slabs

1 Lay the slab carefully on the mortar bed so that its outer edges are in line with the string lines.

2 Place a short length of 100 x 50mm thick timber on the slab to cushion it while you tap it down gently with a club hammer until the surface is level with the height pegs. The slab must be bedded down solidly, with no rocking movement. Ensure the compacted mortar bed is about 25mm thick – adjust the amount if necessary.

3 Use a spirit level and wooden shim to check that the crossfall and lengthways slope of the slab are correct.

4 Lay a row of edge slabs from the corner slab in the same way, in line with the guidelines and pegs. Place wood or plywood spacers at the edge of each slab (unless it has sloped sides) to leave a uniform gap for filling in the joints later.

5 Use a straightedge to check that the surface of each slab in the row is in line with the one before. If a slab is too high, tap it down if possible, or lift it and re-lay it with less mortar. If a slab is too low, lift it, add more mortar, and re-lay it.

6 Lay edge rows out from each corner slab in the same way to form three sides of the area.

7 Fill in between the three edge rows according to your layout pattern. Use a straightedge to check the surface alignment of each slab with its adjoining slabs.

8 Wait for at least two days before removing the spacers and filling in the joints. Mix mortar to a dry stiff mix, using 1 part cement to 2 parts sharp sand. Force the mortar well into the joints with a piece of wood 10mm thick. For a crisp appearance and to aid drainage, tap the mortar down so that it lies a few millimetres below the slab surface.

9 Use a damp sponge to clean off excess mortar from the slabs.

Cutting a slab

1 Lay the slab on soft sand and draw a pencil line all round at the cutting point, using a straightedge and try square.

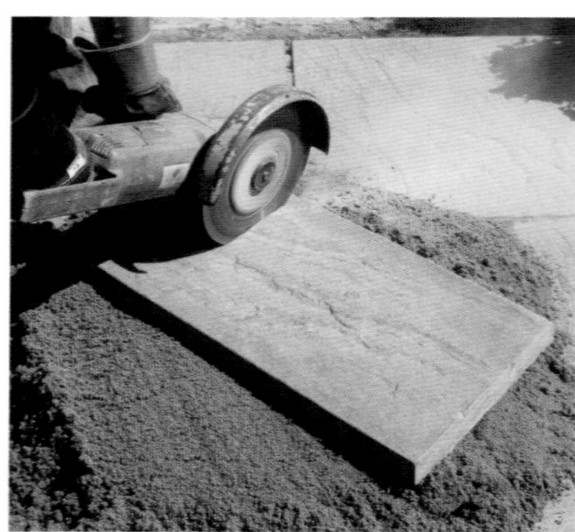

2 Score the pencil line all round, using either a brick bolster or an angle grinder with a masonry cutting disc – which makes a deep groove. Using an angle grinder is less strenuous and more accurate, but handle it carefully to avoid accidents. Wear heavy gloves and protect your eyes from flying particles with safety goggles.

3 To cut the slab, lay it flat (surface upwards). Use the bolster and hammer or the cutting disc to gradually deepen the scored line until the slab breaks cleanly when you tap it.

4 With any cutting method, it is difficult to get a smooth edge. Use cut slabs where the edges will be hidden or not obvious – such as against a lawn edge.

HIRE A BLOCK-CUTTER

If you have a lot of blocks to cut, lay all the whole blocks first, then hire a hydraulic block-cutter (sometimes called a block-splitter) for half a day, and use it to prepare all the cut-to-size pieces you need.

LAYING STONE FLAGS

The instructions on this, and the previous page, are for laying concrete paving slabs that are of a uniform thickness, for which you use the same thickness of mortar for each slab.

If you want to lay natural stone slabs (often called flagstones) – such as sandstone, Yorkstone, slate or granite – you will come across two problems. First, they are very heavy (even heavier than normal paving slabs) and second, they vary in size and shape, but more importantly in thickness (by up to 30mm or more).

You can deal with the weight problem by having a helper and by hiring a two-man paving slab lifter, which allows you to lift slabs without having to bend.

Because you don't want to move slabs more than once, it is not possible to 'mix and match' as with crazy paving (below), so it would be a good idea to measure the length and width of each slab and draw up a paving plan on paper before you start laying actual slabs.

To cope with variable thicknesses, the answer is to lay the mortar bed for each slab individually, making sure that the thinnest slabs have enough motar under them to ensure a compacted thickness of at least 25mm under the thickest slabs. Check the finished surface with spirit level and straightedge.

LAYING CRAZY PAVING

Because crazy paving comes in many shapes and sizes, it is impossible to make a layout plan before you start. Instead, arrange slabs in piles of different colours and sizes, and select from the whole range as you go along. Pick out slabs with a straight edge for the borders.

You will need the same tools as for laying standard paving slabs, except for wooden spacers. It is not practicable to maintain uniform joints between slabs, but they should be no wider than 25mm, for mortar economy and good appearance.
Lay the slabs on a suitable base for a drive or patio and on a full bed of mortar, in the same way as standard slabs.

Not all pieces of crazy paving will be of the same thickness – more mortar will be needed under thinner slabs to maintain a level surface. Check with a straightedge in all directions to make sure that no pieces are tilted.

Constructing a patio

A patio makes a useful sitting or dining area in a garden. Draw a scale plan on graph paper before you begin any work, so that you can work out positions of retaining walls or steps. Make sure your patio will not block any airbricks in the house walls.

Tools *String; wooden pegs; spade; rammer or wooden post; garden roller; spirit level; straightedge board or timber; spacers; brush; hammer or board and mallet; trowel.*

Materials *Suitable paving materials (pages 448-449); hardcore or crushed stone (page 450); dry sand; mortar (page 467).*

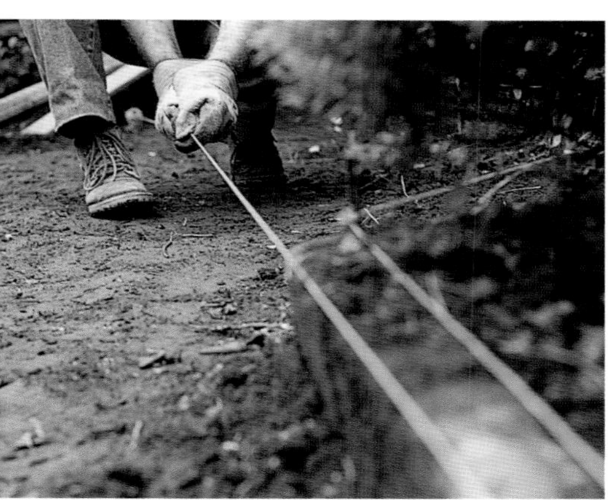

1 Roughly mark out the patio area and clear it. Dig out the soil to a depth of about 150mm, then compact the base with a post or rammer. Measure and mark again, more accurately, using a string line and wooden pegs. Use a spirit level and pegs to establish the final level of the patio surface, ensuring it has a drainage slope (page 451).

2 Cover the excavated area with 100mm of hardcore or crushed stone, spreading it evenly until the surface is level.

3 Compact the hardcore with a garden roller. For awkward corners, or a small area, use an earth rammer (page 451) to ram down the hardcore. Once this layer has been well firmed, cover it with about 80mm of dry sand. Use a board or plank with a straightedge to level and compact it.

4 Starting at a corner, set out the edging bricks in a stacking or soldier bond using a straight-edged plank to use as a guide. Insert spacers to keep the gaps even.

5 Bed the bricks onto a damp mortar mix (or a bed of sand) and use a spirit level to check them. Tamp the bricks into the mortar or sand, using a board and mallet or a hammer, until they are all level.

6 Bed the paving slabs. Spread more sand topped with dry mortar mix so that the slabs will be level with the surface of the bricks. Keep on checking the levels.

7 Sprinkle a dry mortar mix or sand over the bricks and slabs and brush it into the spaces between them. It will give a firmer finish and discourage weeds in the gaps. Make sure you fill the gaps completely.

8 When you have completed the whole area, brush off the excess sand or mortar. Allow the surface to settle for a day or two before walking on it.

Creating an optical illusion

Brick or paver patterns can be used to make the patio's dimensions look different. If bricks run lengthways they will give the impression of extra length; bricks running across a patio will make it look broader. Always keep patterns clear and simple, and avoid mixing them, for the best effects.

Granite setts, laid along the edges, finish off the paved area and provide a hard-wearing surface, unaffected by frost.

Laying block paving using a plate vibrator

Block paving needs to be well bedded to give a stable surface for a drive and carefully planned to create a pleasing finish.

Before you start The only way to lay a large area is with a plate vibrator, a light compacting machine powered by a petrol-driven motor. This compacts an area of blocks laid on sand to a level, rigid surface, compressing the sand bed from about 65mm to 50mm deep.

You can hire a plate vibrator. Be sure to ask for one suitable for compacting paving blocks; some types are too heavy. Pass it over the area as evenly as possible. Do not use it within at least 1m of an unsupported edge, where blocks are still being laid.

Paving to be compacted must be laid between firm edges, otherwise the joints will open and the blocks spread. Where there is no adjoining wall or hard edge, lay edging blocks (right) or a kerb (page 449).

Tools *Straightedge; levelling strips of 65mm wide timber as long as the width of the area to be paved; shovel; rake; kneeling board; either block splitter (see below) or brick bolster and club hammer; plate vibrator; soft broom. Possibly also brick trowel; string line and pegs; builder's square (page 467).*

Materials *Paving blocks, sharp sand – 1m³ covers about 15m² at 65mm deep. Possibly also edging blocks; foundation mix concrete (page 459); water.*

1 Prepare a hardcore base for a drive or patio (page 450), wide enough to accommodate a concrete bedding strip for any edging needed (see right). Allow space above the base for the block depth and for a 50mm layer of sand (the depth after compaction).

2 Lay edging blocks if necessary (see right), allowing for the correct crossfall and any lengthways slope (page 451).

Wait three days for the bedding mortar to harden before laying the paving.

3 Place piles of bedding sand, kept as dry as possible, along the site at about 3m intervals so that you can spread it in sections without having to walk over it.

4 Lay 65mm levelling strips on edge across the site – one where you intend to start laying and one 1–2m farther down the site. Check their crossfall with a spirit level.

5 Spread the sand evenly between the strips, using a shovel and rake. Then lay the straightedge across the strips and use it to rake off excess sand until the surface is level with the tops of the strips.

6 Prepare two or three sections to give a 3–4m² run for laying. Remove the levelling strips as you go along, carefully filling the depressions with sand.

7 Start laying blocks at one corner of the prepared sand bed, but keep off the bed. As you work forwards, lay a kneeling board across the blocks already laid but not yet compacted.

8 Lay the blocks snugly against each other according to the chosen pattern (page 448), leaving no joint gaps. Lay whole blocks first, and cut and fit part blocks later. Check corners with a builder's square. Blocks laid at the edges should stand about 10mm higher than the edging – they should bed down when compacted.

LAYING BRICKS OR BLOCKS WITHOUT A PLATE VIBRATOR

A small area of brick or block paving for a footpath or patio can be laid without using a vibrator, although the surface will not be as stable. Edging can be either paving blocks or timber formwork (page 460) thoroughly coated with wood preservative. The sand layer needs to be about 55mm deep only, as it will not be compressed as much as with a vibrator.

Before levelling the sand bed, dampen it with a fine-rose watering can until it is moist enough to hold together when you squeeze it.

9 After laying a run of about 3–4m², use the plate vibrator over the area two or three times, but keep it at least 1m back from the last row of newly laid blocks. You can then see how much the blocks are bedding down. The actual amount depends on the moisture content of the sand. If the compacted surface is conspicuously too high or too low, lift the blocks and adjust the level of the sand bed.

10 Continue in this way until all the whole blocks have been laid. Then fill in the part blocks and compact the area again with the plate vibrator as before.

11 When all the blocks have been laid and compacted, make sure that the surface is dry, then spread a layer of dry, fine sharp sand on it. Use the plate vibrator to work the sand into the crevices between the blocks to lock them in position. Get a helper to brush sand towards the vibrator, as it will be forced away by the vibrations.

Cutting paving blocks

The easiest and quickest way to cut paving blocks is with a block splitter, a hand-operated hydraulic cutter that can be hired. The alternative is to cut them with a hammer and bolster in the same way as bricks (page 470) – a lengthy job when you are paving a large area.

Laying edging blocks

A common and reliable edging is a row of paving blocks on edge, bedded in stiff sand-and-cement mortar on a layer of concrete (page 467). Use the foundation mix. Allow 200mm space for each line of edging blocks at the edges of the area to be paved.

• Make the concrete layer 75mm thick and 300mm wide, to allow 75mm on the outside and 25mm on the inside of the line of edging blocks. Make the concrete surface at the correct depth to allow the top of the edging to coincide with the finished level of the compacted paving. Generally the depth is about 80mm to accommodate the 60mm deep block and a 20mm layer of bedding mortar.

• Wait 24 hours for the concrete to harden before laying the edging on a bed of 3:1 sand-cement mortar. Use a taut string line to set the surface level, taking into account the crossfall and any lengthways fall. Slope the bedding mortar a little way up the outside of the edging to make a small haunch. Leave no joints between blocks, unless the edging is curved.

For curved edging, use a stiff sand-and-cement mortar (2:1 mix). Make the joints 10–25mm wide and pack them with mortar one day after bedding the blocks. Use a little mortar at a time, packed in with a strip of plywood. Fill to the bottom of the chamfered edge of the block, and sponge off any that smears the surface of the edging.

After completing the edging, wait three days before laying the paving blocks. Check that none of the bedding mortar used for the edging will impede the levelling of the paving blocks. If necessary cut mortar away down to the 25mm ledge of the concrete bed.

LEVELLING THE SAND WITH A NOTCHED BOARD

Where the site has fixed edging on both sides – a footpath, for example – the sand can be levelled with a notched board rested across the edging. Use a length of 100 x 50mm board with a 150mm long notch at each end. To allow for the sand compaction, the depth of the board below the notches should be about 5mm less than the depth of the paving blocks, unless you are using a plate vibrator, in which case it should be about 15mm less.

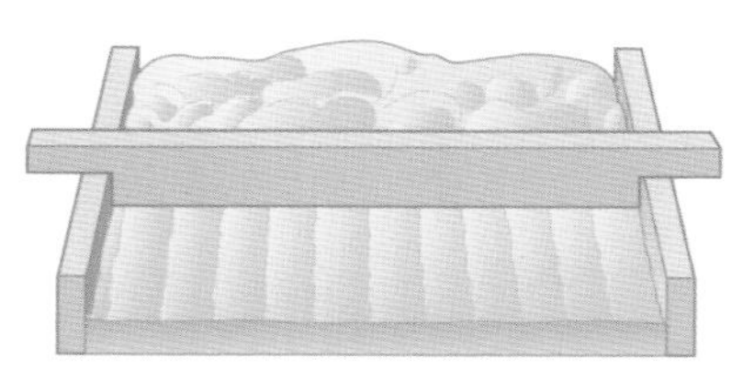

Tools for concreting

Mixing platform If you have no clean, firm surface on which to mix concrete, make one using either boards nailed to cross battens, or a sheet of 12mm thick plywood. Lay it on a large sheet of plastic to catch any spills. For small batches, use a wheelbarrow. Wash the platform or barrow within two hours of use.

Concrete mixer You can hire a small concrete mixer. Most types will mix a load of concrete in about three minutes. The capacity of the drum is usually stated for both the volume of dry materials and the approximate volume of mixed concrete.

A mixer may be electric or petrol driven. An electric type is usually more convenient if you have a long enough extension lead. Make sure you hire a mixer that runs at 230 volts.

A small mixer is likely to be about 750mm wide. It may be a barrow type (with wheels) or be supplied with a mounting frame so that you can stand a wheelbarrow below it. A barrow type should have a safety bar at the front to stop it tipping out of control.

Wheelbarrow A heavy-duty contractor's wheelbarrow – usually 85 litres capacity – can be hired. If it has to be pushed over soft ground or down steps, make a barrow-run – a line of strong planks anchored with pegs or battens. Scaffolding planks about 2.5m long can be hired.

Shovels, buckets and rake Use two shovels and two strong, heavy-duty polythene buckets of identical size. Keep one shovel and one bucket for loading and measuring the cement only so that they stay dry and do not get clogged. Use a garden rake to spread the concrete. Wipe the head clean regularly, before the concrete on it sets.

Tamping beam A length of straight-edged timber 50mm thick used on edge to flatten the concrete and expel air before it sets. Use a beam about 300mm longer than the width of the concrete so that it can rest on the formwork. Tamp a narrow stretch such as a path with a beam about 100mm deep. For broad sections 2–3m across, use a 150mm deep beam with a strong handle at each end. Two people are needed to use a long tamping beam.

Surface-finishing tools For some types of surface finish you will need either a steel plasterer's finishing trowel or a wood or plastic float – tools that you may be able to hire. You can make a suitable wood float with a piece of flat wood 300 x 125mm x 19mm. Screw a D-shaped wooden handle on one side, using two short blocks and one long one with smoothed-off edges.

Arrissing tool A tool resembling a steel float, but with a rounded-over edge. Used to round off the edges of the concrete before it hardens.

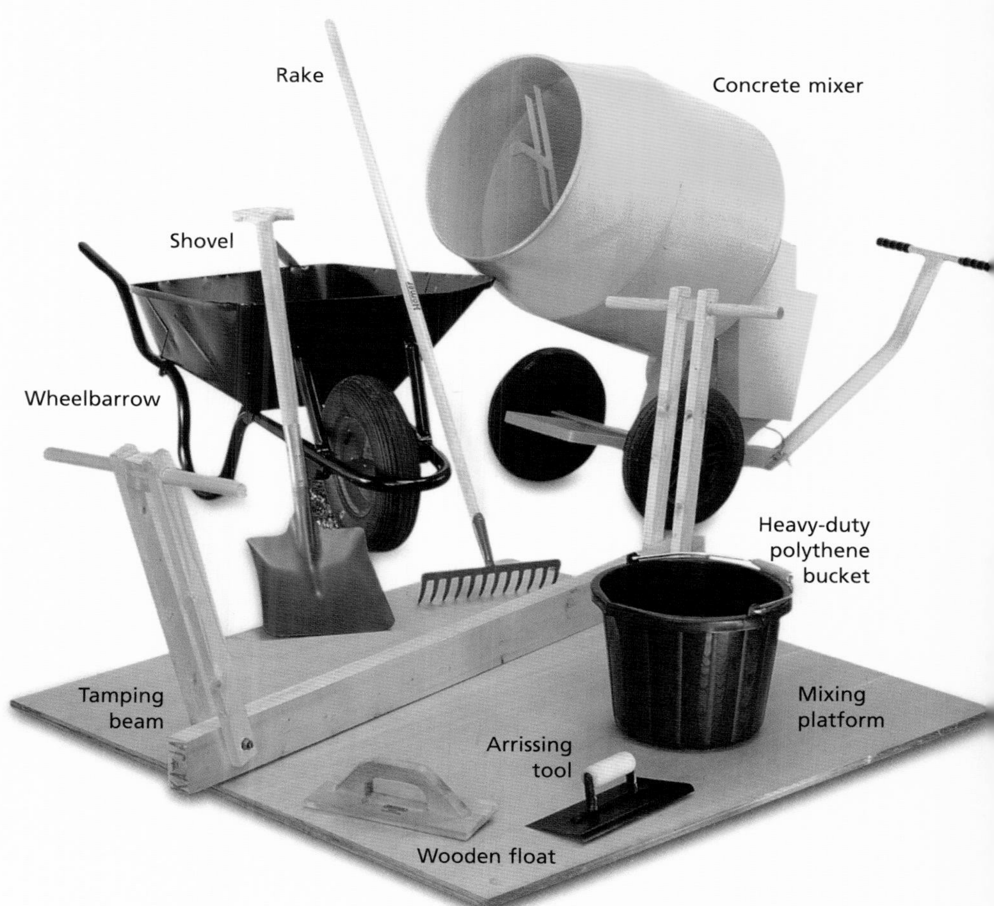

CHOOSING MATERIALS FOR MAKING CONCRETE

Concrete is made by mixing sharp sand and small stones (coarse aggregate) with cement and water. You can make concrete yourself, mixing either by hand or with a concrete mixer. Or you can have it delivered ready-mixed for immediate laying.

Mixing it yourself allows you to work at your own pace and lay sections at different times. If you buy ready-mixed concrete, it must be laid all in one go, and you usually need several helpers. But for large projects – such as paving, a shed base or garden wall foundations – buying ready-mixed concrete can be considerably cheaper and quicker than mixing your own.

Before you decide on whether to mix your own or buy it ready-mixed, it is important to understand the options and make your choice based on various factors – cost, ease of use, the speed with which the mixture must be used and any complications which might occur in the storing of components.

Cement

Mixed lime and clay processed to a powder that sets hard when mixed with water. Grey ordinary Portland cement (OPC) is used for most concrete. White Portland cement for making decorative white concrete or mortar costs twice as much. Sulphate-resisting cement is for concrete that will be exposed to seawater or soils high in sulphates – most likely on reclaimed land or some types of clay (the local Building Control Officer will advise); it is dearer than OPC and not widely available. Do not use masonry cement, which has additives to increase water-holding and plasticity. Rapid-setting cement is for small repairs under water or in wet conditions.

How it is sold Mainly in 50kg bags, but smaller bags – down to about 2.5kg – are available for small jobs or repairs. Always check the condition of bags when buying – do not buy damp bags or bags in which you can feel lumps, which means that the cement has started to harden. To avoid waste because of hardening during storage, buy only as much as you will use in a week.

Storage Keep bags under cover, off the ground on a dry, hard surface, stacked flat and close together so that air cannot circulate round them. Moisture in the air can penetrate the paper of the bag and cause the cement to harden (this is known as air-hardening or air-setting). Once cement has hardened, it is useless, even though it can be crumbled in the hand. If you have to store an opened bag for several days, keep it dry and airtight inside a tightly tied plastic bag. Cement can irritate the skin. If any goes in the eyes, bathe them at once in cold water and get medical advice.

> **HELPFUL TIP**
>
> Delay laying concrete if there is any danger of freezing weather ahead. Do not lay concrete on a frozen base or using frozen aggregate.
>
> If, after you have laid fresh concrete, a light frost is likely, cover the concrete with a polythene sheet (page 462) topped with a layer of earth or sand.

Sand

Use sharp sand for concreting. It is coarser than builder's (or soft) sand, which is used for making mortar (page 467). Silver sand can be used with white Portland cement for making white concrete or mortar. It is finer than sharp sand, so use slightly more cement in the mix to give it sufficient strength.

How it is sold Loose, for large amounts, either by the tonne (1000kg) or the cubic metre (between 1250 and 1750kg, depending on how dry it is. Available from builders' merchants, sand and gravel suppliers or quarries. Sand is cleaned by washing or dry screening. If you buy it from a quarry, make sure this has been done. Small amounts are sold in 50kg and 25kg bags at DIY and garden centres and most builders' merchants.

Storage Store it as clean and dry as possible, on a hard surface or polythene sheeting and with waterproof covering. Sand retains moisture, which increases its bulk. Fully saturated sand has a similar volume to dry sand but weighs a lot more.

Coarse aggregate

Small stones, too big to pass through a 5mm mesh, used to form the bulk of concrete. Well-graded aggregate has a balanced mixture of stone sizes, but is available graded. A 20mm maximum is used for most DIY concreting. Fine concrete is made with 10mm maximum stones.

How it is sold Either by the tonne (1000kg) or cubic metre (1500–1800kg). Available from builders' merchants, sand and gravel suppliers and quarries. Some suppliers sell small amounts such as 50kg in bags; these are easier to keep clean and useful for small jobs, but relatively more expensive than buying in bulk.

Storage Keep on a hard surface or tarpaulin with a covering sheet to keep it clean. If it contains a lot of dirt or debris, the concrete will be weakened. Protect your aggregate from frost – if you use it frozen, ice may form within the concrete.

Ballast

Sometimes known as 'all-in ballast' or as 'all-in aggregate', ballast is a mixture of sand and coarse aggregate. It is used with cement for making concrete (see opposite) and also to fill in gaps on top of a layer of hardcore when laying a sub-base (page 450). Avoid using unwashed ballast.

How it is sold As for coarse aggregate. Tell the supplier you want it for concrete making, as the quality varies. Well-graded material includes 60 per cent of stones bigger than 5mm. One test of the quality is to squeeze the material in your hand – if it leaves a stain because of the high silt content, avoid it.

Storage As for coarse aggregate.

Bagged dry mixes

Mixtures of cement, sand and coarse aggregate (or just cement and sand) to which only water need be added. Available in a range of mixes, with suitable uses normally described on bag – for example foundations, shed bases, post fixing, repair or multi-purpose. Some types set extremely quickly once water has been added.

How it is sold Mainly in 25kg bags by builders' merchants, hardware shops and DIY and garden centres. Convenient for small jobs and repairs, but expensive.

Storage As for cement. When using, tip all the material from the bag and mix the dry ingredients together thoroughly. Keep the amount you need for mixing with water

> **CONCRETE COLOURING AND ADDITIVES**
>
> • You can colour concrete by adding powdered pigment during mixing, or by staining it after laying. However, the finished effect is often disappointing – colours can look patchy, and fade with weathering. This is because most pigments have a maximum percentage (usually 10 per cent) that can be used before the pigment begin to affect the strength of the concrete.
> • Additives for waterproofing and frost protection can also be used, following the manufacturer's instructions.
> • Waterproofers will make the concrete less easy for water to pass through.
> • Frost protectors speed up the reaction between water and cement, and may reduce the risk of frost damage soon after laying, but the concrete should still be protected with sheeting.

to one side and return the remainder to the bag (keep it dry). This ensures that the mix is correctly balanced before you start adding water.

Ready-mixed concrete

For large concreting projects, such as laying a patio or drive, it may be worth getting someone else to do the mixing. You can arrange this in one of two ways.

The first involves the supplier driving to your premises with a lorry carrying the raw materials, a concrete mixer and some builder's barrows which you and your helpers use to transfer the concrete to the site. The operator will mix as much concrete as you need to any mix specification, and will charge you for the number of batches supplied. This method is ideal for jobs where the exact volume needed is hard to calculate – for example, when filling trench foundations for a garden wall.

The second involves ordering a load of ready-mixed concrete from a local supplier. A standard load is about 6m³, and some companies charge more per m³ for smaller deliveries. Tell the supplier what you need the concrete for and how much you need, and he will supply the correct mix.

The concrete can be discharged directly into place if the lorry's delivery chute can reach it – when laying a drive, for example. Otherwise you will have to barrow it to the site – a job for a fleet of helpers, since moving a cubic metre of concrete will take about 30 large wheelbarrow loads.

Note that the concrete must be placed and finished in about two hours; if this is likely to be difficult to achieve, ask for the mix to be made with a retarding agent added to slow down the setting process.

GUIDE TO BATCH MIXING

Always measure the dry materials for each batch of the concrete mix by volume, following the ratios for the three standard mixes given, right. Use a large (15-litre) polythene builder's bucket, filled to the brim.

Hand-mixing concrete is hard work. It is worth hiring a concrete mixer for the duration of the job unless you are mixing only small quantities of it at a time – for example, to set fence posts in place.

A small electric mixer will cope with one batch of any of the three mixes – for example, the six buckets (one of cement, five of aggregate) needed to make the foundation mix.

MEASURING AND MIXING CONCRETE

The ratio of cement to sand and aggregate determines how strong a concrete mix is. If you are mixing concrete yourself, order sharp sand and coarse aggregate combined (known as ballast). This makes ordering materials simpler, and means that you have to find storage space for only one pile instead of two.

Most builders' merchants deliver ballast in a giant reinforced sack, which helps to contain the material on site until you are ready to use it. When the sack is empty, you simply return it to the supplier. These sacks usually contain one cubic metre of ballast, but you can order as little as half a cubic metre if that is all you need.

The volume of concrete you make depends entirely on the volume of ballast you use. The cement does not add to the final volume because the particles fill the voids between the stones and bond them together into a solid mass as the concrete sets. This means that to make one cubic metre (1m³) of concrete you need 1m³ of ballast, plus an amount of cement that is determined by the strength of mix you are intending to make. Three commonly-used standard mixes are given below.

Three standard mixes

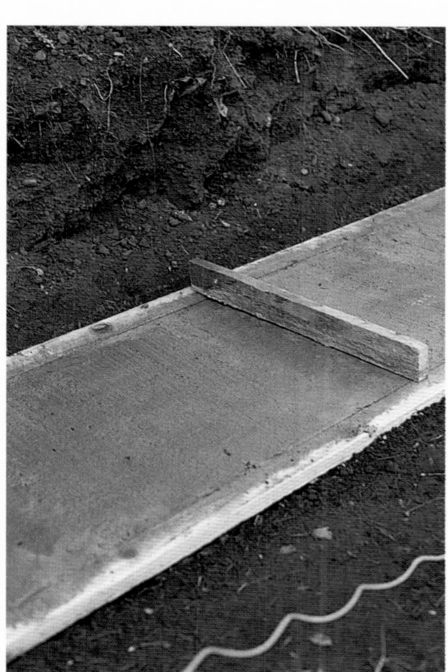

Foundation mix

This consists of 1 part cement to 5 parts ballast (1:2½:3½ cement:sharp sand:coarse aggregate), equivalent to 6 bags of cement per m³ (1850kg) of ballast.

Use this relatively weak mix for any concrete that will be buried underground and not exposed to the weather. Typical jobs include laying a strip foundation for a wall (above), a base for a path or drive that will be surfaced with another paving material, or an anchor for a fence post or rotary clothes line.

General-purpose mix

Make this with 1 part cement to 4 parts ballast (1:2:3 cement:sharp sand:coarse aggregate), equivalent to 7 bags of cement per m³ (1850kg) of ballast.

Use this mix for most jobs other than foundations. Uses include a slab base for an outbuilding or garage, or a new concrete floor indoors.

Paving mix

You will need 1 part cement to 3.5 parts ballast (1:1½:2½ cement:sharp sand:coarse aggregate), equivalent to 8 bags of cement per m³ (1850kg) of ballast. Use this mix for concrete paths, steps, patios and drives, which will be left exposed to the weather.

Estimating quantities

To find the volume of concrete you need, measure the area and multiply this by the thickness needed. Add 10 per cent to the total volume to allow for wastage and the filling of uneven sub-bases.

Laying the concrete

The depth of the concrete you lay depends on its purpose:
- 75mm thick for paths and bases for garden sheds
- 100mm thick for patios
- 125mm thick for drives and garage floors
- 150mm thick for drives that will be used by commercial vehicles.

For example, a drive 10m long, 4m wide and 100mm (0.1m) thick will require 10 x 4 x 0.1 = 4m³ of concrete.
Adding 10 per cent gives a final volume figure (rounded up) of 4.5m³.
If the surface is to be left exposed, paving mix is needed and the material quantities required are 8 x 4.5 = 36 bags of cement, plus 4.5m³ (8325kg) of ballast.

GUIDE TO CONCRETE COVERAGE

Thickness of layer (mm)	Approximate area covered by 1m³
50	18m²
75	13m²
100	10m²
125	8m²
150	6m²

Mixing concrete

Mixing by hand is hard work, suitable only for small jobs or those that can be done in easy stages – a long path laid in sections, for example. The alternative is to hire a concrete mixer.

Mixing by hand

To produce good concrete by hand you need to work carefully and methodically at a steady pace – a rushed job is likely to give disappointing results.

Tools *Mixing platform; two shovels; two heavy-duty polythene buckets of identical size – about 15 litres capacity (keep one for cement only); bucket or watering can.*

Materials *Ballast (sharp sand and coarse aggregate combined); ordinary Portland cement; water (7–10 litres per 15-litre bucket of cement) – use mains water, if possible, as water from a butt or pond will contain organic substances that could affect the concrete.*

1 Set up a mixing platform as near as possible to the laying area.

2 Use one shovel to fill the required number of buckets of ballast and tip them in a pile on the platform.

3 Use the other shovel to fill the cement bucket to the top. To make sure the bucket is properly packed, knock it two or three times as you fill it, because the cement fluffs up as it is shovelled.

4 Make a crater in the top of the pile of ballast and tip in the bucket of cement.

5 Use the ballast shovel to mix the pile thoroughly, turning it over until it looks the same colour throughout.

6 Make a crater in the top of the mixed pile and gradually pour in about half the water. Turn the pile again, moving dry material from the edge to the middle, until the water is well mixed in. Aim for an even colour and a dryish, crumbly consistency.

7 Continue adding and mixing in water a little at a time until the pile is smooth and moist – neither crumbly nor sloppy.

8 Test the consistency by slapping along the top of the pile with the back of the shovel. If water runs out readily it is too wet. Add a small amount of cement and ballast (in the correct proportions) and mix again until you get it right.

Using a concrete mixer

Order the cement and ballast in time for them to be ready for use when the mixer arrives, to save on hiring time. A machine cuts down the amount of heavy work and speeds up mixing. To avoid long breaks between mixing loads, get some helpers. Except for a mixing platform, the tools and materials needed are the same as for hand mixing.

1 Switch on the revolving drum, put in half the ballast, then add half the water. Allow the drum to spin for half a minute, then put in all the cement and the rest of the ballast and water.

2 After two or three minutes more mixing, the concrete is ready for use. Tip it straight onto the site or use a wheelbarrow.

3 When you have finished mixing for the day, wash out the drum by mixing some ballast and plenty of water. Empty the drum, then pull out the electric plug and scrub down the outside of the machine, using plenty of water.

Laying an area of concrete

Freshly mixed concrete sets and starts to harden within about two hours – faster in very hot weather – so it must be laid, levelled and given a surface finish in sections (or bays) so that it can be completed while the concrete is still workable.

Setting up formwork

Timber edging, known as formwork, is needed to contain the concrete when making a path or drive. It can be removed once the concrete has hardened. You can use old timber such as fence boards or floorboards.

Timber can also be used as a permanent edging for other types of path such as gravel, asphalt or paving blocks. If timber edging is to be permanent, it should be well soaked with wood preservative – preferably use wood pre-treated with vacuum-pressure impregnation before purchase.

Tools *Spirit level; mallet; hammer; builder's square (page 467); wooden shim (page 451). Possibly also string and pegs.*

Materials *Timber lengths as wide as the depth of the surface layer; wooden pegs 25mm square and about 300mm long – allow one peg for every 1m of edging; 50mm galvanised nails.*

1 Dig a strip about 150mm wide along each side of the sub-base surface. The strip should be as deep as the surface layer.

2 Stand a timber length on its side along one side of the sub-base, in line with the string marking line, and drive wooden pegs into the soil to support it from outside the base area. The peg tops should be at the right height above ground for the finished path or drive surface, and flush with the top of the timber edging.

3 Use a spirit level to check that the edging strip is laid to the correct lengthways fall, if there is one. Then nail it to the pegs.

4 Butt other timber lengths in the same way to form one side of the edging.

5 To allow a slope for drainage, set the timber edging on one side of the path (the side farthest from the house wall, if it is adjoining it) slightly lower than the other, according to the crossfall required (see Making a sloped surface, page 451).

6 To make a tight corner joint, butt the timbers at right angles, using a builder's square as a check. Nail them together as well as to pegs. There is no need to cut off an overlapping piece of timber on the outside of the corner.

7 On long concrete paths, fit control joints across the path at suitable intervals (see right).

Making a curve in formwork

1 Mark out the shape of the curve on the ground and set up pegs and a string line to follow the curve (see Marking out a curved path, page 451).

2 Use a saw to make cuts in the timber edging for about half its depth on the edge that will form the inside of the curve. Make cuts at about 125mm intervals, or closer for a sharp curve.

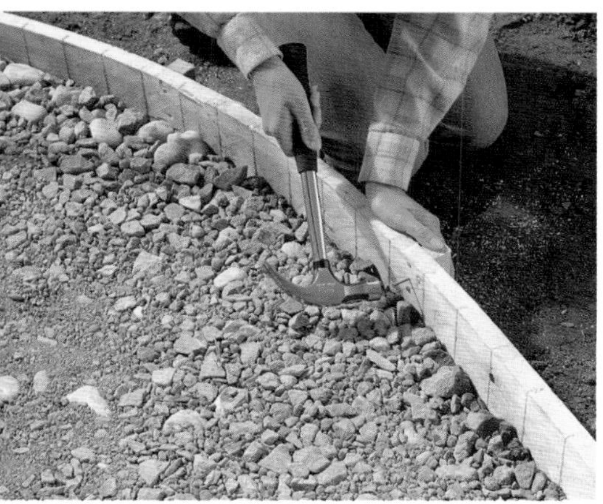

3 Shape the timber by nailing it to the pegs.

4 Check that the timber along each side is at the right height and the correct slope (see Making a sloped surface, page 451). Adjust as necessary by tapping it down or levering it up slightly.

Laying a base for a light building or shed

Set out the formwork in the same way as for a drive, although there is no need to make a drainage slope. Use a spirit level and builder's square to ensure that the formwork is level and that the corners are true right angles.

The size of a workable section

This depends on the rate at which you mix and place the concrete, but is likely to be about 3–4 barrowloads with hand mixing, or 6–8 with machine mixing.

With ready-mixed concrete, two people can generally spread and tamp down an area of roughly 8.5m² of concrete poured directly into the laying area before it sets.

Concrete will crack if it is allowed to dry too fast, so has to be 'cured' – that is, kept moist for three days after laying. It takes about a month to set to its full strength, but you can walk or build on it after three days (wait seven days in winter).

There is a maximum size at which any slab of concrete can be laid in one piece without danger of cracking. A surface larger than this is laid in separate sections (or bays) with control joints between to allow for contraction and expansion of the concrete.

- The maximum intervals between control joints varies according to the thickness of the concrete and the site width (see panel, right).
- In general, joints should be closer as the width gets narrower. So a path, for example, usually needs shorter bays between joints than a drive. Make the bays of equal size and as square as possible. The length can be about one and a half times the width, but no more than twice the width.
- Control joints can be placed at closer intervals to give smaller bays, if this is convenient for laying workable sections when mixing your own concrete.

Making a control joint

Tools *Mallet or club hammer, piece of softwood 25mm thick, as deep as the formwork and long enough to fit across the inside of the formwork; wooden pegs; arrissing tool.*

Materials *Hardboard filler strip as long and as deep as the softwood.*

1 Position a hardboard filler strip between the two sides of the formwork and at right angles to them. If one side of the formwork is curved, bend the filler strip to meet the side at right angles.

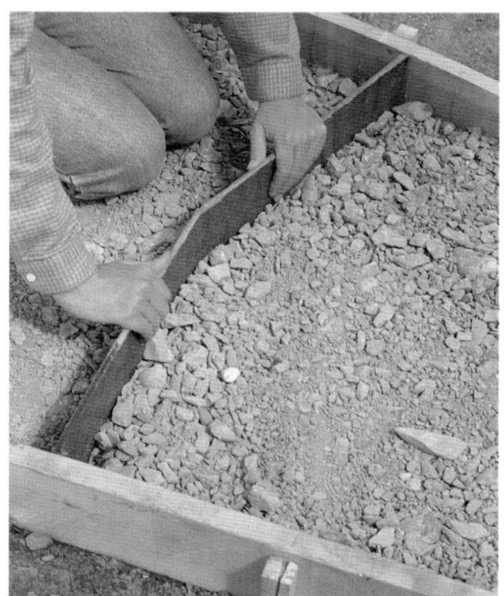

CONTROL JOINT INTERVALS

Width of site	Depth of concrete 75mm	100mm	150mm
3m	3m	4m	5m
1–2m	2.5m	2–3m	3–4m
Under 1m	1.8m	–	–

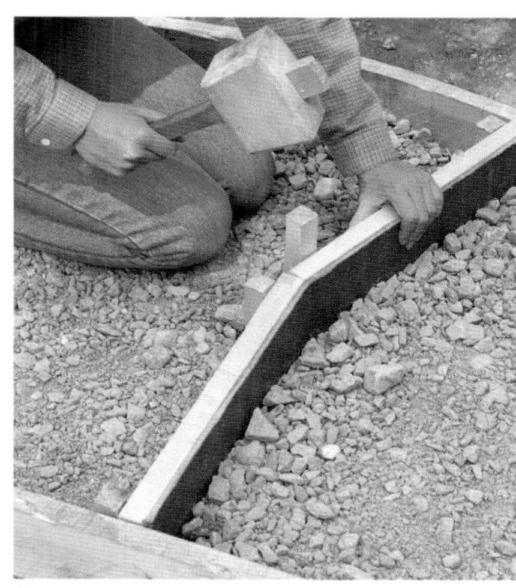

2 Support the filler strip on the outside of the first bay to be concreted, using the piece of softwood held in position by pegs.

3 Concrete the bay (see page 462) right up to the hardboard filler, then concrete about 300mm into the second bay.

4 Lift out the softwood support and pegs but leave the filler strip in position.

5 Push the concrete against the filler strip where you have removed the softwood support, then continue laying the second bay.

6 When finishing the concrete surface (page 462), use an arrissing tool on each side of the hardboard filler strip to smooth the corners.

Making a concrete path or drive

Prepare the sub-base and formwork allowing for a suitable drainage slope (page 450). Make the concrete surface layer 75mm thick for a path, or 100mm thick for a drive. If the drive is on soft soil such as peat, make the surface layer 150mm thick.

Tools *Rake; shovel; wheelbarrow; tamping beam; arrissing trowel; surface-finishing tools; polythene sheeting; bricks. Possibly also watering can; sharp sand.*

Materials *Freshly made concrete of a suitable mix for the job (pages 458, 460).*

1 Pour batches of concrete into the first bay to be laid.

2 Use the back of a rake to draw the batches together so that the concrete is roughly level and about 13mm higher than the top of the timber formwork.

3 Press the concrete into all corners and against all edges of the bay with a shovel or your boot. Make sure all cavities are filled, because air pockets will weaken the concrete.

4 Compact the filled bay with a tamping beam laid across the formwork. Use it with a chopping action, moving it along about half its thickness with each chop. This leaves an undulating surface.

5 Go over the high spots again, using the tamper steadily backwards and forwards with a sawing action to remove excess concrete.

6 If any depressions appear in the surface, scoop fresh concrete into them with a shovel.

7 Give a final tamp over the bay – this can be the final finish or you can apply a different finish (see right). To get a near-smooth tamped finish, pass the tamper slowly backwards and forwards with steady strokes.

For a textured finish, use the tamper with a lift and drop action. Depending on the spacing between drops, the appearance can vary from close rippled to wide rippled, like a washboard.

8 Before the concrete hardens, round off the edges by running an arrissing tool along the slight gap between the formwork and the concrete edge.

9 As soon as the concrete is hard enough not to be marked, cover it with polythene sheeting to stop it drying out too quickly. Weight the edges of the sheeting with bricks to stop it blowing away, and sprinkle some sand over the top, if necessary, to prevent ballooning.

10 Remove the covering after not less than three days, and the formwork a day or so later.

Finishing the surface

A textured finish helps to give the concrete a non-skid surface. If you leave the surface as tamped (see step 7, above), it will have a rippled appearance. Other ways of finishing the surface are shown on the right.

For a narrow path, you can apply the finish from the ground alongside. For a wide area such as a drive, work from a bridge across the formwork – lay the tamping beam across on its side, for example.

For a pathway beside a building, where you cannot stand on either side of the concrete, see Making a path or drive alongside a wall, opposite.

Ways of finishing concrete

Brush finish For a pronounced brush finish, drag a hard-bristled broom over the surface after tamping near-smooth. Hold the broom at a shallow angle so that the surface is indented but not torn up, and make all strokes in the same direction. Rinse the brush bristles if they get clogged, then shake well.

For a smoother brush finish use a soft broom and apply it with gentle strokes.

Float finish Use a wood float in overlapping circles to produce a fish-scale finish. For a plain finish, draw the float across the surface as soon as you have tamped it. If you want to coarsen the texture, let some of the concrete build up on the float face.

For a smooth, unmarked finish, skim the surface with steel plasterer's trowel. For a tight, hard-wearing finish, let the surface stiffen first.

Piped finish/shovel finish A fairly heavy pipe, such as a scaffolding tube, can be rolled over the surface like a rolling pin to give a somewhat stippled appearance. Or it can be rolled, lifted and dropped to give a ridged finish.

For a shovel finish use the back of a shovel to lightly pat the newly tamped surface using a circular movement. This gives an overlapping, fish-scale finish, as with a wood float.

Exposed stone finish Scatter a thin layer of single-sized stones after tamping. Tamp again, making sure the stones are well bedded. Let the concrete harden until the stones are well gripped, then spray the surface lightly with a fine-rose can. Use a soft broom to brush away loose material, leaving the stones partly exposed. Next day clean the surface with a stiff broom and water. Cure for about three days.

HELPFUL TIP

When applying a float finish – whether using a wood float or a steel trowel – be careful not to over-use the float on fresh concrete. If you press on the surface too much, the aggregate will sink and the surface will be left weakened, containing too much water. When the concrete hardens, it will have a permanent film of light grey dust as the surface slowly crumbles away.

Making a path or drive alongside a wall

Instead of fixing formwork along the wall-side of the path, fit a strip of 13mm thick bitumen-impregnated fibreboard against it. It is available in 100mm, 150mm and 200mm strips. This will form a joint between the concrete and the brickwork. Remove it once the concrete has dried.

Lay the concrete in alternate bays so that you and your helper can stand on each side of the bay you are concreting and use the tamping beam parallel with the wall.

After three days, when the concrete has hardened enough to stand on, lay concrete in the empty bays. Remove the stop-ends of the formwork from the laid bays and lay the new concrete up to the hardened edge of the set concrete.

As it dries out, the concrete will shrink and pull away enough to leave a gap sufficient to serve as a control joint.

Laying gravel

Prepare a hardcore sub-base 100mm deep, allowing a depth of about 25mm for the gravel surface. Top the hardcore with a 25mm blinding layer of sharp sand – to fill any gaps and make a close, smooth base for the gravel. Use 10mm or 20mm pea gravel.

Unless there are walls or turf edging to contain the gravel, lay permanent edging such as kerbing (page 449) or timber formwork (page 460).

Spread the gravel with a rake over the whole area to a depth of about 15mm, then roll it with a garden roller. Spread a second layer of about 15mm, then roll again.

The surface will need regular raking or rolling as it becomes disturbed, and will probably need to be treated with weedkiller about once a year.

Alternatively Lay down a semi-permeable membrane before you put down the gravel. This allows rainwater to permeate down into the hardcore and drain away, but prevents the growth of weeds. Known as landscape fabric, it is available in rolls 1m wide and about 20m long from most DIY centres and nurseries.

Repairing paving

Although durable, paths, patios, drives and steps can all develop faults. Loose or damaged paving slabs, broken kerbing, cracked concrete, crumbling path edges and chipped concrete steps may all need to be dealt with. And you need to keep paving clean and looking good.

Before you start It is a waste of time to repair small cracks as soon as they appear. Wait to see if they increase in size and number. They may be caused by a small amount of movement in the ground below. If, after a year or so, there has been little or no increase, it is fair to assume that the ground has settled and repairs can be carried out.

If the surface develops extensive cracking or sunken areas, take it up and lay it again on a new, firm sub-base.

Refitting a loose or damaged paving slab

1 Use a spade to chop through any mortar at edge joints. Push the spade under the slab to lift it and slip a broomstick or pipe under it to roll it out. A sunken or see-sawing slab can be re-laid, but renew a cracked or chipped slab.

2 If the slab was bedded on sand, loosen up the old sand with a trowel, add more sharp sand, and lightly level the surface with a length of wood.

Alternatively If the slab was bedded on mortar, remove the old mortar with a hammer and chisel. Mix new bedding mortar in a dryish mix of one part cement to four parts sharp sand (or use a bagged sand-cement mix) and spread it over the surface with a brick trowel to a thickness of 30–50mm. Roughen the surface with the trowel point.

DEALING WITH A DUST FILM

Light grey dust that forms continually on concrete and cannot be swept away is caused by the surface crumbling. It is usually the result of over-use of the float when smoothing the surface to a finish. Seal the surface by brushing on a priming coat of PVA adhesive and water as instructed on the container, usually with one part adhesive to five parts water.

3 Slab edge joints may be flush or with gaps. If there are gaps, place 10mm thick wooden spacers along one long and one short edge before rolling the slab into position on a broomstick or pipe. Then space other side gaps.

4 Lay a 50mm thick piece of flat wood on the slab as a cushion while you use a club hammer to tap it down flush with the surrounding slabs. Check that it is flush using a length of straight-edged timber.

5 If you cannot tap the slab down flush, lift it again and skim off some of the bedding material. Or, if it sinks down too far, add more of the bedding material.

6 Wait at least two days before filling in the joints in the same way as for laying slabs (page 453).

MAKING A CONCRETE FILLER

Prepare a cement and sharp sand mix in the proportions 1:3 by volume, or for small amounts use a bagged sand-cement mix (page 458).

Separately mix equal parts of water and PVA adhesive – a building adhesive used to seal or bond various building materials is ideal.

Mix the dry material, water and PVA adhesive together in the same way as for making concrete (page 460). Mix until the filler is a smooth, moist consistency – neither crumbly nor too sloppy.

Cleaning up stains

Oil, grease and rust stains, or moss, often occur on paths and drives. Most can be removed with one of the wide range of proprietary removers available from DIY, gardening or motoring stores. Cat litter is a good absorbent for spreading on fresh oil spillages. You can get both acidic and non-acidic liquid patio cleaners; a pressure washer can clean paving very effectively.

Renewing damaged kerbing

1 Use a club hammer to loosen the damaged length of kerbing, then prise it out with a spade.

2 Dig out about 50mm of the sub-base below the removed kerbstone, then ram the surface well down with a thick piece of timber.

3 Mix bedding mortar using a bagged sand-cement mortar mix to a dryish consistency. Spread it about 75mm deep in the gap.

4 Dampen the new kerbstone and lower it into position. Cushion it with a 50mm piece of flat timber and tap it down with a club hammer until it is flush with the adjoining kerbstone.

5 Use a spirit level to check that the sides align with the adjoining kerbstone, and a straightedge to check that the surface is also aligned.

Repairing cracks or holes in concrete

Hairline cracks in concrete can be ignored. They often follow the lines of the contraction joints between sections.

- A hole can be filled if it is at least 15mm deep. If the hole is shallower, deepen it first, or the new layer will be too thin to hold firm.
- Repair concrete with a filler containing PVA adhesive (see panel, page 463) to make a good bond.
- For potholes, proprietary ready-mixed concrete filler can be used instead.

1 Widen the crack or hole below the surface by undercutting the edges with a cold chisel and club hammer. This ensures that the filler will be well anchored.

2 Remove all debris from the hole or crack and brush it with a priming coat of PVA adhesive as instructed on the container – usually one part adhesive to five parts water.

3 When the priming coat is tacky, fill the crack or hole using concrete filler (see panel, page 463). Pack it well down so that there are no air pockets, which will weaken the concrete.

4 Level off the area flush with the surrounding surface using a brick trowel or plasterer's steel finishing trowel.

5 Keep the repair covered with polythene for at least three days.

Repairing crumbling edges on a concrete path

Concrete may crumble at the edges if the edging formwork was removed too soon, or if the wet concrete was not packed well down against the formwork during laying. Air pockets below an apparently solid surface cause the concrete to break up when the edges come under pressure during use.

1 Chip away the damaged concrete back to solid material, using a cold chisel and club hammer.

2 Remove the debris, and if the sub-base is exposed, ram the hardcore well down with a ramming tool or thick length of timber. Add fresh hardcore to any soft spots and ram it well down.

3 Set up timber edging 25mm thick alongside the damaged area so that the top edge is level with the concrete surface. Support it with pegs driven into the ground.

4 Brush the exposed edge of the concrete with a priming coat of PVA adhesive mixed according to the instructions on the container – usually one part adhesive to five parts water.

5 Prepare concrete filler (page 463) and use a brick trowel to press into the exposed area, well down against the edging.

6 Level the surface with the trowel, or use a float (page 462), to give a non-slip finish.

7 Cover the repaired area with polythene to stop it drying too fast. Remove the sheeting after three days. Leave the edging longer if the path is used a lot.

Repairing a concrete step

1 Cut back a crumbling edge using a cold chisel and club hammer. If the surface is worn down, score it with a brick bolster and hammer to provide a good grip (key) for a new layer of concrete.

2 Fix timber edging round the step using pegs and bricks to keep it firmly in place. If renewing a worn surface, set the edging about 15mm higher than the surface, with the side pieces allowing a forward slope of about 10mm for water to run off.

3 Brush away dust and debris.

4 Prime the area with a mixture of PVA adhesive and water according to the container instructions – usually one part adhesive to five parts water.

5 Repair crumbling edges with concrete filler (page 463). Press it will down against the edging.

Alternatively To re-surface the step, use bagged sand-cement mix (page 458) prepared in the normal way, but first coat the surface with a solution of three parts PVA adhesive to one part water. Before it dries, apply the concrete to lie level with top of the edging.

6 Level the area. Cover for three days, as for path repairs.

Buying bricks

Bricks are mostly made from baked clay to a standard size, but some are made from lime mixed with sand or crushed stone or both (these are known as calcium silicate, sandlime or flintlime bricks). There are also concrete bricks made from cement and aggregates. They resemble clay bricks and are about the same price. Blocks are less popular and are usually concrete or stone made in various sizes.

Bricks are usually sold by numbers. Small quantities such as 100, 350 or 500 may be available from DIY stores, but builders' merchants normally sell them by the thousand. If transporting bricks, remember that 350 weigh nearly a tonne.

Grades

Bricks are graded with two letters according to their quality. The first letter takes into account their frost resistance; F indicates frost-resistant, M moderately frost-resistant, O not-resistant. The second letter refers to soluble salt content; L= low, N = normal. Grades are not marked on bricks, but may be on packs. Check when buying.

Internal quality (OL, ON) For indoor use.

Ordinary quality (FN, ML, MN) For outdoor use where conditions are not severe.

Special quality (FL) For severe conditions.

Types

Different types are available in each grade, in both standard and special shapes.

Commons Bricks for use where their appearance does not matter. They may be any grade, and vary widely in quality.

Facings Bricks with an attractive surface finish on one or more sides, and of either ordinary or special grades. They are more expensive than commons, and those faced on more than one side are dearer than one-faced types.

Engineering Dense, strong, highly water- and frost-resistant – and expensive. Often used in garden retaining walls.

Colour and texture

There is a wide range of colours depending on the type of clay used and the manufacturing process; clay varies from area to area. Multi-coloured types are also available. Check the colours stocked by your local brick merchant, and ask to see a catalogue of other colours.

Textures are either imposed or achieved by the choice of material. They include wirecut bricks, sandfaced bricks and rustic bricks, with a mechanically imposed texture.

Using secondhand bricks

Secondhand bricks are generally expensive because they are difficult to clean. Bricks are mixed up during demolition, so it is mostly impossible to know their previous use. Don't use them for paving unless you know they are old paving bricks and are therefore likely to be frost-resistant.

Some manufacturers now produce simulated secondhand bricks. These have a weathered appearance and are safer to use.

The best way to remove the old mortar from bricks is with a bolster chisel and club hammer. Wear heavy gloves and safety goggles. Proprietary brick cleaners are not suitable for removing mortar, except for stubborn stains from brick faces. Wet the brick before applying the cleaner – this reduces surface absorption and prevents acid penetration.

Brick sizes and shapes

The standard size for bricks is 215mm long, 102.5mm wide and 65mm deep – fractionally smaller than the old imperial standard size. The nominal size, which allows for a mortar joint of about 10mm all round, makes it easier to calculate the number of bricks needed. It is 225 x 112.5 x 75mm.

A brick laid with its long face exposed is called a stretcher. A brick laid with its short face exposed is called a header. Part bricks are cut as required. A brick cut across its width is called a bat, and a brick cut lengthways is called a closer. Some bricks are indented or perforated with holes or slits to help to reduce weight.

Corner and end bricks

Shaped corner bricks are known as internal or external returns. Some bricks are designed to lie on edge and others flat. Bricks shaped for special uses – known as specials – are more expensive than bricks of standard shape, and often more difficult to get. They usually have to be ordered.

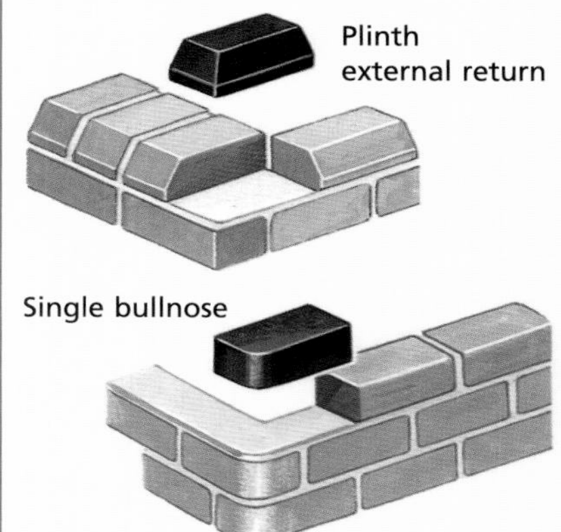

Types of bond for brick walls

Stretcher

All bricks are laid lengthways, with a half brick at the end of every other course so that each vertical joint (perpend) centres on the bricks above and below. The wall is 102.5mm thick and is known as a half-brick wall. It needs to be stiffened with piers (page 471) at each end and at 2m intervals. Insert movement joints as for a Flemish bond. Requires 60 bricks per m², not including piers and capping (top layer).

Flemish

Pairs of parallel stretchers alternated with one header in each course, making a wall 215mm thick. Closers are used on alternate courses to stagger the joints. This is known as a one-brick wall. It is more difficult to build than a half-brick wall, but stronger. Insert movement joints (page 471) every 8m for clay bricks, or every 4m for blocks or calcium-silicate bricks. Requires 120 bricks per m².

English garden wall

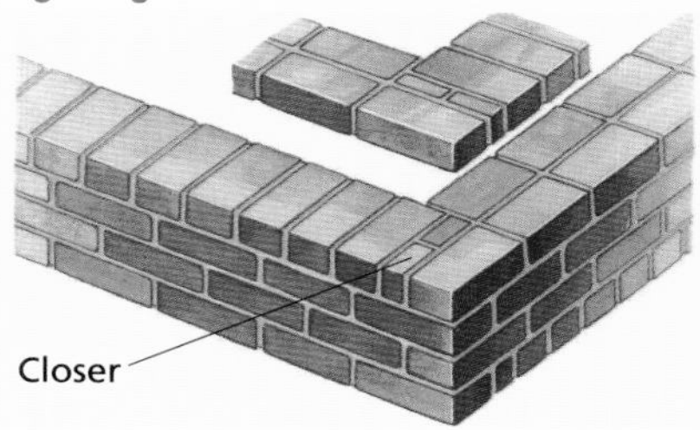

Three courses of parallel stretchers alternated with one header course. Closers are needed on header courses to stagger the joints. It is not quite as strong as a Flemish bond. Insert movement joints as for Flemish bond. Quantity as with Flemish, but cheaper because more of the bricks need be one faced only.

Random

With courses made up of blocks of varying heights fitted together. Can be used with walling blocks only. Insert movement joints (page 471) at 4m intervals. Quantity depends on block sizes and patterns.

Open (or honeycomb)

A decorative stretcher bond with spaces between bricks. The simplest and most solid pattern is with quarter-brick spaces between bricks. Variations are half-brick spaces, or half-brick spaces between header bricks that project about 60mm each side of the wall. Piers are needed as for a stretcher bond. Insert movement joints as for a Flemish bond (left). Requires 50 bricks per m² for the simplest pattern, not including the piers and capping.

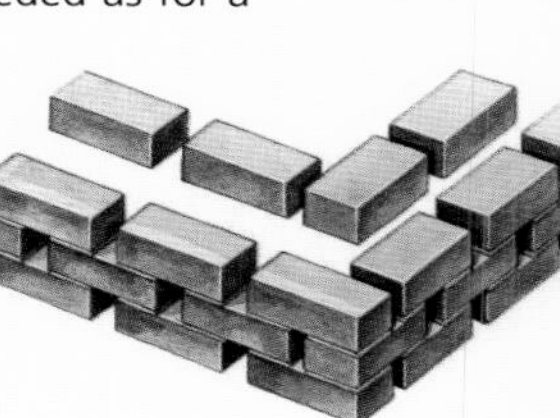

Ways of building a garden wall

A wall is built up of single layers of bricks or blocks, known as courses, cemented together with mortar. The pattern in which the courses are laid is known as a bond.

The arrangement of bricks in a bond is designed to stabilise and strengthen the wall by avoiding vertical mortar joints that run through two or more adjoining courses.

Garden walls built from suitable bricks (page 465) are more expensive than fencing, but last longer, provided that they are built on solid foundations and are given adequate protection from frost.

Even a low wall can be dangerous if it falls down, and frost damage can cause bricks to disintegrate. Use strong mortar and special quality frost-resistant bricks (F grade), at least for the first two courses. Use engineering bricks for any courses in permanent contact with the ground.

If you use mainly ordinary bricks that are only moderately frost-resistant (M grade), protect the top course with a damp-proof membrane, sandwiched under coping stones. Use special shaped bricks (page 465) as a capping for frost-resistant bricks only, and fit a damp-proof membrane at least two courses below the wall top, to throw off any water that seeps down through shrunken mortar joints.

Do not use a damp-proof membrane in the lower part of a free-standing wall, as it affects stability.

You will need to get planning permission from the local authority to build a wall higher than 1m beside a public highway, or for any free-standing wall that is over 2m high. Any wall in the garden of a listed building needs planning permission. If you intend building a wall on a boundary, you will need your neighbour's permission unless the wall is all on your side.

HOW TO STORE BRICKS SAFELY

Keep bricks dry. Bricks that are damp right through do not stick well to mortar. Dampness also leads to efflorescence – a white, powdery deposit (page 408).

Stack bricks on planks laid on a hard surface. Cover the planks with plastic sheeting. Build the stack so that the outer walls lean slightly inwards and will not collapse. Cover the stack with more plastic sheeting.

Building tools you will need

Line pins and building line The flat-bladed steel pins are pushed into the mortar joints at the end of the wall once the ends or corners have been built up. The line stretched between them is raised for each course as a levelling guide while laying bricks or blocks.

Line pins and building line

Plumb line Useful for checking that the wall is vertical. The line can be tied round a piece of board placed on the top course, so that it hangs down the wall as a guide while you work.

Plumb line

Gauge rod Used to check that each course of bricks is the correct height. Make one from a length of 75 x 25mm timber. For brick courses, mark the gauge every 75mm. For screen block walling, mark the gauge every 200mm for pier pilasters, and every 300mm for blocks. If using other types of walling block, mark it to match the course heights (including mortar) required.

Gauge rod

Spirit level

Spirit level Used for checking the alignment of walls. It should have both horizontal and vertical vials, and preferably be about 1m long.

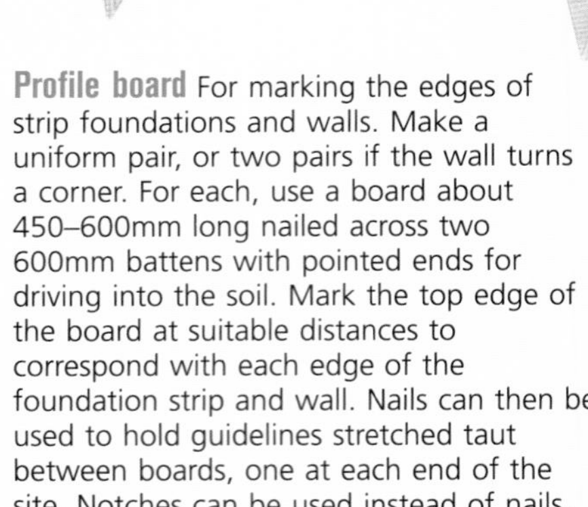

Profile boards

Profile board For marking the edges of strip foundations and walls. Make a uniform pair, or two pairs if the wall turns a corner. For each, use a board about 450–600mm long nailed across two 600mm battens with pointed ends for driving into the soil. Mark the top edge of the board at suitable distances to correspond with each edge of the foundation strip and wall. Nails can then be used to hold guidelines stretched taut between boards, one at each end of the site. Notches can be used instead of nails.

Mortar board (hawk) Useful for holding mortar while working. The wooden, plastic or aluminium surface is about 300mm square, with a central handle underneath. Make one using plywood and a broom handle. It can also be used when plastering.

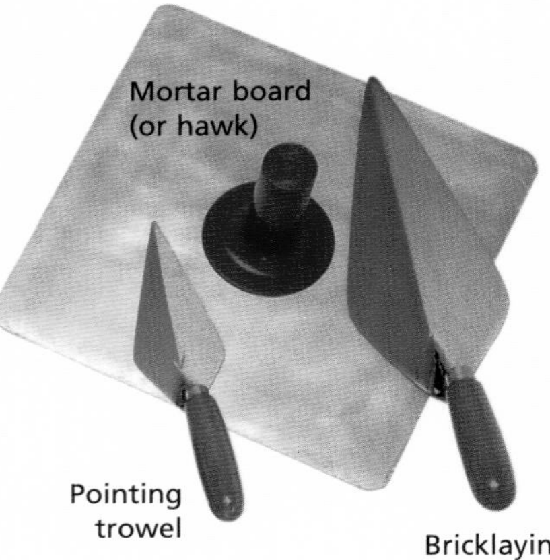

Mortar board (or hawk)

Pointing trowel

Bricklaying trowel

Pointing trowel A small trowel with a blade 75–200mm long, used for shaping mortar joints.

Bricklaying trowel A large trowel with a blade 250–330mm long, for spreading mortar when laying bricks.

Brick bolster and club hammer For cutting bricks. The spade-shaped bolster chisel has a 75mm or 100mm wide blade and can be fitted with a plastic guard to protect your hand. Club hammers come in two main sizes, 1.1kg or 1.8kg (2½ or 4lb). Both are useful.

Club hammer

Brick bolster

Pointing tools For some types of pointing (page 470) you need extra tools for shaping joints. A piece of sacking can be used to smooth flush joints. For concave joints you can use a piece of bent 15mm copper tubing, a piece of garden hosepipe, or something similar. Alternatively, buy a simple brick jointing trowel (see page 470) appropriate to the size of mortar joint you are shaping.

MAKING A BUILDER'S SQUARE

Use three pieces of wood about 50mm wide and 19mm thick, each accurately marked with one of the following lengths: 450mm (A); 600mm (B); 750mm (C).

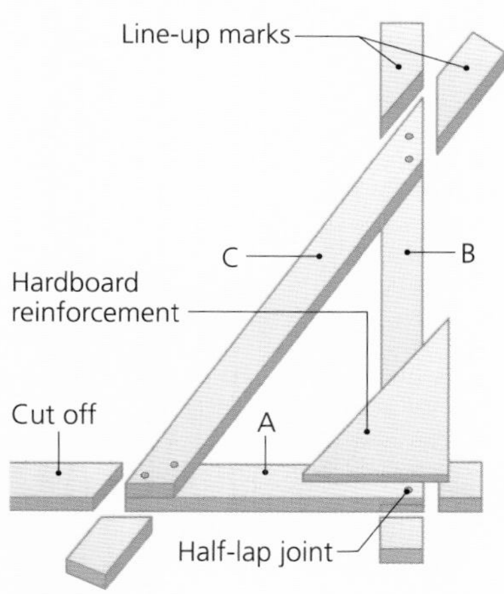

Line up all marks carefully before nailing lengths to each other. Use a half-lap joint for A and B, then overlap C. Check the right angle with a set square, saw off any overlap, then reinforce the corner with a piece of hardboard. (Any three lengths of wood joined in the ratio 3:4:5 must form a right angle. Also a 5:12:13 triangle is useful for restricted areas – a path alongside the house, for example.)

How to handle mortar

Cement, sand and hydrated lime mixed with water make up the mortar used to stick bricks together.

The lime acts as a plasticiser, making the mortar smooth and workable and preventing the sand and cement from shrinking and cracking when the mortar dries. Instead of lime, you can use proprietary liquid plasticiser – usually sold in 2 litre containers.

You can buy ready-mixed bags of dry bricklaying mortar to which only water has to be added. This is more expensive, but convenient for small jobs.

Use strong mortar for a garden wall, to withstand winds and rain. The standard mix is suitable for more sheltered areas.

Preparing a mortar mix

Mortar becomes unusable within two hours of mixing (sooner if the weather is hot). It cannot be enlivened by mixing in a little more water, as this would make it too soft to support a brick. Mix it in small batches to avoid waste. After a time you will be able to gauge how much to make up at a time, according to the rate at which you can lay the bricks.

Tools *Clean mixing surface such as concrete or a mixing board; two clean shovels, one solely for cement; two same-size heavy-duty polythene buckets; watering can with fine spray rose.*

Materials *Ordinary Portland cement; hydrated lime or plasticiser; soft (builder's) sand; water.*

1 Measure out the number of buckets of sand you require on the mixing surface.

2 Use a separate bucket and shovel to measure out the cement and add it to the sand. Do not use the bucket and shovel for other ingredients or mixing, or the cement in the bag could get damp and be spoiled.

3 Mix the sand and cement together thoroughly with the other shovel until they are a consistent greyish colour.

4 Mix in the hydrated lime. Or use a proprietary plasticiser instead, following the instructions on the container for the amount.

5 Make a crater at the top of the pile and pour in a little water from a watering can. Shovel from the outside of the pile into the middle to mix in the water in the crater.

6 Continue adding small amounts of water and turning the pile over with the shovel until the mortar is a stiff mix that falls off the spade cleanly. The mortar is then ready for use.

HELPFUL TIP

Speed up the mixing process by mixing a batch of sand and lime – known as 'coarse stuff' – beforehand and add cement to it as required. Soak the amount of hydrated lime you are likely to need in cold water the night before use. Next morning, pour off the water and mix the lime with the required proportion of sand. Coarse stuff will last a day. It might stiffen up, but can be made workable by adding a little water.

PROPORTIONS FOR MIXING

Ingredient	Strong mix for garden wall	Standard mix	Approximate quantities for strong mix
Ordinary Portland cement (usually grey; white also available)	1 part	1 part	One 50kg bag for 400–500 bricks
Hydrated lime	½ part	1 part	Half a 25kg bag for 400–500 bricks
or			
Mortar plasticiser	As instructed on container		About 0.07 litre for each 50kg bag cement
Clean builder's sand (soft sand)	4 parts	6 parts (bricks) 5 parts (blocks)	Ten 25kg bags for each 50kg bag cement
Bagged bricklaying mortar mix	–	–	One 40kg bag for roughly 150 bricks

Laying strip foundations

Every wall must be built on a firm, level foundation or it will soon crack and fall down.

Before you start The usual foundation is a solid layer of concrete on a bed of hardcore; though you need not use hardcore if you are satisfied that the ground beneath is firm. A low wall can be built on a flat, firm surface such as a patio, as long as it has an adequate sub-base and the slabs are set on a full bed of mortar. Set it back from the edge of the surface by the same distance as its thickness (and by a minimum of 150mm).

Tools *Spade; profile boards (page 466); string; heavy hammer; earth rammer (page 450) or stout length of timber; pencil or chalk; steel tape measure; spirit level; rake; straight-edged board; mixing platform (page 457); brick trowel.*

Materials *Hardcore (page 450); marker pegs 460mm long; concrete (page 458); sharp sand.*

---

1 Mark the edge of each side of the foundation strip using string lines and profile boards (see below).

2 Remove 50–75mm of topsoil and spread it elsewhere in the garden.

3 Measure from the top of each marker peg and mark lines showing the bottom of the concrete layer (page 450). Drive in marker pegs on each side of the strip at about 1m intervals, with their tops at the required height for the surface of the concrete. Generally, the concrete is level with a hard surrounding surface, or 25–50mm below a lawn edge.

4 Level adjacent and opposite pegs using a spirit level, set on a length of board.

5 Dig a trench as wide as the marked lines and to the required overall depth, using the bottom line on the marker pegs as a guide. If the soil is still soft, dig a little deeper.

6 Fill the bottom of the trench with hardcore to the height of the guideline on the marker pegs. Ram the hardcore down well using an earth rammer or a stout length of timber. Cover with a blinding layer of sharp sand, to fill any gaps.

7 Mix the concrete (page 460) on a clean surface and shovel it into the trench. Spread it with a rake, making sure it reaches well into the corners and is level with the tops of the marker pegs. Use the edge of a straight-edged board to tamp across the concrete to expel air.

8 Remove the marker pegs and fill the gaps with concrete, smoothing the surface with the board. Leave the profile boards in position and fit string lines to mark wall edges for bricklaying.

9 Mark the positions of the string guidelines for the walls on the concrete strip. Do this either before the concrete sets (a few hours after laying) using the point of a trowel, or when the concrete is hard, using a chalked string line.

10 Cover the concrete (page 462) and let it cure and harden for at least three days before building on top of it.

Foundation measurements

As a general guide, use a strip 150mm thick and 300mm wide for a half-brick wall up to a maximum of 1m high. Increase this to 225mm thick and 450mm wide for a one-brick wall up to 1m high, and to 300mm thick for a one-brick wall over 1m high (up to a maximum of 2m).

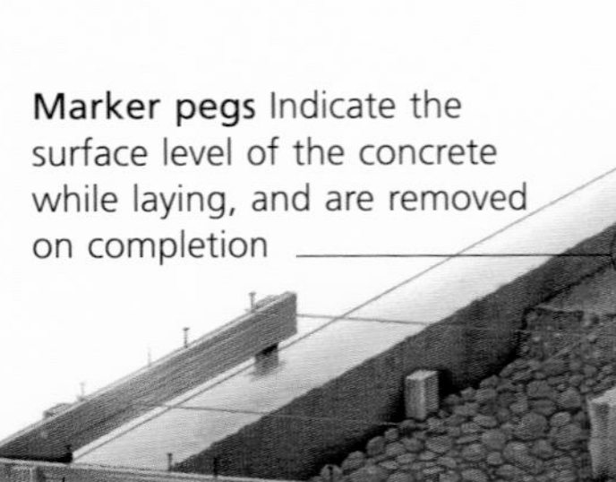

Laying bricks or walling blocks

Take particular care in positioning and laying the first course - it is the most crucial part of the job.

Before you start Work out the bond pattern (page 465) using dry bricks, especially if the wall has any corners or piers (page 470), before laying any bricks or walling blocks on the strip foundation. Make a note of how many part bricks you will need to cut (page 470). Use engineering or special-quality frost-resistant bricks either for the whole wall or at least for the first two courses. For an ordinary (M grade) brick wall, use a damp-proof membrane under the coping.

It takes experience to achieve a 10mm thickness of mortar under a brick every time. If you have never done any bricklaying before, practise laying a few bricks with a pseudo mortar of one part lime and three parts sand. Clean the bricks within two hours so that they can be used again in building the wall. Discard the mortar.

Tools *Brick trowel; spirit level; flat, even length of timber; builder's square; gauge rod with 75mm markings; pointing trowel; line pins and building line; mortar board; jointing tools; straightedge.*

Materials *Bricks or walling blocks; coping or capping bricks; strong mortar (page 467); damp-proof membrane about 20mm narrower than the wall thickness.*

---

1 Leave the profile boards and string lines in position as a guide until you have completed the first course.

2 Shape the mortar with the trowel so that it looks like a fat sausage pointed at both ends.

3 Slide the trowel underneath the mortar to lift it up.

4 Tip the mortar onto the building surface between the marked lines (facing page) in position for laying the first brick.

5 Tap the flat of the trowel blade backwards along the mortar to flatten it to a thickness of about 20mm. The mortar will be pressed down to 10mm thick by the weight of the brick.

6 Lay the first brick in position on the mortar in line with the marked guidelines. If the brick has a frog (indentation on one side) lay it with the frog facing upwards.

7 Lay another brick in the same way a few feet farther along the line. Do not worry about its position in the bond, it is for levelling only and can be removed later.

8 Place a flat board across the tops of the two bricks and use a spirit level to check that it is horizontal. Use the trowel handle to tap down the higher of the two bricks as necessary until both bricks are level.

9 Prepare a mortar bed for the second brick of the course. Before laying the brick, hold it upright and spread mortar for the vertical joint on the end to be butted. Squash the mortar down against all four edges, or it will easily slip off. Lift the levelling brick out of the way.

HELPFUL TIPS

- When levelling bricks, you may have to remove some – either to add more mortar to a low brick, or to scrape some off a high brick that will not tap down to the right level. The replaced brick may not stick well because the mortar has lost some of its adhesion. This does not matter as long as it occurs with only an occasional brick. But if the mortar gives no grip at all, scrape it off and start again.
- On a hot day, dip each brick in water to wet the surface before laying it. This helps to prevent the mortar from drying out too quickly.

Building a freestanding wall

Strip foundation Concrete thickness as required (see opposite)

Builder's square for checking that right-angled corners are true

Profile board Used to stretch string lines for marking edges of strip foundation and position marks for wall edges

Gauge rod For checking that each course is the correct height

Position marks Lines marked to show the wall edges, as a guide to laying the first brick course

Spirit level Use the vertical vial to make sure the wall is upright. Use horizontally to make sure the wall surface is straight

Line pins and building line A line stretched between line pins stuck in the mortar at each end, as a guide for levelling each course

Weather protection Two bottom courses of special quality bricks such as Class B engineering bricks or frost-resistant (F grade) bricks

Stepped end End bricks of the first three or four courses built up in steps before each complete course is laid

10 Lay the next four or five bricks of the course in the same way, then place a spirit level along them to check that they are horizontal. Tap bricks down with a trowel handle as necessary. If a brick is too low, remove it and add more mortar.

11 If the course turns a right-angled corner, use a builder's square to make sure it is true.

12 After completing the first course, build up at each end and corner with three or four stepped courses. Use the gauge rod to check that each course is at the correct height.

13 Insert line pins into the mortar at each built-up end. Use the line between them as a guide to levelling the top of the second course. Move it up progressively to check the levels of following courses as you lay the bricks between the stepped ends.

14 Point the joints after laying three or four courses (page 470)

15 From time to time check that the wall is both upright and straight by using a spirit level against it vertically and horizontally.

16 If using a top course of shaped bricks, sandwich the damp-proof membrane into the mortar two courses from the top. If using coping stones, sandwich it into the mortar bed for the coping.

Cutting a brick

Cutting a brick in half lengthways (called a closer) is tricky, as the brick is likely to fracture. It is generally easier to cut two quarter bricks from a half brick and lay them end on instead of using a closer. The easiest way is with a brick bolster and club hammer.

1 Mark the cutting line round the brick, then score along it with the bolster, tapping it gently with a club hammer.

2 With the brick laid frog down on sand or grass, rest the bolster in the scored line with its handle tilted slightly towards the waste end of the brick. Then strike it hard with the club hammer. The brick should break neatly in two.

Cutting a block A solid walling block can also be cut with a bolster and hammer. Mark the cutting line and continuously score round it, gradually increasing pressure until it breaks in two. As an alternative, you can use a block splitter (page 456).

Using an angle grinder If you have a lot of bricks to cut, hire an angle grinder, but handle it with care to avoid an accident.

Wear safety goggles and heavy gloves as protection from flying fragments.

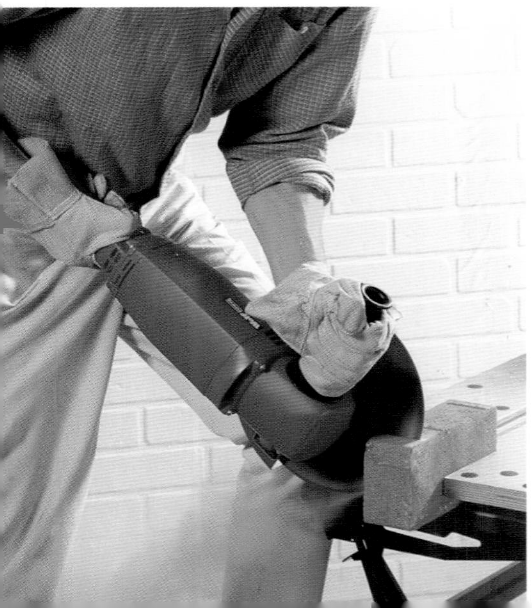

Pointing the joints

Mortar joints between bricks are shaped so that they shed rainwater and look neat. The commonest shapes used are flush, concave, and weatherstruck (sloped outwards from a recess at the top of the joint).

The shaping, generally known as pointing, can be done after each course before the mortar dries, or left until later using fresh mortar – of a different colour if desired. If pointing is to be left until later, when you have laid a few courses, rake out some of the mortar from each joint to leave a 15mm deep recess.

Flush joint Made by trimming off excess mortar with a pointing trowel so that it is in line with the adjoining bricks. Rub the joint smooth with a piece of sacking.

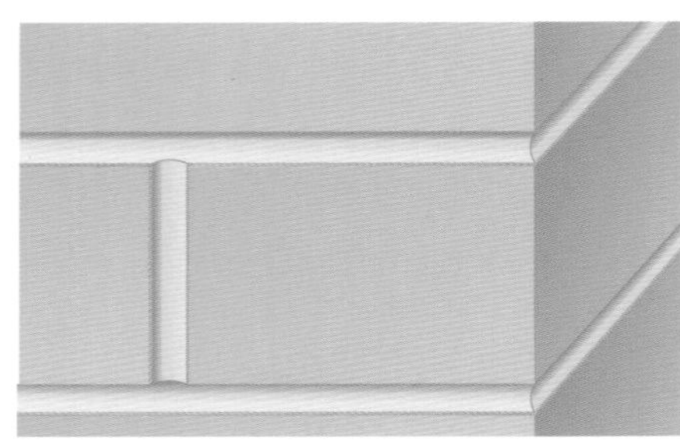

Concave joint Made by trimming off the excess mortar with a trowel, then drawing a rounded piece of metal along the joint to give it an inward curve. You can use a bent piece of 15mm copper pipe, a piece of garden hosepipe or a brick jointing trowel (see top right).

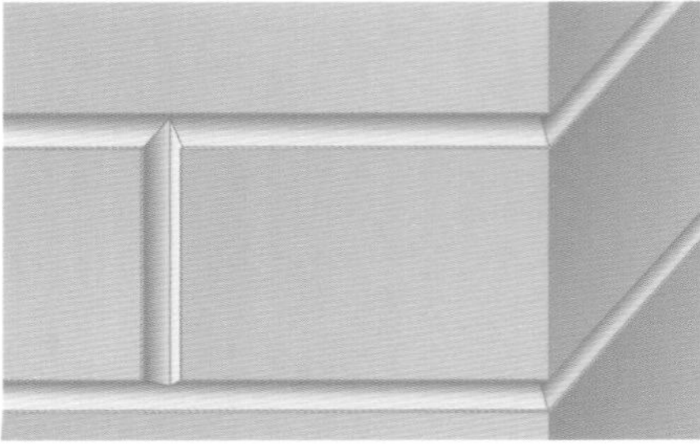

Weatherstruck joint Made by using the pointing trowel to recess the mortar slightly below the upper brick, and then sloping it to project slightly above the lower brick.

Trim off the mortar from the overhang at the base using a straightedge and the trowel. Shape the vertical joints in the same way, but all sloped in the same direction.

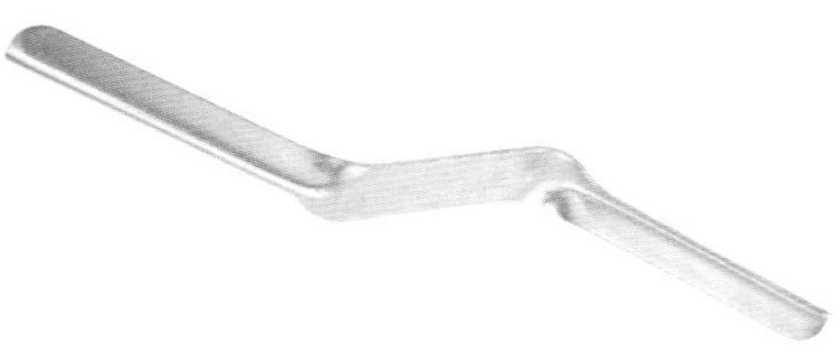

Brick jointing trowel A highly-polished steel tool shaped specifically to produce concave mortar joints between bricks.

Building a brick pier

A pier is not only decorative in a brick wall, but it also adds stability. There are four basic types of pier, as shown below.

End pier on half-brick wall

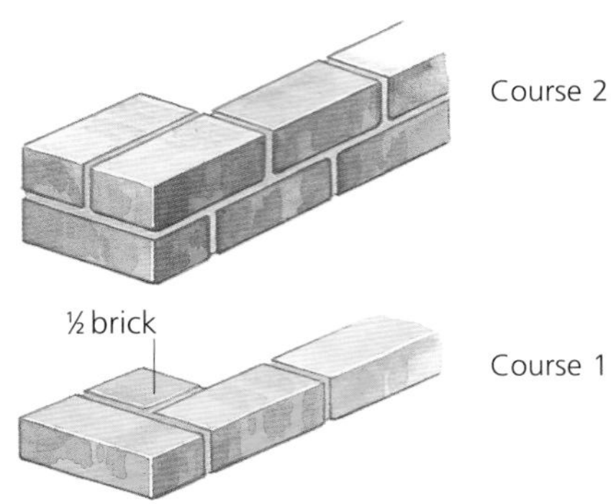

A half-brick (stretcher bond) wall is 102.5mm thick. To make an end pier projecting on one side only, lay a header brick against the end stretcher on the first course, then a half brick in the angle between header and stretcher.

On the second course of the pier, lay two stretcher bricks, then continue the course by laying more stretchers.

Intermediate pier on half-brick wall

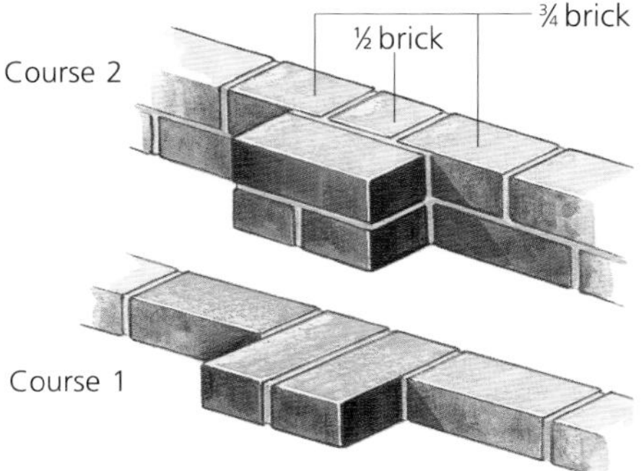

For the first course of an intermediate pier projecting on one side only, lay two header bricks to project from the bond in the place of one of the stretchers at the required positions – usually at 1.8m intervals.

On the second course, the projecting headers are covered with a stretcher, and at the inner end are overlapped by stretchers. To avoid a constant vertical joint on the wall face, use two three-quarter bricks with a half brick in between.

End pier on full-brick wall

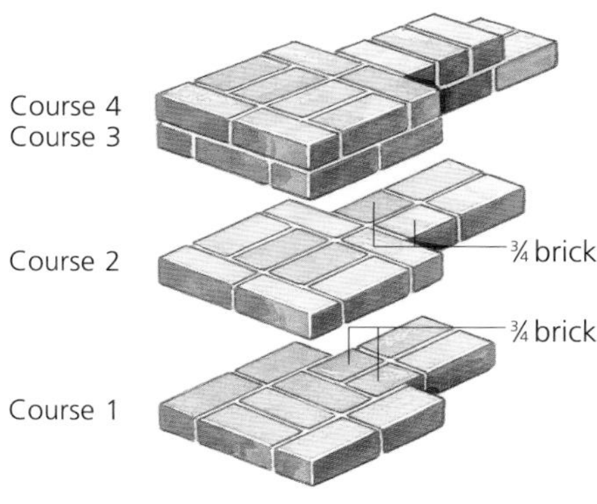

For an end pier on a full-brick wall built with an English garden wall bond, end the course with two three-quarter bricks. Then lay three headers at the end of the wall. Place two head-on stretchers on each side so that the pier projects half a brick length on each side, and runs half a brick beside the three-quarter bricks.

End the second course with three-quarter bricks, then butt headers across the pier at each end, with four parallel stretchers between. Repeat the pattern for alternate courses. On the fourth (header) course, no three-quarter bricks will be needed because this course is all headers.

Intermediate double pier on full-brick wall

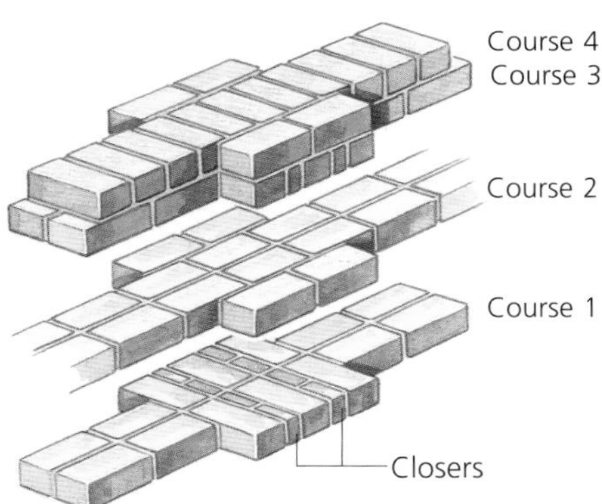

For an intermediate pier projecting from both sides of a wall built with an English garden wall bond, interrupt the first stretcher course with three pairs of head-on headers with two pairs of head-on closers between them. This will project half a brick on each side of the wall.
For the second course, lay two head-on stretchers on each side on the projecting half bricks. Repeat the pattern for alternate courses. The only variation is that on the fourth (header) course the pier stretchers are alongside headers.

Building a brick retaining wall

A retaining wall supports a bank of earth on one side, and may be needed in a sloping garden, or as a base for a boundary fence where the neighbouring garden is at a higher level.

Before you start Your retaining wall can be built of bricks or walling blocks in the usual way, but must be a full-brick wall – 215mm thick – built with a strong bond (page 465) and strong mortar mix (page 467). If the ground behind the wall either slopes upwards or seems unstable, or if you want to build a wall higher than 1m, get the advice of a consulting engineer.

The strip foundations (page 468) should be set in a trench with the top of the concrete surface about 250mm below the level of the lower ground, so that the bottom of the front of the wall is a little below ground level.

To allow for drainage from the banked soil, make drain holes through the wall. One way is to leave out the mortar in every other vertical joint in the second course above the lower ground level. This is simplest to do between headers. Another way is to angle plastic or clay pipes through the wall at 1m intervals.

A RAISED PLANT BED

A hollow bed for planting is simply a wall that completely encloses a small area filled with soil. Build a full-brick wall 215mm thick (page 468) either on a strip foundation surrounding an area of soil, or on a completely solid surface, such as a patio.

Where there is an earth base to the bed, no drainage is needed in the wall. Where the surface is completely solid, make a series of 10mm drain holes round the base by leaving gaps through the wall on the first course. Choose a bond that includes headers, and leave out alternate mortar joints between them.

A useful height for a raised bed is 500mm. If it is any higher, the pressure of the soil as the weather causes it to expand or shrink could force the walls outwards. Do not make the bed wider than about 1m. Not only will it take a lot of soil to fill it, but it will be difficult to reach plants in the centre.

Making movement joints

In a long run of wall, a movement joint is needed to allow for shrinkage or expansion of the materials. The joint is a narrow vertical gap about 10mm wide in the wall and coping, completely separating one length of wall from the next.

Make movement joints at the intervals recommended for the type of wall you are building. Flemish bond walls require movement joints every 8m for clay bricks, and every 4m for blocks or calcium-silicate bricks. This is the most common method and is recommended for stretcher, English garden wall and open or honeycomb patterns. However, random pattern walls should have them no farther apart than every 4m.

Once the wall is complete, fill the gaps with strips of plastic foam and seal them on each side with a generous bead of non-setting exterior-quality mastic.

A brick retaining wall

To last for years and be sturdy and safe, a brick retaining wall needs sound foundations, two or three courses of frost-resistant bricks, good drainage and well-spaced movement joints (above). Check retaining walls regularly, as even a small wall can cause damage or injury should it collapse.

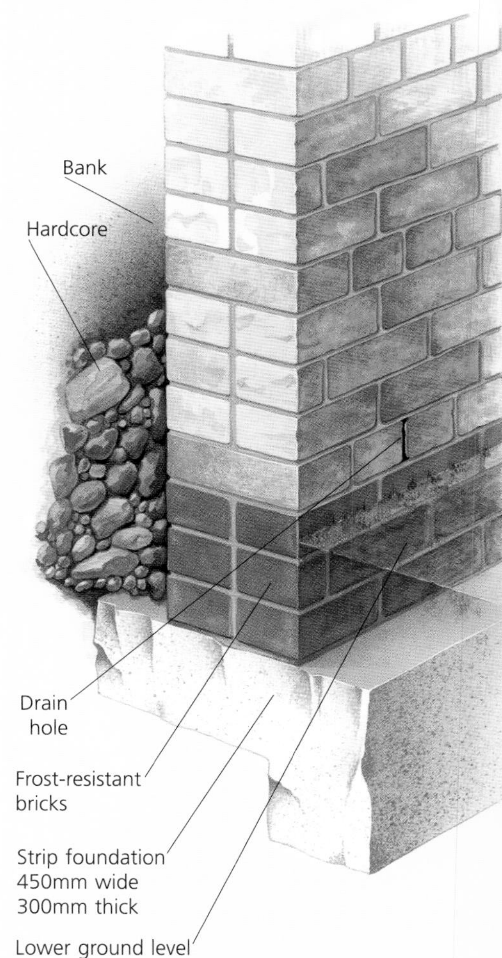

Building garden steps

There are two types of garden step: those built into an existing slope and those that are freestanding – built up from the flat between two different levels of the garden.

Before you start Whichever type you decide to build, for comfort and safety steps should be evenly spaced and not less than 600mm wide. For two people to walk comfortably abreast, the width must be at least 1.5m.

- Steps are easiest to climb comfortably when long treads (the flat parts) are combined with low risers (the upright parts), or when short treads are used with high risers. The best relationship is when the length of the tread plus twice the height of the riser is between 650 and 700mm. See below for possible combinations.
- Choose building materials that blend with their surroundings, and make sure that the treads have a non-slip surface.
- If the steps lead down to a house, make a narrow drainage channel as close as possible to the bottom step (see Building a drainage channel, page 452).

Working out step dimensions

To decide on the number of treads and risers for a flight of steps, measure the following:

- The height difference between the two levels.
- The length of the slope for built-in steps, or the length of ground space available for a freestanding flight to stretch.

For each measurement, calculate the number of steps needed for various combinations of treads and risers until you get more or less the same number for both measurements.

Steps in a slope

For a slope 1.8m long with a 750mm difference in height.

1 Choose a riser height and divide it into the height difference. Try 115mm.
Height difference 750mm divided by 115mm riser = 6½ steps.

2 The best tread for a 115mm riser is about 450mm. Divide this into the slope length:
Slope length 1.8m ÷ 450mm tread = 4 steps.

3 Try again with a higher riser and a shorter tread:
Height 750mm ÷ 150mm = 5
Length 1.8m ÷ 360mm = 5
So 5 steps will fit comfortably.

Freestanding steps

For a flight of freestanding steps with an overall height difference of 950mm and ground space of 1.5m.

1 In a 1.5m stretch of ground, the number of 300mm treads would be 5. But the final tread could be the top of the higher level, so the actual stretch would be 1.2m.

2 Treads 300mm deep from front to back are best with risers of 190mm or 200mm. A riser height of 190 mm looks like the best bet giving exactly five steps, using two courses of brick laid flat with a 30mm paving slab as the step material.

TREAD AND RISER COMBINATIONS

Treads should never be less than 300mm long. Risers should be no lower than 100mm and no higher than 200mm. Their dimensions are governed to some extent by the gradient of the slope and the building material. Long treads are needed for steps up a gentle slope and short treads for a steep slope.

Brick risers, for example, are limited to multiples of 75mm – a brick laid flat – or 112.5mm – a brick laid on edge. Using 50mm clay pavers or 60mm concrete paving blocks gives you more options. When using paving slabs as treads, take into account the slab thickness and its mortar bed when calculating the riser height.

Height of riser	Length of tread	Possible materials
115mm	420-470mm	One course of bricks laid on edge. Or one course of bricks laid flat, topped with 30mm thick slab tread.
125mm	400-450mm	One course of bricks laid flat, topped with 40mm thick slab tread.
135mm	380-430mm	One course of bricks laid flat, topped with 50mm thick slab tread.
142.5mm	365-415mm	One course of bricks laid on edge topped with 30mm thick slab tread.
150mm	350-400mm	Two courses of bricks laid flat. Or one course of bricks laid on edge topped with 40mm paving slab
190mm	300-320mm	Two courses of bricks laid flat, topped with 30mm thick slab tread.
200mm	300-305mm	Two courses of bricks laid flat, topped with 40mm thick slab tread.

Building steps into a slope

Roughly shape the slope before you start building the steps. If it is steep, remove some of the soil. On an irregular slope, build up where necessary with soil from other parts of the garden.

The layout of the slope may suggest two flights of steps at right angles, with a landing in between. On a long flight, make a landing after about every ten steps to provide a resting place. On flights with loose soil at the sides, you may want to build low brick retaining walls (page 471) or mortar in matching paving slabs on edge to follow the line of the slope.

The instructions given here are for steps built with brick risers and concrete paving slab treads, but the method is similar whatever material you use.

Tools *String and pegs; 5m steel tape measure; long length of timber; spirit level; builder's square; spade; club hammer; brick trowel; mortar mixing board; two heavy-duty polythene buckets and two shovels (for mixing concrete); short tamping beam; pointing trowel or joining tool; earth rammer; 10mm thick wooden batten. Possibly also a brick bolster.*

Materials *Hardcore – one barrowload fills about 0.5m² at 150mm deep; concrete foundation mix (page 459); bricks: bricklaying mortar (page 467); paving slabs; bedding mortar; water. Possibly also sharp sand.*

1 Fix two parallel string lines from top to bottom of the slope, as far apart as the required step width.

2 Measure a line to find the length of the slope.

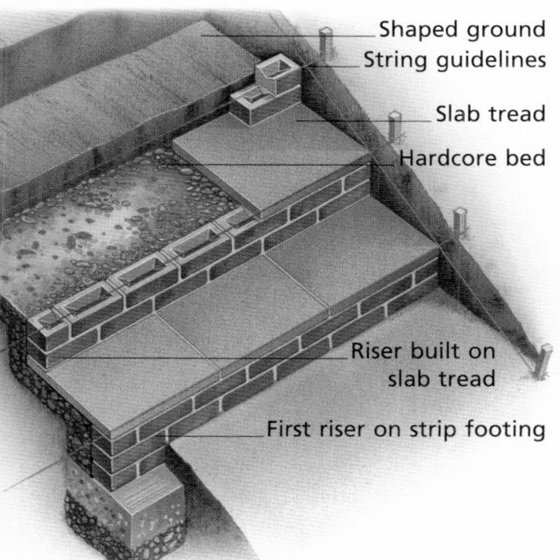

Steps built into a slope The ground is roughly shaped for the treads and risers. The first riser is built on a footing strip, and each following riser on the back of the previous tread. Treads are bedded on hardcore with a built-in drainage slope.

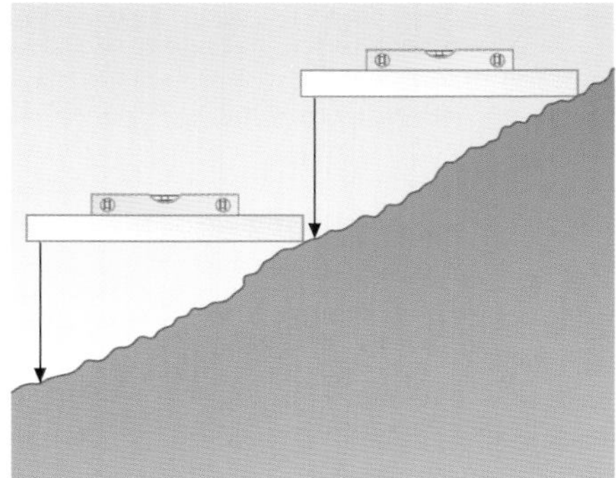

3 To measure the height difference between the levels, rest one end of a length of timber on the top of the slope and place a spirit level on it. Get a helper (with a second spirit level) to hold another piece of timber vertical against the other end so that you can measure the height.

If the timber will not reach the whole way, measure to a point halfway down the slope, then measure from the same point to the lowest level. Add the two heights together for the total fall.

4 Use the height and length measurements to calculate a suitable dimension for treads and risers (see panel).

5 Fix string lines to mark the front edge of each step. Make sure they are evenly spaced, and use a builder's square to check that they are at right angles to the length lines.

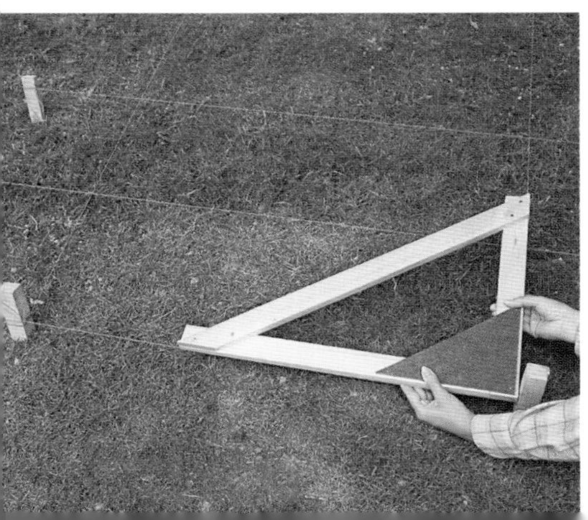

6 Use a spade to shape the ground for each step. Begin at the bottom so you always have a flat area to work from.

7 Dig a trench 125mm deep at the base of the flight to make a footing strip for the first riser.

8 Tip about 25mm of hardcore into the base of the trench and ram it well down.

9 Fill the trench with concrete, tamp level with the ground and cover it with polythene sheet.

10 Wait three days before building the first riser on the footing strip (see Laying bricks, page 468).

11 Wait at least two hours for the mortar to dry before ramming down a layer of hardcore for the first tread behind the riser. Take care not to disturb the bricks and fresh mortar. Slope the hardcore surface to the front for drainage (see right).

12 Lay paving slabs (page 453) to make the surface of the first tread. Use a full bed of mortar and project the slab about 25mm in front of the riser. Leave 9-10mm gaps between slabs using spacers.

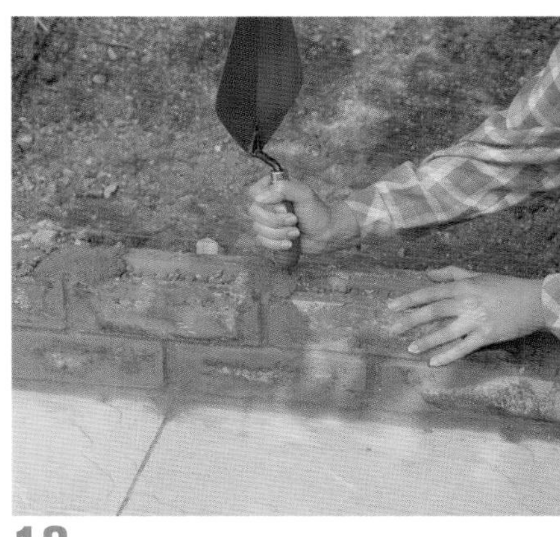

13 Build the next riser on top of the first tread, positioned to match your chosen tread length. Make sure the riser is vertical – use the mortar layer to adjust for the slight drainage slope on the tread.

14 Make sure the top tread is level with the surrounding ground. If necessary, slope the ground towards the tread, or raise the tread slightly – no more than 15mm.

15 Fill the gaps between the tread slabs with mortar and wait about 24 hours before using the steps, to allow the mortar to set.

Sloping a tread for drainage

1 Build up the hardcore surface a little higher at the back of the step. Slope the surface to level with the top of the riser at the front.

2 To check the slope, lay a spirit level from the back to the front with a 10mm thick wooden batten under the front edge, on the riser. Build up the back of the slope until the spirit level is horizontal with the wooden batten in place.

3 Check that the hardcore area is level from side to side.

HELPFUL TIP

To save wear on the lawn at the base of a flight of steps, lay a paving slab in front of the bottom step. Cut out an area of turf of a suitable size and depth, and bed the slab on a layer of 25mm deep sharp sand.

Building freestanding steps

The treads of freestanding steps are supported on side walls, with the area between filled in with hardcore as a base. For a flight of up to about five steps, build the side walls centred on a concrete footing strip. For a higher flight, lay a concrete sub-base for the whole structure.

The risers can be constructed in two ways – either built across the hardcore base or built up from the ground. If they are built across the hardcore base, the hardcore has to be filled in successive layers as a riser and its corresponding side walls are built step by step. This means waiting for the brick mortar to dry out each time, but on a high flight it saves considerably on bricks.

On a low flight, it is generally easier to build up the risers from the ground and fill in all the hardcore at once. Few extra bricks are needed. The method given below is for a small flight with risers built up from the ground.

Steps can be built either at right angles to the higher level, or parallel with it. Or the flight can change direction at a landing about halfway down. A parallel flight often saves space when a lot of steps are needed.

Tools *String and pegs; profile boards (page 466); steel tape measure; spirit level; builder's square (page 467); brick trowel; two heavy-duty polythene buckets and two shovels (for mixing concrete); club hammer; tamping beam; mortar mixing board; earth rammer; pointing trowel; gauge rod; plumb line; line pins and building line; 10mm thick wooden batten. Possibly also: brick bolster.*

Materials *Hardcore – 1 barrowload fills about 0.5m² 150mm deep; concrete foundation mix (page 459); paving slabs; bricks; bedding mortar; bricklaying mortar (page 467); water. Possibly sharp sand.*

1 Measure the height difference and the ground space available, then work out the dimensions of treads and risers (page 472).

2 Prepare a concrete sub-base (page 468) either in strips or for the full area. Use a 50mm layer of hardcore topped with 75mm of concrete. Strip footings should be twice as wide as the thickness of the supporting wall.

3 Wait for three days for the concrete to harden before building the supporting walls.

4 Build supporting walls course by course according to the depths of the risers. The front wall is the riser for the first step. Mark the position of the second and subsequent risers with string and pegs. Anchor courses to an existing wall or terrace as necessary (see below). Check continually that corners are right angles and that walls are vertical, with courses at the right depth.

5 Wait until the brick mortar has set, then fill the areas between the walls and risers with hardcore well rammed down and with a drainage slope from front to back (page 473). Take care not to disturb the newly laid bricks and fresh mortar.

6 Lay the paving slabs for each tread (page 453) on a full mortar bed, ensuring they project 25mm in front of each riser.

7 Fill any gaps between the edges of the slab and the walls with mortar, making sure you don't get any on the slab surface.

Anchoring steps to a wall

The supporting walls of freestanding steps must be anchored – or toothed in – to the wall they are built against. Half of the last brick in every other course of the step's side walls (beginning with the bottom course) is linked into the existing wall. Remove the appropriate bricks (page 408) before you start the steps.

If the flight runs parallel with the existing wall, link in a brick at the end of each riser, and in alternate courses of the back wall.

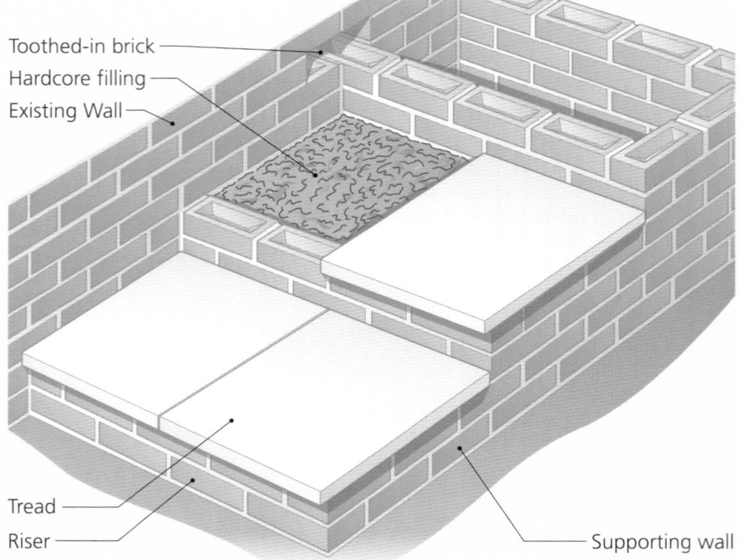

Steps built up from the ground
Steps can be built alongside an existing wall, or outwards from it. The supporting walls of the steps and the risers are built up with bricks, like an open box, and the area between them is filled in with hardcore. The treads rest on the walls and the hardcore bed.

Building a barbecue

A built-in barbecue gives you a custom-made cooking area designed to fit your garden. Think carefully about the right size, the best site and the most suitable design.

The dimensions of a barbecue are dictated by the size of the grill and the charcoal pan. So purchase these first, or buy a built-in barbecue kit to use as a template.

Try to site a barbecue on or near the patio. For convenience it should also be fairly close to the kitchen. Pick a spot that is out of direct view of the house windows, if possible, unless you want to look at the barbecue all the year round, and avoid having any potential fire hazards nearby, such as fences, trellis or pergolas.

Tools *Spirit level; builder's square; stick of chalk; brick trowel; plumb line.*

Materials *Bricks sufficient for ten courses; dry-mix mortar; grill and charcoal pan, or a built-in barbecue kit.*

Before you start A firm, level base is essential. If a suitable area of concrete, slabs or brick is not available, lay a concrete foundation before you begin to build.

1 Use the spirit level to check the ground is level. Without mortar, lay out the first course of bricks in a square U shape. With the builder's square, check the corners are exact right angles and ensure that the charcoal pan will fit correctly. Draw around the bricks with chalk, then move them out of the way.

2 Mix the mortar and, using a brick trowel, put a layer of mortar on the ground. Place the first course of bricks on top. Use the builder's square to check the corners are still at right angles, and ensure the bricks are level.

3 Place a layer of mortar on top of the bricks and lay the second course of bricks so that the joints are staggered. Continue to lay courses of bricks in this way, frequently checking that the courses are horizontal and that the walls are vertical.

4 Once you reach the height convenient for the charcoal pan (about six courses), lay three bricks so they stick out at right angles on each side. These bricks will support the charcoal pan. Lay a further one or two courses of bricks, then repeat the right-angled bricks to provide support for the grill. If you wish to vary the grill height, set short metal bars in the mortar between two or more courses of bricks.

5 Add a further one or two courses of bricks above the highest grill setting. If the barbecue is in an exposed position, you could raise the top by two or three more courses to create a partial windbreak.

Types of barbecue

There is a wide choice of barbecues available, ranging from basic to sophisticated models complete with tools and gadgets. The main differences are in the price and the fuel they use: charcoal or gas.

Charcoal barbecues

These are cheaper to buy than gas barbecues, but less convenient. They use solid fuel in the form of charcoal or briquettes. Check the construction is sturdy and that it has a removable lid to cover the barbecue while it cools, or to quench flames. The main drawback is that charcoal barbecues take time to get going: the coals must be lit about an hour before you want to start cooking. Also, the only way to regulate heat is by raising or lowering the grill. A charcoal barbecue can get smoky: site it where smoke will not billow into neighbours' windows.

Gas barbecues

Fuelled by bottled propane gas, these are essentially outdoor cookers. They are quick and easy to use and have adjustable controls. Gas barbecues are more substantial pieces of equipment than charcoal models and, with the weight of the gas bottle, are heavy to move around. When buying check the size in relation to what you want to cook (larger models will roast a turkey) and how easy it is to clean.

Chimeneas

These Mexican clay ovens make handsome outdoor fireplaces that can be used for cooking. They are fuelled by wood. Buy from a retailer who supplies grills and other cooking accessories to fit.

BARBECUE SAFETY

- For lighting charcoal use only products tailor-made for barbecues.
- Do not pour lighter fluid onto hot coals and never use petrol.
- Keep matches and any combustible materials well away from a barbecue.
- Keep a garden hose and/or a bucket of sand close by, in case the fire gets out of control.
- Buy a barbecue with a hood or lid to quench flames if food catches fire.
- Use long-handled tools and wear oven mitts to protect skin from burns.
- Never leave a lit barbecue unattended.

Installing a flexible pond liner

Making a pond with a flexible liner simply involves digging a hole and placing the liner inside, so that the size and shape of the pond can be to your own design.

Tools *Garden hosepipe; spade; spirit level; straight-edged plank; scissors; sand for marking out the area; bricks to use as temporary weights.*

Materials *Flexible liner; protective underlay of the same size as the liner; edging materials such as rocks, pebbles, coarse gravel, paving slabs; turf.*

Calculating the size of the liner

To find the area of liner required, multiply the length by the width as follows:
Length = maximum overall length
+ (2 x maximum depth) + 300mm
Width = maximum overall width
+ (2 x maximum depth) + 300mm
This formula works for all ponds regardless of shape and size. The extra 300mm is to allow for adequate overlap around the edges of the pond.

CHOOSING A LINER

Flexible liners are available in a range of materials from PVC to butyl rubber. Buy the best you can afford, because cheaper materials have a shorter life. The length of guarantee is a guide to a good liner; the best quality materials will be guaranteed for at least 20 years. Liners come in rolls of varying width – take this into account when planning the dimensions of the pond.

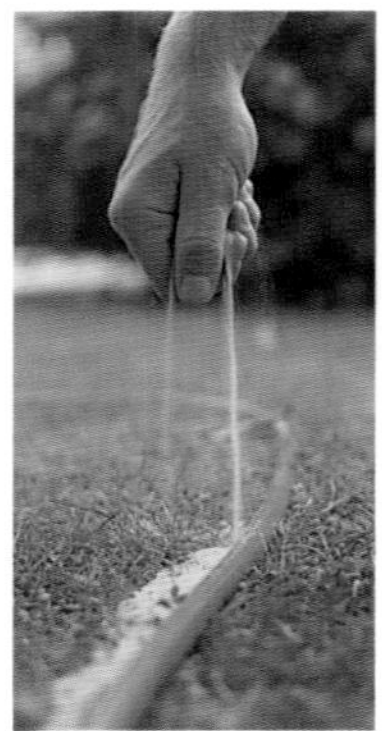

1 Mark out the shape of the pond using a hosepipe. View it from every angle including from an upstairs window. When you are completely happy with the shape and the overall position of the pond, trickle sand onto the ground to mark the outline, then remove the hosepipe.

2 Dig out the pond cavity just inside the sand mark. Make the sides slope outwards by at least 20° to stop the soil crumbling into the hole. Shape underwater shelves around the edge 300mm deep and 250–300mm wide. Outside the sand mark, remove a 450mm strip of soil or turf to a depth of 50mm to accommodate the overlap around the pond edges.

3 Use a spirit level placed on a plank to check that the rim of the pool is level all the way round, as any discrepancies will show up dramatically when the pond is full of water. If you plan to have a bog garden next to the pond, make the adjoining edge 50mm lower than the rest of the rim. Check that the underwater shelves are level, too.

4 Once digging is complete, check over the entire cavity and remove any debris and protruding stones that could damage the liner. Firm the sides with your hands to remove any soft spots that could subside later on. Line the cavity with the recommended protective underlay.

5 Cut the pond liner to size, if necessary. Lay it loosely over the cavity and weigh down the edges temporarily with bricks. When handling the liner, take care that it does not catch on any sharp objects. This part of the job is best done by two people with plenty of time to get things right.

6 Start running in water from a hose once the liner is centred over the hole. The increasing weight of the water will mould the liner to the shape of the cavity. As the liner sinks, move the weights and fold the liner neatly around shelves and corners. Continue filling the pond until the water is just below the rim.

7 Trim the liner to leave an overlap of 150mm all round. Bury the outside edge of the liner in the soil, leaving a rim of exposed liner 50–100mm wide.

8 Edge the pond with materials to conceal the liner rim. Let paving stones project over the water by 50mm to conceal the liner; turf should butt up to the edge.

Installing a rigid pond liner

Rigid liners are made of reinforced plastic. The hole you dig needs to be an accurate match for the shape of the pond: the simpler the shape, the easier this is to achieve.

Marking out and digging the hole for a rigid symmetrical liner is described on this page – making a large shallow hole first to fit the top of the liner, followed by a deeper smaller hole for the bottom of the liner.

With asymmetrical shapes, however, you do it the other way round, first standing the liner on its base to mark (with sand) just the shape of the small deep hole to take the bottom of the liner. When this has been dug (to the full depth of the pond), allowing for tapered sides, put the liner in the hole and mark again for the overall shape of the liner and the shelves, before digging out the larger shallower hole.

Tools *Spade; spirit level; straight-edged plank; earth hammer (page 451).*

Materials *Rigid liner; sand for marking out; hardcore or crushed stone; materials for edging, such as paving slabs. Possibly also coarse sand.*

1 Mark out the shape of the pond. Lay the liner upside down on the site and, using sand, trace the outline of the liner onto the ground. Remove the liner.

2 Cut the outline of the pond into the soil using a sharp spade to ensure straight lines.

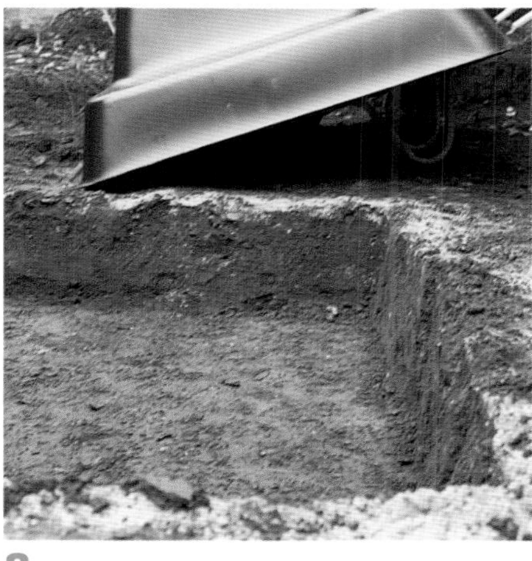

3 Dig out the pond cavity just inside the cut lines, but only as deep as the shallow marginal shelf. Check across the edges using a spirit level and straight-edged plank to ensure that they are level.

4 Place the liner in the hole the right way up and mark around the base of the deepest part of the pond with sand. Remove the liner.

5 Cut the outline for the deep part of the pond in the soil, then dig out the hole to the correct depth. Clear away all loose stones and roots. On stony soil, make the hole a bit deeper, and place a 50mm layer of coarse sand on which the liner can rest.

6 Check that the liner fits in the hole, and dig out more soil if necessary. Ensure the liner is level in each direction by placing the spirit level along each edge. Make any necessary adjustments and back-fill with soil or sand.

7 Slowly fill the liner with water, allowing the mould to settle under its increasing weight. Check for level as it fills and adjust the liner as necessary, otherwise one edge will stand above the water line and be unsightly.

8 As the liner is filling up, back-fill the gaps with soil or sand. When it is level, prepare the ground for paving around the liner, if you are having paved edges. Place a 100mm layer of hardcore or crushed stone and use an earth hammer to compact it.

9 Lay paving slabs on a full bed of mortar, overhanging the edge of the liner slightly. Tap each one into position and check for level before mortaring the gaps.

Installing a wall-mounted water fountain

An electric pump is the basis for all moving water features. The simple installation techniques shown here can be used for pebble fountains, rills, water chutes and many more effects.

Tools *Spirit level; power drill and masonry bit; masonry paintbrush.*

Materials *20–23 litre plastic water tank (available from builders' or plumbers' merchants); length of rigid tubing; flexible piping; pump; low-voltage transformer; wall-mounted spout; wall plug and screw; bricks or slabs to disguise tank; external waterproof paint.*

1 Lift a paving slab next to a wall and dig down to create a hole big enough for the water tank, so that it sits proud of the surrounding surface by an equal amount all the way round. Make sure that the tank sits level in the hole.

2 Surround the tank with a row of bricks or walling blocks to disguise its edge. Butt the bricks tightly together, mortaring them in place if you prefer.

3 Drill a hole in the wall and insert a wall plug and screw to hold the water spout. Hang the spout in place and check with a spirit level that it is level.

4 Attach the flexible piping to the base of the spout and feed the other end into the water tank. Connect it to the pump in the base of the tank.

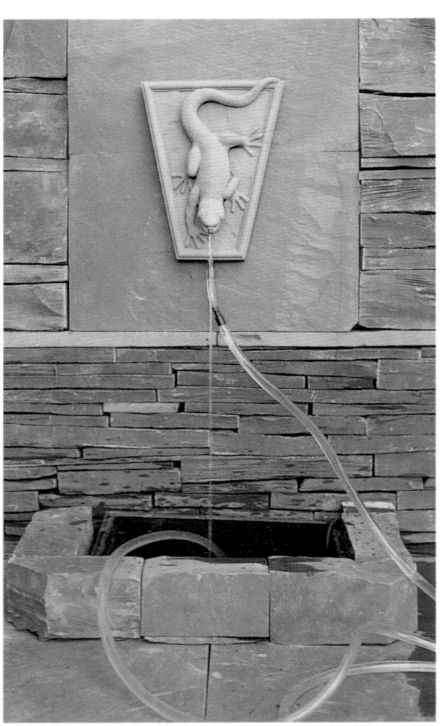

5 Fill the tank with water and connect the pump to the power supply via a low-voltage transformer inside the house. Switch on the fountain to check that it is working. If it is, cut the flexible piping to length so that it runs vertically into the water tank.

6 Paint the rigid tubing, which will enclose the flexible piping, to match the wall behind it. Feed the flexible pipe through the rigid tube and attach it to the pump and water spout at either end.

SAFETY TIP

Mixing electricity with water and the outdoors can be dangerous. If you are installing a water feature that requires a mains power supply, follow the instructions for wiring outdoor electrics on pages 316–19 and always connect the water pump to an RCD.

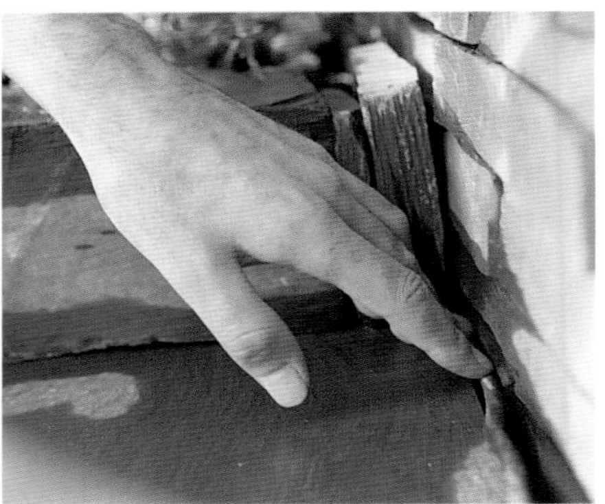

7 Tuck the electric cable running from the pump to the electricity supply along the back of the patio paving, or protect it in a length of metal conduit.

8 Fill the water tank with enough water to cover the pump, connect the power supply and switch on the pump. Add a water-loving plant, such as a fern, with its pot raised above the level of the water to complete the display.

IDEAS FOR WATER FEATURES

- You can hide the workings of a wall-mounted water feature by chasing the pipework into an existing wall or by burying the pipes in a new wall.

- Self-contained pebble fountain kits are easy to install and can be finished in a variety of different ways. They consist of a plastic bucket with a wide lip that catches water sprayed up by the fountain and channels it back into the bucket. A pump sits in the reservoir and is covered by a plastic lid or a metal grille. The surface can be covered with cobbles or a mill-wheel, or the water can be fed from the pump through a flexible pipe to emerge from an urn or ceramic ball.

- A pump can also be used to move water along a shallow rill or garden stream. Dig a gently sloping trench for the rill and bury a water reservoir and pump at one end. Run a length of piping from the far end of the feature back to the reservoir to recycle the water.

Ten ways to keep your property safe

Most break-ins are carried out by casual thieves looking for easy pickings. Burglars are unlikely to persist if they encounter locked doors and windows. Rapid entry and exit are vital for them, and they will not climb in and out of the house through broken glass. The tips on this page will all help to keep your home secure.

GETTING HELP FROM THE POLICE

If you want specific advice on how to protect your home, telephone the Crime Prevention Officer at your local police station. He will visit the house if necessary, point out weak spots in your defences and suggest the most appropriate security devices for your circumstances.

If you see anyone loitering in your street or acting suspiciously, do not disturb them. Call the police, then continue to watch unseen until they arrive.

Neighbourhood Watch groups, run in collaboration with the local police, are intended to encourage neighbours to work together by watching for anything suspicious in the area. They also stress the importance of protecting property, and marking valuables. If you are interested in getting involved in a group, contact your local Crime Prevention Officer.

1 Deliveries Cancel milk and newspapers when you go away. Arrange for a neighbour to push in unexpected items like leaflets and free newspapers. If you have a glazed porch, ask your neighbour to gather up the post each morning so that it is not visible from outside.

2 Garage Add extra security to a back door inside a garage where an intruder could work totally hidden. Ensure that the garage itself is fitted with secure locks. An electronically operated, metal up-and-over door will provide the most security.

3 Ladders Keep ladders locked away. If they must be stored outside, padlock them to a wall with special brackets.

4 Sheds Make sure sheds are securely padlocked. Tools stored there could be used for a break-in. A garden spade, for example, makes a powerful lever for opening windows.

10 Hedges and shrubs Avoid having high hedges and shrubs that will screen an intruder from the road or from neighbours.

9 Keys Never have a name-and-address tag on your keys. At most, use your surname, with a company address or the address of a relative for them to be returned to if you lose them. Be wary of leaving home to go and collect keys from someone who says they have found them. It may be a ruse to get you out of the house while the keys are used for entry. Never leave keys in locks, under the doormat, or hanging inside the letterbox.

5 Security lights Outside lights that switch on automatically when a sensor picks up movement outside the house can be a real deterrent to crime. Site them in areas of the house where a burglar may try to gain access, for example high above French windows at the back or over a garage door. One fitted above a front door will also help you to see who is calling at night. Site the sensor well out of reach of intruders. Bear in mind that most domestic situations do not require high power floodlights, which can be a real nuisance to neighbours.

6 Marking valuables Print your house number and post code on valuable possessions with an ultra-violet marking pen. This will help police to prove they were stolen, and assist in returning them. Metal items can be marked with hammer-and-letter punches. Photograph valuable items together, showing on the photograph where they are marked.

7 Accessible windows Never leave windows open when you go out. Fit locks to all windows, especially those with easy access – near flat roofs, drainpipes and trees. If you live in a 'high-risk' area or have leaded light or louvred windows, consider installing window bars or sliding metal grilles.

8 Driveways A gravel drive or path at the front of the house is a noisy surface that will alert you to the approach of visitors or intruders. Gates at the garden boundary, particularly locked ones, are a very effective deterrent to burglars.

KITCHEN
121
OVEN
PANTRY
122

Rules and regulations 13

Planning and building control

If you are planning to carry out major improvements to your home, such as building an extension, adding a conservatory, rewiring or knocking down a load-bearing wall, you need to know whether you require official approval for the work.

The two most important pieces of legislation that apply to projects of this sort are the Town & Country Planning Acts and the Building Regulations. Before you start work, it is your duty as the householder to find out which rules and regulations apply to the job, to seek prior permission if this is needed, and to make sure that the work complies with the rules when it has been completed. There are financial and other penalties if you do not obtain the required permission, or if you carry out work that does not comply with the rules, and you may be unable to sell a house that has been altered or extended without permission or approval.

The following information gives a general overview of the planning and building rules that apply to home improvements. It explains how to find out if permission or approval is needed, and how to go about applying for it. Specific requirements for individual improvement projects are explained on pages 484–96.

Planning permission

The Town & Country Planning Acts govern what your house looks like from the outside, the impact it has on the street where it is located, and the uses to which the house and the land it occupies are put. Local authorities publish leaflets explaining the Acts and how they apply to home improvements and you will find extensive information available on the Government website www.planningportal.gov.uk.

What you can and cannot do in planning terms is governed by so-called 'permitted development'. This allows certain improvement projects such as home extensions to go ahead if they meet specific requirements. Planning rules were significantly relaxed in 2008, to prevent planning departments being inundated with many similar and minor applications.

LISTED BUILDINGS AND 'DESIGNATED' AREAS

Different planning rules apply if you live in a listed building or your home is in a so-called 'designated' area – conservation areas, the Broads, Areas of Outstanding Natural Beauty, National Parks (National Scenic Areas in Scotland) and World Heritage sites. Check with your local council.

To apply for planning permission, contact your local authority planning department and ask for the relevant forms, plus any guidance notes they publish. You will be told what the current fee is for an application. If you want clarification about whether a particular project needs permission, you can make an appointment with a planning officer to talk over your proposals.

The same form is now used nationwide for all planning applications and you can

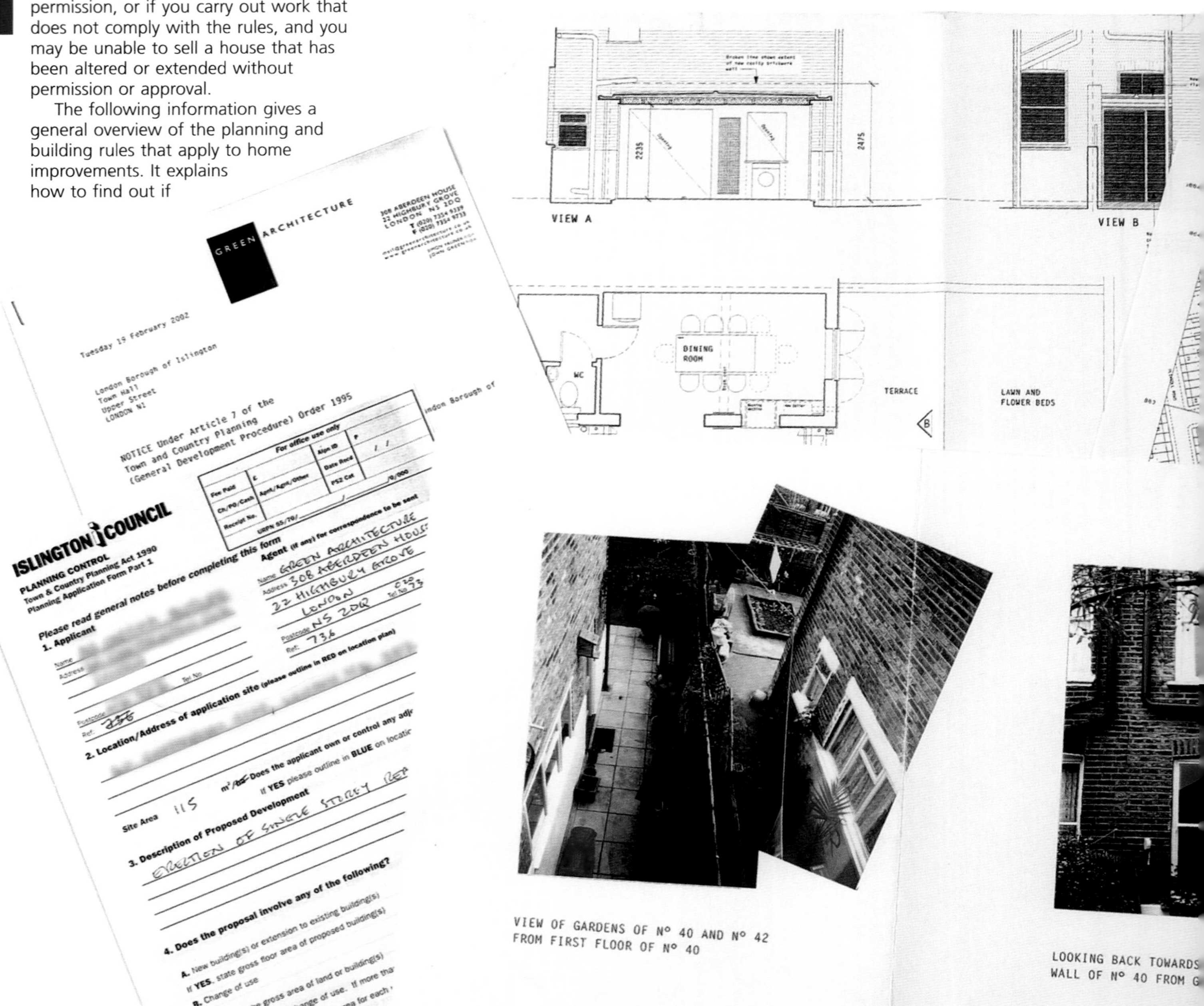

also apply online via the Government Planning Portal, through which you can also buy the site location plan you need. Your application will be considered at a planning meeting, and you should receive a decision within eight weeks. Do not start work without permission if your project needs it.

If permission is granted, it remains valid for three years (extendable to five). If it is refused, or you do not receive a decision within the time limit, you can appeal to the Planning Inspectorate (part of the Department for Communities and Local Goverment) within six months. Details of how to appeal are included in the planning application paperwork.

If you carry out work without planning permission and your local authority becomes aware of this, action is likely to be taken against you. You may be allowed to make a retrospective application for permission, but you are more likely to receive an enforcement notice requiring you to restore the property to its former condition or use. You may also be prosecuted. An enforcement notice must be issued within four years of the unauthorised work being carried out. After that time, no official action can be taken. However, you may still be found out if you try to sell the house, when enquiries before the exchange of contracts are likely to uncover your actions.

Building Regulations approval

The Building Regulations exist to ensure that buildings are structurally sound and are safe and healthy to live in. Unlike planning rules, the Regulations are applied uniformly by every local authority in England and Wales; Scotland and Northern Ireland have their own Regulations, but they are broadly similar in terms of the requirements they contain. The subject areas covered include building structure, fire safety, thermal and sound insulation, ventilation and hygiene, drainage and waste disposal, the use of fuel-burning appliances, the installation of glazing, electrical safety and the provision of facilities for disabled people.

The Regulations themselves contain only general requirements. To find out what these mean in practice, you need to get hold of a copy of the relevant Approved Document which sets out, in detail, what is required to meet the Regulations. There is a separate Approved Document for each part of the Regulations and you can buy these in printed form or download them free from the Government Planning Portal.

To apply for Building Regulations approval for an improvement project, you can take one of two routes. The first is to deliver two copies of the relevant forms and two sets of Full Plans and drawings, plus the appropriate fee, to the local authority Building Control Department. The second is to give the department what is called a Building Notice, and to provide rather less detailed information about the work to be carried out (the application forms will set out what is required).

With either route, you can start work 48 hours after delivering the documents; you no longer have to wait for approval to be granted, although you can do so if you wish. The onus is on you to ensure that the work complies with the requirements of the Regulations, which will be subject to regular inspections as it is carried out.

The advantage of waiting for formal approval of full plans is that you will receive this in writing as firm evidence that the work satisfies the Regulations. The local authority must give a decision within five weeks, unless you agree to an extension. With the building notice route, you only receive oral confirmation of compliance as each stage is inspected.

If you carry out work that does not meet the regulatory requirements and this is uncovered, you will be sent an enforcement notice giving you 28 days to amend the work. Failure to do this may result in the local authority appointing contractors to do the work and charging you. Alternatively, you may be fined a lump sum plus an extra charge for every day until you comply. An enforcement order must be issued within 12 months of the non-complying work being carried out; after that period, no official action will be taken. However, as with work done without planning permission, non-compliance may be discovered when you try to sell the property in the future.

There is a new process for dealing with non-approved work called Regularisation. It allows approval to be sought retrospectively for any work carried out since 1985.

Other restrictions

Your home improvement project may have to comply with other legal requirements apart from planning and building controls. These include restrictive covenants on your property (often inherited or imposed on new developments by the local authority) as well as the special rules for listed buildings and 'designated' areas – see opposite. Local planning authorities can also issue "Article 4 Directions" where specific control over development is required, primarily where the character of an area of acknowledged importance would be threatened. Finally, note that any work involving your plumbing and gas supply may also have to meet individual rules and regulations. These differ in England and Wales, Scotland and Ireland. See pages 496–7 for more details.

ISLINGTON
Environment & Conservation Department
Head of Planning & Transportation
Graham Loveland

Building Control Service
Building Control Manager
The District Surveyor - Parvez Aslam
Development House, 8a Barnsbury Park,
London, N1 1QQ
Tel: 020 7527 5999 (24 hr answer service)
Fax: 020 7527 5998
E-mail: building.control@islington.gov.uk
Web page: www.islington.gov.uk
This matter is being dealt with by:
Zena Blewuada
BN/02/0589

Dear Sir/Madam,

Premises:

We have received notification f... property and would like to brie...

We have a statutory responsi... and safety standards of th... structural stability, fire saf...

We inspect the building w... consultants (i.e. architec... also liaise with your bu... problems may be ove...

Upon satisfactory c... you with a "Comp... Regulations. This... solicitors if you ... on the monies owed.

An information sheet explaining bu... you have any queries do not hesitate to co...

Yours faithfully,

pp The District Surveyor

Director of Environment & Conservation Kevin O'Leary
Greenspace, Planning & Transportation, Public Protection, Street Management

BUILDING CONTROL
BC949

ISLINGTON
Building Control Services
Development House, 8a Barnsbury Park, London N1 1QQ
Tel: 020 7527 5999 Fax: 020 7527 5998

London Building Acts 1930 - 1982 and the London Building (District Surveyors' Fees) By-laws. Building Act 1984 and The Building (Prescribed Fees etc.) Regulations. The Islington Council Charges Scheme (as amended)

OFFICIAL RECEIPT

Value Added Tax (General Regulation 1972 - Regulation 21) 17/06/02

Received from ... Authenticated Receipt No. 12262

nett £ 200.00 the sum of £ 235.00

Building Fee: plus value added tax of £ 35.00

No. BN/02/0589

V.A.T Registration No. 232 7514 79

Account No ... Serial

Signed pp District Surveyor

BUILDING CONTROL

BC58/B

Making internal alterations

The most significant internal alterations you are likely to undertake are those that involve changing the layout or use of existing rooms. You may also plan to create new door or window openings, refurbish a kitchen or bathroom, or install new heating appliances. The rules and regulations that apply to each of these projects are summarised here.

Removing an internal wall

One of the most dramatic changes you can make to the interior layout of your home is to remove one or more of the internal walls to create a new room layout. The most popular choices are removing the wall between the sitting room and dining room to create a large through living room, or the wall between the dining room and kitchen to form a large open-plan cooking and eating area. Other possibilities are removing the wall between the hall and sitting room (advisable only if you have an enclosed porch to maintain an airlock to the outside world), and the wall between adjacent bedrooms to create a large master bedroom suite, perhaps allied with the provision of an en-suite bathroom.

These alterations do not need planning permission. However, Building Regulations approval is essential if the wall to be removed is load-bearing. Ground-floor walls usually support walls and floors in the storey above (or the roof structure in bungalows), and the load must instead be carried on suitable beams – usually rolled steel joists (RSJs) – set on adequate supports at each end. Upstairs walls may be load-bearing, but are more likely to be simple partitions, especially in modern houses with trussed-rafter roofs.

A load-bearing wall does more than carry a superimposed load. It also acts as a transverse brace between the walls at each end of it, and removing it may affect the stability of these walls. Furthermore, transferring the load carried by a solid wall via an RSJ to two small piers or other supports at each end may affect the existing wall foundations, which may need strengthening.

For this reason it is essential to seek professional advice from an architect, surveyor or qualified builder. He or she will ensure that a beam of the correct type, size and cross-section for the job is specified, that it is installed correctly and that it is adequately fire-proofed.

The new through room must also be adequately ventilated, with windows having an openable area equal to at least 5 per cent of the new room's floor area. This is unlikely to be a problem if each original room has a window.

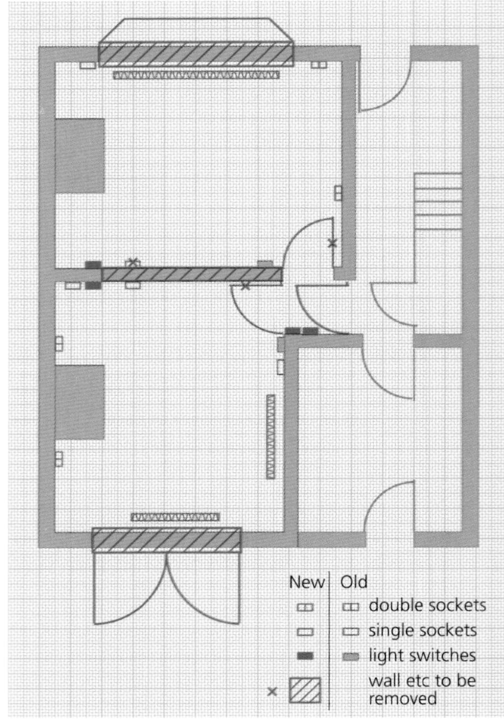

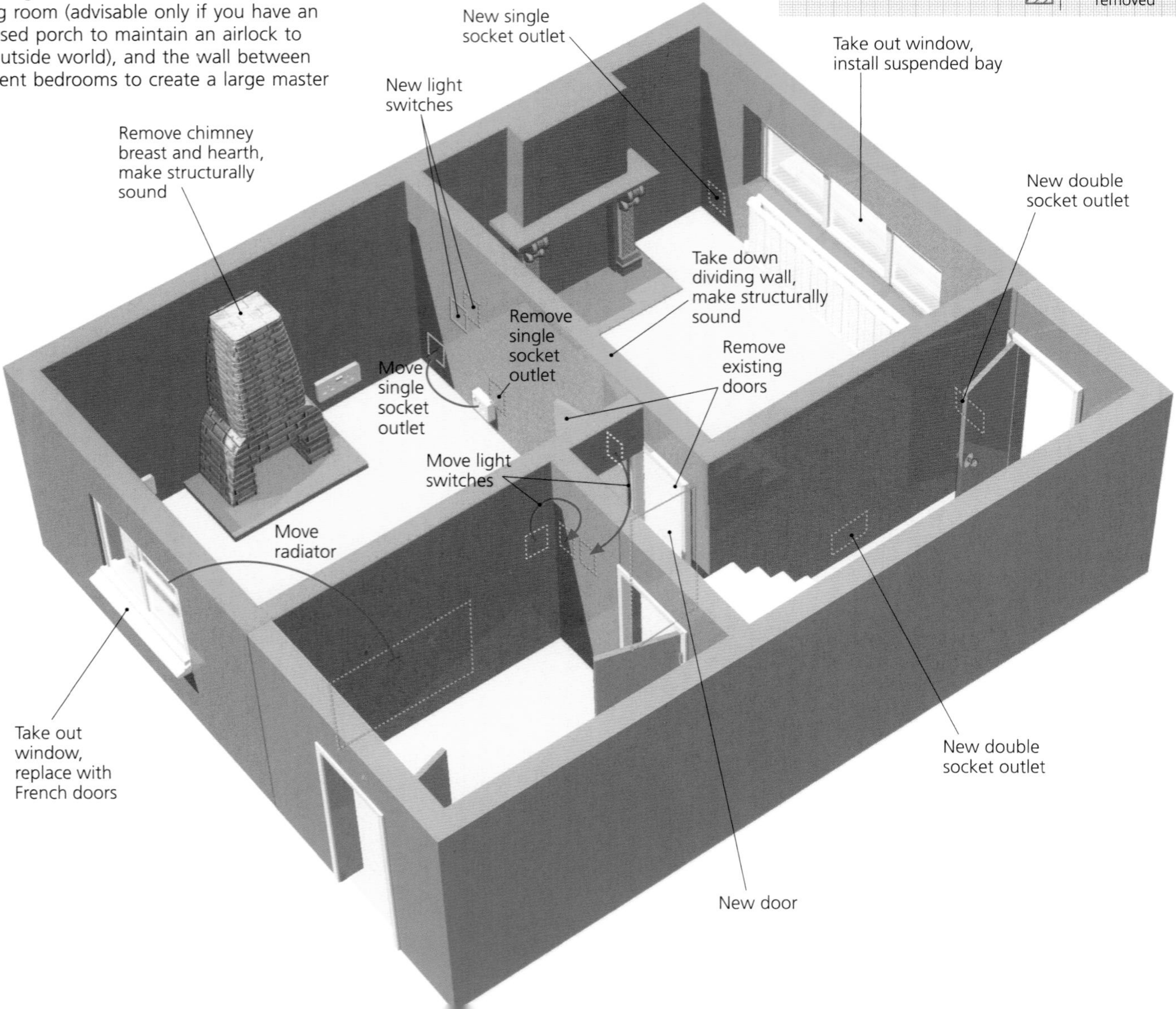

New single socket outlet
Take out window, install suspended bay
New light switches
Remove chimney breast and hearth, make structurally sound
New double socket outlet
Take down dividing wall, make structurally sound
Remove single socket outlet
Move single socket outlet
Remove existing doors
Move light switches
Move radiator
Take out window, replace with French doors
New double socket outlet
New door

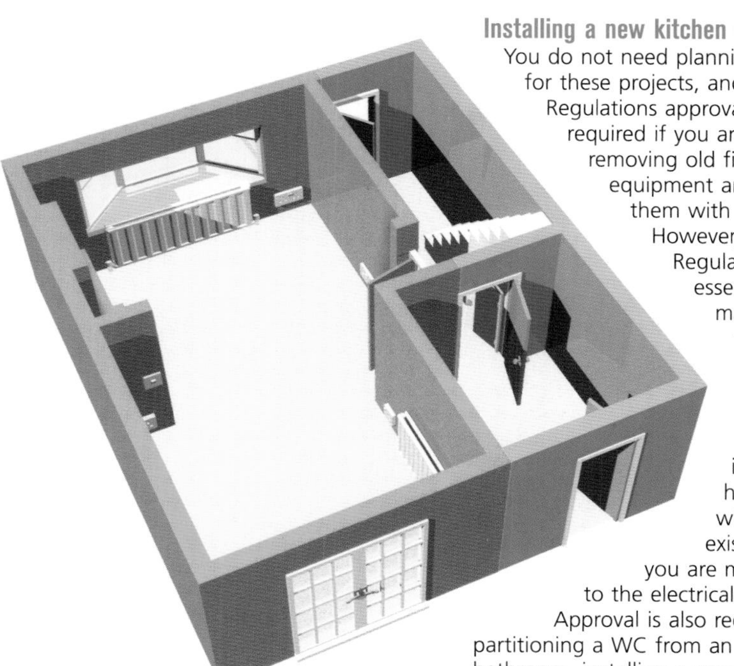

Installing a new kitchen or bathroom

You do not need planning permission for these projects, and Building Regulations approval is also not required if you are merely removing old fittings and equipment and replacing them with new ones.

However, Building Regulations approval is essential if you are making alterations to the existing arrangements for waste water disposal, if you are installing a new heating appliance where none existed before or if you are making changes to the electrical wiring.

Approval is also required if you are partitioning a WC from an existing bathroom, installing a second WC or installing a washbasin or shower cubicle in a bedroom, again because you will have to install new waste water pipes. If the siting of a new WC makes connection to existing soil pipes difficult, the Regulations allow the use of a pumped macerator unit and small-bore pipework to carry the waste water away. Finally, you must also comply with the ventilation requirements of the Regulations for new WC cubicles.

Creating new rooms

If your house has large rooms, you may be able to make better use of the space by building a partition wall across one or more of them. A downstairs room could be partitioned to create a second sitting room or a home office, while an upstairs room could be divided to create an extra bedroom for a child or a second bathroom.

Again, planning permission is not needed, but some requirements of the Building Regulations will have to be met – in particular as far as ventilation of the two new rooms and the provision of sound insulation between them is concerned. Each new room must have a window with an openable area equal to 5 per cent of its floor area. The new rooms are not allowed to share an existing window. If one of the rooms does not need a window (a bathroom, for example), it must be provided with mechanical ventilation via an extractor fan. You will also need Building Regulations approval for the waste water disposal from new bathroom facilities.

Providing access to the new rooms may involve the creation of a corridor in one of them, with some loss of usable floor space. This is essential for bedrooms, which should always have individual access, but may not matter for a home office or similar use.

Changing room layouts

You may be able to make better use of your available floor space by a combination of removing and repositioning walls. If this involves any load-bearing walls, follow the advice given above and consult a professional for advice on finding the best solution. You will need Building Regulations approval for any structural work involved, but planning permission is not required.

Creating a new door or window opening

You may need planning permission for a new door or window opening that will project beyond a wall facing the road. Planning permission will almost certainly be needed if the house is in a conservation area. If the new opening is in a load-bearing wall, you will need Building Regulations approval – this will ensure that the lintel used to span the new opening is the correct type and size. It will also make sure that door and window openings in external walls are correctly damp-proofed, especially if they are of cavity construction.

Fitting new heating appliances

Building Regulations approval is needed for the installation of a new fuel-burning appliance such as a boiler or room heater, but not if it is a direct replacement for an existing appliance. Approval is also needed if its installation requires the building of a new flue and you may have to update the central heating controls. The replacement of an existing vented heating system by an unvented (sealed) system also requires approval. Planning permission may be needed for the construction of a new external chimney or flue, and for the installation of a gas or oil storage tank on the property.

WORK INVOLVING A PARTY WALL

The oddly-named Party Wall etc. Act 1996 covers any construction or repair work carried out on a party wall (one shared with another property, as in a semi-detached or terraced house). It requires you to give your neighbour notice of your intentions, and gives him or her the right to agree or disagree with your proposals. It is best to engage the services of a chartered surveyor, who will take a schedule, or assessment, of the condition of the party wall before work starts, so that any disputes can be resolved over the way the work is carried out and the repair of any damage it causes.

Failure to observe the provisions of the Act can result in an injunction being served on you by your neighbour, preventing work from proceeding until agreement is reached.

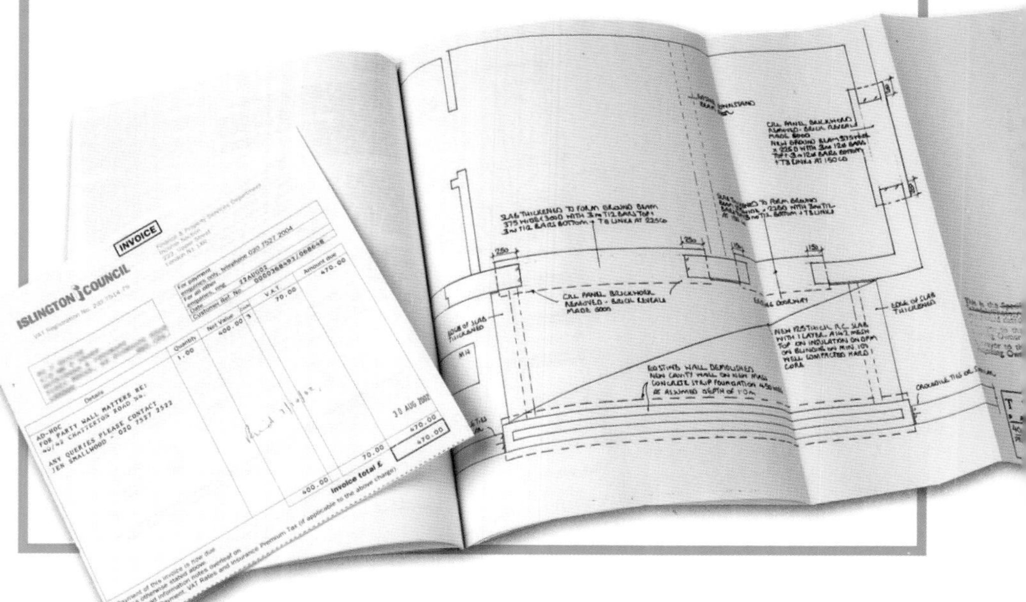

Making external alterations

Changes that affect the outside of your house tend to be rather more dramatic than anything you are likely to undertake indoors, and the rules and regulations affecting what you can and cannot do are much more specific. Here are the things you need to consider for small scale projects and alterations. Larger projects are dealt with on the following pages.

Very old or unusual trees may be protected by a tree preservation order. This prevents you from lopping or cutting down the tree and may restrict your plans for a home extension or conservatory. Your solicitor should tell you about any tree preservation orders on your property when you purchase the house, or you can check with the local planning authority.

Outbuildings

You can put up all sorts of outbuildings such as sheds, summerhouses and greenhouses on your property without the need for planning permission, so long as they meet the following conditions:

- they are not for residential use;
- they are not in front of the building line (any wall of the house facing a highway);
- they are not more than 4m high if they have a dual-pitched roof or 3m for other types of roof;
- have a maximum height of 2.5m if within 2m of the boundary;
- their construction does not result in more than 50 per cent of the total site being occupied by buildings (excluding the house).

Different rules apply for listed buildings and homes in 'designated' areas – see Box on page 482.

Outbuildings are exempt from Building Regulations control so long as their floor area does not exceed $30m^2$ and they contain no sleeping accommodation. Like garages, they should be built of incombustible materials if sited within 1m of a boundary.

Aerials and satellite TV dishes

TV and radio aerials do not need planning permission. Nor do satellite dishes, provided:

- you have no more than two attached to your house;
- a single dish is no more than 1m large (600mm on a chimney stack);
- a second dish is no more than 600mm large if you already have a 1m dish;
- the dish is no higher than the roof (or chimney stack if you have one).

Permission is always needed to install a satellite dish on a listed building or on a house in a 'designated' area see Box on page 482.

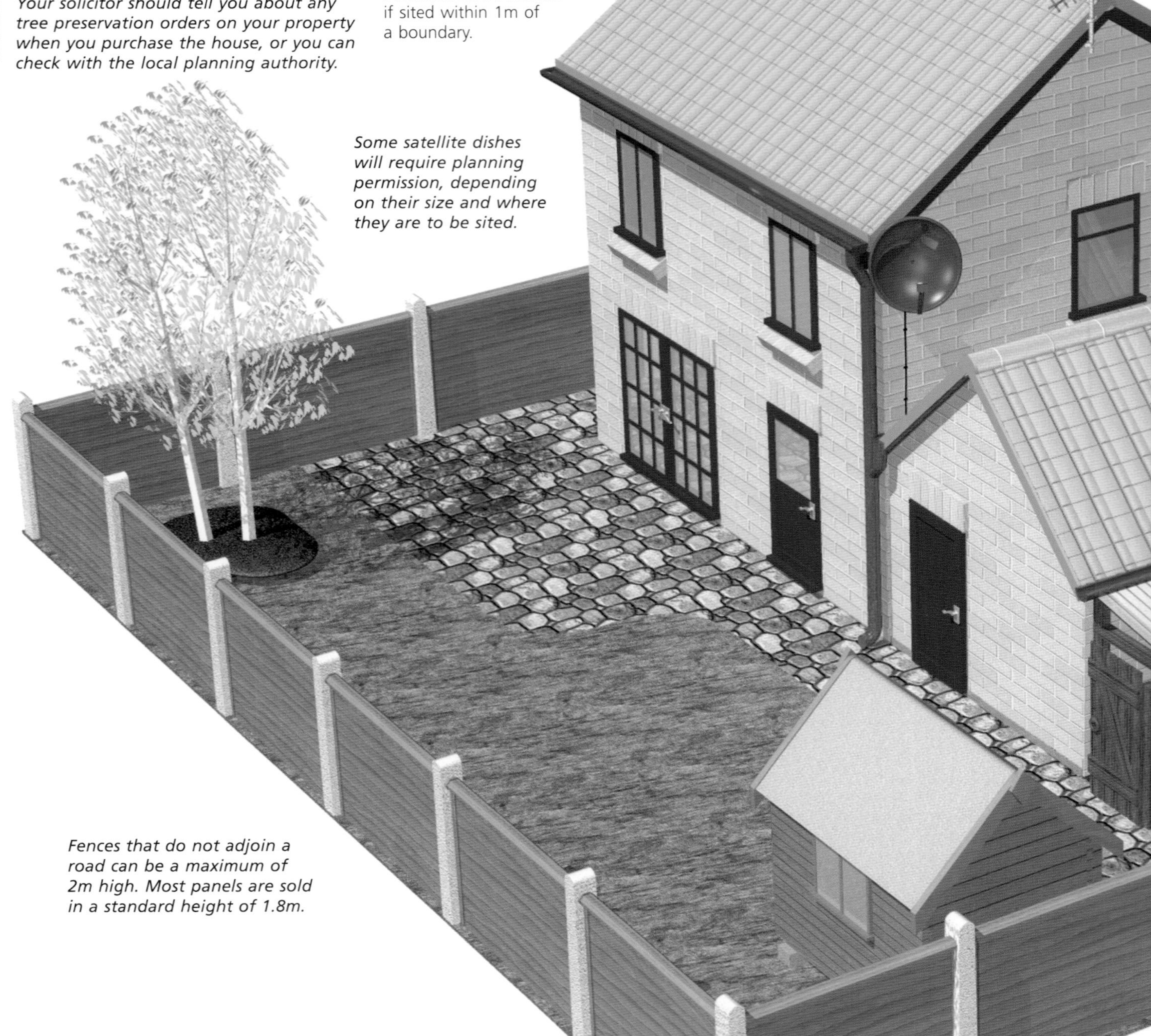

Some satellite dishes will require planning permission, depending on their size and where they are to be sited.

Fences that do not adjoin a road can be a maximum of 2m high. Most panels are sold in a standard height of 1.8m.

Garages

If a new garage is built attached to the house, it counts as an extension and the planning rules on page 488 apply. Garages that are not attached to the house are counted as outbuildings – and the planning rules on the opposite page apply.

A detached garage does not need Building Regulations approval, provided it has a floor area of less than 30m² (or 15m² if less than 1m from a boundary unless constructed from non-combustible materials), but an attached garage will have to meet Building Regulations requirements for foundations, flooring, walls below ground, new electric circuits and provision for disposing of rainwater. Special rules apply to attached carports (open on at least two sides), which are exempt from Building Regulations provided they are less than 30m² in floor area.

Many houses have a garage that is either within the structure of the house or is attached to it. Such a garage is a prime target for conversion into additional living space, especially if it already has access to it direct from the house (see page 495 for more details). You generally do not need planning permission for the conversion, but you may need Building Regulations approval to ensure that it meets the thermal insulation requirements for habitable rooms. The existing building may not have cavity walls, and will certainly have no floor insulation (or roof insulation if it is attached rather than integral). Check with your local authority before proceeding.

Porches

Porches count as home extensions for planning permission purposes. A porch can be built without the need for planning permission if:

- it has a floor area of 3m² or less;
- its roof is no more than 3m high;
- its outermost wall is at least 2m from any boundary between your property and a road or public footpath.

Check with your local authority if you live in a listed building or your home is in a 'designated' area – see Box on page 482. Porches are subject to the safety glazing and electrical safety requirements of the Building Regulations but are otherwise exempt from building control.

Hard paving

There is no restriction on having patios or other hard-paved areas around your houses, provided the rainwater drains off into the surrounding garden. But there are restrictions on paving over front gardens or installing (or replacing) driveways.

For both of these, you will need planning permission for a paved area of more than 5m², unless you use materials that allow the water to pass through the paving into the ground (permeable block paving, porous asphalt or gravel) or arrange the drainage so that rainwater is taken to your garden rather than the road. See page 448 for paving materials.

Note that if you are installing a driveway for the first time, you should inform your local council Highways Department, who may need to strengthen the pavement or arrange for a new dropped kerb.

You may need Building Regulations approval if new paving makes access more difficult – by introducing steps, say.

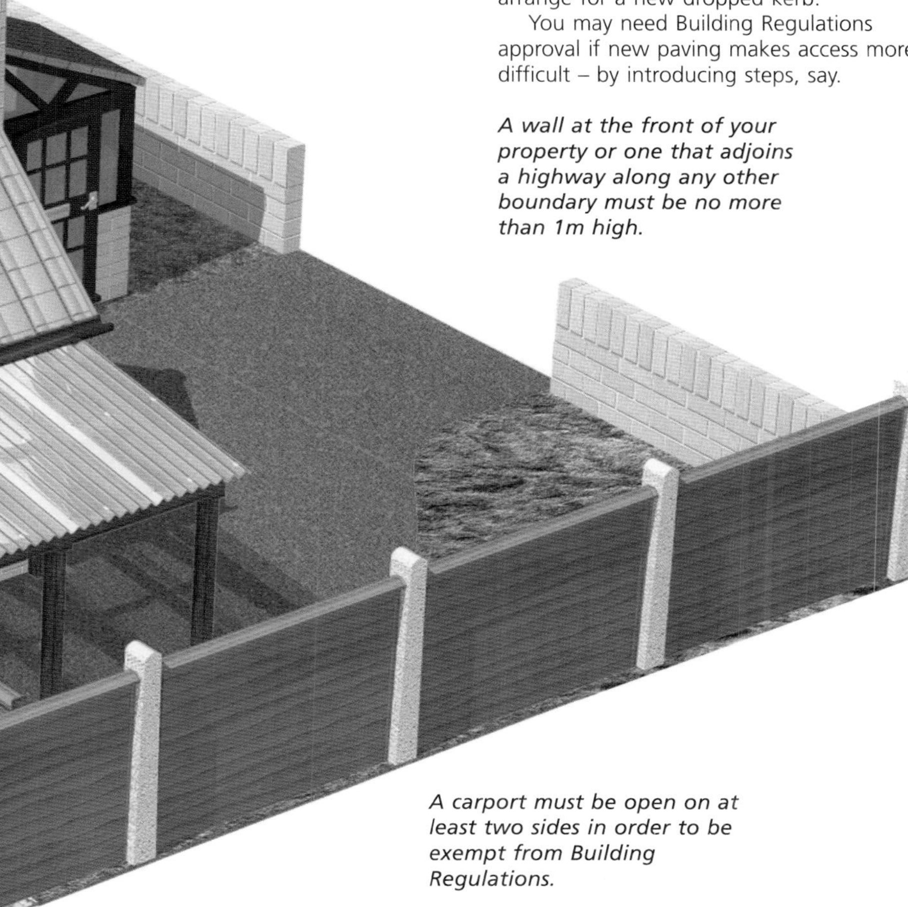

A wall at the front of your property or one that adjoins a highway along any other boundary must be no more than 1m high.

A carport must be open on at least two sides in order to be exempt from Building Regulations.

Fuel storage tanks

Fuel storage tanks do not need planning permission as long as they do not exceed 3500 litres capacity, are not in front of the house and have a maximum height of 3m (2.5m if within 2m of a boundary). Storage tanks for listed building will, however, need permission and there are special rules for 'designated' areas – see Box on page 482.

Building Regulations approval is always required, but new oil and LPG storage tanks are usually installed as part of a complete central heating system, and the work must be carried out by qualified fitters who can ensure that the required safety features are included.

Swimming pools

A swimming pool with any associated structures counts as an outbuilding, so the rules described opposite apply. You will always need planning permission if you live in a listed house or 'designated' area (see Box on page 482), but otherwise only if you want the pool to be in front of the house facing the highway or if it will take up more than half your garden (when added to other extensions and outbuildings).

Building Regulations approval will be needed if you are installing any kind of electric circuit outside (perhaps to provide heating of the pool), but you should inform your water supply company if you intend to install a swimming pool. They will probably insist that you have a water meter installed (if you don't already have one) or will apply an extra charge if your water is unmetered.

Walls and fences

You need planning permission to erect a wall or fence more than 1m high along a boundary adjoining a highway, or more than 2m high along any other boundary. Permission is also needed for any walls or fences round the boundary of a listed building or on land subject to an "Article 4 Direction", which restricts the development permitted (see page 483). However, walls and fences are exempt from Building Regulations control. Hedges are exempt from all control, but the local authority has the right to require the owner to cut back any hedge (or tree) that endangers or obstructs the passage of vehicles or pedestrians, or obstructs or interferes with the view of drivers of vehicles or the light from a street lamp.

Also see:

Annexes – page 486
Basements and cellars – page 494
Conservatories – page 492
Home extensions – page 488
Home offices – page 496
Loft conversions – page 490
Replacement windows – page 211

Home extensions

A home extension is the most popular solution to the problem of a house with insufficient living space. It can provide extra living rooms, extra bedrooms or any other type of space you need such as a bigger kitchen or a home office. The only requirement is that your property has enough free land on which to build it.

Rules and regulations

An extension is probably the biggest home improvement project anyone is likely to consider, and it is more likely to be placed in the hands of a firm of builders than to be tackled as a DIY project. All extensions must comply fully with Building Regulations and it is the householder's responsibility to ensure that proper application for approval has been made, although the actual application may be made by your architect, surveyor or builder – see page 483 for details of application procedures.

As far as planning permission is concerned, a home extension is covered by the rules of permitted development in most circumstances. This means that it can be built without the need to apply for planning permission, so long as the following restrictions are met:

- no more than half the area of land around the original house (as it stood on 1 July 1948 if it was built before that date) should be covered by additions or other buildings;
- the extension must not project in front of any house wall facing a highway;
- the extension must not be higher than the original roof of the house;
- the depth of a single-storey rear extension must be no more than 3m for an attached house and 4m for a detached house;
- the height of a single storey rear extension should be no more than 4m;
- the depth of a rear extension more than one storey high should be no more than 3m, including the ground floor;
- the maximum eaves height should be 3m within 2m of the boundary;
- the maximum eaves and ridge height must be no higher than existing house;
- side extensions must be single storey, no more than 4m in height and no more than half that of the original house in width;
- two-storey extensions must be no closer than 7m to the rear boundary;
- the roof pitch of two-storey extensions must match those of the existing house;
- materials used must be similar in appearance to the existing house;
- no verandas, balconies or raised platforms;
- side facing windows on upper floors must be obscure-glazed with openings 1.7m above the floor;
- for homes in 'designated' areas (see Box on page 482), extensions must be to the rear and single storey only, and exteriors cannot be clad.

Planning permission must be sought for all other kinds of extension. You will need Listed Building Consent to extend a listed building (and also to demolish parts of a building in a conservation area).

Planning points

A successful home extension requires a lot of careful planning. The first stage is to work out what type of extra space you need. The top priority might be more bedroom accommodation, to cope with a new baby or to separate children too old to share a room. You might need more living space so family members can pursue different leisure interests in peace. A bigger kitchen, a separate utility room, an extra bathroom or second WC could all be welcome additions.

Where to build

The site and size of an extension depends on your requirements. An extra living room or a bigger kitchen is best provided by a single-storey extension, added to the side or rear of the property according to where there is the most available space. If you need extra bedrooms, consider a two-storey extension to the side or rear. This could provide extra living space or a garage with a bedroom above, or a second extra

bedroom could be created on the ground floor of the extension.

If you cannot build outwards because of the constraints of the site, your only alternative is to build upwards. A loft conversion (pages 490–1) is the obvious solution, but you may also be able to add a second storey to an existing single-storey extension if its foundations and structure are strong enough. In both cases you will lose some existing floor space in providing access to the new rooms.

Gaining access

The next important consideration is how to gain access to the extension from the house. In the case of a single-storey extension this is unlikely to be a problem. Existing door or window openings can often be used, or new ones created if this suits the room layouts better. In a two-storey extension, access upstairs can be more difficult to plan successfully. Some loss of floor space is inevitable, since access through existing bedrooms is not practicable and may not be allowed. The use of lightweight timber partition walls makes dividing up the existing and new spaces easier, and imposes no restrictions on where the walls are sited.

Professional advice

At this point in the process you may feel that you are not getting the best possible result out of the space available. Now is the time to hand over your preliminary ideas to a professional. An architect or surveyor will be used to finding solutions to apparently intractable problems of space management. He or she will also be adept at making your extension blend in with the structure of the existing house – by matching walling and roofing materials, doors and windows and so on. You can employ a professional just to draw up the plans you will need to submit to your local authority, and leave the building work to your builder.

Alternatively, your architect or surveyor can oversee the entire project from start to finish. This is a more expensive option, but relieves you of the responsibility of finding and managing competent contractors to carry out the work.

When you are adding a major home extension, paying for the services of an architect or surveyor can be money well spent. Taking professional advice may help to smooth the process of obtaining planning permission and pre-empt potential problems throughout the course of the project. See Chapter 14 for more details.

A new extension should blend in with the existing house, mirroring construction methods and using the same materials. Sympathetic designs will be much more likely to win planning approval than proposals that are out of character with the surrounding properties.

Loft conversions

Most homes have a loft, but it is usually used only as storage space. Converting it to habitable rooms could add up to 30 per cent of usable floor area in a two-storey building, and twice as much in a bungalow. A loft conversion will cost less than a home extension of the same floor area, because the shell of the extension – the roof and the loft floor – is already in place.

Rules and regulations

Loft conversions do not need planning permission, provided that the conversion is kept within the existing roof lines. But any extension of the roof (to give extra headroom) is limited to $50m^3$ ($40m^3$ in a terraced house) and dormer windows are not allowed on roofs facing a highway (you must use flat roof windows instead). Roof extensions must match the existing house and not be higher than the existing roof. Roof extensions are not allowed in listed buildings or houses in 'designated' areas – see Box on page 482.

Loft conversions need Building Regulations approval to ensure that the work complies with the requirements for structural stability, safe access, ventilation, wiring, insulation, fireproofing, waste disposal (if it will contain a bathroom or WC) and means of escape in the event of fire. Because of fire safety, you must submit Full Plans for a loft conversion in a two-storey building; you cannot use the Building Notice scheme (although you can for a loft conversion in a bungalow).

Planning points

If you think that a loft conversion is the solution to your space shortage, the first thing you need to do is to assess its feasibility, and this depends on how the roof was constructed.

The importance of roof construction

In houses built before the 1960s, the roof was built up on site from a framework of rafters to support the roof covering, purlins to tie the rafters together, and struts to brace the purlins against the loft floor joists and any internal load-bearing walls. The existing loft area may look awkward and cluttered, but the structure can generally be adapted to make space for a new room. This is done by relocating struts and other supports to create a clear floor area, and by inserting dormer windows if there is not enough full-height headroom over this floor area. You must employ an architect, surveyor or structural engineer to plan this work, so that the alterations do not weaken the roof structure.

Houses built since about 1960 usually have roofs constructed using prefabricated roof trusses. These are triangular frames that span the outer walls of the house, eliminating the need for internal load-bearing walls. Because of the way the roof trusses are assembled and erected, you cannot remove any of their components without seriously weakening the roof structure. Altering the structure to accommodate a loft room is therefore likely to be difficult and expensive, if not impossible. However, you may be fortunate in having a modern house built with loft conversion in mind, using so-called attic trusses instead of conventional ones with their W-shaped bracing. Attic trusses are made from thicker, wider timber components so they can carry floor loads as well as the weight of the roof covering, and they can be adapted readily to allow for the insertion of roof or dormer windows.

Non-habitable or habitable?

The end use to which you want to put a loft conversion will dictate what is involved in creating it. A simple playroom in the loft is deemed to be a 'non-habitable room', and the conversion will involve little more than creating access using a loft ladder or a space-saver staircase, framing and boarding out the roof space and perhaps adding a roof window or two.

Fitting roof windows is an easy way to allow light into a converted loft and, in most cases, does not need planning permission. This kind of conversion leaves you with limited head height towards the edges of the room, but this is useful space for storage or a low seat.

FIRE SAFETY

When you are planning a loft conversion, particularly in a two-storey building, there are fire safety requirements that must be satisfied. The loft windows must provide a means of escape in the event of fire. The Building Regulations require an opening window that is at least 450mm high and 450mm wide, with an openable area of at least $0.33m^2$. The bottom of the openable area must be no more than 1100mm high. This will allow the use of ladders for rescue purposes. In addition, the stairwell leading to the new top storey must be fireproofed, with self-closing devices fitted to any doors opening onto the stairwell and a fire door leading to the new loft rooms. Finally, the loft floor must have 30-minute fire resistance, and interlinked mains-powered smoke detectors must be fitted on each floor of the house.

Conversion to habitable rooms – an extra bedroom and bathroom, a teenager's bedsitter or a home office, for example – is a much more complex project. The conversion will have to comply with all relevant aspects of the Building Regulations. Providing suitable staircase access may involve creating a dormer window over the new staircase to give adequate headroom, or else sacrificing existing floor space in a room below. The existing loft floor will almost certainly have to be strengthened to support the load that the new loft rooms will impose, either by installing deeper joists between the existing ones or by the use of rolled steel joists (RSJs) to support the new floor. The new rooms will require natural light and ventilation (and possibly mechanical ventilation in bathrooms and WCs), thermal, sound and fire insulation and a full range of wiring, plumbing and heating services.

Professional advice

Because of the potential complexity of the job, it is essential to enlist professional help in the design of the conversion at the planning stage. You could employ an architect or surveyor, either just to produce plans for your builder to execute, or to oversee the whole project. Alternatively, you could rely on a builder experienced in loft conversion work, or hand the whole project over to one of the many specialist loft conversion companies now operating nationwide.

A dormer window juts out of the existing roof line (above) and cannot be installed without planning permission. Whatever your window choice, you will need Building Regulations approval for the conversion work, which includes removing supporting struts in the roof (left) and installing a staircase for access (below).

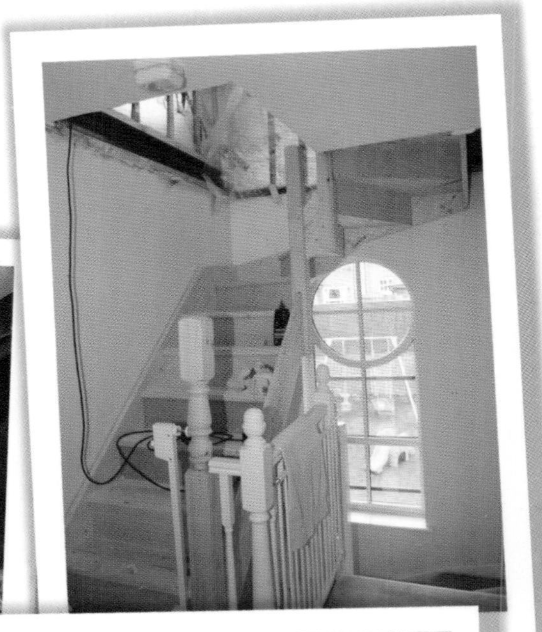

Depending on the construction of your roof, you will need to add new supports (above) to take its weight. Always employ an architect or structural engineer to help you and to make sure that the finished result (right) is in keeping with the rest of the property.

Conservatories

A conservatory is one of the most popular home improvement projects. It can provide extra living space for much less than the cost of a conventional extension – space that can be used as a sitting or dining area, a play area and, of course, somewhere to grow plants that would not thrive in a British garden.

Rules and regulations

For planning purposes, a conservatory counts as an extension and the rules on page 488 apply. The structure of a ground-level conservatory does not need Building Regulations approval, provided it has a floor area of less than 30m² and at least half the walls and three-quarters of the roof is glazed. To be exempt, a conservatory must also be separated from the house by external-quality walls, doors or windows (including French doors) and should have an independent heating system with separate temperature and on/off controls. However, its installation must comply with certain parts of the Regulations:

- any new doorway created in the external wall of the existing house to lead into the conservatory should meet Part A structural requirements;
- glass used for doors (and panels alongside doors) and low-level glazing (up to 800mm) must be safety glass complying with Part N (see page 14);
- a new electric wiring circuit in the conservatory must comply with Part P (see Chapter 9).

Although a conservatory should have adequate ventilation, Building Regulations for this only apply if it has a floor area of more than 30m².

A specialist conservatory company will help you to plan and visualise your project and may also carry out the installation.

Planning points

A conservatory is usually sited at the back of the house. However, the layout of your property, the arrangement of your rooms and the way the house faces may make a site at the side a better choice. The amount of space you have available will dictate how big a conservatory you can build. Size costs, since conservatories are designed on a modular basis, but it is better to err on the large size than to rue the lack of space once you have fitted out and furnished your new room.

Windows

Modern conservatories have developed chiefly from the replacement window business. This means that conservatory style – at the mass-market end of the range, at least – is based on the design of the multiple window frames that make up the walls of the building. These may be made from hardwood or PVCu, and styles range from the plain and unadorned to the elaborate mock-Victorian. There is a wide choice of door and window designs, with a variety of opening mechanisms to allow for ventilation. When choosing them, pay particular attention to the level of security they offer.

Shading

Conservatories can become very hot in summer, and roof and window blinds are essential to keep out the strongest sunlight and reduce glare. They also create privacy if you use your conservatory after dark.

The conservatory walls may be full or part-glazed. Part-glazed walls may have solid PVCu infill panels down to ground level, or may be designed to sit on a dwarf brick cavity wall forming the perimeter of the building. The latter is the only viable option on a sloping site. It also allows for the creating of internal window sills, and provides a convenient mounting surface for radiators or other heaters.

A concrete slab raises the floor level of the conservatory and provides a firm foundation for the structure (above left and left). A cavity tray is inserted into the existing house wall (above) to make a watertight seal where the conservatory will butt up to the house.

HELPFUL TIP

After a heavy snowfall, snow slipping from the roof of the house could damage the conservatory. Before the conservatory is installed, a simple snow guard can be fitted to the eaves of the house to protect the glazed roof.

The roof

The conservatory roof can be transparent or translucent. Glass roofs must be made of safety glass, and sealed unit double glazing is essential if the building is to be used in winter. Translucent polycarbonate roofs use twin or triple-walled sheeting for insulation. Both types can incorporate openable roof lights for ventilation. If possible, the roof should be designed with a slope of at least 25°; shallower slopes than this do not clean themselves very efficiently, and tend to collect algae and wind-blown debris which you will need to remove regularly.

Internal access

Access to the conservatory is likely to be via existing doors leading off a living room. If the siting of the conservatory requires a new opening to be created, it may be possible to turn an existing window into a door opening with a minimum of structural work. If a new opening is needed, you must ensure that its construction meets the requirements of the Building Regulations.

Low cavity brick-and-block walls (below) support the framework for the glazing (below right) and will also provide a fixing for wall-mounted heaters or radiators if required. When it is complete, this conservatory (far right) will connect the house and garage and provide valuable extra living space.

Site and situation

There are several potential site problems with conservatories that will need to be addressed at the planning stage.

A sloping site

If the garden slopes up from the house, a level base will have to be excavated, with retaining walls built to keep the garden at bay. If it slopes down, you could consider building the conservatory floor at a lower level and providing steps down into it from the house. A better solution is to give it a suspended floor (timber, or a concrete post-and-beam floor). This avoids having to back-fill a substantial area of ground to create a traditional solid concrete slab floor.

Obstructions

There may be obstructions, such as a soil pipe or rainwater downpipes, on the house wall against which the conservatory is to be built. Installers can generally get round these by adapting the structure or, in the case of downpipes, by relocating them. Another possible obstruction is a flue from a boiler. Old-style round flue pipes can be accommodated with suitable heat-proofing, but balanced flue boilers will have to be repositioned so their flues do not discharge into the conservatory. Lastly, any manhole covers within the proposed base area will have to be built up to the new floor level and then fitted with special double-seal covers so they can be accessed if necessary.

Access for maintenance

Think about the question of future access for maintenance to walls, windows and gutters above the site of the conservatory. It is worth considering replacing windows above the new structure with a type that can be cleaned from inside the house. Some conservatory glazing bars are strong enough to support crawl boards; if they are not, removable roof panels will have to be incorporated in the design to allow the use of ladders for high-level maintenance work.

Basements and cellars

If your house has a basement or cellar that is at present used solely for storage, it may be possible to convert the space and create some useful extra living room.

A basement space is ideal for recreational uses – as a home workshop, a music room, a gym or a children's playroom – and can also be used to provide valuable storage space or extra facilities such as a utility room or an extra bath or shower room. It could even form an underground garage if providing access to it from the road is feasible.

Rules and regulations

Converting a basement or cellar into a living space will not normally need planning permission unless you live in a listed building or a 'designated' area – see Box on page 482. The exceptions are where you are creating a separate unit, where a new light well is being added or where a domestic cellar is to be put to commercial use.

Building Regulations, on the other hand, apply in full – especially those relating to fire escape, ventilation, ceiling height, damp-proofing, electric wiring and water supply. Foundation or underpinning work may also be needed.

Planning points

Basements were built mainly in town houses to act as service areas – kitchens, sculleries and store areas – for live-in staff. They generally have full-height ceilings and extend beneath the whole ground floor of the building. They receive some natural light and ventilation via an excavated well next to the house walls, and often have an external staircase within the well to allow entry to the below-stairs area for tradesmen's deliveries, as well as an internal one for access to the house. This makes them particularly suitable for conversion to single-storey flats.

Cellars are often built only under part of the house, and have access from within it either via a steep staircase beneath the

Basements often have an existing light well and window (top) and full-height ceilings and may already have internal access from the main house, making them easy to convert into habitable rooms. By echoing the window style of the rest of the house (centre) the space within can be made light and airy, and become a comfortable space for a television room or playroom (right).

main flight of stairs, or through a trap door with steps or a wall ladder below it. In Victorian houses, the cellar often extends beneath the pavement, where a circular coal hole covered by a steel plate allowed coal deliveries to be made directly into the cellar below.

Cellars generally have no natural light or ventilation, low ceilings and often a serious damp problem.

Certificate of Treatment
by
London & Home Counties
TIMBER PRESERVATION
This is to Certify that
Address and Location of Property
Exact Description of Area Treated Ground Floor: Kitchen/Diner
As per Survey Report & Specification dated 23 September 1999 - T5167
has been properly treated in accordance with the schedule submitted, using high grade materials, against rising damp (injection of new DPC only).
and is guaranteed against further attack from this type of
RISING DAMPNESS / [redacted]
(subject to the provisions detailed on the back of this document) for a period of
30 YEARS from 11 October 1999.
Signed on behalf of the Company by
p.p. LONDON & HOME COUNTIES TIMBER PRESERVATION
THIS CERTIFICATE IS TRANSFERABLE.

Dealing with damp

Damp is likely to be the biggest concern when converting a basement or cellar. It is worth having a professional damp survey done to discover the extent of the problem, and to call in expert contractors to tackle it. They will lay a new floor surface over a damp-proof membrane, and will either strip and re-plaster the walls with a damp-resistant three-coat plaster system or (if the damp problem is serious) use a full-scale tanking procedure to waterproof the structure.

Access by stairs

Other parts of a basement that will need attention may include restoring external stairs and stairwells, replacing an internal staircase to comply with the Building Regulations, and replacing old timber windows, door frames and doors. A cellar will almost certainly need a new staircase and a ceiling – cellars rarely had one.

Adding services

As far as services are concerned, a basement may already have wiring and plumbing facilities, but they will probably need updating, and it is unlikely to have central heating. It may be easier to install individual room heaters than to extend the existing heating system. A cellar will probably have just electric lighting, so new circuits will have to be installed. The area will also need heating and some form of mechanical ventilation. In both basements and cellars, pumped macerator units can be used to take waste water from new plumbing appliances to the existing soil pipe or stack.

Garage conversions

If you have an integral or attached garage, there is obvious potential to convert it into additional living space. This is even more attractive if there is already access directly into the garage from the house.

Unless you have space on site to build an additional detached garage or plenty of room for off-street parking, converting your garage may leave you with a parking problem. It is also worth considering that the conversion may deter some buyers when you come to sell your house – most home-buyers say they want a garage. However, this kind of conversion is relatively easy for a buyer to reverse.

Rules and regulations

You do not need planning permission to convert a garage to living accommodation unless you live in a listed building or in a 'designated' area (see Box on page 492) or where there is specific restriction on garage conversions. Nor is Building Regulations approval required if all you intend to create is a non-habitable room – for use as a workshop, as a home for kitchen appliances, or as a playroom for your children.

However, if you intend to create a habitable room, you will need to satisfy the Building Regulations requirements concerning damp-proofing (the floor of an attached garage will probably not incorporate a damp-proof membrane, although an integral garage should have one) and insulation. You will also need approval for new waste water disposal arrangements from a washing machine or other water-using appliance and for new electric wiring. The garage will also need adequate ventilation (openable windows and 'trickle' ventilators).

Planning points

Non-habitable use

If the garage is to be put to non-habitable purposes, the only major job you will need to carry out is to damp-proof the floor and lay some sort of finished surface over the existing concrete slab. The best method is to apply two coats of a liquid damp-proofing compound, and to apply a fine surface screed over it to create a smooth, hard and dry floor surface. Once this has dried out, you can lay any type of floorcovering over it. The garage walls can be given a couple of coats of exterior-quality emulsion paint or masonry paint. You will also need to put up a new plasterboard ceiling in an attached garage, which will not have one.

Habitable use

In order to satisfy the Building Regulations requirements for habitable use, the floor must be damp-proofed in the same way, and must also incorporate some floor insulation. This can be done by applying a liquid damp-proofing treatment as described above, and then placing rigid polystyrene insulation boards 50 or 75mm thick on top of the floor slab. A floating chipboard floor can then be laid over the insulation, ready to receive the new floorcovering.

Integral garages will have cavity walls, so will just need dry-lining with plasterboard to create a suitable surface for decorating. An attached garage is likely to have walls only 100mm thick and these can be insulated by incorporating insulation batts between the dry-lining boards and the garage walls. A vapour barrier must be included behind the plasterboard to prevent condensation from forming in the insulation.

Changing the garage door

Whether you replace the garage door opening with a large window or a wall with window and new door, Building Regulations approval will be needed for the foundations. You may also wish to add other windows to the side or rear walls of the garage, especially if you want to partition the space within the garage. If there is no access directly into the garage, you will have to create an opening at a convenient point in the house wall. Remember that any new openings need Building Regulations approval to ensure that the lintels used are suitable.

Adding services

Finally, you will need to extend your house wiring to provide better lighting and a range of socket outlets in the conversion. You will also need to consider how to heat the new room – ideally by extending the house's downstairs heating circuit, or by using individual room heaters. If plumbing facilities are to be included, supply pipework will have to be extended from the house and provision made for getting rid of waste water.

Home offices

Working from home is becoming increasingly common and more and more people are looking at ways of providing a self-contained office space within their homes. Some of the possible options are outlined below.

Rules and regulations

In principle you need to apply for planning permission to work from home, since this counts as a change from purely residential to part-business use. However, many local authorities are prepared to allow home working without official permission so long as there are no outward signs of a business being run from the premises. Formal permission will be needed only if you have regular deliveries or visitors, if you store or sell goods or materially alter the character of the house or street. It is best to contact your local authority planning department for their views if you plan to start working from home.

Whether any Building Regulations approval is needed depends on the scale of the work proposed. See the options below for cross-references to specific conversions.

Conversion options

These are the most popular choices for creating a home office.

Converting a spare room This is most likely to be a bedroom, but could be another under-used room such as the dining room if there is space elsewhere in the house for meals to be taken. Partitioning a large living room is another option, but may involve creating a new window opening to give light and ventilation to the new work space. See pages 484–5 for more details.

Converting the loft This is an ideal solution if the roof structure is suitable for conversion, since the office will be separate from the rest of the house and no loss of existing living space will be involved (apart from that required for access to the loft). The conversion will need Building Regulations approval. See pages 490–1.

Converting a garage This is a viable option if you are prepared to relegate the car to the driveway or the road. An integral or attached garage is ideal, especially if it has direct access to the house, see page 495. A detached garage is less suitable, especially as far as extending power and telecommunications facilities to the building is concerned.

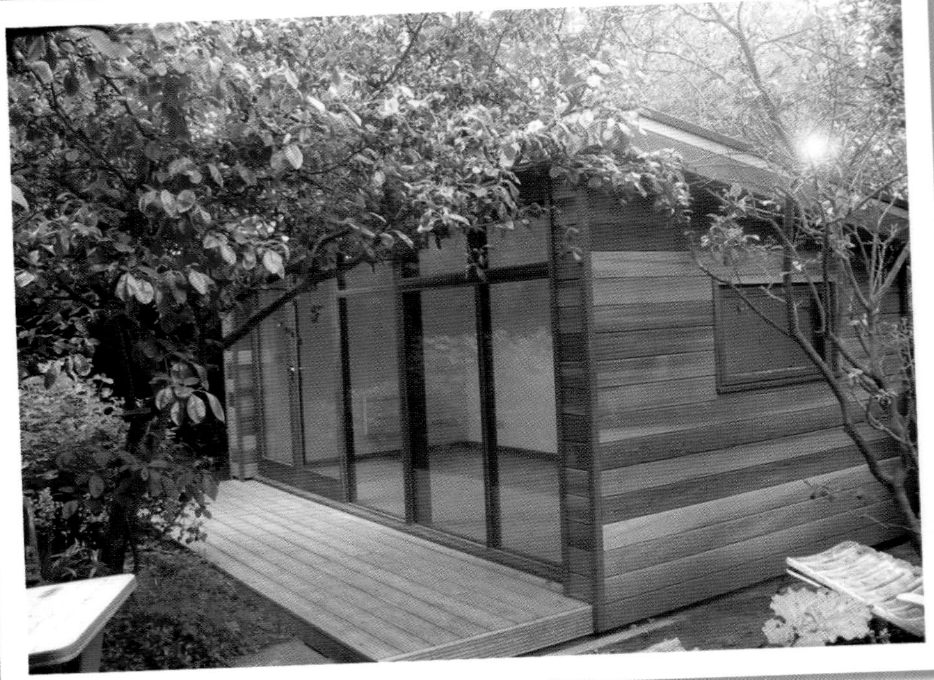

Building a garden office You could simply move to the garden shed, but a more satisfactory solution is to choose one of the growing number of purpose-designed garden office buildings now available (above). The building may need planning permission (check with your local authority) but will be exempt from Building Regulations control (page 486). You will, however, need Building Regulations approval to install a new electricity supply.

Annexes

You may need to provide a 'granny flat' within your home for an elderly or disabled family member. The need is for self-contained living quarters for someone who is semi-independent but needs family support from time to time. The type of accommodation will depend on the type, size and layout of your house; some of the possible options are outlined below.

Rules and regulations

You will almost certainly need planning permission to create a granny flat, because of the change of use involved, although this may be waived if the conversion is wholly internal and has no separate means of external access. Check with your local authority before proceeding.

Building Regulations approval may also be needed, depending on what is involved in the conversion work. See cross-references to other relevant sections of this chapter.

Conversion options

These are the options most likely to be available to you for creating a granny flat.

Using existing rooms Choose adjacent rooms on the ground or first floor, using one as a living room with a kitchenette partitioned off it, and the other as a bedroom with en-suite bath or shower room partitioned off. See pages 484–5 for more details.

Converting the loft If the roof space is suitable for conversion, this is an ideal way of creating self-contained living accommodation. If climbing stairs poses a problem to the intended occupant, consider using the loft conversion yourself and allocating rooms on the floor below to create the granny flat. See pages 490–1.

Converting a basement Originally built to contain servants' quarters, a basement is often ideal for conversion to a granny flat because it will probably have its own entrance and rooms of a reasonable size. A cellar is less likely to be suitable. See page 494.

Converting a garage An integral or attached garage could form the basis for a granny flat, perhaps with an extension to the side or rear to increase the available floor space. An integral garage will be easier to convert than an attached one. See page 495.

Building an extension So long as you have the space and the money, this is the best option because the extension can be tailored to suit the requirements of the occupant. See pages 488–9. Note that if you have a mortgage you should notify the lender of your plans to create a granny flat. You should also inform your household insurance company.

Wiring, plumbing and gas: Safety rules

There are three more sets of rules and regulations that you need to be aware of when planning any home alterations. They deal with your wiring installation, your plumbing system and the gas supply.

Britain is one of the few countries where householders are allowed to carry out their own electrical and plumbing work, but this does not mean you have a free hand to do what you want; you still have to follow some rules. As far as work on your gas supply is concerned, any DIY work is completely out of the question; all work must always be carried out by a qualified gas fitter, and no one else.

Wiring regulations

Since 2006, electrical wiring work has been included in the Building Regulations for England and Wales as Part P: Electrical Safety (it was already part of the Building Regulations in Scotland). All new wiring work (including alterations to existing wiring) must – by law – meet the requirements of Part P and one way of doing this is to use the IEE Wiring Regulations published by the Institution of Engineering and Technology (IET) as British Standard BS7671 – Requirements for Electrical Installations. Part P has its own Approved Document (which can be downloaded at www.planningportal.gov.uk) and this specifically refers to the Wiring Regulations, which have of course existed for years. The Wiring Regulations are being modified in 2011 and you can find out the impact of these modifications on our own website – www.readersdigest.co.uk. You are still allowed to carry out your own wiring work, but for certain jobs you must seek approval from your local Building Control Department. See page 280 for more details. Electrical contractors who are registered under a 'competent persons' scheme can self-certify their own work.

Whenever you employ a professional electrician, choose one who is a member of the Electrical Contractors Association (ECA) or who is on the roll of the National Inspection Council for Electrical Installation Contracting (NICEIC). Full details of both organisations are given on pages 504-505 and they both publish guides on how to interpret and use the Wiring Regulations (the IET publish guides, too).

If you carry out any electrical work yourself, note that your local electricity supply company has the right to inspect and test any electrical work that it thinks may be unsafe. It can also refuse to connect a supply of electricity to an unsafe installation, or one that does not meet the requirements of the Wiring Regulations.

ELECTRICAL RULES FOR THE REPUBLIC OF IRELAND

UK rules for electrical installations do not apply in the Republic of Ireland, where they must comply with Ireland's National Rules for Electrical Installations. Contact the local government office or the Electro-Technical Council of Ireland: www.etci.ie for more information.

Water supply regulations

Plumbing in new houses is covered by the Water Supply (Water Fittings) Regulations enforced by local water companies. The regulations, which also apply to extensions and alterations to existing plumbing systems, are designed to prevent the waste, undue consumption, misuse or contamination of water supplies – and you can be fined if you contravene them.

Provided you follow the regulations, a copy of which (including helpful guidance) can be downloaded from the Department of the Environment (DEFRA) website (www.defra.uk), you do not need to tell anyone what you are doing. But you do have to inform your water supplier if you want to install a a water softener or a bidet with an ascending spray (but not a normal bidet, see page 349). You must wait for their consent before starting work.

There is an illustrated Guide to the Regulations available from the Water Regulations Advisory Scheme (www.wras.co.uk) which also includes guidance to the rules in Scotland (the Water Byelaws 2000, Scotland), which are very similar to the Water Regulations covering England and Wales.

Note that The Water Regulations apply only to water supply. Rules for the disposal of waste water are included in the Building Regulations (page 483).

Gas safety regulations

The Gas Safety (Installation and Use) Regulations make it illegal for anyone to carry out work relating to gas supply and fittings who is not 'competent'. In practice, this means leaving all work on your gas supply system to a qualified gas fitter who is registered on the Gas Safe Register (www.gassaferegister.co.uk) covering Great Britain and the Isle of Man.
See pages 506-507 for details.

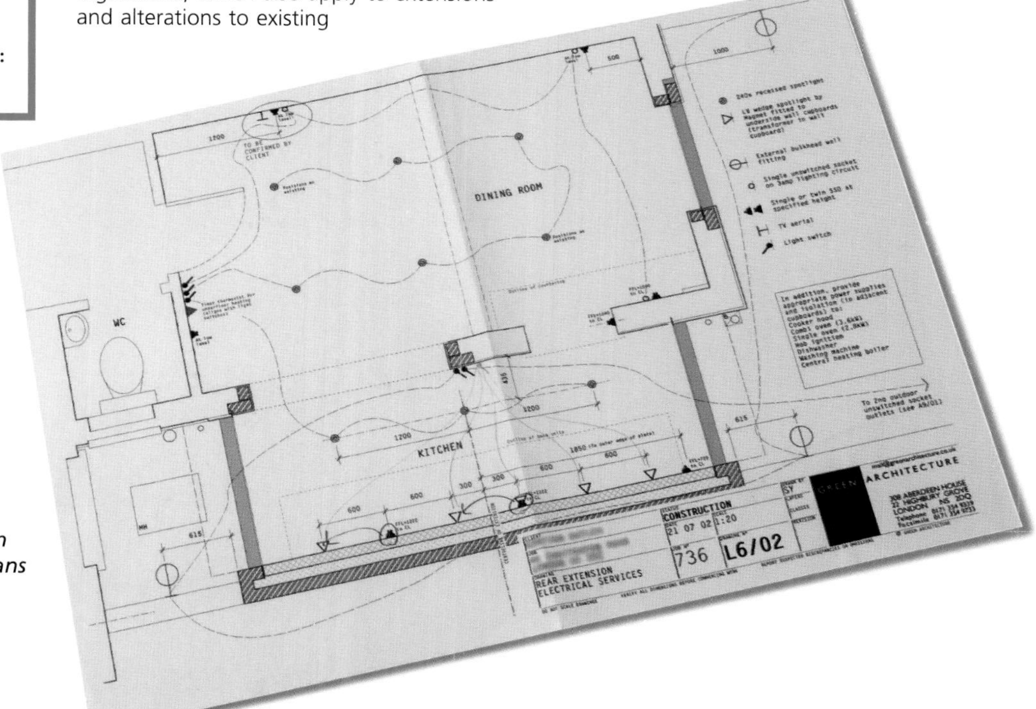

An architect will draw up detailed plans showing the proposed position of any services, such as plumbing or wiring, in a new room or extension. A clear wiring scheme for a network of recessed spotlights in a new kitchen ceiling (right) will enable the electricians and builders to work together on the installation.

Project Management 14

Getting professional help

With any home improvement project, you have to decide who is going to manage it as well as who is going to do the actual work. It could be you, it could be a builder (or other contractor) or it could be an architect or surveyor.

When to call in the professionals

Over the years, the increased availability and improvement of products (especially easy-to-use paints and plumbing materials), the facility to hire specialist tools and equipment and the proliferation of technical advice has made life very much easier for the do-it-yourselfer. But even the more experienced and competent will baulk at many projects – because they are too big (or time-consuming), too dangerous, too strenuous, too skilled or simply illegal. And that's when it's time to call in the professionals.

Too big?

Home extensions and loft conversions come to mind here – both are also included in *Too skilled?* You may be able to lay bricks for simple structures like small garden walls and a bin surround, but laying bricks for a home extension needs the skill of a professional **bricklayer**. The walls will also need the attention of a professional **plasterer**. In short, you need a **builder** – and for larger extensions may need a **surveyor** or an **architect** (or **architectural technician**) as well. Extensions will also need to be designed before they can be approved and built.

Loft conversions will also need professional help – especially that of a **carpenter** to re-arrange the roof timbers and a builder to install supporting steel girders. A **specialist loft conversion firm** will be able to do the whole job.

Unless you want to spend the whole of your summer holiday doing it, painting the outside of your home is another job where you will want to call in a **professional painter and decorator**. Re-decorating inside rooms – one-by-one – is one thing, but the outside could take all of two to three weeks.

Too skilled?

All the building trades will argue that their own particular craft is too skilled for an amateur to learn. But developments in the products available to the do-it-yourselfer have meant that many jobs are now easier:

- modern easy-to-use paints make decorating much simpler than it once was;
- plastic pipe and push-fit fittings remove a lot of the skill needed to make good plumbing connections and pipe runs;
- do-it-yourself plasters and wall fillers make wall repairs very much easier (but a plasterer is still needed for plastering larger areas or a whole wall);
- flat-pack furniture and a huge range of furniture fittings make assembly of cupboards and units much easier;
- cutting services for timber and glass mean that you do not have to be able to cut either accurately yourself (though the ability to trim wood is still necessary).

The degree of skill required for many DIY jobs also depends partly on the kind of house you live in. Modern timber-framed houses tend to have flat level floors, with truly vertical walls and, more importantly, walls that meet at right angles to one another. This makes the fitting of kitchens and bedroom cupboards in particular a much less daunting task, compared with older houses where floors can be sloping and uneven, walls untrue and corners anything but right angles. The skill of **kitchen/bedroom fitters** is to cope with all these irregularities to produce a neat result. Other examples where skill really counts are:

- wallpapering ceilings
- shelving in an irregular alcove
- renovating a bath
- laying stair carpet
- strengthening joists
- replacing sealed double glazing units
- diagnosing central heating faults.

There are some specific projects always best left to specialist firms, who have the skill, the knowledge and the equipment. Examples include:

- replacement windows
- damp-proofing and dry rot treatment
- flooring – especially fitted carpet and hard floorcoverings
- cavity wall (and solid wall) insulation.

You may be able to do small jobs yourself, but major projects are best left to the professionals.

Too strenuous?

Jobs like laying a concrete slab in the garden can be much harder work than you think – especially if you have to move mixed concrete any distance by wheelbarrow – and are almost certainly best left to a builder, as is digging any kind of trench. Paving generally is hard work – a single concrete paving slab can weigh up to 50kg and you will know about it if you have to move 20 or more. Professional **paving contractors** do it all the time.

Fitting a new central heating boiler is also hard work and is best left to a **central heating contractor**. Connecting a gas boiler ***has*** to be left to a professional – it's illegal to do it yourself.

Too dangerous?

Anything involving heights is potentially dangerous – so for pitched roof repairs (and certainly complete roof replacement) you will need a **roofing contractor**. You may also need a professional for working on the outside of large (high) houses (including a **guttering specialist** to repair/replace the gutters). Repairs to chimneys and chimney stacks are certainly best left to a builder who has the proper access equipment. And you should always seek professional help if you are thinking of removing a chimney breast – it might be holding the house up.

Working in a loft space is also potentially dangerous – so you might want to use a **plumber** for work involving the cold water tanks – and you might also want to use an **electrician** for some of the more complicated wiring jobs, such as wiring in bathrooms, wiring garden circuits and replacing a consumer unit.

Sharing the work

There are many instances where it may be possible to share the work – getting the contractor to do the skilled (or strenuous) part of the job, leaving you to do the less skilled part (or parts involving a different skill) or the less strenuous aspects of the work.

For example, you might get a builder to erect a new partition wall to divide one room into two and ask him to stop at the plasterboard stage, leaving you to do the final finishing and decorating. Or you might employ a labourer to dig a trench up the garden, allowing you to lay a water supply or an electrical supply to a garden shed or greenhouse, perhaps getting the labourer back to fill in the trench – after the Building Control Officer or Water Board inspector has been! Or you could agree that you will do all the necessary clearing before work starts – this may be in your interests if there are things you are particularly concerned may be damaged. And it saves you paying a skilled rate for what is essentially labouring work.

Do not be embarrassed about asking to do this – not all tradesmen or tradeswomen are multi-skilled and actually might be quite relieved that they are not expected to do the whole job.

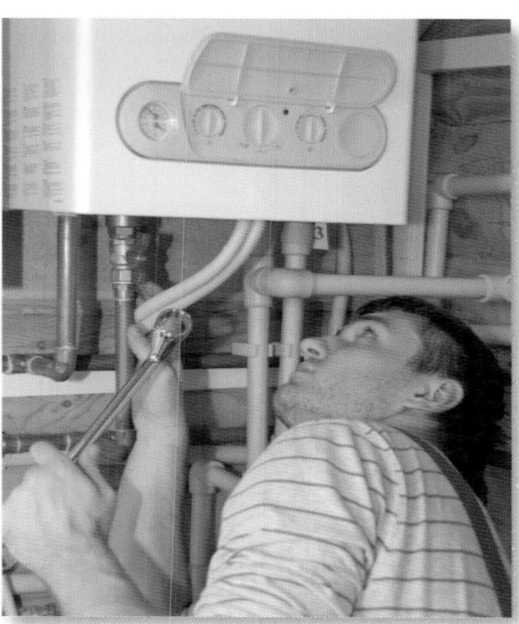

Illegal?

In the UK, the only work you cannot by law do yourself is anything involving the connection of mains gas. You can do anything else, though a lot of building work (including many electrical jobs) has to be notified to the local council Building Control Department to ensure that it complies with Building Regulations. And, for some building work, you may also require planning permission. A professional contractor or advisor can help with both of these.

Costing the project

You should be able to get an idea of how much your proposed project is going to cost by asking other people who have had similar work done. And there are various websites which will give you prices for typical work – bricklaying, plastering, painting, electrical and plumbing jobs – as well as approximate prices for whole jobs like extensions, conservatories and loft conversions. But the cost of home improvement work is notoriously difficult to predict or even estimate and it will not really be until the tendering stage that you will get anything like firm figures.

There are also various books available that set out the cost of various home improvements and building work; the Royal Institution of Chartered Surveyors (RICS) publishes the *Property Makeover Price Guide*, which gives costs related to major property problems, alterations and extensions.

Always allow a contingency in your budget for the unexpected – at least 5 per cent, ideally 10 per cent and perhaps 20 per cent for renovation work on an older property.

Finding the right contractor

The success of a home improvement project may stand or fall according to your choice of contractor.

If you have decided that your project needs outside help, the key to its success will be finding the right contractor to do the job – whether it be a builder, electrician, plumber, roofer or whatever.

If you are using an architect or a surveyor to oversee a large project, he or she may well have their own preferred contractors and, on the whole, you would be wise to use them. The architect or surveyor will have worked with them before so will know the quality of their work and it will be their reputation, not the contractors, that is on the line. The key in this case is to make the right choice of architect or surveyor – and to satisfy yourself that they have no financial interest in the contractor being recommended. See pages 489, 504 and 507 for more about using an architect or a surveyor. Note that whoever signs the contract or written agreement (architect, surveyor or main builder) is responsible for the quality of work of any sub-contractors they may employ. An architect's or surveyor's management fee is in addition to any design fee they may have charged – management fees are typically 10 to 15 per cent of the overall cost of the work, but a good architect or surveyor will go a long way toward paying for themselves by controlling the cost of the building work for you. And they, not you, will have the headache of 'juggling' different trades. Trying to co-ordinate and dovetail the work of (say) builders, plasterers, carpenters, plumbers, electricians and painters can be a nightmare and you can end up with serious overruns. Having a single main contractor will also solve this problem – it is up to them to sort out the work order for their sub-contractors.

For projects you are managing yourself, there are three main choices when it comes to finding the right contractor – personal recommendation, using an advice organisation or contacting a trade association.

Personal recommendation

Every consumer survey carried out on satisfaction with work done on the home comes up with the same result – the people most satisfied have found their contractor through personal recommendation from a friend, relative or neighbour. This has the huge advantage that you can see previous work that has been carried out and talk to whoever is making the recommendation to find out more about how the contractor carried out the job. You just need to be sure that the person is not being paid to make a recommendation – only likely if the recommendation comes out of the blue rather than as a result of you asking around.

You could also ask local letting agents which contractors they use and ask the council planning and building control departments if they have lists of approved contractors. And, of course, keep an eye out for contractors' boards at local sites where they are working.

Using an advice organisation

There are three problems with using friends, family and neighbours to recommend a contractor – you may be new to the area (especially if you have just bought the house), you may not be able to find anyone who has had the kind of work done that you have in mind or the contractor recommended may be based miles away.

For this reason, there has been a huge growth in advice organisations who – in effect – take the personal recommendation based on experience one step further, by maintaining lists of approved contractors and recording feedback from satisfied (and dissatisfied) customers.

Examples include:

www.checkatrade.com
www.findagoodone.com
www.findatrade.com
www.goodbuilderguide.co.uk
www.myhammer.co.uk
www.problemsolved.co.uk
www.ratedpeople.com
www.which.co.uk/local

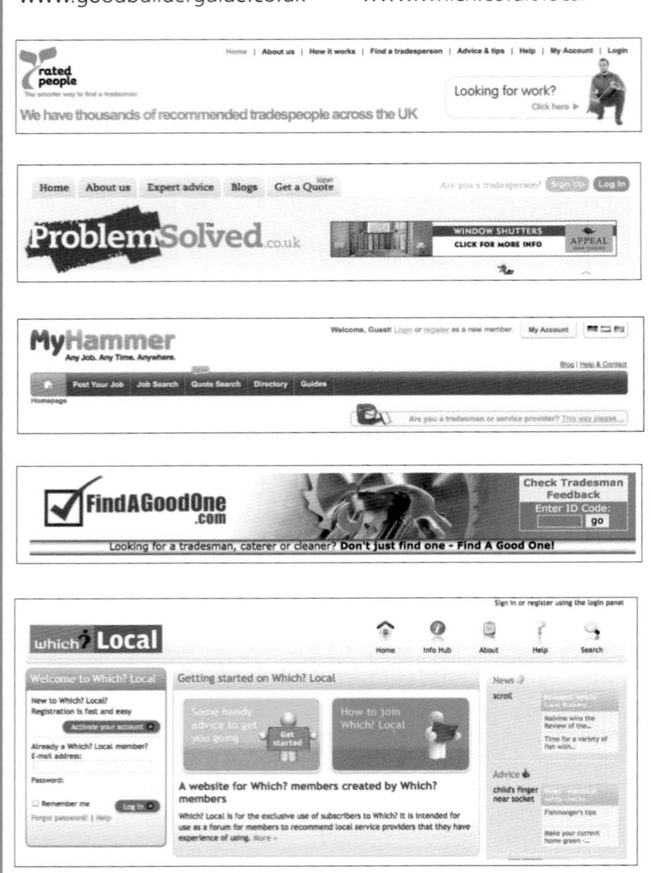

Council and Government schemes

Many local councils run schemes for small independent traders and businesses. These are called Local Authority Assured Trader Schemes and require businesses to comply with all Trading Standards legislation and civil law obligations and to have an effective complaints procedure. Check with the Trading Standards Department of your local council. Participating contractors are prohibited from using high-pressure selling. Many local council Trading Standards Departments have a list of Approved Traders (covering a wide range of trades); for further information, visit www.buywithconfidence.gov.uk

There is a national scheme called Trustmark, supported by the Government, the building industry and consumer protection organisations. It operates across the repair, maintenance and improvement industry and includes trade associations, local government trading standards teams and independent scheme operators. The key benefits are:

- a firm's technical skills have been independently checked through regular on-site inspections, as well as checks on their trading record and financial status;
- firms have signed up to a code of practice that includes insurance, good health and safety practices and customer care;
- the approved scheme operator has checked and will continue to monitor the firm's quality of work, trading practices and customer satisfaction;
- firms are able to offer an insurance-backed guarantee;
- deposit protection insurance is available for consumers in the event of a firm ceasing trading;
- if you have a problem or disagreement with the firm, there will be a clear and user-friendly complaints procedure to help resolve the issue.

Using a trade association

Whatever they may say in their literature, trade associations exist primarily to promote the interests of their members, who pay a fee to belong. The better ones, however, have stringent rules of membership (so membership means more than that the firm has paid the annual fee) plus codes of practice, guarantee schemes and conciliation and arbitration schemes. More importantly at this stage of the project, trade associations can provide a list of their members in your area (often via their website) which gives you an excellent starting list of firms to contact.

The main trade associations covering contractors who might work in, on or around your home are listed on the next four pages with full contact details and an idea of what they offer.

People to avoid

Every firm has to promote or advertise its business in some way, but even so you should be careful when responding to firms who have telephoned you out of the blue or simply knocked on your door because they are 'working in your area'. Certainly be suspicious of any special deals that need signing on the spot or leaflets that have come through the door with only a telephone number on them. Anyone can call themselves a 'builder' or a 'plumber' – but not a 'registered builder' or 'qualified plumber'. Dodgy tarmac cowboys and high-pressure double-glazing or solar heating salesmen are relatively easy to spot, but printing 'official' looking leaflets or brochures is so easy on a home computer these days that it can be more difficult to separate the reputable contractors from the fly-by-night merchants. You should certainly not give your credit card details in response to a 'cold call' over the telephone. If a deal sounds reasonable, ask for it to be put in writing, including any discounts on offer.

Beware, too, of handwritten estimates, only a mobile phone number being given as a contact, discounts offered for cash and a refusal to give references.

Questions to ask a contractor

However you have drawn up your list of contractors, there are several questions you should ask them before putting a firm on your shortlist to ask for a quotation or estimate.

1 Have they done similar work before and, if so, can they give you references and perhaps arrange for you to see the work?

2 How long have they been in business? Most trade associations insist on at least a year's trading before they will accept contractors for membership.

3 Do they have business premises you can visit? There is nothing wrong with a one-man electrician or painter/decorator (say) operating from their own home. But you would expect anyone calling themselves a builder to have something a bit more than this. You do not want a contractor to disappear halfway through a job.

4 Are they members of a trade association? Don't necessarily take their word for it if you are at all suspicious – you can check with the trade association quoted. There have been cases of contractors improperly claiming to be members of trade associations (and even using the relevant logo).

5 Are they insured? They should have public liability insurance that covers them against any personal injury and damage to your property (and also damage to neighbours' property). Ask to see their certificate of insurance if in doubt.

6 Is their work covered by any kind of guarantee and, if so, is the guarantee insurance-backed (see page 513) so that you are covered if they go out of business?

7 Do they charge for giving a quotation and, if so, will the charge be deducted from their bill if they are given the job?

Getting quotes

Unless you are totally happy with a firm that has been recommended by your architect or surveyor or by a friend, relative or neighbour, it is prudent to get quotes from at least three firms. Be aware that an estimate is different from a quotation.

Estimate An estimate is a guess at the overall price (and may well increase at a later date).

Quotation A quotation is a fixed price for the job and should only be altered if mutually agreed. Quotations may legitimately have provisos in them, particularly with reference to the materials chosen (a plumber may have the cheapest taps in mind, whereas you are thinking of snazzy Italian jobs) and with reference to work that is not known – for example, the full extent of rot damage or woodworm attack may not reveal itself until some stripping-out work has been done.

When asking firms for an estimate or a quotation, be as specific as you can (especially about any special materials or fittings you want to use), so that you can compare like with like when you get the quotes back. Make sure that all your specific points have been covered and that you have included things like necessary preparatory work, the need to protect any existing features (fireplaces, for example) and removal of building rubble, so that each contractor knows what they are quoting for.

The cheapest price may not be the best – the price may be tempered by how much the contractor wants the job. Be guided by the quality of what you hear and what you see as well as the price.

Trade and professional associations

The associations listed on the next four pages cover the majority of contractors and advisors in the home maintenance and home improvement industries. Contact them direct for further information.

Architects

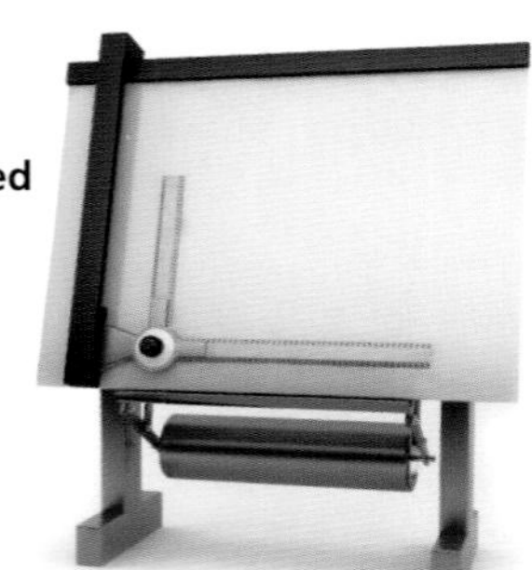

Register of Architects accredited in Building Conservation
AABC Register
No 5 The Parsonage
Manchester M3 2HS

0161 832 0666
www.aabc-register.co.uk
info@aabc-register.co.uk

The AABC Register provides details of architects who have been assessed as to their knowledge and experience in conservation work. All architects on the Register will provide details of their practice and previous projects or assignments. There are two membership categories: **A** and **CA**.
A: Architect knowledgeable and experienced in the conservation of historic buildings, engaged in executive direction of projects of conservation work.
CA: Architect knowledgeable and experienced in the conservation of historic buildings currently acting in a consultant, educational or advisory capacity. The Register is fully searchable online.

Royal Institute of British Architects (RIBA)
66 Portland Place
London W1B 1AD

Public information line Mon-Fri 10am-5pm 0906 302 0400
www.architecture.com
info@inst.riba.org

The RIBA was founded in 1834 and today is the key source of information on architecture and related subjects for architects and the public alike. The RIBA British Architectural Library operates an enquiry and research service available to the public and will answer queries on subjects as diverse as architects' fees, replacement windows and straw bale technology.

All RIBA Chartered Architects or architects in their Chartered Practices have a minimum of seven years' training, and are listed on the RIBA's searchable website, which enables you to browse details and draw up your own shortlist. The Architects Registration Board (ARB) requires Architects to have professional indemnity insurance, which (as a guideline) is set to £250,000.

Building

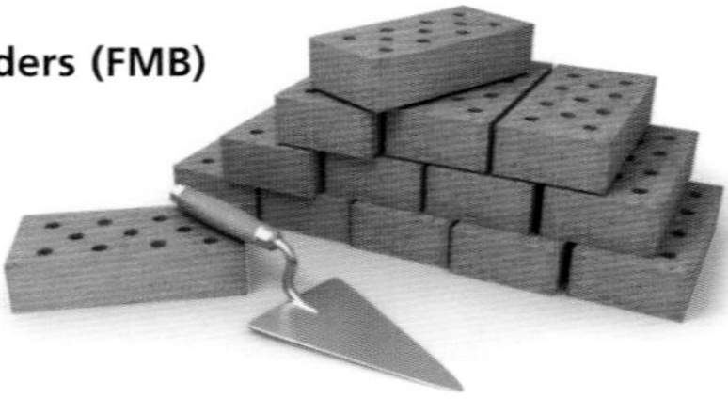

Federation of Master Builders (FMB)
Gordon Fisher House
14-15 Great James Street
London WC1N 3DP

020 7242 7583
www.fmb.org.uk
Email via website

The FMB was established 70 years ago to protect the interests of small and medium-sized building firms – today it is the largest trade association in the UK building industry with 11,000 members and will provide details of local builders via its website. Members must pass FMB vetting and assessment of work in progress. All member firms must sign the FMB Code of Practice. Member firms who have been in business for three years or more have the option (for an additional fee) of joining the National Register of Warranted Builders, which involves additional vetting and inspection (these companies are known as Masterbond members).

FMB offer a complaints procedure via their website and, if the complaint is not sorted out, can offer the services of an independent adjudicator for a fee. The builder has to agree to comply with the adjudicator's findings.

There are also various levels of guarantee scheme, whereby FMB undertake to have the work completed if your (FMB registered) builder goes out of business or fails to complete the job. This costs between 1 and 2.2 per cent of the value of the work, depending on the level of cover you choose.

Carpentry

British Woodworking Federation (BWF)
Royal London House
22-25 Finsbury Square
London EC2A 1DX

0844 209 2610
www.bwf.org.uk
bwf@bwf.org.uk

The BWF represents manufacturers, distributors and installers of joinery and woodworking products such as windows, stairs, doors and fitted furniture, and ensures that all products comply with the highest industry standards. The federation has more than 500 members, committed to meeting the standards set out in the BWF Code of Conduct. Their website provides a fully searchable list of suppliers by postcode, product, service, certifications or keyword. It also promotes the use of wood, notably from sustainably managed forests. The BWF logo is considered by trade and industry specialists to be a guarantee of quality.

Carpet laying

National Institute of Carpet and Floor Layers (NICF)
4c St Mary's Place
The Lace Market
Nottingham NG1 1PH

0115 958 3077
www.nicfltd.org.uk
info@nicfltd.org.uk

Founded in 1979 to promote excellence within the carpet fitting field, the NICF now includes vinyl fitters, wood and laminate fitters and vinyl tile fitters among its members. There are several categories of and criteria for membership, including Trainee Fitter and Master Fitter. The latter are required to demonstrate their skills during an on-site assessment by NICF inspectors.

The website offers a searchable directory by county providing full contact details (including business websites) of members. In the event of a complaint against a NICF member (or non-member), an independent inspection service is available for a fee. The inspector will provide a report which can be used by the customer in the small claims court.

Also at the same address, **Contract Flooring Association (CFA)**, 0115 941 1126, www.cfa.org.uk.

Damp, rot and infestation

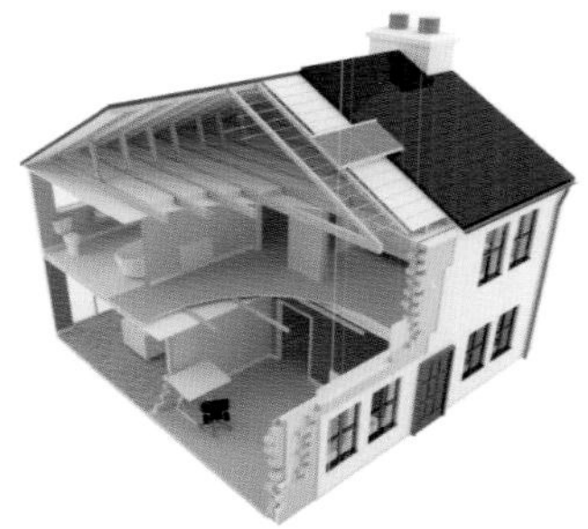

The Property Care Association (PCA)
Lakeview Court
Ermine Business Park
Huntingdon
Cambridgeshire PE29 6XR

0844 375 4301
www.property-care.org
pca@property-care.org

The PCA represents specialists in structural waterproofing, damp proofing, timber preservation, structural maintenance and flooding. Member companies and surveyors are audited on a regular basis. In the case of dispute with a PCA member on quality of work or technical issues, the association will work to resolve it. Members offer Guaranteed Protection Insurance (GPI). The scheme insures the guarantee issued by the contractor and comes into force should the issuing contractor cease to trade. This is backed by the FSA (Financial Services Authority) and is purchased by making a one-off payment at the time of the work being carried out. Cover is usually for a period of 10 or 20 years (dependent on type of work). The PCA website has useful information and FAQs for the public.

Decorating

Painting and Decorating Association (PDA)
32 Coton Road
Nuneaton
Warwickshire CV11 5TW

024 7635 3776
www.paintingdecoratingassociation.co.uk
info@paintingdecoratingassociation.co.uk

The PDA represents 1,800 painters and decorators across the UK. It ensures that members are qualified, fully insured, are conversant with the latest technology and work to a Code of Practice. Each has 5 years' industry experience, public liability insurance, and can offer good references and a clear quotation system. The PDA will investigate all complaints against members and provides a clients' advisory service with conciliation and arbitration arrangements free of charge. The website offers a searchable directory of members.

Electrical

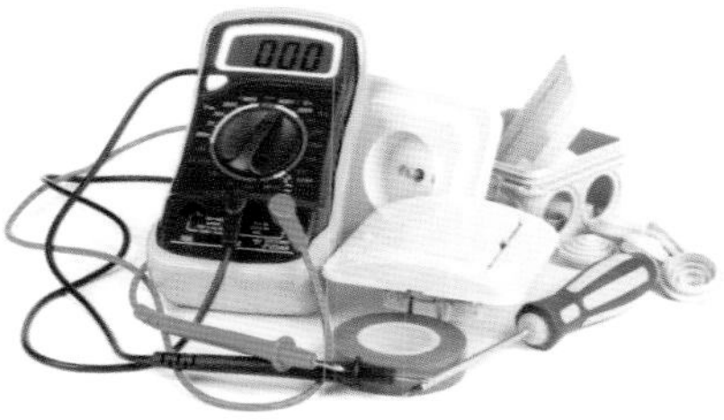

Electrical Contractors Association (ECA)
ESCA House
34 Palace Court
London W2 4HY

020 7313 4800
www.eca.co.uk
Email via website

The ECA represents the interests of contractors who design, install, inspect, test and maintain electrical and electronic equipment and services. Registered Members undergo regular assessments to ensure they carry out safe electrical work, installed to recognised industry standards and practice. Members must comply with the ECA's Code of Fair Trading, the latest Wiring Regulations, be registered with any one of the Government-approved Full Scope Competent Person Schemes for Part P of the Building Regulations, and hold public liability insurance for a minimum of £2 million.

National Inspection Council for Electrical Installation Contracting (NICEIC)
Warwick House
Houghton Hall Park
Houghton Regis
Dunstable LU5 5ZX

0870 013 0382
www.niceic.com
Email via website

NICEIC is a voluntary regulatory body for the electrical contracting industry (with a roll of over 26,000 registered contractors) and is concerned with the safety and technical standard of electrical work carried out by approved contractors. The organisation operates an independent complaints procedure governing the technical standards of its Approved Contractor and Domestic Installer Schemes. If the work of a registered contractor is found to be below the accepted technical standard, NICEIC can require the contractor to correct the work at no additional cost to the customer.

NICEIC contractors must undergo assessment which continues throughout their membership. Additional benefits to the consumer include guaranteed compliance with with (and self-certification to) Part P of the Building Regulations, an insurance-backed warranty and access to an independent complaints procedure, should a problem arise. The website offers a searchable directory of registered electricians by postcode.

Fencing and decking

Fencing Contractors Association Ltd (FCA)
Warren Road
Trellech
Monmouthshire
NP25 4PQ

07000 560722
www.fencingcontractors.org
info@fencingcontractors.org

The FCA was set up in 1942 to help procure timber and other fencing materials to support the war effort. Today, its membership includes fencing contractors, material/product manufacturers and suppliers.

There are currently more than 200 Full and Associate members, ranging from large companies to individual traders. Affiliate Membership is also offered to individuals and companies not directly involved in fencing manufacture, supply or erection. All new members must have a minimum of two years' trading within the fencing industry and must agree to abide by the association's rules.

In the event of a complaint against a member, arbitration is offered free. For complaints against non-members, arbitration is available for a charge. The website offers a searchable directory of contractors.

Timber Decking Association (TDA)
5 Flemming Court
Castleford
West Yorkshire
WF10 5HW

01977 558147
www.tda.org.uk
Email via website

The TDA is an independent advisory and technical organisation and is the UK authority on the quality of design, materials and construction for high performance decks. The Association operates a third party quality assurance scheme called DeckMark™. DeckMark covers both installers and manufacturers of materials. Compliance with DeckMark and the annual verification audits that are part of the scheme is a mandatory requirement of membership. All members are committed to operating by the TDA code and the Dispute Resolution Service. Customers may activate this service by completing a TDA complaint form and sending it with a £25 registration fee to the TDA. This fee is refunded if the complaint is upheld.

TDA installers offer warranties underwritten by Home Pro Insurance that includes deposit protection.

Fireplaces and Flues

National Association of Chimney Engineers (NACE)
PO Box 849
Metheringham
Lincoln LN4 3WU

01526 322555
www.nace.org.uk
info@nace.org.uk

By law, all new flues, for all types of fuels, built since the introduction of the 1965 Building Regulations must have been fitted with an inner lining to protect the chimney structure from flue gases. NACE was formed in 1982 by a group of independent companies specialising in chimney lining and undertakes to ensure the safety of all fuel users through the correct installation and testing of flues and chimneys. There are three categories of membership: Installer members, Associate Members (manufacturers and service providers) and Chimney Registration Inspectors. Building Regulations for England/Wales and Scotland require that a Chimney Data Plate must be placed in a prominent position giving information on any chimney that is constructed or worked upon, and the Chimney Registration Membership is for competent engineers who can inspect and register a chimney not lined by a member of NACE.

In the event of a complaint against a member, an inspector will visit for a deposit of £300 plus VAT, which will be refunded if their complaint is upheld.

NACE does not offer a guarantee scheme, insuring against unfinished work by or bankruptcy of its members, though individual members do offer such schemes.

National Association of Chimney Sweeps (NACS)
Unit 15 Emerald Way
Stone Business Park
Stone
Staffordshire ST15 OSR

01785 811732
www.chimneyworks.co.uk
Email via website

All members of NACS undertake training and on-site assessment prior to enrolment and are also checked for public liability insurance. Members work to the NACS Code of Practice and Code of Conduct for the cleaning of chimneys.

When the work is completed, NACS Sweeps issue a Certificate of Chimney Sweeping and recommend a date for future cleaning. A searchable map on their website enables householders to find a sweep local to them.

Gas

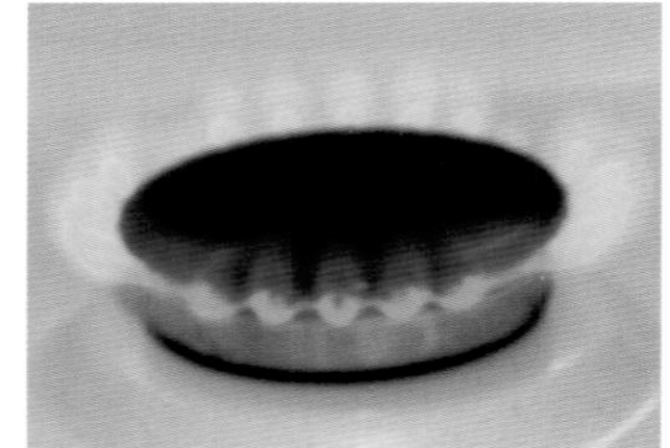

Gas Safe Register
PO Box 6804
Basingstoke RG24 4NB

0800 408 5500 (freephone)
www.gassaferegister.co.uk
Email via website

On 1 April 2009, Gas Safe Register replaced the CORGI gas registration scheme as Britain's gas safety authority. Now, by law, only Gas Safe registered engineers should be employed to carry out work on gas installations or appliances – CORGI gas registration is no longer valid. Gas Safe Register was set up by the government to give consumers a list of gas engineers who are safe and legally allowed to work on gas appliances in your home. There are approximately 125,000 engineers on the Register. You can find one via the website or by phone.

When an engineer comes to your home to do gas work, always check their Gas Safe Register ID card to make sure they're on the Register. Engineers gain different qualifications enabling them to do different types of work, so you need to check the back of the ID card to see which appliances they can legally work on.

After you have gas work done, you can nominate your home for a free gas safety check. You can report any work you suspect has been done illegally, or is dangerous. If your home is chosen, the inspector will check that the gas work has been undertaken safely and legally.

Glass and glazing/replacement windows

Glass & Glazing Federation (GGF)
54 Ayres Street
London SE1 1EU

0207 939 9101
www.ggf.co.uk
Email via website

The GGF represents companies who make, supply or fit glass and glazing related products. Members must have three years' trading, be vetted and undertake to only use products that comply with the relevant British, European and International Standards. Using a member will ensure your deposit is protected via the GGF Deposit Indemnity Fund for up to 25 per cent of the purchase price or £3,000, whichever is the lower, and that any dispute between you and the Member Company is conciliated at no customer cost. All GGF installations will comply with Building Regulations, and you will be supplied with a compliance certificate for all replacement windows and doors. Where replacement window companies are registered with the FENSA (Fenestration Self-Assessment) scheme, they will be able to self-certify that their work complies with Part L of the Building Regulations (page 211). FENSA-registered firms also offer an insurance-backed guarantee.

Insulation

National Insulation Association (NIA)
2 Vimy Court
Vimy Road
Leighton Buzzard
Bedfordshire LU7 1FG

08451 636363
www.nationalinsulationassociation.org.uk
Email via website

The NIA's General Public Site on the internet is a portal for information and advice on home insulation and provides details of government grants, installers (with an online directory), and its code of professional practice in pdf form. It also takes you step-by-step through its complaints procedure. There is a useful page on FAQs covering the various types of insulation. All members are vetted and have public and products liability insurance.

Kitchens/bathrooms

Kitchen Bathroom Bedroom Specialists Association (KBSA)
Unit L4A, Mill 3
Pleasley Vale Business Park
Mansfield
Nottingham NG19 8RL

01623 818808
www.kbsa.org.uk
Email via website

All KBAS retail members must have been trading for two years, be registered with the KBSA's ConsumerCare Plus Insurance Scheme and operate within the scope of Consumer Complaints Service and the KBSA Code of Practice. Arbitration is available and members are bound by an Arbitrator's decision. All certified KBSA retail members must provide customer protection free of charge to cover them if the member they're using stops trading.

Paving

Interlay – The Association of Block Paving Contractors
4th Floor
60 Charles Street
Leicester LE1 1FB

0116 222 9840
www.interlay.org.uk
info@interlay.org.uk

Interlay members install everything from driveways to aircraft hard standings. Its website provides useful information for customers including FAQs and what to expect during an installation. 'Find a Layer' enables you to search for member contractors in your area. All members must abide by the Code of Practice and there is a Complaints Resolution Procedure. The association recommends you check that contractors are registered members to avoid engaging a company making false claims.

Plumbing/heating

Association of Plumbing and Heating Contractors (APHC)
Cranmore Drive
Solihull B90 4SB

0121 711 5030
www.competentpersonsscheme.co.uk
Email via website

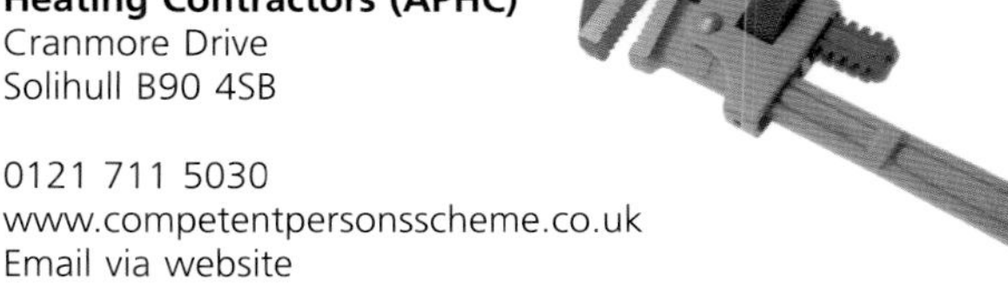

Licensed Membership is open to companies with recognised technical qualifications held over the previous 12 months. Competent Persons Scheme (CPS) and Licensed Membership is open to companies with additional qualifications and these are subject to an extensive vetting procedure and an annual visit by a Certification Officer. CPS and Licensed Members are qualified to self certify, that is they are able to check and certify their own work in the place of a building control officer, saving the cost of employing a separate inspector for the job. They can also offer a six-year warranty on any work undertaken. All members must abide by the Customer Charter and association rules. In the case of a complaint, customers are offered a conciliation service, but both parties need to sign up for arbitration.

Chartered Institute of Plumbing and Heating Engineering (CIPHE)
64 Station Lane
Hornchurch
Essex RM12 6NB

01708 472791
www.ciphe.org.uk
Email via website

The CIPHE has held the Register of Plumbers for over a century and in 2004 expanded its register to include heating professionals. Members must be qualified to a high standard and abide by its Code of Professional Standards. CIPHE inspectors are required to inspect work and investigate complaints where necessary. The Institute operates an Approved Contractor Persons (ACP) scheme, whereby members are able to self-certify their work, and provides a list of ACPs on their website. They also provide details of members able to give expert advice and act as expert witnesses in cases of dispute, for a fee. The website also operates 'Find a plumber', searchable by postcode.

Roofing

National Federation of Roofing Contractors Ltd (NFRC)
Roofing House
31 Worship Street
London
EC2A 2DY

020 7638 7663
www.nfrc.co.uk
Email: info@nfrc.co.uk

All NFRC trade members are vetted before joining and every three years thereafter. They undergo inspections to verify craft skills and technical competence and must have full insurance cover; compliance with Health and Safety Legislation; compliance with the NFRC Code of Practice and British and European Standards and Codes of Practice. Member contractors can offer various tailor-made insurance-backed guarantee packages. In the event of a dispute between a NFRC member contractor and their customer, a free conciliation service is available.

Security

Master Locksmiths Association (MLA)
5D Great Central Way
Woodford Halse
Daventry
Northants NN11 3PZ

0800 783 1498
www.locksmiths.co.uk
enquiries@locksmiths.co.uk

The MLA is recognised as the authoritative body for locksmithing by the police, Home Office and British Standards Institute (BSI), among others. The MLA also has a subsidiary company, Sold Secure, which certifies security products through manual attack testing. MLA licensed locksmith companies undergo strict vetting (including criminal record checks and regular inspections to ensure quality). Personal and company members are encouraged to develop their skills and knowledge through a formal Continued Professional Development (CPD) scheme. In the event of a complaint against a member, the association has a process in place to try to assist and resolve any issues.

Surveyors

Royal Institution of Chartered Surveyors (RICS)
Parliament Square
London
SW1P 3AD

0870 333 1600
www.rics.org
contactrics@rics.org

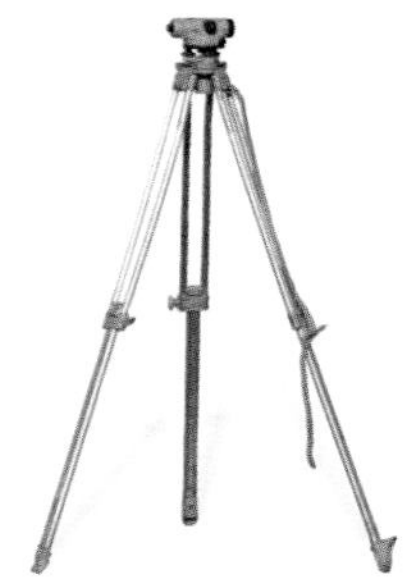

In addition to their professional work (accrediting university courses, training, research and regulation worldwide), the RICS provides a consumer helpline (above), offering up to 30 minutes free advice on issues such as party walls, boundary disputes and compulsory purchase; an online calculator to check the rebuilding cost of your home for insurance purposes, and a searchable database of members. It also offers useful consumer property guides. The libraries and bookshops in London and Edinburgh are mainly for professionals; non-members can enter the libraries for a small fee.

Before work starts

Once you have chosen a contractor, you need to make a formal agreement with them for how the work is to be carried out.

A written agreement (or contract) is best (see below), but even if nothing is written down or agreed you still have some basic legal rights regarding the work that is to be carried out. Specifically, you can expect that the work:

- is carried out with reasonable skill and care (i.e. to a proper standard of workmanship);
- is completed within a reasonable time (unless a longer or shorter time has been agreed);
- costs no more than the agreed price (though additions or subtractions may be agreed along the way) – or, if there is no agreed price, costs no more than is reasonable.

Any goods and materials provided as part of the work must match their description, be of satisfactory quality and be fit for purpose.

A written contract

A contract does not have to be written down to be enforceable in law – what is known as a verbal contract is just as valid as a written contract (but may be more difficult to prove). If you and the contractor agree the work and a price, you have a contract.

But a written agreement is by far the best: there is no argument and both parties have something to refer to during the work if in doubt. There are various forms of contract available that you can use (see Pro-forma contracts) and some contractors may want you to use their own form of contract but, as a minimum, any written agreement should have:

- details of the work to be carried out (including the address where it is to be done);
- the agreed price as far as can be determined at the time the agreement is written (and whether that price includes VAT);
- details of how payments are to be made (see Payments right);
- start and finish dates (a written-down finish date is especially important if the work has to be completed before a special event);
- a clear statement identifying who is applying for Building Regulations approval (and, if required, planning permission);
- the amount of money to be retained (typically 5 or 10 per cent) until you are satisfied that everything has been completed;
- what guarantee is being offered.

Remember that the agreement is binding on you as well as on the contractor. Once you have signed it, you cannot change your mind about using that contractor for that job, though of course in the nature of things, some of the details can be and are frequently changed by agreement during the course of the work. Note that if you ask any of the main builder's sub-contractors to carry out 'extra' work for you, this is not part of the main contract – it is a separate contract between you and the sub-contractor.

PRO-FORMA CONTRACTS

You may find your local council has a form of building contract you can use – or you could download the sample contract from the Federation of Master Builders website – see page 504. Many architects favour the form of minor works contract issued by the JCT (The Joint Contracts Tribunal, page 518), which you can buy from the RIBA shop online (page 514) or at the Building Centre.

Unfair terms

It's possible that a company you ask to carry out work on your home wants you to sign a contract containing unfair terms, weighted in their favour. In law, you are not bound by terms in a contract (usually in the small print) which are unfair. Examples of unfair terms are those which attempt to:

- limit the contractor's responsibility if things go wrong;
- allow the contractor to increase prices (or to change dates) without giving you the right to cancel;
- prevent you holding final payment back if there are faults;
- allow the contractor to keep initial payments if they decide to cancel the contract.

You can get advice on contractual terms from a solicitor or from your local Citizens Advice Bureau or from Community Legal Advice or Consumer Direct (see page 513 for contact details).

Cancellation rights

If you have made a written agreement with a builder or other contractor, you do not normally have any right to cancel it unless the other party breaks the terms of the contract. But you do have cancellation rights if you bought from a door-to-door salesman (a double-glazing salesman, for example) who has arrived at your home uninvited or as the result of an unsolicited telephone call and you should be given a written cancellation notice at the time you sign. You have seven days in which to cancel the contract – known as a 'cooling off' period.

You have similar rights if you buy home improvement services over the telephone, by mail order or via the internet – provided there has been no face-to-face contact – and again you have seven days in which to cancel (provided the work has not actually started in that time).

You may also have the right to cancel if you are using a credit agreement to pay for home improvement work (especially if the credit is arranged though the contractor you are using for the work). And you have the right to cancel if you sign a credit agreement at home – there should be details of this on the credit agreement itself.

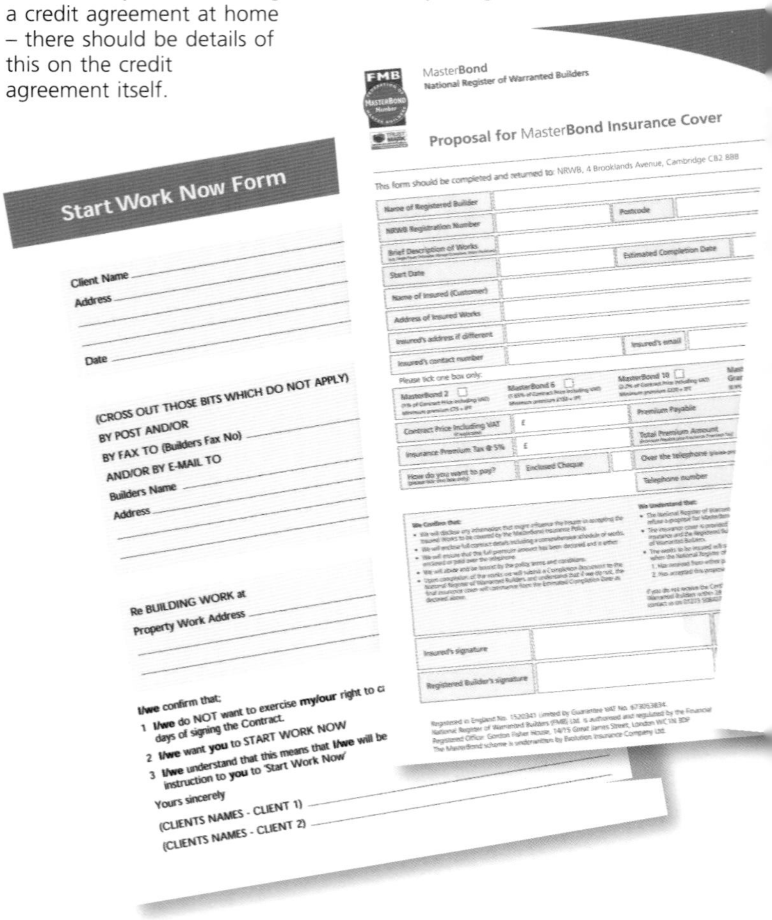

Access and facilities

It is helpful if your written agreement has details of:

- how and when the contractor will have access to your home (many like to start and finish early each day);
- what time deliveries of building materials are likely to be;
- what the arrangements are for storage of building materials;
- what water, electricity and phone facilities the contractor can use;
- which WC the contractor may use;
- arrangements for tidying up (and removing rubbish and unused materials) at the end of the job – and, where applicable, at the end of each working day.

Dispute resolution

It is a good idea to include in any written contract what procedure is to be followed in the event of any dispute.

Payments

For anything other than small one-off jobs, there will be a need for more than one payment and these 'stage' payments should be specified in any written contract.

If there is a written agreement, there should be no need for a deposit, but it is not unreasonable for contractors to ask for one (say 10 or 15 per cent) as reassurance that they have secured the job.

It is also reasonable for contractors to ask for money upfront to pay for materials that they need to buy to get the job started especially if you are having expensive equipment installed in a new bathroom, say – but you should never pay large deposits and certainly not the whole amount before the work starts.

If you agree stage payments, the written agreement should specify the timing of these – you should never agree to a 'day rate' but only payment for specified work.

It is normal for a written agreement to specify that the final payment will not be made in full until you are satisfied that the job has been completed satisfactorily – but this payment should not be withheld 'unreasonably'. Sometimes, building projects can cost more than expected because of things being discovered along the way – more extensive structural damage than first thought, for example – or because of outside influences, especially the weather. Experienced contractors may have allowed for this in their quote, but the additional cost should be agreed (preferably in writing) before any extra work is carried out.

Equally, it is not reasonable if you start adding things without expecting to pay for them (builders hate the words "while you are here...").

The key to all this is agreement in writing. A contract for building work is not cast in stone and can be varied if both parties agree.

Before any payment is made, the contractor should give you a written invoice (including VAT where relevant – see below) plus any receipts for materials, which you should put in your file alongside the contract or written agreement.

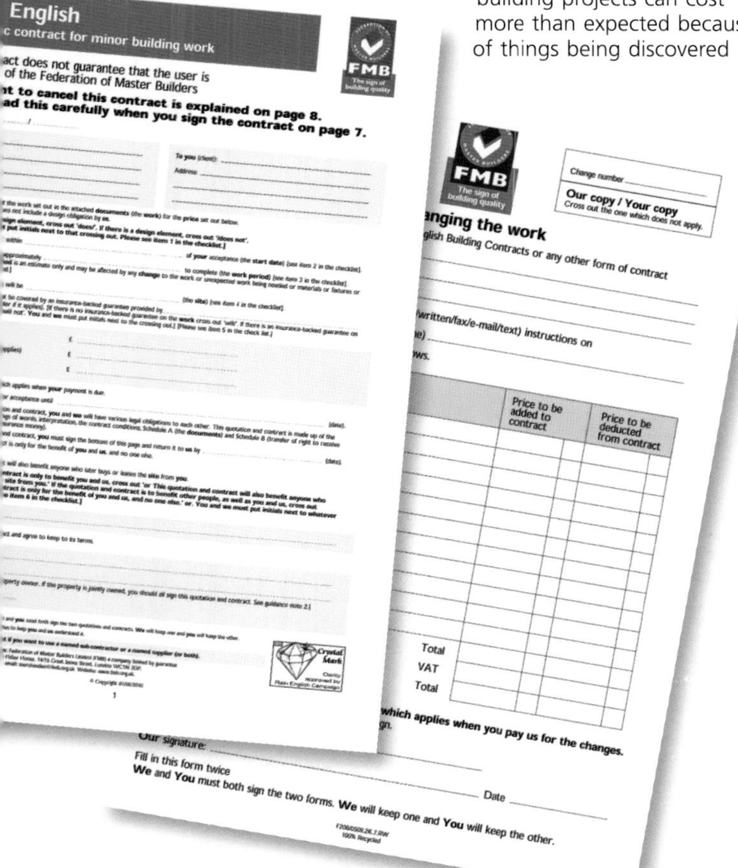

English
...c contract for minor building work
...act does not guarantee that the user is ...of the Federation of Master Builders
...nt to cancel this contract is explained on page 8.
...ad this carefully when you sign the contract on page 7.

FMB The sign of building quality

Change number
Our copy / Your copy
Cross out the one which does not apply.

...nging the work
...glish Building Contracts or any other form of contract

	Price to be added to contract	Price to be deducted from contract
Total		
VAT		
Total		

...hich applies when you pay us for the changes.

Our signature:
Fill in this form twice
We and You must both sign the two forms. We will keep one and You will keep the other.
Date

VAT

Most home improvement work is liable for VAT at the full rate – it is only the building of new homes (and alterations for the disabled) that are zero-rated for VAT. Some improvements (converting houses into flats, renovating an empty house or installing certain energy-saving materials, for example) qualify for VAT at a reduced rate. VAT is always payable on the materials used and on the cost of labour – if the contractor is VAT registered. All large firms will be VAT registered, but some one-man contractors can choose not to register if their turnover is below the VAT limit. They can normally do this only if the customer buys the materials directly – this is perfectly legal since no value is added to the materials.

Make sure you are not being charged VAT by a non-registered trader. All registered firms have a VAT number and you can check the number with HM Revenue and Customs via their website or by ringing 0845 010 9000.

Planning permission and building regulations

It is very important to know whether or not you need planning permission or Building Regulations approval for your project and to agree who is going to make the applications for these. Read Chapter 13 (pages 482 to 496) to see whether you do need planning permission or Building Regulations approval and also for details of how they are obtained. The latest details of legislation are on the government website www.planningportal.gov.uk.

If you are employing an architect or surveyor to oversee the work, they should deal with all this for you, but if you are managing the project yourself, it is vital that it is clear who is doing this part of the job – you or the contractor. It is your responsibility as the householder to ensure the necessary permissions are obtained – if they are not, you could be fined and/or be made to undo the work or there could be problems when it comes to selling the house.

If planning permission is needed, you cannot proceed with the project until it has been granted. If Building Regulations approval is needed, the project can be started without formal approval – and finished if the contractor is able to self-certify the work (true for electrical work and replacement windows, for example).

You will also need to contact the insurance company with whom your buildings insurance is held and to check that there are no restrictive covenants in your house deeds which might prevent you carrying out the project you have in mind.

Planning the work

There are lots of things you need to think about before the builders arrive on site – skip hire, clearing rooms/areas, protecting the house, scaffolding, arranging access, parking and drawing up a schedule of works.

Neighbours

If your project requires planning permission, your neighbours will have an opportunity to comment on your proposals – but they do not have the right of veto and unless (for example) you plan an extension which will seriously affect their right to light, they cannot stop planning permission being granted. This is a decision for the planning committee at your local council whose main concern is to ensure that proposals fit in with the overall plan for the area.

It is, however, always sensible to discuss any building plans you have with your neighbours – and essential if any fences or, especially, walls you have in common will be affected. The Party Wall Act of 1996 is fully explained in a government leaflet which you can order or download for free at www.communities.gov.uk/publications/planningandbuilding/partywall

You should, of course, inform your neighbours when you are having building work done – as they could be affected by the noise and possible mess the work will create. You will need to make sure that piles of building materials (especially sand) do not encroach on their land. Also let neighbours know if you are having any trees felled in the garden.

Skip hire

Any substantial building project will probably mean the hiring of a skip to get rid of building rubble. If the skip is to be left on the road, you need a licence from your local council. This is normally obtained by the skip hire company (who will need to be registered

with your local council) and a licence normally lasts for four weeks. There will be conditions attached – for example, the skip will need lights at night and may also need cones to mark its position. Be prepared for other people putting things into (and taking things out of) your skip (the local council may require you to fit a cover).

Clearing rooms/areas

Before your contractors arrive, clear as much as you can from the work area that is not going to end up in the skip. Store furniture safely and box up valuables or anything that could get broken.

If you are having new carpets laid, clear all the furniture out and remove the old carpets, so you can make any necessary repairs to floorboards (see page 126) before the new carpet is laid (carpet layers will not do these repairs for you). For new floorcoverings in kitchens, you may need to remove all appliances (and possibly the sink and base units if the flooring is to go beneath them). The WC should be removed in a bathroom so that the new flooring can be laid beneath it.

Protecting the house

Building work can create a huge amount of dust, so it is worth buying plenty of plastic sheeting that you can tape over the doors of rooms that are not part of the work to prevent dust getting in – or, perhaps, seal off a whole area of the house. The contractors may provide this – if not, buy it yourself.

Scaffolding

You will not normally have to arrange scaffolding yourself (the builder or roofing contractor will look after this), but when it is erected for a specific job, make sure that your upstairs windows have proper security locks on them. Because scaffolding is so expensive, it is worth considering what other jobs could be done whilst you have it up, if it is necessary for the project in hand. If the budget allows, examples include gutter repairs/replacement, exterior painting and repointing of walls.

Access

The builders should bring heavy-duty plastic runners that can be put down on the floor so that they can walk to where they are working in their work boots. You might also want to protect any doorways they have to pass through carrying tools and materials. If they need to come into 'your' area for anything (to get water or to use the WC), ask them to leave their work boots on their side of the plastic divide.

Materials

Think about where materials are going to be stored during the project and make sure you have enough room for them. Building materials (sand, cement, etc.) are best stored outside with protection against the rain; valuable materials inside. Builders may also want to leave at least some of their tools with you – something you should encourage as you then know they will be coming back the next day.

Make sure that it is clear how and when materials are to be delivered to the site. You do not want building materials dumped in the road (actually it's against the law unless you have permission to do this), nor do you want building materials being delivered at 7am before any builders are on site.

Parking

If you live in a street where only residents parking is allowed, you may need to get an extra permit for the contractor's van – and also to ensure that there is temporary space available for material delivery lorries, some of which can be quite large. A ready-mixed concrete lorry may need to be there for some time.

Schedule of works

A schedule of works is simply a calendar which shows which parts of the work are to be completed in each week (or, for short projects, each day) and when payments are to be made. You may be able to download suitable templates from the internet or you could construct your own schedule – include on it the dates on which specific materials are required and, perhaps, the dates for scheduled site meetings.

During the work

Be prepared for considerable disruption while building work is going on. Your house will not be your own again until it is finished.

Access to house

You will probably need to give your contractors a set of keys (and the code to the burglar alarm if necessary), so that they can let themselves in and out. If you are not going to be there at any time during the day, make sure that they have a telephone number on which they can contact you. You may need to make special arrangements if you have pets.

Material deliveries

Deliveries of building materials may happen nearly every day and quite often are early in the morning – so you may need to move your car (if materials are being left on the drive) or leave it in the road overnight.

If materials are delivered before any contractors are on site, you may be expected to help the driver unload them – not funny if it's sheet lead or full bags of cement that are being delivered. If no one is there, make sure you get the proper paperwork.

Keeping track of progress

When you drew up the contract, you should have produced a schedule of works, so you will be able to use this to compare actual progress with planned progress.

A project 'diary', which records progress each day and also conversations and agreements, can be invaluable if it comes to any dispute at the end. Include things like material deliveries, visits by the Building Control Officer and any 'incidents' (especially those involving any damage or breakage). Use the diary to record changes in the specification – though major changes should be put in writing in a letter to the contractor.

You may want to take photographs as the work proceeds, but try to do this after any contractors have gone home – no one likes having someone looking over their shoulder while working.

Try to arrange regular site meetings (perhaps once a week) – with the main contractor or supervising architect/surveyor – so that you can review progress and adjust payments accordingly.

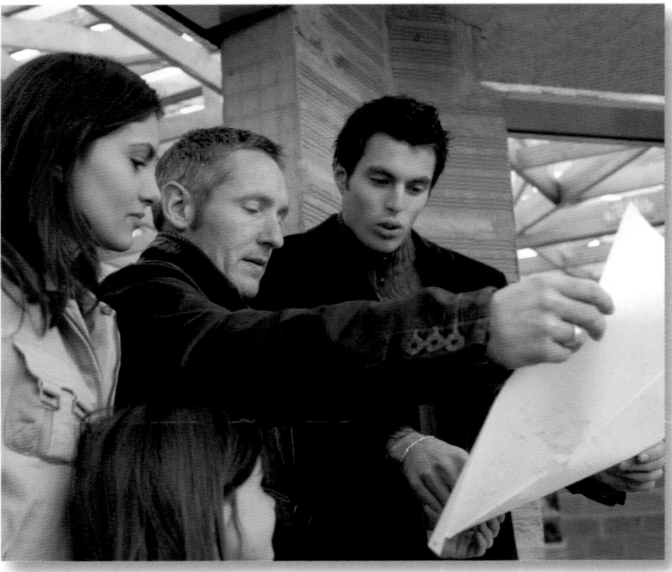

Keep a 'snagging' list – a list of things that are wrong or not quite right, which you can discuss at site meetings and agree when they will be corrected. Cross things off the list as and when they are put right.

Cleanliness

Try to agree with your contractors that the site will be left as clean as possible at the end of each working day. Sweeping up outside is good as it prevents dirt being trodden into the house.

Work not started?

Contractors sometimes take on more work than they can handle – with the result that some jobs do not get started at anything like the scheduled time. If that has happened to you and you are not prepared to wait in an uncertain queue, you should write to the contractor saying that you are cancelling the contract.

If the work has been started, but is nowhere near finished, you can still cancel the contract and you are entitled to claim compensation from the contractor if it subsequently costs you more to employ another contractor to finish the work.

Workers not on site

When faced with a job which involves working outside – and so at the mercy of the weather – many contractors like to have an 'indoor' job running at the same time, so that they have somewhere to work if it is lashing down with rain. If yours is the indoor job and the weather is fine, you may find your workers are missing. There's not a lot you can do about this – except to remind the contractor that you have a contract and that if he expects to get paid, you expect the work to be done on time.

Damage to new fittings

As well as ensuring that existing fittings in the home are not damaged by tools and materials being carted past them, you may need to make sure that new fittings are suitably protected as they are installed. You do not want an expensive bath (for example) being damaged as the walls surrounding it are tiled. Many such fittings will come with some kind of protection precisely for this, but it is often wise to add more.

What to do if things go wrong

Building work can go wrong – sometimes horribly wrong. You need to know what you can do if it happens to you.

As explained on page 508, you have basic legal rights with any work done in your home, even if there is no contract or written agreement with the contractor concerned.

Very often with building work, things will not go to plan. Sometimes this may be the result of outside factors, such as the weather, but you need to know what to do if they go badly wrong.

Amicable settlement

Many disputes can be settled amicably – though it will help if there is a written contract and if you have kept notes and a project diary while the work is in progress. If you make your complaint clear to the contractor, it will give him or her a chance to put things right, without the need for further action. If a friendly conversation does not resolve the problem, it's best to write a more formal letter to the contractor setting out exactly what is wrong, what you expect to be done about it and giving a deadline for things to be put right. Refer to the notes you have taken during the project, especially of any conversations about timing or costs. You can download a suitable letter template on the government website (www.direct.gov.uk); send your letter by recorded delivery and keep a copy of it.

Using Trade Associations

If your contractor is a member of a Trade Association, you may be able to take advantage of the association's conciliation and arbitration schemes, provided both parties agree. Details of the various conciliation and arbitration schemes are given in the Trade and Professional Association section on pages 504-507; conciliation is usually free but you may have to pay to use an arbitration service.

Withholding payment

If you have a contract or a written agreement, you should not withhold payment 'unreasonably'. But you are not expected to pay for work that has not been done satisfactorily nor for work that has not been done at all. And your contract should already contain a 'retention' clause, allowing you to hold back a percentage of the final payment in the event that the work has not been completed satisfactorily. You need to be careful about withholding payments if you have a credit agreement or are paying by credit card – your future credit rating could be affected. But remember that the credit company is jointly liable with the contractor for any breach of the agreement (provided the value of the work is between £100 and £30,000), so you should tell them if there is any dispute.

Work not finished?

If it looks as though the work is not going to be finished within the time stipulated in the contract or written agreement, and there is no good reason for this, you should write to the contractor saying you will cancel the contract unless it is completed within a reasonable time – if you are already at the scheduled finishing point, 28 days would not be unreasonable. Say – explicitly – in your letter that you are now making 'time of the essence'. This is a legal term and, effectively, modifies the contract. Again, send the letter by recorded delivery and keep a copy.

Compensation

If you can show that the work was not carried out with reasonable care and skill, or finished within a reasonable time, or that the contractor has been negligent, you may be entitled to compensation.

You may also be entitled to compensation if you have incurred additional costs (employing someone else to rectify faults, for example) or if you have suffered inconvenience as a result of a breach of contract.

If someone has suffered personal injury as a result of negligent work, always seek legal advice before proceeding with a claim for compensation.

Going to court

This is very much a last resort – but may be necessary if you have tried everything else. The Small Claims Court can hear cases up to a value of £5,000 and you can find out more details of how this works at www.hmcourts-service.gov.uk/infoabout/claims/index.htm.

You can get free legal advice (including advice on legal aid) at your local Citizens Advice Bureau or at Community Legal Advice www.communitylegaladvice.org.uk (0845 345 4 345) and Consumer Direct (08454 04 05 06). Further details of both of these organisations can be found on the extensive Government website www.direct.gov.uk/en/index.htm. Be prepared for the costs of 'expert' opinion when considering court action. If you want to use another contractor (for example) to back up your complaint, they will almost certainly charge for this.

GUARANTEES

Guarantees (sometimes called warrantees) are in addition to your normal legal rights, not in place of them.

Contractor's own guarantee

Many contractors will offer a guarantee on their work for a limited period (say 12 months), during which time they will put right any faults that emerge. Some guarantees are for much longer than that – up to 20 years – but a contractor's guarantee is worthless if they go out of business (however big they are), though you may still have right of redress if you paid for your home improvement project using a credit agreement or if the contractor is a sole trader (even if he has gone out of business).

Trade association guarantees

Many trade associations provide a back-up guarantee on their members' work, so that if one member firm goes out of business, another member firm will finish the job.

Insurance-backed guarantees

An insurance-backed guarantee is underwritten by an insurance company and will protect you if the company goes out of business during the period covered by the guarantee. Insurance-backed guarantees are often tied in with trade associations and association members are usually vetted before they are able to offer such a guarantee. They are particularly important with long-term guarantees and a good example of an insurance-backed guarantee scheme is that offered by Guarantee Protection Insurance covering firms operating within the woodworm/damp control industry (see page 505). Other insurance-backed guarantee providers include the Building Guarantee Scheme (mainly in Northern Ireland), Federation of Master Builders (Masterbond), HomePro, Installations Assured and Quality Assured National Warranties.

As with any insurance, you have to pay a one-off premium to have the insurance cover, but this is tiny (typically 1 to 2 per cent of the overall cost of the project) compared with the possible costs of having more remedial work done.

Glossary

Acrylic Water-based paint or glaze used for walls and ceilings.

Aggregate Small pieces of stone, gravel or similar material; coarse aggregate is mixed with cement to make concrete.

Airbrick Ventilated brick that allows air into a room or under a floor.

Airlock Blockage in a pipe caused by trapped air.

Alkyd paint Most solvent-based paints are now based on alkyd resin.

Ampere (amp) The measure of the rate at which electricity flows through a circuit.

Angle bead A moulding made from expanded metal mesh and galvanised steel. Used as a reinforcement for plaster on external plaster corners.

Apron A flashing of sheet material (such as zinc) with its top edge set into a brickwork joint and its lower edge overlapping the roof below.

Architrave Decorative wooden moulding fitted round a window or door frame, to cover the join between frame and wall.

Armoured cable Electrical cable usually used underground. It is covered in steel wire to protect it from damage.

Arris The sharp edge formed where two surfaces meet at an angle.

Auger Flexible steel spring wire that can be fed along wastepipes to clear blockages. Also a drilling tool, rather like a corkscrew.

Back nut Securing nut for plumbing fittings – e.g. taps and ballvalves.

Back-siphonage Water being drawn back into the mains supply from the house plumbing system, caused by a drop in mains pressure.

Balanced flue A ducting system that allows a boiler, for example, to draw fresh air from outside the house, and also to discharge gases to the outside.

Ball valve Float-operated valve that controls the supply and level of water in a WC cistern or cold water storage cistern.

Ballast Combination of sand and coarse aggregate used for making concrete.

Baluster A turned piece of wood used as a support for the handrail on a staircase.

Balustrade Collective term for the parts of a staircase handrail; it includes balusters and newel posts.

Bargeboard Strip of wood covering the overhanging edge of a pitched roof at a gable.

Basecoat A flat coat of paint over which a decorative coat is applied.

Batten A narrow strip of wood used as a support – e.g. for plasterboard or to support shelving. Useful as a straightedge, too.

Bending spring Metal coil slid into copper pipe, to enable it to be bent without kinking.

Bibtap Wall-mounted tap with horizontal inlet, usually with a threaded outlet for use with a hosepipe.

Blinding The layer of sand or ballast spread over a hardcore base to provide a smooth surface for floors or paving.

Blown When a surface layer such as plaster or cement render comes away from the wall behind. Also used to describe a fuse wire that has melted and broken an electrical circuit, as a result of overloading.

Bond The manner in which bricks are arranged in a wall; bond patterns are chosen to suit particular types of wall.

Bore The hollow part of a pipe or tube.

Bridging debris Earth or building material that covers a damp-proof course and allows water to rise up the wall above the DPC.

Burr Rough edge left after sawing through a copper pipe or a piece of wood.

Came The grooved strip of lead that holds a piece of coloured glass in a leaded light or stained-glass window.

Cap nut The nut used to tighten a compression joint to secure pipework.

Capillary joint Soldered copper connector for joining copper pipes.

Carcass The basic structure of a bathroom or kitchen unit before doors or drawers are added.

Casement Part of a window, or an entire window. Casement windows contain both fixed and opening sections.

Cavity wall A house wall made of two separate leaves, with a gap between them. They are held together with plastic or metal wall ties and the cavity can be insulated.

Cement A powdery binder that bonds with sand to form mortar and sand / coarse aggregate to form concrete.

Chalk line A piece of string, saturated with coloured chalk, used to mark out a straight line on walls, floors and ceilings.

Chamfer A narrow, flat surface along the edge of a piece of wood, normally at 45°.

Chase A groove cut into masonry or plaster, for a run of cable or piping.

Check valve A valve that lets water flow in one direction only.

Chipboard Man-made board made of wood fibres, supplied in sheets.

Circuit The path through which an electric current can flow.

Cistern Open-topped storage vessel for cold water, commonly known as tank.

Cladding Material used to cover a surface – usually a wall or ceiling.

Cleat A short length of timber designed to support a larger piece (e.g. gravel board).

Compression joint Brass connector for plumbing pipe, tightened with spanners.

Conductor Length of wire through which an electric current can pass. Also core.

Control joint Narrow gap in a slab of concrete that is filled with treated fibreboard to limit cracking and relieve pressure.

Cornice Decorative plaster or wood moulding fitted at wall/ceiling joins.

Counterbore An enlargement of a hole.

Countersink To drill a tapered hole that allows the head of a screw to lie flush with the surface.

Coving A plain moulding made of plaster or polystyrene, to cover the join between the walls and ceiling.

Cross cutting Sawing across the grain of the wood, not along it.

Cross-head Type of screw with cross shaped recess in the head, rather than a single slot. The best type to use with a power screwdriver, because the screwdriver bit grips the head better.

Cutting in Careful painting at corners or at junctions on a wall surface, or beside door frames and windowsills.

Dado The lower part of an interior wall, often defined by a dado rail. Because it is more liable to damage it may be covered with wood panelling.

Damp-proof course (DPC) A continuous layer of impervious material (formerly slate, but now usually plastic) which prevents damp rising from the ground into walls.

Damp-proof fluid Used where a DPC has failed or never existed. A silicone-based liquid is injected at regular points into an exterior wall, to form an impermeable layer. Also known as chemical damp-proofing.

Damp-proof membrane (DPM) Plastic sheeting used to form an impermeable layer in concrete floors.

Deadman A temporary brace used to hold up one end of a sheet of ceiling board or a length of timber, while the other end is being worked on.

Dedicated circuit A circuit which runs from the consumer unit to one appliance only, such as a cooker or freezer socket.

Detector Battery-operated electronic device for locating pipes, cables, studs, joists or the presence of electricity.

Distemper A traditional paint which feels powdery and wipes off with a wet cloth. No longer used: to redecorate, old distemper must first be washed off entirely.

Distressing A paint effect used to give an aged appearance to wood.

Diverter valve A valve that diverts water flow from bath taps to a shower head.

Double check valve Backflow prevention device, designed to protect water supplies from contamination.

Dowel A cylindrical wooden peg used to reinforce joints in woodworking.

Dragging A paint effect achieved by dragging a paintbrush in straight lines through wet glaze.

Dry-lining A wall lining formed by fixing sheets of tapered-edge plasterboard to a framework of timber battens. Joints are covered with tape and plastered over.

Dry rot Fungal attack on wood and other materials. First signs are small, silky threads, which spread outwards from a concealed fruiting body.

Earth The safety connection in electric wiring that links all exposed metal parts to the main earthing terminal.

Earth rammer A weighted metal tool for compacting earth and hardcore.

Eaves The lower edge of the roof and rafters, that projects beyond the walls, to protect the walls from rainfall.

Efflorescence White, powdery deposit of soluble salts, left on a wall as it dries out. Must be brushed, not washed, off.

Eggshell Hard-wearing paint with a dull, matt finish. Can be acrylic or solvent-based.

Elbow Plumbing joint that forms a 90° bend in pipework.

Emulsion Water-based paint used for interior walls or ceilings.

Enamel A hard-wearing coating used on baths and sinks. Also a highly-coloured paint with a hard glossy finish.

End-grain The surface of wood exposed after cutting across the grain.

Engineer's vice Bench-mounted vice for holding metal objects.

Escutcheon Small plate used to finish off a keyhole. May have a cover for draught proofing and privacy.

Expanded metal mesh Perforated metal sheet or strip used to support plaster when patching holes in plasterboard.

Expansion joint Gap left to allow for thermal movement – in floors or guttering, for example.

External corner A corner that juts out into a room, for example on a chimney breast.

Face nailing Method of driving in nails through the surface of the wood.

Fascia A strip of wood covering the ends of rafters, to which guttering may be attached.

Feathering Technique used in painting and plastering to smooth away the edges, so that they are undetectable.

Feed-and-expansion cistern Water vessel that stores water to top-up central heating system. Also called header tank.

Finial Decorative piece of wood used to finish the top of a post, usually on a staircase newel. Also the decorative end of a curtain pole.

Flashing Material used to make a weatherproof join between a wall or chimney and a roof.

Flexible filler A filler for wood that sets hard, but allows slight movement.

Flexible sealant Water-based or acrylic sealant, supplied in a tube and applied with a sealant gun, to seal gaps.

Footing A narrow concrete foundation for a brick or block wall.

Formwork Timber boards fixed to pegs in the ground to form a mould when concrete is cast. Also called shuttering.

Foundation Strip of concrete cast in a trench as a base for a masonry wall or other construction.

Frame fixer Long wall plug that can be inserted directly through hole in frame.

Frog The angled depression in one face of some house bricks.

Fuse Weak link in electrical circuit or plug, that fails if current is too high.

Gable The triangular end of a pitched roof.

Galvanised Covered with a protective coating of zinc.

Gate valve On-off control fitted on low-pressure pipework.

Gauge rod A timber batten marked at regular intervals used to check the positioning of tiles or bricks.

Glaze Usually colourless liquid to which paint or pigments can be added. Once applied to the surface of a wall, it is worked in various ways with brushes, sponges and cloths to create paint effects.

Gloss Highly decorative, shiny paint finish. Also paint for wood and metal.

Grommet A flexible ring, used to line a hole to prevent cable, for instance, from chafing against a sharp edge. Blind grommets have a thin membrane that is cut when the cable is ready to be fed through.

Grout Filling compound used in the gaps between ceramic and other hard tiles.

Halving joint Joint formed by cutting away half the depth on two pieces of same-size wood, so that when fitted together the surfaces are flush.

Hardboard Man-made board made of compressed wood pulp and sawdust, supplied in sheets.

Hardcore Crushed or broken bricks, blocks or stone, used as a filler in the construction of foundations and sub-bases.

Hawk Metal or plywood square with a handle underneath, used to hold plaster or mortar while working.

Header Brick laid in a wall with its end visible.

Head plate Timber beam that forms the top frame component in a stud partition wall.

Header tank Popular name for feed-and-expansion cistern.

Hoggin Fine ballast used to form a sub-base for concrete paving.

Hopper head Takes outflow from two rainwater downpipes and directs it into a single pipe.

Housing A long, narrow channel, cut across the grain of wood to receive the edge of a board, when forming a joint.

Instantaneous heater A heater that heats mains-supplied water on demand, as it flows through the heater. Often gas-fired.

Inspection chamber Hole in ground where underground drains are connected or where they change direction.

Insulation Materials used to reduce the transmission of heat or sound. Also non-conductive material surrounding electrical wires or connections to prevent the passage of electricity.

Jamb The vertical side member of a window or door frame.

Jointing trowel Tool used for shaping pointed mortar joints.

Jointing compound Filler used to seal gaps between sheets of plasterboard.

Jointing tape Self-adhesive tape used for covering joins between sheets of plasterboard.

Joist Wooden or steel beam used for supporting floors and ceilings.

Junction box Plastic fitting used for making connections between cables on a power or lighting circuit.

Keying Technique used to roughen a surface in order to provide a better grip when plastering, painting or using adhesive.

Knotting Sealer used to cover knots in bare wood and prevent resin from oozing through decorative finishes

Knock-down fitting Used in flat-pack furniture to join components together.

Lagging Insulating material fitted over hot-water cylinders, as well as pipes and tanks in unheated areas, to prevent freezing.

Laminated Consisting of thin layers. Applies to plywood, safety glass and worktops

Lamp Correct name for light bulb.

Laths Narrow strips of wood to which plaster is stuck, in traditional lath-and¬-plaster walls and ceilings.

Leading edge Vertical edge of door or window farthest from the hinges.

Light Word sometimes used for window.

Lime (hydrated) Ingredient to make mortar more workable.

Live (also known as phase or line) The part of an electrical circuit that carries the flow of current to an appliance.

Lintel Supporting horizontal beam over an opening in masonry, such as a door, window or fireplace.

Louvre vent A grille with downward-pointing slats, used to cover the end of ducting run through a wall.

Manhole cover Removable lud for inspection chamber.

Masonry bolt – see Wall anchor.

MDF (medium density fibreboard) Fine wood-particle board that is easily shaped to a smooth finish.

Melamine Tough, synthetic resin used as facing laminate on man-made boards.

Microporous Describes a finish such as paint or woodstain that permits moisture to escape from wood, allowing it to dry out, at the same time protecting it from rainwater or damp.

Miniature Circuit breaker (MCB) A trip switch on a circuit in a consumer unit that acts automatically to break the circuit in the event of a fault. Once the fault is fixed, the MCB can be reset to restore the power.

Mineral fibre Material used for insulation.

Mitre A corner joint, made by cutting two pieces of material at a 45° angle.

Mortar Mixture of cement, sand and sometimes other additives, used in bricklaying and rendering.

Mortise A rectangular recess cut into wood to allow it to receive a matching tongue or tenon.

Motorised valve A valve controlled by hot water cylinder and room thermostats to direct heating water as required.

Moulding Shaped wood or plaster used as a decorative feature on doors, walls and ceilings and around door frames.

Mouse A small weight used to pass a string-line through a narrow vertical space.

Mullion The vertical dividing piece of a window frame.

Muntin Central vertical frame of a door, fixed to the top and bottom rails.

Nail punch Simple tool used with a hammer, to drive nail heads below the surface of the wood.

Neutral The part of an electrical circuit that carries the flow of current from an appliance.

Newel post Main post fitted at top or bottom of stairs, to support the strings (staircase sides) and the handrail.

Nogging (or noggin) Short horizontal piece of timber fixed between wall studs or ceiling joists, to stiffen the structure.

Nosing The front edge of a stair tread.

Oilstone Flat abrasive stone, lubricated with light oil, used for sharpening tools.

Olive Sealing ring in a brass compression joint for plumbing pipes.

Oxidise To form a layer of metal oxide, as happens in rusting.

Parting bead The strip of wood separating the two sliding sashes in a sash window.

Party wall Shared wall that separates two properties.

Penetrating oil Thin lubricant that seeps between corroded surfaces, allowing them to be eased apart.

Phase (also known as live or line) The part of an electrical circuit that carries the flow of current to an appliance.

Pier Thick column of masonry bonded into a wall to increase the wall's stability.

Pilot hole Small hole drilled to allow a piece of wood to receive a larger screw or nail without splitting.

Pipe/cable detector Electronic device for detecting metal in walls.

Plasterboard Rigid wall-covering material made of gypsum plaster, sandwiched between sheets of paper.

Plinth Detachable panel that covers the supporting legs of self-assembly units such as kitchen cabinets.

Plumb Exactly vertical. A plumb line is used to establish vertical drops.

Plumber's auger See auger.

Plywood Building board made by bonding together thin layers of wood with the grain of alternate layers running at right angles to one another.

Pointing Shaping the mortar joints between bricks with a jointing trowel or other tool.

Pressure-treated timber Wood that has been impregnated with preservative under extreme pressure.

Primer The first coat of paint applied to protect wood and metal. It reduces the absorption of subsequent layers of paint; a metal primer prevents corrosion.

Profile board Board set on edge and nailed to stakes to mark out foundations.

PTFE (polytetrafluoroethylene) Material used to make tape for sealing threaded plumbing fittings.

Push-fit joint Plastic or brass joint for joining pipes without tools.

Purlin A horizontal beam that provides intermediate support for rafters or sheet roofing.

PVA (polyvinyl acetate) General purpose adhesive. Often used as a bonding agent for plaster and mortar. Also used for 'white' wood adhesive.

PVC (polyvinyl chloride) A plastic used for cable insulation and corrugated roofing. The unplasticised form, PVCu, is used for plumbing pipes, exterior cladding and window frames.

Quarry tiles Hard tiles that have been fired in a kiln. Used as a floor covering.

Radial circuit An electrical circuit that starts at the consumer unit and runs from one outlet to another and terminates at the last one.

RCD (residual current device) Fast-acting trip-switch that cuts off the power to prevent electric shock in the event of a fault.

Rebate A L-shaped recess along the edge of a piece of wood.

Reducer Plumbing joint that is used between pipes of different diameter.

Render A thin layer of cement-based mortar. It can be used as a base for plastering on an inside wall, or simply painted over when on an exterior wall.

Reveal Vertical sides of a recessed door or window opening.

Ring circuit An electrical circuit that runs from the consumer unit to each outlet in turn before returning to the consumer unit.

Rip cutting Sawing along the grain of the wood, not across it.

Riser The vertical part of a step.

Rising damp Moisture entering a house from below as a result of the failure of the damp-proof course in a wall or the damp-proof membrane in a concrete floor.

RSJ (rolled steel joist) Used mainly over an opening when a load-bearing wall is removed and two rooms are made into one.

Rubber A pad of cotton wool wrapped in lint-free cloth used to apply stain or polish.

Sash window A type of window with two sliding sections (sashes).

Sashlock Mortise lock fitted to back and side doors containing a handle-operated latch as well as a deadbolt.

Satin Paint with a semi-gloss finish.

Screed A thin layer of mortar applied to give a smooth surface to concrete.

Scribe To score a line with a sharp or pointed instrument. Also to shape tiles or other material to match surface profile.

Sealant See Flexible sealant.

Secret nailing Method of nailing boards through their edges, to conceal the nails.

Self-levelling compound Applied to concrete floors in order to provide a level surface for further floor covering.

Sheath The outer layer of insulation covering an electrical cable or flex.

Shim A thin wooden strip used as a measure to establish a fall across a surface

Shoe Curved outlet at the base of a rainwater downpipe that directs water into a gully.

Short circuit The accidental diversion of electricity between conductors, which increases the flow of current and blows a fuse or trips a miniature circuit breaker (MCB).

Shuttering Wooden framework used to enclose and contain concrete as it is poured. Also known as formwork.

Side light Narrow, non-opening window next to a door.

Silk Paint with a semi-gloss finish.

Size Sealer used to coat plastered or papered surfaces in preparation for wallpapering. It prevents the surface from absorbing too much paste, which makes the paper easier to hang.

Skew Nailing or screwing at an angle through wood in order to provide a fixing.

Skim To apply a thin top coat of plaster to a wall surface.

Snake Common name for a plumber's auger.

Soakaway A pit filled with rubble or gravel into which rainwater is drained.

Soffit The underside of an archway or the eaves of a building.

Soil stack Large-diameter vertical pipe, vented at the top, that carries soil and waste water to the main drainage system.

Sole plate The lowest horizontal frame component of a stud partition wall.

Solvent-weld cement Adhesive used for joining some types of plastic waste pipe.

Spacers Small dividers used between tiles and paving slabs to keep a consistent gap between them during installation.

Spalling Flaking of the outer face of masonry, caused by moisture expanding in freezing conditions.

Spur Branch cable that extends an existing electrical circuit.

Staff bead The innermost strip of wood holding a sliding sash in a sash window frame.

Steam stripper Machine (can be hired) which aids the stripping of wallpaper by applying steam to the paper surface.

Stile The vertical side member of a door or window sash.

Stoptap On-off control fitted on mains-pressure pipework.

Stretcher Brick laid in a wall with its long side visible.

Striker plate Metal plate set in a door frame, containing a cut-out into which the latch fits when the door is shut.

String The sides of a staircase supporting the treads.

Strutting X-shaped metal or timber braces between floor joists that give extra support.

Stud Vertical timber support in a wood-framed partition wall

Stud detector Electronic device that detects presence of studs or joists.

Sub-base A layer of compacted hardcore or hoggin that provides a stable base for a drive, path or patio.

Sugar soap Chemical compound used to degrease paintwork prior to redecorating.

Supplementary bonding The connecting to earth of exposed metal pipework, mainly in bathrooms.

Tail Connection between a tap and its supply pipe. Usually threaded, but plain on some mixer taps. Also connector to fit between radiator and valve.

Tamp To compact soil, hardcore or concrete using an earth rammer or a heavy piece of timber.

Tamping beam Length of timber with a handle at each end, used with a chopping action across shuttering to compact and level concrete.

Tank Storage vessel for cold water.

Tee Plumbing joint that connects a branch pipe to the main pipe run.

Template Cut-out pattern made from metal, wood or paper, to provide a guide to shaping something accurately.

Tenon A projecting tongue on a piece of wood that fits into a corresponding mortise.

Terminals Connections to which the bared conductors of a cable or flex are attached.

Tie Piece of wood or metal that links opposing members and prevents outward movement, such as tie-beams found at the feet of rafters.

Tile spacer See spacer

Tongue-and-groove Type of joint between boards in which a tongue on the edge of one board fits into the groove in another.

Top coat Final coat of paint.

Top light Small opening top window.

Transformer Electrical device that changes the voltage in a circuit.

Transom A horizontal dividing piece of a window frame.

Trap A U-shaped section of pipe below a bath, basin, shower tray, WC or sink. It fills with water to prevent smells coming from the drains into the house.

Tread The horizontal part of a step.

Trowels Tools used for bricklaying and plastering; they come in various shapes to suit their purpose.

Trunking Rectangular-section plastic or metal duct for cables and pipes that protects them as they run along wall surfaces.

Undercoat Layer of paint used to obliterate the colour of the primer and build up a protective layer before applying the top coat.

Underlay Layer of plywood or hardboard applied over a rough floor to provide a smooth surface suitable for tiles or other floor coverings. Also a resilient layer under a carpet or a pond liner.

Valley Rainwater channel, usually of zinc or lead, between two sections of roof.

Vapour barrier Impervious layer that prevents the passage of moisture-laden air.

Veneer Thin layer of hardwood applied over cheaper base wood, for a decorative effect.

Vinyl Plastic material used for easy-to-clean floor coverings. Also protective covering on some wallpapers or an additive used in paint, to increase their hard-wearing and wipeable properties.

Vinyl emulsion Water-based paint ideal for bathrooms as it is easy to wipe down and keep clean.

VOCs Volatile Organic Compounds are chemical compounds found in paints, stains, varnishes, preservatives, carpets and laminated furniture that emit gases, contributing to atmospheric pollution. These gases can cause headaches, nausea and breathing difficulties.

Volt The measure of pressure that causes electric current to flow round a circuit.

Voltage detector Electronic device that detects the presence of electricity.

Wall anchor (masonry bolt) A bolt with a sturdy metal shield that grips the sides of a hole drilled in masonry or concrete.

Wall plate A horizontal timber beam placed along the top of a wall to support and provide attachment for joists and rafters, and to spread their load.

Wallplug Plastic or metal sheath inserted into a pre-drilled hole in a wall to hold a screw

Wall ties Metal or plastic connectors used to bind different sections of a masonry wall together.

Washer A flexible ring that prevents taps from leaking. Also spreads load of nut or bolt head.

Watt The measure of power consumed by an electrical appliance. 1000 watts = 1 kilowatt (kW).

Weatherboard A length of wooden moulding fixed at the base of an external door to direct rainwater away from the door.

Weephole A small hole at the base of a wall that allows moisture to drain to the outside.

Wet rot Fungus that attacks wood with too high a moisture content. Not as serious as dry rot, but leads to the eventual destruction of timber.

Woodworm Generic term for attacks in timber by the larvae of wood-boring beetles.

Further information

ALTERNATIVE TECHNOLOGY

Centre for Alternative Technology
Machynlleth
Powys SY20 9AZ
01654 705950
www.cat.org.uk
Email via website

CAT is an education and visitor centre which demonstrates practical solutions for sustainability. All aspects of green living are featured on the site: environmental building, eco-sanitation, woodland management, renewable energy, energy efficiency and organic growing.

ARCHITECTURAL SALVAGE

SalvoWeb
www.salvo.co.uk

The Salvo Directory lists dealers in architectural salvage, showing yards shops and showrooms where you can buy antique, reclaimed, salvaged and green material.

BUILDING

Building Research Establishment (BRE)
Bucknalls Lane
Watford WD25 9XX
01923 664 000
www.bre.co.uk

Information on building, innovation, testing and refurbishment for the built environment industry. Useful for householders to keep track on developments.

British Standards Institute (BSI)
389 Chiswick High Road
London W4 4AL
020 8996 9001
www.bsigroup.com
Email cservices@bsigroup.com

The BSI provides assessment, certification, and testing of products and services, including electrical and electronic items, windows and doors, aluminium ladders, plumbing and heating products. Certified products are awarded the Kitemark, the BSI's registered certification mark that guarantees quality and safety.

The Building Centre
Store Street
London WC1E 7BT
0207 692 4000
www.buildingcentre.co.uk

The Building Centre is an independent body dedicated to providing information and ideas to all sectors concerned with the built environment. Its Store Street centre is open to everyone involved in architecture and construction and has exhibition and product galleries, plus a bookshop which sells a wide range of construction and architecture related titles.

CONTRACTS

The Joint Contracts Tribunal Ltd
JCT Contracts
Sweet & Maxwell
Cheriton House
North Way
Andover SP10 5BE
0845 600 9355
www.jctcontracts.com
jct.support@thomson.com

JCT Contracts provides standard forms of building contracts which you can buy for a small fee. While the contracts are mainly used by professionals, they may be useful if you are project managing your own building work.

HEATING, WATER AND SEWERAGE

Heating and Hot Water Information Council (HHIC)
Camden House
Warwick Road
Kenilworth CV8 1TH
www.centralheating.co.uk
Email via website

The HHIC provides consumers with independent advice for their heating systems. You can search FAQs on their website or email them with questions.

Ofwat
Centre City Tower
7 Hill Street
Birmingham B5 4UA
0121 644 7500
www.ofwat.gov.uk
enquiries@ofwat.gsi.gov.uk

Ofwat is the economic regulator of the water and sewerage industry in England and Wales and ensures that water companies provide household and business customers with a good service and value for money. Visit their website for information on all aspects of household water from understanding your bill to meters and complaints.

Waterwatch Scotland
Corporate Office
Forrester Lodge
Inglewood
Alloa FK10 2HU
0845 850 3344 (local rate number)
01259 725335
www.waterwatchscotland.org
Email info@waterwatchscotland.org

Waterwatch Scotland is the complaints handling authority for all domestic and non-domestic water customers. It is also the consumer representative body for the water industry in Scotland.

TREES

Arboricultural Association
Ullenwood Court
Ullenwood
Cheltenham
Gloucestershire GL53 9QS
01242 522152
www.trees.org.uk
admin@trees.org.uk

The Arboricultural Association promotes care and knowledge of trees. Its website provides a Directory of Tree Advisors who can offer specialist opinion on tree health, safety, preservation, trees and buildings, planning and law.They do not plant, prune or fell but can provide a schedule and work specification for a tree surgeon. Their website offers a list of approved contractors searchable by area or postcode, and a useful page of FAQs for the public.

WASTE AND RECYCLING

Dulux Customer Care Centre
ICI Paints
Wexham Road
Slough SL2 5DS
www.dulux.co.uk/advice

Provides information on reducing and recycling the paint you buy, plus donating unused paint.

www.direct.gov.uk

The UK government's official website has a section on the hazardous waste disposal under Environment and greener living. It details what is considered hazardous and directs you to your local authority website so you can find out about disposal facilities in your area.

WRAP (Waste & Resources Action Programme)
01295 819900
www.wrap.org.uk/individuals

WRAPs mission statement is to help businesses and individuals reap the benefits of reducing waste, develop sustainable products and use resources in an efficient way. Their website www.recyclenow.com offers advice and tips on recycling and disposing of DIY items such as carpets, paint and small electrical items.

ADVICE ON THE INTERNET

There are many sites offering DIY advice on the Internet, but quite a few are linked to specific products or outlets. Make sure a website is based on UK products and building standards. Many American sites give advice – particularly on plumbing and electrics – that does not conform with British safety standards. For impartial UK-based advice, these are some of the best.

www.bbc.co.uk/homes/diy Very informative, with advice on most DIY jobs plus a calculations facility that helps you to work out how much paint, wallpaper, etc you will need for your specific project.

www.diydoctor.org.uk Tips and tricks of the trade, information on products, and details of local tradespeople and specialists.

www.diyfixit.co.uk Information on general building, plumbing, electrics, woodworking, decorating, insulation and central heating.

www.finddiy.co.uk A very good starting point as it offers links to other sites as well as information on tools, equipment and tradespeople.

www.homepro.com Unusual style ideas as well as down-to-earth DIY, legal and financial advice, and a guide to contractors.

www.ukdiyforum.co.uk A resource for DIY enthusiasts, builders and industry professionals with videos, DIY guides and an active forum.

www.ultimatehandyman.co.uk A site dedicated to all kinds of DIY, plus an active forum for DIY help.

MAKING DIY GREENER

The following websites offer information and advice on saving energy and sourcing environmentally friendly materials for your DIY needs. Some also provide links to key products and services.

www.direct.gov.uk/en/Environmentandgreenerliving

www.green-solutions.com

www.livingethically.co.uk

www.greenchoices.org

CONVERSION FOR LINEAR MEASUREMENTS

Metric	Imperial	Metric	Imperial
1mm	1/32in	320mm	12½in
2mm	1/16in	330mm	13in
3mm	⅛in	340mm	13½in
6mm	¼in	360mm	14in
10mm	⅜in	370mm	14½in
13mm	½in	380mm	15in
15mm	⅝in	390mm	15½in
20mm	¾in	400mm	16in
25mm	1in	420mm	16½in
30mm	1¼in	430mm	17in
40mm	1½in	440mm	17½in
50mm	2in	460mm	18in
55mm	2¼in	480mm	19in
60mm	2½in	500mm	19½in
70mm	2¾in	510mm	20in
75mm	3in	530mm	21in
80mm	3¼in	560mm	22in
90mm	3½in	580mm	23in
100mm	4in	600mm	23½in
110mm	4¼in	610mm	24in
115mm	4½in	660mm	26in
130mm	5in	700mm	27½in
140mm	5½in	710mm	28in
150mm	6in	750mm	29½in
160mm	6¼in	760mm	30in
170mm	6½in	800mm	31½in
180mm	7in	810mm	32in
190mm	7½in	850mm	33½in
200mm	8in	860mm	34in
215mm	8½in	900mm	35½in
230mm	9in	910mm	36in
240mm	9½in	960mm	38in
250mm	10in	990mm	39in
260mm	10½in	1000mm (1m)	39½in
270mm	10¾in	1.2m	4ft
280mm	11in	1.5m	5ft
290mm	11½in	2m	6ft 6in
300mm	12in	5m	16ft 6in

TEMPERATURE CONVERSIONS

Rough guide

°C	°F
0	32
5	41
10	50
15	59
20	68
25	77
30	86
35	95
40	104
45	113
50	122
55	131
60	140
65	149
70	158
75	167
80	176
85	185
90	194
95	203
100	212

For exact temperature conversions:
°F = (°C x 1.8) + 32
°C = (°F – 32) ÷ 1.8

HOW TO CONVERT UNITS OF MEASUREMENT

Metric to Imperial

	To convert	into	multiply by
Length	millimetres	inches	0.0394
	metres	feet	3.2808
	metres	yards	1.0936
Area	square metres	square feet	10.764
	square metres	square yards	1.196
Volume	cubic metres	cubic feet	35.315
	cubic metres	cubic yards	1.308
	litres	pints	1.76
	litres	gallons	0.22
Weight	kilograms	pounds	2.2046

Imperial to metric

	To convert	into	multiply by
Length	inches	millimetres	25.4
	feet	metres	0.3048
	yards	metres	0.9144
Area	square feet	square metres	0.0929
	square yards	square metres	0.836
Volume	cubic feet	cubic metres	0.0283
	cubic yards	cubic metres	0.7646
	pints	litres	0.568
	gallons	litres	4.55
Weight	pounds	kilograms	0.45359

Index

A

B

C

Q

R

S

T

Acknowledgments

All images in this book are copyright of the Reader's Digest Association Limited, with the exception of those in the following list. The position of photographs and illustrations on each page is indicated by letters after the page number:

T = Top; **B** = Bottom; **L** = Left;
R = Right; **C** = Centre
Cover Getty Images

1 ShutterStock, Inc/zentilia
2 Frieze no. 1 ShutterStock, Inc/DJM-photo; Frieze no. 2 iStockphoto.com/Darren Wise; Frieze no. 3 ShutterStock, Inc/Lisa F. Young; Frieze no. 4 iStockphoto.com/Sabrina dei Nobili; Frieze no. 5 Alamy Images/Oote Boe Photography 2; Frieze no. 6 ShutterStock, Inc/Agphotographer
3 Frieze no. 1 iStockphoto.com/Dejan Nikolic; Frieze no. 2 ShutterStock, Inc/Villedieu Christophe; Frieze no. 3 ShutterStock, Inc/Vonkara; Frieze no. 4 ShutterStock, Inc/Monika23; Frieze no. 5 ShutterStock, Inc/Scott Rothstein; Frieze no. 6 ShutterStock, Inc/Jim Lopes
4-5 iStockphoto.com/Skip ODonnell
6 **L** ShutterStock, Inc/Gilmanshin; **C** ShutterStock, Inc/Pack-Shot; **R** ShutterStock, Inc/Kristin Smith
7 **L** ShutterStock, Inc/Lukiyanova Natalia/frenta
C ShutterStock, Inc/Invisible;
R iStockphoto.com/Levent Ince
15 **TC** www.magnettrade.co.uk
TR www.magnettrade.co.uk
BC Red Cover/Nick Carter
26 **T** Science Photo Library/Agema Infrared Systems
27 Monodraught/www.sunpipe.co.uk
28 **L** ShutterStock, Inc/Chris Hellyar
C ShutterStock, Inc/Jim Lopes
R ShutterStock, Inc/BelleMedia
29 **L** iStockphoto.com/Eric Delmar
C ShutterStock, Inc/Joe Gough
R iStockphoto.com/Luis Pedrosa
43 **BR** GE Fabbri Limited
68 **L** iStockphoto.com/Janice Richard;
C ShutterStock, Inc/Mona Makela;
R iStockphoto.com/Christine Balderas
69 **L** ShutterStock, Inc/Scott Rothstein
C ShutterStock, Inc/Dewayne Flowers
R ShutterStock, Inc/Monika Wisniewska
71 **BR** Punchstock/Blend Images
73 GE Fabbri Limited
75 **TR, C, CR** GE Fabbri Limited
79 **TR, C, BC, BR** GE Fabbri Limited
81 **BL** With thanks to Dulux (www.dulux.co.uk/paintpod)
82 **BL** GE Fabbri Limited
85 **C, BR** GE Fabbri Limited
93 **TC, TR, BL, BC** GE Fabbri Limited
96 **TR, CR, BR** GE Fabbri Limited
97 **BR** GE Fabbri Limited
98 **T, B** GE Fabbri Limited
104 **CR, BR** GE Fabbri Limited
106 **TR, BR** GE Fabbri Limited
107 **TL, CL** GE Fabbri Limited
109 **TC, TR, BL, BC, BR** GE Fabbri Limited
118 **TL, TC, TR, BL, BC** GE Fabbri Limited
120 **T, TL, TR, C, BL, BC, BR** GE Fabbri Limited
121 **TR, BC, BR** GE Fabbri Limited
122 **L** Corbis/Con Tanasiuk/Design Pics; **C** ShutterStock, Inc/photobeps, **R** ShutterStock, Inc/Monika23
123 **L** ShutterStock, Inc/Endi Sukma Dewata
C ShutterStock, Inc/Michael Pettigrew
R Alamy Images/Laura S. Goodman
124 **T, B** Fired Earth
130 **L** Witex/Floorbrand Ltd/Floorbrand Ltd
TR Elizabeth Whiting & Associates/David Giles
BR Elizabeth Whiting & Associates/Mark Luscombe-Whyte
131 **TR, BL, BC, BR** GE Fabbri Limited
132 **CL, BL** GE Fabbri Limited
137 **TC, TR, C, CR, BL, BC, BR** GE Fabbri Limited
138 **TL, TR, CL, C, BL, BC** GE Fabbri Limited
139 **TL, TC, TR, C, CR, BL, BR** GE Fabbri Limited
156 **L** iStockphoto.com/Chris Schmidt; **C** ShutterStock, Inc/Colin Nixon; **R** ShutterStock, Inc/Baloncici
157 **L** ShutterStock, Inc/Vonkara
C iStockphoto.com/Kristian Septimius
R ShutterStock, Inc/Monkey Business Images
161 **TR** www.CotswoldCo.com
164 **TR, CR, BC** GE Fabbri Limited
168 **BL** Red Cover/Nick Carter
173 GE Fabbri Limited
176 **TC, TR, C, CR, BL, BR** GE Fabbri Limited
177 **TC, TR, C, BL, BC, BR** GE Fabbri Limited
178 **TL, TC, TR, CR, BL, BC** GE Fabbri Limited
186 **L** ShutterStock, Inc/grynka
C ShutterStock, Inc/Villedieu Christophe
R ShutterStock, Inc/Vera Bogaerts
187 **L** ShutterStock, Inc/Wendy Keveney Photography,
C ShutterStock, Inc/Dariusz Gora
R Corbis/Neil C. Robinson
198 **TR, BR** GE Fabbri Limited
199 **TL, BL** GE Fabbri Limited
216 **TR, C, BR** GE Fabbri Limited
220 **L** iStockphoto.com/Gunay Mutlu
C iStockphoto.com/Howard Oates
R ShutterStock, Inc/Lisa F. Young
221 **L** iStockphoto.com/Dejan Mikolic
C ShutterStock, Inc/HANA, **R** iStockphoto.com
226 **L, TC, TR, C, BC** GE Fabbri Limited
233 **TR, CR, BR** GE Fabbri Limited
240 **TL, TC, TR, BL, BC, BR** GE Fabbri Limited
251 **T** Elizabeth Whiting & Associates/David Giles
B Red Cover/Jake Fitzjones
252 **L** ShutterStock, Inc/Lisa Turay
C iStockphoto.com/Carol Gering
R Punchstock/Brand X Pictures
253 **L** ShutterStock, Inc/Agphotographer
C ShutterStock, Inc/Chris Rodenberg Photography
R ShutterStock, Inc/robcocquyt
260 **TC, TR, CR, BC, BR** GE Fabbri Limited
262 **L** iStockphoto.com/Jonathan Moddock
C Alamy Images/Oote Boe Photography 2
R ShutterStock, Inc/Thorsten Rust
263 **L** Alamy Images/David J. Green; **C** Alamy Images/Urban Zone; **R** ShutterStock, Inc/TVR
271 **L, TR** GE Fabbri Limited
272 **C, BL, BR** GE Fabbri Limited
273 **L, TC, C, BC** www.screwfix.com
277 **TL** HL Studios, Oxford.
298 **T** HL Studios, Oxford.
299 **TR** GE Fabbri Limited, **CL** HL Studios, Oxford.
C, BC, BR GE Fabbri Limited
302 **TL** www.screwfix.com
TR www.ring.ltd.uk, **BL** Electric Light Company
BR www.ring.ltd.uk
303 **TL, TC, TR, C, CR, BL, BC,**
BR GE Fabbri Limited
309 **CR** GE Fabbri Limited
314 **BR** www.screwfix.com
315 **TL** Cooper Security Ltd, **TC, TR, CR** www.screwfix.com, **BL** www.Fireangel.co.uk
BC www.screwfix.com, **BR** www.screwfix.com
316 HL Studios, Oxford
320 **L** ShutterStock, Inc/rfx
C ShutterStock, Inc/Yuganov Konstantic
R iStockphoto.com/Sabrina Dei Nobili
321 **L** iStockphoto.com/Howard Oates
C ShutterStock, Inc/Suzanne Tucker
R ShutterStock, Inc/Lisa F. Young
348 **T** www.bathstore.com/'XT' wash basin mixer
TL 'Cliveden' pillar taps by Armitage Shanks; **TR** 'Tratto' by Ideal Standard; **CL** 'Superspa' by Armitage Shanks; **CR** 'Palladian' by Ideal Standard
BL 'Hathaway' by Armitage Shanks; **BC** 'Academy' by Ideal Standard; **BR** 'Millenia QT' by Armitage Shanks
349 **T** 'Academy & Kyomi' by Ideal Standard, **TC** 'Plaza' by Ideal Standard; **TR** www.bathstore.com/' Square' designer basin; **CL** 'Kyomi' by Ideal Standard; **C** 'Meadow' handrinse basin by Ideal Standard; **BR** 'The Space Studio Bidet' by Ideal Standard
353 **BR** Red Cover/Dan Duchars
359 **BL** 'Calista' Trevi showers by Ideal Standard
361 **T, C** GE Fabbri Limited
371 **L** Worcester, Bosch Group
376 **BR** GE Fabbri Limited
377 **TL, BL** GE Fabbri Limited
383 **TL** www.bisque.co.uk, **TC** www.bisque.co.uk
TR www.bisque.co.uk, **B** Myson Radiators
384 **L** Alamy Images/Jurgen Muller
C iStockphoto.com/Frances Twitty
R ShutterStock, Inc/tkemot
385 **L** ShutterStock, Inc/Bonita R. Cheshier
C ShutterStock, Inc/Lisa F. Young
R ShutterStock, Inc/bezmaski
416 **L** ShutterStock, Inc/Jerry Horbert
C ShutterStock, Inc/Videowokart
R ShutterStock, Inc/Elena Elisseeva
417 **L** iStockphoto.com/Thomas Polen
C iStockphoto.com/Jesse Karjalainen
R iStockphoto.com/Darren Wise
418 **T** Clive Nichols/Joe Swift/Thamasin Marsh
421 **TC** Clive Nichols/Designer: Jill Billington
BL Clive Nichols/Designer: Olivia Clarke
BC Clive Nichols/Wollerton Old Hall, Shropshire
431 **TR** www.wickes.co.uk, **BR** www.screwfix.com
446 **TL, B** www.magnettrade.co.uk
447 **T** www.magnettrade.co.uk
448 **TR, BL** www.marshalls.co.uk
449 **T, B** www.marshalls.co.uk
452 **TL** ©Elaine Denne
470 **TR** Draper Tools Ltd
480 **L** ShutterStock, Inc/DJM-photo
C iStockphoto.com/Sean Locke
R ShutterStock, Inc/Charles Taylor
481 **L** ShutterStock, Inc/Baris Turan **C** ShutterStock, Inc/Franck Boston, **R** ShutterStock, Inc/Marcin Balcerzak
490 www.econoloft.co.uk
491 www.econoloft.co.uk
492 **TL, R, BL, B** Images courtesy of www.nuglas.co.uk
493 **TR, BL, BC, BR** Images courtesy of www.nuglas.co.uk
494 **T, C, B** The London Basement Company Ltd
496 www.thegardenescape.co.uk
498 **L** ShutterStock, Inc, **C** ©Natasha Bourne
R ShutterStock, Inc/©Dmitry Kalinovsky
499 **L, C** ©Natasha Bourne, **R** ShutterStock, Inc/©Stanislav Komogorov
500 **L, R** ©Natasha Bourne
501 **L** ShutterStock, Inc/©nikkytok, **R** ShutterStock, Inc/©Nomad Soul
502 **L** ShutterStock, Inc
504 **TL** ShutterStock, Inc/©Serhio Grey,
TR ShutterStock, Inc/©Andrijuss,
BL ShutterStock, Inc/©Zelfit
BR ShutterStock, Inc/©Gualtiero Boffi
505 **TL** ShutterStock, Inc/©Jaddingt
CL ShutterStock, Inc/©Peter Wollinga
R ShutterStock, Inc/©Sashkin
BL ShutterStock, Inc/©Dmitry Melnikov
506 **TL** iStockphoto.com/©John Cave
TR ShutterStock, Inc/©kristin Smith
CR iStockphoto.com/©Don Nichols
BL ShutterStock, Inc/©Silver-john
BR ShutterStock, Inc/©Milos Luzanin
507 **TL** iStockphoto.com/©Sister Sarah
TR ShutterStock, Inc/©Simon krzic
CL ShutterStock, Inc/©Alaettin Yildirim
CR ShutterStock, Inc/©Llin Sergey
BR ShutterStock, Inc/©prism68
509 **TR** ShutterStock, Inc/©Dmitry Kalinovsky
510-511 ©Natasha Bourne
512 **L** ShutterStock, Inc/©Auremar
R ShutterStock, Inc/Sergey Fedenko

Reader's Digest DIY Manual Published in 2011 in the United Kingdom by
Vivat Direct Limited (t/a Reader's Digest), 157 Edgware Road, London W2 2HR

This edition has been fully revised, updated and expanded. It is based on material previously published in *Reader's Digest New D-I-Y Manual* (1987), *Reader's Digest Complete DIY Manual* (1994) and *Reader's Digest DIY Manual* (2004, 2007 and 2009)

Editor Jo Bourne

Art Editor Simon Webb

Editorial Consultant David Holloway, Mike Lawrence, Simon Gilham, Roger Bisby

Additional editorial material David Holloway

Additional photography Martin Cameron

Additional artworks HL Studios, Long Hanborough

Proofreader Barry Gage

Indexer Marie Lorimer

For Vivat Direct
Editorial Director Julian Browne
Art Director Anne-Marie Bulat
Managing Editor Nina Hathway
Picture Resource Manager Sarah Stewart-Richardson
Prepress Technical Manager Dean Russell
Production Controller Jan Bucil
Product Production Manager Claudette Bramble

Vivat Direct Limited would like to thank the following people for their help in producing the book:
Ian Atkinson, Martin Bennett, Tony Eastwood, John Lister, Debbie Robertson, Pete Simmons, Alan Smytherman, Jill Tucker, Kelly Woodgate

Vivat Direct Limited would like to thank the following organisations for the loan of tools, props and other materials for photographic shoots:
Draper Tools (www.drapertools.com), Rogers Ceramics

We are committed both to the quality of our products and the service we provide to our customers. We value your comments, so please do contact us on **0871 351 1000**, or via our website at www.readersdigest.co.uk
If you have any comments about the content of our books, email us at **gbeditorial@readersdigest.co.uk**

Origination by FMG
Printed in China

ISBN 978 1 78020 038 5
BOOK CODE 400-541 UP0000-1